The 1988–89 WORLD COIN CATALOG

Coin World
● THE WEEKLY NEWSPAPER OF THE ENTIRE NUMISMATIC FIELD ●

WORLD COIN CATALOG
twentieth century

Günter Schön
Sixth edition

Amos Press Incorporated

Copyright © 1969, 1978, 1982, 1985, 1988 by Ernst Battenberg Verlag, München

Translated from the 19th edition of **Weltmünzkatalog, XX. Jahrhundert,**
by Günter Schön

Designed by Battenberg Verlag, Munich
Manufactured in West-Germany
Printed by Presse-Druck Augsburg
Bound by AIB, Augsburg

Published by Amos Press, Inc., Post Office Box 150, Sidney, Ohio 45365. Publishers
of Coin World, the weekly newspaper for the entire numismatic field; Linn's Stamp
News, the world's largest weekly stamp newspaper; Cars and Parts, the magazine
serving the car hobbyist; and the Scott Publishing line of philatelic catalogs and
albums.

Copyright © 1988 by Amos Press Inc.

Library of Congress Cataloging in Publication Data
ISBN: 0 944 945 007

Contents

Afars and Issas	*595*
Afghanistan	15
Ajman	28
Aksu	*376*
Albania	31
Algeria	40
Andorra	45
Angola	47
Anguilla	51
Anhalt	*604*
Anhwei	*314, 383*
Annam	*591*
Antigua	53
Antigua and Barbuda	54
Argentina	55
Armarwir Money	*1318*
Aruba	62
Ascension	63
Australia	65
Austria	77
Azores	125
Baden	*606*
Bahamas	126
Bahawalpur	*834*
Bahrain	134
Bangladesh	137
Barbados	140
Barbuda	*54*
Bavaria	*608*
Belgian Congo	144
Belgium	147, 707
Belize	156
Bermuda	161
Bhutan	166
Biafra	172
Bikanir	*895*
Bohemia and Moravia	*707*
Bolivia	174
Botswana	179
Brazil	183
Bremen	*611*
British Caribbean Territories	196
British Guiana	198
British Honduras	199
British North Borneo	202
British Virgin Islands	203
British West Africa	207
Brunei	210
Brunswick	*611*

Bulgaria	213
Bundi	*896*
Burma	232
Burundi	234
Cambodia	236
Cameroon	238
Canada	241
Cap Verde Islands	282
Cayman Islands	285
Central African Republic	290
Central African States	292
Ceylon	293
Chad	297
Chekiang	*315, 362*
Chihli	*316*
Chile	300
China	308
Chinese Turkestan	*339, 375*
Chingkiang	*318*
Colombia	396
Communist People's Republic of	
China	*382*
Comoro Islands	405
Congo-Brazzaville	407
Congo-Kinshasa	409
Cook Islands	411
Costa Rica	418
Crete	425
Croatia	426
Cuba	427
Curaçao	437
Cyprus	439
Czechoslovakia	447
Dahomey	471
Danish West Indies	473
Danzig	*701*
Datia	*896*
Denmark	475
Denmark Greenland	489
Dire Daoua	*555*
Djibouti	490
Dominica	491
Dominican Republic	493
Dungarpur	*837*
East Africa	499
East Caribbean States	502
Ecuador	505

Egypt	507	Honduras		848
Equatorial African States	539	Hong Kong		851
Equatorial Guinea	540	*Hopei*		*326, 366*
Eritrea	544	*Hunan*	*323, 347, 364*	
Estonia	545	Hungary		856
Ethiopia	548	*Hupeh*		*326, 368*
		Hyderabad		*838*
Falkland Islands	556			
Fiji Islands	561	Iceland		877
Finland	567	India		883
Fookien	*318, 363*	Indonesia		905
France	575	*Indore*		*840*
French Equatorial Africa	588	*Inner Mongolia*		*374*
French Indo-China	589	Iran		910
French Oceania	592	Iraq		923
French Polynesia	593	Ireland		931
French Somaliland	594	*Isle of Man*		*777*
French Territory of the Afars		Israel		934
and Issas	595	Italian Somaliland		973
French West Africa	596	Italy		974
Friendly Islands	*1385*	Ivory Coast		987
Fujairah	597			
Fukien	*318, 363*	*Jaipur*		*841*
Fungtien	*321*	Jamaica		988
		Japan		998
Gaboon	599	*Jersey*		*770*
Gambia	601	Jordan		1018
German Democratic Republic	*671*			
German East Africa	*704*			
German Federal Republic	*651*	*Kansu*		*329, 369*
German New Guinea	*703*	*Kashgar*		*322, 357*
Germany	604	Katanga		1022
Ghana	710	Keeling-Cocos Islands		1023
Ghurfah	712	Kenya		1024
Gibraltar	713	*Khmer*		*223*
Great Britain	716	*Kiangnan*		*310*
Greece	814	*Kiangsee*		*331, 369*
Greenland	*489*	*Kiangsi*	*312, 331, 350, 363*	
Grenada	823	*Kiangsoo*		*332*
Guadeloupe	824	*Kiaochow*		*706*
Guatemala	825	Kiribati		1025
Guernsey	*764*	*Kirin*		*334*
Guinea	830	Korea		1028
Guinea-Bissau	836	*Kutch*		*842*
Guyana	837	Kuwait		1030
Gwalior	*837*	*Kwangsea*		*370*
		Kwangsi		*370*
Haiti	839	*Kwangtung*		*337, 371*
Hamburg	*612*	*Kweichow*		*372*
Heilungkiang	*322*			
Hejaz	847	Laos		1032
Hessen	*613*	Latvia		1034
Honan	*322, 365*	Lebanon		1035

Lesotho	1038	*North China*	*374*
Liberia	1040	North Korea	1180
Libya	1045	North Vietnam	1181
Liechtenstein	1047	Norway	1183
Lippe	*572*		
Lithuania	1049	*Oldenburg*	*575*
Lodz Ghetto	*708*	Oman	1192
Luxembourg	1051		
Lübeck	*572*	Pakistan	1194
		Palestine	1199
Macao	1056	Panama	1200
Madagascar	1058	Papua New Guinea	1209
Madeira	1060	Paraguay	1212
Malawi	1061	*People's Republic of China*	*385*
Malaya	1063	Peru	1219
Malaya and British Borneo	1064	Philippines	1228
Malaysia	1065	Poland	1237
Maledive Islands	1071	Portugal	1265
Mali	1075	Portuguese Guinea	1275
Malta	1076	Portuguese India	1277
Manchukuo	1082	*Prussia*	*576*
Manchuria	*338, 373*		
Martinique	1085	Qatar	1279
Mauritania	1086	Qatar and Dubai	1280
Mauritius	1087		
Mecklenburg-Schwerin	*616*	Ras Al Khaima	1281
Mecklenburg-Strelitz	*617*	Reunion	1282
Mewar Udaipur	*843*	*Reuss, elder branch*	*580*
Mexico	1091	*Reuss, younger branch*	*581*
Monaco	1107	Rhodesia	1283
Mongolian People's Republic		Rhodesia and Nyasaland	1285
	1111	*Riau Archipelago*	*849*
Montenegro	1117	Rumania	1287
Montserrat	1119	Russia	1296
Morocco	1120	Rwanda	1320
Mozambique	1126	Rwanda and Burundi	1322
Muscat and Oman	1130		
		Saarland	*703*
Nejd	1131	*Sailana*	*843*
Nepal	1134	St. Christopher-Nevis-	
Netherlands	1148	Anguilla	1323
Netherlands Antilles	1154	St. Christopher and Nevis	1324
Netherlands East Indies	1157	St. Helena	1325
New Caledonia	1158	St. Helena-Ascension	1328
Newfoundland	1160	St. Kitts and Nevis	1329
New Guinea	1162	St. Lucia	1330
New Hebrides	1164	St. Pierre and Miquelon	1332
New Zealand	1166	St. Thomas	
Nicaragua	1173	and Prince Islands	1333
Niger	1177	St. Vincent	1336
Nigeria	1178	Salvador	1338
North Borneo	*192*	San Marino	1341

Santander	379
Sarawak	1350
Saudi Arabia	1352
Saxe-Altenburg	629
Saxe-Coburg-Gotha	629
Saxe-Meiningen	630
Saxe-Weimar	631
Saxony	625
Schaumburg-Lippe	633
Schwarzburg-Rudolstadt	633
Schwarzburg-Sondershausen	633
Senegal	1357
Serbia	1358
Seychelles	1360
Shangtung	339, 374
Shansi	339, 374
Shantung	374
Sharjah	1363
Shensi	375
Sierra Leone	1365
Singapore	1369
Sinkiang	339, 375
Slovakia	1373
Solomon Islands	1375
Somalia	1377
South Africa	1381
South Arabia	1390
Southern Rhodesia	1391
South Vietnam	1402
Southern Yemen	1394
South Korea	1390
Spain	1396
Spitsbergen	1404
Sri Lanka	1409
Straits Settlements	1411
Sudan	1413
Sungarei	322
Surinam	1417
Swaziland	1419
Sweden	1423
Switzerland	1433
Syria	1445
Szechuan	344, 377
Taiwan	1449
Tanzania	1452
Territory of the Eastern Kommandantur	707

Thailand	1455
Tibet	1467
Tihwa	324, 358
Timor	1474
Togo	1475
Tokelau Islands	1476
Tonga	1477
Tonkin	548
Transvaal	1483
Travancore	843
Trinidad and Tobago	1485
Tristan da Cunha	1487
Tsingkiang	299
Tsungarei	322
Tunisia	1488
Turkey	1502
Tuks and Caicos Islands	1516
Tuva	1520
Tuvalu	1521
Uganda	1522
Umm Al Qiwain	1525
United Arab Emirates	1526
United States of America	1527
Uruguay	1585
Urumchi	324, 358
Vanuatu	1591
Vatican City	1592
Venezuela	1604
Vizcaya	1320
Waldeck and Pyrmont	634
West African States	1608
Western Samoa	1609
West Irian	849
Württemberg	634
Yemen	1614
Yugoslavia	1620
Yunnan	346, 379
Yunnan-Burma	381
Zaire	1628
Zambia	1629
Zanzibar	1632
Zimbabwe	1633

Introduction

Yeoman Numbers

In order to help collectors and dealers, we have added after most Schön numbers the corresponding number assigned by R.S. Yeoman in his well-known works entitled »A Catalog of Modern World Coins« and »Current Coins of the World«.

Hints for Quick Understanding of the Book

The coins described in this catalogue are arranged in the alphabetical order of issuing countries. Certain territories have, however, been classified under those countries with which they are, or were formerly, linked, as for instance the Faroe Islands and Greenland come under Denmark; the Riau Islands and West Irian under Indonesia, etc. In the case of Germany, all the territories linked with it, which have issued their own coinage since the foundation of the German Reich on 18th January 1871, have been grouped together in date order.

The issues are listed systematically in chronological order; coins of the same type are nevertheless given together in the increasing order of their nominal value. The catalogue begins, broadly speaking, with 1900; but care has been taken not to break artificially the series with issues going back to an earlier date; for example, in the case of an issue dated 1874–1906, the listing in the catalogue covers all the coins of the same type struck between those two extreme dates.

In spite of intensive care taken throughout in quest of accuracy, this catalogue cannot pretend to be exhaustive. The compilers will, therefore, be glad to receive any additional information that might contribute to make it more complete and more perfect.

Illustrations and Descriptions

All the coins which are illustrated are reproduced in actual size and are placed above the text which refers to them. Whenever this proved impossible, the relative catalogue numbers are given with the illustrations. These illustrations are intended to help to recognize the coins, and can under no circumstances be used for comparison in the case of an expertise.

In view of the greatly increasing interest in commemorative issues, the author has sought to give a more complete description of them, whilst usually only the bare essentials are offered when ordinary current coins are under consideration.

For the amateurs of »collections with a theme« a very complete documentation can be found in the works by Dieter Fassbender entitled »Gedenkmünzen« (»Commemorative Coins«), and by Anton von Ziegésar entitled »Tiermotivkatalog« (»Thematic Catalogue of Animals on Coins«).

Abbreviations Used in the Text

CD	= Cyclical Date	R	= reverse
EE	= Ethiopian Era	Rev.	= reverse
EF	= Extremely Fine (XF)	S-HC	= Solar-Hidshra Calendar
FAO	= Food and Agricultural Organization of the United Nations	Unc	= Uncirculated
		VF	= Very Fine
		XF	= Extremely Fine
H-C	= Hidshra Calendar	Y	= Yeoman Numbers
ND	= No Date	pcs.	= pieces
No.	= number		

Abbreviations Used for Metal Contents

Acm	= Acmonital (Italian coinage)	Fe	= Iron
		Mg	= Magnesium
Ag	= Silver	Ni	= Nickel
Al	= Aluminium	Pb	= Lead
Au	= Gold	Pd	= Palladium
Bi	= Billon	Sn	= Zinc
Bra	= Brass	St	= Steel
Br	= Bronze	Ti	= Tin
Cu	= Copper	Z, Zi	= Zinc
E	= Iron	Zn	= Tin

State of Preservation of the Coins

In the case of both buying and selling coins it is all important to know the terms which are used by the numismatists to define the grades of preservation. There are eight main grades, but the first two are best left out as far as coins of the 20th century are concerned.

Good = gut erhalten (German) = bien conservé (French) = mediocre (Italian) = goed (Dutch) = regular (Spanish), and *Very Good* = sehr gut erhalten = très bien conservé = discreto = zeer goed = bien conservada: these grades are less and less in use as dealers and buyers have turned more and more quality conscious; such terms describe coins which have long been in circulation and have suffered much from wear, leaving types and inscriptions rather flat and unrecognizable. Such coins should not be found in good collections.

Fine = schön = beau = bello = fraai = bien conservada: is used to describe coins which, in spite of having been much in circulation, still show clearly the contours of the types in fairly high relief. This is the lowest grade which should be acceptable to collectors.

Very Fine = sehr schön = très beau = bellissimo = zeer fraai = muy bien conservada: the coins in this state show some traces of wear on the portions in high relief and the legends.

Extremely Fine = vorzüglich = superbe = splendido = prachtig = extraordinariamente bien conservada: all the details of the engraving are seen; there is almost no wear at all even on the portions of the type in high relief, and in the deeper parts the original shine is still preserved.

Uncirculated = Stempelglanz = fleur de coin = fior di conio: there is no trace of wear at all, the coin looks fresh from the mint. Coins issued after 1950 must, broadly speaking, be in this state of preservation to be really worth having. It is since about that date that, at the request of the collecting public, the various mints have often made the new coinage available for sale in special containers. It must, however, be pointed out that, as the coins are struck by machines in great quantities, the handling and transport in bags often cause slight scratches or marks on the surface. These coins are sometimes struck on specially prepared flans.

Proof = Spiegelglanz or polierte Platte = flan bruni = fondo specchio = proefslag = flor de cuño: This term defines no longer the state of preservation, but a special form of production. The flans are previously polished and struck with polished dies, and meticulous care is taken.

Valuations

The prices given in the catalogue are, broadly speaking, for coins in the best condition obtainable, generally in an extremely fine state of preservation (EF). Coins in VF (very fine) condition may only be worth half, and those in F (fine) might be worth very little. Top prices are always paid for top quality pieces. Scratched or damaged coins command very low figures.

It should be also said that there is a general tendency for collectors to demand VF-EF condition in the case of coins struck between 1900–1939, and EF-FDC for the more recent issues. Coins which have circulated for years or even decades are seldom to be found in a state of preservation better than VF. The quality of a coin will make its price; so also will its rarity.

It must be evident to all that it is very difficult in a catalogue like this to quote prices; these depend largely on the law of offer and demand and can fluctuate widely over the years and in various parts of the world. It is accepted that US material fetches higher prices in the United States, and British coins are much more in demand in Britain than in the rest of Europe, for instance; prices depend, therefore, largely on the interest attached to the coins by the collecting public. It is a well-known fact that sometimes at an auction sale certain objects fetch exorbitant or unrealistic prices; only two amateurs are needed to send the prices rocketing sky high.

Commemorative coins, or coins issued for a special purpose (patterns, coronation sets, etc.) call for a separate consideration. The state of preservation required here is, as a rule, EF, even better EF-FDC. The reason for this is that commemorative issues are generally preserved with great care and seldom come into circulation.

As coins cannot keep "fresh" indefinitely (even in a box or case), it is necessary to look after them. Much information as to how to do this will be found in the work by Horst Winskowsky entitled "Münzen pflegen" ("How to Look after Your Coins").

All valuations in the SCHÖN are stated in U.S. Dollars.

There is the occasional criticism that so-called not-collectable pseudo coins are entered indiscriminately; in this respect it must be mentioned that when listing new coins it depends on the completeness of the information and it is frequently difficult to determine whether the minting in question concerns an authentic current coin. The listing of a coin therefore does not purport anything regarding its essence as a genuine coin in circulation and does not embrace any opinion in the sense of such persons who do not consider the »pseudo coins« as collectable.

FAO COIN PLAN

The FAO COIN PLAN with its subject "Produce More Food" which was commenced by the World Food Council in 1968, is the first issue of coins in the history of money coming under international patronage. The main object of the plan centers around the spreading of the message of the FAO over the greatest possible area; in order that this message will appear on coins in many languages and with many symbols. The only objects which will change hands daily for a generation and more.

Our sincerest thanks are due to:

Dr. Walter Alexander-Katz, Lisbon; Mrs. Maryam Avida, Jerusalem; Nikolaus J. Bachmayer, Maria Enzersdorf; M. I. Bathia, Muscat; Roland Becker, Avellino; Dr. Francisca Bernheimer, Munich; David Boehm, New York; W. Ernst Boehm, Ludwigshafen; Dr. Lore Börner, Berlin; Professor Dr. Klaus Brehme, Weilheim; Tim J. Browder, San Marino, California; J. F. Cartier, Chambéry; Peter A. Clayton, Hemel Hempstead; Ernst Debrunner, Zürich; Joachim Düster, Pforzheim; Holger Dombrowski, Münster; Rainer Erdmann, Fulda; Barbara Ernst, Korntal; Dieter Fassbender, Bonn; Enrique Franke, San Salvador; D. A. Grischin, Odessa; H. Häberling, Zürich; Herbert S. Halm, Montevideo; Robert E. Herwegh (†), Frankfurt am Main; Burt Hobson, New York; Octavian Iliescu, Bukarest; Dr. Jørgen Steen Jensen, Copenhagen; Karel Junek, Bratislava; Ewald Junge, London; Willy Kisskalt, Munich; Melvin J. Kohl, Mission Place, California; Hermann Krause, Minneiska, Minn.; Dr. Ottfried Neubecker, Wiesbaden; Miss Gerda Paehlke, Ludwigshafen; Bernard Poindessault, Paris; Ralf Ring, Jena; Prof. Dr. Günther Röblitz, Leipzig; Dr. Bernard Schaaf, Dubuque, Iowa; Peter-M. Schiller, Offenbach; Hans Schlumberger, Stuttgart; Gerhard Schön, Munich; P. N. Schulten, Cologne; Dr. Gregor Schwirtz, Jena; Adam Czopko, Warsaw; J. B. Desai, Ahmedabad; Günther Frank, Nürnberg; Dennis A. Kurir, Longwood, Florida; Rajesh Kumar Lodha, Kathmandu; Reinhold Meckel, Erkrath; G. F. Medrano, Bonn; Hans Meyer, Stolberg; Richard H. Ponterio, San Diego, California; Romain Probst, Luxemburg; Scott Semans, Seattle, Washington; Heinz Senger, Berlin; Robert L. Steinberg, Boca Raton, Florida; V. K. Thacker, Bhuj; Robert M. F. Vogeleer, Brüssel; Anton Freiherr von Ziegésar, Frankfurt am Main. Artexport, Tirana; Artia, Prague; Arve Uruguay Coin, Montevideo; Banco Nacional de Cuba; Havana; Bank of Ghana, Accra; Bank of Jamaica, Kingston; Banque Centrale du Liban, Beirut; Banque Centrale de Madagascar, Antanarivo; Banque du Maroc, Rabat; Banque Nationale de Yougoslavie, Belgrade; Bernhardt Inc., Geneva; British Bank of Middle East, Muscat; Bundesstelle für Außenhandelsinformation, Cologne; Caisse Générale de l'Etat, Luxembourg; Casa da Moeda, Lisbon; Central Bank of Cyprus, Nicosia; Central Bank of Ireland, Dublin; Central Mint of China, Taipeh; Chase Manhattan Bank, New York; Consulado de la Republica Argentina, Munich; Consulado-Geral do Brasil, Munich; Consulat de Monaco, Munich; Consulate-General of South Africa, Munich; Crown Agents, Sutton, Surrey; Currency Board, Suva; Department of Archaeology, Katmandu; Der Bundesminister für Finanzen, Bonn; DESA Foreign Trade Company, Warsaw; Deutsche Bundesbank, Frankfurt am Main; Dresdner Bank AG, Numismatischer Handel, Frankfurt am Main; Eidgenössische Münzstätte Bern; Embassy of Cyprus; Bonn-Bad Godesberg; Embassy of Ireland, Bonn-Bad Godesberg; Etablissement Evolena, Vaduz; Euronummis, Milan; Financial Secretary Treasury Department, Apia; Hemus, Sofia; Heraldischer Verein »Zum Kleeblatt«, Hannover; International Numismatic Promotion, Brussels; Israel Government Coins and Medals Corporation Ltd., Jerusalem; Italcambio, Milan; Karl-May-Verlag, Bamberg; Landsbanki Islands, Reykjavik; Magyar Nemzeti Bank, Budapest; Mecattaf Bank, Beirut; Merkur Bank, Munich; Mint Bureau Ministry of Finance, Osaka; Monnaies Or Agent, Chiasso; Münzzentrum, Cologne; Nationalmuseet, Copenhagen; Numismatica Italiana, Milan; Numismatic Section Treasury, Nuku'alofa; Österreichisches Hauptmünzamt, Vienna; Paramount Internationale Münzgesellschaft, Karlsruhe; Pobjoy Mint, Sutton, Surrey; Royal Australian Mint, Canberra; Royal Canadian Mint, Ottawa; Services Commerciaux Français en Allemagne, Munich; Staatliche Münzsammlung, Munich; Staatliche Museen (Münzkabinett), Berlin; Suomen Kansallismuseo, Helsinki; The Treasury, Wellington.

Area: 250,000 sq. mi. Population: 17,600,000.
Emirate; independent kingdom since 1919, constitutional monarchy since 1926; republic since 17th July 1973; it was then proclaimed a People's Republic. Capital: Kabul.
Monetary unit until 1925 the Rupee-Kabuli; since 1926 decimal system, i. e. 100 Puls = 1 Afghani. During the currency conversion of 1926, the factor was 11 Rupees for 10 Afghani.

60 Paisa = 1 Rupee, 5 Paisa = Shahi, 10 Paisa = Senar, 6 Senar = 1 Rupee, 20 Paisa = 1 Abbasi, 3 Abbasi = 1 Rupee, 30 Paisa = 1 Quiran, 2 Quiran = 1 Rupee, 30 Rupees = 1 Habibi, 1 Amani, 1 Tilla
30 Rupees = 1 Habibi, 1 Amani, 1 Tilla. These coins weighed 1 Musqual = 4.6 grams. After the currency conversion to Afghani, the weight system was also changed over to grams. Since 1933 a Tilla possesses a coin weight of only 4 grams. Gold coins are not in circulation and are not being dealt with at any Afghan bank.

HABIB ULLAH KHAN 1901–1919

National arms: mosque flanked by tilted flags and rifles with fixed bayonets, underneath crossed swords, rifles, flags and cannons. In one instance Star of David below mosque in a wreath of light rays. In many instances there are, however, only crossed canons below the mosque.

			VF	XF
1 (15)	1 Abbasi (Ag) H–C 1320 (1902). Toughra and date in wreath. ℞ national arms; mosque with flags on either side; below, crossed sabres, the whole within wreath of corn-ears		30.00	50.00
2 (16)	1 Quiran (Ag) H–C 1320, 1321, 1325 (1902, 1903, 1907)		12.00	20.00
3 (17)	1 Rupee (Ag) H–C 1319–1321, 1325 (1901–1903, 1907)		12.00	20.00
4 (18)	5 Rupees (Ag) H–C 1319 (1901)		70.00	125.00
5 (19)	1 Tilla (Au) H–C 1319–1320 (1901–1902)		130.00	220.00
6 (20)	1 Paisa (Bra) H–C 1329 (1911). Inscription in circle. ℞ national arms.		18.00	30.00
7 (21)	1 Senar (Ag) H–C 1325–1329 (1907–1911). Inscription in wreath, above star. ℞ national arms in wreath.		10.00	18.00
8 (22)	1 Abbasi (Ag) H–C 1324–1329 (1906–1911)		16.00	25.00

		VF	XF
9 (23)	1 Quiran (Ag) H–C 1323–1329 (1905–1911)	10.00	15.00
10 (24)	1 Rupee (Ag) H–C 1321–1329 (1903–1911)	12.00	20.00
11 (25)	5 Rupees (Ag) H–C 1322–1329 (1904–1911)	50.00	85.00
A11	1 Tilla (Au) H–C 1325 (1907)	600.00	900.00
12 (26)	1 Paisa (Cu) H–C 1329–1337 (1911–1919). Inscription. ℞ national arms in octagon	7.00	12.00
13 (27)	1 Senar (Ag) H–C 1329–1337 (1911–1919). Inscription in wreath, above star. ℞ national arms in octagon, in wreath	8.00	15.00
14 (28)	1 Abbasi (Ag) H–C 1329–1337 (1911–1919)	7.00	12.00
15 (29)	1 Quiran (Ag) H–C 1329–1337 (1911–1919)	6.00	10.00
16 (30)	1 Rupee (Ag) H–C 1329–1337 (1911–1919)	8.00	15.00
17 (31)	1 Tilla (Au) H–C 1335–1337 (1917–1919)	175.00	260.00

AMAN ULLAH KHAN 1919–1929

National arms: mosque flanked by tilted flags, below crossed swords, all within a partly round or oval wreath of light rays.

18 (32)	1 Paisa (Cu) H–C 1337 (1919)	8.00	15.00
19 (34)	1 Shahi (Cu) H–C 1337 (1919)	15.00	30.00
20 (35)	1 Senar (Cu) H–C 1337 (1919)	12.00	20.00
21 (36)	3 Shahi (Cu) H–C 1337 (1919). With date according to Solar-Hidshra calendar: No. 26	5.00	10.00
22 (39)	½ Rupee (Ag) H–C 1337 (1919). With date according to Solar-Hidshra calendar: No. 29	4.00	8.00
23 (40)	1 Rupee (Ag) H–C 1337 (1919). With date according to Solar-Hidshra calendar: No. 30	10.00	18.00
24 (41)	1 Tilla (Au) H–C 1337 (1919). Star above, inscription and date below, all within a wreath of leaves. ℞ mosque crossed swords below, wreath of light rays surrounded by wreath of leaves. 4.6 grams; 21 mm dia.	140.00	220.00

			VF	XF
A24 (41)	1	Tilla (Au) H–C 1337 (1919). Type similar to No. 24, but Star of David in place of the crossed swords	140.00	220.00
B24	4	Tilla (Au) H–C 1337 (1919). Type similar to No. A24. 18.53 grams, 32 mm dia.	–.–	–.–

After the introduction of the Solar-Hidshra calendar (hidshri shamsi) on the strength of a decree of 1920, the dates 1298–1307 given on the coins correspond to the years 1920–1929 of the Christian calendar. Coins of same types, but bearing different dates, are listed separately.

A25	1	Paisa (Cu) S–HC 1298 (1920). Type as No. 18	12.00	25.00
25 (33)	1	Paisa (Cu) S–HC 1299–1303 (1921–1925)	5.00	10.00
26 (36)	3	Shahi (Cu) S–HC 1298–1300 (1920–1922). Type as No. 21	6.00	12.00
27 (37)	1	Abbasi (Bi) S–HC 1298 (1920)	50.00	85.00
28 (38)	1	Abbasi (Bi) S–HC 1299 (1921). Type as No. 27, yet with a diameter now of 25 mm instead of 20 mm	28.00	40.00
29 (39)	½	Rupee (Ag) S–HC 1298–1300 (1920–1922). Type as No. 22	6.00	10.00
30 (40)	1	Rupee (Ag) S–HC 1298–1299 (1920–1921). Type as No. 23	10.00	18.00

31 (42)	2	Tilla (Au) S–HC 1298 (1920). Type as No. 24	160.00	240.00
32 (43)	3	Shahi (Cu) S–HC 1300–1303 (1922–1925). Toughra surrounded by stars. ℞ national arms in octagon, surrounded by stars.	6.00	8.00
33 (44)	1	Abbasi (Cu) S–HC 1299–1303 (1921–1925)	5.00	10.00
34 (45)	½	Rupee (Ag) S–HC 1300–1303 (1922–1925). Toughra in wreath. ℞ national arms in oval, septagon, the whole within wreath	7.00	11.00
35 (46)	1	Rupee (Ag) S–HC 1299–1303 (1921–1925)	10.00	16.00
36 (47)	2½	Rupees (Ag) S–HC 1298–1303 (1920–1925)	25.00	40.00
37 (48)	½	Amani (Au) S–HC 1299 (1921)	90.00	140.00

38 (49) 1 Amani (Au) S–HC 1299 (1921). Toughra, date below, all within a wreath of leaves. ℞ Amani above, mosque below and crossed swords, in an oval wreath of light rays, all within a wreath of leaves. 4.6 grams; 22.5 mm dia.

39 (50) 2 Amani (Au) S–HC 1299–1303 (1921–1925)

	VF	XF
38	90.00	140.00
39	140.00	220.00

40 (51) 5 Amani (Au) S–HC 1299 (1921). Denomination above, Toughra and date below, all within a wreath of leaves. ℞ Amani above, mosque, crossed swords below, in oval wreath of light rays, all within wreath of leaves. 23 grams, 33.5 mm dia.   700.00   1100.00

A40 (51) 5 Amani (Au) S–HC 1299 (1921). Type as No. 40, but in place of the numeral 5, a star; ℞ in place of Amani, a '5'   750.00   1200.00

NEW VALUE: 100 Puls = 1 Afghani

				VF	XF
41 (52)	2	Puls (Cu) S–C 1304–1305 (1926–1927). Toughra within circle, the whole within wreath. ℞ value in circle, the whole within wreath.		3.00	6.00
42 (53)	5	Puls (Cu) S–HC 1304–1305 (1926–1927)		3.00	6.00
43 (54)	10	Puls (Cu) S–HC 1304–1306 (1926–1928)		3.00	5.00
44 (55)	20	Puls (Ag) S–HC 1304 (1926)		55.00	100.00
45 (56)	½	Afghani (Ag) S–HC 1304–1307 (1926–1929). National arms in wreath. ℞ Toughra within wreath, above value.		4.00	7.00
46 (57)	1	Afghani (Ag) S–HC 1304–1307 (1926–1929)		5.00	10.00
47 (58)	2½	Afghani (Ag) S–HC 1305–1306 (1927–1928)		25.00	40.00
48 (59)	½	Amani (Au) S–HC 1304–1306 (1926–1928)		80.00	130.00

49 (60)	1	Amani (Au) S–HC 1304–1306 (1926–1928). Denomination above, Toughra below, date, all within a wreath of leaves. ℞ Great Mosque without wreath of rays of light. Number of the years of the reign, all within a wreath of leaves. 4.6 grams, 23 mm dia.		100.00	160.00
50 (61)	2½	Amani (Au) S–HC 1306 (1928)		700.00	1300.00

HABIB ULLAH GHAZI (Bātschä-ji Saqqa) 1929

National arms: mosque flanked by tilted flags in a round wreath of light rays. Pulpit at left.

51 (66)	10	Paisa (Cu) H–C 1348 (1929). Denomination in Pashtu, between two stars. Legend partly arranged in a circle, and date within a wreath of leaves. ℞ denomination in Dari, between two stars. Mosque within wreath of rays of light, pulpit at left		18.00	30.00
52 (62)	20	Paisa (Cu) H–C 1347 (1929). Denomination in Pashtu, between two stars, legend and date within a wreath of			

leaves. ℞ denomination in Dari, between two stars. Mosque in a wreath of light rays, pulpit at left 7.00   15.00

53 (67) 1 Quiran (Ag) H–C 1347 (1929). Star above, legend partly arranged in a circle, date below, all within a wreath of leaves. ℞ 1 Quiran, mosque in a wreath of light rays, date below 35.00   50.00

54 (63) 1 Quiran (Ag) H–C 1348 (1929). Similar to No. 53, but legend arranged horizontally 12.00   18.00

55 (68) 1 Rupee (Ag) H–C 1347 (1929). Star above, legend partly arranged in a circle, date below, all within a wreath of leaves. ℞ mosque in a wreath of light rays 60.00   90.00

56 (64) 1 Rupee (Ag) H–C 1348 (1929). Similar to No. 55, but legend arranged horizontally on left in the national arms 16.00   30.00

57 (65) 1 Habibi (Au) H–C 1347 (1929). Denomination 30 Rupees, legend, date below, surrounded by wreath of leaves. ℞ 1 Habibi, below mosque in a wreath of light rays, pulpit at left. 4.6 grams, 21 mm dia. 240.00   350.00

A57 (65) 1 Habibi (Au) H–C 1347 (1929). Type similar to No. 57, but a star in place of the denomination of 30 Rupees 240.00   350.00

MOHAMMED NADIR SHAH 1929–1933

National arms: mosque flanked by flags, within a wreath of corn ears or of leaves. Pulpit at left.

58 (69) 1 Pul (Cu) H–C 1349 (1930). Inscription surrounded by stars. ℞ value in circle, the whole surrounded by stars 1.50   2.50

A58 1 Pul (Cu) H–C 1349 (1930). Toughra surrounded by stars. Rev. Value 200.00   300.00

59 (70) 2 Puls (Cu) H–C 1348 (1929). Toughra and date in circle, the whole within wreath 2.00   4.00

60 (71) 5 Puls (Cu) H–C 1349–1350 (1930–1931) 2.50   4.00

61 (72) 10 Puls (Cu) H–C 1348–1349 (1929–1930) 3.00   5.00

62 (73) 20 Puls (Cu) H–C 1348–1349 (1929–1930) 4.00   6.00

			VF	XF
63 (74)	25 Puls (Cu) H–C 1349 (1930)		3.00	5.00
64 (75)	½ Afghani (Ag) H–C 1348–1350 (1929–1931)		3.00	5.00

65 (76)	1 Afghani (Ag) H–C 1348–1350 (1929–1931)		8.00	14.00

66 (78) 20 Afghani (Au) H–C 1348–1350 (1929–1931). Toughra, name and title within the wreath of leaves; denomination in brackets above. ℞ mosque and date within wreath of leaves, pulpit at left. 21.8 mm dia. — 170.00 / 240.00

In the type similar to No. 66 there is another 1 Tilla gold coin (H–C 1348–1350). This coin probably weighs 4.6 grams, diameter unknown, and must be described as extremely rare.

67 (80) 2 Puls (Bra) S–HC 1311–1314 (1932–1935). Inscription in dotted circle, within wreath. ℞ value in dotted circle, within wreath — 2.00 / 4.00

68 (81) 5 Puls (Bra) S–HC 1311–1314 (1932–1935) — 2.00 / 4.00

69 (82) 10 Puls (Bra) S–HC 1311–1314 (1932–1935) — 2.00 / 4.00

As can be seen from the dates given, the coins listed under Nos. 67–69 were still issued during the reign of King Mohammed Sahir Shah.

70 (83) ½ Afghani (Ag) S–HC 1310–1312 (1931–1933). Inscription in dotted circle, within wreath. Rev. Arms within wreath — 3.00 / 5.00

71 (84) 1 Afghani (Ag) S–HC 1310, 1311 (1931, 1932); 27 mm dia. — 55.00 / 90.00

National arms: mosque between flags, within the wreath of corn ears.
Pulpit at left.

			VF	XF
72 (90)	2 Puls (Br) S–HC 1316 (1937). National arms within wreath. ℞ value in circle, within wreath.		0.50	1.00
73 (91)	3 Puls (Br) S–HC 1316 (1937)		1.00	2.00
74 (92)	5 Puls (Br) S–HC 1316 (1937)		0.50	1.00
75 (93)	10 Puls (Cu-Ni) S–HC 1316 (1937)		0.50	1.00
76 (85)	25 Puls (Cu) S–HC 1312–1316 (1933–1937). Inscription in dotted circle, within wreath. ℞ value in dotted circle, within wreath		3.00	7.00
77 (94)	25 Puls (Cu-Ni) S–HC 1316 (1937). National arms in wreath. ℞ inscription in circle, the whole surrounded by legend		0.50	1.00
78 (95)	25 Puls (Br) S–HC 1330–1332 (1951–1953)		0.50	1.00
79 (95a)	25 Puls (Ni–St) S–HC 1331–1334 (1952–1955)		0.50	1.00
80 (95b)	25 Puls (Al) S–HC 1331 (1952). Denomination in Pashtu in the circle. The word Afghanistan in the outer circle. ℞ national arms in the dotted circle, date below. 24 mm dia.		0.40	0.60
81 (86)	1 Quiran (Ag) H–C 1312–1314 (1933–1935). Legend in the dotted circle (60 dots), surrounded by wreath of corn ears; the word Afghanistan above. ℞ denomination 1 Quiran, date below, all within the wreath of ears of corn		3.00	5.00
A81 (86)	1 Quiran (Ag) H–C 1315–1316 (1936–1937). Type as No. 81, but dotted circle with 40 dots		3.00	5.00

			VF	XF
82 (97)	50 Puls (Ni–St) S–HC 1331 (1952). National arms within wreath. ℞ value in circle, the whole surrounded by inscription		0.90	1.50

Values are given for each coin in U.S. Dollars and reference to Yeoman-numbers.

				VF	XF
83 (96)	50	Puls (Br) S–HC 1330 (1951). National arms in wreath. ℞ value in circle, the whole within legend		0.50	1.00
84 (96a)	50	Puls (Ni-St) S–HC 1331–1334 (1952–1955)		0.50	1.00
85 (98)	2	Afghani (Al) S–HC 1337 (1958). National arms in dotted circle, the whole surrounded by stars and legend. ℞ value in dotted circle, the whole surrounded by stars		1.60	3.00
86 (99)	5	Afghani (Al) S–HC 1337 (1958). National arms, value. Rev. Toughra		2.20	4.00
A86	10	Afghani (Al) S–HC 1336 (1957). Type similar to No. 86		–.–	–.–

87 (88)	4	Grami = 1 Tilla (Au) S–HC 1315, 1317 (1936, 1938). Legend in dotted circle, surrounded by corn ears, the word Afghanistan above. R denomination 4 Grami, national arms and date belowe, 4 grams, 19 mm dia.		120.00	175.00
88 (87)	6	Grami = 1½ Tilla (Au) S–HC 1313 (1934). Type similar to No. 87, but 6 grams and 22.2 mm dia.		180.00	260.00
89 (89)	8	Grami = 2 Tilla (Au) S–HC 1314, 1315, 1317 (1935, 1936, 1938). Type similar to No. 87, but 8 grams and 22.2 mm dia.		190.00	280.00

				XF	Unc
90 (100)	1	Afghani (Ni-St) S–HC 1340 (1961). 3 ears of corn and date. ℞ value surrounded by stars		0.20	0.30

91 (101) 2 Afghani (Ni–St) S–HC 1340 (1961). Above inscription "Afghanistan", in the center the fabulous eagle in front of the sun who is reputed to have placed a gold crown on the head of the legendary first King Yamma, below the date 1340. ℞ numeral of value below the word "two" and above the word "Afghani" between an ear of corn and three stars

	XF	Unc
	0.30	0.40

92 (102) 5 Afghani (Ni–St) S–HC 1340, H–C 1381 (1961). King Mohammed Sahir Shah (* 1914), in uniform between the dates 1340 and 1381, above the legend "Mohammed Sahir – asterisk – Afghanistan's – asterisk – King". ℞ numeral of value below the word "five" and above the word "Afghani" between two ears of corn

0.70 1.20

93 (A 102) 4 Grami = 1 Tilla (Au) S–HC 1339, HC 1380 (1960). The king's name in Thoughra shape, to the right invocation of God, below: "De Afghanistan Padshahi Daulat" (= Royal Afghan Government). ℞ above "four Grami", below "Kabul", left 1339, right 1380, in the center an emblem above crossed ears of corn formed of the mosque of the national arms and historico-religious beasts (Eagle of Zarathustra and the Bull of Mithras). 4 grams

Proof –.–

Values are given for each coin in U.S. Dollars and reference to Yeoman-numbers.

94 (B 102)   8 Grami = 2 Tilla (Au) S–HC 1339,
HC. 1380 (1960). Type similar to
No. 93, but 8 grams, 22.2 mm dia.   Proof   650.00

REPUBLIC

		XF	Unc
95 (103) 25 Puls (Brass-clad steel) S-HC 1352 (1973). Coat of arms. *R* value		1.00	2.50
96 (104) 50 Puls (Cu-clad steel) S-HC 1352 (1973). Type as No. 95		2.50	5.00
97 (105) 5 Afghani (Cu-Ni-clad steel) S-HC 1352 (1973). *R* value between two ears		4.00	8.00

CONSERVATION COMMEMORATIVE (3)

		Unc	Proof
98 (106) 250 Afghani (Ag) 1978. Coat of arms. Rev. Snow Leopard:			
a) .500 silver, 25.31 g		25.00	
b) .925 silver, 28.28 g			
99 (107) 500 Afghani (Ag) 1978. Rev. Siberian Crane:			
a) .500 silver, 31.65 g		35.00	
b) .925 silver, 35.00 g			50.00
100 (108) 10000 Afghani (Au) 1978. Rev. Marco Polo Sheep		550.00	750.00

DEMOCRATIC REPUBLIC

		XF	Unc
101 (109) 25 Puls (Al-Br) S-HC 1357 (1978). Coat of arms. R value		1.00	2.00
102 (110) 50 Puls (Al-Br) S-HC 1357 (1978). Same type as No. 101		1.00	2.00
103 (111) 1 Afghani (Cu-Ni) S-HC 1357 (1978). Same type as No. 101		–.–	–.–
104 (A112) 2 Afghani (Cu-Ni) S-HC 1357 (1978). Same type as No. 101		–.–	–.–
105 (111) 5 Afghani (Cu-Ni) S-HC 1357 (1978). Same type as No. 101		2.00	4.00

		XF	Unc
106 (115)	25 Puls (Al-Br) S-HC 1359 (1980). New coat of arms. Rev. value, inscription, stars	1.00	2.00
107 (116)	50 Puls (Al-Br) S-HC 1359 (1980). Type as No. 106	2.00	4.00
108 (117)	1 Afghani (Cu-Ni) S-HC 1359 (1980). Type as No. 106	5.00	8.00
109 (118)	2 Afghani (Cu-Ni) S-HC 1359 (1980). Type as No. 106	8.00	12.00
110 (119)	5 Afghani (Cu-Ni) S-HC 1359 (1980). Type as No. 106	12.00	18.00

WORLD FOOD DAY (2)

		XF	Unc
111 (113)	5 Afghani (Bra) S-HC 1360 (1981)	1.00	2.00
112 (114)	500 Afghani (Ag) S-HC 1360 (1981)	Proof	26.00

CENTENARY OF THE AUTOMOBILE (2)

113	2 Afghani (Cu-Ni) 1986. Arms. Rev. Ferrari Testarossa	–.–
114	500 Afghani (Ag) 1986. Type as No. 113	30.00

WORLD SOCCER CHAMPIONSHIP 1986 IN MEXICO

No. 115 omitted.

116	500 Afghani (Ag) 1986	–.–

Nos. 117–119 omitted.

DEFENSE OF NATURE

120	500 Afghani (Ag) 1986. Rev. Leopard	30.00

Nos. 121–122 omitted.

123	500 Afghani (Ag) ND (1986)	35.00

Nos. 124–125 omitted.

OLYMPIC GAMES 1988 IN SEOUL

126	500 Afghani (Ag) 1987. Rev. Volleyball	30.00

Yeoman Numbers

In order to help collectors and dealers, we have added after most SCHÖN-numbers the corresponding number assigned by R.S. Yeoman in his wellknown works entitled »A Catalog of Modern World Coins« and »Current Coins of the World«.

Previous issues, see »Weltmünzkatalog 19. Jahrhundert« (World Coin Catalogue of the 19th Century)

Area: 96 sq. mi. Population: 5,000 (1971).
The sheikdom of Ajman belonged to the seven Trucial States in the Pacified Oman. Ajman also administratively includes the territory of Manama. Since December 2, 1971 Ajman is a member state of the »United Arab Emirates« (UAE). In addition to the Ajman-Riyal, the Qatar and Dubai-Riyal was legal tender. Capital: Ajman.

100 Dirham = 1 Ajman-Riyal

RASHID BIN HUMAID 1928–1981

		Unc	Proof
1	1 Riyal (Ag) 1969. Crossed flags and jambijas, underneath Arabian sand-hen or May's partridge (Ammoperdix hayi – Fam. Phasianidae). ℞ value and name of country	*10.00*	*10.00*
2	2 Riyals (Ag) 1969. Type as No. 1	*14.00*	*14.00*

| 3 | 5 Riyals (Ag) 1969. Type as No. 1 | *25.00* | *25.00* |

| 4 | 7½ Riyals (Ag) AH 1389/1970. Rev. Bone-fish (or Ladyfish) (Albula vulpes – Albuliae), stylized | 30.00 | 70.00 |

			Unc	Proof
5	7½	Riyals (Ag) AH 1389/1970. Rev. Berber falcon (or Peregrine falcon) (Falco peregrinoides – Falconidae)	30.00	70.00
6	7½	Riyals (Ag) AH 1389/1970. Rev. Gazelle (Gazella sp. – Bovidae)	30.00	70.00

A 7	100	Dirhams (Cu-Ni) 1970. Arms, value. Rev. Dove. Pattern!	280.00	
7	1	Riyal (Ag) 1970. Type as No. 1, but three dates	18.00	
8	2	Riyals (Ag) 1970. Type as No. 7	25.00	
9	5	Riyals (Ag) 1970. Type as No. 7	40.00	

LENIN BIRTH CENTENNIAL (2)

10	10	Riyals (Ag) ND (1970). Arms. Rev. Head of Lenin:		
		a)	–.–	
		b) with inscription »PROOF«	150.00	
11	100	Riyals (Au) ND (1970). Type similar to No. 10	400.00	

DEATH OF GAMAL ABD EL NASSER (4)

12	5	Riyals (Ag) 1970. Gamal Abd el Nasser (1918–1970), President of the United Arab Republic 1958–1970; head facing left in front of Sphinx and Pyramid. R national emblem, denomination	50.00	

13	7½	Riyals (Ag) 1970. Type similar to No. 12	30.00	
14	25	Riyals (Au) 1970. Type similar to No. 12	100.00	
15	50	Riyals (Au) 1970. Type similar to No. 12	200.00	

16	5 Riyals (Ag) ND (1970). Dag Hammerskjöld	50.00
17	25 Riyals (Au) ND (1970). Type as No. 16	100.00
18	5 Riyals (Ag) ND (1970). Mahatma Gandhi	50.00
19	25 Riyals (Au) ND (1970). Type as No. 18	100.00
20	5 Riyals (Ag) ND (1970). Martin Luther King	50.00
21	25 Riyals (Au) ND (1970). Type as No. 20	100.00
22	5 Riyals (Ag) ND (1970). George C. Marshall	50.00
23	25 Riyals (Au) ND (1970). Type as No. 22	100.00
24	5 Riyals (Ag) ND (1970). Bertrand A. Russel	50.00
25	25 Riyals (Au) ND (1970). Type as No. 24	100.00
26	5 Riyals (Ag) ND (1970). Albert Schweitzer	50.00
27	25 Riyals (Au) ND (1970). Type as No. 26	100.00
28	5 Riyals (Ag) ND (1970). Jan Palac	50.00
29	25 Riyals (Au) ND (1970). Type as No. 28	100.00
30	5 Riyals (Ag) ND (1970). Albert J. Luthuli	50.00
31	25 Riyals (Au) ND (1970). Type as No. 30	100.00

FAO COIN PLAN (2)

Proof

32	5 Riyals (Ag) 1970. Ears of corn supported by two hands. R national emblem, denomination	40.00
33	75 Riyals (Au) 1970. Fish	300.00

These issues (No. 32 and 33) are not recognized by the FAO.

SAVE VENICE (4)

34	5 Riyals (Ag) ND (1971). Motto: SAVE VENICE and symbolical representation. R national emblem, above denomination in Arabic. Portrait of the Sheik	30.00
34	25 Riyals (Au) ND (1971). Type as No. 34	100.00
36	50 Riyals (Au) ND (1971). Type as No. 34	190.00
37	100 Riyals (Au) ND (1971). Type as No. 34	380.00

All valuations in the SCHÖN are stated in U.S. Dollars.

Albanien   # Albania   **Albanie**

Shqipëri

Area: 11,057 sq. mi. Population: 3,000,000.

After a long struggle under the leadership of the national hero Prince Skanderbeg, Albania fell under Turkish domination in the 15th century. The country did not regain its independence until 28th November 1912. As it was occupied by the warring powers, it began its independent political life only after the First World War. In 1925 Ahmet Zogu founded a dictatorship with himself as President. On 1st September 1928 he proclaimed himself King as Zog I. After the military occupation of Albania by Italy in April 1939, the country was linked to the Italian State in a close union. After the War of Liberation, successfully fought first against the Italian domination, and then from 1943 against the German occupation, the new Peoples's State was formed on 24th May 1944 with a provisional Government under Enver Hodja, which was able to exercise full control over the whole country from 29th November 1944 onward. On 11th January 1946 a People's Republic was proclaimed. Capital: Tirana.

100 Qindarka Leku = 1 Lek, 100 Qindarka Ari = 1 Franka Ari, 5 Lek = 1 Franka Ari; since 1939–1944: 1 Lek = 1 Lire; since 1947 only Lekë; since 1964: 100 Qindarka = 1 Lek

			VF	XF
1 (1)	5	Qindarka Leku (Br) 1926. Lion's head. ℞ value above oak leaves	40.00	80.00
2 (2)	10	Qindarka Leku (Br) 1926. Eagle's head to right. ℞ value between olive branches (Olea europaea – Oleaceae)	40.00	80.00
3 (3)	¼	Leku (Ni) 1926–1927. Lion (Panthera leo – Felidae). ℞ oak branch above value	6.00	10.00
4 (4)	½	Lek (Ni) 1926. Double eagle. ℞ Hercules fighting the Nemean lion	7.00	12.00
5 (5)	1	Lek (Ni) 1926–1927, 1930–1931. Classical head. ℞ horseman	7.00	12.00

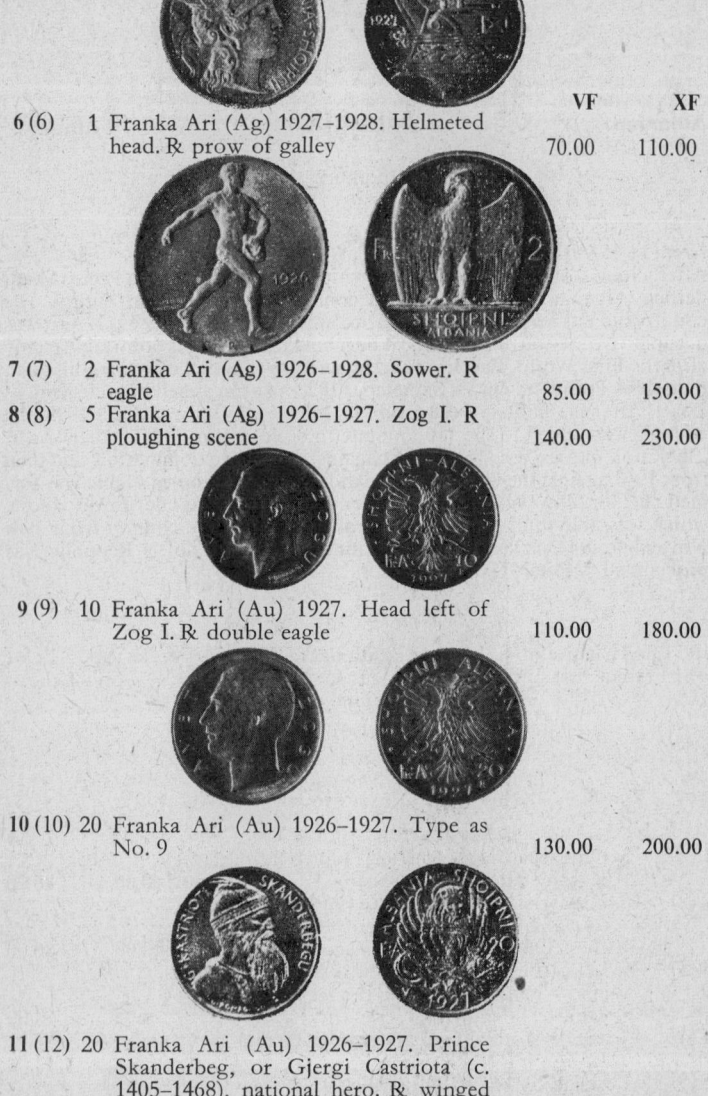

		VF	XF
6 (6)	1 Franka Ari (Ag) 1927–1928. Helmeted head. ℞ prow of galley	70.00	110.00
7 (7)	2 Franka Ari (Ag) 1926–1928. Sower. ℞ eagle	85.00	150.00
8 (8)	5 Franka Ari (Ag) 1926–1927. Zog I. ℞ ploughing scene	140.00	230.00
9 (9)	10 Franka Ari (Au) 1927. Head left of Zog I. ℞ double eagle	110.00	180.00
10 (10)	20 Franka Ari (Au) 1926–1927. Type as No. 9	130.00	200.00
11 (12)	20 Franka Ari (Au) 1926–1927. Prince Skanderbeg, or Gjergi Castriota (c. 1405–1468), national hero. ℞ winged lion facing (lion of St. Mark)	150.00	230.00

			VF	XF
12 (11)	100	Franka Ari (Au) 1926–1927. Zog I. ℞ Biga. Variants: at the cut of the neck, no star; sometimes one or two stars	700.00	900.00
13 (13)	½	Lek (Ni) 1930–1931. National arms. ℞ as No. 4	4.00	8.00
14 (14)	1	Qindarka Ari (Br) 1935. Double eagle. ℞ value	7.00	12.00
15 (15)	2	Qindarka Ari (Br) 1935. Double eagle. ℞ value	9.00	15.00
16 (16)	1	Franka Ari (Ag) 1935–1937. Zog I. (1895–1961). ℞ national arms	12.00	18.00
17 (17)	2	Franka Ari (Ag) 1935. Type as No. 16	22.00	32.00

ISSUES (4) COMMEMORATING THE 25th ANNIVERSARY OF INDEPENDENCE ON 28th NOVEMBER 1937

18 (18)	1	Franka Ari (Ag) 1937. Zog I. ℞ national arms with inscription and dates 28th November 1912 to 1937	20.00	35.00
19 (19)	2	Franka Ari (Ag) 1937	25.00	50.00

20 (20)	20	Franka Ari (Au) 1937	185.00	280.00
21 (21)	100	Franka Ari (Au) 1937	900.00	1500.00

ISSUES (2) COMMEMORATING THE MARRIAGE OF KING ZOG TO COUNTESS GERALDINE APPONYI ON 27th APRIL 1938

		VF	XF
22 (22)	20 Franka Ari (Au) 1938. Zog I. ℞ national arms with inscription and date 27th April 1938	220.00	320.00
23 (23)	100 Franka Ari (Au) 1938	1200.00	1700.00

ISSUES (3) COMMEMORATING THE 10th JUBILEE OF THE REIGN OF KING ZOG I ON 1st SEPTEMBER 1938

24 (24)	20 Franka Ari (Au) 1938. Zog I. ℞ national arms with inscription and date 1st September 1928–1938	200.00	300.00
25 (25)	50 Franka Ari (Au) 1938	420.00	650.00
26 (26)	100 Franka Ari (Au) 1938	650.00	1100.00

CLOSE UNION WITH ITALY (ITALIAN DOMINATION) UNDER VICTOR EMMANUEL III 1939–1943

27 (27)	0,05 Lek (Al–Br) 1940–1941, Victor Emmanuel III (1869–1947), King of Italy 1900–1946, Emperor of Ethiopia 1939–1941. King of Albania 1939–1943. ℞ oak branch above value	4.00	7.00

28 (28)	0,10 Lek (Al–Br) 1940–1941. Victor Emmanuel III. ℞ olive branch (Olea europaea – Oleaceae) above value	6.00	10.00
29 (29)	0,20 Lek (Ac) 1939–1941. Helmeted bust to right. ℞ double eagle with fasces	1.50	3.00

			VF	XF
30 (30)	0.50	Lek (Ac) 1939–1941. Helmeted bust to left	2.00	3.50
31 (31)	1	Lek (Ac) 1939–1941. Helmeted bust to right	3.00	5.00
32 (32)	2	Lek (Ac) 1939–1941. Helmeted bust to left	4.00	6.00
33 (33)	5	Lek (Ag) 1939. Head of Victor Emmanuel to left	15.00	22.00
34 (34)	10	Lek (Ag) 1939. Head of Victor Emmanuel to right	50.00	80.00

PEOPLE'S REPUBLIC since 1946

35 (35)	½	Lek (Zi) 1947–1957. National arms of the People's Republic with name of country and stars. ℞ value surrounded by stars	0.50	1.00
36 (36)	1	Lek (Zi) 1947–1957	0.60	1.20

37 (37)	2	Lekë (Zi) 1947–1957	1.00	1.80
38 (38)	5	Lekë (Zi) 1947–1957	1.40	2.40
39 (39)	5	Qindarka (Al) 1964. National arms with name of country, stars and date. ℞ value, ears of corn, stars	0.20	0.40
40 (40)	10	Qindarka (Al) 1964	0.20	0.40
41 (41)	20	Qindarka (Al) 1964	0.40	0.80
42 (42)	50	Qindarka (Al) 1964	0.70	1.20

43 (43)	1	Lek (Al) 1964	0.90	1.60

44   5 Lekë (Ag) 1968-1970. Helmet with ram's
horns, arms of the Skanderbeg family
(Castriota) with swords in saltire. *R*
national arms, value

Proof

25.00

45   10 Lekë (Ag) 1968-1970. Equestrian statue of
Skanderbeg in Tirana. *R* as No. 44   40.00

46   20 Lekë (Au) 1968–1970. Helmet with ram's
horns. Oak wreath and sword of the Prince. Rev. as No. 44:
  a) 1968–1970, yellow gold,
     narrow edge milling   85.00
  b) 1968, red gold, wide edge milling
     (c. 24 pcs.) (see ill.)   300.00

47   25 Lekë (Ag) 1968-1970. Sword dancers with
mountains in background. *R* as No. 44   Proof   100.00

48   50 Lekë (Au) 1968-1970. View of Argirocas-
trum. *R* as No. 44   Proof   150.00

49   100 Lekë (Au) 1968-1970. Grape-picking scen-
ce. Rev. as No. 44   Proof   300.00

50 200 Lekë (Au) 1968–1970. Butrinto (Buthrotum), in Epirus: the Apollo head of the so-called »Goddess of Butrinto«, in background Odeon theatre. The coin type refers to Greco-Roman times. It is reported that in the former city of Augusta Buthrotum (in Albanian Butrinti, in Italian Butrinto) the Romans had already placed the head of a young man on top of a headless Greek marble stature – probably that of a goddess. When discovered, this archaeological work of art was therefore described as »the Apollo-like head of the goddess of Butrinto«; it is now in the Archaeological Museum in Tirana. R as No. 44

580.00

51 500 Lekë (Au) 1968–1970. Prince Skanderbeg. R̸ as No. 44   Proof   1 500.00

25th ANNIVERSARY OF LIBERATION (5)

			VF	XF
52 (44)	5	Qindarka (Al) 1969. National emblem; below, date 1944–1969. R̸ value between ears of corn; above, five stars	0.15	0.30
53 (45)	10	Qindarka (Al) 1969. Same type as No. 52	0.25	0.50
54 (46)	20	Qindarka (Al) 1969. Same type as No. 52	0.50	1.00

			VF	XF
55 (47)	50	Qindarka (Al) 1969. Obverse as No. 52. R̸ armed warrior holding torch; below, value	1.00	2.00
56 (48)	1	Lek (Al) 1969. Obverse as No. 52. R̸ battle scene; below, value	1.20	2.40

2600th ANNIVERSARY OF DURAZZO SEAPORT (3)

			Unc	Proof
57	5	Lekë (Cu-Ni) 1987. Sailing vessel	5.00	
58	50	Lekë (Ag) 1987. Type as No. 57		120.00
59	100	Lekë (Au) 1987. Type as No. 57		180.00

Algerien　　　　　　# Algeria　　　　　　**Algérie**

Area: 916,150 sq. mi. Population: 22,000,000.

In ancient times what is now Algeria was part of the Roman Province of Numidia and Mauretania Caesariensis. In the 5th century A. D. it belonged to the Vandalic Empire and towards the end of the 7th century was conquered by the Arabs. The country was then ruled by the Beys of Algeria who had been chosen as sovereigns by the Turkish Janissaries, until the French conquered Algiers in 1830. Later it became a French Department; then, since 1st July 1962 an indepedent republic and finally a People's Republic since 15th September 1963.
Capital: Algiers.

100 Centimes = 1 France
since 1st April 1964: 100 Centimes = 1 Algerian Dinar

FRENCH DEPARTMENT AS PART OF THE FRENCH STATE

			VF	XF
1 (1)	20 Francs (Cu-Ni) 1949, 1956. Marianne, symbol of the French Republic. ℞ value between ears of corn		3.00	6.00

		VF	XF
2 (2)	50 Francs (Cu-Ni) 1949	4.00	7.00
3 (3)	100 Francs (Cu-Ni) 1950, 1952	6.00	10.00

REPUBLIC since 1962

		VF	XF
4 (4)	1 Centime (Al) 1964. National arms within wreath. ℞ value	0.05	0.10
5 (5)	2 Centimes (Al) 1964	0.05	0.10
6 (6)	5 Centimes (Al) 1964	0.10	0.15
7 (7)	10 Centimes (Al-Br) 1964	0.15	0.30
8 (8)	20 Centimes (Al-Br) 1964	0.20	0.40
9 (9)	50 Centimes (Al-Br) 1964	0.25	0.50

		VF	XF
10 (10) 1 Dinar (Cu-Ni) 1964		0.60	1.00

COMMEMORATIVE ISSUE FOR THE
FIRST FOUR-YEAR PLAN 1970/73 AND FOR THE
FAO COIN PLAN

		VF	XF
11 (11) 5 Centimes (Al-Mg) 1970/1973		0.30	0.40

12 (16) 50 Centimes (Al-Br) 1971, 1973. Motto: Reconstruction, Education, Progress — 1.00 | 2.00

COMMEMORATIVE ISSUE (2)
FOR THE AGRICULTURAL REVOLUTION OF 1972
AND FOR THE FAO COIN PLAN

13 (13) 20 Centimes (Bra) 1972. Horn of Plenty with local fruit, date. ℞ denomination — 0.30 | 0.50

				XF	**Unc**

14 (14) 1 Dinar (Cu-Ni) 1972. Tractor between branches. Clasped hands, date. R denomination:

	XF	**Unc**
a) legend far from inner circle (as ill.)	1.00	2.50
b) legend touches inner circle	0.60	1.50

10th ANNIVERSARY OF INDEPENDENCE

15 (15) 5 Dinar 1972. Ear of corn in front of oil derrick between 10 stars. Symbol for 10 years of independence. Dates. *R* denomination between rosettes

a) (Ag)	8.00	12.00
b) (Ni)	4.50	8.00

COMMEMORATIVE ISSUE FOR THE SECOND FOUR-YEAR PLAN 1974/77 AND FOR THE FAO COIN PLAN

16 (12) 5 Centimes (Al-Mg) 1974/1977. Similar to No. 11   0.20   0.35

20th ANNIVERSARY OF REVOLUTION

17 (17) 5 Dinar (Ni) 1974. Revolutionist. *R* as No. 15   4.50   8.00

	XF	Unc
18 (18) 50 Centimes (Bra) 1975. Inscription. *R* value	1.00	1.50

19 (19) 20 Centimes (Cu-Ni) 1975. Head of ram. Rev. value. F.A.O. Issue:

	XF	Unc
a) without rosette above value (as ill.)	0.30	1.00
b) with rosette above value	0.30	1.00

	Unc	Proof
20 (20) 10 Dinar (Al-Br) 1979, 1981. Arabic legend. Rev. value and date	5.00	
21 (20a) 10 Dinar (Ag) 1979. Type as No. 20; .925 silver	25.00	
22 (20b) 10 Dinar (Au) 1979. Type as No. 20; 900 gold		650.00

FOR THE FIVE-YEAR PLAN 1980/84

	XF	Unc
23 5 Centimes (Al) ND (1980/1984). Similar to No. 16, but inscription inside emblem	1.00	2.50

1400th ANNIVERSARY OF MOHAMMED'S FLIGHT

	XF	Unc
24 (21) 50 Centimes (Bra) 1980. Mosque of Medina and Kaaba	0.70	1.50

No. 25 omitted.

20th ANNIVERSARY OF INDEPENDENCE

	XF	Unc
26 (22) 1 Dinar (Cu-Ni) ND (1982). Rising sun. Rev. value	0.90	1.50
27 10 Centimes (Al) 1984. Palm tree. Rev. Valne	0.25	0.50

30th ANNIVERSARY OF REVOLUTION

	XF	Unc
28 5 Dinars (Cu-Ni) 1984	4.00	10.00

FOR THE FIVE-YEAR PLAN 1985/89

	XF	Unc
29 5 Centimes (Al) 1985/1989. Type as No. 16	0.20	0.35

Yeoman Numbers

In order to help collectors and dealers, we have added after most SCHÖN-numbers the corresponding number assigned by R. S. Yeoman in his wellknown works entitled »A Catalog of modern World Coins« and »Current Coins of the World«.

Previos issues, see »Weltmünzkatalog 19. Jahrhundert« (World Coin Catalogue of the 19th Century)

Andorra   # Andorra   **Andorre**

Area: 175 sq. mi. Population: 21,000.
The tiny republic of Andorra in the Pyrenees is under the mutual protection (co-principate) of the North Spanish Bishop of Urgel and the President of the day of the French Republic as legal heir to the Comte de Foix. Capital: Andorra la Vella.
In Andorra French francs and Spanish pesetas are exclusively legal tender. The coinage in Diners are not current coins and are also not in circulation. The designation »Diner« is the Catalan version of the Spanish Dinero or Denario.

1	25 Diners (Ag) 1960. Bust of Carolus Magnus (742–814). ℞ arms	Proof	40.00

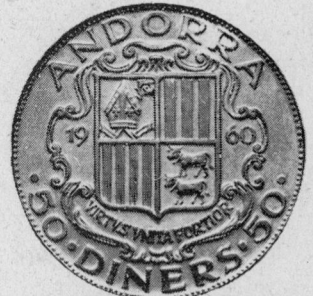

2	50 Diners (Ag) 1960	Proof	50.00

3	25 Diners (Ag) 1963. Bust of J. Benlloch (1864–1926), Bishop of Urgel. ℞ arms	Proof	35.00

| 4 | 50 Diners (Ag) 1963 | Proof | 45.00 |
| 5 | 25 Diners (Ag) 1964. Napoleon I (1769–1821). R arms | Proof | 30.00 |

6   7

6	50 Diners (Ag) 1964. Type as No. 5	Proof	40.00
7	25 Diners (Ag) 1965. House of Council of Justice. R value	Proof	35.00
8	50 Diners (Ag) 1965. Type as No. 7	Proof	50.00

100 Pesetas = 1 Diner

		Unc
9	1 Diner (Bra) 1983. Bust. Rev. arms, value, date	2.50
10	1 Diner (Br) 1984. Bust. Rev. crowned and supported arms, value, date	2.00

11	5 Diners (Cu-Ni) 1984. Type as No. 10	4.00
12	10 Diners (Ag) 1984. Type as No. 10	10.00
13	25 Diners (Ag) 1984. Type as No. 10	20.00

Angola

Area: 481,350 sq. mi. Population: 7,000,000.

In 1483 the Portuguese navigator Diego Cão discovered Angola, in 1485 the estuary of the Congo river and during the years up to 1488 explored the adjacent coastline. By recognizing the local rulers, Portugal organized from here a slave trade to Brazil, founded Luanda (Loanda) in 1576 (the full name: São Paulo de Luanda) and from there extended its rule into the interior which was successfully contested by the Dutch between 1641 and 1648. In the course of the international partitioning of Africa by the European colonial powers (Congo Conference of 1885), the present-day Angola together with Cabinda was awarded to Portugal. The attempt in 1951 of hushing up the colonial regime by redesignating the colonies as (overseas) provinces, eventually miscarried. Three independence movements, hostile among each other, formed in Angola: Frente Nacional de Libertação de Angola (FNLA) (National Liberation Front of Angola), Movimento Popular de Libertação de Angola (People's Movement for the Liberation of Angola), União Nacional de Independencia Total de Angola (UNITA) (National Union for the total independence of Angola). Indepedence was proclaimed on November 11th 1975, and then a People's Republic. Capital: Luanda.

5 Centavos = 1 Macuta; 100 Centavos = 1 Angola-Escudo
since January 10th 1977: 100 Lwei = 1 Kwanza

There was a legal parity with the escudo of the motherland in respect of the escudos circulating in Angola of 1 :1.

COLONY

			VF	XF
1 (12)	1	Centavo (Br) 1921. Arms. ℞ value	10.00	20.00
2 (13)	2	Centavos (Br) 1921	30.00	50.00
3 (14)	5	Centavos (Br) 1921–1924	10.00	16.00
4 (15)	10	Centavos (Cu-Ni) 1921–1923. Liberty head. ℞ arms and value	6.00	10.00
5 (16)	20	Centavos (Cu-Ni) 1921-1922	7.00	11.00
6 (17)	50	Centavos (Ni) 1922, 1923. Liberty head. Rev. arms, value:		
		a) 1922, 1923	6.00	10.00
		b) 1923 KN (King's Norton)		220.00

NEW CURRENCY:

5 Centavos = 1 Macuta, 100 Centavos = 1 Angolar

			VF	XF
7 (18)	5 Centavos = 1 Macuta (Ni-Br) 1927. Liberty head, symbol of the Republic. Rev. arms and value		2.00	5.00
8 (19)	10 Centavos = 2 Macuta (Ni-Br) 1927, 1928		2.00	5.00

		VF	XF
9 (20)	20 Centavos = 4 Macuta (Ni-Br) 1927–1928	4.00	8.00
10 (21)	50 Centavos = 10 Macuta (Ni-Br) 1927–1928	5.00	10.00
11 (22)	10 Centavos (Br) 1948–1949. Arms with mural crown. ℞ value	1.00	2.00
12 (23)	20 Centavos (Br) 1948–1949	1.00	2.00

		VF	XF
13 (24)	50 Centavos (Ni-Br) 1948–1950	1.00	2.00

OVERSEAS PROVINCE

NEW CURRENCY: 100 Centavos = 1 Angola-Escudo

		VF	XF
14 (23a)	20 Centavos (Br) 1962	0.10	0.20
15 (25)	50 Centavos (Br) 1953–1955, 1958, 1961	0.20	0.40
16 (26)	1 Escudo (Br) 1953–1974	0.40	0.60
17 (27)	2½ Escudos (Cu-Ni) 1953–1974. Arms and cross in background. Rev. arms with mural crown and value	0.50	1.00

			XF	Unc
18 (28)	10 Escudos (Ag) 1952, 1955. Type as No. 17		4.00	7.00
19 (29)	20 Escudos (Ag) 1952, 1955. Type as No. 17		4.00	8.00

		XF	Unc
20 (22a)	10 Centavos (Al) 1974. Type as No. 14		10.00
21 (25a)	50 Centavos (Cu-Ni) 1972, 1974. Type as No. 14:		
	1972	–.–	–.–
	1974	90.00	150.00
22 (26a)	1 Escudo (Cu-Ni) 1972, 1974. Type as No. 14	–.–	–.–
23 (A28)	5 Escudos (Cu-Ni) 1972, 1974. Type as No. 17	10.00	15.00
24 (28a)	10 Escudos (Cu-Ni) 1969, 1970. Type as No. 17	4.00	7.00
25 (30)	20 Escudos (Ni) 1971, 1972	2.00	4.00

PEOPLE'S REPUBLIC

NEW CURRENCY: 100 Lwei = 1 Kwanza

		XF	Unc
26 (31)	50 Lwei (Cu-Ni) 1975. Arms, commemorative legend. Rev. value	0.40	1.00
27 (32)	1 Kwanza (Cu-Ni) 1975. Type as No. 26	0.50	1.00
28 (33)	2 Kwanzas (Cu-Ni) 1975. Type as No. 26	0.70	1.40
29 (34)	5 Kwanzas (Cu-Ni) 1975. Type as No. 26	1.00	2.00
30 (35)	10 Kwanzas (Cu-Ni) 1975. Type as No. 26	2.00	3.00

31 (31)	50 Lwei (Cu-Ni) 1979. Arms, commemorative legend. Rev. value, date	0.40	1.00
32 (32)	1 Kwanza (Cu-Ni) 1978, 1979. Type as No. 31	0.50	1.00
35 (35)	10 Kwanzas (Cu-Ni) 1978. Type as No. 31	2.00	3.00
36 (36)	20 Kwanzas (Cu-Ni) 1978. Type as No. 31	2.00	4.00

Values are given each coin in U.S. Dollars and reference to Yeoman-numbers.

Anguilla

Area: 35 sq. mi. Population: 6,000.
Anguilla, also called Snake Island, belongs to the group of the Leeward
Islands (The Lesser Antilles) and administratively is part of the Federa-
tion formed by St. Christopher (St. Kitts), Nevis and Anguilla. On
30th May 1967 it severed all links with the other islands and British
Naval forces had to intervene in 1969.
Capital: The Valley.

100 Cents = 1 Anguilla Dollar

		Proof
1	½ Dollar (Ag) 1969, 1970. Arms, value. Rev. Church of St. Mary	10.00

2	1 Dollar (Ag) 1969, 1970. Topographical map of the island; compass-card, sea-horse (Hippocampus sp. – Syngnathidae), Caribbean silver lobster (Panulirus argus – Panuliridae) and shell of a water-snail or murex (family of the spiny snails = Muricidae). Rev. as No. 1	12.00
3	2 Dollars (Ag) 1969, 1970. Rev. Flag over topographical map	20.00

4   4 Dollars (Ag) 1969, 1970. Rev. The One-and-a-half-master »Atlantic Star«   90.00

5   5 Dollars (Au) 1969, 1970. Rev. West End Methodist Church   50.00

6   10 Dollars (Au) 1969, 1970. Rev. Caribbean silver lobster, common dolphin (Delphinus delphis – Delphinidae) and starfish (Asterias sp. – Asteridae)   90.00

7   20 Dollars (Au) 1969, 1970. Rev. Mermaids, stylized scallop (Pectinidae family), starfish and watersnail shell   180.00

8 100 Dollars (Au) 1969, 1970. Rev. Popular uprising   900.00

All valuations in the SCHÖN are stated in U.S. Dollars.

Antigua

Area: 108 sq. mi. Population: 57,000 (1980).
Belongs to the Lesser Antilles; a member of the Caribbean Free Trade Area
(CARIFTA). Antigua is linked with the other countries of Barbados, Domini-
ca, Grenada, Montserrat, St. Christopher (St. Kitts), Nevis and Anguilla, St.
Lucia and St. Vincent in the Monetary Union of the East Caribbean Dollar.
The issuing authority for the whole Monetary Union is the East Caribbean
Currency Authority with headquarters in Bridgetown, Barbados. Capital: St.
John's.

100 Cents = 1 East Caribbean Dollar

COMMEMORATIVE ISSUE FOR THE INAUGURATION OF THE CARIBBEAN DEVELOPMENT BANK AND FOR THE FAO COIN PLAN

			Unc	Proof
1 (1*)	4	Dollars (Cu-Ni) 1970. Arms with shields held by two ibexes, and helmet decoration. R bananas, sugar-cane and value		
			8.00	25.00

*This number refers to Yeoman's East Caribbean Territories listings.

Antigua and Barbuda

Antigua und Barbuda   **Antigua et Barbuda**

Area: 443 sq. km. Population: 77,000.
In 1981 the Associated State of Antigua, together with Barbuda, became independent as Antigua and Barbuda. Capital: St. John's.

100 Cents = 1 East Caribbean Dollar

250th ANNIVERSARY OF BIRTH OF GEORGE WASHINGTON (3)

			Unc	Proof
1 (2)	30	Dollars (Ag) 1982. Arms. Rev. Yorktown 1781 (battle scene)		50.00
2 (3)	30	Dollars (Ag) 1982. Rev. Washington for Inaugural (1789)		50.00
3 (4)	30	Dollars (Ag) 1982. Washington near Verplanck's Point (1790)		50.00

ROYAL VISIT (2)

		Unc	Proof
4	10 Dollars 1985. Queen Elizabeth II. Rev. arms:		
	a) (Ag)		35.00
	b) (Cu-Ni)	5.00	
5	500 Dollars (Au) 1985. Type as No. 4		900.00

Argentinien # Argentina **Argentine**
República Argentina

Area: 1,554,800 sq. mi. (including the Antarctic possessions). Population: 28,500,000.
The Republic of Argentina consists of 22 provinces, and in addition the federal district of Buenos Aires and the national territory of Tierra del Fuego.
Capital: Buenos Aires.

100 Centavos = 1 Argentine Peso

			VF	XF
1 (7)	5	Centavos (Cu-Ni) 1896–1942. Liberty head facing left (head of Argentina, symbol of the Republic). ℞ value within wreath	0.30	0.80
2 (8)	10	Centavos (Cu-Ni) 1896–1942	0.20	1.00
3 (9)	20	Centavos (Cu-Ni) 1896–1942	0.20	1.00
4 (14)	50	Centavos (Ni) 1941. Of similar description: Nos. 17–21	1.20	2.00
5 (12)	1	Centavo. National arms. ℞ value within wreath		
		a) (Br) 1939–1944	0.20	0.50
		b) (Cu) 1945–1948	0.30	0.80
6 (13)	2	Centavos. National arms. ℞ value within wreath		
		a) (Br) 1939–1947	0.30	0.70
		b) (Cu) 1947–1950	0.30	0.70
7 (15)	5	Centavos (Al-Br) 1942–1950. Head of Argentina, symbol of the Republic, facing right. ℞ value, with ears of corn and ox-head	0.20	0.50
8 (16)	10	Centavos (Al-Br) 1942–1950. Type as No. 7	0.20	0.50
9 (17)	20	Centavos (Al-Br) 1942–1950. Type as No. 7	0.30	0.60
10 (18)	5	Centavos (Cu-Ni) 1950. Bust of General José de San Martin (1778–1850). ℞ value	0.50	1.00

			VF	XF
11 (19)	10	Centavos (Cu-Ni) 1950	0.50	1.00
12 (20)	20	Centavos (Cu-Ni) 1950	0.60	2.00
13 (21)	5	Centavos. bust of José de San Martin. R value, as No. 10 but without commemorative inscription		
		a) (Cu-Ni) 1951–1953	0.20	0.40
		b) (Cu-Ni-St) 1953–1956	0.10	0.20
14 (22)	10	Centavos		
		a) (Cu-Ni) 1951–1952	0.20	0.35
		b) (Cu-Ni-St) 1952–1956	0.10	0.20
15 (23)	20	Centavos		
		a) (Cu-Ni) 1951–1952	0.20	0.40
		b) (Cu-Ni-St) 1952–1956	0.10	0.20
16 (24)	50	Centavos (Cu-Ni-St) 1952–1956	0.50	0.80
17 (25)	5	Centavos (Ni-St) 1957–1959. Head of Argentina, symbol of the Republic, facing left; below, LIBERTAD. R value within wreath, date	0.10	0.20
18 (26)	10	Centavos (Ni-St) 1957–1959	0.10	0.20
19 (27)	20	Centavos (Ni-St) 1957–1961	0.10	0.20
20 (28)	50	Centavos (Ni-St) 1957–1961	0.20	0.40

21 (29)	1	Peso (Ni-St) 1957–1962	0.30	0.50

COMMEMORATIVE ISSUE FOR THE 150th ANNIVERSARY OF THE REMOVAL OF THE SPANISH VICEROY 25th MAI 1810

22 (30)	1	Peso (St) 1960. The old townhall in Buenos Aires. R national arms and value	0.50	1.00

		VF	XF
23 (31)	5 Pesos (St) 1961–1968. The sail training ship "Presidente Sarmiento". ℞ value	0.30	0.50

24 (32)	10 Pesos (St) 1962–1968. Gaucho. ℞ value	0.30	0.50

ISSUE COMMEMORATING THE 1st ISSUE OF NATIONAL COINAGE IN 1813

25 (33)	25 Pesos (St) 1964–1968. Representation of the 8-Reales piece of 1813. ℞ reverse of the same coin	0.50	1.00

ISSUE COMMEMORATING THE 150th ANNIVERSARY OF THE DECLARATION OF INDEPENDENCE

26 (34)	10 Pesos (St) 1966. The National Museum in Tucumán. It was in this building that the Declaration of Independence for the United Province of Rio de la Plata was read on 9th July 1816. ℞ value	0.30	0.60

ISSUE COMMEMORATING THE 80th ANNIVERSARY OF THE DEATH OF D. F. SARMIENTO

27 (35) 25 Pesos (Ni) 1968. Head of Domingo Faustino Sarmiento (1811–1888), politician, writer, pedagogue, President of State 1868–1874. ℞ value (dodecagonal)

	XF	Unc
27 (35)	0.60	1.00

CURRENCY REFORM:
1st January 1970: 100 old Pesos = 1 new Peso

		XF	Unc
28 (36)	1 Centavo (Al-Mg) 1970–1975. Head of Argentina, symbol of the Republic, facing left. Rev. laurel branch, value, date	0.05	0.10
29 (37)	5 Centavos (Al-Mg) 1970–1975. Type as No. 28	0.10	0.20
30 (38)	10 Centavos (Cu-Ni) 1970, 1971, 1973–1976. Type as No. 28	0.10	0.20
31 (39)	20 Centavos (Cu-Ni) 1970–1976. Type as No. 28	0.12	0.25
32 (40)	50 Centavos (Cu-Ni) 1970–1976. Type as No. 28	0.20	0.40

		XF	Unc
33 (41)	1 Peso (Bra) 1974–1976. Sun with rays. Rev. value	0.25	0.50
34 (42)	5 Pesos (Al-Br) 1976–1978. Type as No. 33	0.30	0.60
35 (43)	10 Pesos (Al-Br) 1976–1979. Type as No. 33	0.35	0.70

Values are given for each coin in U.S. Dollars and reference to Yeoman-numbers.

			XF	Unc
36 (44)	20	Pesos (Ni-Bra) 1977, 1978. World Cup emblem, value. *R* two soccer players	0.50	1.00

			XF	Unc
37 (45)	50	Pesos (Ni-Bra) 1977, 1978, *R* soccer player. Global grid background	0.50	1.00

38 (46)	100	Pesos (Ni-Bra) 1977, 1978. *R* soccer stadium. Global grid background	1.00	1.50

			Unc	Proof
39 (47)	1000	Pesos (Ag) 1977, 1978. *R* radiant sun face. Legend "ARGENTINA 78, BUENOS AIRES, CORDOBA, MAR DEL PLATA, MENDOZA, ROSARIO"	5.00	20.00
40 (48)	2000	Pesos (Ag) 1977, 1978. *R* large Argentinian coat of arms in center and 5 small coats of arms of cities above	10.00	25.00
41 (49)	3000	Pesos (Ag) 1977, 1978. *R* globe featuring South America in center above laurel sprigs	15.00	35.00

		XF	Unc
42 (50)	5 Pesos (Al-Br) 1977. Guillermo Brown (1777-1857), admiral	0.25	0.50
43 (51)	10 Pesos (Al-Br) 1977. Type as No. 42	0.40	0.80

200th BIRTHDAY OF GENERAL JOSE DE SAN MARTIN (2)

44 (52)	50 Pesos (Al-Br) 1978. General José de San Martin (1778–1850)	0.50	1.00
45 (53)	100 Pesos (Al-Br) 1978. Type as No. 44	0.80	1.50

46 (54)	50 Pesos (Al-Br) 1979, 1980. Type as No. 44, but laurel branch instead of dates behind head	0.50	1.00
47 (55)	100 Pesos (Al-Br) 1979–1981. Type as No. 46	0.80	1.50

CONQUEST OF PATAGONIA CENTENNIAL (2)

48 (56)	50 Pesos (Al-Br) 1979	0.50	1.00

				XF	Unc

49 (57) 100 Pesos (Al-Br) 1979. Type as No. 48   0.80   1.50
50 (54a) 50 Pesos (Bronze-clad steel) 1980, 1981.
    Type as No. 46   0.50   1.00
51 (55a) 100 Pesos (Bronze-clad steel) 1980, 1981.
    Type as No. 47   0.40   0.60

CURRENCY REFORM:
1st June 1983: 10,000 old Pesos = 1 (new) Peso Argentino

52 (58) 1 Centavo (Al) 1983. Head of Argentina,
    symbol of the Republic. Rev. value,
    date   0.05   0.10
53 (59) 5 Centavos (Al) 1983. Type as No. 52   0.05   0.10
54 (60) 10 Centavos (Al) 1983. Type as No. 52   0.05   0.10
55 (61) 50 Centavos (Al) 1983. Type as No. 52   0.10   0.15

56 (62) 1 Peso (Al) 1984. Building of National
    Congress. Rev. value, date   0.10   0.20
57 (63) 5 Pesos (Bra) 1984, 1985. Buenos Aires
    city hall. Rev. value, date   0.20   0.40
58 (64) 10 Pesos (Bra) 1984, 1985. The National
    Museum in Tucumán (see No. 26).
    Rev. value, date   0.30   0.50

5Oth ANNIVERSARY OF CENTRAL BANK

59 (65) 50 Pesos (Al-Ni-Br) 1985. Emblem of the
    Central Bank   0.60   1.00

NEW CURRENCY: 100 Centavos = 1 Austral

60 ½ Centavo (Bra) 1985   0.10
61 1 Centavo (Bra) 1985, 1987   0.10
62 5 Centavos (Bra) 1985   0.15
63 10 Centavos (Bra) 1985, 1986   0.30
64 50 Centavos (Bra) 1985   1.00

Values are given for each coin in U.S. Dollars and reference to Yeoman-numbers.

Aruba

193 sq. km.; Population: 30,000.
Aruba, part of the Netherlands Antilles, on Jan. 1, 1986 achieved a special
status "Status aparte" of self-government, but constitutes part of the Kingdom of the Netherlands. Capital: Oranjestad.
100 Cent = 1 Aruba-Gulden (Aruba-Florin)

BEATRIX since 1980

		XF	Unc
1	5 Cent (Nickel-clad steel) 1986, 1987	0.10	0.15
2	10 Cent (Nickel-clas steel) 1986, 1987	0.10	0.25
3	25 Cent (Nickel-clad steel) 1986, 1987	0.20	0.50
4	50 Cent (Nickel-clad steel) 1986, 1987	0.40	1.00
5	1 Florin (Nickel-clad steel) 1986, 1987	0.80	2.00
6	2½ Florin (Nickel-clad steel) 1986, 1987	2.00	4.00
7	5 Florin		–.–

SELF-GOVERNMENT COMMEMORATIVE

		Unc	Proof
8	25 Florin (Ag) 1986. Rev. Arms, value, commemorative legend	30.00	40.00

Area 38 sq. mi. Population: 1,231.
Ascension Island owes its name to the same Portuguese explorer, Joao da
Nova, who discovered it on Ascension Day, 1501. Exactly two centuries later William Dampier was wrecked on its shore, but it remained uninhabited
until 1815 when it was garrisoned by British troops, to forestall any attempts
by Bonapartists to rescue Napoleon from St. Helena 700 miles to the south-
east. Until 1922 it was transferred to the Colonial Office and became a dependency of St. Helena. In addition to the cable station operated by Cable
and Wireless Ltd., it has a BBC relay station and a NASA tracking station.

100 Pence = 1 £; 25 Pence = 1 Crown

25th ANNIVERSARY OF THE CORONATION OF HER MAJESTY QUEEN ELIZABETH II

	Unc	Proof
1 (1) 1 Crown 1978.		
The Lion of England superimposed on the		
Green Turtle of Ascension:		
a) (Ag)	15.00	25.00
b) (Cu-Ni)	2.50	

WEDDING OF PRINCE CHARLES AND LADY DIANA

2 (2) 25 Pence 1981:		
a) (Ag)		40.00
b) (Cu-Ni)	3.00	

			Unc	Proof
3 (3)	25	Pence (Ag) 1982. Rev. Lord Baden-Powell	20.00	30.00
4 (4)	2	£ (Au) 1982. Rev. Boy Scout viewing landscape	250.00	300.00

VISIT OF PRINCE ANDREW (2)

			Unc	Proof
5 (5)	50	Pence 1984. Prince Andrew:		
		a) (Ag)		30.00
		b) (Ag), Pièfort		100.00
		c) (Cu-Ni)	3.00	
6 (6)	50	Pence (Au) 1984. Type as No. 5		–.–

For later issues, see under St. Helena.

Values are given for each coin in U.S. Dollars and reference to Yeoman-numbers.

Australien   # Australia   **Australie**

Area: 2,574,980 sq. mi. Population: 14,800,000.

First discovered by 17th century Dutch navigators, later claimed for Great Britain by Captain Cook, who first landed south of what is today Sidney (1770). Colonised for the next 50 years mainly as an English penal settlement. The discovery of gold in 1851 led to much more extensive exploration of the continent (population increase during 50 years from 405,000 in 1850 to 3,770,000 by 1900. Today comprises 6 states within the independent Commonwealth of Australia. Until 1927 the capital was Melbourne, since when it has been Canberra.

Until decimalisation of the coinage in Feb. 1966, when the Canberra Mint opened, Australian coins were mainly struck at various English mints, more occasionally at Bombay and Calcutta.

Capital: Canberra.

12 Pence = 1 Shilling. 2 Shillings = 1 Florin. 20 Shillings = 1 £.
Since 14th February 1966: 100 Cents = 1 Australian Dollar.

EDWARD VII 1901–1910

		VF	XF
1 (1)	3 Pence (Ag) 1910. Edward VII (1841–1910). Crowned bust of Edward VII to right. ℞ arms supported by great red kangaroo (Macropus = Megaleia rufus – Macropodidae) and emu (Dromaeus novaehollandiae – Dromaiidae or Dromiceidae)	12.00	35.00
2 (2)	6 Pence (Ag) 1910. Type as No. 1	22.00	55.00
3 (3)	1 Shilling (Ag) 1910. Type as No. 1	35.00	100.00

			VF	XF
4 (4)	1 Florin = 2 Shillings (Ag) 1910. Type as No. 1		180.00	400.00
5 (A 5)	½ £ (Au) 1902–1910. Edward VII. ℞ St. George and the Dragon		85.00	110.00

		VF	XF
6 (B5)	1 £ (Au) 1902–1910. Type as No. 5	135.00	150.00
7 (C5)	2 £ (Au) 1902. Type as No. 5	–.–	–.–
8 (D5)	5 £ (Au) 1902. Type as No. 5	–.–	–.–

Coins Nos. 5–8 differ only from similar pieces issued at the same time in Great Britain because of the mint marks. M = Melbourne, P = Perth or S = Sydney.

GEORGE V 1910–1936

		VF	XF
9 (5)	½ Penny (Br) 1911–1936. Head of George V (1865–1936). ℞ value in circle	1.00	10.00

				VF	XF
10 (6)	1	Penny (Br) 1911–1936		1.00	10.00
		a) 1930		3500.00	6000.00
11 (9)	3	Pence (Ag) 1911–1936. Head of George			
			V. Rev. arms	3.00	15.00
12 (10)	6	Pence (Ag) 1911–1936		5.00	15.00
13 (11)	1	Shilling (Ag) 1911–1936		10.00	30.00
14 (12)	1	Florin (Ag) 1911–1936		15.00	40.00
		a) 1932		*500.00*	*2000.00*

				VF	XF
15 (A13)	½ £ (Au) 1911–1918. Head of George V.				
	R St. George and the Dragon:				
		a) 1911, 1912, 1914–1916		100.00	150.00
		b) 1918 P		*600.00*	*1000.00*
16 (B13)	1 £ (Au) 1911–1931			120.00	150.00

Coins Nos. 15 and 16 differ only from similar pieces issued at the same time in Great Britain because of the mint marks. M = Melbourne, P = Perth or S = Sydney. The Sydney mint was closed in 1926. There are no mint marks on silver coins after 1921.

ISSUE COMMEMORATING THE OPENING OF PARLIAMENT IN CANBERRA

			VF	XF
17 (7)	1 Florin (Ag) 1927. Bust of George V.			
	R Parliament buildings in Canberra		10.00	22.00
			Proof	1600.00

ISSUE COMMEMORATING THE CENTENARY OF VICTORIA AND MELBOURNE

			VF	XF
18 (8)	1	Florin (Ag) 1934–1935. Bust of George V. ℞ horseman holding torch	180.00	250.00

GEORGE VI 1936–1952

			VF	XF
19 (13)	½	Penny (Br) 1938–1939. Head of George VI (1895–1952). R value in circle:		
		a) 1938	0.50 Proof	3.00 350.00
		b) 1939	1.00 Proof	5.00 400.00
20 (14)	½	Penny (Br) 1939–1948. Head of George VI. ℞ great red kangaroo (Macropus = Megaleia rufus – Macropodidae)	0.40 Proof	2.00 300.00

			VF	XF
21 (15)	1	Penny (Br) 1938–1948. ℞ great red kangaroo	0.40 Proof	2.00 350.00

In the period 1942–1944 Australian silver coins were struck in the cities of Denver and San Francisco, U.S.A. From this period come the coins which bear on reverse the mintmark "D" or "S".

			VF	XF
22 (16)	3	Pence (Ag) 1938–1948. ℞ ears of wheat	0.50	1.00
23 (17)	6	Pence (Ag) 1938–1948. ℞ arms	1.00	3.00
24 (18)	1	Shilling (Ag) 1938–1948. ℞ head of a Merino ram (Ovis ammon aries – Bovidae)	3.00	6.00
25 (19)	1	Florin (Ag) 1938–1947. ℞ crowned arms	4.00	7.00

				VF	XF
26 (20)	1	Crown (Ag) 1937–1938. Rev. crown:			
		a) 1937		12.00	25.00
				Proof	2500.00
		b) 1938		75.00	150.00
				Proof	2000.00
27 (21)	½	Penny (Br) 1949–1952. ℞ great red kangaroo to right		0.30	2.00
28 (22)	1	Penny (Br) 1949–1952		0.30	1.00
29 (24)	3	Pence (Ag) 1949–1952. ℞ ears of wheat		0.50	2.00
30 (25)	6	Pence (Ag) 1950–1952. ℞ arms		1.00	3.00
31 (26)	1	Shilling (Ag) 1950–1952. ℞ head of a Merino ram		3.00	6.00
32 (27)	1	Florin (Ag) 1951–1952. ℞ crowned arms		5.00	10.00

COMMEMORATIVE ISSUE FOR THE 50th ANNIVERSARY OF THE COMMONWEALTH OF AUSTRALIA

			VF	XF
33 (23)	1	Florin (Ag) 1951. Head of George VI to l. ℞ crown above sceptre and sword in saltire, as well as stars in the form of the "Southern Cross"	4.00	8.00

ELIZABETH II since 1952

			VF	XF
34 (28)	½	Penny (Br) 1953–1955. Bust of Elizabeth II (*1926). ℞ great red kangaroo to right	0.30	1.00
35 (29)	1	Penny (Br) 1953. Great red kangaroo to left	0.50	2.00

			VF	XF
36 (30)	3 Pence (Ag) 1953–1954. ℞ ears of wheat		2.00	5.00
37 (31)	6 Pence (Ag) 1953–1954. ℞ arms		1.00	3.00

| 38 (32) | 1 Shilling (Ag) 1953–1954. ℞ Merino ram | | 3.00 | 5.00 |

| 39 (33) | 1 Florin (Ag) 1953–1954. ℞ crowned arms | | 5.00 | 8.00 |

ISSUE COMMEMORATING THE VISIT OF THE BRITISH ROYAL COUPLE

| 40 (34) | 1 Florin (Ag) 1954. Bust of Elizabeth II. ℞ great red kangaroo and lion, animals representative of Australia and Great Britain | | 3.00 | 6.00 |

Coins Nos. 40–46 have the letters F: D: added to the obverse legend.

41 (35)	½ Penny (Br) 1959–1964		0.15	0.50
42 (36)	1 Penny (Br) 1955–1964		0.20	0.50
43 (37)	3 Pence (Ag) 1955–1964. ℞ ears of weath		0.40	0.80

		VF	XF
44 (38)	6 Pence (Ag) 1955–1963. ℞ arms	0.60	1.00
45 (39)	1 Shilling (Ag) 1955–1963. ℞ head of a Merino ram	1.00	2.00
46 (40)	1 Florin (Ag) 1956–1963. ℞ crowned arms	2.50	5.00

NEW VALUE: 100 Cents = 1 Australian Dollar

		XF	Unc
47 (41)	1 Cent (Br) 1966–1984. Bust of the Queen right. Rev. Australian ring-tailed opossum or pigmy flying phalanger (Acrobates pygmaeus – Phalangeridae)	0.05	0.10
48 (42)	2 Cent (Br) 1966–1984. Rev. frilled lizard (Chlamydosaurus kingii – Agamidae)	0.05	0.10
49 (43)	5 Cents (Cu-Ni) 1966–1984. Rev. Australian short-beaked spiny ant-eater (Tachyglossus aculeatus – Tachyglossidae)	0.10	0.20

50 (44) 10 Cents (Cu-Ni) 1966–1984. Rev. Superb

		XF	Unc
lyre-bird (Menura novaehollandiae – Menuridae)		0.15	0.30

51 (45) 20 Cents (Cu-Ni) 1966–1984. Rev. Duck-billed platypus (Duckbill) (Ornithorhynchus anatius – Ornithorhynchidae)   0.20   0.40

52 (46) 50 Cents (Ag) 1966. Crowned bust of Elizabeth II facing right. Rev. arms   4.00   7.00

53 (47) 50 Cents (Cu-Ni) 1969, 1971–1976, 1978–1981, 1983, 1984 (dodecagonal)   0.40   1.00

Yeoman Numbers

In order to help collectors and dealers, we have added after most SCHÖN-numbers the corresponding number assigned by R.S. Yeoman in his wellknown works entitled »A Catalog of Modern World Coins« and »Current Coins of the World«.

ISSUE COMMEMORATING THE 200th ANNIVERSARY OF COOK'S SEA VOYAGE ALONG THE EAST COAST OF AUSTRALIA

		XF	Unc
54 (48) 50	Cents (Cu-Ni) 1970. James Cook (1728–1779), famous English world sailor; inscription; sketch of Australia and sea route (dodecagonal)	2.00	5.00
		Proof	50.00

SILVER JUBILEE OF HER MAJESTY QUEEN ELIZABETH II

55 (49) 50 Cents (Cu-Ni) 1977	0.60	1.50
	Proof	18.00

	Unc	Proof
56 (50) 200 Dollars (Au) 1980–1984. Koala Bear. .917 gold, 10.000 g:		
a) 1980	200.00	350.00
b) 1983	180.00	250.00
c) 1984	180.00	250.00

			Unc	Proof
57 (51)	50	Cents (Cu-Ni) 1981. Rev. Conjoined heads	1.50	
58 (52)	200	Dollars (Au) 1981. Typ as No. 57	160.00	

XII COMMONWEALTH GAMES BRISBANE (3)

			Unc	Proof
59 (53)	50	Cents (Cu-Ni) 1982	2.00	10.00
60 (54)	10	Dollars (Ag) 1982	25.00	40.00
61 (55)	200	Dollars (Au) 1982	160.00	180.00
62	1	Dollar (Cu-Ni-Al) 1984. Rev. Five kangaroos	1.50	12.00
63	1	Dollar (Ag) 1984. Typ as No. 62		20.00

			XF	Unc
64	1	Cent (Br) 1985–. New bust of Elizabeth II. Rev. as No. 47	0.05	0.10
65	2	Cents (Br) 1985–. Rev. as No. 48	0.05	0.10
66	5	Cents (Cu-Ni) 1985–. Rev. as No. 49	0,10	0.20
67	10	Cents (Cu-Ni) 1985–. Rev as No. 50	0.15	0.30
68	20	Cents (Cu-Ni) 1985–. Rev. as No. 51	0.20	0.40
69	50	Cents (Cu-Ni) 1985–. Rev. as No. 53	0.50	1.00
70	1	Dollar (Cu-Ni-Al) 1985–. Rev. as No. 62	1.00	1.50
71	200	Dollars (Au) 1985–1987. Rev. as No. 56	170.00	240.00

150th ANNIVERSARY OF THE STATE OF VICTORIA

		Unc	Proof
72	10 Dollars (Ag) 1985	15.00	30.00

INTERNATIONAL YEAR OF PEACE 1986

73	1 Dollar (Cu-Ni-Al) 1986	1.50	20.00

150th ANNIVERSARY OF SOUTH AUSTRALIA

74	10 Dollars (Ag) 1986	15.00	30.00

BULLION ISSUES »NUGGETS« (4)

75	10 Dollars (Au) 1986–1988. Elizabeth II, value. Rev. Nugget »Little Hero« (1890); .999.9 gold, 3.11 g:	
	1986	100.00
	1987, 1988	–.–
76	25 Dollars (Au) 1986–1988. Rev. Nugget »Golden Eagle« (1931); .999.9 gold, 7.77 g:	
	1986	250.00
	1987, 1988	–.–
77	50 Dollars (Au) 1986–1988. Rev. Nugget »Hand of Faith« (1980); .999.9 gold, 15.55 g:	
	1986	450.00
	1987, 1988	–.–
78	100 Dollars (Au) 1986–1988. Rev. Nugget »Welcome Stranger« (1869); .999.9 gold, 31.10 g:	
	1986	900.00
	1987, 1988	–.–

NEW SOUTH WALES

		Unc	Proof
79	10 Dollars (Ag) 1987	15.00	30.00

BULLION ISSUES »NUGGETS« (4)

80	10 Dollars (Au) 1987. Rev. Nugget »Golden Aussie«; .999.9 gold, 3.11 g	–.–
81	25 Dollars (Au) 1987. Rev. Nugget »Father's Day«; .999.9 gold, 7.77 g	–.–
82	50 Dollars (Au) 1987. Rev. Nugget »Bobby Dazzler«; .999.9 gold, 15.55 g	–.–

83 100 Dollars (Au) 1987. Rev. Nugget »Posei-
don«; .999.9 gold, 31.10 g   –.–
84 200 Dollars 1987

200th ANNIVERSARY OF IMMIGRATION (4)

85 50 Cents 1988
86   1 Dollar 1988
87   2 Dollars (Cu-Ni-Al) 1988
88 10 Dollars (Ag) 1988

89 200 Dollars (Au) 1988

                                                            Proof

90   5 Dollars (Cu-Ni-Al) 1988. New Parliament
building   –.–

BULLION ISSUES »NUGGETS« (4)

91 10 Dollars (Au) 1988   –.–
92 25 Dollars (Au) 1988   –.–
93 50 Dollars (Au) 1988   –.–
94 100 Dollars (Au) 1988   –.–

Österreich **Austria** **Autriche**

Area: 32,374 sq. mi. Population: 7,570,000.
For centuries the history of Austria and that of Germany as parts of the Holy
Roman Empire were very closely connected. Until the disintegration of the
Holy Roman Empire in 1806, the House of Habsburg provided a long line of
remarkable rulers. After the breakdown of the Danube Monarchy into indi-
vidual states and the renunciation of the throne by Emperor Karl, a republic
was created.
Capital: Vienna.

100 Heller = 1 Krone, 10 000 Kronen = 1 Schilling,
100 Groschen = 1 Schilling

FRANZ JOSEPH 1848–1916

1 (23c) 1 Ducat (Au) 1872–1915. Laureate head
facing right of Franz Joseph (1830–1916).

	Vf	SF
R double eagle:		
a) 1872-1914	80.00	100.00
b) 1915. Proof restrike		50.00
c) 1951. Mint error for 1915	120.00	150.00

2 (25c) 4 Ducats (Au) 1872-1915. Type as No. 1,
but laureate bust:

a) 1872-1914	250.00	300.00
b) 1915. Proof restrike	110.00	120.00

	VF	XF

3 (26) 1 Heller (Cu) 1892–1916. Double eagle
with shield. ℞ value 0.40 0.80
4 (28) 2 Heller (Cu) 1892–1915 0.35 0.70

5 (29) 10 Heller (Ni) 1892–1911 0.50 0.80
6 (30) 20 Heller (Ni) 1892–1914 0.80 1.60

7 (35) 1 Krone (Ag) 1892–1907. Laureate bust
facing right of Franz Joseph (1830–
1916). ℞ crown above value 2.50 6.00

8 (39) 5 Kronen (Ag) 1900, 1907. ℞ eagle
within circle, the whole surrounded
by crowns and laurel branches 12.00 25.00
9 (42) 10 Kronen (Au) 1892–1906. Rev. double
eagle:
a) 1892   1500.00
b) 1896, 1897, 1905, 1906 40.00 50.00
10 (43) 20 Kronen (Au) 1892–1905 85.00 100.00

				VF	XF
11 (36)	1	Krone (Ag) 1908. Head of Franz Joseph facing right. R crown above monogram, dates 1848–1908		3.00	5.00

12 (40)	5	Kronen (Ag) 1908. R running figure of Fame, dates 1848–1908		12.50	18.00

13 (44)	10	Kronen (Au) 1908. R double eagle, dates 1848–1908		50.00	60.00
14 (45)	20	Kronen (Au) 1908. Type as No. 13		140.00	180.00

15 (46)	100	Kronen (Au) 1908. R resting figure of Fame with coat of arms		750.00	1000.00
16 (41)	5	Kronen (Ag) 1909		15.00	25.00

		VF	XF
17 (47)	10 Kronen (Au) 1909	35.00	50.00
18 (48)	20 Kronen (Au) 1909	650.00	800.00
19 (37)	1 Krone (Ag) 1912–1916. Head of Franz Joseph facing right, signature: St. Schwartz. ℞ crown above value	1.80	2.40
20 (38)	2 Kronen (Ag) 1912–1913	3.00	5.00
21 (A 41)	5 Kronen (Ag) 1909. Type as No. 16, but smaller head	12.50	20.00

		VF	XF
22 (49)	10 Kronen (Au)		
	a) 1909–1911	35.00	50.00
	b) 1912, mostly re-strikes	25.00	30.00
23 (50)	20 Kronen (Au)		
	a) 1909–1916	130.00	160.00
	b) 1915, mostly re-strikes	50.00	60.00

		VF	XF
24 (51)	100 Kronen (Au)		
	a) 1909–1916	600.00	750.00
	b) 1915, mostly re-strikes	200.00	250.00

There are official re-strikes of coins Nos. 22–24, which are very difficult to differentiate from the originals.

		VF	XF
25 (31)	10 Heller (Cu–Zi) 1915–1916. Double eagle. ℞ value within wreath	0.25	0.50

		VF	XF
26 (27)	1 Heller (Cu) 1916. Type as No. 3, but double eagle now with filleted shield	5.00	10.00

			VF	**XF**
27 (32)	10	Heller (Cu–Zi) 1916. Type as No. 5, but double eagle now with filleted shield	0.60	1.00
28 (52)	20	Kronen (Au) 1916. Type as No. 23, but double eagle now with filleted shield	500.00	600.00
29 (33)	2	Heller (Fe) 1916. Double eagle with filleted shield. ℞ value surrounded by laurel branches	0.90	2.50

For coin No. 29, as first issue of Karl I, see under No. 31

30 (34)	20	Heller (Fe) 1916. Double eagle. ℞ value within wreath	0.70	1.20

For coin No. 30, as first issue of Karl I, see under No. 32

KARL I 1916–1918

31 (33)	2	Heller (Fe) 1917–1918. Type as No. 29	0.40	0.80
32 (34)	20	Heller (Fe) 1917–1918. Type as No. 30	0.40	0.80
33	20	Kronen (Au) 1918. Head to right of Karl I (1887–1922). ℞ double eagle with filleted shield	——	——

Of No. 33 there is only one known specimen left in existence, which is found in the Münzkabinett in Vienna.

1st REPUBLIC 1918–1938

Austria: Federal Provinces

Burgenland	Carinthia	Lower Austria	Upper Austria	Salzburg

| | | Styria | Tyrol | Vorarlberg | Vienna |

			VF	XF
34 (56)	100	Kronen (Br) 1923–1924. Head of eagle. Rev. value and oak leaves:		
		a) 1923	12.00	20.00
		b) 1924	0.60	1.00
35 (57)	200	Kronen (Br) 1924. Kruckenkreuz (similar to the cross of Jerusalem). ℞ value	1.00	1.60
36 (58)	1000	Kronen (Cu–Ni) 1924. Tyrolese woman's head. ℞ value within wreath	2.00	4.00
37 (80)	20	Kronen (Au) 1923–1924. Crowned eagle bearing national arms and holding symbols of agricultural and industrial workers in its claws. ℞ value within wreath	750.00	900.00
38 (81)	100	Kronen (Au) 1923–1924. Type as No. 37	1300.00	1750.00

Values are given for each coin in U.S. Dollars and reference to Yeoman-numbers.

		VF	XF
39 (60)	1 Groschen (Br) 1925–1938. Head of eagle. ℞ value	0.40	0.80
40 (61)	2 Groschen (Br) 1925–1938. Kruckenkreuz. Rev. value	0.40	0.80

41 (62)	5 Groschen (Cu-Ni) 1931–1938. Krukkenkreuz. Rev. value:		
	a) 1931, 1932, 1934, 1936, 1937	0.60	1.00
	b) 1938	200.00	300.00

42 (63)	10 Groschen (Cu–Ni) 1925–1929. Tyrolese woman's head. ℞ value within wreath	1.00	1.60
43 (67)	½ Schilling (Ag) 1925–1926. Arms. ℞ value	3.00	5.00

44	1 Schilling (Ag) Parliament building in Vienna. R arms with national colours between laurel branches, value		
	a) (Y 59) 1924	4.00	8.00
	b) (Y 68) 1925–1926; smaller dia.	2.50	4.00
	c) (Y 68) 1932; smaller dia.	65.00	100.00

45 (82) 25 Schilling (Au) 1926–1934. Crowned
eagle bearing national arms and hold-
ing symbols of agricultural and industrial workers in its claws. ℞ value and
laurel branches

	VF	XF
	80.00	100.00

46 (83) 100 Schilling (Au) 1926–1934. Type as No. 45   320.00   400.00

COMMEMORATIVE ISSUE FOR THE CENTENARY OF THE DEATH OF F. SCHUBERT

47 (69) 2 Schilling (Ag) 1928. Bust left of Franz
Schubert (1797–1828), composer. ℞
value within wreath of shields: these
are the armorial shields of the nine
Federal Provinces, surmounted by a
shield with the Austrian national col-
ours   7.00   10.00

COMMEMORATIVE ISSUE FOR THE CENTENARY OF THE BIRTH OF BILLROTH

			VF	XF
48 (70)	2 Schilling (Ag) 1929. Bust facing left of Prof. Dr. Theodor Billroth (1829–1894), surgeon. ℞ as No. 47		12.00	22.00

COMMEMORATIVE ISSUE FOR THE 700th ANNIVERSARY OF THE DEATH OF WALTHER VON DER VOGELWEIDE

49 (71)	2 Schilling (Ag) 1930. Walther von der Vogelweide (c. 1170–1230), minstrel. R as No. 47	8.00	12.50

COMMEMORATIVE ISSUE FOR THE 175th ANNIVERSARY OF THE BIRTH OF MOZART

50 (72)	2 Schilling (Ag) 1931. Bust facing right of Wolfgang Amadeus Mozart (1756–1791), composer. ℞ as No. 47	20.00	32.00

COMMEMORATIVE ISSUE FOR THE 200th ANNIVERSARY OF THE BIRTH OF HAYDN

			VF	XF
51 (73)	2	Schilling (Ag) 1932. Bust facing left of Joseph Haydn (1732–1809), composer. ℞ as No. 47	50.00	80.00

COMMEMORATIVE ISSUE FOR THE CENTENARY OF THE DEATH OF DR. SEIPEL

52 (74)	2	Schilling (Ag) 1933. Bust facing right of Dr. Ignaz Seipel (1876–1932), Federal Chancellor from 1922 to 1924 and from 1926 to 1929. ℞ as No. 47	28.00	40.00

53 (64)	50	Groschen (Cu-Ni) 1934. Double-headed eagle with haloes and national arms, without symbols in its claws; date. ℞ value within square ("Nacht-schilling")	40.00	70.00

54 (65) 50 Groschen (Cu–Ni) 1935–1936. Double-headed eagle as No. 53, surrounded by name of country. ℞ value

	VF	XF
	2.50	6.00

55 (66) 1 Schilling (Cu–Ni) 1934–1935. Obverse as No. 53. ℞ value and ears of corn

	2.00	4.00

56 (79) 5 Schilling (Ag) 1934–1936. The Madonna of Mariazell. ℞ double-headed eagle, value

	28.00	40.00

57 (85) 100 Schilling (Au) 1935–1938. Obverse as No. 56. Rev. similar to No. 56

a) 1935–1937	800.00	1000.00
b) 1938	5000.00	6500.00

COMMEMORATIVE ISSUE FOR DR. E. DOLLFUSS

58 (75) 2 Schilling (Ag) 1934. Bust right of Dr. Engelbert Dollfuss (1892–1934), Federal Chancellor from 1932 to 1934. ℞ double-headed eagle with haloes and national arms, without symbols in its claws; value, date

	VF	XF
	16.00	25.00

COMMEMORATIVE ISSUE FOR DR. K. LUEGER

59 (76) 2 Schilling (Ag) 1935. Bust facing right of Dr. Karl Lueger (1844–1910). politician, social reformer. R as No. 58   18.00   32.00

60 (84) 25 Schilling (Au) 1935–1938. Facing bust of St. Leopold. Rev. as No. 57:
a) 1935–1937   420.00   550.00
b) 1938   4000.00   5000.00

200th ANNIVERSARY OF THE DEATH OF PRINCE EUGEN

	VF	XF
61 (77) 2 Schilling (Ag) 1936. Prince Eugen of Savoy (1663–1736), Imperial Austrian Field-Marshal	14.00	20.00

COMMEMORATIVE ISSUE FOR J. B. FISCHER VON ERLACH

62 (78) 2 Schilling (Ag) 1937. The Karlskirche (St. Charles Church) in Vienna	15.00	22.00

2nd REPUBLIC since 1945

63 (86) 1 Groschen (Zinc) 1947. Arms. Rev. Value	0.20	0.30

64 (89) 2 Groschen (Al) 1950–1952, 1954, 1957, 1962, 1964–1988	0.10	0.15

	VF	XF
65 (87) 5 Groschen (Zinc) 1948, 1950, 1951, 1953, 1955, 1957, 1961–1988	0.10	0.15

66 (88) 10 Groschen (Zi) 1947–1949	0.80	2.00

67 (90) 10 Groschen (Al) 1951–1953, 1955, 1957, 1959, 1961–1988	0.10	0.15

68 (95) 20 Groschen (Al–Br) 1950, 1951, 1954	0.60	1.00

69 (91) 50 Groschen (Al) 1946, 1947, 1952, 1955	0.70	1.50

		VF	XF
70 (92) 1	Schilling (Al) 1946, 1947, 1952, 1957. ℞ peasant sowing	0.80	1.50

		VF	XF
71 (93) 2	Schilling (Al) 1946, 1947, 1952. ℞ grapes and ears of corn:		
	a) 1946, 1947	1.80	3.00
	b) 1952	130.00	200.00
72 (94) 5	Schilling (Al) 1952, 1957.		
	a) 1952	5.00	7.00
	b) 1957	200.00	300.00

COMMEMORATIVE ISSUE FOR THE REOPENING OF THE FEDERAL THEATRES

		XF	Unc
73 (96) 25	Schilling (Ag) 1955. Muse with mask and lyre. The theatre curtain is drawn aside by two attendants. ℞ value within wreath made of the shields of the nine Federal Provinces; below, laurel branches	15.00	25.00

200th ANNIVERSARY OF THE BIRTH OF MOZART

74 (97)   25 Schilling (Ag) 1956. Monument to Wolfgang Amadeus Mozart (1756–1791) in the Burggarten in Vienna. ℞ as No. 73

	XF	Unc
	6.00	8.00

8th CENTENNIAL OF MARIAZELL BASILICA

75 (98)   25 Schilling (Ag) 1957. Mariazell. R as No. 73

	6.00	8.00

76 (103) 50 Groschen (Al-Br) 1959–1988. Arms. Rev. Value, date

	VF	XF
	0.10	0.15

77 (104)   1 Schilling (Al–Br) 1959–. Edelweiss (Leontopodium alpinum-Compositae). ℞ value

	0.10	0.15

78 (106) 5 Schilling (Ag) 1960–1968. The Spanish Riding School in Vienna: rider on horse in levade. ℞ arms and value

	VF	XF
	1.50	2.00

For coin of similar type, see under No. 98

79 (99) 10 Schilling (Ag) 1957–1959, 1964–1973. Head of a woman from the Wachau district with a golden bonnet in profile. ℞ arms

	VF	XF
	2.00	3.00

COMMEMORATIVE ISSUE FOR THE CENTENARY OF THE BIRTH OF AUER VON WELSBACH

80 (100) 25 Schilling (Ag) 1958. Bust facing right of Carl Freiherr Auer von Welsbach (1858–1929), chemist. ℞ as No. 73

	XF	Unc
	6.00	8.00

COMMEMORATIVE ISSUE FOR THE LIBERATION OF TYROL

81 (101) 50 Schilling (Ag) 1959. Bust facing of Andreas Hofer (1767–1810), leader of the revolt against the occupation of Tyrol. ℞ Tyrolese eagle surrounded by shields of the other eight Federal Provinces

	XF	Unc
	9.00	12.00

COMMEMORATIVE ISSUE FOR THE CENTENARY OF THE DEATH OF ARCHDUKE JOHANN

82 (102) 25 Schilling (Ag) 1959. Head facing right of Archduke Johann (1782–1859), military leader in the French Wars, encouraged the cultural and economic development, especially of Steiermark; founder of the Joanneum in Graz. ℞ lion of Styria

	6.00	8.00

Yeoman Numbers

In order to help collectors and dealers, we have added after most Schön numbers the corresponding number assigned by R.S. Yeoman in his well-known works entitled »A Catalog of Modern World Coins« and »Current Coins of the World«.

COMMEMORATIVE ISSUE FOR THE 40th ANNIVERSARY OF THE CARINTHIAN PLEBISCITE

		XF	Unc
83 (105)	25 Schilling (Ag) 1960. Couple wearing Carinthian traditional costumes standing by voting urn. ℞ as No. 73	6.00	8.00

COMMEMORATIVE ISSUE FOR THE 40th ANNIVERSARY OF BURGENLAND

84 (107)	25 Schilling (Ag) 1961. The Haydnkirche in Eisenstadt. ℞ as No. 73	9.00	12.50

COMMEMORATIVE ISSUE FOR A. BRUCKNER

85 (108)	25 Schilling (Ag) 1962. Head right of Anton Bruckner (1824–1896), composer. ℞ as No. 73	5.00	8.00

COMMEMORATIVE ISSUE FOR THE 300th ANNIVERSARY OF THE BIRTH OF PRINCE EUGEN

			XF	Unc
86 (109)	25	Schilling (Ag) 1963. Half-length figure of Prince Eugen of Savoy (1663–1736), Imperial Austrian General Field-Marshal. ℞ as No. 73	5.00	8.00

COMMEMORATIVE ISSUE FOR THE 600th ANNIVERSARY OF THE UNION OF TYROL WITH AUSTRIA

87 (110)	50	Schilling (Ag) 1963. The two coats of arms of Austria and Tyrol united by a chain. ℞ as No. 73	7.00	10.00

COMMEMORATIVE ISSUE FOR THE 9th OLYMPIC WINTER GAMES IN INNSBRUCK

88 (111) 50 Schilling (Ag) 1964. Ski-jumper with
mountain scenery in background;
above, Olympic rings. ℞ as No. 73

	XF	Unc
	9.00	12.00

COMMEMORATIVE ISSUE FOR F. GRILLPARZER

89 (112) 25 Schilling (Ag) 1964. Bust threequar-
ters facing of Franz Grillparzer (1791–
1872), poet. ℞ value within shield of
arms: these are the arms of the nine
Federal Provinces, surmounted by the
national arms
  a) ℞ of new design   6.00   8.00
  b) ℞ as on Nos. 83–86. **Proof only**   400.00

COMMEMORATIVE ISSUE FOR THE 600th ANNIVERSARY OF THE FOUNDATION OF VIENNA UNIVERSITY

90 (114) 50 Schilling (Ag) 1965. Bust threequar-
ters facing of Rudolf IV, "The Found-
er", Duke of Austria from 1358 to
1365. ℞ as No. 89a   8.00   12.00

COMMEMORATIVE ISSUE FOR THE 150th ANNIVERSARY
OF THE TECHNICAL HIGH SCHOOL

		XF	Unc
91 (113) 25 Schilling (Ag) 1965. Head facing left of Joh. Jos. Ritter von Prechtl (1778–1854), technologist, Director of the Polytechnic Institute in Vienna. ℞ as No. 89a		5.00	8.00

COMMEMORATIVE ISSUE FOR THE 150th ANNIVERSARY
OF THE AUSTRIAN NATIONAL BANK

92 (116) 50 Schilling (Ag) 1966. National Bank building in Vienna. ℞ as No. 89a	8.00	12.00

COMMEMORATIVE ISSUE FOR F. RAIMUND

93 (115) 25 Schilling (Ag) 1966. Facing half portrait of Ferdinand Raimund (1790–
1836), poet. ℞ as No. 89a

	XF	Unc
	5.00	8.00

COMMEMORATIVE ISSUE FOR THE 250th ANNIVERSARY OF THE BIRTH OF MARIA THERESIA

94 (117) 25 Schilling (Ag) 1967. Bust facing right
of Maria Theresia (1717–1780), Em-
press, reigned from 1740–1780. ℞ as
No. 89a

5.00   8.00

COMMEMORATIVE ISSUE FOR THE CENTENARY OF THE "BLUE DANUBE" WALTZ

95 (118) 50 Schilling (Ag) 1967. Facing half portrait of Johann Strauss the Younger
(1825–1899), from a bronze statue in
the monument to Strauss (marble arch
of the Muses), unveiled in 1923 in the
Vienna City Park (Park-Ring); the
sculptor was Edmund Hellmer. ℞ as
No. 89a

8.00   12.00

COMMEMORATIVE ISSUE FOR THE 50th ANNIVERSARY OF THE REPUBLIC OF AUSTRIA

96 (120) 50 Schilling (Ag) 1968. Parliament building in Vienna, built by Theophil Hansen, Danish architect; in front, the Pallas-Athena fountain by Karl Kundmann. ℞ as No. 89a

	XF	Unc
	8.00	12.00

COMMEMORATIVE ISSUE FOR THE 300th ANNIVERSARY OF THE BIRTH OF LUKAS VON HILDEBRANDT (1668–1745)

97 (119) 25 Schilling (Ag) 1968. Main gateway to the Belvedere castle in Vienna with the upper Belvedere gardens. ℞ as No. 89a

	7.00	10.00

 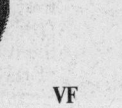

	VF	XF
98 (106a) 5 Schilling (Cu-Ni) 1968–. Type as No. 78, plain edge	0.20	0.30

450th ANNIVERSARY OF DEATH OF EMPEROR MAXIMILIAN I

		XF	Unc
99 (122) 50 Schilling (Ag) 1969. Bust right of Maximilian I (1459–1519), Emperor, reigned from 1493 to 1519		7.00	11.00

COMMEMORATIVE ISSUE FOR PETER ROSEGGER

100 (121) 25 Schilling (Ag) 1969. Head facing left of Peter Rosegger (1843–1918), poet and writer   5.00   7.00

CENTENARY OF THE BIRTH OF FRANZ LEHAR

101 (123) 25 Schilling (Ag) 1970. Bust three-quarters facing of Franz Lehár (1870–1948), composer, successful exponent of Viennese operetta   5.00   7.00

COMMEMORATIVE ISSUE FOR THE 300th ANNIVERSARY OF THE LEOPOLD FRANZENS UNIVERSITY IN INNSBRUCK

102 (124) 50 Schilling (Ag) 1970. The oldest seal of the university dating from 1673, the year of completion of all four Faculties (1669 Philosophy, 1671 Theology and Law, 1673 Medicine). In the centre, the Margrave of Babenberg, Leopold III the Saint, after whom Leopold I, the Founder of the University, was named. In his right hand he holds a model of the monastery Klosterneuburg; in his left, the five-eagle banner half rolled-up. On his right, shield with the eagle of Tyrol, and in front of it the inscription: LEVPOLDO FELICI; on his left, the imperial double eagle in the chain of the Golden Fleece, surmounted by the imperial crown of Rudolf. In the background, canopy on which dove, symbol of the Holy Spirit.

	XF	Unc
	7.00	11.00

COMMEMORATIVE ISSUE FOR THE CENTENARY OF THE BIRTH OF DR. KARL RENNER

103 (125) 50 Schilling (Ag) 1970. Dr. Karl Renner (1870–1950), Federal President 1945 to 1950

	7.00	11.00

200th ANNIVERSARY OF VIENNA BOURSE

XF   Unc

104 (126) 25 Schilling (Ag) 1971. General view of
building of Vienna Bourse   4.00   6.00

COMMEMORATIVE ISSUE FOR THE 80th BIRTHDAY OF DR. J. RAAB

105 (127) 50 Schilling (Ag) 1971. Dr. Julius Raab
(1891–1964), Federal Chancellor from
1953 to 1961   7.00   11.00

COMMEMORATIVE ISSUE FOR THE 350th ANNIVERSARY OF THE UNIVERSITY IN SALZBURG

106 (129) 50 Schilling (Ag) 1972. Great Seal of
Salzburg University. The pair of letters

"PA" and "SF" refer to the founder PARIS Lodron, Archbishop (ARCHI-EPISCOPUS) of Salzburg (SALZBURGENSIS), FUNDATOR. The left-hand Roman numeral in the seal signifies the year of its foundation in 1622, the right-hand Roman numeral 1962 indicates the year of its re-establishment

	XF	Unc
	7.00	11.00

COMMEMORATIVE ISSUE FOR THE 50th ANNIVERSARY OF THE DEATH OF CARL MICHAEL ZIEHRER

107 (128) 25 Schilling (Ag) 1972. Carl Michael Ziehrer (1843–1922). Composer of operettas; also composed dance music and march tunes. He possessed the Imperial title of a "Court Ball Music Director"   4.00   6.00

COMMEMORATIVE ISSUE FOR 100 YEARS OF THE INSTITUTE OF AGRICULTURE IN VIENNA

108 (130) 50 Schilling (Ag) 1972. General view of the institute building. Coats of arms are part of the legend, symbolizing the faculties of "Agriculture", "Forestry and Timber Management", "Cultivation Technology and Water Manage-

	XF	Unc
ment" and "Food and Fermentation Technology"	7.00	11.00

COMMEMORATIVE ISSUE FOR THE 500th ANNIVERSARY OF THE BUMMERL HOUSE IN STEYR

109 (132) 50 Schilling (Ag) 1973. A former public house built in the Gothic style which was called the "Golden Lion". Since, however, the figure of a lion located above the entrance had turned out very small, and rather resembled a small dog, called a "Bummerl" in the vernacular, the house has been traditionally known as the Bummerl House   7.00   11.00

COMMEMORATIVE ISSUE FOR THE 100th BIRTHDAY OF MAX REINHARDT

110 (131) 25 Schilling (Ag) 1973. Max Reinhardt (1873–1943), distinguished producer and theatrical manager   4.00   6.00

Values are given for each coin in U.S. dollars and reference to Yeoman-numbers.

COMMEMORATIVE ISSUE FOR THE 100th ANNIVERSARY
OF THE BIRTH OF THEODOR KÖRNER

		XF	Unc
111 (133) 50 Schilling (Ag) 1973. Theodor Körner (1873–1957), Federal President 1951 to 1957		7.00	11.00

		VF	XF
112 (A 99) 10 Schilling (Cu–Ni) 1974–. Head of a woman from the Wachau district with a golden bonnet in profile, denomination, date. ℞ federal arms and legend **"REPUBLIK ÖSTERREICH"**		0.50	0.70

VIENNA INTERNATIONAL GARDEN EXHIBITION
(April 18 to October 14, 1974)

		XF	Unc
113 (134) 50 Schilling (Ag) 1974. Artist's impression of plant-life shapes		4.00	6.00

COMMEMORATIVE ISSUE FOR THE 125th ANNIVERSARY
OF THE AUSTRIAN POLICE FORCE
(1849 to 1974)

114 (135) 50 Schilling (Ag) 1974. The federal coat
of arms with a wreath of oak leaves as
an emblem of the police force, above
two flaming hand grenades which refer
to the corps badge of the police force

	XF	Unc
	4.00	6.00

COMMEMORATIVE ISSUE FOR THE 1200th ANNIVERSARY
OF SALZBURG CATHEDRAL

115 (136) 50 Schilling (Ag) 1974. Two saints holding church over arms

4.00   6.00

50th ANNIVERSARY OF AUSTRIAN BROADCASTING

116 (137) 50 Schilling (Ag) 1974. Symbol of Austrian
Broadcasting

4.00   6.00

150th ANNIVERSARY OF BIRTH OF JOHANN STRAUSS

		XF	Unc
117 (138) 100 Schilling (Ag) 1975. Johann Strauss the Younger (1825-1899), composer		6.50	9.00

20th ANNIVERSARY OF STATE TREATY

118 (139) 100 Schilling (Ag) 1975.   6.50   9.00

50th ANNIVERSARY OF SCHILLING

119 (140) 100 Schilling (Ag) 1975. A modernistic version of a sower in a plowed field   6.50   9.00

	XF	Unc
120 (141) 100 Schilling (Ag) 1976. Emblem of the Olympic Winter Games 1976	6.50	9.00

	XF	Unc
121 (142) 100 Schilling (Ag) 1976. Buildings with tower against background of 5 Olympic rings. *R* coat of arms and value. A small arms-emblem below, for the mint, in Vienna	6.50	9.00
122 (142) 100 Schilling (Ag) 1976. Type as No. 121, but a small Tyrolian eagle, for the mint, in Hall	6.50	9.00

	XF	Unc
123 (143) 100 Schilling (Ag) 1976.	6.50	9.00

				XF	Unc
124 (143)	100	Schilling (Ag) 1976. Type as No. 123, but a small Tyrolian eagle, for the mint, in Hall		6.50	9.00
125 (144)	100	Schilling (Ag) 1976		6.50	9.00

			XF	Unc
126 (144)	100	Schilling (Ag) 1976. Type as No. 125, but a small Tyrolian eagle, for the mint, in Hall	6.50	9.00

200th ANNIVERSARY OF BURGTHEATER

			XF	Unc
127 (145)	100	Schilling (Ag) 1976. General view of the Burgtheater	6.50	9.00—

1000th ANNIVERSARY OF CARINTHIA

			XF	Unc
128 (146)	100	Schilling (Ag) 1976. Herzogstuhl and Carinthian arms	6.50	9.00

1000th ANNIVERSARY OF THE INSTALLATION OF THE BABENBERGER IN AUSTRIA

			XF	Unc
129 (148)	1000	Schilling (Au) 1976. The seal of the Duke Friedrich II (yellow gold or red gold)		200.00

175th ANNIVERSARY OF BIRTH OF JOHANN NESTROY

130 (147)	100	Schilling (Ag) 1976. Johann Nestroy (1801-1862), singer	6.50	9.00

1200th ANNIVERSARY OF STIFT KREMSMÜNSTER

131 (149)	100	Schilling (Ag) 1977	6.50	9.00

900th ANNIVERSARY OF FORTRESS HOHENSALZBURG

	XF	Unc
132 (150) 100 Schilling (Ag) 1977. View of the fortress Hohensalzburg	6.50	9.00

500th ANNIVERSARY OF THE MINT IN HALL/TYROL

133 (151) 100 Schilling (Ag) 1977	6.50	9.00

700th ANNIVERSARY OF GMUNDEN

134 (153) 100 Schilling (Ag) 1978. Orth, castle in Gmunden	6.50	9.00

700th ANNIVERSARY OF THE BATTLE OF DÜRNKRUT AND JEDENSPEIGEN

			XF	Unc
135 (154)	100	Schilling (Ag) 1978. Bust of Rudolf I, landscape of the Marchfield, battle-scene	6.50	9.00

1100th ANNIVERSARY OF VILLACH

136 (155)	100	Schilling (Ag) 1978. View of the city of Villach and arms	6.50	9.00

150th ANNIVERSARY OF BIRTH OF FRANZ SCHUBERT

137 (152)	50	Schilling (Ag) 1978. Franz Schubert (1797-1828), composer	4.00	6.00

OPENING OF ARLBERG TUNNEL

138 (156)	100	Schilling (Ag) 1978	6.00	8.00

CATHEDRAL OF WIENER NEUSTADT CENTENNIAL

139 (157)	100	Schilling (Ag) 1979	6.00	8.00

Values are given for each coin in U.S. Dollars and reference to Yeoman-numbers.

200th ANNIVERSARY OF INN DISTRICT

			XF	Unc
140 (158)	100 Schilling (Ag) 1979		6.00	8.00

VIENNA INTERNATIONAL CENTER

141 (159)	100 Schilling (Ag) 1979		6.00	8.00

FESTIVAL AND CONGRESS HALL AT BREGENZ

142 (160)	100 Schilling (Ag) 1979		6.00	8.00

MILLENIUM OF THE CITY OF STEYR

143 (161)	500 Schilling (Ag) 1980		40.00	55.00

25th ANNIVERSARY OF STATE TREATY

144 (162)	500 Schilling (Ag) 1980. Belvedere castle in Vienna		38.00	42.00

BICENTENNIAL OF THE DEATH OF MARIA THERESIA

145 (163)	500 Schilling (Ag) 1980. Maria Theresia (1717–1780), Empress, reigned from 1740–1780		38.00	42.00

CENTENNIAL OF AUSTRIAN RED CROSS

			XF	Unc
146 (164)	500 Schilling (Ag) 1980. Henri Dunant (1828–1910), philanthropist		38.00	42.00

			VF	XF
147 (165)	20 Schilling (Al-Br) 1980, 1981.		1.25	1.75

800th ANNIVERSARY OF THE VERDUN ALTAR

			XF	Unc
148 (166)	500 Schilling (Ag) 1981		38.00	42.00

100th ANNIVERSARY OF THE BIRTH OF ANTON WILDGANS

			XF	Unc
149 (167)	500 Schilling (Ag) 1981. Anton Wildgans (1881–1932), writer		38.00	42.00

100th ANNIVERSARY OF THE BIRTH OF OTTO BAUER

			XF	Unc
150 (168)	500	Schilling (Ag) 1981. Otto Bauer (1881–1938), Socialdemocrat politician	38.00	42.00

200th ANNIVERSARY OF RELIGIOUS TOLERANCE

151 (169)	500	Schilling (Ag) 1981. Cross, bible and chalice	38.00	42.00

1500th ANNIVERSARY OF THE DEATH OF ST. SEVERIN

152 (170)	500	Schilling (Ag) 1982. St. Severin standing	38.00	42.00

500 YEARS OF AUSTRIAN PRINTING

153 (172)	500	Schilling (Ag) 1982. Printing-press, about 1500	38.00	42.00

250th ANNIVERSARY OF THE BIRTH OF J. HAYDN

			VF	XF
154 (171)	20 Schilling (Al-Br) 1982. Joseph Haydn (1732–1809), composer		1.25	1.75

825 YEARS OF MARIAZELL

			XF	Unc
155 (173)	500 Schilling (Ag) 1982. Madonna of Mariazell		38.00	42.00

80th ANNIVERSARY OF THE BIRTH OF L. FIGL

156 (174)	500 Schilling (Ag) 1982. Leopold Figl (1902–1965), politician		40.00	50.00

			VF	XF
157 (175)	20 Schilling (Al-Br) 1983. Hochosterwitz Castle		1.25	1.75

WORLD CUP HORSE JUMPING CHAMPIONSHIP

			VF	**XF**
158 (176)	500	Schilling (Ag) 1983. Horse jumping	38.00	42.00

CENTENNIAL OF VIENNA CITY HALL

			XF	**Unc**
159 (177)	500	Schilling (Ag) 1983. City Hall, Vienna	38.00	42.00

AUSTRIAN CATHOLIC DAY – POPE'S VISIT

160 (178)	500	Schilling (Ag) 1983. Pope John Paul II	38.00	42.00

CENTENNIAL OF PARLIAMENT BUILDING, VIENNA

			XF	Unc
161 (179)	500 Schilling (Ag) 1983. Parliament building		38.00	42.00

		VF	XF
162	20 Schilling (Al-Br) 1984. Grafenegg Castle	1.25	1.75

175th ANNIVERSARY OF TYROLEAN UPRISING

		XF	Unc
163 (180)	500 Schilling (Ag) 1984. Andreas Hofer (1767–1810), leader of the revolt against the occupation of Tyrol	36.00	40.00

CENTENNIAL OF BODENSEE-NAVIGATION

		XF	Unc
164	500 Schilling (Ag) 1984. Passenger-ship »Vorarlberg«	36.00	40.00

700 YEARS OF STIFT STAMS

		XF	Unc
165	500 Schilling (Ag) 1984. Stift Stams, Tyrol	36.00	40.00

100th ANNIVERSARY OF THE DEATH OF F. ELSSLER

		VF	XF
166	500 Schilling (Ag) 1984. Fanny Elssler (1810–1884), dancer	36.00	40.00

200 YEARS OF DIOCESE LINZ

		VF	XF
167	20 Schilling (Al-Br) 1985. Rosette and arms of Upper Austria	1.25	1.75

400th ANNIVERSARY OF THE KARL-FRANZENS-UNIVERSITY IN GRAZ

		XF	Unc
168	500 Schilling (Ag) 1985. Archduke Karl, founder of the University	36.00	40.00

40 YEARS OF PEACE IN AUSTRIA

			XF	Unc
169	500	Schilling (Ag) 1985	36.00	40.00

2000 YEARS OF THE CITY OF BREGENZ

170	500	Schilling (Ag) 1985	36.00	40.00

500th ANNIVERSARY OF THE CANONIZATION
OF MARGRAVE LEOPOLD III

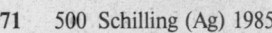

171	500	Schilling (Ag) 1985	38.00	42.00

800th ANNIVERSARY OF GEORGENBERGER TREATY

		VF	XF
172	20 Schilling (Cu-Ni-Al) 1986	1.25	1.75

250th ANNIVERSARY OF DEATH OF PRINCE EUGEN

173	500 Schilling (Ag) 1986. Prince Eugen of Savoy	38.00	42.00

FIRST THALER COIN STRUCK AT HALL MINT

174	500 Schilling (Ag) 1986	38.00	42.00

300th ANNIVERSARY OF ST. FLORIAN'S STIFT

		XF	Unc
175	500 Schilling (Ag) 1986	38.00	42.00

176 500 Schilling (Ag) 1986. Map of Europe   38.00   42.00

177 20 Schilling (Cu-Ni-Al) 1987. Seal of Johann Ernst von Thun und Hohenstein, archbishop of Salzburg   1.25   1.75

400th ANNIVERSARY OF ACCESSION

178 500 Schilling (Ag) 1987. Wolf Dietrich von Raitenau (1559–1617), archbishop of Salzburg 1587–1617   38.00   42.00

150th ANNIVERSARY OF RAILROAD IN AUSTRIA

179 500 Schilling (Ag) 1987   38.00   42.00

STIFT HEILIGENKREUZ

180 500 Schilling (Ag) 1987   38.00   42.00

Previous issues, see »Weltmünzkatalog 19. Jahrhundert« (World Coin Catalogue of the 19th Century)

Azoren

Azores

Açores

Area: 922 sq. mi. Population: 330,000.
The island group in the Atlantic was (re?)-discovered 1432 by the Portuguese, Cabral, named after the birds found on the islands the »Hawk Islands«, taken possession of in 1445 in the name of Portugal and since then considered to be an integrated part of the motherland, on which legitimate and exile governments set up bases and from where they were able to regain the motherland. The strategically important location of the island group should be able to prevent a fundamental change in this situation also in future.
Capital: Ponte Delgada.

CARLOS I 1889–1908

			VF	XF
1 (4)	5	Reis (Cu) 1901. Crowned arms. ℞ value in wreath	6.00	10.00
2 (5)	10	Reis (Cu) 1901. Type as No. 1	8.00	15.00

AUTONOMOUS TERRITORY

100 Centavos = 1 Escudo

			Unc	Proof
3 (6)	25	Escudos 1980. Arms, date. Rev. value:		
		a) (Ag)		12.00
		b) (Cu-Ni)	2.50	
4 (7)	100	Escudos 1980. Type as No. 3:		
		a) (Ag)		40.00
		b) (Cu-Ni)	5.00	

Previous issues, see »Weltmünzkatalog 19. Jahrhundert« (World Coin Catalogue of the 19th Century)

Bahama-Inseln   # Bahamas   **Bahames**

Area: 4,387 sq. mi. Population: 245,000.
Group of islands in the West Indies including Watlings Island, the former Guanahani or San Salvador. Christopher Columbus landed in Guanahani on 12th October 1492, setting foot for the first time on American soil. Independence 10th July 1973.
Capital: Nassau.

100 Cents = 1 Bahama Dollar

			XF	Unc
1 (1)	1 Cent (Ni-Bra) 1966-1970. Head of Queen Elizabeth II to right; inscription around: ELIZABETH II BAHAMA ISLANDS. *R* great netted starfish (Oreaster reticulatus - Oreasteridae):			
	a) 1966, 1969, 22,5 mm dia.		0.10	0.20
	b) 1968, 22,5 mm dia.		0.20	0.40
	c) 1970, 19 mm dia.		0.25	0.50

2   3

		XF	Unc
2 (2)	5 Cents (Cu-Ni) 1966-1970. *R* pineapple (Ananas comosus - Bromeliaceae):		
	a) 1966, 1969, 1970	0.10	0.25
	b) 1968	0.10	0.25
3 (3)	10 Cents (Cu-Ni) 1966-1970. *R* king mackerels (Scomberomorus cavalla - Scombridae):		
	a) 1966, 1969, 1970	0.15	0.30
	b) 1968	1.50	5.00

4 (4) 15 Cents (Cu–Ni) 1966–1970. ℞ Chinese
       hibiscus (Hibiscus rosa-sinensis – Mal-
       vaceae)

	XF	Unc
	0.20	0.40

5 (5) 25 Cents (Ni) 1966–1970. ℞ sloop

	XF	Unc
	0.30	0.60

6 (6) 50 Cents (Ag) 1966–1970. ℞ blue marlin
       (Makaira indica = Makaira ampla –
       Istiophoridae)

	XF	Unc
	3.00	4.00

Yeoman Numbers

**In order to help collectors and dealers, we have added after most SCHÖN-
numbers the corresponding number assigned by R.S. Yeoman in his wellknown
works entitled »A Catalog of modern World Coins« and »Current Coins of the
World«.**

		XF	**Unc**
7 (7)	1 Dollar (Ag) 1966–1970. ℞ queen conch (Strombus gigas – Strombidae)	3.00	5.00

8 (8)	2 Dollars (Ag) 1966–1970. ℞ greater flamingos (Phoenicopterus ruber ruber – Phoenicopteridae)	6.00	9.00

9 (9)	5 Dollars (Ag) 1966–1970. ℞ arms	9.00	12.00

COMMEMORATIVE ISSUES (4) ON THE OCCASION OF THE 1st GENERAL ELECTION FOR THE ADOPTION OF THE NEW CONSTITUTION

			Unc	Proof
10 (10)	10	Dollars (Au) 1967. Head of Queen Elizabeth II. ℞ fort, two palm branches and value	60.00	90.00
11 (11)	20	Dollars (Au) 1967. ℞ lighthouse and value	120.00	165.00
12 (12)	50	Dollars (Au) 1967. ℞ The "Santa Maria", flagship of Christopher Columbus	275.00	325.00
13 (13)	100	Dollars (Au) 1967. ℞ Christopher Columbus (1451–1506) setting foot on American soil at Guanahani (San Salvador) on 12th October 1492	550.00	625.00
14 (14)	1	Cent (Ni–Bra) 1971–1973. Type as No. 1, but inscription COMMONWEALTH OF THE BAHAMA ISLANDS ELIZABETH II	0.20	0.50
15 (15)	5	Cents (Cu–Ni) 1971–1973. ℞ pineapple	0.30	0.50
16 (16)	10	Cents (Cu–Ni) 1971–1973. ℞ king mackerels	0.50	0.50
17 (17)	15	Cents (Cu–Ni) 1971–1973. ℞ Chinese hibiscus	0.35	0.50
18 (18)	25	Cents (Ni) 1971–1973. ℞ sloop	0.50	0.80
19 (19)	50	Cents (Ag) 1971–1973. Rev. blue marlin	3.00	4.50
20 (20)	1	Dollar (Ag) 1971–1973. Rev. queen conch	4.50	6.00
21 (21)	2	Dollars (Ag) 1971–1973. ℞ greater flamingos	9.00	10.00
22 (22)	5	Dollars (Ag) 1971. ℞ arms	12.00	15.00
23 (23)	10	Dollars (Au) 1971, 1972. Type as No. 10:		
		a) 1971, 3.99 grams	50.00	60.00
		b) 1972, 3.19 grams	50.00	60.00
24 (24)	20	Dollars (Au) 1971, 1972. Type as No. 11:		
		a) 1971, 7.99 grams	130.00	150.00
		b) 1972, 6.38 grams	110.00	140.00
25 (25)	50	Dollars (Au) 1971, 1972. Type as No. 12:		
		a) 1971, 19.97 grams	250.00	300.00
		b) 1972, 15.97 grams	210.00	260.00
26 (26)	100	Dollars (Au) 1971, 1972. Type as No. 9:		
		a) 1971, 39.94 grams	500.00	600.00
		b) 1972, 31.95 grams	475.00	525.00

Values are given for each coin in U.S. Dollars and reference to Yeoman-numbers.

			Unc	Proof
27 (22a)	5 Dollars (Ag) 1972, 1973. Type as No. 22, but new coat of arms, since December 7, 1971 (rising sun with thirteen rays in the upper field)		11.00	12.50

COMMEMORATIVE ISSUES (6) ON THE OCCASION OF INDEPENDENCE ON 10th JULY 1973

28 (27)	10 Dollars (Ag) 1973. Head of Queen Elizabeth II. R The »Santa Maria«, flagship of Christopher Columbus		20.00	22.50
29 (29)	10 Dollars (Au) 1973. R tobacco dove (Columbigallina passerina – Columbidae)		30.00	40.00
30 (30)	20 Dollars (Au) 1973. R greater flamingos		35.00	60.00
31 (28)	50 Dollars (Au) 1973. R greater flamingos before rising sun		125.00	125.00
32 (31)	50 Dollars (Au) 1973. R lobster (Palinurus argus – Palinuridae)		85.00	100.00
33 (32)	100 Dollars (Au) 1973. R Coat of arms		130.00	160.00

			XF	Unc
A33 (15a)	5 Cents (Cu-Ni) 1973. Type as No. 15, but THE COMMONWEALTH		0.20	0.40
B33 (16a)	10 Cents (Cu-Ni) 1973. Type as No. 16, but THE COMMONWEALTH		0.20	0.40

			Unc	Proof
34 (33)	1 Cent (Bra) 1974–1985. Coat of arms since 7th December 1971. Rev. great netted starfish		0.15	0.50
35 (34)	5 Cents (Cu-Ni) 1974–1984. Rev. pineapple		0.25	0.50
36 (35)	10 Cents (Cu-Ni) 1974–1984. Rev. king mackerels		0.25	0.50
37 (36)	15 Cents (Cu-Ni) 1974–1984. Rev. Chinese hibiscus		0.35	0.50
38 (37)	25 Cents (Ni) 1974–1984. Rev. sloop		0.50	0.80
39 (38)	50 Cents 1974–1984. Rev. blue marlin:			
	a) (Ag) 1974–1980			5.00
	b) (Cu-Ni) 1974–1984		1.20	4.00
40 (39)	1 Dollar 1974. Rev. queen conch:			
	a) (Ag) 1974–1980			6.00
	b) (Cu-Ni) 1974–1978 2.50		2.50	
41 (40)	2 Dollar 1974–. Rev. greater flamingos:			
	a) (Ag) 1974–1980			10.00
	b) (Cu-Ni) 1974–1978		4.00	
42 (41)	5 Dollars 1974–1981, Rev. new national flag since 10th July 1973:			
	a) (Ag) 1974–1980, .925 silver			12.00
	b) (Cu-Ni) 1974–1978		6.00	
	c) (Ag) 1981, .500 silver			25.00

43 (42)   10 Dollars 1974. Sir Milo B. Butler, Governor
General:
a) (Ag)   20.00
b) (Cu-Ni)   12.00

			Unc	Proof
44 (44)	50	Dollars (Au) 1974–1977. R tobacco dove	50.00	50.00
45 (45)	100	Dollars (Au) 1974–1977. R greater flamingos	100.00	100.00
46 (43)	100	Dollars (Au) 1974. R greater flamingos and fully circular inscription; 33 mm dia.	140.00	150.00

47 (46)	150	Dollars (Au) 1974–1977. Rev. lobster	150.00	150.00

48 (47)	200	Dollar (Au) 1974–1977. Rev. arms	200.00	200.00
49 (57)	2500	Dollars (Au) 1974, 1977. Rev. greater flamingos; 72 mm dia., .917 gold, 407.26 g:		
		a) 1974 (204 pieces)		7000.00
		b) 1977 (168 pieces)		8000.00

2nd ANNIVERSARY OF INDEPENDENCE (2)

50 (48)   10 Dollars 1975–1977. R flower:
a) (Ag)   20.00
b) (Cu-Ni)   10.00

51 (49) 100 Dollars (Au) 1975–1977. R parrot
(Amazona leucocephala – Psittacidae)   175.00   175.00

FIFTH ANNIVERSARY OF INDEPENDENCE (4)

		Unc	Proof
52 (50)	10 Dollars (Ag) 1978. Portrait of H.R.H. Prince Charles		18.00
53 (51)	100 Dollars (Au) 1978		225.00
54 (52)	10 Dollars (Ag) 1978. Sir Milo B. Butler		16:00
55 (53)	100 Dollars (Au) 1978		200.00

250th ANNIVERSARY OF PARLIAMENT (2)

56 (54)	25 Dollars (Ag) 1979	45.00
57 (55)	250 Dollars (Au) 1979	250.00

10th ANNIVERSARY OF CARIBBEAN DEVELOPMENT BANK

58 (56)	10 Dollars (Ag) 1980	25.00

WEDDING OF PRINCE CHARLES AND LADY DIANA (3)

59 (58)	10 Dollars (Ag) 1981	20.00

60 (59)	100 Dollars (Au) 1981	125.00
61 (60)	500 Dollars (Au) 1981	500.00
62 (61)	50 Dollars (Au) 1981. Arms. Rev. flamingos	70.00
63 (62)	1 Dollar (Cu-Ni) 1982. Rev. Poinciana flower	8.00
64 (63)	2 Dollars (Cu-Ni) 1982. Rev. Bahama swallows	12.50
65 (64)	5 Dollars (Ag) 1982. Rev. Columbus Memorial in front of the »Santa Maria«	25.00
66 (65)	50 Dollars (Au) 1982. Rev. Blue Marlin	70.00

30th ANNIVERSARY OF CORONATION OF QUEEN ELIZABETH II

67 (66)	10 Dollars (Ag) 1983	25.00

10th ANNIVERSARY OF INDEPENDENCE (7)

			Unc	Proof
68 (67)	1	Dollar (Cu-Ni) 1983. Rev. Allamanda		9.00
69 (68)	2	Dollars (Cu-Ni) 1983. Rev. Hummingbird		12.50
70 (69)	5	Dollars (Ag) 1983. Rev. Flamingo		30.00
71 (71)	10	Dollars (Ag) 1983. Prince Charles standing in front of national flag		40.00
72 (70)	50	Dollars (Au) 1983. Rev. Flamingo		70.00
73 (72)	100	Dollars (Au) 1983. Rev. Bust of Charles in an oval and national flag		150.00
74 (73)	2500	Dollars (Au) 1983. Rev. Arms		8000.00

AMERICA'S CUP CHALLENGE

			Unc	Proof
75 (74)	1000	Dollars (Au) 1983. Rev. Sailboats		1000.00

LOS ANGELES XXIII OLYMPIAD

			Unc	Proof
76 (75)	10	Dollars (Ag) 1984. Rev. Sprinter		40.00
77 (76)	1	Dollar (Cu-Ni) 1984, 1985. Rev. Bougainvillea flower		6.00
78 (77)	2	Dollars (Cu-Ni) 1984, 1985, Rev. Flying flamingos		10.00
79 (78)	5	Dollars (Ag) 1984. Rev. 15th century map of the Bahamas		30.00
80	50	Dollars (Au) 1984. Rev. Golden Allamanda		70.00
81	5	Dollars (Ag) 1985. Rev. Bust of Christopher Columbus		20.00
82	50	Dollars (Au) 1985. Rev. »Santa Maria«		70.00

ROYAL VISIT (2)

			Unc	Proof
83	10	Dollars 1985. Rev. Arms:		
		a) (Ag)		30.00
		b) (Cu-Ni)	18.00	
84	250	Dollars (Au) 1985		1500.00

COLUMBUS' DISCOVERY OF AMERICA (3)

			Unc	Proof
85	25	Dolars (Ag) 1985		85.00
86	100	Dollars (Au) 1985		200.00
87	2500	Dollars (Au) 1985		9000.00

200th ANNIVERSARY OF THE BIRTH OF JOHN JAMES AUDUBON

			Unc	Proof
88	25	Dollars (Ag) 1985. Rev. Flamingos		80.00

Bahrain-Inseln # Bahrain **(Iles) Bahrain**

Amarat al-Bahrain

Area: 250 sq. mi. Population: 445,000.

Arab Sheikdom on the Persian Gulf; a British Protectorate since 1861; independent since 14th August 1971. The Bahrain Dinar has been legal tender since October 16, 1965; in parallel with it, the socalled Gulf Rupee (1 BD = 10 Gulf Rupees) still remained legal tender until October 25, 1969. The Bahrain Dinar was also temporarily legal tender in Abu Dhabi. The monetary union with Abu Dhabi has been dissolved in the meantime.

Capital: Manama.

1000 Fils = 1 Bahrain Dinar

ISA BEN SULMAN BEN HAMAD AL KHALIFA since 1961

			XF	Unc
1 (1)	1	Fils (Br) 1965, 1966. Date palm (Phoenix dactylifera – Palmae). ℞ value	0.60	1.50
2 (2)	5	Fils (Br) 1965	0.15	0.25
3 (3)	10	Fils (Br) 1965	0.15	0.35
4 (4)	25	Fils (Cu–Ni) 1965	0.25	0.50
5 (5)	50	Fils (Cu–Ni) 1965	0.35	0.70

6 (6)	100	Fils (Cu–Ni) 1965	0.50	0.90

Values are given for each coin in U.S. Dollars and reference to Yeoman-numbers.

COMMEMORATIVE ISSUES (2) FOR THE DEDICATION OF ISA TOWN ON 6th NOVEMBER 1968

			XF	Unc
7 (7)	500	Fils (Ag) 1968. Bust right of Sheik Isa. R national arms and value	8.50	12.50
8 (8)	10	Dinars (Au) 1968. Type as No. 7	Proof	300.00

ISSUE FOR THE FAO COIN PLAN

			Unc	Proof
9 (9)	250	Fils (Cu-Ni) 1969, 1983. Date palm with fishing boat, name of country, date. R the FAO emblems and motto FIAT PANIS; value	3.00	5.00

INDEPENDENCE COMMEMORATIVE (14th August 1971)

10 (10)	10	Dinars (Au) 1971	300.00

5th ANNIVERSARY OF THE BAHRAIN MONETARY AGENCY (2)

11 (11)	50	Dinars (Au) 1978. Bust of Sheik Isa. R arms	300.00
12 (12)	100	Dinars (Au) 1978	600.00

10th ANNIVERSARY OF THE BAHRAIN MONETARY AGENCY (8)

Proof

13	1 Fils (Ag) 1983. Type as No. 1	–.–
14	5 Fils (Ag) 1983. Type as No. 1	–.–
15	10 Fils (Ag) 1983. Type as No. 1	–.–
16	25 Fils (Ag) 1983. Type as No. 1	–.–
17	50 Fils (Ag) 1983. Type as No. 1	–.–
18	100 Fils (Ag) 1983. Type as No. 1	–.–
19	250 Fils (Ag) 1983. Type as No. 9 (FAO issue)	–.–
20	500 Fils (Ag) 1983. Type as No. 7	–.–

Set (15,000 pieces) 110.00

25th ANNIVERSARY OF WORLD WILDLIFE FUND

21 5 Dinars (Ag) 1986. Sheik Isa. Rev. Gazelle   40.00
(Gazella subgutturosa marica – Bovidae)

All valuations in the SCHÖN are stated in U.S. Dollars.

Area: 54,501 sq. mi. Population: 104,000,000.

Upon the partition of British India based on the British law of independence, West Bengal came under Indian rule, and East Bengal became a part of the Islamic Republic of Pakistan. With the aid of Indian troops the independence of Bangladesh (Land of the Bengalis), proclaimed on December 17th, 1971 was realized. In December 1971 the »Bank of Bangladesh« was established which took over the funtion of the Pakistan State Bank in the territory of the former territory of East Pakistan.

Capital: Dacca.

100 Paise (Poisha) = 1 Taka

			VF	Unc
1 (A 1)	1	Paisa (Al) 1974. State emblem (National flower Shapla or water lily above wavy lines between ears of padi, crowned by tea leaves and stars). R value, date	0.10	0.20
2 (1)	5	Paise (Al) 1973, 1974. Rev. Plough, date and denomination within a cogwheel	0.10	0.20

3 (2)	10	Paise (Al) 1973. Rev. Leaf, date. Denomination (scalloped edge)	0.15	0.30
4 (3)	25	Paise (St) 1973. Rev. Fish	0.20	0.40
5 (4)	50	Paise (Cu-Ni) 1973. Rev. Bird	1.00	3.00

ISSUE FOR THE FAO COIN PLAN (7)

6 (5)	5	Paise (Al) 1974–1976. Type similar to No. 2, but motto »Grow More Food«	0.10	0.20

		VF	Unc

7 (6) 10 Paise (Al) 1974–1979. R Rice: grains, jute saplings, plant, tractor; motto: »Green Revolution« (scalloped edge) 0.20 0.40

8 (7) 25 Paise (St) 1974–1978. R carp fish, egg, bananas, pumpkin; motto: »Food for All« 0.25 0.50

9 (8) 1 Taka (Cu-Ni) 1975–1977. Rev. Family 0.40 0.75

10 (9) 5 Paise (Al) 1977–1980. Rev. Cogwheel, tractor, plough 0.10 0.20

11 (10) 10 Paise (Al) 1977–1983. Rev. Family (scalloped edge):
a) 1977–1980 0.15 0.30
b) 1983, smaller dia. 0.15 0.30

	VF	Unc
12 (11) 25 Paise (Cu-Ni) 1977–1980, 1983, 1984. Rev. Head of a tiger	0.20	0.40

ISSUE FOR THE FAO COIN PLAN

	VF	Unc
13 (12) 50 Paise (St) 1977–1981, 1983, 1984. Rev. Fish, ananas, hen, fruit	0.25	0.50

Yeoman Numbers

In order to help collectors and dealers, we have added after most SCHÖN-numbers the corresponding number assigned by R.S. Yeoman in his wellknown works entitled »A Catalog of Modern World Coins« and »Current Coins of the World«.

Barbados

Area: 165 sq. mi. Population: 266,640.
The most eastern of the Lesser Antilles, Barbados was discovered in 1519 by the Spaniards, but has been a British possession since 1625. The colonial status came to an end when independence was proclaimed on 30th November 1966. Barbados is a member of the Caribbean Free Trade Area (CARIFTA) and is linked with the countries of Antigua, Dominica, Grenada, Montserrat, St. Christopher (St. Kitts), Nevis and Anguilla, St. Lucia and St. Vincent to form the Monetary Union of the East Caribbean Dollar. The issuing authority for the whole Monetary Union is the East Caribbean Currency Authority with headquarters in Bridgetown, Barbados.
Capital: Bridgetown.

100 Cents = 1 East Caribbean Dollar;
since 3rd December 1973: 100 Cents = 1 Barbados Dollar

COMMEMORATIVE ISSUE FOR THE INAUGURATION
OF THE CARIBBEAN DEVELOPMENT BANK
AND FOR THE FAO COIN PLAN

			Unc	Proof
1 (2*)	4 Dollars (Cu–Ni) 1970. Arms with shield bearers and ornamented helmet. ℞ bananas, sugar-cane and value		5.00	12.50

*This number refers to Yeoman's East Caribbean Territories listings.

			Unc	Proof
2 (1)	1	Cent (Br) 1973–. Coat of arms, name of country, date. R broken trident, symbol of Barbados	0.20	0.50
3 (2)	5	Cents (Bra) 1973–. R South Point lighthouse, built in 1852	0.25	0.80
4 (3)	10	Cents (Cu-Ni) 1973–. R Bonaparte tern (Larus philadelphia – Laridae)	0.30	1.00
5 (4)	25	Cents (Cu-Ni) 1973–. R Morgan Lewis sugar mill	0.75	1.50
6 (5)	1	Dollar (Cu-Ni) 1973–. R flying fish (Hirundichthys affinis – Exocoëtidae)	1.00	1.80
7 (6)	2	Dollars (Cu-Ni) 1973–. R Staghorn coral (Acropora cervicornis – Madroporaria)	2.25	3.00
8 (7)	5	Dollars 1973–1984. Rev. Shell fountain in Bridgetown's Trafalgar square:		
		a) (Ag)		10.00
		b) (Cu-Ni)	5.00	
9 (8)	10	Dollars 1973–1981. Rev. Neptune, god of the sea with trident		
		a) (Ag)		12.50
		b) (Cu-Ni)	10.00	

350th ANNIVERSARY COMMEMORATIVE

			Unc	Proof
10 (9)	100	Dollars (Au) 1975. Rev. sailing vessel »Olive Blossom«	60.00	70.00

10th ANNIVERSARY OF INDEPENDENCE (8)

			Unc	Proof
11 (10)	1	Cent (Br) 1976	0.15	0.50
12 (11)	5	Cents (Bra) 1976	1.00	1.50
13 (12)	10	Cents (Cu-Ni) 1976	0.85	1.50
14 (13)	25	Cents (Cu-Ni) 1976	1.00	1.75
15 (14)	1	Dollar (Cu-Ni) 1976	2.00	2.50
16 (15)	2	Dollars (Cu-Ni) 1976	2.50	3.00
17 (16)	5	Dollars:		
		a) (Ag)		15.00
		b) (Cu-Ni)	12.50	
18 (17)	10	Dollars 1976:		
		a) (Ag)		22.00
		b) (Cu-Ni)	20.00	

		Unc	Proof

CORONATION JUBILEE

			Unc	Proof
19 (18)	25 Dollars (Ag) 1978		60.00	30.00
20 (19)	100 Dollars (Au) 1978. Human Rights:			
	a) .900 gold, dia. 20 mm, 4.06 gm		100.00	
	b) .900 gold, dia. 21 mm, 5.05 gm			100.00

YEAR OF THE CHILD

		Unc	Proof
21 (20)	200 Dollars (Au) 1979. Children, stylized:		
	a) .900 gold, dia. 24 mm, 8.12 gm	200.00	
	b) .900 gold, dia. 27 mm, 10.10 gm		250.00

10th ANNIVERSARY OF CARIBBEAN DEVELOPMENT BANK

		Proof
22 (21)	25 Dollars (Ag) 1980	30.00

CARIBBEAN FESTIVAL OF ARTS

		Proof
23 (22)	25 Dollars (Ag) 1981	30.00

WORLD FOOD DAY

		Unc	Proof
24 (24)	50 Dollars (Ag) 1981. Rev. Black Belly Sheep	25.00	
25 (23)	150 Dollars (Au) 1981. Poinciana, national flower and map		185.00

10th ANNIVERSARY OF THE CENTRAL BANK OF BARBADOS

		Unc	Proof
26 (25)	10 Dollars 1982. Rev. Sea-horse, emblem of the Central Bank:		
	a) (Ag)		40.00
	b) (Cu-Ni)	18.00	

250th ANNIVERSARY OF BIRTH OF GEORGE WASHINGTON

		Proof
27 (26)	250 Dollars (Au) 1982. Head of George Washington in front of a building	185.00

30th ANNIVERSARY OF THE CORONATION
OF HER MAJESTY QUEEN ELIZABETH II

			Unc	Proof
28 (27)	25 Dollars (Ag) 1983			35.00
29 (28)	10 Dollars 1983. Rev. Pelican:			
	a) (Ag)			50.00
	b) (Cu-Ni)		18.00	
30 (29)	100 Dollars (Au) 1983. Neptune with trident			150.00
31 (31)	10 Dollars (Ag) 1984. Rev. Three dolphins			50.00

FAO WORLD FISHERIES CONFERENCE

		Unc	Proof
32	50 Dollars (Ag) 1984	30.00	
33	100 Dollars (Au) 1984. Triton, sea god		130.00
34	100 Dollars (Au) 1985. Amphitrite, sea goddess		110.00

ROYAL VISIT (2)

		Unc	Proof
35	25 Dollars 1985. Elizabeth II. Rev. Arms:		
	a) (Ag) .925 silver, 28.28 g		40.00
	b) (Cu-Ni)	10.00	
36	500 Dollars (Au) 1985. Type as No. 35; .916⅔ gold, 47.54 g (250 pieces)		900.00

UNITED NATIONS DECADE FOR WOMEN

		Unc	Proof
37	20 Dollars (Ag) 1985. Arms. Rev. Woman teacher; .925 silver, 23.33 g		–.–

COMMONWEALTH GAMES IN EDINBURGH (2)

		Unc	Proof
38	25 Dollars (Ag) 1986. Rev. Discus thrower:		
	a) .500 silver, 28.28 g	20.00	
	b) .925 silver, 28.28 g		50.00
39	250 Dollars (Au) 1986; .916⅔ gold, 47.54 g (150 pieces)		–.–

Belgisch-Kongo **Belgian Congo** **Congo Belge**

This former Belgian Colony in Central Africa was originally the personal property of King Leopold II, under the name of "State of Congo". It secured independence on 30th June 1960.

Capital: Leopoldville, renamed Kinshasa on 1st July 1966.

100 Centimes = 1 Franc

STATE OF CONGO 1885–1908

			VF	XF
1 (9)	5	Centimes (Cu–Ni) 1906–1908. Crown and monogram of King Leopold II repeated five times in the form of a star. ℞ star and value (with central hole)	3.00	6.00
2 (10)	10	Centimes (Cu–Ni) 1906–1908	4.00	8.00
3 (11)	20	Centimes (Cu–Ni) 1906–1908	5.00	9.00

COLONY since 18th October 1908

4 (12)	5	Centimes (Cu–Ni) 1909. Type as No. 1, but with inscription CONGO BELGE – BELGISCH CONGO	5.00	10.00
5 (13)	10	Centimes (Cu–Ni) 1909	5.00	10.00
6 (14)	20	Centimes (Cu–Ni) 1909	6.50	15.00

ALBERT I 1909–1934

7 (15)	1	Centime (Cu) 1910–1919. Crown and monogram of King Albert I repeated five times in the form of a star. ℞ star and value (with central hole)	4.00	7.50
8 (16)	2	Centimes (Cu) 1910–1919	4.00	7.50
9 (17)	5	Centimes (Cu–Ni) 1910–1928	2.50	5.00
10 (18)	10	Centimes (Cu–Ni) 1910–1928	3.00	6.00
11 (19)	20	Centimes (Cu–Ni) 1910–1911	3.00	6.00
12 (20)	50	Centimes (Cu–Ni) 1921–1929. Laureate head l. of King Albert I (1875–1934). ℞ oil palm (Elaeis guineensis – Palmae)		
		a) Belgisch Congo	2.50	4.00
		b) Congo Belge	2.50	4.00

			VF	XF
13 (21)	1	Franc (Cu–Ni) 1920–1930		
		a) Belgisch Congo, 1920–1929	3.00	5.00
		b) Congo Belge, 1920–1930	3.00	5.00

LEOPOLD III 1934–1950

14 (22) 1 Franc (Bra) 1944–1949. African elephant (Loxodonta africana – Elephantidae). ℞ value — 1.50 / 2.50

15 (24) 2 Francs (Bra) 1943 (hexagonal). Issue of the mint of Philadelphia — 9.00 / 16.00

16 (23) 2 Francs (Bra) 1946–1947 — 2.50 / 5.00

17 (26) 5 Francs (Ni-Br) 1936–1937. Head l. of King Leopold III (1901–1983). Rev. Lion — 16.00 / 32.00

18 (25) 5 Francs (Bra) 1947–1948. African elephant. R value — 5.50 / 10.00

All valuations in the SCHÖN are stated in U.S. Dollars.

	VF	XF
19 (27) 50 Francs (Ag) 1944. African elephant. ℞ value	50.00	85.00

Nos. 14, 16, 17, 18 and 19 were struck at Pretoria, South Africa, because of World War II.

COMBINED ISSUES FOR THE BELGIAN CONGO AND RWANDA-URUNDI

BAUDOUIN 1950–1960

	VF	XF
20 (28) 5 Francs (Al–Br) 1952. Oil palm (Elaeis guineensis – Palmae). ℞ value in star	3.50	7.00
21 (29) 50 Centimes (Al) 1954–1955. Oil palm. ℞ arms	0.40	1.00

	VF	XF
22 (30) 1 Franc (Al) 1957–1960	1.00	1.80
23 (31) 5 Francs (Al) 1956–1959	1.50	2.50

For later issues, see under Congo-Kinshasa, Katanga, Burundi, Rwanda and Zaïre.

Belgien   # Belgium   **Belgique**

Belgie

Area: 11,779 sq. mi. Population: 9,880,000.
Since the Congress of Vienna in 1815, the territory of Belgium as we know it today was part of the kingdom of the United Low Countries. Following the revolution of September 1830, the Belgians obtained their independence and elected Prince Leopold of Saxe-Coburg as their king. Since 1921 there is an economic union and the monetary agreement with Luxemburg.
Capital: Brussels.
Most Belgian coins were issued with French as well as Flemish inscriptions. In the case of inscriptions in the two languages, there are usually two varieties, either »Belgie-Belgique« (Flemish = Fl) or »Belgique-Belgie« (French = Fr).

100 Centimes = 1 Belgian Frank (Franc)

LEOPOLD II 1865–1909

			VF	XF
1 (1)	1	Centime (Cu) 1869–1902, 1907. Crown above monogram of King Leopold II. ℞ lion and shield		
		a) Fl., 1882–1907	1.00	2.00
		b) Fr., 1869–1907	0.90	1.80
2 (2)	2	Centimes (Cu) 1869–1876, 1902–1909		
		a) Fl., 1902–1909	1.50	2.50
		b) Fr., 1869–1909	1.50	2.50
3 (3)	5	Centimes (Cu–Ni) 1894–1901. Lion emblem. ℞ value		
		a) Fl., 1894–1901	6.00	10.00
		b) Fr., 1894–1901	6.00	10.00
4 (4)	10	Centimes (Cu–Ni) 1894–1901		
		a) Fl, 1894–1901	5.00	10.00
		b) Fr., 1894–1901	5.00	10.00
5 (12)	5	Centimes (Cu–Ni) 1901–1907. Monogram with crown. ℞ value and laurel branch (with central hole)		
		a) Fl., 1902–1907	0.50	2.00
		b) Fr., 1901–1907	0.50	2.00
6 (13)	10	Centimes (Cu–Ni) 1901–1906		
		a) Fl., 1902–1906	0.40	1.00
		b) Fr., 1901–1906	0.40	1.00

	VF	XF
7(14) 25 Centimes (Cu–Ni) 1908–1909		
a) Fl., 1908	2.00	3.50
b) Fr., 1908–1909	2.00	3.50
8(15) 50 Centimes (Ag) 1901. Leopold II (1835–		
1909). ℞ lion and value		
a) Fl., 1901	5.00	10.00
b) Fr., 1901	5.00	10.00
9(16) 50 Centimes (Ag) 1907–1909. Leopold II.		
℞ value within wreath		
a) Fl., 1907–1909	4.50	10.00
b) Fr., 1907–1909	4.50	10.00

	VF	XF
10(17) 1 Franc (Ag) 1904–1909		
a) Fl., 1904–1909	5.00	10.00
b) Fr., 1904–1909	5.00	10.00
11(18) 2 Francs (Ag) 1904–1909		
a) Fl., 1904–1909	8.00	12.50
b) Fr., 1904–1909	8.00	12.50

ALBERT I 1909–1934

	VF	XF
12(22) 1 Centime (Cu) 1912–1914. Crown above		
monogram of King Albert I. ℞ lion		
with shield		
a) Fl., 1912	1.00	3.00
b) Fr., 1912–1914	1.00	3.00
13(23) 2 Centimes (Cu) 1910–1919		
a) Fl., 1910–1919	1.00	2.50
b) Fr., 1911–1919	1.00	2.50
14(24) 5 Centimes (Cu–Ni) 1910–1932. Mono-		
gram with crown. ℞ value and branch		
(with central hole)		
a) Fl., 1910–1928	0.60	1.00
b) Fl., 1930 (very rare)	60.00	120.00
c) Fr., 1910-1928	0.60	1.00
d) Fr., 1932 (very rare)	60.00	120.00

				VF	XF
15 (25)	10	Centimes (Cu–Ni) 1920–1929			
		a) Fl., 1920–1929		0.60	1.20
		b) Fr., 1920–1929		0.60	1.20

Of the same type: Nos. 24 and 25

			VF	XF
16 (26)	25	Centimes (Cu–Ni) 1910–1929		
		a) Fl., 1910–1929	0.60	1.20
		b) Fr., 1913–1929	0.60	1.20
17 (33)	50	Centimes (Ag) 1910–1914. King Albert I (1875–1934). ℞ value within wreath		
		a) Fl., 1910–1912	2.50	4.50
		b) Fr., 1910–1914	2.50	4.50
18 (34)	1	Franc (Ag) 1910–1914		
		a) Fl., 1910–1914	2.50	4.50
		b) Fr., 1910–1914	2.50	4.50
19 (35)	2	Francs (Ag) 1910–1912		
		a) Fl., 1911–1912	7.00	12.50
		b) Fr., 1910–1912	7.00	12.50
20 (37)	20	Francs (Au) 1914. King Albert I in uniform. ℞ national arms		
		a) Fl., 1914	120.00	140.00
		b) Fr., 1914	120.00	140.00

The coins issued during the German Occupation of Belgium in 1915–1918 are listed in the German section of this catalogue.

			VF	XF
21 (27)	50	Centimes (Ni) 1922–1934. Type: female figure representing Belgium, wounded but triumphant. ℞ caduceus		
		a) Fl., 1923–1934	0.40	0.80
		b) Fr., 1922–1934	0.40	0.80
22 (28)	1	Franc (Ni) 1922–1935		
		a) Fl., 1922–1935	0.50	0.90
		b) Fr., 1922–1935	0.50	0.90
23 (29)	2	Francs (Ni) 1923–1930		
		a) Fl., 1923–1930	2.00	4.00
		b) Fr., 1923–1930	2.00	4.00
24 (24a)	5	Centimes (Ni–Bra) 1930–1932. Type as No. 14, but with star		
		a) Fl., 1930–1931	1.20	2.00
		b) Fr., 1932	1.20	2.00
25 (25a)	10	Centimes (Ni–Bra) 1930–1932. Type as No. 15		
		a) Fl., 1930–1931	2.50	4.50
		b) Fr., 1930–1932	2.50	4.50
26 (30)	5	Francs = 1 Belga (Ni) 1930–1934. King Albert I. ℞ value within wreath; above, crown		
		a) Fl., 1930–1933	4.50	9.00
		b) Fr., 1930–1934	4.50	9.00

COMMEMORATIVE ISSUES (2) FOR THE CENTENNIAL OF INDEPENDENCE

27 (31) 10 Francs = 2 Belgas (Ni) 1930. Heads
left of Leopold I, reigned 1831–1865,
Leopold II, reigned 1865–1909 and
Albert I, reigned 1909–1934. ℞ value
between laurel branches

	VF	XF
a) Fl., 1930	110.00	200.00
b) Fr., 1930	110.00	200.00

28 (32) 20 Francs = 4 Belgas (Ni) 1931–1932.
Head left of Albert I. ℞ national arms

a) Fl., 1931–1932	95.00	150.00
b) Fr., 1931–1932	95.00	150.00

29 (36) 20 Francs (Ag) 1933–1934. Type as No. 28,
but without Belga denomination:

a) Fl., 1933–1934	8.00	12.50
b) Fr., 1933–1934	8.00	12.50

LEOPOLD III 1934–1950

30 (42) 5 Centimes (Ni–Bra) 1938–1940. Crown
above monogram of Leopold III. ℞
three shields of arms and value (with
central hole)

a) Belgie-Belgique, 1939–1940	0.40	1.00
b) Belgique-Belgie, 1938	0.40	1.00

31 (43) 10 Centimes (Ni–Bra) 1938–1939. Type
similar to No. 31, but arms of Namur
(Fl. Namen), Antwerp and Hasselt:

a) Belgie – Belgique, 1939	0.40	0.90
b) Belgique – Belgie, 1938–1939	0.40	0.90

32 (44) 25 Centimes (Ni–Bra) 1938–1939. Type

similar to No. 31, but arms of Mons
(Fl. Bergen), Brussels and Bruges:

		VF	XF
a) Belgie-Belgique, 1938		0.40	0.90
b) Belgique-Belgie, 1938–1939		0.40	0.90

Of the same type: Nos. 39–41

33 (45) 1 Franc (Ni) 1939–1940. Stylized tree
with three shields in foreground. (West
Flanders, Namur, Limburg). ℞ lion
and value:

a) Belgie-Belgique, 1939–1940	0.40	0.80
b) Belgique-Belgie, 1939	0.40	0.80

34 (46) 5 Francs (Ni) 1938–1939. Type as No. 33,
but arms of Ghent, Province of Ant-
werp and Liege:

a) Belgie-Belgique, 1938–1939	1.60	3.00
b) Belgique-Belgie, 1938	1.60	3.00

35 (47) 5 Francs (Ni) 1936–1937. Leopold III
(1901–1983). Rev. value:

a) Fl., 1936	25.00	40.00
b) Fr., 1936–1937	25.00	40.00

36 (49) 20 Francs (Ag) 1934–1935. Leopold III.
℞ crown, value, branches; inscription
in two languages

	6.00	10.50

37 (50) 50 Francs (Ag) 1939–1940. Leopold III.
℞ crown above shields of arms of the
nine provinces (Antwerp, Brabant,
West Flanders, East Flanders, Henne-
gau, Liege, Limburg, Luxemburg and
Namur):

a) Belgie-Belgique, 1939–1940	12.50	22.00
b) Belgique-Belgie, 1939–1940	12.50	22.00

				VF	XF
38 (48)	50	Francs (Ag) 1935. The Exhibition Hall. ℞ St. Michael, patron saint of the city of Brussels, and dragon			
		a) Fl., 1935		260.00	400.00
		b) Fr., 1935		260.00	400.00
39 (51)	5	Centimes (Zi) 1941–1943. As No. 30			
		a) Belgie-Belgique, 1941–1942		0.80	1.50
		b) Belgique-Belgie, 1941–1943		0.80	1.50
40 (52)	10	Centimes (Zi) 1941–1946. As No. 31			
		a) Belgie-Belgique, 1941–1946		0.90	2.00
		b) Belgique-Belgie, 1941–1943		0.90	2.00
41 (53)	25	Centimes (Zi) 1942–1946. As No. 32			
		a) Belgie-Belgique, 1942–1946		0.90	2.00
		b) Belgique-Belgie, 1942–1946		0.90	2.00
42 (54)	1	Franc (Zi) 1941–1947. Crowned shield of arms. ℞ crowned monogram, value, date			
		a) Belgie-Belgique, 1942–1947		0.90	2.00
		b) Belgique-Belgie, 1941–1943		0.90	2.00
43 (55)	5	Francs (Zi) 1941–1947. Head of Leopold III r. ℞ crown above value, and date			
		a) Fl., 1941–1947		1.50	3.50
		b) Fr., 1941–1947		1.50	3.50
44 (56)	2	Francs (zinc-coated steel) 1944. Name of countries in French and Flemish, laurel branches, above star. ℞ value between laurel branches. Philadelphia mint issue		3.00	4.50
45 (57)	1	Franc (Cu–Ni) 1950–. Head of goddess Ceres, cornucopia. ℞ crown over laurel branch, value			
		a) Fl., 1950–		0.10	0.20
		b) Fr., 1950–		0.10	0.20

46 (58) 5 Francs (Cu–Ni) 1948–

		VF	XF
a) Fl., 1948–		0.15	0.30
b) Fr., 1948–		0.15	0.30

47 (59) 20 Francs (Ag) 1949–1955. Head r. of Mercury, the messenger of the gods, with caduceus. ℞ lion with shield

a) Fl., 1949–1955	6.00	10.00
b) Fr., 1949–1955	6.00	10.00

48 (60) 50 Francs (Ag) 1948–1954

a) Fl, 1948–1954	10.00	16.00
b) Fr., 1948–1954	10.00	16.00

49 (61) 100 Francs (Ag) 1948–1954. Conjoined heads l. of Leopold I, Leopold II, Albert I and Leopold III, facing left. ℞ crowned shield of arms, encircled by the chain of the Order of Leopold:

a) Fl., 1948–1951	12.00	15.00
b) Fr., 1948–1954	12.00	15.00

BAUDOUIN I since 1950

50 (62) 20 Centimes (Br) 1953–1963. Head of miner. ℞ crown and value

a) Fl., 1954–	0.10	0.20
b) Fr., 1953–	0.10	0.20

51 (66) 25 Centimes (Cu–Ni) 1964–. Crown over monogram of Baudouin I. ℞ value

a) Fl., 1964–	0.08	0.16
b) Fr., 1964–	0.08	0.16

52 (63) 50 Centimes (Br) 1952–

a) Fl., 1952–	0.10	0.20
b) Fr., 1952–	0.10	0.20

Values are given for each coin in U.S. Dollars and reference to Yeoman-numbers.

COMMEMORATIVE ISSUE FOR THE BRUSSELS WORLD FAIR IN 1958

		VF	XF
53 (64)	50 Francs (Ag) 1958. Head of King Baudouin I l. ℞ emblem of "Expo 58" above the gothic Town Hall of Brussels built in 1402–1454; the tower is 90 m. high.		
	a) Fl., 1958	10.00	16.00
	b) Fr., 1958	10.00	16.00

COMMEMORATIVE ISSUE FOR THE MARRIAGE OF KING BAUDOUIN I AND DOÑA FABIOLA DE MORA Y ARAGON

54 (65) 50 Francs (Ag) 1960. Conjoined heads l. of Baudouin I (*1930) and Doña Fabiola (*1928), ℞ crown over arms of Belgium and Aragón; inscriptions in Latin   10.00   16.00

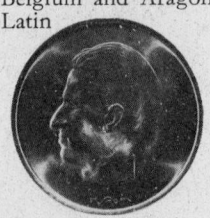 

55 (67) 10 Francs (Ni) 1969–1979. Head l. of Baudouin I. Rev. complete large national arms:
a) Fl., 1969–1979   0.30   0.60
b) Fr., 1969–1979   0.30   0.60

25th ANNIVERSARY OF THE SILVER JUBILEE OF
KING BAUDOUIN I

56 (68) 250 Francs (Ag) 1976. Head left of Baudouin I.
R crowned monogram:

		Unc	Proof
a) Fl.		15.00	
b) Fl., proof, stars on edge			20.00
c) Fr.		15.00	
d) Fr., proof, stars on edge			20.00

57 (A67) 20 Francs (Cu-Ni-Al) 1980–1982. Head left of Baudouin I. Rev. Laurel branch, value:

	XF	Unc
a) Fl.	0.60	0.80
b) Fr.	0.60	0.80

150th ANNIVERSARY OF INDEPENDENCE

58 (69) 500 Francs (Ag) 1980:

	Unc	Proof
a) Silver Clad Copper-Nickel, Fl.	15.00	
b) Silver Clad Copper-Nickel, Fr.	15.00	
c) (Ag) .510 silver, Fl.		25.00
d) (Ag) .510 silver, Fr.		25.00

59   5 Francs (Cu-Ni-Al) 1986. Head of Baudouin I. Rev. value, name of country:

	XF	Unc
a) Fl.	0.30	0.40
b) Fr.	0.30	0.40

61   50 Francs

Previous issues, see »Weltmünzkatalog 19. Jahrhundert« (World Coin Catalogue of the 19th Century)

Belize

Area: 8,867 sq. mi. Population: 165,000.

Since 1st June, 1973 when attaining full autonomy, British Honduras ist now called Belize. The place of the former capital of the same name is now taken by the newly built capital of Belmopan.

100 Cents = 1 British Honduras Dollar;
100 Cents = 1 Belize Dollar

			XF	Unc
1 (1)	1 Cent (Br) 1973–1976. Elizabeth II, crowned head facing right, R numeral of value in wreath, as legend name of the country BELIZE, denomination in letters, date		0.10	0.20
2 (2)	5 Cents (Ni-Bra) 1973–1976. R denomination in circle of dots, as legend name of the country BELIZE, date		0.10	0.20

		XF	Unc
3 (3)	10 Cents (Cu-Ni) 1974–1976, 1979, 1980. Type similar to No. 2	0.20	0.40
4 (4)	25 Cents (Cu-Ni) 1974–1976, 1979, 1980. Type similar to No. 2	0.40	0.80
5 (5)	50 Cents (Cu-Ni) 1974–1976, 1979, 1980. Type similar to No. 2	0.80	1.00

		Unc	Proof
6 (6)	1 Cent (Br) 1974. Arms. Rev. Swallow-tailed Kite (Elanoides forficatus – Accipitriade)	0.30	1.00

			Unc	Proof
7 (7)	5 Cents (Ni-Bra) 1974. Rev. Fork-tailed Flycatcher (Muscivora tyrannus – Tyrannidae)		0.40	1.00
8 (8)	10 Cents (Cu-Ni) 1974. Rev. Long-tailed Hermit Bird (Phaetornis superciliosus – Trochilidae)		1.00	1.50
9 (9)	25 Cents (Cu-Ni) 1974. Rev. Blue-crowned Motmot (Momotus momota – Momotidae)		2.00	2.50
10 (10)	50 Cents (Cu-Ni) 1974. Rev. Magnificent Frigate Bird (Fregata magnificens – Fregatidae)		2.80	3.50
11 (11)	1 Dollar (Cu-Ni) 1974–1985. Rev. Scarlet Macaw (Ara macao – Psittacidae)		5.00	7.00
12 (12)	5 Dollars (Cu-Ni) 1974–1985. Rev. Keel-billed Toucan (Ramphastos sulfuratus – Ramphastidae)		7.50	8.50
13 (13)	10 Dollars (Cu-Ni) 1974–1978. Rev. Great Curassow (Crax rubra – Cracidae)		15.00	15.00

			Proof
14 (6a)	1 Cent (Ag) 1974. Type as No. 6		3.00
15 (7a)	5 Cents (Ag) 1974. Type as No. 7		3.00
16 (8a)	10 Cents (Ag) 1974. Type as No. 8		3.50
17 (9a)	25 Cents (Ag) 1974. Type as No. 9		5.00
18 (10a)	50 Cents (Ag) 1974. Type as No. 10		8.00
19 (11a)	1 Dollar (Ag) 1974–1983. Type as No. 11		12.00
20 (12a)	5 Dollars (Ag) 1974–1983. Type as No. 12		15.00
21 (13a)	10 Dollars (Ag) 1974–1978. Type as No. 13		22.00

			Unc	Proof
22 (14)	1 Cent (Br) 1975, 1976. Type as No. 6, but value »1 CENT« (scalloped edge)		0.50	1.00
23 (15)	5 Cents (Ni-Bra) 1975, 1976. Type as No. 7, but value »5 CENTS«		1.00	1.20
24 (16)	10 Cents (Cu-Ni) 1975–1985. Type as No. 8, but value »10 CENTS«		1.50	2.00
25 (17)	25 Cents (Cu-Ni) 1975–1985. Type as No. 9, but value »25 CENTS«		2.50	3.00
26 (18)	50 Cents (Cu-Ni) 1975–1985. Type as No. 10, but value »50 CENTS«		3.00	3.50

			Proof
27 (14a)	1 Cent (Ag) 1975–1985. Type as No. 22		2.00
28 (15a)	5 Cents (Ag) 1975–1985. Type as No. 23		2.00
29 (16a)	10 Cents (Ag) 1975–1985. Type as No. 24		2.50
30 (17a)	25 Cents (Ag) 1975–1985. Type as No. 25		3.50
31 (18a)	50 Cents (Ag) 1975–1985. Type as No. 26		6.50

30th ANNIVERSARY OF UNITED NATIONS (24th Oct. 1975)

			XF	Unc
32 (19)	100 Dollars (Au) 1975. Coat of arms, date, fineness. R council-room, value		65.00	75.00

MAYAN COMMEMORATIVE

		Unc	Proof
33 (20)	100 Dollars (Au) 1976. R Mayan number and day heiroglyphs	200.00	75.00

		XF	Unc
34 (1a)	1 Cent (Al) 1976, 1979, 1980, 1982. Type as No. 1	0.10	0.20

		Unc	Proof
35 (14b)	1 Cent (Al) 1977–1985. Type as No. 22	0.10	1.00

		Unc	Proof
36 (2a)	5 Cents (Al) 1976, 1979, 1980, 1986. Type as No. 2	0.10	0.20

		Unc	Proof
37 (15b)	5 Cents (Al) 1977–1985. Type as No. 23	0.50	1.50
38 (21)	100 Dollars (Au) 1977. Carved jade head of the Mayan god Kinich Ahau	250.00	75.00
39 (22)	100 Dollars (Au) 1978. Itzamna, Lord of the Heavens and ruler of all the Mayan gods	185.00	75.00

CORONATION JUBILEE

40 (24)	25 Dollars (Ag) 1978	60.00	30.00
41 (23)	250 Dollars (Au) 1978. Jaguar	300.00	300.00
42 (25)	10 Dollars 1979. Flying Jabirus:		
	a) (Ag)		40.00
	b) (Cu-Ni)	18.00	25.00
43 (26)	100 Dollars (Au) 1979. Queen Angel-fish	125.00	80.00

CHRISTMAS 1979

44 (27)	100 Dollars (Au) 1979. Star of Bethlehem	120.00	90.00
45 (28)	10 Dollars 1980. Scarlet Ibis:		
	a) (Ag)		42.00
	b) (Cu-Ni)	22.00	
46 (30)	100 Dollars (Au) 1980. Moorish Idols (fishes)	150.00	80.00

		Unc	Proof
47 (31)	100 Dollars (Au) 1980. Orchids	150.00	80.00

10t ANNIVERSARY OF CARIBBEAN DEVELOPMENT BANK

| **48** (29) | 25 Dollars (Ag) 1980 | | 30.00 |

WORLD FOOD DAY

49 (32)	5 Cents (Al) 1981	0.40	
50 (33)	10 Dollars 1981. Roseate Spoonbill:		
	a) (Ag)		60.00
	b) (Cu-Ni)	28.00	30.00
51 (34)	50 Dollars (Au) 1981. White-necked Jacobin Hummingbird	75.00	40.00
52 (35)	100 Dollars (Au) 1981. Yellow Swallowtail Butterfly	200.00	150.00

NATIONAL INDEPENDENCE

53 (36)	100 Dollars (Au) 1981. National map	300.00	110.00
54 (37)	10 Dollars 1982. Yellow-headed Parrot:		
	a) (Ag)		50.00
	b) (Cu-Ni)	30.00	30.00
55 (38)	100 Dollars (Au) 1982. Kinkajou		150.00

30th ANNIVERSARY OF CORONATION OF QUEEN ELIZABETH II

56 (39)	25 Dollars (Ag) 1983		30.00
57 (40)	10 Dollars 1983. Ringed King Fisher:		
	a) (Ag)		50.00
	b) (Cu-Ni)	25.00	25.00
58 (41)	100 Dollars (Au) 1983, Margay Jungle Cat	400.00	135.00
59	100 Dollars (Au) 1984. White-tail Deer		100.00

		Unc	Proof
60	20 Dollars (Ag) 1984		40.00
61	10 Dollars 1984. Rev. Laughing Falcon:		
	a) (Ag) .925, 25,50 g		50.00
	b) (Cu-Ni)		25.00

FOR THE FAO COIN PLAN

		Unc	Proof
62	25 Cents (Cu-Ni) 1985	1.00	
63	100 Dollars (Au) 1985. Rev. Ocelot		135.00
64	10 Dollars 1985:		
	a) (Ag)		–.–
	b) (Cu-Ni)	–.–	

UNITED NATIONS DECADE FOR WOMEN 1976–1985

		Unc	Proof
65	20 Dollars (Ag) 1985		60.00

ROYAL VISIT (2)

		Unc	Proof
66	25 Dollars 1985. Elizabeth II. Rev. Arms:		
	a) (Ag) .925 silver, 28,28 g		25.00
	b) (Cu-Ni)	10.00	
67	500 Dollars (Au) 1985. Type as No. 66;		
	916⅔ gold, 47,54 g (250 pieces)		1000.00

200th ANNIVERSARY OF THE BIRTH OF JOHN JAMES AUDUBON

		Unc	Proof
68	50 Dollars (Ag) 1985. Arms. Rev. Red-		
	footed Booby; .925, 129,60 g		50.00

Area: 21 sq. mi. Population: 60,000.
The islands of Bermuda were discovered in 1522 by the Spaniard Juan de Bermúdez, then occupied and colonized by the English nearly one hundred years later. This group of islands, which number about 300, is situated about 677 miles south-east of Cape Hatteras, facing the North American Continent; it is the oldest self-governing British Colony (self-goverment granted 1888).
Capital: Hamilton.

12 Pence = 1 Shilling, 5 Shillings = 1 Crown, 20 Shillings = £ 1; since 6th February 1970: 100 Cents = 1 Bermuda Dollar

ISSUE COMMEMORATING THE 350th ANNIVERSARY OF THE FOUNDING OF THE COLONY

			XF	Unc
1 (1)	1 Crown (Ag) 1959. Crowned bust r. of Queen Elizabeth II. ℞ map between the sailing ship "Sea Venture" of Sir George Somer and a sailing boat of the Islands' Administration		10.00	15.00

2 (2) 1 Crown (Ag) 1964. Crowned bust r. of
        Queen Elizabeth II. ℞ arms of the
        Bermuda islands; lion holding shield

	Unc	Proof
	4.00	6.00

NEW CURRENCY: 100 Cents = 1 Bermuda Dollar

3 (3) 1 Cent (Br) 1970–. Head of Queen Eliza-
        beth II. ℞ wild boar (Sus scrofa domes-
        ticus – Suidae), reproduced from the
        reverse of pieces of 2, 3, 6 and 12 pence
        called »swine money«, which were
        current in the years 1616 to 1624, as
        the first coins issued in the New World
        by the English Colonists

	XF	Unc
	0.05	0.10

4 (4) 5 Cents (Cu-Ni) 1970–. ℞ banded
        imperial fish or Queen angel fish
        (Holacanthus ciliaris – Chaetodontidae)

	XF	Unc
	0.10	0.20

Values are given for each coin in U.S. Dollars and reference to Yeoman-numbers.

			XF	**Unc**

5 (5) 10 Cents (Cu-Ni) 1970–. R Bermuda lily or Easter lily (Lilium longiflorum – Liliaceae) — 0.15 — 0.30

6 (6) 25 Cents (Cu-Ni) 1970–. R white-tailed or yellow-billed tropical bird (Phaëthon lepturus – Phaënthontidae) — 0.30 — 0.60

7 (7) 50 Cents (Cu-Ni) 1970–. R arms of the Bermuda islands; lion holding shield — 0.75 — 1.00

8 (8) 1 Dollar (Ag) 1970. R map between two fishes — **Proof** — 25.00

9 (9) 20 Dollars (Au) 1970. R bird — **Proof** — 300.00

COMMEMORATIVE ISSUE FOR THE SILVER WEDDING OF THE BRITISH ROYAL COUPLE ON 20th NOVEMBER 1972

			Unc	**Proof**

10 (10) 1 Dollar (Ag) 1972. R map between crowned monograms:
a) .500 fine silver — 8.00
b) .925 fine silver — — 12.50

ROYAL VISIT COMMEMORATIVE (2)

11 (11) 25 Dollars 1975. Royal scepter and crowned monograms:
a) (Ag) — — 30.00
b) (Cu-Ni) — 20.00

12 (12) 100 Dollars (Au) 1975. Type as No. 11 — 130.00 — 150.00

25th ANNIVERSARY OF THE SILVER JUBILEE OF HER MAJESTY QUEEN ELIZABETH II (3)

13 (13) 25 Dollars (Ag) 1977. R depicts Bermuda's 18th century "ship penny" sailing vessel — 40.00 — 50.00

14 (14) 50 Dollars (Au) 1977. R Dinghy — 80.00 — 90.00

15 (15) 100 Dollars (Au) 1977. R "Deliverance", the first ship to be built in Bermuda — 150.00 — 170.00

WEDDING OF PRINCE CHARLES AND LADY DIANA (2)

			Unc	Proof
16 (16)	1	Dollar 1981. Rev. Conjoined heads:		
		a) (Ag)		25.00
		b) (Cu-Ni)	2.50	

			Unc	Proof
17 (17)	250	Dollars (Au) 1981. Type as No. 16:		
		a) Normal thickness, .917 gold, 15.97 g	350.00	350.00
		b) Pièfort		950.00
18 (18)	1	Dollar (Al-Br) 1983. Rev. Albatross and map	2.00	6.00

			Unc	Proof
19 (19)	5	Dollars (Al-Br) 1983. Rev. Onion and map	5.00	8.00

375th ANNIVERSARY OF THE SETTLEMENT OF BERMUDA (22)

			XF	Unc
20 (20)	25	Cents (Cu-Ni) 1984. Rev. Arms of the Bermudas	1.50	2.00
21 (21)	25	Cents (Cu-Ni) 1984. Rev. City of Hamilton	1.50	2.00
22 (22)	25	Cents (Cu-Ni) 1984. Rev. Town of St. George	1.50	2.00
23 (23)	25	Cents (Cu-Ni) 1984. Rev. Warwick	1.50	2.00
24 (24)	25	Cents (Cu-Ni) 1984. Rev. Smith's	1.50	2.00
25 (25)	25	Cents (Cu-Ni) 1984. Rev. Devonshire	1.50	2.00

			XF	Unc
26 (26)	25 Cents (Cu-Ni) 1984. Rev. Sandy's		1.50	2.00
27 (27)	25 Cents (Cu-Ni) 1984. Rev. Hamilton Parish		1.50	2.00
28 (28)	25 Cents (Cu-Ni) 1984. Rev. Paget		1.50	2.00
29 (29)	25 Cents (Cu-Ni) 1984. Rev. Pembroke		1.50	2.00
30 (30)	25 Cents (Cu-Ni) 1984. Rev. Southampton		1.50	2.00

		BU	Proof
31 (20a)	25 Cents (Ag) 1984. Type as No. 20		20.00
32 (21a)	25 Cents (Ag) 1984. Type as No. 21		20.00
33 (22a)	25 Cents (Ag) 1984. Type as No. 22		20.00
34 (23a)	25 Cents (Ag) 1984. Type as No. 23		20.00
35 (24a)	25 Cents (Ag) 1984. Type as No. 24		20.00
36 (25a)	25 Cents (Ag) 1984. Type as No. 25		20.00
37 (26a)	25 Cents (Ag) 1984. Type as No. 26		20.00
38 (27a)	25 Cents (Ag) 1984. Type as No. 27		20.00
39 (28a)	25 Cents (Ag) 1984. Type as No. 28		20.00
40 (29a)	25 Cents (Ag) 1984. Type as No. 29		20.00
41 (30a)	25 Cents (Ag) 1984. Type as No. 30		20.00

FOR THE TOURISM

42	1 Dollar 1985:		
	a) (Ag) .925 silver, 28,28 g		30.00
	b) (Ag) .500 silver, 28,28 g	20.00	
	c) (Cu-Ni)	3.00	

		XF	Unc
43	1 Cent (Br) 1986	0.20	2.50
44	5 Cents (Cu-Ni) 1986	0.20	2.50
45	10 Cents (Cu-Ni) 1986	0.30	5.00
46	25 Cents (Cu-Ni) 1986	0.75	10.00
47	50 Cents (Cu-Ni) 1986	1.50	12.00
48	1 Dollar (Ni-Bra) 1986	2.00	15.00
49	5 Dollars (Ni-Bra) 1986	6.00	17.50

25th ANNIVERSARY OF WORLD WILDLIFE FUND

		BU	Proof
50	1 Dollar 1986:		
	a) (Ag) .925 silver, 28,28 g	18.00	25.00
	b) (Cu-Ni)	3.00	

50th ANNIVERSARY OF COMMERCIAL AIR TRAVEL TO THE BERMUDAS

51	1 Dollar (Ag) 1987. Disembarking from a flying boat	–.–	–.–
52	25 Dollars (Pd) 1987. Rev. Sailing ship »Sea Venture«	–.–	

Bhutan　　　　　　　　# Bhutan
　　　　　　　　Druk-jul　　　　　　　　Bhoutan

Area: 18.077 sq. mi Population: 1,420,000.
Constitutional monarchy in the eastern Himalayas. Treaty of protection
with British India (8. 1. 1910) and with the Indian Union (8. 8. 1949). Summer residence: Thimphu, winter residence: Punakha.

64 Pice (Paise) = 1 Rupee; since 1957: 100 Naye Paise = 1 Rupee, 100 Rupees
= 1 Sertum; since 1974: 100 Chetrum (Paise) = 1 Ngultrum (Rupee)

Weight and fineness of the Sertum (gold) correspond to that of the
British Pound Sterling.
The Indian Rupee is commonly used as legal tender.

MAHARAJAH JIGME WANGCHUK 1926-1952

			VF	XF
1 (5)	1	Pice (Cu/Bra) 1875-1930. Inscription on both sides, irregular flan	3.00	6.00

MAHARAJAH JIGME DORJI WANGCHUK 1952–1972

			VF	XF
2 (3)	1	Pice (Br) undated (1951, 1954). Buddhist symbols	1.60	3.00

3 (1) 1 Pice (Br) 1928. Bust l. of Maharajah Jigme
Wangchuk. Rev. Buddhist symbols   25.00   40.00

			VF	XF
4 (4)	½ Rupee (Ag) 1928. Type as No. 3		22.00	30.00
5	½ Rupee (Ni) 1928, 1950. Type as No. 4:			
	a) (Y 4a) 1928, 1950; 5.83 gm.		2.50	5.00
	b) (Y 4b) 1950; 5.00 gm.		1.00	2.00

COMMEMORATIVE ISSUES (7) FOR THE 40th ANNIVERSARY OF THE BEGINNING OF THE REIGN OF MAHARAJAH JIGME WANGCHUK

		XF	Unc
6 (6)	25 Naye Paise (Cu–Ni) 1966. Bust l. of Sir Jigme Wangchuk. ℞ arms	0.30	0.60
7 (7)	50 Naye Paise (Cu–Ni) 1966	0.80	1.60
8 (8)	1 Rupee (Cu–Ni) 1966	1.00	2.00
9 (9)	3 Rupees (Cu–Ni) 1966		
	a) (Cu-Ni)	3.00	6.00
	b) (Ag)	Proof	45.00

		Unc	Proof
10 (40)	1 Sertum (Au) 1966	125.00	150.00
11 (41)	2 Sertum (Au) 1966	225.00	250.00
12 (42)	5 Sertum (Au) 1966	550.00	650.00

There are also off-metal strikes in platinum of Nos. 10-12.

Unc

13 (43)   1 Sertum (Au) 1970   130.00

MARHARAJAH JIGME SINGH WANGCHUK since 1972

ISSUES (2) FOR THE FAO COIN PLAN

		Unc	Proof
14 (10)	20 Chetrum (Bra) 1974. Rice cultivation. R national emblem, name of country, denomination	0.50	1.50

15 (11)   15 Ngultrum (Ag) 1974. Type as No. 14   8.00   35.00

16 (12)   5 Chetrums (Al) 1974, 1975   0.20   1.00

168   **Bhutan**

17   18

| 17 (13) | 10 Chetrums (Al) 1974 | 0.40 | 1.00 |
| 18 (14) | 25 Chetrums (Cu-Ni) 1974, 1975 | 0.60 | 2.50 |

| 19 (15) | 1 Ngultrum (Cu-Ni) 1974, 1975 | 1.00 | 4.00 |

INTERNATIONAL WOMEN'S YEAR 1975 (2)

		Unc	Proof
20 (16)	10 Chetrums (Al) 1975, 1976	0.70	–.–
21 (17)	30 Ngultrums (Ag) 1975, 1976	10.00	18.00

22 (18)	5 Chhertum (Br) 1979		0.60	1.00
23 (19)	10 Chhertum (Br) 1979		1.20	2.00
24 (20)	25 Chhertum (Cu-Ni) 1979		2.00	4.00
25 (21)	50 Chhertum (Cu-Ni) 1979		2.50	5.00
25 (22)	1 Ngultrum (Cu-Ni) 1979		3.00	6.00
27 (23)	3 Ngultrum 1979:			
	a) (Ag)			30.00
	b) (Cu-Ni)		3.00	7.50
28 (24)	1 Sertum 1979:			
	a) (Au)		140.00	160.00
	b) (Pt)			250.00
29 (25)	2 Sertum 1979:			
	a) (Au)		225.00	250.00
	b) (Pt)			500.00
30 (26)	5 Sertum 1979:			
	a) (Au)		600.00	700.00
	b) (Pt)			1000.00

WORLD FOOD DAY 1981

31 (27)	50 Ngultrums (Ag) 1981. Rev. Muruk (Bos mutus grunniens – Bovidae)	25.00	35.00

INTERNATIONAL YEAR OF DISABLED PERSONS 1981

32 (30)	200 Ngultrum (Ag) 1981:			
	a) .925 silver, 28.28 g	25.00	30.00
	b) Piéfort, .925 silver, 56.56 g		120.00

75th ANNIVERSARY OF MONARCHY (2)

33 (28)	200 Ngultrum (Ag) 1982. Bust of Maharajah Wangchuk (1907–1926)	25.00	35.00
34 (29)	1 Sertum (Au) 1982. Type as No. 33	185.00	185.00

INTERNATIONAL GAMES 1984

35   25 Ngultrum (Cu-Ni) 1984. Rev. Boxing   35.00

Note: The above is not an official issue.

UNITED NATIONS DECADE FOR WOMEN 1976–1985

36   100 Ngultrum (Ag) 1984. Arms. Rev. Rice
         cultivation; .925 silver, 23.33 g   35.00

Biafra

Area: 29,370 sq. mi. Population: 12,802,000 (1970).

On 30th May 1967, on the strength of a request from the Consultative Assembly of the region inhabited predominantly by the Ibos, the Military Governor of the Eastern region of Nigeria proclaimed independence as "The Republic of Biafra". Following a war which lasted 2½ years, and the slow occupation of the country by the Nigerian Federal troops, Biafra surrendered in January 1970. As a result of this the country is again part of Nigeria.

12 Pence = 1 Shilling, 20 Shillings = 1 £

			VF	XF
1 (1)	3 Pence (Al) 1969. Coconut palm (Cocos nucifera – Palmae); in background, rising sun; the whole in a bow of U-shape; inscription around: PEACE. UNITY. FREEDOM. ℞ Name of country: REPUBLIC OF BIAFRA. Mark of value, date		12.00	35.00

2 (2)	1 Shilling (Al) 1969. ℞ crowned hawk eagle (Stephanoaëtus coronatus – Accipitridae) standing on elephant's tusk. Name of country: REPUBLIC OF BIAFRA. Value, date		10.00	30.00
A2	1 Shilling (Al) 1969. Type as No 2, but value: ONE SHILLING		–.–	–.–
3 (3)	2½ Shillings (Al) 1969. Rev. Leopard		18.00	40.00

| 4 | 1 £ (Ag) 1969 | Unc | 100.00 |

COMMEMORATIVE ISSUES (5) FOR THE 2nd ANNIVERSARY OF THE PROCLAMATION OF INDEPENDENCE

| 5 | 1 £ (Au) 1969. National arms. ℞ imperial eagle standing on parchment; in the background, rising sun, value | Proof | 90.00 |
| 6 | 2 £ (Au) 1969. Type as No. 5 | Proof | 160.00 |

7	5 £ (Au) 1969. Type as No. 5	Proof	320.00
8	10 £ (Au) 1969. Type as No. 5	Proof	750.00
9	25 £ (Au) 1969. Type as No. 5	Proof	1600.00

Bolivien   # Bolivia   **Bolivie**

Area: 422,538 sq. mi. Population: 6,550,000.
Bolivia covers mostly the high areos of Ancient Peru, which formerly
belonged to the Empire of the Incas and had been part of the Viceroyality of
Peru since the 16th century. In 1825 Bolivia became a Republic.
Capital: La Paz, though according to the Constitution it should be the
town of Sucre.

100 Centavos = 1 Boliviano; since 1st January 1963:
100 Centavos = 1 Peso Boliviano

			VF	**XF**
1 (47a)	5	Centavos (Ag) 1885–1900. National arms. R value	4.00	8.00
2 (48a)	10	Centavos (Ag) 1885–1900	6.00	10.00
3 (49a)	20	Centavos (Ag) 1885–1907	5.00	8.00
4 (51b)	50	Centavos (Ag) 1891–1900	6.00	11.00
5	5	Centavos (Cu-Ni) 1893–1919, 1935. Sun rising over the mount Potosi, vicuña (Lama vicugna – Camelidae). R caduceus and value		
		a) (Y 45) 1893–1919	1.00	4.00
		b) (Y 57) 1935, smaller diameter	0.60	1.00

6	10	Centavos (Cu-Ni) 1893–1919, 1935–1936		
		a) (Y 46) 1893–1919	1.00	4.00
		b) (Y 58) 1935–1936, smaller diameter	0.60	1.20
7 (55)	20	Centavos (Ag) 1909	3.00	6.00

8 (54)   50 Centavos (Ag) 1900–1908. National

		VF	**XF**
	arms with Andean condor (Vultur gryphus – Cathartidae). ℞ value in wreath (3 types)	6.00	12.00
9 (60)	10 Centavos (Cu–Ni) 1937. Sun rising over mount Potosi, vicuña. ℞ hand holding torch.	1.00	2.50
10 (61)	50 Centavos (Cu–Ni) 1937	40.00	80.00
11	10 Centavos. Same type as No. 6		
	a) (Y 58) (Cu–Ni) 1939	0.30	0.60
	b) (Y 57a) (Zi) 1942	1.00	2.00
12 (58a)	20 Centavos (Zi) 1942. Same type as No. 7	1.00	2.00
13	50 Centavos. Same type as No. 5		
	a) (Y 59) (Cu–Ni) 1939	1.30	2.50
	b) (Y 59a) (Br) 1942	0.40	0.60

| 14 (62) | 1 Boliviano (Br) 1951. Sun rising over mount Potosi, vicuña. ℞ value in wreath | 0.50 | 1.00 |

| 15 (63) | 5 Bolivianos (Br) 1951. National arms. ℞ value in wreath | 0.80 | 1.50 |

| 16 (64) | 10 Bolivianos (Br) 1951. Head r. of Simón Bolívar (1783–1830), President of the State of Bolivia 1825–1826. ℞ value in wreath | 1.50 | 3.00 |

		VF	XF
17	5 Bolivianos (Au) 1952. Agricultural worker	60.00	75.00

18	10 Bolivianos (Au) 1952. Miner	130.00	140.00

19	20 Bolivianos (Au) 1952. Head of Germán Busch	220.00	280.00

20	50 Bolivianos (Au) 1952. Head of Gualberto Villarroel	500.00	650.00

CURRENCY REFORM:
1000 old Bolivianos = 1 Peso Boliviano

			VF	XF
21 (66)	5	Centavos (Cu-St) 1965–. Sun rising over mount Potosi, vicuña. R value and date between branches	0.08	0.16
22 (67)	10	Centavos (Cu-St) 1965–. Same type as No. 21	0.10	0.20
23 (68)	20	Centavos (Ni-St) 1965–. Same type as No. 21	0.12	0.25
24 (71)	25	Centavos (Cu-Ni) 1971, 1972, 1974. Type as No. 21 (dodecagonal)	0.15	0.30

			VF	XF
25 (69)	50	Centavos (Ni-St) 1965, 1967, 1972–1974, 1978, 1980. Same type as No. 21	0.25	0.50
26 (70)	1	Peso Boliviano (Cu-Ni) 1968–1970, 1972–1974, 1978, 1980. Same type as No. 21	0.40	0.80

COMMEMORATIVE ISSUE FOR THE FAO COIN PLAN AND FOR THE 23rd ANNIVERSARY OF THE FAO
(16th October 1968)

			XF	Unc
27 (72)	1	Peso Boliviano (Ni) 1968. Obverse as No. 25. R under the value: the date 16–10–68 and the legend: GUERRA CONTRA EL HAMBRE	18.00	30.00

150th ANNIVERSARY OF INDEPENDENCE (3)

28 (73)	100	Pesos Bolivianos (Ag) 1975. Coat of arms. R conjoined heads left of Simón Bolívar and Hugo Banzer Suarez	10.00

29 (74) 250 Pesos Bolivianos (Ag) 1975. Type as No. 28 — 15.00

30 (75) 500 Pesos Bolivianos (Ag) 1975. Type as No. 28 — 20.00

31 (76) 5 Pesos Bolivianos (Cu-Ni) 1976, 1978, 1980 — 1.00 — 3.00

INTERNATIONAL YEAR OF THE CHILD (2)

Proof

32 (77) 200 Pesos Bolivianos (Ag) 1979:
  a) .925 silver, 23.32 g — 40.00
  b) Piéfort, .925 silver, 46.65 g (135 pieces) — 180.00

33 (78) 4000 Pesos Bolivianos (Au) 1979.
  a) .900 gold, 17,17 g — 260.00
  b) Piéfort, .900 gold, 34.35 g (40 pieces) — 2000.00

Yeoman Numbers

In order to help collectors and dealers, we have added after most SCHÖN-numbers the corresponding number assigned by R.S. Yeoman in his wellknown works entitled »A Catalog of Modern World Coins« and »Current Coins of the World«.

Previous issues, see »Weltmünzkatalog 19. Jahrhundert« (World Coin Catalogue of the 19th Century)

Area: 221,146 sq. mi. Population: 1,100,000.
Under the name of Bechuanaland it was a British Protectorate since 1885; it obtained internal autonomy in 1965; since 30th September 1966 it has been an independet Republic with the name of Botswana.
Capital: Gaborone.

100 Cents = 1 Rand; since 23th August 1976: 100 Thebe = 1 Pula

Until 30th November 1976 Botswana belonged to the monetary area of the South African Rand.

COMMEMORATIVE ISSUE (2) FOR THE DECLARATION OF INDEPENDENCE ON 30th SEPTEMBER 1966

			Unc	Proof
1 (1)	50	Cents (Ag) 1966. Head l. of Sir Seretse Khama (*1921), Head of State. ℞ national arms supported by Chapman's zebras (Equus quagga chapmani – Equidae)	8.00	
2 (2)	10	Thebes (Au) 1966		220.00

ISSUE FOR THE FAO COIN PLAN (6)

			Unc	Proof
3 (3)	1	Thebe (Al) 1976, 1981, 1983, 1984. Arms, date. Rev. Turako	0.20	1.00
4 (4)	5	Thebe (Br) 1976, 1977, 1979–1981, 1984. Rev. Toko	0.40	1.00
5 (5)	10	Thebe (Cu-Ni) 1976, 1977, 1979–1981, 1984. Rev. South African Oryx	0.50	1.50
6 (6)	25	Thebe (Cu-Ni) 1976, 1977, 1980, 1981, 1984. Rev. Zebu	1.00	2.00
7 (7)	50	Thebe (Cu-Ni) 1976, 1977, 1980, 1981, 1984. Rev. African fish eagle	2.00	3.00
8 (8)	1	Pula (Cu-Ni) 1976, 1977, 1981. Rev. Zebra (scalloped edge)	3.00	5.00

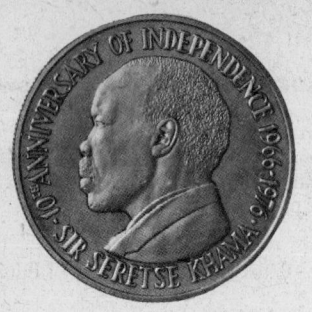 

			Unc	Proof
9 (9)	5 Pula (Ag) 1976. Bust left of Sir Seretse Khama (1921–1980). Rev. The Botswana National Assembly Building, with value above and country name below:			
	a) .500 silver, 28.5 g		15.00	
	b) .925 silver, 28.28 g			25.00
10 (10)	150 Pula (Au) 1976. Type as No. 9; .916⅔ gold, 15.98 g		260.00	300.00

CONSERVATION COMMEMORATIVE (3)

11 (11)	5 Pula (Ag) 1978. Rev. South African Oryx:			
	a) .925 silver, 25.31 g		25.00	
	b) .925 silver, 28.28 g			35.00
12 (12)	10 Pula (Ag) 1978. Rev. Klipspringer:			
	a) .925 silver, 31.65 g		30.00	
	b) .925 silver, 35 g			45.00
13 (13)	150 Pula (Au) 1978. Rev. Brown Hyaena; .900 gold, 33.437 g		550.00	650.00

WORLD FOOD DAY

14 (16)	2 Thebe (Al-Br) 1981. Millet		0.50	2.00

Values are given for each coin in U.S. Dollars and reference to Yeoman numbers.

INTERNATIONAL YEAR OF DISABLED PERSONS (2)

		Unc	Proof
15 (14)	5 Pula (Ag) 1981:		
	a) .925 silver, 28.28 g	20.00	
	b) Piéfort, .925 silver, 56.56 g		30.00

16 (15)	150 Pula (Au) 1981:		
	a) .916 ⅔ gold, 15.98 g	250.00	300.00
	b) Piéfort, 916 ⅔ gold, 31.95 g		1100.00

COMMONWEALTH GAMES IN EDINBURGH

17	2 Pula (Ag) 1986. Rev. Runner with flag:		
	a) .500 silver, 28.28 g	12.00	
	b) .925 silver, 28.28 g		20.00

25th ANNIVERSARY OF WORLD WILDLIFE FUND (2)

18	2 Pula (Ag) 1986. Rev. Slaty Egret; .925 silver, 28.28 g		25.00

Proof

19   5 Pula (Au) 1986. Rev. Lechwe Water-
bucks; .916 ⅔ gold, 15.98 g   280.00

Brasilien   # Brazil   **Brésil**
Estados Unidos do Brasil

Area: 3,273,832 sq. mi. Population: 138,000,000.
The largest country in South America, it was discovered in the year 1500 by
Pedro Alvares Cabral who took possession in the name of Portugal. In 1822
Brazil freed itself from the colonial yoke by the Declaration of Independ-
ence. First an Empire, it has been a Republic since 15th November 1889.
Capital: Rio de Janeiro; since 21st April 1960: Brasilia.

1000 Reis = 1 Milreis
Since 1942 100 Centavos = 1 Cruzeiro
From 1964 to 1967 only Cruzeiros
Since 1967 100 Centavos = 1 Cruzeiro Novo
Since 15th May 1970: 100 Centavos = 1 Cruzeiro

			VF	**XF**
1 (1)	20	Reis (Br) 1889–1912. Arms. ℞ value in circle	1.50	3.00
2 (2)	40	Reis (Br) 1889–1912. "Southern Cross" within circle of stars	1.50	3.00
3 (3)	100	Reis (Cu–Ni) 1889–1900	1.50	3.00
4 (4)	200	Reis (Cu–Ni) 1889–1900	3.00	10.00

COMMEMORATIVE ISSUES (4) FOR THE 400th ANNIVERSARY
OF THE DISCOVERY OF BRAZIL

5 (8)	400	Reis (Ag) 1900. Cross within circle. ℞ value in wreath	50.00	70.00
6 (9)	1000	Reis (Ag) 1900. Liberty head between symbols of progress: steamer, railway line and plough. ℞ value in wreath	70.00	150.00
7 (10)	2000	Reis (Ag) 1900. Sailing ship of the time of discovery	150.00	250.00
8 (11)	4000	Reis (Ag) 1900. Pedro Alvares Cabral (c. 1468–1526), explorer and seaman	350.00	600.00
9 (12)	100	Reis (Cu–Ni) 1901. Liberty head r. ℞ arms	1.00	3.00
10 (13)	200	Reis (Cu–Ni) 1901	1.00	3.00
11 (14)	400	Reis (Cu–Ni) 1901	2.00	5.00
12 (15)	500	Reis (Ag) 1906–1912. Liberty head l. ℞ value	5.00	10.00
13 (16)	1000	Reis (Ag) 1906–1912	6.00	12.00
14 (17)	2000	Reis (Ag) 1906–1912	10.00	22.00

			VF	XF
15 (25)	10000 Reis (Au) 1889–1922. Liberty head l. Rev. Arms		350.00	650.00
16 (26)	20000 Reis (Au) 1889–1922. Liberty head l. Rev. »Southern Cross«		450.00	700.00
17 (B14)	400 Reis (Cu-Ni) 1914. Statue of Liberty holding shield with inscription LEX		90.00	150.00
18 (18)	500 Reis (Ag) 1912. Liberty head r. ℞ arms		8.50	12.00
19 (19)	1000 Reis (Ag) 1912–1913		8.50	14.00
20 (20)	2000 Reis (Ag) 1912–1913		14.00	22.00
21 (21)	500 Reis (Ag) 1913. Same type as No. 18. ℞ inscription over arms		6.00	12.00
22 (22)	1000 Reis (Ag) 1913. Same type as No. 19. ℞ inscription over arms		9.00	16.50
23 (23)	2000 Reis (Ag) 1913. Same type as No. 20. ℞ inscription over arms		10.00	18.00
24 (27)	20 Reis (Cu-Ni) 1918–1935. Liberty head r. ℞ value		0.80	1.50
25 (28)	50 Reis (Cu-Ni) 1918–1935		0.80	1.50
26 (29)	100 Reis (Cu-Ni) 1918–1935		0.80	1.80
27 (30)	200 Reis (Cu–Ni) 1918–1935		0.80	1.80
28 (31)	400 Reis (Cu–Ni) 1918–1935		0.80	1.80
29 (32)	500 Reis (Al–Br) 1924–1930. Symbolic figure of the Republic holding horn of plenty. ℞ value in wreath		0.80	1.80
30 (33)	1000 Reis (Al–Br) 1924–1931		1.20	2.00
31 (24)	2000 Reis (Ag) 1924–1934. Liberty head. ℞ value in wreath		5.00	9.00

COMMEMORATIVE ISSUES (3) FOR THE CENTENARY OF INDEPENDENCE

32 (34)	500 Reis (Al–Br) 1922. Conjoined busts of Dom Pedro I (1798–1834), Emperor of Brazil 1822–1831, and Epitácio da Silva Pessòa (1865–1942), President from 1919 to 1922. ℞ torch between crown and Liberty cap		1.00	2.00
33 (35)	1000 Reis (Al–Br) 1922		2.00	5.00

34 (38) 2 Milreis (Ag) 1922. ℞ arms of the Empire and the Republic:

	VF	XF
a) Fine silver content 900	7.00	12.00
b) Fine silver content 500	7.00	12.00

COMMEMORATIVE ISSUES (6) FOR THE 400th ANNIVERSARY OF COLONIZATION 1532–1932

35 (39) 100 Reis (Cu–Ni) 1932. Bust facing of Kazike Tibiriçá. († 1562). ℞ value   2.60   5.00

36 (40) 200 Reis (Cu–Ni) 1932. Globe. ℞ sailing ship of the time of discovery   2.60   5.00

37 (41) 400 Reis (Cu–Ni) 1932. Map of South America. ℞ Lusinian cross   6.00   11.00

38 (42) 500 Reis (Al–Br) 1932. João Ramalho (1494–1584), a Portuguese colonist and founder of the town of Santo Andre; he married the daughter of Kazike Tibiriçá. ℞ cuirass   7.00   12.00

39 (43) 1000 Reis (Al–Br) 1932. Standing figure facing of Martim Affonso da Sousa (c. 1500–1571), general, seaman and colonist. ℞ arms   7.00   12.00

40 (44) 2000 Reis (Ag) 1932. Bust three-quarters to
r. of John III (1502 to 1557), King of
Portugal from 1521 to 1557. ℞ arms

	VF	XF
	5.00	10.00

41 (45) 100 Reis (Cu–Ni) 1936–1938. Bust facing
of Admiral Marques Tamandaré (1807
–1897), founder of the Brazilian Navy.
℞ anchor

	1.20	2.00

42 (46) 200 Reis (Cu–Ni) 1936–1938. Bust facing
of Viscount de Mauá (1813–1889), his
family name was Irineu Evangelista de
Souza, builder of the first railway line
Rio de Janeiro to Queimados. ℞ engine

	1.60	3.00

43 (47) 300 Reis (Cu–Ni) 1936–1938. Head facing
of Antonio Carlos Gomes (1836–
1896), composer. ℞ lyre

	2.00	3.50

			VF	XF
44 (48)	400	Reis (Cu–Ni) 1936–1938. Head facing of Oswaldo Cruz (1872–1917), microbiologist, well-known for his research into yellow fever. ℞ lamp	2.00	3.00

45	500	Reis (Al-Br) 1935–1938. Bust facing of Diego Antônio Feijó (1784–1843), Regent of Brazil 1835–1837. ℞ column		
		a) (Y 49) 1935; 4 gm.	7.00	12.50
		b) (Y 50) 1936–1938; 5 gm.	2.00	4.00

46	1000	Reis (Al-Br) 1935–1938. Fr. José de Anchieta (1534–1597). ℞ open Bible		
		a) (Y 51) 1935, diameter 26 mm	4.00	8.00
		b) (Y 52) 1936–1938, diameter 24 mm	2.00	4.00
47 (55)	2000	Reis (Ag) 1935. Portrait l. of Field-Marshal Luiz Alves de Lima, Duke of Caxias (1803 to 1880), Commanding Officer of the troops of the Emperor of Brazil. ℞ sword	3.00	6.00

			VF	XF

48   2000 Reis (Al-Br) 1936–1938. Portrait r. of Duke of Caxias. R sword

a) (Y 53) 1936–1938, round   3.00   6.00

b) (Y 54) 1938, dodecagonal   4.00   8.00

49 (56) 5000 Reis (Ag) 1936–1938. Head l. of Alberto Santos Dumont (1873–1932), pioneer aviator; on 23–10–1906 he flew 60 m. in France. R eagle's wing   4.00   7.00

50 (57) 100 Reis (Cu–Ni) 1938–1942. Dr. Getúlio Dornelles Vargas (1883–1954), President of State from 1930 to 1945 and from 1951 to 1954. R value   0.80   1.50

51 (58) 200 Reis (Cu–Ni) 1938–1942   0.80   1.50

52 (59) 300 Reis (Cu–Ni) 1938–1942   0.90   1.80

53 (60) 400 Reis (Cu–Ni) 1938–1942   1.50   3.00

Values are given for each coin in U.S. Dollars and reference to Yeomannumbers.

54 (61) 500 Reis (Al–Br) 1939. Bust facing of Joaquim Maria Machado de Assis (1839–1908), author and poet. ℞ value in wreath

	VF	XF
	1.00	3.00

55 (62) 1000 Reis (Al–Br) 1939. Bust facing of Tobias Barreto de Menezes (1839–1889), philosopher and poet. ℞ value in wreath

1.00	3.00

56 (63) 2000 Reis (Al–Br) 1939. Bust facing of Field-Marshal Floriano Peixoto (1842–1895). President of State from 1891 to 1894. ℞ value in wreath — 1.00 | 4.00

57 (64)   10 Centavos (Cu–Ni) 1942–1943. Getúlio D. Vargas. ℞ value — 0.50 | 1.00

58 (64a) 10 Centavos (Al–Br) 1943–1947. Same type as No. 57 — 0.50 | 1.00

59 (65)   20 Centavos (Cu–Ni) 1942–1943 — 0.70 | 1.50

60 (65a) 20 Centavos (Al–Br) 1943–1948. Same type as No. 59 — 0.70 | 1.50

Values are given for each coin in U.S. Dollars and reference to Yeomann numbers.

		VF	XF
61 (66)	50 Centavos (Cu–Ni) 1942–1943	0.80	1.60
62 (66a)	50 Centavos (Al–Br) 1943–1947. Same type as No. 61	0.40	0.80
63 (67)	1 Cruzeiro (Al–Br) 1942–1956. Map of Brazil. ℞ value	0.80	1.20
64 (68)	2 Cruzeiros (Al–Br) 1942–1956	0.80	1.50
65 (69)	5 Cruzeiros (Al–Br) 1942–1943	2.50	5.00

66 (73) 10 Centavos (Al–Br) 1947–1955. Bust l. of José Bonifacio de Andrada e Silva (1763 to 1838), fighter for independence, so-called "Patriarch of Independence", Paulistan politician. ℞ value   0.40   0.80

67 (74) 20 Centavos (Al–Br) 1948–1956. Bust l. of Ruy Barbosa (1849–1923), jurist, author, politician. ℞ value   0.50   1.00

68 (75) 50 Centavos (Al–Br) 1948–1956. Bust l. of General Eurico Gaspar Dutra (*1885), President of State from 1946 to 1951. ℞ value   0.50   1.00

			VF	XF
69 (76)	10	Centavos (Al) 1956–1961. National arms. ℞ value	0.10	0.20
70 (77)	20	Centavos (Al) 1956–1961	0.15	0.30
71 (78)	50	Centavos (Al–Br) 1956	0.35	0.70
72 (81)	50	Centavos (Al) 1957–1962	0.25	0.50
73 (79)	1	Cruzeiro (Al–Br) 1956	1.20	2.40
74 (82)	1	Cruzeiro (Al) 1957–1962	0.35	0.70
75 (80)	2	Cruzeiros (Al–Br) 1956	1.40	2.40
76 (83)	2	Cruzeiros (Al) 1957–1962	0.35	0.70
77 (84)	10	Cruzeiros (Al) 1965. Map of Brazil. ℞ value	0.10	0.20

78 (85)	20	Cruzeiros (Al) 1965	0.15	0.30

79 (86)	50	Cruzeiros (Cu–Ni) 1965. Liberty head l. ℞ value, branch of a coffee tree, date	0.40	0.80

NEW CURRENCY: 100 Centavos = 1 Cruzeiro Novo

			XF	Unc
80 (87)	1	Centavo (St). Liberty head l. R value, date:		
		a) 1967	0.05	0.10
		b) 1969, 1975; thinner planchet	0.05	0.10

81 (88)	2	Centavos (St). Same type as No. 80:		
		a) 1967	0.05	0.10
		b) 1969, 1975; thinner planchet	0.05	0.10

			XF	Unc
82 (89)	5 Centavos (St). Same type as No. 80:			
	a) 1967		0.10	0.20
	b) 1969, 1975, thinner planchet		0.08	0.16

83 (90)	10 Centavos (Cu-Ni). Factory:			
	a) 1967		0.15	0.30
	b) 1970, thinner planchet		0.10	0.20

84 (91)	20 Centavos (Cu-Ni) Oil-derrick:			
	a) 1967		0.25	0.35
	b) 1970, thinner planchet		0.10	0.20

85 (92)	50 Centavos. Steamship at quay-side:			
	a) (Ni) 1967		0.50	1.00
	b) (Cu–Ni) 1970		0.30	0.70

86 (93)	1 Cruzeiro (Ni) 1967–1970. Value, date, branch of a coffee tree:			
	a) 1967, pattern		–.–	–.–
	b) 1970		0.50	1.00

COMMEMORATIVE ISSUES (3) FOR THE
150th ANNIVERSARY OF INDEPENDENCE

		XF	Unc
87 (94)	1 Cruzeiro (Ni) 1972	0.75	1.50
88 (95)	20 Cruzeiros (Ag) 1972	4.00	8.00
89 (96)	300 Cruzeiros (Au) 1972		300.00

10th ANNIVERSARY OF CENTRAL BANK

		XF	Unc
90 (97)	10 Cruzeiros (Ag) 1975. Bust left. Rev. value, emblem		55.00

FOR THE FAO COIN PLAN (3)

		XF	Unc
91 (98)	1 Centavo (St) 1975–1979. Rev. sugar-cane	0.10	0.20
92 (99)	2 Centavos (St) 1975–1978. Rev. soja	0.10	0.20
93 (100)	5 Centavos (St) 1975–1978. Rev. zebu	0.10	0.20
94 (90b)	10 Centavos (St) 1974–1979. Type as No. 83; plain edge	0.10	0.20
95 (91b)	20 Centavos (St) 1975–1979. Type as No. 84; plain edge	0.10	0.20
96 (92b)	50 Centavos (St) 1975–1979. Type as No. 85; plain edge	0.30	0.70
97 (93a)	1 Cruzeiro 1975–1979. Type as No. 86:		
	a) (Cu-Ni) 1975, 1976	0.40	1.00
	b) (St) 1977–1979	0.40	1.00

FOR THE FAO COIN PLAN (3)

		XF	Unc
98 (101)	1 Centavo (St) 1979–1982. Rev. Soja	0.10	0.20

			XF	Unc
99 (102)	1 Cruzeiro (St) 1979–1984. Sugar-cane		0.20	0.30
100 (103)	5 Cruzeiros (St) 1980–1984. Coffee		0.25	0.40
101 (104)	10 Cruzeiros (St) 1980–1986. Map of Brazil		0.30	0.50

102 (105)	20 Cruzeiros (St) 1981–1985. Church	0.30	0.70

103 (106)	50 Cruzeiros (St) 1981–1986. View of the Paranoã dam, Brasilia	0.40	0.80
104	100 Cruzeiros (St) 1985, 1986. Arms. Rev. Value, date	0.40	0.80
105	200 Cruzeiros (St) 1985, 1986. Type as No. 104	0.50	0.90
106	500 Cruzeiros (St) 1985, 1986. Type as No. 104	0.60	1.00

FOR THE FAO COIN PLAN (2)

107	1 Cruzeiro (St) 1985. Sugar-cane	0.10	0.40
108	5 Cruzeiros (St) 1985. Coffee	0.35	0.85

NEW CURRENCY: 100 Centavos = 1 Cruzado

		Unc
109	1 Centavo (St) 1986. Arms. Rev. Value, name of country	0.10
110	5 Centavos (St) 1986. Type as No. 109	0.10
111	10 Centavos (St) 1986. Type as No. 109	0.10
112	20 Centavos (St) 1986. Type as No. 109	0.10
113	50 Centavos (St) 1986, 1987. Type as No. 109	0.10
114	1 Cruzado (St) 1986. Type as No. 109	0.20
115	5 Cruzados (St) 1986. Type as No. 109	0.75

Values are given for each coin in U.S. Dollars and reference to Yeomannumbers.

Previous ussues, see »Weltmünzkatalog 19. Jahrhundert« (World Coin Catalogue of the 19th Century)

British Caribbean Territories

Britisch-Karibische Gebiete   **Antilles Britanniques**

This economic and monetary area comprised the following territories: Barbados, British Guiana (up to 1962), the Leeward Islands (Antigua, the British Virgin Islands, Montserrat, St. Kitts-Nevis-Anguilla), Trinidad and Tobago (up to 1962), the Windward Islands (Dominica, Grenada, St. Lucia, St. Vincent). On 6th October 1965 the British West Indian Dollar was replaced by the new monetary unit, the East Caribbean Dollar.

100 Cents = 1 British West Indian Dollar

ELIZABETH II since 1952

			XF	Unc
1 (1)		½ Cent (Br) 1955–1958. Crowned bust r. of Queen Elizabeth II. ℞ value	0.60	1.20
2 (2)		1 Cent (Br) 1955–1965	0.15	0.25

		XF	Unc
3 (3)	2 Cents (Br) 1955–1965. ℞ value in wreath	0.20	0.40
4 (4)	5 Cents (Ni–Bra) 1955–1965. ℞ "The Golden Hind", flagship of Sir Francis Drake	0.25	0.50
5 (5)	10 Cents (Cu–Ni) 1955–1965	0.30	0.60

			XF	Unc
6 (6)	25 Cents (Cu–Ni) 1955–1965		0.70	1.20

			XF	Unc
7 (7)	50 Cents (Cu-Ni) 1955, 1965. Rev. Arms		1.50	3.00

Further issues see Antigua, Barbados, Dominica, Grenada, Montserrat, St. Christopher-Nevis-Anguilla, St. Lucia, St. Vincent (all 1970) and East Caribbean States (since 1980).

Britisch-Guiana   # British Guiana   Guyane Britannique

Area: 82,680 sq. mi. Population: 647,000 (1966).
A British Crown Colony since the 17th century on the North-East
coast of South America. Since 26th June 1966 the country has been
independent under the name of The Republic of Guyana.
Capital: Georgetown.

50 Pence = 1 British Guiana Dollar

EDWARD VII 1901–1910

			VF	XF
1 (2)	4 Pence (Ag) 1903–1910. Crowned bust r. of King Edward VII. ℞ value in wreath; above, crown		11.00	20.00

GEORGE V 1910–1936

		VF	XF
2 (3)	4 Pence (Ag) 1911–1916. Crowned bust l. of King George V. ℞ circular legend reading BRITISH GUIANA AND WEST INDIES. Value in wreath; above, crown	11.00	20.00
3 (4)	4 Pence (Ag) 1917–1936. Same type as No. 2, but the legend now reads only BRITISH GUIANA	3.00	6.00

GEORGE VI 1936–1952

		VF	XF
4 (5)	4 Pence (Ag) 1938–1945. Crowned bust l. of King George VI. ℞ value in wreath; above, crown	1.50	2.50

For later issues, see under *Guyana*.

Britisch-Honduras British Honduras Honduras Britannique

Area: 8,867 sq. mi. Population: 120,000.

This British Colony on the eastern shore of Central America obtained in 1960 a new Constitution with full internal selfgovernment. Since 1st June 1973, upon attaining full autonomy, the country is called Belize. The previous capital of the same name is now replaced by the newly built capital of Belmopan.

The British Honduras Dollar was declared the monetary unit in 1894.

100 Cents = 1 British Honduras Dollar

EDWARD VII 1901–1910

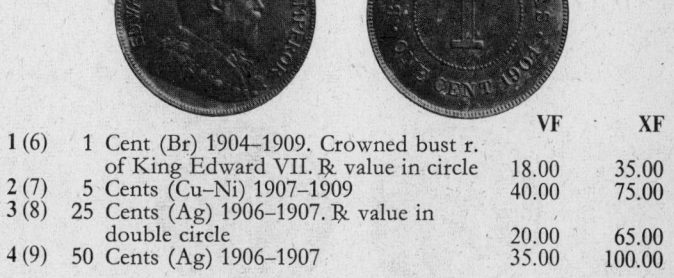

			VF	XF
1 (6)	1	Cent (Br) 1904–1909. Crowned bust r. of King Edward VII. ℞ value in circle	18.00	35.00
2 (7)	5	Cents (Cu–Ni) 1907–1909	40.00	75.00
3 (8)	25	Cents (Ag) 1906–1907. ℞ value in double circle	20.00	65.00
4 (9)	50	Cents (Ag) 1906–1907	35.00	100.00

Values are given for each coin in U.S. Dollars and reference to Yeomannumbers.

GEORGE V 1910–1936

			VF	XF
5 (10)	1	Cent (Br) 1911–1913. Crowned bust l. of King George V. ℞ value in dotted circle	100.00	200.00
6 (11)	1	Cent (Br) 1914–1936. Same type as No. 5. ℞ value in wreath	8.00	18.00
7 (12)	5	Cents (Cu–Ni) 1911–1936	5.00	12.00
8 (13)	10	Cents (Ag) 1918–1936. ℞ value in double circle	6.00	15.00
9 (14)	25	Cents (Ag) 1911–1919	15.00	50.00

10 (15)	50	Cents (Ag) 1911–1919	20.00	65.00

GEORGE VI 1936–1952

11 (16)	1	Cent (Br) 1937–1947. Crowned head l. of King George VI. ℞ value in wreath	1.50	5.00
12 (17)	5	Cents (Cu-Ni) 1939. ℞ value in dotted circle	5.00	12.00
13 (17a)	5	Cents (Ni-Bra) 1942-1945, 1947. Type as No. 12	5.00	12.00

	VF	XF
14 (18) 10 Cents (Ag) 1939–1946. ℞ value in double circle	4.00	15.00
15 (19) 1 Cent (Br) 1949–1951. Same type as No. 11, but the legend now reads only KING GEORGE THE SIXTH	1.00	2.00
16 (20) 5 Cents (Ni–Bra) 1949–1952	1.00	3.00
17 (21) 25 Cents (Cu–Ni) 1952	4.00	16.00

ELIZABETH II since 1952

18 (22) 1 Cent (Br) 1954. Crowned head r. of Queen Elizabeth II. ℞ value in wreath	0.75	1.50

19 (23) 1 Cent (Br) 1956–1973. Same type as No. 17, but dodecagonal	0.10	0.20
20 (24) 5 Cents (Ni-Bra) 1956–1973. R value in circle	0.10	0.20
21 (25) 10 Cents (Cu-Ni) 1956–1970. R value in double circle	0.20	0.40

22 (26) 25 Cents (Cu-Ni) 1955-1973	0.30	0.60
23 (27) 50 Cents (Cu-Ni) 1954-1971.	0.75	1.50

For later issues, see under Belize.

British North Borneo

Britisch-Nordborneo   **Bornéo du Nord Britannique**

The Chartered British North Borneo Company formed with effect of
1st Nov. 1881 administered as the only colonial company existing into
the 20th century the territory of a state in its power until its dissolution
on 15th July 1946. In exercising its rights it was hampered due to the
disastrous consequences of World War II, during the course of which
the real rule was exercised from 1942–1945 by the Japanese and then by
the British military administration. To the now existing Crown Colony
of British North Borneo, the small island of Labuan was added after
the severance of the administrative connection with the Straits Settlements which had existed since the thirties. With the revived name of
"Sabah", North Borneo joined the new state of Malaysia as a founder
member on 16th Sept. 1963 and together with Sarawak constitutes the
territory of East Malaysia.
Capital: Jesselton.

100 Cents = 1 Straits Dollar

			VF	XF
1 (1)	½ Cent (Br) 1885–1907. Coat of arms. ℞ value within wreath		5.00	12.00

2 (2)	1 Cent (Br) 1882–1907. Coat of arms of the North Borneo Company, a privileged company protected by charter. ℞ value within wreath		4.00	10.00
3 (3)	1 Cent (Cu–Ni) 1904–1941. Same type as No. 2. ℞ value in circle, legend: STATE OF NORTH BORNEO		2.50	6.00
4 (4)	2½ Cents (Cu–Ni) 1903–1920		3.00	10.00
5 (5)	5 Cents (Cu–Ni) 1903–1941		2.00	5.00
6 (6)	25 Cents (Ag) 1929		9.00	18.00

British Virgin Islands

Britische Jungferninseln   **Iles de la Vierge Britanniques**

Area: 41 sq. mi. Population: 14,000.
The British Virgin Islands include the islands of Tortola, Virgin Gorda, Anegada, Jost van Dyke and numerous islets. The British colony of the "Leeward Islands" (cf. British Caribbean Territories) was dissolved into the four presidencies, of which it consisted at the time: Antigua, St. Kitts-Nevis-Anguilla, Montserrat and the Virgin Islands. After the breakup of the West Indian Federation, which they had joined as individual colonies on 3rd January 1958, the status of these islands was somewhat obscure; the Virgin Islands reverted to the former status of a British Colony. Even after the introduction of their own currency on 30th June 1973, the monetary units of the USA have remained in use. Capital: Road Town.

100 Cents = 1 East Caribbean Dollar

			Unc	Proof
1 (1)	1	Cent (Br) 1973–. Greenthroated Caribbean humming bird (Sericotes holosericeus) and Antillean crested humming bird (Orthorhynchus cristatus), both Trochilidae	0.30	1.00
2 (2)	5	Cents (Cu-Ni) 1973–. Zenaida turtledove (Zenaida aurita – Columbidae)	0.50	1.20
3 (3)	10	Cents (Cu-Ni) 1973–. Ringed kingfisher (Ceryle torquata – Alcedinidae)	0.70	1.50
4 (4)	25	Cents (Cu-Ni) 1973–. Mangrove cuckoo (Coccysus minor – Cuculidae)	1.00	1.70
5 (5)	50	Cents (Cu-Ni) 1973–. Brown or sea pelican (Pelecanus occidentalis – Pelecanidae)	1.50	2.50
6 (6)	1	Dollar 1973–. Magnificent frigate bird (Fregata magnificens - Fregatidae):		
		a) (Ag)		10.00
		b) (Cu-Ni)	6.00	
7 (7)	100	Dollars (Au) 1975. Royal Tern (Sterna maxima – Sternidae)	100.00	130.00

50th BIRTHDAY OF HER MAJESTY QUEEN ELIZABETH II

		Unc	Proof
8 (8)	100 Dollars (Au) 1976. R Coat of arms, with crowned monogram above. Commemorative inscription, value	140.00	110.00

SILVER JUBILEE OF HER MAJESTY QUEEN ELIZABETH II (7)

9 (9)	1 Cent (Ag) 1977	2.50
10 (10)	5 Cents (Ag) 1977	3.50
11 (11)	10 Cents (Ag) 1977	5.00
12 (12)	25 Cents (Ag) 1977	7.00
13 (13)	50 Cents (Ag) 1977	10.00
14 (14)	1 Dollar (Ag) 1977	15.00
15 (15)	100 Dollars (Au) 1977. Queen. R crown	150.00

25th ANNIVERSARY OF THE CORONATION OF HER MAJESTY QUEEN ELIZABETH II (8)

16 (16)	1 Cent (Ag) 1978		3.50
17 (17)	5 Cents (Ag) 1978		4.00
18 (18)	10 Cents (Ag) 1978		5.00
19 (19)	25 Cents (Ag) 1978		7.50
20 (20)	50 Cents (Ag) 1978		12.00
21 (21)	1 Dollar (Ag) 1978		18.00
22 (22)	25 Dollars (Ag) 1978		25.00
23 (23)	100 Dollars (Au) 1978		150.00
24 (24)	5 Dollars 1979. Snowy Egret:		
	a) (Ag)		28.00
	b) (Cu-Ni)	25.00	
25 (25)	100 Dollars (Au) 1979. Sir Francis Drake		175.00
26 (26)	5 Dollars 1980. Great Blue Heron:		
	a) (Ag)		25.00
	b) (Cu-Ni)	25.00	
27 (27)	25 Dollars (Au) 1980. Diving Osprey		40.00
28 (28)	50 Dollars (Au) 1980. Golden Dove of Christmas		65.00

400th ANNIVERSARY OF DRAKE'S VOYAGE

29 (29)	100 Dollars (Au) 1980. Rev. »The Golden Hind«, flagship of Sir Francis Drake		150.00

400th ANNIVERSARY OF KNIGHTING OF SIR FRANCIS DRAKE

30 (30)	100 Dollars (Au) 1981		150.00
31 (31)	5 Dollars 1981. Rev. Royal Tern:		
	a) (Ag)		30.00
	b) (Cu-Ni)	25.00	

			Unc	Proof
32 (32)	25 Dollars (Au) 1981. Caribbean Sparrow Hawk			40.00
33 (33)	5 Dollars 1982. Rev. White-tailed Tropic Birds:			
	a) (Ag)			30.00
	b) (Cu-Ni)		25.00	
A 33	25 Dollars (Au) 1982. Hawk			40.00

30th ANNIVERSARY OF QUEEN EILIZABETH II REIGN

			Unc	Proof
34 (34)	100 Dollars (Au) 1982. Rev. Crowned monogram			150.00
35 (36)	5 Dollars 1983. Rev. Yellow Warblers:			
	a) (Ag)			50.00
	b) (Cu-Ni)		25.00	

30th ANNIVERSARY OF CORONATION OF QUEEN ELIZABETZ II (2)

			Unc	Proof
36 (35)	10 Dollars (Ag) 1983			25.00
37 (37)	100 Dollars (Au) 1983			180.00
38 (38)	25 Dollars (Au) 1983. Rev. Merlin Hawk			40.00
39	25 Dollars (Au) 1984. Rev. Peregrine Falcon			40.00
A 39	100 Dollars (Au) 1984. Rev. Ginger Thomas			400.00

			Unc	Proof
40	1 Cent (Br) 1985. Portrait of Queen Elizabeth II facing right. Rev. Hawksbill Turtle			–.–
41	5 Cents (Cu-Ni) 1985. Rev. Bonitos			–.–
42	10 Cents (Cu-Ni) 1985. Rev. Barracuda			–.–
43	25 Cents (Cu-Ni) 1985. Rev. Blue Marlin			–.–
44	50 Cents (Cu-Ni) 1985. Rev. Dolphin			–.–
45	1 Dollar (Cu-Ni) 1985. Rev. School of Butterfly Fish			–.–

Set containing 6 pieces 25.00

			Unc	Proof
46	1 Cent (Ag) 1985. Type as No. 40			–.–
47	5 Cents (Ag) 1985. Type as No. 41			–.–
48	10 Cents (Ag) 1985. Type as No. 42			–.–
49	25 Cents (Ag) 1985. Type as No. 43			–.–
50	50 Cents (Ag) 1985. Type as No. 44			–.–
51	1 Dollar (Ag) 1985. Type as No. 45			–.–

Set containing 6 pieces 85.00

		Proof
52	20 Dollars (Ag) 1985. Rev. Crossed Cannons; .925 silver, 19.09 g	25.00
53	20 Dollars (Ag) 1985. Rev. Porcelain Cup	25.00
54	20 Dollars (Ag) 1985. Rev. Sextant	25.00
55	20 Dollars (Ag) 1985. Rev. Emerald and Gold Ring	25.00
56	20 Dollars (Ag) 1985. Rev. Gold Doubloon (8 Escudos) of 1702	25.00
57	20 Dollars (Ag) 1985. Rev. Anchor	25.00
58	20 Dollars (Ag) 1985. Rev. Noctural	25.00
59	20 Dollars (Ag) 1985. Rev. Sword Guillon	25.00
60	20 Dollars (Ag) 1985. Rev. Gold Bar	25.00
61	20 Dollars (Ag) 1985. Rev. Gold Escudo of 1733	25.00
62	20 Dollars (Ag) 1985. Rev. Ivory Sundial	25.00
63	20 Dollars (Ag) 1985. Rev. Gold Monstrance	25.00
64	20 Dollars (Ag) 1985. Rev. Teapot	25.00
65	20 Dollars (Ag) 1985. Rev. Brass Religious Medallion	25.00
66	20 Dollars (Ag) 1985. Rev. Astrolable	25.00
67	20 Dollars (Ag) 1985. Rev. Bell	25.00
68	20 Dollars (Ag) 1985. Rev. Porcelain Bottle	25.00
69	20 Dollars (Ag) 1985. Rev. Dutch Cannon	25.00
70	20 Dollars (Ag) 1985. Rev. Gold Inca Figurine	25.00
71	20 Dollars (Ag) 1985. Rev. Gold Locket	25.00
72	20 Dollars (Ag) 1985. Rev. Clay Pipe Bowls	25.00
73	20 Dollars (Ag) 1985. Rev. Gold Cross	25.00
74	20 Dollars (Ag) 1985. Rev. Perfume Bottle	25.00
75	20 Dollars (Ag) 1985. Rev. Pocket Watch	25.00
76	20 Dollars (Ag) 1985. Rev. Gold Bracelet and Button	25.00
77	25 Dollars (Au) 1985. Rev. Marsh Hawk	40.00

SIR FRANCIS DRAKE'S WEST INDIAN VOYAGE

78	100 Dollars (Au) 1985. Rev. „Elizabeth Bonaventure", flagship of Sir Francis Drake	200.00

British West Africa

Until they issued their own currencies the territories of the British Cameroons (since 1961 part of the Cameroons), British Togoland (since 1957 linked with Ghana), Gambia, the Gold Coast (since 1957 called Ghana), Nigeria and Sierra Leone formed together an administrative grouping under the name of British West Africa. Coinage now obsolete.

$$12 \text{ Pence} = 1 \text{ Shilling}$$
$$20 \text{ Shillings} = £ 1$$

EDWARD VII 1901–1910

			VF	XF
1 (3)	$1/_{10}$	Penny (Al) 1907–1908. Star within inscription around reading NIGERIA – BRITISH WEST AFRICA. ℞ crown over value (central hole)	3.00	6.00
2 (1)	$1/_{10}$	Penny (Cu–Ni) 1908–1910	1.00	2.00

3 (2)	1	Penny (Cu–Ni) 1907–1910	3.00	6.00

GEORGE V 1910–1936

4 (4)	$1/_{10}$	Penny (Cu–Ni) 1911. Star. ℞ crown over value (central hole)	3.00	6.00
5 (5)	$1/_{2}$	Penny (Cu–Ni) 1911	8.00	15.00

6 (6)	1	Penny (Cu–Ni) 1911	30.00	55.00
7 (7)	$1/_{10}$	Penny (Cu–Ni) 1912–1936. Same type as No. 4. ℞ the legend now reads only BRITISH WEST AFRICA (central hole)	0.50	2.00

			VF	XF
8 (8)	¹/₂	Penny (Cu–Ni) 1912–1936	2.50	6.00
9 (9)	1	Penny (Cu–Ni) 1912–1936	2.00	5.00
10 (14)	3	Pence (Ag) 1913–1920. ℞ value in wreath	3.00	6.00
11 (15)	6	Pence (Ag) 1913–1920	4.00	8.00
12 (16)	1	Shilling (Ag) 1913–1920. Crowned bust l. of King George V. ℞ oil palm (Elaeis guineensis — Palmae)	6.00	10.00

13 (17)	2	Shillings (Ag) 1913–1920	12.50	18.00
14 (14a)	3	Pence (Bra) 1920–1936	3.00	6.00
15 (15a)	6	Pence (Bra) 1920–1936	4.00	9.00
16 (16a)	1	Shilling (Bra) 1920–1936	5.00	10.00
17 (17a)	2	Shillings (Bra) 1920–1936	5.50	12.00

EDWARD VIII 1936

			VF	XF
18 (18)	¹/₁₀	Penny (Cu–Ni) 1936. Star. ℞ crown over value (central hole)	1.00	2.00
19 (19)	¹/₂	Penny (Cu–Ni) 1936	1.00	2.00

20 (20)	1	Penny (Cu–Ni) 1936	1.20	2.50

GEORGE VI 1936–1952

			VF	XF
21 (22)	1/10	Penny (Cu–Ni) 1938–1947. Star. R crown over value (central hole). Legend reading GEORGIUS VI REX ET IND IMP	0.50	1.00

			VF	**XF**
22 (23)	$^1/_2$ Penny (Cu–Ni) 1937–1947	1.00	2.00
23 (24)	1 Penny (Cu–Ni) 1937–1947	0.75	1.50

24 (25)	3 Pence (Cu–Ni) 1938–1948. ℞ value in wreath	1.50	3.00
25 (26)	6 Pence (Bra) 1938–1947	1.20	2.50
26 (27)	1 Shilling (Bra) 1938–1948. ℞ oil palm	2.00	4.00
27 (28)	2 Shillings (Bra) 1938–1948	2.50	5.00
28 (29)	$^1/_{10}$ Penny (Cu–Ni) 1949–1950. Same type as No. 21, but reverse legend reads only GEORGIUS SEXTUS REX (central hole)	1.00	2.00
29 (30)	$^1/_2$ Penny (Cu–Ni) 1949–1951	4.00	8.00
30 (31)	1 Penny (Cu–Ni) 1951	14.00	26.00
31 (29a)	$^1/_{10}$ Penny (Br) 1952	1.60	3.20
32 (30a)	$^1/_2$ Penny (Br) 1952	0.50	1.00
33 (31a)	1 Penny (Br) 1952	1.50	3.00
34 (32)	6 Pence (Ni–Bra) 1952	7.50	15.00
35 (33)	1 Shilling (Ni–Bra) 1949–1952	1.20	2.50
36 (34)	2 Shillings (Ni–Bra) 1949–1952	3.00	6.00

ELIZABETH II since 1952

| 37 (38) | 1/10 Penny (Br) 1954–1957. Star. R crown over value (central hole) | 1.00 | 2.00 |
| 38 (39) | 1 Penny (Br) 1956–1958 | 1.50 | 3.00 |

| 39 (40) | 3 Pence (Cu–Ni) 1957. Elizabeth II. ℞ value in wreath | 25.00 | 55.00 |

Yeoman Numbers

**In order to help collectors and dealers, we have added after most SCHÖN–
numbers the corresponding number assigned by R. S. Yeoman in his wellknown
works entitled »A Catalog of modern World Coins« and »Current Coins of the
World«.**

Brunei

Area: 2,217 sq. mi. Population: 250,000.
The Mohammedan sultanate on the north coast of the Island of Borneo was still so powerful in the early 19th century that the Sultan of Brunei was considered as the Sultan of Borneo, resulting in the name of the whole island of Borneo having been formed from the name Brunei. Mineral resources which have become a matter of interest lately, have induced the Sultan of Brunei not to join the Federation of Malaysia, but to allow the protectorate arranged by treaty with Great Britain in 1886 to 1983. On 1st January 1984 the sultanate became independent. Capital: Brunei, since 4th October 1970 renamed Bandar Seri Begawan.
The Mexican Piaster was initially the most common trade coin. From 25th Juni 1903 the Straits Dollar was in circulation and from 1th April 1946 the Malaya Dollar became legal tender. The new currency, the Brunei Dollar, was introduced on 12th Junie 1967. The Brunei Dollar is on a par with the Malaysia and the Singapore Dollar.

100 Sen = 1 Brunei Dollar

OMAR ALI SAIFUDDIN III 1950–1967

			XF	Unc
1 (2)	1 Sen (Br) 1967. Head l. of Sultan Sir Omar Ali Saifuddin Wasa'dul Khairi Waddin (*1916). ℞ ornamental design		0.15	0.30

2 (3)	5 Sen (Cu–Ni) 1967. ℞ ornamental design		0.20	0.40

			XF	Unc

3 (4) 10 Sen (Cu–Ni) 1967. R ornamental design 0.20 0.40

4 (5) 20 Sen (Cu–Ni) 1967. R ornamental design 0.35 0.70

5 (6) 50 Sen (Cu-Ni) 1967. R national arms 0.60 1.00

HASSANAL BOLKIAH I since 1967

6 (7) 1 Sen (Br) 1968–1977. Head r. of Hassanal Bolkiah Muizzuddin Waddaulah (*1946). son of Omar Ali who abdicated on 4th October 1967. R as No. 1 0.10 0.20

7 (8) 5 Sen (Cu-Ni) 1968–1977. R as No. 2 0.15 0.30

8 (9) 10 Sen (Cu-Ni) 1968–1977. R as No. 3 0.20 0.40

9 (10) 20 Sen (Cu-Ni) 1968–1977. R as No. 4 0.35 0.70

10 (11) 50 Sen (Cu-Ni) 1968–1977. R as No. 5 0.45 0.90

11 (12) 1 Dollar (Cu-Ni) 1970 Proof 40.00

		XF	Unc
12 (7a)	1 Sen (Br) 1977–. Type as No. 6, but without numeral »I« in title	0.10	0.20
13 (8a)	5 Sen (Cu-Ni) 1977–	0.10	0.20
14 (9a)	10 Sen (Cu-Ni) 1977–	0.10	0.20
15 (10a)	20 Sen (Cu-Ni) 1977–	0.20	0.30
16 (11a)	50 Sen (Cu-Ni) 1977–	0.50	0.80

		Unc	Proof
17 (12a)	1 Dollar (Cu-Ni) 1979, 1984–1986. Type as No. 11, but without numeral »I« in title	6.00	15.00

10th ANNIVERSARY OF BRUNEI CURRENCY BOARD

18 (13)	10 Dollars (Ag) 1977. Rev. Mosque		40.00

10th ANNIVERSARY OF SULTAN'S CORONATION

19 (15)	1000 Dollars (Au) 1978. Rev. Crown; .916⅔ gold, 50 g		900.00

YEAR OF HIJRAH 1400 (3)

20 (14)	5 Dollars (Cu-Ni) 1980	10.00	
21 (16)	50 Dollars (Ag) 1980		75.00
22 (17)	750 Dollars (Au) 1980		500.00

INDEPENDENCE DAY (3)

23	10 Dollars (Cu-Ni) 1984	10.00	30.00
24	100 Dollars (Ag) 1984	100.00	140.00
25	1000 Dollars (Au) 1984	750.00	800.00

All valuations in the SCHÖN are stated in U.S. Dollars.

Bulgarien   **Bulgaria**   **Bulgarie**

БЪЛГАРИЯ

Area: 42,823 sq. mi. Population: 8,970,000.
Created in 1879, this principality was declared an independent Kingdom on
22nd September (5th October) 1908 by Ferdinand I in Tirnowo. Initially the
Julian Calendar continued to be used by the Bulgarian people, hence the
different dates given for example for Independence Day. A People's Republic since 15th September 1946.
Capitel: Sofia.

100 Stotinki (СТОТИНКИ) = 1 Lew (ЛЕВ)

FERDINAND I 1887–1918

			VF	XF
1 (16)	1 Stotinka (Br) 1901, 1912. National arms. ℞ value in wreath			
	a) 1901 (Paris)		3.00	6.00
	b) 1912 (Vienna)		2.50	5.00
2 (17)	2 Stotinki (Br) 1901, 1912		1.50	3.00
3 (18)	5 Stotinki (Cu-Ni) 1906–1913		0.70	1.20
4 (18a)	5 Stotinki (Zi) 1917		2.50	4.00
5 (19)	10 Stotinki (Cu-Ni) 1906–1913		0.40	0.80
6 (19a)	10 Stotinki (Zi) 1917		1.50	3.00

		VF	XF
7 (20)	20 Stotinki (Cu-Ni) 1906–1913	0.60	1.20
8 (20a)	20 Stotinki (Zi) 1917	2.00	4.00
9 (24)	50 Stotinki (Ag) 1910. Head r. of Ferdinand I. ℞ value in wreath	3.50	6.00
10 (25)	1 Lew (Ag) 1910	4.00	6.50
11 (26)	2 Lewa (Ag) 1910	5.00	11.00

COMMEMORATIVE ISSUES (2) FOR THE DECLARATION OF INDEPENDENCE AND THE CREATION OF THE KINGDOM OF BULGARIA ON 22nd SEPTEMBER (5th OCTOBER) 1908

		VF	XF
12 (30)	20 Lewa (Au) 1912. Head l. of Ferdinand of Saxe-Coburg-Gotha (1861–1948), Prince of Bulgaria 1887–1908, as Ferdinand I, 1908–1918 King of Bulgaria	200.00	280.00

		VF	XF
13 (31)	100 Lewa (Au) 1912	1000.00	1600.00

Later restrikes in gold (4 ducats), also with countermark, are medallic
issues for the same occasion.

		VF	XF
14 (27)	50 Stotinki (Ag) 1912–1916. Head l. of Ferdinand I		
	a) 1912, 1913	3.00	7.00
	b) 1916	30.00	45.00
15 (28)	1 Lew (Ag) 1912–1916		
	a) 1912, 1913	3.50	6.00
	b) 1916	60.00	100.00
16 (29)	2 Lewa (Ag) 1912–1916		
	a) 1912, 1913	5.00	9.00
	b) 1916	175.00	300.00

BORIS III 1918–1943

17 (32)	1 Lew (Al) 1923. National arms. ℞ value in wreath	6.00	15.00
18 (34)	1 Lew (Cu-Ni) 1925	0.60	1.20
19 (33)	2 Lewa (Al) 1923	14.00	28.00

20 (35)	2 Lewa (Cu-Ni) 1925	0.40	1.00
21 (36)	5 Lewa (Cu-Ni) 1930. Relief figure of Czar Krum (reigned from 802 to 814) as a horseman on the rock at Madara (district of Kolarovgrad, in northeast Bulgaria), dating from the 9th century A. D. ℞ value in wreath	1.50	3.00

			VF	XF
22 (37)	10	Lewa (Cu-Ni) 1930. Same type as No. 21	3.00	6.00
23 (38)	20	Lewa (Ag) 1930. Head l. of Boris III (1894–1943). ℞ value in wreath	2.50	4.00
24 (39)	50	Lewa (Ag) 1930	4.00	8.00
25 (40)	100	Lewa (Ag) 1930	8.00	16.00
26 (41)	50	Stotinki (Al-Br) 1937. National arms. ℞ value in wreath	0.60	2.00
27 (42)	20	Lewa (Cu-Ni) 1940. Same type as No. 23	1.50	2.50
28 (44)	50	Lewa (Ag) 1934. Head l. of Boris III. ℞ value between ears of wheat; below, rose and tobacco plants	3.50	7.00
29 (43)	50	Lewa (Cu-Ni) 1940. Same type as No. 24	1.50	2.50
30 (43a)	50	Lewa (Fe, Ni-St, plated) 1943	2.00	3.50
31 (45)	100	Lewa (Ag) 1934, 1937. Same type as No. 28	4.50	10.00
32 (34a)	1	Lew (Fe) 1941. Same type as No. 18	4.00	10.00
33 (35a)	2	Lewa (Fe) 1941. Same type as No. 20	1.50	2.50

34 (A45)	2	Lewa (Fe) 1943	2.50	5.00
35 (36a)	5	Lewa (Fe) 1941. Same type as No. 21	3.00	6.00
36 (36b)	5	Lewa (Fe, Ni-St, plated) 1943	2.50	5.00
37 (37a)	10	Lewa (Fe) 1941. Same type as No. 22	11.00	20.00
38 (37b)	10	Lewa (Fe, Ni-St, plated) 1943	2.00	4.00

PEOPLE'S REPUBLIC since 1946

39 (46)	1	Stotinka (Bra) 1951. Arms of the People's Republic. ℞ ears of wheat and value	0.10	0.20
40 (47)	3	Stotinki (Bra) 1951	0.15	0.30
41 (48)	5	Stotinki (Bra) 1951	0.20	0.40
42 (49)	10	Stotinki (Cu-Ni) 1951	0.30	0.60

			VF	XF
43 (A49)	20	Stotinki (Cu-Ni) 1952–1954		
		a) 1952	10.00	20.00
		b) 1954	0.35	0.70
44 (50)	25	Stotinki (Cu-Ni) 1951	0.40	0.80
45 (51)	50	Stotinki (Cu-Ni) 1959	0.60	1.00

46 (52)	1	Lew (Cu-Ni) 1960. ℞ value in wreath	1.00	1.80

CURRENCY REFORM: 100 old Lewa = 1 new Lew

47 (53)	1	Stotinka (Bra) 1962. National arms. ℞ value between ears of wheat	0.10	0.20

48 (54)	2	Stotinki (Bra) 1962	0.10	0.20
49 (55)	5	Stotinki (Bra) 1962	0.15	0.25
50 (56)	10	Stotinki (Cu-Ni) 1962	0.20	0.35
51 (57)	20	Stotinki (Cu-Ni) 1962	0.30	0.50
52 (58)	50	Stotinki (Cu-Ni) 1962	0.60	1.00
53 (59)	1	Lew (Cu-Ni) 1962	1.00	2.00

COMMEMORATIVE ISSUES (4)
FOR 1100 YEARS OF THE CYRILLIC ALPHABET

			Unc	Proof
54 (60)	2	Lewa (Ag) 1963. Cyril (826–869) and Methodios (c. 815–885), Slavic apostles and propagators of the Cyrillic alphabet. ℞ value	7.00	8.00
55 (61)	5	Lewa (Ag) 1963	10.00	15.00

56 (62)	10	Lewa (Au) 1963		120.00
57 (63)	20	Lewa (Au) 1963		250.00

COMMEMORATIVE ISSUE (4) FOR THE 80th BIRTHDAY OF G. DIMITROV AND FOR THE 20th ANNIVERSARY OF THE PROCLAMATION OF THE PEOPLE'S REPUBLIC

			Unc	Proof
58 (64)	2 Lewa (Ag) 1964. Georgi Dimitrov (1882–1949), printer and politician, Prime Minister 1946–1949. R flags over value		5.00	6.00
59 (65)	5 Lewa (Ag) 1964. Type as No. 58		8.00	12.00

60 (66)	10 Lewa (Au) 1964. Type as No. 58			120.00
61 (67)	20 Lewa (Au) 1964. Type as No. 58			225.00

COMMEMORATIVE ISSUE FOR THE 1050th ANNIVERSARY OF THE DEATH OF KLIMENT OCHRIDSKI

		XF	Unc
62 (68)	2 Lewa (Cu-Ni) 1966. St. Kliment Ochridski (✝ 916), rationalist, he perfected the Bulgarian-Slavonic (Cyrillic) alphabet	1.50	3.00

COMMEMORATIVE ISSUES (2) FOR THE 25th ANNIVERSARY OF THE SOCIALIST REVOLUTION OF 9th SEPTEMBER 1944

63 (69)	1 Lew (Cu-Ni) 1969. Monument to the fighters of the Resistance. R value between ears of wheat	1.00	1.50

64 (70)	2 Lewa (Cu-Ni) 1969. Monument to the Soviet soldiers in Plovdiv (Philippopolis. ℞ as No. 63	**XF**	**Unc**
		1,25	2.50

COMMEMORATIVE ISSUES (2) FOR THE 90th ANNIVERSARY OF THE LIBERATION OF BULGARIA FROM THE OTTOMAN DOMINATION

65 (71)	1 Lew (Cu-Ni) 1969. Sofia: equestrian statue of Alexander II, Czar of Russia, on a plinth (43 ft high) with effigies from Bulgarian history (1877–1879). Created in the years 1901 to 1907 by the Italian sculptor Arnoldo Zocchi ℞ value in tied laurel wreath	1.00	1.50

66 (72)	2 Lewa (Cu–Ni) 1969. "The Battle on the Orlovo Gnesdo" (Eagle's Nest), by the Russian painter Popov; section of a painting. ℞ as No. 65	1.50	2.50

Values are given for each coin in U.S. Dollars and reference to Yeomannumbers.

120th BIRTHDAY OF IVAN VASOV

67 (73)　　5 Lewa (Ag) 1970. Ivan Vasov, (1850–1921), poet; his best known work is "Under the Yoke", written in 1889/90. ℞ emblem of state, value

	Unc	Proof
	8.50	12.00

150th BIRTHDAY OF G. RAKOVSKI

68 (74)　　5 Lewa (Ag) 1971. Georgi Rakovski (1821–1867), patriot, revolutionary, writer, author of the constitution for the provisional Bulgarian Government. ℞ emblem of state, value　　　　　12.00

250th BIRTHDAY OF PAISSII HILENDARSKI

69 (76)　　5 Lewa (Ag) 1972. Paissii Hilendarski, called "Otez Paissii", Bulgarian monk,

born 1722 in the town of Bansko,
wrote the history of the Bulgarian
people and thus roused national con-
sciousness

	Unc	Proof
		12.00

COMMEMORATIVE ISSUE FOR THE 150th BIRTHDAY OF DOBRI TCHINTULOV

70 (75) 2 Lewa (Cu–Ni) 1972. Dobri Tchintulov
(1822–1886), distinguished Bulgarian
pioneer of progress 1.25 2.50

COMMEMORATIVE ISSUE FOR THE 100th ANNIVERSARY OF THE DEATH OF VASIL LEVSKI

71 (77) 5 Lewa (Ag) 1973. Vasil Levski (1837–
6th February 1873), organizer of the
Bulgarian national freedom movement
against the Turks, founded a revolutionary central committee; executed by the
Turks in Sofia

Proof

12.00

Values are given for each coin in U.S. Dollars and referance to Yeomannumbers.

COMMEMORATIVE ISSUE FOR THE 50th ANNIVERSARY OF THE SEPTEMBER RISING (23. 9. 1923) UNDER THE LEADERSHIP OF G. DIMITROV AND V. KOLAROV

			Proof
72 (78)	5 Lewa (Ag) 1973		10.00

COMMEMORATIVE ISSUE FOR THE 50th ANNIVERSARY OF THE DEATH OF ALEXANDER STAMBULIJSKI

		Proof
73 (79)	5 Lewa (Ag) 1974. Alexander Stambulij- ski (1879–1923), politician	10.00

COMMEMORATIVE ISSUE FOR THE 30th ANNIVERSARY OF THE SOCIALIST REVOLUTION OF 9th SEPTEMBER 1944

		Proof
74 (80)	5 Lewa (Ag) 1974. Two soldiers and factory. R coat of arms, date, value	10.00

			Unc	Proof
75 (53a)	1 Stotinka (Bra) 1974–1980. Type as No. 47, but new coat of arms, since 14th May 1971:			
	a) 1974		0.10	
	b) 1979, 1980			4.00
76 (54a)	2 Stotinki (Bra) 1974–1980. Type as No. 75:			
	a) 1974		0.15	
	b) 1979, 1980			4.00
77 (55a)	5 Stotinki (Bra) 1974–1980. Type as No. 75:			
	a) 1974		0.25	
	b) 1979, 1980			4.00

78 (56a) 10 Stotinki (Cu-Ni) 1974–1980. Type as   **Unc**   **Proof**
No. 75:
a) 1974   0.30
b) 1979, 1980   4.00

79 (57a) 20 Stotinki (Cu-Ni) 1974–1980. Type as
No. 75:
a) 1974   0.50
b) 1979, 1980   4.00

80 (58a) 50 Stotinki (Cu-Ni) 1974–1980. Type as
No. 75:
a) 1974   1.00
b) 1979, 1980   4.00
81 (59a) 1 Lew (Cu-Ni) 1979, 1980. Type as No. 75   12.50

10th OLYMPIC CONGRESS IN VARNA

82 (81) 10 Lewa (Ag) 1975. Ancient Greek coin with
boxer, and olympic rings below. R coat of   **Unc**   **Proof**
arms, value, date:
a) with edge inscription in Cyrillic   40.00
b) with edge inscription in Latin   40.00

Proof

83 (82)   1 Lew (Cu) 1976   2.00

84 (83)   2 Lewa (Cu-Ni) 1976   4.00

85 (85)   5 Lewa (Ag) 1976   12.00

Yeoman Numbers

In order to help collectors and dealers, we have added after most SCHÖN-
numbers the corresponding number assigned by R.S. Yeoman in his wellknown
works entitled »A Catalog of Modern World Coins« and »Current Coins of
the World«.

100th ANNIVERSARY OF THE DEATH OF KHRISTO BOTEV

		Unc	Proof

86 (84)   5 Lewa (Ag) 1976. Khristo Botev (1848-1876), revolutionary and poet   10.00

UNIVERSADE IN SOFIA

87 (86)   50 Stotinki (Cu-Ni) 1977. Runner with torch, commemorative inscription. R coat of arms, value, date   1.50

150th ANNIVERSARY OF THE BIRTH OF P. R. SLAVEYKOV

88 (87)   5 Lewa (Ag) 1977. Petko Racev Slaveykov (1827-1895), poet   10.00

100th ANNIVERSARY OF THE BIRTH OF P. K. YAVOROV

89 (88)   5 Lewa (Ag) 1978. Peijo Yavorov, real name Kracholov, lyric poet and dramatist   10.00

100th ANNIVERSARY OF LIBERATION

90 (89)   10 Lewa (Ag) 1978. Monument   17.50

Values are given for each coin in U.S. Dollars and reference to Yeomannumbers.

100th ANNIVERSARY OF NATIONAL LIBRARY

			Unc	Proof
91 (90)	5 Lewa (Ag) 1978. National Library			10.00

100th ANNIVERSARY OF COMMUNICATIONS SYSTEMS

			Unc	Proof
92 (91)	5 Lewa (Ag) 1979		12.50	12.50

CENTENNIAL OF SOFIA AS CAPITAL

93 (93) 20 Lewa (Ag) 1979:
    a) .500 silver, dia. 37 mm   50.00
    b) .900 silver, dia. 42 mm   30.00

BULGARIAN-SOVIET COSMONAUT FLIGHT

94 (97) 10 Lewa (Ag) 1979:
    a) .500 silver, dia. 32 mm   25.00
    b) .900 silver, dia. 38 mm   20.00

INTERNATIONAL YEAR OF THE CHILD

95 (92) 10 Lewa (Ag) 1979:
    a) .925 silver, 23.32 gm.   25.00
    b) Piéfort   150.00

WORLD CUP SOCCER GAMES IN SPAIN 1982 (3)

		Unc	Proof
96 (94)	1 Lew (Cu-Ni) 1980	3.00	3.00
97 (95)	2 Lewa (Cu-Ni) 1980	4.00	4.00
98 (96)	5 Lewa (Cu-Ni) 1980	8.00	8.00

100th ANNIVERSARY OF THE BIRTH OF YORDAN YOVKOV

99 (98)	2 Lewa (Cu-Ni) 1980. Yordan Yovkov (1880–1937), writer	4.00

1300th YEARS OF BULGARIA (11)

100 (53b)	1 Stotinka (Bra) 1981. Arms, legend. R value and date between ears	0.30	1.00
101 (54b)	2 Stotinki (Bra) 1981. Type as No. 100	0.30	1.00

102 (55b)	5 Stotinki (Bra) 1981. Type as No. 100	0.30	1.00
103 (56b)	10 Stotinki (Cu-Ni) 1981. Type as No. 100	0.30	1.00
104 (57b)	20 Stotinki (Cu-Ni) 1981. Type as No. 100	1.00	2.00
105 (58b)	50 Stotinki (Cu-Ni) 1981. Type as No. 100	2.00	4.00
106 (59b)	1 Lew (Cu-Ni) 1981. Type as No. 100	3.00	6.00

			Unc	Proof
107	(102)	2 Lewa (Cu-Ni) 1981. Relief figure on the rock at Madara (see also No. 21)	4.00	
108	(103)	50 Lewa (Ag) 1981. Type as No. 107		40.00

| **109** | (113) | 2 Lewa (Cu-Ni) 1981. Statue of a woman. Rev. portrait of Georgi Dimitrov | 7.00 | 7.50 |
| **110** | (104) | 50 Lewa (Ag) 1981. Type as No. 109 | | 40.00 |

WORLD HUNTING EXPOSITION »EXPO 81« (3)

111	(99)	1 Lew (Cu-Ni) 1981. Emblem of »Expo 81« and head of a stag	4.00	6.00
112	(100)	2 Lewa (Cu-Ni) 1981. Falconer	4.00	8.00
113	(101)	5 Lewa (Cu-Ni) 1981. Large stag skull with horns (Hunting trophy)	8.00	12.00

1300th YEARS OF BULGARIA AND RUSSO-BULGARIAN FRIENDSHIP

| **114** | (105) | 1 Lew (Cu-Ni) 1981. Flags above clasped hands | 5.00 | 7.00 |

1300th YEARS OF BULGARIA (6)

| **115** | (106) | 2 Lewa (Cu-Ni) 1981. Mother and child | | 8.00 |

			Unc	**Proof**
116 (108)	25	Lewa (Ag) 1981. Type as No. 115		25.00
117 (118)	50	Lewa (Ag) 1981. Type as No. 115		45.00
A117	1000	Lewa (Au) 1981. Type as No. 115		500.00

118 (114)	2	Lewa (Cu-Ni) 1981. Czar Ivan Assen II (reigned from 1218 to 1241)		7.50
119 (121)	50	Lewa (Ag) 1981. Type as No. 118		40.00

1300th YEARS OF BULGARIA AND HUNGARIAN-BULGARIAN FRIENDSHIP

120 (115)	5	Lewa (Cu-Ni) 1981. Portraits of Khristo Botev (1848–1876), Bulgarian poet and Alexander Petöfi (1823–1849), Hungarian poet		8.50

1300th YEARS OF BULGARIA (2)

121 (116)	2	Lewa (Cu-Ni) 1981		7.50
122 (117)	2	Lewa (Cu-Ni) 1981		7.50

1300th YEARS OF BULGARIA (4)

123 (125)	2	Lewa (Cu-Ni) 1981. Rila Monastery		7.50
124 (124)	2	Lewa (Cu-Ni) 1981. Cyrillic alphabet		7.50
125 (126)	2	Lewa (Cu-Ni) 1981. Woman holding flag and sword next to lion (Russky Monument)		7.50

126	2	Lewa (Cu-Ni) 1981. Fresco in the Boyana Church near Sofia		7.50

100th ANNIVERSARY OF BIRTH OF
VLADIMIR DIMITROV MAJSTORA

				Unc	Proof
127 (107)	5 Lewa (Cu-Ni) 1982. Vladimir Dimitrov Majstora (1882–1960), painter				10.00

40th ANNIVERSARY OF BIRTH OF L. JIVKOVA (2)

128 (108)	5 Lewa (Cu-Ni) 1982. Ljudmila Jivkova (1942–1981), politician				8.50
129 (118)	20 Lewa (Ag) 1982. Type as No. 128				32.00

2nd INTERNATIONAL CHILDREN'S ASSEMBLY

130 (109)	5 Lewa (Cu-Ni) 1982				8.00

WORLD SOCCER CHAMPIONSHIP GAMES IN SPAIN 1982 (2)

131 (111)	10 Lewa (Ag) 1982				25.00
132 (112)	10 Lewa (Ag) 1982				25.00

100th ANNIVERSARY OF BIRTH OF G. DIMITROV

133 (110)	25 Lewa (Ag) 1982. George Dimitrov (1882–1949), printer and politician			30.00	30.00

OLYMPIC WINTER GAMES

134 (123)	10 Lewa (Ag) 1984. Skier				40.00

LOS ANGELES XXIII. OLYMPIAD

135 (128)	10 Lewa 1984.				
	a) (Ag) .925 silver (50 pcs.), Pattern				400.00
	b) (Ag) .640 silver (300 pcs.), Pattern				100.00
	c) (Cu-Ni) (2000 pcs.), Pattern				40.00

Proof

136 (127) 25 Lewa (Ag) 1984. A bunch of roses, construction scaffolding and an atom nucleus — 25.00

BULGARIA

UNITED NATIONS DECADE FOR WOMEN 1976–1985

137   10 Lewa (Ag) 1984 — 25.00

138   100 Lewa (Au) 1984 — 200.00

3rd INTERNATIONAL CHILDREN'S ASSEMBLY

139 (132)   5 Lewa (Cu-Ni) 1985 — 7.50

90th ANNIVERSARY OF TOURISMOVEMENT

140 (133)   5 Lewa (Cu-Ni) 1985. Aleka Konstantinov, head left — 7.50

UNESCO CONFERENCE GENERALE IN SOFIA

141   5 Lewa (Cu-Ni) 1985 — 7.50

YOUNG INVENTORS EXPOSITION

142   5 Lewa (Cu-Ni) 1985 — 7.50

SOVIET-BULGARIAN SPACE FLIGHT

143   10 Lewa (Ag) 1985 — 35.00

230   **Bulgaria**

		Unc	Proof
144	2 Lewa (Cu-Ni) 1986	8.00	25.00
145	25 Lèwa (Ag) 1986		50.00
146	25 Lewa (Ag) 1986		50.00

Birma # Burma **Birmanie**

Area: 260,800 sq. mi. Population: 38,750,000.

In historical times several kingdoms have been in control of the territory of the present state, among them the Mon and the Shan Kingdoms, but also the Burmese. In the 19th century Burma was occupied gradually by the English and until 1897 was part of the Union of States of British India. After temporary occupation by the Japanese during World War II, Burma obtained its independence on 4th January 1948 and became an independent Republic.
Capital: Rangoon.

16 Annas = 1 Rupee; since 1st July 1952: 100 Pyas = 1 Kyat

			VF	XF
1 (13)	½ Anna (Cu-Ni) 1949. Lion, mythological guardian figure. ℞ value in wreath (square)		0.60	1.00
2 (14)	1 Anna (Cu-Ni) 1949–1951 (dodecagonal)		0.70	1.20
3 (15)	2 Annas (Cu-Ni) 1949–1951 (square)		1.00	2.00
4 (16)	4 Annas (Ni) 1949–1950 (round)		2.50	4.00

5 (17)	8 Annas (Ni) 1949–1950 (round)		3.00	6.00

NEW CURRENCY : 100 Pyas = 1 Kyat

6 (18)	1 Pya (Br) 1952–1966. Lion, mythological guardian figure. R value in wreath (round)		0.10	0.20
7 (19)	5 Pyas (Cu-Ni) 1952–1966 (dodecagonal)		0.10	0.20
8 (20)	10 Pyas (Cu-Ni) 1952–1965 (square)		0.15	0.30
9 (21)	25 Pyas (Cu-Ni) 1952–1965 (hexagonal)		0.25	0.40
10 (22)	50 Pyas (Cu-Ni) 1952–1966 (round)		0.40	0.80
11 (23)	1 Kyat (Cu-Ni) 1952–1965 (round)		1.00	2.00

			VF	XF
12 (24)	1 Pya (Al) 1966. General Aung San (1915–1947), liberator and politician; murdered by political enemies. ℞ value in wreath (round)		0.10	0.20
13 (25)	5 Pyas (Al) 1966 (scalloped edge)		0.12	0.25

14 (26)	10 Pyas (Al) 1966 (square)		0.15	0.30

15 (27)	25 Pyas (Al) 1966 (hexagonal)		0.25	0.50

16 (28)	50 Pyas (Al) 1966 (round)		0.50	1.00

ISSUE FOR THE FAO COIN PLAN (4)

			XF	Unc
17 (36)	10 Pyas (Al-Br) 1983. Rice plant		0.20	0.30
18 (35)	25 Pyas (Al-Br) 1980. Type as No. 17		0.25	0.35

19 (33)	50 Pyas (Br) 1975, 1976. Type as No. 17		0.30	0.50
20 (34)	1 Kyat (Cu-Ni) 1975. Type as No. 17		0.70	1.00

Burundi

Area: 10,780 sq. mi. Population: 4,700,000.

Belonging at first to German East Africa, it later became part of the Belgian Trust Territory of Rwanda-Urundi. An independent kingdom since 1st July 1962, a republic since 1966. Burundi formed an economic union with Rwanda; the unit of currency was the Rwanda-Burundi franc; see also Rwanda and Burundi (for joint issues) as well as the issues dating from before the independence, under Belgian Congo, years 1952–1960.

Capital: Bujumbura (Usumbura).

100 Centimes = 1 Burundi Franc

MWAMBUTSA IV 1915–1966
COMMEMORATIVE ISSUES (4) FOR INDEPENDENCE

			Proof
1	10 Francs (Au) 1962		70.00
2	25 Francs (Au) 1962		140.00
3	50 Francs (Au) 1962		260.00
4	100 Francs (Au) 1962		500.00

COMMEMORATIVE ISSUES (4)
FOR THE FIFTY YEAR JUBILEE OF THE GOVERNMENT

5	10 Francs (Au) 1965		70.00
6	25 Francs (Au) 1965		140.00
7	50 Francs (Au) 1965		260.00
8	100 Francs (Au) 1965		500.00

		XF	Unc
9 (1)	1 Franc (Bra) 1965. National arms. ℞ value in circle	0.30	0.60
10	500 Francs (Ag) 1966		100.00

NTARE V 1966

A 11	100 Francs (Ag) 1966		60.00
11	500 Francs (Ag) 1966		100.00

COMMEMORATIVE ISSUES (5)
FOR THE FIRST ANNIVERSARY OF THE REPUBLIC

			XF	Unc
12	10	Francs (Au) 1967. Head of Michel Micombero, President of State. R national arms		
13	20	Francs (Au) 1967. Same type as No. 12	–,–	–,–
14	25	Francs (Au) 1967. Same type as No. 12	–,–	–,–
15	50	Francs (Au) 1967. Same type as No. 12	–,–	–,–
16	100	Francs (Au) 1967. Same type as No. 12	–,–	–,–

17 (2)	5	Francs (Al) 1968–1971. National motto: Unity, Work, Progress, in two languages in concentric circles, date. Rev. value between laurel branches	0.50	1.00

ISSUE FOR THE FAO COIN PLAN

18 (3)	10	Francs (Cu-Ni) 1968, 1971. Inscription as No. 17, but arranged differently. R farm produce set in form of a wheel, with value in centre, symbolizing the dynamic improvement of the agrarian structure:		
		a) 1968	0.60	1.50
		b) 1971	1.50	2.50

19 (A2)	1	Franc (Al) 1970	1.00	3.00
20 (4)	1	Franc (Al) 1976, 1980. Arms Rev. value	0.50	1.00
21	5	Francs (Al) 1976, 1980. Arms. Rev. value	1.00	2.00

Kambodscha   **Cambodia (Khmer)**   **Cambodge**

Preah Reach Ana Chak Kampuchea

Area: 69,629 sq. mi. Population: 7,350,000.

Cambodia was a constitutional monarchy with a parliamentary form of government. After leaving the French Union, the country achieved full independence in 1955. The Khmer Republic proclaimed on 8th October 1970 removed the reference to the myth of royalty from the existing coat of arms. April 17th 1975, the Khmer rouge took control of the government and renamed the country Democratic Cambodia.

Capital: Pnom-Penh.

100 Centimes = 1 Piastre (Franc);
since 1955: 100 Sen = 1 Riel

NORODOM SIHANOUK 1953–1955

			VF	XF
1 (11)	10	Centimes (Al–Mg) 1953. Garuda, mythological bird and mount of the god Vishnu. ℞ value within wreath	1.00	2.50
2 (12)	20	Centimes (Al–Mg) 1953. Goblet. ℞ value within wreath	1.20	2.50
3 (13)	50	Centimes (Al–Mg) 1953. National arms. ℞ value within wreath	1.50	3.00

NORODOM SURAMARIT 1955–1960

NEW CURRENCY: 100 Sen = 1 Riel

4 (11a)	10	Sen (Al–Mg) 1959. Type as No. 1, but with new indication of value	0.50	1.00
5 (12a)	20	Sen (Al–Mg) 1959. Type as No. 2, but with new indication of value	0.60	1.20
6 (13a)	50	Sen (Al–Mg) 1959. Type as No. 3, but with new indication of value	0.70	1.40

FOR THE FAO COIN PLAN

			Unc
7 (14)	1	Rial (Cu-Ni) 1970. Temple of Angkor-Vath. Rev. Rice plant	35.00

REPUBLIC

			Unc	**Proof**
8	5000	Riels (Ag) 1974. Temple of Angkor-Vath. R new coat of arms	30.00	30.00
9	5000	Riels (Ag) 1974. Three Cambodian dancers	30.00	30.00
10	10000	Riels (Ag) 1974. Portrait of Marshall Lon Nol	50.00	50.00
11	10000	Riels (Ag) 1974. Basrelief of celestial dancer (Apsara)	50.00	50.00

12	50000	Riels (Au) 1974. Type as No. 9	125.00	125.00

13	50000	Riels (Au) 1974. Type as No. 11	160.00	160.00
14	100000	Riels (Au) 1974. Type as No. 10	320.00	400.00

PEOPLE'S REPUBLIC OF KAMPUCHEA

			XF	**Unc**
15 (15)	5	Sen (Al) 1979. Arms. Rev. value, date	15.00	20.00

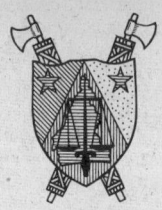

Kamerun   # Cameroon   **Cameroun**

Area: 182,863 sq. mi. Population: 10,000,000.

A German protectorate from 14th July 1884; it was enlarged by further acquisitions of territories in the east and south of the country (New Cameroon) on 4th November 1911; it was then occupied by the French and the British in the years 1914–1916. The part of Cameroon which then became French was made a Trust Territory, the English part was joined with Nigeria. The reunification took place only in 1961; the former French part has been a republic since 1960. Like the countries of Gaboon, Congo-Brazzaville, Chad and the Central African Republic, Cameroon is part of the Monetary Union of Equatorial Africa; such joint issues are treated separately under Equatorial Africa.
Capital: Yaoundé.

100 Centimes = 1 CFA Franc

				VF	**XF**
1 (1)	50	Centimes (Al-Br) 1924–1926. Laureate head of Marianne, symbol of the French Republic. Rev. value between shoots		4.00	12.00
2 (2)	1	Franc (Al-Br) 1924–1926		4.00	12.00
3 (3)	2	Francs (Al-Br) 1924–1925		8.00	25.00
4 (4)	50	Centimes (Br) 1943. Gallic cockerel, inscription CAMEROUN FRANÇAIS. R Croix de Lorraine		6.00	12.00
5 (5)	1	Franc (Br) 1943. Type as No. 4		6.00	12.00
6 (6)	50	Centimes (Br) 1943. Gallic cockerel, inscription now reading CAMEROUN FRANÇAIS LIBRE. R Croix de Lorraine		6.00	12.00

7 (7)	1	Franc (Br) 1943. Type as No. 6		6.00	12.00

				VF	XF

8 (8) 1 Franc (Al) 1948. Head of Marianne. ℞ head of a slender-horned gazelle (Gazella leptoceros — Bovidae)   0.50   0.90

9 (9) 2 Francs (Al) 1948. Type as No. 8   0.60   1.10

10 (5) 5 Francs (Al–Br) 1958. Addax antelope (Addax nasomaculatus — Bovidae). ℞ value within wreath • 0.50   0.90

11 (6) 10 Francs (Al–Br) 1958. Type as No. 10   0.60   1.10

12 (7) 25 Francs (Al–Br) 1958. Type as No. 10   1.20   2.00

COMMEMORATIVE ISSUE FOR THE PROCLAMATION OF INDEPENDENCE ON 1st JANUARY 1960

13 (13) 50 Francs (Cu–Ni) 1960. Addax antelope. Inscription ETAT DU CAMEROUN/ 1er JANVIER 1960/PAIX – TRAVAIL – PATRIE. ℞ value within wreath   3.00   5.00

For coins of 5, 10, and 25 Francs with reproductions of Addax antelopes and inscription ETATS DE L'AFRIQUE EQUATORIALE/CAMEROUN/BANQUE CENTRALE with dates from 1961–1962, ℞ value within wreath, see under Equatorial African States Nos. 1–4.

14 (14) 100 Francs (Ni) 1966–1968. Addax antelope. Inscription ETAT DU CAMEROUN/ BANQUE CENTRALE/PAIX – TRAVAIL – PATRIE/PEACE – WORK – FATHERLAND. R value   2.00   4.00

COMMEMORATIVE ISSUES (5) FOR THE 10th ANNIVERSARY OF INDEPENDENCE

			Proof

15 1000 Francs (Au) 1970. El Haj Ahmadou Ahijo (*1922), politician, leader of the Union Camerounaise since 1958 and President of State since 1960. Motto: Peace – Work – Fatherland. ℞ geometrical design in centre, value   70.00

16 3000 Francs (Au) 1970. ℞ antlers of eland (Taurotragus oryx congolanus — Bovidae), stylized. Value **Proof** 165.00

17 5000 Francs (Au) 1970. ℞ head of a young native (= national seal), surrounded with branch of the coffee tree (Coffea canephora — Rubiaceae) and five cocoa beans (Theobroma cacao — Sterculiaceae). Value 285.00

18 10000 Francs (Au) 1970. ℞ heads of elands. Value 550.00

19 20000 Francs (Au) 1970. ℞ national arms. Value 1000.00

		VF	XF
20 (15) 100	Francs (Ni) 1971, 1972, Mendes antelopes, name of country. Rev. Value	2.00	5.00

		VF	XF
21 (15a)100	Francs (Ni) 1972. Type as No. 20, but name of country CAMEROUN - CAMEROON	10.00	18.00
22 (16) 100	Francs (Ni) 1975, 1980, 1982, 1983, 1986. Type as No. 21, but inscription "Banque des Etats de l'Afrique Centrale"	2.00	4.00
23 (17) 500	Francs (Cu-Ni) 1985	3.00	6.00

Area: 3,836,991 sq. mi. Population: 25,000,000.

The Canadian coast was first explored by John Cabot, who sailed from Bristol in 1797 to discover Newfoundland. The French were next, Champlain colonising Quebec in 1608. Much greater expansion came with the Hudson's Bay Company in 1670; disputes between the British and French became more frequent, and France finally ceded Canada to England in 1763. Nonetheless, 30% of the population remains French to this day, and Montreal is the biggest French-speaking city ouside France. Various divisions (e.g. Upper and Lower Canada) happened from 1791 onwards; certain parts of the country (e.g. Alberta, British Columbia) were not developed until the second half of 19th century. Canada's position as a full member of the Commonwealth was ratified by the Statute of Westminster in 1981; a more independent constitution still was signed in April 1982, with a French minority again dissatisfied.

The Royal Canadian Mint at Ottawa was opened in 1908 and has since then struck the greater part of the country's coins. The mintmark C is, however, by no means always used, and is mentioned in the catalogue where it is to be found.

Canadian gold coins since 1976 are notable for being struck (when .916 fine) in an alloy entirely of silver, with no addition of copper; they are thus paler than others, e.g. the sovereign. The most recent Canadian gold coin, known from its reverse type as the »maple leaf« is a bullion piece struck to the standard of .999 fine, and thus the purest gold coin since medieval times.
Capital: Ottawa.

100 Cents = 1 Canadian Dollar

Mintmarks:
C = Ottawa
H = Heaton

Yeoman Numbers

In order to help collectors and dealers, we have added after most SCHÖN-numbers the corresponding number assigned by R.S. Yeoman in his wellknown works entitled »A Catalog of Modern World Coins« and »Current Coins of the World«.

1 (10) 1 Cent (Br) 1902-1910. Crowned bust right
of King Edward VII. R value

	Mintage	Fine	VF	XF
1902	3,000,000	1.50	2.50	4.50
1903	4,000,000	2.00	3.50	5.00
1904	2,500,000	2.50	3.50	6.00
1905	2,000,000	5.00	7.00	10.00
1906	4,100,000	2.00	3.50	5.00
1907	2,400,000	3.00	4.00	7.00
1907 H	800,000	12.00	15.00	30.00
1908	2,401,506	2.00	3.50	6.00
1909	3,973,339	1.50	2.50	4.00
1910	5,146,487	1.50	2.50	4.00

2 (11) 5 Cents (Ag) 1902-1910. Crowned bust right
of King Edward VII. R value within wreath,
above crown:

	Mintage			
1902	2,120,000	3.00	5.00	9.00
1902 H	2,200,000	3.50	6.00	11.00
1903	1,000,000	5.00	10.00	20.00

	Mintage	Fine	VF	XF
1903 H	2,640,000	3.00	6.00	12.00
1904	2,400,000	4.00	6.00	12.00
1905	2,600,000	4.00	6.00	12.00
1906	3,100,000	2.00	5.00	9.00
1907	5,200,000	2.00	5.00	9.00
1908	1,220,524	7.00	12.00	25.00
1909	1,983,725	4.00	7.00	14.00
1910	3,850,325	2.50	5.00	9.00

3 (12) 10 Cents (Ag) 1902–1910. Type as No. 2:

	Mintage	Fine	VF	XF
1902	720,000	5.00	10.00	32.00
1902 H	1,100,000	4.00	8.00	25.00
1903	500,000	10.00	30.00	75.00
1903 H	1,320,000	5.00	12.00	35.00
1904	1,000,000	8.00	25.00	60.00
1905	1,000,000	8.00	18.00	50.00
1906	1,700,000	5.00	10.00	30.00
1907	2,620,000	5.00	10.00	25.00
1908	776,666	8.00	20.00	50.00
1909	1,697,200	6.00	12.00	40.00
1910	4,468,331	4.00	6.00	20.00

4 (13) 25 Cents (Ag) 1902–1910. Type as No. 2:

	Mintage			
1902	464,000	10.00	20.00	60.00
1902 H	800,000	6.00	15.00	45.00
1903	846,150	10.00	22.00	70.00
1904	400,000	40.00	65.00	160.00
1905	800,000	10.00	25.00	90.00
1906	1,237,843	12.00	30.00	60.00
1907	2,088,000	10.00	26.00	55.00
1908	495,016	15.00	40.00	100.00
1909	1,335,929	7.00	25.00	70.00
1910	3,577,569	5.50	20.00	45.00

5 (14) 50 Cents (Ag) 1902–1910. Type as No. 2:

	Mintage			
1902	120,000	25.00	85.00	200.00
1903 H	140,000	35.00	120.00	260.00
1904	60,000	150.00	320.00	750.00
1905	40,000	180.00	400.00	950.00
1906	350,000	25.00	60.00	180.00
1907	300,000	20.00	50.00	150.00

	Mintage	Fine	VF	XF
1908	128,119	40.00	110.00	275.00
1909	302,118	28.00	80.00	240.00
1910	649,521	20.00	50.00	150.00

6 (A14) 1 Sovereign (Au) 1908–1910. Head right of King Edward VII. R St. George and the Dragon:

	Mintage	Proof		
1908 C	636			2800.00
1909 C	16,273	250.00	320.00	450.00
1910 C	28,012	185.00	250.00	300.00

Coin No. 6 can only be distinguished from similar issues made at the same time in Great Britain by the mintmark C for Ottawa.

GEORGE V 1910–1936

		VF	XF
7 (15a)	1 Cent (Br) 1911. Crowned bust left of King George V. R value (4,663,486 pieces)	2.00	5.00
8 (17a)	5 Cents (Ag) 1911. R value within wreath, above crown (3,692,350 pieces)	5.00	12.00
9 (18a)	10 Cents (Ag) 1911. Type as No. 8 (2,737,584 pieces)	18.00	50.00
10 (19a)	25 Cents (Ag) 1911. Type as No. 8 (1,721,341 pieces)	45.00	110.00
11 (20a)	50 Cents (Ag) 1911. Type as No. 8 (209,972 pieces)	240.00	600.00

12 (15) 1 Cent (Br) 1912-1920. Type as No. 7, but with added inscription DEI GRA:

	Mintage	Fine	VF	XF
1912	5,107,642	1.00	2.00	3.50
1913	5,735,405	1.00	2.00	3.50
1914	3,405,958	1.20	2.50	5.00
1915	4,932,134	1.00	2.00	4.00
1916	11,022,367	0.90	1.80	3.00
1917	11,899,254	0.90	1.80	3.00
1918	12,970,798	0.90	1.80	3.00
1919	11,279,634	0.90	1.80	3.00
1920	6,762,247	1.00	2.00	3.50

13 (17)   5 Cents (Ag) 1912-1921. Type as No. 12:

	Mintage	Fine	VF	XF
1912	5,863,170	2.00	4.00	7.00
1913	5,488,048	2.00	4.00	7.00
1914	4,202,179	2.50	4.00	7.00
1915	1,172,258	9.00	16.00	40.00
1916	2,481,675	3.00	6.00	15.00
1917	5,521,373	2.00	3.00	6.00
1918	6,052,298	2.00	3.00	6.00
1919	7,835,400	2.00	3.00	6.00
1920	10,649,851	1.50	2.50	5.00
1921	2,582,495	1800.00	2800.00	4600.00

The 5-cent-piece of 1921 had been struck when it was decided to use a nickel coin for this denomination. The silver pieces were then melted down. Approximately 100 pieces known.

14 (18)   10 Cents (Ag) 1912-1936. Type as No. 12:

	Mintage			
1912	3,235,557	3.00	6.00	18.00
1913	3,613,937	2.00	5.00	15.00
1914	2,549,811	3.00	6.00	18.00
1915	688,057	10.00	30.00	120.00
1916	4,218,114	2.00	4.00	10.00
1917	5,011,988	2.00	4.00	10.00
1918	5,133,602	2.00	4.00	10.00
1919	7,877,722	2.00	4.00	10.00
1920	6,305,345	2.00	4.00	10.00
1921	2,469,562	2.50	5.00	12.00
1928	2,458,602	3.00	5.00	10.00
1929	3,253,888	2.50	5.00	11.00
1930	1,831,043	2.50	5.50	12.00
1931	2,067,421	2.50	5.00	11.00
1932	1,154,317	3.00	6.50	15.00
1933	672,368	4.00	8.00	30.00
1934	409,067	4.00	12.00	45.00
1935	384,056	6.00	18.00	60.00
1936	2,460,871	2.00	4.00	10.00

The 10-cent piece of 1936 are also known with raised dot below date (only 4 pieces known).

15 (19)   25 Cents (Ag) 1912-1936. Type as No. 12:

	Mintage			
1912	2,544,199	5.00	10.00	40.00
1913	2,213,595	5.00	10.00	35.00
1914	1,215,397	5.00	12.50	50.00

	Mintage	Fine	VF	XF
1915	242,382	25.00	90.00	260.00
1916	1,462,566	5.00	10.00	30.00
1917	3,365,644	4.00	8.00	20.00
1918	4,175,649	4.00	8.00	20.00
1919	5,852,262	4.00	8.00	20.00
1920	1,975,278	4.00	9.00	25.00
1921	597,337	20.00	50.00	200.00
1927	468,096	35.00	90.00	220.00
1928	2,114,178	4.00	8.00	25.00
1929	2,690,562	4.00	8.00	25.00
1930	968,748	5.00	10.00	32.00
1931	537,815	6.00	12.00	35.00
1932	537,994	6.00	15.00	40.00
1933	421,282	7.00	16.00	45.00
1934	384,350	7.00	18.00	55.00
1935	537,772	6.50	15.00	45.00
1936	972,094	4.00	8.00	22.00
1936 dot	153,322	50.00	150.00	350.00

16 (20) 50 Cents (Ag) 1912-1936. Type as No. 12:

	Mintage			
1912	285,867	15.00	55.00	200.00
1913	265,889	15.00	55.00	180.00
1914	160,128	55.00	180.00	400.00
1916	459,070	12.00	45.00	125.00
1917	752,213	10.00	30.00	100.00
1918	754,989	10.00	22.00	90.00
1919	1,113,429	9.00	20.00	80.00
1920	584,691	10.00	28.00	130.00
1921	206,398	6000.00	9000.00	20000.00
1929	228,328	12.00	30.00	110.00
1931	57,581	20.00	60.00	180.00
1932	19,213	80.00	200.00	450.00
1934	39,539	30.00	85.00	250.00
1936	38,550	20.00	60.00	200.00

Most of the 50-cent-piece of 1921 were melted. Only about 50 pieces known.

Yeoman Numbers

In order to help collectors and dealers, we have added after most SCHÖN-numbers the corresponding number assigned by R.S. Yeoman in his wellknown works entitled »A Catalog of Modern World Coins« and »Current Coins of the World«.

		VF	XF
17 (A 22) 1 Dollar (Ag) 1936. Rev. Indian canoe (306,100 pieces)		13.00	18.00

18 (23) 5 Dollars (Au) 1912-1914. Crowned bust left of King George V. Rev. arms:

	Mintage	**Fine**	**VF**	**XF**
1912	165,680	125.00	140.00	185.00
1913	98,832	125.00	145.00	190.00
1914	31,122	200.00	300.00	450.00

19 (24) 10 Dollars (Au) 1912-1914. Type as No. 18:

	Mintage			
1912	74,759	225.00	360.00	450.00
1913	149,232	215.00	375.00	480.00
1914	140,068	240.00	450.00	550.00

20 (25) 1 Sovereign (Au) 1911-1919. Head left of King George V. Rev. St. George and the Dragon:

	Mintage			
1911 C	256,946	110.00	130.00	150.00
1913 C	3,715	350.00	500.00	700.00
1914 C	14,871	175.00	275.00	400.00

	Mintage	Fine	VF	XF
1916 C	6,111		17000.00	22000.00
1917 C	58,845	110.00	130.00	150.00
1918 C	106,516	110.00	130.00	140.00
1919 C	135,889	110.00	130.00	140.00

Most of the sovereigns of 1916 C were melted. Only about 10 pieces known.

Coin No. 20 can only be distinguished from similar issues made at the same time in Great Britain by the mintmark C for Ottawa.

21 (16) 1 Cent (Br) 1920-1936. Rev. value between maple leaves (Acer saccharum – Aceraceae):

	Mintage			
1920	15,483,923	0.25	1.00	2.00
1921	7,601,627	0.50	2.00	6.00
1922	1,243,635	10.00	15.00	25.00
1923	1,019,002	15.00	20.00	35.00
1924	1,593,195	5.00	8.00	12.00
1925	1,000,622	12.00	18.00	30.00
1926	2,143,372	2.00	3.00	8.00
1927	3,553,928	1.00	2.00	5.00
1928	9,144,860	0.25	0.75	2.00
1929	12,159,840	0.25	0.75	2.00
1930	2,538,613	2.00	3.00	6.00
1931	3,842,776	1.00	2.00	4.00
1932	21,316,190	0.25	0.50	2.00
1933	12,079,310	0.25	0.60	2.00
1934	7,042,358	0.25	0.60	2.00
1935	7,526,400	0.25	0.60	2.00
1936	8,768,769	0.25	0.60	2.00

The 1-cent piece of 1936 are also known with raised dot below date (only 8 pieces known).

22 (21) 5 Cents (Ni) 1922-1936. Rev. value and maple leaves:

	Mintage	Fine	VF	XF
1922	4,794,119	0.50	2.00	6.00
1923	2,502,279	1.00	3.00	9.00
1924	3,105,839	0.50	3.00	7.00
1925	201,921	30.00	50.00	160.00
1926 near6	938.162	4.00	12.50	48.00
1926 far6		95.00	140.00	300.00
1927	5,285,627	0.50	2.00	5.00
1928	4,577,712	0.50	2.00	5.00
1929	5,611,911	0.50	2.00	5.00
1930	3,704,673	0.50	2.00	6.00
1931	5,100,830	0.50	2.00	5.00
1932	3,198,566	0.50	2.00	5.00
1933	2,597,867	1.00	3.00	10.00
1934	3,827,304	0.40	2.00	5.00
1935	3,900,000	0.40	2.00	5.00
1936	4,400,450	0.40	2.00	5.00

25th ANNIVERSARY OF REIGN OF KING GEORGE V

		VF	XF
23 (22)	1 Dollar (Ag) 1935. Crowned bust left of King George V, inscription GEORGIUS V. REX IMPERATOR ANNO REGNI XXV. R Indian canoe	14.00	18.00

GEORGE VI 1936-1952

24 (26) 1 Cent (Br) 1937-1947. Head left of King George VI. Rev. maple leaves:

	Mintage	Fine	VF	XF
1937	10,040,231	0.40	0.80	1.50
1938	18,365,608	0.25	0.50	1.00
1939	21,600,319	0.25	0.50	1.00
1940	85,740,532	0.20	0.40	0.70
1941	56,336,011	0.10	0.40	0.70
1942	76,113,708	0.10	0.40	0.60
1943	89,111,969	0.10	0.40	0.60
1944	44,131,216	0.10	0.40	1.50
1945	77,268,591	0.10	0.25	0.50
1946	56,662,071	0.10	0.25	0.50
1947	31,093,901	0.10	0.25	0.50
1947 ML	47,855,448	0.10	0.25	0.50

ML means Maple Leaf. The year 1947 also has a variety with a small maple leaf behind the date.

25 (27) 5 Cents (Ni) 1937-1942. Rev. Canadian beaver (Castor fiber canadensis – Castoridae):

	Mintage	Fine	VF	XF
1937 dot	4,593,263	0.50	1.75	3.00
1938	3,898,974	0.75	2.50	8.00
1939	5,661,123	0.50	1.50	5.00
1940	13,920,197	0.25	0.75	3.00
1941	8,681,785	0.25	1.00	3.00
1942	6,847,544	0.25	1.00	3.00

26 (28) 5 Cents Rev. Canadian beaver (dodecagonal):

	Mintage	Fine	VF	XF
1942 (Bra)	3,396,234	0.50	1.00	2.00
1946 (Ni)	6,952,684	0.25	0.50	2.00
1947 (Ni)	7,603,724	0.20	0.40	1.50
1947 (Ni) dot		12.00	25.00	50.00
1947 (Ni) ML	9,595,124	0.20	0.50	2.00

ML means Maple Leaf.

27 (29) 5 Cents. Rev. large »V« and torch, along the border Morse characters reading »We Win When We Work Willingly« (dodecagonal):

	Mintage	Fine	VF	XF
1943 (Bra)	24,760,256	0.25	0.50	1.00
1944 (St)	11,532,784	0.25	0.40	0.75
1945 (St)	18,893,216	0.20	0.35	0.75

28 (30) 10 Cents (Ag) 1937-1947. Rev. schooner "Bluenose"

	Mintage	Fine	VF	XF
1937	2,500,095	2.00	4.00	8.00
1938	4,197,323	2.00	4.00	9.00
1939	5,501,748	2.00	4.00	9.00
1940	16,526,470	1.00	2.00	4.00
1941	8,716,386	1.00	3.00	8.00
1942	10,214,011	1.00	2.00	6.00
1943	21,143,229	1.00	2.00	5.00
1944	9,383,582	1.00	2.00	6.00
1945	10,979,570	1.00	2.00	5.00
1946	6,300,066	1.00	3.00	6.00
1947	4,431,926	1.50	3.00	8.00
1947 ML	9,638,793	1.00	2.00	4.00

29 (31) 25 Cents (Ag) 1937-1947. Rev. head of caribou (Rangifer tarandus – Cervidae):

	Mintage			
1937	2,690,176	3.00	5.00	8.00
1938	3,149,245	3.00	5.00	10.00
1939	3,532,495	3.00	5.00	10.00
1940	9,583,650	2.00	3.00	5.00
1941	6,654,672	2.00	3.00	5.00
1942	6,935,871	2.00	3.00	5.00
1943	13,559,575	2.00	3.00	5.00
1944	7,216,237	2.00	3.00	6.00
1945	5,296,495	2.00	3.00	5.00
1946	2,210,810	2.50	4.00	9.00
1947		2.50	5.00	10.00
1947 dot after 7	1,524,554	35.00	65.00	100.00
1947 ML	4,393,938	2.00	3.00	5.00

30 (32) 50 Cents (Ag) 1937-1947. Rev. crowned coat of arms, shield supporters: lion and unicorn:

	Mintage			
1937	192,016	5.00	8.00	15.00
1938	192,018	9.00	20.00	40.00
1939	287,976	6.00	12.00	22.00
1940	1,996,566	3.00	4.00	8.00
1941	1,714,874	3.00	4.00	8.00
1942	1,974,164	3.00	4.00	8.00
1943	3,109,583	3.00	4.00	8.00
1944	2,460,205	3.00	4.00	8.00

ML means Maple Leaf.

	Mintage	**Fine**	**VF**	**XF**
1945	1,959,528	3.00	4.00	8.00
1946		4.00	5.00	10.00
1946 Hoof in 6	950,235	18.00	35.00	110.00
1947 straight 7	424,885	4.00	8.00	15.00
1947 curved 7		4.00	8.00	15.00
1947 ML, straight 7		18.00	40.00	65.00
1947 ML, curved 7	738,433	1200.00	1500.00	2200.00

31 (33) 1 Dollar (Ag) 1937-1947. Rev. Indian canoe:

	Mintage			
1937	241,002	10.00	15.00	20.00
1938	90,304	22.00	32.00	45.00
1945	38,391	65.00	100.00	130.00
1946	93,055	15.00	30.00	45.00
1947 pointed 7	65,595	75.00	115.00	165.00
1947 blunt 7		35.00	65.00	80.00
1947 ML	21,135	85.00	155.00	200.00

VISIT OF THE ROYAL COUPLE TO CANADA

			VF	**XF**

32 (34) 1 Dollar (Ag) 1939. Rev. Parliament building in Ottawa (1,363,816 pieces) — VF 8.00, XF 12.50

33 (35) 1 Cent (Br) 1948-1952. Type as No. 24, but without IND: IMP:

	Mintage	**Fine**	**VF**	**XF**
1948	25,767,779	0.25	0.40	0.50
1949	33,128,933	0.15	0.20	0.30
1950	60,444,992	0.05	0.10	0.20
1951	80,430,379	0.05	0.10	0.20
1952	67,631,736	0.05	0.10	0.20

34 (36) 5 Cents. Rev. Canadian beaver (dodecagonal):

	Mintage	**Fine**	**VF**	**XF**
1948 (Ni)	1,810,789	0.70	1.50	4.00
1949 (Ni)	13,037,090	0.20	0.40	0.75
1950 (Ni)	11,970,521	0.20	0.40	0.75
1951 (St)	4,313,410	0.20	0.40	1.00
1952 (St)	10,891,148	0.20	0.40	0.65

35 (38) 10 Cents (Ag) 1948-1952. Rev. schooner "Bluenose":

	Mintage			
1948	422,741	5.00	10.00	25.00
1949	11,336,172	1.00	2.00	3.00
1950	17,823,075	1.00	2.00	3.00
1951	15,079,265	1.00	2.00	3.00
1952	10,474,455	1.00	2.00	3.00

36 (39) 25 Cents (Ag) 1948-1952. Rev. head of caribou:

	Mintage			
1948	2,564,424	2.50	4.00	9.00
1949	7,988,830	2.00	3.00	5.00
1950	9,673,335	2.00	3.00	5.00
1951	8,290,719	2.00	3.00	5.00
1952	8,859,642	2.00	3.00	5.00

37 (40) 50 Cents (Ag) 1948-1952. Rev. crowned coat of arms, shield supporters: lion and unicorn:

	Mintage			
1948	37,784	40.00	60.00	90.00
1949	858,991	4.00	6.00	10.00
1950	2,384,179	3.00	4.00	7.00
1951	2,421,730	3.00	4.00	7.00
1952	2,596,465	3.00	4.00	7.00

38 (41) 1 Dollar (Ag) 1948-1952. Rev. Indian canoe:

	Mintage			
1948	18,780	300.00	500.00	650.00
1950	261,002	6.00	8.00	12.50
1951	416,395	4.00	7.00	10.00
1952	406,148	4.00	7.00	12.00

COMMEMORATIVE ISSUE FOR THE ENTRY OF NEW-FOUNDLAND AS A PROVINCE IN THE CANADIAN CONFEDERATION on 11th December 1948

		VF	XF
39 (42)	1 Dollar (Ag) 1949. Rev. The "Matthew", sailing ship of the discoverer John Cabot (672,218 pieces)	12.00	17.50

COMMEMORATIVE ISSUE FOR THE 200th ANNIVERSARY OF THE NICKEL INDUSTRY

		VF	XF
40 (37)	5 Cents (Ni) 1951. Rev. nickel preparation plant, maple leaves (dedecagonal) (9,028,507 pieces)	0.25	0.75

ELIZABETH II since 1952

41 (43)   1 Cent (Br) 1953-1964. Head right of Queen Elizabeth II. Rev. maple leaves:

	Mintage	VF	XF	Unc
1953	67,806,016	0.10	0.20	0.60
1954	22,181,760	0.05	0.40	1.60
1955	56,403,193	0.05	0.10	0.60
1956	78,658,535	0.05	0.10	0.50
1957	100,601,792	0.05	0.10	0.20
1958	59,385,679	0.05	0.10	0.20
1959	83,615,343	0.05	0.10	0.20
1960	75,772,775	0.05	0.10	0.20
1961	139,598,404	0.05	0.10	0.15
1962	227,244,069	0.05	0.10	0.15
1963	279,076,334	0.05	0.10	0.15
1964	484,655,322	0.05	0.10	0.10

5 Cents 1953–1962. Rev. Canadian beaver (dodecagonal) (Y 44: St, Y 45: Ni):

	Mintage	VF	XF	Unc
1953 (St)	16,635,552	0.20	0.50	2.00
1954 (St)	6,998,662	0.50	1.00	4.00
1955 (Ni)	5,355,028	0.30	1.00	2.00
1956 (Ni)	9,399,854	0.20	0.50	1.50
1957 (Ni)	7,387,703	0.20	0.50	1.00
1958 (Ni)	7,607,521	0.20	0.50	1.00
1959 (Ni)	11,552,523	0.10	0.20	0.50
1960 (Ni)	37,157,433	0.10	0.20	0.40
1961 (Ni)	47,889,051	0.10	0.20	0.40
1962 (Ni)	46,307,305	0.10	0.20	0.40

43 (45a) 5 Cents (Ni) 1963-1964. Rev. Canadian beaver (round):

	Mintage			
1963	43,970,320	0.10	0.20	0.30
1964	78,075,068	0.10	0.20	0.30

44 (46) 10 Cents (Ag) 1953-1964. Rev. schooner "Bluenose":

	Mintage			
1953	17,706,395	0.60	1.00	5.00
1954	4,493,150	1.00	3.00	10.00
1955	12,237,294	0.70	1.20	5.50
1956	16,732,844	0.50	0.80	4.00
1957	16,110,229	0.50	0.60	2.00
1958	10,621,236	0.60	0.70	2.00
1959	19,691,433	0.50	0.60	1.50
1960	45,446,835	0.20	0.40	0.75
1961	26,850,859	0.25	0.50	0.75
1962	41,864,335	0.25	0.50	0.75
1963	41,916,208	0.25	0.50	0.75
1964	49,518,549	0.25	0.50	0.75

45 (47) 25 Cents (Ag) 1953-1964. Rev. head of caribou:

	Mintage			
1953	10,546,769	2.00	3.00	8.00
1954	2,318,891	4.00	9.00	35.00
1955	9,552,505	1.00	2.00	6.00
1956	11,269,353	0.90	1.75	5.00
1957	12,770,190	0.80	1.25	3.00

	Mintage	VF	XF	Unc
1958	9336,910	0.80	1.25	2.50
1959	13,503,461	0.75	1.00	2.00
1960	22,835,327	0.60	0.80	1.75
1961	18,164,368	0.60	0.80	1.75
1962	29,559,266	0.60	0.80	1.75
1963	21,180,652	0.60	0.80	1.75
1964	36,479,343	0.50	0.75	1.75

46 (48) 50 Cents (Ag) 1965-1958. Rev. crowned coat of arms, shield supporters: lion and unicorn:

	Mintage			
1953	1,630,429	3.00	4.00	10.00
1954	506,305	5.00	9.00	30.00
1955	753,511	4.00	6.00	20.00
1956	1,379,499	2.00	4.00	8.00
1957	2,171,689	1.00	3.00	5.00
1958	2,957,266	1.00	3.00	5.00

47 (51) 50 Cents (Ag) 1959–1964. Type as No. 47, but redesigned reverse:

	Mintage			
1959	3,095,535	1.50	2.50	4.00
1960	3,488,897	1.00	1.50	3.00
1961	3,584,417	1.00	1.50	3.00
1962	5,208,030	1.00	1.50	3.00
1963	8,348,871	1.00	1.50	3.00
1964	9,377,676	0.90	1.50	3.00

48 (49) 1 Dollar (Ag) 1953–1963. Rev. Indian canoe:

	Mintage			
1953	1,074,578	6.00	8.00	10.00
1954	246,606	9.00	12.00	15.00
1955	268,105	9.00	12.00	15.00
1956	209,092	10.00	12.00	17.50
1957	496,389	7.00	12.50	18.00
1959	1,443,502	3.00	5.00	8.00
1960	1,420,486	3.00	5.00	8.00
1961	1,262,231	3.00	5.00	8.00
1962	1,884,789	3.00	5.00	8.00
1963	4,179,981	2.00	5.00	8.00

CENTENARY OF BRITISH COLUMBIA

		XF	Unc
49 (50)	1 Dollar (Ag) 1958. Rev. totem pole (3,039,630 pieces)	6.00	9.00

CONFERENCES AT CHARLOTTETOWN (PRINCE EDWARD ISLAND) AND QUEBEC IN 1864

50 (52) 1 Dollar (Ag) 1964. Rev. Within a circle: the French fleur-de-lis, the Irish shamrock, the Scottish thistle and the English rose (7,296,832 pieces) 5.00 8.00

51 (53) 1 Cent (Br) 1965–1988. Rev. maple leaves (reduced weight since 1980, 12 sided planched since 1982):

	Mintage	VF	XF	Unc
1965	304,441,082	0.05	0.10	0.20
1966	184,151,087	0.05	0.10	0.40
1968	329,695,772	0.05	0.10	0.20
1969	335,240,929	0.05	0.10	0.20
1970	311,145,010	0.05	0.10	0.20
1971	298,228,936	0.05	0.10	0.20
1972	451,304,591	0.03	0.05	0.10
1973	457,059,852	0.03	0.05	0.10
1974	692,058,489	0.03	0.05	0.10
1975	642,318,000	0.03	0.05	0.10
1976	701,122,890	0.03	0.05	0.10
1977	453,762,670	0.03	0.05	0.10
1978	911,170,647	0.03	0.05	0.10
1979	754,394,064	0.03	0.05	0.10

REDUCED WEIGHT (Y 53a)

	Mintage	VF	XF	Unc
1980	911,800,000	0.03	0.05	0.10
1981	1,219,465,254	0.03	0.05	0.10

12 SIDED PLANCHET (Y 116)

	Mintage	VF	XF	Unc
1982	876,036,898	0.02	0.05	0.10
1983	975,510,000	0.02	0.05	0.10
1984	838,225,000	0.02	0.05	0.10
1985	771,772,500	0.02	0.05	0.10
1986		0.02	0.05	0.10
1987		0.02	0.05	0.10
1988		0.02	0.05	0.10

52 (54)   5 Cents (Ni, since 1982 Cu-Ni) 1965–
1985. Rev. Canadian beaver:

	Mintage	VF	XF	Unc
1965	84,876,018	0.08	0.10	0.20
1966	27,976,648	0.08	0.10	0.30
1968	101,930,379	0.08	0.10	0.20
1969	27,830,229	0.08	0.10	0.20
1970	5,726,010	0.15	0.25	0.70
1971	27,312,609	0.08	0.10	0.20
1972	62,417,387	0.08	0.10	0.20
1973	53,507,435	0.08	0.10	0.20
1974	94,704,645	0.08	0.10	0.20
1975	138,882,000	0.08	0.10	0.20
1976	55,140.213	0.08	0.10	0.20
1977	89,120,791	0.08	0.10	0.15
1978	137,079,273	0.07	0.08	0.15
1979	186,706,667	0.07	0.08	0.15
1980	134,878,000	0.07	0.08	0.15
1981	99,107,900	0.07	0.08	0.15

		VF	XF	Unc
1982	105,539,898	0.07	0.08	0.15
1983	72,596,000	0.07	0.08	0.15
1984	84,088,000	0.07	0.08	0.15
1985	126,560,000	0.07	0.08	0.15
1986		0.07	0.08	0.15
1987		0.07	0.08	0.15
1988		0.07	0.08	0.15

53 (55) 10 Cents (Ag) 1965-1968. Rev. schooner "Bluenose":

	Mintage			
1965	56,965,392	0.50	0.75	1.00
1966	34,567,898	0.50	0.75	1.00
1968	70,460,000	0.40	0.75	1.00

Values are given for each coin in U.S. Dollars and reference to Yeomannumbers.

54 (56) 25 Cents (Ag) 1965-1968. Rev. head of caribou:

	Mintage	VF	XF	Unc
1965	44,708,869	0.75	1.50	2.00
1966	25,626,315	0.75	1.50	2.00
1968	71,464,000	0.60	1.00	1.25

55 (57) 50 Cents (Ag)1965-1966. Arms:

	Mintage			
1965	12,629,974	1.00	2.00	2.50
1966	7,920,496	1.25	2.00	2.50

56 (58) 1 Dollar (Ag) 1965-1972. Indian canoe:

	Mintage			
1965	10,768,569	4.00	6.00	9.00
1966	9,912,178	3.00	5.00	8.00
1972	341,598			17.50

COMMEMORATIVE ISSUES (7) FOR THE CENTENARY OF THE EXISTENCE OF THE CANADIAN CONFEDERATION

		XF	Unc
57 (59)	1 Cent (Br) 1967. Rev. common pigeon (Columba livia domestica – Columbidae) (345,140,645 pieces)	0.10	0.20
58 (60)	5 Cents (Ni) 1967. Rev. snoshoe-rabbit or varying hare (Lepus americanus – Leporidae) (36,876,574 pieces)	0.20	0.30
59 (61)	10 Cents (Ag) 1967. Rev. Atlantic mackerel (Scomber scombrus - Scombridae) (63,012,417 pieces)	0.75	1.00

60 (62) 25 Cents (Ag) 1967. Rev. lynx (Lynx lynx – Felidae) (48,855,500 pieces) — 1.50 — 2.50

			XF	Unc
61 (63)	50	Cents (Ag) 1967. Rev. wolf (Canis lupus – Canidae) 4,211,395 pieces)	3.00	4.00

			XF	Unc
62 (64)	1	Dollar (Ag) 1967. Rev. Canada goose (Branta canadensis – Anatidae) (6,767,496 pieces)	9.00	12.00
63 (65)	20	Dollar (Au)1967. Rev. arms (337,688 pieces)	Proof	260.00
64 (55)	10	Cents (Ni) 1968-1988. Type as No. 53:		

	Mintage	XF	Unc
1968 Ottawa	87,412,930	0.20	0.30
1968 Philadelphia	85,170,000	0.20	0.30
1969	55,833,929	0.20	0.30
1970	5,249,296	0.40	0.70
1971	41,016,968	0.20	0.30
1972	60,169,387	0.20	0.30
1973	167,715,435	0.15	0.20
1974	201,566,565	0.15	0.20
1975	207,680,000	0.15	0.20
1976	95,018,533	0.15	0.20
1977	128,452,206	0.15	0.20
1978	170,366,431	0.15	0.20

	Mintage	XF	Unc
1979	236,910,479	0.15	0.20
1980	169,910,479	0.12	0.15
1981	123,912,900	0.12	0.15
1982	93,960,898	0.12	0.15
1983	111,501,710	0.12	0.15
1984	119,080,000	0.12	0.15
1985	142,800,000	0.12	0.15
1986		0.12	0.15
1987		0.12	0.15
1988		0.12	0.15

65 (56a) 25 Cents (Ni) 1968-1988. Type as No. 54:

	Mintage		
1968	88,686,931	0.40	0.80
1969	133,037,929	0.35	0.70
1970	10,302,010	0.65	1.20
1971	48,170,428	0.40	0.80
1972	43,743,387	0.40	0.80
1974	192,360,598	0.35	0.60
1975	141,148,000	0.35	0.60
1976	86,898,261	0.35	0.60
1977	99,634,555	0.35	0.60
1978	176,475,408	0.35	0.60
1979	131,042,905	0.35	0.60
1980	76,178,000	0.35	0.60
1981	131,583,900	0.35	0.60
1982	167,421,898	0.30	0.50
1983	13,162,000	0.30	0.50
1984	121,668,000	0.30	0.50
1985	154,400,000	0.30	0.50
1986		0.30	0.50
1987		0.30	0.50
1988		0.30	0.50

66 (57a) 50 Cents (Ni) 1968-1988. Type as No. 55,
but reduced size:

	Mintage		
1968	3,966,932	0.80	1.20
1969	7,113,929	0.80	1.20
1970	2,429,526	1.00	1.60
1971	2,166,444	0.80	1.20
1972	2,515,632	0.80	1.20
1973	2,546,096	0.80	1.20
1974	3,436,650	0.80	1.00

	Mintage	XF	Unc
1975	3,710,000	0.80	1.00
1976	2,940,719	0.80	1.00
1977	709,839	2.00	3.50
1978	3,341,892	0.80	1.00
1979	3,425,000	0.80	1.00
1980	1,574,000	0.80	1.00
1981	2,588,900	0.80	1.00

	Mintage	XF	Unc
1982	2,884,572	0.60	0.80
1983	1,205,000	0.60	0.80
1984	1,502,989	0.60	0.80
1985	2,188,374	0.60	0.80
1986		0.60	0.80
1987		0.60	0.80
1988		0.60	0.80

67 (58a) 1 Dollar (Ni) 1968-1988. Type as No. 56, but reduced size:

	Mintage	XF	Unc
1968	5,579,714	1.50	2.40
1969	4,809,313	2.00	3.00
1972	2,193,000	1.50	2.40
1975	3,256,000	1.40	2.00
1976	2,498,204	1.40	2.00
1977	1,393,745	1.40	2.00
1978	2,948,488	1.40	2.00
1979	2,544,000	1.40	2.00
1980	2,922,000	1.40	2.00
1981	2,778,900	1.40	2.00
1982	1,544,398	1.40	2.00
1983	2,267,525	1.40	2.00
1984	1,223,486	1.40	2.00
1985	3,104,092	1.40	2.00
1986		1.40	2.00
1987		1.40	2.00

Values are given for each coin in U.S. Dollars and reference to Yeomannumbers.

ISSUE FOR THE ENTRY OF
MANITOBA INTO THE CANADIAN CONFEDERATION IN 1870

		XF	Unc
68 (66)	1 Dollar (Ni) 1970. Manitoba pasque flower (Pulsatilla ludoviciana – Ranunculaceae) (4,140,058 pieces)	1.50	2.00

ISSUES (2) FOR THE ENTRY OF
BRITISH COLUMBIA INTO THE CANADIAN CONFEDERATION 1871

69 (68)	1 Dollar (Ag) 1971. Rev. coat of arms of British Columbia (conferred on 31st March 1906) and shield bearers. Jubilee dates (585,674 pieces)	Proof	15.00
70 (67)	1 Dollar (Ni) 1971. Rev. coat of arms and national flower of British Columbia (4,260,781 pieces)	1.50	2.00

COMMEMORATIVE ISSUE
FOR THE ENTRY OF PRINCE EDWARD ISLAND
IN THE CANADIAN FEDERATION IN 1873

			XF	**Unc**
71 (69)	1 Dollar (Ni) 1973. ℞ building of the Legislative Assembly in Charlottetown (3,196,452 pieces)		1.60	2.00

CENTENARY OF THE ROYAL CANADIAN MOUNTED POLICE (2)

72 (70)	25 Cents (Ni) 1973. ℞ member of the Royal Canadian Mounted Police in dress uniform on horseback, on a patch of lawn (134,958,587 pieces)	0.50	0.70

73 (71)	Dollar (Ag) 1973. Rev. Officer oft the Northwest Mounties on horseback, on a patch of prairie (1,031,271 pieces)	Proof	12.50

74   75

		Unc	Proof
74 (73)	5 Dollars (Ag) 1973. Elizabeth II. head facing right. R map of North America	7.50	10.00
75 (72)	5 Dollars (Ag) 1973. R sailing boats in front of skyline of Kingston, Ontario	7.50	10.00

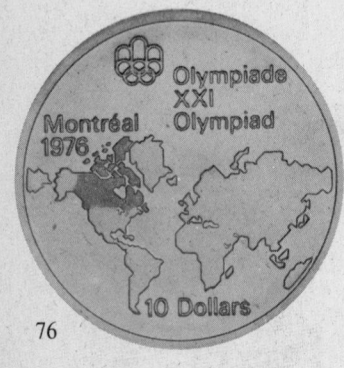 

76   77

		Unc	Proof
76 (74)	10 Dollars (Ag) 1973. R map of the world	12.50	16.00
	1974 (date error)	450.00	
77 (75)	10 Dollars (Ag) 1973. R city skyline of Montreal	12.50	16.00

COMMEMORATIVE ISSUE (2) FOR THE CENTENARY OF THE FOUNDING OF THE CITY OF WINNIPEG

			Unc	Proof
78 (100)	1 Dollar (Ni) 1974, Rev. View of Main Street in 1874 and the same location in 1984 (2,799,363), dia. 32 mm		2.00	
79 (100a)	1 Dollar (Ag) 1974 Type as No. 78, (728, 947), dia. 36 mm			10.00

COMMEMORATIVE ISSUES (4) FOR THE OLYMPIC GAMES 1976 IN MONTREAL (2nd ISSUE)

80   82

		Unc	Proof
80 (77)	5 Dollars (Ag) 1974. Rev. athlete and torch	7.50	10.00
81 (76)	5 Dollars (Ag) 1974. Rev. olympic rings	7.50	10.00
82 (78)	10 Dollars (Ag) 1974. Rev. head of Zeus	12.50	16.00
83 (79)	10 Dollars (Ag) 1974. Rev. temple of Zeus	12.50	16.00

84   86

			Unc	Proof
84 (81)	5	Dollars (Ag) 1974. Rev. Indian paddling canoe	7.50	10.00
85 (80)	5	Dollars (Ag) 1974. Rev. olympic rower	7.50	10.00
86 (83)	10	Dollars (Ag) 1974. Rev. Indians playing Lacrosse	12.50	16.00
87 (82)	10	Dollars (Ag) 1974. Rev. high wheel bicycles	12.50	16.00

100th ANNIVERSARY OF CALGARY

88 (101)	1	Dollar (Ag) 1975. Rev. cowboy on horse with oil weells and city skyline in background (930,956 pieces)		10.00

89   90

			Unc	Proof
89 (85)	5	Dollars (Ag) 1975. Rev. women's javelin	7.50	10.00
90 (84)	5	Dollars (Ag) 1975. Rev. marathon runner	7.50	10.00

91   92

			Unc	Proof
91 (86)	10	Dollars (Ag) 1975. Rev. men's high hurdles	12.50	16.00
92 (87)	10	Dollars (Ag) 1975. Rev. women's shot put	12.50	16.00

COMMEMORATIVE ISSUES (4) FOR THE OLYMPIC GAMES 1976 IN MONTREAL (5th ISSUE)

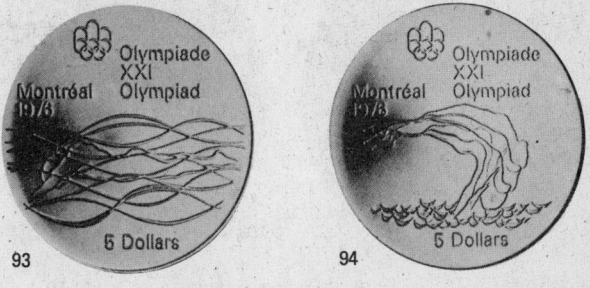

93   94

			Unc	Proof
93 (88)	5	Dollars (Ag) 1975. Rev. swimmer	7.50	10.00
94 (89)	5	Dollars (Ag) 1975. Rev. diver	7.50	10.00

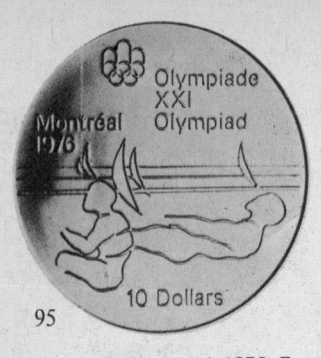

95   96

	Unc	Proof
95 (90) 10 Dollars (Ag) 1975. Rev. sailing	12.50	16.00
96 (91) 10 Dollars (Ag) 1975. Rev. paddler	12.50	16.00

COMMEMORATIVE ISSUES (4) FOR THE OLYMPIC GAMES 1976 IN MONTREAL (6th ISSUE)

97 (92) 5 Dollars (Ag) 1976. Rev. fencing	7.50	10.00
98 (93) 5 Dollars (Ag) 1976. Rev. boxing	7.50	10.00

99   100

99 (94) 10 Dollars (Ag) 1976. Rev. soccer	12.50	16.00
100 (95) 10 Dollars (Ag) 1976. Rev. field hockey	12.50	16.00

COMMEMORATIVE ISSUES (4) FOR THE OLYMPIC GAMES 1976 IN MONTREAL (7th ISSUE)

101 (96) 5 Dollars (Ag) 1976. Rev. olympic village	7.50	11.00

		Unc	Proof
102 (97)	5 Dollars (Ag) 1976. Rev. olympic flame	7.50	11.00
103 (98)	10 Dollars (Ag) 1976. Rev. olympic stadium	12.50	18.00
104 (99)	10 Dollars (Ag) 1976. Rev. olympic velo- drome	12.50	18.00

COMMEMORATIVE ISSUE FOR THE OLYMPIC GAMES 1976 IN MONTREAL (8th ISSUE)

105   100 Dollars (Au) 1976. Rev. Athena,
Greek goddes and ancient athlete:
a) (Y A 100) .583 gold, dia. 27 mm;
beaded borders (650,000)   140.00
b) (Y A 100a) .917 gold, dia. 25 mm;
plain borders (350,000) (as ill.)   250.00

100th ANNIVERSARY OF THE LIBRARY OF PARLIAMENT

106 (102)   1 Dollar (Ag) 1976. Rev. Library of Parliament in Ottawa (578,708 pieces)   15.00

Proof

107 (103)   1 Dollar (Ag) 1977. Rev. The throne of the
Senate (744,848 pieces)   10.00

108 (104)   100 Dollars (Au) 1977. Rev. bouquet of
twelve flowers representing the twelve
Canadian provinces and territories
(180,396 pieces)   300.00

COMMEMORATIVE ISSUE FOR THE 11th COMMONWEALTH GAMES IN EDMONTON (August 3-12, 1978)

109 (106)   1 Dollar (Ag) 1978. Rev. the official symbols of the ten sports which comprise
the Commonwealth Games (709,602
pieces)   10.00

CANADIA UNITY COIN

Proof

110 (105) 100 Dollars (Au) 1978. Twelve flying
gooses
(200,000 pieces)   250.00

Values are given for each coin in U.S. Dollars and reference to Yeoman-numbers.

300th ANNIVERSARY OF GRIFFON

111 (107) 1 Dollar (Ag) 1979. The »Griffon«
(826,695 pieces)   16.00

YEAR OF THE CHILD

112 (108) 100 Dollars (Au) 1979. Children encircling
a globe (250,000 pieces)   250.00

Unc

113 (118) 5 Dollars (1/10 troy ounce) (Au)
1982–. Maple leaf; 3.131 g, .9999
gold:
a) 1982 (184,000 pieces) 45.00
b) 1983 (224,000 pieces) 45.00
c) 1984 (476,000 pieces) 45.00
d) 1985 (480,000 pieces) 45.00
e) 1986– 45.00

114 (119) 10 Dollars (¼ troy ounce) (Au) 1982–
1988.
Type as No. 113; 7.797 g, .9999
gold:
a) 1982 (246,000 pieces) 100.00
b) 1983 (130,000 pieces) 100.00
c) 1984 (607,200 pieces) 100.00
d) 1985 100.00
e) 1986– 100.00

A 114 20 Dollars (½ troy ounce) (Au) 1986–
1988.
Type as No. 113; 15.575 g, .9999
gold:
a) 1986 200.00
b) 1987 200.00
c) 1988 200.00

115 (109) 50 Dollars (1 troy ounce) (Au) 1979–   **Unc**
        1988.
        Type as No. 113:
        a) 1979–1982, 31.150 g, fineness
        .999   400.00
        b) 1983–1988, 31.150 g, fineness
        .9999   400.00

ARCTIC TERRITORIES CENTENNIAL (2)

                                               BU

116 (110) 1 Dollar (Ag) 1980. Polar bear
        (539,617 pieces)   22.00

                                           Proof

117 (111) 100 Dollars (Au) 1980. Rev. Eskimo
        Hunter (300,000 pieces)   280.00

100th ANNIVERSARY OF TRANS-CANADA RAILROAD

		Unc	Proof
118 (112)	1 Dollar (Ag) 1980. Rev. Train engine (699,494 pieces)	18.50	50.00

CANADA NATIONAL ANTHEM »O CANADA«

119 (113) 100 Dollars (Au) 1981. Rev. Map and scroll (100,950 pieces)   280.00

100th ANNIVERSARY OF THE CITY OF REGINA

120 (114)	1 Dollar (Ag) 1982. Rev. Bison skull (903,888 pieces)	15.00	20.00

CANADA'S OLD CONFEDERATION (1867) AND NEW CONSTITUTION (1982)

		Unc	Proof
121 (115)	1 Dollar (Ni) 1982. »Fathers of Confederation« from a painting by Robert Harris	2.00	
122 (117)	100 Dollars (Au) 1982. Rev. An open book bearing the coat of arms of Canada and a maple leaf (121,706 pieces)		260.00

EDMONTON UNIVERSITY GAMES 1983

		Unc	Proof
123 (120)	1 Dollar (Ag) 1983. Rev. Athlete	12.00	22.00

400th ANNIVERSARY OF THE LANDING OF SIR HUMPHRY GILBERT IN ST. JOHN'S, NEWFOUDLAND

124 (121)	100 Dollars (Au) 1983 (83,128 pieces)		280.00

150th ANNIVERSARY OF TORONTO

125	1 Dollar (Ag) 1984	10.00	18.00

450th ANNIVERSARY OF THE LANDING OF
JACQUES CARTIER IN QUEBEC (2)

		Unc	Proof
126	1 Dollar (Ni) 1984 (7,009,323 pieces and 87,760 proofs)	2.00	9.00

127	100 Dollars (Au) 1984. Rev. Jacques Cartier and a ship of his era (67,601 pieces)		300.00

100th ANNIVERSARY OF BANFF NATIONAL PARK (2)

128	1 Dollar (Ag) 1985. Rev. Moose wading in a lake (584,440 pieces)	10.00	15.00

129	100 Dollars (Au) 1985. Rev. Bighorn Sheep (59,745 pieces)		300.00

		Unc	Proof
130	20 Dollars (Ag) 1985. Rev. Downhill Skiing. .925 silver, 33.63 g (142,914 pieces)		30.00
131	20 Dollars (Ag) 1985. Rev. Speed Skating (134,600 pieces)		30.00

VANCOUVER FOUNDATION CENTENARY

132	1 Dollar (Ag) 1986. Rev. Canadian Pacific Engine No. 371, Vancouver skyline in background	10.00	14.00

INTERNATIONAL YEAR OF PEACE 1986

133	100 Dollars (Au) 1986. Rev. Branch of maple leaves intertwined with a branch of olive leaves (100,000 pieces)	Unc	Proof
			250.00

XV OLYMPIC WINTER GAMES CALGARY 1988
2nd ISSUE (2)

134	20 Dollars (Ag) 1986. Rev. Hockey		30.00
135	20 Dollars (Ag)1986. Rev. Biathlon		30.00

Canada

3rd ISSUE (2)

136	20 Dollars (Ag) 1986. Rev. Cross-Country Skiing		30.00
137	20 Dollars (Ag) 1986. Rev. Free-Style Skiing		30.00

400th ANNIVERSARY OF JOHN DAVIS' THIRD EXPEDITION IN SEARCH OF THE NORTH WEST PASSAGE

138	1 Dollar (Ag) 1987. Rev. Brigg »Sunshine«	10.00	14.00

4th ISSUE (2)

		Unc	Proof
139	20 Dollars (Ag) 1987. Rev. Figure Skating		30.00
140	20 Dollars (Ag) 1987. Rev. Curling		30.00

5th ISSUE

		Unc	Proof
141	20 Dollars (Ag) 1987. Rev. Ski-Jumping		30.00
142	20 Dollars (Ag) 1987. Rev. Bobsleigh		30.00

6th ISSUE

143	100 Dollars (Au) 1987. Rev. Hand with torch		–.–

		XF	Unc
144	1 Dollar (Aureate Nickel) 1987, 1988. Elizabeth II. Rev. Loon (Gavia immer) (eleven-sided)	1.00	1.50

Kap Verde   # Cape Verde Islands   **Cap Vert**

Area: 1,557 sq. mi. Population: 327,000.

The Portuguese navigators, Diego Gomes and Antonio Nola, discovered this island group in 1460; unil then it had been uninhabited and was settled with Negro slaves by Portugal. The colonial status was formally transferred in 1951 to that of an (overseas-) province; this, however, was unable to call a halt to the movements of independence. Mainly on the mainland opposite (Portuguese Guinea) the P(artido) A(fricano) (de) I(ndependencia) (de) G(uiné e) C(abo Verde) (African Party for the Independence of Guinea and the Cape Verde Islands) was operating. After the declaration of independence of Guinea-Bissau (on the mainland) the Cape Verdes became independent on July 5, 1975.

Capital: Praia.

100 Centavos = 1 Escudo; 100 Centavos = 1 Cape Verde Escudo

			VF	**XF**
1 (1)	5	Centavos (Br) 1930. Allegorical figure of the Republic. ℞ value	3.00	6.00
2 (2)	10	Centavos (Br) 1930. Type as No. 1	2.50	5.00
3 (3)	20	Centavos (Br) 1930. Type as No. 1	2.50	5.00
4 (4)	50	Centavos (Ni–Br) 1930. ℞ arms within wreath above value	8.00	15.00

5 (5)	1	Escudo (Ni–Br) 1930. Type as No. 4	12.00	20.00
6 (6)	50	Centavos (Ni–Br) 1949. Arms with mural crown. ℞ value		
7 (7)	1	Escudo (Ni–Br) 1949. Type as No. 6	4.00	6.00
8 (A 8)	50	Centavos (Br) 1968. Type as No. 6, but without COLONIA DE in the inscription	5.00	9.00
9 (8)	1	Escudo (Br) 1953, 1968. Type as No. 8	0.80	1.40
10 (9)	2½	Escudos (Cu–Ni) 1953, 1967. Type as No. 8	0.80	1.40
11 (A 10)	5	Escudos (Cu–Ni) 1968. Type as No. 8	1.00	2.00
12 (10)	10	Escudos (Ag) 1953. Type as No. 8	1.50	3.00
			3.00	5.00

1th ANNIVERSARY OF INDEPENDENCE (2)

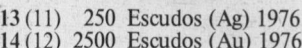

			Unc	Proof
13 (11)	250	Escudos (Ag) 1976	18.00	45.00
14 (12)	2500	Escudos (Au) 1976		200.00

			XF	Unc
15 (13)	20	Centavos (Al) 1977. Arms. Rev. value	0.40	0.80
16 (14)	50	Centavos (Al) 1977. Type as No. 15	0.50	1.00

ISSUE FOR THE FAO COIN PLAN (2)

17 (15)	1 Escudo (Cu-Al-Ni) 1977, 1980. Rural education	0.50	1.00
18 (16)	2,50 Escudos (Cu-Al-Ni) 1977, 1982. Planting coffee	0.50	1.00
19 (17)	10 Escudos (Cu-Ni) 1977, 1982. Eduardo Mondlane (1920–1969), patriot	1.00	2.00
20 (18)	20 Escudos (Cu-Ni) 1977, 1982. Domingos Ramos (1935–1966), patriot	1.50	2.50
21 (19)	50 Escudos (Cu-Ni) 1977, 1980, 1982. Amilcar Cabral (1924–1973), patriot	2.00	4.00

No. 22 omitted.

FAO WORLD FISHERIES CONFERENCE

23	50 Escudos 1984. Rev. White Seabream (Diplotus sargis lineatus):	
	a) (Ag), .925 Silver, 16 g		30.00
	b) (Ag), .925 Silver, 32 g (Piéfort)		65.00
	c) (Cu-Ni)	5.00	

| 24 | 50 Escudos (Au) 1984. Type as No. 23, .916⅔ gold, 27 g (100 pcs.) | | 1200.00 |

10th ANNIVERSARY OF INDEPENDENCE (6)

		Unc	Proof
25	1 Escudo (Cu-Al-Ni) 1985. Arms, value. Rev. Parliament building	2.00	–.–
26	10 Escudos (Cu-Ni) 1985. Rev. Emblem	2.00	–.–
27	1 Escudo (Ag) 1985. Type as No. 25, .925 silver, 4 g		–.–
28	10 Escudos (Ag) 1985. Type as No. 26, .925 silver, 6 g		–.–
29	1 Escudo (Au) 1985. Type as No. 25, .750 gold, 6 g (50 pcs.)		–.–
30	10 Escudos (Au) 1985. Type as No. 26, .750 gold, 9 g (50 pcs.)		–.–

Kaiman-Inseln **Cayman Islands** **Caïmanes (Iles)**

Area: 68 sq. mi. Population: 13,000.
The coral islands of Grand Cayman, Little Cayman and Cayman Brac,
situated in the Caribbean Ocean, were under the administration of
Jamaica until 1959, were under a Governor General from 1959–62
and since 1962 enjoy limited autonomy. Until the introduction of a
local currency on 1st May 1972, the Jamaica Dollar was legal tender.
Capital: Georgetown.

100 Cents = 1 Cayman Dollar

			Unc	Proof
1 (1)	1	Cent (Bro) 1972–. Queen Elisabeth II. R Great Caiman thrush (Mimocichla ravida – Turtidae), denomination	0.20	0.50
2 (2)	5	Cents (Cu–Ni) 1972–. R Prawn (Penaeus setiferus – Penaeidae) denomination	0.20	0.50
3 (3)	10	Cents (Cu–Ni) 1972–. R green turtle (Chelonia mydas – Cheloniidae) = the heraldic animal of the islands, denomination	0.50	0.75
4 (4)	25	Cents (Cu–Ni) 1972–. R Caiman schooner	1.00	1.00
5 (5)	50	Cents (Ag) 1972–. R Caribbean emperor fish (Holacanthus tricolor – Chaetodontidae), denomination		3.00
6 (6)	1	Dollar (Ag) 1972–. R Flamboyant (Delonix regia – Leguminosae), denomination		6.00
7 (7)	2	Dollars (Ag) 1972–. R Silver Heron (Casmerodius albus – Ardeidae), denomination		9.00
8 (8)	5	Dollars (Ag) 1972–. R coat of arms, denomination		12.00

Values are given for each coin in U.S. Dollars and reference to Yeomannumbers.

COMMEMORATIVE ISSUES (2) FOR THE SILVER WEDDING OF THE BRITISH ROYAL COUPLE ON 20th NOVEMBER 1972

			Unc	Proof
9 (9)	25	Dollars (Ag) 1972. British Royal Couple, overlapping heads, facing right	30.00	35.00
10 (9a)	25	Dollars (Au) 1972. Type as No. 9	140.00	125.00

COMMEMORATIVE ISSUES (2) FOR THE CENTENARY OF THE BIRTH OF SIR WINSTON CHURCHILL

11 (10)	25	Dollars (Ag) 1974. Bust of Sir Winston Churchill (1874–1965). R Coat of arms, value	35.00	32.50
12 (11)	100	Dollars (Au) 1974. Type as No. 11	200.00	175.00

SOVEREIGN QUEENS OF ENGLAND (2)

13 (12)	50	Dollars (Ag) 1975-1977. Bust of Queen Elizabeth II. Rev. the Queens Mary I, Elizabeth I, Mary II, Anne, and Victoria. Value in centre	60.00	65.00
14 (13)	100	Dollars (Au) 1975-1977. Type as No. 13	175.00	175.00

SILVER JUBILEE OF HER MAJESTY QUEEN ELIZABETH (12)

15 (14)	25	Dollars (Ag) 1977. Elizabeth II. Rev. Coat of arms	35.00	35.00
16 (15)	100	Dollars (Au) 1977. Type as No. 15	250.00	175.00

			Proof
17 (16)	25 Dollars (Ag) 1977. Mary I		40.00
18 (17)	25 Dollars (Ag) 1977. Elizabeth I		40.00
19 (18)	25 Dollars (Ag) 1977. Mary II		40.00
20 (19)	25 Dollars (Ag) 1977. Anne		40.00
21 (20)	25 Dollars (Ag) 1977. Victoria		40.00
22 (21)	50 Dollars (Au) 1977. Type as No. 17		125.00
23 (22)	50 Dollars (Au) 1977. Type as No. 18		125.00
24 (23)	50 Dollars (Au) 1977. Type as No. 19		125.00
25 (24)	50 Dollars (Au) 1977. Type as No. 20		125.00
26 (25)	50 Dollars (Au) 1977. Type as No. 21		125.00

25th ANNIVERSARY OF THE CORONATION OF HER MAJESTY QUEEN ELIZABETH II (22)

27 (1a)	1 Cent (Br) 1978. Type as No. 1, but Coronation Anniversary legend		2.00
28 (2a)	5 Cents (Cu-Ni) 1978		3.00
29 (3a)	10 Cents (Cu-Ni) 1978		3.50
30 (4a)	25 Cents (Cu-Ni) 1978		4.00
31 (5a)	50 Cents (Ag) 1978		8.00
32 (6a)	1 Dollar (Ag) 1978		12.00
33 (7a)	2 Dollars (Ag) 1978		22.00
34 (8a)	5 Dollars (Ag) 1978		28.00
35 (38)	50 Dollars (Ag) 1978		80.00
36 (39)	100 Dollars (Au) 1978		250.00
37 (26)	25 Dollars (Ag) 1978. Rev. the Ampulla		40.00
38 (27)	25 Dollars (Ag) 1978. Rev. the Orb		40.00
39 (28)	25 Dollars (Ag) 1978. Rev. St. Edward's crown		40.00
40 (29)	25 Dollars (Ag) 1978. Rev. the Coronation chair		40.00
41 (30)	25 Dollars (Ag) 1978. Rev. the Royal scepter		40.00
42 (31)	25 Dollars (Ag) 1978. Rev. the Spoon		40.00
43 (32)	50 Dollars (Au) 1978. Type as No. 37		125.00
44 (33)	50 Dollars (Au) 1978. Type as No. 38		125.00
45 (34)	50 Dollars (Au) 1978. Type as No. 39		125.00
46 (35)	50 Dollars (Au) 1978. Type as No. 40		125.00
47 (36)	50 Dollars (Au) 1978. Type as No. 41		125.00
48 (37)	50 Dollars (Au) 1978. Type as No. 42		125.00

KINGS OF GREAT BRITAIN (20)

49 (40)	25 Dollars (Ag) 1980. Saxon Kings		35.00
50 (41)	25 Dollars (Ag) 1980. House of Normandy		35.00

51 (42)	25 Dollars (Ag) 1980. House of Plantagenet I	35.00
52 (43)	25 Dollars (Ag) 1980. House of Plantagenet II	35.00
53 (44)	25 Dollars (Ag) 1980. House of Lancaster	35.00
54 (45)	25 Dollars (Ag) 1980. House of York	35.00
55 (46)	25 Dollars (Ag) 1980. House of Tudor	35.00
56 (47)	25 Dollars (Ag) 1980. House of Stuart & Orange	35.00
57 (48)	25 Dollars (Ag) 1980. House of Hanover	35.00
58 (49)	25 Dollars (Ag) 1980. House of Saxe-Coburg and Windsor	35.00
59 (50)	50 Dollars (Au) 1980. Type as No. 49	120.00
60 (51)	50 Dollars (Au) 1980. Type as No. 50	120.00
61 (52)	50 Dollars (Au) 1980. Type as No. 51	120.00
62 (53)	50 Dollars (Au) 1980. Type as No. 52	120.00
63 (54)	50 Dollars (Au) 1980. Type as No. 53	120.00
64 (55)	50 Dollars (Au) 1980. Type as No. 54	120.00
65 (56)	50 Dollars (Au) 1980. Type as No. 55	120.00
66 (57)	50 Dollars (Au) 1980. Type as No. 56	120.00
67 (58)	50 Dollars (Au) 1980. Type as No. 57	120.00
68 (59)	50 Dollars (Au) 1980. Type as No. 58	120.00

WEDDING OF PRINCE CHARLES AND LADY DIANA (2)

69 (68)	10 Dollars (Ag) 1981	20.00
70 (69)	100 Dollars (Au) 1981	175.00

150th ANNIVERSARY OF PARLIAMENTARY GOVERNMENT (2)

71 (70)	5 Dollars (Ag) 1982	30.00
72 (71)	50 Dollars (Au) 1982	130.00

INTERNATIONAL YEAR OF THE CHILD

73 (72)	10 Dollars (Ag) 1982	25.00

QUEEN'S ROYAL VISIT (7)

74 (73)	50 Cents (Ag) 1983, 1984, 1986. Rev. Morning glory flower	10.00
75 (74)	1 Dollar (Ag) 1983, 1984, 1986. Rev. Pineapple	12.50
76 (75)	2 Dollars (Ag) 1983, 1984. Parrot	25.00

77 (76)	5 Dollars (Ag) 1983	30.00
78 (77)	10 Dollars (Ag) 1983	40.00
79 (78)	25 Dollars (Ag) 1983	50.00
80 (79)	50 Dollars (Au) 1983	200.00

250th ANNIVERSARY OF ROYAL LAND GRANT (2)

81	5 Dollars (Ag) 1985. Rev. Map of Grand Cayman, Little Cayman and Cayman Brac	40.00
82	250 Dollars (Au) 1985. Type as No. 81, .916⅔ gold, 47.54 g (250 pcs)	1100.00

200th ANNIVERSARY OF THE BIRTH OF JOHN JAMES AUDUBON

83	50 Dollars (Ag) 1985. Rev. Snowy Egret, .925 silver, 129.6 g	80.00

COMMONWEALTH GAMES IN EDINBURGH (2)

84	5 Dollars (Ag) 1986. Rev. Long-jumper:		
	a) .500 silver, 28.28 g	12.50	
	b) .925 silver, 28.28 g		15.00
85	250 Dollars (Au) 1986. Type as No. 84, .916⅔ gold, 47.54 g (150 pcs.)		1100.00

All valuations in the SCHÖN are stated in U.S. Dollars.

Central African Republic
Zentralafrikanische Republik   **République Centrafricaine**

Area: 239,609 sq. mi. Population: 2,600,000.
The Central African Republic, part of French Equatorial Africa under the
name of Oubangui-Chari, obtained its autonomy on 1st December 1958
within the French Community; on 12th August 1960 it gained independece.
The Central African Republic belongs to the Monetary Union of Equatorial
Africa; see under this heading for the joint issues by the Community.
Capital: Bangui.

100 Centimes = 1 CFA Franc

COMMEMORATIVE ISSUES (5) FOR THE 10th ANNIVERSARY OF INDEPENDENCE

1	1000	Francs (Au) 1970. Jean Bédel Bokassa (*1921), 3rd President of State. Commemorative inscription. Motto: Unity – Honour – Work. R national arms, neck decoration: the national order of service, and legend: Zo Kwe Zo (Man is Man = All men are equal). Value	Proof 60.00
2	3000	Francs (Au) 1970. R Dr. Martin Luther King (1929–1968), clergyman, American civil rights campaigner, winner of the Nobel Prize for Peace (1964). Legend in German: "Wir müssen Haß mit tätiger Liebe begegnen" (We must meet hate with active love). Value	160.00
3	5000	Francs (Au) 1970. R representation of a wrestler, from an ancient model, a reference to the 1972 Olympic Games in Munich and Kiel. Value	260.00
4	10000	Francs (Au) 1970. Emblem for the jubilee of the UN, a reference to the 25th anniversary of the World Organization. Value	480.00

5 20 000 Francs (Au) 1970. Agricultural and industrial design with the legend "Operation Bokassa". Gearwheels, symbol of industrialisation, and farm produce: wild oat plants (Panicum miliaceum — Gramineae) above; on the right, corn cobs (Zea mays — Gramineae) and cattle horns; on the left, cotton plants (Gossypium sp. — Malvaceae). Value   Proof

1000.00

			XF	Unc
6 (1)	100	Francs (Ni) 1971, 1972, 1974. Mendes antelopes (Addax nasomaculatus – Bovidae). Name of country. R inscription: Banque Centrale, value, date	5.00	12.00
7 (2)	100	Francs (Ni) 1975, 1976. Type as No. 6, but inscription »Banque des Etats de l'Afrique Centrale«	4.00	8.00

CENTRAL AFRICAN EMPIRE BOKASSA I 1976–1979

8	100	Francs (Ni) 1978. Typ as No. 6, but legend EMPIRE CENTRAFRICAINE	–.–	–.–
9	10000	Francs (Au) undated (1979). Bust of Bokassa. Rev. Busts of Caesar, Carolus Magnus and Napoleon		125.00
10	25000	Francs (Au) undated (1979). Rev. eagle and sun		275.00

No. 11 omitted.   **CENTRAL AFRICAN REPUBLIC**

12 (2)	100	Francs (Ni) 1979, 1983, Type as No. 7	2.00	5.00
13 (4)	500	Francs (Cu-Ni) 1985	5.00	8.00

Central African States

The institution covering the issues of currency for the territories of Central Africa is the Banque des Etats de l'Afrique Centrale. This Monetary Union comprises the states of Gabon, Cameroon, the People's Republic of the Congo, Chad, and the Central African Republic (Central African Empire).

100 Centimes = 1 CFA Franc

		EF	Unc
1 (6)	1 Franc (Al) 1974, 1976, 1978, 1979, 1982. Addax antelopes (Addax nasomaculatus – Bovidae), inscription BANQUE DES ETATS DE L'AFRIQUE CENTRALE. Rev. value within wreath of fruits	0.20	0.30

2 (7)	5 Frances (Cu-Al-Ni) 1973, 1975–1979, 1985. Type as No. 1	0.20	0.40
3 (8)	10 Francs (Cu-Al-Ni) 1974–1979, 1983–1985. Type as No. 1	0.30	0.70
4 (9)	25 Francs (Cu-Al-Ni) 1975, 1978, 1982, 1983, 1985. Type as No. 1	0.40	1.00
5 (10)	50 Francs (Ni) 1976, 1977, 1979, 1980, 1982, 1986. Rev. value within a rosette of fruits	0.80	1.50

6 (11)	500 Francs (Cu-Ni) 1976, 1977, 1984	5.00	7.00

Note (No. 5 and 6): Coins have letter A, B, C, D or E.

All valuations in the SCHÖN are stated in U.S. Dollars.

Ceylon

Area: 25,384 sq. mi. Population: 13,000,000 (1972).

Island in the Indian Ocean off the southern tip of India, Ceylon became a sovereign member of the British Commonwealth on 4th February 1948. As of 22nd May 1972 Ceylon has declared itself a republic and declared its former name, in Singhalese, to be Sri Lanka, the latter also to be used exclusively on an international basis. As of 16th December 1929 the Ceylon Rupee substituted the Indian Rupee, with which it, however, remained at par until 1966. Since 22nd May 1972 the monetary unit is called the Sri Lanka Rupee.

Capital: Colombo.

100 Cents = 1 Rupee

EDWARD VII 1901–1910

			VF	XF
1 (11)	¼	Cent (Br) 1904. Crowned bust r. of Edward VII. ℞ value and coconut palm (Cocos nucifera — Palmae)	4.00	9.00
2 (12)	½	Cent (Br) 1904–1909	2.50	5.00
3 (13)	1	Cent (Br) 1904–1910	1.00	2.00
4 (14)	5	Cents (Cu–Ni) 1909–1910. ℞ value (square)	1.50	3.00
5 (15)	10	Cents (Ag) 1902–1910. ℞ coconut palm between value	4.00	7.00
6 (16)	25	Cents (Ag) 1902–1910	4.50	9.00
7 (17)	50	Cents (Ag) 1902–1910	10.00	20.00

GEORGE V 1910–1936

			VF	XF
8 (18)	½	Cent (Br) 1912–1926. Crowned bust l. of George V. ℞ value and coconut palm	0.80	2.00
9 (19)	1	Cent (Br) 1912–1929	0.60	1.50
10 (20)	5	Cents (Cu–Ni) 1912–1926. ℞ value	1.00	2.00
11 (21)	10	Cents (Ag) 1911–1928. Crowned bust r. of George V. ℞ value and coconut palm	2.50	4.00
12 (22)	25	Cents (Ag) 1911–1926	4.00	6.00
13 (23)	50	Cents (Ag) 1913–1929	6.00	10.00

GEORGE VI 1936–1952

			VF	XF
14 (24)	½	Cent (Br) 1937–1940. Crowned bust l. of George VI. ℞ coconut palm	0.70	2.00

			VF	XF
15 (25)	1	Cent (Br) 1937–1942	0.80	2.00
16 (25a)	1	Cent (Br) 1942–1945. Same as No. 15, but larger type	0.20	0.50
17 (27)	2	Cents (Ni–Bra) 1944 (octagonal)	0.80	1.50
18 (28)	5	Cents (Ni–Bra) 1942–1943 (square)	0.80	1.50

			VF	XF
19 (28a)	5	Cents (Ni–Bra) 1944–1945. Same as No. 18, but lighter in weight and thinner	0.20	0.50
20 (32)	10	Cents (Ag) 1941. ℞ coconut palm and value (round)	2.50	4.00

			VF	XF
21 (29)	10	Cents (Ni–Bra) 1944 (octagonal)	0.40	1.00

			VF	XF
22 (30)	25	Cents (Ni–Bra) 1943–1945. ℞ crown above value (round)	0.40	1.00
23 (33)	50	Cents (Ag) 1942. ℞ coconut palm and value (round)	7.00	12.00
24 (31)	50	Cents (Ni–Bra) 1943 (round)	0.60	1.20
25 (34)	2	Cents (Ni–Bra) 1951. Same type as No. 17, but now inscription reads only: KING GEORGE THE SIXTH	0.15	0.30
26 (35)	5	Cents (Ni–Bra) 1951. Not put into circulation	Proof	20.00
27 36)	10	Cents (Ni–Bra) 1951 (octagonal)	0.20	0.40
28 (37)	25	Cents (Ni–Bra) 1951 (round)	0.30	0.60
29 (38)	50	Cents (Ni–Bra) 1951 (round)	0.70	1.40

ELIZABETH II 1952–1972

			VF	XF
30 (39)	2	Cents (Ni–Bra) 1955–1957. Head r. of Elizabeth II. ℞ value	0.25	0.50

COMMEMORATIVE ISSUES (2) FOR 2500 YEARS OF BUDDHISM

			Unc	Proof
31 (40)	1 Rupee (Cu–Ni) 1957. Stupa (= dome-shaped Buddhist shrine) in front of the dhamachakr (= the Buddhists' wheel of the law). ℞ legend and value		2.50	18.00

| **32** (41) | 5 Rupees (Ag) 1957. Circular design of elephant, horse, lion, humped bull, each with a symbolic meaning: the elephant representing the East, Indra's steed; the horse, for the North, symbol of strength; the lion, for the South, emblem of the sun; the bull, for the West, Shiva's steed. ℞ legend | | 25.00 | 75.00 |

			VF	XF
33 (43)	1 Cent (Al–Mg) 1963–1971. National arms. ℞ value (round)		0.05	0.10
34 (44)	2 Cents (Al–Mg) 1963–1971 (octagonal)		0.05	0.10

| **35** (45) | 5 Cents (Ni–Bra) 1963–1971 (sqare shape) | | 0.10 | 0.20 |

		VF	XF
36 (46)	10 Cents (Ni–Bra) 1963–1971 (octagonal)	0.15	0.25
37 (47)	25 Cents (Cu–Ni) 1963–1971 (round)	0.15	0.30
38 (48)	50 Cents (Cu–Ni) 1963, 1965, 1968–1972 (round)	0.25	0.50

39 (49)	1 Rupee (Cu–Ni) 1963, 1965, 1969–1972 (round)	0.40	0.80

ISSUE FOR THE FAO COIN PLAN

40 (50)	2 Rupees (Cu–Ni) 1968. Parakramabahu I, The Great, King of Ceylon 1153 to 1186, copied from the statue in Polonnaruva. Under the reign of this Buddhist king, an important system of irrigation was created	1.50	2.50

For later issues, see under Sri Lanka.

Values are given for each coin in U.S. Dollars and reference to Yeoman-numbers.

Tschad

Chad

Tchad

République du Tchad

Area: 493,849 sq. mi. Population: 5,100,000.
Formerly a part of French Equatorial Africa. Chad became an autonomous republic within the French Community on 28th November 1958, and gained independence on 11th August 1960.
Capital: N'djamena (formerly, until 4th Sept. 1973 known as Fort Lamy).

100 Centimes = 1 CFA Franc

COMMEMORATIVE ISSUES (5) FOR THE 10th ANNIVERSARY OF INDEPENDENCE

			Proof
1	1 000	Francs (Au) 1970. Commandant Lamy (†1900), leader of the French military expedition, defeated the armies of Rabeh near Kuseri in 1900. ℞ a woman of Chad with decorative hair-style; chains; national arms, value	65.00
2	3 000	Francs (Au) 1970. Felix Eboué (1885 to 1944), colonial official from Cayenne, Governor of Chad in 1939; on 26th August 1940 he rallied to the side of de Gaulle. ℞ map of the country, national arms, value	200.00
3	5 000	Francs (Au) 1970. Leclerc de Haute-cloque (1902–1947), Maréchal de France. Chad became, under Leclerc, in 1941, the basis of operations for the conquest of the Fessan with the goal "From Chad to the Rhine". ℞ coconut palm, Strasbourg cathedral and the Arc de Triomphe in Paris. National arms, value	320.00
4	10 000	Francs (Au) 1970. General Charles de Gaulle (1890–1970), French President of State, fought for the independence of Chad. ℞ Croix de Lorraine and sun rays over broken chains. National arms, value	650.00

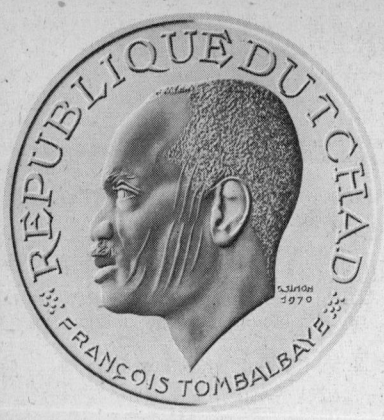

5 20000 Francs (Au) 1970. François Tombal-
baye (1918–1975), Head of State and
Prime Minister. ℞ national arms, commemorative inscription, value

Proof

1200.00

COMMEMORATIVE ISSUES (3) FOR PERSONALITIES FROM THE UNITED STATES OF AMERICA

6 100 Francs (Ag) 1970. Outline of Africa
with Chad clearly marked. ℞ Robert F.
Kennedy (1925–1968), Attorney-Gen-
eral, candidate for the Presidency in
1968. Value

60.00

7 200 Francs (Ag) 1970. ℞ Dr. Martin Luther King (1929–1968), clergyman, civil rights campaigner, and winner of the Nobel Prize for Peace in 1964. Value   **Proof**

           80.00

8 300 Francs (Ag) 1970, ℞ John F. Kennedy (1917–1963), 35th President of the U.S.A. Space capsule over section of the moon. Value   400.00

COMMEMORATIVE ISSUE (2) FOR THE DEATH OF GAMAL ABD EL NASSER

9 200 Francs (Ag) 1970. Gamal Abd el Nasser (1918–70), President of the United Arab Republic 1958–70; head. ℞ outline of Africa with marking of the Chad. Denomination   200.00

10 10 000 Francs (Au) 1970. Type as No. 9   –.–

COMMEMORATIVE ISSUE (2) FOR THE DEATH OF GENERAL CHARLES DE GAULLE

11 200 Francs (Ag) 1970. General Charles de Gaulle (1890–1970), French President; head. ℞ outline of Africa with marking of the Chad. Denomination   –.–

12 10 000 Francs (Au) 1970. Type as No. 11   –.–

			VF	**XF**
13 (1)	100	Francs (Ni) 1971, 1972. Mendes antelopes (Addax nasomaculatus – Bovidae). Name of country. R inscription: Banque Centrale, value, date	7.50	12.00

			VF	**XF**
14 (2)	100	Franc (Ni) 1975, 1978, 1980. Type as No. 13, but inscription »Banques des Etats de l'Afrique Centrale«	3.50	6.00
15 (3)	500	Francs (Cu-Ni) 1985. Native woman		3.00

Chile

Area: 285,295 sq. mi. Population: 12,200,000.
A Republic on the western coastline of South America.
Capital: Santiago de Chile.
N. B.: Because of inflationary tendencies which have been experienced in this part of the world for decades, size, weight and metal content of the coins vary for individual pieces of same nominal value.

100 Centavos = 1 Peso
10 Pesos = 1 Condor;
since 1st January 1960: 100 Centesimos = 1 Escudo; since 1975:
100 Centavos = 1 Chilean Peso

			VF	XF
1 (38)	5	Pesos (Au) 1898, 1900. Rev. national arms: shield with star supported by a Chilean Andes mountain deer or Huë-mul (Hippocamelus bisulcus – Cervi-dae) and an Andean condor (Vultur gryphus – Cathartidae)	60.00	90.00
2 (39)	10	Pesos (Au) 1896–1901. Same type as No. 1	85.00	120.00

3 (40)	20	Pesos (Au) 1896–1917. Same type as No. 1	140.00	200.00
4 (27)		UN (1) Centavo (Cu) 1904–1919. Bust of Liberty l. with cape. ℞ value in wreath	1.80	3.50
5 (28)		DOS (2) Centavos (Cu) 1919	6.00	12.00
6 (29)	2½	Centavos (Cu) 1904–1908	4.00	8.00
7 (30)		CINCO (5) Centavos (Ag) 1899–1919. Andean condor (Vultur gryphus — Cathartidae) on rock to l. ℞ value in wreath	2.00	3.00
8 (41)	5	Centavos (Cu–Ni) 1920–1938	0.40	0.80

			VF	XF
9 (31)		DIEZ (10) Centavos (Ag) 1899–1920	1.00	2.00
10 (42)	10	Centavos (Cu–Ni) 1920–1941	0.25	0.50
11 (32)		VEINTE (20) Centavos (Ag) 1899 to 1920	2.00	3.50
12 (43)	20	Centavos (Cu–Ni) 1920–1941	0.30	0.70
13 (33)	40	Centavos (Ag) 1907–1908		
		a) 1907	12.00	20.00
		b) 1908	2.00	4.00
14 (34)	50	Centavos (Ag) 1902–1906		
		a) 1902–1905	6.50	11.00
		b) 1906	25.00	32.00
15 (35)		UN (1) Peso (Ag) 1902–1932		
		a) 1902–1905, diameter 32 mm	15.00	20.00
		b) 1910, diameter 31.5 mm	7.50	10.00
		c) 1915, 1917, diameter 27.5 mm	6.50	9.00
		d) 1921–1925, diameter 29 mm	4.00	6.00
		e) 1932, diameter 26 mm	6.00	8.00
16 (35e)	1	= UN Peso (Ag) 1927	5.00	7.00

			VF	XF
17 (35)	1	Peso (Cu–Ni) 1933–1940	0.50	1.00
18 (45)	2	= DOS Pesos (Ag) 1927	8.50	12.00
19 (46)	5	= CINCO Pesos (Ag) 1927	17.50	35.00
20 (47)	20	Pesos = DOS Condores (Au) 1926. Date below Liberty head. ℞ national arms	65.00	80.00
21 (48)	50	Pesos = CINCO Condores (Au) 1926	140.00	170.00

			VF	XF
22 (49)	100	Pesos = DIEZ Condores (Au) 1926 to 1960	260.00	300.00
23 (50)	20	Centavos (Cu) 1942–1953. Bust r. of General Bernardo O'Higgins (1778 to 1842), Dictator of Chile 1817–1823. ℞ Copihue flowers (Lapageria rosea — Liliaceae)	0.20	0.40

		VF	XF
24 (51)	50 Centavos (Cu) 1942	1.00	2.00

		VF	XF
25 (52)	1 Peso (Cu) 1942–1954	0.40	0.80
26 (52a)	1 Peso (Al) 1954–1958	0.40	0.80
27 (53)	5 Pesos = Medio Condor (Al) 1956. Andean condor flying. ℞ value between ears of wheat	0.60	1.20

		VF	XF
28 (54)	10 Pesos = UN Condor (Al) 1956–1959	0.50	1.00

CURRENCY REFORM: 100 Centesimos = 1 Escudo

		VF	XF
29 (55)	½ Centesimo (Al) 1962–1963. Andean condor. ℞ value between ears of wheat	0.10	0.20
30 (56)	1 Centesimo (Al) 1960–1963	0.15	0.30
31 (57)	2 Centesimos (Al–Br) 1964–1970	0.20	0.40
32 (58)	5 Centesimos (Al–Br) 1960–1970	0.25	0.50

		VF	XF
33 (59)	10 Centesimos (Al–Br) 1960–1970	0.30	0.60

COMMEMORATIVE ISSUE FOR 150 YEARS OF THE MILITARY ACADEMY

34   50 Pesos (Au) 1968. Arms. Rev. Bust r. of   **Proof**
General Bernardo O'Higgins (1778 to
1842), founder of the Military Acade-
my   175.00

COMMEMORATIVE ISSUE FOR 150 YEARS OF CHILEAN COINAGE

35   100 Pesos (Au) 1968. Rev. Laureate bust of
Liberty to l.; coin press   350.00

COMMEMORATIVE ISSUE FOR THE 150th ANNIVERSARY OF THE CROSSING OF THE ANDES

36   200 Pesos (Au) 1968. Rev. »Paso de los

Andes« – »The Crossing of the
Andes« from a painting by Vila
Prades; the Liberation Army under
San Martin and O'Higgins passing ac-
ross the Andes, February 1817

700.00

COMMEMORATIVE ISSUE FOR 150 YEARS OF THE NATIONAL FLAG

37   500 Pesos (Au) 1968. Rev. Laureate head
of Liberty to l. In background, national flag

2000.00

COMMEMORATIVE ISSUE FOR 150 YEARS OF THE NAVAL SCHOOL

38   5 Pesos (Ag) 1968. Rev. Bust facing of
Arturo Prat Chacon (1848–1879), Admiral, hero of the naval battle of Iq-
uique

25.00

304   **Chile**

39		10 Pesos (Ag) 1968. Rev. Naval squadron under the command of Lord Cochrane		**Proof**
				75.00

			XF	Unc
40 (60)	10	Centesimos (Al-Br) 1971. Bernardo O'Higgins (1778–1842), Dictator of Chile 1817–1823	0.10	0.20
41 (61)	20	Centesimos (Al-Br) 1971, 1972. José Manuel Balmaceda (1838–1891), President of State 1886–1891	0.10	0.20
42 (62)	50	Centesimos (Al-Br) 1971. Manuel Rodriguez (1786–1819), advocate and freedom fighter	0.15	0.30
43 (63)	1	Escudo (Cu-Ni) 1971, 1972. José Miguel Carrera (1785–1821), Dictator 1811–1813	0.20	0.40
44 (64)	2	Escudos (Cu-Ni) 1971. Caupolicán (died 1558), Chief of the Araucanian Indians, fought together with Lautaro against the Spaniards. Rare. About 110 pieces		150.00
45 (65)	5	Escudos (Cu-Ni) 1971, 1972. Lautaro (1535? to 1557), an Araucanian Indian, served as prisoner under Valdivia, the conqueror of Chile, fled and led an initially successful uprising against the Spaniards; fall in the battle of Mataquito; symbolizes the freedom movement of the Chilean original inhabitants	0.30	0.80

				XF	Unc

46 (65a) 5 Escudos (Al) 1972, 1974. Type as No. 45 0.15 0.25

47 (66) 10 Escudos (Al) 1974, 1975. Rising Andean
condor. Rev. value, date 0.20 0.40

48 (67) 50 Escudos (Ni-Bra) 1974, 1975. Type as
No. 47 0.30 0.60

49 (68) 100 Escudos (Ni-Bra) 1974, 1975. Type as
No. 47 0.40 0.80

CURRENCY REFORM: 1000 Escudos = 1 Chilean Peso

50 (69) 1 Centavo (Al) 1975. Rising Andean
condor. Rev. value and date between
laurel branches 0.10 0.20

51 (70) 5 Centavos (Al-Br) 1975, 1976. Type as
No. 50 (twelve-sided) 0.10 0.20

52 (71) 10 Centavos (Al-Br) 1975, 1976.
Type as No. 50 0.10 0.20

53 (72) 50 Centavos (Cu-Ni) 1975–1977.
Type as No. 55 0.15 0.30

54 (73) 1 Peso (Cu-Ni) 1975. Bust right of Bernardo O'Higgins. In the field BER-
NARDO/O' Higgins. Rev. value and
date between laurel branches 0.25 0.50

55 (70a) 5 Centavos (Al) 1976. Type as No. 50
(twelve-sided) 0.10 0.20

56 (71a) 10 Centavos (Al) 1976–1979. Type as No.
50 0.10 0.20

57 (73a) 1 Peso (Cu-Ni) 1976–1978, 1980. Type
as No. 54, but in the field LIBERTA-
DOR/B. O'HIGGINS 0.25 0.50

			XF	Unc
58 (74)	5	Pesos (Cu-Ni) 1976–1980. »Chilena« with broken chains	0.30	0.60
59 (75)	10	Pesos (Cu-Ni) 1976–1981. Type as No. 58	0.40	0.80

			Unc	Proof
60 (75a)	10	Pesos (Ag) 1976. »Chilena«. R̸ Arms	–.–	100.00
61 (76)	50	Pesos (Au) 1976. Type as No. 60	–.–	260.00

62 (77)	100	Pesos (Au) 1976. Type as No. 60	350.00	850.00
63 (78)	500	Pesos (Au) 1976. Type as No. 60	1500.00	1700.00

			XF	Unc
64 (72a)	50	Centavos (Al-Br) 1978, 1979. Type as No. 50	0.10	0.20
65 (73b)	1	Peso (Al-Br) 1978, 1979. Type as No. 50	0.15	0.30
66 (79)	1	Onza (Au) 1978–1983. Trade Coin »Pillar Dollar«:		
		a) 1978 (8 pieces)		2000.00
		b) 1979–1981, 1983		500.00
67 (73c)	1	Peso (Al-Br) 1981. Type as No. 57, but dia. 17 mm	0.15	0.30
68 (74a)	5	Pesos (Ni-Bra) 1981, 1982, 1984. Type as No. 58	0.25	0.60
69 (80)	10	Pesos (Ni-Bra) 1981, 1982. Type as No. 58	0.80	1.20

70 (81)	50	Pesos (Cu-Ni-Al) 1981, 1982, 1986. Type as No. 57	0.75	1.25
71 (85)	100	Pesos (Cu-Ni-Al) 1981, 1983–1986, 1987. Arms. Rev. Value	1.00	2.50

China

Chung Kuo 中國

The Chinese Empire, which existed long before our chronology, became the Republic of China in 1912. After the successful operations of the Communist People's Army, the People's Republic of China was proclaimed on 1st October 1949.

During the period of the Empire, and during the time of the Republic, various provinces were temporarily authorized to issue money. For convenience' sake the provincial issues have been listed separately; but in each case they have been coordinated with the issues of both the Empire and the Republic.

Capital: Peking.

10 Cash (Wen 文) = 1 Cent (Fen 分); 10 cents = 1 Chiao (角)

100 Cents = 1 Dollar (Yuan 圓)

10 Li (釐) = 1 Candareen (Fen)

10 Candareens = 1 Mace (Chien 錢)

10 Mace = 1 Tael (Liang 兩)

1 Dollar = 7 Mace and 2 Candareens

EMPIRE (until 1911)

The coins of the Empire bear a description of the Emperor's reign, rather than his name. Dates were reckoned from the beginning of each reign, and these are sometimes indicated, as are the dates according to the Chinese Calendar (sexagenary system – cycles of 60 years). The reigns of the last two Emperors fall within the period covered in this catalogue:

Te Tsung, Kuang Hsü era 光緒 (1875–1908) and

Pu Yih, Hsüan Tung era 宣統 (1909–1911)

Abbreviation: CD = Cyclical Date

			VF	XF
1	5	Candareens (Ag) 1903. Dragon and inscription 29TH YEAR OF KUANG HSÜ. HU POO. ℞ Chinese and Manchu characters, among which denomination and value. Trial piece (pattern)		450.00
2	1	Mace (Ag) 1903. Type as No. 1 Pattern		150.00
3	2	Mace (Ag) 1903. Type as No. 1 Pattern		200.00
4	5	Mace (Ag) 1903. Type as No. 1 Pattern		300.00
5	1	Tael (Ag) 1903. Type as No. 1 Pattern		600.00
6	1	Cash (Cu) 1905 (undated). Dragon. Chinese and Manchu characters, among which denomination and value	1.00	2.00
7	2	Cash (Cu) 1905 (undated). Type as No. 6	2.00	4.00
8 (3)	5	Cash (Cu) 1905 (undated). Dragon in dotted circle and inscription HU POO FIVE CASH. ℞ Chinese and Manchu characters, among which denomination, mint, and value	12.00	25.00
9 (4)	10	Cash (Cu) 1905 (undated). Type as No. 8, but obverse without dotted circle, and the inscription around giving the value TEN CASH	1.50	3.00
10 (5a)	20	Cash (Cu) 1905 (undated). Type as No. 8, but in the obverse legend the value 20 CASH	25.00	60.00

			VF	XF
11 (5)	20	Cash (Cu) 1905 (undated). Type as No. 10, but the obverse without dotted circle	1.00	2.00
12 (5.1)	20	Cash (Cu) 1905 (undated). Type as No. 11, but rosette added	6.00	12.00

			VF	XF
13 (7)	1	Cash (Bra) 1980. Dragon. R. Chinese characters, among which denomination, date, and value	2.50	5.00
14 (8)	2	Cash (Cu) 1905–1907. Dragon. R Chinese and Manchu characters, among which denomination, date, and value	4.00	8.00
15 (9)	5	Cash (Cu) 1905–1907. Dragon in dotted circle and iscription TAI-CHING-TI-KUO COPPER COIN as well as four Chinese characters. Rev. same as No. 14	10.00	20.00
16 (10)	10	Cash (Cu) 1905–1907 (CD). Type as No. 15	1.50	2.50
17 (11)	20	Cash (Cu) 1905–1907 (CD). Type as No. 15	18.00	32.00
18	1	Mace (Ag) 1906. Dragon in dotted circle and inscription TAI-CHING-TI-KUO SILVER COIN as well as four Chinese characters. R Chinese and Manchu characters, among which denomination, date, and value	5.00	8.00
19	2	Mace (Ag) 1906. Type as No. 18	9.00	14.00
20	5	Mace (Ag) 1906. Type as No. 18	16.00	22.00
21	1	Tael (Ag) 1906. Type as No. 18, but the reverse with lined triangel border	380.00	700.00
22	1	Tael (Au) 1906, 1907. Dragon. R Chinese characters, among which denomination, date, and value	2000.00	3500.00
23	10	Cents (Ag) 1907. Dragon in dotted circle and inscription TAI-CHING-TI-KUO SILVER COIN as well as four Chinese characters. R Chinese and Manchu characters, among which denomination, date, and value	70.00	115.00
24	20	Cents (Ag) 1907 (CD). Type as No. 23	70.00	110.00
25	50	Cents (Ag) 1907 (CD). Type as No. 23	175.00	220.00
26	1	Dollar (Ag) 1907, 1908 (CD). Type as No. 23, but the reverse with lined triangle border	220.00	360.00
27 (12)	10	Cents (Ag) 1908 (undated). Dragon in dotted circle and inscription TAI-CHING-TI-KUO SILVER COIN as well as four Chinese characters. R Chinese characters and, in centre, four Manchu characters, among which denomination and value	30.00	50.00
28 (13)	20	Cents (Ag) 1908 (undated). Type as No. 27	40.00	70.00

All valuations in the SCHÖN are stated in U.S. Dollars.

			VF	XF
29 (14)	1	Dollar (Ag) 1908 (undated). Type as No. 27	30.00	45.00
30 (18)	1	Cash (Cu) 1909. Type as No. 13, but on the reverse the Chinese characters read Hsüan Tung instead of Kuang Hsü	26.00	50.00
31 (A18)	2	Cash (Cu) 1909. Dragon. R Dynasty and coin description in Chinese characters in the circle of dots. In the legend four Manchu characters, including year and denomination in Chinese characters	–.–	–.–
32 (19)	5	Cash (Cu) 1909. Type as No. 15, but the obverse inscription has Chinese characters reading Hsüan Tung instead of Kuang Hsü		*400.00*

			VF	XF
33 (20)	10	Cash (Cu) 1909. Type as No. 32	1.50	2.50
33a (20.1)	10	Cash (Cu) 1909. Type as No. 33, but with a rosette in the centre on R	25.00	40.00
34 (20x)	10	Cash (Cu) 1909 (CD). Type as No. 33, but rosette added	15.00	30.00
35 (21)	20	Cash (Cu) 1909 (CD). Type as No. 32	1.20	2.00
36	1	Cash (Cu) (undated). Dragon. R Chinese characters, among which value	1.50	2.50

			VF	XF
37	5	Li (Cu) 1910 (undated). Dragon in dotted circle and inscription of four Chinese characters. Rev. Chinese characters, among which value	–.–	–.–
38	1	Cent (Cu) 1910 (undated). Type as No. 37	–.–	–.–
39	2	Cents (Cu) 1910 (undated). Type as No. 37	–.–	–.–
40	1/10	Dollar (Ag) 1910 (undated). Dragon in dotted circle and inscription 1/10 DOL. as well as four Chinese characters. R Chinese and Manchu characters, among which denomination and value	80.00	140.00
41	¼	Dollar (Ag) 1910 (undated). Type as No. 40, but in the obverse inscription ¼ DOL.	75.00	100.00
42	½	Dollar (Ag) 1910 (undated). Type as No. 40, but in the obverse inscription ½ DOLLAR	50.00	80.00
43	1	Dollar (Ag) 1910 (undated). Type as No. 40, but in the obverse inscription $ 1	185.00	250.00
44 (25)	1	Cash (Cu) (undated). Denomination in Chinese characters. R value in Chinese characters. With centre round hole	2.20	4.00
45 (26)	5	Cash (Cu) 1911. Dragon in circle and inscription of four Chinese characters. R Chinese characters, among which date and value	160.00	200.00

46 (27)	10	Cash (Cu) 1911. Type as No. 41	5.00	8.00
47	20	Cash (Cu) 1911. Type as No. 41	265.00	350.00
48	1	Dollar (Ag) 1911. Dragon, inscription below ONE DOLLAR. R Chinese and Manchu characters, among which denomination, date, and value. Pattern	–.–	–.–

No. 49 omitted.

			VF	XF
50 (28)	10	Cents (Ag) 1911. Dragon (new design); in the centre, value in Chinese characters. R Chinese characters, among which denomination, date, and value	10.00	15.00
51 (29)	20	Cents (Ag) 1911. Type as No. 50	15.00	25.00
52 (30)	50	Cents (Ag) 1911. Type as No. 50	160.00	250.00

53 (31)	1	Dollar (Ag) 1911. Dragon (again of different design); in the centre, value in Chinese characters, below, ONE DOLLAR. R Chinese and Manchu characters, among which denomination and date	14.00	20.00

54	1	Cash (Bra) 1909–1911 (undated). Four Chinese characters. R on right and left one Manchu character. In the centre, square hole. Cast	6.00	10.00

All valuations in the SCHÖN are stated in U.S. Dollars.

Anhwei 安徽 (肙完)

			VF	XF
1 (35)	5	Cash (Cu) (undated). Dragon in dotted circle, inscription above ANHWEI. ℞ Chinese characters and two Manchu characters, among which province and denomination as well as value	85.00	150.00
2 (36a)	10	Cash (Cu) (undated). Dragon in circle of dots and legend AN-HWEI. ℞ government era and coin description in the way of four Chinese characters in the circle of dots. In the centre a rosette. In the legend name of province and denomination by way of nine Chinese characters. In addition two Manchu characters in the legend	1.50	2.50
2a (36a5)	10	Cash (Cu) (undated). As type No. 2, but denomination in the legend of ℞ only by way of six Chinese characters	4.50	9.00
2b	10	Cash (Cu) (undated). Dragon in the circle of dots and legend AN-HWEI TEN CASH. ℞ government era and coin designation by way of four Chinese characters in the circle of dots. In the centre two Manchu characters. In the legend description of province and denomination by way of eleven Chinese characters	–.–	–.–
2c	10	Cash (Cu) (undated). Dragon (changed design, without circle of dots) and legend AN-HWEI 10 CASH. ℞ as type No. 2a	4.50	9.00
2d	10	Cash (Cu) (undated). Obverse as type No. 2c, ℞ as type No. 2	–.–	–.–
3	10	Cash (Cu) (undated). Dragon in the circle of dots and legend AN-HWEI ONE CEN. ℞ as type No. 2b	35.00	55.00
3a	10	Cash (Cu) (undated). As type No. 3, but legend of the obverse. AN-HWEI ONE SEN	40.00	60.00
4 (37)	20	Cash (Cu) (undated). Similar to type No. 1	300.00	550.00
5	10	Cash (Cu) 1906. Dragon in dotted circle and legend TAI-CHING-TI-KUO COPPER COIN, including four Chinese characters	2.00	4.00
6 (11a)	20	Cash (Cu) 1906. Type as No. 5	70.00	125.00
7	10	Cash (Cu) 1909. Type as No. 5, but in		

			VF	XF
		the obverse legend the Chinese characters read Hsüan Tung instead of Kuang Hsü	20.00	40.00
8	20	Cash (Cu) 1909. Type as No. 7	25.00	50.00

Chekiang 浙江 (浙)

			VF	XF
1 (49.1)	10	Cash (Cu) (undated). Dragon. ℞ Chinese characters, among which province and denomination as well as value	1.20	2.40
2 (49)	10	Cash (Cu) (undated). As type No. 1, in centre of ℞, however, a circle	3.00	6.00
3	10	Cash (Cu) (undated). As type No. 1, but the centre of ℞ level	–.–	–.–
4 (49a)	10	Cash (Cu) (undated). As type No. 1, but in the legend of ℞ instead of six, eight Chinese characters	4.00	8.00
5 (50)	20	Cash (Cu) (undated). Type as No. 1	60.00	130.00
6 (51)	5	Cents (Ag) 1902 (undated). Dragon and inscription CHE-KIANG PROVINCE 3,2 CANDAREENS. ℞ Chinese characters, among which province and denomination as well as value. In the centre, four Manchu characters	12.00	20.00
7	5	Cents (Ag) 1902 (undated). Type as No. 6, but now in the legend on obverse with the denomination 3.6 CANDAREENS. Trial strike!	–.–	–.–
8 (52)	10	Cents (Ag) 1902 (undated). Type as No. 6, but value in the obverse inscription 7,2 CANDAREENS	30.00	60.00
9 (53)	20	Cents (Ag) 1902 (undated). Type as No. 6, but value in the obverse inscription 1 MACE AND 4,4 CANDAREENS	80.00	160.00

			VF	XF
10 (54)	50	Cents (Ag) 1902 (undated). Type as No. 6, but the value in the obverse inscription 3 MACE AND 6 CANDAREENS	200.00	350.00
11	1	Dollar (Ag) 1902 (undated). Type as No. 6, but value in the obverse inscription 7 MACE AND 2 CANDAREENS		3000.00
12	1	Dollar (Ag) 1902 (undated). Type as No. 11, but obverse legend CHE-KIANG		3400.00
13 (8b)	2	Cash (Cu) 1906. Dragon R Chinese and Manchu characters, among which denomination, date, and value; in the centre, Chinese character for Chekiang	14.00	20.00
14 (9b)	5	Cash (Cu) 1906. Dragon in dotted circle and inscription TAI-CHING-TI-KUO COPPER COIN as well as four Chinese characters. R as type No. 13	8.50	14.00
15 (10b)	10	Cash (Cu) 1906 (CD). Type as No. 14	5.00	9.00
16 (11b)	20	Cash (Cu) 1906 (CD). Type as No. 14	42.00	75.00

Chihli 智利 (直)

			VF	XF
1 (66)	1	Cash (Cu) 1896–1908 (undated). Chinese characters in dotted circle and ornamental border. R name of province and value in Chinese characters	3.50	7.00
2 (67)	10	Cash (Cu) 1896–1908 (undated). Dragon in dotted circle and inscription PEI YANG TEN CASH. R Chinese and Manchu characters, among which name of province and denomination as well as value	3.00	6.00
3	10	Cash (Cu) (undated). Type as No. 2, but in the centre of R additionally a rosette	–.–	–.–
4 (68)	20	Cash (Cu) 1896–1908 (undated). Type as No. 2	20.00	40.00
5 (69)	5	Cents (Ag) 1900. Dragon and inscription 26th YEAR OF KUANG HSÜ PEI YANG. R Chinese characters, among which name of province and denomination as well as value; in the centre, four Manchu characters	25.00	50.00
6	10	Cents (Ag) 1900. Type as No. 5	–.–	–.–
7 (71)	20	Cents (Ag) 1900, 1903. Type as No. 5	60.00	100.00

			VF	XF
8 (72)	50	Cents (Ag) 1899. Type as No. 5, but in the obverse inscription 25th YEAR OF KUANG HSÜ PEI YANG	60.00	90.00

9 (73)	1	Dollar (Ag) 1900, 1903, 1907, 1908. Type as No. 5	15.00	25.00
10	5	Cents (Ag) 1900. Dragon and inscription PEKING 3,6 CANDAREENS. R Chinese characters, among which name of province and denomination as well as date and value. In the centre, four Manchu characters. Pattern	200.00	250.00
11	10	Cents (Ag) 1900. Type as No. 10, but in the obverse inscription PEKING 7,2 CANDAREENS. Pattern.	–.–	–.–
12	20	Cents (Ag) 1900. Type as No. 10, but in the obverse inscription PEKING 1 MACE AND 4,4 CANDAREENS. Pattern.	–.–	–.–
13	50	Cents (Ag) 1900. Type as No. 10, but in the obverse inscription PEKING 3 MACE AND 6 CANDAREENS. Pattern.	–.–	–.–
14	1	Dollar (Ag) 1900. Type as No. 10, but in the obverse inscription PEKING 7 MACE AND 2 CANDAREENS. Pattern.	–.–	–.–
15 (74)	1	Tael (Ag) 1907. Dragon and inscription 33RD YEAR OF KUANG HSÜ PEI YANG. R Chinese and Manchu characters, among which name of province and denomination as well as value	1500.00	2000.00
16 (7c)	1	Cash (Cu) 1908. Dragon. R name of province, date, and value in Chinese characters	4.00	8.00

			VF	XF
17 (9c)	5 Cash (Cu) 1906. Dragon in dotted circle and inscription TAI-CHING-TI-KUO COPPER COIN as well as four Chinese characters. R Chinese and Manchu characters, among which denomination and value, in the centre, Chinese characters for Chihli		5.00	10.00
18 (10c)	10 Cash (Cu) 1906 (CD). Type as No. 17		1.20	2.00
19 (11c)	20 Cash (Cu) 1906 (CD). Type as No. 17		35.00	70.00

Chingkiang or Tsingkiang 清江 (淮)

			VF	XF
1 (77)	10 Cash (Cu) (undated). Dragon and inscription CHING-KIANG. R Chinese characters and two Manchu characters, among which name of province and denomination as well as value		1.50	3.00
2 (77.6)	10 Cash (Cu) (undated). Type as No. 1, but centre of Rev. without rosette		2.50	5.00
3	10 Cash (Cu) (undated). Type as No. 1, but dragon in dotted circle		–.–	–.–
4 (78)	10 Cash (Cu) 1905 (undated). Dragon and inscription TSING-KIANG TEN CASH. R Chinese and Manchu characters, among which name of province and denomination as well as value		3.00	6.00
5 (78.4)	10 Cash (Cu) (undated). Type as No. 4, but centre of Rev. without rosette		3.00	6.00
6 (10d6)	10 Cash (Cu) 1906. Dragon in dotted circle and inscription TAI-CHING-TI-KUO COPPER as well as four Chinese characters. R Chinese and Manchu characters, among which denomination, date, and value. In the centre, Chinese characters for »Huai« incused on raised disc		–.–	–.–
7 (10d)	10 Cash (Cu) (CD). Type as No. 6, but centre of Rev. without raised disc		20.00	40.00
8	20 Cash (Cu) 1906 (CD). Type as No. 7		–.–	–.–

Fookien (Fukien) 福建 (閩)

			VF	XF
1 (99)	5 Cash (Cu) undated. Dragon in dotted circle and inscription FOO-KIEN as well as value. R name of province and denomination as well as value in Chinese characters		8.00	15.00

			VF	XF
2 (100)	10	Cash (Cu) undated. Dragon in dotted circle and inscription FOO-KIEN 10 CASH. R Chinese characters and two Manchu characters, among which name of province and denomination as well as value	1.50	3.00
3 (100.3)	10	Cash (Cu) (undated). Type as No. 1, but legend of obverse FOO-KIEN 10 CASHES	11.00	20.00
4 (101)	20	Cash (Cu) undated. Type as No. 1	24.00	40.00
5 (97)	10	Cash (Cu) 1896–1908 (undated). Dragon in dotted circle and inscription F. K. CUSTOM-HOUSE 10 CASH. R name of province and denomination as well as value in Chinese characters and two Manchu characters	1.20	2.50
6	10	Cash (Cu) 1896–1908 (undated). Type as No. 5, but in the obverse inscription FOO-KIEN CUSTOM HOUSE	1.75	3.00
7 (98)	10	Cash (Cu) (undated). Dragon in circle of dots and legend FOO-KIEN CUSTOM 10 CASH. R government era and coin designation by way of four Chinese characters in circle of dots. In the centre two Manchu characters. In the legend Chinese characters, among other province designation and denomination	85.00	150.00
8 (102.1)	5	Cents (Ag) 1902 (undated). Dragon and inscription FOO-KIEN PROVINCE 3,6 CANDAREENS. R name of province and denomination as well as value in Chinese characters. In the centre, four Manchu characters. In the reverse legend, above, four characters instead of the five on the 1898 issue	4.50	6.50
9 (103.2)	10	Cents (Ag) 1902 (undated). Type as No. 8, but in the obverse legend FOO-KIEN PROVINCE 7,2 CANDAREENS	6.50	10.00

			VF	XF
10 (104.2)	20 Cents (Ag) 1902 (undated). Type as No. 6, but in the obverse legend FOO-KIEN PROVINCE 1 MACE AND 4,4 CANDAREENS		6.00	9.00
11 (8f)	2 Cash (Cu) 1906, 1908. Dragon. R Chinese and Manchu characters, among which denomination, date and value. In the centre, Chinese characters for FOO-KIEN		4.00	9.00
12 (99)	5 Cash (Cu) 1906, 1908. Dragon in dotted circle and inscription TAI-CHING-TI-KUO COPPER COIN as well as four Chinese characters. Rev. as type No. 11		6.00	11.00

13 (10f)	10 Cash (Cu) 1906, 1908. Type as No. 12		1.50	2.50
14	20 Cash (Cu) 1906, 1908. Type as No. 12		3.00	6.50
15 (20f)	10 Cash (Cu) 1909. Type as No. 12, but in the obverse legend the Chinese characters read Hsüan Tung instead of Kuang Hsü		45.00	90.00
16	1 Cash (Bra) 1909–1911 (undated). Government era and coin designation by way of four Chinese characters. R left and right one Manchu character each. In the centre square hole. Casting		–.–	–.–
17 (106)	1 Cash (Bra) 1909–1911 (undated). Type as No. 14, but embossed and in the centre a round hole in a squareborder		25.00	50.00

				VF	XF
1 (88)	10	Cash (Bra) 1903 (CD). Dragon and inscription FEN-TIEN PROVINCE TEN CASH. R name of province and denomination as well as date and value in Chinese characters		65.00	120.00
1a	10	Cash (Bra) undated. Dragon and legend FEN-TIEN PROVINCE TEN CASH. R two Chinese characters. Pseudo coin?		–.–	–.–
1b	10	Cash (Cu) undated. Government era and coin designation in four Chinese characters. R sixteen Chinese characters as legend, among others province designation and denomination. With central square hole.		35.00	70.00
2	1	Tael (Cu) 1903. Dragon and inscription FEN-TIEN PROVINCE ONE TAEL. R Chinese characters and, in the centre, four Manchu characters, among which name of province and denomination as well as date and value. Pattern. Only 3 specimens known!		–.–	–.–

3 (89)	10	Cash (Cu) 1903–1906 (CD). Dragon and inscription FUNG-TIEN PROVINCE TEN CASH. Rev. as type No. 1		5.00	10.00
4 (90)	20	Cash (Cu) 1903–1905 (CD). Dragon and inscription FUNG-TIEN PROVINCE 20 CASH. Rev. as type No. 1		15.00	25.00
5 (91)	20	Cents (Ag) 1904. Dragon and inscription FUNG-TIEN PROVINCE 1 MACE AND 4,4 CANDAREENS. R name of province and denomination as well as date and value in Chinese characters. In the centre, two Manchu characters		12.00	20.00

			VF	**XF**
6 (92)	1	Dollar (Ag) 1903. Dragon and inscription FUNG-TIEN PROVINCE 7 MACE AND 2 CANDAREENS. ℞ as type No. 5	70.00	110.00
7 (86)	50	Cents (Ag) 1906. Dragon and inscription in Chinese characters (name of province and date). ℞ in the centre, value in Chinese characters; around, inscription in Manchu characters	90.00	150.00
8 (10e)	10	Cash (Cu) 1905, 1907. Dragon in dotted circle and inscription TAI-CHING-TI-KUO COPPER COIN, as well as four Chinese characters. ℞ Chinese and Manchu characters, among which denomination, date, and value. In the centre, Chinese character for Fungtien	5.50	9.00
9 (11e)	20	Cash (Cu) 1905, 1907. As type No. 8	8.50	12.50
10 (19e)	5	Cash (Cu) 1909. As type No. 8, but in the obverse legend the Chinese characters read Hsüan Tung instead of Kuang Hsü	70.00	120.00
11 (20e)	10	Cash (Cu) 1909. As type No. 10	8.00	15.00
12 (21e)	20	Cash (Cu) 1909. As type No. 10	42.00	80.00

Heilungkiang 黑龍江

1	50	Cents (Ag) 1903 (undated). Dragon and inscription HEILUNGKIANG PROVINCE 3 MACE AND CANDAREENS 6. ℞ Chinese characters, among which name of province and denomination as well as value. Pattern	–.–	–.–

Honan 河南 (汴)

1 (7g)	1	Cash (Bra) 1908. Dragon. ℞ government era, date and denomination in Chinese characters. In the Centre a Chinese character for Honan in the circle of dots	20.00	35.00
2 (108)	10	Cash (Cu) 1896–1908 (undated). Dragon in dotted circle and inscription HO-NAN TEN CASH. ℞ Chinese characters, among which name of province and denomination as well as value. In the centre, Yin-Yang symbol	3.00	6.00

			VF	XF
3 (108a1)	10	Cash (Cu) 1896–1908 (undated). Dragon and inscription HO-NAN TEN CASH as well as 8 stars. ℞ name of province and denomination as well as value in Chinese characters. In the centre, Yin-Yang symbol	2.00	4.00
3a (108a)	10	Cash (Bra) (undated). Dragon and legend HOU-NAN TEN CASH. ℞ government era and coin designation by way of four Chinese characters in the circle of dots. In the centre the Yin-Yang symbol. In the legend province designation and denomination in Chinese characters. In addition in the legend, right and left, one Manchu character each.	–.–	–.–
4	20	Cash (Cu) 1896–1908 (?) (undated). Type as No. 3	3.00	6.00
5 (10g)	10	Cash (Cu) 1906. Dragon in dotted circle and inscription TAI-CHING-TI-KUO COPPER COIN as well as four Chinese characters. ℞ Chinese and Manchu characters, among which denomination, date and value. In the centre, Chinese character for Honan	1.00	2.00
6 (20g)	10	Cash (Cu) 1909, 1911. Type as No. 5, but in the obverse legend the Chinese characters read Hsüan Tung instead of Kuang Hsü	5.00	10.00
7 (21g)	20	Cash (Cu) 1909 (CD). Type as No. 6	–.–	–.–

Hunan 湖 南 (湘)

1 (112.8)	10	Cash (Cu) 1896–1908 (undated). Dragon in dotted circle and inscription HU-NAN TEN CASH. ℞ Chinese characters and, in the centre, two Manchu characters, among which name of province and denomination as well as value	5.00	10.00
1a (112.9)	10	Cash (Cu) undated. Type similar to No. 1, but on ℞ the two Manchu characters not in the centre, but in the legend and in centre a rosette	5.00	10.00
2	10	Cash (Cu) 1896–1908 (undated). Type as No. 1, but different design for the dragon	3.50	7.00
2a	10	Cash (Cu) 1896–1908 (undated). Type similar to No. 2, but design of the dragon changed once more, as well as	3.50	7.00

			VF	XF
		in the legend of ℞ nine instead of eight Chinese characters	2.50	5.00
2b	10	Cash (Cu) (undated). Type similar to No. 2a, but in the legend of ℞ ten instead of nine Chinese characters	4.50	9.00
2c	10	Cash (Cu) (undated). Type similar to No. 2, but on ℞ the two Manchu characters in the legend and in the centre a rosette	1.25	2.50
3	5	Cents (Ag) 1902 (undated). Dragon and inscription HU-NAN PROVINCE 3,6 CANDAREENS. ℞ Chinese characters and, in the centre, four Manchu characters, among which name of province and denomination as well as value	–.–	–.–
4 (115.1)	10	Cents (Ag) 1902 (undated). Type as No. 3, but in the obverse legend HU-NAN PROVINCE 7,2 CANDA-REENS	12.50	22.00
5 (116)	20	Cents (Ag) 1902 (undated). Type as No. 3, but in the obverse legend HU-NAN PROVINCE 1 MACE 4,4 CANDAREENS	30.00	45.00
6 (10h)	10	Cash (Cu) 1906. Dragon in dotted circle and inscription TAI-CHING-TI-KUO COPPER COIN as well as four Chinese characters. ℞ Chinese and Manchu characters, among which denomination, date, and value. In the centre, Chinese character for Hunan	15.00	30.00
7	1	Mace (Ag) 1906 (undated). Two lines each with two Chinese characters, among which name of province. ℞ value in two Chinese characters. The border of the obverse and the reverse is made up of one dotted circle between two circles of elongated dots. There are three variants due to different arrangement of characters; partial use of new characters	–.–	–.–
8	2	Mace (Ag) 1906 (undated). Type as No. 7, but on the reverse two lines of two Chinese characters each; also two variants	20.00	35.00
9	3	Mace (Ag) 1906 (undated). Type as No. 7, but on the obverse and reverse two horizontal lines of three Chinese characters each; also two variants	20.00	35.00
10	4	Mace (Ag) 1906 (undated). Type as No. 9; but also two variants	20.00	35.00

			VF	**XF**
11	5	Mace (Ag) 1906 (undated). Type as No. 9; also two variants	20.00	35.00
12	6	Mace (Ag) 1906 (undated). Type as No. 9; also two variants	20.00	35.00
13	7	Mace (Ag) 1906 (undated). Type as No. 9; also two variants	20.00	35.00
14	8	Mace (Ag) 1906 (undated). Type as No. 9; also two variants	20.00	35.00
15	9	Mace (Ag) 1906 (undated). Type as No. 9; also two variants	20.00	35.00
16	1	Tael (Ag) 1906 (undated). Type as No. 9; also two variants	70.00	100.00
16a	1	Tael (Ag) 1906 (undated). Three horizontal rows at four Chinese characters each, among others province designation and denomination. ℞ smooth	–.–	–.–
17	1	Mace (Ag) 1908 (undated). Two lines of two Chinese characters each, among which name of province. ℞ value in two Chinese characters. The border of the obverse and the reverse is made up of one dotted circle between two circles of elongated dots. Similar to type No. 7	–.–	–.–
18	2	Mace (Ag) 1908 (undated). Type as No. 17, but also on the reverse two lines of two Chinese characters each. Similar to type No. 8	–.–	–.–
19	1	Mace (Ag) 1908 (?) (undated). Two horizontal lines of three Chinese characters, each among which name of province. ℞ value in two Chinese characters. The border of the obverse and the reverse is made up of one dotted circle between two circles of elongated dots Coins 19–28 were issued by the mint of Chien-Y in Changsha.	–.–	–.–
20	2	Mace (Ag) 1908 (?) (undated). Type as No. 19, but on the ℞ two lines of two Chinese caracters each	–.–	–.–
21	3	Mace (Ag) 1908 (?) (undated). Type as No. 19, but on the ℞ two horizontal lines of three Chinese characters each	–.–	–.–
22	4	Mace (Ag) 1908 (?) (undated). Type as No. 21	–.–	–.–
23	5	Mace (Ag) 1908 (?) (undated). Type as No. 21	–.–	–.–
24	6	Mace (Ag) 1908 (?) (undated). Type as No. 21	–.–	–.–
25	7	Mace (Ag) 1908 (?) (undated). Type as No. 21	–.–	–.–

			VF	XF
26	8 Mace (Ag) 1908 (?) (undated). Type as No. 21		–.–	–.–
27	9 Mace (Ag) 1908 (?) (undated). Type as No. 21		–.–	–.–
28	1 Tael (Ag) 1908 (?) (undated). Type as No. 21		–.–	–.–
29	1 Mace (Ag) 1909 (undated). Two vertical lines of three Chinese characters each, among which name of province. ℞ two horizontal lines of three Chinese characters each, among which value. The border of the obverse and the reverse is made up of one dotted circle between two circles of elongated dots. (Coins Nos. 29–38 were issued by the Ta Ching Government Bank in Changsha).		–.–	–.–
30	2 Mace (Ag) 1909 (undated). Type as No. 29		–.–	–.–
31	3 Mace (Ag) 1909 (undated). Type as No. 29		–.–	–.–
32	4 Mace (Ag) 1909 (undated). Type as No. 29		–.–	–.–
33	5 Mace (Ag) 1909 (undated). Type as No. 29		–.–	–.–
34	6 Mace (Ag) 1909 (undated). Type as No. 29		–.–	–.–
35	7 Mace (Ag) 1909 (undated). Type as No. 29		–.–	–.–
36	8 Mace (Ag) 1909 (undated). Type as No. 29		–.–	–.–
37	9 Mace (Ag) 1909 (undated). Type as No. 29		–.–	–.–
38	1 Tael (Ag) 1909 (undated). Type as No. 29		95.00	150.00

Hupeh 湖北 (鄂)

1 (121)	1 Cash (Cu) 1896–1908 (undated). Dragon and inscription HU-PEH PROVINCE ONE CASH. ℞ name of province and denomination as well as value in Chinese characters		4.00	8.00

			VF	**XF**
2 (120a)	10	Cash (Cu) 1896–1908 (undated). Dragon and inscription HU-PEH PROVINCE TEN CASH. ℞ name of province and denomination as well as value in Chinese characters and two Manchu characters. In the centre, a rosette (several variants)	4.00	8.00
2a (120a9)	10	Cash (Cu) 1896–1908 (undated). Type similar to No. 2, but on ℞ in place of the rosette, a square in a circle	2.00	4.00
2b (122)	10	Cash (Cu–Bra) undated. Type as No. 2, but changed design of the dragon	1.25	2.50
2c (120)	10	Cash (Cu) undated. Type similar to No. 2, but dragon in circle of dots	4.50	9.00

3 (128)	1	Tael (Ag) 1904. Value in Chinese characters between two dragons and inscription HU-PEH PROVINCE ONE TAEL as well as two Manchu characters. ℞ Chinese characters and, in the centre, four Manchu characters, among which name of province and denomination as well as date and value	120.00	170.00
4	1	Cash (Cu) 1906. Dragon. ℞ Chinese characters	3.00	6.00

			VF	XF
5 (8j)	2	Cash (Cu) 1906. Dragon. ℞ Chinese and Manchu characters, among which denomination, date, and value. In the centre, Chinese character for Hupeh	45.00	70.00
6 (9j)	5	Cash (Cu) 1906–1908. Dragon in dotted circle and inscription TAI-CHING-TI-KUO COPPER COIN as well as four Chinese characters. ℞ Chinese and Manchu characters, among which denomination, date, and value. In the centre, Chinese character for Hupeh	4.50	9.00

7 (10j)	10	Cash (Cu) 1906–1908. Type as No. 6	1.25	2.50
8 (11j)	20	Cash (Cu) 1906–1908. Type as No. 6	70.00	100.00
9 (7j)	1	Cash (Bra) 1908. Dragon. ℞ Chinese characters, among which date and value	7.00	12.00
10	5	Cash (Cu) 1909, 1911. Type as No. 6, but in the obverse legend the Chinese characters read Hsüan Tung instead of Kuang Hsü	3.50	7.00
11 (20j)	10	Cash (Cu) 1909, 1911. Type as No. 10	2.00	4.00
12	20	Cash (Cu) 1909–1911. Type as No. 10	3.50	7.00
13 (129)	10	Cents (Ag) 1909 (undated). Dragon and inscription HU-PEH PROVINCE 7,2 CANDAREENS. ℞ Chinese characters and, in the centre, four Manchu characters, among which name of province and denomination as well as value	30.00	40.00
14 (130)	20	Cents (Ag) 1909 (undated). Dragon and inscription HU-PEH PROVINCE 1 MACE AND 4,4 CANDAREENS. ℞ as type No. 13	160.00	225.00
15 (131)	1	Dollar (Ag) 1909 (undated). Dragon and inscription HU-PEH PROVINCE 7 MACE AND 2 CANDAREENS. ℞ as type No. 13	30.00	40.00
16	10	Cents (Ag) 1911. Dragon. ℞ Chinese characters, among which name of province and denomination as well as date	7.00	10.00

1   1 Tael (Ag) 1905. Dragon. ℞ Chinese characters, among which name of province and denomination as well as date and value   –.–   –.–

Kiangnan 江 南 (甯)

1 (141a)   5 Cents (Ag) 1900, 1901. Dragon and legend KIANG NAN PROVINCE 3,6 CANDAREENS. ℞ Chinese characters and, in centre, four Manchu characters, among which name of province and denomination as well as date and value   7.00   10.00

2 (142a4) 10 Cents (Ag) 1900, 1901, 1905 (CD). Dragon and inscription KIANG NAN PROVINCE 7,2 CANDAREENS. R as type No. 1   5.00   7.00

3 (143a4) 20 Cents (Ag) 1900, 1901, 1905 (CD). Dragon and inscription KIANG NAN PROVINCE 1 MACE AND 4,4 CANDAREENS. R as type No. 1   8.00   12.00

4 (144a) 50 Cents (Ag) 1900. Dragon and inscription KIANG NAN PROVINCE 3 MACE AND 6 CANDAREENS. ℞ as type No. 1   170.00   250.00

5 (145a2)   1 Dollar (Ag) 1900, 1901. Dragon and inscription KIANG NAN PROVINCE 7 MACE AND 2 CANDAREENS. ℞ as type No. 1   30.00   40.00

6 (142a7) 10 Cents (Ag) 1901–1903. As type No. 2, but the reverse legend has in addition the letters HAH   8.00   10.50

7 (143a7) 20 Cents (Ag) 1901–1903. As type No. 3, but the reverse legend has in addition the letters HAH   6.00   8.50

8 (145a4)   1 Dollar (Ag) 1901–1903. As type No. 5,

			VF	**XF**
	but the reverse legend has in addition the letters HAH	26.00	38.00
9	10 Cents (Ag) 1904. As type No. 2, but the reverse legend has in addition the letters HAH and TH	4.00	6.00
10	20 Cents (Ag) 1904. As type No. 3, but the reverse legend has in addition the letters HAH and TH	9.00	15.00
11	1 Dollar (Ag) 1904. As type No. 5, but the reverse legend has in addition the letters		
	a) HAH and TH	40.00	50.00
	b) HAH and CH	32.00	40.00
12 (142a14)	10 Cents (Ag) 1905. As type No. 2, but the reverse legend has in addition the letters SY	4.00	6.00
13 (143a13)	20 Cents (Ag) 1905. As type No. 3, but the reverse legend has in addition the letters SY	15.00	20.00
14 (145a15)	1 Dollar (Ag) 1905. As type No. 5, but the reverse legend has in addition the letters SY	30.00	40.00

15 (135)	10 Cash (Cu) 1902–1905. Dragon in dotted circle and inscription KIANG-NAN TEN CASH. ℞ Chinese characters and, in centre, two Manchu characters, among which name of province, date, and denomination as well as value	1.25	2.50
15a	10 Cash (Cu) (undated). As type No. 15, but undated	–.–	–.–
16	10 Cash (Cu) 1902–1905. Dragon (new design) and inscription KIANG-NAN TEN CASH; a Manchu character on right and left. ℞ Chinese characters, among which name of province and denomination as well as date and value. In centre, rosette	–.–	–.–
16a	10 Cash (Cu) 1906. Obverse as type No. 16. ℞ Chinese and Manchu characters, among which denomination, date, and value	2.50	5.00

			VF	XF
16b	10	Cash (Cu) 1905. Dragon (repeated change in design) in the circle of dots and legend KIANG NAN TEN CASH. ℞ Type as No. 16a	–.–	–.–
17	20	Cash (Cu) 1902–1905. As type No. 16	50.00	90.00
18 (7k)	1	Cash (Bra) 1908. Dragon. ℞ date and value in Chinese characters. In centre, Chinese character for Kiangnan	5.00	10.00
19 (9k1)	5	Cash (Cu) 1906–1908. Dragon in dotted circle and inscription TAI-CHING-TI-KUO COPPER COIN as well as four Chinese characters. ℞ Chinese and Manchu characters, among which denomination, date, and value. In centre, Chinese character for Kiangnan	55.00	100.00
20	10	Cash (Cu) 1906–1908. As type No. 19	1.00	2.00
21	10	Cash (Cu) 1909. As type No. 20, but the Chinese characters in the obverse inscription read Hsüan Tung instead of Kuang Hsü	2.00	4.00
22	20	Cash (Cu) 1909. As type No. 21	–.–	–.–
23 (146)	10	Cents (Ag) 1909 (undated). Dragon and inscription KIANG NAN PROVINCE 7,2 CANDAREENS. ℞ Chinese characters and, in centre, four Manchu characters, among which name of province and denomination as well as value	12.50	25.00
24 (147)	20	Cents (Ag) 1909 (undated). Dragon and inscription KIANG NAN PROVINCE 1 MACE 4,4 CANDAREENS. ℞ as type No. 23	20.00	40.00

Kiangsee (Kiangsi) 江 西 (贑)

1 (150.2)	10	Cash (Cu) 1896–1908 (undated). Dragon and inscription KIANG SI 10 CASH as well as two stars on right

			VF	XF
		and on left. ℞ Chinese characters and two Manchu characters, among which name of province and denomination as well as value. In centre, rosette	4.00	7.00
2	10	Cash (Cu) (undated). Type similar to No. 1, but dragon of varied type	–.–	–.–
3	10	Cash (Cu) undated. Type similar to No. 2, but in the centre in place of the rosette, two Manchu characters	–.–	–.–
4	10	Cash (Cu) undated. Type similar to No. 1, but on ℞ the two Manchu characters in the centre	–.–	–.–
5	10	Cash (Cu) 1896–1908 (undated). Dragon and legend KIANG-SEE PROVINCE TEN CASH. ℞ Chinese and two Manchu characters, among others province and coin designation as well as denomination. In the centre a rosette	2.00	4.00
6	10	Cash (Cu) undated. Obverse Type as No. 5, but changed design of the dragon. ℞ government era and coin designation by way of four Chinese characters in the circle of dots. In the centre two Manchu and in the legend eight Chinese characters, among others province designation and denomination	–.–	–.–
7	20	Cash (Cu) undated. Type as No. 5	50.00	90.00
8 (10m)	10	Cash (Cu) 1906. Dragon in dotted circle and legend TAI-CHING TI-KUO COPPER COIN as well as four Chinese characters. ℞ Chinese and Manchu characters, among others coin designation, year and denomination. In the centre Chinese character for Kiang-See	6.00	10.00
9 (154)	10	Cash (Cu) undated. Dragon (changed design) and legend KIANG-SI 10 CASH. ℞ province and coin designation as well as denomination in Chinese characters	40.00	60.00

Kiangsoo 江蘇 (蘇)

1	2	Cash (Cu) undated. Dragon. ℞ value in Chinese characters	135.00	200.00
2 (158)	5	Cash (Cu) undated. Dragon and inscription KIANG-SOO. ℞ name of province and value in Chinese characters	40.00	70.00

			VF	XF
2a	5	Cash (Cu) undated. Type similar to No. 2, but with changed design of the dragon	–.–	–.–
3 (160)	10	Cash (Cu) undated. Dragon of varied type and inscription KIANG-SOO as well as value. ℞ name of province and value in Chinese characters	2.50	5.00
3a (162.4)	10	Cash (Cu) undated. Dragon (new type) in dotted circle and inscription KIANG-SOO TEN CASH. ℞ Chinese characters and two Manchu characters, right and left, among which name of province, denomination, and value. In centre, rosette	0.60	1.20
3b (162)	10	Cash (Cu) undated. Type as No. 3a, but on ℞ the two Manchu characters in the centre in place of the rosette	1.50	3.00
3c	10	Cash (Cu) undated. Type as No. 3a, but the centre of ℞ smooth	–.–	–.–
3d	10	Cash (Cu) 1902, 1903. Type similar to No. 3a, but with two Manchu characters in the centre of ℞ as well as additionally in the legend the date in Chinese characters	–.–	–.–
4	10	Cash (Cu) 1902, 1903, 1905. As type No. 3, but in centre of reverse two Manchu characters instead of rosette. Date in Chinese characters	2.00	4.00
4a	10	Cash (Cu) 1905. Type as No. 4, but on ℞ the two Manchu characters in the legend and a rosette in the centre	–.–	–.–
5 (163)	20	Cash (Cu) undated. As type No. 3a	25.00	50.00
6	2	Cash (Cu) 1906. Dragon. ℞ Chinese and Manchu characters, among which denomination, date, and value. In centre, Chinese character for Kiangsoo	70.00	100.00
7 (9n)	5	Cash (Cu) 1906. Dragon in dotted circle and inscription TAI-CHING-TI-KUO COPPER COIN as well as four Chinese characters. ℞ Chinese and Manchu characters, among which denomination, date, and value. In centre, Chinese character for Kiangsoo	70.00	110.00
8 (10n)	10	Cash (Cu) 1906. As type No. 7	4.00	8.00
9 (11n1)	20	Cash (Cu) 1906. As type No. 7	30.00	55.00

Values are given for each coin in U.S. Dollars and reference to Yeoman-numbers.

Kirin 吉林 (吉)

			VF	XF
1 (175)	2	Cash (Cu) 1883–1908 (undated). Four Chinese characters, among which denomination. In centre, two Manchu characters. ℞ value in Chinese characters. In centre, Chinese character for Kirin	100.00	200.00
2 (177)	10	Cash (Cu) 1883–1908 (undated). Dragon in dotted circle and inscription KIRIN 10 CASHES. ℞ Chinese characters and, in centre, two Manchu characters, among which name of province and denomination as well as value. Variants	5.00	10.00
2a	10	Cash (Cu) undated. As type No. 2, but dragon of varied type	–.–	–.–

			VF	XF
3 (178)	20	Cash (Cu) 1883–1908 (undated). As type No. 2. Variants	50.00	90.00
3a	20	Cash (Cu) 1883–1908 (undated). As type No. 2a	–.–	–.–
4 (179.1)	5	Cents (Ag) 1900, 1906–1908. Dragon and inscription KIRIN-PROVINCE 36 CANDAREENS, one Manchu character to right and left. ℞ Chinese characters, among which name of province and denomination as well as date and value. In centre, bundle of leaves. Variants	7.00	10.00
5 (180.1)	10	Cents (Ag) 1900, 1906–1908. As type No. 4, but value in obverse inscription CANDARINS. 72. Variants	7.00	10.00
6 (181)	20	Cents (Ag) 1900, 1906–1908. As type No. 4, but value in obverse inscription 1 MACE AND 44 CANDAREENS. Variants	16.00	24.00

			VF	XF
7 (182.2)	50	Cents (Ag) 1900, 1906–1908. As type No. 4, but value in obverse inscription 3. CANDARINS. 6. Variants	22.00	30.00
8 (183)	1	Dollar (Ag) 1900, 1906–1908. As type No. 4, but value in obverse inscription 7. CANDARINS. 2. Variants	45.00	60.00
9 (179a)	5	Cents (Ag) 1900–1905. As type No. 4, but in centre of reverse the Yin Yang symbol instead of the bundle of leaves. Variants	12.00	20.00
10 (180a)	10	Cents (Ag) 1900–1905. As type No. 5, but in centre of reverse the Yin Yang symbol instead of the bundle of leaves. Variants	10.00	15.00
11 (181a)	20	Cents (Ag) 1900–1905. As type No. 6, but in centre of reverse the Yin Yang symbol instead of the bundle of leaves. Variants	12.00	20.00

12 (182a)	50	Cents (Ag) 1900–1905. As type No. 7, but in centre of reverse the Yin Yang symbol instead of the bundle of leaves. Variants	25.00	40.00
13 (183a)	1	Dollar (Ag) 1900–1905. As type No. 8, but in centre of reverse the Yin Yang symbol instead of the bundle of leaves. Variants	50.00	80.00

			VF	XF

14 (181b) 20 Cents (Ag) 1908. Dragon (new design) and inscription KIRIN PROVINCE 1 MACE AND 44 CANDAREENS. ℞ Chinese characters, and, in centre, two Manchu characters, among which name of province and denomination as well as date and value — 65.00 / 100.00

15 (182b) 50 Cents (Ag) 1908. As type No. 14, but value in obverse inscription 3. CANDARINS. 6 — 100.00 / 200.00

16 (183b) 1 Dollar (Ag) 1908. As type No. 14, but value in obverse inscription. 7. CANDARINS. 2 — 200.00 / 360.00

17 (180c) 10 Cents (Ag) 1908. Dragon and inscription KIRIN-PROVINCE CANDARINS 72. ℞ Chinese characters, among which name of province and denomination as well as date and value. In centre, the figure 1 — 50.00 / 70.00

18 (181c) 20 Cents (Ag) 1908. As type No. 17, but value in obverse inscription 1 MACE AND 44 CANDAREENS and in centre of reverse the figure 2 — 40.00 / 60.00

19 (183c) 1 Dollar (Ag) 1908. As type No. 17, but value in obverse inscription 7. CAINDARINS. 2 and in centre of reverse the figure 11 — 250.00 / 400.00

20 1 Tael (Ag) 1908. Dragon and inscription KWANG-SHU KUOPING ONE TAEL. ℞ Chinese and Manchu characters, among which denomination, date, and value. In centre, Chinese character for Kirin — –.– / –.–

21 (22) 20 Cents (Ag) 1909. Dragon in dotted circle and inscription TAI-CHING-TI-KUO SILVER COIN as well as four Chinese characters. ℞ Chinese and Manchu characters, among which denomination, date, and value. In centre, Chinese character for Kirin — 30.00 / 50.00

22 (20p) 10 Cash (Cu) 1909. Dragon in dotted circle and inscription TAI-CHING-TI-KUO COPPER COIN as well as four Chinese characters. ℞ Chinese and Manchu characters, among which denomination, date, and value. In centre, Chinese character for Kirin — 25.00 / 40.00

23 (21p) 20 Cash (Cu) 1909. As type No. 22 — 100.00 / 175.00

All valuations in the SCHÖN are stated in U.S. Dollars.

			VF	XF
1 (193)	10	Cash (Cu) undated. Dragon in dotted circle and inscription KWANG-TUNG TEN CASH. ℞ Chinese characters and, in centre, two Manchu characters, among which name of province and denomination as well as value	1.00	2.00
2 (192)	10	Cash (Cu) undated. Dragon in dotted circle and inscription KWANG-TUNG ONE CENT. ℞ Chinese characters, among which value	2.50	4.00
3	1	Tael (Ag) 1904 (undated). Chinese characters in dotted circle. Border formed by two dragons. ℞ Chinese characters, among which name of province and denomination as well as value. In centre, four Manchu characters. Pattern	–.–	–.–
4 (10r)	10	Cash (Cu) 1906–1908. Dragon in dotted circle and inscription TAI-CHING-TI-KUO COPPER COIN as well as four Chinese characters. ℞ Chinese and Manchu characters, among which denomination as well as date and value. In centre, Chinese character for Kwangtung	1.00	2.00
5 (20r)	10	Cash (Cu) 1909. As type No. 4, but the Chinese characters in the obverse inscription read Hsüan Tung instead of Kuang Hsü	1.30	2.50
6 (204)	1	Cash (Bra) 1909–1911 (undated). Four Chinese characters. ℞ two Manchu characters. In centre, round hole within square frame	0.60	1.20
7 (205)	20	Cents (Ag) 1909 (undated). Dragon and inscription KWANG-TUNG PROVINCE 1 MACE AND 4,4 CANDAREENS. ℞ Chinese characters, among which name of province and denomination as well as value. In centre, four Manchu characters	7.00	11.00

			VF	XF
8 (206)	1	Dollar (Ag) 1909 (undated). As type No. 7, but value in the obverse inscription 7 MACE and 2 CANDAREENS	20.00	35.00

Manchuria 東 三 省

			VF	XF
1 (209)	10	Cents (Ag) 1907. Dragon and inscription 33rd YEAR OF KUANG HSU MANCHURIAN PROVINCES. ℞ Chinese characters and, in centre, four Manchu characters, among which name of province and denomination as well as value	11.00	15.00
2 (210)	20	Cents (Ag) 1907. As type No. 1	7.00	11.00
3 (211)	50	Cents (Ag) 1907. As type No. 1	110.00	165.00
4 (212)	1	Dollar (Ag) 1907. As type No. 1	130.00	180.00
5 (213a)	20	Cents (Ag) 1909 (undated). Dragon and inscription MANCHURIAN PROVIENCES 1 MACE AND 44 CANDAREENS. ℞ Chinese characters and, in centre, three Manchu characters, among which name of province and denomination as well as value	5.00	8.50
6 (213)	20	Cents (Ag) 1909. As type No. 5, but obverse inscription FIRST YEAR OF HSUEN TUNG MANCHURIAN PROVINCES	5.00	8.50
7 (213.2)	20	Cents (Ag) 1909. As type No. 5, but obverse inscription 1st YEAR OF HSUEN TUNG MANCHURIAN PROVINCES	5.00	8.50
8 (213a.1)	20	Cents (Ag) 1910 (undated). Dragon and inscription MANCHURIAN PROVINCES 1 MACE AND 44 CANDAREENS. ℞ Chinese characters, among which name of province and denomination as well as value. In centre, a five-leaved rosette	4.50	8.00
9 (213a4)	20	Cents (Ag) 1910 (undated). As type No. 8, but no rosette in centre of the reverse	6.50	10.00
10 (213a5)	20	Cents (Ag) 1910 (undated). As type No. 9, but in the obverse inscription read PROVIENCES instead of PROVINCES	7.00	10.50

Shansi　ㄕ (山)

1 (217)　20 Cents (Ag) 1911 (undated). Dragon
and inscription NIACEURAN PROV-
INCES 1 MACE AND 4,4 CIN-
DARRNS (faulty legend). ℞ Chinese
characters, among which name of province and denomination as well as
value. Variants through other mis-
takes in the obverse legend

	VF	XF
	100.00	180.00

Shantung (Shangtung)　山東 (東)

1 (221a)　10 Cash (Cu) undated. Dragon in dotted
circle and inscription SHANG-TUNG
TEN CASH. ℞ Chinese characters and,
in centre, two Manchu characters,
among which name of province and
denomination as well as value　　　2.00　4.00

2 (221)　10 Cash (Cu) undated. As type No. 1, but
in the obverse inscription read SHAN-
TUNG instead of SHANG-TUNG　　4.00　8.00

3 (220)　10 Cash (Cu) undated. Dragon (new
type) and inscription. ℞ Chinese characters　　　　　　　　　　　　　10.00　20.00

4 (8s)　2 Cash (Cu) 1906. Dragon. ℞ Chinese
and Manchu characters, among which
denomination as well as date and value. In centre, Chinese character for
Shantung　　　　　　　　　　　25.00　40.00

5 (10s)　10 Cash (Cu) 1906. Dragon in dotted
circle and inscription TAI-CHING-
TI-KUO COPPER COIN as well as
four Chinese characters. ℞ as type
No. 2　　　　　　　　　　　　　6.00　10.00

Sinkiang (Chinese Turkestan)　新疆

10 Miscals (Mace) = 1 Tael

General issues for Sinkiang:

1 (1)　1½ Cents (Cu) (undated). ℞ dragon. Four
Chinese characters in dotted circle and
legend in Chinese characters, among
others province and coin designation
as well as denomination. In the centre
one and in the legend two fiveleafed
rosettes　　　　　　　　　　　　–.–　　–.–

1a　1 Mace (Ag) 1905 (undated). Dragon. ℞
denomination and value in four Chinese
characters in dotted circle. Legend in
four Arabic characters　　　　170.00　260.00

			VF	**XF**
2	1	Mace (Ag) 1905 (undated). Dragon and four Arabic characters as legend. ℞ denomination and value in four Chinese characters in dotted circle	170.00	260.00
2a	2	Mace (Ag) 1905 (undated). As type No. 2, but no legend on obverse	–.–	–.–
3	2	Mace (Ag) 1905 (undated). Dragon. ℞ denomination and value in four Chinese characters in dotted circle	40.00	75.00
4	2	Mace (Ag) 1905 (undated). Dragon. Denomination and value in four Chinese characters in dotted circle. Legend in four Arabic characters	40.00	75.00
4a	2	Mace (Ag) 1905 (undated). As type No. 4, but ℞ in the legend, the Arabic characters only in the lower half	30.00	50.00
5 (5)	4	Mace (Ag) 1905 (undated). As type No. 4	60.00	100.00
6 (6)	5	Mace (Ag) 1905 (undated). As type No. 4	35.00	60.00
6a (6.1)	5	Mace (Ag) 1905 (undated). Type as No. 6, but dragon within the dotted circle	40.00	70.00
7 (7)	1	Tael (Ag) 1905 (undated). Dragon. To left and right, rosette. ℞ denomination and value in four Chinese characters in dotted circle	80.00	140.00
8 (7.3)	1	Tael (Ag) 1905 (undated). As type No. 7, but legend in four Arabic characters and, in centre of reverse, rosette	90.00	170.00
9 (7.2)	1	Tael (Ag) 1905 (undated). Dragon and legend in four Arabic characters. ℞ denomination and value in four Chinese characters in dotted circle	200.00	320.00
9a (7.1)	1	Tael (Ag) 1905 (undated). Type as No. 9, but dragon within the dotted circle	160.00	220.00
10	1	Mace (Ag) 1907 (undated). Dragon. ℞ denomination and value in four Chinese characters in dotted circle. As legend, above and below, one Chinese character; to right and left, one Arabic character. In centre, six-pointed star	–.–	–.–
11 (8)	1	Gold Mace (Au) 1907 (undated). Dragon and inscription in Arabic characters. ℞ value in Chinese characters in dotted circle. (Rate of exchange: 1 Gold Mace = 3 Silver Taels)	500.00	750.00
12 (9)	2	Gold Mace (Au) 1907 (undated). As type No. 11	385.00	500.00
13 (2.3)	10	Cash (Cu) 1910–1911 (undated). Dragon and inscription above in Chinese		

<table>
<tr><td></td><td></td><td></td><td>VF</td><td>XF</td></tr>
</table>

			VF	XF
		characters, and below in Arabic characters. ℞ denomination and value in Chinese characters. In centre, five-pointed star in double circle	8.00	15.00
14 (2.1)	10	Cash (Cu) 1910, 1911. Type as No. 13, but a six-leafed rosette in centre of ℞	70.00	120.00
15 (2)	10	Cash (Cu) 1910–1911 (undated). Dragon and inscription below in Arabic characters. ℞ as type No. 11, but in centre, six-pointed star without circle	70.00	120.00

Issues for the Sungarei territory (Tsungarei):

1 (10)	1	Mace (Ag) 1906 (undated). Dragon and inscription SUNGAREI 1 MACE. ℞ Chinese characters and, in centre, four Manchu characters, among which name of province and denomination as well as value. Pattern	120.00	200.00
2 (11)	2	Mace (Ag) 1906 (undated). As type No. 1, but obverse inscription SUNGAREI 2 MACE. Pattern	160.00	260.00
3	4	Mace (Ag) 1906 (undated). As type No. 1. Pattern	–.–	–.–
4 (6.9)	5	Mace (Ag) 1906 (undated). As type No. 1, but the obverse inscription SUNGAREI 5 MACE. Pattern	–.–	–.–
5	1	Dollar (Ag) 1906 (undated). Dragon and inscription SUNGAREI 7 MACE 2 CANDAREENS. R as type No. 1. Pattern	–.–	–.–
6	2	Gold Mace (Au) 1906 (undated). Draggon and inscription SUNGAREI 2 MACE. ℞ Chinese and Manchu characters, among which name of province and denomination as well as value	–.–	–.–

Issues for Kashgar: 喀什

1 (B16)	1	Mace (Ag) 1904. Eight Chinese characters, among which mint, denomination and value. ℞ Arabic characters within wreath of ten rosettes	80.00	120.00
2 (C16)	1	Mace (Ag) 1904. Mint and denomination by way of four Chinese characters. ℞ Arabic characters in the wreath. Top and bottom one rosette each	80.00	120.00

			VF	XF
3 (17a)	2	Mace (Ag) 1901, 1902. As type No. 1	40.00	70.00
4 (18a)	3	Mace (Ag) 1901, 1902. As type No. 1	15.00	20.00
5 (19a)	5	Mace (Ag) 1901, 1902. Obverse as type No. 1. R Arabic characters within wreath of two twigs. Above, rosette	16.50	25.00
6 (17a1)	2	Mace (Ag) 1902–1904. As type No. 1, but some different characters on obverse	12.50	20.00
7 (18a1)	3	Mace (Ag) 1902–1904. As type No. 6	12.50	20.00
8 (19a1)	5	Mace (Ag) 1903, 1904. As type No. 5, but some different characters on obverse	16.00	26.00
9 (A20)	1	Mace (Ag) 1905. Dragon. R Chinese and Arabic characters, among which value	–.–	–.–
10 (B20)	2	Mace (Ag) 1905. Dragon. R Four Chinese characters in dotted circle and inscription in Chinese and Arabic characters, among which mint and denomination as well as value	130.00	180.00
11 (20)	3	Mace (Ag) 1905. As type No. 10	–.–	–.–
12 (21)	5	Mace (Ag) 1905. As type No. 10, but in centre of reverse, in addition, rosette	60.00	100.00
13 (25.1)	5	Mace (Ag) 1907–1910. Dragon in dotted circle, border made of two differing twigs; above, rosette. R Chinese and Arabic characters, among which mint, denomination, and value	40.00	75.00
14 (25)	5	Mace (Ag) 1908 (undated). Type as No. 13, but Arabic characters without year date	45.00	80.00
15 (26.1)	1	Tael (Ag) 1907. Dragon in dotted circle, border made of two differing twigs; above, rosette. R Chinese and Arabic characters, among which mint, denomination and value. In centre, rosette	60.00	100.00
16 (23)	2	Mace (Ag) 1907. As type No. 10, but some different characters	40.00	75.00
17 (25.4)	5	Mace (Ag) 1907. As type No. 10	–.–	–.–
18 (26.0)	1	Tael (Ag) 1907. As type No. 10, but some different characters	65.00	85.00
19 (29)	2	Mace (Ag) 1911. Dragon in dotted circle. Outside border of arabesques. In between, ring of 3 mm width. R Chinese and Arabic characters, among which denomination and value	50.00	80.00
20 (29.1)	2	Mace (Ag) 1911. Dragon in wider circle and inscription in Arabic characters. R as type No. 36, but without Arabic characters	–.–	–.–

			VF	XF
21 (30)	3	Mace (Ag) 1911. Dragon in wider circle and inscription below in Arabic characters. R four Chinese characters (denomination and value). In centre, rosette	125.00	180.00
22 (27.6)	5	Mace (Ag) 1909–1911. Dragon in dotted circle. Outside border of arabesques. In between, ring of 3 mm width. R Chinese and Arabic characters, among which mint, denomination and value. In centre, five-pointed star	40.00	65.00
23	5	Mace (Ag) 1910. Type as No. 22, but on R partly different characters	–.–	–.–
24 (31.1)	5	Mace (Ag) 1911–1913. Dragon in wider circle and, as inscription, two Chinese characters above and Arabic characters below. In the legend, three five-pointed stars. R denomination and value in four Chinese characters in dotted circle. In centre, one five-pointed star, in outside border, four five-pointed stars	40.00	65.00
25	1	Tael (Ag) 1911	–.–	–.–

Issues for Tihwa (Urumchi): 迪化

1 (33)	2	Mace (Ag) 1903–1905. 8 Chinese characters, among which mint, denomination and value. R in border, decoration of 8 rosettes and leaves	40.00	50.00
2 (34)	3	Mace (Ag) 1903–1905. As type No. 1	50.00	75.00
3 (35)	5	Mace (Ag) 1903, 1904. As type No. 1, but the reverse inscription has a border of two branches, between which rosette above	30.00	40.00
4 (33.1)	2	Mace (Ag) 1905–1907. As type No. 1, but on obverse a different Chinese character for 2	40.00	60.00
5 (34a)	3	Mace (Ag) 1904–1907. As type No. 2, but on obverse a different Chinese character for 3	48.00	75.00
6 (35a)	5	Mace (Ag) 1904–1907. As type No. 3, but on obverse a different Chinese character for 5	30.00	45.00

All valuations in the SCHÖN are stated in U.S. Dollars.

			VF	XF
1 (225)	5	Cash (Cu) undated. Dragon in dotted circle and inscription SZE CHUEN as well as value. R Chinese characters and two Manchu characters, among which name of province and denomination as well as value	100.00	150.00
2 (226)	10	Cash (Cu) (undated). Similar to type No. 1	40.00	60.00
3 (227)	20	Cash (Cu-Bra) undated. As type No. 1, but changed denomination	80.00	150.00
4 (228)	5	Cash (Cu) undated. As type No. 5, but changed denomination	80.00	150.00
5 (229)	10	Cash (Cu) undated. Dragon in dotted circle and inscription SZE CHUEN 10 CASH. R Chinese characters and two Manchu characters, among which name of province and denomination as well as value. In centre, circular symbol	6.00	10.00

6 (230)	20	Cash (Cu) undated. As type No. 5	20.00	35.00
6a (A234)	30	Cash (Cu) undated. As type No. 5	–.–	–.–
7 (231)	10	Cash (Cu) undated. As type No. 5, but design of the dragon changed again	100.00	165.00
8 (232)	20	Cash (Cu) undated. As type No. 7	–.–	–.–
9 (233.1)	30	Cash (Cu) undated. As type No. 7	–.–	–.–
10 (234)	5	Cents (Ag) 1902 (undated). Dragon and inscription SZECHUAN PROVINCE 3,6 CANDAREENS. R Chinese characters and, in centre, four Manchu characters, among which name of province and denomination as well as value	12.50	20.00
11 (235)	10	Cents (Ag) 1902 (undated). As type No. 10, but obverse legend SZECHUAN PROVINCE 7,2 CANDAREENS	12.50	20.00
12 (236)	20	Cents (Ag) 1902 (undated). As type No. 10, but obverse legend SZECHUEN PROVINCE 1 MACE AND 4,4 CANDAREENS	12.50	20.00

			VF	XF
13 (237)	50	Cents (Ag) 1901, 1902 (undated). As type No. 10, but obverse legend SZE-CHUEN PROVINCE 3 MACE AND 6 CANDAREENS	28.00	40.00
14 (238)	1	Dollar (Ag) 1901, 1902 (undated). As type No. 10, but obverse legend SZE-CHUEN PROVINCE 7 MACE AND 2 CANDAREENS	25.00	32.00
15 (10t)	10	Cash (Cu) 1906. Dragon in dotted circle and inscription TAI-CHING-TI-KUO COPPER COIN as well as four Chinese characters. R Chinese and Manchu characters, among which denomination, date, and value. In centre, Chinese character for Szechuan	1.00	2.00
16 (11t)	20	Cash (Cu) 1906. As type No. 15	8.50	14.00
17	5	Cash (Cu) 1909. As type No. 15, but the Chinese characters in obverse legend read Hsüan Tung instead of Kuang Hsü	9.00	15.00
18 (20t1)	10	Cash (Cu) 1909. As type No. 17	1.50	3.00
19 (21t1)	20	Cash (Cu) 1909. As type No. 17	17.00	25.00
20 (239a)	5	Cents (Ag) 1909 (undated). As type No. 10, but the Chinese characters on reverse read Hsüan Tung instead of Kuang Hsü	22.00	35.00
21 (240)	10	Cents (Ag) 1909 (undated). As type No. 11, but the Chinese characters on reverse read Hsüan Tung instead of Kuang Hsü	20.00	35.00
22	20	Cents (Ag) 1909 (undated). As type No. 12, but the Chinese characters on reverse read Hsüan Tung instead of Kuang Hsü	–.–	–.–
23 (242)	50	Cents (Ag) 1909 (undated). As type No. 13, but the Chinese characters on reverse read Hsüan Tung instead of Kuang Hsü	80.00	125.00
24 (243)	1	Dollar (Ag) 1909 (undated). As type No. 14, but the Chinese characters on reverse read Hsüan Tung instead of Kuang Hsü	22.00	40.00

For Szechuan Rupees, see under Tibet.

Values are given for each coin in U.S. Dollars and reference to Yeoman-numbers.

			VF	XF
1 (10u)	10	Cash (Cu) 1906. Dragon in dotted circle and inscription TAI-CHING-TI-KUO COPPER COIN as well as four Chinese characters. R Chinese and Manchu characters, among which denomination, date, and value. In centre, Chinese character for Yunnan	15.00	25.00
2 (11u)	20	Cash (Cu) 1906. As type No. 1	45.00	80.00
3 (10w)	10	Cash (Cu) 1906. As type No. 1, but in centre of reverse, the Chinese characters for Yunnan and Szechuan	3.00	5.00
4 (11w)	20	Cash (Cu) 1906. As type No. 3	4.00	7.00
5 (10v)	10	Cash (Cu) 1906. As type No. 1, but in the centre of R the Chinese character Tien	25.00	40.00
6 (11v1)	20	Cash (Cu) 1906. As type No. 5	60.00	110.00
7 (252)	20	Cents (Ag) 1907 (undated). Dragon and inscription YUN-NAN-PROVINCE 1 MACE AND 4,4 CANDAREENS. R Chinese characters and, in centre, four Manchu characters, among which name of province and denomination as well as value	15.00	22.00
8 (253)	50	Cents (Ag) 1907 (undated). As type No. 7, but obverse legend YUN-NAN-PROVINCE 3 MACE AND 6 CANDAREENS	9.00	12.00
9 (254)	1	Dollar (Ag) 1907 (undated). As type No. 7, but obverse legend YUN-NAN PROVINCE 7 MACE AND 2 CANDAREENS	40.00	60.00
10	1	Rupee (Ag) 1907 (undated). Tsen Yuing, Governor of Yun-Nan Province. Head with cap, facing left, as well as inscription on left YUN-NAN and on right. R the inscription SILVER COIN surrounded by leaf ornamentations. Trial minting or pseudo coin?	–.–	–.–
11 (255)	10	Cents (Ag) 1908 (undated). Dragon in dotted circle. To left and right, rosette. R similar to type No. 7	16.00	25.00
12 (256)	20	Cents (Ag) 1908 (undated). As type No. 11	16.00	25.00
13 (257)	50	Cents (Ag) 1908 (undated). As type No. 11	7.00	10.50
14 (258)	1	Dollar (Ag) 1908 (undated). As type No. 11	22.00	30.00

			VF	XF

15 (259)   50 Cents (Ag) 1909 (undated). As type No.
8, but the Chinese characters on reverse
read Hsüan Tung instead of Kuang Hsü   8.00   12.50

16 (260)   1 Dollar (Ag) 1909 (undated). As type No.
9, but the Chinese characters on reverse
read Hsüan Tung instead of Kuang Hsü   24.00   32.00

17 (260.1)   1 Dollar (Ag) 1910. As type No. 16, but
in the reverse legend (in the mention of
the date) 13 Chinese characters instead
of 10   750.00   1200.00

18   1 Cash (Bra) 1909–1911 (undated). Government are and coin designation by
way of four Chinese characters. ℞ on
left and right one Manchu character
each. With square hole. Casting!   3.50   6.00

REPUBLIC (1912–1949)

中華民國

The dates given on the coins of the Republic are reckoned from the
foundation of the Republic (1912 = 1st year).
Central Government Issues:

1 (305)   10 Cash (Cu) 1912–1915 (undated). Leaf
decoration and rosette in circle and
legend THE REPUBLIC OF CHINA
TEN CASH. ℞ crossed flags   10.00   15.00

2 (301)   10 Cash (Cu) 1912–1915 (undated). Value
in Chinese characters in circle between
ears of wheat, with legend THE RE-
PUBLIC OF CHINA TEN CASH. ℞
crossed flags (with tassels) and legend
in Chinese characters, among which
name of country   1.00   2.00

3 (303)   10 Cash (Cu) 1912–1915 (undated). Value
in Chinese characters in circle between

			VF	XF
		ears of wheat, with legend THE RE-PUBLIC OF CHINA TEN CASH. ℞ crossed flags (without tassels) in dotted circle and legend in Chinese characters, among which name of country	1.50	2.50
4	10	Cash (Cu) 1912–1915 (undated). Value in Chinese characters in dotted circle between ears of wheat; border of leaf decoration. ℞ crossed flags (with tassels) and legend in Chinese characters, among which name of country	1.50	2.50
4a	10	Cash (Cu) undated. Obv. as type No. 4, ℞ as type No. 3	16.00	30.00
5	10	Cash (Cu) 1912 (undated). Bust l. of Dr. Sun Yat Sen (1866–1925), first President of the Republic of China 1912. ℞ value in Chinese characters in dotted circle between ears of wheat, legend above in Chinese characters, among which name of country, below, TEN CASH. Pattern	–.–	–.–
5a	10	Cash (Cu) 1912 (undated). Bust turned half to l. of Li Yuan Hung (without cap). ℞ value in Chinese characters between ears of wheat in dotted circle; legend. Similar to type No. 13	–.–	–.–
5b	10	Cash (Cu) 1912 (undated). As type No. 5a, but Li Yuan Hung wearing cap. Similar to type No. 14	–.–	–.–
5c	10	Cash (Cu) 1912 (undated). Bust turned half to l. of Yuan Shih Kai in uniform with plumed cap. ℞ value in Chinese characters between rice plants, legend. Similar to type No. 16	–.–	–.–
5d (309)	10	Cash (Cu) 1912–1915 (undated). Value in Chinese characters between rice plants. Below, legend TEN CASH. ℞ crossed flags (new design) and legend in Chinese characters, among which name of country	12.00	20.00
6	20	Cash (Cu) 1912–1915 (undated). Value in Chinese characters between rice plants, below TWENTI CASH. ℞ crossed flags; in the legend THE RE-PUBLIC OF CHINA as well as name of country in Chinese characters. Obv. and ℞ similar to type No. 5a	2.00	4.00
6a (310)	20	Cash (Cu) (undated). As type No. 6, but inscription on obverse TWENTY CASH	22.00	40.00

				VF	XF
7 (307)	10	Cash (Cu) 1912–1915, 1919 (undated). Value in Chinese characters between ears of wheat. ℞ crossed flags (ribbons without tassels) in circle; in the legend, name of country and denomination as well as value in Chinese characters		2.00	4.00
8 (308)	20	Cash (Cu) 1919. As type No. 7, but in the reverse legend, date instead of value		2.00	4.00
9	10	Cents (Ag) 1912 (undated). Bust l. in circle of Dr. Sun Yat Sen, legend in Chinese characters, among which name of country. ℞ value in Chinese characters in circle between ears of wheat, inscription MEMENTO BIRTH OF REPUBLIC OF CHINA		–.–	–.–
10 (317)	20	Cents (Ag) 1912 (undated). Bust l. of Dr. Sun Yat Sen with inscription MEMENTO BIRTH OF REPUBLIC OF CHINA. ℞ crossed flags in dotted circle and inscription in Chinese characters, among which name of country		17.50	25.00
11 (318)	1	Dollar (Ag) 1912 (undated). As type No. 9		85.00	140.00

For same type, see No. 45

12 (319)   1 Dollar (Ag) 1912 (undated). Bust l. in

	VF	XF

circle of Dr. Sun Yat Sen; legend in Chinese characters, among which name of country. ℞ value in Chinese characters in circle between ears of wheat, and legend THE REPUBLIC OF CHINA ONE DOLLAR

60.00 100.00

13 (321) 1 Dollar (Ag) 1912 (undated). Bust (without cap) turned half to l. in dotted circle of Li Yuan Hung (1864–1930), Vice-President 1912 – 1916, President of the Republic of China 1916 – 1918 and 1922 – 1923; legend in Chinese characters, among which name of country. ℞ value in Chinese characters in circle between ears of wheat, and legend THE REPUBLIC OF CHINA ONE DOLLAR. There are also trial strikes in gold of this coin!

40.00 70.00

14 (320) 1 Dollar (Ag) 1912 (undated). As type No. 13, but Li Yuan Hung wears military cap

110.00 165.00

350   China

			VF	XF
14a	1	Dollar (Ag) 1912 (undated). Bearded bust half turned to l. of Chin Teh Chuen, Governor of the province Kiangsoo; legend in Chinese characters, among which name of country. ℞ value in Chinese characters in circle between ears of wheat, and legend THE REPUBLIC OF CHINA ONE DOLLAR. Pattern	–.–	–.–
15	1	Dollar (Ag) 1914. Bust turned half to l. of Yuan Shih Kai (1859–1916), President of the Republic of China 1912 to 1916; above, name of country and date in Chinese characters. ℞ value in Chinese characters between rice plants	–.–	–.–

			VF	XF
16 (322)	1	Dollar (Ag) 1914 (undated). Bust turned half to l. of Yuan Shih Kai in uniform with plumed cap. ℞ value in Chinese characters in dotted circle between rice plants; in the legend, ONE DOLLAR and Chinese characters, among which name of country	80.00	130.00
17 (326)	10	Cents (Ag) 1914, 1916. Bust l. of Yuan Shih Kai in uniform; above, name of country and date in Chinese characters. ℞ value in Chinese characters between, above, rice plants	3.00	4.00
18 (327)	20	Cents (Ag) 1914, 1916, 1920. As type No. 17	4.00	5.00
19 (328)	50	Cents (Ag) 1914. As type No. 17	10.00	18.00

Values are given for each in U.S. Dollars and reference to Yeoman-numbers.

			VF	XF

20 (329) 1 Dollar (Ag) 1914, 1919–1921. Obv. as type No. 17, ℞ as type No. 15 — **7.50** / **15.00**

20a 5 Cents (Ni) 1914. Bust l. of Yuan Shih Kai; above, name of country and date in Chinese characters. ℞ in centre, value in Chinese characters within wreath opened above; above, inscription in Chinese characters. Pattern — **–.–** / **–.–**

21 (332) 1 Dollar (Ag) 1916 (undated). Bust turned half to l. of Yuan Shih Kai in uniform with plumed cap. ℞ winged dragon and legend in Chinese characters, among which name of country — **160.00** / **250.00**

22 (323) ½ Cent (Cu) 1916. Wreath of rice plants and four-pointed star. ℞ within circle, value in Chinese characters, legend in Chinese characters, among which name of country, date, and value. Round hole in centre — **11.00** / **20.00**

23 (324) 1 Cent (Cu) 1916. As type No. 22
a) with round hole in centre — **4.00** / **6.00**
b) without hole — **–.–** / **–.–**

24 (325) 2 Cents (Cu) 1916. As type No. 22 — **35.00** / **60.00**

			VF	XF
25	5	Dollars (Au) 1914, 1916. Bust l. of Yuan Shih Kai in uniform. ℞ winged dragon and legend in Chinese characters, among which name of country and date. Pattern	–.–	–.–
26 (333)	10	Dollars (Au) 1916. As type No. 25, but not a pattern	2000.00	2400.00
27 (330)	10	Dollars (Au) 1919. Bust l. of Yuan Shih Kai in uniform. ℞ name of country, date and value in Chinese characters between, and above, rice plants	1000.00	1200.00
28 (331)	20	Dollars (Au) 1919. As type No. 27	1750.00	2000.00
28a (307a)	10	Cash (Cu) 1921 (undated). As type No. 7, but new design for flags and ribbons with tassels	2.00	4.00
29 (308a)	20	Cash (Cu) 1921, 1922. As type No. 8, but new design for flags and ribbons with tassels	3.00	6.00
30	1	Dollar (Ag) 1921. Bust turned half to l. of Hsü Chih Chang (1858–1936) in mufti, President of the Republic of China 1918–1922. ℞ pavilion within circle; name of country, date, and value in Chinese characters, as legend above	300.00	380.00
31	1	Dollar (Ag) 1921. As type No. 30, but the reverse legend is also repeated below the type	300.00	380.00
32	1	Dollar (Ag) 1923 (undated). Bust facing of Tsao Kun (1862–1938) in mufti, President of the Republic of China 1923–1924. ℞ crossed flags; above, legend of six Chinese characters	200.00	280.00
33	1	Dollar (Ag) 1923 (undated). Bust facing of Tsao Kun in uniform. ℞ crossed flags, two Chinese characters in ancient seal-script between the flag-staffs. Six stars within circular border	110.00	160.00
34 (311)	10	Cash (Cu) 1924. Name of country, date, and value in Chinese characters between, and above, rice plants. ℞ four Chinese characters in dotted circle. In the legend, THE REPUBLIC OF CHINA as well as four Manchu characters	100.00	165.00
35 (312)	20	Cash (Cu) 1924. As type No. 34	8.00	15.00
36	1	Dollar (Ag) 1924 (undated). Bust facing of Tuan Chi Yui (1864–1936) in mufti, General, politician and Minister of the Republic of China; above, nine Chinese characters, among which name of country. ℞ two Chinese char-		

			VF	XF

acters in ancient seal-script between
rice plants — 135.00 — 180.00

37   1 Dollar (Ag) 1926. Bust facing of Dr. Sun Yat Sen. In the legend, name of country and date in seven Chinese characters. ℞ value in Chinese characters between rice plants. Pattern — –.– — –.–

38 (334)   10 Cents (Ag) 1926. Symbol of long life between dragon and phoenix. ℞ value in Chinese characters in dotted circle between rice plants. In the legend, name of country, date, and value in Chinese characters — 7.00 — 9.00

39 (335)   20 Cents (Ag) 1926. As type No. 38 — 7.00 — 9.00

40 (336)   1 Dollar (Ag) 1923. Symbol of long life between dragon and phoenix; above, name of country and date in Chinese characters. ℞ value in Chinese characters between rice plants — 200.00 — 350.00

41   1 Dollar (Ag) 1927. Bust facing of Chu Yu Pu in uniform, Military and Civil Governor of the Hopei province 1926. ℞ crossed flags and legend in Chinese characters, among which name of country and date — 750.00 — 900.00

42 (339)   10 Cents (Ag) 1927. Bust facing of Dr. Sun Yat Sen and legend of 13 Chinese characters, among which name of country and date. ℞ crossed flags and value in Chinese characters above, between flag-staffs. Below, value in six Chinese characters — 25.00 — 40.00

43 (340)   20 Cents (Ag) 1927. As type No. 42 — 22.00 — 35.00

44   20 Cents (Ag) 1927. Head l. of Dr. Sun Yat Sen. Legend comprising name of country and date in Chinese characters.

R crossed flags and value in Chinese characters between flag-staffs. Below, value in six Chinese characters

45 (318.1) 1 Dollar (Ag) 1927 (undated). As type No. 11, but the rosettes in the reverse legend are not round but elliptical   8.00   15.00

46 1 Dollar (Ag) 1927. Head facing of Dr. Sun Yat Sen and legend of eight Chinese characters, among which name of country. R in centre, value in Chinese characters; to right, mausoleum and to left, sun with rays; below, date in Chinese characters   450.00   650.00

47 1 Dollar (Ag) 1926. Bust facing of Chang Tso Lin (1876–1928) in uniform, General and Commander-in-Chief of land and naval forces of the Republic of China 1927. Above, inscription of six Chinese characters. R Chinese characters in dotted circle between ears of wheat; above the characters, sun. In the legend ONE DOLLAR as well as name of country and date in Chinese characters. Pattern   420.00   600.00

48 1 Dollar (Ag) 1927. Bust facing of Chang Tso Lin in uniform; above, name of country and date in Chinese characters. R dragon and phoenix within circle. In the legend ONE DOLLAR as well as name of country and date in Chinese characters. Pattern   550.00   700.00

49 1 Dollar (Ag) 1927 (undated). Obverse as type No. 47. R as type No. 48. Pattern   -.-   -.-

50 1 Dollar (Ag) 1928. Bust facing of Chang Tso Lin in mufti; above, six Chinese characters. R crossed flags. In the leg-

			VF	XF
		end ONE DOLLAR as well as name of country and value in Chinese characters. Pattern	190.00	250.00
50a (337)	1	Cent (Bra) 1928. 12-rayed sun. ℞ value	200.00	300.00
50b (338)	2	Cents (Bra) 1928. As type No. 50a	400.00	600.00
51	10	Cents (Ag) 1929. Head l. of Dr. Sun Yat Sen; above, name of country and date in Chinese characters. ℞ junk under sail (with three sails) as well as value in Chinese characters to right and left. Pattern	–.–	–.–
52	20	Cents (Ag) 1929. As type No. 51. Pattern	–.–	–.–
53	50	Cents (Ag) 1929. As type No. 51. Pattern	–.–	–.–
54	1	Dollar (Ag) 1929. As type No. 51. Several variants for reverse. Not a pattern	–.–	–.–
55	10	Cents (Cu–Ni) 1929. As type No. 51, but on reverse below, five Chinese characters. Pattern	–.–	–.–
56	20	Cents (Cu–Ni) 1929. As type No. 55. Pattern	–.–	–.–
57	50	Cents (Cu–Ni) 1929. As type No. 55. Pattern	–.–	–.–
58	1	Dollar (Ag) 1929. As type No. 54, but on reverse, junk without eye ornament. Pattern	–.–	–.–
59	1	Dollar (Ag) 1929. Bust facing of Dr. Sun Yat Sen; above, name of country and date in seven Chinese characters. ℞ as type No. 51. Pattern	–.–	–.–
60	20	Cents (Ag) 1929. Bust turned half to l. of Dr. Sun Yat Sen; above, name of country and date in Chinese characters. ℞ value in Chinese characters between, and above, rice plants. Pattern	–.–	–.–
61	1	Dollar (Ag) 1929. Bust turned half to l. of Dr. Sun Yat Sen; above, name of country and date in seven Chinese characters. ℞ crossed flags on globe with legend THE REPUBLIC OF CHINA; below, value in Chinese characters. Pattern	–.–	–.–
62	1	Dollar (Ag) 1929. Obv. as type No. 61. ℞ value in Chinese characters between rice plants. Pattern	–.–	–.–
63	1	Dollar (Ag) 1929 (undated). Head facing of Dr. Sun Yat Sen. ℞ as type No. 45. Pattern	–.–	–.–
64	1	Dollar (Ag) 1929 (undated). Obv. as		

type No. 63. ℞ value in Chinese characters between rice plants. Pattern   –.–   –.–

65   2 Cents (Ni) 1932. Branch in blossom and inscription in Chinese characters, among which value. ℞ sun (national emblem of the Chinese Republic) as well as name of country and date in Chinese characters. Round hole in centre. Pattern   –.–   –.–

65a   2 Cents (Ni) 1932. As type No. 65, but without hole in centre. Pattern   –.–   –.–

66   5 Cents (Ni) 1932. As type No. 65. Pattern   –.–   –.–

66a   5 Cents (Ni) 1932. As type No. 66, but without hole in centre. Pattern   –.–   –.–

67 (344)   1 Dollar (Ag) 1932. Head l. of Dr. Sun Yat Sen; above, name of country and date in Chinese characters. ℞ junk under sail (only two sails); above, three birds in flight; on r., rising sun; to l. and to r., value in Chinese characters   65.00   110.00

67a   1 Dollar (Ag) 1932. As type No. 67, but indication of mint in five Chinese characters within circular border   –.–   –.–

68   10 Cents ($^1/_{10}$ Sun) (Ag) 1932. Head l. of Dr. Sun Yat Sen; above, name of country and date in Chinese characters. ℞ junk under sail (two sails); on r., rising sun; two birds on the water; above, value in Chinese characters. Diameter 16 mm. Pattern   –.–   –.–

A "Sun" is a monetary unit based on gold.

69   20 Cents ($^1/_5$ Sun) (Ag) 1932. As type No. 68. Diameter 26 mm. Pattern   –.–   –.–

70   50 Cents (½ Sun) (Ag) 1932. As type No. 68. Diameter 34 mm. Pattern   –.–   –.–

			VF	XF
71	1	Dollar (1 Sun) (Ag) 1932. As type No. 68. Diameter 39 mm. Pattern	-.-	-.-
71a (324a)	1	Cent (Br) 1933. Similar to No. 22	20.00	50.00
71b (325a)	2	Cents (Br) 1933. Similar to No. 22	90.00	150.00

72 (345)	1	Dollar (Ag) 1933, 1934. As type No. 67, but reverse without birds and without sun	10.00	12.50
73	50	Cents (Ag) 1935. As type No. 72. Pattern	-.-	-.-
74	50	Cents (Ag) 1935. As type No. 73, but on the reverse, different character on right. Pattern	-.-	-.-
75	1	Dollar (Ag) 1935. As type No. 72. Pattern	-.-	-.-
76	50	Cents (Ag) 1936. As type No. 74, but diameter only 26 mm. Pattern	-.-	-.-
77	1	Dollar (Ag) 1936. As type No. 72, but diameter only 32 mm. Pattern	-.-	-.-
78	50	Cents (Ag) 1936, 1937. Bust l. of Dr. Sun Yat Sen; above, name of country and date in legend of Chinese characters. Meander pattern border. ℞ ancient Pu coin, value to right and left in Chinese characters	-.-	-.-
79	1	Dollar (Ag) 1936, 1937. As type No. 78	-.-	-.-
79a	50	Cents (Ag) 1936. As type No. 78, but obv. and ℞ without the meander pattern border	-.-	-.-
79b	1	Dollar (Ag) 1936. As type No. 79, but obv. and ℞ without the meander pattern border	-.-	-.-
80	1	Dollar (Ag) 1936. Bust l. of Chiang Kai-shek (1886–1975) in uniform with cap, President of the Republic of China 1928–1931 and 1948–1949; President of Nationalist China (Taiwan) since 1950. Border of meander pattern. R ancient Pu coin; above, name of country and		

		VF	XF

date in eight Chinese characters. Meander pattern border. Pattern   –.–   –.–

81   1 Dollar (Ag) 1936. Bust facing of Chiang Kai-shek in uniform without cap. Above, five Chinese characters. Meander pattern border. ℞ ancient Pu coin as well as name of country and date in Chinese characters. Meander pattern border. Pattern   –.–   –.–

82 (346)   ½ Cent (Br) 1936, 1937, 1939 (?) 1940 (?). In centre, sun (national emblem of the Republic); above, name of country and date in Chinese characters as legend. Meander pattern border. ℞ ancient Pu coin, value to right and left in Chinese characters. Meander pattern border   2.50   5.00

83 (347)   1 Cent (Br) 1936–1940. As type No. 82   1.20   2.40
84 (353)   1 Cent (Bra) 1939. As type No. 82, but the border on obverse and ℞ is composed of T-shaped elements   22.00   40.00
85 (354)   2 Cents (Bra) 1939. As type No. 84   5.50   10.00

86 (348)   5 Cents (Ni) 1935–1939, 1941. Bust l. of Dr. Sun Yat Sen; above, name of country and date in Chinese characters. Border of meander pattern. ℞ ancient Pu coin, value in Chinese characters on right and left. Border of meander pattern. The 1935 and 1937 issues are only patterns   0.50   1.00
87 (349)   10 Cents (Ni) 1935, 1936, 1938, 1939. As type No. 86. The 1935 issue is a pattern   0.40   0.80
88 (350)   20 Cents (Ni) 1935–1939. As type No. 86. The 1935 and 1937 issues are patterns   0.80   1.60
89 (348.3)   5 Cents (Ni) 1936. As type No. 86, but on the obverse, two additional Chinese characters for Tientsin. Pattern   45.00   65.00

			VF	XF
90 (348.2)	5	Cents (Ni) 1936. As type No. 86, but on the obverse, two additional Chinese characters for Peiping. Pattern	45.00	65.00
91 (349.4)	10	Cents (Ni) 1936. As type No. 87, but in the obverse legend another additional Chinese character for Tientsin. Pattern	45.00	65.00
92 (349.5)	10	Cents (Ni) 1936. As type No. 87, but in the obverse legend another additional Chinese character for Peiping. Pattern	55.00	85.00
93	10	Cents (Ni) 1936. As type No. 87, but in the obverse legend, two additional Chinese characters for Tientsin. Pattern	–.–	–.–
94	10	Cents (Ni) 1936. As type No. 87, but in the obverse legend, two additional Chinese characters for Peiping. Pattern	–.–	–.–
95	10	Cents (Ni) 1936. As type No. 87, but on the ℞ an additional Chinese character for Tientsin. Pattern	–.–	–.–
96	10	Cents (Ni) 1936. As type No. 87, but on the ℞ an additional Chinese character for Peiping. Pattern	–.–	–.–
97	10	Cents (Ni) 1936. As type No. 87, but on the obverse, on the robe of Dr. Sun Yat Sen, an additional character for Tientsin. Pattern	–.–	–.–
98	10	Cents (Ni) 1936. As type No. 87, but on the obverse, on the robe of Dr. Sun Yat Sen, an additional character for Peiping. Pattern	–.–	–.–
98a (348.1)	5	Cents (Ni) 1936. As type No. 86, but on ℞ underneath the Pu coin, additionally the letter A	1.50	3.00
98b	10	Cents (Ni) 1936. As type No. 87, but on ℞ underneath the Pu coin additionally the letter A. Trial strike!	–.–	–.–
98c (350.1)	20	Cents (Ni) 1936. As type No. 88, but on ℞ underneath the Pu coin additionally the letter A	1.25	2.50
99 (359)	5	Cents (Ni) 1940, 1941. As type No. 86, but smaller diameter (17.5 mm)	0.50	1.00
100 (360)	10	Cents (Ni) 1940–1942. As type No. 87, but smaller diameter (21 mm)	0.40	0.80
101 (361)	20	Cents (Ni) 1941, 1942. As type No. 88, but smaller diameter (24 mm)	0.80	1.50
102 (362)	½	Dollar (Ni) 1941–1943. As type No. 101, but diameter of 28 mm. The 1941 issue is a pattern	2.00	4.00

			VF	XF
102a (362.1)	50	Cents (Ni) 1942. As type No. 102, but on the reverse, beneath the Pu coin, an additional Chinese character for Kweilin	–.–	–.–
103	1	Cent (Ni) 1940. Chinese characters between wings within circle; name of country and date forming circular legend in Chinese characters. ℞ bundle of rice plants; value to right and left in Chinese characters. Hua Shing Bank issue	–.–	–.–
104	5	Cents (Ni) 1940. Obv. as type No. 103. ℞ pagoda and value in Chinese characters. Hua Shing Bank issue	–.–	–.–
105 (522)	10	Cents (Ni) 1940. Obv. as type No. 103. ℞ in centre, Chinese characters for long life in ancient seal-script; value to right and left in Chinese characters. Border of meander pattern. Hua Shing Bank issue	5.50	10.50
106	20	Cents (Ni) 1940. Obv. as type No. 103. ℞ junk with three sails, value to right and left in Chinese characters. Hua Shing Bank pattern	–.–	–.–
107	1	Cent (Al) 1939. Value in centre and in the legend, name of country and date in Chinese characters. Dotted border. ℞ ancient Pu coin. Dotted border. Pattern	–.–	–.–
108	5	Cents (Al) 1939. As type No. 107, but on obverse and reverse, meander pattern border. Pattern	–.–	–.–
109	10	Cents (Al) 1940. As type No. 108. Pattern	–.–	–.–
110 (355)	1	Cent (Al) 1940. As type No. 107, but not a pattern	0.40	0.60
111	2	Cents (Al) 1940. As type No. 108. Pattern	–.–	–.–
111a	2	Cents (Al) 1940. As type No. 111, but on obverse and reverse, no meander pattern, but only a dotted border. Pattern	–.–	–.–
112 (356)	5	Cents (Al) 1940. As type No. 108, but new Chinese character for 5	0.50	1.00
113	10	Cents (Ni) 1941 (undated). Head half turned to left of Chiang Kai-shek. ℞ ancient Pu coin, value to right and left in Chinese characters. Border of meander pattern	–.–	–.–
114	50	Cents (Ni) 1941 (undated). As type No. 113	–.–	–.–

			VF	XF
115	50	Cents (Ag) 1941. Bust facing of Chiang Kai-shek; above, name of country and date in Chinese characters. Border of meander pattern ℞ ancient Pu money, value in Chinese characters to right and left. Meander pattern border. Pattern	–.–	–.–
116 (357)	1	Cent (Bra) 1940. In centre, sun (national emblem of the Republic), name of country and date forming legend of Chinese characters. ℞ ancient Pu money, value in Chinese characters to right and left	0.40	0.80
117 (358)	2	Cents (Bra) 1940. As type No. 116	0.50	1.00
118 (363)	1	Cent (Br) 1948. As type No. 116	11.00	20.00
119	1	Dollar (Ag) 1948. Head l. of Dr. Sun Yat Sen; above, name of country and date forming legend in Chinese characters. ℞ ancient Pu money, value in Chinese characters to right and left	–.–	–.–
120	2	Dollars (Ag) 1948. As type No. 119	–.–	–.–
121	50	Cents (Ag) 1948. Bust r. of Chiang Kai-shek in uniform; above, legend in Chinese characters giving name of country and date. ℞ value in Chinese characters within wreath of rice stalks	–.–	–.–
122	(–)	No face value (Ag?) 1949. Flower with five petals within circle, legend in Chinese characters, among which name of country and date. ℞ above, wreath of rice stalks opened above. No characters	–.–	–.–

For further issues, see under the People's Republic of China and Taiwan (Nationalist China, Formosa).

PROVINCIAL ISSUES DURING THE REPUBLIC

Chekiang 浙江

1 (371)	10	Cents (Ag) 1924. Denomination and value in four Chinese characters within circle. Legend CHE-KIANG PROVINCE TEN CENTS. ℞ crossed flags within circle as well as legend in Chinese characters giving names of country and province, and date	5.00	8.00
2 (372)	20	Cents (Ag) 1924. As type No. 1, but the obverse legend reads CHE-KIANG PROVINCE TWENTY CENTS	–.–	–.–

			VF	XF
3 (373)	20	Cents (Ag) 1924. 20 in dotted circle with legend CHE-KIANG PROVINCE TWENTY CENTS. ℞ denomination and value in four Chinese characters within dotted circle. Circular legend giving names of country and province as well as date in Chinese characters	280.00	380.00

Fookien (Fukien) 福建

			VF	XF
1 (374)	1	Cash (Bra) 1911. Value given by a Chinese character above and below. Flag to right and left. ℞ Chinese characters. Round hole in centre	125.00	240.00
2 (375)	2	Cash (Bra) 1911. As type No. 1	25.00	50.00
3 (379)	10	Cash (Cu) 1912–1922, 1924. Three flags with ribbons and legend FOO-KIEN COPPER COIN TEN CASH. ℞ Chinese characters, among which denomination and value. In centre, rosette	5.00	9.00
4	20	Cents (Ag) 1912 (undated). Crossed flags in dotted circle and legend THERMEEMEA CBCERO 1 MACE AND 44 CANDAREENS. ℞ denomination in four Chinese characters within dotted circle. Legend in Chinese characters giving name of country and value	–.–	–.–
5 (377)	20	Cents (Ag) 1912. In centre, Chinese characters for Fukien in rosette; around, two circles of nine dots each (the dots on the inner and outer circle are connected by straight lines). Legend FOO-KIEN 1 MACE AND 44 CANDAREENS. ℞ Chinese characters, among which name of province and denomination as well as date and value. In centre, Chinese character for Fukien	17.50	30.00
6	20	Cents (Ag) 1912. As type No. 5, but the obverse legend FOO-KIEN GOVERNOR 1 MACE AND 44 CANDAREENS. Pattern	–.–	–.–
7 (380)	10	Cents (Ag) 1912 (undated). Three flags with ribbons and legend MADE IN FOO-KIEN MINT 7,2 CANDAREENS. ℞ denomination and name of province as well as value in Chinese characters. In centre, twelve-pointed star	40.00	70.00

			VF	**XF**
8 (A381)	20	Cents (Ag) 1912 (undated). As type No. 7, but value in the obverse legend 1 MACE AND 4,4 CANDAREENS	8.00	15.0
9 (382)	10	Cents (Ag) 1913 (undated). 10 in dotted circle and legend FOO-KIEN PROVINCE 7,2 CANDAREENS. ℞ names of country and province, and denomination as well as value in Chinese characters	5.00	8.0
10 (383)	20	Cents (Ag) 1913 (undated). 20 in dotted circle and legend. FOO-KIEN PROVINCE 1 MACE AND 44 CANDAREENS. ℞ as type No. 9	8.00	12.0
11 (381)	20	Cents (Ag) 1923. Three flags with ribbons and legend MADE IN FOO-KIEN MINT 1 MACE AND 44 CANDAREENS. ℞ names of country and province, and denomination as well as date and value in Chinese characters. In centre, twelve-pointed star	7.00	10.0
12 (380a)	10	Cents (Ag) 1924. As type No. 11, but the value on the obverse 7,2 CANDAREENS and name of country on reverse in different Chinese characters	15.00	26.0
13 (381.4)	20	Cents (Ag) 1924. As type No. 12, but value on the obverse 1 MACE AND 44 CANDAREENS	12.50	20.0
14 (383a)	20	Cents (Ag) 1924. 20 in dotted circle and legend FOO-KIEN PROVINCE TWENTY CENTS. ℞ Chinese characters, among which name of province and denomination as well as date and value	17.50	30.0
15 (385)	20	Cents (Ag) 1927. Two crossed flags within circle and legend in Chinese characters, among which value. ℞ Chinese characters, among which name of country, mint, and date. To right and left a large figure 2; in centre, twelve-pointed star. Issued by the Army	600.00	900.0
16	20	Cents (Ag) 1927. Head l. of Dr. Sun Yat Sen and legend in Chinese characters, among which name of country and date. ℞ two crossed flags and value in Chinese characters. Pattern	–.–	
17 (384)	20	Cents (Ag) 1927. Abacus, axe, sickle, gun, and book in the middle; on r. and l. a figure 2; circular inscription in Chinese characters, among which name of country and date as well as legend for National Government. ℞ crossed		

			VF	XF
		flags and legend in Chinese characters, among which value	260.00	400.00
18	20	Cents (Ag) 1927. As type No. 17, but no figure "2" in the obverse and in the reverse nine instead of thirteen Chinese characters	–.–	–.–
19 (388)	10	Cents (Ag) 1928, 1931. Sun with figure 10 in centre; around, dotted circle. Legend in Chinese characters giving names of country and province as well as date and value. ℞ memorial monument to the Huang Hwa massacre. Above, inscription in Chinese characters	12.00	20.00
20 (389)	20	Cents (Ag) 1928, 1931. As type No. 19, but figure 20 within sun	9.00	17.50
21 (390)	10	Cents (Ag) 1932. Two crossed flags, value in two Chinese characters between flag-staffs. Legend in Chinese characters. R as type No. 19	150.00	250.00
22 (391)	20	Cents (Ag) 1932. As type No. 19	70.00	125.00

Honan 河 南

			VF	XF
1 (A392)	10	Cash (Cu) 1912 (undated). Crossed flags (with tassels) and legend HO-NAN TEN CASH. ℞ value in Chinese characters between ears of corn in dotted circle. Legend in Chinese characters giving names of country and province	2.50	5.00
2 (392)	10	Cash (Cu) 1912 (undated). Obv. as type No. 1, but flags different. ℞ rosette between ears of corn in dotted circle. Legend in Chinese characters giving name of country and value	1.00	2.00
3 (392.2)	10	Cash (Cu) 1912 (undated). Obv. as type No. 1. Rev. as type No. 2	–.–	–.–
4 (393)	20	Cash (Cu) 1912 (undated). As type No. 2, but value in obverse legend 20 CASH	2.50	5.00
5 (393.1)	20	Cash (Cu) (undated). As type No. 4, but denomination in the legend of R in different Chinese characters	2.00	4.00
6 (394)	50	Cash (Cu) 1912 (undated). As type No. 2, but legend of obverse HO-NAN 50 CASH	8.00	15.00
7 (395)	100	Cash (Cu) 1912 (undated)	12.00	20.00
8 (396)	200	Cash (Cu) 1912 (undated). Crossed flags (with tassels) and legend HO-NAN 200 CASH	12.50	20.00

			VF	XF
9 (393.2)	20	Cash (Cu) undated. As type No. 4, but in the inscription of the obverse the name of country CHINA instead of the name of province HO-NAN	30.00	50.00
10 (394a)	50	Cash (Cu) undated. As type No. 9	18.00	30.00
11 (397)	50	Cash (Cu) 1931. Similar to No. 12	80.00	150.00
12 (398)	100	Cash (Cu) 1931. Value in Chinese characters between ears of corn; above, five-pointed star. ℞ in centre, sun (national emblem of the Republic). Legend in Chinese characters giving names of country and province as well as date	40.00	75.00
13 (A397)	20	Cash (Cu) 1931. Crossed flags with tassels, star above. Rev. rosette in dotted circle	–.–	–.–

Hopei 河北

1 (516)	½	Cent (Cu) 1937. Type as No. 2	15.00	25.00
2 (517)	1	Cent (Cu) 1937. Starred flags in dotted circle and legend in Chinese characters, among which name of country and date as well as inscription for Chi Tung Government. ℞ value in Chinese characters between ears of corn	4.50	8.00
3 (518)	5	Cents (Ni) 1937. As type No. 2	5.50	10.00
4 (519)	10	Cents (Ni) 1937. Pagoda in dotted circle and legend in Chinese characters, among which name of country and date as well as inscription for Chi Tung Government. ℞ value in Chinese characters between ears of corn	4.00	7.50
5 (520)	20	Cents (Ni) 1937. As type No. 4	7.00	13.00

Hunan 湖南

1 (400.2) 20 Cash (Cu) 1912–1921 (undated). Ears of corn and leaf decoration within circle. Inscription THE REPUBLIC OF CHINA TWENTY CASH. R crossed flags in circle; above, rosette between flag-staffs. Legend in Chinese characters giving name of country and value. Several variants .... VF 2.50 XF 4.00

2 (400) 20 Cash (Cu) (undated). As type No. 1, but the reverse legend in different Chinese characters 4.00 7.00

2a (400a) 20 Cash (Cu) (undated). As type No. 2, but the obverse legend 20 CASH ... 150.00 220.00

3 (399) 10 Cash (Cu) 1914 (undated). Nine-pointed star in dotted circle and legend HU-NAN TEN CASH. R Chinese characters, among which name of country and value. In centre, rosette ... 3.50 6.00

4 (401) 10 Cash (Cu) 1916 (undated). Ears of corn and leaf decoration within circle. Legend THE FIRST YEAR OF HUNG SHUAN TEN CASH. R Chinese characters, among which name of province and date 25.00 35.00

5 10 Cents (Ag) 1916. Dragon and value in Chinese characters. R Chinese characters, among which name of province and denomination as well as date. Pattern. .... –.– –.–

6 (404) 1 Dollar (Ag) 1922. Chinese character (three horizontal lines) between leaf ornaments in dotted circle. Legend in Chinese characters, among which names of country and province as well as date and value. R crossed flags in dotted

Values are given for each coin in U.S. Dollars and reference to Yeoman-numbers.

			VF	XF
		circle; above, rosette between flag-staffs. Legend THE REPUBLIC OF CHINA ONE DOLLAR	275.00	380.00
7	1	Dollar (Ag) 1922. Head half turned to l. of General Chao Heng Ti between branches in dotted circle. Legend in Chinese characters. ℞ as type No. 6. Pattern	–.–	–.–
8 (402)	10	Cash (Cu) 1922. Type similar to No. 6	20.00	30.00
9 (403)	20	Cash (Cu) 1922. Type similar to No. 6	25.00	40.00
10 (402.1)	10	Cash (Cu) 1922. Type similar to No. 6, but, above, a five-pointed star between flag-staffs	12.00	20.00
11 (400.9)	20	Cash (Cu) undated. Type as No. 1, but, above, a five-pointed star between flag-staffs	2.50	3.50

Hupeh 湖北 (鄂)

			VF	XF
1	5	Cents (Ni) 1915 (undated). Value in Chinese characters within sun (national emblem of the Republic). Border of meander pattern. ℞ name of country in Chinese characters within 16-pointed star. Pattern	–.–	–.–
2	10	Cents (?) 1916. Dragon and value in Chinese characters. ℞ Chinese characters, among which name of province and denomination as well as date. (Issue possibly in white metal?)	–.–	–.–
3 (406)	20	Cents (Ag) 1920. Bust l. of Yuan Shih Kai; above, names of country and province as well as date forming inscription in Chinese characters. ℞ value in Chinese characters between, and above, rice stalks	150.00	220.00

All valuations in the SCHÖN are stated in U.S. Dollars

4 (405) 50 Cash (Cu–Bra) 1914, 1918. Inscription in ancient Chinese 'seal writing' in the circle, all surrounded by eighteen rings arranged in a circle. Above designation of the country and date as inscription in Chinese characters. ℞ province and coin designation by way of four Chinese characters in the dotted circle. In the centre a stylized flower. In the legend Chinese characters, among others denomination 450.00 750.00

5 (A405) 20 Cash (Bra) undated. Denomination in four Chinese characters. Rev. value in four Chinese characters. In centre of obverse as well as of reverse a Chinese character in circle 100.00 160.00

Kansu 甘 肅

1 (407) 1 Dollar (Ag) 1914. Bust l. of Yuan Shih Kai in uniform. Legend in Chinese characters giving names of country and province as well as date. ℞ value in Chinese characters between rice stalks 240.00 450.00

2 (408) 50 Cash (Cu) 1926. Crossed flags. R in centre, Chinese character for Kansu 160.00 250.00

3 (409) 100 Cash (Cu) 1926. Crossed flags; above, large rosette between flag-staffs, four small rosettes at the edge. ℞ Chinese characters, among which names of country and province as well as date and value 90.00 160.00

4 (410) 1 Dollar (Ag) 1928. Bust facing of Dr. Sun Yat Sen; legend in Chinese characters giving name of country and date. ℞ in centre, sun within dotted circle. Legend in Chinese characters giving name of province and value, as well as two Manchu characters 280.00 500.00

Kiangsee (Kiangsi) 江 西

1 (412a) 10 Cash (Cu) 1912. Nine-pointed star in dotted circle and legend KIANG-SEE TEN CASH. R names of country, province, and denomination as well as date and value in eight Chinese characters ... 2.50 5.00

2 (412) 10 Cash (Cu) 1912. Obverse as No. 1. Rev. value in eleven Chinese characters 200.00 350.00

3 1 Dollar (Ag) 1912. Similar to No. 1, but value in the obverse legend ONE DOLLAR .... –.– –.–

Kwangsea (Kwangsi) 廣西

			VF	XF
1 (413)	1	Cent (Bra) 1919. The figure 1 in dotted circle and legend KWANG SEA PROVINCE ONE CENT. ℞ names of country, province, and denomination as well as date and value in Chinese characters	70.00	125.00
2 (413a)	1	Cent (Bra) 1919. As type No. 1, but in the obverse legend the name of the province reads KWANGSI	25.00	40.00
3 (414)	10	Cents (Ag) 1920, 1921. The figure 10 in circle and legend KWANG-SI PROVINCE TEN CENTS. ℞ name of province and denomination as well as date and value. The 1921 issue was only a pattern issue	80.00	150.00
4 (415)	20	Cents (Ag) 1919, 1920, 1924. As type No. 3, but on the obverse the figure 20 and the inscription KWANG-SEA PROVINCE TWENTY CENTS	60.00	90.00
5 (415a)	20	Cents (Ag) 1919–1923. As type No. 4, but in the obverse legend the name of the province KWANG-SI. The 1921 issue was only a pattern issue	20.00	30.00
6 (415a1)	20	Cents (Ag) 1924. As type No. 5, but in addition, in centre of reverse, a Chinese character for Kweilin	60.00	100.00
7	20	Cents (Ag) 1924. As type No. 6, but for the name of the province read KWANG-SEA instead of KWANG-SI	6.00	9.00
8	20	Cents (Ag) 1925. As type No. 5, but in addition, in centre of reverse, the Chinese character Si	–.–	–.–
9 (415b)	20	Cents (Ag) 1926, 1927. Similar to No. 7, but the figure 20 on obverse is surrounded by ears of corn	14.00	25.00
10	5	Cents (Ni) 1923. Figure 5 within wreath and legend KWANG-SI PROVINCE FIFE CENTS. ℞ name of country and province as well as date and value in Chinese characters. Pattern	–.–	–.–
11 (416)	20	Cents (Ag) 1949. Scenery with junk surrounded by 24 rosettes. ℞ Chinese characters, among which names of country and province as well as date and value	110.00	180.00

Values are given for each coin in U.S. Dollars and reference to Yeoman-numbers.

			VF	XF
1		10 Cents (Ag) 1912. Two crossed flags and five spears in dotted circle. Legend KWANG-TUNG PROVINCE TEN CENTS. ℞ names of country and province as well as date and value in Chinese characters. Pattern	–.–	–.–
2		10 Cents (Ag) 1912. Crossed flags with swords and guns in dotted circle. Legend KWANG-TUNG PROVINCE TEN CENTS. ℞ Chinese characters, among which name of province, date and value. Pattern	–.–	–.–
3 (417)		1 Cent (Bra) 1912, 1914–1916, 1918. Figure 1 in dotted circle and legend KWANG-TUNG PROVINCE ONE CENT. ℞ Chinese characters, among which names of country, province, and denomination as well as date and value	2.00	4.00
4 (418)		2 Cents (Bra) 1918. Type as No. 3	45.00	80.00
5 (422)		10 Cents (Ag) 1913, 1914, 1922. The figure 10 in dotted circle and legend KWANG-TUNG PROVINCE TEN CENTS. ℞ Chinese characters, among which name of province, date and value	4.00	6.00

			VF	XF
6 (423)		20 Cents (Ag) 1912–1915, 1918–1924. As type No. 5, but value in obverse in form of figure 20 and in the legend TWENTY CENTS	4.00	6.00
7 (420)		5 Cents (Ni) 1919. The figure 5 in wreath within dotted circle. Legend KWANG-TUNG PROVINCE FIVE CENTS. R names of country and province as well as date and value in Chinese characters	2.25	4.50
8 (420a)		5 Cents (Ni) 1923. Type similar to No. 7, but different Chinese characters	4.00	6.00

			VF	**X**

9 (421) 5 Cents (Ni) 1921. Flags in dotted circle and legend KWANG-TUNG PROVINCE FIVE CENTS. R names of country and province as well as date and value in Chinese characters — 4.50 — 8.C

10 (424) 20 Cents (Ag) 1924. Head l. of Dr. Sun Yat Sen. R Chinese characters, among which name of province, date and value — 18.00 — 30.C

11 (426) 20 Cents (Ag) 1928–1930. Head l. of Dr. Sun Yat Sen. Value in Chinese characters within wreath and legend in Chinese characters, among which name of province and date. The 1930 issue was only a pattern issue — 3.50 — 6.C

12 (425) 10 Cents (Ag) 1929. Head l. of Dr. Sun Yat Sen. R value in Chinese characters in dotted circle as well as names of country, province, and date forming legend in Chinese characters. Twelve-pointed sun to left and right — 2.50 — 4.C

13 (427) 1 Cent (Cu) 1936. Landscape with animals, country and province designation as well as the year, as an inscription, above in Chinese characters. R rice panicle as well as denomination in Chinese characters. A round hole in the centre — 200.00 — 320.C

Kweichow 貴州

COMMEMORATIVE ISSUE FOR THE FIRST ROAD IN KWEICHOW

1 (428) 1 Dollar (Ag) 1928. Automobile in dotted circle and legend in Chinese characters, among which name of province and value. R Chinese characters,

				VF	XF

among which name of country, date and value — 260.00 — 450.00

2 (429) 10 Cents (Antimony) 1931. Twelve-pointed sun in circle. ℞ four Chinese characters in circle and inscription in Chinese characters, among which names of country and province as well as date and value — 300.00 — 500.00

3 (431) 20 Cents (Ag) 1949. The figure 20 within circle made of 28 figures of 20. Meander pattern border. ℞ Chinese characters, among which names of country and province as well as date and value. Meander pattern border. Pattern — 250.00 — 400.00

4 (430) 20 Cents (Ag) 1949. Value in old Chinese seal characters within circle made of 30 figures of 20. ℞ similar to No. 2. Pattern — 250.00 — 350.00

5 (432) 50 Cents (Ag) 1949. The figure 50 within circle made of 32 figures of 50. Meander pattern border. ℞ similar to No. 2. Pattern — 350.00 — 700.00

6 (433) 1 Dollar (Ag) 1949. Bamboo stems (Gramineae family) in dotted circle; value to right and left in Chinese characters. ℞ pavilion within wreath and legend in Chinese characters, among which names of country and province as well as date. Pattern — 1000.00 — 1800.00

Manchuria 東三省

1 (434) 1 Cent (Cu) 1929. Sun composed of twelve rays in the floral wreath. ℞ denomination in Chinese characters in dotted circle. Country and province designation in Chinese characters — 3.00 — 5.00

2 1 Tael (Au) 1932 (undated). Chinese character "Fuh". ℞ inscription "24 K 1000" — –.– — –.–

3 1 Teal (Au) 1932 (undated). Chinese character "Hsih". ℞ inscription "24 K 1000" — –.– — –.–

4 1 Tael (Au) 1932 (undated). In the centre the character "Fuh" in ancient Chinese 'seal writing' in square border. Legend by way of four Chinese characters. ℞ "24 K 1000" and four Chinese characters in square border — –.–

5 1 Tael (Au) 1932 (?) (undated). Chinese character "Shou" in ancient Chinese 'seal writing'. ℞ inscription "24 K 1000" — –.– — –.–

Inner Mongolia 內蒙古

			VF	XF
1 (521)	50	Cents (Ni) 1938. Value in Chinese characters between stylized dragons. Above, seven Mongolian characters. ℞ Chinese characters between floral ornaments, among which name of country, mint, and date	8.00	15.00

North China

The provinces of Honan, Hopei, Hupeh, Shansi and Shantung were integrated into the Government territory of North China under the Japanese Occupation.

1 (523)	1	Cent (Al) 1941–1943. Sun temple; value to right and left in Chinese characters. ℞ in centre, three interlocking circles within double circle. Inscription in Chinese characters, among which legend reading "The Federal Reserve Bank", and date	0.60	1.20
2 (524)	5	Cents (Al) 1941–1943. As type No. 1	2.00	4.00
3 (525)	10	Cents (Al) 1941–1943. As type No. 1	1.50	3.00

Shansi 山西

1 (A435)	10	Cash (Cu) undated. Crossed flags within circle and legend in Chinese characters, among which names of country and province as well as value. ℞ value in Chinese characters between ears of corn	160.00	250.00
2	5	Cents (Ni) 1925. Crossed flags in dotted circle and legend in Chinese characters, among which name of country, date and value. ℞ name of province and denomination in Chinese characters within wreath	–.–	–.–

Shantung (Shangtung) 山東

1	10	Dollars (Au) 1926. Dragon and phoenix. ℞ value in Chinese characters within wreath. Legend in Chinese characters, among which name of country and date. Pattern		3500.00

			VF	XF
2	20	Dollars (Au) 1926. As type No. 1. Pattern		4000.00
3	2	Cents (Ni) 1933. Value in Chinese characters within ring of several rosettes. Above, value in Chinese characters; below, inscription TWO CENTS. ℞ crossed flags and legend in Chinese characters, among which names of country and province as well as date. Pattern	–.–	–.–

Shensi 陝 西

			VF	XF
1 (435)	1	Cent (Cu) 1924 (?) (undated). Crossed flags; inscription IMTYPIF	150.00	220.00
2 (436.1)	2	Cents (Cu) undated. Value in Chinese characters and ears of corn in dotted circle. In centre, dot within circle. Legend in Chinese characters, among which name of province and value. ℞ crossed flags in dotted circle. In centre, dot within circle. Legend above giving name of country in Chinese characters, and below, IMTYPEF	60.00	100.00
3 (436)	2	Cents (Cu) undated. Type as No. 2, but star between flags	75.00	110.00

Sinkiang (Chinese Turkestan) 新 疆

General issues for Sinkiang:

			VF	XF
1 (41a)	5	Mace (Ag) 1912. Crossed flags, date in Chinese characters between flag-staffs. ℞ Chinese characters, among which name of country and denomination as well as value	50.00	85.00
2 (42a)	1	Tael (Ag) 1912. As type No. 1	280.00	400.00
2a (41)	5	Mace (Ag) 1912. As type No. 1, but in the flags only two strips with arabesques	100.00	160.00
2b (42)	1	Tael (Ag) 1912. As type No. 2, but in the flags only two strips with arabesques	280.00	400.00
2c (39)	20	Cash (Cu) 1912 (undated). Crossed flags. ℞ province and coin designation by way of four Chinese characters in the dotted circle. In the legend, country designation and denomination in Chinese characters	100.00	125.00

			VF	XF
3 (46.2)	1	Dollar (Ag) 1949. The figure 1 and Arabic characters in dotted circle. In the legend, Arabic characters and date 1949. R value in Chinese characters within wreath of ears of corn. Legend in Chinese characters, among which names of country and province as well as value	–.–	–.–

Issues for Aksu: 阿 廾式

1 (37)	10	Cash (Cu) ND. Crossed flags and Arabic characters. Rev. Chinese characters. Cast (dia: 32 mm, and smaller dia: 29 mm	150.00	260.00
2 (40.2)	10	Cash (Cu) 1930 (CD). Crossed flags, Chinese characters. Rev. Chinese characters, in the centre a rosette	160.00	275.00

Issues for Kashgar: 喀 什

1 (36)	5	Cash (Cu) H-C 1331 (1913). Crossed flags, Arabic characters between flagstaffs. Rev. Chinese characters, among which name of country and value	120.00	200.00
2 (38)	10	Cash (Cu) H-C 1331, 1332 (1913, 1914). Type as No. 1	70.00	120.00
2a (38.3)	10	Cash (Cu) H-C 1334 (1916). Type similar to No. 2	–.–	–.–
3 (43)	5	Mace (Ag) H-C 1331, 1332, 1334 (1913, 1914, 1916). Crossed flags, between the flagstaffs Arabic characters. Rev. Chinese characters, among others name of country and province as well as denomination	30.00	50.00
4 (A36)	5	Cash (Cu) ND. Chinese characters. Rev. flag in dotted circle.	400.00	700.00
5 (B36)	10	Cash (Cu) ND. Type as No. 4	400.00	700.00
6 (38a)	10	Cash (Cu) 1921, 1922. Crossed flags, top and bottom between the flagstaffs Arabic characters. Rev. name of country in Chinese characters in the dotted circle. In the legend name of province, mint, date and denomination in Chinese characters	45.00	80.00
7 (44.6)	10	Cash (Cu) 1929, 1930. Crossed flags, above Chinese characters between the flagstaffs. Rev. Chinese characters, among others name of country and province as well as mint and denomination. In the centre a rosette	–.–	–.–

Issues for Tihwa (Urumchi): 廸化

			VF	XF
1 (45.1)	1	Tael (Ag) 1917. Arabic characters in dotted circle and border of leaf decoration and ears of corn. ℞ Chinese and Arabic characters in dotted circle as well as legend in Chinese characters, among which name of country, mint, date, and value	100.00	165.00
2 (45)	1	Tael (Ag) 1917. Type as No. 1, but in border decoration of leaves on obverse, in addition a rosette above (several variants through changes in the decoration of leaves)	100.00	165.00
3 (45.2)	1	Tael (Ag) 1918. Type as No. 1, but border decoration of leaves on obverse is of varied type (not in the form of corn-ears)	160.00	220.00

Szechuan 四川

1 (446)	5	Cash (Cu or Bra) 1912–1914. Inscription in old Chinese seal characters within circle, the whole surrounded by 18 rings. ℞ Chinese characters, among which name of province and denomination as well as value	80.00	125.00
2 (447)	10	Cash (Cu or Bra) 1912–1914. Similar to No. 1	3.00	5.00
3 (448)	20	Cash (Cu or Bra) 1912–1914. Similar to No. 1	3.00	5.00
4 (449)	50	Cash (Cu or Bra) 1912–1914. Similar to No. 1	4.00	6.00
5 (450)	100	Cash (Cu or Bra) 1912–1914. Similar to No. 1	6.00	11.00
6 (443)	5	Cash (Cu or Bra) 1912. Crossed flags. ℞ Chinese characters for Szechuan in centre	50.00	90.00

7 (441)	5	Cash (Cu or Bra) 1912. Lion and cloud	55.00	90.00
8	10	Cash (Cu or Bra) 1912	–.–	–.–
9	100	Cash (Cu or Bra) 1913	–.–	–.–
10 (459)	200	Cash (Cu or Bra) 1913. Crossed flags within dotted circle and legend THE REPUBLIC OF CHINA 200 CASH. ℞ Value in Chinese characters between ears of corn and flower decoration within dotted circle. Legend in Chinese characters, among which names of country and province	22.00	30.00
11	500	Cash (Cu) undated	–.–	–.–
12 (453)	10	Cents (Ag) 1912. In centre, Chinese characters in old Chinese seal characters, surrounded by 18 rings; above, name of country and date in Chinese characters. ℞ Chinese characters, among which name of province and value	20.00	35.00
13 (454)	20	Cents (Ag) 1912. Type as No. 12	35.00	55.00
14 (455)	50	Cents (Ag) 1912, 1913. Type as No. 12	22.00	40.00
15 (456)	1	Dollar (Ag) 1912, 1914. Type as No. 12	15.00	25.00
16	20	Cents (Ag) 1912. Lion above cloud. ℞ crossed flags within dotted circle; name of country and date above in Chinese characters	–.–	–.–
17	10	Cents (Ag) 1912. Value in Chinese characters within wreath of corn-ears. ℞ four Chinese characters with star in centre	–.–	–.–
19	5	Cents (Ni) 1925. Value in Chinese characters within circle; in centre, two circles. Name of country, date, and value forming legend in Chinese characters. ℞ four-pointed star between rice stalks	–.–	–.–
20 (468)	10	Cents (Ni) 1926 (undated). Value in Chinese characters surrounded by leaf ornaments. R crossed flags; dia. 23.7 mm	–.–	–.–
21 (468a)	10	Cents (Ag) 1926. Type as No. 20, but dia. 23 mm	–.–	–.–
22 (462)	50	Cash (Cu or Bra) 1926	35.00	55.00
23 (463)	100	Cash (Cu or Bra) 1926	10.00	18.00
24 (464)	200	Cash (Cu or Bra) 1926. In centre, Chinese character for Szechuan within circle. Legend with name of country, date, and value in Chinese characters. ℞ figure 200 in four-pointed star between rice stalks	12.00	20.00
25 (473)	50	Cents (Ag) 1928. Head facing of Dr. Sun Yat Sen within circle. Legend with name of province and date in Chinese characters. ℞ value in Chinese charac-		

			VF	XF
		ters between rice stalks and decoration of leaves	250.00	400.00
26 (474)	1	Dollar (Ag) 1928. Type as No. 25	450.00	700.00
27 (466)	100	Cash (Bra) 1926, 1930. Obverse similar to No. 22. Rev. twelve Chinese characters in four lines	160.00	250.00
28 (476)	2	Cents (Cu) 1930. In the centre a sun composed of 12 rays in a wreath of branches of buds; open at the top. Above inscription 2 CENTS. R Chinese characters (partly in ornamental border), among others name of country and province as well as date and denomination	200.00	350.00
29	20	Cents (Ag) 1932. Bust facing of Liu Wen Hwei (*1895), General and Governor of the Szechuan province, in uniform with cap. Legend in Chinese characters, among which name of province. R crossed flags and Chinese characters. Below the flags the date 1932	110.00	160.00
30	10	Fen (Cu) ND. Value between branches. Rev. Character Chuan in circle	–.–	–.–

Yunnan 雲南

			VF	XF
1 (478)	50	Cash (Bra) 1912 (undated). Bust turned half to l. of T'ang Chi-yao (1882 to 1927), General and Governor of the Yunnan province, within dotted circle. Border of leaf ornaments and, above, four Chinese characters. R crossed flags and legend in Chinese characters, among which name of province and value	20.00	35.00
2 (480)	50	Cents (Ag) 1916 (undated). Bust r. of General T'ang Chi-yao; above, legend of seven Chinese characters. R crossed flags in dotted circle; above, star between flag-staffs. Legend in Chinese characters, among which value	15.00	35.00
3 (479)	50	Cents (Ag) 1917 (undated). Bust turned half to l. of General T'ang Chi-yao within dotted circle. Border of leaf ornaments and, above, seven Chinese characters. R as No. 2	12.00	20.00
4	5	Dollars (Au) 1917 (undated). Value given by five Chinese characters arranged vertically. To right and left, a group of five dots. R blank	–.–	–.–
5	10	Dollars (Au) 1917 (undated). Type as No. 4	–.–	–.–

			VF	XF
6 (481.1)	5	Dollars (Au) 1919 (undated). Bust turned half to l..of General T'ang Chi-yao; above, legend of Chinese characters. ℞ crossed flags in dotted circle; above, five-pointed star between flag-staffs. Legend in Chinese characters, among which value	–.–	–.–
7 (482)	10	Dollars (Au) 1919 (undated). Type as No. 6	600.00	900.00
8 (481)	5	Dollars (Au) 1919 (undated). Type as No. 6, but figure 2 between flag-staffs on the reverse	600.00	900.00
9 (482.1)	10	Dollars (Au) 1919 (undated). Type as No. 7, but figure 1 between flag-staffs on the reverse	500.00	850.00
10 (485)	5	Cents (Ni) 1923. Flags within dotted circle and legend YUN-NAN PROVINCE FIFE CENTS. ℞ Chinese characters, among which name of country, date, and value	40.00	70.00
11 (486)	10	Cents (Ni) 1923. Type as No. 10, but value 10 CENTS in the obverse inscription	3.50	6.00
12	5	Dollars (Au) 1925 (undated). Value in four Chinese characters. In centre, rosette. ℞ Chinese character for Yunnan between ears of corn	750.00	1000.00
13	10	Dollars (Au) 1925 (undated). Type as No. 12, but dot in centre of obverse	850.00	1200.00
14	20	Cents (Ag) 1926. Crossed flags; above, five-pointed star, below, leaf ornament. ℞ Chinese characters, among which name of country and denomination as well as date and value. Pattern	–.–	–.–
14a (488)	1	Cent (Bra) 1932. Crossed flags in dotted circle. Rev. value	–.–	–.–
15 (489)	2	Cents (Bra) 1932. Type as No. 14a	300.00	450.00
16 (490)	5	Cents (Bra) 1932. Crossed flags within dotted circle. In centre, dot surrounded by circle. Above, figure 5 between flag-staffs. Legend in Chinese characters, among which name of country and date. R Chinese characters, among which name of province and value. In centre, dot surrounded by circle	200.00	320.00
17 (491)	20	Cents (Ag) 1932. Crossed flags within dotted circle; above, name of country and date in Chinese characters. R Chinese characters, among which name of province and denomination as well as value	10.00	18.00
18 (492)	50	Cents (Ag) 1932. Type as No. 17	7.50	12.00

			VF	**XF**

19 (493) 20 Cents (Ag) 1949. Building. R names of country and province as well as date and value in Chinese characters. In centre, rosette 25.00 40.00

Yunnan - Burma

Special coins were issued occasionally during the 2nd World War for the Chinese troops on the Yunnan-Burma Front. According to more recent information, this is supposed to concern issues by the troops of Chiang Kai-shek who had been forced on to Burmese territory by the Red Army of China.

1 (495) ½ Tael (Ag) 1949? (undated). Denomination in four Chinese characters, above a semicircle of Burmese characters. R characters in the so-called small 'seal writing', meaning "Luck" 35.00 60.00

2 (496) 1 Tael (Ag) 1949 (undated). Type as No. 1 ..... 40.00 70.00

			VF	**XF**
3 (497)	1 Tael (Ag) ND (1943?). Value in Burmese characters (one line) and in Chinese characters (two lines) within circle. Rev. head of stag within circle		45.00	80.00
4 (497.1)	1 Tael (Ag) 1943 (undated). Type as No. 3, but larger stag's head and longer antlers		–.–	–.–

Issues of the Communist People's Army

The Red Army of China (Communist People's Army) was established in 1928 during the Chinese civil war until the fall of the Central Government. Under the command of Mao Tse-tung and Chou Teh, this army occupied and governed, at different times, different provinces of China where it issued its own coins between 1931 and 1934. From 1947 to 1949 the Red Army of China occupied the whole of the Chinese mainland, so that the Central Government under General Chiang Kai-shek had to withdraw to Taiwan.

On the mainland, the People's Republic of China was formed in 1949, and in 1950, in Taiwan, the National Republic of China.

Issues for Kiangsee (Kiangsi).

1 (506)	1 Cent (Cu) 1932 (undated). Figure 1 in front of hammer and sickle; above, legend in Chinese characters. ℞ value in Chinese characters between ears of corn; above, five-pointed star		30.00	50.00
2 (507)	5 Cents (Cu) 1932 (undated). Hammer and sickle; in background, sketch of the land of China in dotted circle. Legend in Chinese characters. ℞ value in Chinese characters between ears of corn; above, five-pointed star		55.00	100.00

			VF	**XF**
3 (508)	20	Cents (Ag) 1932, 1933. Hammer and sickle in front of globe placed between ears of corn. Above, five-pointed star and Chinese characters. ℞ value and legend in Chinese characters, among which date	70.00	120.00

Issues for Hunan:

1 (501)	1	Dollar (Ag) 1930 (undated). Head right of Lenin (?) within circle. Above, inscription in Chinese characters. ℞ value in Chinese characters between hammer and sickle in double circle	–.–	–.–
2 (502)	1	Dollar (Ag) 1931. Hammer and sickle in front of five-pointed star within circle. Legend in Chinese characters. ℞ value in Chinese characters within wreath	–.–	–.–

Issues for Hupeh, Anhwei and Honan:

1 (503)	1	Dollar (Ag) 1932. Hammer and sickle in front of globe and legend in Chinese characters. ℞ value in Chinese characters within circle. Above, date in Chinese characters and, below, legend in pseudo-cyrillic characters	450.00	700.00
2 (504)	1	Dollar (Ag) 1932. Hammer and sickle in front of globe within dotted circle. In the legend, twelve Chinese characters. ℞ value in Chinese characters within circle. Legend in Chinese characters, among which date	300.00	500.00

Issues for Szechuan and Shensi:

1	20	Cents (Ag) 1932 (undated). In centre, a linear and a dotted circle. Legend in Chinese characters. ℞ crossed flags within dotted circle. Legend in Chinese characters	–.–	–.–
2 (510)	200	Cash (Cu) 1933. Hammer and sickle; above, three five-pointed stars. Chinese characters forming inscription above, and below, CCZC. ℞ figure 200 within wreath and legend in Chinese characters, among which date	150.00	250.00

3 (511) 200 Cash (Cu) 1934. Five-pointed star with hammer and sickle. Four Chinese characters between the points and the date 1934. ℞ figure 200 within circle and legend in Chinese characters, among which value

	VF	EF
	85.00	150.00

4 (512) 500 Cash (Cu) 1934. Hammer and sickle in front of five-pointed star and legend in Chinese characters, among which date. ℞ figure 500 within circle and legend in Chinese characters, among which value — 150.00 — 250.00

5 (513) 1 Dollar (Ag) 1934. Hammer and sickle in front of globe. Legend in Chinese characters, among which date. ℞ value in dotted circle and legend in Chinese characters — 200.00 — 320.00

Values are given for each coin in U.S. Dollars and reference to Yeoman-numbers.

People's Republic of China

Chinesische Volksrepublik　　**République populaire du Chine**

Chung Hua Ren Min Gung Ho Kuo

中 華 人 民 共 和 國

Area: 3,700,000 sq. mi. Population: 1,025,000,000.

The Red Army of China (Communist People's Army) which was formed in 1928 during the Chinese civil war, occupied the whole of the Chinese mainland from 1947 to 1949 whilst fighting against the troops of the Central Government of the Republic of China, so that the Central Government under General Chiang Kai-shek had to withdraw to Taiwan. On 1st October 1949, the People's Republic of China was set up in Peking.

Capital: Peking.

100 Fen 分 = 1 Yuan 圓 or 元
since June 1969: 100 Fen = 10 Chiao = 1 Renminbi Yuan

			XF	Unc
1 (1)	1 Fen (Al) 1955–. National arms of the People's Republic of China; above, name of country in Chinese characters. ℞ value in Chinese characters between ears of corn; above, value and below, date in Arabic figures		0.10	0.25
2 (2)	2 Fen (Al) 1955–. Type as No. 1		0.20	0.35

3 (3)	5 Fen (Al) 1955–. Type as No. 1		0.25	0.40

Proof

4 (4)	400 Yuan (Au) 1979. Tian An Men	250.00
5 (5)	400 Yuan (Au) 1979. People's Heroes Monument	250.00
6 (6)	400 Yuan (Au) 1979. Chairman Mao Tse Tung Memorial Hall	250.00
7 (7)	400 Yuan (Au) 1979. Great Hall of the People	250.00

INTERNATIONAL YEAR OF THE CHILD 1979 (2)

8 (8)	35 Yuan (Ag) 1979. Girl and boy watering flower	35.00
9 (9)	450 Yuan (Ag) 1979. Type as No. 8:	
	a) 17.2 gm.	225.00
	b) 34,4 gm., Piéfort	1200.00

13th OLYMPIC WINTER GAMES IN LAKE PLACID (6)

10 (15)	1 Yuan (Bra) 1980. Speed Skating	6.00
11 (14)	1 Yuan (Bra) 1980. Alpine Skiing	6.00
12 (16)	1 Yuan (Bra) 1980. Figure Skating	6.00
13 (17)	1 Yuan (Bra) 1980. Biathlon	6.00
14 (21)	30 Yuan (Ag) 1980. Type as No. 10:	
	a) .800 silver, 15 g	20.00
	b) Piéfort	100.00
A14	30 Yuan (Ag) 1980. Type as No. 11. Piéfort	100.00
B14	30 Yuan (Ag) 1980. Type as No. 12. Piéfort	100.00
C14	30 Yuan (Ag) 1980. Type as No. 13. Piéfort	100.00
15 (22)	250 Yuan (Au) 1980. Type as No. 11:	
	a) .916⅔ gold, 8 g	150.00
	b) Piéfort	1000.00

				Proof
16 (11)	1	Yuan (Bra) 1980. Wrestling		6.00
17 (12)	1	Yuan (Bra) 1980. Equestrian		6.00
18 (13)	1	Yuan (Bra) 1980. Soccer		6.00
19 (10)	1	Yuan (Bra) 1980. Archery		6.00
20 (18)	20	Yuan (Ag) 1980. Type as No. 16		15.00
21 (19)	30	Yuan (Ag) 1980. Type as No. 17		25.00
22 (20)	30	Yuan (Ag) 1980. Type as No. 18		25.00
23 (23)	300	Yuan (Au) 1980. Type as No. 19		250.00

				Unc
24 (24)	1	Chiao (Bra) 1980–. Arms. Rev. value		0.50
25 (25)	2	Chiao (Bra) 1980–. Type as No. 24		0.60
26 (26)	5	Chiao (Bra) 1980–. Type as No. 24		0.80

27 (27)	1	Yuan (Cu-Ni) 1980–. Great Wall of China		1.80

CHINESE BRONZE AGE FINDS (4)

				Proof
28 (29)	200	Yuan (Au) 1981. Dragon		250.00
29 (28)	200	Yuan (Au) 1981. Leopard		250.00
30 (30)	400	Yuan (Au) 1981. Rhinocerous		400.00
31 (31)	800	Yuan (Au) 1981. Elephant		800.00

YEAR OF THE ROOSTER (2)

			Proof
32 (32)	30	Yuan (Ag) 1981. Pagoda. Rev. Rooster	80.00
33 (33)	250	Yuan (Au) 1981. Type as No. 32	400.00

70th ANNIVERSARY OF THE REVOLUTION (2)

34 (46)	35	Yuan (Ag) 1981. Statue of Dr. Sun Yat Sen. Rev. Monument	60.00
35 (47)	400	Yuan (Au) 1981. Bust of Dr. Sun Yat Sen. Rev. Revolutionary	300.00

WORLD SOCCER CHAMPIONSHIP GAMES 1982 IN SPAIN (4)

36 (34)	1	Yuan (Bra) 1982. Soccer	6.00
37 (35)	25	Yuan (Ag) 1982. Two soccers, emblem above	20.00
38 (36)	25	Yuan (Ag) 1982. Two soccers, emblem right	20.00
39 (37)	200	Yuan (Au) 1982. Soccer	200.00

YEAR OF THE DOG (2)

40 (38)	20	Yuan (Ag) 1982. Pagoda. Rev. Dog	50.00
41 (39)	200	Yuan (Au) 1982. Type as No. 40	350.00

No. 42 omitted.

BULLION ISSUE (4)

43 (40)	1/10	Ounce (Au) 1982. Pagoda. Rev. Panda; 3.11 g	–.–
44 (41)	¼	Ounce (Au) 1982. Type as No. 43; 7.77 g	–.–
45 (42)	½	Ounce (Au) 1982. Type as No. 43; 15.55 g	–.–
46 (43)	1	Ounce (Au) 1982. Type as No. 43; 31.10 g	–.–

YEAR OF THE PIG (2)

		Proof
47 (44)	10 Yuan (Ag) 1983. Palace. Rev. Two pigs	40.00
48 (45)	150 Yuan (Au) 1983. Type as No. 47	300.00

BULLION ISSUE (5)

		P/L
49 (48)	5 Yuan (Au) 1983. Pagoda. Rev. Panda; 1.55 g	–.–
50 (49)	10 Yuan (Au) 1983. Type as No. 49; 3.11 g	–.–
51 (50)	25 Yuan (Au) 1983. Type as No. 49; 7.77 g	–.–
52 (51)	50 Yuan (Au) 1983. Type as No. 49; 15.55 g	–.–
53 (52)	100 Yuan (Au) 1983. Type as No. 49; 31.10 g	–.–

		Proof
54 (58)	1 Yuan (Bra) 1983, 1984. Arms. Rev. Panda	8.00
55 (57)	10 Yuan (Ag) 1983. Pagoda. Rev. Two pandas	100.00

660th ANNIVERSARY OF THE DEATH OF MARCO POLO (4)

56 (53)	5 Chiao (Ag) 1983. Great Wall of China. Rev. Marco Polo (1254–1324), Venecian merchant and globe-trotter	6.00
57 (54)	5 Yuan (Ag) 1983. Rev. Marco Polo and sailing vessel »Epopea«	40.00
58 (55)	10 Yuan (Au) 1983. Type as No. 56	50.00
59 (56)	100 Yuan (Au) 1983. Type as No. 57	300.00

YEAR OF THE RAT (2)

60 (59)	10 Yuan (Ag) 1984. Palace. Rev. »Rat« from a painting by Qi Baishi	50.00
61 (60)	150 Yuan (Au) 1984. Type as No. 60	300.00

OLYMPIC WINTER GAMES

62 (64)	10 Yuan (Ag) 1984. Speed Skating	40.00

		Proof
63 (61)	5 Yuan (Ag) 1984. High jumper	25.00
64 (63)	10 Yuan (Ag) 1984. Volleyball	40.00

U.N. DECADE OF WOMEN 1976–1985 (2)

65 (62)	10 Yuan (Ag) ND (1984). Women heads	35.00
66 (89)	200 Yuan (Ag) ND (1985)	200.00

CHINESE CULTURE – 1st ISSUE

67 (68)	5 Yuan (Ag) 1984	40.00
68 (69)	5 Yuan (Ag) 1984	40.00
69 (70)	5 Yuan (Ag) 1984	40.00
70 (71)	5 Yuan (Ag) 1984	40.00
71 (72)	100 Yuan (Au) 1984	320.00
72 (67)	10 Yuan (Ag) 1984. Pagoda. Rev. Panda	90.00

BULLION ISSUE (6)

		Unc
73 (73)	5 Yuan (Au) 1984. Pagoda. Rev. Panda; 1,55 g	40.00
74 (74)	10 Yuan (Au) 1984. Type as No. 73; 3,11 g	70.00
75 (75)	25 Yuan (Au) 1984. Type as No. 73; 7,77 g	175.00
76 (76)	50 Yuan (Au) 1984. Type as No. 73; 15,55 g	300.00
77 (77)	100 Yuan (Au) 1984. Type as No. 73; 31,10 g	900.00
78 (66)	1000 Yuan (Au) 1984; 373,24 g	16.000.00

35th ANNIVERSARY OF PEOPLE'S REPUBLIC (3)

			Proof
79 (85)	1	Yuan (Cu-Ni) 1984. Rev. Proclamation of the Republic by Mao Tse-Tung	4.50
80 (86)	1	Yuan (Cu-Ni) 1984. Rev. Folklore Dancers, T'ien-an men in background	4.50
81 (87)	1	Yuan (Cu-Ni) 1984. Rev. T'ien-an men Tower, flying cranes	4.50
82 (88)	10	Yuan (Ag) 1984. Jie-Mei scool. Rev. Dr. Cheng Jiageng, .925 silver, 27 g	70.00

YEAR OF THE OX (2)

83 (78)	10	Yuan (Ag) 1985	60.00
84 (79)	150	Yuan (Au) 1985	300.00

BULLION ISSUE (5)

			P/L
85 (80)	5	Yuan (Au) 1985. Temple of Heaven. Rev. Panda	35.00
86 (81)	10	Yuan (Au) 1985	55.00
87 (82)	25	Yuan (Au) 1985	125.00
88 (83)	50	Yuan (Au) 1985	240.00
89 (84)	100	Yuan (Au) 1985	900.00

20th ANNIVERSARY OF TIBET AUTONOMOUS REGION (2)

			BU	Proof
90 (96)	1	Yuan (Cu-Ni) 1985. Potala Palace at Lhasa, residence of the Dalai Lama	5.00	7.50
91 (97)	10	Yuan (Ag) 1985. Type as No. 90		45.00

92 (109)	1 Yuan (Cu-Ni) 1985. Great Hall of the People. Rev. Female farm worker and harvest scene	5.00		7.50
93 (110)	10 Yuan (Ag) 1985. Type as No. 92			45.00
94	5 Ounces Fine Silver (Ag) 1985. Type as No. 92			180.00

CHINESE CULTURE – 2nd ISSUE (5)

95 (90)	5 Yuan (Ag) 1985. Rev. Lao-Tse		50.00
96 (91)	5 Yuan (Ag) 1985. Rev. Qu-Yuan		50.00
97 (92)	5 Yuan (Ag) 1985. Rev. Sun-Wu		50.00
98 (93)	5 Yuan (Ag) 1985. Rev. Cheng-Sheng and Wu-Guang		50.00
99 (94)	100 Yuan (Au) 1985. Rev. Confucius		265.00
		BU	**Proof**
100 (95)	10 Yuan (Ag) 1985. Rev. Female panda with cub		

YEAR OF THE TIGER (2)

101 (98)	10 Yuan (Ag) 1986		40.00
102 (99)	150 Yuan (Au) 1986		300.00

103 (106) 5 Yuan (Ag) 1986. Rev. Giant Panda (Ailuropoda melanoleuca – Procyonidae), .900 silver, 22,22 g   50.00

104 (107) 100 Yuan (Au) 1986. Rev. Wild Yak (Bos grunniens – Bovidae), .9167 gold, 11,31 g   250.00

BULLION ISSUE (6)

			P/L
105 (101)	5 Yuan (Au) 1986. Temple of Heaven. Rev. Panda in bamboo forest		35.00
106 (102)	10 Yuan (Au) 1986		55.00
107 (103)	25 Yuan (Au) 1986		125.00
108 (104)	50 Yuan (Au) 1986		240.00
109 (105)	100 Yuan (Au) 1986		500.00

No. 105–109, presentation set with »P« mintmark, proof (10.000 Ex.) –.–

Proof

110 (118) 1000 Yuan (Au) 1986. Rev. Female panda with cub   9.000.00

WORLD SOCCER CHAMPIONSHIP GAMES 1986 IN MEXICO (2)

			Proof
111 (112)	5 Yuan (Ag) 1986. Rev. Soccer player in action		35.00
112	5 Yuan (Ag) 1986		35.00

INTERNATIONAL YEAR OF PEACE (2)

113 (119)	5 Yuan (Ag) 1986. Rev. Goddess of Peace with doves		35.00
114 (120)	100 Yuan (Au) 1986. Type as No. 113		300.00

No. 115 omitted.

CHINESE CULTURE – 3rd ISSUE (5)

116 (116)	5 Yuan (Ag) 1986. Rev. Si Ma Quain	35.00
117 (113)	5 Yuan (Ag) 1986. Rev. Cai Lun	35.00
118 (114)	5 Yuan (Ag) 1986. Rev. Zhang Heng	35.00
119 (115)	5 Yuan (Ag) 1986. Rev. Zu Chang Zhi	35.00
120 (117)	100 Yuan (Au) 1986. Rev. Liu Bang on A horseback	300.00

120th ANNIVERSARY OF BIRTH OF DR. SUN-YAT-SEN (2)

121 (111)	10 Yuan (Ag) 1986. Portrait. Rev. Sun-Yat-Sen's residence, .999 silver, 27 g	40.00
122 (108)	50 Yuan (Ag) 1986. Arms. Rev. Dr. Sun-Yat-Sen, .999 silver, 155.5 g	200.00

		BU	**Proof**
123	5 Yuan (Ag) 1986. The Great Wall of China. Rev. Sailing ship	40.00	

YEAR OF THE RABBIT (3)

124	10 Yuan (Ag) 1987. The Yellow Pavillon at Wuhan. Rev. Two rabbits, .900 silver, 15 g	45.00
125	50 Yuan (Ag) 1987. Type as No. 124, .999 silver, 155,5 g	200.00
126	150 Yuan (Au) 1987. Type as No. 124, .9167 gold, 8 g	300.00

RAILWAY COMMEMORATIVE

A126	100 Yuan (Ag) 1987	400.00

P/L

127 (124)   5 Yuan (Au) 1987. Temple of Heaven. Rev. Panda   35.00
128 (125) 10 Yuan (Au) 1987   55.00
129 (126) 25 Yuan (Au) 1987   125.00
130 (127) 50 Yuan (Au) 1987   240.00
131 (128) 100 Yuan (Au) 1987   500.00

No. 127–131 come with »S« mintmark (for Shanghai) or »Y« mintmark (for Shengyang).

Presentation Proof sets of No. 127–131 bear a »P« mintmark.

Kolumbien   # Colombia   **Colombie**

Area: 437,822 sq. mi. Population: 29,000,000.

After the discovery by Hojeda and Vespucci in the year 1499 and the conquest, the kingdom of the Chibcha was made a Spanish Viceroyalty, which also included Ecuador. The Wars of Independence against the Spanish domination began in 1810. The state of Colombia, also known for a long time as New Grenada, also included, temporarily, the countries of Panama and Venezuela as well as Ecuador.

Capital: Bogotá.

100 Centavos = 1 Colombian Peso

REPUBLIC OF COLOMBIA

			VF	XF
1 (23)	2½ Centavos (Cu-Ni) 1900, 1902. Cap of Liberty. R value within circle		125.00	200.00
2 (25)	5 Centavos (Cu-Ni) 1886, 1902. Head of Liberty to left. R value between branches		1.00	2.00
3 (28a)	50 Centavos (Ag) 1889, 1898–1899, 1906 to 1908. Head of Liberty to left. R national arms, value in letters		10.00	20.00
4 (42)	1 Peso (Cu-Ni) 1907–1916. Head of Liberty to right. R value within wreath		2.00	3.00
5 (43)	2 Pesos (Cu-Ni) 1907–1914. Type as No. 4		4.00	8.00
6 (44)	5 Pesos (Cu-Ni) 1907–1914. Type as No. 4		2.00	4.50
7 (45)	5 Centavos (Ag) 1902. Head of Liberty to left. R national arms and value in letters		3.00	5.00
8 (46)	50 Centavos (Ag) 1902. Head of Liberty to left. R national arms and value in letters		25.00	35.00
9 (47)	10 Centavos (Ag) 1911–1942. Simón Bolívar (1783–1830), President of State 1810–1812. R national arms with Andean condor (Vultur gryphus — Cathartidae)		2.00	4.00
10 (48)	20 Centavos (Ag) 1911–1942. Type as No. 9		4.00	6.00
11 (49)	50 Centavos (Ag) 1912–1934. Type as No. 9		8.00	12.50

			VF	XF
12 (50)	2½	Pesos (Au) 1913. Workman cutting stone. R national arms	75.00	100.00
13 (51)	5	Pesos (Au) 1913–1919. Type as No. 12	110.00	150.00
14 (52)	2½	Pesos (Au) 1919–1920. Large head to right of Simón Bolívar, reaching almost to the border above and below. R national arms	60.00	90.00
15 (53)	5	Pesos (Au) 1919–1924. Type as No. 14	110.00	145.00
16 (54)	10	Pesos (Au) 1919–1924. Type as No. 14	225.00	320.00
17 (55)	2½	Pesos (Au) 1924–1928. Smaller head to right of Simón Bolívar. R national arms		
18 (56)	5	Pesos (Au) 1924–1930. Type as No. 17	60.00	90.00
19 (57)	1	Centavo (Cu–Ni) 1918–1948. Head of Liberty to right. R value within wreath	100.00 0.20	125.00 0.50
20 (57a)	1	Centavo (Ni–St) 1952–1958. Type as No. 19	0.10	0.20
21 (61)	1	Centavo. Cap of Liberty within wreath. R value between branches		
		a) (Br) 1942–1966	0.20	0.30
		b) (Br–St) 1967–	0.10	0.20
22 (59)	2	Centavos (Cu–Ni) 1918–1947. Head of Liberty to right. R value within wreath	0.30	0.50
23 (62)	2	Centavos (Br) 1948–1950. Cap of Liberty within wreath. R value between branches	1.00	2.00
24 (60)	5	Centavos (Cu–Ni) 1918–1950. Head of Liberty to right. R value within wreath	0.50	1.00
25 (63)	5	Centavos (Br) 1942–1966. Phrygian cap between branches tied below. R branches of the coffee tree, denomination	0.35	0.60
26 (64)	10	Centavos. Head right of Francisco de Paula Santander (1792–1840), President of State of New Grenada (1832-1836). R value within wreath		
		a) (Ag) 1945–1952	1.00	2.00
		b) (Ni–St) 1967–1969	0.20	0.30
27 (65)	20	Centavos		
		a) (Ag) 1945–1952 (1952 very rare)	1.40	2.50
		b) (Ni–St) 1967–1969	0.30	0.50
28 (66)	50	Centavos (Ag) 1947–1948. Head left of Simón Bolívar. R value within wreath	5.00	10.00
29 (A 65)	50	Centavos (Ni–St) 1967–1969. Type as No. 26	0.50	0.80
30 (67)	2	Centavos (Al–Br) 1952–1965. Head of Liberty to left. R value within wreath	0.25	0.40
A30 (67a)	2	Centavos (Al-Br) 1955, 1959, 1961, 1963, 1964, 1965. Type as No. 30, but full circular inscription	0.25	0.40

All valuations in the SCHÖN are stated in U.S. Dollars.

			VF	**XF**
31 (68)	10	Centavos (Cu–Ni) 1952–1966. National arms. ℞ head right of the Indian Chief Calarcá; value		
		a) 1952, 1953, diameter 18 mm	0.30	0.60
		b) 1954–1966, diameter 18.5 mm	0.15	0.30

32 (69)	20	Centavos (Ag) 1953. National arms. ℞ bust left of Simón Bolívar	1.70	3.00
33 (70)	20	Centavos (Cu–Ni) 1956–1966. Head right of Simón Bolívar. ℞ national arms	0.30	0.60
34 (71)	50	Centavos (Cu–Ni) 1958–1966. Type as No. 33	0.70	1.20

COMMEMORATIVE ISSUE FOR THE 200th ANNIVERSARY OF THE EXISTENCE OF THE MINT AT POPAYÁN

35 (72)	1	Peso (Ag) 1956. Mint building surrounded by laurel branches, inscription CASA DE MONEDA 1756–1956. ℞ national arms and value	10.00	18.00

COMMEMORATIVE ISSUES (6) FOR THE 150th ANNIVERSARY OF THE BEGINNING OF THE WARS OF INDEPENDENCE

36 (73)	1	Centavo (Br). Dates 1810–1960	1.60	3.00
37 (74)	2	Centavos (Al–Br). Dates 1810–1960	2.00	3.60
38 (A 74)	5	Centavos (Br). Dates 1810–1960	2.60	4.80
39 (75)	10	Centavos (Cu–Ni). Dates 1810–1960	2.00	3.00
40 (76)	20	Centavos (Cu–Ni). Dates 1810–1960	2.00	3.00
41 (77)	50	Centavos (Cu–Ni). Dates 1810–1960	2.50	4.00

COMMEMORATIVE ISSUES (2) FOR JORGE ELIECER GAITAN

			VF	XF
42 (78)	20	Centavos (Cu-Ni) 1965. Jorge Eliecer Gaitán (1898–1948), attorney, liberal politician. R national arms	0.30	0.60
43 (79)	50	Centavos (Cu-Ni) 1965. Type as No. 42	0.60	1.00
44 (80)	1	Peso (Cu-Ni) 1967. Simón Bolívar. R value within wreath	0.50	0.80
45 (63a)	5	Centavos (Br-St) 1967–1979. Jacobean cap, or Liberty cap, surrounded by branches. Rev. branches of the coffee tree (Coffea arabica – Rubiaceae) with blossom and fruit; cornucopia	0.10	0.20

COMMEMORATIVE ISSUES (6) FOR THE 39th EUCHARISTIC WORLD CONGRESS IN BOGOTÁ
from 22nd to 24th August 1968

			VF	XF
46 (81)	5	Pesos (Cu–Ni) 1968. Emblem of the World Congress, by Dr. Dicken Castro: a cross made of fishes representing the mission work extending to all four corners of the earth. R value within wreath	1.20	1.80

			Unc	Proof
47	100	Pesos (Au) 1968. Pope Paul VI (1897–1978); the cathedral on Plaza de Bolivar in Bogotá; emblem of the World Congress. R national arms, value	65.00	75.00
48	200	Pesos (Au) 1968. Type as No. 47	120.00	150.00
49	300	Pesos (Au) 1968. Type as No. 47	175.00	200.00
50	500	Pesos (Au) 1968. Type as No. 47	280.00	350.00
51	1500	Pesos (Au) 1968. Type as No. 47	1000.00	1000.00

COMMEMORATIVE ISSUES (5) FOR THE 150th ANNIVERSARY OF THE BATTLE OF BOYACÁ

| **52** | 100 | Pesos (Au) 1969. Simón Bolívar (1783 to 1830), national hero of Latin Ameri- |

| | | ca. ℞ Joaqín París y Ricaurte (1795 to 1868), Colombian General; national arms, value | **Proof** 80.00 |
| 53 | 200 | Pesos (Au) 1969. ℞ Carlos Soublette (†1870), Venezuelan General; national arms, value | 160.00 |

54	300	Pesos (Au) 1969. ℞ José Antonio Anzoátegui (1789–1819), Venezuelan General; national arms, value		240.00
55	500	Pesos (Au) 1969. ℞ Juan José Rondón (c. 1780–1822), Colombian General; national arms, value		400.00
56	1500	Pesos (Au) 1969. ℞ Francisco de Paula Santander (1792–1840), General, President of State of New Grenada 1832 to 1836; national arms, value		1100.00
57 (82)	10	Centavos (Ni-clad steel) 1969–1971. Type as No. 26, but legend divided after REPUBLICE DE	**VF** 0.10	**XF** 0.20
A57 (82.1)	10	Centavos (Ni-clad steel) 1970, 1971. Type as No. 57, but legend divided after REPUBLICA	0.10	0.20
B57 (82.2)	10	Centavos (Ni-clad steel) 1972–1979. Type as No. 57, but legend continuous	0.10	0.20
58 (83)	20	Centavos (Ni-clad steel) 1969, 1970. Type as No. A 57	0.10	0.20
A58 (83.1)	20	Centavos (Ni-clad steel) 1971. Type as No. 57	0.10	0.20
B58 (83.2)	20	Centavos (Ni-clad steel) 1971–1978. Type as No. B57	0.10	0.20
59 (84)	50	Centavos (Ni-clad steel) 1970–1973, 1975–1979. Type as No. B57	0.15	0.30
60 (84)	50	Centavos (Ni-clad steel) 1974. Type as No. 59, but large date	0.20	0.35

			VF	XF
61 (85)	5 Pesos (Cu-Ni) 1971. Emblem of the games		0.75	1.50

			Proof
62 (86)	100 Pesos (Au) 1971. Indian throwing spear		80.00
63 (87)	200 Pesos (Au) 1971. Indian running		160.00
64 (88)	300 Pesos (Au) 1971. Indian prophet and teacher		250.00
65 (89)	500 Pesos (Au) 1971. Indian goddes with son		380.00
66 (90)	1500 Pesos (Au) 1971. Figures on raft		1200.00

COMMEMORATIVE ISSUE FOR THE 50th ANNIVERSARY OF THE GOLD MUSEUM (MUSEO DE ORO) OF THE CENTRAL BANK OF BOGOTÁ

67 (91)	1500 Pesos (Au) 1973. Pre-Columbian urn, rare archeological treasure, made by Chibcha Indians. ℞ value		300.00

100th ANNIVERSARY OF THE BIRTH OF GUILLERMO VALENCIA (3)

68 (92)	1000 Pesos (Au) 1973. Guillermo Valencia (1873-1943), bust right. ℞ coat of arms, value, date		100.00
69 (93)	1500 Pesos (Au) 1973. Type as No. 68		160.00
70 (94)	2000 Pesos (Au) 1973. Type as No. 68		250.00

			VF	XF
71 (95)	1 Peso (German silver) 1974–1981. Bust of Simón Bolívar (1783-1830), statesman and general, liberator of South America from Spanish rule. Rev. corn cob (Zea mays – Gramineae) and value		0.15	0.40

Proof

72 (96) 1000 Pesos (Au) 1975. Explorer Rodrigo de
Bastidas. Rev. Indian sculpture 90.00
73 (97) 2000 Pesos (Au) 1975. Type as No. 72 ...... 175.00

300th ANNIVERSARY OF THE CITY MEDELLIN (2)

74 (98) 1000 Pesos (Au) 1975. Arms of the city.
Rev. Orchids 85.00
75 (99) 2000 Pesos (Au) 1975. Type as No. 74 ...... 175.00

			XF	Unc
76 (100)	2 Pesos (Cu-Ni) 1977–1981, 1983. Simón Bolívar. Rev. value within wreath. Composition: Cu 92%, Ni 8%		0.20	0.50

No. 77 omitted.

CONSERVATION COMMEMORATIVE (3)

			Unc	Proof
78 (101)	500 Pesos (Ag) 1978. Head of Tomas Cipriano de Mosquera. Rev. Orinoco crocodile:			
	a) .925 silver, 25.31 g		25.00	
	b) .925 silver, 28.28 g			30.00
79 (102)	750 Pesos (Ag) 1978. Rev. Chestnut-bellied hummingbird:			
	a) .925 silver, 31.65 g		35.00	
	b) .925 silver, 35.00 g			45.00
80 (103)	15000 Pesos (Au) 1978. Rev. Ocelot, .900 gold, 33.43 g		500.00	700.00

			XF	Unc
81 (83.3)	20 Centavos (Cu-Ni) 1979, 1980. Head of Santander		0.10	0.20

			XF	Unc
82 (104)	25 Centavos (Al-Br) 1979, 1980. Head of Santander		0.30	0.60

	XF	Unc
83 (105) 5 Pesos (Cu-Ni) 1980, 1981, 1983. Policarpa Salavarrieta (1795–1817), patriot, Rev. factory. Composition: Cu 90%, Ni 10%	1.00	1.80

DEATH OF SIMON BOLIVAR

	XF	Unc
84 (106) 30000 Pesos (Au) 1980. Fasces between cornucopias. Rev. Simón Bolivar on death-bed	Proof	700.00
85 (107) 10 Pesos (Cu-Ni) 1981, 1983. Cordoba on horseback. Rev. San Andres and Providencia, islands	0.60	1.00
86 (108) 20 Pesos (Al-Br) 1982. Pre-Columbian urn. Rev. value within wreath	1.00	2.00

CONSTUTION CENTENARY AND 50th ANNIVERSARY OF THE CONSTITUTION REFORM

	XF	Unc
87 50 Pesos (Al-Br) 1987. Arms. Rev. Capitol in Bogotá	1.00	2.00

Previous issues, see "Weltmünzkatalog 19. Jahrhundert" (World Coin Catalogue of the 19th Century)

Santander

During the revolt, the province of Santander was governed by General Ramon Gonzales Valencia, at whose instigation provisional issues were struck in 1902. (These were made from the brass of old cartridges, and are in relief on one side and intaglio on the other).

			VF	XF
1 (S 1)	10	Centavos (Bra) (1902). Undated. Inscription SANTANDER, value 10/C. ℞ no inscription	20.00	30.00
2 (S 2)	20	Centavos (Bra) 1902. Inscription SANTANDER, the figure 20 within the C of Centavos; below, date	22.00	32.00
3 (S 3)	50	Centavos (Bra) 1902. Type as No. 2	18.00	30.00

Area: 835 sq. mi. Population: 370,000.

The group of islands with the main islands of Anjouan, Great Comoro, Mayotte and Moheli (or Mohilla), situated in the Indian Ocean facing the coast of Africa, East of Mozambique, were governed until 1912 by the four sultans, deposed after this date. The island of Mayotte had been a French protectorate since 1841, the whole group of islands since 1886; since 1912 administered from Madagascar; self-governing since 1925. The autonomy awarded on 9th May 1946 was converted in 1961 to the status of an overseas territory within the framework of the French Community. The franc system was introduced in 1889 on all the islands and the coins brought into circulation were struck in Paris. In 1975 the Comoro Islands became the independent Republic of the Comoros. Mayotte retained the option of determining its future ties.

Capital: Moroni.

100 Centimes = 1 Franc

COLONY

			VF	XF
1 (1)	5	Centimes (Br) H. C. 1308, 1319 (1890, 1901). Arabic inscription	12.00	20.00
2 (2)	10	Centimes (Br) H. C. 1308, 1319	13.00	22.00

OVERSEAS TERRITORY

3 (4)	1	Franc (Al-Mg) 1964. Allegorical figure of the French Republic. ℞ coconut palm (Cocos nucifera – Palmae) and value	0.60	1.50
4 (5)	2	Francs (Al-Mg) 1964	0.30	0.60

5 (6)	5	Francs (Al-Mg) 1964	0.45	0.80
6 (7)	10	Francs (Ni-bra) 1964. ℞ Pacific trumpet shell (Charonia tritonis – Cymatiidae or Tritonidae, family of the mantled creatures), fruit and Coelacanth fish (Latimeria chalumnae – Latimeriidae or Coelacanthidae)	0.75	1.50
7 (8)	20	Francs (Ni-Bra) 1964. Type as No. 6	0.85	1.75

REPUBLIC
FOR THE INDEPENDENCE

		XF	Unc
8 (9)	50 Francs (Ni) 1975. Mosque. Rev. value, date, above arms	0.75	1.25

		Unc	Proof
9	5000 Francs (Ag) 1976. Cluster of flowers	45.00	45.00
10	10000 Francs (Au) 1976. Hummingbird	65.00	65.00
11	20000 Francs (Au) 1976. Coelacanth fish	150.00	150.00

FOR THE FAO COIN PLAN

		XF	Unc
12 (10)	100 Francs (Ni) 1977. Fishing cutter	1.20	2.00

ISLAMIC FEDERAL REPUBLIC OF THE COMOROS

13 (11)	25 Francs (Ni) 1981, 1982. Chickens. Rev. value, date (FAO issue)	0.65	1.00

WORLD FISHERIES CONFERENCE

14 (12)	5 Francs (Al) 1984. Coelacanth fish (Latimeria chalumnae – Latimeriidae or Coelacanthidae). Rev. Palms and value	0.75	1.00

Previous issue, see »Weltmünzkatalog 19. Jahrhundert« (World coin Catalogue of the 19th Century)

Congo (Brazzaville)

Volksrepublik Kongo   **Congo (République populaire du)**
People's Republic of the Congo

Area: 132,000 sq. mi. Population: 1,300,000.
Under the designation of Central Congo, the country was formerly part of French Equatorial Africa. On 28th November, 1958 the country received limited autonomy and on 15th August, 1960, Congo-Brazzaville became independent. Transformation into a People's Republic took place on 31st December 1969. Congo-Brazzaville belongs to the currency area of Equatorial Africa; concerning mutual issues, please refer to Equatorial Africa.
Capital: Brazzaville.

100 Centimes = 1 CFA-Franc

		XF	Unc
1 (1) 100 Francs (Ni) 1971, 1972. Mendes antelopes (Addax nasomaculatus – Bovidae). Name of country. R inscription: Banque Centrale, value, date		5.00	10.00

		XF	Unc
2 (2) 100 Francs (Ni) 1975, 1982, 1983. Type as No. 1, but inscription »Banque des Etats de l'Afrique Centrale«		4.00	7.50

			Proof
			–.–
3	100 Francs (Cu-Ni) 1984	**XF**	**Unc**
4	500 Francs (Cu-Ni) 1985	–.–	–.–

Republik Saire   **Congo (Kinshasa)** République du Zaïre

République du Zaïre

Area: 902,080 sq. mi. Population: 22,600,000 (1971).
On 30th June 1960, the colony of the Belgian Congo became inde-
pendent under the name of Congo (Leopoldville). The temporary
secession of the Katanga province was brought to an end by a United
Nations police operation in the interests of the unity of the Congo.
Capital: Leopoldville, renamed Kinshasa since 1st July 1966.

100 Centimes = 1 Congo Franc. Since 24th June 1967:
100 Sengi = 1 Likuta, 100 Makuta = 1 Zaïre
(Makuta = plural of Likuta)

		XF	Unc
1 (1)	10 Francs (Al) 1965. Head of a lion (Panthera leo – Felidae). ℞ value	1.20	2.00

COMMEMORATIVE ISSUES (5) FOR THE 5th ANNIVERSARY OF THE REPUBLIC

		Proof
2	10 Francs (Au) 1965. Joseph Kasavubu (1913–1968), Head of State from 1960 to 1965. Rev. Palm trees	60.00
3	20 Francs (Au) 1965. Type as No. 2	120.00
4	25 Francs (Au) 1965. Rev. African elephant	150.00
5	50 Francs (Au) 1965. Type as No. 4	300.00
6	100 Francs (Au) 1965. Type as No. 4	600.00

		XF	Unc
7 (2)	10 Sengi (Al) 1967. Leopard (Panthera pardus – Felidae)	0.40	0.75
8 (3)	1 Likuta (Al) 1967–1969. National arms. ℞ value	0.70	1.00

		XF	Unc

9 (4) 5 Makuta (Cu–Ni) 1967–1969. Bust left
       of Joseph Désiré Mobutu (*1930),
       Head of State since 1965. ℞ value   1.00   1.75

10th ANNIVERSARY OF INDEPENDENCE (4)

10 10 Sengi (Au) 1970. Joseph Désiré Mobutu.
        Rev. Arms, value; .900 gold, 3.11 g   85.00

11 25 Makutas (Au) 1970. Type as No. 10; .900
        gold, 7.77 g   175.00
12 50 Makutas (Au) 1970. Type as No. 10; .900
        gold, 15.55 g   350.00
13   1 Zaïre (Au) 1970. Type as No. 10; .900
        gold, 31.88 g   700.00

Values are given for each coin in U.S. Dollars and reference to Yeomann numbers.

410   Congo (Kinshasa)

Area: 90 sq. mi. Population: 21,000.

The Cook Islands, discovered by James Cook in 1773 during his second voyage and named after him, comprise the following 15 islands: Aitutaki, Atiu, Mangaia, Manuae, Manihiki, Mauke, Mitiaro, Nassau, Palmerston Atoll (Avarua), Penrhyn (Tongareva), Pukapuka, Rakahanga, Rarotonga, Suwarrow and Te Au O Tu (Hervey Islands). On 16th September 1965, the islands obtained complete internal autonomy as a dependency of New Zealand.

100 Cents = 1 New Zealand Dollar

200th ANNIVERSARY OF THE VOYAGE OF JAMES COOK AND THE VISIT OF THE BRITISH ROYAL COUPLE TO AUSTRALIA AND NEW ZEALAND IN 1970

			Unc	Proof
1 (46*)	1	Dollar (Cu-Ni) 1970. Bust right of Queen Elizabeth II; legend ELIZA-BETH II – NEW ZEALAND, and date. ℞ bust of the English explorer James Cook (1728–1779) and his ship, H. M. S. "Endeavour"; legend COOK ISLANDS – ONE DOLLAR	25.00	90.00

*This number refers to Yeoman's New Zealand listing.

2 (1)	1	Cent (Br) 1972–. Elizabeth II facing right. ℞ Taro (Colocasia sp. – Araceae)	0.20	0.50
3 (2)	2	Cents (Br) 1972–. ℞ pineapple (Ananas comosus – Bromeliaceae)	0.30	0.80

4   6   7

		Unc	Proof
4 (3)	5 Cents (Cu-Ni) 1972–1977, 1979, 1983. Rev. Hibiscus flower (Hibiscus rosa-sinensis – Malvaceae)	0.40	1.00
5 (4)	10 Cents (Cu-Ni) 1972–1977, 1979, 1983. Rev. Orange (Citrus sinensis – Rita-ceae)	0.50	1.20
6 (5)	20 Cents (Cu-Ni) 1972–1975, 1983. Rev. Fairy Tern (Gygis alba – Sternidae)	0.75	1.50
7 (6)	50 Cents (Cu-Ni) 1972–1977, 1983. Rev. Bonito (Katsuwonus pelamis – Scom-bridae)	1.20	2.00

8 (7)	1 Dollar (Cu-Ni) 1972–. Rev. Tangaroa, ancient Polynesian deity surrounded by fifteen stars, symbolizing the number of islands which are also displayed in the flag	3.00	6.00

Values are given for each coin in U.S. Dollars and reference to Yeoman-numbers.

20th ANNIVERSARY OF THE CORONATION
OF QUEEN ELIZABETH II (2nd JUNE 1953)

		Unc	Proof
9 (8)	2 Dollars (Ag) 1973. ℞ Elizabeth II in coronation robes. Commemorative legend, denomination	12.50	12.50

COMMEMORATIVE ISSUES (2)
FOR THE 2nd WORLD CIRCUMNAVIGATION
BY JAMES COOK AND THE DISCOVERY OF THE
ISLANDS OF MANUAE AND TE AU O TU (23. 9. 1773)

10   11

		Unc	Proof
10 (9)	2½ Dollars (Ag) 1973, 1974	17.50	17.50
11 (10)	7½ Dollars (Ag) 1973, 1974	22.50	22.50

COMMEMORATIVE ISSUES (3) FOR THE CENTENARY
OF BIRTH OF SIR WINSTON CHURCHILL

12 (11)	50 Dollars (Ag) 1974	60.00	75.00
13 (11a)	50 Dollars (Ag, gold-plated) 1974		120.00
14 (12)	100 Dollars (Au) 1974	350.00	280.00

200th ANNIVERSARY OF COOK'S RETURN TO ENGLAND FROM 2nd VOYAGE

			Unc	Proof
15 (13)	100	Dollars (Au) 1975. Ship between busts of James Cook and King Georg III	175.00	160.00

U.S. BICENTENNIAL COMMEMORATIVE

			Unc	Proof
16 (14)	100	Dollars (Au) 1976. Conjoined heads left of Benjamin Franklin and James Cook	200.00	175.00
17 (15)	20	Cents (Cu-Ni) 1976–1979. Rev. Triton seashell	0.80	1.50
18 (16)	5	Dollars (Ag) 1976. Rev. Mangaia Kingsfisher	15.00	12.50

SILVER JUBILEE OF HER MAJESTY QUEEN ELIZABETH II (2)

19 (17)	25	Dollars (Ag) 1977. Royal Cipher, flanked by Hibiscus and Frangipani flowers	30.00	25.00
20 (18)	100	Dollars (Au) 1977. Type as No. 19	200.00	200.00
21 (19)	5	Dollars (Ag) 1977. Flying birds	15.00	15.00

200th ANNIVERSARY OF REDISCOVERY OF HAWAII BY CAPTAIN JAMES COOK

22 (22)	200	Dollars (Au) 1978. James Cook and two shipmates going ashore	300.00	300.00

CORONATION JUBILEE

23 (21)	10	Dollars (Ag) 1978. The Lion of Mortimer and the Yale of Beaufort as supporter of royal crown	20.00	20.00
24 (20)	5	Dollars (Ag) 1978. Wildlife Conservation	15.00	15.00

250th ANNIVERSARY OF THE BIRTH OF JAMES COOK (8)

25 (1a)	1	Cent (Br) 1978. Type as No. 1, but edge: »1728 CAPTAIN COOK 1978«	1.00	1.00
26 (2a)	2	Cents (Br) 1978	0.50	1.00
27 (3a)	5	Cents (Cu-Ni) 1978	0.50	1.00
28 (4a)	10	Cents (Cu-Ni) 1978	0.60	1.20
29 (15a)	20	Cents (Cu-Ni) 1978	0.80	1.50
30 (6a)	50	Cents (Cu-Ni) 1978	1.20	2.00
31 (7a)	1	Dollar (Cu-Ni) 1978	5.00	6.00
32 (23)	250	Dollars (Au) 1978. Head of James Cook	300.00	300.00

LEGACY OF CAPTAIN COOK

			Unc	**Proof**
33 (24)	200	Dollars (Au) 1979. Pacific flora and fauna	350.00	300.00

COOK ISLAND CONSERVATION DAY

34 (25)	5	Dollars (Ag) 1979. Rev. pigeons	22.50	20.00

MEMBERSHIP IN THE COMMONWEALTH OF NATIONS

35 (26)	100	Dollars (Au) 1979. Tangaroa (see also No. 8)	200.00	180.00

FOR THE FAO COIN PLAN (2)

36 (4b)	10	Cents (Cu-Ni) 1979. Type as No. 5, but »FAO« added	0.80	1.50
37 (6b)	50	Cents (Cu-Ni) 1979. Type as No. 7, but »FAO« added	2.00	2.00

WEDDING OF PRINCE CHARLES AND LADY DIANA (8)

38 (1b)	1	Cent (Br) 1981. Type as No. 1, but edge: »THE ROYAL WEDDING 29 JULY 1981«	0.40	0.50
39 (2b)	2	Cents (Br) 1981	0.40	0.80
40 (3b)	5	Cents (Cu-Ni) 1981	0.50	1.00
41 (4c)	10	Cents (Cu-Ni) 1981	0.60	1.20
42 (15b)	20	Cents (Cu-Ni) 1981	0.80	1.50
43 (6c)	50	Cents (Cu-Ni) 1981	1.20	2.00
44 (7b)	1	Dollar (Cu-Ni) 1981	5.00	8.00
45 (27)	50	Dollars (Au) 1981. Crown and plumes above a monogram of the letters C and D	85.00	65.00

INTERNATIONAL YEAR OF THE SCOUT (2)

46 (28)	20	Dollars (Ag) 1983. Boy Scouts in landscape, .925 silver, 28.28 g	20.00	20.00
47 (29)	200	Dollars (Au) 1983. .917 gold, 15.98 g		250.00

16th FORUM, 2nd P.I.C. AND MINI GAMES (2)

		Unc	Proof
48 (30)	1 Dollar 1985: Type as No. 8, but inscription 16th FORUM/2nd P.I.C./& MINI GAMES:		
	a) .925 silver, 27.22 g		20.00
	b) Piéfort, .925 silver, 54.44 g (250 pcs.)		150.00
	c) (Cu-Ni) reeded edge	5.00	
49	1 Dollar (Au) 1985. Type as No 48; .916⅔ gold, 39.8 g (25 pcs.)		1000.00

60th BIRTHDAY OF QUEEN ELIZABETH II (2)

		Unc	Proof
50 (31)	1 Dollar 1986. Elizabeth II (Maklouf Type). Rev. Members of the Royal Family:		
	a) .925 silver, 27.22 g		22.50
	b) Piéfort, .925 silver, 54.44 g		175.00
	c) (Cu-Ni)	3.00	
51	1 Dollar (Au) 1986. Type as No. 50, .916 ⅔ gold, 44.00 g (60 pcs.)		1200.00

PRINCE ANDREW'S MARRIAGE (2)

		Unc	Proof
52 (32)	1 Dollar 1986		
	a) .925 silver, 27.22 g		20.00
	b) Piéfort, .925 silver, 54.44 g		–.–
	c) (Cu-Ni)	3.00	
53	1 Dollar (Au) 1986. Type as No. 52, .916⅔ gold, 44.00 g (75 pcs.)		900.00

Nos. 54 and 55 omitted.

		XF	Unc
56	5 Cents (Cu-Ni) 1987. Elizabeth II, new portrait by R.D. Maklouf. Rev. Hibiscus flower, as No. 4	0.20	0.40
57	10 Cents (Cu-Ni) 1987. Rev. oranges, as No. 5	0.20	0.50
58	20 Cents (Cu-Ni) 1987. Rev. Fairy tern, as No. 6	0.40	0.75
59	50 Cents (Cu-Ni) 1987. Revc. Bonito, as No. 7	0.65	0.90
60	1 Dollar (Cu-Ni) 1987. Rev. Tangaroa, as No. 8 (scalloped)	2.00	3.00

61   2 Dollars (Cu-Ni) 1987. Rev. »Kumete«, traditionally used to pound root foods such as arrowroot, from the island of Atiu (triangular)   3.00   4.50

62   5 Dollars (Cu-Al-Ni) 1987. Rev. Conch shell, as No. 17 (dodecagonal)   6.50   9.00

Nos. 56–62, Proof set 30.00

Costa Rica

Area: 19,500 sq. mi. Population: 2,800,00.
An independent Republic since 1821, part of the Central American Confederation from 1824 to 1838.
Capital: San José.

100 Centavos or Centimos = 1 Colon

			VF	XF
1 (46)	2 Centimos (Cu-Ni) 1903. Value. ℞ value and wreath		2.00	4.00

For No. 1 with countermark, see under No. 23.

			VF	XF
2 (39)	5 Centimos (Ag) 1905–1914. National arms. ℞ value within wreath		2.00	4.00
3 (40)	10 Centimos (Ag) 1905–1914. Type as No. 2. Fine silver content 900		5.00	10.00
4 (42)	10 Centavos (Ag) 1917. Type as No. 2. Fine silver content 500		4.00	7.00
5 (41)	50 Centimos (Ag) 1902–1903, 1914. Type as No. 2. Fine silver content 900		30.00	55.00
6 (A 42)	50 Centimos (Ag) 1917–1918. Type as No. 5. Fine silver content 500. Very rare			850.00

No. 6 was almost exclusively countermarked: see No. 19

			VF	XF
7 (35)	DOS (2) Colones (Au) 1897–1928. Head of Christopher Columbus (1451–1506). ℞ national arms		50.00	70.00

			VF	XF
8 (36)	Cinco (5) Colones (Au) 1899–1900. Type as No. 7		60.00	75.00
9 (37)	Diez (10) Colones (Au) 1897–1900. Type as No. 7		110.00	140.00
10 (38)	Veinte (20) Colones (Au) 1897–1900. Type as No. 7		250.00	320.00
11 (47)	5 Centavos (Bra) 1917–1919. National arms. ℞ value within wreath, but without the inscription AMERICA CENTRAL		2.50	6.00

			VF	XF
12 (49)	5	Centimos (Bra) 1920–1941. National arms. ℞ value within wreath; inscription G. C. R. = Gobierno Costa Rica	1.00	3.00
13 (51)	5	Centimos (Br) 1929. Type as No. 12	2.00	4.00
14 (48)	10	Centavos (Bra) 1917–1919. Similar to No. 12	3.00	6.00
15 (50)	10	Centimos (Bra) 1920–1922. Type No. 12	1.00	3.00
16 (52)	10	Centimos (Br) 1929. Type as No. 12	1.00	3.00
17 (45)	25	Centavos (Ag) 1924. Type as No. 12	6.00	10.00
18 (43)	50	Centavos on 25 C. 1923. Countermarked on various 25 Centavos coins of previous issues	4.00	8.00
19 (44)	1	Colon on 50 Centimos 1923. Countermarked on No. 6 and various previous issues	5.00	12.00
A19 (54)	10	Centimos (Bra) 1936, 1941. Type as No. 16	1.00	2.00
20 (55)	25	Centimos (Cu-Ni) 1935. National arms. ℞ value within wreath; inscription B. I. C. R. = Banco Internacional de Costa Rica	2.00	4.00
21 (56)	50	Centimos (Cu-Ni) 1935. Type as No. 20	3.00	6.00
22 (57)	1	Colon (Cu-Ni) 1935. Type as No. 20	4.00	7.00
23 (58)	5	Centimos on 2 C. 1942. Countermarked on No. 1	3.00	7.00
24 (A 58)	5	Centimos (Bra) 1942–1947. National arms. ℞ value within wreath; inscription B. N./C. R. = Banco Nacional de Costa Rica	1.00	2.00
25 (B 58)	10	Centimos (Bra) 1942–1947. Type as No. 24	0.80	1.50
26 (59)	25	Centimos (Cu-Ni) 1937–1967	0.50	1.00
27 (63)	25	Centimos (Bra) 1944–1946	0.80	1.80
28 (63a)	25	Centimos (Br) 1945	1.30	3.00
29 (60)	50	Centimos (Cu-Ni)		
		a) 1937	1.20	2.00
		b) 1948	0.50	1.20

30 (61)	1	Colon (Cu-Ni) 1937–1948	1.00	2.00
31 (62)	2	Colones (Cu-Ni) 1948	0.75	1.50
32 (A 64)	5	Centimos (Cu-Ni) 1951. National arms. ℞ value within wreath; inscrip-		

			VF	**XF**

tion B. C./C. R. = Banco Central de Costa Rica — 0.50 1.10

33 (64.1) 5 Centimos (Cu-Ni) 1951. Arms (5 stars in shield). Rev. value within wreath, B.C.C.R. not divided — 0.15 0.30

34 (66) 5 Centimos (St) 1953, 1958, 1967. Type as No. 33 — 0.15 0.30

35 (65) 10 Centimos (Cu-Ni) 1951. Type as No. 33 — 0.20 0.50

36 (67) 100 Centimos (St) 1953, 1958, 1967, 1979. Type as No. 33 — 0.15 0.25

37 (68) 1 Colon (St) 1954. Type as No. 33 — 0.40 1.00

38 (68a) 1 Colon (Cu-Ni) 1961. Type as No. 33 — 0.25 0.60

39 (69) 2 Colones (St) 1954. Type as No. 33 — 0.90 2.00

40 (69a) 2 Colones (Cu-Ni) 1961. Type as No. 33 — 0.50 1.00

41 (64) 5 Centimos (Cu-Ni) 1969–1978. Arms (7 stars in shield). Rev. value within wreath, B.C.C.R. not divided:
a) 1969 (small ship) — 0.10 0.20
b) 1972, 1973, 1976–1978 (large ship) — 0.10 0.20

42 (65) 10 Centimos (Cu-Ni) 1969–1979. Type as No. 41:
a) 1969, 1975, 1976, 1979 (small ship) — 0.10 0.15
b) 1972, 1975 1976, 1979 (large ship) — 0.10 0.15

43 (70) 25 Centimos (Cu-Ni) 1967–1978. Type as No. 41:
a) 1967, 1969, 1970, 1974, 1976, 1978 (small ship) — 0.15 0.30
b) 1972, 1974, 1976–1978 (large ship) — 0.15 0.30

44 (71) 50 Centimos (Cu-Ni) 1965–1978. Type as No. 41:
a) 1965, 1968, 1970, 1978 (small ship) — 0.20 0.40
b) 1972, 1975–1977 (large ship) — 0.20 0.40

45 (68) 1 Colon (Cu-Ni) 1965–1978. Type as No. 41:
a) 1965, 1968, 1970, 1974, 1976, 1977 (small ship) — 0.30 0.60
b) 1972, 1975–1978 (large ship) — 0.30 0.60

			VF	**XF**
46 (69)	2	Colones (Cu-Ni) 1961–1978. Type as No. 41:		
		a) 1968, 1970, 1972, 1978 (small ship)	0.40	0.80
		b) 1961 (large ship)	0.40	0.80
47	2	Colones (Ag) 1970. National arms. Rev. building in San José of the Central Bank founded in 1950		**Proof** 9.00
48	5	Colones (Ag) 1970. Rev. head of Juan Vazquez de Coronado, founder of the city of Cartago in Costa Rica (1564)		15.00
49	10	Colones (Ag) 1970. Rev. kapok tree (Ceiba pentandra – Bombaceae) in front of 5 volcanoes, symbol of the efforts for reunification of the five states of Guatemala, Honduras, Salvador, Nicaragua and Costa Rica		22.50
50	20	Colones (Ag) 1970. Rev. marble statue of the »Venus of Milo«, made in 150 B.C., the Greek Aphrodite of the island of Melos (found in 1820). It is now in the Louvre, Paris (symbol of universal art)		45.00
51	25	Colones (Ag) 1970. Rev. »Motherhood«, a sculpture by F. Zuñiga (25 years of social legislation – law of 15th September 1943)		60.00
52	50	Colones (Au) 1970. Rev. Allegorical representation of human rights – Inter-American Convention		150.00

53   100   Colones (Au) 1970. Rev. Pendant in

			Unc	Proof
		the form of a vulture, repoussé work in gold of the Chibcha people, according to an original in the San José National Museum		260.00
54	200	Colones (Au) 1970. Rev. Head of Juan Santamaria, national hero		500.00
55	500	Colones (Au) 1970. Rev. head of Jesús Jiménez (1823–1897), politician, introduced general compulsory education into Costa Rica in 1869		1200.00
56	1000	Colones (Au) 1970. Rev. national arms with volcanoes, Central American symbol for the efforts for reunification of the five Republics (see No. 49), combined with a geographical sketch of the 5 countries. The national arms refer back to the date of 15th September 1821 and therefore to the »Provincias Unidas del Centro de Américo«		3000.00

SPECIAL ISSUE (3) CONSERVATION COIN COLLECTION

			Unc	Proof
57 (82)	50	Colones (Ag) 1974. Coat of arms, name of country, date. Rev. green turtle (Chelonia mydas – Cheloniidae):		
		a) .500 silver, 25.31 g	18.00	
		b) .925 silver, 28.28 g		20.00
58 (83)	100	Colones (Ag) 1974. Rev. manatee (Trichechus manatus – Trichechidae):		
		a) .500 silver, 31.65 g	25.00	
		b) .925 silver, 35.00 g		30.00
59 (84)	1500	Colones (Au) 1974. Rev. Giant Anteater (Myrmecophaga tridactyla – Myrmecophagidae); .900 gold, 33.43 g	500.00	650.00

25th ANNIVERSARY OF THE CENTRAL BANK (3)

			Unc	Proof
60 (85)	5	Colones (Ni) 1975	1.00	2.50
61 (86)	10	Colones (Ni) 1975	2.00	5.00
62 (87)	20	Colones (Ni) 1975	4.00	8.00

INTERNATIONAL YEAR OF THE CHILD

			Unc	Proof
63 (88)	100	Colones (Ag) 1979	15.00	22.50

Values are given for each coin in U.S. Dollars and reference to Yeomannumbers.

	XF	Unc
64 (64.3) 5 Centimos (Bra) 1979. Type as No. 41	0.10	0.20
65 (70.1) 25 Centimos (St) 1980. Type as No. 43	0.15	0.30

125th ANNIVERSARY OF THE DEATH OF JUAN SANTAMARIA (2)

		Proof
66 (89) 300 Colones (Ag) 1981. Juan Santamaria, patriot		20.00
67 (90) 5000 Colones (Au) 1981. Type as No. 66	300.00	400.00

200th ANNIVERSARY OF FOUNDING OF ALAJUELA

A 68 300 Colones (Ag) 1981. Arms. Rev. Head of Gregorio José Ramirez; .925 silver, 10.97 g — 15.00

68 (91) 250 Colones (Ag) 1982. Rev. Head of a Jaguar — 35.00

69 (92) 1500 Colones (Au) 1982. Rev. Busts of Francisco Vásquez de Coronado and Christopher Columbus — 175.00

	XF	Unc
71 (70a) 25 Centimos (Al) 1982, 1983, 1986. Type as No. 65:		
a) 1982, dia. 23 mm	0.20	0.30
b) 1983, 1986, dia. 17 mm	0.20	0.30
72 (93) 50 Centimos (St) 1982, 1983. Arms (7 stars in shield). Rev. value within wreath, large figures	0.25	0.50
73 (94) 1 Colon (St) 1982–1984. Type as No. 72	0.30	0.60
74 (95) 2 Colones (St) 1982, 1983. Type as No. 72	0.40	0.80
75 (98) 5 Colones (St) 1983, 1985. Arms. Rev. value	1.00	2.00
76 (99) 10 Colones (St) 1983, 1985. Type as. No. 76	2.00	4.00
77 (100) 20 Colones (St) 1983. Type as. No. 76	3.00	6.00

78 (96) 250 Colones (Ag) 1983. Flower 70.00
79 (97)1500 Colones (Au) 1983. Indian statue;
.500 gold, 6.98 g 250.00

Previous issues, see »Weltmünzkatalog 19. Jahrhundert« (World Coin Catalogue of the 19th Century)

Kreta   # Crete   **Crète**

ΚΡΗΤΗ

Area: 3,220 sq. mi. Population: 483,000 (1913).

This island, which had been under Turkish domination since 1669, obtained self-government in 1898 under the aegis of Greece, and was reunited with the motherland on 30th May 1913, after a previous resolution in the Cretan National Assembly.

Capital: Canea.

100 Lepta = 1 Drachma

			VF	XF
1 (1)	1 Lepton (Br) 1900–1901. Crown. ℞ value within wreath			
	a) 1900		25.00	60.00
	b) 1901		16.00	30.00

			VF	XF
2 (2)	2 Lepta (Br) 1900–1901			
	a) 1900		15.00	30.00
	b) 1901		26.00	50.00
3 (3)	5 Lepta (Cu–Ni) 1900		5.00	11.00
4 (4)	10 Lepta (Cu–Ni) 1900		5.00	9.00
5 (5)	20 Lepta (Cu–Ni) 1900		7.00	12.00
6 (6)	50 Lepta (Ag) 1901. Head right of Prince George of Greece (1869–1957) 1st High Commissioner of Crete 1898–1906. ℞ arms with crown on drapery		12.00	22.00
7 (7)	1 Drachma (Ag) 1901		18.00	30.00
8 (8)	2 Drachmai (Ag) 1901		40.00	75.00
9 (9)	5 Drachmai (Ag) 1901		80.00	125.00

Values are given for each coin in U.S. Dollars and reference to Yeomannumbers.

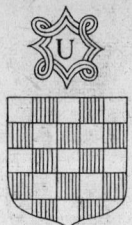

Area: 21,726 sq. mi. Population: 4,250,000.
From 1867 until November 1918 Croatia formed a united kingdom
with Hungary, and later was part of the kingdom of the Serbians,
Croatians and Slovaks, later known as Yugoslavia. After the occupation
of Yugoslavia by German troops, Croatia declared its independence on
10th April 1941. Since 1945 Croatia has been an integral part of the
Republic of Yugoslavia.
Capital: Zagreb (Agram).

100 Banica = 1 Kuna

			VF	XF
1 (1)	2 Kune (Zi) 1941. National arms. ℞ value		5.00	10.00

2   500   Kune (Au) 1941. Ante Pavelić (1889 to
1959), Head of State 1941–1945. ℞ national arms and value   2600.00

3   500   Kune (Ag) 1941. Kneeling female figure with corn ears, personifying Croatia.
℞ as No. 2   3500.00

Area: 44,048 sq. mi. Population: 10,150,000.

Discovered by Christopher Columbus on 28th October 1492 and taken possession of by Spain in 1511, under the name of Fernandina. When the various continental Latin-American states obtained their independence at the beginning of the 19th century, the West Indian island of Cuba remained the most important colony of Spain. After several revolts and the formation of a provisional government, and after the end of the Spanish-American War in 1898, Cuba was at first occupied by the United States, and later in 1902 gained independence as a republic, but it remained under the aegis of the United States of America until 1934 (the U. S. dollar was the official currency). As a result of the revolution from 1956 to 1959, Dr. Fidel Castro became Prime Minister on 13th February 1959.

Capital: Havana.

100 Centavos = 1 Peso

PROVISIONAL GOVERNMENT

		VF	XF
1 (1)	Souvenir Peso (Ag) 1897. Liberty head to right, inscription PATRIA Y LIBERTAD and SOUVENIR. ℞ national arms. Several variants	100.00	180.00

WAR OF INDEPENDENCE

2 (2)	1 Peso (Ag) 1898. Type as No. 1, but date below head instead of "SOUVENIR". ℞ national arms and value	380.00	750.00

THE MEDIATIZED REPUBLIC

3 (3)	1 Centavo (Cu–Ni) 1915–1938. National arms, value in letters. ℞ five-pointed star with value in Roman figures; indication of weight "2.5 G"	0.50	1.20
	For coins of same or slightly different description, see Nos. 16, 17 and 29		
4 (4)	2 Centavos (Cu–Ni) 1915–1916. Type as No. 3	0.60	1.50

			VF	XF
5 (5)	5	Centavos (Cu–Ni) 1915–1920. Type as No. 3; indication of weight "5.0 G" *For coins of same or slightly different description, see Nos. 18, 19 and 30*	0.70	3.00
6 (6)	10	Centavos (Ag) 1915–1949. Five-pointed star with rays. ℞ national arms and value in letters	1.50	4.00
7 (7)	20	Centavos (Ag) 1915–1949. Type as No. 6		
		a) 1915–1920, 1948–1949	3.00	5.00
		b) 1932	40.00	90.00

			VF	XF
8 (8)	40	Centavos (Ag) 1915–1920. Type as No. 6	7.00	15.00
9 (9)	1	Peso (Ag) 1915–1934. Type as No. 6	15.00	30.00
10 (10)	1	Peso (Au) 1915–1916. Head right of José Julián Marti y Perez (1853–1895), patriot and writer. ℞ national arms and value in letters	140.00	220.00
11 (11)	2	Pesos (Au) 1915–1916. Type as No. 10	80.00	90.00
12 (12)	4	Pesos (Au) 1915–1916. Type as No. 10	125.00	160.00
13 (13)	5	Pesos (Au) 1915–1916. Type as No. 10	140.00	175.00
14 (14)	10	Pesos (Au) 1915–1916. Type as No. 10	240.00	265.00
15 (15)	20	Pesos (Au) 1915–1916. Type as No. 10		
		a) 1915	480.00	550.00
		b) 1916, Proof only (10 pes.)		–.–
16 (3a)	1	Centavo (Bra) 1943. Type as No. 3	0.40	0.80
17 (3b)	1	Centavo (Cu–Ni) 1946–1961. Type as No. 3, but indication of weight "2.5 GR"	0.40	0.90

The last year, 1961, is to be considered as a Castro issue.

18 (5a)	5	Centavos (Bra) 1943. Type as No. 5	1.50	4.00
19 (5b)	5	Centavos (Cu–Ni) 1946–1961. Type as No. 5, but indication of weight "5.0 GR"	0.40	0.80

All valuations in the SCHÖN are stated in U.S. Dollars.

20 (16) 1 Peso (Ag) 1934–1939. Head of Liberty **VF** **XF**
with laureate cap of Liberty, five-
pointed star with rays, legend: PA-
TRIA Y LIBERTAD. ℞ national arms
and value 40.00 65.00

COMMEMORATIVE ISSUES (3) FOR THE 50th ANNIVERSARY OF THE REPUBLIC

21 (17)10 Centavos (Ag) 1952. Ruins of la Dema-
jagna sugar-mill. Rev. Flag in front of
the fortress »El Morro« in Havana 3.00 5.00
22 (18) 20 Centavos (Ag) 1952. Type as No. 21 4.50 7.50
23 (19) 40 Centavos (Ag) 1952. Type as No. 21 11.00 15.00

COMMEMORATIVE ISSUES (4) FOR THE CENTENARY OF THE BIRTH OF J. J. MARTI

24 (20) 1 Centavo (Bra) 1953. José Julián Marti
y Perez (1853–1895), patriot and writer,
inscription CENTENARIO DE
MARTI. ℞ star of Cuba on triangle,
value 0.30 0.80

For coin of similar design, see No. 28

25 (21) 25 Centavos (Ag) 1953. Type as No. 24.
℞ cap of Liberty and value 4.00 6.00
26 (22) 50 Centavos (Ag) 1953. Type as No. 24.
℞ inscribed scroll and value 8.00 12.50
27 (23) 1 Peso (Ag) 1953. Type as No. 24. ℞ key
with rising sun in background – part of
the national arms 22.00 30.00
28 (24) 1 Centavo (Cu–Ni) 1958. José J. Marti;
type as No. 24, but without commemorative inscription. ℞ star of Cuba on
triangle, and value 0.30 0.50

SOCIALIST REPUBLIC

XF **Unc**

29 (27) 1 Centavo (Al) 1963, 1966, 1969–1972,
1978, 1979, 1981, 1982. Type as No. 3 0.30 0.50

				XF	Unc

30 (28) 5 Centavos (Al) 1963, 1966, 1968, 1969, 1971, 1972. Type as No. 5   0.25   0.70

31 (25) 20 Centavos (Cu–Ni) 1962, 1968. Bust left of José J. Marti, legend: PATRIA O MUERTE. ℞ national arms   0.90   1.60

32 (26) 40 Centavos (Cu–Ni) 1962. Bust right of Camilo Cienfuegos y Gorriarian (1933–1959), revolutionary hero, legend: PATRIA O MUERTE. ℞ national arms   2.20   4.00

33 (29) 20 Centavos (Al) 1969, 1970, 1971, 1972. Type as No. 29   0.50   1.00

In order to help collectors and dealers, we have added after most SCHÖN-numbers the corresponding number assigned by R.S. Yeoman in his wellknown works entitled »A Catalog of Modern World Coins« and »Current Coins of the World«.

		Proof
34 (30)	5 Pesos (Ag) 1975. General view of National bank	12.00
35 (31)	10 Pesos (Ag) 1975. Type as No. 34	20.00
36 (32)	20 Pesos (Ag) 1977. Ignacio Agramonte	25.00
37 (33)	20 Pesos (Ag) 1977. Maximo Gomez	25.00
38 (34)	20 Pesos (Ag) 1977. Antonio Maceo	25.00
39 (35)	100 Pesos (Au) 1977. Carlos Manuel de Céspedes	200.00

60th ANNIVERSARY OF THE OCTOBER REVOLUTION (2)

40 (A34)	20 Pesos (Ag) 1977. Lenin (1870–1924), Russian politician (30 pcs.)	850.00
A40 (A35)	100 Pesos (Au) 1977. Type as No. 40 (10 pieces), 916⅔ gold, 12 g	–,–

NONALIGNED NATIONS CONFERENCE (2)

41 (36)	20 Pesos (Ag) 1979. Arms. Rev. Emblem	40.00
42 (37)	100 Pesos (Au) 1979. Type as No. 41	200.00

FIRST SOVIET-CUBAN SPACE FLIGHT (3)

43 (38)	5 Pesos (Ag) 1980 (30 pcs.)	18.00
44 (39)	10 Pesos (Ag) 1980	30.00
45 (40)	100 Pesos (Au) 1980	300.00

			Proof
46 (41)	5 Pesos (Ag) 1980		18.00
47 (42)	10 Pesos (Ag) 1980		30.00

CUBAN FLOWERS (9)

		Unc	Proof
A47 (A43)	1 Peso (Cu-Ni) 1980. Rev. Mariposa	3.50	
B47 (A44)	1 Peso (Cu-Ni) 1981. Rev. Azahar	3.50	
C47 (A45)	1 Peso (Cu-Ni) 1981. Rev. Orquidea	3.50	
48 (43)	5 Pesos (Ag) 1981. Type as No. A47	12.50	16.50
49 (44)	5 Pesos (Ag) 1981. Type as No. B47	12.50	16.50
50 (45)	5 Pesos (Ag) 1981. Type as No. C47	12.50	16.50
A50	100 Pesos (Au) 1980. Type as No. A47		–.–
B50	100 Pesos (Au) 1981. Type as No. B47		–.–
C50	100 Pesos (Au) 1981. Type as No. C47		–.–

DISCOVERY OF AMERICA (9)

51	1 Peso (Cu-Ni) 1981. Rev. »Nina«		4.00
52	1 Peso (Cu-Ni) 1981. Rev. »Pinta«		4.00
53	1 Peso (Cu-Ni) 1981. Rev. »Santa Maria«		4.00
54 (46)	5 Pesos (Ag) 1981. Type as No. 51	15.00	20.00
55 (47)	5 Pesos (Ag) 1981. Type as No. 52	15.00	20.00
56 (48)	5 Pesos (Ag) 1981. Type as No. 53	15.00	20.00
A56 (49)	100 Pesos (Au) 1981. Type as No. 51		250.00
B56 (50)	100 Pesos (Au) 1981. Type as No. 52		250.00
C56 (51)	100 Pesos (Au) 1981. Type as No. 53		250.00

CUBAN FAUNA – First Issue (9)

57 (52)	1 Peso (Cu-Ni) 1981. Rev. Crocodile	3.50	
58 (53)	1 Peso (Cu-Ni) 1981. Rev. Colibri	3.50	
59 (54)	1 Peso (Cu-Ni) 1981. Rev. Zunzun	3.50	
60 (55)	5 Pesos (Ag) 1981. Type as No. 57	12.50	16.50
61 (56)	5 Pesos (Ag) 1981. Type as No. 58	12.50	16.50
62 (57)	5 Pesos (Ag) 1981. Type as No. 59	12.50	16.50
A62	100 Pesos (Au) 1981. Type as No. 57		–.–
B62	100 Pesos (Au) 1981. Type as No. 58		–.–
C62	100 Pesos (Au) 1981. Type as No. 59		–.–

WORLD SOCCER CHAMPIONSHIP GAMES (2)

		Unc	Proof
63 (58)	1 Pesos (Cu-Ni) 1981. Rev. Soccer player	5.00	
64 (59)	5 Pesos (Ag) 1981. Type as No. 63		25.00
65 (60)	1 Peso (Cu-Ni) 1981. Rev. Sugar Production	4.00	
66 (61)	5 Pesos (Ag) 1981. Type as No. 65	15.00	22.50

XIV CENTRAL AMERICAN AND CARIBBEAN GAMES (6)

67 (62)	1 Peso (Cu-Ni) 1981. Rev. »Alligator«, emblem of the games	4.00	
68 (63)	1 Peso (Cu-Ni) 1981. Rev. Three athlets	4.00	
69 (64)	1 Peso (Cu-Ni) 1981. Rev. Three boxer	4.00	
70 (65)	5 Pesos (Ag) 1981. Type as No. 67	15.00	22.50
71 (66)	5 Pesos (Ag) 1981. Type as No. 68	15.00	22.50
72 (67)	5 Pesos (Ag) 1981. Type as No. 69	15.00	22.50

CUBAN FAUNA – Second Issue (9)

73 (68)	1 Peso (Cu-Ni) 1981. Rev. Tocororo	4.00	
74 (69)	1 Peso (Cu-Ni) 1981. Rev. Almiqui	4.00	
75 (70)	1 Peso (Cu-Ni) 1981. Rev. Manjuari	4.00	
76 (71)	5 Pesos (Ag) 1981. Type as No. 73	15.00	22.50
77 (72)	5 Pesos (Ag) 1981. Type as No. 74	15.00	22.50
78 (73)	5 Pesos (Ag) 1981. Type as No. 75	15.00	22.50
A78	100 Pesos (Au) 1981. Type as No. 73		–.–
B78	100 Pesos (Au) 1981. Type as No. 74		–.–
C78	100 Pesos (Au) 1981. Type as No. 75		–.–

		Unc	Proof
79 (74)	1 Peso (Cu-Ni) 1982. Rev. Ernest Hemingway (1898–1961), writer, Nobel prize winner in 1954	4.00	
80 (76)	1 Peso (Cu-Ni) 1982. Rev. »El Viejo y el Mar«	4.00	
81 (75)	1 Peso (Cu-Ni) 1982. Rev. »Pesca de la Aguja«	4.00	
82 (77)	5 Pesos (Ag) 1982. Type as No. 79	15.00	25.00
83 (79)	5 Pesos (Ag) 1982. Type as No. 80	15.00	25.00
84 (78)	5 Pesos (Ag) 1982. Type as No. 81	15.00	25.00

435th ANNIVERSARY OF THE BIRTH OF MIGUEL DE CERVANTES (6)

		Unc	Proof
85 (80)	1 Peso (Cu-Ni) 1982. Rev. Miguel de Cervantes y Saavedra (1547–1616), poet	4.00	
86 (81)	1 Peso (Cu-Ni) 1982. Rev. Don Quixote on horseback	4.00	
87 (82)	1 Peso (Cu-Ni) 1982. Rev. Don Quixote and Sancho Panza	4.00	
88 (83)	5 Pesos (Ag) 1982. Type as No. 85	12.00	20.00
89 (84)	5 Pesos (Ag) 1982. Type as No. 86	12.00	20.00
90 (85)	5 Pesos (Ag) 1982. Type as No. 87	12.00	20.00

FOR THE FAO COIN-PLAN (4)

91 (88)	1 Peso (Cu-Ni) 1982. Rev. Cow	4.00	
92 (86)	1 Peso (Cu-Ni) 1982. Rev. Citrus fruit	4.00	
93 (89)	5 Pesos (Ag) 1982. Type as No. 91	12.00	20.00
94 (87)	5 Pesos (Ag) 1982. Type as No. 92	12.00	20.00

		XF	Unc
95	2 Centavos (Al) 1983. Arms. Rev. fivepointed star with value	0.30	0.50
96 (90)	1 Peso (Bra) 1983, 1984, 1987. Arms., value. Rev. five-pointed star, date	1.00	2.00

RAILROAD (2)

		Unc	Proof
97 (95)	1 Peso (Cu-Ni) 1983. rev. engine »La Junta«	4.00	
98 (96)	5 Pesos (Ag) 1983 1983. Type as No. 97	20.00	25.00

XIV OLYMPIC WINTER GAMES IN SARAJEVO (3)

99 (92)	5 Pesos (Ag) 1983. Rev. Ice-hockey players		25.00
100	5 Pesos (Ag) 1983. Rev. Olympic flame		25.00
101	5 Pesos (Ag) 1983. Rev. Skier, national flag		25.00

XIII OLYMPIC SUMMER GAMES IN LOS ANGELES (3)

Proof

102 (94)	5 Pesos (Ag) 1983. Rev. Runner	25.00
103	5 Pesos (Ag) 1983. Rev. Discus thrower	25.00
104	5 Pesos (Ag) 1983. Rev. Judo fighter	25.00

TOURIST TOKEN ISSUES

		Unc
TN 1	5 Centavos (Cu-Ni) 1981. Rev. shell	1.00
TN 2	10 Centavos (Cu-Ni) 1981. Rev. hummingbird	1.00
TN 3	25 Centavos (Cu-Ni) 1981. Rev. orchid	1.50
TN 4	50 Centavos (Cu-Ni) 1981. Rev. palm	2.00
TN 5	1 Peso (Cu-Ni) 1981. Rev. fortress »El Morro« in Havana	4.00
TN 6	5 Centavos (Cu-Ni) 1981. Denomination written in cipher. Rev. shell	1.00
TN 7	10 Centavos (Cu-Ni) 1981. Rev. hummingbird	1.00
TN 8	25 Centavos (Cu-Ni) 1981. Rev. orchid	1.50

Values are given for each coin in U.S. Dollars and reference to Yeoman-numbers.

Area: 172 sq. mi. Population: 127,900.

Curaçao was discovered in 1499 and first occupied by the Spaniards, then in 1634 by the Dutch. Since 1952 the island forms part of the Dutch East Indies (Netherlands Antilles).

Capital: Willemstad.

100 Cents = 1 Gulden

WILHELMINA 1890–1948

			VF	XF
1 (1)	$^1/_{10}$ Gulden (Ag) 1901. Head left of Wilhelmina (1880–1962), Queen of the Netherlands. ℞ crowned arms and value		25.00	55.00
2 (2)	¼ Gulden (Ag) 1900. Type as No. 1		25.00	55.00
3 (3)	1 Cent (Br) 1944–1947. National arms (lion). ℞ value within wreath		1.00	2.00

4 (4)	2½ Cents (Br) 1944–1948. Type as No. 3	1.50	3.00

5 (9)	5 Cents (Cu–Ni) 1948. Flower. ℞ value	1.00	3.00
6 (5)	$^1/_{10}$ Gulden (Ag) 1944–1947. Head of Queen Wilhelmina. ℞ value	2.00	4.00
7 (8)	$^1/_{10}$ Gulden (Ag) 1948. Diademed head left of Queen Wilhelmina	2.00	4.00

8 (6)	¼ Gulden (Ag) 1944–1947. Type as No. 6	3.00	6.00

				VF	XF
9 (7)	1	Gulden (Ag) 1944. Head left of Queen Wilhemina. ℞ crowned arms		8.00	20.00

10 (10)	2½ Gulden (Ag) 1944. Type as No. 9			9.00	12.00

For other issues, see under NETHERLANDS ANTILLES.

Values are given for each coin in U.S. Dollars and reference to Yeoman-numbers.

Cyprus

Zypern   **Chypre**

Area: 3,558 sq. mi. Population: 710,000.

Cyprus became a British possession in 1878 and in 1925 obtained the status of a Crown Colony; it has been an independent republic since 16th August 1960.

Capital: Nicosia.

9 Piastres = 1 Shilling; since 1st August 1955: 1000 Millièmes = £ 1

EDWARD VII 1901–1910

		VF	XF
1 (8)	¼ Piastre (Br) 1902–1908, Crowned bust right of King Edward VII ℞ value within circle		
	a) 1902, 1905	17.50	30.00
	b) 1908	50.00	110.00
2 (9)	½ Piastre (Br) 1908. Type as No. 1	125.00	180.00

3 (10)	1 Piastre (Br) 1908	165.00	220.00
4 (11)	9 Piastres (Ag) 1907. ℞ crowned arms	85.00	200.00
5 (12)	18 Piastres (Ag) 1907	90.00	200.00

GEORGE V 1910–1936

6 (13)	¼ Piastre (Br) 1922–1926. Crowned bust left of King George V. ℞ value within circle	12.50	25.00
7 (14)	½ Piastre (Br) 1922–1931. Type as No. 6:		
	a) 1922	22.00	40.00
	b) 1927, 1930, 1931	18.00	30.00
8 (15)	1 Piastre (Br) 1922-1931	40.00	65.00
9 (18)	4½ Piastres (Ag) 1921. R crowned arms	12.00	20.00
10 (19)	9 Piastres (Ag) 1913-1921:		
	a) 1913	22.00	40.00
	b) 1919, 1921	15.00	25.00

11 (20)	18 Piastres (Ag) 1913-1921:	VF	XF
	a) 1913	100.00	250.00
	b) 1921	40.00	100.00

COMMEMORATIVE ISSUE FOR THE 50th ANNIVERSARY OF BRITISH OCCUPATION

		Unc	Proof
12 (21)	45 Piastres (Ag) 1928. Crowned bust left of King George V. ℞ arms of Cyprus	175.00	650.00

		VF	XF
13 (16)	½ Piastre (Cu–Ni) 1934. Crowned bust left of King George V. ℞ value (scalloped edge)	4.00	6.00
14 (17)	1 Piastre (Cu–Ni) 1934	3.00	5.50

GEORGE VI 1936–1952

15 (22)	½ Piastre (Cu–Ni) 1938. Crowned head left of King George VI (scalloped edge)	2.00	4.00
16 (23)	1 Piastre (Cu–Ni) 1938. Type as No. 15	2.50	6.00
17 (28)	4½ Piastres (Ag) 1938	6.00	15.00
18 (29)	9 Piastres (Ag) 1938-1940	15.00	30.00
19 (30)	18 Piastres (Ag) 1938-1940	18.00	25.00
20 (22a)	½ Piastre (Br) 1942-1945. Type as No. 15	1.00	3.00
21 (23a)	1 Piastre (Br) 1942-1946. Type as No. 16	1.00	3.00
22 (26)	1 Shilling (Cu–Ni) 1947	2.00	6.00

23 (27)	2 Shillings (Cu–Ni) 1947	3.00	10.00
24 (31)	½ Piastre (Br) 1949. Type as No. 15, but inscription now GEORGIUS SEXTUS DEI GRATIA REX	0.75	1.50
25 (32)	1 Piastre (Br) 1949	0.60	1.25
26 (33)	1 Shilling (Cu–Ni) 1949	2.00	6.00
27 (34)	2 Shillings (Cu–Ni) 1949	4.00	10.00

NEW CURRENCY: 1000 Millièmes = £ 1

	XF	Unc

28 (35) 3 Mils (Br) 1955. Crowned head right of Queen Elizabeth II. ℞ flying fish in two-tone style, dating from the Cypriot archaic period (Iron Age II), 7th century B. C.   0.10   0.20

29 (36) 5 Mils (Br) 1955–1956. ℞ "Male figure carrying copper bar", from a bronze group from Curium, dating back to the late Bronze Age, c. 1200 B. C.; the original is in the British Museum, London   0.20   0.40

30 (37) 25 Mils (Cu–Ni) 1955. ℞ head of bull l.   0.25   0.50
31 (38) 50 Mils (Cu–Ni) 1955. ℞ fern leaves   0.50   1.20

		XF	Unc
32 (39)	100 Mils (Cu-Ni) 1955, 1957. Rev. merchant ship, c. 6th century B. C.:		
	a) 1955	1.00	2.00
	b) 1957	30.00	65.00

REPUBLIC

33 (41)	1 Mil (Al-Mg) 1963, 1971, 1972. National arms of the Republic. Rev. value in figure within wreath	0.10	0.20
34 (42)	5 Mils (Br) 1963, 1970–1974, 1977–1980. Rev. merchant ship, c. 6th century B. C.	0.10	0.20
35 (43)	25 Mils (Cu-Ni) 1963, 1968, 1971–1974, 1976–1982. Rev. cedar of Lebanon (Cedrus libani – Pinaceae)	0.15	0.30

36 (44)	50 Mils (Cu-Ni) 1963–1982. Rev. Bunch of grapes (Vitis vinifera – Vitaceae)	0.30	0.50

37 (45)	100 Mils (Cu-Ni) 1963–1982. Rev. Cyprus mouflon (Ovis ammon ophion – Bovidae)	0.50	1.00

COMMEMORATIVE MEDALS FOR ARCHBISHOP MAKARIOS III. (3)

38	½ £ (Au) 1966. Head left of Makarios III. (1913-1977), President of State 1959-1977. R double eagle		150.00

39	1 £ (Au) 1966. Type as No. 38	280.00
40	5 £ (Au) 1966. Type as No. 38	1400.00

FOR THE FAO COIN PLAN

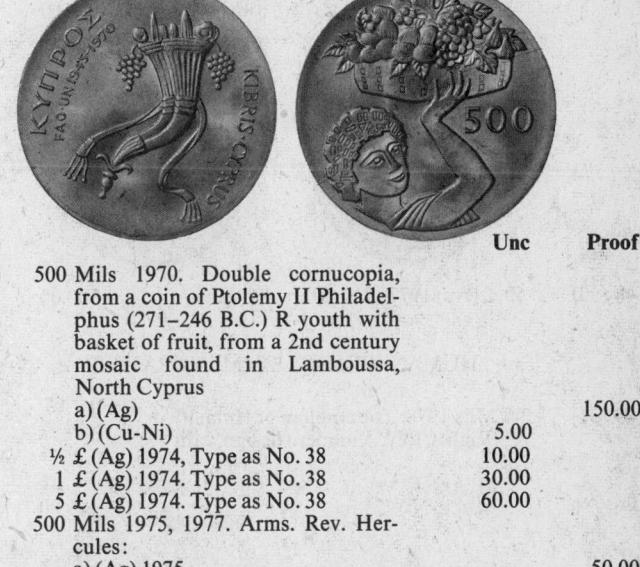

		Unc	Proof

		Unc	**Proof**
41 (46)	500 Mils 1970. Double cornucopia, from a coin of Ptolemy II Philadelphus (271–246 B.C.) R youth with basket of fruit, from a 2nd century mosaic found in Lamboussa, North Cyprus		
	a) (Ag)		150.00
	b) (Cu-Ni)	5.00	
42	½ £ (Ag) 1974, Type as No. 38	10.00	
43	1 £ (Ag) 1974. Type as No. 38	30.00	
44	5 £ (Ag) 1974. Type as No. 38	60.00	
45 (47)	500 Mils 1975, 1977. Arms. Rev. Hercules:		
	a) (Ag) 1975		50.00
	b) (Cu-Ni) 1975, 1977	3.00	

REFUGEE COMMEMORATIVE (2)

46 (48)   500 Mils 1976. Rev. Mother and child
with a damaged house in the back-
ground:
a) (Ag)   18.00
b) (Cu-Ni)   3.00

47 (49)   1 £ 1976. Rev. Mother and children
with tents in the background:
a) (Ag)   30.00
b) (Cu-Ni)   4.00

48 (50)   50 £ (Au) 1977. Rev. Map of Cyprus   300.00   350.00

HUMAN RIGHTS COMMEMORATIVE

49 (51)   500 Mils 1978. The emblem of Human
Rights. Rev. A modern design, valu
e:
a) (Ag)   75.00
b) (Cu-Ni)   3.00

OLYMPIC GAMES 1980 IN MOSCOW

50 (52)   500 Mils 1980. Rev. Olympic rings:
a) (Ag)   70.00
b) (Cu-Ni)   4.00

COMMEMORATIVE ISSUE FOR ARCHBISHOP MAKARIOS III

		XF	Unc
51 (53)	5 Mils (Al) 1981, 1982. Arms. Rev. merchant ship, c. 6th century B.C.	0.10	0.20

WORLD FOOD DAY

		XF	Unc
52 (54)	500 Mils 1981. Rev. Swordfish and ear of weath: .		
	a) (Ag)		35.00
	b) (Cu-Ni)	3.00	

CURRENCY REFORM: 100 Cents = 1£

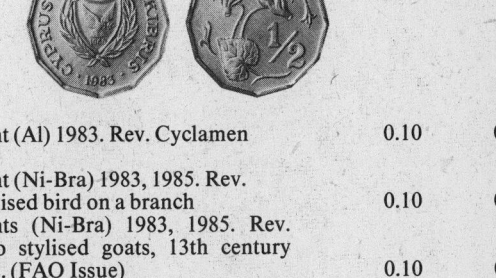

		XF	Unc
53 (55)	½ Cent (Al) 1983. Rev. Cyclamen	0.10	0.20
54 (56)	1 Cent (Ni-Bra) 1983, 1985. Rev. Stylised bird on a branch	0.10	0.20
55 (57)	2 Cents (Ni-Bra) 1983, 1985. Rev. Two stylised goats, 13th century B.C. (FAO Issue)	0.10	0.25
56 (58)	5 Cents (Ni-Bra) 1983, 1985. Rev. Silver bowl with a wishbone handle	0.15	0.30
57 (59)	10 Cents (Ni-Bra) 1983, 1985. Rev. Modern clay vase of Phini village	0.20	0.50
58 (60)	20 Cents (Ni-Bra) 1983, 1985. Rev. Pied Wheatear on an olive branch	0.40	0.75

INTERNATIONAL YEAR OF THE FOREST

		XF	Unc
59 (61)	50 Cents 1985. Rev. Dryad:		
	a) (Ag) .925 silver, 14.14 g		25.00
	b) (Cu-Ni)	3.00	

60   1 £ 1986. Rev. Cyprus Mouflons:
           a) (Ag) .925 silver, 28.28 g   20.00
           b) (Cu–Ni)   4.00

Tschechoslowakei   # Czechoslovakia   **Tchécoslovaquie**

Republika Ceskoslovenská
since 11th July 1960:

Ceskoslovenská socialistická republika

Area: 49,370 sq. mi. Population: 15,580,000.
On 28th October 1918 a republic was proclaimed in the states of Bohemia, Moravia, and Slovakia, which had previously been part of the joint kingdom of Austria-Hungary; the independent state of Czechoslovakia was founded. After the creation of the protectorates of Bohemia and Moravia (Čechy a Morava) on 15th March 1939, Slovakia obtained temporarily the status of an independent state and started issuing its own currency. In May 1945 the Republic of Czechoslovakia was reestablished; in 1960 it was made a Socialist Republic.
Capital: Prague.

100 Halere = 1 Koruna

			VF	XF
1 (1)	2	Halere (Zi) 1923–1925. Lion coat of arms. ℞ the Karlsbrücke in Prague	5.00	12.00

2 (2)	5	Halere (Br) 1923–1932, 1938. Type as No. 1	0.30	0.60
3 (3)	10	Halere (Br) 1922–1938. Type as No. 1	0.40	0.80
4 (4)	20	Halere (Cu–Ni) 1921–1922, 1924–1931, 1933, 1937–1938. Lion coat of arms. ℞ sheaf of wheat	0.50	1.00
5 (5)	25	Halere (Cu–Ni) 1933. Lion coat of arms. ℞ value in figures	1.20	2.20
6 (6)	50	Halere (Cu–Ni) 1921–1922, 1924–1927, 1931. Lion coat of arms. ℞ value over linden branch and sheaf of wheat	0.40	0.90
7 (7)	1	Koruna (Cu–Ni) 1922–1925, 1929–1930, 1937–1938. Lion coat of arms. ℞ harvest scene: female agricultural worker kneeling, holding sheaf and sickle	1.00	1.80

			VF	XF
8 (8)	5	Korun (Cu-Ni) 1925-1927. Lion coat of arms. R factory, value; diameter 30 mm	5.50	9.00
9 (8a)	5	Korun (Ag) 1928-1932. Type as No. 8; diameter 27 mm	3.00	6.00
10 (12)	10	Korun (Ag) 1930–1933. National arms. R allegorical figure of the Republic holding linden shoot	7.50	10.50
11 (13)	20	Korun (Ag) 1933–1934. National arms. R three standing figures	9.50	12.50

5th ANNIVERSARY OF THE REPUBLIC

			VF	XF
A12 (A15)	1	Ducat (Au) 1923. Type as No. 12, but serially numbered next to date (1,000 pcs.)		700.00
12 (15)	1	Ducat (Au) 1923–1939, 1951. National arms. Rev. facing half figure of St. Wenceslas (907–929), national hero and national saint	75.00	100.00

			VF	XF
13 (16)	2	Ducats (Au) 1923–1938, 1951. Type as No. 12	225.00	350.00

			VF	XF
14 (17)	5	Ducats (Au) 1929-1938, 1951. St. Wenceslas on horseback. Riv. lion within coat of arms; linden shoot on right	500.00	700.00

15 (18)   10 Ducats (Au) 1929-1938, 1951. Type
          as No. 14   1100.00   1400.00

10th ANNIVERSARY OF THE REPUBLIC

16 (11)   10 Korun (Ag) 1928, Bust right of To-
          más Garrigue Masaryk (1850–1937),
          1st President of State. ℞ national
          arms: Bohemian lion in centre of
          coat of arms of heart shape; in upper
          field left, the emblem of Slovakia; in
          upper field right, the emblem of Car-
          pathian Ukraine (Russian Carpathi-
          an mountains); below, Moravian ea-
          gle on left, Silesian eagle on right   6.00   11.00

MEDALLIC ISSUES FOR THE 10th ANNIVERSARY OF THE REPUBLIC (2)

17   2 Ducats (Au) 1928. St. Prokop guid-
          ing plough drawn by demon   200.00   250.00

18   4 Ducats (Au) 1928. Type as No. 17   400.00   500.00

MEDALLIC ISSUES FOR THE 1000th ANNIVERSARY OF THE CHRISTIANISATION OF BOHEMIA AND THE MURDER OF ST. WENCESLAS IN ALTBUNZLAU (3)

19	1 Ducat (Au) 1929. St. Wenceslas holding banner and sword. ℞ St. Wenceslas on horseback; angel		350.00
20	3 Ducats (Au) 1929. Type as No. 19		800.00
21	5 Ducats (Au) 1929. Type as No. 19		1200.00

COMMEMORATIVE ISSUE FOR THE 100th ANNIVERSARY THE BIRTH OF TYRŠ

		VF	XF
22	1 Ducat (Au) 1932. Dr. Miroslav Tyrš (1832–1884), founder of the Sokol movement		360.00

COMMEMORATIVE ISSUE FOR ANTONIN ŠVEHLA

23	1 Ducat (Au) 1933. Bust left of Dr. Antonin Svehla (1873–1933), politician and statesman. R peasant sowing		
	a)		300.00
	b) Cross above date		360.00

COMMEMORATIVE ISSUES (4) FOR THE REOPENING OF THE MINT IN KREMNITZ (KREMNICE)

24	1 Ducat (Au) 1934. St. Elizabeth. ℞ mining scene		900.00
25	2 Ducats (Au) 1934. Type as No. 24		1800.00
26	5 Ducats (Au) 1934. Type as No. 24		3600.00
27	10 Ducats (Au) 1934. Type as No. 24		7200.00

COMMEMORATIVE MEDALS (2) FOR THE 300th ANNIVERSARY OF THE DEATH OF ALBRECHT VON WALLENSTEIN

		VF	XF
28	5 Ducats (Au) 1934. Albrecht Eusebius Wenceslas von Wallenstein, known as Waldstein (1583–1634), Imperial Generalissimo in the Thirty Years' War. ℞ crowned arms	–.–	–.–
29	10 Ducats (Au) 1934. Type as No. 28	–.–	–.–
30 (8b)	5 Korun (Ni) 1937, 1938. Type as No. 8; diameter 27 mm:		
	a) 1937		100.00
	b) 1938	2.00	4.00

COMMEMORATIVE ISSUE FOR THE DEATH OF PRESIDENT MASARYK

		VF	XF
31 (14)	20 Korun (Ag) 1937. Bust right of T. Garrigue Masaryk (1850–1937), 1st President of State. ℞ national arms	9.00	12.00

For the coins of the protectorates of Bohemia and Moravia, which were current from 1939 to 1945 (and even later), see under German Occupation in the 2nd World War.

The Slovakian coins issued between 1939 and 1944 are dealt with separately under Slovakia.

		VF	XF
32 (33)	20 Halere (Br) 1947–1950. Lion coat of arms. ℞ sheaf and sickle; diameter 18 mm	0.30	0.60
33 (35)	50 Halere (Br) 1947–1950. Lion coat of arms. ℞ value above linden branch and sheaf; diameter 20 mm	0.40	0.80
34 (37)	1 Koruna (Cu-Ni) 1946, 1947. Lion coat of arms. R harvest scene: female agricultural worker kneeling, holding sheaf of wheat and sickle	0.50	1.00

		VF	XF
35 (39)	2 Korun (Cu–Ni) 1947–1948. Lion coat of arms. ℞ bust right of Juraj Jánošik (1688–1713), Slovakian national hero	0.80	1.50

COMMEMORATIVE ISSUE FOR THE 3rd ANNIVERSARY OF THE SLOVAKIAN UPRISING ON 29th AUGUST 1944

			VF	XF
36 (40)	50	Korun (Ag) 1947. National arms. ℞ Female fighter holding gun and linden branch	5.00	6.00
37 (34)	20	Halere (Al) 1951, 1952. Type as No. 32; diameter 16 mm	0.30	0.70
38 (36)	50	Halere (Al) 1951-1953. Type as No. 33; diameter 18 mm	0.40	0.80
39 (38)	1	Korun (Al) 1947-1953. Type as No. 34:		
		a) 1947, pattern		200.00
		b) 1950-1953	0.40	0.80
40 (A 39)	5	Korun (Al) 1952. Type as No. 8; diameter 24 mm	18.00	32.00

No. 40 did not come into circulation. The coins were melted down again; only very few of them came into collectors' hands.

COMMEMORATIVE ISSUE FOR THE 3rd ANNIVERSARY OF THE MAY REVOLUTION

41 (41)	50	Korun (Ag) 1948. Lion coat of arms. ℞ male figure holding sword and laurel branch	5.00	6.50

COMMEMORATIVE ISSUE FOR 600 YEARS OF THE KARL UNIVERSITY IN PRAGUE

42 (42) 100 Korun (Ag) 1948. Lion coat of arms. ℞ St. Wenceslas (907–929) holding banner and sword; kneeling in front of him, Karl I (1316–1378), Count of Luxembourg, from 1346 Karl IV, King of Bohemia, from 1347 also Emperor of the Holy Roman Empire, founder of the first German-speaking university, holding foundation documents; on left, coats of arms: Bohemian lion and eagle of St. Wenceslas   7.00   8.50

COMMEMORATIVE ISSUE FOR THE 30th ANNIVERSARY OF LIBERATION FROM AUSTRIA

		VF	XF

43 (43) 100 Korun (Ag) 1948. Lion coat of arms. ℞ male figure holding laurel branch   6.50   9.00

COMMEMORATIVE ISSUE FOR 700 YEARS OF THE CODE OF MINING RIGHTS OF JIHLAVA (IGLAU)

44 (44) 100 Korun (Ag) 1949. Lion coat of arms. ℞ coal miner in traditional costume emerging from pit. The Jihlava code of mining rights goes back to King Wenceslas I (he reigned from 1230 to 1253) and is applied in the regions of the Sudetenland and the Carpathian mountains, as well as in Upper Hungary   6.50   9.00

COMMEMORATIVE ISSUES (2) FOR THE 70th ANNIVERSARY OF THE BIRTH OF STALIN

Values are given for each coin un U.S. Dollars and reference to Yeomannumbers.

			VF	XF
45 (45)	50	Korun (Ag) 1949. Lion coat of arms. R Generalissimo J. V. Stalin (1879–1953), Soviet statesman	5.00	9.00
46 (46)	100	Korun (Ag) 1949. Type as No. 45	7.00	12.00

COMMEMORATIVE ISSUE FOR THE 30th ANNIVERSARY OF THE CZECHOSLOVAKIAN COMMUNIST PARTY

			VF	XF
47 (47)	100	Korun (Ag) 1951. Lion coat of arms. R Klement Gottwald (1896–1953), President of State 1948–1953	5.00	9.00
48 (48)	1	Haleru (Al) 1953–1960. Lion coat of arms. R value within wreath	0.10	0.20
49 (49)	3	Halere (Al) 1953–1954. Type as No. 44	0.10	0.20
50 (50)	5	Halere (Al) 1953–1955. Type as No. 44	0.20	0.40
51 (51)	10	Halere (Al) 1953–1956, 1958. Type as No. 44	0.20	0.35
52 (52)	25	Halere (Al) 1953–1954. Type as No. 44	0.40	0.80
53 (61)	1	Koruna (Al–Br) 1957–1960. Lion coat of arms. R female agricultural worker holding plant	0.60	1.20

COMMEMORATIVE ISSUES (2) FOR THE 10th ANNIVERSARY OF THE SLOVAKIAN UPRISING

54 (53)	10	Korun (Ag) 1954. Lion coat of arms. R partisan with factory and railway in background	6.00	7.50
55 (54)	25	Korun (Ag) 1954. Type as No. 54	7.50	10.00

COMMEMORATIVE ISSUES (4) FOR THE 10th ANNIVERSARY OF LIBERATION ON 9th MAY 1945

56 (55)	10	Korun (Ag) 1955. Lion coat of arms. R soldier kneeling to left, holding child	6.00	7.50

All valuations in the SCHÖN are stated in U.S. Dollars.

			VF	XF
57 (56)	25	Korun (Ag) 1955. Lion coat of arms. ℞ "The return of the soldier": scene with mother holding child in arms, and soldier	8.00	10.50
58 (57)	50	Korun (Ag) 1955. Lion coat of arms. ℞ Soviet soldier	17.00	22.00
59 (58)	100	Korun (Ag) 1955. Lion coat of arms. ℞ scenes of rejoicing at barricade in May 1945	28.00	35.00

300th ANNIVERSARY OF THE PUBLICATION OF THE BOOK »OPERA DIDACTICA OMNIA«

60 (60)	10	Korun (Ag) 1957. Bust right of Jan Amos Komenský, called Comenius (1592–1670), preacher and Bishop of the Moravian Brotherhood, educational reformer and theologian	6.00	9.00

250th ANNIVERSARY OF THE EXISTENCE OF THE TECHNICAL HIGH SCHOOL IN PRAGUE

61 (59)	10	Korun (Ag) 1957. Lion coat of arms. ℞ bust left of Christian Josef Willenberg (1676–1731), founder of the School of Engineering; in background, the Slapy dam near Prague	11.00	15.00

CZECHOSLOVAKIAN SOCIALIST REPUBLIC – CSSR
Ceskoslovenská socialistická republika

		VF	XF
62 (62)	1 Haleru (Al) 1962–1963. Coat of arms. R value within wreath	0.10	0.20
63 (63)	3 Halere (Al) 1962, 1963. Type as No. 62		
	a) 1962		100.00
	b) 1963	0.15	0.25
64 (64)	5 Halere (Al) 1962–1963, 1966–1968, 1970, 1972–1976. Type as No. 62	0.15	0.25
65 (65)	10 Halere (Al) 1961–1971. Type as No. 62	0.20	0.35
66 (66)	25 Halere (Al) 1962–1964. Type as No. 62	0.20	0.40

67 (67)	50 Halere (Br) 1963–1965, 1969–1974. Type as No. 62	0.25	0.50

68 (68)	1 Koruna (Al-Br) 1961–1971, 1975–1977, 1980–1982, 1984. Coat of arms. Rev. female agricultural worker holding plant	0.20	0.40

COMMEMORATIVE ISSUE FOR THE 20th ANNIVERSARY OF THE SLOVAKIAN UPRISING

69 (69)	10 Korun (Ag) 1964. Coat of arms. R three hands raised holding the symbols of industry, agriculture and science	6.00	7.50

COMMEMORATIVE ISSUE FOR THE 20th ANNIVERSARY OF LIBERATION

70 (70)	25 Korun (Ag) 1965. Coat of arms. R girl's head to left, with dove of peace holding linden branch; in background, the Karlsbrücke in Prague	7.50	10.00

COMMEMORATIVE ISSUE FOR THE 550th ANNIVERSARY OF THE DEATH OF JAN HUS

				VF	XF
71 (71)	10	Korun (Ag) 1965. Coat of arms. ℞ Jan Hus (1369–1415), rector of the Karl university, religious reformer and martyr		25.00	32.00
72 (72)	3	Korun (Cu–Ni) 1965–1969. Coat of arms. ℞ stylized flower surrounded with ribbons, symbol of liberty and progress		0.50	0.80
73 (73)	5	Korun (Cu-Ni) 1966–1970, 1973–1975, 1978, 1980–1982, 1984. Coat of arms. Rev. representation of cranes with star and flower, symbol of reconstruction		0.70	1.20

COMMEMORATIVE ISSUE FOR THE 1100th ANNIVERSARY OF THE FOUNDING OF GREATER MORAVIA

				VF	XF
74 (74)	10	Korun (Ag) 1966. Coat of arms. ℞ hawking scene: falconer on horseback; silversmith work of the 9th century found at Staré Mesto in Moravia		7.00	9.00

COMMEMORATIVE ISSUE FOR THE 500th ANNIVERSARY OF THE FOUNDING OF PRESSBURG UNIVERSITY

				VF	XF
75 (75)	10	Korun (Ag) 1967. Coat of arms above the spurs of the Carpathian mountains with the castle of Pressburg (Bratislava) and the Danube river, stylized, symbol of the City. ℞ university buildings, and seal of the city, with inscription SIGILLUM CIVITATIS BRATISLAVENSIS		20.00	25.00

COMMEMORATIVE ISSUE FOR THE CENTENARY OF THE LAYING OF THE FOUNDATION STONE OF THE PRAGUE NATIONAL THEATRE

		VF	XF
76 (76)	10 Korun (Ag) 1968. Triga. ℞ coat of arms	25.00	40.00

COMMEMORATIVE ISSUE FOR THE 150th ANNIVERSARY OF THE EXISTENCE OF THE NATIONAL MUSEUM

77 (77)	25 Korun (Ag) 1968. Coat of arms. ℞ the National Museum building in Prague	12.00	17.00

COMMEMORATIVE ISSUE FOR THE 50th ANNIVERSARY OF THE REPUBLIC AND THE 20th ANNIVERSARY OF THE PEOPLE'S REPUBLIC

78 (78)	50 Korun (Ag) 1968. Head left of the Republic crowned with linden leaves, a project by Jiri Harcuba. Around, dates 1918, 1968. ℞ coat of arms, dates 1948, 1968. Name of country and value	60.00	85.00

COMMEMORATIVE ISSUE FOR THE CENTENARY OF THE DEATH OF J. E. PURKINJE

79 (79)	25 Korun (Ag) 1969. Bust right of Jan Evangelista, Knight of Purkinje (1787–

	VF	XF

1869), professor of physiology and
pathology. ℞ national arms and value   8.00   12.00

Medal upon the same occasion with the
use of the obverse die, approx. 25.3 g fine
gold   480.00

COMMEMORATIVE ISSUE FOR THE 25th ANNIVERSARY OF THE SLOVAKIAN UPRISING

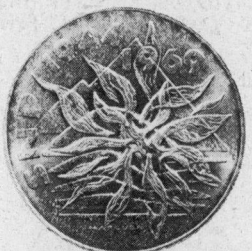

80 (80) 25 Korun (Ag) 1969. Allegorical representation with letters S N P (=
Slovenské národni povstáni) 1944/1969
℞ coat of arms, name of country and
value   40.00   50.00

COMMEMORATIVE ISSUE FOR THE 50th ANNIVERSARY OF THE SLOVAKIAN NATIONAL THEATRE IN PRESSBURG

81 (81) 25 Korun (Ag) 1970. Facing head of muse
crowned with laurel leaves. ℞ coat of
arms and value   7.50   10.00

COMMEMORATIVE ISSUE FOR THE 25th ANNIVERSARY OF LIBERATION

			VF	XF
82 (82)	25 Korun (Ag) 1970. Coat of arms. ℞ star above landscape. Dates, value		6.00	9.00

COMMEMORATIVE ISSUE FOR THE CENTENARY OF THE BIRTH OF LENIN

83 (83)	50 Korun (Ag) 1970. Vladimir Ilyich Lenin (1870–1924), real name Ulyanov; Soviet-Russian statesman, leader of the world proletariat	8.00	11.00

COMMEMORATIVE ISSUE FOR THE 50th ANNIVERSARY OF THE CZECHOSLOVAKIAN COMMUNIST PARTY

84 (84)	50 Korun (Ag) 1971. Hammer and sickle in front of people, above star	8.00	12.00

COMMEMORATIVE ISSUE FOR THE 50th ANNIVERSARY OF THE DEATH OF P. O. HVIEZDOSLAV

85 (85)	50 Korun (Ag) 1971. Pavel Országh Hviezdoslav (1849–1921), poet and writer	9.00	12.50

COMMEMORATIVE ISSUE FOR THE CENTENARY OF THE DEATH OF J. MÁNES

86 (86)	100 Korun (Ag) 1971. Josef Mánes (1820–1871), painter	12.00	17.00

COMMEMORATIVE ISSUE FOR THE CENTENARY
OF THE DEATH OF A. SLÁDKOVIČ

			VF	XF
87 (87)	20 Korun (Ag) 1972. Andrej Sládkovič, Slovakian poet		5.00	7.50

COMMEMORATIVE ISSUE FOR THE 50th ANNIVERSARY
OF THE DEATH OF J. V. MYSLBEK

88 (88)	50 Korun (Ag) 1972. J. V. Myslbek (1848 to 1922), Czechoslovakian sculptor		9.00	12.00

89 (91)	20 Halere (Al–Br) 1972–		0.10	0.20

90 (94)	2 Korun (Cu–Ni) 1972–1983		0.25	0.50

COMMEMORATIVE ISSUE FOR THE 25th ANNIVERSARY
OF THE PEOPLE'S REPUBLIC

91 (96)   50 Korun (Ag) 1973. Soldier and factory   8.00   10.50

COMMEMORATIVE ISSUE FOR THE 200th ANNIVERSARY
OF THE BIRTH OF J. JUNGMANN

92 (97)   50 Korun (Ag) 1973. Josef Jungmann,
        writer and philologist   9.00   12.00

COMMEMORATIVE ISSUE FOR THE 150th BIRTHDAY
OF FRIEDRICH SMETANA

93 (99)   100 Korun (Ag) 1974. Friedrich Smetana
        (1824–1884), composer   13.00   17.00

COMMEMORATIVE ISSUE FOR THE 100th BIRTHDAY
OF JANKO JESENSKY

94 (98)   50 Korun (Ag) 1974. Janko Jesensky (30.
        12. 1874 to 27. 12. 1945), Slovakian
        writer   9.00   12.00
95 (90)   10 Halere (Al) 1974–1986. Type as No.
        89   0.10   0.20

100th ANNIVERSARY OF THE BIRTH OF S. K. NEUMANN

			VF	XF
96 (100)	50	Korun (Ag) 1975. Stanislav Kostka Neumann (1875-1947), Czech poet	10.00	12.50

100th ANNIVERSARY OF THE DEATH OF JANKO KRAL

97 (101)	100	Korun (Ag) 1976. Janko Král (1822-1876), Slovakian poet	15.00	18.00

100th ANNIVERSARY OF THE BIRTH OF VIKTOR KAPLAN

98 (102)	100	Korun (Ag) 1976. Viktor Kaplan (1876-1934), engineer, inventor of the Kaplan-turbine	15.00	18.00

125th ANNIVERSARY OF THE DEATH OF JAN KOLLÁR

			VF	XF
99 (103)	50	Korun (Ag) 1977. Jan Kollár (1793-1852), Slovakian poet	9.00	12.00

300th ANNIVERSARY OF THE DEATH OF WENZEL HOLLAR

			VF	XF
100 (104)	100	Korun (Ag) 1977. Wenzel Hollar (1607–1677), engraver and designer	12.00	18.00

			VF	XF
101 (89)	5	Halere (Al) 1977–1983. Type as No. 89	0.10	0.20

100th ANNIVERSARY OF THE BIRTH OF ZDENĚK NEJEDLÝ

			VF	XF
102 (105)	50	Korun (Ag) 1978. Dr. Zdeněk Nejedlý	9.00	12.00

75th ANNIVERSARY OF THE BIRTH OF JULIUS FUČIK

			VF	XF
103 (107)	100 Korun (Ag) 1978. Julius Fučik (1903–1943), journalist		9.00	12.50

650th ANNIVERSARY OF THE MINT OF KREMNICA

104 (106)	50 Korun (Ag) 1978. Coins strack at Kremnica Mint	7.00	10.00

600th ANNIVERSARY OF THE DEATH OF KARL IV (5)

105 (108)	100 Korun (Ag) 1978. Karl IV (1316–1378), Count of Luxembourg, from 1346 King of Bohemia, from 1347 also Emperor of the Holy Roman Empire	11.00	15.00

106 (110)	1 Ducat (Au) 1978–1982	130.00	150.00

107 (111)	2 Ducats (Au) 1978	250.00	280.00
108 (112)	5 Ducats (Au) 1978	450.00	500.00
109 (113)	10 Ducats (Au) 1978	900.00	1000.00

110 (92) 50 Halere (Cu-Ni) 1978–1986. Type as   0.15   0.50
No. 89

150th ANNIVERSARY OF THE BIRTH OF JAN BOTTO

		Unc	**Proof**
111 (109)	100 Korun (Ag) 1979. Ján Botto (1829–1881), Slovakian poet	12.50	15.00

30th ANNIVERSARY OF THE 9th CONGRESS OF THE CZECHOSLOVAKIAN COMMUNIST PARTY

112 (114)	50 Korun (Ag) 1979. Hammer and sickle as well as gear-wheel	10.00	40.00

650th ANNIVERSARY OF THE BIRTH OF PETER PARLER

113 (115)	100 Korun (Ag) 1980. Peter Parler (1330–1399), architect	12.50	22.50

100th ANNIVERSARY OF THE BIRTH OF B. SMERAL

114 (117)	100 Korun (Ag) 1980. Dr. Bohumir Smeral (1880–1941), writer and politician	12.50	20.00

SPARTAKIADE GAMES 1980

		Unc	Proof
115 (116)	100 Korun (Ag) 1980	12.50	20.00

100th ANNIVERSARY OF THE BIRTH OF O. SPANIEL

			Unc	Proof
116 (120)	100 Korun (Ag) 1981. Otakar Spaniel (1881–1955), sculptor and medallist		12.50	20.00

125th ANNIVERSARY OF THE DEATH OF L. STUR

		Unc	Proof
117 (118)	500 Korun (Ag) 1981. Ludovit Stur (1815–1856), Slovakian poet and politician	35.00	50.00

20th ANNIVERSARY OF MANNED SPACES FLIGHT

		Unc	Proof
118 (119)	100 Korun (Ag) 1981. Juri A. Gagarin (1934–1968), Soviet cosmonaut	12.00	18.00

100th ANNIVERSARY OF THE BIRTH OF I. OLBRACHT

		Unc	Proof
119 (121)	100 Korun (Ag) 1982. Ivan Olbracht (1882–1952), writer	12.00	18.00

150th ANNIVERSARY OF HORSE DRAWN TRAM (BUDWEIS – LINZ)

		Unc	Proof
120 (122)	100 Korun (Ag) 1982	12.00	20.00

100th ANNIVERSARY OF PRAGUE THEATRE (2)

			Unc	Proof
121 (126)	100 Korun (Ag) 1983. General view of the Theatre		12.00	20.00
122 (127)	500 Korun (Ag) 1983		50.00	70.00

100th ANNIVERSARY OF THE DEATH OF KARL MARX

123 (123)	100 Korun (Ag) 1983. Karl Marx (1818–1883), social ideologist	12.50	20.00

100th ANNIVERSARY OF THE BIRTH OF J. HASEK

124 (124)	100 Korun (Ag) 1983. Jaroslav Hašek (1883–1923), writer	12.50	20.00

100th ANNIVERSARY OF THE DEATH OF S. CHALUPKA

125 (125)	100 Korun (Ag) 1983. Samo Chalupka (1812–1883), poet	12.50	20.00

300th ANNIVERSARY OF THE BIRTH OF MATHIAS BEL

126	100 Korun (Ag) 1983. Mathias Bél (1684–1749), savant, geographer	12.50	20.00

150th ANNIVERSARY OF THE BIRTH OF J. NERUDA

127	100 Korun (Ag) 1984. Jan Neruda (1834–1891), poet and journalist	12.50	20.00

100th ANNIVERSARY OF THE BIRTH OF A. ZAPOTOCKY

128	100 Korun (Ag) 1984. Antonín Zápotocký (1884–1957) politician and writer	12.50	20.00

125th ANNIVERSARY OF THE BIRTH OF M. KUKUCIN

		Unc	**Proof**
129	100 Korun (Ag) 1985. Martin Kukučin (1860–1928), writer	12.50	20.00

200th ANNIVERSARY OF THE BIRTH OF J. HOLLY

130	100 Korun (Ag) 1985. Jan Hollý (1785–1849), poet	12.50	20.00

WORLD ICE-HOCKEY CHAMPIONSHIP GAMES IN PRAGUE

131	100 Korun (Ag) 1985. Ice-hockey player	15.00	25.00

250th ANNIVERSARY OF THE DEATH OF P. J. BRANDL

132	100 Korún (Ag) 1985. Petr Jan Brandl (1668–1735), painter	12.50	20.00

10th ANNIVERSARY OF THE HELSINKI CONFERENCE

133	100 Korún (Ag) 1985. Dove superimposed on map of Europe	15.00	22.50

134	100 Korún (Ag) 1986. Karel Hynek Mácha (1810–1836), poet and writer		12.50	20.00

Dahome   # Dahomey   **Dahomey**

Benin

Area: 44,524 sq. mi. Population: 4,000,000.
In the 17th century the powerful kingdom of Dahomey existed in the territory of the present state of Dahomey. One after another, neighbouring tribes were subjected to rigidly organised military power, either through conquest or through voluntary submission. After occupation by, and submission to the French, and the inclusion of Abomey (1894), the country became a colony and part of French West Africa. In 1957 it obtained further internal autonomy within the framework of the Communauté Française. On 4th December 1958 the Republic was proclaimed. Since 1st August 1960 Dahomey has been independent. Dahomey joined up with the countries of the Ivory Coast, Mauretania, Nigeria, Upper Volta, Senegal and Togo in order to form the Union Monétaire Ouest-Africaine; the issuing authority for the whole of the monetary union is the Banque Centrale des Etats de l'Afrique de l'Quest. See also under the heading »West African States«. In 1974, the republic began a transition to a socialist society with Marxism-Leninism as its revolutionary philosophy. On November 30, 1975 the name of the Republic Dahomey was changed to the People's Republic of Benin.
Capital: Porto Novo.

$$100 \text{ Centimes} = 1 \text{ CFA Franc}$$

COMMEMORATIVE ISSUES (8) FOR THE 10th ANNIVERSARY
OF INDEPENDENCE ON 1st AUGUST 1970

1	100	Francs (Ag) 1971–. Buildings on stilts on Lake Ganvié. ℞ national arms, name of country, commemorative inscription, value	**Proof** 20.00

		Proof
2	200 Francs (Ag) 1971–. Abomey woman. Ŗ same as No. 1	30.00
3	500 Francs (Ag) 1971–. Ouémé woman. Ŗ same as No. 1	60.00
4	1000 Francs (Ag) 1971–. Somba woman. Ŗ same as No. 1	100.00
5	2500 Francs (Au) 1971–. Group of religious dancers. Ŗ same as No. 1	225.00

6	5000 Francs (Au) 1971–. African buffaloes (Syncerus caffer – Bovidae). Ŗ same as No. 1	500.00
7	10000 Francs (Au) 1971–. Hippopotami (Hippopotamus amphibius – Hippopotamidae). Ŗ same as No. 1	950.00
8	25000 Francs (Au) 1971–. Busts of Sourou-Migan Apithy (*1913), Prime Minister 1957–1959, President of State from 1964 to 1965, Justin Ahomadegbé-Tometin (*1917) and Hubert Maga (*1916), Prime Minister 1959–1961, President of State 1961–1963; present President of State. Ŗ same as No. 1	1850.00

All valuations in the SCHÖN are stated in U.S. Dollars.

Danish West Indies

This group of about 50 islands in the West Indies became a Danish possession in the 17th century and was sold to the United States of America on 31st March 1971 for $ 25,000,000. Since then, these islands have been known as the U. S. Virgin Islands.
Capital: Charlotte Amalie.

5 Bit = 1 Cent, 20 Cents = 1 Franc, 5 Francs = 1 Daler

		CHRISTIAN IX 1863–1906	VF	XF
1 (5)	½ Cent = 2½ Bit (Br) 1905. Crown above monogram. ℞ sickle, herald's staff and trident		16.00	30.00
2 (6)	1 Cent = 5 Bit (Br) 1905. Same type as No. 1		15.00	25.00

3 (7)	2 Cents = 10 Bit (Br) 1905. Same type as No. 1		20.00	35.00

4 (8)	5 Cents = 25 Bit (Ni) 1905. Same type as No. 1		10.00	20.00

5 (9)	10 Cents = 50 Bit (Ag) 1905. Head l. of Christian IX. ℞ value and laurel branch		16.00	25.00

			VF	**XF**
6 (10)	20	Cents = 1 Franc (Ag) 1905. Bust l. of Christian IX. ℞ 3 female figures	35.00	60.00
7 (11)	40	Cents = 2 Francs (Ag) 1905. Same type as No. 6	100.00	180.00
8 (12)	4	Daler = 20 Francs (Au) 1904, 1905. Head l. of Christian IX. Rev. Seated female figure:		
		a) 1904	400.00	550.00
		b) 1905	500.00	700.00

			VF	**XF**
9 (13)	10	Daler = 50 Francs (Au) 1904. Same type as No. 8	4000.00	5000.00

FREDERIK VIII 1906–1912

			VF	**XF**
10 (14)	20	Cents = 1 Franc (Ag) 1907. Head l. of Frederik VIII. ℞ three female figures	40.00	80.00
11 (15)	40	Cents = 2 Francs (Ag) 1907. Same type as No. 10	130.00	210.00

CHRISTIAN X 1912–1917

			VF	**XF**
12 (16)	1	Cent = 5 Bit (Br) 1913. Crown above monogram. ℞ sickle, herald's staff and trident	22.00	40.00

Previous issues, see "Weltmünzkatalog 19. Jahrhundert" (World Coin Catalogue of the 19th Century)

Denmark
Danmark

Area: 16,629 sq. mi. Population: 5,200,000.
The kingdom of Denmark includes the Jutland peninsula and about 50 islands between the Baltic and the North Sea. The Faroe Islands in the Atlantic Ocean are administered by Denmark, but enjoy limited autonomy.
Capital: Copenhagen.
Greenland, on the other hand, has been an integral part of the kingdom since 1953, with equal rights, under a governor.

100 Øre = 1 Krone

CHRISTIAN IX 1863–1906

			VF	XF
1 (8)	1	Øre (Br) 1874–1904. Monogram. ℞ common dolphin (Delphinus delphis – Delphinidae), ear of wheat and value	4.00	7.50
2 (9)	2	Øre (Br) 1874–1904. Same type as No. 1	5.00	8.00
3 (10)	5	Øre (Br) 1874–1906. Same type as No. 1	10.50	17.00

			VF	XF
4 (11)	10	Øre (Ag) 1874–1905. Head r. of Christian IX. (1818–1906). ℞ common dolphin, ear of wheat, star and value	6.00	11.00
5 (12)	25	Øre (Ag) 1874–1905. Same type as No. 4	10.50	18.50
6 (13)	1	Krone (Ag) 1875–1898. Head of Christian IX. ℞ crowned arms between common dolphin and ear of wheat	20.00	36.00
7 (14)	2	Kroner (Ag) 1875–1899. Same type as No. 6	20.00	38.00
8 (18)	10	Kroner (Au) 1873–1900. Head of Christian IX. ℞ allegorical representation of Denmark	110.00	140.00
9 (19)	20	Kroner (Au) 1873–1900. Head of Christian IX. ℞ allegorical figure	125.00	150.00

			VF	**XF**
10 (17)	2	Kroner (Ag) 1903. Bust r. of King Christian IX. ℞ allegorical figure, inscription, value	30.00	50.00

FREDERIK VIII 1906–1912

COMMEMORATIVE ISSUE FOR THE DEATH OF CHRISTIAN IX AND THE ACCESSION TO THE THRONE OF FREDERIK VIII

11 (25)	2	Kroner (Ag) 1906. Bust l. of Frederik VIII (1843–1912). ℞ Bust l. of Christian IX	20.00	30.00
12 (20)	1	Øre (Br) 1907–1912. Monogram. ℞ value	4.00	5.00
13 (21)	2	Øre (Br) 1907–1912. Monogram. ℞ value	4.00	6.00
14 (22)	5	Øre (Br) 1907–1912. Monogram. ℞ value	8.00	14.00
15 (23)	10	Øre (Ag) 1907–1912. Head of Frederik VIII. ℞ value	8.00	14.00
16 (24)	25	Øre (Ag) 1907, 1911. Head of Frederik VIII. ℞ value	7.50	12.50
17 (26)	10	Kroner (Au) 1908–1909. Head of Frederik VIII. ℞ crowned arms and value	110.00	150.00

			VF	**XF**
18	(27)	20 Kroner (Au) 1908–1912. Same type as No. 17	130.00	165.00

CHRISTIAN X 1912–1947

COMMEMORATIVE ISSUE FOR THE DEATH OF FREDERIK VIII AND THE ACCESSION TO THE THRONE OF CHRISTIAN X

19	(40)	2 Kroner (Ag) 1912. Head of Christian X. R head of Frederik VIII	25.00	40.00
20	(28)	1 Øre (Br) 1913–1923. Monogramm CX with crown, date. R value	1.50	3.00
21	(29)	2 Øre (Br) 1913–1923. Type as No. 20	2.00	4.00

22	(30)	5 Øre (Br) 1913-1923. Type as No. 20	5.00	10.00
23	(36)	10 Øre (Ag) 1914-1919. Type similar to No. 20	4.00	6.00

24	(37)	25 Øre (Ag) 1913-1919. Type as No. 23	4.50	7.50

25 (38)	1 Krone (Ag) 1915–1916. Head r. of Christian X. R crowned arms between common dolphin and ear of wheat	**VF**	**XF**
		7.00	12.00

26 (39)	2 Kroner (Ag) 1915-1916. Type as No. 25	14.00	22.00
27 (44)	10 Kroner (Au) 1913, 1917. Head of Christian X. R crowned arms	125.00	145.00
28 (45)	20 Kroner (Au) 1913-1931. Type No. 27	135.00	160.00
29 (28a)	1 Øre (Fe) 1918, 1919. Type as No. 20	3.50	7.00
30 (29a)	2 Øre (Fe) 1918, 1919. Type as No. 21	3.50	7.00
31 (30a)	5 Øre (Fe) 1918, 1919. Type as No. 22	10.00	20.00
32 (31)	10 Øre (Cu-Ni) 1920-1923. Type as No. 23	4.00	8.00
33 (32)	25 Øre (Cu-Ni) 1920-1922. Type as No. 24	3.50	7.00

COMMEMORATIVE ISSUE FOR THE SILVER WEDDING OF THE ROYAL COUPLE

34 (41)	2 Kroner (Ag) 1923. Conjoined busts r. of Christian X and Queen Alexandrine (1879–1952). R crowned arms	12.00	18.00

35 (46) 1 Øre (Br) 1926–1940. Monogram CX
with crown. ℞ value (with central
hole) · · · · · · 0.60 1.10

36 (47) 2 Øre (Br) 1926–1940. Same type as No.
35 · · · · · · · · 0.60 1.10

37 (48) 5 Øre (Br) 1927–1941. Same type as No.
35 · · · · · · · · 0.80 1.50

38 (49) 10 Øre (Cu-Ni) 1924-1947. Monogramm CX
and ℞ above, crown. ℞ value (central hole) 1.60 3.20

39 (50) 25 Øre (Cu-Ni) 1924-1927. Type as No. 38 2.00 4.00

For similar coins to Nos. 35–39, but without any mintmark, see under
Faroe Islands.

40 (33) ½ Krone (Al-Br) 1924-1940. Monogramm
CX with crown dividing date. ℞ crown and
value · · · · · · 6.00 11.00

41 (34) 1 Krone (Al-Br) 1924–1941.
Type as No. 40:
a) 1924 · · · · · 85.00 150.00
b) 1925–1941 · · · 3.00 6.00

42 (35) 2 Kroner (Al-Br) 1924-1941. Same type as
No. 40 · · · · · · 3.00 6.00

60th BIRTHDAY OF THE KING

		VF	XF
43 (42)	2 Kroner (Ag) 1930. Head r. of Christian X (1870–1947). ℞ crowned arms and shield supported by two figures	10.00	15.00

COMMEMORATIVE ISSUE FOR 25 YEARS' REIGN

44 (43)	2 Kroner (Ag) 1937. Head r. of Christian X. ℞ crowned arms, value and inscription 15 Mai 1912–1937	12.00	16.50
45 (51)	1 Øre (Zi) 1941–1946. Monogram CX with crown. ℞ value in wreath	0.70	2.00
46 (52a)	2 Øre (Zi) 1942-1947. Type as No. 45	0.80	1.60
47 (53a)	5 Øre (Zi) 1942-1945. Type as No. 45	1.20	2.50
48 (49a)	10 Øre (Zi) 1941-1945. Type as No. 38	1.50	3.50
49 (50a)	25 Øre (Zi) 1941-1945. Type as No. 39	4.00	8.00
50	1 Øre (Al) 1941. Type as No. 45. Trial strike!	–.–	–.–
51 (52)	2 Øre (Al) 1941. Type as No. 46	1.20	2.50
52 (53)	5 Øre (Al) 1941. Type as No. 47	2.00	5.00

53 (54) 1 Krone (Al-Br) 1942–1947. Head r. of Christian X. ℞ value and ears of wheat in saltire   1.50   3.00

COMMEMORATIVE ISSUE FOR THE 75th BIRTHDAY OF THE KING

54 (55) 2 Kroner (Ag) 1945. Head r. of Christian X. ℞ dates 1870–1945 within wreath   20.00   30.00

FREDERIK IX 1947–1972

		VF	XF
55 (56)	1 Øre (Zi) 1948–1972. Monogram FR; crown above. R value	0.10	0.20
56 (57)	2 Øre (Zi) 1948–1972. Same type as No. 55	0.10	0.20

57 (58)	5 Øre (Zi) 1950–1964. Same type as No. 55	0.40	0.80
58 (59)	10 Øre (Cu-Ni) 1948–1960. Monogram FR; crown above. R value	0.40	0.80
59 (60)	25 Øre (Cu-Ni) 1948–1960. Same type as No. 58	0.50	0.80

60 (61) 1 Krone (Al-Br) 1947-1960. Head r. of
Frederik IX. (1899-1972). R crowned arms:

          a) 1947-1959   1.50   3.00

          b) 1960   –.–   –.–

61 (62) 2 Kroner (Al-Br) 1947-1959. Same type as
No. 60   3.00   5.00

COMMEMORATIVE ISSUE FOR GREENLAND FOR THE ANTI-TUBERCULOSIS CAMPAIGN

62 (63) 2 Kroner (Ag) 1953. Conjoined heads r.
of Frederik IX and Queen Ingrid
(*1910). R map of Greenland   30.00   50.00

COMMEMORATIVE ISSUE FOR THE 18th BIRTHDAY OF PRINCESS MARGRETHE ON 16th APRIL 1958

		VF	XF
63 (64)	2 Kroner (Ag) 1958. Head r. of Frederik IX. R Head l. of Princess Margrethe (*1940), Queen since 1972	11.00	15.00

COMMEMORATIVE ISSUE FOR THE SILVER WEDDING OF
THE ROYAL COUPLE

64 (65) 5 Kroner (Ag) 1960. Conjoinded heads r.
            of Frederik IX and Queen Ingrid   11.00   15.00

65 (66) 1 Øre (Br) 1960–1964. Crowned mono-
            gram. ℞ value between ears   4.00
66 (67) 2 Øre (Br) 1960–1966. Same type as
            No. 65   3.50
67 (68) 5 Øre (Br) 1960–1972. Same type as
            No. 65   0.10   0.20

		VF	XF
68 (69)	10 Øre (Cu-Ni) 1960–1972. R value between oak leaves	0.10	0.20
69 (70)	25 Øre (Cu-Ni) 1960–1967. Same type as No. 68	0.40	0.60
70 (71)	1 Krone (Cu-Ni) 1960–1972. Head r. of Frederik IX. R crowned arms	0.40	0.80

71 (72)   5 Kroner (Cu-Ni) 1960-1972. Type as No. 70,
but coat of arms between oak leaves   1.20   2.00

COMMEMORATIVE ISSUE FOR THE WEDDING OF PRINCESS
ANNE-MARIE ON 18th SEPTEMBER 1964

72 (73)   5 Kroner (Ag) 1964. Head r. of Frederik
IX. ℞ head l. of Princess Anne-Marie
(*1947)   10.00   15.00

		VF	**XF**
73 (76)	25 Øre (Cu–Ni) 1966–1972. Monogram FR; above, crown; and twig of hornbeam (Carpinus bétulus). ℞ value and ears of barley (Hordeum sp. – Graminae)		
		0.15	0.25

COMMEMORATIVE ISSUE FOR THE WEDDING OF PRINCESS MARGRETHE ON 10th JUNE 1967

74 (74) 10 Kroner (Ag) 1967. Head r. of Frederik
IX. ℞ heads r. of Crown Princess
Margrethe and Count Henry de
Montpezat   10.00   15.00

COMMEMORATIVE ISSUE FOR THE WEDDING OF PRINCESS BENEDIKTE ON 3th FEBRUARY 1968

75 (75) 10 Kroner (Ag) 1968. Head r. of Frederik
IX. ℞ head l. of Princess Benedikte
(*1944)   10.00   15.00

			VF	XF
76 (77)	10	Kroner (Ag) 1972. Margrethe II. R Frederik IX	8.50	12.50

77 (78)	5	Øre (St, Br-plated) 1973-. Crowned monogramm, year date. R value	0.05	0.10

78 (79)	10	Øre (Cu-Ni) 1973-. Type similar to No. 69	0.05	0.10
79 (80)	25	Øre (Cu-Ni) 1973-. Crowned monogram, oak branch, year date. R denomination (with hole)	0.10	0.20
80 (81)	1	Krone (Cu-Ni) 1973-. Margrethe II, bust with legend, facing right. R crowned coat of arms (introduced 16. 11.1972), year date, denomination	0.15	0.30
81 (82)	5	Kroner (Cu-Ni) 1973-. R crowned coat of arms between oak leaves, year date, denomination	0.90	1.50
82 (83)	10	Kroner (Cu-Ni) 1979-	1.20	2.00

83 (84) 10 Kroner 1986. Rev. Crown Prince Frederik André Henrik Christian, head left:
    a) (Ag) .800 silver, 12.5 g   50.00
    b) (Cu-Ni)   3.00   –.–

Faroe Islands (Faerøerne)

Area: 538 sq. mi. Population: 34,500.
All the coins were struck in London and, unlike Nos. 35–39 of Denmark, show no mintmark.
Capital: Thorshavn.

100 Øre = 1 Krone

			VF	XF
1 (1)	1 Øre (Br) 1941. Monogram CX with crown. ℞ value (with central hole)		30.00	65.00
2 (2)	2 Øre (Br) 1941. Same type as No. 1		7.50	12.50
3 (3)	5 Øre (Br) 1941. Same type as No. 1		7.50	12.50
4 (4)	10 Øre (Cu-Ni) 1941. Monogram CX and R, above which, crown. ℞ value (with central hole)		12.00	20.00
5 (5)	25 Øre (Cu-Ni) 1941. Same type as No. 4		12.50	22.00

Values are given for each coin in U.S. Dollars and reference to Yeomannumbers.

Greenland (Grønland)

Area: 836,538 sq. mi. Population: 48,000.
According to the Danish Constitution of 5th June 1953, Greenland is an integral part of the kingdom of Denmark, with equal rights.
Capital: Godthaab.

100 Øre = 1 Krone

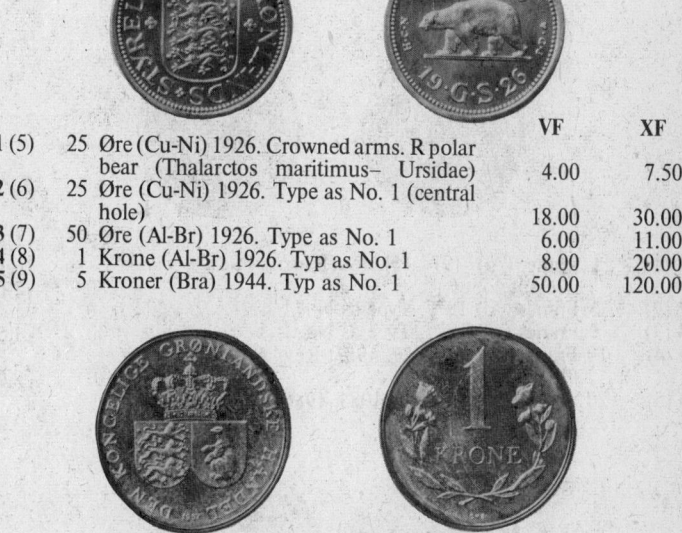

			VF	XF
1 (5)	25	Øre (Cu-Ni) 1926. Crowned arms. R polar bear (Thalarctos maritimus– Ursidae)	4.00	7.50
2 (6)	25	Øre (Cu-Ni) 1926. Type as No. 1 (central hole)	18.00	30.00
3 (7)	50	Øre (Al-Br) 1926. Type as No. 1	6.00	11.00
4 (8)	1	Krone (Al-Br) 1926. Typ as No. 1	8.00	20.00
5 (9)	5	Kroner (Bra) 1944. Typ as No. 1	50.00	120.00
6 (10)	1	Krone (Al-Br) 1957. Crown over shields of Denmark and Greenland. R value within wreath	12.50	25.00
7 (10a)	1	Krone (Cu-Ni) 1960, 1964. Type as No. 6	6.00	12.50

Dschibuti   # Djibouti   **Djibouti**

Area: 8,462 sq. mi. Population: 280,000.
The former French Territory of the Afars and Issas was renamed Djibouti and became independent on June 27, 1977.
Capital: Djibouti.

100 Centimes = 1 Djibouti Franc

			XF	Unc
1 (1)	1	Franc (Al) 1977. National arms. Rev. lyre antelope	0.50	1.00
2 (2)	2	Francs (Al) 1977. Type as No. 1	0.50	1.00
3 (3)	5	Francs (Al) 1977. Type as No. 1	1.00	1.50
4 (4)	10	Francs (Al-Br) 1977, 1983. Rev. Arab dhow	1.50	2.00
5 (5)	20	Francs (Al-Br) 1977, 1983, 1986. Type as No. 4	2.00	3.00

6 (6)	50	Francs (Cu-Ni) 1977, 1983. Rev. dromedaries	4.00	5.00
7 (7)	100	Francs (Cu-Ni) 1977, 1983. Type as No. 6	6.00	8.00

Dominica   # Dominica   **Dominique**

Area: 304 sq. mi. Population: 87,000.

Dominica, the largest island of the Lesser Antilles, was discovered by Christopher Columbus on 3rd November 1493. British since 1783, it became in 1968 an associate member of the United Kingdom of Great Britain. Dominica is a member of the Caribbean Free Trade Area (CARIFTA) and is linked with the countries of Antigua, Barbados, Grenada, Montserrat, St. Christopher- (Kitts-) Nevis-Anguilla, St. Lucia and St. Vincent to form the monetary union of the East Caribbean Dollar. The issuing authority for the whole monetary union is the East Caribbean Currency Authority with headquarters in Bridgetown, Barbados. Full independence was attained on 3rd November 1978. Capital: Roseau.

100 Cents = 1 East Caribbean Dollar

COMMEMORATIVE ISSUE FOR THE INAUGURATION OF THE CARIBBEAN DEVELOPMENT BANK AND THE FAO COIN PLAN

			Unc	Proof
1 (4*)	4 Dollars (Cu-Ni) 1970. Arms with eagles holding shield, and lion as helmet decoration. ℞ bananas, sugarcane and value		10.00	30.00

*This number refers to Yeoman's East Caribbean Territories listings.

INDEPENDENCE COMMEMORATIVE (4)

		Unc	Proof
2	10 Dollars (Ag) 1978. History of Carnival	25.00	30.00
3	20 Dollars (Ag) 1978. 50th Anniversary		
	Graf Zeppelin	70.00	85.00
4	150 Dollars (Au) 1978. Parrot and map	200.00	225.00
5	300 Dollars (Au) 1978. Arms	400.00	400.00

VISIT OF POPE JOHN PAUL II (2)

		Unc	Proof
6	10 Dollars (Ag) 1979. Portrait of Pope John		
	Paul II	25.00	30.00
7	300 Dollars (Au) 1979	375.00	450.00

ISRAEL AND EGYPT PEACE TREATY (2)

		Unc	Proof
8	20 Dollars (Ag) 1979	80.00	90.00
9	150 Dollars (Au) 1979	250.00	280.00

ROYAL VISIT (2)

		Unc	Proof
10	10 Dollars 1985. Rev. Arms:		
	a) (Ag) .925 silver, 28.28 g		40.00
	b) (Cu-Ni)	5.00	
11	500 Dollars (Au) 1985. Type as No. 10;		
	.916⅔ gold, 47.54 g		1000.00

Dominican Republic
Dominikanische Republik   **Dominicaine**

Area: 18,744 sq. mi. Population: 6,250,000.
State on the east side of the island of Haiti. After the discovery of the island
in 1492 the eastern part became a Spanish colony under the name of Santo
Domingo; it was ceded to the French in 1795, but was returned to Spain in
1808 with the help of Britain. It was declared independent in 1844.
Captial: Santo Domingo, renamed Ciudad Trujillo during the Trujillo regime.

100 Centavos = 1 Peso

			VF	XF
1 (15)	1	Centavo (Br) 1937–1961. Coconut palm (Cocos nucifera – Palmae). ℞ national arms	0.40	0.80
2 (16)	5	Centavos (Cu–Ni) 1937–1972. Taino Indian with feather headdress. ℞ national arms	0.30	0.60
3 (16a)	5	Centavos (Bi) 1944. Type as No. 2, but oblique stroke through the C of the denomination	4.00	7.50
4 (17)	10	Centavos (Ag) 1937–1961	1.20	2.50
5 (18)	25	Centavos (Ag) 1937–1961	3.00	5.00
6 (19)	½	Peso (Ag) 1937–1961	6.00	8.00
7 (20)	1	Peso (Ag) 1939, 1952:		
		a) 1939	25.00	60.00
		b) 1952	10.00	15.00

COMMEMORATIVE ISSUES (2) FOR THE 25th YEAR OF THE TRUJILLO REGIME

8 (21)	1	Peso (Ag) 1955. Bust right of Dr. Rafael Leonidas Trujillo y Molina (1891–1961), Head of State and Dictator 1930–1961. ℞ national arms	22.50	35.00

			VF	XF
9 (22)	30	Pesos (Au) 1955. Head left of Dr. Rafael L. Trujillo. ℞ national arms	350.00	425.00

			XF	Unc
10 (23)	1	Centavo (Br) 1963. Type as No. 2. ℞ national arms and commemorative inscription CENTENARIO DE LA RESTAURACION DE LA REPUBLICA 1863–1963	0.20	0.40
11 (24)	5	Centavos (Bi) 1963. Type as No. 10	0.50	0.80
12 (25)	10	Centavos (Ag) 1963. Type as No. 10	1.20	1.70
13 (26)	25	Centavos (Ag) 1963. Type as No. 10	3.00	4.00

14 (27)	½	Peso (Ag) 1963. Type as No. 10	6.00	9.00
15 (28)	1	Peso (Ag) 1963. Type as No. 10	12.50	17.50
16 (A 16)	1	Centavo (Br) 1968, 1971, 1972, 1975. National arms. ℞ Taino Indian with feather headdress, value, date	0.10	0.20
17 (17a)	10	Centavos (Cu-Ni) 1967, 1973, 1975. Type as No. 16	0.10	0.20
18	25	Centavos (Cu-Ni) 1967–1974. Type as No. 16:		
		a) (Y 18a) 1967, 1972; plain edge	0.50	1.00
		b) (Y 18b) 1974; reeded edge	0.40	0.80

19	½	Peso (Cu-Ni) 1967–1975. Type as No. 16:		
		a) (Y 19a) 1967, 1968; plain edge	1.00	2.00
		b) (Y 19b) 1973, 1975; reeded edge	0.60	1.20

ISSUE FOR THE FAO COIN PLAN

		XF	Unc
20 (29)	1 Centavo (Br) 1969. Inscription: PRODUZCAMOS MAS ALIMENTOS	0.10	0.30

COMMEMORATIVE ISSUE FOR THE 125th ANNIVERSARY OF THE REPUBLIC

21 (30)	1 Peso (Cu–Ni) 1969. National arms, commemorative inscription. ℞ old fort	2.00	4.00

COMMEMORATIVE ISSUE FOR THE 25th ANNIVERSARY OF THE EXISTENCE OF THE CENTRAL BANK OF THE DOMINICAN REPUBLIC

		Unc	Proof
22 (31)	1 Peso (Ag) 1972. State coat of arms, commemorative legend, year dates 1947–1972. ℞ main portal of the Mint (Casa de la Moneda); denomination	10.00	20.00

XII CENTRAL AMERICAN AND CARIBBEAN SPORTS GAMES IN SANTO DOMINGO (27. 2.–13. 3. 1974) (3)

23 (32)	1 Peso (Ag) 1974. State arms. Coat of arms of the city of Santo Domingo on a map outline of the Dominican Republic and 23 rays, symbolizing the participating nations, .900 silver, 26,7 g	10.00	20.00
A 23	1 Peso (Au) 1974. Type as No. 23, .900 gold, 26,7 g		–.–

24 (33) 30 Pesos (Au) 1974. R emblem of the
Sports Games   180.00   225.00

INTERNATIONAL BANKER'S CONFERENCE

25 (34) 10 Pesos (Ag) 1975. Reproduction of an old
coin. R coat of arms, value, commemora-
tive inscription   15.00   20.00

PUEBLO VIEJO MINE COMMEMORATIVE (2)

26 (35) 10 Pesos (Ag) 1975. Coat of arms, date,
inscription PLATA INICIAL EXPLO-
TACION MINA PUEBLO VIEJO. R
Taino-work of art   15.00   20.00
27 (36) 100 Pesos (Au) 1975. Coat of arms, date,
inscription ORO INICIAL EXPLO-
TATION MINA PUEBLO VIEJO. R
Taino-work of art   175.00   200.00

CENTENNIAL OF THE DEATH OF JUAN PABLO DUARTE (6)
1st Issue

28 (37) 1 Centavo (Br) 1976. Bust of Juan Pablo
Duarte (1813-1876), national hero, date. R
coat of arms, memorial legend.   0.40   1.00
29 (38) 5 Centavos (Cu-Ni) 1976. Type as No. 28   0.50   2.00
30 (39) 10 Centavos (Cu-Ni) 1976. Type as No. 28   0.80   2.00
31 (40) 25 Centavos (Cu-Ni) 1976. Type as No. 28   1.25   2.50
32 (41) ½ Peso (Cu-Ni) 1976. Type as No. 28   2.00   3.00
33 (42) 1 Peso (Cu-Ni) 1976. Type as No. 28   3.00   9.00

30th ANNIVERSARY OF CENTRAL BANK

34 (43) 30 Pesos (Ag) 1977. The new building of
the Banco Central in Santo Domingo   60.00   85.00

DUARTE CENTENNIAL
2nd Issue

35 (44) 200 Pesos (Au) 1977. Rev. Juan Pablo
Duarte, .800 gold, 31 g   500.00   500.00

		XF	Unc
36 (45)	1 Centavo (Br) 1978–1981. Type as No. 28, but without commemorative inscription	0.10	0.15
37 (46)	5 Centavos (Cu-Ni) 1978–1981. Type as No. 36	0.10	0.20
38 (47)	10 Centavos (Cu-Ni) 1978–1981. Type as No. 36	0.15	0.25
39 (48)	25 Centavos (Cu-Ni) 1978–1981. Type as No. 36	0.30	0.50
40 (49)	½ Peso (Cu-Ni) 1978–1981. Type as No. 36	0.80	1.00
41 (50)	1 Peso (Cu-Ni) 1978–1981. Type as No. 36	1.50	2.50

Silver strikes of Nos. 36–41 exist.

POPE JOHN PAUL II'S VISIT (3)

		Unc	Proof
42 (51)	25 Pesos (Ag) 1979. Pope John Paul II and cathedral	70.00	80.00
43 (52)	100 Pesos (Au) 1979. Type as No. 42	300.00	350.00
44 (53)	250 Pesos (Au) 1979. Type as No. 42	700.00	750.00

INTERNATIONAL YEAR OF THE CHILD (2)

45 (54)	10 Pesos (Ag) 1982:	
	a) normal thickness	35.00
	b) Pièfort	200.00
46 (55)	200 Pesos (Au) 1982:	
	a) normal thickness	350.00
	b) Pièfort	–.–

HUMAN RIGHTS (6)

		XF	Unc
47 (61)	1 Centavo (Bro) 1986. Arms. Rev. Caonabo		
48 (59)	5 Centavos (Cu-Ni) 1983, 1984, 1986. Rev. conjoined heads of Sanchez and Mella:		
	a) normal thickness	0.20	12.00
	b) Piéfort, 1983		22.50
49 (60)	10 Centavos (Cu-Ni) 1983, 1984, 1986. Rev. head of P. Duarte:		
	a) normal thickness	0.25	12.00
	b) Piéfort, 1983		22.50
50 (56)	25 Centavos (Cu-Ni) 1983, 1984, 1986. Rev. heads of sisters Mirabal:		
	a) normal thickness	0.60	12.00
	b) Piéfort, 1983		22.50

51 (57)   ½ Peso (Cu-Ni) 1983, 1984, 1986. Rev.
              heads of Bono, Espaillat and Rojas:
              a) normal thickness   1.50   12.00
              b) Piéfort, 1983   22.50
52 (58)   1 Peso (Cu-Ni) 1983, 1984. Rev. heads
              of Montesinos, Enriquillo and Lem-
              ba:
              a) normal thickness   2.50   12.00
              b) Piéfort, 1983   22.50

Silver strikes of Nos. 47–51 exist.

XV CENTRAL AMERICAN AND CARIBBEAN GAMES
SANTIAGO 1986

		XF	**Unc**
53 (62)	1 Peso (Ni bonded St) 1986. Arms, val-		
	ue. Rev. Rider and Santiago arms	1.50	2.50

The East African Monetary Union comprising the now independent states of Kenya (gained independence in 1963), Uganda (1962) and Tanzania (formed by the union of Tanganyika and Zanzibar in 1964) included also British Somaliland until the Republic of Somalia was set up in 1960. The coins issued between 1907 and 1919 have the inscription EAST AFRICA & UGANDA PROTECTORATES.

100 Cents = 1 Rupee (Florin);
since 1921: 100 Cents = 1 Shilling

EDWARD VII 1901–1910

			VF	XF
1 (2)	½ Cent (Al) 1908. Crown above value. Ornamental decoration. ℞ elephants' tusks (central hole)		28.00	60.00
2 (3)	1 Cent (Al) 1907–1908		5.00	12.00
3 (2a)	½ Cent (Cu-Ni) 1909		18.00	40.00
4 (3a)	1 Cent (Cu-Ni) 1908–1910:			
	1908		–.–	–.–
	1909, 1910		1.50	3.00
5	5 Cents (Cu-Ni) 1908, pattern!		60.00	110.00
6 (6)	10 Cents (Cu-Ni) 1907–1910		3.50	7.00
7 (7)	25 Cents (Ag) 1906–1910. Crowned bust right of King Edward VII. ℞ lion (Panthera leo – Felidae) with mountains in background		10.00	25.00
8 (8)	50 Cents (Ag) 1906–1910. Type as No. 7		18.00	45.00

GEORGE V 1910–1936

9 (9)	1 Cent (Cu-Ni) 1911–1918. Crown above value, ornamental decoration. ℞ elephants' tusks (central hole)		1.50	3.00
10 (10)	5 Cents (Cu-Ni) 1913–1919		2.50	6.00
11 (11)	10 Cents (Cu-Ni) 1911–1918		3.00	8.00
12 (12)	25 Cents (Ag) 1912–1918. Crowned bust left of King George V. ℞ lion with mountains in background		8.00	15.00
13 (13)	50 Cents (Ag) 1911–1919		12.50	25.00
14 (14)	1 Cent (Cu-Ni) 1920–1921. Type as No. 9, but inscription now reads only EAST AFRICA:			
	1920		55.00	125.00
	1921			–.–
15 (15)	5 Cents (Cu–Ni) 1920. Type as No. 10, but inscription now reads only EAST AFRICA		100.00	165.00

			VF	**XF**
16 (16)	10	Cents (Cu–Ni) 1920	125.00	225.00
17 (17)	25	Cents (Ag) 1920–1921	35.00	70.00
18 (18)	50	Cents = 1 Shilling (Ag) 1920	650.00	1100.00
19 (19)	1	**Florin (Ag)** 1920–1921:		
		1920	30.00	75.00
		1921, Proof only		–.–
20 (20)	1	Cent (Br) 1922–1935. Type as No. 14, but smaller diameter	0.40	1.00
21 (21)	5	Cents (Br) 1921–1936. Type as No. 15, but smaller diameter	0.80	2.00
22 (22)	10	Cents (Br) 1921–1936. Type as No. 16, but smaller diameter	1.00	3.00
23 (23)	50	Cents = ½ Shilling (Ag) 1921–1924. Type as No. 18, but smaller diameter	2.50	6.00

24 (24)	1	Shilling (Ag) 1921–1925. Lion with mountains in background	2.50	4.00

EDWARD VIII 1936

25 (25)	5	Cents (Br) 1936. Crown above value, ornamental decoration. ℞ elephants' tusks	1.00	2.00
26 (26)	10	Cents (Br) 1936. Type as No. 25	1.60	3.20

GEORGE VI 1936–1952

27 (27)	1	Cent (Br) 1942. Crown above value, ornamental decoration. ℞ elephants' tusks	0.30	1.00
28 (28)	5	Cents (Br) 1937–1943	1.00	2.00
29 (29)	10	Cents (Br) 1937–1945	1.00	2.00
30 (30)	50	Cents (Ag) 1937–1944. Crowned head left of King George VI. ℞ lion with mountains in background	2.00	4.00
31 (31)	1	Shilling (Ag) 1937–1946	2.50	5.00
32 (32)	1	Cent (Br) 1949–1952. Type as No. 27, but inscription now reads GEORGIUS SEXTUS REX	0.25	0.60
33 (33)	5	Cents (Br) 1949–1952. Type as No. 28, but inscription now reads GEORGIUS SEXTUS REX	0.50	2.00

34 (34)	10 Cents (Br) 1949–1952. Type as No. 29, but inscription now reads GEORGIUS SEXTUS REX	**VF**	**XF**
		0.60	2.00
35 (35)	50 Cents (Cu–Ni) 1948–1952. Type as No. 30, but inscription now reads GEORGIUS SEXTUS REX	0.60	1.50
36 (36)	1 Shilling (Cu–Ni) 1948–1952. Type as No. 31, but inscription now reads GEORGIUS SEXTUS REX	1.00	2.00

ELIZABETH II 1952–1963

37 (37)	1 Cent (Br) 1954–1962. Crown above value, ornamental decoration. ℞ elephants' tusks (central hole)	0.20	0.40

38 (38)	5 Cents (Br) 1955–1963	0.25	0.50
39 (39)	10 Cents (Br) 1956	0.80	2.00
40 (40)	50 Cents (Cu–Ni) 1954–1963. Crowned head right of Queen Elizabeth II	0.40	0.80

JOINT ISSUES OF THE INDEPENDENT STATES

41 (41)	5 Cents (Br) 1964. Ornamental decoration, value also in Swahili. ℞ elephants' tusks	0.10	0.30

42 (42)	10 Cents (Br) 1964	0.20	0.40

Yeoman Numbers

In order to help collectors and dealers, we have added after most SCHÖN-numbers the corresponding number assigned by R.S. Yeoman in his wellknown works entitled »A Catalog of Modern World Coins« and »Current Coins of the World«.

East Caribbean States

Westindische Assoziierte Staaten   **Antilles Britanniques**

The East Caribbean Territories, renamed East Caribbean States, comprise the territories of Montserrat, Antigua, St. Christopher-Nevis-Anguilla as well as the independent States of Dominica, Grenada, St. Lucia and St. Vincent.

100 Cents = 1 East Caribbean Dollar

East Caribbean Territories

The 1970 issues are listed under the respective territories Anguilla, Barbados, Dominica, Grenada, Montserrat, St. Christopher-Nevis-Anguilla, St. Lucia and St. Vincent.

10th ANNIVERSARY OF THE CARIBBEAN DEVELOPMENT BANK

			Unc	Proof
1 (1*)	10 Dollars 1980. »The Golden Hind«. Rev. map and commemorative legend:			
	a) (Ag)			30.00
	b) (Cu-Ni)		5.00	

ROYAL WEDDING

2 (2*)	10 Dollars 1981. Elizabeth II. Rev. »The Golden Hind«:		
	a) (Ag)		35.00
	b) (Cu-Ni)	5.50	

*These numbers refer to Yeoman's East Caribbean Territories listings.

3 (2) 1 Cent (Al) 1981, 1983, 1984, 1986. Rev. value within branches 0.10

4 (3) 2 CENTS (Al) 1981, 1984, 1986. Type as No. 3 (square) 0.15

5 (4) 5 Cents (Al) 1981, 1984, 1986. Type as No. 3 (scalloped) 0.20

6 (5) 10 Cents (Cu-Ni) 1981, 1986. Rev. »The Golden Hind« 0.25

7 (6) 25 Cents (Cu-Ni) 1981, 1986. Type as No. 6 .... 0.40

8 (7) 1 Dollar (Al-Br) 1981, 1986. Type as No. 6 .... 1.50

WORLD FOOD DAY

9 (1) 10 Dollars 1981:
   a) (Ag) 35.00
   b) (Cu-Ni) 6.50

INTERNATIONAL YEAR OF THE DISABLED PERSONS (2)

10 (10) 50 Dollars (Ag) 1981:
   a) 25.00   35.00
   b) Piéfort 120.00

11 (11)   500 Dollars (Au) 1981:   –.–   –.–
                a)
                b) Piéfort   –.–

INTERNATIONAL YEAR OF THE SCOUT (2)

12 (8)   50 Dollars (Ag) 1982   20.00   25.00
13 (9)   500 Dollars (Au) 1982   300.00   350.00

Area: 104,306 sq. mi. Population: 9,500,000.

Formerly part of the Inca Empire. After the conquest by the Spaniards, the country became first a part of the Vice-Kingdom of Peru and later a part of the Vice-Kingdom of New Granada. It belonged to Great Colombia from the time of the revolt against Spain until 1830, when it became an independent republic.

Capital: Quito.

10 Centavos = 1 Decimo

100 Centavos or 10 Decimos = 1 Sucre (Peso)

25 Sucres = 1 Condor

			VF	XF
1 (27)	½	Decimo (Ag) 1893–1915. Head left of Antonio José de Sucre (1795–1830), Grand Marshal of Ayacucho, Mayor of Quito, President of the State of Bolivia 1826–1828, President of the Congress which gave its constitution to Colombia in 1830. ℞ national arms	2.50	4.00
2 (28)	1	Decimo (Ag) 1884–1916	3.00	5.00

3 (29)	2	Decimos (Ag) 1884–1916. ℞ national arms with Andean condor (Vultur gryphus — Cathartidae)	4.00	6.00
4 (32)	10	Sucres (Au) 1899–1900	150.00	225.00
5 (33)	½	Centavo (Cu–Ni) 1909. National arms. ℞ value within wreath	4.00	10.00
6 (34)	1	Centavo (Cu–Ni) 1909	5.50	12.00
7 (35)	2	Centavos (Cu–Ni) 1909	7.00	15.00
8 (36)	2½	Centavos (Cu–Ni) 1917	9.00	20.00
9 (37)	5	Centavos (Cu–Ni)		
		a) 1909	10.00	20.00
		b) 1917–1918	2.00	4.00
A9 (38)	5	Centavos (Cu–Ni) 1919. Type as No. 9, but smaller diameter and denomination 5 CENTAVOS	2.00	4.00

			VF	XF
10 (39)	10	Centavos (Cu–Ni) 1918. Value in letters	9.00	15.00
11 (40)	10	Centavos (Cu–Ni) 1919	1.25	2.50
12 (41)	5	Centavos (Cu–Ni) 1924. Bust left of Simón Bolívar (1783–1830), President of the State of Colombia 1810–1821. ℞ national arms	1.50	3.00
13 (42)	10	Centavos (Cu–Ni) 1924	1.00	2.50
14 (44)	1	Centavo (Br) 1928. National arms. ℞ value within wreath	1.00	2.00
15 (45)	2½	Centavos (Ni) 1928. Type as No. 14	1.50	3.50
16 (46)	5	Centavos (Ni) 1928. National arms. ℞ bust right in wreath of A. J. de Sucre	0.80	1.60
17 (47)	10	Centavos (Ni) 1928. Type as No. 16	0.80	1.60
18 (48)	50	Centavos (Ag) 1928, 1930. Head left of A. J. de Sucre. ℞ national arms and value	3.00	5.00
19 (49)	1	Sucre (Ag) 1928–1934	4.00	6.00
20 (50)	2	Sucres (Ag) 1928, 1930	6.00	10.00
21 (43)	1	Condor (Au) 1928	275.00	375.00
22 (51)	5	Centavos. National arms. ℞ value within wreath		
		a) (Ni) 1937	0.40	0.80
		b) (Bra) 1942–1944	1.80	2.50
		c) (Cu–Ni) 1946	0.15	0.20
		d) (Ni–St) 1970	0.10	0.20
23 (52)	10	Centavos. Type as No. 22		
		a) (Ni) 1937	0.60	1.20
		b) (Bra) 1942	1.25	2.50
		c) (Cu–Ni) 1946	0.20	0.40
		d) (Ni-St) 1964, 1968, 1972, 1976	0.10	0.20
24 (53)	20	Centavos. Type as No. 22		
		a) (Ni) 1937	0.80	2.00
		b) (Bra) 1942–1944	1.25	2.50
		c) (Cu–Ni) 1946	0.20	0.40
		d) (Ni-St) 1959, 1962, 1966, 1969, 1971, 1972	0.30	0.80
		e) (Cu–Ni) 1974, 1975	0.10	0.20
		f) (Ni-St) 1975, 1978, 1980	0.10	0.20
25 (57)	50	Centavos (Ni-St) 1963, 1971, 1974, 1975, 1977, 1979. Type as No. 22	0.25	0.50
26 (54)	1	Sucre. National arms. R A. J. de Sucre		
		a) (Ni) 1937	0.90	1.80
		b) (Ni) 1946	0.60	1.20
		c) (Cu-Ni) 1959	0.40	0.80
		d) (Ni-St) 1964, 1970, 1971, 1974–1981	0.25	0.50
27 (55)	2	Sucres (Ag) 1944. A. J. de Sucre. R national arms and value	6.00	9.00
28 (56)	5	Sucres (Ag) 1943–1944. Type as No. 27	8.50	12.00
29 (58)	2	Sucres (Cu-Ni) 1973. National arms. Rev. A. J. de Sucre, value	–.–	–.–

Ägypten   # Egypt   **Égypte**

Misr

Area: 1,000,000 sq. km. Population: 45,000,000.
Governed by a Turkish viceroy from 8th July 1867. On 18th December 1914
it became a British Protectorate, but from 15th March 1922 Egypt was recog-
nized as a kingdom independent of Great Britain. On 18th June 1953 it was
proclaimed a Republic. Since 1st March 1958 Egypt has been called The
United Arab Republic. This official description was maintained even after
Syria had left the Union in 1961.
Capital: Cairo.

40 Para = 1 Guerche (Piastre)
1000 Millièmes = 100 Piastres
100 Piastres = 1 Egyptian £

ABD UL-HAMID II (1876–1909)

			VF	XF
1 (12)	1	Para (Br) 1885–1908. Toughra. ℞ in- scription with star on either side	2.00	6.00
2 (13)	2	Para (Br) 1885–1909	2.50	8.00
3 (14)	4	Para (Cu–Ni) 1885–1909. Toughra in wreath. ℞ value surrounded by inscrip- tion	2.00	8.00
4 (15)	8	Para (Cu–Ni) 1885–1909	2.50	8.00
5 (16)	20	Para (Cu–Ni) 1885–1909. Of same type: Nos. 13 to 17	3.00	9.00
6 (18)	1	Guerche (Ag) 1885–1908. Toughra in wreath. ℞ inscription within wreath	5.00	12.50
7 (19)	2	Guerche (Ag) 1885–1908	6.00	17.50
8 (20)	5	Guerche (Ag) 1885–1908	10.00	22.50
9 (21)	10	Guerche (Ag) 1885–1908	12.50	30.00
10 (22)	20	Guerche (Ag) 1885–1908 Of same type: Nos. 18 to 22	40.00	80.00
11 (A22)	5	Guerche (Au) 1880–1909. Toughra. ℞ inscription	40.00	60.00

Other gold coins of the same type were exclusively minted before 1900.

			VF	XF
12 (17)	1	Guerche (Cu–Ni) 1898–1908. Toughra in wreath. ℞ inscription surrounded by stars. Of same type: No. 23	3.00	6.00

MOHAMMED V 1909–1915

			VF	XF
13 (23)	1	Para (Br) 1910–1914. Toughra. ℞ inscription with star on either side	3.00	6.00
14 (24)	2	Para (Br) 1910–1914	2.00	5.00
15 (25)	4	Para (Cu–Ni) 1910–1914	3.00	6.00
16 (26)	8	Para (Cu–Ni) 1910–1914	5.00	10.00
17 (27)	20	Para (Cu–Ni) 1910–1914	3.00	6.00
18 (29)	1	Guerche (Ag) 1910–1911	6.00	12.00
19 (30)	2	Guerche (Ag) 1910–1911	22.00	45.00
20 (31)	5	Guerche (Ag) 1911–1914	8.00	20.00
21 (32)	10	Guerche (Ag) 1910–1914	25.00	55.00
22 (33)	20	Guerche (Ag) 1911–1914	50.00	100.00
23 (28)	1	Guerche (Cu–Ni) 1912–1914. Toughra in wreath. ℞ inscription surrounded by stars	8.00	16.00

SULTAN HUSSEIN KAMIL (1915–1917)

			VF	XF
24 (34)	½	Millième (Br) 1917. Inscription. ℞ value	8.00	15.00
25 (35)	1	Millième (Cu–Ni) 1917. Inscription. ℞ value (with hole)	5.00	10.00
26 (36)	2	Millièmes (Cu–Ni) 1916–1917. As No. 25	3.00	10.00
27 (37)	5	Millièmes (Cu–Ni) 1916–1917. As No. 25	3.00	8.00
28 (38)	10	Millièmes (Cu–Ni) 1916–1917. As No. 25	3.00	8.00
29 (39)	2	Piastres (Ag) 1916–1917. Inscription in wreath. ℞ value within wreath	5.00	16.00
30 (40)	5	Piastres (Ag) 1916–1917	8.00	17.50
31 (41)	10	Piastres (Ag) 1916–1917	18.00	50.00
32 (42)	20	Piastres (Ag) 1916–1917	30.00	65.00

			VF	XF
33 (43)	100	Piastres (Au) 1916	150.00	200.00

SULTAN FUAD I (1917–1922)

			VF	XF
34 (44)	2	Piastres (Ag) 1920. Inscription. ℞ inscription and value	65.00	160.00
35 (45)	5	Piastres (Ag) 1920	70.00	180.00
36 (46)	10	Piastres (Ag) 1920	60.00	130.00
A36 (A42)	20	Piastres (Ag) (2 pcs. known)		–.–

KING FUAD I (1922–1936)

			VF	**XF**
37 (47)	½	Millième (Br) 1924. Portrait of Fuad I (1868–1936). Rev. value with inscription	4.00	10.00
38 (48)	1	Millième (Br) 1924	6.00	15.00
39 (49)	2	Millièmes (Cu-Ni) 1924	5.00	12.50
40 (50)	5	Millièmes (Cu-Ni) 1924	6.00	16.50
41 (51)	10	Millièmes (Cu-Ni) 1924	7.00	20.00
42 (52)	2	Piastres (Ag) 1923–1924. R inscription in circle	6.00	12.50
43 (53)	5	Piastres (Ag) 1923–1926	8.00	22.00
44 (54)	10	Piastres (Ag) 1923–1926	16.00	40.00

45 (55)	20	Piastres (Ag) 1923–1925	40.00	80.00
46 (56)	20	Piastres (Au) 1923	60.00	80.00
47 (57)	50	Piastres (Au) 1923	80.00	110.00

48 (58)	100	Piastres (Au) 1922	175.00	275.00

Coins were struck in both red and yellow gold

			VF	XF
49 (59)	500	Piastres (Au) 1922		
		a) White gold	900.00	1400.00
		b) Red gold	900.00	1400.00
50 (60)	½	Millième (Br) 1929–1932. Portrait of Fuad I in uniform, to left. ℞ value	5.00	10.00
51 (61)	1	Millième (Br) 1929–1935	3.00	11.00
52 (62)	2	Millièmes (Cu–Ni) 1929	3.00	11.00

			VF	XF
53 (63)	2½	Millièmes (Cu–Ni) 1933 (octagonal)	3.00	7.00
54 (64)	5	Millièmes (Cu–Ni) 1929–1935	2.50	6.00
55 (65)	10	Millièmes (Cu–Ni) 1929–1935	3.00	11.00
56 (66)	2	Piastres (Ag) 1929	4.00	8.00
57 (67)	5	Piastres (Ag) 1929–1933	10.00	22.00
58 (68)	10	Piastres (Ag) 1929–1933	12.50	30.00

			VF	XF
59 (69)	20	Piastres (Ag) 1929–1933	45.00	75.00
60 (70)	20	Piastres (Au) 1929–1930	60.00	85.00
61 (71)	50	Piastres (Au) 1929–1930	90.00	120.00

			VF	XF
62 (72)	100	Piastres (Au) 1929–1930	125.00	175.00
63 (73)	500	Piastres (Au) 1929–1930	850.00	1300.00

			VF	XF
64 (74)	½	Millième (Br) 1938. Portrait to l. of Faruk I (1920 - 1965). ℞ value	3.00	9.00
65 (75)	1	Millième (Br) 1938–1950	3.00	9.00

			VF	XF
66 (79)	1	Millième (Cu–Ni) 1938 (with hole)	3.00	7.00
67 (80)	2	Millièmes (Cu–Ni) 1938	2.00	6.00
68 (77)	5	Millièmes (Br) 1938–1943	2.00	5.00
69 (81)	5	Millièmes (Cu–Ni) 1938–1941	2.50	6.00

			VF	XF
70 (78)	10	Millièmes (Br) 1938–1943 (scalloped)	2.00	5.00

			VF	XF
71 (82)	10	Millièmes (Cu-Ni) 1938–1943	2.50	6.00
72 (83)	2	Piastres (Ag) 1937–1948	5.00	10.00
73 (87)	2	Piastres (Ag) 1942–1944 (hexagonal)	2.50	6.00
74 (84)	5	Piastres (Ag) 1937–1939	8.00	15.00
75 (85)	10	Piastres (Ag) 1937–1939	11.00	22.00
76 (86)	20	Piastres (Ag) 1937–1939	45.00	75.00
77 (88)	20	Piastres (Au) 1938	55.00	90.00
78 (89)	50	Piastres (Au) 1938	100.00	130.00

			VF	XF
79 (90)	100	Piastres (Au) 1938	125.00	185.00
80 (91)	500	Piastres (Au) 1938	950.00	1400.00

		VF	XF
81 (92)	1 Millième (Al-Br) 1954–1958. Head of the Sphinx of Chephren, 4th Dynasty, about 2620 BC, in Gizeh, near Cairo. R value:		
	a) 1954–1956, small sphinx	1.00	3.00
	b) 1957–1958, large sphinx	0.30	1.00

		VF	XF
82 (93)	5 Millièmes (Al-Br) 1954–1958:		
	a) 1954–1956, small sphinx	5.00	11.00
	b) 1957–1958, large sphinx	1.00	2.00
83 (94)	10 Millièmes (Al-Br) 1954–1958:		
	a) 1954–1955, small sphinx	6.00	15.00
	b) 1956–1958, large sphinx	1.00	2.50

		VF	XF
84 (95)	5 Piastres (Ag) 1955–1959. Sphinx. R sun winged and value	4.00	8.00
85 (96)	10 Piastres (Ag) 1955–1957. Type as No. 84. Varieties exist.	6.00	12.50
86 (97)	20 Piastres (Ag) 1956. Type as No. 84	10.50	20.00

ISSUES (2) COMMEMORATING THE 3rd ANNIVERSARY OF THE REVOLUTION

		VF	XF
87 (103)	1 £ (Au) 1955. The Pharaoh Rameses II in war-chariot. R sun winged and inscription	140.00	175.00

		VF	**XF**
88 (104) 5 £ (Au) 1955		600.00	800.00

Of similar type: Nos. 92 and 93

ISSUE COMMEMORATING THE EVACUATION OF THE BRITISH TROOPS

89 (99) 50 Piastres (Ag) 1956. Pharaoh holding torch of liberty and broken chains. ℞ sun winged and value   17.00   25.00

Yeoman Numbers

In order to help collectors and dealers, we have added after most SCHÖN-numbers the corresponding number assigned by R.S. Yeoman in his wellknown works entitled »A Catalog of Modern World Coins« and »Current Coins of the World«.

NATIONALIZATION OF THE SUEZ CANAL

		VF	XF
90 (98)	25 Piastres (Ag) 1956. The Headquarters of the Suez Canal Company in Port Said. ℞ sun winged and value	12.00	16.50

NATIONAL ASSEMBLY INAUGURATION

| **91** (102) | 25 Piastres (Ag) 1957. National Assembly building | 12.50 | 16.50 |

5th ANNIVERSARY OF THE REVOLUTION (2)

| **92** (103) | 1 £ (Au) 1957. Type as No. 87, but red gold | 160.00 | 220.00 |
| **93** (104) | 5 £ (Au) 1957. Type as No. 88, but red gold | 700.00 | 1000.00 |

UNITED ARAB REPUBLIC (1958–1971)
1st INDUSTRIAL AND AGRICULTURAL FAIR IN CAIRO, 1958

| **94** (105) | 20 Millièmes (Al–Br) 1958. Gear-wheel and land produce. ℞ value | 1.70 | 5.00 |

ISSUE COMMEMORATING THE FOUNDATION OF THE UNITED ARAB REPUBLIC

95 (106) ½ £ (Au) 1958. Pharaoh Rameses II in war-chariot. ℞ sun winged and inscription

Unc

175.00

ISSUE COMMEMORATING THE 1st ANNIVERSARY OF THE UNITED ARAB REPUBLIC

			VF	XF
96 (107)	10	Piastres (Ag) 1959. Emblem of State. R value	12.00	18.00
97 (111)	1	Millième (Al-Br) 1960, 1966. Emblem of State. R value	0.10	0.20
98 (112)	2	Millièmes (Al-Br) 1962, 1966	0.20	0.40
99 (113)	5	Millièmes (Al-Br) 1960, 1966	0.50	1.00
100 (113a)	5	Millièmes (Al) 1967	1.00	2.00
101 (A 113)	10	Millièmes (Al-Br) 1960, 1966	1.00	2.50
102 (A 113a)	10	Millièmes (Al) 1967	0.60	1.50
103 (114)	5	Piastres (Ag) 1960, 1966	3.00	7.00
104 (115)	10	Piastres (Ag) 1960, 1966	5.00	8.00
105 (116)	20	Piastres (Ag) 1960, 1966	8.50	20.00

ISSUES (2) COMMEMORATING THE BEGINNING OF THE BUILDING OF THE ASWAN DAM

				VF	XF

106 (108) 1 £ (Au) 1960. Reproduction of the projected Aswan Dam Sadd el-Ali; agricultural produce, rising sun. ℞ sun winged and inscription — 110.00 — 160.00

107 (109) 5 £ (Au) 1960 — 600.00 — 750.00

ISSUE COMMEMORATING THE 3rd YEAR OF THE NATIONAL ASSEMBLY

108 (110) 25 Piastres (Ag) 1960. National Assembly building — 12.00 — 16.00

ISSUES (6) COMMEMORATING THE END OF THE FIRST STAGE OF CONSTRUCTION OF THE SADD EL-ALI DAM

109 (117) 5 Piastres (Ag) 1964. Sadd el-Ali Dam, high voltage pylons and rising sun — 3.00 — 3.50

110 (118) 10 Piastres (Ag) 1964 — 4.00 — 6.00

111 (119) 25 Piastres (Ag) 1964 — 7.50 — 10.00

112 (120) 50 Piastres (Ag) 1964 — 12.00 — 16.50

				VF	XF
113	(121)	5	£ (Au) 1964. Type as No. 109. ℞ inscription	300.00	400.00
114	(122)	10	£ (Au) 1964	600.00	700.00
115	(123)	5	Piastres (Cu–Ni) 1967. Emblem of State. ℞ value	0.60	2.50
116	(124)	10	Piastres (Cu–Ni) 1967. Type as No. 115	1.20	5.00

ISSUE COMMEMORATING THE INTERNATIONAL INDUSTRIAL FAIR IN CAIRO

				VF	XF
117	(125)	5	Piastres (Cu–Ni) 1968. Globe and inscription in Arabic. ℞ value	1.00	2.00

ISSUE COMMEMORATING THE INAUGURATION OF THE POWER STATION FOR THE ASWAN DAM

				VF	XF
118	(126)	1	£ (Ag) 1968. View of the power station. ℞ inscription and dates in Arabic	10.00	16.00

ISSUE COMMEMORATING THE 1400th ANNIVERSARY OF THE KORAN

				Unc
119	(127)	5	£ (Au) 1968. The Holy Book of Islam, the Koran, open; in background rising sun; globe between arabesques	650.00

120   10 Piastres (Cu–Ni) 1968. Agricultural scene   **VF**   **XF**
copied from an old Egyptian bas-relief.
R value, date inscription. Not released for
circulation.   –.–   –.–
Of similar type: No. 132

ISSUE COMMEMORATING THE INTERNATIONAL AGRICULTURAL FAIR IN CAIRO 1969

121 (139) 10 Piastres (Cu–Ni) 1969. Ears of corn
over stylized globe, and the word
CAIRO; on right, inscription. ℞ value
surrounded by circular inscription   1.70   2.50

ISSUE COMMEMORATING THE 50th ANNIVERSARY OF THE INTERNATIONAL LABOUR ORGANIZATION (ILO)

122 (131) 5 Piastres (Cu–Ni) 1969. Two hands
holding screw wrench (emblem of the
ILO). ℞ value   1.20   1.80

ISSUES (2) COMMEMORATING THE JUBILEE OF THE EL AZHAR UNIVERSITY IN CAIRO

			VF	XF
123 (130)	1 £ (Ag) 1970. University building		12.50	16.00
124 (A131)	5 £ (Au) 1979		265.00	300.00

ISSUE COMMEMORATING THE CAIRO FAIR

			VF	XF
125 (133)	10 Piastres (Cu–Ni) 1970. Emblem. ℞ value		1.25	2.50

ISSUE COMMEMORATING 50 YEARS OF BANK MISR

			VF	XF
126 (132)	10 Piastres (Cu–Ni) 1970. Sun rising over Bank building. ℞ emblem and value		1.25	2.50

ISSUES (5) COMMEMORATING THE DEATH OF GAMAL ABD EL NASSER

			VF	XF
127 (134)	25 Piastres (Ag) 1970. Head to right of Gamal Abd el Nasser (1918–1970), President of the United Arab Republic 1958–1970. ℞ Arabic inscription and date		3.50	5.00
128 (135)	50 Piastres (Ag) 1970. Type as No. 127		6.00	10.00

			VF	XF
129 (136)	1 £ (Ag) 1970. Type as No. 127		8.00	12.00
130 (137)	1 £ (Au) 1970. Type as No. 127			175.00
131 (138)	5 £ (Au) 1970. Type as No. 127			500.00

COMMEMORATIVE ISSUE FOR THE FAO COIN PLAN AND THE 18th ANNIVERSARY OF THE AGRICULTURAL REFORM

			XF	**Unc**
132 (128)	10	Piastres (Cu–Ni) 1970. Type as No. 120, but above the old Egyptian bas-relief now the state emblem	3.00	6.00

COMMEMORATIVE ISSUE FOR THE CAIRO FAIR 1971

133 (133a)	10	Piastres (Cu–Ni) 1971. Emblem of Cairo Fair 71 (type similar to No. 125)	1.50	3.00

ARAB REPUBLIC OF EGYPT since 1971/72

134 (157)	1	Millième (Al) 1972. Type as No. 103, but without stars in the breast plate of the redesigned arms falcon and with new inscription (translated: Federation of Arab Republics and Arab Republic Egypt)	0.20	0.60
135 (141a)	5	Millièmes (Al) 1972. Type as No. 134	0.25	0.80
136 (142a)	10	Millièmes (Al) 1972. Type as No. 134	0.30	0.80
137 (158)	5	Piastres (Cu-Ni) 1972. Type as No. 134	0.70	1.30
138 (159)	10	Piastres (Cu-Ni) 1972. Type as No. 134	1.00	1.60

25th ANNIVERSARY OF UNICEF

			XF	Unc
139(139)	5 Piastres (Cu-Ni) 1972. Mother and child	1.00	2.00

ISSUE FOR THE CAIRO FAIR 1972

140(140)	10 Piastres (Cu-Ni) 1972. Type similar to No. 133	1.40	2.50

COMMEMORATIVE ISSUES (2) FOR THE COMPLETION OF THE HIGH DAM SADD EL-ALI ON 15th JANUARY 1971 AND FOR THE FAO COIN PLAN

141(144)	5 Millièmes (Al) 1973. High Dam Sadd el-Ali between ears of wheat	0.25	0.50
142(145)	1 £ (Ag) 1973. Type as No. 141	8.00	12.00

ISSUE FOR THE CAIRO FAIR 1973

			XF	Unc
143 (143)	5	Piastres (Cu-Ni) 1973. Emblem of Cairo Fair 1973. R name of country, value	0.80	1.50

75th ANNIVERSARY OF THE EGYPTIAN NATIONAL BANK (4)

			XF	Unc
144 (146)	5	Piastres (Cu-Ni) 1973. Building of the Egyptian National Bank and globe. R inscription, value	1.00	1.50
145 (147)	25	Piastres (Ag) 1973. Type as No. 144	5.00	11.00
146 (148)	1	£ (Au) 1973. Type as No. 144		175.00
147 (149)	5	£ (Au) 1973. Type as No. 144		500.00

148 (141)	5	Millièmes (Al-Br) 1973. Type as No. 136	0.25	0.50
149 (142)	10	Millièmes (Al-Br) 1973. Type as No. 148	0.40	1.00

1th ANNIVERSARY OF YOM KIPPUR WAR (4)

			XF	Unc
150 (150)	5	Piastres (Cu-Ni) 1974. Soldier, laurel branch. R value, dates	0.50	0.80
151 (151)	10	Piastres (Cu-Ni) 1974. Type as No. 150	0.80	1.30
152 (152)	1	£ (Ag) 1974. Type as No. 150	9.00	13.00
153 (A 152)	5	£ (Au) 1974. Type as No. 150		600.00

INTERNATIONAL WOMEN'S YEAR 1975 (2)

154 (153)	5	Millièmes (Al-Br) 1975. Bust right of Nefertiti. R name of country, value	0.15	0.30

155 (155)	5	Piastres (Cu-Ni) 1975. Type as No. 154	0.60	1.00

ISSUE FOR THE FAO COIN PLAN (2)

156 (154)	10	Millièmes (Bra) 1975. Classical Egyptian family	0.15	0.30
157 (156)	10	Piastres (Cu-Ni) 1975. Type as No. 156	0.80	1.50

ISSUE FOR THE CAIRO FAIR 1976

			XF	Unc
158 (162)	5 Piastres (Cu-Ni) 1976. Emblem of Cairo Fair 1976		0.60	1.00

ISSUE FOR THE FAO COIN PLAN (2)

159 (160)	10 Millièmes (Bra) 1976. The god Osiris seated facing an enlarged ear of grain		0.15	0.30
160 (161)	1 £ (Ag) 1976. Type as No. 159		7.50	12.00

RE-OPENING OF THE SUEZ CANAL (3)

161 (163)	10 Piastres (Cu-Ni) 1976. Ships bow at right with two wheat ears and world globe sailing left in Suez Canal towards large building and laurel leaves. All under radiant sun		1.00	1.50
162 (164)	1 £ (Ag) 1976. Type as No. 161		7.00	10.00
163 (165)	5 £ (Au) 1976. Type as No. 161			500.00

FIRST ANNIVERSARY OF THE DEATH OF KING FAISAL (3)

164 (166)	1 £ (Ag) 1976. King Faisal of Saudi Arabia		7.00	10.00
165 (167)	1 £ (Au) 1976. Type as No. 164			175.00
166 (168)	5 £ (Au) 1976. Type as No. 164			550.00

FIRST ANNIVERSARY OF THE DEATH OF OM KALSOUM (3)

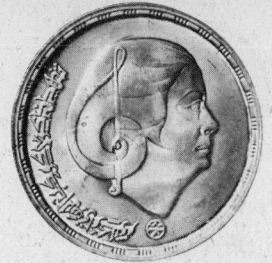 

		XF	Unc
167 (169)	1 £ (Ag) 1976. Om Kalsoum 1898–1975), singer	7.00	10.00
168 (170)	1 £ (Au) 1976. Type as No. 167		180.00
A 169 (171)	5 £ (Au) 1976. Type as No. 167		550.00

50th ANNIVERSARY OF THE EGYPTIAN TEXTILE INDUSTRY

170 (184)   5 Piastres (Cu-Ni) 1977. Classical Egyptian figure holding spindle. R emblem and value   0.60   1.25

FOR THE FAO COIN PLAN (2)

171 (179)   5 Millièmes (Bra) 1977. Classical Egyptian rural scene   0.20   0.40

172 (181)   5 Piastres (Cu-Ni) 1977. Type as No. 171   0.70   1.00

			XF	Unc
173 (172)	5	Millièmes (Al-Br) 1977, 1979. Egyptian god	0.25	0.40
174 (173)	10	Millièmes (Al-Br) 1977, 1979. Type as No. 173	0.30	0.60
175 (174)	5	Piastres (Cu-Ni) 1977, 1979. Type as No. 173	0.50	1.00
176 (175)	10	Piastres (Cu-Ni) 1977, 1979. Type as No. 173	0.60	0.85
177 (176)	1	£ (Ag) 1977, 1979. Type as No. 173	7.00	10.00

FOR THE FAO COIN PLAN (3)

178 (180)	10	Millièmes (Bra) 1977. Classical Egyptian professions	0.30	0.60
179 (182)	10	Piastres (Cu-Ni) 1977. Type as No. 178	0.60	1.30
180 (183)	1	£ (Ag) 1977. Type as No. 178	7.00	10.00

20th ANNIVERSARY OF ARABIC ECONOMIC UNION (3)

181 (177)	10	Piastres (Cu-Ni) 1977. Clasped hands	0.60	1.30
182 (178)	1	£ (Ag) 1977. Type as No. 181	7.00	10.00
183 (178a)	1	£ (Au) 1977. Type as No. 181		200.00

SADAT'S PEACE INITIATIVE (4)

			Proof
184	5	£ (Ag) 1977. Bust of President Sadat, rock cathedral of Jerusalem	–.–
185	10	£ (Ag) 1977. Type as No. 184	–.–
186	50	£ (Au) 1977. Type as No. 184	–.–
187	100	£ (Au) 1977. Type as No. 184	–.–

50th ANNIVERSARY OF PORTLAND CEMENT (2)

		XF	Unc
188 (187)	5 Piastres (Cu-Ni) 1978. Industrial district	0.50	0.70
189 (188)	1 £ (Ag) 1978. Type as No. 188	7.00	10.00

CAIRO FAIR 1978

190 (185)	10 Piastres (Cu-Ni) 1978. Emblem of Cairo Fair 1978	0.60	1.00

25th ANNIVERSARY OF AIN SHAMS UNIVERSITY

191 (186)	1 £ (Ag) 1978. Obelisk and falcons	6.00	10.00

FOR THE FAO COIN PLAN (3)

192 (189)	10 Millièmes (Al-Br) 1978. Assistant with microscop	0.30	0.40
193 (190)	5 Piastres (Cu-Ni) 1978. Type as No. 192	0.60	0.80

194 (191)	1 £ (Ag) 1978. Type as No. 192	7.00	10.00

			Unc	Proof
195 (192)	10	Piastres (Cu-Ni) 1979. Mint building	1.00	
196 (193)	1	£ (Ag) 1979. Type as No. 195	10.00	35.00

INTERNATIONAL YEAR OF THE CHILD AND FAO COIN PLAN (3)

			XF	Unc
197 (194)	10	Millièmes (Al-Br) 1979. Mother and child	0.20	0.30
198 (195)	5	Piastres (Cu-Ni) 1979. Type as No. 197	0.50	0.65

199 (196)	1	£ (Ag) 1979. Type as No. 197	10.00	50.00

NATIONAL EDUCATION DAY (2)

			Unc	Proof
200 (197)	10 Piastres (Cu-Ni) 1979. Classroom		0.80	

			Unc	Proof
201 (198)	1 £ (Ag) 1979. Type as No. 200		9.00	30.00

100th ANNIVERSARY OF THE BANK OF LAND REFORM (3)

			Unc	Proof
202 (199)	1 £ (Ag) 1979. Writer and rural scene		10.00	35.00
203 (200)	1 £ (Au) 1979. Type as No. 202			450.00
204 (201)	5 £ (Au) 1979. Type as No. 202			1100.00

1400th ANNIVERSARY OF MOHAMMED'S FLIGHT (3)

			Unc	Proof
205 (202)	1 £ (Ag) 1979. Two birds in their nest		10.00	25.00
206 (203)	1 £ (Au) 1979. Type as No. 205			250.00
207 (204)	5 £ (Au) 1979. Type as No. 205			700.00

FOR THE FAO COIN PLAN (3)

		XF	Unc
208 (222)	10 Millièmes (Al-Br) 1980. Kneeling woman with Egyptian landscape background	0.30	0.60

		XF	Unc
209 (223)	10 Piastres (Cu-Ni) 1980. Type as No. 208	0.60	1.00

		Unc	Proof
210 (224)	1 £ (Ag) 1980. Type as No. 208	10.00	50.00

EGYPTIAN-ISRAELI PEACE TREATY (5)

		XF	Unc
211 (217)	10 Piastres (Cu-Ni) 1980. Head of President Sadat, dove, palm branch	0.60	1.00

		Unc	Proof
212 (218)	1 £ (Ag) 1980. Type as No. 211	15.00	55.00
213 (219)	1 £ (Au) 1980. Type as No. 211		200.00
214 (220)	5 £ (Au) 1980. Type as No. 211		1000.00
215 (221)	10 £ (Au) 1980. Type as No. 211		2000.00

DOCTER'S DAY (4)

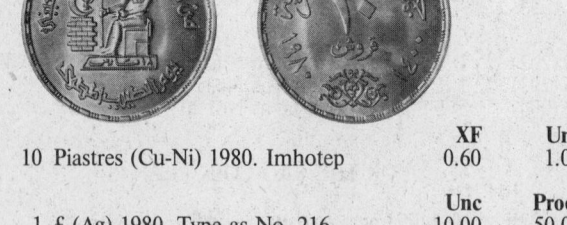

		XF	Unc
216 (213)	10 Piastres (Cu-Ni) 1980. Imhotep	0.60	1.00

		Unc	Proof
217 (214)	1 £ (Ag) 1980. Type as No. 216	10.00	50.00
218 (215)	1 £ (Au) 1980. Type as No. 216		200.00
A218 (216)	5 £ (Au) 1980. Type as No. 216		500.00

HANDICRAFT IN CLASSICAL EGYPT (3)

		XF	Unc
219 (210)	5 Piastres (Cu-Ni) 1980. Applied professions	0.60	1.00

		Unc	Proof
220 (221)	1 £ (Ag) 1980. Type as No. 219	10.00	50.00
221 (212)	1 £ (Au) 1980. Type as No. 219		–.–

SADAT'S CORRECTIVE REVOLUTION OF MAY, 15 1971 (5)

			XF	Unc
222 (205)	5	Millièmes (Al-Br) 1980. Sadat's hand holding palm branch	–.–	–.–
223 (206)	10	Millièmes (Al-Br) 1980. Type as No. 222	0.20	0.40
224 (207)	5	Piastres (Cu-Ni) 1980. Type as No. 222	0.60	1.25
225 (208)	10	Piastres (Cu-Ni) 1980. Type as No. 222	0.60	1.25

			Unc	Proof
226 (209)	1	£ (Ag) 1980. Type as No. 222	10.00	50.00

CAIRO UNIVERSITY LAW FACILITY (2)

				Unc
227 (225)	1	£ (Ag) 1980	10.00	40.00
228 (226)	1	£ (Au) 1980		250.00

			XF	Unc
229 (239)	2	Piastres (Al-Br) 1980. Type as No. 134	0.30	1.00
230 (245)	20	Piastres (Cu-Ni) 1980. Type as No. 134	1.00	1.60

WORLD FOOD DAY

		Unc	Proof
231 (231)	1 £ (Ag) 1981. Ancient figures representing agriculture	12.00	35.00

SCIENTIST'S DAY (2)

		XF	Unc
232 (227)	10 Piastres (Cu-Ni) 1981. Communications satellite radio antenna, oil derricks, rising sun. Rev. Thoth, ancient deity	0.60	1.25

		Unc	Proof
233 (228)	1 £ (Ag) 1981. Type as No. 232	10.00	50.00

5th ANNIVERSARY OF SUEZ CANAL REOPENING (3)

234 (233)	1 £ (Ag) 1981. Stylized ships	10.00	40.00
235 (246)	1 £ (Au) 1981. Type as No. 234		200.00
236 (247)	5 £ (Au) 1981. Type as No. 234	600.00	1250.00

			Unc	Proof
237 (240)	1 £ (Ag) AH 1401/1981. Ancient Egyptian ship		10.00	50.00
238 (241)	1 £ (Au) AH 1401/1981. Type as No. 237			200.00
239 (256)	5 £ (Au) AH 1401/1981. Type as No. 237			500.00

FOR THE FAO COIN PLAN

240 (244)	1 £ (Ag) AH 1401/1981. Ancient weaver's loom	10.00

INTERNATIONAL YEAR OF THE CHILD

241 (229) 5 £ (Ag) AH 1401/1981. Children
encircling a globe:
a) .925 silver, 24 g   35.00
b) Piéfort, .925 silver, 48 g (152 pes.)   350.00

242 (235)	1 £ (Ag) AH 1402/1981. Oil derrick, cog wheel, factory		10.00	50.00
243 (248)	5 £ (Au) AH 1402/1981. Type as No. 242			500.00
244 (255)	10 £ (Au) AH 1402/1981. Type as No. 242		600.00	650.00

25th ANNIVERSARY OF EGYPTIAN TRADE UNION (2)

		XF	Unc
245 (237)	10 Piastres (Cu-Ni) AH 1402/1981. Trade Union symbol	0.60	1.25

		Unc	Proof
246 (238)	1 £ (Ag) AH 1402/1981. Type as No. 245	10.00	50.00

No. 247 omitted.

100th ANNIVERSARY OF ARABI REVOLUTION (3)

248 (242) 1 £ (Ag) AH 1402/1981. Ahmed Arabi on horseback in front of revolutionary crowd   10.00   50.00
249 (243) 1 £ (Au) AH 1402/1981. Type as No. 248   180.00
250 (254) 5 £ (Au) AH 1402/1981. Type as No. 248   500.00

GOLDEN JUBILEE OF THE CIVIL AIRLINE »EGYPT AIR«

251 (250) 1 £ (Ag) AH 1402/1982. Eagle and globe   10.00

1000th ANNIVERSARY OF AL AZHAR MOSQUE (4)

252 (251) 1 £ (Ag) AH 1402/1982. Mosque and rising sun   10.00   35.00
253 (257) 1 £ (Au) AH 1402/1982. Type as No. 252   225.00

		Unc.	Proof
254 (258)	5 £ (Au) AH 1402/1982. Type as No. 252	500.00	
255 (259)	10 £ (Au) AH 1402/1982. Type as No. 252	700.00	

50th ANNIVERSARY OF LARGEST DEPARTMENT STORE (2)

		XF	Unc
256	10 Piastres (Cu-Ni) AH 1402/1982. Emblem of the »Egyptian Sales Products Company«	1.00	2.00

		Unc	Proof
257 (253)	1 £ (Ag) AH 1402/1982. Type as No. 256	20.00	30.00

RETURN OF SINAI TO EGYPT (4)

258 (263)	1 £ (Ag) AH 1402/1982. Dove and map of Sinai	10.00
259	1 £ (Au) AH 1402/1982. Type as No. 258	–.–
260	5 £ (Au) AH 1402/1982. Type as No. 258	–.–
261	10 £ (Au) AH 1402/1982. Type as No. 258	–.–

50th ANNIVERSARY OF EGYPTIAN AIR FORCE (3)

262 (252)   1 £ (Ag) AH 1403/1982. Emblem of Air Force, above arms   10.00   –.–

263 (260)   1 £ (Au) AH 1403/1982. Type as No. 262   225.00

264 (261)   5 £ (Au) AH 1403/1982. Type as No. 262   550.00

265 (262) 100 £ (Au) 1983. Queen Nefertiti. Rev. Kufic legend   500.00

50th ANNIVERSARY OF DEATHS OF AHMED SHAWKY AND IBRAHIM HAFEZ

266 (264)   1 £ (Ag) AH 1403/1983. Ahmed Shawky (1868–1932) and Ibrahim Hafez (1873–1932), Egyptian poets   12.00

25th ANNIVERSARY OF CAIRO UNIVERSITY

	Unc	Proof
267 5 £ (Ag) 1983. Cairo University and emblem	20.00	–.–

	XF	Unc
268 1 Piastre (Al-Br) 1984. Pyramids. Rev. Name of country within toughra:		
a) 1984/1404	0.30	0.50
b) 1404/1984 (as ill.)	0.10	0.20

269	2 Piastres (Al-Br) 1984. Type as No. 268:		
	a) 1984/1404	0.30	0.50
	b) 1404/1984	0.40	0.85
270	5 Piastres (Al-Br) 1984. Type as No. 268:		
	a) 1984/1404	0.40	0.85
	b) 1404/1984	0.30	0.60
271	10 Piastres (Cu-Ni) AH 1404/1984. Mohamad Ali Mosque, Cairo. Rev. Kufic legend	0.50	0.85
272	20 Piastres (Cu-Ni) AH 1404/1984. Type as No. 271	0.60	1.00

Nos. 273 and 274 omitted.

50th ANNIVERSARY OF MISR INSURANCE COMPANY

| 275 (265) | 1 £ (Ag) AH 1404/1984. Emblem of the Misr Insurance Company | 15.00 | –.– |

Previous issues, see »Weltmünzkatalog 19. Jahrhundert« (World Coin Catalogue of the 19th Century).

Equatorial African States

Äquatorialafrikanische Staaten   **Afrique Equatoriale**

The institution covering the issue of currency for the territories of Equatorial Africa is the Banque Centrale des Etats de l'Afrique Equatoriale. This Monetary Union comprises the states of Gabon, Cameroon, Congo-Brazzaville, Chad and the Central African Republic.

100 Centimes = 1 CFA Franc

		VF	XF
1 (Al)	1 Franc (Al) 1969, 1971. Addax antelopes (Addax nasomaculatus – Bovidae), inscription ETATS DE L'AFRIQUE EQUATORIALE / CAMEROUN / BANQUE CENTRALE. Rev. value within wreath of fruits	0.20	0.60
2 (1)	5 Francs (Al-Br) 1961, 1962, 1965, 1967– 1970, 1972–1974. Type as No. 1	0.40	0.60
3 (2)	10 Francs (Al-Br) 1961, 1962, 1965, 1967– 1969, 1972–1974. Type as No. 1	0.50	1.00
4 (3)	25 Francs (Al-Br) 1962, 1968–1970, 1972– 1974. Type as No. 1	1.00	2.00

5 (4)	50 Francs (Cu–Ni) 1961, 1963. Antelopes, names of states: Gabon, Congo (Brazzaville), Chad and Central African Republic. ℞ value within wreath of fruits	3.50	5.00

6 (5)	100 Francs (Ni) 1966-1968. Antelopes without mention of the participating countries. R value	2.00	3.00

For later issues, see under Central African States.

Äquatorialguinea　**Equatorial Guinea**　Guinée Equatoriale

Area: 10,789 sq. mi. Population: 340,000.

The Republic of Equatorial Guinea, the only Spanish-speaking state in Africa, obtained its independence on 10th October 1968. The territory covers the mainland strip of Rio Muni and the islands Fernando Poo, Elobey, Annobón and Corisco. On 10th October 1969 the country secured its own currency with parity with the Spanish peseta. Until the issue of the separate currency Spanish coins were exclusively in use. Capital: Santa Isabel.

100 Centimos = 1 Guinea Peseta; since 1975:
100 Céntimos = 1 Ekuele, new currency: Epkwele, plural Bipkwele

			VF	XF
1 (1)	1 Peseta (Al–Br) 1969		2.00	3.50
2 (2)	5 Pesetas (Cu–Ni) 1969		3.00	6.00
3 (3)	25 Pesetas (Cu–Ni) 1969		5.00	9.00
4 (4)	50 Pesetas (Cu–Ni) 1969		6.00	12.00

		Proof
5	25 Pesetas (Ag) 1970–. Emblem of the United Nations. ℞ national arms, value	9.00
6	25 Pesetas (Ag) 1970–. Emblem of the World Bank	9.00

7	50 Pesetas (Ag) 1970–. "Hands joined of an Apostle praying", from a drawing by Albrecht Dürer (1471–1528)	15.00

8	75	Pesetas (Ag) 1970–. Pope John XXIII, Roncalli (1881–1963)	25.00
9	75	Pesetas (Ag) 1970–. Abraham Lincoln (1809–1865), 16th President of the United States of America	25.00
10	75	Pesetas (Ag) 1970–. Mohandas Karamchand Gandhi (1869–1948), called Mahatma ("Sublime Soul"), advocator of the non-violent resistance movement "Satyagraha"	25.00
11	75	Pesetas (Ag) 1970–. Vladimir Ilyich Lenin (1870–1924), real name Ulyanov; Soviet statesman, leader of the world proletariat, name	25.00
12	100	Pesetas (Ag) 1970–. "The Nude Maya", from the painting by Francisco José Goya y Lucientes (1746–1828), Prado Museum, Madrid	50.00
13	100	Pesetas (Ag) 1970–. Type as No. 7	35.00
14	150	Pesetas (Ag) 1970–. Roma Aeterna – (centenary of Rome as capital of Italy)	40.00
15	150	Pesetas (Ag) 1970–. Forum (centenary of Rome as capital of Italy)	40.00

16	150	Pesetas (Ag) 1970–. Caput Mundi (centenary of Rome as capital of Italy)	40.00
17	150	Pesetas (Ag) 1970–. Dea Roma (centenary of Rome as capital of Italy)	40.00
18	200	Pesetas (Ag) 1970–. The Jules Rimet Trophy (World Cup) surrounded by names of places of presentation, indication of dates and names of winners of all the world football championships	65.00
19	200	Pesetas (Ag) 1970–. Francisco Macias Nguema, 1st Head of State	65.00
20	250	Pesetas (Au) 1970–. Type as No. 12	125.00

					Proof
21	250	Pesetas (Au)	1970. Type as No. 7			100.00
22	500	Pesetas (Au)	1970. Type as No. 8			150.00
23	500	Pesetas (Au)	1970. Type as No. 9			150.00
24	500	Pesetas (Au)	1970. Type as No. 10			150.00
25	500	Pesetas (Au)	1970. Type as No. 11			150.00
26	750	Pesetas (Au)	1970. Type as No. 14			225.00
27	750	Pesetas (Au)	1970. Type as No. 15			225.00
28	750	Pesetas (Au)	1970. Type as No. 16			225.00
29	750	Pesetas (Au)	1970. Type as No. 17			225.00
30	1000	Pesetas (Au)	1970. Type as No. 18			350.00
31	5000	Pesetas (Au)	1970. Type as No. 19			1400.00

NEW CURRENCY: 100 Céntimos = 1 Ekuele

32   33   **XF**   **Unc**

			XF	Unc
32 (5)	1	Ekuele (Al-Br) 1975	0.50	1.50
33 (6)	5	Ekuele (Cu-Ni) 1975	1.00	2.50

34 (7)	10	Ekuele (Cu-Ni) 1975	1.50	4.00

10th ANNIVERSARY OF REIGN OF PRESIDENT NGUEMA (4)

35 (8)	1000	Ekuele (Ag) 1978. Central Bank	22.50
36 (9)	2000	Ekuelle (Ag) 1978. President Nguema. Rev. arms	45.00
37 (10)	5000	Ekuele (Au) 1978. Central Bank	160.00
38 (11)	10000	Ekuele (Au) 1978. Type as No. 36	320.00

WORLD SOCCER CHAMPIONSHIP IN ARGENTINA (2)

39 (13)	2000 Ekuele (Ag) 1978	200.00
40 (14)	10000 Ekuele (Au) 1978	550.00

OLYMPIC GAMES 1980 IN MOSCOW

41 (12)	2000 Ekuele (Ag) 1980. Man throwing a discus	40.00
42	2000 Ekuele (Ag) 1980. Zebra	35.00
43	2000 Ekuele (Ag) 1980. Impalas	35.00
44	2000 Ekuele (Ag) 1980. Head of a Tiger	35.00
45	2000 Ekuele (Ag) 1980. Cheetah	35.00

NEW CURRENCY: 100 Céntimos = 1 Ekwele, plural Bipkwele

VISIT OF THE ROYAL COUPLE OF SPAIN
TO EQUATORIAL GUINEA (4)

46 (15)	1000 Bipkwele (Ag) 1979	15.00	25.00
47 (16)	2000 Bipkwele (Ag) 1979	22.50	30.00
48 (17)	5000 Bipkwele (Au) 1979	85.00	100.00
49 (18)	10000 Bipkwele (Au) 1979	175.00	200.00

VISIT OF KING JUAN CARLOS I TO EQUATORIAL GUINEA (4)

50 (19)	1000 Bipkwele (Ag) 1970	15.00	25.00
51 (20)	2000 Bipkwele (Ag) 1979	22.50	30.00
52 (21)	5000 Bipkwele (Au) 1979	85.00	100.00
53 (22)	10000 Bipkwele (Au) 1979	175.00	200.00

		VF	XF
54 (23)	1 Ekwele (Al-Br) 1980	–.–	–.–
55 (24)	5 Bipkwele (Cu-Ni) 1980	–.–	–.–
56 (25)	25 Bipkwele (Cu-Ni) 1980	–.–	–.–
57 (26)	50 Bipkwele (Cu-Ni) 1980	–.–	–.–

VISIT OF POPE JOHN PAUL II

58	1 Ekwele (Au) 1982. Arms. Rev. Head of Pope John Paul II; dia. 50 mm, 62.29 g, .999 gold	1600.00

Eritrea

This former Italian colony on the coast of the Red Sea was part of
Italian East Africa from 1936 to 1941, and was occupied by the British
in 1941. On 15th September 1952 Eritrea was federated with Ethiopia as an autonomous territory and later in 1960 became an Ethiopian
province.
Capital: Asmara.

100 Centesimi = 1 Lira, 5 Lire = 1 Tallero

VICTOR EMMANUEL III

		VF	XF
1 (5)	1 Tallero (Ag) 1918. Diademed bust right of Italia. ℞ crowned eagle with breast shield with arms of Savoy	50.00	80.00

Estland
Estonia
Estonie
Eesti

At the beginning of the 13th century the Estonians were converted to Christianity by the Germans and the Danes. In the year 1346 the northern part of the territory, hitherto Danish, was sold to a German crusading Order called the Knights of the Sword. Estonia became Swedish in 1561, and a Russian province in 1721. On 24th February 1918 the Estonian Republic was proclaimed, but it was occupied by Russian troops in June 1940 and since then, apart from a short period of time (1941–1944), it has belonged to the Confederation of States of the Soviet Union.

Capital: Reval (Tallinn).

100 Penni = 1 Estonian Mark; from 1st January 1928:
100 Senti = 1 Kroon (Crown)

		VF	XF
1 (4)	1 Mark (Cu-Ni) 1922. Arms: three leopards left dividing date. R Value	4.00	7.00
2 (5)	3 Marka (Cu-Ni) 1922. Type as No. 1	4.50	9.00
3 (6)	5 Marka (Cu-Ni) 1922. Type as No. 1	5.00	10.00
4 (4a)	1 Mark (Ni-Br) 1924. Type as No. 1	6.00	11.00

		VF	XF
5 (5a)	3 Marka (Ni-Br) 1925. Type as No. 2	6.00	11.00
6 (6a)	5 Marka (Ni-Br) 1924. Type as No. 3	7.00	12.00
7 (7)	10 Marka (Ni-Br) 1925. Type as No. 1	11.00	20.00
8 (8)	1 Mark (Ni-Br) 1926. Arms with three leopards (national arms), within wreath. R value	10.00	18.00
9 (9)	3 Marka (Ni-Br) 1926. Type as No. 7	40.00	80.00
10 (10)	5 Marka (Ni-Br) 1926. Type as No. 7	250.00	450.00
11 (A 10)	10 Marka (Ni-Br) 1926. Type as No. 7	2000.00	4000.00
12 (B 10)	25 Marka (Ni-Br) 1926. Type as No. 7. Not released for circulation. Very rare!	–.–	–.–

			VF	XF
13 (1)	1 Sent (Br) 1929. National arms. R Value over oak leaves		2.00	4.00

			VF	XF
14 (1a)	1 Sent (Br) 1939. National arms. R figure 1 with legend EESTI VABARIIK and value in letters		20.00	40.00
15 (2)	2 Senti (Br) 1934. Type as No. 13		3.00	6.00
16 (3)	5 Senti (Br) 1931. Type as No. 13		4.00	7.00

17 (11)	10 Senti (Ni-Br) 1931. National arms. R value		3.00	5.00
18 (12)	20 Senti (Ni-Br) 1935. Type as No. 17		4.00	6.00

19 (13)	25 Senti (Ni-Br) 1928. National arms within wreath. R value		7.50	12.50
20 (14)	50 Senti (Ni-Br) 1936. Coat of arms dividing date. R value		7.50	12.00

		VF	**XF**
21 (15)	1 Kroon (Al–Br) 1934. National arms within wreath. ℞ Viking ship	8.50	15.00

22 (16)	2 Krooni (Ag) 1930. National arms. ℞ castle of Reval (Tallinn) originally built in 1227, renovated many times	9.00	17.00

TERCENTENARY OF THE UNIVERSITY OF DORPAT

23 (17)	2 Krooni (Ag) 1932. National arms within wreath. ℞ middle section of University buildings of Dorpat (Tartu)	20.00	40.00

FOR THE TENTH SINGING FESTIVAL FROM 23rd–25th JUNE 1933 IN REVAL

		VF	**XF**
24 (18)	1 Kroon (Ag) 1933. National arms within crossed oak branches. R lyre with view of open-air staircase	30.00	50.00

Äthiopien   # Ethiopia   **Éthiopie**

Area: 455,538 sq. mi. Population: 33,000,000.
A Christian empire in North Africa. Apart from the ruling Amharen people,
among others living in Ethiopia are the predominantly Mohammedan tribes
of the Galla, Danakil and Somali. During the years 1936-1941 Ethiopia
formed part of the Italian Empire. The emperor was deposed by a military
committee in 1974. As of July 1976, Ethiopia's present rule is by a military
provisional government which refers to the country as Socialist Ethiopia.
Capital: Addis Ababa.

16 Gersh = 1 Talari = 100 Matoñas (Cents) = 1 Talari (Dollar; since 1945:
100 Cents = 1 Ethiopian Dollar; since 1976: new currency was named Birr

EMPEROR MENELIK II 1889–1913

				VF	XF
1 (1)	¹/₁₀₀	Talari (Cu) Ethiopian Era (EE) 1889 (1897). Bust of Menelik II. ℞ inscription in dotted circle. 25.5 mm dia.		15.00	25.00

2 (5)	1 Gersh (Ag) EE 1889–1895 (1897 to 1903). Crowned head of Menelik II (1844–1913) to right. ℞ lion of Judah (= national arms), its left foreleg raised. 16.5 mm dia.:		
	a) EE 1889, 1891 (1897, 1898)	9.00	12.00
	b) EE 1895 (1903)	6.00	8.50

3 (6)	⅛ Talari (Ag) EE 1887, 1888 (1894, 1896). Type as No. 2. 20 mm dia.:	**VF**	**XF**
	a) EE 1887 (1894)	35.00	60.00
	b) EE 1888 (1896) (200 pieces)	–.–	–.–

4 (7)	¼ Talari (Ag) EE 1887–1895 (1894–1903). Type as No. 2. 25 mm dia.:		
	a) EE 1887 (1894)	26.00	50.00
	b) EE 1888 (1896) (200 pieces)	–.–	–.–
	c) EE 1889, 1895 (1897, 1903)	12.50	18.00

5 (8)	½ Talari (Ag) EE 1887–1889 (1894–1897). Type as No. 2. 30.5 mm dia.:		
	a) EE 1887 (1894)	40.00	60.00
	b) EE 1888 (1896) (200 pieces)	–.–	–.–
	c) EE 1889 (1897)	25.00	35.00

6 (9) 1 Talari (Ag) EE 1887–1889 (1894–1897).   **VF**   **XF**
Type as No. 2. 40 mm dia.:
a) EE 1887 (1894)   45.00   65.00
b) EE 1888 (1896) (200 pieces)   –.–   –.–
c) EE 1889 (1897)   30.00   50.00

7 (17) 1 Besa (Cu) EE 1889 (1897). ℞ lion of
Judah, its right foreleg raised. 20 mm
dia.   15.00   20.00

8 (18) 1 Gersh (Ag) EE 1889 (1897). Type as
as No. 7. 17 mm dia.   30.00   65.00

9 (19) ¼ Talari (Ag) EE 1889 (1897). Type as
No. 7. 25.5 mm dia.   40.00   70.00

		VF	**XF**
10 (20)	½ Talari (Ag) EE 1889 (1897). Type as No. 7. 30.2 mm dia.	55.00	80.00

| **11** (10) | 1 Talari (Ag) EE 1892, 1895 (1899, 1903). Type as No. 7. 40 mm dia. | 35.00 | 45.00 |
| **12** | ⅛ Wark (Au) undated | 110.00 | 140.00 |

13 (11)	¼ Wark (Au) undated	260.00	300.00
14 (12)	½ Wark (Au) undated	320.00	360.00
15 (13)	1 Wark (Au) undated	550.00	600.00
16	2 Wark (Au) undated	600.00	700.00

Coins Nos. 12–16 were first issued in 1916

EMPRESS ZAUDITU 1917–1930

17	1 Wark (Au). Bust, crowned and veiled, to left of Empress Zauditu = Judith, also called Woisero, (1876–1930). ℞ national arms. Diameter 20 mm	350.00	400.00
18	2 Wark (Au). Diameter 25 mm	1000.00	1250.00
19	4 Wark (Au). Diameter 31 mm	1350.00	1500.00

		VF	XF
20	4 Wark (Au) 1930. Bust of Haile Selassie I (1892–1975), crowned, to right. R national arms, lion to right	350.00	400.00

21 (23)	1 Matoña (Cu) 1931. Crowned bust of Haile Selassie to right. R national arms, lion to right	4.00	6.00
22 (24)	5 Matoñas (Cu) 1931	5.00	8.00
23 (25)	10 Matoñas (Ni) 1931	4.00	6.00
24 (26)	25 Matoñas (Ni) 1931	3.00	4.50
25 (27)	50 Matoñas (Ni) 1931	6.00	9.00
26 (28)	½ Wark (Au) 1931. Crowned bust of Haile Selassie to left. R St. George and the Dragon	270.00	320.00
27 (29)	1 Wark (Au) 1931. Type as No. 26	400.00	450.00

28 (30)	1 Cent (Br) 1944. Bust of Haile Selassie to left. R national arms	0.10	0.30
29 (31)	5 Cents (Br) 1944	0.20	0.40
30 (32)	10 Cents (Br) 1944	0.25	0.50
31 (33)	25 Cents (Br) 1944	22.00	35.00

32 (35)	25 Cents (Br) 1952. Shape of edge scalloped	0.70	1.10

	VF	XF
33 (34) 50 Cents (Ag) 1944	3.50	6.00

COMMEMORATIVE ISSUES (5) FOR THE 75th ANNIVERSARY OF THE BIRTH AND THE 50th JUBILEE OF THE REIGN OF EMPEROR HAILE SELASSIE I

		Unc	Proof
34	10 Dollars (Au) 1966. Bust of Haile Selassie almost facing, between Imperial crown and monogram, commemorative inscription. ℞ national arms and value		100.00
35	20 Dollars (Au) 1966. Type as No. 34		175.00
36	50 Dollars (Au) 1966. Type as No. 34		400.00
37	100 Dollars (Au) 1966. Type as No. 34		700.00
38	200 Dollars (Au) 1966. Type as No. 34		1500.00

39	5 Dollars (Ag) 1972. Theodoros II	30.00	50.00
40	5 Dollars (Ag) 1972. John IV	30.00	50.00

		Unc	Proof
41	5 Dollars (Ag) 1972. Menelik II	30.00	50.00
42	5 Dollars (Ag) 1972. Zewditu	30.00	50.00
43	10 Dollars (Ag) 1972. Haile Selassie	50.00	65.00
44	50 Dollars (Au) 1972. Type as No. 39		400.00
45	50 Dollars (Au) 1972. Type as No. 40		400.00
46	50 Dollars (Au) 1972. Type as No. 41		400.00
47	50 Dollars (Au) 1972. Type as No. 42		400.00
48	100 Dollars (Au) 1972. Type as No. 43		700.00
49 (41)	5 Dollars (Ag) 1972. Haile Selassie		12.50

NEW CURRENCY: 100 Cent = Birr

ISSUE FOR THE FAO COIN PLAN

		Unc	Proof
50 (36)	1 Cent (Al) EE 1969 (1977). Head of a lion. Rev. ploughing	1.00	–.–
51 (37)	5 Cents (Br) EE 1969 (1977).	1.00	–.–
52 (38)	10 Cents (Br) EE 1969 (1977).	1.50	–.–
53 (39)	25 Cents (Cu-Ni) EE 1969 (1977).	2.50	–.–
54 (40)	50 Cents (Cu-Ni) EE 1969 (1977).	3.00	–.–

CONSERVATION COMMEMORATIVE (3)

		Unc	Proof
55 (42)	10 Birr (Ag) 1979. Bearded Vulture	20.00	30.00
56 (43)	25 Birr (Ag) 1979. Mountain Nyala	30.00	40.00
57 (44)	600 Birr (Au) 1979. Walia Ibex	550.00	800.00

INTERNATIONAL YEAR OF THE CHILD (2)

		Unc	Proof
58 (45)	20 Birr (Ag) 1980	25.00	25.00
59 (46)	400 Birr (Au) 1980		300.00

WORLD SOCCER CHAMPIONSHIP GAMES 1982 IN SPAIN (3)

		Unc	Proof
60 (47)	2 Birr (Cu-Ni) 1981. Head of a lion. Rev. soccers in front of globes		
61 (48)	20 Birr (Ag) 1981. Type as No. 60	6.00	35.00
62 (49)	200 Birr (Au) 1981. Type as No. 60		250.00

INTERNATIONAL YEAR OF DISABLED PERSONS (2)

		Unc	Proof
63 (50)	50 Birr (Ag) 1982	20.00	25.00
64 (51)	500 Birr (Au) 1982	300.00	400.00

U. N. DECADE FOR WOMEN (2)

65 (52)   20 Birr (Ag) 1984

Proof
50.00

66 (53)   200 Birr (Ag) 1984. .900 gold, 7.13 g

300.00

EMERGENCY ISSUE OF DIRE DAOUA

Issued by a commercial syndicate in Dire Daoua.

		VF	XF
1	1 Piastre 16 au Taler (Al) 1922	35.00	65.00

EMERGENCY ISSUE OF ADDIS ABABA
Issued by P. P. Trohalis in Addis Ababa.

1	1 Piastre 16 au Thaler (Al) undated	40.00	70.00

Falklandinseln   **Falkland Islands**   **Falkland (Iles)**

Area: 6,430 sq. mi. Population: 2,260.
Group of islands in the South Atlantic, east of the Straits of Magellan.
Discovered 1592, British since 1833.
Capital: Stanley.

100 Pence = 1 Falkland Pound

		Unc	Proof
1 (1)	½ Penny (Br) 1974, 1980, 1982. Rev. Salmon (Salmo trutta – Salmonidae)	0.20	1.50

2 (2)	1 Penny (Br) 1974, 1980, 1982, 1985, 1987. Rev. Gentoo penguins (Pygoscelis papua – Spheniscidae)	0.25	2.00

3 (3)	2 Pence (Br) 1974, 1980, 1982, 1985, 1987. Rev. Upland goose (Chloephaga picta leucoptera – Anatidae)	0.40	2.50

		Unc	Proof

4 (4) 5 Pence (Cu-Ni) 1974, 1980, 1982, 1983, 1985, 1987. Rev. blackbrowed albatross (Diomedea melanophris – Diomedeidae)   0.60   4.00

5 (5) 10 Pence (Cu-Ni) 1974, 1980, 1982, 1983, 1985, 1987. Rev. ursine seal (Arctocephalus australis – Otariidae)   1.00   5.00

6 (6) ½ Sovereign (Au) 1974. R Corriedale/Romney marsh sheep (Ovis ammon aries-Bovidae)   250.00

7 (7) 1 Sovereign (Au) 1974. Type as No. 6   350.00

8 (8) 2 Sovereign (Au) 1974. Type as No. 6   750.00

9 (9) 5 Sovereign (Au) 1974. Type as No. 6   1400.00

SILVER JUBILEE OF HER MAJESTY QUEEN ELIZABETH II

10 (10) 50 Pence 1977:
     a) (Ag)   30.00
     b) (Cu-Ni)   2.00

CONSERVATION COMMEMORATIVE (3)

11 (11) 5 £ (Ag) 1979. Humback whale:
     a) .925 silver, 25.31 g   25.00
     b) .925 silver, 28.28 g   30.00

12 (12) 10 £ (Ag) 1979. Flightless steamer duck:
     a) .925 silver, 31.65 g   30.00
     b) .925 silver, 35.00 g   45.00

13 (13) 150 £ (Au) 1979. Falkland fur seal   600.00   900.00

	Unc	Proof
14 (14) 50 Pence (Cu-Ni) 1980, 1982, 1985, 1987. Rev. Fox	2.00	6.50

80th ANNIVERSARY OF BIRTH OF QUEEN MOTHER

15 (15) 50 Pence 1980:		
a) (Ag)		30.00
b) (Cu-Ni)	2.00	

WEDDING OF PRINCE CHARLES AND LADY DIANA

16 (16) 50 Pence 1981:		
a) (Ag)		25.00
b) (Cu-Ni)	3.50	

LIBERATION FROM ARGENTINE FORCES (2)

17 (17) 50 Pence 1982. Arms, Union Jack, inscription »LIBERATION 14th JUNE 1982«:		
a) (Ag)		30.00
b) (Cu-Ni)	3.00	
18 (17b) 50 Pence (Au) 1982. Type as No. 17 (25 pcs.)		7000.00

			Unc	Proof

19 18   20 Pence (Cu-Ni) 1982, 1983, 1985, 1987.
Rev. Rommey marsh sheep   1.00   5.00

150th ANNIVERSARY OF BRITISH RULE (2)

20 (19)   50 Pence 1983. Sailing vessel »H.M.S.
Desire«:
a) (Ag)   35.00
b) (Cu-Ni)   3.00

21 (19b)   50 Pence (Au) 1983. Type as No. 20   2000.00

100 YEARS OF SELF SUFFICIENCY

22 (20)   25 £ (Ag) 1985. New portrait of Queen Elizabeth II. Rev. steam and sailing ship
»SS Great Britain«   185.00

OPENING OF MOUNT PLEASANT AIRPORT

23 (21)   50 Pence 1985. Rev. Portrait of Prince
Andrew:
a) (Ag)   35.00
b) Cu-Ni)   3.00

COMMONWEALTH GAMES IN EDINBURGH

24 (22)   2 £ (Ag) 1986:
a) .500 silver, 28.28 g   15.00
b) .925 silver, 28.28 g   30.00

PRINCE ANDREW'S WEDDING

25 (23)   25 £ (Ag) 1986   125.00

| 26 | 50 Pence (Ag) 1987. Rev. Penguins | | 40.00 |

Nos. 27–32 omitted.

		XF	**Unc**
33	1 £ (Ni-Bra) 1987. Elizabeth II (Mak-louf Type). Rev. Arms	2.00	4.00
			Proof
34	1 £ (Ag) 1987. Type as No. 33:		
	a) .925 silver, 9.5 g		25.00
	b) .925 silver, 19 g		125.00

Fidschi-Inseln **Fiji Islands** **Fidji (Iles)**

Area: 7,039 sq. mi. Population: 715,000.
A group of islands in the Pacific Ocean. It was discovered in 1643 by Abel
Janszoon Tasman, visited in 1774 by James Cook and explored in 1827 by
Dumont d'Urville. After the abdication of King Cakobau on 10th October
1874 it became a British possession. The islands have had a large measure of
internal autonomy since 1965.
Capital: Suva

12 Pence = 1 Shilling, 2 Shillings = 1 Florin, 20 Shillings = £ 1;
since 13th January 1969: 100 Cents = 1 Fiji Dollar

GEORGE V 1910–1936

			VF	XF
1 (1)	½	Penny (Cu–Ni) 1934. Crown above inscription GEORGE V · KING · EMPEROR. ℞ value in letters (with central hole)	4.00	9.00
2 (2)	1	Penny (Cu–Ni) 1934–1936. Type as No. 1	2.00	6.00
3 (3)	6	Pence (Ag) 1934–1936. Crowned bust left of King George V. ℞ sea turtle, stylized (family of the Cheloniidae)	4.00	18.00
4 (4)	1	Shilling (Ag) 1934–1936. ℞ native boat	10.00	30.00
5 (5)	1	Florin (Ag) 1934–1936. ℞ coat of arms	15.00	40.00

EDWARD VIII 1936

6 (6)	1	Penny (Cu–Ni) 1936. Crown above inscription EDWARD VIII · KING · EMPEROR. ℞ value in letters (with central hole)	2.50	5.00

			VF	XF
7 (7)	½	Penny (Cu–Ni) 1940–1941. Crown above inscription GEORGE VI · KING · EMPEROR. ℞ value in letters	3.00	6.00
8 (7a)	½	Penny (Bra) 1942–1943. Type as No. 7	1.50	4.00
9 (8)	1	Penny (Cu–Ni) 1937, 1940, 1941, 1945. Type as No. 7	1.50	4.00
10 (8a)	1	Penny (Bra) 1942–1943. Type as No. 9	2.00	7.00
11 (11)	6	Pence (Ag) 1937. Crowned head of King George VI to left; to the right of the portrait the inscription EMPEROR. ℞ sea turtle	10.00	30.00
12 (12)	1	Shilling (Ag) 1937. ℞ outrigger	12.00	40.00
13 (13)	1	Florin (Ag) 1937. ℞ coat of arms	20.00	65.00
14 (17)	3	Pence (Ni–Bra) 1947. Crowned head of King George VI to left; to the right of the portrait the inscription KING · EMPEROR (scalloped). ℞ native hut	2.00	5.00
15 (11a)	6	Pence (Ag) 1938–1943. Type as No. 11, but to the right of the portrait the inscription KING · EMPEROR	10.00	30.00
16 (12a)	1	Shilling (Ag) 1938–1943. Type as No. 12, but to the right of the portrait the inscription KING · EMPEROR:		
		a) .500 silver, 5.6552 g, 1938, 1941	10.00	30.00
		b) .900 silver, 5.6552 g, 1942, 1943	3.00	6.00
17 (13a)	1	Florin (Ag) 1938–1945. Type as No. 13, but with inscription KING · EMPEROR:		
		a) .500 silver, 11.3104 g, 1938, 1941, 1945	25.00	65.00
		b) .900 silver, 11.3104 g, 1942, 1943	7.00	10.00
18 (18)	½	Penny (Cu–Ni) 1949–1952. Crown above inscription KING GEORGE THE SIXTH. ℞ value in letters (with hole)	0.50	1.00
19 (19)	1	Penny (Cu–Ni) 1949–1952. Type as No. 18	0.50	1.20
20 (20)	3	Pence (Ni–Bra) 1950–1952. Type as No. 14, but with inscription KING GEORGE THE SIXTH	1.00	3.00

ELIZABETH II since 1952

			VF	XF
21 (21)	½	Penny (Cu–Ni) 1954. Crown above inscription QUEEN ELIZABETH THE SECOND. ℞ value in letters (with hole)	0.30	0.70

		VF	XF
22 (22)	1 Penny (Cu–Ni) 1954–1968. Type as No. 21	0.20	0.40
23 (23)	3 Pence (Ni–Bra) 1955–1967. Head right of Queen Elizabeth II. R. native hut	0.20	0.50
24 (24)	6 Pence (Cu–Ni) 1953–1967. R. sea-turtle	0.25	0.60

		VF	XF
25 (25)	1 Shilling (Cu–Ni) 1957–1965. R. out-rigger	0.40	0.90
26 (26)	1 Florin (Cu–Ni) 1957–1965. R. coat of arms	0.60	1.20

CURRENCY REFORM: 100 Cents = 1 Fiji Dollar

27 (27)	1 Cent (Br) 1969, 1973, 1975, 1983, 1984. Rev. kava dish	0.10	0.20

28 (28)	2 Cents (Br) 1969, 1973, 1975–1985	0.10	0.20

29 (29)	5 Cents (Cu–Ni) 1969, 1973–1984	0.10	0.25

				VF	**XF**
30 (30)	10 Cents (Cu-Ni) 1969, 1973, 1975–1985			0.15	0.40
31 (31)	20 Cents (Cu-Ni) 1969, 1973–1985. Rev. ceremonial chain			0.30	0.50

			Unc	**Proof**
32 (32)	1 Dollar 1969, 1976. Rev. arms and value:			
	a) (Cu-Ni) 1969, 1976		5.00	
	b) (Ag) 1976			35.00

COMMEMORATIVE ISSUE TO MARK INDEPENDENCE

			Unc	**Proof**
33 (33)	1 Dollar 1970. Bust r. of Queen Elizabeth II. R large seal of state			
	a) (Ag)			250.000
	b) (Cu-Ni)		6.00	10.00

1ooth ANNIVERSARY OF CESSION TO GREAT BRITAIN

34 (34) 25 Dollars (Ag) 1974. Elizabeth II. R Cakobau, King of the Fiji Islands up the
1874; 45 mm dia   30.00   40.00

	Unc	Proof
35 (35) 100 Dollars (Au) 1974. Type as No. 34; 38 mm dia.	300.00	325.00
36 (A32) 50 Cents Elizabeth II. Rev. outrigger:		
a) (Cu-Ni) 1975, 1976, 1978, 1980–1983	1.00	10.00
b) (Ag) 1976		25.00
37 (36) 25 Dollars (Ag) 1975. Type similar to No. 34	60.00	50.00
38 (37) 100 Dollars (Au) 1975. Type similar to No. 35	300.00	325.00

Nos. 39–45 omitted.

SILVER JUBILEE OF HER MAJESTY QUEEN ELIZABETH II

46 (39) 10 Dollars (Ag) 1977. R coat of arms,
value, memorial legend   55.00

ISSUE FOR THE FAO COIN PLAN

47 (38) 1 Cent (Br) 1977–1982. Rev. rice   0.20   2.00

CONSERVATION COMMEMORATIVE (3)

48 (40) 10 Dollars (Ag) 1987. Pink-billed parrot
finch   25.00   30.00

49 (41)	20 Dollars (Ag) 1978. Golden cowrie	30.00	35.00
50 (42)	250 Dollars (Au) 1978. Banded Iguana	600.00	750.00

FIRST INDIANS IN FIJI CENTENNIAL AND FOR THE FAO COIN PLAN

51 (43)	50 Cents (Cu-Ni) 1979. Rev. sugar-cane	2.50	12.50

10th ANNIVERSARY OF INDEPENDENCE (3)

52 (44)	50 Cents (Cu-Ni) 1980. Prince Charles	5.00	
53 (45)	10 Dollars (Ag) 1980. Type as No. 52	25.00	35.00
54 (46)	200 Dollars (Ag) 1980. Type as No. 52	280.00	325.00

WEDDING OF PRINCE CHARLES AND LADY DIANA

55 (47)	10 Dollars (Ag) 1981. Head of Prince Charles, commemorative legend	35.00

25th ANNIVERSARY OF WORLD WILDLIFE FUND (2)

56 (48)	10 Dollars (Ag) 1986. Rev. Fijian Ground Frog	40.00
57 (49)	200 Dollars (Au) 1986. Rev. Ogmodon Cobra	350.00

Finnland　　　　　**Finland**　　　　　**Finlande**

Suomi

Area: 130,160 sq. mi. Population: 4,900,000.
Made a duchy in 1284 and a principality in 1581, Finland was part of the
Swedish kingdom until 1809. Later it became an autonomous principality
within the Russian Union of States. On 6th December 1917 the country declared its independence and on 17th July 1919 it was granted a Republican
constitution.
Capital: Helsinki.

100 Penniä = 1 Markka

PRINCIPALITY

			VF	XF
1 (13)	1	Penni (Cu) 1895–1916. Filleted crown over monogram of Czar Nicolas II. ℞ value within wreath	1.50	4.00
2 (14)	5	Penniä (Cu) 1896–1917. Type as No. 1	2.00	4.00

3 (15)	10	Penniä (Cu) 1895–1917. Type as No. 1	3.50	7.50
4 (1a)	25	Penniä (Ag) 1897–1917. Crowned double eagle. ℞ value within wreath	2.50	4.50
5 (2a)	50	Penniä (Ag) 1907–1917. Type as No. 4	3.00	6.00
6 (3a)	1	Markka (Ag) 1907–1915. Crowned double eagle and inscription. ℞ value within wreath	6.00	11.00
7 (4a)	2	Markkaa (Ag) 1905–1908. Type as No. 6	18.00	35.00

			VF	**XF**
8 (5)	10	Markkaa (Au) 1904–1913. Crowned double eagle, inscription FINLAND/ SUOMI. ℞ value and date, inscription	250.00	300.00
9 (6)	20	Markkaa (Au) 1903–1913. Type as No. 8	200.00	275.00

INDEPENDENCE

10 (16)	1	Penni (Cu) 1917. Double eagle without crown. ℞ value within wreath	3.00	6.00
11 (17)	5	Penniä (Cu) 1917–1918. Type as No. 10	4.00	8.00
12 (18)	10	Penniä (Cu) 1917. Type as No. 10	6.00	11.00
13 (19)	25	Penniä (Ag) 1917. Double eagle without crown. ℞ value within wreath	3.00	6.00
14 (20)	50	Penniä (Ag) 1917. Type as No. 13	4.00	9.00

RED GOVERNMENT IN SOUTHERN FINLAND

15 (21)	5	Penniä (Cu) 1918. Three trumpets with banner within wreath and inscription. ℞ value	60.00	95.00

REPUBLIC since 1918

16 (22)	1	Penni (Cu) 1919–1924. Arms (lion). ℞ value	1.60	3.00
17 (23a)	5	Penniä (Fe) 1918. Type as No. 16	2000.00	3500.00
18 (23)	5	Penniä (Cu) 1918-1940. Type as No. 17	1.50	3.00

19 (24)	10	Penniä(Cu) 1919-1940.Type as No. 16	1.50	3.00
20 (25)	25	Penniä (Ni) 1921-1940. Arms (lion) dividing date. Rev. value between ears	2.00	6.00
21 (26)	50	Penniä (Ni) 1921-1940. Type as No. 20	2.50	6.00
22 (27)	1	Markka (Ni) 1921-1924. Arms (lion). R value within wreath, diameter 24 mm	3.00	6.00
23 (27a)	1	Markka (Ni) 1928-1940. Type as No. 22; diameter 21 mm	2.00	4.00
24 (28)	5	Markkaa (Al-Br) 1928-1942. Coat of arms within wreath, date. R value within wreath, inscription	2.50	4.00

			VF	**XF**

25 (29)   10 Markkaa (Al-Br) 1928-1939. Type as No. 24   3.00   5.00

26 (30)   20 Markkaa (Al-Br) 1931-1939. Type as No. 24   4.00   9.00

27 (31) 100 Markkaa (Au) 1926. Arms (lion) dividing
date. R value between branches   600.00   900.00

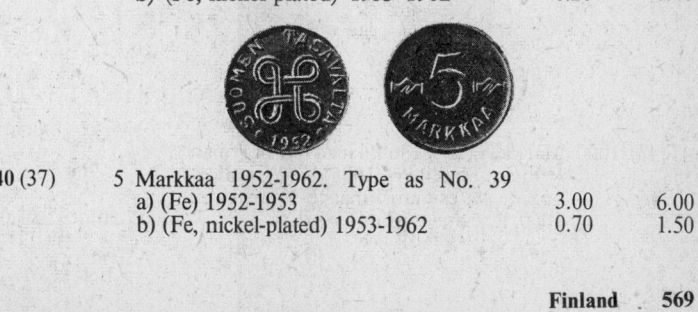

28 (32) 200 Markkaa (Au) 1926. Type as No. 27   750.00   1000.00

29 (33)   5 Penniä (Cu) 1941-1943. Fir-branches,
divided date. R value (with center hole)   1.00   2.00

30 (34)   10 Penniä (Cu) 1941-1943. Type as No. 29   1.50   2.50

Nos. 29 and 30 are also know without punched hole (rare)

31 (25a)   25 Penniä (Cu) 1940-1943. Type as No. 20   2.00   3.50

32 (26a)   50 Penniä (Cu) 1940-1943. Type as No. 21   2.50   4.00

33 (27b)   1 Markkaa (Cu) 1940-1951. Type as No. 22:
   a) 1940-1943, 1950, 1951   2.00   4.00
   b) 1949 (about 250 pieces)   1000.00   1300.00

34 (34b)   10 Penniä (Fe) 1943-1945. Type as No. 30,
but smaller diameter   2.00   4.00

No. 34 are also known without punched hole (rare)

35 (25b)   25 Penniä (Fe) 1943–1945. Type as No. 20   1.50   3.50

36 (26b)   50 Penniä (Fe) 1943–1948. Type as No. 21   3.00   6.00

37 (27c)   1 Markka (Fe) 1943-1952. Type as No. 22   2.50   4.00

38 (28a)   5 Markkaa (Bra) 1946-1952. Type as No. 24:
   a) 1946-1951   2.00   3.50
   b) 1952   8.00   11.00

39 (36)   1 Markkaa 1952-1962. Ornamental pattern.
R value, two clasped hands, a subject from
the national saga "The Kalevala"
   a) (Fe) 1952–1953   2.00   4.00
   b) (Fe, nickel-plated) 1953–1962   0.20   0.40

40 (37)   5 Markkaa 1952-1962. Type as No. 39
   a) (Fe) 1952-1953   3.00   6.00
   b) (Fe, nickel-plated) 1953-1962   0.70   1.50

				VF	XF

41 (38) 10 Markkaa (Al–Br) 1952–1962. Arms (lion) and inscription. ℞ fir-tree and value — **1.20** / **3.00**

42 (39) 20 Markkaa (Al–Br) 1952–1962. Type as No. 41 — **1.50** / **8.00**

43 (40) 50 Markkaa (Al–Br) 1952–1962. Type as No. 41 — **2.50** / **7.00**

44 (41) 100 Markkaa (Ag) 1956–1960. Coat of arms. ℞ value — **3.50** / **6.00**

45 (42) 200 Markkaa (Ag) 1956–1959. Type as No. No. 44 — **4.00** / **9.00**

15th OLYMPIC SUMMER GAMES IN HELSINKI
FROM 19. 7. – 3. 8. 1952

46 (35) 500 Markkaa (Ag) 1951, 1952. Olympic rings. ℞ value within wreath
    a) 1951 — **300.00** / **420.00**
    b) 1952 — **40.00** / **60.00**

MARKKA CURRENCY SYSTEM CENTENNIAL

47 (43) 1000 Markkaa (Ag) 1960. Head left of Johan Vilhelm Snellman (1806–1881), philosopher, statesman, Finance Minister in 1860. ℞ value within wreath — **17.50** / **25.00**

CURRENCY REFORM 1st January 1963:
100 old Markkaa = 1 new Markka

		VF	XF
48 (44)	1 Penni (Cu) 1963–1969. Type as No. 39	0.15	0.35
49 (45)	5 Penniä (Cu) 1963–1977. Type as No. 48	0.12	0.25
50 (46)	10 Penniä (Al-Br) 1963–1982. Arms (lion).	0.12	0.30
51 (47)	20 Penniä (Al-Br) 1963–. Type as No. 50	0.18	0.35

52 (48)	50 Penniä (Al-Br) 1963–. Arms (lion). R fir-tree and value	0.20	0.40

53 (49)	1 Markka (Bi) 1964–1968. R value in front of stylized trees	1.00	2.50

COMMEMORATIVE ISSUE FOR 50 YEARS OF INDEPENDENCE

54 (51)	10 Markkaa (Ag) 1967. Five whooper swans in flight (Cygnus cygnus — Anatidae). R buildings and bridges in course of construction, symbol of recovery; value	10.00	12.50
55 (44a)	1 Penni (Al) 1969–1979. Type as No. 48	0.05	0.10
56 (49a)	1 Markkaa (Cu-Ni) 1969–1987. Type as No. 53	0.20	0.40

			XF	Unc
57 (50)	5 Markkaa (Cu-Ni) 1972–1978. Ice-breaker. R value:			
	a) 1972		1.00	3.00
	b) 1973–1978		0.80	1.50

COMMEMORATIVE ISSUE FOR THE CENTENARY OF THE BIRTH OF JUHO KUSTI PAASIKIVI

58 (52)	10 Markkaa (Ag) 1970. Head facing of Juho Kusti Paasikivi (1870–1956), Head of State 1946–1956. R date, value, names of country on brick wall background	6.00	10.00

COMMEMORATIVE ISSUE FOR THE 10th EUROPEAN ATHLETICS CHAMPIONSHIPS IN HELSINKI
(10th to 15th August 1971)

59 (53)	10 Markkaa (Ag) 1971	6.00	10.00

75th ANNIVERSARY OF THE BIRTH OF URHO KEKKONEN

		XF	Unc
60 (54)	10 Markkaa (Ag) 1975. Urho Kekkonen (*1900), President of State since 1956	6.00	10.00
61 (45a)	5 Penniä (Al) 1977-. Type as No. 49	0.05	0.10

60th ANNIVERSARY OF INDEPENDENCE

62 (55)	10 Markkaa (Ag) 1977	9.00	12.50

ISSUE FOR THE SKI CHAMPIONSHIPS IN LAHTI

63 (56)	25 Markkaa (Ag) 1978	8.00	12.00

750th ANNIVERSARY OF TURKU

			XF	**Unc**
64 (58)	25 Markkaa (Ag) 1979		8.00	12.50

65 (57)	5 Markkaa (Al-Br) 1979–. Ice-breaker		0.80	1.50

80th ANNIVERSARY OF THE BIRTH OF URHO KEKKONEN

66 (59)	50 Markkaa (Ag) 1981. President Urho Kekkonen	9.00	13.00

WORLD ICE-HOCKEY CHAMPIONSHIP GAMES

67 (60)	50 Markkaa (Ag) 1982. Ice-hockey player	9.00	13.00
68 (46a)	10 Penniä (Al) 1983–. Type as No. 50	0.05	0.10

WORLD ATHLETICS CHAMPIONSHIPS

69 (61)	50 Markkaa (Ag) 1983	9.00	12.00

NATIONAL SAGA KALEVALA

70 (62)	50 Markkaa (Ag) 1984	9.00	12.00

Frankreich   **France**   **France**

Area: 212,974 sq. mi. Population: 54,335,000.

After the fall of Emperor Napoleon III in 1870 the Third Republic was created, which lasted until 1940. After the Armistice of 22nd June 1940, the Government was in the hands of Marshal Pétain in Vichy, in the part of France which was not occupied by German troops. After the referendum of 13th October 1946 a new Constitution was formulated which established the Fourth Republic. The constitution of the Fifth Republic was granted by popular vote in 1958.

Capital: Paris.

Since 1879, in general no mintmarks appear on French coins, although there are a few exceptions: the mintmark B indicates the striking of coins in Brussels in 1939, and during the years 1943–1958 it refers to issues made by the mint at Beaumont le Roger in the Eure department. The mintmark C indicates special circumstances resulting from the two World Wars, when the mint at Castelsarrasin (Tarn et Garonne) issued coins in 1914 as well as in 1943–1946.

$$100 \text{ Centimes} = 1 \text{ Franc}$$

THE THIRD REPUBLIC 1870–1940

			VF	XF
1 (58)	1 Centime (Br) 1898–1904, 1908–1914, 1916, 1919–1920. Head of Marianne wearing cap of liberty, symbol of the Republic. ℞ value and date between olive branches		2.00	4.00

			VF	XF
2 (59)	2 Centimes (Br) 1898–1904, 1907–1914, 1916, 1919–1920. Type as No. 1		2.50	4.50
3 (60)	5 Centimes (Br) 1898–1917, 1920–1921. ℞ allegorical representation: the Republic protecting her child; value and date		1.50	3.00

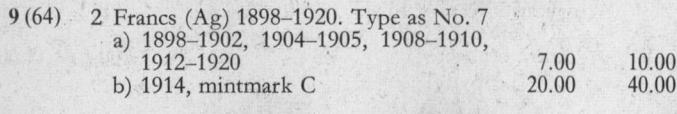

				VF	XF

4 (61) 10 Centimes (Br) 1898–1917, 1920 to
1921. Type as No. 3 — 3.00 7.00

5 (69) 25 Centimes (Ni) 1903. Head left of Marianne. ℞ value within square frame — 3.00 6.00

6 (70) 25 Centimes (Ni) 1904–1905. ℞ fasces, oak leaves (Quercus sp. – Fagaceae), value — 1.50 4.00

7 (62) 50 Centimes (Ag) 1897–1920. Female figure sowing with rising sun in background. ℞ value and olive branch (Olea europea — Oleaceae) — 2.50 3.00

8 (63) 1 Franc (Ag) 1898–1920. Type as No. 7
  a) 1898–1920 — 3.00 5.00
  b) 1914, mintmark C — 300.00 500.00

9 (64) 2 Francs (Ag) 1898–1920. Type as No. 7
  a) 1898–1902, 1904–1905, 1908–1910, 1912–1920 — 7.00 10.00
  b) 1914, mintmark C — 20.00 40.00

10 (65) 10 Francs (Au) 1899–1901, 1905–1912, 1914. Head right of Marianne. ℞ Gallic cockerel — 60.00 70.00

11 (66) 20 Francs (Au) 1899–1914. Type as No. 10   **VF**   **XF**
a) 1899–1906, circular inscription
DIEU PROTÈGE LA FRANCE   110.00   120.00
b) 1907–1914, circular inscription
LIBERTÉ ÉGALITÉ FRATERNITÉ   110.00   120.00

12 (56) 50 Francs (Au) 1878–1904. Standing geni-
us writing the Constitution on tablet;
on left, fasces; on right, Gallic cockerel.
℞ value and date within oak wreath
a) 1878, 1904   750.00   1250.00
b) 1887, 1889, 1896, 1900   1500.00   2500.00

13 (57) 100 Francs (Au) 1878–1914. Type as No.
12
a) 1878–1906, circular inscription
DIEU PROTÈGE LA FRANCE   500.00   600.00
b) 1907–1913, circular inscription LI-
BERTÉ ÉGALITÉ FRATERNITÉ   500.00   600.00
c) 1914, as 13b (1281 pieces issued) 4500.00   6500.00

14 (71) 5 Centimes (Cu–Ni) 1917–1920. Initials
RF below cap of liberty and between
oak branches. ℞ olive branch between
value; no line under CMES. Diameter
19 mm (with central hole)   1.00   2.00

15 (72) 5 Centimes. Type as No. 14, but diameter 17 mm
a) (Cu–Ni) 1920–1927, 1930–1938   0.40   0.80
b) (Cu–Ni) 1929   –.–   –.–
c) (Ni–Br) 1938–1939   1.20   2.50

16 (73) 10 Centimes (with hole)
a) (Ni) 1914, CMES with line   1800.00
b) (Cu–Ni) 1917–1938. CMES with-
out line   0.20   0.40
c) (Ni–Br) 1938–1939, as 16 b   0.60   1.20

17 (76) 25 Centimes (with hole)
a) (Ni) 1914–1915. CMES with line   5.00   10.00
b) (Ni) 1916–1917, as 17a   35.00   60.00
c) (Cu–Ni) 1917–1938. CMES with-
out line   0.30   0.60
d) (Ni–Br) 1938–1940. CMES without line   1.00   2.00

18 (77)   50   Centimes (Al–Br) 1921–1929. Mercury, the messenger of the gods, seated to left. Inscription COMMERCE IN-DUSTRIE. ℞ value with indication BON POUR. Inscription around: CHAMBRES DE COMMERCE DE FRANCE (token issued by the Chamber of Commerce)   1.00   2.00

19 (78)   1   Franc (Al–Br) 1920–1928. Type as No. 18   1.00   2.00

20 (79)   2   Francs (Al–Br) 1920–1927. Type as No. 18   1.60   4.00

21 (80)   50   Centimes. Head left of Marianne. ℞ value and date between horns of plenty

     a) (Al–Br) 1931–1941   0.80   3.00
     b) (Al–Br) 1939, mintmark B   6.00   12.50
     c) (Al) 1941-1947   0.60   1.20

22 (81)   1   Franc. Type as No. 21

     a) (Al–Br) 1931–1941   0.30   0.60
     b) (Al) 1941, 1944–1950, 1957–1959   0.40   0.60
     c) (Al) 1943, struck in Algiers   1500.00
     d) (Zi) 1943, struck in Algiers   1600.00

23 (82)   2   Francs. Type as No. 21

     a) (Al–Br) 1931–1941   0.80   1.60
     b) (Al) 1941, 1944–1950, 1958–1959   0.30   0.60

24 (83)   5   Francs (Ni) 1933. Head right of Mari-anne. ℞ ears of corn (Triticum sati-vum — Gramineae), laurel branch, oak twig and bunch of grapes (Vitis vini-fera — Vitaceae); value   6.00   9.00

			VF	XF
25 (84)		5 Francs. Laureate head of Marianne to left. ℞ value within wreath, above which initials RF		
	a)	(Ni) 1933, 1935	2.40	5.00
	b)	(Ni) 1936	–.–	–.–
	c)	(Ni) 1937, 1938	40.00	55.00
	d)	(Al-Br) 1938-1940, 1945-1946	7.00	15.00
	e)	(Al) 1945-1950, 1952	0.60	1.00
26 (86)		10 Francs. Laureate head of Marianne to right. ℞ value between ears of corn		
	a)	(Ag) 1929–1934, 1938–1939; diameter 28 mm	5.00	7.00
	b)	(Ag) 1937; diameter 28 mm	90.00	170.00
	c)	(Cu–Ni) 1945–1947; diameter 26 mm	2.50	4.00
27 (86b)		10 Francs (Cu–Ni) 1947–1949. Type as No. 26, but with smaller head of Marianne	1.00	4.00
28 (87)		20 Francs (Ag) 1929–1938. Type as No. 26		
	a)	1929, 1933–1934, 1937–1938	12.50	15.00
	b)	1936	300.00	400.00

			VF	XF
29 (88)		100 Francs (Au) 1929, 1933, 1935–1936. Winged head. ℞ ears of corn between laurel and oak branches, value	500.00	700.00

Coins of type 29 with dates 1929 and 1933 are patterns, of which only very few specimens came on the market.

			VF	XF
30 (73b)		10 Centimes (Zi) 1941. Type as No. 16	0.50	1.50
31 (74)		10 Centimes (Zi) 1945–1946. Type as No. 16, but diameter 17.5 mm	2.50	4.00

32 (75) 20 Centimes (Zi) 1945–1946. Type as No.   **VF**   **XF**
17, but diameter 24.5 mm
a) 1945–1946   8.50   18.00
b) 1945, mintmark B   75.00   140.00

ISSUES OF THE VICHY GOVERNMENT
Legend: ÉTAT FRANÇAIS

33 (V 91) 10 Centimes (Zi) 1941–1943. Ears of
wheat. ℞ oak leaves, value (with hole)
a) 1941–1942, diameter 21.5 mm   0.60   3.50
b) 1943, diameter 21.2 mm   0.60   3.50
34 (V 93) 10 Centimes (Zi) 1943–1944. Type as No.
33, but diameter 17.2 mm   2.00   4.50
35 (V 90) VINGT (20) Centimes (Zi) 1941. Value
in letters (with hole)   3.00   6.00
36 (V 92) 20 Centimes
a) (Zi) 1941–1944   1.10   3.50
b) (Fe) 1944   90.00   125.00
37 (V 94) 50 Centimes (Al) 1942–1944. Battle axe
between ears of corn. ℞ value between
oak twigs   0.80   2.50
38 (V 95) 1 Franc (Al) 1942–1944. As No. 37   0.80   3.00

39 (V 96) 2 Francs (Al) 1943–1944. As No. 37:
a) 1943, 1944   0.50   1.50
b) 1943 B   10.00   22.00

40 (V 97) 5 Francs (Ni–Br) 1941. Head left of
Marshal Henri Philippe Pétain (1856 to
1951), Head of State 1940–1944. ℞
battle axe and value (not put into circulation)   240.00

	VF	XF

41 (89) 2 Francs (Bra) 1944. FRANCE within circle. ℞ value, date and legend LIBERTÉ – ÉGALITÉ – FRATER-NITÉ (struck at Philadelphia; circulated mostly in Algeria and Southern France as Allied Occupation money) 5.00 10.00

THE FOURTH REPUBLIC 1947–1958

Many issues of the period of the Third Republic still appear with dates until 1959.

42 (98) 10 Francs (Al–Br) 1950–1958. Head left of Marianne. ℞ Gallic cockerel, laurel branch, value 0.30 0.60

43 (99) 20 Francs (Al–Br). Type as No. 42
  a) 1950. Name of the designer in two lines: Georges/Guiraud 3.50 6.00
  b) 1950–1954. Name of the designer in one line: G. Guiraud 0.40 0.80

44 (100) 50 Francs (Al–Br) 1950–1954, 1958. Type as No. 42 0.70 1.40

45 (101) 100 Francs (Cu–Ni) 1954–1958. Head of Marianne to right with hand holding torch. ℞ value and olive branches 1.20 2.20

Numbers 46–59 omitted.

			XF	Unc
60 (102)	1 Centime (St) 1962–. Ear of wheat. R value		0.10	0.25

61 (103)	5 Centimes (St) 1961–1964. Type as No. 60		0.20	0.40
62 (A 104)	5 Centimes (Al-Br) 1965–. Head of Marianne to left. R value, olive branch and ear of wheat		0.05	0.10

63 (104)	10 Centimes (Al-Br) 1962–. Type as No. 62		0.05	0.10
64 (105)	20 Centimes (Al-Br) 1962–. Type as No. 62		0.10	0.20

65 (106)	50 Centimes (Al-Br) 1962–1964. Type as No. 62		1.00	2.00
66 (107)	½ Franc (Ni) 1965–. Female figure sowing with rising sun in background. R olive branch and value		0.15	0.25

67 (108)	1 Franc (Ni) 1960–1962, 1964–. Type as No. 66		0.25	0.40

			XF	Unc
68	(110)	5 Francs (Ag) 1960–1969. Type as No. 66	4.00	8.50
69	(110a)	5 Francs (Cu-Ni) 1970–. Type as No. 68	1.50	2.00

70 (111) 10 Francs (Ag) 1964, 1965–1973. Group of three, standing, comprising Hercules and two female figures. R value within wreath. The issue of 1964 is a very rare pattern. 15.00 20.00

71 (A 112) 10 Francs (Cu-Al-Ni) 1974–1984, 1987. Map and letters RF. Rev. factories, value 1.50 2.50

72 (112) 50 Francs (Ag) 1974–1980. Type as No. 70 20.00

73 (109) 2 Francs (Ni) 1979–. Type similar to No. 68 0.25 0.50

100th ANNIVERSARY OF DEATH OF GAMBETTA

			XF	Unc
74 (113)	10 Francs (Cu-Ni) 1982. Léon Gambetta (1838–1882), statesman		1.50	2.50

75 (114)	100 Francs (Ag) 1982–. Pantheon			22.00

200th ANNIVERSARY OF MONTGOLFIER BALLOON

76 (115)	10 Francs (Cu-Ni) 1983. Montgolfier Balloon		1.50	2.50

200th ANNIVERSARY OF BIRTH OF STENDHAL

77 (116)	10 Francs (Cu-Ni) 1983. Stendhal (1783–1842), writer		1.50	2.50

50th ANNIVERSARY OF DEATH OF MARIE CURIE (2)

		Unc	Proof
78 (117)	100 Francs (Ag) 1984. Marie Curie (1867–1934), 1903 Nobel Prize winner für physics and chemistry 1911; .900 silver, 15 g	20.00	
79	100 Francs (Ag) 1984. Type as No. 78; .999 silver, 15 g (1000 pcs.)		600.00
80	100 Francs (Au) 1984. Type as No. 78; .920 gold, 17 g (5000 pcs.)		700.00

200th ANNIVERSARY OF BIRTH OF F. RUDE

		XF	Unc
81 (118)	10 Francs (Cu–Al–Ni) 1984. François Rude (1784–1855), sculptor	1.50	2.00

100th ANIVERSARY OF DEATH OF V. HUGO (2)

		XF	Unc
82 (119)	10 Francs (Cu–Ni) 1985. Victor Hugo (1802–1885), poet	1.50	2.00

		Unc	Proof
83	10 Francs (Ag) 1985. Type as No. 82;		
	a) .900 silver, 12 g	20.00	
	b) .999 silver, 12 g (8000 pcs.)		50.00

CENTENARY OF »GERMINAL« BY EMILE ZOLA (3)

		Unc	Proof
84 (121)	100 Francs (Ag) 1985. Emile Zola (1840–1902), writer; .900 silver, 15 g	20.00	
85	100 Francs (Ag 1985. Type as No. 84; .999 silver, 15 g (5000 pcs.)		100.00
86	100 Francs (An) 1985. Type as No. 84; .920 gold, 17 g (5000 pcs.)		600.00

		XF	Unc
87 (123)	10 Francs (Ni) 1986. Head of Marianne and map of France. Rev. Gallic cockerel	1.50	2.50

88 (122)	10 Francs (Ni) 1986. Robert Schumann (1886–1963), politician	1.50	2.50
		XF	**Unc**
89	10 Francs (Ag) 1986. Type as No. 88:		
	a) .900 silver, 7 g	20.00	
	b) .905 silver, 7 g (6000 pcs.)		50.00
90	10 Francs (An) 1986. Type as No. 88; .920 gold, 7 g (5000 pcs)		250.00

STATUE OF LIBERTY (3)

		Unc	**Proof**
91 (120)	100 Francs (Ag) 1986. Statue of Liberty „Liberty Lighting The World". Rev. Motto „Liberté Egalité Fraternité":		
	a) .900 silver, 15 g	30.00	
	b) Piéfort, .900 silver, 30 g (Struck for the American market)	50.00	
92	100 Francs (Ag) 1986. Type as No. 91; .999 silver, 15 g		50.00
93	100 Francs (An) 1986. Type as No. 91; .920 gold, 17 g		900.00

MILLENNIUM OF THE CORONATION OF HUGO CAPET AS KING OF FRANCE (4)

94	10 Francs (Cu–Al–Ni) 1987. Hugo Capet (939/941–996)	3.00	
95	10 Francs (Ag) 1987. Type as No. 94	–.–	–.–
96	10 Francs (An) 1987. Type as No. 94		–.–
97	10 Francs (Pt) 1987. Type as No. 94		–.–

		Unc	Proof
98	100 Francs (Ag) 1987:		
	a) .900 Silver, 15 g	30.00	
	b) Piéfort, .900 Silver, 30 g (struck for the American market)	50.00	
99	100 Francs (Ag) 1987; .999 fine, 15 g		–.–
100	100 Francs (An) 1987; .920 fine, 17 g	–.–	–.–
101	100 Francs (Pt) 1987; .999 fine, 20 g		–.–
102	100 Francs (Pd) 1987; .900 fine, 17 g		–.–

French Equatorial Africa

Französisch-Äquatorial-Afrika · Afrique Equatoriale Française

On 15th January 1910 the French colonies of Gaboon, Central Congo and Ubangi-Chari-Chad were united to form the administration territory of French Equatorial Africa. Gaboon and Central Congo (renamed Congo Brazzaville) became independent in 1960, so also Chad and the Central African Republic (formerly Ubangi-Chari). The individual states remained as self-governing republics within the Communauté Française.
Capital: Brazzaville.

100 Centimes = 1 Franc

			VF	XF
1 (1)	50 Centimes (Bra) 1942. Gallic cockerel. R. Lorraine cross		2.50	7.00

2 (1a)	50 Centimes (Br) 1943. Type as No. 1	2.50	7.00
3 (2)	1 Franc (Bra) 1942. Type as No. 1	3.00	8.00
4 (2a)	1 Franc (Br) 1943. Type as No. 1	4.00	10.00
5 (3)	1 Franc (Al) 1948. Head of Marianne. R. head of a Loder's gazelle (Gazella leptoceros — Bovidae) and value	0.40	1.00

6 (4)	2 Francs (Al) 1948. Type as No. 5	0.60	1.50

French Indo-China

Area: 272,355 sq. mi. Population: 30,000,000.
The French colonies and protectorates of Annam, Cochinchina, Cambodia and Tonkin were originally joined to form this colonial territory. Laos was added to it in 1893 and Kouang-Tchéou-Wan in 1898.

5 Sapek = 1 Centième, 100 Centièmes = 1 Piastre

			VF	XF
1 (1)	2	Sapek (Br) 1887–1902. Name of country, date. ℞ value (with square hole in centre)	3.00	6.00
2 (2)	1	Centième (Br) 1895–1908. Allegorical figure of the French Republic, value. ℞ value in Chinese. Diameter 27.5 mm (with hole)	2.50	3.50
3 (4)	1	Centième (Br) 1908–1939. Type as No. 2, but diameter now 26 mm (with hole)	0.40	0.60

4 (5)	5	Centièmes. Marianne. ℞ ears of rice and value		
		a) (Cu–Ni) 1923–1938	0.60	0.80
		b) (Ni–Br) 1938–1939	0.60	0.80
5 (14)	10	Centièmes (Ag). Allegorical figure of the French Republic, fasces. ℞ value within wreath		
		a) 1898–1922. Fine silver content 835	3.50	5.50
		b) 1923–1937. Fine silver content 630	2.00	3.50
6 (15)	20	Centièmes (Ag). Type as No. 5		
		a) 1898–1922. Fine silver content 835	4.00	7.50
		b) 1923–1937. Fine silver content 630	2.00	4.00

Coins 5a and 6a dated 1920 also exist without mention of the fine silver content and weight.

7 (8a)	50	Centièmes (Ag) 1896–1936. Type as No. 5	4.00	8.00
8 (9a)	1	Piastre (Ag) 1895–1928. Type as No. 5	16.00	25.00
9 (18)	1	Piastre (Ag) 1931, 1932. Crowned head of the Republic to left. ℞ value within ornamented oval centre	12.50	22.00

			VF	XF
10 (20)	½	Centième. Cap of Liberty, initials RF and oak wreath. ℞ value and ears of rice (with hole)		
		a) (Br) 1936–1939	0.60	0.80
		b) (Zi) 1940	16.00	25.00
11 (21)	10	Centièmes. Laureate bust of Marianne. ℞ rice plants (Oryza sativa — Gramineae) and value (with hole)		
		a) (Ni) 1939	0.40	0.60
		b) (Cu–Ni) 1939–1941	0.40	0.60

No. 11b with date 1941 and mintmark S was struck in San Francisco.

12 (22)	20	Centièmes. Type as No. 11		
		a) (Ni) 1939	11.00	18.00
		b) (Cu-Ni) 1939–1941. Scalloped border	0.40	0.80

ISSUES OF THE VICHY GOVERNMENT

13 (V 30)	1	Centième (Zi) 1940, 1941. Cap of Liberty, laurel, value. ℞ ears of corn, value (with hole):		
		a) 1940; with circles on Phrygian cap	8.00	14.00
		b) 1940, 1941; with rosette on Phrygian cap	1.25	2.50
14 (V 31)	¼	Centième (Zi) 1942. Name of country ÉTAT FRANÇAIS/INDOCHINE. ℞ value (with hole)	9.00	12.50
15 (V 32)	1	Centième (Al) 1943. Name of country ÉTAT FRANÇAIS. ℞ name of country INDOCHINE, value	0.40	1.20
16 (V 33)	5	Centièmes (Al) 1943. Type as No. 15	0.40	0.80

ISSUES OF THE FRENCH REPUBLIC

17 (26)	5	Centièmes (Al) 1945–1946. Type as No. 11	0.35	0.50

18 (27)	10	Centièmes (Al) 1945–1946. Type as No. 17	0.40	0.60
19 (28)	20	Centièmes (Al) 1945–1946. Type as No. 17	0.50	0.80
20 (23)	50	Centièmes (Cu–Ni) 1946–1947. Type as No. 7, but in addition the inscription BRONZE DE NICKEL	3.50	5.50

21 (24) 1 Piastre (Cu-Ni). Type as No. 19, but   **VF**   **XF**
with inscription UNION FRANÇAISE
instead of REPUBLIQUE FRANÇAISE
a) 1946–1947   8.00   12.50
b) 1947. Reeded edge   2.00   4.00

ISSUES FOR THE TERRITORY OF ANNAM (CENTRAL VIETNAM)

5 Sapek = 1 Centièmes, 100 Centièmes = 1 Piastre,
600 Sapek = 1 Quan-qui

1   1 Sapek (Br) 1889–1907 (Emperor
Thanh–Thai). Four hieroglyphs. ℞ no
inscription, but square hole in centre   6.00   11.00
2   10 Sapek 1889–1907. Four hieroglyphs.
℞ two hieroglyphs (square hole)
a) (Cu)   3.50   5.00
b) (Br)   4.00   6.00

3   10 Sapek (Br) 1907–1916 (Emperor Duy-
Tan). Four hieroglyphs. ℞ two hieroglyphs (square hole)   5.00   8.00
4   1 Sapek 1916–1925 (Emperor Khai-
Dinh). Four hieroglyphs. ℞ no inscription (square hole)
a) (Cu)   10.00   12.50
b) (Br)   11.00   15.00
5   1 Sapek (Br) 1926–1945 (Emperor Bao-
Dai). Four hieroglyphs. ℞ no inscription (square hole); diameter 23 mm   2.50   4.00
6   1 Sapek (Br) 1926–1945. Type as No. 5,
but diameter 17.5 mm   5.00   8.00
7   10 Sapek (Br) 1926–1945. Four hieroglyphs. ℞ two hieroglyphs (square
hole)   6.50   9.00

ISSUES FOR THE TERRITORY OF TONKIN

1 (1)   1 Sapek (Sn–Pb) 1905. Five small hieroglyphs (three above, two below) and
two large hieroglyphs. ℞ inscription
PROTECTORAT DU TONKIN and
date (square hole)   5.00   8.00

Französisch-Ozeanien French Oceania   Océanie

A French colony in the Pacific Ocean comprising the Society, Marquesas, Tuamotu, Tubuai, Gambier, Austral, Leeward, and Rapa islands and Clipperton island. Renamed French Polynesia in 1958. For further issues see under this name.

Capital: Papeete.

100 Centimes = 1 Franc

			VF	XF
1 (1)	50 Centimes (Al) 1949. Allegorical figure of the French Republic. ℞ harbour scenery		1.00	3.00
2 (2)	1 Franc (Al) 1949. Type as No. 1		1.00	3.00

3 (3)	2 Francs (Al) 1949. Type as No. 1		3.00	8.00
4 (4)	5 Francs (Al) 1952. Type as No. 1		3.00	7.00

Values are given for each coin in U.S. Dollars and reference to Yeoman-numbers.

French Polynesia

Französisch-Polynesien   **Polynésie Française**

Area: 1560 sq. mi. Population: 88,000.
A French overseas territory with limited self-government. First known
as French Oceania, but renamed French Polynesia in 1958.
Capital: Papeete.

100 Centimes = 1 Franc

			VF	XF
1 (1)	50	Centimes (Al–Bra) 1965. Allegorical figure of the French Republic. R harbour scenery	0.30	1.00
2 (2)	1	Franc (Al–Bra) 1965. Type as No. 1	0.20	0.50
3 (3)	2	Francs (Al–Bra) 1965. Type as No. 1	0.40	0.70
4 (4)	5	Francs (Al–Bra) 1965. Type as No. 1	0.70	1.50

5 (5)	10	Francs (Ni) 1967. Head of Marianne to left. R upper part of a ceremonial pole	1.00	2.00
6 (6)	20	Francs (Ni) 1967, 1969, 1970. Rev. breadfruit (Artocarpus communis – Moraceae); Frangipani flowers (Plumeria sp. – Apocynaceae); vanilla shoots (Vanilla planifolia – Orchidaceae)	1.50	3.00
7 (7)	50	Francs (Ni) 1967. R view of Mooréa, an island of the Society group near Tahiti; outrigger canoes, huts and coconut palms (Cocos nucifera – Palmae)	2.50	4.00
8 (2a)	1	Franc (Al) 1975, 1977, 1979, 1981–1983. Type as No. 2, but I.E.O.M. added	0.20	0.40
9 (3a)	2	Francs (Al) 1973, 1975, 1977, 1979, 1982, 1983. Type as No. 8	0.20	0.40
10 (4a)	5	Francs (Al) 1975, 1977, 1979, 1982. Type as No. 8	0.60	1.20
11 (5a)	10	Francs (Ni) 1972, 1973, 1975, 1979, 1982, 1983. Type as No. 5, but I.E.O.M. added	0.80	1.10
12 (6a)	20	Francs (Ni) 1972, 1973, 1975, 1977, 1979, 1983. Type as No. 6, but I.E.O.M. added	1.20	1.50
13 (7a)	50	Francs (Ni) 1975, 1979, 1982. Type as No. 7, but I.E.O.M. added	2.00	2.50
14 (8)	100	Francs (Ni) 1976, 1979, 1982. Type as No. 13	3.00	4.00

French Somaliland

Area: 8,900 sq. mi. Population: 81,000 (1977).
A French overseas territory with limited self-government on the Gulf of
Aden in North East Africa. Renamed Afar and Issa Territories on 19th
March 1967.
Capital: Djibouti.

100 Centimes = 1 Franc

			VF	XF
1 (1)	1	Franc (Al) 1948, 1949. Head of Marianne to left. Rev. lyre antelope (Damaliscus – Bovidae):		
		a) 1948	2.50	7.00
		b) 1949	6.00	20.00
2 (2)	2	Francs (Al) 1948, 1949. Type as No. 1:		
		a) 1948	2.50	6.00
		b) 1949	8.00	18.00
3 (3)	5	Francs (Al) 1948. Type as No. 1	3.00	7.00

			VF	XF
4 (4)	20	Francs (Al–Br) 1952. Head fo Marianne to left. Ŗ Arabian dhow and transatlantic liner, value	3.00	7.00
5 (5)	1	Franc (Al) 1959, 1965. Type as No. 1, but inscription reads only RÉPUBLIQUE FRANÇAISE instead of RÉPUBLIQUE FRANÇAISE/UNION FRANÇAISE	0.40	1.00
6 (6)	2	Francs (Al) 1959–1965. Type as No. 5	0.40	1.00
7 (7)	5	Francs (Al) 1959–1965. Type as No. 5	1.00	2.50
8 (8)	10	Francs (Al–Br) 1965. Head of Marianne to left Ŗ Arabian dhow and transatlantic liner, value	2.50	6.50
9 (9)	20	Francs (Al–Br) 1965. Type as No. 8	2.50	6.50

All valuations in the SCHÖN are stated in U.S. Dollars.

French Territory of the Afars and Issas

Afar- und Issagebiet   Territoire Français des Afars et des Issas

Area: 8,462 sq. mi. Population: 125,000 (1977).
On 19th March 1967, on the strength of a referendum, the name of French Somaliland was changed into French Territory of the Afars and Issas. The new name was derived from the locally predominant population of the Afars (Danakil) and the Issas. The former French Territory was renamed Djibouti and became independent on June 27, 1977.
Capital: Djibouti.

100 Centimes = 1 Djibouti Franc

			VF	XF
1 (1)	1	Franc (Al) 1969, 1971, 1975. Marianne, design by L. Bazor. R. lyre antelope (Damaliscus lunatus – Bovidae), denomination	0.50	2.00
2 (2)	2	Francs (Al) 1968, 1975. Type as No. 1	3.00	15.00
3 (3)	5	Francs (Al) 1968, 1975. Type as No. 1	0.50	2.00
4 (4)	10	Francs (Al-Br) 1969, 1970, 1975. R Arab dhow in front of a ocean liner, denomination	0.50	2.00
5 (5)	20	Francs (Al-Br) 1968, 1975. Type as No. 4	1.00	3.50
6 (6)	50	Francs (Cu-Ni) 1970, 1975. Marianne, design by L. Joly. R dromedaries (Camelus dromedarius – Camelidae), denomination	1.00	3.50

7 (7)	100	Francs (Cu-Ni) 1970, 1975. Type as No. 6	2.50	3.50

French West Africa

Area: 1,753,100 sq. mi. Population: 17,375,000 (1960).
French West Africa comprises the territories of Dahomey, the Ivory
Coast, French Guinea, French Sudan, Mauritania, Niger, Upper Volta
and Senegal. French West Africa was reorganized in 1946 as part of the
Union Française, and at the end of 1958 the individual territories, apart
from French Guinea, became autonomous republics within the Communauté Française, and in 1960, fully independent. French Sudan took the
name of Mali. Since 1957 Togoland is also part of the Monetary Territory of French West Africa.
Capital: Dakar.

100 Centimes = 1 Franc

			VF	XF
1 (1)	50	Centimes (Al–Br) 1944. Head of Marianne to left. ℞ value between horns of plenty	6.00	12.00
2 (2)	1	Franc (Al–Br) 1944	6.00	12.00
3 (3)	1	Franc (Al) 1948–1955. Head of Marianne to left. ℞ head of a Loder's gazelle (Gazella leptoceros — Bovidae) and value	0.20	0.40

4 (4)	2	Francs (Al) 1948–1955. Type as No. 3	0.30	1.00
5 (5)	5	Francs (Al–Br) 1956	0.40	1.00
6 (6)	10	Francs (Al–Br) 1956	2.00	4.00
7 (7)	25	Francs (Al–Br) 1956	1.00	2.50

INTEGRATED COINAGE FOR FRENCH WEST AFRICA AND TOGOLAND

8 (8)	10	Francs (Al–Br) 1957. Head of a Loder's gazelle. ℞ Ashanti gold weight, and inscription INSTITUT D'ÉMISSION AFRIQUE OCCIDENTALE FRANÇAISE – TOGO	1.00	2.50
9 (9)	25	Francs (Al–Br) 1957. Type as No. 8	1.00	2.50

Fudschairah   # Fujairah   **Fujeira**

Area: 454 sq. mi. Population: 10,000.
This Sheikdom situated on the Gulf of Oman was one of the seven
Trucial States in the Pacified Oman. Since 2nd December 1971 Fujairah
is a member state of the United Arab Emirates (UAE).
Capital: Fujairah.

100 Dirham = 1 Fujairah Ryal

MOHAMMED BIN HAMAD AL SHARQI since 1952

1	1	Ryal (Ag) 1969–. Desert fort; in exergue, national arms between olive branches. ℞ national arms, date, value and name of country	**Proof** 9.00
2	2	Ryals (Ag) 1969–. Head of Richard M. Nixon (*1913), 37th President of the U.S.A. ℞ as No. 1	20.00

3   4

3	5	Ryals (Ag) 1969–. Distant view of Munich with flaming torch; Olympic rings, within which arms of city and Olympic medal. Inscription: OLYMPIA MÜNCHEN 1972. ℞ as No. 1	60.00
4	10	Ryals (Ag) 1969–. United States moon research programme, third stage "Manned Landing". Apollo programme. Astronauts: M. Collins, N. Armstrong and E. Aldrin in front of lunar globe	45.00
5	10	Ryals (Ag) 1969–. Astronauts Charles Conrad, Richard Gordon, Alan Bean. Apollo XIII. ℞ as No. 1	45.00
6	10	Ryals (Ag) 1969–. Three winged	

		horses ascending before sun with rays. Apollo XIII. ℞ as No. 1	**Proof** 45.00
7	25	Ryals (Au) 1969. Type as No. 2	100.00
8	50	Ryals (Au) 1969–. Type as No. 3	200.00
9	100	Ryals (Au) 1969–. Type as No. 4	350.00
10	100	Ryals (Au) 1969–. Type as No. 5	350.00
11	100	Ryals (Au) 1969–. Type as No. 6	350.00
12	200	Ryals (Au) 1969–. Sheikh Mohammed Bin Hamad Al Sharqi. ℞ as No. 1	700.00

COMMEMORATIVE ISSUES (4) FOR THE VISIT OF POPE PAUL VI TO THE PHILIPPINES AND AUSTRALIA

13	10	Ryals (Ag) 1969. Head of Pope Paul VI wearing pileolus (cap). Above, St. Peter's Cathedral, Rome. Below, Manila Cathedral, dedicated in 1958. ℞ as No. 1	45.00
14	10	Ryals (Ag) 1969. Pope Paul VI wearing pileolus; papal arms and coastal outline of Australia with giant red kangaroo. ℞ as No. 1	45.00
15	100	Ryals (Au) 1969. Type as No. 13	320.00
16	100	Ryals (Au) 1969. Type as No. 14	320.00

COMMEMORATIVE ISSUES (2) FOR THE MOON LANDING OF APOLLO 14 ON 4th FEBRUARY 1971

17	10	Ryals (Ag) 1970–. Representation of the flight of the space-ship "Apollo 14" from the earth to the moon. In field, stars	**Proof** 45.00
18	100	Ryals (Au) 1970–. Type as No. 17	320.00

Gabun   # Gaboon   **Gabon**

Area: 102,290 sq. mi. Population: 1,160,000.
After the French had founded their first settlement in 1839 by the River Gaboon, the whole territory came under French domination and was governed
as a part of French Equatorial Africa. In 1958 the country obtained limited
autonomy, and became independent on 17th august 1960. Gaboon belongs
to the Monetary Territory of Equatorial Africa; for the community coins issues, see under this name. Capital: Libreville.

100 Centimes = 1 CFA Franc

COMMEMORATIVE ISSUES (4) FOR INDEPENDENCE

1	10	Francs (Au) 1960. Head of Léon M'Ba (1902–1967), Head of State 1960–1967. Rev. national arms, value	**Proof** 80.00
2	25	Francs (Au) 1960. Type as No. 1	200.00
3	50	Francs (Au) 1960. Type as No. 1	400.00
4	100	Francs (Au) 1960. Type as No. 1	800.00

COMMEMORATIVE ISSUES (5) FOR THE FIRST MANNED MOON LANDING ON 20th JULY 1969

5	1000	Francs (Au) 1969. Head left of Albert Bernard Bongo, Head of State since 1967. ℞ Gaboon scenery with stump of okume tree, above which national arms; value	150.00
6	3000	Francs (Au) 1969. ℞ national arms and legend: UNION – TRAVAIL – JUSTICE; value	200.00

7   5000 Francs (Au) 1969. ℞ three-headed
          reliquary figure of the Bakota (Kota

tribe of Gaboon). The Kota tribe places this »spirit of the dead«, known as mbulu-ngulu, on the reliquary basket, the family body, which contains the ancestral skulls, as a symbol of vigilance and meditation

500.00

8 10000 Francs (Au) 1969. R American space programme, third stage: »manned landing«. Apollo programme. Lunar module and astronaut in lunar landscape – 20th July 1969

850.00

9 20000 Francs (Au) 1969. Rev. view of Cape Kennedy: departure of "Apollo 11" on 16th July 1969; value, dia. 53 mm

1800.00

VISIT OF PRESIDENT GEORGES POMPIDOU

10 5000 Francs (Au) 1971. Georges Pompidou, head left. Rev. arms, date, value

800.00

		VF	XF
11 (1)	100 Francs (Ni) 1971, 1972. Mendes antelopes. Rev. value, date	6.00	10.00
12 (2)	100 Francs (Ni) 1975, 1977, 1978, 1982–1984. Type similar to No. 11	2.50	6.00
13 (3)	500 Francs (Cu–Ni) 1985	5.00	8.00

The Gambia

Area: 4,003 sq. mi. Population: 720.000.

Since 1843 Gambia was first a British possession, then a Crown Colony, and at one time was part of the British West Africa Currency Board. Since 18th February 1965 it has been an independent republic within the British Commonwealth.

Capital: Banjul (formerly named Bathurst).

12 Pence = 1 Shilling, 20 Shillings = £ 1;
since 1st July 1971: 100 Bututs = 1 Dalasi

			XF	Unc
1 (1)	1	Penny (Br) 1966. Head right of Queen Elizabeth II. ℞ sailing boat	0.15	0.30
2 (2)	3	Pence (Bra) 1966. ℞ double-spurred francolin (Francolinus bicalcaratus — Phasianidae)	0.15	0.30
3 (3)	6	Pence (Cu-Ni) 1966. ℞ ground nuts (Arachis hypogaea — Leguminosae)	0.25	0.50
4 (4)	1	Shilling (Cu-Ni) 1966. ℞ oil palm (Elaeis guineensis — Palmae)	0.40	0.80
5 (5)	2	Shillings (Cu-Ni) 1966. ℞ African domestic ox (Bos primigenius taurus — Bovidae)	0.70	1.50
6 (6)	4	Shillings (Cu-Ni) 1966. ℞ slender-snouted crocodile (Crocodilus cataphractus — Crocodilidae)	2.00	4.00

		Unc	Proof
7 (7)	8 Shillings 1970. ℞ hippopotamus (Hippopotamus amphibius — Hippopotamidae)		
	a) (Ag)		40.00
	b) (Cu-Ni)	8.00	

CURRENCY REFORM: 100 Bututs = 1 Dalasi

		XF	Unc
8 (8)	1 Butut (Br) 1971, 1973–1975	0.10	0.30
9 (9)	5 Bututs (Bra) 1971, 1977	0.10	0.20
10 (10)	10 Bututs (Cu-Ni) 1971, 1977	0.15	0.30

11 (11)	25 Bututs (Cu–Ni) 1971	0.40	0.90

12 (12)	50 Bututs (Cu–Ni) 1971	0.60	1.50
13 (13)	1 Dalasi (Cu–Ni) 1971	1.60	3.00

ISSUE FOR THE FAO COIN PLAN

				XF	Unc
14 (14)	1	Butut (Br) 1974. Type as No. 8, but inscription FOOD FOR MANKIND added		0.10	0.20

10th ANNIVERSARY OF INDEPENDENCE

				Unc	Proof
15 (15)	10	Dalasis (Ag) 1975. Head of Sir Dawda Kairaba Jawara. Rev. coat of arms, commemorative inscription, value:			
		a) .500 silver, 28.28 g		10.00	
		b) .925 silver, 28.28 g			17.50

CONSERVATION COMMEMORATIVE (3)

16 (16)	20	Dalasis (Ag) 1977. Rev. Spur-winged Goose:			
		a) .925 silver, 25.31 g		20.00	
		b) .925 silver, 28.28 g			30.00
17 (17)	40	Dalasis (Ag) 1977. Rev. Aardvark:			
		a) .925 silver, 31.65 g		30.00	
		b) .925 silver, 35.00 g			40.00
18 (18)	500	Dalasis (Au) 1977. Rev. Sitatunga. .900 gold, 33.43 g		500.00	650.00

WORLD FOOD DAY

19 (19)	20	Dalasis (Ag) 1981. Rev. cotton		25.00	30.00

The great variety of German coins which have appeared since the foundation of the Reich on 18th January 1871 is a clear reflection of most recent German history. The issues of provinces and cities are placed before the small denominations of the Empire and arranged in alphabetical order, each with its own numbering. The coins of the German principalities, Duchies, Grand Duchies and Kingdoms, as well as of the Free Cities and Hanseatic States of Bremen, Hamburg and Lübeck are plainly recognizable as coins of the Reich by the representation of the imperial eagle and by the inscription DEUTSCHES REICH. After the small denominations of the Empire follows the listing in chronological order of the issues of the Weimar Republic, those of the Third Reich, those of the Allied Occupation, of the Bank Deutscher Länder and of the German Federal Republic, simply divided under corresponding headings.

The coins of the GDR are catalogued under yet another system of numbering. It is evident that Danzig and the Saar enjoyed temporary autonomy. German New Guinea, German East Africa and Kiaochow remind us of the short-lived German colonial period. The Occupation issues of the First and Second World War form the close of the German section.

100 Pfennig = 1 Mark (Reichsmark, Rentenmark, Deutsche Mark)

Anhalt (Duchy)

FRIEDRICH I 1871–1904

			VF	XF
1 (1)	2 Mark (Ag) 1876. Head right of Friedrich I (1831–1904). R imperial eagle		200.00	600.00

		VF	**XF**
2 (2)	20 Mark (Au) 1875. Type as No. 1	600.00	1200.00

COMMEMORATIVE ISSUES (4) FOR THE 25th YEAR OF REIGN

3 (3)	2 Mark (Ag) 1896. Head right of Friedrich I	180.00	400.00
4 (4)	5 Mark (Ag) 1896. Type as No. 3	500.00	1150.00

5 (5)	10 Mark (Au) 1896. Type as No. 3	550.00	1000.00
6 (6)	20 Mark (Au) 1896. Type as No. 3	600.00	1100.00

COMMEMORATIVE ISSUES (2) FOR THE 70th BIRTHDAY OF THE DUKE on 29th April 1901

7 (5)	10 Mark (Au) 1901. Type as No. 5	550.00	1000.00
8 (6)	20 Mark (Au) 1901. Type as No. 6	600.00	1100.00

FRIEDRICH II 1904–1918

9 (7)	2 Mark (Ag) 1904. Head left of Friedrich II (1856–1918). ℞ imperial eagle	180.00	400.00
10 (8)	3 Mark (Ag) 1909, 1911	40.00	90.00
11 (9)	20 Mark (Au) 1904	500.00	1000.00

COMMEMORATIVE ISSUES (2) FOR THE SILVER WEDDING OF THE DUKE AND THE DUCHESS

12 (10)	3 Mark (Ag) 1914. Conjoined heads of Friedrich II and Marie, Duchess of Anhalt, née Princess of Baden	35.00	70.00
13 (11)	5 Mark (Ag) 1914. Type as No. 12	150.00	250.00

Baden (Grand Duchy)

FRIEDRICH I 1852–1907

			VF	XF
1 (15)	10	Mark (Au) 1872–1873. Head left of Friedrich I (1826–1907). ℞ imperial eagle	150.00	220.00

			VF	XF
2 (16)	20	Mark (Au) 1872–1873	150.00	220.00
3 (12)	2	Mark (Ag) 1876–1888	65.00	600.00
4 (13)	5	Mark (Ag) 1874–1888. Type as No. 3	55.00	600.00
5 (14)	5	Mark (Au) 1877	200.00	350.00
6 (15a)	10	Mark (Au) 1875–1888	120.00	200.00
7 (16a)	20	Mark (Au) 1874	300.00	500.00
8 (12a)	2	Mark (Ag) 1892–1902	45.00	165.00
9 (13)	5	Mark (Ag)		
		a) 1891–1902	45.00	200.00
		b) BADEN (A = without cross-line)	350.00	700.00

			VF	XF
10 (15b)	10	Mark (Au) 1890–1901	130.00	225.00
11 (16b)	20	Mark (Au) 1894–1895	140.00	250.00

COMMEMORATIVE ISSUES (2) FOR THE 50th YEAR OF REIGN

			VF	XF
12 (20)	2	Mark (Ag) 1902. Head right with laurel branch below	18.00	30.00

		VF	**XF**
13 (21)	5 Mark (Ag) 1902. As type No. 12	80.00	150.00

14 (17)	2 Mark (Ag) 1902–1907. Similar to No. 12, but without laurel branch	22.00	65.00
15 (18)	5 Mark (Ag) 1902–1907. Similar to No. 13, but without laurel branch	40.00	130.00

16 (19)	10 Mark (Au) 1902–1907	150.00	220.00

COMMEMORATIVE ISSUES (2) FOR THE GOLDEN WEDDING

17 (22)	2 Mark (Ag) 1906	15.00	30.00
18 (23)	5 Mark (Ag) 1906	80.00	150.00

COMMEMORATIVE ISSUES (2) FOR THE DEATH OF THE GRAND DUKE

19 (24)	2 Mark (Ag) 1907	22.00	45.00
20 (25)	5 Mark (Ag) 1907	100.00	180.00

		VF	XF
21 (26)	2 Mark (Ag) 1911–1913	150.00	300.00
22 (27)	3 Mark (Ag) 1908–1915	15.00	22.00
23 (28)	5 Mark (Ag) 1908–1913	40.00	125.00

| 24 (29) | 10 Mark (Au) 1909–1913 | 400.00 | 650.00 |
| 25 (30) | 20 Mark (Au) 1911–1914 | 130.00 | 200.00 |

Bavaria (Kingdom)

LUDWIG II 1864–1886

1 (34)	10 Mark (Au) 1872–1873. Head right of Ludwig II (1845–1886). R imperial eagle	115.00	185.00
2 (35)	20 Mark (Au) 1872–1873. Type as No. 1	115.00	215.00
3 (31)	2 Mark (Ag) 1876–1883	65.00	250.00
4 (32)	5 Mark (Ag) 1874–1876	50.00	200.00
5 (33)	5 Mark (Au) 1877–1878	200.00	275.00
6 (34a)	10 Mark (Au) 1874–1881	110.00	165.00
7 (35a)	20 Mark (Au) 1874–1878	130.00	210.00

OTTO 1886–1913. Under Regency of Prince Regent Luitpold

| 8 (36) | 2 Mark (Ag) 1888. Head left of Otto (1848–1916). R imperial eagle | 300.00 | 750.00 |

All valuations in the SCHÖN are stated in U.S. Dollars.

			VF	**XF**
9 (38)	5 Mark (Ag) 1888. Type as No. 8	260.00	800.00

		VF	**XF**
10 (39)	10 Mark (Au) 1888. Type as No. 8	160.00	300.00
11 (36a)	2 Mark (Ag) 1891–1913	13.00	30.00
12 (37)	3 Mark (Ag) 1908–1913	10.00	18.00
13 (38a)	5 Mark (Ag) 1891–1913	20.00	50.00
14 (39a)	10 Mark (Au) 1890–1900	100.00	160.00
15 (40)	20 Mark (Au) 1895–1913	105.00	160.00

		VF	**XF**
16 (39b)	10 Mark (Au) 1900–1912	110.00	150.00

COMMEMORATIVE ISSUES (3) FOR THE 90th BIRTHDAY OF PRINCE REGENT LUITPOLD

		VF	**XF**
17 (41)	2 Mark (Ag) 1911. Head right of Prince Regent Luitpold (1821–1912). ℞ imperial eagle	13.00	25.00
18 (42)	3 Mark (Ag) 1911	13.00	25.00
19 (43)	5 Mark (Ag) 1911	60.00	120.00

		VF	XF
20 (44)	2 Mark (Ag) 1914. Head left of Ludwig III (1845–1921). ℞ imperial eagle	45.00	85.00
21 (45)	3 Mark (Ag) 1914	20.00	40.00

22 (46)	5 Mark (Ag) 1914	80.00	185.00

23 (47)	20 Mark (Au) 1914	2400.00	

COMMEMORATIVE ISSUE FOR THE GOLDEN WEDDING

24 (48)	3 Mark (Ag) 1918. Conjoined heads of Ludwig III and Marie Therese of Bavaria	15 000.00	25 000.00

Of No. 24 electrotypes are also on the market.

Bremen (Free Hanseatic City)

			VF	XF
1(49)	2	Mark (Ag) 1904. Arms of the city. R imperial eagle	40.00	80.00
2(50)	5	Mark (Ag) 1906	120.00	225.00

3(51)	10	Mark (Au) 1907	500.00	750.00
4(52)	20	Mark (Au) 1906	600.00	900.00

Brunswick (Duchy)

WILHELM 1831–1884

1(53)	20	Mark (Au) 1875–1876. Head left of Wilhelm (1806–1884). R imperial eagle	600.00	1000.00

ERNST AUGUST 1913–1918

COMMEMORATIVE ISSUES (4) FOR THE ACCESSION AND WEDDING OF THE DUKE

2(54)	3	Mark (Ag) 1915. Conjoined heads to r. of Ernst August and Viktoria Luise	800.00	1200.00
3(55)	5	Mark (Ag) 1915. Type as No. 2	1000.00	1500.00
4(54a)	3	Mark (Ag) 1915. Type as No. 2, but with additional inscription U. LÜNEB	100.00	150.00
5(55a)	5	Mark (Ag) 1915. Type as No. 4	225.00	480.00

		VF	XF
1 (56)	10 Mark (Au) 1873. Arms of the city. R imperial eagle	900.00	1300.00

		VF	XF
2 (56a)	10 Mark (Au) 1874	650.00	1000.00
3 (57)	2 Mark (Ag) 1876–1888	40.00	200.00
4 (59)	5 Mark (Ag) 1875–1888. Type as No. 3	40.00	300.00
5 (60)	5 Mark (Au) 1877	230.00	300.00
00. **6** (61)	10 Mark (Au) 1875–1888	110.00	165.00
00. **7** (62)	20 Mark (Au) 1875–1889	100.00	130.00

		VF	XF
8 (57a)	2 Mark (Ag) 1892–1914. Arms of the city. R imperial eagle	20.00	45.00
9 (58)	3 Mark (Ag) 1908–1914	15.00	22.00
10 (59a)	5 Mark (Ag) 1891–1913	26.00	65.00
11 (61a)	10 Mark (Au) 1890–1913	100.00	130.00
12 (62a)	20 Mark (Au) 1893–1913:		
	a) 1893–1900, 1913	125.00	165.00
	b) 1908 (14 pieces)		30 000.00

All valuations in the SCHÖN are stated in U.S. Dollars.

Hessen (Grand Duchy)

LUDWIG III 1848–1877

			VF	XF
1 (66)	10 Mark (Au) 1872–1873. Head right of Ludwig III (1806–1877). R imperial eagle		260.00	450.00
2 (67)	20 Mark (Au) 1872–1873. Type as No. 1		250.00	500.00
3 (63)	2 Mark (Ag) 1876–1877		260.00	2000.00
4 (64)	5 Mark (Ag) 1875–1876		170.00	1500.00
5 (65)	5 Mark (Au) 1877		450.00	800.00

6 (66a)	10 Mark (Au) 1875–1877		150.00	250.00
7 (67a)	20 Mark (Au) 1874		420.00	700.00

LUDWIG IV 1877–1892

8 (68)	2 Mark (Ag) 1888. Head right of Ludwig IV (1837–1892). R imperial eagle		650.00	1500.00
9 (69)	5 Mark (Ag) 1888		650.00	2000.00
10 (70)	5 Mark (Au) 1877		500.00	750.00
11 (71)	10 Mark (Au) 1878–1888		350.00	650.00
12 (68a)	2 Mark (Ag) 1891		400.00	800.00
13 (69a)	5 Mark (Ag) 1891		450.00	1200.00
14 (71a)	10 Mark (Au) 1890		600.00	850.00
15 (72)	20 Mark (Au) 1892		900.00	1300.00

			VF	**XF**
16 (73)	10	Mark (Au) 1893. Head left of Ernst Ludwig (1866–1937). R imperial eagle	500.00	800.00
17 (74)	20	Mark (Au) 1893. Type as No. 16	600.00	900.00
18 (75)	2	Mark (Ag) 1895–1900. Head of the Grand Duke to left	200.00	500.00
19 (79)	3	Mark (Ag) 1910	45.00	80.00
20 (76)	5	Mark (Ag) 1895–1900	130.00	500.00
21 (77)	10	Mark (Au) 1896–1898	400.00	650.00

22 (78)	20	Mark (Au) 1896–1903	220.00	320.00

23 (78a)	20	Mark (Au) 1905–1911	230.00	320.00

COMMEMORATIVE ISSUES (2) FOR THE 400th ANNIVERSARY OF THE BIRTH OF PHILIP I, THE MAGNANIMOUS (1504–1567)

24 (80)	2	Mark (Ag) 1904. Conjoined heads to l. of Philip, Landgrave of Hessen, and Ernst Ludwig	30.00	60.00
25 (81)	5	Mark (Ag) 1904	85.00	180.00

26 (82)　　3 Mark (Ag) 1917. Head left of the
　　　　　　　Grand Duke; laurel branch below　　Proof　2500.00

Lippe (Principality)

LEOPOLD IV 1905–1918

		VF	XF
1 (83)	2 Mark (Ag) 1906. Head left of the Prince	165.00	260.00
2 (84)	3 Mark (Ag) 1913	180.00	300.00

Lübeck (Free Hanseatic City)

		VF	XF
1 (85)	2 Mark (Ag) 1901. Arms of the city	135.00	225.00
2 (85a)	2 Mark (Ag) 1904–1912	60.00	100.00
3 (86)	3 Mark (Ag) 1908–1914	50.00	90.00
4 (87)	5 Mark (Ag) 1904–1913	180.00	325.00

5 (88)　　10 Mark (Au) 1901–1904　　　　450.00　　650.00

		VF	XF
6 (88a)	10 Mark (Au) 1905–1910	450.00	650.00

Mecklenburg-Schwerin (Grand Duchy)

FRIEDRICH FRANZ II 1842–1883

		VF	XF
1 (90)	10 Mark (Au) 1872. Head right of Friedrich Franz II (1823–1883) ℞ imperial eagle	1000.00	1850.00
2 (91)	20 Mark (Au) 1872. Type as No. 1	700.00	1000.00

3 (89)	2 Mark (Ag) 1876	180.00	800.00
4 (90a)	10 Mark (Au) 1878	500.00	800.00

FRIEDRICH FRANZ III 1883–1897

5 (92)	10 Mark (Au) 1890. Head right of Friedrich Franz III (1851–1897). ℞ imperial eagle	350.00	550.00

FRIEDRICH FRANZ IV 1897–1918

COMMEMORATIVE ISSUES (3) FOR THE COMING OF AGE OF THE GRAND DUKE ON 9th APRIL 1901

6 (93)	2 Mark (Ag) 1901	200.00	350.00
7 (94)	10 Mark (Au) 1901	1000.00	1400.00
8 (95)	20 Mark (Au) 1901	1750.00	2800.00

COMMEMORATIVE ISSUES (2) FOR THE WEDDING OF THE GRAND DUKE, 7th JUNE 1904

			VF	XF
9 (96)	2 Mark (Ag) 1904. Conjoined heads to l. of Friedrich Franz IV (1882–1945) and Alexandra		35.00	60.00
10 (97)	5 Mark (Ag) 1904. Type as No. 9		90.00	170.00

COMMEMORATIVE ISSUES (2) FOR THE CENTENARY OF THE GRAND DUCHY AND THE ACCESSION TO THE TITLE OF GRAND DUKE OF FRIEDRICH FRANZ ON 9th JUNE 1815

11 (98)	3 Mark (Ag) 1915. Conjoined busts left of Friedrich Franz I (1765–1837) and Friedrich Franz IV	115.00	150.00
12 (99)	5 Mark (Ag) 1915. Type as No. 11	250.00	500.00

Mecklenburg-Strelitz (Grand Duchy)

FRIEDRICH WILHELM 1860–1904

1 (101)	10 Mark (Au) 1873. Head left of Friedrich Wilhelm (1819–1904). R imperial eagle	4000.00	5500.00

2 (102)   20 Mark (Au) 1873. Type as No. 1   3000.00   4000.00

3 (100)   2 Mark (Ag) 1877   260.00   1300.00
4 (101a)   10 Mark (Au) 1874, 1880   2600.00   4000.00
5 (102a)   20 Mark (Au) 1874   2200.00   4000.00

ADOLF FRIEDRICH V 1904–1914

6 (103)   2 Mark (Ag) 1905. Head left of the
                   Grand Duke (1848–1914)   230.00   500.00
7 (106)   3 Mark (Ag) 1913   300.00   650.00
8 (104)   10 Mark (Au) 1905   4000.00   5500.00

9 (105)   20 Mark (Au) 1905   4000.00   5500.00

Oldenburg (Grand Duchy)

NICOLAUS FRIEDRICH PETER 1853–1900

1 (107)   10 Mark (Au) 1874. Head left of Nico-
                   laus Friedrich Peter (1827–1900).
                   ℞ imperial eagle   2800.00   3500.00

2 (108)   2 Mark (Ag) 1891. Head right of
                   Nicolaus Friedrich Peter   200.00   400.00

			VF	XF
3 (109)	2	Mark (Ag) 1900–1901. Head of the Grand Duke to left	150.00	400.00
4 (110)	5	Mark (Ag) 1900–1901	300.00	1000.00

Prussia (Kingdom)

WILHELM I 1861–1888

			VF	XF
1 (114)	10	Mark (Au) 1872–1873. Head right of Wilhelm I (1797–1888). R imperial eagle	100.00	140.00
2 (115)	20	Mark (Au) 1871–1873. Type as No. 1	120.00	150.00
3 (111)	2	Mark (Ag) 1876–1884	28.00	150.00
4 (112)	5	Mark (Ag) 1874–1876	30.00	210.00

5 (113)	5	Mark (Au) 1877–1878	175.00	230.00
6 (114a)	10	Mark (Au) 1874–1888	110.00	150.00
7 (115a)	20	Mark (Au) 1874–1888	110.00	140.00

FRIEDRICH 1888

8 (116)	2	Mark (Ag) 1888. Head right of Friedrich (1831–1888). R imperial eagle	25.00	50.00
9 (117)	5	Mark (Ag) 1888	50.00	115.00

				VF	XF
10 (118)	10	Mark (Au) 1888		100.00	130.00
11 (119)	20	Mark (Au) 1888		110.00	130.00

WILHELM II 1888–1918

12 (120)	2	Mark (Ag) 1888. Head right of Wilhelm II (1859–1941). R imperial eagle	250.00	600.00
13 (122)	5	Mark (Ag) 1888	350.00	1000.00
14 (123)	10	Mark (Au) 1889	1650.00	2800.00

15 (124)	20	Mark (Au) 1888, 1889	105.00	130.00
16 (120a)	2	Mark (Ag) 1891–1912	12.50	30.00
17 (121)	3	Mark (Ag) 1908–1912	10.00	20.00
18 (122a)	5	Mark (Ag) 1891–1908	20.00	45.00

19 (123a)	10	Mark (Au) 1890–1912	100.00	130.00
20 (124a)	20	Mark (Au) 1890–1913	110.00	130.00

COMMEMORATIVE ISSUES (2) FOR THE 2nd CENTENARY OF THE PRUSSIAN KINGDOM

		VF	XF
21 (128)	2 Mark (Ag) 1901. Conjoined busts left of Friedrich I and Wilhelm II	10.00	17.50

22 (129)	5 Mark (Ag) 1901. Type as No. 21	45.00	75.00

COMMEMORATIVE ISSUE FOR THE CENTENARY OF BERLIN UNIVERSITY

23 (130)	3 Mark (Ag) 1910. Conjoined heads left of Friedrich Wilhelm III and Wilhelm II	35.00	60.00

COMMEMORATIVE ISSUE FOR THE CENTENARY OF BRESLAU UNIVERSITY

		VF	XF
24 (131)	3 Mark (Ag) 1911. Conjoined heads of Friedrich Wilhelm III and Wilhelm II	45.00	70.00

COMMEMORATIVE ISSUES (2) FOR THE CENTENARY OF THE WAR OF LIBERATION

25 (132)	2 Mark (Ag) 1913. Friedrich Wilhelm III on horseback surrounded by a rejoicing crowd. ℞ eagle holding serpent in its claws	12.50	18.00
26 (133)	3 Mark (Ag) 1913. Type as No. 25	15.00	20.00

COMMEMORATIVE ISSUES (2) FOR THE 25th YEAR OF REIGN

27 (134)	2 Mark (Ag) 1913. Wilhelm II in the uniform of a cuirassier with the

		VF	XF
	chain of the Order of the Black Eagle; laurel branch	12.50	18.00
28 (135)	3 Mark (Ag) 1913. Type as No. 27	15.00	20.00

		VF	XF
29 (125)	3 Mark (Ag) 1914. Type as No. 28, but without laurel branch	12.50	20.00
30 (126)	5 Mark (Ag) 1913, 1914. Type as No. 29	22.50	35.00
31 (127)	20 Mark (Au) 1913-1915. Type as No. 29:		
	a) 1913, 1914	110.00	140.00
	b) 1915	2000.00	3000.00

COMMEMORATIVE ISSUE FOR THE CENTENARY OF THE UNITING OF THE EARLDOM OF MANSFELD TO PRUSSIA

		VF	XF
32 (136)	3 Mark (Ag) 1915. St. George to r. fighting the dragon; on the saddle-cloth of his horse the arms of Mansfeld	250.00	450.00

Reuss, elder branch (Principality)

HEINRICH XXII 1859–1902

		VF	XF
1 (137)	2 Mark (Ag) 1877. Head right of Heinrich XXII (1846–1902). ℞ imperial eagle	300.00	1200.00

			VF	XF
2 (138)	20 Mark (Au) 1875		9000.00	1300.00
3 (137a)	2 Mark (Ag) 1892		230.00	600.00

4 (139)   2 Mark (Ag) 1899, 1901. Head of the Prince to right   150.00   260.00

HEINRICH XXIV 1902–1918

5 (140)   3 Mark (Ag) 1909. Head of the Prince to right   175.00   330.00

Reuss, younger branch (Principality)

HEINRICH XIV 1867–1913

1 (141)   2 Mark (Ag) 1884. Head left of Heinrich XIV (1832–1913). ℞ imperial eagle   200.00   650.00

2 (142)   10 Mark (Au) 1882   3000.00   5000.00

		VF	XF
3 (143)	20 Mark (Au) 1881	1500.00	2200.00

Saxony (Kingdom)

JOHANN 1854–1873

1 (178)	10 Mark (Au) 1872, 1873. Head left of Johann (1801–1873). R imperial eagle	110.00	180.00
2 (179)	20 Mark (Au) 1872, 1873. Type as No. 1	130.00	200.00

3 (180)	2 Mark (Ag) 1876–1888. Head right of Albert (1828–1902). R imperial eagle	80.00	330.00
4 (181)	5 Mark (Ag) 1875–1889	40.00	400.00

5 (182)	5 Mark (Au) 1877	200.00	265.00
6 (183)	10 Mark (Au) 1874–1888	110.00	150.00
7 (184)	20 Mark (Au) 1874–1878	160.00	250.00

COMMEMORATIVE MEDAL FOR THE 8th CENTENARY OF THE HOUSE OF WETTIN IN 1889

		VF	XF
8	(–) 1889. Head to right of Albert. ℞ Saxonia seated on throne surrounded by a crowd		
	a) (Ag)	1100.00	1600.00
	b) (Cu)	250.00	300.00
9 (180a)	2 Mark (Ag) 1891–1902	28.00	80.00
10 (181a)	5 Mark (Ag) 1891–1902	35.00	125.00
11 (183a)	10 Mark (Au) 1891–1902	110.00	160.00
12 (184a)	20 Mark (Au) 1894, 1895	160.00	200.00

COMMEMORATIVE MEDAL FOR THE VISIT OF THE KING TO THE MINT AT MULDNER HÜTTE ON 16th JULY 1892

13	(–) (Ag) 1892. Head of the King to right. ℞ commemorative inscription	650.00

GEORG 1902–1904

COMMEMORATIVE ISSUES (2) FOR THE DEATH OF KING ALBERT ON 19th JUNE 1902

14 (185)	2 Mark (Ag) 1902	25.00	55.00
15 (186)	5 Mark (Ag) 1902	55.00	130.00
16 (187)	2 Mark (Ag) 1903, 1904	30.00	125.00
17 (188)	5 Mark (Ag) 1903, 1904	40.00·	175.00

18 (189)	10 Mark (Au) 1903–1904	125.00	180.00
19 (190)	20 Mark (Au) 1903	170.00	250.00

COMMEMORATIVE MEDAL FOR THE VISIT OF THE KING TO THE MINT AT MULDNER HÜTTE ON 7th MAY 1903

			VF	XF
20		(–) (Ag) 1903. Head of the King to right. ℞ commemorative inscription		650.00

FRIEDRICH AUGUST III 1904–1918
FOR THE DEATH OF KING GEORG ON 15th OCTOBER 1904 (2)

21	(191)	2 Mark (Ag) 1904	26.00	50.00
22	(192)	5 Mark (Ag) 1904	85.00	170.00
23	(193)	2 Mark (Ag) 1905–1914	25.00	55.00
24	(194)	3 Mark (Ag) 1908–1913	9.00	18.00
25	(195)	5 Mark (Ag) 1907–1914	20.00	55.00
26	(196)	10 Mark (Au) 1905–1912	130.00	200.00

| 27 | (197) | 20 Mark (Au) 1905–1914 | 135.00 | 200.00 |

MEDAL FOR THE VISIT OF THE KING TO THE MINT AT MULDNER HÜTTE ON 6th ARPIL 1905

| 28 | | (–) (Ag) 1905. Head of the King to right. ℞ commemorative inscription | | 650.00 |

5th CENTENARY OF LEIPZIG UNIVERSITY (2)

| 29 | (198) | 2 Mark (Ag) 1909. Conjoined heads left of Crown Prince Friedrich the Pugnacious (1370–1428) and Friedrich August III | 30.00 | 85.00 |
| 30 | (199) | 5 Mark (Ag) 1909 | 85.00 | 200.00 |

COMMEMORATIVE ISSUE FOR THE CENTENARY OF THE BATTLE OF LEIPZIG

		VF	XF
31 (200)	3 Mark (Ag) 1913. National battle monument at Leipzig	18.00	30.00

COMMEMORATIVE ISSUE FOR THE 4th CENTENARY OF THE REFORMATION

32 (201) 3 Mark (Ag) 1917. Bust right of Friedrich the Wise (1463–1525) with close-fitting cap and mantle; advocator of the imperial reform, protected Luther who taught at the University of Wittenberg which had been founded by the former in 1502, and granted him asylum at the Wartburg after the Reichstag at Worms 50 000.00

Modern copies of No. 32 in the shape of Klippen are known to exist, as well as electrotypes.

Values are given for each coin in U.S. Dollars and reference to Yeoman-numbers.

Saxe-Altenburg (Duchy)

ERNST 1853–1908

			VF	XF
1 (146)	20 Mark (Au) 1887. Head right of Ernst (1826–1908). ℞ imperial eagle		1000.00	1500.00

FOR THE 75th BIRTHDAY OF THE DUKE ON 16th SEPTEMBER 1901 (2)

2 (144)	2 Mark (Ag) 1901	200.00	300.00
3 (145)	5 Mark (Ag) 1901	350.00	650.00

FOR THE 50th YEAR OF REIGN ON 3rd AUGUST 1903

4 (147)	5 Mark 1903	150.00	265.00

Saxe-Coburg and Gotha (Duchy)
ERNST II 1844–1893

1 (148)	20 Mark (Au) 1872. Head left of Ernst II (1818–1893). ℞ imperial eagle	11 000.00	16 000.00
2 (148a)	20 Mark (Au) 1886	850.00	1400.00

ALFRED 1893–1900

3 (149)	2 Mark (Ag) 1895. Head right of Alfred (1844–1900). ℞ imperial eagle	260.00	750.00
4 (150)	5 Mark (Ag) 1895	1000.00	1600.00
5 (151)	20 Mark (Au) 1895	1000.00	1600.00

CARL EDUARD 1900–1918

6 (152)	2 Mark (Ag)		
	a) 1905	225.00	400.00
	b) 1911	3500.00	6000.00

			VF	XF
7 (153)	5 Mark (Ag) 1907		500.00	800.00
8 (154)	10 Mark (Au) 1905		700.00	1000.00

			VF	XF
9 (155)	20 Mark (Au) 1905		800.00	1100.00

Saxe-Meiningen (Duchy)

GEORG II 1866–1914

			VF	XF
1 (156)	20 Mark (Au) 1872. Head right of Georg II (1826–1914). ℞ imperial eagle		6000.00	8000.00
2 (156a)	20 Mark (Au) 1882		3500.00	5000.00
3 (158)	20 Mark (Au) 1889		3000.00	4600.00

COMMEMORATIVE ISSUES (2) FOR THE 75th BIRTHDAY OF THE DUKE

			VF	XF
4 (159)	2 Mark (Ag) 1901		250.00	400.00
5 (160)	5 Mark (Ag) 1901		225.00	425.00
6 (157)	10 Mark (Au) 1890–1898		1800.00	2800.00
7 (158a)	20 Mark (Au) 1900–1905		3000.00	5000.00
8 (161)	2 Mark (Ag) 1902–1913		130.00	225.00
9 (162)	3 Mark (Ag) 1908–1913		55.00	100.00
10 (163)	5 Mark (Ag) 1902–1908		100.00	180.00

			VF	XF
11 (164)	10 Mark (Au) 1902–1914		1600.00	2500.00
12 (165)	20 Mark (Au) 1910–1914		3000.00	5000.00

BERNHARD III 1914–1918
COMMEMORATIVE ISSUES (2) FOR THE FIRST ANNIVERSARY OF THE DEATH OF DUKE GEORG II ON 25th JUNE 1915

		VF	XF
13 (166)	2 Mark (Ag) 1915	70.00	140.00
14 (167)	3 Mark (Ag) 1915	80.00	150.00

Saxe-Weimar (Grand Duchy)

CARL ALEXANDER 1853–1901
COMMEMORATIVE ISSUES (2) FOR THE GOLDEN WEDDING

1 (168)	2 Mark (Ag) 1892. Head left of Carl Alexander (1818–1901). ℞ imperial eagle	120.00	220.00
2 (169)	20 Mark (Au) 1892. Type as No. 1	1000.00	1500.00
3 (169)	20 Mark (Au) 1896. Type as No. 2	800.00	1200.00

COMMEMORATIVE ISSUE FOR THE 80th BIRTHDAY OF THE GRAND DUKE ON 24th JUNE 1898

4 (168)	2 Mark (Ag) 1898	125.00	300.00

WILHELM ERNST 1901–1918

5 (170)	2 Mark (Ag) 1901	180.00	350.00

6 (171)	20 Mark (Au) 1901	1300.00	2000.00

COMMEMORATIVE ISSUES (2) FOR THE FIRST MARRIAGE ON 30th APRIL 1903

			VF	**XF**
7 (172)	2 Mark (Ag) 1903. Conjoined heads left of Wilhelm Ernst and the Grand Duchess Caroline		60.00	100.00
8 (173)	5 Mark (Ag) 1903		100.00	225.00

COMMEMORATIVE ISSUES (2) FOR 350 YEARS OF THE UNIVERSITY OF JENA

9 (174)	2 Mark (Ag) 1908. Bust facing of Johann Friedrich I the Magnanimous (1503–1554), founder of the University of Jena in 1547 which was ratified by Emperor Ferdinand I in 1558		50.00	100.00
10 (175)	5 Mark (Ag) 1908		125.00	200.00

COMMEMORATIVE ISSUE FOR THE SECOND MARRIAGE OF WILHELM ERNST ON 4th JANUARY 1910

11 (176)	3 Mark (Ag) 1910. Conjoined heads left of Wilhelm Ernst and the Grand Duchess Feodora		35.00	75.00

COMMEMORATIVE ISSUE FOR THE CENTENARY OF THE GRAND DUCHY

12 (177)	3 Mark (Ag) 1915. Conjoined busts right of Wilhelm Ernst and Carl August (1757–1828), Duke until his coming of age in 1758 under his mother, Duchess Anna Amalia, also his guardian; he called Goethe and Herder to Weimar, and also Schiller to Jena		75.00	150.00

Schaumburg-Lippe (Principality)

ADOLF GEORG 1860–1893

		VF	XF
1 (202)	20 Mark (Au) 1874. Head left of Adolf Georg (1817–1893). ℞ imperial eagle	5000.00	6500.00

GEORG 1893–1911

2 (203)	2 Mark (Ag) 1898–1904	270.00	500.00
3 (204)	5 Mark (Ag) 1898–1904	650.00	1000.00
4 (205)	20 Mark (Au) 1898–1904	900.00	1400.00

COMMEMORATIVE ISSUE FOR THE DEATH OF THE PRINCE

5 (206)	3 Mark (Ag) 1911	70.00	110.00

Schwarzburg-Rudolstadt (Principality)

GÜNTHER VIKTOR 1890–1918

1 (207)	2 Mark (Ag) 1898. Head left of Günther Viktor. ℞ imperial eagle	250.00	500.00

2 (208)	10 Mark (Au) 1898	950.00	1500.00

Schwarzburg-Sondershausen (Principality)

KARL GÜNTHER 1880–1909

1 (209)	2 Mark (Ag) 1896. Head right of Karl Günther (1830–1909). ℞ imperial eagle	250.00	450.00
2 (210)	20 Mark (Au) 1896	1350.00	2200.00

COMMEMORATIVE ISSUE FOR THE 25th YEAR OF REIGN ON 17th JULY 1905

3 (211)	2 Mark (Ag) 1905. Head of the Prince to right; laurel branch.		
	a) thin rim	35.00	90.00
	b) thick rim	90.00	200.00

COMMEMORATIVE ISSUE FOR THE DEATH OF THE PRINCE ON 28th MARCH 1909

4 (212)	3 Mark (Ag) 1909	50.00	90.00

Waldeck and Pyrmont (Principality)

FRIEDRICH ADOLPH 1893–1918

			VF	XF
1 (213)	5 Mark (Ag) 1903		1300.00	2500.00

2 (214)	20 Mark (Au) 1903	1750.00	2500.00

Württemberg (Kingdom)

KARL 1864–1891

1 (218)	10 Mark (Au) 1872–1873. Head right of Karl (1823–1891). R imperial eagle	90.00	200.00
2 (219)	20 Mark (Au) 1872–1873	100.00	250.00
3 (215)	2 Mark (Ag) 1876–1888	70.00	400.00
4 (216)	5 Mark (Ag) 1874–1888	50.00	420.00
5 (217)	5 Mark (Ag) 1877–1878	200.00	260.00
6 (218a)	10 Mark (Au) 1874–1888	110.00	170.00
7 (219a)	20 Mark (Au) 1874–1876	140.00	250.00
8 (218b)	10 Mark (Au) 1890–1891	125.00	220.00

WILHELM II 1891–1918

9 (220)	2 Mark (Ag) 1892–1914	15.00	32.00
10 (221)	3 Mark (Ag) 1908–1914	9.00	16.00
11 (222)	5 Mark (Ag) 1892–1913	20.00	30.00

12 (223)	10 Mark (Au) 1893–1913	100.00	165.00
13 (224)	20 Mark (Au) 1894–1914	110.00	175.00

		VF	XF
14 (225)	3 Mark (Ag) 1911		
	a) normal H in Charlotte	20.00	50.00
	b) the bar of the H is placed higher than normal	250.00	450.00

COMMEMORATIVE ISSUE FOR THE 25th YEAR OF REIGN

15 (226)	3 Mark (Ag) 1916		
Of No. 15 electrotypes are also on the market.		Proof	4000.00

German Empire

Small-denomination coins were also in general circulation throughout the Empire.

1 (1)	1 Pfennig (Cu) 1873–1889. Imperial eagle. ℞ value	2.50	10.00
2 (2)	2 Pfennig (Cu) 1873–1877. Type as No. 1	2.50	15.00
3 (5)	5 Pfennig (Cu-Ni) 1874–1889. Type as No. 1	1.25	6.50
4 (6)	10 Pfennig (Cu-Ni) 1873–1889. Type as No. 1	1.50	7.00
5 (12)	20 Pfennig (Ag) 1873–1877. Type as No. 1	5.00	10.00
6 (13)	50 Pfennig (Ag) 1875–1877. Type as No. 1	15.00	30.00
7 (17)	1 Mark (Ag) 1873–1887	5.00	22.50
8 (7)	20 Pfennig (Cu-Ni) 1887–1888	20.00	45.00
9 (14)	50 Pfennig (Ag) 1877–1878	40.00	95.00

10 (3)	1 Pfennig (Cu) 1890–1916. Large

			VF	XF
		imperial eagle with small breast-shield	0.30	1.00
11 (4)	2	Pfennig (Cu) 1904–1908, 1910–1916. Large imperial eagle with small breast-shield	0.30	1.00
12 (8)	5	Pfennig (Cu-Ni) 1890–1915. Large imperial eagle with small breast-shield	0.30	0.60
13 (9)	10	Pfennig (Cu-Ni) 1890–1894, 1896–1916. Large imperial eagle with small breast-shield	0.25	0.60
14 (10)	20	Pfennig (Cu-Ni) 1890, 1892. Large imperial eagle with small breast-shield within oak wreath. ℞ value in large figures	30.00	60.00

			VF	XF
15 (11)	25	Pfennig (Ni) 1909–1912	6.00	12.00

			VF	XF
16 (15)	50	Pfennig (Ag) 1896, 1898, 1900–1903. Large imperial eagle with small breast-shield within oak wreath	180.00	300.00
17 (16)	½	Mark (Ag) 1905–1909, 1911–1919.	2.00	4.00

			VF	XF
18 (18)	1	Mark (Ag) 1891–1894, 1896, 1898–1916. Large imperial eagle with small breast-shield. ℞ value within oak wreath	3.00	5.00

In the years 1916–1924 various states, municipalities and provinces issued numerous emergency coins (Notgeld) of very pleasing and widely varied design and finish. An exhaustive study of this very popular sideline of numismatics must, however, remain outside the scope of this catalogue. There is a special catalogue by Funck entitled »Die Notmünzen der deutschen Städte, Gemeinden, Kreise, Länder etc.« (The Emergency Issues of the German States, Minicipalities, Districts and Provinces etc.)

			VF	XF
19 (19)	1	Pfennig (Al) 1916–1918. Small imperial eagle with large breast-shield	0.40	0.60
20 (21)	5	Pfennig (Fe) 1915–1922. Large imperial eagle with small breast-shield. ℞ date below denomination	0.30	0.60
21 (22)	10	Pfennig (Fe) 1915–1918, 1921–1922. Large imperial eagle with small breast-shield within dotted circle. ℞ date below denomination. The 1915 issue is a pattern	0.30	0.80
22 (22a)	10	Pfennig (Zi) 1917. Imperial eagle within dotted circle. ℞ date below denomination	100.00	225.00
23 (22.1)	10	Pfennig (Zi) 1917–1922. Imperial eagle similar to No. 13, but without mark of value. ℞ date below denomination	0.30	0.60

WEIMAR REPUBLIC 1919–1933

24 (26)	50	Pfennig (Al) 1919–1922. Wheat sheaf with legend in 2 lines. ℞ value	0.30	0.60

25 (28)	3	Mark (Al) 1922–1923. Imperial eagle with legend VERFAS-SUNGSTAG 11. AUGUST 1922 (date of promulgation of the Weimar Constitution). R value	1.00	2.50
26 (29)	3	Mark (Al) 1922. Type as No. 25, but without obverse inscription	4.00	10.00
27 (30)	200	Mark (Al) 1923	0.50	1.00
28 (31)	500	Mark (Al) 1923	0.60	1.20
29 (32)	1	Rentenpfennig (Br) 1923–1925, 1929. Sheaf between date. R value in large figures within circle		

		VF	XF
	a) 1923, 1924	0.80	4.00
	b) 1925, 1929	300.00	450.00

In the case of No. 29 b, these are errors in striking.

			VF	XF
30 (33)	2 Rentenpfennig (Br) 1923–1924. Type as No. 29		1.00	3.00
31 (34)	5 Rentenpfennig (Al-Br) 1923–1924. Crossed ears of corn. ℞ value within square surrounded by oak leaves		1.50	2.00
32 (35)	10 Rentenpfennig (Al-Br) 1923–1925. Type as No. 31:			
	a) 1923–1924		0.80	3.00
	b) 1925, mis-strike		500.00	850.00
33 (36)	50 Rentenpfennig (Al-Br) 1923–1924. Type as No. 31		10.00	25.00

100 Reichspfennig = 1 Reichsmark

			VF	XF
34 (37)	1 Reichspfennig (Br) 1924–1925, 1927–1936. Sheaf between date. ℞ value in large figures within circle		0.30	1.00
35 (38)	2 Reichspfennig (Br) 1923–1925, 1936. Type as No. 34			
	a) 1923		700.00	1500.00
	b) 1924, 1925, 1936		0.60	2.50

			VF	XF
36 (39)	4 Reichspfennig (Cu) 1932. Imperial eagle. ℞ value in large figures within circle		6.00	12.50
37 (40)	5 Reichspfennig (Al-Br) 1924–1926, 1930, 1935, 1936. Crossed ears of corn. ℞ value within square surrounded by oak leaves		0.50	1.60
38 (41)	10 Reichspfennig (Al-Br) 1924–1926, 1928–1936. Type as No. 37		0.80	3.00
39 (42)	50 Reichspfennig (Al-Br) 1924–1925. Type as No. 37		850.00	1500.00
40 (43)	50 Reichspfennig (Ni) 1927–1933, 1935–1938. Imperial eagle within circle. ℞ value in large figures		1.60	3.00
41 (44)	1 Mark (Ag) 1924–1925. Imperial eagle. ℞ value		8.00	20.00
42 (47)	3 Mark (Ag) 1924–1925. Imperial eagle. ℞ value		35.00	85.00

			VF	**XF**
43 (45)	1	R-Mark (Ag) 1925–1927. Imperial eagle, legend DEUTSCHES REICH and date. ℞ value within oak wreath	10.00	25.00
44 (46)	2	R-Mark (Ag) 1925–1927, 1931. Imperial eagle. ℞ value within oak wreath	15.00	38.00
45 (49)	5	R-Mark (Ag) 1927–1933. Oak tree. ℞ imperial eagle and value	70.00	140.00

COMMEMORATIVE ISSUES (2) FOR THE THOUSANDTH YEAR OF THE RHINELAND

46 (50)	3	R-Mark (Ag) 1925. Knight with right arm raised in oath, holding shield on which imperial eagle. ℞ value within oak wreath	35.00	55.00
47 (51)	5	R-Mark (Ag) 1925	80.00	140.00

COMMEMORATIVE ISSUE FOR THE 700th YEAR OF THE GRANTING OF IMPERIAL FREEDOM TO LÜBECK

48 (52)	3	R-Mark (Ag) 1926. On a Gothic shield, the double eagle of Lübeck with divided breast-shield. Commemorative legend. ℞ value	110.00	200.00

COMMEMORATIVE ISSUES (2) FOR THE HUNDREDTH ANNIVERSARY OF BREMERHAVEN

			VF	XF
49 (53)	3 R-Mark (Ag) 1927. Three-master and arms of Bremen. ℞ eagle on shield, eight-sided scrollwork in background		125.00	200.00
50 (54)	5 R-Mark (Ag) 1927		400.00	650.00

COMMEMORATIVE ISSUE FOR THE THOUSANDTH ANNIVERSARY OF THE FOUNDING OF NORDHAUSEN

51 (55)	3 R-Mark (Ag) 1927. The Emperor Heinrich I (876–936), reigned 919–936, and his wife Mathilde, great granddaughter of Widukind		110.00	200.00

COMMEMORATIVE ISSUES (2) FOR THE 450th ANNIVERSARY OF THE UNIVERSITY OF TÜBINGEN

52 (57)	3 R-Mark (Ag) 1927. Count Eberhard The Bearded (1445–1496); he founded the University of Tübingen in 1477 and endowed it with a library. ℞ imperial eagle	**VF**	**XF**
		300.00	500.00
53 (58)	5 R-Mark (Ag) 1927	400.00	600.00

COMMEMORATIVE ISSUE FOR THE 400th ANNIVERSARY OF THE PHILIP UNIVERSITY IN MARBURG

54 (56)	3 R-Mark (Ag) 1927. Arms of Philip I the Magnanimous (1504–1567), Landgrave of Hessen; in 1527 he founded the university in his home town. On the centre shield, the Hessian lion. ℞ imperial eagle	100.00	180.00

COMMEMORATIVE ISSUE FOR THE 400th ANNIVERSARY OF THE DEATH OF ALBRECHT DÜRER

* 55 (59)	3 R-Mark (Ag) 1928. Bust left of Albrecht Dürer (1471–1528), painter, engraver and writer on art subjects. ℞ imperial eagle	300.00	500.00

All valuations in the SCHÖN are stated in U.S. Dollars

COMMEMORATIVE ISSUE FOR THE 900th ANNIVERSARY OF THE FOUNDING OF NAUMBURG/SAALE

		VF	XF
56 (60)	3 R-Mark (Ag) 1928. Margrave Hermann, founder of the city, holding shield with the arms of Naumburg. ℞ imperial eagle	125.00	200.00

COMMEMORATIVE ISSUE FOR THE THOUSANDTH ANNIVERSARY OF THE FOUNDING OF DINKELSBÜHL

57 (61)	3 R-Mark (Ag) 1928. Half figure holding sickle and sheaf of wheat between two towers; below, arms of Dinkelsbühl. ℞ imperial eagle	400.00	650.00

COMMEMORATIVE ISSUES (2) FOR THE 200th ANNIVERSARY OF THE BIRTH OF LESSING

58 (62)	3 R-Mark (Ag) 1929. Gotthold Ephraim Lessing (1729–1781), poet. ℞ imperial eagle	40.00	65.00
59 (63)	5 R-Mark (Ag) 1929	90.00	175.00

COMMEMORATIVE ISSUE FOR THE UNION OF WALDECK WITH PRUSSIA

			VF	XF
60 (64)	3 R-Mark (Ag) 1929. Prussian eagle with arms of Waldeck. ℞ imperial eagle		100.00	185.00

COMMEMORATIVE ISSUES (2) FOR THE THOUSANDTH ANNIVERSARY OF THE CASTLE AND CITY OF MEISSEN

		VF	XF
61 (67)	3 R-Mark (Ag) 1929. Armed figure holding the triangular shields of the Margrave and of the Burgrave of Meissen. ℞ imperial eagle	40.00	75.00
62 (68)	5 R-Mark (Ag) 1929	300.00	550.00

COMMEMORATIVE ISSUES (2) FOR THE 10th ANNIVERSARY OF THE WEIMAR CONSTITUTION

63 (65)   3 R-Mark (Ag) 1929. Hand raised in

		VF	XF

oath. ℞ Paul von Beneckendorff und von Hindenburg (1847–1934), President of the German Reich from 1925–1934   30.00   50.00

64 (66)   5 R-Mark (Ag) 1929   90.00   150.00

COMMEMORATIVE ISSUES (2) FOR THE ROUND-THE-WORLD FLIGHT OF THE AIRSHIP "GRAF ZEPPELIN" IN 1929

65 (69)   3 R-Mark (Ag) 1930. The airship in front of globe. ℞ imperial eagle   60.00   120.00

66 (70)   5 R-Mark (Ag) 1930   125.00   225.00

COMMEMORATIVE ISSUE FOR THE 700th ANNIVERSARY OF THE DEATH OF VON DER VOGELWEIDE

67 (71)   3 R-Mark (Ag) 1930. Walther von der Vogelweide (c. 1170–1230), minnesinger. ℞ eagle on shield on three-sided scrolled background   70.00   125.00

Yeoman Numbers

In order to help collectors and dealers, we have added after most SCHÖN-numbers the corresponding number assigned by R.S. Yeoman in his wellknown works entitled »A Catalog of Modern World Coins«– and »Current Coins of the World«.

COMMEMORATIVE ISSUES (2) FOR THE EVACUATION OF THE RHINELAND BY THE ALLIES IN 1930

			VF	**XF**
68 (72)	3 R-Mark (Ag) 1930. Eagle standing on bridge. ℞ eagle on shield on three-sided scrolled background		35.00	65.00
69 (73)	5 R-Mark (Ag) 1930		125.00	225.00

COMMEMORATIVE ISSUE FOR THE 300th ANNIVERSARY OF THE BURNING OF MAGDEBURG

70 (74)	3 R-Mark (Ag) 1931. Arms of the city over view of the old city. ℞ eagle on shield on eight-sided scrolled background	165.00	300.00

COMMEMORATIVE ISSUE FOR THE CENTENARY OF THE DEATH OF VON STEIN

71 (75)	3 R-Mark (Ag) 1931. Karl Reichs-freiherr vom und zum Stein (1757–1831), statesman. ℞ imperial eagle	120.00	200.00

		VF	**XF**
72 (48)	3 R-Mark 1931–1933. Imperial eagle, legend DEUTSCHES REICH and date. ℞ value within oak wreath:		
	a) 1931–1932	200.00	350.00
	b) 1933	1200.00	2200.00

COMMEMORATIVE ISSUES (2) FOR THE CENTENARY OF THE DEATH OF GOETHE

73 (76)	3 R-Mark (Ag) 1932. Johann Wolfgang von Goethe (1749–1832), poet and writer.	60.00	125.00
74 (77)	5 R-Mark (Ag) 1932	1750.00	2800.00

THIRD REICH 1933–1945
COMMEMORATIVE ISSUES (2) FOR THE 450th ANNIVERSARY OF THE BIRTH OF MARTIN LUTHER

75 (78)	2 R-Mark (Ag) 1933. Head left of Dr. Martin Luther (1483–1546), reformer. ℞ imperial eagle. Edge inscription: EIN FESTE BURG IST UNSER GOTT (a mighty fortress is our God) and date.	15.00	30.00

76 (79)   5 R-Mark (Ag) 1933. Type as No. 75   85.00   140.00

77 (81)   1 R-Mark (Ni) 1933–1939. Imperial eagle. ℞ value within oak wreath   1.60   3.00

COMMEMORATIVE ISSUES (2) FOR THE FIRST ANNIVERSARY OF THE OPENING OF THE REICHSTAG

78 (83)   2 R-Mark (Ag) 1934. Potsdam Military Church and date 21 March 1933. ℞ imperial eagle, edge inscription: GEMEINNUTZ GEHT VOR EIGENNUTZ (the common good comes before personal interest)   7.00   20.00

79 (84)   5 R-Mark (Ag) 1934. Type as No. 78   10.00   35.00
80 (85)   5 R-Mark (Ag) 1934–1935. Type as No. 79, but no date   6.00   12.50

COMMEMORATIVE ISSUES (2) FOR THE 175th ANNIVERSARY OF THE BIRTH OF FRIEDRICH VON SCHILLER

81 (86)   2 R-Mark (Ag) 1934. Head of Friedrich von Schiller (1759–1805), poet. ℞ imperial eagle, edge inscription: ANS VATERLAND ANS TEURE SCHLIESS DICH AN (cling to the fatherland, the precious fatherland)   35.00   60.00

			VF	**XF**
82 (87)	5	R-Mark (Ag) 1934. Type as No. 81	175.00	285.00

83 (82)	5	R-Mark (Ag) 1935–1936. Head right of Paul von Beneckendorff und von Hindenburg. ℞ imperial eagle	5.00	10.00
84 (88)	1	Reichspfennig (Br) 1936–1940. Imperial eagle with swastika	0.30	1.00
85 (89)	2	Reichspfennig (Br) 1936–1940. Imperial eagle with swastika	0.50	1.60
86 (90)	5	Reichspfennig (Al-Br) 1936–1939. Imperial eagle with swastika	0.40	1.00
87 (91)	10	Reichspfennig (Al-Br) 1936–1939. Imperial eagle with swastika	0.60	1.30

88 (93)	50	Reichspfennig (Ni) 1938–1939. Imperial eagle with swastika within circle. ℞ value in large figures within circle	20.00	40.00
89 (96)	2	R-Mark (Ag) 1936–1939. Paul von Beneckendorff und von Hindenburg, head r. ℞ imperial eagle with swastika	2.60	5.00
90 (97)	5	R-Mark (Ag) 1936–1939. Type as No. 89	6.00	15.00

		VF	XF
91 (A 92)	1 Reichspfennig (Zi) 1940–1945. Imperial eagle with swastika. ℞ value	0.30	0.60
92 (B 92)	5 Reichspfennig (Zi) 1940–1944	0.40	1.00
93 (C 92)	10 Reichspfennig (Zi) 1940–1945	0.40	1.00

94 (80)	50 Reichspfennig (Al) (issued 1939) 1935. Imperial eagle. ℞ value. This coin was only put into circulation in 1939	0.80	3.00
95 (92)	50 Reichspfennig (Al) 1939–1944. Type as No. 94, but imperial eagle with swastika	0.60	2.50

ALLIED OCCUPATION 1945–1948

96 (98)	1 Reichspfennig (Zi) 1944–1946. Eagle ℞ value.		
	a) (issued 1945) 1944. Imperial eagle (swastika omitted); only with mintmark D for Munich	–.–	–.–
	b) 1945–1946. New style imperial eagle (without swastika)	9.00	28.00
97 (99)	5 Reichspfennig (Zi) 1945, 1947, 1948:		
	a) 1945 (extremely rare)		–.–
	b) 1947, 1948	4.00	12.50

98 (100)	10 Reichspfennig (Zi). 1945–1948:

	VF	XF
a) 1945–1948	3.00	8.50
b) 1947 with »slavonic cross-line« (little line crossing the stem of the seven)	1100.00	2000.00

BANK DEUTSCHER LÄNDER

99 (101) 1 Pfennig (Bronze-clad steel) 1948–1949. Oak twig. R value   0.40   4.00

100 (102) 5 Pfennig (Brass-clad steel) 1949   0.60   4.00

101 (103) 10 Pfennig (Brass-clad steel) 1949   0.40   4.00

102 (104) 50 Pfennig (Cu-Ni) 1949–1950. Girl holding sapling

	VF	XF
a) 1949	2.00	12.50
b) 1950	120.00	200.00

No. 102b is available only with the G mintmark and is often a forgery.

Yeoman Numbers

In Order to help collectors and dealers, we have added after most SCHÖN-numbers the corresponding number assigned by R.S. Yeoman in his wellknown works entitled »A Catalog of Modern World Coins« and »Current Coins of the World«.

Federal Republic of Germany

			XF	Unc
103 (105)	1 Pfennig (Bronze-clad steel) 1950–		0.02	0.05
104 (106)	2 Pfennig			
	a) (Br) 1950–1968		0.15	0.25
	b) (Bronze-clad steel) 1968–		0.02	0.05
105 (107)	5 Pfennig (Brass-clad steel) 1950–		0.05	0.10
106 (108)	10 Pfennig (Brass-clad steel) 1950–		0.10	0.20

		XF	Unc
107 (109)	50 Pfennig (Cu-Ni) 1950-:		
	a) 1950, 1966-1971; reeded edge	0.35	0.80
	b) 1972 -; plain edge	0.35	0.50
108 (110)	1 D-Mark (Cu-Ni) 1950–	0.65	0.90
109 (111)	2 D-Mark (Cu-Ni) 1951. Value between wheat ears, grapes and vine leaves	18.00	35.00
110 (112)	5 D-Mark (Ag) 1951–1974. On the edge, legend reading:		
	a) EINIGKEIT UND RECHT UND FREIHEIT (Unity and Right and Freedom)	3.50	6.50
	b) GRÜSS DICH DEUTSCHLAND AUS HERZENSGRUND (Greetings to Germany with deepest feelings) (1957 J)	1100.00	1700.00

COMMEMORATIVE ISSUE FOR THE CENTENARY OF THE GERMAN NATIONAL MUSEUM IN NÜRNBERG

111 (113)   5 D-Mark (Ag) 1952. Representation of an Ostro-Gothic fibula in the form of an eagle from North Italy, gold cloisonné work dating from the 5th century A. D. Length 4.7 inches. Now in the German National Museum

	Unc	Proof
	800.00	3000.00

COMMEMORATIVE ISSUE FOR THE 150th ANNIVERSARY OF THE DEATH OF FRIEDRICH VON SCHILLER

112 (114)   5 D-Mark (Ag) 1955. Head right of Friedrich von Schiller (1759–1805), poet. Edge inscription: SEID EINIG EINIG EINIG (Be united, united, united)

	600.00	2000.00

Yeoman Numbers

In order to help collectors and dealers, we have added after most SCHÖN-numbers the corresponding number assigned by R.S. Yeoman in his wellknown works entitled »A Catalog of Modern World Coins« and »Current Coins of the World«.

COMMEMORATIVE ISSUE FOR THE 300th ANNIVERSARY OF THE BIRTH OF THE MARGRAVE VON BADEN

		Unc	Proof
113 (115)	5 D-Mark (Ag) 1955. Bust right of Ludwig Wilhelm I von Baden (1655–1707), Margrave since 1677, Imperial Field-Marshal, won the battle over the Turks at Novi Slankamen in 1691; known as the Turkish Louis	600.00	2000.00

COMMEMORATIVE ISSUE FOR THE CENTENARY OF THE DEATH OF EICHENDORFF

		Unc	Proof
114 (116)	5 D-Mark (Ag) 1957. Head left of Joseph Freiherr von Eichendorff (1788–1857), poet	600.00	2000.00

		XF	Unc
115 (117)	2 D-Mark (Cu–Ni) 1957–1971. Head left of Max Planck (1858–1947), physicist, creator of the Quantum Theory, Nobel prize winner in 1918	1.75	3.00

COMMEMORATIVE ISSUE FOR THE 150th ANNIVERSARY OF THE DEATH OF FICHTE

			Unc	Proof
116 (118)	5 D-Mark (Ag) 1964. Head left of Johann Gottlieb Fichte (1762–1814), philosopher		200.00	650.00

COMMEMORATIVE ISSUE FOR THE 250th ANNIVERSARY OF THE DEATH OF LEIBNIZ

117 (119)	5 D-Mark (Ag) 1966. Gottfried Wilhelm Leibniz (1646–1716), philosopher and savant		40.00	100.00

COMMEMORATIVE ISSUE FOR WILHELM AND ALEXANDER VON HUMBOLDT

118 (120)	5 D-Mark (Ag) 1967. Heads of Wilhelm von Humboldt (1767–1835), statesman and philologist, and Alexander von Humboldt (1769–1859), natural philosopher		50.00	185.00

COMMEMORATIVE ISSUE FOR THE 150th ANNIVERSARY OF THE BIRTH OF RAIFFEISEN

			Unc	**Proof**
119 (121)	5 D-Mark (Ag) 1968. Bust facing of Friedrich Wilhelm Raiffeisen (1818–1888), society founder and social reformer		9.00	35.00

COMMEMORATIVE ISSUE FOR THE 500th ANNIVERSARY OF THE DEATH OF GUTENBERG

120 (122)	5 D-Mark (Ag) 1968. Bust to r. of Johannes Gutenberg, actually Gensfleisch (c.1400–1468), he introduced printing with movable letters		22.50	85.00

COMMEMORATIVE ISSUE FOR THE 150th ANNIVERSARY OF THE BIRTH OF PETTENKOFER

121 (123)	5 D-Mark (Ag) 1968. Bust l. of Max von Pettenkofer (1818–1901), hygienist and natural scientist		20.00	55.00

COMMEMORATIVE ISSUE FOR THE 150th ANNIVERSARY OF THE BIRTH OF THEODOR FONTANE

			Unc	Proof
122 (124)	5 D-Mark (Ag) 1969. Bust l. of Theodor Fontane (1819–1898), writer and poet		22.50	40.00

COMMEMORATIVE ISSUE FOR THE 375th ANNIVERSARY OF THE DEATH OF GERHARD MERCATOR

123 (125)	5 D-Mark (Ag) 1969. Bust facing of Gerhard Mercator, actually Kremer (1512–1594), cartographer and geographer, in front of a map projection; on the orders of Emperor Charles V he made a terrestrial globe and a celestial globe			
	a) on the edge: TERRAE DESCRIPTIO AD USUM NAVIGANTIUM (description of the earth for the use of navigators)		8.00	25.00
	b) on the edge: EINIGKEIT UND RECHT UND FREIHEIT (Unity and Right and Freedom)			1000.00
	c) no inscription on edge			–.–

			XF	Unc
124 (A 117)		2 D-Mark (Cu–Ni) 1969–. Head left of Dr. Konrad Adenauer (1876–1967), first German Federal Chancellor	1.50	2.00

			XF	Unc
125 (B 117)		2 D-Mark (Cu–Ni) 1970–. Head left of Prof. Dr. Theodor Heuss (1884–1963), first German Federal President	1.50	2.00

COMMEMORATIVE ISSUE FOR THE 200th ANNIVERSARY OF THE BIRTH OF LUDWIG VAN BEETHOVEN

			Unc	Proof
126 (131)		5 D-Mark (Ag) 1970. Head left of Ludwig van Beethoven (1770–1827), composer	9.00	22.50

COMMEMORATIVE ISSUE FOR THE FOUNDATION OF THE REICH ON 18th JANUARY 1871

	Unc	Proof
127 (132) 5 D-Mark (Ag) 1971. Reichstag building in Berlin	9.00	22.50

COMMEMORATIVE ISSUE FOR THE 500th ANNIVERSARY OF THE BIRTH OF ALBRECHT DÜRER

	Unc	Proof
128 (133) 5 D-Mark (Ag) 1971. Monogram of Albrecht Dürer (1471 – 1528), painter, engraver and writer on art subjects	6.00	40.00

COMMEMORATIVE ISSUES (6)
FOR THE 1972 OLYMPIC GAMES HELD IN MUNICH
(26th August to 11th September 1972)

	Unc	Proof
129 (126) 10 D-Mark (Ag) 1972. Spiral of rays (Emblem of the 1972 Olympic Games)	9.00	22.50

| 130 (127) | 10 D-Mark (Ag) 1972. Entwined arms in front of a fan-like background as a symbolical representation of the Olympic theme | **Unc** 7.50 | **Proof** 10.00 |

| 131 (128) | 10 D-Mark (Ag) 1972. Delicately drawn group of a youth and a girl | 7.50 | 10.00 |

132 (129)	10 D-Mark (Ag) 1972. Representation of buildings put up for the Olympic Games in Munich	7.50	10.00
133 (126a)	10 D-Mark (Ag) 1972. Type as No. 129, but inscription SPIELE DER XX. OLYMPIADE 1972 IN MÜNCHEN	7.50	10.00
134 (130)	10 D-Mark (Ag) 1972. Olympic flame, spiral of rays and 5 interlocking rings	7.50	10.00

COMMEMORATIVE ISSUE FOR THE 500th BIRTHDAY OF NIKOLAUS COPERNICUS (1473–1543)

			Unc	Proof
135 (134)	5 D-Mark (Ag) 1973. Representation of the fundamental idea of the Copernican Theory, the Earth and other planets revolving around the central celestial body, the Sun		5.50	12.50

COMMEMORATIVE ISSUE FOR THE 125th RETURN OF THE MEETING OF THE FRANKFURT NATIONAL ASSEMBLY IN THE CHURCH OF PAUL

136 (135)	5 D-Mark (Ag) 1973. Considerably simplified representation of the interior of the Church of Paul, in the centre the year 1848; inscription FRANKFURTER NATIONALVERSAMMLUNG		5.50	12.50

COMMEMORATIVE ISSUE FOR THE 25th ANNIVERSARY OF THE CONSTITUTIONAL LAW

137 (136)	5 D-Mark (Ag) 1974		5.50	12.50

COMMEMORATIVE ISSUE FOR THE 250th BIRTHDAY OF IMMANUEL KANT

138 (137)	5 D-Mark (Ag) 1974. Immanuel Kant (1724–1804), philosopher		5.50	27.50

COMMEMORATIVE ISSUE FOR THE 50th ANNIVERSARY
OF THE DEATH OF FRIEDRICH EBERT

		Unc	Proof
139 (138)	5 D-Mark (Ag) 1975. Friedrich Ebert (1871–1925), President of the German Reich from 1919 to 1925	5.50	22.50

		XF	Unc
140 (139)	5 D-Mark (Cu–Ni) 1975-. Federal eagle, year date, mintmark. ℞ name of country, denomination	3.50	4.50

COMMEMORATIVE ISSUE FOR THE CENTENARY OF BIRTH
OF ALBERT SCHWEITZER

		Unc	Proof
141 (141)	5 D-Mark (Ag) 1975. Albert Schweitzer (1875-1965), philosopher and Doctor of Medicine	5.50	20.00

EUROPEAN MONUMENT PROTECTION YEAR 1975

	Unc	Proof
142 (140) 5 D-Mark (Ag) 1975	5.50	12.50

300th ANNIVERSARY OF THE DEATH OF HANS JACOB CHRISTOPH VON GRIMMELSHAUSEN

143 (142) 5 D-Mark (Ag) 1976. Hans Jacob Christoph von Grimmelshausen (1621–1676), poet; his best known work is »Der abenteuerliche Simplicissimus Teutsch«   5.50   35.00

200th ANNIVERSARY OF THE BIRTH OF CARL FRIEDRICH GAUSS

144 (143) 5 D-Mark (Ag) 1977. Carl Friedrich Gauss (1777-1855), mathematician and astronomer   5.50   36.00

200th ANNIVERSARY OF THE BIRTH OF HEINRICH VON KLEIST

		Unc	Proof
145 (144) 5 D-Mark (Ag) 1977. Heinrich von Kleist (1777-1811), poet		5.50	25.00

100th ANNIVERSARY OF THE BIRTH OF GUSTAV STRESEMANN

146 (145) 5 D-Mark (Ag) 1978. Gustav Stresemann (1878-1929), politician and Nobel Prize winner for peace		5.50	12.50

225th ANNIVERSARY OF THE DEATH OF BALTHASAR NEUMANN

147 (146) 5 D-Mark (Ag) 1978. Balthasar Neumann (1687-1753), architect		5.50	12.50

		XF	Unc
148 (148) 2 D-Mark (Cu-Ni) 1979-. Dr. Kurt Schumacher (1895-1952), politician		1.50	2.00

150th ANNIVERSARY OF GERMAN ARCHEOLOGICAL INSTITUTE

		Unc	Proof
149 (147)	5 D-Mark (Ag) 1979	5.50	22.50

100th ANNIVERSARY OF THE BIRTH OF OTTO HAHN

150 (149)	5 D-Mark (Cu-Ni) 1979	7.50	10.00

750th ANNIVERSARY OF THE DEATH OF WALTHER VON DER VOGELWEIDE

151 (150)	5 D-Mark (Cu-Ni) 1980. Walther von der Vogelweide (c. 1170–1230), minnesinger	6.00	10.00

100th ANNIVERSARY OF COLOGNE CATHEDRAL

						Unc	Proof
152 (151)	5 D-Mark (Cu-Ni) 1980. Cologne cathedral					9.00	12.50

200th ANNIVERSARY OF THE DEATH OF G.E. LESSING

		Unc	Proof
153 (152)	5 D-Mark (Cu-Ni) 1981. Gotthold Ephraim Lessing (1729–1781), poet	5.00	10.00

150th ANNIVERSARY OF THE DEATH OF VON STEIN

		Unc	Proof
154 (153)	5 D-Mark (Cu-Ni) 1981. Carl Reichsfreiherr vom und zum Stein (1757–1831), statesman	5.00	10.00

ENVIRONMENT PROTECTION

		Unc	Proof
155 (155)	5 D-Mark (Cu-Ni) 1982. Emblem	5.00	10.00

150th ANNIVERSARY OF THE DEATH OF GOETHE

		Unc	Proof
156 (154)	5 D-Mark (Cu-Ni) 1982. Johann Wolfgang von Goethe (1749–1832), poet and writer	5.00	11.00

100th ANNIVERSARY OF THE DEATH OF K. MARX

157 (156)	5 D-Mark (Cu-Ni) 1983. Karl Marx (1818–1883), social ideologist	5.00	10.00

500th ANNIVERSARY OF BIRTH OF MARTIN LUTHER

158 (157)	5 D-Mark (Cu-Ni) 1983. Martin Luther (1483–1546), reformer	5.00	12.50

150th ANNIVERSARY OF THE ZOLLVEREIN

			Unc	Proof
159 (158)	5 D-Mark (Cu-Ni) 1984. Stage coach and customs-barrier		4.50	10.00

175th ANNIVERSARY OF THE BIRTH OF FELIX MENDESSOHN-BARTHOLDY

160 (159)	5 D-Mark (Cu-Ni) 1984. Felix Mendels-sohn-Bartholdy (1809–1847), composer	4.50	10.00

EUROPEAN YEAR OF MUSIC

161 (160)	5 D-Mark (Cu-Ni) 1985. Emblem	4.50	10.00

150th ANNIVERSARY OF RAILROAD IN GERMANY

		Unc	Proof
162 (161) 5 D-Mark (Cu-Ni) 1985. Winged wheel		4.50	10.00

600th ANNIVERSARY OF HEIDELBERG UNIVERSITY

163 5 D-Mark (Cu-Ni) 1986. Crowned lion	4.50	10.00

200th ANNIVERSARY OF THE DEATH OF FRIEDRICH II, THE GREAT

164 5 D-Mark (Cu-Ni) 1986. Friedrich II, the Great (1712–1786), King of Prussia 1740–1786	4.50	10.00

750th ANNIVERSARY OF THE CITY OF BERLIN

		Unc	Proof
165	10 D-Mark (Ag) 1987	9.00	15.00

30th ANNIVERSARY OF EUROPEAN ECONOMIC COMMUNITY

166	10 D-Mark (Ag) 1987	9.00	15.00

200th ANNIVERSARY OF THE BIRTH OF A. SCHOPENHAUER

167	2 D-Mark (Cu-Ni bounded on a Ni core) 1988. Ludwig Erhard (1897–1977), politician, German Federal Chancellor 1963–1966	–.–	–.–

200th ANNIVERSARY OF THE BIRTH OF A. SCHOPENHAUER

168	10 D-Mark (Ag) 1988. Arthur Schopenhauer (1788–1860), philosopher	9.00	15.00

100th ANNIVERSARY OF THE DEATH OF CARL ZEISS

169	10 D-Mark (Ag) 1988. Carl Zeiss (1816–1888), scientist and founder of Zeiss-Works	9.00	15.00

670   **Germany**

German Democratic Republic

		VF	XF
1 (1)	1 Pfennig (Al) 1948–1950. Ear of corn with cog wheel. Ŗ value	1.00	6.00

2 (2)	5 Pfennig (Al) 1948–1950. Ear of corn with cog wheel. Ŗ value	1.00	4.00

3 (3)	10 Pfennig (Al) 1948–1950. Ear of corn with cog wheel. Ŗ value	1.25	3.00

4 (4)	50 Pfennig (Al-Br) 1949, 1950. Plough and factory in background. R value:		
	a) 1949, rare		1500.00
	b) 1950	4.00	10.00

			VF	XF
5 (5)	1 Pfennig (Al) 1952–1953. Hammer and compasses between ears of corn. ℞ value		1.00	4.00

6 (6)	5 Pfennig (Al) 1952–1953. Hammer and compasses between ears of corn. ℞ value		1.00	4.00

7 (7)	10 Pfennig (Al) 1952–1953. Hammer and compasses between ears of corn. ℞ value		1.00	4.00

8 (8)	1 Pfennig (Al) 1960–1965, 1968, 1972, 1973, 1975, 1977–1987. Hammer and compasses within wreath of corn ears, Rev. value between oak leaves		0.10	0.20

9 (9)	5 Pfennig (Al) 1968, 1972, 1975, 1978–1987		0.10	0.20

		VF	XF

10 (10)   10 Pfennig (Al) 1963, 1965, 1967, 1968, 1970–1973, 1978–1987. Rev. oak leaf above value — 0.15 | 0.25

11 (A11)   20 Pfennig (Bra) 1969–:
a) without mintmark: 1969, 1971 — 0.25 | 0.50
b) with mintmark A: 1972–1974, 1979–1987 — 0.20 | 0.30

12 (11)   50 Pfennig (Al) 1958, 1968, 1971–1973, 1979–1987 — 0.25 | 0.50

13 (12)   1 D-Mark (Al) 1956, 1962, 1963, R. value between oak leaves — 0.50 | 2.50

14 (13)   2 D-Mark (Al) 1957 — 1.00 | 2.50

COMMEMORATIVE ISSUE FOR THE 250th ANNIVERSARY OF THE DEATH OF LEIBNIZ

Unc

15 (15)   20 MDN (Ag) 1966. Bust right of Gottfried Wilhelm Leibniz (1646–1716), philosopher and savant — 65.00

COMMEMORATIVE ISSUE FOR THE 125th ANNIVERSARY OF THE DEATH OF SCHINKEL

16 (14)   10 MDN (S) 1966. Head right of Karl Friedrich Schinkel (1781–1841), architect and painter.
Of No. 16 there is also a pattern in aluminium. No. 16 also has a variety with no inscription on edge.

Unc

60.00

COMMEMORATIVE ISSUE FOR THE 200th ANNIVERSARY OF THE BIRTH OF HUMBOLDT

17 (17)   20 MDN (Ag) 1967. Bust left of Wilhelm von Humboldt (1767–1835), statesman and philologist
a) on the edge: * 20 MARK DER DEUTSCHEN NOTENBANK (20 Marks issued by the Deutschen Notenbank)
b) on the edge: * 20 MARK * 20 MARK * 20 MARK

35.00

155.00

COMMEMORATIVE ISSUE FOR THE 100th ANNIVERSARY OF THE BIRTH OF K. KOLLWITZ

18 (16)   10 MDN (Ag) 1967. Head left of Käthe Kollwitz (1867 – 1945), etcher, painter and sculptor
    a) on the edge: * 10 MARK DER DEUTSCHEN NOTENBANK (10 Marks issued by the Deutschen Notenbank)
    b) on the edge: * 10 MARK * 10 MARK * 10 MARK

	Unc
a)	22.50
b)	125.00

COMMEMORATIVE ISSUE FOR THE 150th ANNIVERSARY OF THE BIRTH OF KARL MARX

19 (20)   20 Mark (Ag) 1968. Head left of Karl Marx (1818–1883), social ideologist   30.00

COMMEMORATIVE ISSUE FOR THE 500th ANNIVERSARY OF THE DEATH OF GUTENBERG

20 (19) 10 Mark (Ag) 1968. Monogram for Johannes Gutenberg, actually Gensfleisch (c. 1400–1468); he introduced printing with movable letters

Unc

22.50

COMMEMORATIVE ISSUE FOR THE 125th ANNIVERSARY OF THE BIRTH OF KOCH

21 (18) 5 Mark (German silver) 1968. Bust left of Dr. Robert Koch (1843 to 1910), physician, bacteriologist; he discovered the tubercule bacillus (1882)

20.00

COMMEMORATIVE ISSUE FOR 20 YEARS OF THE GERMAN DEMOCRATIC REPUBLIC

22 (21) 5 Mark 1969. National arms. ℞ commemorative inscription, value and date
  a) (Cu–Ni)   2.00   3.00
  b) (Ni) Pattern (12,741 pieces)   45.00

COMMEMORATIVE ISSUE FOR THE 220th ANNIVERSARY OF THE BIRTH OF GOETHE

23 (24)   20 Mark (Ag) 1969. Bust left of Johann Wolfgang von Goethe (1749–1832), poet and writer

Unc

35.00

COMMEMORATIVE ISSUE FOR THE 75th ANNIVERSARY OF THE DEATH OF HEINRICH HERTZ

24 (22)   5 Mark (German silver) 1969. Head right of Heinrich Hertz (1857 to 1894), physicist; the Hertzian waves, named after him, form the basis of modern radio

9.00

COMMEMORATIVE ISSUE FOR THE 250th ANNIVERSARY OF THE DEATH OF JOHANN FRIEDRICH BÖTTGER (1682–1719)

25 (23)   10 Mark (Ag) 1969. Porcelain jug; the curved swords in saltire are the trademark of the porcelain works, founded and directed in Meissen by Böttger (also known as Böttiger)

22.50

COMMEMORATIVE ISSUE FOR THE 125th ANNIVERSARY OF THE BIRTH OF WILHELM CONRAD RÖNTGEN

26 (25)   5 Mark (German silver) 1970. Prof. Wilhelm Conrad Röntgen (1845 to 1923), physicist; in 1895 he discovered X-rays, which are named after him; in 1901 he won the first Nobel prize for physics   9.00

COMMEMORATIVE ISSUE FOR THE 200th ANNIVERSARY OF THE BIRTH OF LUDWIG VAN BEETHOVEN

27 (26)   10 Mark (Ag) 1970. Bust left of Ludwig van Beethoven (1770–1827), composer   25.00

COMMEMORATIVE ISSUE FOR THE 150th ANNIVERSARY OF THE BIRTH OF FRIEDRICH ENGELS

28 (27) 20 Mark (Ag) 1970. Head left of   **XF**   **Unc**
Friedrich Engels (1820–1895), pol-
itician and socialist theoretician   32.00

29 (31) 20 Mark (German silver) 1971. Heinrich Mann (1871–1950), writer   7.00   12.00

COMMEMORATIVE ISSUE FOR KEPLER

30 (28) 5 Mark (German silver) 1971. Johannes Kepler (1571–1630), impe-
rial mathematician and court astronomer; in 1596 he published his
writings on "Mysterium cosmo-
graphicum"; his pricipal work was
"Astronomia nova", in 1611   9.00

COMMEMORATIVE ISSUE FOR DÜRER

31 (29) 10 Mark (Ag) 1971. Albrecht Dürer

(1471–1528), painter, engraver and
writer on art subjects. Monogram
of Albrecht Dürer

	XF	Unc
		22.50

COMMEMORATIVE ISSUE FOR ROSA LUXEMBURG AND KARL LIEBKNECHT

32 (30) 20 Mark (Ag) 1971. Rosa Luxemburg
(1870–1919), Socialist politician,
and Karl Liebknecht (1871–1919),
politician, founder of the Spartacus
Association   30.00

COMMEMORATIVE ISSUE FOR THE 85th BIRTHDAY OF ERNST THÄLMANN

33 (32) 20 Mark (German silver) 1971. Ernst
Thälmann (1886–1944), politician   ·6.00   12.00

COMMEMORATIVE ISSUE BRANDENBURG GATE

34 (A29) 5 Mark (German silver) 1971,
1979–1982, 1984, 1986, 1987.
Brandenburg Gate   2.00   4.00

COMMEMORATIVE ISSUE FOR FRIEDRICH VON SCHILLER

35 (38) 20 Mark (German silver) 1972. Friedrich von Schiller (1759–1805), poet   6.00   12.00

COMMEMORATIVE ISSUE
FOR THE BUCHENWALD MEMORIAL

			XF	**Unc**
36 (35)	10 Mark (German silver) 1972. Group of figures taken from Buchenwald memorial, near Weimar		4.00	7.00

COMMEMORATIVE ISSUE FOR THE 500th BIRTHDAY OF
LUCAS CRANACH

37 (37)   20 Mark (Ag) 1972. Lucas Cranach the Elder (1472–1553), painter and graphic artist. Having received his patent for bearing arms from the Elector Friedrich the Wise in 1508, Cranach exclusively used as his signature the serpent with raised wings and the crown as well as the ring   32.00

COMMEMORATIVE ISSUE FOR THE 75th ANNIVERSARY
OF THE DEATH OF JOHANNES BRAHMS (1833–1897)

38 (33)   5 Mark (German silver) 1972. Quotation of score from the 4th movement of Symphony No. 1 by Brahms. The third note must be "c" instead of "b".   17.50

COMMEMORATIVE ISSUE FOR WILHELM PIECK

		XF	Unc
39 (39)	20 Mark (German silver) 1972. Wilhelm Pieck (1876–1960), President of the GDR	6.00	12.00

COMMEMORATIVE ISSUE FOR THE 175th BIRTHDAY OF HEINRICH HEINE

40 (36)	10 Mark (Ag) 1972. Heinrich Heine (1797 to 1856), lyric poet and satirist		20.00

COMMEMORATIVE ISSUE FOR MEISSEN

41 (34)	5 Mark (German silver) 1972, 1981, 1983. View of the Meissen castle hill with cathedral (Gothic hall church of the 13th/14th century) and Albrechtsburg (built 1471–1485)	3.00	7.00

42 (67)	1 Mark (A1) 1972, 1973, 1975, 1977–1987. Type as No. 13, but MARK instead of DEUTSCHE MARK	0.50	1.00
43 (68)	2 Mark (A1) 1974, 1975, 1977–1987. Type as No. 42	1.00	2.00

COMMEMORATIVE ISSUE FOR THE 75th BIRTHDAY OF BERTOLT BRECHT

44 (42)	10 Mark (Ag) 1973. Bertolt Brecht (1898–1956), eminent Socialist lyric poet, epic poet and theatrical director		22.50

			XF	Unc
45 (41)	10	Mark (German silver) 1973. Emblem of the World Festival Games, surrounded by functional inscription. ℞ denomination, national emblem	4.00	10.00

125th BIRTHDAY OF OTTO LILIENTHAL

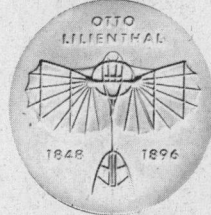 

46 (40)	5	Mark (German silver) 1973. Otto Lilienthal (1848–1896), pioneer of German aviation, since 1891 performed flights with selfconstructed gliders over distances of several hundred meters.		8.00

60th ANNIVERSARY OF THE DEATH OF A. BEBEL

47 (43)	20	Mark (Ag) 1973. August Bebel (1840–1913), Socialdemocrat politician and member of the German parliament		32.00
48 (44)	20	Mark (German silver) 1973. Otto Grotewohl (1894–1964), Socialdemocrat politician, took a decisive part in the amalgamation of the Communist Party of Germany and the Socialist Party of Germany forming the "SED" (Socialist Unity Party)	6.00	12.50

COMMEMORATIVE ISSUE FOR THE 250th BIRTHDAY
OF IMMANUEL KANT

		Unc	Proof
49 (49)	20 Mark (Ag) 1974. Immanuel Kant (1724–1804), philosopher	30.00	100.00

COMMEMORATIVE ISSUE FOR THE CENTENARY
OF THE DEATH OF PHILIPP REIS

50 (45)	5 Mark (German silver) 1974. Philipp Reis (1834–1874), physicist, inventor of the first telephone	8.50

COMMEMORATIVE ISSUE (2) 25 YEARS GDR

51 (46)	10 Mark 1974. Arms, date:		
	a) German silver	5.00	
	b) .500 silver (1,500 pieces)		1000.00
52 (47)	10 Mark (Ag) 1974. Significant buildings	28.00	2500.00

COMMEMORATIVE ISSUE FOR THE 200th BIRTHDAY OF C. D. FRIEDRICH

Unc

53 (48)   10 Mark (Ag) 1974. Caspar David Friedrich (1774–1840), painter   30.00

COMMEMORATIVE ISSUE FOR THE CENTENARY OF BIRTH OF ALBERT SCHWEITZER

54 (52)   10 Mark (Ag) 1975. Albert Schweitzer (1875–1965), philosopher and Doctor of Medicine:
    a) .625 silver (100,000 pieces)   25.00
    b) .500 silver; proof (1,040 pieces)   1400.00
    c) pattern; .500 silver; reverse like No. 56 (8,810 pieces)   85.00

225th ANNIVERSARY OF THE DEATH OF J. S. BACH

55 (54)	20 Mark (Ag) 1975. Johann Sebastian Bach (1685-1750), composer:	**XF**	**Unc**
	a) raised notes		30.00
	b) incused notes (pattern)		90.00

20th ANNIVERSARY OF THE WARSAW PACT

56 (53)	10 Mark (German silver) 1975.	12.50

100th ANNIVERSARY OF THE BIRTH OF THOMAS MANN

57 (50)	5 Mark (German silver) 1975. Thomas Mann (1875-1955), writer	9.00

INTERNATIONAL WOMEN'S YEAR 1975

58 (51)	5 Mark (German silver) 1975. Conjoined women heads, emblem, commemorative legend	8.00

200th ANNIVERSARY OF THE BIRTH OF FERDINAND VON SCHILL

59 (55)	5 Mark (German silver) 1976. Ferdinand von Schill (1776-1809), Prussian officer	10.00

20th ANNIVERSARY OF NATIONAL PEOPLE'S ARMY

		XF	Unc
60 (56)	10 Mark (German silver) 1976. Bust of a soldier	4.00	10.00

150th ANNIVERSARY OF THE BIRTH OF WILHELM LIEBKNECHT

		Unc	Proof
61 (58)	20 Mark (Ag) 1976. Wilhelm Liebknecht 1826–1900), Socialdemocrat politician	35.00	120.00

150th ANNIVERSARY OF THE DEATH OF CARL MARIA VON WEBER

62 (57)	10 Mark (Ag) 1976. Carl Maria von Weber (1786–1826), composer; one of his most famous works is entitled »Der Frei-schütz«	25.00	80.00

200th ANNIVERSARY OF THE BIRTH OF CARL FRIEDRICH GAUSS

63 (61)	20 Mark (Ag) 1977. Carl Friedrich Gauss (1777-1855), mathematician and astro-nomer	35.00	

	Unc	Proof
64 (60) 10 Mark (Ag) 1977. Otto von Guericke (1602–1686), burgomaster of the city of Magdeburg, inventor:		
a) as illustrated above	30.00	85.00
b) pattern; with horses	100.00	

125th ANNIVERSARY OF THE DEATH OF FRIEDRICH LUDWIG JAHN

65 (59) 5 Mark (German silver) 1977. Friedrich Ludwig Jahn (1778–1852), founder of the gymnastics movement in Germany, know as »Turnvater Jahn« (father of the gymnastics)   9.00   35.00

175th ANNIVERSARY OF THE DEATH OF G. F. KLOPSTOCK

			Unc	**Proof**
66 (62)	5 Mark (German silver) 1978. Friedrich Gottlieb Klopstock (1724-1803), poet:		10.00	70.00

175th ANNIVERSARY OF THE BIRTH OF J. VON LIEBIG

67 (64)	10 Mark (Ag) 1978. Justus von Liebig (1803-1873), chemist:	25.00	75.00

175th ANNIVERSARY OF THE DEATH OF J. G. HERDER

68 (66)	20 Mark (Ag) 1978. Johann Gottfried Herder (1744-1803), philosopher:	35.00	85.00

SOVIET-GERMAN SPACE FLIGHT

			Unc	Proof
69 (65)	10 Mark (German silver) 1978		15.00	400.00

ANTI-APARTHEID YEAR

			Unc	Proof
70 (63)	5 Mark (German silver) 1978		8.00	85.00

100th ANNIVERSARY OF THE BIRTH OF ALBERT EINSTEIN

71 (69)	5 Mark (German silver) 1979. Albert Einstein (1879-1955), physicist	9.00	85.00

175th ANNIVERSARY OF THE BIRTH OF L. FEUERBACH

72 (70)	10 Mark (Ag) 1979. Ludwig Feuerbach (1804-1872), philosopher	25.00	70.00

250th ANNIVERSARY OF THE BIRTH OF G. E. LESSING

		Unc	Proof
73 (71)	20 Mark (Ag) 1979. Gotthold Ephraim Lessing (1729–1781), poet	35.00	85.00

30th ANNIVERSARY OF THE GDR

| **74** (72) | 20 Mark (German silver) 1979 | 15.00 | |

225th ANNIVERSARY OF THE BIRTH OF J.D. SCHARNHORST

| **75** (74) | 10 Mark (Ag) 1980. Gerhard J. D. von Scharnhorst (1755–1813), general and military theoretician | 25.00 | 55.00 |

75th ANNIVERSARY OF THE DEATH OF ADOLPH VON MENZEL

| **76** (73) | 5 Mark (German silver) 1980. Adolph von Menzel (1815–1905), engraver and drawer | 9.00 | 35.00 |

75th ANNIVERSARY OF THE DEATH OF ERNST ABBE

		Unc	Proof
77 (75)	20 Mark (Ag) 1980. Ernst Abbe (1840–1905), physicist	30.00	80.00

25th ANNIVERSARY OF NATIONAL PEOPLE'S ARMY

		Unc	Proof
78 (77)	10 Mark (German silver) 1981	10.00	60.00

150th ANNIVERSARY OF THE DEATH OF VON STEIN

		Unc	Proof
79 (76)	20 Mark (Ag) 1981. Carl Reichsfreiherr vom und zum Stein (1757–1831), statesman	35.00	85.00

150th ANNIVERSARY OF THE DEATH OF G.W. HEGEL

		Unc	Proof
80 (79)	10 Mark (Ag) 1981. Georg Wilhelm Hegel (1770–1831), philosopher	30.00	65.00

450th ANNIVERSARY OF THE DEATH OF RIEMENSCHNEIDER

	Unc	Proof
81 (78) 5 Mark (German silver) 1981. Tilman Riemenschneider (c. 1455–1531), sculptor and wood-carver	12.50	30.00

700th ANNIVERSARY OF THE BERLIN MINT

82 (80) 10 Mark (German silver) 1981. Old bear pfennig design	20.00	65.00

NEUES GEWANDHAUS LEIPZIG

83 (82) 10 Mark (Ag) 1982	27.50	65.00

200th ANNIVERSARY OF THE BIRTH OF FRIEDRICH FRÖBEL (1782–1852)

			Unc	**Proof**
84 (81)	5 Mark (German silver) 1982. Three nude children with large building blocks and balls		12.50	35.00

125th ANNIVERSARY OF THE BIRTH OF C. ZETKIN

85 (83)	20 Mark (Ag) 1982. Clara Zetkin (1857–1933), politician		40.00	85.00

86 (85)	5 Mark (German silver) 1982, 1983. Wartburg Castle			
87 (84)	5 Mark (German silver) 1982. Goethe's Weimar Cottage		12.00 / 15.00	55.00 / 60.00

100th ANNIVERSARY OF THE DEATH OF RICHARD WAGNER

88 (88)	10 Mark (Ag) 1983		30.00	65.00

500th ANNIVERSARY OF THE BIRTH OF MARTIN LUTHER (3)

		Unc	Proof
89 (87)	5 Mark (German silver) 1983. Martin Luther's Birth Place in Eisleben	12.00	55.00
90 (86)	5 Mark (German silver) 1983. Wittenberg Church	12.00	55.00

91 (89)	20 Mark (Ag) 1983. Dr. Martin Luther (1483–1546), reformer	65.00	100.00

100th ANNIVERSARY OF THE DEATH OF KARL MARX

92 (90)	20 Mark (German silver) 1983. Karl Marx (1818–1883), social ideologist	17.50	60.00

125th ANNIVERSARY OF THE BIRTH OF MAX PLANCK

93 (91)	5 Mark (German silver) 1983. Max Planck (1858–1947), physicist, creator of the Quantum Theory, Nobel prize winner in 1918	12.00	35.00

30th ANNIVERSARY OF WORKERS MILITIA

94 (92)	10 Mark (German silver) 1983	8.00	50.00

225th ANNIVERSARY OF THE DEATH OF G.F. HÄNDEL

		Unc	Proof
95 (93)	20 Mark (Ag) 1984. Georg Friedrich Händel (1685–1759), composer	40.00	85.00

100th ANNIVERSARY OF THE DEATH OF ALFRED BREHM (1829–1884)

96	10 Mark (Ag) 1984. Marabu (Leptoptilus crumeniferus)	30.00	65.00

150th ANNIVERSARY OF THE DEATH OF A. FREIHERR V. LÜTZOW

97	5 Mark (German silver) 1984. Adolf Freiherr von Lützow (1782–1834), Prussian officer	12.00	35.00
98	5 Mark (German silver) 1984. Old townhall, Leipzig	8.00	35.00
99	5 Mark (German silver) 1984. Thomas Church, Leipzig	9.00	35.00

REOPENING OF THE SEMPEROPER

		Unc	Proof
100	10 Mark (Ag) 1984. »Semperoper«, opera house in Dresden	30.00	65.00

125th ANNIVERSARY OF THE DEATH OF E.M. ARNDT

101	20 Mark (Ag) 1985. Ernst Moritz Arndt (1769–1860), writer and poet	35.00	80.00

175th ANNIVERSARY OF THE HUMBOLDT UNIVERSITY

102	10 Mark (Ag) 1985	30.00	70.00

225th ANNIVERSARY OF THE DEATH OF F.C. NEUBER

103	5 Mark (German silver) 1985. Friederike Caroline Neuber (1697–1760), actress and theatre manager	10.00	35.00
104	5 Mark (German silver) 1985. The Wall Pavilion with its Baroque architecture (Zwinger, Dresden)	9.00	35.00

		Unc	Proof
105	5 Mark (German silver) 1985. The ruins of the Frauenkirche in Dresden	9.00	35.00

40th ANNIVERSARY OF LIBERATION

		Unc	Proof
106	10 Mark (German silver) 1985. Statue of a soldier	10.00	40.00

200th ANNIVERSARY OF THE BIRTH OF JACOB AND WILHELM GRIMM

		Unc	Proof
107	20 Mark (Ag) 1986	35.00	80.00

275th ANNIVERSARY OF CHARITÉ BERLIN

		Unc	Proof
108	10 Mark (Ag) 1986	25.00	55.00

100th ANNIVERSARY OF THE BIRTH OF E. THÄLMANN

		Unc	Proof
109	10 Mark (German silver) 1986. Ernst Thälmann (1886–1944), politician	10.00	40.00

175th ANNIVERSARY OF THE DEATH OF H. VON KLEIST

110 5 Mark (German silver) 1986. Heinrich von
Kleist (1777–1811), poet   12.50   35.00

		Unc	Proof
111	5 Mark (German silver) 1986. Sanssouci, Potsdam	9.00	35.00
112	5 Mark (German silver) 1986. Neues Palais, Potsdam	9.00	35.00

750th ANNIVERSARY OF THE CITY OF BERLIN (5)

113	5 Mark (German silver) 1987. Nikolai Quarter	6.00	30.00
114	5 Mark (German silver) 1987. Red City Hall	6.00	30.00
115	5 Mark (German silver) 1987. Universal Time Clock	6.00	30.00
116	10 Mark (German silver) 1987. Theatre (Schauspielhaus)	25.00	55.00
117	20 Mark (Ag) 1987. Old City Seal	35.00	75.00

Danzig

100 Pfennig(e) = 1 Gulden; since 1923: 100 Pfennig(e) = 1 Danzig Gulden

		VF	XF
1 (1)	10 Pfennig (Zi) 1920. Arms of the city and date. ℞ value on panel	25.00	40.00
2 (2)	10 Pfennig (Zi) 1920. Arms of the city and date. ℞ value in large figures	175.00	280.00

3 (3)	1 Pfennig (Br) 1923–1937. Arms of the city. ℞ value	3.00	4.00
4 (4)	2 Pfennige (Br) 1923–1937	3.00	5.00
5 (5)	5 Pfennige (Cu–Ni) 1923–1928	4.00	6.00

6 (6)	10 Pfennige (Cu–Ni) 1923	5.00	7.00

7 (7)	½ Gulden (Ag) 1923–1927. Small galley	15.00	25.00
8 (8)	1 Gulden (Ag) 1923	25.00	45.00

		VF	XF
9 (9)	2 Gulden (Ag) 1923	45.00	70.00

10 (10)	5 Gulden (Ag) 1923–1927. The Marienkirche in Danzig	100.00	170.00

11 (11)	25 Gulden (Au) 1923. Neptune brandishing trident, from the famous Neptune fountain in Danzig	2000.00	3000.00

12 (13)	5 Pfennig (Al–Br) 1932. East Atlantic flounder or turbot (Bothus = Rhombus = Scophthalmus maximus – Bothidae). ℞ value	2.20	4.00

			VF	XF
13 (14)	10	Pfennig (Al–Br) 1932. Atlantic codfish (Gadus morrhua – Gadidae). ℞ value	3.00	5.00
14 (15)	½	Gulden (Ni) 1932	18.00	26.00
15 (16)	1	Gulden (Ni) 1932	17.00	26.00
16 (17)	2	Gulden (Ag) 1932	125.00	265.00
17 (18)	5	Gulden (Ag) 1932. The Marienkirche	250.00	450.00

18 (19)	5	Gulden (Ag) 1932. Grain elevator	350.00	650.00

19 (20)	5	Gulden (Ni) 1935. Small galley	200.00	350.00

20 (21)	10	Gulden (Ni) 1935. The Town Hall	550.00	900.00

		XF	Unc
21 (12)	25 Gulden (Au) 1930. Neptune brandishing trident, from the famous Neptune fountain	8000.00	11 000.00

Saarland

100 Centimen = 1 Franken

1 (1)	10 Franken (Al–Br) 1954. Pit head and arms	1.50	3.50
2 (2)	20 Franken (Al–Br) 1954	2.00	4.00
3 (3)	50 Franken (Al–Br) 1954	10.00	15.00
4 (4)	100 Franken (Cu–Ni) 1955	4.00	6.00

German New Guinea

1 (1)	1 New Guinea Pfennig (Cu) 1894	22.00	42.00
2 (2)	2 New Guinea Pfennig (Cu) 1894. Type as No. 1	30.00	50.00

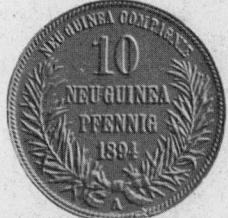

3 (3)   10 New Guinea Pfennig (Cu) 1894. Great bird of paradise (Paradisea

			VF	**XF**

apoda – Paradiseaidae). ℞ value between palm branches — 30.00 — 52.00

4 (4) ½ New Guinea Mark (Ag) 1894. Type as No. 3 — 80.00 — 115.00

5 (5) 1 New Guinea Mark (Ag) 1894. Type as No. 3 — 80.00 — 130.00

6 (6) 2 New Guinea Mark (Ag) 1894. Type as No. 3 — 130.00 — 220.00

7 (7) 5 New Guinea Mark (Ag) 1894. Type as No. 3 — 450.00 — 1200.00

8 (8) 10 New Guinea Mark (Au) 1895. Type as No. 3 — 3500.00 — 6000.00

9 (9) 20 New Guinea Mark (Au) 1895. Type as No. 3 — 3500.00 — 6000.00

German East Africa

ISSUES OF THE GERMAN EAST AFRICA COMPANY
64 Pesa = 1 Rupie, 100 Heller = 1 Rupie

1 (1) 1 Pesa (Cu) 1890–1892. Imperial eagle, inscription DEUTSCH-OSTAFRIKANISCHE GESELLSCHAFT. ℞ inscription in Swahili — 4.00 — 8.00

2 (2) ¼ Rupie (Ag) 1891–1901. Bust left of Kaiser Wilhelm II (1859–1941) wearing helmet surmounted by eagle. ℞ arms with palm tree and lion walking to left — 15.00 — 26.00

3 (3) ½ Rupie (Ag) 1891–1901. Type as No. 2 — 26.00 — 45.00

4 (4) 1 Rupie (Ag) 1890–1902. Type as No. 2 — 18.00 — 35.00

			VF	**XF**
5 (5)	2 Rupien (Ag) 1893–1894. Type as No. 2		280.00	400.00

ISSUES OF THE MINISTRY OF FOREIGN AFFAIRS

6 (6)	½ Heller (Br) 1904–1906. Crown		5.00	10.00
7 (7)	1 Heller (Br) 1904–1913		1.50	3.00
8 (8)	5 Heller (Br) 1908–1909		16.00	40.00
9 (11)	5 Heller (Cu–Ni) 1913–1914 (with hole)		12.50	20.00

10 (12)	10 Heller (Cu–Ni) 1908–1914		10.00	15.00

11 (13)	¼ Rupie (Ag) 1904–1914. Bust left of Kaiser Wilhelm II wearing helmet surmounted by eagle		12.00	20.00
12 (14)	½ Rupie (Ag) 1904–1914		30.00	50.00
13 (15)	1 Rupie (Ag) 1904–1914		12.50	22.00

EMERGENCY ISSUES

			VF	XF
14 (16)	15	Rupien (Au) 1916. African elephant (Loxodonta africana — Elephantidae)	850.00	1100.00

15 (9)	5	Heller (Bra) 1916. Filleted crown, date and abbreviation D. O. A. for Deutsch-Ostafrika. ℞ value between crossed branches	4.00	10.00
16 (10)	20	Heller 1916. Type as No. 15. Filleted crown of large type		
		a) (Cu)	130.00	160.00
		b) (Bra)	10.00	15.00
17 (10)	20	Heller 1916. Type as No. 16, but only one leaf on each branch below HELLER		
		a) (Cu)	130.00	225.00
		b) (Bra)	6.50	10.00
18 (10)	20	Heller 1916. Type as No. 16, but filleted crown of small type		
		a) (Cu)	90.00	130.00
		b) (Bra)	9.00	16.00
19 (10)	20	Heller 1916. Type as No. 18, but only one leaf on each branch below HELLER		
		a) (Cu)	6.50	12.50
		b) (Bra)	5.00	10.00

Kiaochow

1 (1)	5	Cents (Cu–Ni) 1909. Imperial eagle standing on anchor. ℞ Chinese characters	30.00	40.00

2 (2)	10	Cents (Cu–Ni) 1909	26.00	35.00

GERMAN OCCUPATION ISSUES IN THE OCCUPIED TERRITORIES 1914–1918

Belgium

100 Centimes = 1 Franc

		VF	XF
1 (38)	5 Centimes (Zi) 1915–1916. Arms (lion). ℞ value	2.00	3.00
2 (39)	10 Centimes (Zi) 1915–1917	2.00	3.00
3 (40)	25 Centimes (Zi) 1915–1918	3.00	5.00
4 (41)	50 Centimes (Zi) 1918 (with hole)	10.00	18.00

Territory of the Eastern Kommandantur

100 Kopeks = 1 Rouble

1 (A 18)	1 Kopek (Fe) 1916. Inscription: GEBIET DES OBERBEFEHLSHABERS OST, oak twigs. ℞ value and date in iron cross	3.50	6.50
2 (B 18)	2 Kopeks (Fe) 1916	3.50	6.50
3 (C 18)	3 Kopeks (Fe) 1916	3.00	6.50

GERMAN OCCUPATION ISSUES IN THE OCCUPIED TERRITORIES 1939–1945

General Issues

1 (94)	5 Pfennig (Zi) 1940–1941. Swastika. ℞ imperial eagle, value (with hole)	12.50	18.00
2 (95)	10 Pfennig (Zi) 1940–1941 (with hole)	12.50	20.00

Bohemia and Moravia

1 (B 29)	10 Heller (Zi) 1940–1944. Arms (lion). ℞ the Karl bridge in Prague	1.50	3.00

			VF	XF

2 (B 30)	20 Heller (Zi) 1940–1944. Arms (lion). ℞ sheaf of wheat	0.80	1.60
3 (B 31)	50 Heller (Zi) 1940–1944. Arms (lion). ℞ lime-tree branches and ears of wheat	2.50	4.00
4 (B 32)	1 Krone (Zi) 1941–1944. Arms (lion). ℞ lime-tree branches	1.50	2.50

Government General

1 (34)	1 Grosz (Zi) 1939. Polish eagle. ℞ value	2.50	4.00

There exists a zinc pattern piece from 1939 of identical design and denomination.

2 (35)	5 Groszy (Zi) 1939 (with hole) (also known without hole)	5.00	10.00

There exists a zinc pattern piece with hole from 1939 of identical design and denomination.

3 (36)	10 Groszy (Zi) dated 1923 but issued in 1939–45	0.80	1.50
4 (37)	20 Groszy (Zi) dated 1923 but issued in 1939–45	0.80	1.50
5 (38)	50 Groszy (Fe–Ni) 1938. Polish eagle. ℞ value within wreath	4.00	6.50

These coins exist in nickel-plated iron with and without mint mark, as well as an iron without mint mark. Three pattern pieces from 1938 exist, two of which are in nickel-plated iron, and one in aluminium, all of identical design and denomination.

A further pattern piece from 1938 exists in nickel-plated iron, of different design, but of identical denomination.

Issues for the Lodz Ghetto (Litzmannstadt)

Coins were issued by the Jewish camp authorities in the ghetto of Lodz during 1942–1943 for their own use.

Owing to lack of technical facilities at the time of striking, numerous varieties of dies and legends are encountered. There is also a difference in the thickness of the flans. Since hardly any survivors were left at the time of the closing of the ghetto very little is known about the history of the production of these coins, so that many questions – especially as to patterns – still remain unanswered.

1	10 Pfennig (Al–Mg) 1942. Star of David with ears of corn surrounded by in-		

scription: Litzmannstadt-Getto · 1942.
℞ value and inscription DER ÄLTE-
STE DER JUDEN (the elder of the
Jews); also oak leaves with small star
of David. Diameter 21 mm.

	VF	XF
	140.00	200.00

These coins were withdrawn because the authorities of the Government General took offence at the reverse side, which resembled the German 10 Pfennig piece.

2   10 Pfennig (Al–Mg) 1942. Star of David with date within circle; around, inscription as No. 1. ℞ value and circular inscription QUITTUNG ÜBER · PFENNIG (payment for · Pfennig). Diameter 19 mm — **45.00** — **65.00**

3   5 Mark. Large star of David over circular decoration; next to it inscription GETTO 1943. ℞ value on which inscription reading QUITTUNG ÜBER (denomination); circular inscription DER ÄLTESTE DER JUDEN · IN LITZMANNSTADT ·
a) 1943 (Al–Mg) — 6.50 — 12.50
b) 1943 (Al) — 8.00 — 17.50

4   10 Mark. Type as No. 3, but of larger diameter
a) 1943 (Al–Mg) — 10.00 — 20.00
b) 1943 (Al) — 10.00 — 20.00

5   20 Mark (Al) 1943. Type as No. 3, but of even larger diameter — 40.00 — 75.00

There is a specimen pattern of No. 3 in silver as well as a trial piece of a 5-Pfennig.

All valuations in the SCHÖN are stated in U.S. Dollars.

Area: 238,537 sq. km. Population: 14,000,000.

The West African country of Ghana was formed by an Act of Independence of 7th February 1957 passed by the British Parliament from the former British Crown Colony of the Gold Coast and the League of Nations mandate territory of Togoland (West Togo). Independence was proclaimed on 6th March 1957. Though a republic since 1st July 1960, Ghana is a member of the British Commonwealth and previously formed part of the British West Africa Currency Board.

Capital: Accra.

12 Pence = 1 Shilling, 20 Shillings = £ 1; since 19th July 1965:
100 Pesewas = 1 Cedi

			XF	Unc
1 (1)	½ Penny (Br) 1958. Head right of Dr. Kwame Nkrumah (1909–1972), Prime Minister 1957–1960, Head of State 1960–1966. ℞ star (emblem of state)		0.20	0.50
2 (2)	1 Penny (Br) 1958. Type as No. 1		0.20	0.50
3 (3)	3 Pence (Cu–Ni) 1958 (scalloped edge)		0.25	0.50
4 (4)	6 Pence (Cu–Ni) 1958		0.30	0.60
5 (5)	1 Shilling (Cu–Ni) 1958		0.50	0.80
6 (6)	2 Shillings (Cu–Ni) 1958		1.00	1.50

		Proof
7 (7)	10 Shillings (Ag) 1958	25.00

COMMEMORATIVE ISSUE FOR REPUBLIC DAY ON
1st JULY 1960

			Proof
8	2	£ (Au) 1960. Head right of Dr. Kwame Nkrumah. ℞ national arms, inscription 1st JULY 1960/REPUBLIC DAY	250.00

CURRENCY REFORM: 100 Pesewas = 1 Cedi

			XF	Unc
9 (8)	5	Pesewas (Cu–Ni) 1965. Head right of Dr. Kwame Nkrumah. ℞ national emblem (scalloped edge)	0.20	0.30
10 (9)	10	Pesewas (Cu–Ni) 1965. Type as No. 9	0.20	0.40
11 (10)	25	Pesewas (Cu–Ni) 1965. Type as No. 10	0.50	1.00
12 (11)	50	Pesewas (Cu–Ni) 1965. Type as No. 10	1.00	1.50
13 (12)	½	Pesewa (Br) 1967. Bush drums. ℞ emblem of state	0.10	0.30

14 (13)	1	Pesewa (Br) 1967, 1975, 1979. Type as No. 13	0.30	0.60
15 (14)	2½	Pesewas (Cu-Ni) 1967. Cocoa beans on stem (Theobroma cacao – Sterculiaceae). R arms (scalloped edge)	0.20	0.50
16 (15)	5	Pesewas (Cu-Ni) 1967, 1973, 1975. Type as No. 15 (round)	0.20	0.40
17 (16)	10	Pesewas (Cu-Ni) 1967, 1975, 1979. Type as No. 16	0.30	0.60
18 (17)	20	Pesewas (Cu-Ni) 1967, 1975, 1979. Type as No. 16	0.70	1.50

20th ANNIVERSARY OF INDEPENDENCE (2)

			Proof
19	2	£ (Au) 1977	350.00
20	4	£ (Au) 1977	850.00

FOR THE FAO COIN PLAN (3)

			XF	Unc
21 (18)	50	Pesewas (Al-Br) 1979. Type as No. 15	0.60	1.00
22 (19)	1	Cedi (Al-Br) 1979. Cauri	1.00	1.50

INTERNATIONAL YEAR OF DISABLED PERSONS

			Unc	Proof
23	50	Cedis (Ag) 1981. Rev. Emblem:		
		a)	25.00	35.00
		b) Pièfort		80.00

		Unc	Proof
24 (21)	50 Cedis 1983. Bush drums:		
	a) (Ag)		40.00
	b) (Ag), Pièfort		–.–
	c) (Cu-Ni)	6.00	
25	50 Cedis (Au) 1983. Type as No. 24		2000.00

YEAR OF THE SCOUT (2)

26 (22)	50 Cedis (Ag) 1983	20.00	35.00
27 (23)	500 Cedis (Au) 1983		350.00

Ghuraf	**Ghurfah**	Ghourfah

A town sheikhdom called itself the Ghurfah sheikhdom after the town of Al-Ghuraf situated in the wadi Hadramaut slightly to the West of Tarim (in Arabic: Ghurfah). The town is situated near the border between the two parts of the Sultanate of Kathiri, the territory of Seiwun (Seyyun) and that of Tarim, that is on the Tarim side. The fate of the Sultanate of Kathiri was that also of Ghuraf; the Sultanate of Kathiri first belonged to the Aden Protectorate, then to the eastern Protectorate of Aden and was then conquered by the South Yemen rebels without appreciable resistance on 2nd October 1967. On 27th November the People's Republic was proclaimed which in the meantime has been renamed the Democratic People's Republic Yemen.

120 Shomsih = 1 Riyal

			VF	XF
1 (4)	4	Shomsih (Ag) A. H. 1344 (1925). Arabic inscription and date in circle, the whole surrounded by ears of corn crossed below. ℞ numeral of value in the circle, the whole surrounded by ears of corn crossed below.	40.00	60.00
2 (6)	8	Shomsih (Ag) A. H. 1344 (1925). Type as No. 1	35.00	50.00
3 (8)	15	Shomsih (Ag) A. H. 1344 (1925). Type as No. 1	15.00	25.00
4 (10)	30	Shomsih (Ag) A. H. 1344 (1925). Type as No. 1	20.00	30.00
5 (11)	45	Shomsih (Ag) A. H. 1344 (1925). Type as No. 1	200.00	350.00
6 (12)	60	Shomsih (Ag) A. H. 1344 (1925). Type as No. 1	40.00	75.00

Area: 440 acres. Population: 30,000 (without the garrison).
In 1704 siege and capture by the British. Since 1830 a British Crown
Colony, since 1964 limited self-government; extended autonomy since
1st June 1969.

12 Pence = 1 Shilling, 5 Shillings = 1 Crown, 20 Shillings = 1 £;
  since February 15th, 1971: 100 New Pence = 1 Gibraltar Pound

ELIZABETH II since 1952

			Unc	**Proof**
1 (1)	1 Crown 1967. Head right of Queen Elizabeth II. R arms (castle and key)			
	a) (Ag) 1967			20.00
	b) (Cu-Ni) 1967–1970		2.50	

NEW CURRENCY (Decimal System): 100 New Pence = 1 £

2 (2)	25 New Pence 1971. R Magot (Macaca sylvana-Cercophitecidae):			
	a) (Ag)			20.00
	b) (Cu-Ni)		2.50	

COMMEMORATIVE ISSUE FOR THE SILVER WEDDING OF THE BRITISH ROYAL COUPLE ON 20th NOVEMBER 1972

3 (3)	25 New Pence 1972. R coats of arms of the alliance:			
	a) (Ag)			20.00
	b) (Cu-Ni)		2.00	

250th ANNIVERSARY OF INTRODUCTION OF THE BRITISH STERLING IN THE COLONY (3)

			Unc	Proof
4 (4)	25 £ (Au) 1975. Rev. lion with key		140.00	180.00

5 (5)	50 £ (Au) 1975. Rev. "Our Lady of Europa"		280.00	300.00

6 (6)	100 £ (Au) 1975. Rev. coat of arms		550.00	600.00

25th ANNIVERSARY OF THE SILVER JUBILEE OF HER MAJESTY QUEEN ELIZABETH II

7 (7)	25 Pence 1977:		
	a) (Ag)		20.00
	b) (Cu-Ni)	2.00	

80th ANNIVERSARY OF THE BIRTHDAY OF QUEEN MOTHER

8 (8)	1 Crown 1980:		
	a) (Ag)		22.00
	b) (Cu-Ni)	2.00	

175th ANNIVERSARY OF THE DEATH OF NELSON (2)

		Unc	Proof
9 (9)	1 Crown 1980:		
	a) (Ag)		20.00
	b) (Cu-Ni)	1.50	
10 (10)	50 £ (Au) 1980	250.00	300.00

WEDDING OF PRINCE CHARLES AND LADY DIANA (2)

		Unc	Proof
11 (11)	1 Crown 1981:		
	a) (Ag)		20.00
	b) (Cu-Ni)	2.00	
12 (12)	50 £ (Au) 1981	250.00	250.00

Values are given for each coin in U.S. Dollars and reference to Yeomannumbers.

Großbritannien   **Great Britain**   **Grande Bretagne**

Area: 94,284 sq. mi. Population: 56,400,000
The United Kingdom of Great Britain and Northern Ireland comprises England, Wales, Scotland, the northern part of Ireland and the adjacent islands. Capital: London.

4 Farthings = 1 Penny, 12 Pence = 1 Shilling,
2 Shillings = 1 Florin, 5 Shillings = 1 Crown,
20 Shillings = £ 1 or 1 Sovereign (Gold);
since 15th February 1971: 100 (New) Pence = £ 1

Mintmarks: H-Heaton;   KN – King's Norton

When no mint-mark is shown, coins were struck by the Royal Mint (London, or since 1970 at Llantrisant in Wales).

EDWARD VII 1901–1910

1 (46)   1 Farthing (Br) 1902–1910. Head right of King Edward VII (1841–1910).
℞ Britannia seated:

	Mintage	Fine	VF	XF
1902	5,125,120	0.50	1.20	4.00
1903	5,331,200	0.60	1.50	6.50
1904	3,628,800	1.50	4.00	9.00
1905	4,076,800	0.50	2.00	6.00
1906	5,340,160	0.50	1.50	5.50
1907	4,399,360	0.50	1.20	6.00
1908	4,264,960	0.50	1.80	7.00
1909	8,852,480	0.50	1.20	6.00
1910	2,298,400	2.50	6.00	9.00

2 (47) ½ Penny (Br) 1902–1910:

	Mintage	Fine	VF	XF
1902	13,672,960	0.50	1.80	6.00
1903	11,450,880	0.75	2.50	10.00
1904	8,131,200	1.50	4.00	15.00
1905	10,124,800	0.75	2.50	12.00
1906	11,101,440	0.75	2.50	10.00
1907	16,849,280	0.75	2.50	8.00
1908	16,620,800	0.80	2.00	8.00
1909	8,279,040	1.00	4.00	12.00
1910	10,769,920	1.00	3.00	10.00

3 (48) 1 Penny (Br) 1902–1910:

	Mintage	Fine	VF	XF
1902	26,976,768	0.50	1.50	6.00
1903	21,415,296	0.60	2.00	12.50
1904	12,913,152	1.00	3.00	18.50
1905	17,783,808	0.70	1.80	16.00
1906	37,989,504	0.60	1.50	12.00
1907	47,322,240	0.50	1.50	12.00
1908	31,506,048	0.60	2.00	12.00
1909	19,617,024	0.70	2.00	12.00
1910	29,549,184	0.50	1.60	10.00

Values are given for each coin in U.S. Dollars and reference to Yeoman-numbers.

4 (49) 3 Pence (Ag) 1902–1910. ℞ value
within wreath:

	Mintage	Fine	VF	XF
1902	8,283,603	0.70	1.00	5.00
1903	5,227,200	0.90	1.50	16.00
1904	3,627,360	3.00	9.00	45.00
1905	3,548,160	2.50	8.00	40.00
1906	3,152,160	1.50	6.50	32.00
1907	4,831,200	0.80	1.20	16.00
1908	8,157,600	0.80	1.20	16.00
1909	4,055,040	0.80	1.20	16.00
1910	4,563,380	0.70	1.00	13.00

5 (50) 6 Pence (Ag) 1902–1910. ℞ value
within wreath:

	Mintage	Fine	VF	XF
1902	6,382,501	0.80	2.00	30.00
1903	5,410,096	1.30	5.00	50.00
1904	4,487,098	3.00	8.00	75.00
1905	4,235,556	1.50	5.00	55.00
1906	7,641,146	1.20	4.00	35.00
1907	8,733,673	1.20	4.00	45.00
1908	6,739,491	1.50	7.50	55.00
1909	6,584,017	1.20	4.00	45.00
1910	12,490,724	0.80	2.00	25.00

6 (51) 1 Shilling (Ag) 1902–1910. Rev. Lion on
crown:

Prices for strictly unc. coins will be considerably higher.

	Mintage	Fine	VF	XF
1902	7,822,604	1.20	4.00	35.00
1903	2,061,823	4.00	18.00	100.00
1904	2,040,161	3.00	12.00	80.00
1905	488,390	40.00	150.00	600.00
1906	10,791,025	1.20	4.00	40.00
1907	14,083,418	1.75	6.00	50.00
1908	3,806,969	2.50	12.00	125.00
1909	5,664,982	2.00	9.00	100.00
1910	26,547,236	1.20	3.50	30.00

7 (52)　1 Florin (Ag) 1902–1910. ℞ Britannia standing:

	Mintage	Fine	VF	XF
1902	2,204,698	3.50	10.00	70.00
1903	1,995,298	5.50	18.00	110.00
1904	2,769,932	7.50	22.00	130.00
1905*	1,187,596	16.00	70.00	380.00
1906	6,910,128	4.00	18.00	140.00
1907	5,947,895	5.00	20.00	150.00
1908	3,280,010	7.00	30.00	200.00
1909	3,482,829	6.00	20.00	160.00
1910	5,650,713	3.00	18.00	110.00

* N. B. Beware of recent forgeries.

8 (53)　½ Crown (Ag) 1902–1910. Rev. crowned shield in Garter:

	Mintage	Fine	VF	XF
1902	1,331,131	4.00	15.00	70.00
1903	274,840	50.00	160.00	650.00
1904	709,652	26.00	90.00	400.00
1905*	166,008	100.00	400.00	1500.00
1906	2,886,206	4.50	18.00	130.00
1907	3,93,930	5.00	20.00	140.00
1908	1,758,889	6.00	25.00	185.00
1909	3,051,592	6.00	20.00	150.00
1910	2,557,685	4.00	16.00	110.00

* N. B. Beware of recent forgeries.

		VF	XF
9 (54)	1 Crown (Ag) 1902. Rev. St. George and the Dragon (271,143 pieces)	75.00	150.00

A 9   Maundy money: 1 Penny, 2 Pence, 3 Pence and 4 Pence (1 Groat), 1902 to 1910. These sets of silver coins are not intended for circulation. Such coins have been issued in Britain since 1660 for the Sovereign to perform the age-old ceremony of making a gift of money to the poor on Maundy Thursday (Y A 55–D 55):

	Mintage	VF	XF	FDC
1902	8,976	–	70.00	90.00
1903	8,976	–	70.00	90.00
1904	8,976	–	70.00	90.00
1905	8,976	–	70.00	90.00
1906	8,800	–	70.00	90.00
1907	8,760	–	70.00	90.00
1908	8,760	–	70.00	90.00
1909	1,983	–	80.00	110.00
1910	1,440	–	90.00	120.00

Maundy sets in the original dated cases are worth approximately $ 10.00 more than the above prices quoted.

10 (56) ½ Sovereign (Au) 1902–1910. Rev. St. George and the Dragon. **London mint:**

	Mintage	Fine	VF	XF
1902	4,259,580	55.00	70.00	100.00
1903	2,522,057	55.00	70.00	100.00
1904	1,717,440	55.00	70.00	100.00
1905	3,023,993	55.00	70.00	100.00
1906	4,245,437	55.00	70.00	100.00
1907	4,233,421	55.00	70.00	100.00
1908	3,996,992	55.00	70.00	100.00
1909	4,010,715	55.00	70.00	100.00
1910	5,023,881	55.00	70.00	100.00

11 (57) 1 Sovereign (Au) 1902–1910. Type as No. 10. **London mint:**

	Mintage	Fine	VF	XF
1902	4,752,919	90.00	100.00	135.00
1903	8,888,627	90.00	100.00	135.00
1904	10,041,369	90.00	100.00	135.00
1905	5,910,403	90.00	100.00	135.00
1906	10,466,981	90.00	100.00	135.00
1907	18,458,663	90.00	100.00	135.00

	Mintage	Fine	XF	Unc
1908	11,729,006	90.00	100.00	135.00
1909	12,157,099	90.00	100.00	135.00
1910	22,379,624	90.00	100.00	135.00

		VF	XF
12 (58)	2 £ (Au) 1902. Type as No. 10 (53,873 pieces)	350.00	550.00

13 (59)	5 £ (Au) 1902. Type as No. 10 (42,977 pieces)	700.00	1200.00

Branches of the Royal Mint were set up in Australia at Sydney (mintmark S), Melbourne (mintmark M), and Perth (mintmark P), as well as in Canada at Ottawa (mintmark C), for coining gold of imperial type. These coins are listed in the Australian and Canadian section of this catalogue.

GEORGE V 1910-1936

14 (60)   1 Farthing (Br) 1911-1936. Head left of King George V (1865-1936). Rev. Britannia seated:

	Mintage	Fine	VF	XF
1911	5,196,800	0.50	1.00	3.50
1912	7,669,760	0.30	0.75	2.20
1913	4,184,320	0.50	1.00	2.50
1914	6,126,988	0.30	0.75	2.50
1915	7,129,254	0.50	1.00	5.00
1916	10,993,325	0.30	0.75	3.00
1917	21,434,844	0.15	0.40	1.30
1918	19,362,818	0.15	0.40	1.30
1919	15,089,425	0.20	0.40	1.30
1920	11,480,536	0.20	0.40	1.30
1921	9,469,097	0.20	0.40	1.30
1922	9,956,983	0.20	0.40	1.30
1923	8,034,457	0.20	0.40	1.30
1924	8,733,414	0.20	0.40	1.30
1925	12,634,697	0.20	0.40	1.30
1926	9,792,397	0.20	0.40	1.20
1927	7,868,355	0.20	0.40	1.20
1928	11,625,600	0.20	0.40	1.20
1929	8,419,200	0.20	0.40	1.20
1930	4,195,200	0.20	0.40	1.80
1931	6,595,200	0.20	0.40	1.20
1932	9,292,800	0.20	0.40	0.60
1933	4,560,000	0.20	0.40	1.50
1934	3,052,800	0.30	0.60	2.20
1935	2,227,200	0.50	1.20	2.80
1936	9,734,400	0.15	0.30	0.80

15 ½ Penny (Br) 1911–1936. Type as No. 14.
Since 1925 the portrait has been slightly
modified (Y 61,62):

	Mintage	Fine	VF	XF
1911	12,570,880	0.75	1.80	6.00
1912	21,185,920	0.50	1.20	6.00
1913	17,476,480	0.80	2.00	7.00
1914	20,289,111	0.75	1.80	7.00
1915	21,563,040	0.75	1.80	7.00
1916	39,386,143	0.70	1.50	6.00
1917	38,245,436	0.70	1.50	6.00
1918	22,321,072	0.70	1.50	6.00
1919	28,104,001	0.60	1.50	6.00

	Mintage	Fine	VF	XF
1920	35,146,793	0.50	1.50	6.00
1921	28,027,293	0.60	1.50	6.00
1922	10,734,964	0.75	2.50	10.00
1923	12,266,282	0.60	1.50	8.00
1924	13,971,038	0.60	1.50	7.00
1925	12,216,123	0.60	1.60	8.00
1926	6,172,306	1.00	2.00	10.00
1927	15,589,622	0.60	1.50	6.00
1928	20,935,200	0.30	0.75	4.00
1929	25,680,000	0.25	0.75	4.00
1930	12,532,800	0.25	0.75	4.00
1931	16,137,600	0.25	0.75	4.00
1932	14,448,000	0.25	0.75	4.50
1933	10,560,000	0.25	0.75	4.00
1934	7,704,000	0.50	1.50	6.00
1935	12,180,000	0.25	0.75	4.00
1936	23,008,800	0.20	0.60	2.00

16 1 Penny (Br) 1911–1936. Type as No. 14
Since 1926 the portrait has been slightly
modified (Y 63, 64):

	Mintage	Fine	VF	XF
1911	23,079,168	0.30	1.00	9.00
1912	48,306,048	0.30	1.00	9.00
1912H	16,800,000	1.00	3.00	50.00
1913	65,497,812	0.50	1.00	9.00
1914	50,820,997	0.40	1.00	10.00
1915	47,310,807	0.50	1.00	10.00
1916	86,411,165	0.50	1.00	9.00
1917	107,905,436	0.40	0.80	7.00
1918	84,227,372	0.40	0.80	9.00
1918H	3,660,800	2.00	15.00	150.00
1918KN	3,660,800	2.50	17.00	185.00
1919	113,761,090	0.40	1.00	7.00
1919H	113,761,090	1.50	11.00	125.00
1919KN	5,209,600	3.00	22.00	240.00
1920	24,693,485	0.40	1.00	5.00

	Mintage	Fine	VF	XF
1921	29,717,693	0.30	0.80	5.00
1922	16,346,711	1.00	3.00	20.00
1926	4,498,519	1.50	4.00	30.00
1927	60,989,561	0.40	1.00	4.00
1928	50,178,000	0.25	0.50	3.00
1929	49,132,800	0.25	0.50	3.00
1930	29,097,600	0.40	1.00	5.50
1931	19,843,200	0.40	1.00	10.00
1932	8,277,600	0.80	2.50	25.00
1933*	very rare	–	–	–
1934	13,965,600	0.50	1.50	15.00
1935	56,070,000	0.25	0.60	2.50
1936	154,296,000	0.20	0.40	1.80

17 (65) 3 Pence (Ag) 1911-1926. Since 1926 the portrait has been slightly modified:

	Mintage	Fine	VF	XF
1911	5,841,084	0.50	0.70	5.00
1912	8,932,825	0.50	0.70	5.00
1913	7,143,242	0.50	0.70	5.00
1914	6,733,584	0.50	0.70	5.00
1915	5,450,617	0.50	0.70	5.00
1916	18,555,201	0.50	0.70	4.00
1917	21,662,490	0.50	0.70	4.00
1918	20,630,909	0.50	0.70	4.00
1919	16,845,687	0.50	0.70	4.00
1920	16,703,597	0.50	0.70	5.50
1921	8,749,301	0.50	0.70	4.00
1922	7,979,998	0.50	0.70	8.00
1925	3,731,859	0.90	2.00	18.00
1926	4,107,910	1.20	2.50	20.00

18 (66) 6 Pence (Ag) 1911-1927. Since 1926 the portrait has been slightly modified:

	Mintage	Fine	VF	XF
1911	9,161,317	1.50	2.50	18.00
1912	10,984,129	1.50	5.00	30.00
1913	7,499,833	1.70	6.00	40.00
1914	22,714,602	1.20	2.50	18.00

* An extremely fine specimen sold at auction for £ 15,000 in November 1985.

	Mintage	Fine	VF	XF
1915	15,694,597	1.50	2.50	18.00
1916	22,207,178	1.20	2.50	18.00
1917	7,725,475	2.00	4.00	30.00
1918	27,553,743	1.00	2.00	18.00
1919	13,375,447	1.50	2.50	20.00
1920	14,136,287	1.50	2.50	20.00
1921	30,339,741	0.80	2.00	20.00
1922	16,878,890	1.00	2.50	22.00
1923	6,382,793	1.50	5.00	30.00
1924	17,444,218	1.00	2.00	20.00
1925	12,720,558	1.00	2.00	28.00
1926	21,809,621	0.90	1.80	20.00
1927	8,924,873	1.20	2.00	25.00

19 (67) 1 Shilling (Ag) 1911–1927 Rev. Lion on crown, inner circles. Since 1926 the portrait has been slightly modified:

	Mintage	Fine	VF	XF
1911	20,071,908	1.00	3.00	20.00
1912	15,594,009	1.00	3.50	40.00
1913	9,011,509	2.50	12.00	55.00
1914	23,415,843	1.00	3.00	15.00
1915	39,279,024	1.00	3.00	15.00
1916	35,862,015	1.00	3.00	15.00
1917	22,202,608	1.00	4.00	25.00
1918	34,915,934	1.00	3.00	15.00
1919	10,823,824	1.00	4.50	25.00
1920	22,825,142	1.00	3.50	30.00
1921	22,648,763	1.00	8.00	45.00
1922	27,215,738	1.00	3.00	30.00
1923	14,575,243	1.00	3.00	28.00
1924	9,250,095	1.00	8.00	45.00
1925	5,418,764	3.00	15.00	80.00
1926	22,516,453	1.00	5.00	30.00
1927	9,247,344	1.50	4.00	35.00

Values are gives for each coin in U.S. Dollars and reference to Yeoman-numbers.

20 (68) 1 Florin (Ag) 1911–1926. ℞ the four crowned shields of the United Kingdom in cross pattern with sceptres in *saltire*:

	Mintage	Fine	VF	XF
1911	5,957,291	4.00	8.00	50.00
1912	8,571,731	4.50	13.00	55.00
1913	4,545,278	5.00	15.00	80.00
1914	21,252,701	2.50	6.00	28.00
1915	12,367,939	2.50	5.00	28.00
1916	21,064,337	2.50	5.00	28.00
1917	11,181,617	3.00	6.00	40.00
1918	29,211,792	2.50	5.00	28.00
1919	9,469,792	3.50	6.00	35.00
1920	15,387,833	3.00	7.00	45.00
1921	34,863,895	2.00	7.00	45.00
1922	23,861,044	2.00	7.00	35.00
1923	21,546,533	2.00	7.00	30.00
1924	4,582,372	3.00	8.50	70.00
1925	1,404,136	10.00	24.00	180.00
1926	5,125,410	3.00	8.50	65.00

21 (69) ½ Crown (Ag) 1911–1927. Rev. Crowned shield in Garter:

	Mintage	Fine	VF	XF
1911	2,920,580	4.50	9.00	55.00
1912	4,700,789	5.00	10.00	70.00
1913	4,090,169	6.00	12.00	80.00

	Mintage	Fine	VF	XF
1914	18,333,003	2.50	6.00	25.00
1915	32,433,066	2.00	5.00	25.00
1916	29,530,020	2.00	5.00	25.00
1917	11,172,052	2.50	6.00	40.00
1918	29,079,592	2.50	6.00	25.00
1919	10,266,737	3.00	9.00	45.00
1920	17,982,077	2.50	6.00	50.00
1921	23,677,889	2.50	7.00	70.00
1922	16,396,724	2.50	6.00	60.00
1923	26,308,526	2.00	5.00	28.00
1924	5,866,294	3.00	8.00	70.00
1925	1,413,461	10.00	40.00	250.00
1926	4,473,516	3.00	12.00	75.00
1927	6,837,872	2.50	6.00	35.00

22 (77) ½ Sovereign (Au) 1911–1915. Rev. St. George and the Dragon. **London mint:**

	Mintage	Fine	VF	XF
1911	6,107,870	55.00	70.00	100.00
1912	6,224,316	55.00	70.00	100.00
1913	6,094,290	55.00	70.00	100.00
1914	7,251,124	55.00	70.00	100.00
1915	2,042,747	55.00	70.00	100.00

23 (78) 1 Sovereign (Au) 1911–1925. Type as No. 22. **London mint:**

	Mintage	Fine	VF	XF
1911	30,047,869	80.00	90.00	150.00
1912	30,317,921	80.00	90.00	150.00
1913	24,539,672	80.00	90.00	150.00
1914	11,501,117	80.00	90.00	150.00

	Mintage	Fine	VF	XF
1915	20,295,280	80.00	90.00	150.00
1916	1,554,120	90.00	100.00	180.00
1917*	1,014,714	–	6000.00	–
1925	4,406,431	80.00	90.00	150.00

* Counterfeits exist of these and of most other dates.

Coins of imperial type (Nos. 22 and 23) with mintmark C (Ottawa), I (Bombay), M (Melbourne), P (Perth), S (Sydney) or SA (South Africa) are listed in the Australian, Canadian, Indian and South African Section of this catalogue.

Proof

24 (79) 2 £ (Au) 1911. Type as No. 22 (2,812 pieces) Forgeries exist. 1000.00

25 (80) 5 £ (Au) 1911. Type as No. 22 (2,812 pieces). Forgeries exist. 2200.00

26 (70) 3 Pence (Ag) 1927–1936. Rev. Three oak sprigs with three acorns:

	Mintage	Fine	VF	XF
1927	15,022	Proof only	–	70.00
1928	1,302,106	1.00	3.00	20.00
1930	1,319,412	0.80	2.00	15.00
1931	6,251,936	0.50	1.00	2.00
1932	5,887,325	0.50	1.00	2.00
1933	5,578,541	0.50	1.00	2.00
1934	7,405,954	0,40	1.00	2.00
1935	7,027,654	0.40	1.00	2.00
1936	3,328,670	0.50	1.00	2.00

27 (71)   6 Pence (Ag) 1927–1936. Rev. Six oak
sprigs with six acorns:

	Mintage	Fine	VF	XF
1927	15,000	Proof only	–	35.00
1928	23,123,384	0.50	0.90	10.00
1929	28,319,326	0.50	0.90	8.00
1930	16,990,289	0.50	1.00	10.00
1931	16,873,268	0.50	1.00	18.00
1932	9,406,117	1.00	2.00	30.00
1933	22,185,083	0.50	0.90	15.00
1934	9,304,009	0.50	0.90	20.00
1935	13,995,621	0.50	0.90	12.50
1936	24,380,171	0.50	0.80	7.00

28 (72)   1 Shilling (Ag) 1927-1936. Rev. lion
standing over crown:

	Mintage	Fine	VF	XF
1927	15,000	Proof only	–	35.00
1928	18,136,778	0.80	1.50	12.00
1929	19,343,006	0.80	1.50	12.00
1930	3,172,092	1.00	5.00	40.00
1931	6,993,926	0.80	1.50	16.00
1932	12,168,101	0.80	1.50	16.00
1933	11,511,624	0.80	1.50	15.00
1934	6,138,463	1.00	2.00	30.00
1935	9,183,462	0.80	1.50	15.00
1936	11,910,613	0.80	1.50	12.00

29 (73)   1 Florin (Ag) 1927–1936. ℞ the four
crowned shields of the United King-
dom in cross pattern with sceptres in
saltire

	Mintage	Fine	VF	XF
1927	101,497	Proof only	–	75.00
1928	11,087,186	1.00	2.50	15.00
1929	16,397,279	1.00	2.50	15.00
1930	5,753,568	1.20	3.00	20.00
1931	6,556,331	1.00	2.50	15.00
1932	717,041	8.50	25.00	160.00

	Mintage	Fine	VF	XF
1933	8,685,303	0.90	2.00	18.00
1935	7,540,546	0.90	2.00	15.00
1936	9,897,448	0.90	2.00	12.00

29   30

30 (74) ½ Crown (Ag) 1927–1936. Rev. Shield:

	Mintage	Fine	VF	XF
1927	15,000	Proof only		60.00
1928	18,762,727	2.00	3.00	16.00
1929	17,632,636	2.00	3.00	16.00
1930	809,051	8.00	35.00	180.00
1931	11,264,468	2.00	3.00	18.00
1932	4,793,643	3.00	8.00	50.00
1933	10,311,494	2.00	3.00	18.00
1934	2,422,399	4.00	9.00	70.00
1935	7,022,216	2.00	3.00	16.00
1936	7,039,423	2.00	3.00	15.00

31 (75) 1 Crown (Ag) 1927-1936. Rev. crown:

	Mintage	Fine	VF	XF
1927	15,030	Proof only		250.00
1928	9,034	30.00	100.00	220.00
1929	4,994	35.00	120.00	260.00
1930	4,847	35.00	120.00	260.00
1931	4,056	40.00	130.00	320.00
1932	2,395	45.00	160.00	400.00
1933	7,132	35.00	120.00	260.00
1934	932	300.00	850.00	1600.00
1936	2,473	60.00	165.00	400.00

Values are given for each coin in U.S. Dollars and reference to Yeomannumbers.

| A31 | Maundy money: 1 Penny, 2 Pence, 3 Pence and 4 Pence, 1911–1936 (Y A81–H81): |

	Mintage	XF	Unc	Proof
1911	1,786	70.00	110.00	125.00
1912	1,246	70.00	100.00	
1913	1,228	70.00	100.00	
1914	982	70.00	100.00	
1915	1,293	70.00	100.00	
1916	1,128	70.00	100.00	
1917	1,237	70.00	100.00	
1918	1,375	70.00	100.00	
1919	1,258	70.00	100.00	
1920	1,399	70.00	100.00	
1921	1,386	70.00	100.00	
1922	1,373	70.00	100.00	
1923	1,430	70.00	100.00	
1924	1,515	70.00	100.00	
1925	1,438	70.00	100.00	
1926	1,504	70.00	100.00	
1927	1,647	70.00	100.00	
1928	1,642	80.00	100.00	
1929	1,761	75.00	100.00	
1930	1,724	75.00	100.00	
1931	1,759	75.00	100.00	
1932	1,835	75.00	100.00	
1933	1,872	75.00	100.00	
1934	1,887	75.00	100.00	
1935	1,928	80.00	100.00	
1936	1,323	85.00	110.00	

Values are given for each coin in U.S. Dollars and reference to Yeoman-numbers.

	VF	XF
32 (76) 1 Crown (Ag) 1935. Rev. St. George and the Dragon:		
a) incuse lettering on edge (714, 769)	7.00	20.00
b) similar. Specimen striking issued in box.	Unc	60.00
c) raised lettering on edge (2,500) (.925 silver)	Proof	450.00

GEORGE VI 1936-1952

33 (82) 1 Farthing (Br) 1937–1948. Head left of King George VI (1895–1952). ℞ wren (Troglodytes troglodytes — Troglodydidae):

	Mintage	VF	XF	Unc
1937	8,157,602	0.20	0.40	1.50
1938	7,449,600	0.30	0.80	3.00
1939	31,440,000	0.10	0.40	0.90
1940	18,360,000	0.10	0.40	1.60
1941	27,312,000	0.10	0.20	1.00
1942	28,857,600	0.10	0.20	1.00
1943	33,345,600	0.10	0.20	0.90
1944	25,137,600	0.10	0.20	0.90
1945	23,736,000	0.10	0.20	0.90
1946	24,364,800	0.10	0.20	0.90
1947	14,745,600	0.10	0.20	0.90
1948	16,622,400	0.10	0.20	1.00

34 (83) ½ Penny (Br) 1937–1948. ℞ "The Golden Hind", flagship of Sir Francis Drake:

	Mintage	VF	XF	Unc
1937	24,530,402	0.25	0.80	3.00
1938	40,320,000	0.25	1.50	6.00
1939	28,924,800	0.25	1.50	8.00
1940	32,162,400	0.50	1.80	12.00
1941	45,120,000	0.25	1.00	10.00
1942	71,908,800	0.20	0.60	3.00
1943	76,200,000	0.20	1.00	3.00
1944	81,840,000	0.20	1.00	3.00
1945	57,000,000	0.20	1.00	5.00
1946	22,725,600	0.50	2.00	12.00
1947	21,266,400	0.20	1.50	5.00
1948	26,947,200	0.20	0.80	3.00

35 (84) 1 Penny (Br) 1937–1948. ℞ Britannia seated:

	Mintage	VF	XF	Unc
1937	88,922,402	0.30	1.20	3.00
1938	121,560,000	0.30	1.20	3.00
1939	55,560,000	0.50	2.00	10.00
1940	42,284,400	0.50	2.00	12.00
1944	42,600,000	0.50	2.50	14.00
1945	79,531,200	0.50	1.50	10.00
1946	66,855,600	0.30	1.20	3.00
1947	52,220,400	0.25	1.00	3.00
1948	63,961,200	0.25	1.00	3.00

36 (85) 3 Pence (Ni-Bra) 1937–1948. Rev. Thrift
(Allium porrum – Liliaceae) – em-
blem of Wales (dodecagonal):

	Mintage	VF	XF	Unc
1937	45,734,359	0.50	1.00	2.50
1938	14,532,332	0.80	3.00	12.00
1939	5,603,021	1.50	5.00	30.00
1940	12,636,018	0.80	2.00	10.00
1941	60,239,489	0.35	0.80	5.00
1942	103,214,400	0.30	0.70	3.00
1943	101,702,400	0.25	0.70	3.00
1944	69,760,000	0.25	0.80	4.00
1945	33,942,466	0.50	1.20	8.00
1946	620,734	6.00	60.00	250.00
1948	4,230,400	2.00	6.00	30.00

37 (86) 3 Pence (Ag) 1937–1944. ℞ shield on
rose:

	Mintage	VF	XF	Unc
1937	8,174,558	0.50	0.90	2.50
1938	6,402,473	0.50	0.90	2.50
1939	1,355,860	1.50	6.00	15.00
1940	7,914,401	0.30	1.00	5.00
1941	7,979,411	0.30	1.00	5.00
1942*	4,144,051	2.00	10.00	22.00
1943*	1,397,220	3.00	15.00	30.00
1944*	2,005,533	5.00	22.00	50.00

* For colonial use only.

Values are given for each coin in U.S. Dollars and reference to Yeomannumbers.

38   6 Pence 1937–1948. Rev. crown above
      monogram (Y 87, 95):

	Mintage	VF	XF	Unc
1937 (Ag)	22,328,926	0.60	1.00	6.00
1938 (Ag)	13,402,701	1.00	2.00	12.00
1939 (Ag)	28,670,304	0.60	1.00	8.00
1940 (Ag)	20,875,196	0.50	1.00	8.00
1941 (Ag)	23,086,616	0.50	1.00	8.00
1942 (Ag)	44,942,785	0.40	0.80	8.00
1943 (Ag)	46,927,111	0.40	0.80	3.00
1944 (Ag)	36,952,600	0.35	0.70	3.00
1945 (Ag)	39,939,259	0.30	0.60	3.00
1946 (Ag)	43,466,407	0.30	0.60	3.00
1947 (Cu-Ni)	29,993,263	0.15	0.60	4.00
1948 (Cu-Ni)	88,323,540	0.15	0.50	3.00

39   1 Shilling 1937–1948. Rev. Lion on
      large crown »English»
      type (Y 88, 96):

	Mintage	VF	XF	Unc
1937 (Ag)	8,385,524	0.70	1.60	10.00
1938 (Ag)	4,833,436	1.25	4.00	30.00
1939 (Ag)	11,052,677	0.50	1.20	10.00
1940 (Ag)	11,099,126	0.60	1.50	10.00
1941 (Ag)	11,391,883	0.60	1.50	10.00
1942 (Ag)	17,453,643	0.40	1.00	7.50
1943 (Ag)	11,404,213	0.40	1.00	7.50
1944 (Ag)	11,586,751	0.40	1.00	7.50
1945 (Ag)	15,143,404	0.30	0.80	5.00
1946 (Ag)	18,663,797	0.30	0.80	5.00
1947 (Cu-Ni)	12,120,611	0.25	0.90	8.00
1948 (Cu-Ni)	45,576,923	0.15	0.50	5.00

40   1 Shilling 1937–1948. Rev. Lion seated
facing on crown »Scottish«
type (Y 89, 97):

	Mintage	VF	XF	Unc
1937 (Ag)	6,775,277	0.70	1.60	10.00
1938 (Ag)	4,797,852	1.25	4.00	30.00
1939 (Ag)	10,263,892	0.60	1.50	10.00
1940 (Ag)	9,913,089	0.60	1.50	12.00
1941 (Ag)	8,086,030	0.60	1.60	12.00
1942 (Ag)	13,676,759	0.60	1.50	10.00
1943 (Ag)	9,824,214	0.60	1.50	10.00
1944 (Ag)	10,990,167	0.60	1.50	10.00
1945 (Ag)	15,106,270	0.30	0.80	5.00
1946 (Ag)	16,381,501	0.30	0.80	5.00
1947 (Cu-Ni)	12,283,223	0.20	0.60	7.50
1948 (Cu-Ni)	45,351,937	0.15	0.50	4.00

41   2 Shillings 1937–1948. Rev. crown above
rose, thistle and shamrock (Y 90, 98):

	Mintage	VF	XF	Unc
1937 (Ag)	13,033,183	0.80	1.60	12.00
1938 (Ag)	7,909,388	1.50	6.00	30.00
1939 (Ag)	20,850,607	0.70	1.50	10.00
1940 (Ag)	18,700,338	0.70	1.50	10.00
1941 (Ag)	24,451,079	0.70	1.50	8.00
1942 (Ag)	39,895,243	0.50	1.25	8.00
1943 (Ag)	26,711,987	0.50	1.25	8.00
1944 (Ag)	27,560,005	0.50	1.25	8.00
1945 (Ag)	25,858,049	0.50	1.25	8.00
1946 (Ag)	22,300,254	0.50	1.25	8.00

	Mintage	VF	XF	Unc
1947 (Cu-Ni)	22,910,085	0.25	0.80	5.00
1948 (Cu-Ni)	67,553,636	0.25	0.70	4.50

42   ½ Crown 1937–1948. Rev. Shield (Y 91, 99):

	Mintage	VF	XF	Unc
1937 (Ag)	9,132,842	1.00	2.00	12.00
1938 (Ag)	6,426,478	2.00	6.00	30.00
1939 (Ag)	15,478,635	0.80	1.80	10.00
1940 (Ag)	17,948,439	0.80	1.80	10.00
1941 (Ag)	15,773,984	0.80	1.80	10.00
1942 (Ag)	31,220,090	0.70	1.70	10.00
1943 (Ag)	15,462,875	0.70	1.80	12.00
1944 (Ag)	15,255,165	0.70	1.70	7.50
1945 (Ag)	19,849,242	0.70	1.70	7.50
1946 (Ag)	22,724,873	0.70	1.70	7.50
1947 (Cu-Ni)	21,911,484	0.40	0.90	7.50
1948 (Cu-Ni)	71,164,703	0.30	0.60	5.00

		VF	XF
43 (92)	1 Crown (Ag) 1937. Crowned shield supported by lion for England and unicorn for Scotland (445,101 pieces)	10.00	25.00

A43

Maundy money: 1 Penny, 2 Pence,
3 Pence and 4 Pence, 1937–1948
(Y A93–D93):

	Mintage	XF	Unc	Proof
1937	1,325	45.00	100.00	100.00
1938	1,275	45.00	100.00	
1939	1,234	45.00	100.00	
1940	1,277	45.00	100.00	
1941	1,253	45.00	100.00	
1942	1,231	45.00	100.00	
1943	1,239	45.00	100.00	
1944	1,259	45.00	100.00	
1945	1,355	45.00	100.00	
1946	1,365	45.00	100.00	
1947	1,375	45.00	100.00	
1948	1,385	45.00	100.00	

44 (100) ½ Sovereign (Au) 1937. St. George and
the Dragon (5,501 pieces)   Proof   350.00

45 (101) 1 Sovereign (Au) 1937. Type as No. 44
(5,501 pieces)   Proof   750.00

Proof

46 (102) 2 £ (Au) 1937. Type as No. 44
(5,501 pieces)   800.00

47 (103) 5 £ (Au) 1937. Type as No. 44
(5.501 pieces)   1300.00

48 (104) 1 Farthing (Br) 1949-1952. Type as No. 33,
but shorter inscription:

	Mintage	XF	Unc	Proof
1949	8,424,000	0,50	1.80	
1950	10,342,313	0,25	1.00	8.00
1951	14,036,000	0,25	1.00	6.00
1952	5,251,200	0,50	1.20	

NB. The coins dated 1952 were issued during the reign of Elizabeth II.

Values are given for each coin in U.S. Dollars and reference to Yeoman-numbers.

49 (105) ½ Penny (Br) 1949–1952. Type as No. 34, but shorter inscription:

	Mintage	XF	Unc	Proof
1949	24,744,000	1.00	7.50	
1950	524,171,113	1.00	6.00	8.00
1951	14,888,000	1.00	7.50	8.00
1952	33,278,400	0.85	3.50	

50 (106) 1 Penny (Br) 1949–1951. Type as No. 35, but shorter inscription:

	Mintage	XF	Unc	Proof
1949	14,324,400	1.00	2.50	
1950	257,513	12.50	40.00	32.00
1951	140,000	16.00	35.00	30.00

51 (107) 3 Pence (Ni-Bra) 1949–1952. Type as No. 36, but shorter inscription (dodecagonal):

	Mintage	XF	Unc	Proof
1949	464,000	70.00	250.00	
1950	1,617,513	12.00	45.00	50.00
1951	1,204,000	12.00	50.00	50.00
1952	25,494,400	0.80	5.00	

52 (108) 6 Pence (Cu-Ni) 1949-1952. Type similar to
No. 38; shorter inscription:

	Mintage	XF	Unc	Proof
1949	41,335,515	0.80	5.50	
1950	32,759,468	0.80	5.50	7.50
1951	40,419,491	0.80	5.50	7.00
1952	1,013,477	16.00	55.00	

53 (109) 1 Shilling (Cu–Ni) 1949–1951. Type as
No. 39, but shorter inscription:

	Mintage	XF	Unc	Proof
1949	19,328,405	1.00	10.00	
1950	19,261,385	1.00	10.00	12.00
1951	9,976,930	1.25	10.00	12.00

54 (110) 1 Shilling (Cu–Ni) 1949–1951. Type as
No. 40, but shorter inscription:

	Mintage	XF	Unc	Proof
1949	21,243,074	1.00	10.00	
1950	14,317,114	1.00	9.00	10.00
1951	10,981,174	1.00	9.00	10.00

55 (111) 2 Shillings (Cu-Ni) 1949-1951. Type as
No. 41, but shorter inscription:

	Mintage	XF	Unc	Proof
1949	28,614,939	1.00	11.00	
1950	24,375,003	1.00	10.50	16.00
1951	27,431,747	1.00	11.00	16.00

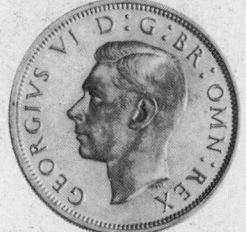

56 (112) ½ Crown (Cu–Ni) 1949–1952. Type as
No. 42, but shorter inscription:

	Mintage	XF	Unc	Proof
1949	28,272,512	1,50	10.00	
1950	28,353,013	1.50	11.00	18.00
1951	9,023,520	1.50	12.50	18.00

1952, extremely rare (1 specimen known).

COMMEMMORATIVE ISSUE FESTIVAL OF BRITAIN

57 (114) 1 Crown (Cu-Ni) 1951. Type as No. 44,
but shorter inscription (1,983,540 pieces; Proof 10.00
A57 Maundy money: 1 Penny, 2 Pence,
3 Pence and 4 Pence, 1949–1952
(Y A113–D113):

	Mintage	VF	XF	Unc
1949	1,395	40.00	45.00	100.00
1950	1,405	40.00	45.00	100.00
1951	1,468	40.00	45.00	100.00
1952	1,012	45.00	50.00	110.00

ELIZABETH II since 1952

		Unc	Proof
58 (116)	1 Farthing (Br) 1953. Head right of Queen Elizabeth II (*1926). Rev. wren (6,171,037 pieces)	1.00	6.00
59 (117)	½ Penny (Br) 1953. Rev. »The Golden Hind« (8,966,366 pieces)	3.00	8.00

		Unc	Proof
60 (118)	1 Penny (Br) 1953. Rev. Britannia seated (1,348,400 pieces)	8.00	12.00
61 (119)	3 Pence (Ni-Bra) 1953. Rev. portcullis with chains (30,658,000 pieces)	2.00	8.00
62 (120)	6 Pence (Cu–Ni) 1953 R rose (Rosa gallica – Rosaceae), emblem of England; thistle (Cirsium vulgare – Compositae), emblem of Scotland; shamrock (Trifolium repens – Leguminosae), emblem of Northern Ireland; thrift plant (Allium porrum – Liliaceae), emblem of Wales (70,363,876 pieces)	1.00	5.00

Values are given for each coin in U.S. Dollars and reference to Yeoman-numbers.

		Unc	Proof

63 (121) 1 Shilling (Cu-Ni) 1953. Rev. arms of England (41,982,894 pieces)   1.50   8.00

64 (122) 1 Shilling (Cu-Ni) 1953. Rev. arms of Scotland (20,703,528 pieces)   1.50   8.00

65 (123) 2 Shillings (Cu-Ni) 1953. Rev. rose within circle, the border made of horse-thistle, white clover leaves and thrift plant (11,998,710 pieces)   5.00   12.50

66 (124) ½ Crown (Cu-Ni) 1953. Rev. crowned arms (4,373,214 pieces)   6.00   15.00

CORONATION OF QUEEN ELIZABETH II

67 (125) 1 Crown (Cu–Ni) 1953. Queen Elizabeth II on horseback. R crown surrounded by the arms and emblems of England, Scotland, Northern Ireland and Wales (6,002,621 pieces)   5.00   50.00

A67   Maundy money: 1 Penny, 2 Pence, 3 Pence and 4 Pence, 1953 (1,025 sets)   500.00
(Y A126–D126):

Gold coins of nominal value £ ½, 1, 2 and 5 with date 1953 were issued as sets in very limited quantities for special purposes.

68 (127)   1 Farthing (Br) 1954-1956. Type as No. 58, but shorter inscription:

	Mintage	VF	XF	Unc
1954	6,566,400	0.15	0.40	1.50
1955	5,779,200	0.15	0.40	1.50
1956	1,996,800	0.40	0.70	4.00

69 (128)   ½ Penny (Br) 1954–1967. Type as No. 59, but shorter inscription:

	Mintage	VF	XF	Unc
1954	19,375,000	0.30	1.00	6.00
1955	18,799,200	0.20	0.80	5.00
1956	21,799,200	0.20	0.80	5.50
1957	43,684,888		0.20	1.00
1958	62,318,400			0.50
1959	79,176,000			0.30
1960	41,340,000			0.30
1962	41,779,200			0.20
1963	45,036,000			0.20
1964	78,583,200			0.20
1965	98,083,200			0.20
1966	95,289,600			0.20
1967	146,491,200			0.20

70 (A128)   1 Penny (Br) 1954, 1961–1967. Type as No. 60, but shorter inscription:

	Mintage	VF	XF	Unc
1954			extremely rare	
1961	48,313,400	0.15	0.30	0.80
1962	143,308,600	0.10	0.15	0.30
1963	125,235,600		0.15	0.30
1964	153,294,000			0.20
1965	121,310,400			0.20
1966	165,739,200			0.20
1967	654,564,000			0.20

Values are given for each coin in U.S. Dollars and reference to Yeoman-numbers.

71 (129) 3 Pence (Ni–Bra) 1954–1967. Type as
No. 61, but shorter inscription:

	Mintage	VF	XF	Unc
1954	41,720,000	0.20	0.60	8.00
1955	41,075,200	0.20	0.60	10.00
1956	36,801,600	0.20	0.60	10.00
1957	24,294,500	0.20	0.60	6.00
1958	20,504,000	0.30	1.00	12.00
1959	28,499,200	0.20	0.50	6.00
1960	83,078,400	0.15	0.40	6.00
1961	41,102,400		0.15	0.50
1962	51,545,600		0.15	0.50
1963	39,482,866			0.30
1964	44,867,200			0.30
1965	27,160,000			0.30
1966	53,160,000			0.30
1967	151,780,800			0.20

72 (130) 6 Pence (Cu–Ni) 1954–1967. Type as
No. 62, but shorter inscription:

	Mintage	VF	XF	Unc
1954	105,241,150	0.20	0.50	6.00
1955	109,929,554	0.10	0.25	1.20
1956	109,841,555		0.25	1.20
1957	105,654,290		0.20	1.00
1958	123,518,527		0.80	8.00
1959	93,089,441		0.15	0.50
1960	103,283,346		0.70	8.00
1961	115,052,017		0.50	6.00
1962	166,483,637		0.10	0.40
1963	120,056,000		0.10	0.30
1964	152,336,000		0.10	0.25
1965	129,644,000		0.10	0.25

	Mintage	VF	XF	Unc
1966	175,676,000		0.10	0.25
1967	240,788,000		0.10	0.25

73 (131) 1 Shilling (Cu-Ni) 1954–1966. Type as No. 63 (»English« type), but shorter inscription:

	Mintage	VF	XF	Unc
1954	30,262,032	0.20	0.40	4.00
1955	45,259,908	0.20	0.40	4.00
1956	44,907,008	0.40	1.00	15.00
1957	42,774,217		0.30	2.00
1958	14,392,305		3.00	30.00
1959	19,442,778		0.25	2.00
1960	27,027,914		0.25	1.20
1961	39,816,907		0.20	1.00
1962	36,704,379		0.20	0.70
1963	49,433,607		0.10	0.30
1964	8,590,900		0.15	0.40
1965	9,216,000		0.15	0.40
1966	15,002,000		0.15	0.40

74 (132) 1 Shilling (Cu-Ni) 1954–1966. Type as No. 64 (»Scottish« type), but shorter inscription:

	Mintage	VF	XF	Unc
1954	26,771,735	0.15	0.60	4.00
1955	27,950,906	0.15	0.60	6.00
1956	42,853,639	0.20	1.00	15.00
1957	17,959,988	0.50	3.00	30.00
1958	40,822,557	0.15	0.30	2.00
1959	1,012,988	1.00	3.00	30.00
1960	14,376,932		0.30	2.00
1961	2,762,558		0.80	10.00
1962	17,475,310		0.30	1.50
1963	32,300,000		0.15	0.30
1964	5,239,100		0.20	0.70
1965	2,774,000		0.20	0.70
1966	15,604,000		0.20	0.40

Values are given for each coin in U.S. Dollars and reference to Yeoman-numbers.

75 (133) 2 Shillings (Cu–Ni) 1954–1967. Type as No. 65, but shorter inscription:

	Mintage	VF	XF	Unc
1954	13,085,422	1.00	4.00	60.00
1955	25,887,253	0.15	0.80	5.00
1956	47,824,500	0.15	0.80	5.00
1957	33,071,282	0.70	3.00	40.00
1958	9,564,580	0.20	1.50	20.00
1959	14,080,319	0.30	3.50	50.00
1960	13,831,782		0.60	3.00
1961	37,735,315		0.25	3.00
1962	35,147,903		0.20	2.00
1963	26,471,000		0.20	1.00
1964	16,539,000		0.15	0.80
1965	48,163,000		0.15	0.70
1966	83,999,000		0.15	0.70
1967	39,718,000		0.15	0.70

76 (134) ½ Crown (Cu–Ni) 1954–1967. Type as No. 66, but shorter inscription:

	Mintage	VF	XF	Unc
1954	11,614,953	0.90	4.00	30.00
1955	23,628,726	0.40	1.00	8.00
1956	33,934,909	0.40	1.20	10.00
1957	34,200,563	0.30	0.80	3.00
1958	15,745,668	0.90	4.00	22.00

	Mintage	VF	XF	Unc
1959	9,028,844	0.90	4.00	30.00
1960	19,929,191	0.50	1.00	5.00
1961	25,887,897	0.20	0.50	2.00
1962	24,013,312	0.20	0.50	2.00
1963	17,625,200	0.20	0.50	2.00
1964	5,973,600	0.50	1.00	6.00
1965	9,778,440	0.20	0.50	2.00
1966	13,375,200	0.15	0.40	1.00
1967	33,058,400	0.15	0.40	1.00

BRITISH EXHIBITION IN NEW YORK

		Unc	Proof
77 (136)	5 Shillings (Cu–Ni) 1960. Head right of Queen Elizabeth II. ℞ crown surrounded by the arms and emblems of England, Scotland, Northern Ireland and Wales (1,094,038 pieces)	10.00	30.00

A77 Maundy money: 1 Penny, 2 Pence, 3 Pence and 4 Pence, 1954– (Y A135–D135):

	Mintage		XF	Unc
1954	1,020	Westminster	35.00	110.00
1955	1,036	Southwark	35.00	110.00

	Mintage		XF	Unc
1956	1,088	Westminster	35.00	110.00
1957	1,094	St. Albans	35.00	110.00
1958	1,100	Westminster	35.00	110.00
1959	1,106	Windsor	35.00	110.00
1960	1,112	Westminster	35.00	110.00
1961	1,118	Rochester	35.00	110.00
1962	1,125	Westminster	35.00	110.00
1963	1,131	Chelmsford	35.00	110.00
1964	1,137	Westminster	35.00	110.00
1965	1,143	Canterbury	35.00	110.00
1966	1,206	Westminster	35.00	110.00
1967	986	Durham	35.00	110.00
1968	964	Westminster	35.00	110.00
1969	1,002	Selby	35.00	110.00
1970	980	Westminster	35.00	110.00
1971	1,018	Tewkesbury Abbey	35.00	110.00
1972	1,026	York Minster	35.00	110.00
1973	1,004	Westminster Abbey	35.00	110.00
1974	1,042	Salisbury Cathedral	35.00	110.00
1975	1,050	Peterborough Cathedral	35.00	110.00
1976	1,158	Hereford Cathedral	35.00	110.00
1977	1,138	Westminster Abbey	80.00	130.00
1978	1,138	Carlisle Cathedral	35.00	110.00
1979	1,188	Winchester Cathedral	35.00	110.00
1980	1,198	Worcester Cathedral	35.00	110.00
1981	1,208	Westminster Abbey	35.00	110.00
1982	1,218	St. David's Cathedral	35.00	110.00
1983	1,218	Exeter Cathedral	35.00	110.00
1984	1,243	Southwell Minster	90.00	150.00
1985	1,248	Ripon Cathedral	90.00	150.00
1986		Chichester Cathedral	90.00	150.00
1987		Ely Cathedral	110.00	170.00
1988			–.–	–.–

78 (137) 1 Sovereign (Au) 1957-1959, 1962-1968.
Head right of Queen Elizabeth II. Rev.
St. George and the Dragon:

	XF	Unc
	90.00	150.00

79 (138) 1 Crown (Cu–Ni) 1965. Head right of Queen Elizabeth II. ℞ Head of Sir Winston Churchill (1874–1965), statesman (19,640,000 pieces)

	XF	Unc
	0.60	1.00

NEW CURRENCY (Decimal System): 100 New Pence = £ 1

80 (139) ½ New Penny (Br) 1971–1981. Bust right of Queen Elizabeth II by Arnold Machin. Rev. the Tudor crown, crown of King Henry VII, founder of the House of Tudor:

	Mintage	XF	Unc	Proof
1971	1,394,188,250	0.05	0.10	3.00
1972	127,000	Proof only		3.00
1973	365,680,000	0.05	0.10	2.00
1974	365,448,000	0.05	0.10	2.00
1975	197,600,000	0.05	0.10	2.00
1976	256,000,000	0.05	0.10	2.00
1977	103,420,000	0.05	0.10	2.00
1978	59,650,000	0.05	0.10	2.00
1979	217,600,000	0.05	0.10	2.00
1980		0.05	0.10	2.00
1981		0.05	0.10	2.00

81 (140) 1 New Penny (Br) 1971–1981. Rev. portcullis with chains surmounted by royal crown, from the badge of King Henry VII (1457–1509):

	Mintage	XF	Unc	Proof
1971	1,521,666,250	0.05	0.10	3.50
1972	127,000	Proof only		2.50
1973	280,196,000	0.05	0.15	2.00
1974	330,892,000	0.05	0.15	2.00
1975	221,604,000	0.05	0.15	2.00
1976	241,800,000	0.05	0.15	2.00
1977	544,512,000	0.05	0.15	2.00
1978	292,888,000	0.05	0.15	2.00
1979	387,000,000	0.05	0.15	2.00
1980		0.05	0.15	2.00
1981		0.05	0.15	2.00

82 (141) 2 New Pence (Br) 1971–1981. Rev. Plumes over Prince's crown with fillets inscribed with motto »Ich dien«, badge of the Prince of Wales:

	Mintage	XF	Unc	Proof
1971	1,454,856,250	0.05	0.10	4.00
1972	127,000	Proof only		3.00
1973	102,000	Proof only		2.00
1974	104,000	Proof only		2.00
1975	144,406,000	0.10	0.15	2.00
1976	135,772,000	0.10	0.15	2.00
1977	109,533,000	0.10	0.15	2.00
1978	189,776,000	0.10	0.15	2.00
1979	157,600,000	0.10	0.15	2.00
1980		0.10	0.15	2.00
1981		0.10	0.15	2.00

83 (142)　　5 New Pence (Cu-Ni) 1968–1981. Rev.
horse-thistle, emblem of Scotland,
surmounted by royal crown:

	Mintage	XF	Unc	Proof
1968	98,868,250	0.15	0.20	
1969	119,270,000	0.15	0.20	
1970	225,948,525	0.15	0.20	
1971	81,783,475	0.15	0.20	5.00
1972	231,000	Proof only		3.00
1973	102,000	Proof only		3.00
1974	104,000	Proof only		3.00
1975	86,550,000	0.15	0.20	3.00
1976	108,000	Proof only		3.00
1977	24,366,000	0.15	0.20	3.00
1978	61,000,000	0.15	0.20	3.00
1979	133,056,000	0.15	0.20	3.00
1980		0.15	0.20	3.00
1981		Proof only		3.00

84 (143)　　10 New Pence (Cu-Ni) 1968–1981. Rev. lion
passant guardant wearing royal crown,
part of the English arms:

	Mintage	XF	Unc	Proof
1968	336,143,250	0.20	0.30	
1969	314,008,000	0.20	0.40	
1970	133,571,000	0.20	0.40	
1971	63,205,000	0.25	0.50	5.50
1972	65,000	Proof only		3.00
1973	152,174,000	0.20	0.30	3.00
1974	92,741,000	0.20	0.30	3.00
1975	181,559,000	0.20	0.30	3.00
1976	196,745,000	0.20	0.30	3.00
1977	12,920,000	0.20	0.30	3.00

	Mintage	XF	Unc	Proof
1978	118,000	Proof only		3.00
1979	64,289,000	0.20	0.30	3.00
1980		0.20	0.30	3.00
1981		0.20	0.30	3.00

85 (144) 50 New Pence (Cu-Ni) 1969–1981. Rev. Britannia seated (seven-sided):

	Mintage	XF	Unc	Proof
1969	188,400,000	0.90	2.50	
1970	19,461,000	1.25	5.00	
1971	191,000	Proof only		7.00
1972	65,000	Proof only		5.00
1973	42,000	Proof only		5,00
1974	41,000	Proof only		5,00
1975	37,000	Proof only		5,00
1976	51,396,000	0.90	1.50	5.00
1977	49,788,000	0.90	1.50	5.00
1978	72,214,000	0.90	1.25	5.00
1979	40,345,000	0.90	1.25	5.00
1980		0.90	1.25	5.00
1981		0.90	1.25	5.00

Values are given for each coin in U.S. Dollars and reference to Yeoman-numbers.

SILVER WEDDING OF THE BRITISH ROYAL COUPLE
ON 20th NOVEMBER 1972

			Unc	Proof
86 (145)	25 New Pence 1972. R Crowned monogram:			
	a) (Ag); (100,000 pieces)			25.00
	b) (Cu-Ni); (7,452,100 pieces)		1.50	

ACCESSION TO EUROPEAN ECONOMIC COMMUNITY

	Unc	Proof
87 (146) 50 New Pence (Cu-Ni) 1973. Rev. value and clasped hands (80,306,000 pieces)	2.00	7.50

88 (B137) ½ Sovereign (Au) 1980, 1982–1984. Rev. St. George and the dragon, like No. 78:

	Mintage	Unc	Proof
1980	10,000		110.00
1982	23,000	90.00	110.00
1983	23,000		110.00
1984	23,000		110.00

89 (A137) 1 Sovereign (Au) 1974–1984.
      Type as No. 88:

	Mintage	Unc	Proof
1974	5,002,566	150.00	
1976	4,150,000	150.00	
1978	6,685,000	150.00	
1979	50,000	150.00	170.00
1980	100,000	150.00	160.00
1981	5,055,000	150.00	160.00
1982	23,000	150.00	160.00
1983	23,000		160.00
1984	23,000		180.00

90 (C137) 2 £ (Au) 1980, 1982, 1983.
      Type as No. 88:

		Unc	Proof
1980	10,000		450.00
1982	2,500		550.00
1983	12,500		450.00

91 (D137) 5 £ (Au) 1980–1982, 1984.
      Type as No. 88:

1980	10,000		950.00
1981	15,000		850.00
1982			950.00
1984			850.00
1984 U			600.00

SILVER JUBILEE OF HER MAJESTY QUEEN ELIZABETH II

92 (147) 25 Pence 1977. Queen Elizabeth II on
    horseback. Rev. Ampulla and spoon:
    a) (Ag); (473,000 pieces) — 20.00
    b) (Cu-Ni); (37,453,000 pieces) — 1.00

80th BIRTHDAY OF QUEEN MOTHER

93 (148) 25 Pence 1980:
    a) (Ag)   35.00
    b) (Cu-Ni)   1.00

WEDDING OF PRINCE CHARLES AND LADY DIANA

	Unc	Proof
94 (149) 25 Pence 1981. Rev. Conjoined heads 1.:		
a) (Ag)		30.00
b) (Cu-Ni)	1.25	
95 (150) ½ Penny (Br) 1982–1984.		
Type as No. 80	0.10	1.00
96 (151) 1 Penny (Br) 1982–1984.		
Type as No. 81	0.15	1.25

97 (152) 2 Pence (Br) 1982–1984. Type as No. 82	0.75	1.50

		Unc	Proof
98 (153)	5 Pence (Cu-Ni) 1982–1984. Type as No. 83	0.20	1.50

		Unc	Proof
99 (154)	10 Pence (Cu-Ni) 1982–1984. Type as No. 84	0.60	2.00

		Unc	Proof
100 (155)	20 Pence (Cu-Ni) 1982–1984. Rev. rose, emblem of England, surmounted by royal crown	0.50	6.00
101 (156)	50 Pence (Cu-Ni) 1982–1984. Type as No. 85	1.00	3.50

		Unc	Proof
102 (157)	1 £ (Ni-Bra) 1983. U. K. type. Edge DE-CUS ET TUTAMEN	2.00	6.00
103 (155a)	20 Pence (Ag) 1982. Type as No. 100		40.00
104 (157a)	1 £ (Ag) 1983. Type as No. 102:		
	a) normal thickness		50.00
	b) Pièfort		180.00

				Unc	Proof
105 (158)	1 £ (Ni-Bra) 1984. Scottish type. Edge NEMO ME IMPUNE LACESSIT			2.00	6.00
106 (158a)	1 £ (Ag) 1984. Type as No. 105:				
	a) normal thickness				40.00
	b) Pièfort				110.00
107 (159)	1 Penny (Br) 1985–. Elizabeth II, new portrait, after Raphael David Maklouf. Rev. Portcullis with chains			0.05	

108 (160)	2 Pence (Br) 1985–. Rev. Plumes			0.05	
109 (161)	5 Pence (Cu-Ni) 1985–. Rev. Crowned thistle			0.10	
110 (162)	10 Pence (Cu-Ni) 1985–. Rev. Lion passant guardant			0.15	

111 (163)	20 Pence (Cu-Ni) 1985–. Rev. Crowned double rose			0.30	
112 (164)	50 Pence (Cu-Ni) 1985–. Rev. Britannia seated			0.80	
113 (165)	1 £ (Ni-Bra) 1985. Rev. Thrift plant (Welsh type). Edge PLEIDIOL WYF I'M GWLAD			2.00	
114 (165a)	1 £ (Ag) 1985. Type as No. 113:				
	a) normal thickness				40.00
	b) Piéfort				110.00
115 (166)	½ Sovereign (Au) 1985–. Rev. St. George and the dragon				120.00
116 (167)	1 Sovereign (Au) 1985–. Type as No. 115				200.00

	Unc	Proof
117 (168) 2 £ (Au) 1985, 1987. Type as No. 115		450.00
118 (169) 5 £ (Au) 1985, 1986. »U« in a circle to left of date. Type as No. 115:		
a) 1985		650.00
b) 1985 U, 1986 U	600.00	

Note: For the uncouped portrait version see No. 125.

119	1 £ (Ni-Bra) 1986. Rev. Shamrock (Northern Ireland type). Edge DE-CUS ET TUTAMEN	2.00	
120	1 £ (Ag) 1986. Type as No. 119:		
	a) normal thickness		40.00
	b) Piéfort		110.00

XIII COMMONWEALTH GAMES IN EDINBURGH (2)

121	2 £ 1986. Rev. St. Andrew's cross surmounted by a thistle and laurel branches:		
	a) (Ag) 925 fine		60.00
	b) (Ag) 500 fine	30.00	
	c) (Ni-Bra)	5.00	

		Unc	Proof
122	2 £ (Au) 1986. Type as No. 121. 916⅔ fine, 15.98 g		450.00
123	1 £ (Ni-Bra) 1987. Rev. Oak tree (English type). Edge DECUS ET TUTAMEN	2.00	
124	1 £ (Ag) 1987. Type as No. 123:		
	a) 925 fine, 9.5 g		40.00
	b) Piéfort		80.00

		Unc	Proof
125	5 £ (Au) 1987 U. Type as No. 118, but uncouped portrait of Queen Elizabeth II, »U« in a circle to left of date		900.00

BULLION ISSUE »BRITANNIA« (4)

		Unc	Proof
126	10 £ (Au) 1987. Elizabeth II. Rev. Britannia; .916⅔ gold, ¹/₁₀ ounce:		
	a) »NATHAN«	–.–	
	b) »P. NATHAN«, Proof only		–.–
127	25 £ (Au) 1987. Type as No. 126, ¼ ounce:		
	a) »NATHAN«	–.–	
	b) »P. NATHAN«, Proof only		–.–
128	50 £ (Au) 1987. Type as No. 126, ½ ounce:		
	a) »NATHAN«	–.–	
	b) »P. NATHAN«, Proof only		–.–
129	100 £ (Au) 1987. Type as No. 126, 1 ounce:		
	a) »NATHAN«	–.–	
	b) »P. NATHAN«, Proof only		–.–

130	1 £ (Ni-Bra) 1988. Rev. the Royal Arms, surmounted by the crown of Queen Elizabeth II.	2.00	
131	1 £ (Ag) 1988. Type as No. 130:		
	a) 925 fine, 9.5 g	30.00	40.00
	b) Piéfort		80.00

TERCENTENARY OF THE BILL OF RIGHTS OF 1689

132	2 £ (Ni-Bra) 1989	–.–	

BRITISH TRADE DOLLAR

The Trade Dollar was destined for the Far East. The issues were made mostly in Bombay and Calcutta, less frequently by the Royal Mint in London.

			VF	XF
T1 (T1)	1	Dollar (Ag) 1895–1935. Standing Britannia with spear and shield, date and value. ℞ value in Chinese and Malay	16.50	28.00

Guernsey

Area: 31 sq. mi. Population: 54,000.
The Bailiwick of Guernsey also comprises, in addition to the more important island bearing this name, the islands of Alderney, Brechon, Herm, Jethou, Lihou and Sark (Sercq).
Capital: St. Peter Port.

8 Doubles = 1 Penny, 12 Pence = 1 Shilling,
20 Shillings = 1 £; 100 New Pence = 1 £

EDWARD VII 1901–1910

			VF	XF
1 (1)	1 Double (Br) 1902, 1903. Three leaves of the Guernsey lily above shield. ℞ value		1.00	2.00
2 (2)	2 Doubles (Br) 1902, 1903, 1906, 1908. Type as No. 1		12.00	20.00
3 (3)	4 Doubles (Br) 1902, 1903, 1906, 1908, 1910. Type as No. 1		3.50	7.00
4 (4)	8 Doubles (Br) 1902, 1903, 1910. Type similar to No. 1		3.00	6.00

GEORGE V 1910–1936

5 (1)	1 Double (Br) 1911. Type as No. 1	2.00	4.50
6 (2)	2 Doubles (Br) 1911. Type as No. 2	10.00	20.00
7 (3)	4 Doubles (Br) 1911. Type as No. 3	7.50	15.00
8 (4)	8 Doubles (Br) 1911. Type as No. 4	10.00	22.00

9 (1a)	1 Double (Br) 1911, 1914, 1929, 1933. Type similar to No. 5	1.00	2.00
10 (2a)	2 Doubles (Br) 1914, 1917, 1918, 1920, 1929. Type as No. 9	3.00	6.00
11 (3a)	4 Doubles (Br) 1914, 1918, 1920. Type as No. 9	2.00	4.00
12 (5)	8 Doubles (Br) 1914, 1918, 1920, 1934. Type similar to No. 8	2.00	4.50

GEORGE VI 1936–1952

13 (1a)	1 Double (Br) 1938. Type as No. 9	1.00	2.00
14 (3a)	4 Doubles (Br) 1945, 1949. Type as No. 11	1.50	3.00
15 (5)	8 Doubles (Br) 1938, 1945, 1947, 1949. Type as No. 12	1.00	2.50

ELIZABETH II since 1952

16 (6)	4 Doubles (Br) 1956–1966. Arms, inscription for the first time BALLIVIE

	VF	XF

(BAILIWICK) INSULE DE GERNE-
REVE. ℞ Guernsey lily, value in letters   1.00   2.00

17 (7)   8 Doubles (Br) 1956–1966. Arms. ℞ three
flowers of the Guernsey lily (Nerine
sarniensis – Amaryllidaceae)   0.50   1.00

18 (8)   3 Pence (Cu–Ni) 1956. Arms. ℞ Guernsey cow (Bos primigenius taurus –
Bovidae)   0.50   1.00

19 (8a)   3 Pence (Cu–Ni) 1959–1966. Type as
No. 18, but thicker flan   0.25   0.50

COMMEMORATIVE ISSUE FOR THE 900th
ANNIVERSARY OF THE BATTLE OF HASTINGS

20 (9)   10 Shillings (Cu–Ni) 1966. Head of Queen
Elizabeth II. ℞ head of William the
Conqueror (1027–1087), Duke of Nor-
mandy, as William I, King of England
1066–1087   1.00   2.00

NEW CURRENCY (Decimal System): 100 New Pence = 1 £

		XF	Unc

21 (10)   ½ New Penny (Br) 1971. Arms. ℞ value,
date   0.10   0.20

22 (11)   1 New Penny (Br) 1971. Gannet   0.10   0.20

23 (12)   2 New Pence (Br) 1971. Old windmill
(1571) from the island of Sark   0.10   0.20

			XF	Unc
24 (13)	5	New Pence (Cu-Ni) 1968, 1971. Arms. Rev. value, date; flower of the Guernsey lily	0.15	0.30

			XF	Unc
25 (14)	10	New Pence (Cu-Ni) 1968, 1970, 1971. Obverse as No. 24. Rev. value, date; Guernsey cow	0.30	0.50

			XF	Unc
26 (15)	50	New Pence (Cu-Ni) 1969, 1970, 1971. Obverse as No. 24. Rev. The Ducal Cap of the Duke of Normandy, value and date (sevensided)	1.20	1.80

COMMEMORATIVE ISSUE FOR THE SILVER WEDDDING OF THE BRITISH ROYAL COUPLE ON 20th NOVEMBER 1972

			Unc	Proof
27 (16)	25	New Pence 1972. Rev. Eros, the God of Love		20.00
		a) (Ag)		
		b) (Cu-Ni)	6.00	

SILVER JUBILEE OF HER MAJESTY QUEEN ELIZABETH II

			Unc	Proof
28 (17)	25	Pence 1977. Rev. Caste Cornet:		15.00
		a) (Ag)		
		b) (Cu-Ni)	1.75	

			XF	Unc
29 (18)	½ Penny (Br) 1979. Type as No. 21		0.10	0.20
30 (19)	1 Penny (Br) 1977, 1979, 1981. Type as No. 22		0.15	0.25

			XF	Unc
31 (20)	2 Pence (Br) 1977, 1979, 1981. Type as No. 23		0.15	0.25
32 (21)	5 Pence (Cu-Ni) 1977, 1979, 1981, 1982. Type as No. 24		0.25	0.40
33 (22)	10 Pence (Cu-Ni) 1977, 1979, 1981, 1982. Type as No. 25		0.40	0.70
34 (23)	50 Pence (Cu-Ni) 1979, 1981–1983. Type as No. 26		1.20	1.80

ROYAL VISIT

		Unc	Proof
35 (24)	25 Pence 1978:		
	a) (Ag)		15.00
	b) (Cu-Ni)	1.50	

80th BIRTHDAY OF QUEEN MOTHER

		Unc	Proof
36 (25)	25 Pence 1980:		
	a) (Ag)		17.50
	b) (Cu-Ni)	1.50	

					Unc	Proof
37 (26)	1 £ (Ni-Bra) 1981. Arms. Rev. Guernsey lily				2.50	
38 (26a)	1 £ (Au) 1981. Type as No. 37:					
	a) 8.00 gm.					200.00
	b) 16.00 gm. (Pièfort)					500.00

WEDDING OF PRINCE CHARLES AND LADY DIANA

			Unc	Proof
39 (27)	25 Pence 1981. Rev. Heads of Prince Charles and Lady Diana Spencer:			
	a) (Ag)			27.50
	b) (Cu-Ni)		2.00	

			XF	Unc
40 (28)	20 Pence (Cu-Ni) 1982, 1983. Rev. Guurnsey milk can		0.50	0.75
41 (29)	1 £ (Ni-Bra) 1983		2.00	2.50
42	1 Penny (Br) 1985, 1986		0.10	0.20
43	2 Pence (Br) 1985, 1986		0.10	0.20
44	5 Pence (Cu-Ni) 1985, 1986		0.15	0.25
45	10 Pence (Cu-Ni) 1985, 1986		0.20	0.35
46	20 Pence (Cu-Ni) 1985, 1986		0.50	0.75
47	50 Pence (Cu-Ni) 1985, 1986		1.10	1.50
48	1 £ (Ni-Bra) 1985, 1986		2.00	2.50

40th ANNIVERSARY OF THE END OF WORLD WAR II

			Unc	Proof
49	2 £ 1985. Rev. Two doves with olive branch:			
	a) (Ag)			40.00
	b) (Cu-Ni)		5.00	

		Unc	Proof
50	2 £ 1986:		
	a) (Ag) .925 silver, 28.28 g		30.00
	b) (Ag) .500 silver, 28.28 g	15.00	
	c) (Cu-Ni)	6.00	

900th ANNIVERSARY OF THE DEATH OF WILLIAM THE CONQUEROR

51	2 £ 1987. Rev. William the Conqueror (1027–1087), Duke of Normandy:		
	a) (Ag) .925 silver, 28.28 g		30.00
	b) (Cu-Ni)	6.00	
52	2 £ (Au) 1987. Type as No. 51; .916⅔ gold, 47.54 g (90 pcs.)		2000.00

Jersey

Area: 45 sq. mi. Population: 74,000.

The Bailiwick of Jersey also comprises, in addition to the main island of the same name, the islands of Les Boeuftins, Les Dironilles, Les Ecrehos and Les Minquiers. The group of islands of Jersey, like those of Guernsey, has an autonomous government with its own Constitution. It is a dependency of the British Crown, but does not form part of the United Kingdom.

Capital: St. Hélier.

12 Pence = 1 Shilling, 20 Shillings = 1 £;
100 New Pence = 1 £

EDWARD VII 1901–1910

			VF	XF
1 (9)	$^1/_{24}$	Shilling (Br) 1909. Crowned bust right of King Edward VII. ℞ arms	5.00	12.00
2 (10)	$^1/_{12}$	Shilling (Br) 1909. Type as No. 1	4.50	15.00

GEORGE V 1910–1936

3 (11)	$^1/_{24}$	Shilling (Br) 1911–1923. Crowned bust left of King George V. ℞ pointed shield	5.00	12.50
4 (12)	$^1/_{12}$	Shilling (Br) 1911–1923. Type as No. 3	2.50	8.00
5 (13)	$^1/_{24}$	Shilling (Br) 1923–1926. ℞ blunter shield	3.00	6.00
6 (14)	$^1/_{12}$	Shilling (Br) 1923–1926. Type as No. 5	2.00	4.00
7 (15)	$^1/_{24}$	Shilling (Br) 1931–1935	2.50	5.00
8 (16)	$^1/_{12}$	Shilling (Br) 1931–1935	1.50	3.00

GEORGE VI 1936–1952

9 (17)	$^1/_{24}$	Shilling (Br) 1937–1947. Crowned head left of King George VI. ℞ arms	2.50	5.00
10 (18)	$^1/_{12}$	Shilling (Br) 1937–1947	1.00	2.00
11 (19)	$^1/_{12}$	Shilling (Br) 1949–1952. Type as No. 11, but with inscription LIBERATED 1945	0.40	0.80

ELIZABETH II since 1952

			VF	XF
12 (20)	$\frac{1}{12}$	Shilling (Br) 1954. Crowned head right of Queen Elizabeth II. ℞ arms, inscription LIBERATED 1945	0.40	0.80
13 (21)	$\frac{1}{12}$	Shilling (Br) 1957–1964. ℞ arms, inscription for the first time BAILIWICK OF JERSEY	0.20	0.40
14 (22)	$\frac{1}{4}$	Shilling (Ni–Bra) 1957–1960	0.20	0.40

COMMEMORATIVE ISSUE FOR KING CHARLES II
(reigned 1660–1685)

15 (23)	$\frac{1}{12}$	Shilling (Br) 1960. Crowned head r. of Queen Elizabeth II. ℞ arms and date 1660–1960	0.20	0.50
16 (24)	$\frac{1}{4}$	Shilling (Ni-Br) 1964 (dodecagonal)	0.20	0.50

COMMEMORATIVE ISSUES (3) FOR THE 900th ANNIVERSARY OF THE BATTLE OF HASTINGS

17 (25)	$\frac{1}{12}$	Shilling (Br) 1966. ℞ arms and date 1066–1966	0.20	0.50
18 (26)	$\frac{1}{4}$	Shilling (Ni–Bra) 1966. Type similar to No. 16, but with date 1066–1966	0.20	0.50
19 (27)	5	Shillings (Cu–Ni) 1966. ℞ arms and date 1066–1966	1.00	2.00

NEW CURRENCY (Decimal System): 100 New Pence = 1 £

			XF	Unc
20 (28)	½	New Penny (Br) 1971, 1980	0.10	0.20
21 (29)	1	New Penny (Br) 1971, 1980	0.10	0.20
22 (30)	2	New Pence (Br) 1971, 1975, 1980	0.10	0.20

23 (31)	5	New Pence (Cu-Ni) 1968, 1980. Head of Queen Elizabeth II. Rev. arms, value and date	0.15	0.25

					XF	Unc
24 (32)	10	New Pence (Cu-Ni) 1968, 1975, 1980. Type as No. 23			0.30	0.70
25 (33)	50	New Pence (Cu-Ni) 1969, 1980. Type as No. 23, but seven-sided			1.00	2.00

COMMEMORATIVE ISSUES (9) FOR THE SILVER WEDDING OF THE BRITISH ROYAL COUPLE

			Unc	Proof
26 (34)	50	Pence (Ag) 1972. ℞ Royal Mace and map	6.00	8.00
27 (35)	1	£ (Ag) 1972. ℞ Belladonna lily (Amaryllis belladonna – Amaryllidaceae)	10.00	15.00
28 (36)	2	£ (Ag) 1972. ℞ the sailing ship Alexandra	35.00	35.00

29 (37)	2½	£ (Ag) 1972. R lobster (Homarus gammarus – Homaridae)	20.00	35.00
30 (38)	5	£ (Au) 1972. R garden shrew (Crocidura suaveolens – Soricidae)	50.00	80.00
31 (39)	10	£ (Au) 1972. R a magnificent Gold Torque weighing 746 gms used as jewelry ab. 1500 B.C. was excavated 1889 in St. Hélier, Jersey	85.00	110.00
32 (40)	20	£ (Au) 1972. R the Ormer Shell (Haliotis tuberculata – Haliotidae)	150.00	175.00

			Unc	Proof
33 (41)	25 £ (Au) 1972. ℞ the Royal Arms of England 1593, are cut in granite above the Main Gate of Elizabeth Castle, where King Charles II found refuge		200.00	220.00
34 (42)	50 £ (Au) 1972. ℞ the Arms of Jersey, Three Golden Lions, are derived from the Arms of King Edward I through a Seal granted to Jersey in 1279		400.00	425.00

SILVER JUBILEE OF HER MAJESTY QUEEN ELIZABETH II

			Unc	Proof
35 (43)	25 Pence 1977:			
	a) (Ag)			17.50
	b) (Cu-Ni)		2.00	
36 (44)	½ Penny (Br) 1981. Elizabeth II. Rev. Arms between devided date		0.10	1.00
37 (45)	1 Penny (Br) 1981. Type as No. 36		0.15	1.25
38 (46)	2 Pence (Br) 1981. Type as No. 36		0.20	1.50
39 (47)	5 Pence (Cu-Ni) 1981. Type as No. 36		0.25	2.00
40 (48)	10 Pence (Cu-Ni) 1981. Type as No. 36		0.60	2.50
41 (49)	50 Pence (Cu-Ni) 1981. Type as No. 36		2.00	3.50

BICENTENNIAL BATTLE OF JERSEY (2)

42 (50)	1 £ 1981:			
	a) (Ag)			15.00
	b) (Cu-Ni)		3.00	
43 (50b)	1 £ (Au) 1981			400.00

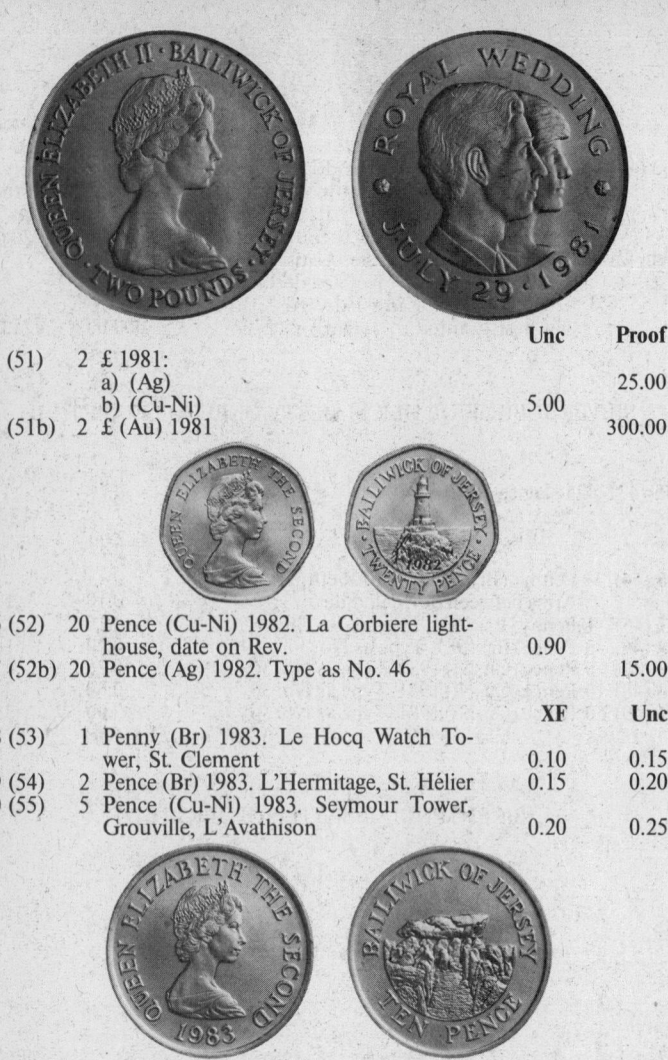

			Unc	Proof
44 (51)	2 £ 1981:			
	a) (Ag)			25.00
	b) (Cu-Ni)		5.00	
45 (51b)	2 £ (Au) 1981			300.00

			Unc	Proof
46 (52)	20	Pence (Cu-Ni) 1982. La Corbiere light-house, date on Rev.	0.90	
47 (52b)	20	Pence (Ag) 1982. Type as No. 46		15.00

			XF	Unc
48 (53)	1	Penny (Br) 1983. Le Hocq Watch Tower, St. Clement	0.10	0.15
49 (54)	2	Pence (Br) 1983. L'Hermitage, St. Hélier	0.15	0.20
50 (55)	5	Pence (Cu-Ni) 1983. Seymour Tower, Grouville, L'Avathison	0.20	0.25

			XF	Unc
51 (56)	10	Pence (Cu-Ni) 1983. La Hougue Bie, Faldouet, St. Martin	0.50	0.60
52 (52)	20	Pence (Cu-Ni) 1983. La Corbiere Light-house, date on obv.	0.70	0.90

			Unc	Proof
53 (57)	50 Pence (Cu-Ni) 1983, 1984. Grosnez Castle		1.20	1.50
54–59	No. 48–53, in silver, proof only			–.–

Nos. 60–65 omitted.

66	1 £ (Ni-Bra) 1983. St. Hélier		2.50	
67	1 £ (Ag) 1983. Type as No. 66			25.00
68	1 £ (Au) 1983. Type as No. 66			400.00
69	1 £ (Ni-Bra) 1984. St. Saviour		2.50	
70	1 £ (Ag) 1984. Type as No. 69			25.00
71	1 £ (Au) 1984. Type as No. 69			400.00
72	1 £ (Ni-Bra) 1984. St. Brelade		2.50	
73	1 £ (Ag) 1984. Type as No. 72			25.00
74	1 £ (Au) 1984. Type as No. 72			400.00

40th ANNIVERSARY OF LIBERATION (3)

75	50 Pence (Cu-Ni) 1985. Rev. Union Jack and flag of Jersey		2.00	
76	2 £ 1985. Rev. H.M.S. Beagle:			
	a) (Ag)			45.00
	b) (Cu-Ni)		6.00	
77	2 £ (Au) 1985. Type as No. 76			1600.00
78	1 £ (Ni-Bra) 1985. St. Clement		2.50	
79	1 £ (Ag) 1985. Type as No. 78			25.00
80	1 £ (Au) 1985. Type as No. 78			400.00
81	1 £ (Ni-Bra) 1985. St. Lawrence		2.50	
82	1 £ (Ag) 1985. Type as No. 81			25.00
83	1 £ (Au) 1985. Type as No. 81			400.00

COMMONWEALTH GAMES IN EDINGBURGH

84	2 £ 1986. Rev. Two sprinters:		
	a) (Ag). 925 silver, 28.28 g		27.50
	b) (Ag). 500 silver, 28.28 g	17.50	
	c) (Cu-Ni) with edge inscription	5.00	
	d) (Cu-Nr) without edge inscription	10.00	
85	1 £ (Ni-Bra) 1986. St. Peter	2.50	
86	1 £ (Ag) 1986. Type as No. 85		25.00
87	1 £ (Au) 1986. Type as No. 85		400.00
88	1 £ (Ni-Bra) 1986. Grouville	2.50	
89	1 £ (Ag) 1986. Type as No. 88		25.00
90	1 £ (An) 1986. Type as No. 88		400.00

25 th ANNIVERSARY OF WORLD WILDLIFFE FUND

91	2 £ 1986. Rev. Dove:		
	a) (Ag) .925 silver, 28.28 g		50.00
	b) (Cu-Ni)	6.00	
92	1 £ (Ni-Bra) 1987. St. Martin	2.50	
93	1 £ (Ag) 1987. Type as No. 92		25.00
94	1 £ (Au) 1987. Type as No. 92		400.00
95	1 £ (Ni-Bra) 1987. St. Ouen	2.50	
96	1 £ (Ag) 1987. Type as No. 95		25.00
97	1 £ (Au) 1987. Type as No. 95		400.00

Due to issue within the next years:
1 £ coins showing the parish arms of Trinity, St. John and St. Mary.

Isle of Man

Area: 227 sq. mi. Population: 68,000.
Since the 14th century this island in the Irish Sea has belonged to
England. It has had its own constitution and judical system since 1866.
The PM mintmark is that of the Pobjoy Mint in Sutton, England. Capital:
Douglas.

12 Pence = 1 Shilling, 20 Shillings = 1 £;
100 New Pence = 1 £

200th ANNIVERSARY OF THE REVESTMENT ACT (3)

		Unc	Proof
1	½ £ (Au) 1965. Crowned head right of Queen Elizabeth II. R triskelion (three legs joined in centre), emblem of the Isle of Man with circular motto QUOCUMQUE JECERIS STABIT (how ever you throw him he will stand):		
	a) .917 gold	85.00	
	b) .980 gold		90.00

		Unc	Proof
2	1 £ (Au) 1965. Type as No. 1:		
	a) .917 gold	150.00	
	b) .980 gold		175.00
3	5 £ (Au) 1965. Type as No. 1:		
	a) .917 gold	600.00	
	b) .980 gold		700.00

4 (1) 1 Crown 1970. Crowned bust right of
        Queen Elizabeth II. R manx cat, in
        exergue value and date:

	Unc	Proof
a) (Ag)		27.50
b) (Cu-Ni)	4.00	

NEW CURRENCY (Decimal System): 100 New Pence = 1 £

5 (2) ½ New Penny (Br) 1971. Elizabeth II,
        head right. R St. James's weed (Senecio
        jacobaea – Compositae). National flow-
        er (Cushag). This medicinal herb blos-
        soms around St. James's Day (25th
        July), key date for the second mowing

	Unc	Proof
a) 1971	0.15	2.00
b) 1972 PM - 1975 PM	0.20	

6 (3) 1 New Penny (Br) 1971. R Celtic cross
        (chain cross)

	Unc	Proof
a) 1971	0.40	2.00
b) 1972 PM - 1975 PM	0.30	

7 (4) 2 New Pence (Br) 1971. R falcon (Falco
        rusticolus – Falconidae) originally
        given to a feudal lord on the occasion
        of his coronation

	Unc	Proof
a) 1971	0.50	2.00
b) 1972 PM - 1975 PM	0.30	

8 (5) 5 New Pence (Cu–Ni) 1971. R "Tower
        of Refuge" at the harbour entrance of
        the capital Douglas, on the east side of
        the island. The tower was built in 1832,
        by the founder of the "Royal National
        Lifeboat Institution", Sir William
        Hillary (1771–1847):

	Unc	Proof
a) 1971	0.60	4.00
b) 1972 PM-1975 PM	0.40	

9 (6) 10 New Pence (Cu–Ni) 1971. ℞ triskelion, emblem of the Isle of Man. Originating in Sicily, this old emblem appeared for the first time on the arms of Henry de Bello Monte in 1310, and on those of the Earl of Moray in 1313

	Unc	Proof
a) 1971	0.80	3.50
b) 1972 PM - 1975 PM	0.50	

10 (7) 50 New Pence (Cu–Ni) 1971. ℞ Viking ship. Vikings on the Isle of Man: two Viking periods are to be distinguished: a) around 800 to the battle of Hastings (1066) and b) 1079 to 1266. The Viking ship under full sails is documented on 12th and 13th century seals

a) 1971	1.50	8.00
b) 1972 PM–1975 PM	1.20	

11 (2a) ½ New Penny (Ag) 1975 PM. Type as No. 5 — 15.00

12 (3a) 1 New Penny (Ag) 1975 PM. Type as No. 6 — 18.00

13 (4a) 2 New Pence (Ag) 1975 PM. Type as No. 7 — 20.00

14 (5a) 5 New Pence (Ag) 1975 PM. Type as No. 8 — 25.00

15 (6a) 10 New Pence (Ag) 1975 PM. Type as No. 9 — 30.00

16 (7a) 50 New Pence (Ag) 1975 PM. Type as No. 10 — 40.00

17 (2b) ½ New Penny (Platinum) 1975 PM. Type as No. 5 — *165.00*

18 (3b) 1 New Penny (Platinum) 1975 PM. Type as No. 6 — *200.00*

19 (4b) 2 New Pence (Platinum) 1975 PM. Type as No. 7 — *220.00*

			Unc	Proof

20 (5b) · 5 New Pence (Platinum) 1975 PM. Type as
No. 8 .... *260.00*

21 (6b) 10 New Pence (Platinum) 1975 PM. Type as
No. 9 .... *330.00*

22 (7b) 50 New Pence (Platinum) 1975 PM. Type as
No. 10 .... *400.00*

COMMEMORATIVE ISSUE FOR THE SILVER WEDDING OF THE BRITISH ROYAL COUPLE

23 (8) 25 New Pence 1972:
a) (Ag) 35.00
b) (Cu-Ni) 6.00

24 (9) ½ Sovereign (Au) 1973–1978. Head right.
Rev. Viking warrior on horseback:
a) 1973 A, 1974 A 100.00
b) 1974 B (1,798 pieces) 120.00
c) 1975–1978, without die mark ... 100.00
d) 1973–1978; Proof 120.00

25 (10) 1 Sovereign (Au) 1973–1978. Type as
No. 24:
a) 1973 A, 1974 A 135.00
b) 1973 B, 1974 B 120.00
c) 1973 C, 1974 C 135.00
d) 1973 X (1 piece) *400.00*
e) 1975–1978, without die mark ... 120.00
f) 1973–1978; Proof 150.00

26 (11) 2 £ (Au) 1973–1978. Type as No. 24:
a) 1973 A, 1974 A 265.00
b) 1974 B (120 pieces) 350.00
c) 1975–1978, without die mark ... 265.00
d) 1973–1978; Proof 300.00

27 (12) 5 £ (Au) 1973–1978. Type as No. 24:
a) 1973 A, 1974 A 600.00
b) 1973 B, 1974 B 600.00
c) 1973 C (712 pieces) 550.00
d) 1973 D (809 pieces) 550.00
e) 1973 E (33 pieces) 1000.00
f) 1975–1978, without die mark ... 550.00
g) 1973–1978; Proof 600.00

COMMEMORATIVE ISSUE FOR THE CENTENARY OF BIRTH
OF SIR WINSTON CHURCHILL

				Unc	Proof
28 (13)	1	Crown 1974. Full-face portrait of Sir Winston Churchill, after Yousef Karsh:			
		a) (Ag)		12.50	17.50
		b) (Cu-Ni)		2.50	
29 (14)	25	Pence 1975. Manx cat:			
		a) (Ag)		12.50	17.50
		b) (Cu-Ni)		2.50	

BICENTENARY OF AMERICAN INDEPENDENCE (3)

			Unc	Proof
30 (21)	1	Crown 1976. Profile of George Washington (1732-1799), 1st President of the United States of America, after Jean-Antoine Houdon:		
		a) (Ag)	12.50	17.50
		b) (Cu-Ni)	2.50	

A 30	1 Crown (Au) 1976. Type as No. 30		–.–
B 30	1 Crown (Platinum) 1976. Type as No. 30		–.–

CENTENARY OF THE HORSE-DRAWN TRAMS

			Unc	Proof
31 (22)	1	Crown 1976. Horse-drawn Tram, Douglas Promenade:		
		a) (Ag)	12.50	17.50
		b) (Cu-Ni)	2.50	
32 (15)	½	Penny (Br) 1976, 1978. Atlantic herring (Clupes harengus – Clupeidae)	0.20	
33 (16)	1	Penny (Br) 1976–1978. Loaghtyn sheep (Capra aegagrus hircus – Bovidae)	0.20	
34 (17)	2	Pence (Br) 1976–1978. Manx shearwater (Puffinus puffinus – Procellariidae)	0.30	

				Unc	Proof
35 (18)	5	Pence (Cu-Ni) 1976–1978. Laxey Wheel	0.50	
36 (19)	10	Pence (Cu-Ni) 1976–1978. Triskelion	1.00	
37 (20)	50	Pence (Cu-Ni) 1976–1978. Viking long-ship	2.20	
38 (18.1)	5	Pence (Cu-Ni) 1976. Type as No. 35, but Rev. without mintmark PM	0.80	
39 (19.2)	10	Pence (Cu-Ni) 1976. Type as No. 36, but Rev. without mintmark PM	1.10	
40 (15a)	½	Penny (Ag) 1976, 1978. Type as No. 32		18.00
41 (16a)	1	Penny (Ag) 1976–1978. Type as No. 33		22.00
42 (17a)	2	Pence (Ag) 1976–1978. Type as No. 34		28.00
43 (18a)	5	Pence (Ag) 1976–1978. Type as No. 35		30.00
44 (19a)	10	Pence (Ag) 1976–1978. Type as No. 36		38.00
45 (20a)	50	Pence (Ag) 1976–1978. Type as No. 37		50.00
46 (15b)	½	Penny (Platinum) 1976, 1978. Type as No. 32		*200.00*
47 (16b)	1	Penny (Platinum) 1976, 1978. Type as No. 33		*250.00*
48 (17b)	2	Pence (Platinum) 1976, 1978. Type as No. 34		*270.00*
49 (18b)	5	Pence (Platinum) 1976, 1978. Type as No. 35		*320.00*
50 (19b)	10	Pence (Platinum) 1976, 1978. Type as No. 36		*400.00*
51 (20b)	50	Pence (Platinum) 1976, 1978. Type as No. 37		*500.00*

SILVER JUBILEE OF HER MAJESTY QUEEN ELIZABETH II (3)

52 (23) 1 Crown 1977. Triskelion surrounded by three St. Edward's crowns and cushag; commemorative legend:

	Unc	Proof
a) (Ag)	15.00	20.00
b) (Cu-Ni)	3.00	

A 52 1 Crown (Au) 1977. Type as No. 52   –.–
B 52 1 Crown (Platinum) 1977. Type as No. 52   –.–

53 (25) 1 Crown 1977. Crowned monogram and coat of arms between laurel branches:

	Unc	Proof
a) (Ag)	15.00	20.00
b) (Cu-Ni)	2.50	

ISSUE FOR THE FAO COIN PLAN (2)

54 (24) ½ Penny (Br) 1977. Elizabeth II, inscription ELIZABETH THE SECOND. Rev. as No. 32, but inscription F.A.O./FOOD FOR ALL added:

a) map with mintmark PM	0.20
b) map without mintmark	0.20

55 (24a) ½ Penny (Ag) 1977. Type as No. 54a   15.00

			Unc	Proof
56 (26)	1	Crown 1978. Rev. falcons:		
		a) (Ag)	15.00	20.00
		b) (Cu-Ni)	2.50	
57 (27)	1	£ (Virenium) 1978–1981. Rev. triskelion and map:		
		a) 1978, 1979, 1981 AA	3.00	
		b) 1978, 1979 AB	3.00	
		c) 1978, 1979 AC	3.00	
		d) 1978 AD (3,780 pieces)	12.00	
		e) 1980, without die mark	3.00	
		f) 1978, 1980; proof		20.00
58 (27a)	1	£ (Ag) 1978–1980. Type as No. 57		*25.00*
A58 (27c)	1	£ (Au) 1980. Type as No. 57, .917 gold, 8 gm.		*350.00*
59 (27b)	1	£ (Platinum) 1978–1980. Type as No. 57		*400.00*

300th ANNIVERSARY OF MANX COINAGE

			Unc	Proof
60 (28)	1	Crown 1979. Rev. different coins:		
		a) (Ag)	15.00	20.00
		b) (Cu-Ni)	2.50	

MILLENIUM OF TYNWALD (40)
(different coins with Millenium symbol)

			XF	Unc
61 (15.1)	½ Penny (Br) 1979. Type as No. 32, but with Millenium symbol (circle containing stylized triskelion)		0.10	0.15
62 (16.1)	1 Penny (Br) 1979. Type as No. 33		0.10	0.15
63 (17.1)	2 Pence (Br) 1979. Type as No. 34		0.15	0.20
64 (18.2)	5 Pence (Cu-Ni) 1979. Type as No. 35		0.25	0.40
65 (19.3)	10 Pence (Cu-Ni) 1979. Type as No. 36		0.50	0.80
66 (20.1)	50 Pence (Cu-Ni) 1979. Type as No. 37		1.50	1.85
67 (27.1)	1 £ (Virenium) 1979. Type as No. 57:			
	a) 1979 AA		2.00	2.50
	b) 1979 AB		2.00	2.50
	c) 1979 AC		2.00	2.50

		Unc	Proof
68 (15.1a)	½ Penny (Ag) 1979. Type as No. 40		15.00
69 (16.1a)	1 Penny (Ag) 1979. Type as No. 41		18.00
70 (17.1a)	2 Pence (Ag) 1979. Type as No. 42		22.00
71 (18.2a)	5 Pence (Ag) 1979. Type as No. 43		25.00
72 (19.3a)	10 Pence (Ag) 1979. Type as No. 44		30.00
73 (20.1a)	50 Pence (Ag) 1979. Type as No. 45		40.00

No. 74, 75 omitted.

76 (15.1b)	½ Penny (Platinum) 1979. Type as No. 46		*165.00*
77 (16.1b)	1 Penny (Platinum) 1979. Type as No. 47		*200.00*
78 (17.1b)	2 Pence (Platinum) 1979. Type as No. 48		*220.00*
79 (18.2b)	5 Pence (Platinum) 1979. Type as No. 49		*260.00*
80 (19.3b)	10 Pence (Platinum) 1979. Type as No. 50		*330.00*
81 (20.1b)	50 Pence (Platinum) 1979. Type as No. 51		*400.00*

No. 82 omitted.

83 (35)	½ Sovereign (Au) 1979. Type as No. 24		*135.00*
84 (36)	1 Sovereign (Au) 1979. Type as No. 25		*175.00*
85 (37)	2 £ (Au) 1979. Type as No. 26		*330.00*
86 (38)	5 £ (Au) 1979. Type as No. 27		*650.00*

87 (34.2)	50 Pence 1979. Viking ship »Odin's Raven« with Millenium symbol and inscription »DAY OF TYNWALD/JULY 5th«; plain edge:		
	a) (Ag)	40.00	50.00
	b) (Cu-Ni)	3.00	

88 (34b)   50 Pence (Platinum) 1979. Type as No. 87   *1000.00*

89 (29)   1 Crown 1979. Viking warrior and Viking
longship:
    a) (Ag)   15.00   20.00
    b) (Cu-Ni)   3.00

90 (30)   1 Crown 1979. English cog:
    a) (Ag)   15.00   20.00
    b) (Cu-Ni)   3.00

91 (31)   1 Crown 1979. Flemish carrack:
    a) (Ag)   15.00   20.00
    b) (Cu-Ni)   3.00

92 (32)   1 Crown 1979. Loyalist and English Man-
of-War:
    a) (Ag)   15.00   20.00
    b) (Cu-Ni)   3.00

93 (33)   1 Crown 1979. Lifeboat and Sir William
Hillary portrait:
    a) (Ag)   15.00   20.00
    b) (Cu-Ni)   3.00

94 (29b)   1 Crown (Au) 1979. Type as No. 89   *800.00*
95 (30b)   1 Crown (Au) 1979. Type as No. 90   *800.00*
96 (31b)   1 Crown (Au) 1979. Type as No. 91   *800.00*
97 (32b)   1 Crown (Au) 1979. Type as No. 92   *800.00*
98 (33b)   1 Crown (Au) 1979. Type as No. 93   *800.00*

99 (29c)   1 Crown (Platinum) 1979. Type as No. 89   *1800.00*
100 (30c)   1 Crown (Platinum) 1979. Type as No. 90   *1800.00*
101 (31c)   1 Crown (Platinum) 1979. Type as No. 91   *1800.00*

			Unc	Proof

102 (32c) 1 Crown (Platinum) 1979. Type as No. 92 .... *1800.00*
103 (33c) 1 Crown (Platinum) 1979. Type as No. 93 .... *1800.00*

ROYAL VISIT (2)

104 (34) 50 Pence 1979. Type as No. 87, but edge inscription: »H.M.Q.E. II/ROYAL/VI-SIT/I.O.M./JULY/1979«:
   a) (Ag) .... 22.00 / 30.00
   b) (Cu-Ni) 3.00

105 (34b) 50 Pence (Platinum) 1979. Type as No. 104 .... *1000.00*

HENLEY REGATTA

106 1 £ (Virenium) 1979. Type as No. 57, but with crossed rudders 6.00 8.00

13th OLYMPIC WINTER GAMES IN LAKE PLACID (3)

107 (40) 1 Crown 1980. Triskelion and different athletes:
   a) (Ag), without dot between OLYMPICS and LAKE 50.00 80.00
   b) (Ag), with dot between OLYMPICS and LAKE 50.00 80.00
   c) (Cu-Ni), without dot between OLYMPICS and LAKE 2.00
   d) (Cu-Ni), with dot between OLYMPICS and LAKE 2.00

			Unc	Proof
108 (40b)	1 Crown (Au) 1980. Type as No. 107b		*1000.00*	*1100.00*
109 (40c)	1 Crown (Platinum) 1980. Type as No. 107b			*1500.00*

22nd OLYMPIC GAMES 1980 IN MOSCOW (9)

110 (43) 1 Crown 1980. Triskelion and different
athletes: Judo match at top:

a) (Ag)		40.00
b) (Cu-Ni)	4.00	

111 (41) 1 Crown 1980. Triskelion and different
athletes: Runner at top:

a) (Ag), without dot between
OLYMPIAD and MOSCOW and
without dots to right and left of ONE
CROWN (see illustration) 40.00

b) (Ag), without dot between
OLYMPIAD and MOSCOW and
with dots to right and left of ONE
CROWN 40.00

c) (Ag), with dot between OLYMPIAD
and MOSCOW and with dots to right
and left of ONE CROWN 40.00

d) (Cu-Ni), Type as No. 111a	4.00	
e) (Cu-Ni), Type as No. 111b	4.00	
f) (Cu-Ni), Type as No. 111c	4.00	

			Unc	Proof
112 (42)	1 Crown 1980. Triskelion and different athletes: Javelin thrower at top:			
	a) (Ag)			40.00
	b) (Cu-Ni)		4.00	
113 (43b)	1 Crown (Au) 1980. Type as No. 110		*1000.00*	*1100.00*
114 (41b)	1 Crown (Au) 1980. Type as No. 111c		*1000.00*	*1100.00*
115 42b)	1 Crown (Au) 1980. Type as No. 112		*1000.00*	*1100.00*
116 (43c)	1 Crown (Platinum) 1980. Type as No. 110			*1500.00*
117 (41c)	1 Crown (Platinum) 1980. Type as No. 111c			*1500.00*
118 (42c)	1 Crown (Platinum) 1980. Type as No. 112			*1500.00*

			XF	Unc
119 (44)	½ Penny (Br) 1980–1983. Atlantic herring		0.05	0.10

			XF	Unc
120 (45)	1 Penny (Br) 1980–1983. Manx cat		0.10	0.15
121 (46)	2 Pence (Br) 1980–1983. Manx shearwater		0.15	0.20

			XF	Unc
122 (47)	5 Pence (Cu-Ni) 1980–1983. Loagthyn sheep		0.25	0.40
123 (48)	10 Pence (Cu-Ni) 1980–1983. Falcon		0.50	0.80

			XF	Unc
124 (49)	50	Pence (Cu-Ni) 1980–1983. Viking long-ship	1.50	2.00

			Proof
125 (44a)	½ Penny (Ag) 1980, 1983. Type as No. 119		5.00
126 (45a)	1 Penny (Ag) 1980, 1983. Type as No. 120		6.50
127 (46a)	2 Pence (Ag) 1980, 1983. Type as No. 121		8.00
128 (47a)	5 Pence (Ag) 1980, 1983. Type as No. 122		8.50
129 (48a)	10 Pence (Ag) 1980, 1983. Type as No. 123		12.50
130 (49a)	50 Pence (Ag) 1980, 1983. Type as No. 124		18.00

Note: No. 125–130, 1980 date of .500 silver,
1983 date of .925 silver.

131 (44b)	½ Penny (Au) 1980, 1983. Type as No. 119		*60.00*
132 (45b)	1 Penny (Au) 1980, 1983. Type as No. 120		*125.00*
133 (46b)	2 Pence (Au) 1980, 1983. Type as No. 121		*200.00*
134 (47b)	5 Pence (Au) 1980, 1983. Type as No. 122		*200.00*
135 (48b)	10 Pence (Au) 1980, 1983. Type as No. 123		*325.00*
136 (49b)	50 Pence (Au) 1980, 1983. Type as No. 124		*500.00*
137 (44c)	½ Penny (Platinum) 1980, 1983. Type as No. 119		*90.00*
138 (45c)	1 Penny (Platinum) 1980, 1983. Type as No. 120		*150.00*
139 (46c)	2 Pence (Platinum) 1980, 1983. Type as No. 121		*250.00*
140 (47c)	5 Pence (Platinum) 1980, 1983. Type as No. 122		*250.00*
141 (48c)	10 Pence (Platinum) 1980, 1983. Type as No. 123		*400.00*
142 (49c)	50 Pence (Platinum) 1980, 1983. Type as No. 124		*650.00*

DAILY MAIL IDEAL HOME EXHIBITION, LONDON AND MANCHESTER (2)

			XF	Unc
143 (27.2)	1 £ (Virenium) 1980. Type as No. 57, but inscription D.M.I.H.E.:			
	a) 1980 AA		5.00	6.50
	b) 1980 AB		5.00	6.50
	c) 1980 AC		5.00	6.50
144 (27.3)	1 £ (Virenium) 1980. Type as No. 57, but inscription D.M.I.H.E.N.:			
	a) 1980 AA		5.00	6.50
	b) 1980 AB		5.00	6.50

		Unc	Proof
145 (39)	1 Crown 1980:		
	a) (Ag)	17.50	22.50
	b) (Cu-Ni)	2.50	
146	1 Crown (Platinum) 1980. Type as No. 145		*1250.00*

80th BIRTHDAY OF QUEEN MOTHER (6)

147 (50)	1 Crown 1980. Queen Elizabeth the Queen Mother:		
	a) (Ag) .925 silver		30.00
	b) (Ag) .500 silver	20.00	
	c) (Cu-Ni)	2.50	
148	1 Crown (Au) 1980. Type as No. 147:		
	a) 22 carat, 7.28 gm.		200.00
	b) 9 carat, 5.00 gm.		80.00

			Unc	Proof

149 (9a)   ½ Sovereign (Au) 1980. Viking warrior on horseback, Queen Mother's portrait at top (countermark)   *350.00*

150 (10a)   1 Sovereign (Au) 1980. Type as No. 149   *350.00*

151 (11a)   2 £ (Au) 1980. Type as No. 149   *500.00*

152 (12a)   5 £ (Au) 1980. Type as No. 149 (250 pieces)   1300.00

TOURIST TROPHY 1980 (2)

153 (27.4)   1 £ 1980. Type as No. 57, but inscription T.T.:
  a) (Ag)   22.00
  b) (Virenium), AA, AB   4.00

A153 (27,6)   1 £ (Au) 1980. Type as No. 153   *260.00*

VIKING EXHIBITION, NEW YORK (3)

154 (34d)   50 Pence 1980. Type as No. 87, but edge inscription »ODINS/RAVEN/VIKING/EXHIBN/NEW/YORK/1980«:
  a) (Ag)   20.00   50.00
  b) (Cu-Ni)   5.00

155 (34f)   50 Pence (Au) 1980. Type as No. 154   *700.00*

156 (34g)   50 Pence (Platinum) 1980. Type as No. 154   *1000.00*

CHRISTMAS 1980 (3)

157 (51)   50 Pence 1980:
  a) (Ag)   30.00   50.00
  b) (Cu-Ni)   2.00   8.00
  c) (Cu-Ni), mule with obv. of No. 154   –.–

158 (51b)   50 Pence (Au) 1980. Type as No. 157   *700.00*

		Unc	Proof
159 (51 c)	50 Pence (Platinum) 1980. Type as No. 157		*1000.00*

DUKE OF EDINBURGH AWARD SCHEME (12)

		Unc	Proof
160 (53)	1 Crown 1981:		
	a) (Ag)	17.50	25.00
	b) (Cu-Ni)	2.50	8.00
161 (54)	1 Crown 1981:		
	a) (Ag)	17.50	25.00
	b) (Cu-Ni)	2.50	8.00
162 (55)	1 Crown 1981:		
	a) (Ag)	17.50	25.00
	b) (Cu-Ni)	2.50	8.00

		Unc	Proof
163 (56)	1 Crown 1981:		
	a) (Ag)	17.50	25.00
	b) (Cu-Ni)	2.50	8.00
164 (53b)	1 Crown (Au) 1981. Type as No. 160:		
	a) .916 gold, 7.96 gm.		*150.00*
	b) .375 gold, 5.1 gm.		*80.00*
165 (54b)	1 Crown (Au) 1981. Type as No. 161:		
	a) .916 gold, 7.96 gm.		*150.00*
	b) .375 gold, 5.1 gm.		*80.00*
166 (55b)	1 Crown (Au) 1981. Type as No. 162:		
	a) .916 gold, 7.96 gm.		*150.00*
	b) .375 gold, 5.1 gm.		*80.00*
167 (56b)	1 Crown (Au) 1981. Type as No. 163:		
	a) .916 gold, 7.96 gm.		*150.00*
	b) .375 gold, 5.1 gm.		*80.00*
168 (53d)	1 Crown (Platinum) 1981. Type as No. 160		*1250.00*
169 (54d)	1 Crown (Platinum) 1981. Type as No. 161		*1250.00*
170 (55d)	1 Crown (Platinum) 1981. Type as No. 162		*1250.00*
171 (56d)	1 Crown (Platinum) 1981. Type as No. 163		*1250.00*

			Unc	Proof
172 (63)	1	Crown 1981. Conjoined busts:		
		a) (Ag)	17.50	25.00
		b) (Cu-Ni)	2.50	
A172 (63b)	1	Crown (Au) 1981. Type as No. 172:		
		a) 22 ct, 7.96 g		150.00
		b) 9 ct, 5.1 g		80.00
173 (63d)	1	Crown (Platinum) 1981. Type as No. 172		*1250.00*
174 (62)	1	Crown 1981. Two arms:		
		a) (Ag)	17.50	25.00
		b) (Cu-Ni)	2.50	
A174 (62b)	1	Crown (Au) 1981. Type as No. 174:		
		a) 22 ct, 7.96 g		150.00
		b) 9 ct, 5.1 g		80.00
175 (62d)	1	Crown (Platinum) 1981. Type as No. 174		*1250.00*
176 (64)	½	Sovereign (Au) 1981. Conjoined busts and two arms		*120.00*
177 (65)	1	Sovereign (Au) 1981. Type as No. 176		*220.00*
178 (66)	2	£ (Au) 1981. Type as No. 176		*400.00*
179 (67)	5	£ (Au) 1981. Type as No. 176		*1100.00*

INTERNATIONAL YEAR OF THE DISABLED (12)

			Unc	**Proof**
180 (58)	1 Crown 1981. Louis Braille, inventor of the reading system for the blind:			
	a) (Ag)		17.50	25.00
	b) (Cu-Ni)		2.50	8.00
181 (59)	1 Crown 1981. Ludwig van Beethoven, composer:			
	a) (Ag)		17.50	25.00
	b) (Cu-Ni)		2.50	8.00
182 (60)	1 Crown 1981. Sir Douglas Bader, aviator:			
	a) (Ag)		17.50	25.00
	b) (Cu-Ni)		2.50	8.00

183 (61)	1 Crown 1981. Sir Francis Chichester, sailor:			
	a) (Ag)		17.50	25.00
	b) (Cu-Ni)		2.50	8.00
184 (58b)	1 Crown (Au) 1981. Type as No. 180:			
	a) .375 gold			80.00
	b) .916 gold			150.00
185 (59b)	1 Crown (Au) 1981. Type as No. 181:			
	a) .375 gold			80.00
	b) .916 gold			150.00
186 (60b)	1 Crown (Au) 1981. Type as No. 182:			
	a) .375 gold			80.00
	b) .916 gold			150.00
187 (61b)	1 Crown (Au) 1981. Type as No. 183:			
	a) .375 gold			80.00
	b) .916 gold			150.00
188 (58d)	1 Crown (Platinum) 1981. Type as No. 180			1250.00
189 (59d)	1 Crown (Platinum) 1981. Type as No. 181			1250.00
190 (60d)	1 Crown (Platinum) 1981. Type as No. 182			1250.00
191 (61d)	1 Crown (Platinum) 1981. Type as No. 183			1250.00

TOURIST TROPHY 1981 (3)

			Unc	Proof
192 (57)	50	Pence 1981. Joey Dunlup, winner of Tourist Trophy, TT at top:		
		a) (Ag)		30.00
		b) (Cu-Ni)	2.00	
193 (57b)	50	Pence (Au) 1981. Type as No. 192		*900.00*
194 (57c)	50	Pence (Platinum) 1981. Type as No. 192		*1000.00*
195 (52)	5	£ (Virenium) 1981, 1983. Rev. triskelion superimposed on island map	12.00	60.00
196 (52a)	5	£ (Ag) 1981, 1983. Type as No. 195		70.00
197 (52b)	5	£ (Au) 1981, 1983. Type as No. 195		*1200.00*
198 (52c)	5	£ (Platinum) 1981, 1983. Type as No. 195		*1300.00*

CHRISTMAS 1981 (3)

199 (68)	50	Pence 1981:		
		a) (Ag)		30.00
		b) (Cu-Ni)	2.00	8.00
200 (68b)	50	Pence (Au) 1981. Type as No. 199		*700.00*
201 (68c)	50	Pence (Platinum) 1981. Type as No. 199		*800.00*

FOR THE FAO-COIN-PLAN

			XF	Unc
202 (82)	½	Penny (Br) 1981. Type as No. 54, but Obv. inscription reads ELIZABETH II ISLE OF MAN	0.20	0.30

			XF	Unc
203 (69)	20	Pence (Cu-Ni) 1982, 1983	0.80	1.00
204 (69a)	20	Pence (Ag) 1982, 1983		40.00

			Unc	Proof
205 (69b)	20	Pence (Au) 1982, 1983		200.00
206 (69c)	20	Pence (Platinum) 1982, 1983		250.00

WORLD SOCCER CHAMPIONSHIP GAMES 1982 IN SPAIN (12)

207 (70)	1 Crown 1982. Passarella holding aloft the World Cup:		
	a) (Ag)	25.00	30.00
	b) (Cu-Ni)	2.50	
208 (71)	1 Crown 1982. A soccer ball covered by the national arms of the championship winners:		
	a) (Ag)	25.00	30.00
	b) (Cu-Ni)	2.50	
209 (73)	1 Crown 1982. Dramatic actions, goal-keeper at bottom:		
	a) (Ag)	25.00	30.00
	b) (Cu-Ni)	2.50	
210 (72)	1 Crown 1982. Dramatic actions:		
	a) (Ag), Rev. three balls	25.00	30.00
	b) (Cu-Ni), Rev. three balls	2.50	
	c) (Cu-Ni), Rev. four balls	4.00	

			Unc	Proof
211		1 Crown (Au) 1982. Type as No. 207		80.00
212		1 Crown (Au) 1982. Type as No. 208		80.00
213		1 Crown (Au) 1982. Type as No. 209		80.00
214		1 Crown (Au) 1982. Type as No. 210a		80.00
215 (70d)		1 Crown (Platinum) 1982. Type as No. 207		*1250.00*
216 (71d)		1 Crown (Platinum) 1982. Type as No. 208		*1250.00*
217 (73d)		1 Crown (Platinum) 1982. Type as No. 209		*1250.00*
218 (72d)		1 Crown (Platinum) 1982. Type as No. 210a		*1250.00*

TOURIST TROPHY 1982 (3)

			Unc	Proof
219 (74)	50	Pence 1982:		
		a) (Ag)		30.00
		b) (Cu-Ni)	2.00	
220–221		Same in gold and platinum.		

ITALY WORLD SOCCER CHAMPIONSHIP WINNER (3)

			Unc	Proof
222 (75)		1 Crown 1982. Type as No. 208, but date 1982 above Italian arms:		
		a) (Ag)		35.00
		b) (Cu-Ni)	3.00	10.00
223–224		Same in gold 9 ct, 22 ct and platinum.		

BIRTH OF PRINCE WILLIAM ALBERT PHILIP LOUIS (38)

225–231		No. 119–124, 203 with baby crib mark, standard metals.

No. 232, 233 omitted.

			Unc	Proof
234–242		No. 119–124, 203, 57, 195 with baby crib mark, sterling silver.		
243–251		Same in gold.		
252–260		Same in platinum.		
261 (9b)	½	Sovereign (Au) 1982. Type as No. 24, but with baby crib mark		80.00
262 (10b)	1	Sovereign (Au) 1982. Type as No. 261		150.00
263 (11b)	2	£ (Au) 1982. Type as No. 261		300.00
264 (12b)	5	£ (Au) 1982. Type as No. 261		700.00

		Unc	Proof
265 (78)	1 Crown 1982. H.M.S. Victory, Captain John William:		
	a) (Ag)		35.00
	b) (Cu-Ni)	2.00	8.00
266 (77)	1 Crown 1982. H.M.S. Bounty, Lieutenant Fletcher Christian:		
	a) (Ag)		35.00
	b) (Cu-Ni)	2.00	8.00

		Unc	Proof
267 (79)	1 Crown 1982. P.S. Mona's Queen II, Captain William Cain:		
	a) (Ag)		35.00
	b) (Cu-Ni)	2.00	8.00
268 (76)	1 Crown 1982. Mayflower, Captain Myles Standish:		
	a) (Ag)		35.00
	b) (Cu-Ni)	2.00	8.00
269–272	Same in gold 9 ct and 22 ct, dia. 22.1 mm.		
273–276	Same in platinum.		

CHRISTMAS 1982 (3)

		Unc	Proof
277 (80)	50 Pence 1982. Christmas singers in front of Castle Rushen:		
	a) (Ag)		30.00
	b) (Cu-Ni)	2.50	10.00
278–279	Same in gold and platinum.		

			Unc	Proof
A280 (81)	1 £ 1983, Peel city arms; dia. 22.12 mm:			20.00
	a) (Ag) 4.6 g			
	b) (Virenium)		3.00	
B280–				
C280	Same in gold, 7.96 g and platinum, 9 g.			
280 (81)	1 £ (S) 1983. Type as No. A280, but dia. 22.5 mm:			
	a) 9.5 g			35.00
	b) Pièfort, 19 g			–.–
281–282	Same in gold 9 ct, 9.5 g; Pièfort 19 g; gold 22 ct, 9.5 g; Pièfort 19 g; platinum 9.5 g and Pièfort 19 g.			

BICENTENARY OF MANNED FLIGHT (12)

			Unc	Proof
283 (86)	1 Crown 1983. Montgolfièr Balloon, 1783:			
	a) (Ag)		25.00	30.00
	b) (Cu-Ni)		2.50	8.00
284 (87)	1 Crown 1983. Wright Brothers Flyer, 1903:			
	a) (Ag)		25.00	30.00
	b) (Cu-Ni)		2.50	8.00
285 (88)	1 Crown 1983. Gloster Whittle Jet, 1941:			
	a) (Ag)		25.00	30.00
	b) (Cu-Ni)		2.50	8.00

			Unc	Proof
286 (89)	1 Crown 1983. Orbiter Space Shuttle, 1983:			
	a) (Ag)		25.00	30.00
	b) (Cu-Ni)		2.50	8.00
287–290	Same in gold 9 ct and 22 ct, dia. 22.1 mm.			
291–294	Same in platinum.			

		Unc	Proof
A295	1/10 Noble (Platinum) 1984. Viking long-ship; 1/10 troy ounce		*60.00*

295 (97)	1 Noble (Platinum) 1983, 1984. Type as No. A295; 1 troy ounce:		
	1983	600.00	1600.00
	1984	600.00	1000.00

TOURIST TROPHY 1983 (3)

296 (96)	50 Pence 1983. Ron Haslam, TT 1982 winner:		
	a) (Ag)		30.00
	b) (Cu-Ni)	2.00	
297–298	Same in gold and platinum.		

CHRISTMAS 1983 (3)

299 (95)	50 Pence 1983. Ford Model T, »Tin Lizzy«:		
	a) (Ag)		30.00
	b) (Cu-Ni)	2.00	
300–301	Same in gold and platinum.		

CITY ARMS 1984 – CENTENARY OF CASTLETOWN INCORPORATION (3)

302 (83)	1 £ (Ag) 1984. Castletown city arms; dia. 22.5 mm:		
	a) 9.5 g		25.00
	b) Pièfort, 19 g		–.–
303–304	Same in gold 9 ct, 9.5 g; Pièfort 19 g; gold 22 ct, 9.5 g; Pièfort 19 g; platinum 9.5 g and Pièfort 19 g.		

See also No. 324, 333, 342, 351.

305   306

			Unc	Proof
305 (91)	1 Crown 1984. Figure skating couple; Jayne Torvill and Christopher Dean:			
	a) (Ag)		25.00	30.00
	b) (Silverclad)			–.–
	c) (Cu-Ni)		2.50	
306 (94)	1 Crown 1984. Horse jumping:			
	a) (Ag)		25.00	30.00
	b) (Silverclad)			–.–
	c) (Cu-Ni)		2.50	
307 (92)	1 Crown 1984. Pair of runners:			
	a) (Ag)		25.00	30.00
	b) (Silverclad)			–.–
	c) (Cu-Ni)		2.50	
308 (93)	1 Crown 1984. Female gymnast:			
	a) (Ag)		25.00	30.00
	b) (Silverclad)			–.–
	c) (Cu-Ni)		2.50	
309–312	Same in gold 9 ct and 22 ct, dia. 22.1 mm.			
313–316	Same in platinum.			

QUINCENTENARY OF COLLEGE OF ARMS (52)

317   318   319

			XF	Unc
317 (98)	½ Penny (Br) 1984. Fuchsia blossom	0.05	0.30
318 (99)	1 Penny (Br) 1984. Puffin (Manx shearwater)	0.10	0.30
319 (100)	2 Pence (Br) 1984. Falcon	0.15	0.30
320 (101)	5 Pence (Cu-Ni) 1984. Cushag	0.20	0.30
321 (102)	10 Pence (Cu-Ni) 1984. Loagthyn ram	0.25	0.50
322 (103)	20 Pence (Cu-Ni) 1984. Atlantic herrings	0.30	0.65

		XF	Unc
323 (104)	50 Pence (Cu-Ni) 1984. Viking longship	0.60	1.25
324 (83)	1£ (Virenium) 1984. Type as No. 302; dia. 22.1 mm	2.00	3.00
325 (106)	5 £ (Virenium) 1984. Viking warrior on horseback	8.00	12.00
326–334	Same in silver.		
335–343	Same in gold.		
344–352	Same in platinum.		

		Unc	Proof
353	1 Crown 1984:		
	a) (Ag)		30.00
	b) (Silverclad)		–.–
	c) (Cu-Ni)	2.50	
354	1 Crown 1984:		
	a) (Ag)		30.00
	b) (Silverclad)		–.–
	c) (Cu-Ni)	2.50	
355	1 Crown 1984:		
	a) (Ag)		30.00
	b) (Silverclad)		–.–
	c) (Cu-Ni)	2.50	
356	1 Crown 1984:		
	a) (Ag)		30.00
	b) (Silverclad)		–.–
	c) (Cu-Ni)	2.50	
357–360	Same in gold 9 ct and 22 ct; dia. 22.1 mm.		
361–364	Same in platinum.		

365	½ Sovereign (Au) 1984. Four arms with Fuchsia blossoms in angles, motto QUOCUNQUE JECERIS STABIT	–.–	80.00
366	1 Sovereign (Au) 1984. Type as No. 365	–.–	150.00
367	2 £ (Au) 1984. Type as No. 365	–.–	285.00
368	5 £ (Au) 1984. Type as No. 365	–.–	700.00

TOURIST TROPHY 1984 (3)

369	50 Pence 1984. Motorcycle with sidecar:		
	a) (Ag)		30.00
	b) (Cu-Ni)	2.00	
370–371	Same in gold and platinum.		

30th COMMONWEALTH CONFERENCE (12)

		Unc	Proof
372	1 Crown 1984. Queen Elizabeth II and Prince Philip:		
	a) (Ag)		30.00
	b) (Silverclad)		–.–
	c) (Cu-Ni)	2.50	
373	1 Crown 1984. Princess Anne:		
	a) (Ag)		30.00
	b) (Silverclad)		–.–
	c) (Cu-Ni)	2.50	
374	1 Crown 1984. Rev. Tynwald Hall:		
	a) (Ag)		30.00
	b) (Silverclad)		–.–
	c) (Cu-Ni)	2.50	
375	1 Crown 1984. Rev. State Sword of Manx and the Speaker's chair:		
	a) (Ag)		30.00
	b) (Silverclad)		–.–
	c) (Cu-Ni)	2.50	
376–379	Same in gold 9 ct and 22 ct; dia. 22.1 mm.		
380–383	Same in platinum.		

GOLD BULLION ISSUE »ANGEL« (2)

384	¹⁄₁₀ Angel (Au) 1984		–.–
A384	1 Angel (Au) 1984. Archangel Michael slaying the dragon; 1 troy ounce		450.00

CHRISTMAS 1984 (3)

385	50 Pence 1984. Railway line Douglas-Peel: steam engine »Sutherland«, constructed in 1873, with snow-plough, shoved against by another engine, passenger-train in background:		
	a) (Ag)		40.00
	b) (Cu-Ni)	2.50	
386–387	Same in gold and platinum.		

CITY ARMS 1985 – RAMSEY (3)

		Unc	Proof
388 (84)	1 £ (Ag) 1985. Ramsey city arms; dia. 22.5 mm:		
	a) 9.5 g		25.00
	b) Pièfort, 19 g		–.–
389–390	Same in gold 9 ct, 9.5 g; Pièfort 19 g; gold 22 ct, 9.5 g; Pièfort 19 g; platinum		

See also No. 398, 407, 416, 425.

YEAR OF SPORTS 1985 (36)

		Unc	Proof
391	½ Penny (Br) 1985. New portrait of the Queen by R.D. Maklouf. Rev. as No. 317	0.10	0.30
392	1 Penny (Br) 1985. Rev. as No. 318	0.10	0.30
393	2 Pence (Br) 1985. Rev. as No. 319	0.15	0.30
394	5 Pence (Cu-Ni) 1985. Rev. as No. 320	0.15	0.30
395	10 Pence (Cu-Ni) 1985. Rev. as No. 321	0.25	0.50
396	20 Pence (Cu-Ni) 1985. Rev. as No. 322	0.30	0.65
397	50 Pence (Cu-Ni) 1985. Rev. as No. 323	0.60	1.25
398 (84)	1 £ (Virenium) 1985. Rev. as No. 388; dia. 22.1 mm	1.50	3.00
399	5 £ (Virenium) 1985. Rev. as No. 325	8.00	12.00
400–408	Same in silver.		
409–417	Same in gold.		
418–426	Same in platinum.		

GOLD BULLION ISSUE »ANGEL« (8)

		Unc	Proof
A427	¹⁄₂₀ Angel (Au) 1986. Elizabeth II, portrait by R.D. Maklouf. Rev. Archangel Michael haying the dragon, as No. 384; ¹⁄₂₀ troy ounce		–.–
427	¹⁄₁₀ Angel (Au) 1985, 1986; ¹⁄₁₀ troy ounce:		
	a) long wings, 1985	50.00	75.00
	b) clipped wings, 1985, 1986	50.00	75.00
428	¼ Angel (Au) 1985, 1986. ¼ troy ounce		–.–
429	½ Angel (Au) 1985, 1986. ½ troy ounce		–.–

		Unc	Proof
430	1 Angel (Au) 1985, 1986. 1 troy ounce		450.00

		Unc	Proof
431	5 Angels (Au) 1985–1987. 5 troy ounces	–.–	
432	10 Angels (Au) 1985–1987. 10 troy ounces	–.–	
A432	15 Angels (Au) 1987; 15 troy ounces	–.–	

PLATINUM BULLION ISSUE »NOBLE« (6)

		Unc	Proof
433	¹⁄₁₀ Noble (Platinum) 1985, 1986. Obv. as No. 391. Rev. as No. A295; ¹⁄₁₀ troy ounce	60.00	80.00
A433	¼ Noble (Platinum) 1986; ¼ troy ounce		160.00
B433	½ Noble (Platinum) 1986; ½ troy ounce		240.00

		Unc	Proof
434	1 Noble (Platinum) 1985–1987; 1 troy ounce	600.00	900.00
435	5 Nobles (Platinum) 1986; 5 troy ounces		–.–
436	10 Nobles (Platinum) 1986; 10 troy ounces		–.–

1985 EXPOSITION ANGELS (4)

		Unc	Proof
437	¹⁄₁₀ Angel (Au) 1985 »A«. 94th convention of the American Numismatic Association, Baltimore	–.–	
438	¹⁄₁₀ Angel (Au) 1985 »L«. 8th Long Beach International Coin and Stamp Exposition	–.–	
439	¹⁄₁₀ Angel (Au) 1985 »H«. Hong Kong International Coin Exposition	–.–	
440	¹⁄₁₀ Angel (Au) 1985 »C«. Coinex International Coin Fair, London	–.–	

		Unc	Proof
441–458	Sets of six crowns depicting The Life & Times of The Queen Mother in Cu-Ni, silverclad, silver, gold 9ct, gold 22ct and platinum.		

CHRISTMAS 1985

459	50 Pence 1985, Ronalds way Airport;		
	a) (Ag)		–.–
	b) (cu-Ni)	2.50	
460–461	Same in gold and platinum.		

CITY ARMS – DOUGLAS (3)

462	(85) 1 £ (Ag) 1986. Douglas city arms; dia. 22.5 mm:		
	a) 9.5 g	25.00	
	b) Piéfort, 19 g		–.–
463–464	Same in gold 9 ct, 9.5 g; Piéfort 19 g; gold 22 ct, 9.5 g; Piéfort 19 g; platinum 9.5 g and Piéfort 19 g.		

1986 EXPOSITION ANGELS (4)

A464	¹⁄₁₀ Angel (Au) 1986 »T«. Toronto Exposition		
			–.–
A465	¹⁄₁₀ Angel (Au) 1986 »X«. American International Philatelic Exhibition, Chicago		–.–
465	¼ Angel (Au) 1986 »L«. 9th Long Beach International Coin and Stamp Exposition	200.00	
A466	¹⁄₁₀ Angel (Au) 1986 »A«. 95th convention of the American Numismatic Association, Milwaukee	–.–	

XIII WORLD SOCCER CHAMPIONSHIP GAMES MEXICO (18)

466–483   Sets of six crowns in Cu-Ni, silverclad, silver, gold 9ct, gold 22 ct and platinum.

60th BIRTH DAY OF H.R.M. QUEEN ELIZABETH (3)

484–486   1 Crown 1986 in Cu-Ni, Silverclad, silver, gold 9 ct, gold 22 ct and platinum.

No. 487 omitted.

		XF	Unc
488–494	Base metal circulation coinage like Nos. 392–398, but w/boat privy mark		
495	2 £ (Virenium) 1986. Rev. Tower of Refuge	3.50	5.50

Nos. 496–526 omitted.

WEDDING OF PRINCE ANDREW AND MISS SARAH FERGUSON (6)

527–532   Sets of two crowns in Cu-Ni, silverclad, silver, gold 9 ct, gold 22 ct, platinum.

CHRISTMAS 1986 (4)

		Unc	Proof
A533	¹⁄₂₀ Angel (Au) 1986 with stylized christmas tree	50.00	
533	50 Pence 1986. Christmas parcel service:		
	a) (Ag)		25.00
	b) (Cu-Ni)	2.50	
534–535	Same in gold and platinum.		

1987 EXPOSITION ANGEL

536	¹⁄₁₀ Angel (Au) 1987 »F«. Florida United Numismatists Coin Convention, Orlando	–.–	

		Unc	Proof
537	½ Crown (Ag) 1987. Rev. 1887 »America's Cup« regatta Scene at New York harbour with Statue of Liberty in background, .999 silver, 15.63 g (20 pcs.)		–.–
538	½ Crown (Au) 1987, .999 gold, 15.55 g		
539	1 Crown 1987. Rev. George Steers, Yacht »America«, 1851:		
	a) (Ag) .925 fine, 28.28 g		–.–
	b) (silverclad)		–.–
	c) (Cu-Ni)	2.50	
540	1 Crown 1987. Rev. Sir Thomas Lipton:		
	a) (Ag)		–.–
	b) (silverclad)		–.–
	c) (Cu-Ni)	2.50	
541	1 Crown 1987. Rev. The Victorious »Stars and Stripes« and »Kookaburra II« and map of Australia:		
	a) (Ag)		–.–
	b) (silverclad)		–.–
	c) (Cu-Ni)	2.50	
542	1 Crown 1987. Rev. The Cup in front of sailing ships:		
	a) (Ag)		
	b) (silverclad)		–.–
	c) (Cu-Ni)	2.50	
543	1 Crown 1987. Type as No. 537:		
	a) (Ag)		–.–
	b) (silverclad)		–.–
	c) (Cu-Ni)	2.50	
544	1 Crown (Palladium) 1987. Type as No. 541, .999 fine, 31.1 g		–.–
545	5 Crowns (Ag) 1987. Type as No. 537, .9995 silver, 155.5 g (200 pcs.)		–.–
546	5 Crowns (Ag) 1987. Type as No. 542		–.–
547	10 Crowns (Ag) 1987. Type as No. 542, .9995 silver, 311 g (50 pcs.)		–.–
548	10 Crowns (Ag) 1987. Type as No. 537		–.–

BICENTENARY OF AMERICA'S CONSTITUTION (5)

		Unc	Proof
549	½ Crown (Au) 1987		–.–
550	1 Crown 1987:		

		Unc	Proof
	a) (Ag)		−.−
	b) (silverclad)		−.−
	c) (Cu-Ni)	2.50	
551	1 Crown (Palladium) 1987		−.−
552	5 Crowns (Ag) 1987		−.−
553	10 Crowns (Ag) 1987		−.−

Nos. 554–559 omitted.

		XF	Unc
560	1 £ (Virenium) 1987. Rev. Viking warrior on horseback, Celtic legend »ellan vannin«	1.50	2.50

Nos. 561–589 omitted.

1987 EXPOSITION ANGELS (5)

		Unc	Proof
590	¼ Angel (Au) 1987 »Golden Gate Bridge 50th«. San Francisco International Numismatic and Philatelic Exposition		−.−
591	¹⁄₁₀ Angel (Au) 1987 »A«. 96th Convention of the American Numismatic Association, Atlanta	−.−	
592	1 Angel (Au) 1987 »Hong Kong«. 6th International Coin Exposition, Hong Kong		−.−
593	¼ Angel (Au) 1987 »Big Ben Tower«. Coinex International Coin Fair, London		−.−
594	¼ Angel (Au) 1987 »Saint Louis Arch«. Saint Louis Silver Dollar Conventions		200.00

1987 EXPOSITION NOBLE

595	¼ Noble (Platinum) 1987 »Statue of Liberty«. New York International Numismatic Convention		−.−

CHRISTMAS 1987 (4)

596	¹⁄₂₀ Angel (Au) 1987 with mistletoe privy mark		−.−

810   **Great Britain/Isle of Man**

597   50 Pence 1987:
a) (Ag)
b) (Cu-Ni)   –.–

598–599   Same in gold and platinum.

		XF	**Unc**
600	1 Penny (Br) 1988. Rev. The toolmaker's high-speed precision toolroom lathe, superimposed an a cog-wheel	0.10	0.15
601	2 Pence (Br) 1988. Rev. Celtic stone cross with Hiberno-Norse ring-chain ornament, a traditional Manx jug on a potter's wheel, hand-knitting, weaver's bobbin, reel of yearn and woodcarving tools	0.15	0.20
602	5 Pence (Cu-Ni) 1988. Rev. wind-surfer	0.25	0.40

603	10 Pence (Cu-Ni) 1988. Rev. Map of the Island on globe, encircled by a band with a star pointing at Douglas financial centre	0.50	0.80

		XF	**Unc**
604	20 Pence (Cu-Ni) 1988. Rev. modern combine harvester, framed by cass of wheat (seven-sided)	0.80	1.00
605	50 Pence (Cu-Ni) 1988. Rev. Personal computer showing a triskelion on screen (seven-sided)	1.50	2.00

606

607

		XF	**Unc**
606	1 £ (Virenium) 1988. Rev. digital cordless telephone, flanked by a communications space satellite and a receiving-station with parabolic reflector	2.00	3.00
607	2 £ (Virenium) 1988. Rev. the latest turboprop airliner, brought into service by Manx Airlines in 1987	4.00	6.00

		XF	**Unc**
608	5 £ (Virenium) 1988. Rev. modern inshore fishing vessel, triskelion in a roundel above, lobster and herrings below	10.00	14.00

Nos. 609–635 omitted.

GOLD BULLION ISSUE »ANGEL« (9)

		Unc	Proof
636	¹⁄₂₀ Angel (Au) 1988. Modified version of R.D. Maklouf's portrait of the Queen prepared by the Pobjoy Mint. Rev. Archangel Michael slaying the dragon, as No. 384	–.–	–.–
637	¹⁄₁₀ Angel (Au) 1988	–.–	–.–
638	¼ Angel (Au) 1988		–.–
639	½ Angel (Au) 1988		–.–
640	1 Angel (Au) 1988	–.–	–.–
641	5 Angel (Au) 1988		–.–
642	10 Angel (Au) 1988		–.–
643	15 Angel (Au) 1988	–.–	
644	20 Angel (Au) 1988		–.–

PLATINUM BULLION ISSUE »NOBLE« (6)

		Unc	Proof
645	¹⁄₁₀ Noble (Platinum) 1988	–.–	–.–
646	¼ Noble (Platinum) 1988		–.–
647	½ Noble (Platinum) 1988		–.–
648	1 Noble (Platinum) 1988	–.–	–.–
649	5 Noble (Platinum) 1988		–.–
650	10 Noble (Platinum) 1988		–.–

Griechenland   **Greece**   **Grèce**

Hellas, ΕΛΛΑΣ

Area: 50,547 sq. mi. Population: 9,980,000.
The Greek War of Liberation in the years 1921–1830 brought to an end the
Turkish domination which had existed since the 15th century. On gaining
independence the country became a kingdom, and in the years 1924–1935
was ruled as a republic. After the successful National Revolution of 21st
April 1967, King Constantine left the country; republic since 1973.
Capital: Athens.

100 Lepta = 1 Drachma

GEORGE I 1863–1913

			VF	XF
1 (19)	5	Lepta (Ni) 1912. Crown, date. ℞ screech owl (Athene noctua — Strigidae) and value (with hole in centre)	1.50	3.00

2 (20)	10	Lepta (Ni) 1912. Type as No. 1	1.25	2.50
3 (21)	20	Lepta (Ni) 1912. National arms, date. ℞ Athena and olive branch (Olea europea — Oleaceae)	2.00	4.50
4 (22)	1	Drachma (Ag) 1910–1911. Head left of King George I (1845–1913). ℞ Thetis, goddess of the·sea, seated on sea-horse	9.00	20.00
5 (23)	2	Drachmai (Ag) 1911. Type as No. 4	15.00	35.00

Under King Constantine I 1913–1917, King Alexander 1917–1920 and
King Constantine I 1920–1922 there was no issue of coinage.

GEORGE II 1922–1923

6 (29)	10	Lepta (Al) 1922. Crown, date. ℞ olive branch and value	2.50	4.00
7 (30)	50	Lepta (Ni–Br) 1921. Inscription, arms, date. ℞ olive branch		
		a) mintmark H (Heaton)		1100.00
		b) mintmark KN (King's Norton)		2000.00

8 (31) 20 Lepta (Cu–Ni) 1926. Helmeted head
left of Athena, patrones of heroes,
cities, agriculture, science and the
arts. ℞ inscription and value

	VF	XF
	1.60	4.00

9 (32) 50 Lepta (Cu–Ni) 1926. Type as No. 8   1.50   3.00
10 (33)   1 Drachma (Cu–Ni) 1926. Type as No. 8   1.50   4.00
11 (34)   2 Drachmai (Cu–Ni) 1926. Type as No. 8   2.00   4.50

12 (35)   5 Drachmai (Ni) 1930. Phoenix, above
High Cross next to rays of light. ℞
value between laurel branches tied
underneath   2.00   6.00

13 (36) 10 Drachmai (Ag) 1930. Head left of
Demeter. Greek goddess of the earth
and all its fruits. ℞ ears of wheat   9.00   30.00
14 (37) 20 Drachmai (Ag) 1930. Head of Poseidon, god of the sea. ℞ prow of galley   11.00   32.00

GEORGE II 1935–1947

COMMEMORATIVE ISSUES (3) FOR THE RESTORATION OF THE MONARCHY

15 (B 37) 20 Drachmai (Au) 1935. Head left of King
George II (1890–1947). Inscription. ℞
value within wreath; above, crown

Proof

4500.00

A 15 (A 37) 100 Drachmai (Ag) 1935. Type as No. 15   1000.00
16 (C 37) 100 Drachmai (Au) 1935. Type as No. 15   8000.00

PAUL I 1947–1964

		VF	XF
17 (38)	5 Lepta (Al) 1954. Olive branches; above, crown. ℞ ears of corn and value	0.20	0.35
18 (39)	10 Lepta (Al) 1954–1969. ℞ bunches of grapes and value	0.20	0.35
19 (40)	20 Lepta (Al) 1954–1959. ℞ olive branch and date	0.25	0.40

20 (41)	50 Lepta (Cu–Ni) 1954–1965. Head left of Paul I (1901–1964). ℞ national arms. Occurring with different mint marks!	0.80	1.50
21 (42)	1 Drachma (Cu–Ni) 1954–1965. Type as No. 20. Occurring with different mint marks!	0.60	1.50
22 (43)	2 Drachmai (Cu–Ni) 1954–1965. Type as No. 20. Occurring with different mint marks!	1.10	1.80
23 (44)	5 Drachmai (Cu–Ni) 1954, 1965. Type as No. 20	1.30	2.00
24 (45)	10 Drachmai (Ni) 1959, 1965. Type as No. 20	1.80	2.60
25 (46)	20 Drachmai (Ag) 1960–1965. ℞ Selene, the moon goddess, rising from the sea	4.50	8.00

COMMEMORATIVE ISSUE FOR THE CENTENARY OF THE ROYAL GREEK DYNASTY

26 (47) 30 Drachmai (Ag) 1963. Heads of George I, reigned 1863–1913; Con-

stantine I, reigned 1913–1917, 1920 to
1922; Alexander, reigned 1917–1920;
George II, reigned 1922–1923, 1935 to
1947; Paul I, reigned 1947–1964. ℞
map representing the Kingdom of
Greece; value

	VF	XF
	8.00	15.00

CONSTANTINE II 1964–1973

COMMEMORATIVE ISSUE FOR THE WEDDING OF KING CONSTANTINE II AND PRINCESS ANNE-MARIE OF DENMARK

				VF	XF
27 (48)	30	Drachmai (Ag) 1964. Conjoined heads of the Royal couple. ℞ double eagle and value		7.00	10.50
28 (49)	50	Lepta (Cu–Ni) 1966–1970. Head left of King Constantine II (*1940). ℞ national arms and value		0.20	0.40
29 (50)	1	Drachma (Cu–Ni) 1966–1970. Type as No. 28		0.40	0.80
30 (51)	2	Drachmai (Cu–Ni) 1966–1970. Type as No. 28		0.60	1.20

31 (52)	5	Drachmai (Cu–Ni) 1966–1970. Type as No. 28	1.00	2.00
32 (53)	10	Drachmai (Cu–Ni) 1968. Type as No. 28	1.80	2.50

COMMEMORATIVE ISSUES (4) FOR THE NATIONAL REVOLUTION OF 21st APRIL 1967

			Unc
33 (56)	20	Drachmai (Au) 1967. Soldier standing in front of a phoenix rising from flames, emblem of the military régime. ℞ national arms and value	300.00
34 (54)	50	Drachmai (Ag) 1967. Type as No. 33	35.00

				Unc
35 (55)	100	Drachmai (Ag) 1967. Type as No. 33		50.00
36 (57)	100	Drachmai (Au) 1967. Type as No. 33		900.00
37 (38)	5	Lepta (Al) 1971. Type as No. 17, but hole with smaller diameter	**VF** 0.10	**XF** 0.20

38 (39)	10	Lepta (Al) 1971. Type as No. 18, but hole with smaller diameter	0.10	0.20
39 (40)	20	Lepta (Al) 1971. Type as No. 19, but hole with smaller diameter	0.20	0.40

40 (58)	50	Lepta (Cu–Ni) 1971. Constantine II, bust facing left. ℞ emblem of the military government, value	0.30	0.60
41 (59)	1	Drachma (Cu–Ni) 1971, 1973. Type as No. 40	0.50	0.80
42 (60)	2	Drachmai (Cu–Ni) 1971, 1973. Type as No. 40	0.60	1.20
43 (61)	5	Drachmai (Cu–Ni) 1971, 1973. Type as No. 40	0.80	1.50
44 (62)	10	Drachmai (Cu-Ni) 1971, 1973. Type as No. 40	1.00	2.50
45 (A 58)	10	Lepta (Al) 1973. Emblem of the military government, name of country (translated: Kingdom of Greece), date. ℞ trident between two dolphins, value	0.20	0.70
46 (B 58)	20	Lepta (Al) 1973. ℞ fruit branch, value	0.20	0.70

				VF	XF
47 (63)	20	Drachmai (Cu–Ni) 1973. Selene (moon-goddess), rising from the sea. ℞ emblem of the military government		2.00	3.50

REPUBLIC since 1973

48 (64)	10	Lepta (Al) 1973. Phoenix rising from the flames, above rays of light (arms of the Republic), name of country, date. ℞ trident between two dolphins, value		0.10	0.20
49 (65)	20	Lepta (Al) 1973. ℞ fruit branch, value		0.10	0.20
50 (66)	50	Lepta (Br) 1973. ℞ ornament, value		0.10	0.20
51 (67)	1	Drachma (Al–Br) 1973. ℞ screech-owl (Athene noctua – Strigidae), value		0.15	0.25
52 (68)	2	Drachmai (Al–Br) 1973. Type as No. 51		0.20	0.40
53 (69)	5	Drachmai (Cu–Ni) 1973. ℞ Pegasus, value		0.50	1.00

54 (70)	10	Drachmai (Cu–Ni) 1973. Type as No. 53		1.20	1.80
55 (71)	20	Drachmai (Cu–Ni) 1973. ℞ Athene		1.50	2.50

56 (72)	10	Lepta (Al) 1976, 1978. Coat of arms. Rev. bull, value		0.10	0.20

	XF	Unc

57 (73) 20 Lepta (Al) 1976, 1978. Rev. head of a
horse, value — 0.10 — 0.20

58 (74) 50 Lepta (Al–Br) 1976, 1978, 1982, 1984.
Markos Botsaris. Rev. value, date — 0.10 — 0.20

59 (75) 1 Drachma (Al–Br) 1976, 1978, 1980,
1982, 1984. Konstantinos Kanaris.
Rev. sailing ship, value, date — 0.20 — 0.40

60 (76) 2 Drachmai (Al–Br) 1976, 1978, 1980.
Georgios Karaiskakes. Rev. crossed
rifles, value, date — 0.25 — 0.50

61 (77) 5 Drachmai (Cu-Ni) 1976, 1978, 1980.
Head left of Aristotle. Rev. value, date — 0.40 — 0.90

62 (78) 10 Drachmai (Cu-Ni) 1976, 1978, 1980.
Head left of Democritos. Rev. symbolic
representation of an atom; value, date — 0.70 — 1.00

820   **Greece**

			XF	**Unc**
63 (79)	20	Drachmai (Cu-Ni) 1976, 1978, 1980. Head left of Pericles. Rev. temple in the Acropolis; value, date	0.80	1.20

50th ANNIVERSARY OF BANK OF GREECE

			Proof
64 (82)	100	Drachmai (Ag) 1978	75.00

COMMON MARKET MEMBERSHIP (2)

			Proof
65 (80)	500	Drachmai (Ag) 1979	85.00
66 (81)	10000	Drachmai (Au) 1979	650.00

			XF	**Unc**
67 (83)	50	Drachmai (Cu-Ni) 1980. Portrait left of Solon (c. 640–560 B.C.), statesman and poet of Athens	1.00	2.00

		Unc	Proof
68 (84)	100 Drachmai (Ag) 1981	6.00	10.00
69 (85)	250 Drachmai (Ag) 1981	10.00	15.00
70 (86)	500 Drachmai (Ag) 1981	15.00	25.00

71 (87)	2500 Drachmai (Au) 1981		150.00

		Unc	Proof
72 (88)	5000 Drachmai (Au) 1981		300.00
73 (89)	100 Drachmai (Ag) 1982	6.00	10.00
74 (90)	250 Drachmai (Ag) 1982	10.00	15.00
75 (91)	500 Drachmai (Ag) 1982	15.00	25.00
76 (92)	2500 Drachmai (Au) 1982		175.00
77 (93)	5000 Drachmai (Au) 1982		275.00
78 (94)	100 Drachmai (Ag) 1982	6.00	10.00
79 (95)	250 Drachmai (Ag) 1982	10.00	15.00
80 (96)	500 Drachmai (Ag) 1982	15.00	25.00
81 (97)	2500 Drachmai (Au) 1982		175.00
82 (98)	5000 Drachmai (Au) 1982		275.00

		XF	Unc
83 (99)	2 Drachmes (Al–Br) 1982, 1984, 1986	0.20	0.30
84 (100)	5 Drachmes (Cu–Ni) 1982, 1984, 1986	0.30	0.50
85 (101)	10 Drachmes (Cu–Ni) 1982, 1984, 1986	0.40	0.60
86 (102)	20 Drachmes (Cu–Ni) 1982, 1984, 1986	0.80	1.20
87 (103)	50 Drachmes (Cu–Ni) 1982, 1984	1.25	1.75

XXIII. OLYMPIC SUMMER GAMES IN LOS ANGELES (2)

		Proof
88 (104)	500 Drachmes (Ag) 1984. Rev. Runner with torch	40.00
89 (105)	5000 Drachmes (Au) 1984. Rev. Portrait of Apollon	275.00

Grenada

Area: 133 sq. mi. Population: 110,000.
Part of the Lesser Antilles; a member of the Caribbean Free Trade Area (CARIFTA). Since 1967 an associate member of the United Kingdom of Great Britain. Together with the countries of Antigua, Barbados, Dominica, Montserrat, St. Christopher- (St. Kitts-) Nevis-Anguilla, St. Lucia and St. Vincent, Grenada forms part of the Monetary Union of the East Caribbean Dollar. The issuing authority for the whole Monetary Union is the East Caribbean Currency Authority with headquarters in Bridgetown, Barbados.
Capital: St. George's.

100 Cents = 1 East Caribbean Dollar

COMMEMORATIVE ISSUE FOR THE INAUGURATION OF THE CARIBBEAN DEVELOPMENT BANK AND FOR THE FAO COIN PLAN

		Unc	Proof
1 (5*)	4 Dollars (Cu–Ni) 1970. Emblem of state. ℞ bananas, sugar-cane and value	10.00	25.00

*This number refers to Yeoman's East Caribbean Territories listing.

ROYAL VISIT (2)

		Unc	Proof
2	10 Dollars 1985:		
	a) (Ag) .925 silver, 28.28 g		35.00
	b) (Cu–Ni)	5.00	
3	500 Dollars (Au) 1985. Type as No. 2; .916⅔ gold, 47.54 g (250 pcs.)		900.00

Guadeloupe

Area: 812 sq. mi. Population: 306,000.

Guadeloupe has been a French possession since 1635. Merely in the years 1759–63, 1794, 1810–13 and 1815/16 the island was in British hands. The Overseas Department formed in 1958 comprising the islands of Marie Galante, Désirade, two-thirds of of Saint Martin (the remaining part of Saint Martin belongs to the Netherlands Antilles) and Saint Barthélémy has since then been a part of the French motherland.

Capital: Basse-Terre.

100 Centimes = 1 Franc

			VF	XF
1 (1)	50	Centimes (Cu–Ni) 1903–1921. Head of native to left. ℞ palm branch	8.00	15.00
2 (2)	1	Franc (Cu–Ni) 1903–1921	12.00	24.00

Guatemala **Guatemala** **Guatemala**

Area: 42,045 sq. mi. Population: 8,000,000.
The Maya tribes were brought under submission in 1524 by the Spaniard Pedro de Alvaredo and their country absorbed into the Captaincy-General of Guatemala. After independence in 1821 Guatemala came temporarily under Mexican domination. In 1823 the country joined up with the other states of Central America to form the »Provincias Unidas del Centro de Améri-co«. After the break-up of the Confederation and warlike conflicts, Guatemala became independent again in 1839.
Capital: Guatemala City.

100 Centavos or 8 Reales = 1 Peso
100 Centavos = 1 Quetzal

			VF	XF
1 (85)	¼	Real (Cu–Ni) 1900–1901. Mountain range. ℞ value within wreath	0.80	1.60
2 (86)	½	Real (Cu–Ni) 1900–1901. National arms. ℞ seated allegorical figure of the Republic and value	1.50	3.00
3 (81)	1	Real (Ag) 1899–1900	3.50	6.00
4 (87)	1	Real (Cu–Ni) 1900–1912	2.00	3.50
5 (89)	12½	Centavos (Br) 1915. Name of country, date and inscription PROVISIONAL. ℞ value within circle	3.50	6.00
6 (90)	25	Centavos (Br) 1915. Type as No. 5	5.00	7.00
7 (91)	50	Centavos (Al–Br) 1922. Stylized sun. ℞ value within circle	2.50	5.00
8 (92)	1	Peso (Al–Br) 1923. Bust left of Miguel Garcia Gránados (1809–1878), provisional Head of State 1871–1873. ℞ value	3.00	6.50

9 (93)   5 Pesos (Al–Br) 1923. Bust right of Justo

			VF	XF
		Rufino Barrios (1835–1885), Head of State 1873–1885	5.00	9.00

CURRENCY REFORM on 16th November 1924

			VF	XF
10 (94)	½	Centavo (Bra) 1932, 1946. National arms. ℞ value	0.80	1.60
11 (95)	1	Centavo (Br) 1925. Type as No. 10	4.00	7.00
12 (96)	1	Centavo (Br) 1929. Type as No. 11, but arms larger	2.50	4.00
13 (97)	1	Centavo (Bra) 1932, 1939, 1946–1949	0.40	1.20
14 (98)	2	Centavos (Bra) 1932	0.80	1.60
15 (99)	5	Centavos (Ag) 1925, 1944–1949. National arms with long-tailed quetzal. ℞ quetzal (Pharomachrus mocinno–Trogonidae) on column, value	1.50	2.50
16 (99a)	5	Centavos (Ag) 1928–1943. Type as No. 15, but national arms with short-tailed quetzal	1.50	2.50
17 (100)	10	Centavos (Ag) 1925, 1944–1949. Type as No. 15	1.00	2.00
18 (100a)	10	Centavos (Ag) 1928–1947. Type as No. 16	2.00	3.00
19 (101)	¼	Quetzal (Ag) 1925. With lettered edge	6.00	11.00
20 (102)	¼	Quetzal (Ag) 1926–1929	3.50	5.00
21 (102a)	¼	Quetzal (Ag) 1946–1949. Reeded edge	3.50	5.00
22 (103)	½	Quetzal (Ag) 1925	20.00	30.00
23 (104)	1	Quetzal (Ag) 1925	500.00	850.00
24 (105)	5	Quetzales (Au) 1926	275.00	360.00
25 (106)	10	Quetzales (Au) 1926	450.00	750.00

			VF	XF
26 (107)	20	Quetzales (Au) 1926	600.00	900.00
27 (108)	1	Centavo (Bra) 1943–1944. Quetzal with outstretched wings. ℞ value in letters	1.50	2.50
28 (109)	2	Centavos (Bra) 1943–1944	0.80	1.60
29 (110)	25	Centavos (Ag) 1943. Quetzal and map of Guatemala. ℞ Parliament buildings in Guatemala City	6.50	11.00

				VF	XF
30 (111)	1	Centavo (Bra) 1949–1954. National arms. ℞ Bust left of Bartolomé de las Casas (1474–1566), Missionary to the Indians, value in letters		0.40	0.80
31 (112)	1	Centavo (Bra) 1954–1958. Type as No. 30, but head of Bartolomé de las Casas larger and close to the circular inscription		0.40	0.80
32 (113)	1	Centavo (Bra) 1958–1964. ℞ head of Bartolomé de las Casas, slimmer portrait		0.10	0.20
33 (114)	5	Centavos (Ag) 1949. National arms. ℞ kapok tree (Ceiba pentandra – Bombaceae) and value		4.00	8.00
34 (115)	5	Centavos (Ag) 1950–1959. ℞ kapok tree with bare crown. Heavy figure 5		0.80	1.60
35 (116)	5	Centavos (Ag) 1960–1964. ℞ kapok tree with somewhat lighter foliage; low relief, smaller figures and inscription		0.70	1.20

36 (117)	10	Centavos (Ag) 1949–1959. National arms. ℞ the monolith at Quiriguà, stele with figures and calendar dates from the Maya culture, c. 750–800; value		2.00	5.00
37 (117a)	10	Centavos (Ag) 1957–1958. ℞ monolith of larger size		3.00	6.00
38 (118)	10	Centavos (Ag) 1960–1964. ℞ monolith even larger		2.00	3.50

| **39** (119) | 25 | Centavos (Ag) 1950–1959. National arms. ℞ bust of an Indian woman wearing costume of Santiago Atitlan; value | | 3.50 | 7.00 |
| **40** (120) | 25 | Centavos (Ag) 1960–1964. Type similar to No. 39 | | 2.00 | 3.50 |

			VF	**XF**
41 (121)	50	Centavos (Ag) 1962–1963. National arms. ℞ "White Nun" orchid (Lycaste skinneri var. alba – Orchidaceae), the national emblem	3.00	5.00

42 (122)	1	Centavo (Bra) 1965–1970. Type similar to No. 32, but diameter 9 mm instead of 11 mm	0.10	0.15

43 (123)	5	Centavos (Ni–Bra) 1965–1970. Type similar to No. 35	0.10	0.20
44 (124)	10	Centavos (Ni–Bra) 1965–1970. Type similar to No. 38	0.20	0.40
45 (125)	25	Centavos (Ni-Bra) 1965–1970. Type similar to No. 40	0.60	0.90

46 (122a)	1	Centavo (Bra) 1972, 1973	0.10	0.15
47 (123a)	5	Centavos (Ni-Bra) 1971, 1974–1977	0.10	0.20
48 (124a)	10	Centavos (Ni-Bra) 1971	0.20	0.40
49 (124b)	10	Centavos (Cu-Ni) 1973–1976. Type similar to No. 48	0.15	0.30

		VF	XF
50 (125b) 25 Centavos (Ni-Bra) 1971, 1975, 1976		0.50	0.80
51 (122b) 1 Centavo (Bra) 1974–1982, 1987		0.10	0.20

52 (123b) 5 Centavos (Cu-Ni) 1977–1981, 1985, 1987. Type as No. 47, but fully circular inscription on the obverse   0.10   0.20

53 (124c) 10 Centavos (Cu-Ni) 1977–1981, 1983, 1986, 1987   0.15   0.25

54 (125c) 25 Centavos (Cu-Ni) 1977–1979, 1981, 1984, 1987.   0.50   0.80

55 25 Centavos (Cu-Ni) 1982. Type as No. 54, but smaller dia.   0.60   1.00

Guinea **Guinea** **Guinée**

Area: 98,344 sq. mi. Population: 6,100,000.
From 1904 onwards Guinea was part of French West Africa. The inhabitants voted against joining the French Community in a referendum of 28th September 1958, and as a result independence was declared as soon afterwards as 2nd October 1958.
Capital: Conakry.

100 Centimes = 1 Guinea Franc; since 2nd October 1972:
100 Cauris = 1 Syli

			VF	XF
1 (1)	5	Francs (Al-Br) 1959. Head right of Ahmed Sékou Touré (1922–1984), Head of State and Prime Minister since 1958. Rev. value between coconut palms	3.00	10.00
2 (2)	10	Francs (Al-Br) 1959. Head left of Ahmed Sékou Touré	6.00	12.50
3 (3)	25	Francs (Al-Br) 1959	10.00	20.00
4 (4)	1	Franc (Cu-Ni) 1962. Rev. value between palm branches	3.00	8.00

5 (5)	5	Francs (Cu–Ni) 1962. ℞ value between palm branches and coconuts	4.00	8.00
6 (6)	10	Francs (Cu-Ni) 1962. ℞ value within wreath	3.00	8.00
7 (7)	25	Francs (Cu-Ni) 1962. ℞ value within wreath	5.00	10.00
8 (8)	50	Francs (Cu-Ni) 1969. Type as No. 6		75.00
9 (9)	100	Francs (Cu-Ni) 1971. Type similar to No. 7		100.00

COMMEMORATIVE ISSUES (11)
FOR THE 10th ANNIVERSARY OF INDEPENDENCE

10	100	Francs (Ag) 1968–. Head of Dr. Martin Luther King (1929–1968), evangelist, American Civil Rights Leader and winner of the Nobel prize for peace in 1964. ℞ national arms, value	**Proof** 10.00
11	200	Francs (Ag) 1968–. Head of John F. Kennedy (1917–1963), 35th President of the United States of America, and Robert F. Kennedy (1925–1968), Minister of Justice, Presidential Candidate in 1968. Rev. as No. 10	15.00
12	200	Francs (Ag) 1968–. Head of Almamy Samory Touré (1830–1900), Chief of the Bisandugu and leader of the struggle against the French. ℞ as No. 10	15.00

13	250	Francs (Ag) 1968–. U.S. moon research programme, third stage "Manned Landing". Apollo programme. Lunar module and lunarnauts carrying out studies of the moon surface; in background, moon scenery; diagram of the lunar orbits showing the Apollo capsule; on left, terrestrial globe. R as No. 10	20.00

14	250	Francs (Ag) 1968–. Bust facing of Alpha Yaya Diallo (1850–1912), local ruler. R as No. 10	20.00

| 15 | 500 Francs (Ag) 1968–. Masked bird-man dancer from the Macenta district (South Guinea). R as No. 10 | **Proof** 30.00 |

16	500 Francs (Ag) 1968–. Distant view of the city of Munich; medals of the Olympic Games in Helsinki 1952, Melbourne 1956, Rome 1960, Tokyo 1964 and Mexico 1968, each set in one of the five Olympic rings; below, flaming torch. R as No. 10	35.00
17	1000 Francs (Au) 1968–. John F. Kennedy and Robert F. Kennedy. R as No. 10	100.00
18	2000 Francs (Au) 1968–. Type as No. 13	150.00
19	5000 Francs (Au) 1968–. Type as No. 16	350.00

20 10 000 Francs (Au) 1968–. Head left of Ahmed
    Sékou Touré. ℞ as No. 10

Proof

700.00

COMMEMORATIVE ISSUES (4) FOR SPACE RESEARCH

21   250 Francs (Ag) 1970. Rev. Three winged
       horses ascending before sun with rays
       in background. Apollo XIII, and part
       of moon surface.

20.00

22   250 Francs (Ag) 1970. Rev. »Soyuz«, the
       Soviet space-ship

20.00

23   2000 Francs (Au) 1970. Type as No. 21

150.00

24   2000 Francs (Au) 1970. Type as No. 22

150.00

25   31

25	500	Francs (Ag) 1970–. Rameses III (1198–1167 B. C.), Pharaoh of the 20th Dynasty. ℞ as No. 10	**Proof** 40.00
26	500	Francs (Ag) 1970–. Chephren, Pharaoh of the 4th Dynasty; he built the second highest pyramid near Gizeh, which is today still 136.5 metres high	40.00
27	500	Francs (Ag) 1970–. Ikhnaton (Amenophis IV), Pharaoh of the 18th Dynasty; he introduced the sun-worship as the State religion	40.00
28	500	Francs (Ag) 1970–. Tutankhamen, Pharaoh of the 18th Dynasty	40.00
29	500	Francs (Ag) 1970–. Queen Nefertiti	40.00
30	500	Francs (Ag) 1970–. Queen Teyi	40.00
31	500	Francs (Ag) 1970–. Queen Cleopatra	40.00
32	500	Francs (Ag) 1970–. Gamal Abd al Nasser (1918–1970), Egyptian Head of State 1956–1970	40.00
33	5 000	Francs (Au) 1970–. Type as No. 23	300.00
34	5 000	Francs (Au) 1970–. Type as No. 24	300.00
35	5 000	Francs (Au) 1970–. Type as No. 25	300.00
36	5 000	Francs (Au) 1970–. Type as No. 26	300.00
37	5 000	Francs (Au) 1970–. Type as No. 27	300.00
38	5 000	Francs (Au) 1970–. Type as No. 28	300.00
39	5 000	Francs (Au) 1970–. Type as No. 29	300.00
40	5 000	Francs (Au) 1970–. Type as No. 30	300.00

	NEW CURRENCY: 100 Cauris = 1 Syli	**XF**	**Unc**
41 (10)	50 Cauris (Al) 1971.	5.00	10.00
42 (11)	1 Syli (Al) 1971	6.00	12.00
43 (12)	2 Sylis (Al) 1971	6.00	12.00
44 (13)	5 Sylis (Al) 1971	6.00	12.00

All valuations in the SCHÖN are stated in U.S. Dollars.

			Unc	Proof
45	500	Sylis (Ag) 1977. Miriam Makeba	50.00	55.00
46	500	Sylis (Ag) 1977. Patrice Lumumba	70.00	75.00
47	1000	Sylis (Au) 1977. Miriam Makeba	100.00	100.00
48	1000	Sylis (Au) 1977. Nkrumah	100.00	100.00
49	2000	Sylis (Au) 1977. Sekou Touré	200.00	200.00
50	2000	Sylis (Au) 1977. Mao Tse Tung	200.00	200.00

INTERNATIONAL GAMES (2)

51	200 Sylis (Cu-Ni) 1984. Rev. Walking	-.-
52	500 Sylis (Ag) 1984. Type as No. 51	-.-

NEW CURRENCY: Guinea Francs only

		XF	Unc
53	5 Francs (Brass-clad steel) 1985	0.60	1.50
54	10 Francs (Brass-clad steel)1985	1.00	2.50

Guinea-Bissau   **Guinea-Bissau**   **Guiné Bissau**

Area: 13,948 sq. mi. Population: 895,000.
The former Portuguese colony and overseas territory Portuguese Guinea became independent on Sept. 10th 1974. The new republik took the name of Guinea-Bissau.
Capital: Bissau.

100 Centavos = 1 Guinea Peso

ISSUES FOR THE FAO COIN PLAN (5)

			XF	Unc
1 (1)	50	Centavos (Al) 1977, 1978. Coconut	1.00	2.50
2 (2)	1	Peso (Ni-Bra) 1977, 1978. Oil palm	1.00	2.50
3 (3)	2,50	Pesos (Ni-Bra) 1977, 1978. Cassava	2.50	5.00
4 (4)	5	Pesos (Cu-Ni) 1977, 1978. Groundnuts	5.00	10.00
5 (5)	20	Pesos (Cu-Ni) 1977, 1978. Rice	10.00	15.00

Area: 83,00 sq. mi. Population: 955,000.
The former British Crown Colony of British Guiana, situated in the north-eastern part of South America, has considerable deposits of diamonds and aluminium. The country became independent under the name of Guyana on 26th June 1966, but remained within the British Commonwealth; since 23rd February 1970 the country has been a republic.
Capital: Georgetown.

100 Cents = 1 Guyana Dollar

			VF	EF
1 (1)	1	Cent (Bra) 1967–. Stylized lotus flowers (Nelumbo sp. – Nymphaeaceae). ℞ value within circle, date between two hoatzins (Opisthocomus hoazin – Opisthocomidae)	0.05	0.10

			VF	EF
2 (2)	5	Cents (Bra) 1967–. Type as No. 1	0.10	0.20
3 (3)	10	Cents (Cu-Ni) 1967. National arms with jaguars ((Panthera onca – Felidae) as supporters and hoatzin as emblem. R as No. 1	0.15	0.30
4 (4)	25	Cents (Cu-Ni) 1967–. Type as No. 3	0.20	0.40

			VF	EF
5 (5)	50	Cents (Cu-Ni) 1967. Type as No. 3	0.40	0.80

			Unc	Proof
6 (6)	1 Dollar (Cu–Ni) 1970. Cuffy, an African slave who organized a revolt on 23rd February 1763 and captured from the Dutch governor a territory bordering the Berbice river. The Revolutionary Government, subsequently set up, was defeated after initial successes. The "Berbice Revolt" was the first step towards independence. ℞ motto FOOD FOR ALL above figure 1, with head of cow and ears of corn on either side		3.00	6.00

10th ANNIVERSARY OF INDEPENDENCE (10)

			Unc	Proof
7 (7)	1 Cent (Br) 1976–1980		0.25	0.50
8 (8)	5 Cents (Bra) 1976–1980.		0.30	0.75
9 (9)	10 Cents (Cu–Ni) 1976–1980.		0.40	1.00
10 (10)	25 Cents (Cu–Ni) 1976–1980.		1.00	1.50
11 (11)	50 Cents (Cu–Ni) 1976–1980.		5.00	2.00
12 (12)	1 Dollar (Cu–Ni) 1976–1980.		4.00	5.00
13 (13)	5 Dollars 1976–1980			
	a) (Ag)			12.50
	b) (Cu–Ni)		15.00	
14 (14)	10 Dollars 1976–1980:			
	a) (Ag)			20.00
	b) (Cu–Ni)		30.00	
15 (15)	50 Dollars (Ag) 1976		125.00	100.00
16 (16)	100 Dollars (Au) 1976. Arawak Indian		125.00	100.00
17 (17)	100 Dollars (Au) 1977. Legendary golden Man		125.00	100.00

Area: 10,714 sq. mi. together with the islands La Tortuga and Gonave.
Population: 5,000,000.
Haiti (Indian: mountain) was discovered in 1492 by Columbus, and called
Hispaniola, in some parts also San(to) Domingo. The Republic of Haiti
comprises the western part of the Island of Haiti.
Capital: Port-au-Prince.

100 Centimes = 1 Gourde

The medium of exchange of the United States is also used as legal tender.

			VF	XF
1 (14)	5	Centimes (Cu–Ni) 1904. Coat of arms. ℞ value and date	5.00	10.00
2 (10)	5	Centimes (Cu–Ni) 1904–1906. General Pedro Nord-Alexis (1820–1910), president 1902–1908. ℞ coat of arms and value	0.80	1.50
3 (11)	10	Centimes (Cu–Ni) 1905, 1906	1.00	1.80
4 (12)	20	Centimes (Cu–Ni) 1907, 1908	1.50	2.50
5 (13)	50	Centimes (Cu–Ni) 1907–1908	3.00	5.00
6 (15)	5	Centimes (Cu–Ni) 1949. Dumarsais Estimé (1900–1953), President 1946–1950. ℞ coat of arms and value	0.30	0.60
7 (16)	10	Centimes (Cu–Ni) 1949	0.50	0.90
8 (17)	5	Centimes (Ni–St) 1953. Paul E. Magloire (*1907), President 1951–1956. ℞ coat of arms and value	0.25	0.50
9 (18)	10	Centimes (Ni–St) 1953	0.40	0.70
10 (19)	20	Centimes (Ni–St) 1956	0.50	0.90
11 (20)	5	Centimes (Ni–St) 1958, 1970. François Duvalier (1909–1971), President 1957–1971	0.10	0.20

12 (21)	10	Centimes (Ni–St) 1958, 1970	0.16	0.30
13 (22)	20	Centimes (Ni–St) 1970	0.30	0.60

			Proof
14	5	Gourdes (Ag) 1967–. Map of the Haiti Island (Hispaniola) and Columbus' fleet: "Nina", "Santa Maria", and "Pinta"	15.00
15	10	Gourdes (Ag) 1967–. François Dominique Toussaint-Louverture (1745–1803), descendant of the kings of Allada (Dahomey), Haitian general and politician	25.00
16	25	Gourdes (Ag) 1967–. Art objects	80.00
17	20	Gourdes (Au) 1967–. Mackandal, one of the first revolutionaries of Haiti, with machete	85.00
18	50	Gourdes (Au) 1967–. Voodoo dancer, surrounded by symbols	175.00

19	100	Gourdes (Au) 1967–. Marie Jeanne, wife of General Lamatinière, fought at his side in 1803 for the liberation of Haiti	325.00
20	200	Gourdes (Au) 1967–. Revolt of Santo Domingo during the years 1791–1803 against French domination. Design: liberated slave with machete and torch	650.00
21	1000	Gourdes (Au) 1967–. Dr. François Duvalier, President. ℞ coat of arms	3000.00

Proof

22   30 Gourdes (Au) 1967–. Citadel of St. Christopher   125.00

23   40 Gourdes (Au) 1967–. Jean Jacques Dessalines (1758–1806), who overthrew the republic in December 1804, had himself crowned emperor of Haiti, with the title of Jacob I   175.00

24   60 Gourdes (Au) 1967–. Alexander Sabès Pétion (1770–1818), President of Southern Haiti 1808–1818   300.00

25 250 Gourdes (Au) 1969. Henri Christophe (1767–1820), President of Northern Haiti 1808–1810, emperor of Haiti, with the title of Henry I, 1811–18.20. Citadel of St. Christopher   1000.00

26 500 Gourdes (Au) 1967–. Handicraft   2000.00

27   5 Gourdes (Ag) 1970. Vacation land Haiti: beach scene   25.00

28   10 Gourdes (Ag) 1970. Billy Bowlegs, deputy chief of the Seminoles. During the Indian War of 1812, he fought with the chieftain King Paine near the border of Georgia, against American troops commanded by Andrew Jackson, who was later to become president. He was wounded in combat   40.00

29   10 Gourdes (Ag) 1970. Geronimo (Goy-

athlay = "One who yawns") (January 1829–17th February 1909), a dreaded warrior, medicine man, and prophet of the Chiricahua Apaches. In 1875, when Cochise (whose image inspired Karl May's creation of "Winnetou") made peace with the Americans, he left his tribe. Together with devoted warriors and some younger Indian chiefs he terrorized Mexican territory. He died as a prisoner in Fort Hill, Oklahoma.

40.00

30 10 Gourdes (Ag) 1970. Sitting Bull (Ta-tanka Yotanka) (c. 1834–15th December 1890), one of the most important personalities of the Dakota (Sioux) tribe. The last Indian massacre at Little Big Horn in the Black Hills perpetuated his fame: during this battle (1876) General Custer (the Indians called him Long Hair) and his troops were wiped out to the last man. Sitting Bull died from a bullet shot by an Indian sheriff near his birthplace on the Grand River in South Dakota.   40.00

31 10 Gourdes (Ag) 1970. Chief Joseph (Hin-maton-Yalatkit = "The-thunder-that-rushes-over-the-hills") (1840–21st September 1904), impressive, peace-loving character, from the Nez Perzé tribe, who owes his occidental name to his teacher, a white missionary. He died in the Colville Reservation of Nespelem, in the federated state of Washington.   40.00

32 10 Gourdes (Ag) 1970. War Eagle, chief of the Yankton Sioux   40.00

33 10 Gourdes (Ag) 1970. Red Cloud (Mach-piya-Luta) (c. 1822–8th October 1909), important Dakota chief from the Oglala tribe, who tried by force to prevent the start of road construction at Fort Laramie in 1865. The road was intended to provide an easy approach to the gold fields of Montana. In 1868 he abandoned his warlike activities and did not even take part in the Sioux War of 1876 (battle at Little Big Horn). He died in the Indian Reservation of Pine Ridge in South Dakota.

			Proof
34	10	Gourdes (Ag) 1970. Stalking Turkey, chief of the Cherokee	40.00
35	10	Gourdes (Ag) 1970. Osceola (As-se-he-ho-lar) (1804–30th January 1838), famous chief of the Seminoles, outstanding strategist. Successfully fought the American troops during the Seminole War. During a peace conference he was unjustly arrested, and taken prisoner to Fort Moultrie in South Carolina, where he died.	40.00
36	10	Gourdes (Ag) 1970. Playing Fox, chief of the Fox (also Sauk or Sac)	40.00
37	25	Gourdes (Ag) 1970. International air port "François Duvalier", main building	40.00
38	50	Gourdes (Au) 1970. Héros de Vertières	175.00
39	100	Gourdes (Au) 1970. Same type as No. 28	225.00
40	100	Gourdes (Au) 1970. Same type as No. 29	350.00
41	100	Gourdes (Au) 1970. Same type as No. 30	350.00
42	100	Gourdes (Au) 1970. Same type as No. 31	350.00
43	100	Gourdes (Au) 1970. Same type as No. 32	350.00
44	100	Gourdes (Au) 1970. Same type as No. 33	350.00
45	100	Gourdes (Au) 1970. Same type as No. 34	350.00

46	100	Gourdes (Au) 1970. Same type as No. 35	350.00
47	100	Gourdes (Au) 1970. Same type as No. 36	350.00
48	200	Gourdes (Au) 1970. "Le Marron inconnu", the unkonwn rebel of San Domingo	550.00

			XF	Unc
49 (23)	5	Centimes (Cu-Ni) 1975. President Jean-Claude Duvalier	0.20	0.30
50 (24)	10	Centimes (Cu-Ni) 1975, 1983. Type as No. 49	0.25	0.40

			XF	Unc
51 (25)	20	Centimes (Cu-Ni) 1972, 1975, 1983. Type as No. 49	0.50	0.70
52 (26)	50	Centimes (Cu-Ni) 1972, 1975, 1979, 1983, 1985. Type as No. 49	0.60	0.85

WORLD SOCCER CHAMPIONSHIP GAMES 1974 (3)

			Proof
53	25	Gourdes (Ag) 1973. Emblem of the World Cup 1974. R arms of Haiti, value, date	8.00
54	50	Gourdes (Ag) 1973. Type as No. 53	20.00
55	200	Gourdes (Au) 1973. Type as No. 53	80.00
56	25	Gourdes (Ag) 1973. Christopher Columbus	8.00
57	50	Gourdes (Ag) 1973, 1974. Mother and child	15.00
58	50	Gourdes (Ag) 1973. Beauty on the beach	15.00
59	100	Gourdes (Au) 1973. Christopher Columbus (1451–1506), discoverer of the New World	30.00
60	500	Gourdes (Au) 1973. Type as No. 57	125.00
61	500	Gourdes (Au) 1973. Type as No. 58	125.00
62	1000	Gourdes (Au) 1973. President Jean-Claude Duvalier	300.00

HOLY YEAR 1975 (2)

			XF	Unc
63	50	Gourdes (Ag) 1974		20.00
64	200	Gourdes (Au) 1974	60.00	75.00

BICENTENARY OF THE UNITED STATES (2)

		Unc	Proof
65	25 Gourdes (Ag) 1974–1976. U. S. Bicentennial/Savannah:		
	a) 1974; inscription BICENTENAIRE DES U.S.A.		12.00
	b) 1974–1976; inscription REPUBLIQUE D'HAITI		12.00
66	1000 Gourdes (Au) 1974, 1975. U. S. Bicentennial/Savannah:		
	a) 1974; as No. 65a	225.00	
	b) 1974, 1975; as No. 65b	200.00	225.00

OLYMPIC GAMES 1976 IN MONTREAL (2)

		Unc	Proof
67	50 Gourdes (Ag) 1974, 1976		20.00
68	500 Gourdes (Au) 1974, 1975		185.00

INTERNATIONAL WOMEN'S YEAR (1975) (2)

		Unc	Proof
69	25 Gourdes (Ag) 1975	7.00	12.50
70	200 Gourdes (Au) 1975	60.00	75.00

WORLD SOCCER CHAMPIONSHIP GAMES (2)

		Unc	Proof
71	50 Gourdes (Ag) 1977	12.50	22.50
72	500 Gourdes (Au) 1977	120.00	200.00

OLYMPIC GAMES 1980 IN MOSCOW (2)

		Unc	Proof
73	50 Gourdes (Ag) 1977, 1979	12.50	22.50
74	500 Gourdes (Au) 1977/1978, 1979	180.00	220.00

HUMAN RIGHTS (2)

		Unc	Proof
75	50 Gourdes (Ag) 1977	12.50	17.50
76	250 Gourdes (Au) 1977	60.00	65.00

LINDBERGH'S NEW YORK TO PARIS FLIGHT 1927 (2)

		Unc	Proof
77	100 Gourdes (Ag) 1977	27.50	30.00
78	250 Gourdes (Au) 1977	60.00	65.00

STATUE OF LIBERTY

			Unc	Proof
79	100	Gourdes (Ag) 1977. Statue of Liberty and city skyline of New York	40.00	50.00

20th ANNIVERSARY OF EUROPEAN MARKET – 1st ISSUE (2)

80	50	Gourdes (Ag) 1977, 1977/1978, 1979. Map of Europe	20.00	30.00
81	500	Gourdes (Au) 1977/1978, 1979	200.00	225.00

No. 82 omitted.

ECONOMIC CONNECTIONS (2)

83	50	Gourdes (Ag) 1977	20.00	30.00
84	500	Gourdes (Au) 1977	200.00	225.00

DUVALIER 1957–1977

85	500	Gourdes (Au) 1977	200.00	225.00

PEACE INITIATIVE (2)

86	100	Gourdes (Ag) 1977. Facing portraits of Sadat and Begin	70.00	85.00
87	250	Gourdes (Au) 1977	150.00	185.00

20th ANNIVERSARY OF EUROPEAN MARKET – 2nd ISSUE (2)

88	100	Gourdes (Ag) 1977	70.00	80.00
89	250	Gourdes (Au) 1977	150.00	185.00

QUEEN OF THE SUGAR

90	50	Gourdes (Ag) 1978	25.00	35.00

WORLD FOOD DAY 1981 (5)

			XF	Unc
91 (27)	5	Centimes (Cu-Ni) 1981	0.15	0.30
92 (28)	10	Centimes (Cu-Ni) 1981	0.15	0.30
93 (29)	20	Centimes (Cu-Ni) 1981	0.30	0.65
94 (30)	50	Centimes (Cu-Ni) 1981	0.50	1.00
			Unc	Proof
95 (31)	50	Gourdes (Ag) 1981	20.00	30.00

FOR THE FAO-COIN-PLAN (3)

			XF	Unc
96	10	Centimes (Cu-Ni) 1984	0.30	0.35
97	20	Centimes (Cu-Ni) 1984	0.60	1.00
98	50	Centimes (Cu-Ni) 1984	1.00	1.60
99	50	Gourdes (Ag) 1984. Type as No. 57	Proof	40.00

Hedschas   # Hejaz   **Hedjaz**

Area: 180,000 sq. mi. Population: 3,000,000.
This kingdom, situated on the west of the Arabian peninsula, declared
its independence on 30th May 1916. It has been part of the sultanate of
Nejd since 1925, and of Saudi Arabia since 1932.
Capital: Mecca.

$$40 \text{ Paras} = 1 \text{ Gersh}, \quad 20 \text{ Gersh} = 1 \text{ Rial},$$
$$100 \text{ Gersh} = 1 \text{ Dinar}$$

HUSEIN IBN ALI 1916–1924

			VF	XF
1 (16)	5 Paras (Br) 1923. (Solar Calendar dating 1334). Arabic inscription in five oval patterns. ℞ similar		16.00	25.00
2 (17)	10 Paras (Br) 1923 (S. C. 1334)		8.00	16.00
3 (18)	20 Paras (Br) 1923 (S. C. 1334)		9.00	18.00
4 (19)	40 Paras (Br) 1923 (S. C. 1334)		12.00	25.00
5 (20)	¼ Gersh (Br) 1923 (S. C. 1334)		8.00	15.00
6 (22)	1 Gersh (Br) 1923 (S. C. 1334)		10.00	18.00
7 (23)	¼ Rial (Ag) 1923 (S. C. 1334)		30.00	50.00
8 (24)	½ Rial (Ag) 1923 (S. C. 1334)		100.00	150.00

9 (25)	1 Rial (Ag) 1923 (S. C. 1334)		55.00	75.00
10 (26)	1 Dinar (Au) 1923 (S. C. 1334)		300.00	400.00

All valuations in the SCHÖN are stated in U.S. Dollars.

Honduras

Area: 44,836 sq. mi. Population: 4,540,000.
Honduras is a democratic republic with a President. After leaving the Confederation of Central American States (Provincias Unidas del Centro de América) the country declared its independence in 1838.
Capital: Tegucigalpa.

100 Centavos or 8 Reales = 1 Peso;
since 1926: 100 Centavos = 1 Lempira

1 (14)	1 Centavo (Br) 1881–1907. National arms within circle. ℞ value within wreath	9.00	20.00
2 (15)	1 Centavo (Br) 1890–1908. National arms. ℞ value within circle, inscription PROGRESO * LIBERTAD * PAZ	5.00	10.00
3 (17)	1 Centavo (Br) 1890–1908. National arms within wreath. ℞ value within circle, inscription PROGRESO * LIBERTAD * PAZ	10.00	25.00
4 (19)	5 Centavos (Ag) 1883–1902. National arms within wreath. R value within circle	20.00	50.00
5 (21)	10 Centavos (Ag) 1883–1900. National arms within circle, the whole within wreath. ℞ value within circle, inscription PROGRESO * LIBERTAD * PAZ	22.50	40.00
6 (23)	25 Centavos (Ag) 1898–1913. National arms within wreath. ℞ allegorical figure of Liberty	8.00	20.00
7 (24a)	50 Centavos (Ag) 1908	120.00	250.00
8 (25a)	UN (1) Peso (Ag) 1881–1914	45.00	85.00
9 (27)	1 Peso (Au) 1887–1922. Head of Liberty. ℞ national arms	350.00	550.00
	Coin No. 9 with date 1912 commands a very high price		
10 (28)	5 Pesos (Au) 1883–1913. Type as No. 9	700.00	1100.00
11 (32)	1 Centavo (Br) 1910–1911	20.00	40.00
12 (37)	1 Centavo (Br) 1919–1920. National arms within circle. ℞ value within wreath; but 'Centavo' not mentioned	5.00	10.00
13 (31)	2 Centavos (Br) 1907–1908. National arms within circle. ℞ value within wreath	80.00	135.00
14 (33)	2 Centavos (Br) 1910–1913	3.00	6.00

			VF	XF
15 (38)	2 Centavos (Br) 1919–1920. National arms within circle. ℞ value within wreath; but 'Centavos' not mentioned		2.00	3.50

CURRENCY REFORM: 100 Centavos = 1 Lempira

16 (39)	1 Centavo (Br) 1935–1957. National arms. ℞ value within circle, the whole within wreath		0.15	0.25
17 (40)	2 Centavos (Br) 1939–1956. Type as No. 16		0.20	0.30
18 (41)	5 Centavos (Cu-Ni) 1931, 1932, 1949, 1954, 1956, 1972. Type as No. 16		0.20	0.40
19 (42)	10 Centavos (Cu-Ni) 1932–1956, 1967. Type as No. 16		0.30	0.60
20 (43)	20 Centavos (Ag) 1931–1958. Lempira, Indian Chieftain (1497–1537), resisted occupation by the first Spanish conquerors. The unit of currency was named after him by an act of Parliament of 3rd April 1926		3.00	5.00
21 (44)	50 Centavos (Ag) 1931–1951. Type as No. 20		5.00	8.00

22 (45)	1 Lempira (Ag) 1931–1937. Type as No. 20		8.00	12.50
23 (46)	20 Centavos (Cu-Ni) 1967, 1973. Type as No. 20		0.20	0.30
24 (47)	50 Centavos (Cu-Ni) 1967, 1978. Type as No. 21		0.30	0.60

ISSUE FOR THE FAO COIN PLAN

25 (48)	50 Centavos (Cu–Ni) 1973		0.50	1.50

		XF	Unc
26 (39a)	1 Centavo (Bronze-clad steel) 1974. Type as No. 16	0.15	0.25
27 (40a)	2 Centavos (Bronze-clad steel) 1974. Type as No. 17	0.15	0.25
28 (41a)	5 Centavos (Brass-clad steel) 1975. Type as No. 18	0.15	0.25
29 (42a)	10 Centavos (Brass-clad steel) 1976. Type as No. 19	0.20	0.40
30 (49)	20 Centavos (Cu-Ni) 1978. Type as No. 20	0.30	0.60
31 (50)	50 Centavos (Cu-Ni) 1978. Type as No. 21	0.30	1.00

Yeoman Numbers

In order to help collectors and dealers, we have added after most numbers the corresponding number assigned by R.S. Yeoman in his wellknown works entitled »A Catalog of Modern World Coins« and »Current Coins of the World«.

Hongkong # Hong Kong **Hong Kong**

Area: 392 sq. mi. Population: 4,800,000.
This British possession on the south coast of China comprises the island of Hong Kong, the Kowloon peninsula and a small part of the mainland. Since 1956 Hong Kong has been self-governing.
Capital: Victoria.

100 Cents = 1 Hong Kong Dollar

EDWARD VII 1901–1910

			VF	XF
.1 (9)	1	Cent (Br) 1902–1905. Crowned bust right of King Edward VII. ℞ value	1.50	3.00

			VF	XF
2 (10)	5	Cents (Ag) 1903–1905	1.50	2.50
3 (11)	10	Cents (Ag) 1902–1905	2.00	4.00
4 (12)	20	Cents (Ag) 1902–1905	45.00	65.00
5 (13)	50	Cents (Ag) 1902–1905	22.00	35.00

GEORGE V 1910–1936

			VF	XF
6 (14)	1	Cent (Br) 1919–1926. Crowned bust left of King George V. ℞ value	1.00	2.00

			VF	XF
7 (15)	1	Cent (Br) 1931–1934. Type as No. 6, but diameter 22 mm instead of 28 mm	0.40	1.00
8 (18)	5	Cents (Ag) 1932–1933	1.00	2.00
9 (16)	5	Cents (Cu–Ni) 1935	3.00	6.00
10 (17)	10	Cents (Cu–Ni) 1935–1936	0.50	1.00

GEORGE VI 1936–1952

11 (19)	1	Cent (Br) 1941	900.00	1500.00
12 (20)	5	Cents (Ni) 1937	1.00	1.60
13 (22)	5	Cents (Ni) 1938–1941. Type as No. 12, but head larger	0.40	0.90
14 (21)	10	Cents (Ni) 1937	0.60	1.20
15 (23)	10	Cents (Ni) 1938–1939. Type as No. 14, but head larger	0.30	0.60
16 (24)	5	Cents (Ni–Bra) 1949–1950. Inscription now KING GEORGE THE SIXTH	0.15	0.25
17 (25)	10	Cents (Ni–Bra) 1948–1951. Inscription now KING GEORGE THE SIXTH	0.20	0.40

18 (26)	50	Cents (Cu–Ni) 1951. Inscription now KING GEORGE THE SIXTH	1.50	3.00

ELIZABETH II since 1952

19 (27)	5	Cents (Ni-Bra) 1958–1979. Crowned head right of Queen Elizabeth II:		
		a) 1958–1968, security edge	0.10	0.20
		b) 1971–1979, reeded edge	0.08	0.15
20 (28)	10	Cents (Ni-Bra) 1955–1979:		
		a) 1955–1968, security edge	0.12	0.25
		b) 1971–1979, reeded edge	0.10	0.20
21 (29)	50	Cents (Cu-Ni) 1958–1975:		
		a) 1958–1970, security edge	0.20	0.40
		b) 1971–1975, reeded edge	0.20	0.35

			VF	**XF**
22 (30)	1	Dollar (Cu-Ni) 1960–1975:		
		a) 1960, 1970, security edge	0.40	0.80
		b) 1971–1975, reeded edge	0.30	0.60
23 (33)	20	Cents (Ni-Bra) 1975–1980. Portrait of the Queen and legend. Rev. value, date (scalloped)	0.15	0.30
24 (34)	50	Cents (Bra) 1977–1980. Typ as No. 23 (round)	0.30	0.60
25 (36)	2	Dollars (Cu-Ni) 1975, 1978–1980, 1982. Type as No. 23 (scalloped)	0.70	1,20
26 (37)	5	Dollars (Cu-Ni) 1976, 1978, 1979. Type as No. 23 (decagon)	1.00	1.50

ROYAL VISIT 1975

			Unc	**Proof**
27 (31)	1000	Dollars (Au) 1975. Rev. coat of arms	300.00	1100.00

YEAR OF THE DRAGON

28 (32)	1000	Dollars (Au) 1976. Rev. dragon	450.00	1100.00

YEAR OF THE SNAKE

29 (38)	1000	Dollars (Au) 1977. Rev. snake	300.00	400.00

YEAR OF THE HORSE

30 (39)	1000	Dollars (Au) 1978. Rev. horse	300.00	500.00

			XF	Unc
31 (35)	1	Dollar (Cu-Ni) 1978–1981. Type as No. 22, but diameter 25 mm	0.30	0.50

YEAR OF THE GOAT

			Unc	Proof
32 (40)	1000	Dollars (Au) 1979. Rev. goat	250.00	350.00

YEAR OF THE MONKEY

			Unc	Proof
33 (42)	1000	Dollars (Au) 1980. Rev. monkey	250.00	300.00

			XF	Unc
34 (41)	5	Dollars (Cu-Ni) 1980–1982	1.00	1.50

YEAR OF THE COCKEREL

			Unc	Proof
35 (43)	1000	Dollars (Au) 1981. Rev. cockerel	250.00	300.00

YEAR OF THE DOG

			Unc	Proof
36 (44)	1000	Dollars (Au) 1982. Rev. dog	285.00	350.00

			XF	Unc
37 (46)	10	Cents (Bra) 1982, 1983. Type as No. 34	0.20	0.30

			Unc	Proof

38 (45) 1000 Dollars (Au) 1983. Rev. pig 500.00 800.00

YEAR OF THE RAT

39 (46) 1000 Dollars (Au) 1984. Rev. rat 300.00 500.00

YEAR OF THE OX

40 (47) 1000 Dollars (Au) 1985. Rev. ox 400.00 650.00

YEAR OF THE TIGER

41 1000 Dollars (Au) 1986 400.00 650.00

ROYAL VISIT

42 1000 Dollars (Au) 1986 350.00 650.00

YEAR OF THE RABBIT

43 1000 Dollars (Au) 1987 350.00 650.00

Ungarn   # Hungary   **Hongrie**

Magyarország

Area: 35,918 sq. mi. Population: 10,500,000.
From 1867 to 1918 the country was one of the two component states of
the Austro-Hungarian Empire. In 1918 it was declared a republic, and
on 21st March 1919 the Republic of Revolutionary Councils was created,
which only had a short existence. The National Assembly, which was
called together at the beginning of 1920, decided in favour of the re-
institution of the kingdom, and elected Admiral Horthy as Regent on 1st
March 1920. At the end of the Second World War Hungary again
became a republic, which was changed into a People's Republic by
parliamentary resolution on 20th August 1949.
Capital: Budapest.

100 Filler = 1 Korona, from 1925 to 1945: 100 Filler = 1 Pengö,
since 1946: 100 Filler = 1 Forint

			VF	XF
1 (23)	1	Filler (Br) 1892–1914. Crown of St. Stephen. R value within wreath:		
		a) 1892–1903, 1906	0.80	2.00
		b) 1914	–.–	–.–
2 (24)	2	Filler (Br) 1892–1915. Type as No. 1	0.50	1.00
3 (25)	10	Filler (Ni) 1892–1909. Type as No. 1:		
		a) 1892–1895, 1908, 1909	0.50	0.80
		b) 1906	100.00	200.00
4 (27)	20	Filler (Ni) 1892–1914. Type as No. 1:		
		a) 1892–1894, 1907, 1908, 1914	5.00	8.00
		b) 1906	300.00	600.00
5 (32)	1	Korona (Ag) 1892–1916. Head right of Emperor Franz Joseph (1830–1916). R crown of St. Stephen above value:		
		a) large head, 1892–1896	4.00	6.00
		b) large head, 1906	160.00	300.00
		c) small head, 1912, 1914–1916	3.50	5.50
		d) small head, 1913	50.00	100.00
6 (33)	2	Korona (ag) 1912–1914. Crown of St. Stephen held by angels:		
		a) 1912, 1913	6.00	7.50
		b) 1914	20.00	50.00

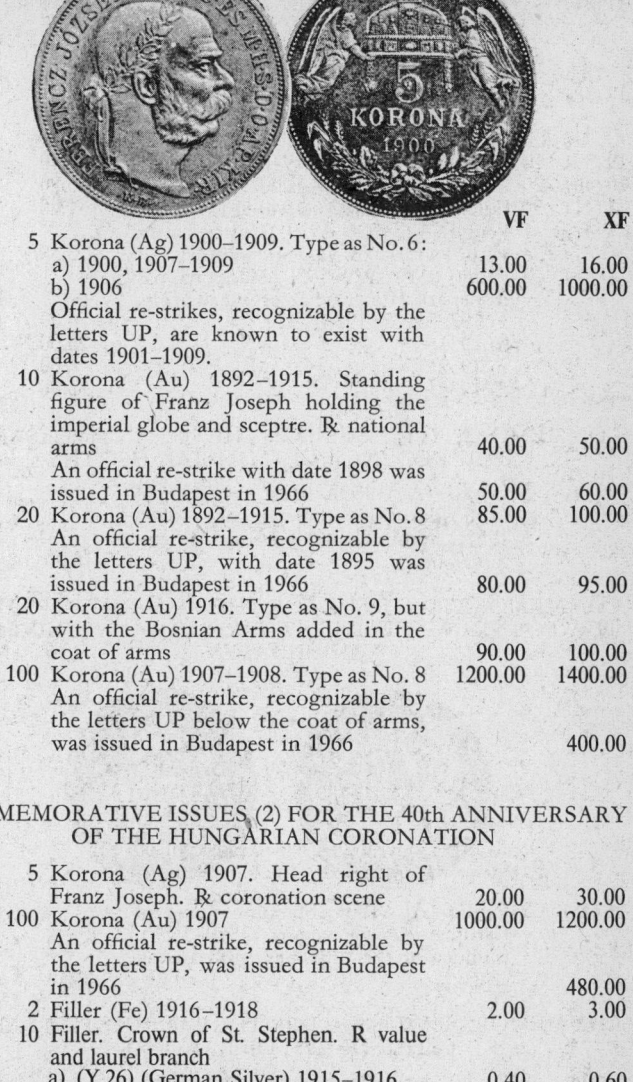

			VF	XF
7 (34)	5	Korona (Ag) 1900–1909. Type as No. 6:		
		a) 1900, 1907–1909	13.00	16.00
		b) 1906	600.00	1000.00

Official re-strikes, recognizable by the letters UP, are known to exist with dates 1901–1909.

8 (36)	10	Korona (Au) 1892–1915. Standing figure of Franz Joseph holding the imperial globe and sceptre. ℞ national arms	40.00	50.00

An official re-strike with date 1898 was issued in Budapest in 1966 — 50.00 — 60.00

9 (A 36)	20	Korona (Au) 1892–1915. Type as No. 8	85.00	100.00

An official re-strike, recognizable by the letters UP, with date 1895 was issued in Budapest in 1966 — 80.00 — 95.00

10 (B 36)	20	Korona (Au) 1916. Type as No. 9, but with the Bosnian Arms added in the coat of arms	90.00	100.00
11 (D 36)	100	Korona (Au) 1907–1908. Type as No. 8	1200.00	1400.00

An official re-strike, recognizable by the letters UP below the coat of arms, was issued in Budapest in 1966 — 400.00

COMMEMORATIVE ISSUES (2) FOR THE 40th ANNIVERSARY OF THE HUNGARIAN CORONATION

12 (35)	5	Korona (Ag) 1907. Head right of Franz Joseph. ℞ coronation scene	20.00	30.00
13 (C 36)	100	Korona (Au) 1907	1000.00	1200.00

An official re-strike, recognizable by the letters UP, was issued in Budapest in 1966 — 480.00

14 (28)	2	Filler (Fe) 1916–1918	2.00	3.00
15	10	Filler. Crown of St. Stephen. ℞ value and laurel branch		
		a) (Y 26) (German Silver) 1915–1916	0.40	0.60
		b) (Y 29) (Fe) 1915, 1918, 1920	12.00	16.00
16 (30)	20	Filler (Fe) 1916–1921. Type as No. 15	0.80	1.00

				VF	XF
17 (37)	1	Filler (Br) 1926–1939. Crown of St. Stephen. ℞ value:			
		a) 1926–1936, 1938, 1939		0.40	0.70
		b) 1929		2.50	5.00
18 (38)	2	Filler (Br) 1926–1940:			
		a) 1926–1931, 1934–1940		0.40	0.70
		b) 1932, 1933		2.50	4.00
19 (39)	10	Filler (Cu–Ni) 1926–1940		0.40	0.70
20 (40)	20	Filler (Cu–Ni) 1926–1940		0.80	1.20
21 (41)	50	Filler (Cu–Ni) 1926–1940		1.20	1.80
22 (42)	1	Pengö (Ag) 1926–1939. Crowned arms within wreath. ℞ value in wreath		3.50	5.00
23 (43)	2	Pengö (Ag) 1929–1939. Madonna, patroness of Hungary. ℞ crowned arms:			
		a) 1929, 1933, 1936–1939		4.00	6.00
		b) 1931		25.00	40.00
		c) 1932		6.00	9.00
		d) 1935		35.00	100.00

COMMEMORATIVE ISSUE FOR THE 10th ANNIVERSARY OF THE REGENCY OF ADMIRAL HORTHY

24 (44) 5 Pengö (Ag) 1930. Bust to right of Miklós Horthy von Nagybánya (1868–1957), admiral and statesman. ℞ national arms   10.00   15.00

COMMEMORATIVE ISSUE FOR THE 300th ANNIVERSARY OF THE FOUNDING OF THE PETER PÁZMÁNY UNIVERSITY IN BUDAPEST

25 (45) 2 Pengö (Ag) 1935. Standing figure of Cardinal Peter Pázmány (1570–1637), founder of the university. ℞ national arms   12.50   20.00

COMMEMORATIVE ISSUE FOR THE 200th ANNIVERSARY OF THE DEATH OF RÁKOCZI

26 (46) 2 Pengö (Ag) 1935. Bust to right of Francis II Rákóczi (1676–1735), Prince of Hungary and Transylvania 1694–1711;

	VF	XF

leader of the War of Independence
1703–1711. ℞ national arms   6.00   12.00

COMMEMORATIVE ISSUE FOR THE 50th ANNIVERSARY OF THE DEATH OF LISZT

27 (47)   2 Pengö (Ag) 1936. Head right of Franz von Liszt (1811–1886), pianist and composer. ℞ national arms   6.00   10.00

COMMEMORATIVE ISSUE FOR THE 900th ANNIVERSARY OF THE DEATH OF ST. STEPHEN

28 (48)   5 Pengö (Ag) 1938. Bust to right with halo of Stephen I the Saint (969–1038), King of Hungary 995–1038. ℞ national arms   10.00   15.00

COMMEMORATIVE ISSUE FOR ADMIRAL HORTHY

29 (49)   5 Pengö (Ag) 1939. Bust to left of Miklós Horthy von Nagybánya. ℞ national arms   9.00   12.00

30 (50)   2 Filler (St). Type as No. 18
   a) 1940, plain edge   1.80   4.00
   b) 1940–1942, reeded edge   0.40   0.80

31 (51)   2 Filler (Zi) 1943–1944   0.30   0.50

32 (52)   10 Filler (St) 1940–1942. Type as No. 19   0.80   1.20

			VF	XF
33 (53)	20	Filler (St) 1941–1944. Crown of St. Stephen. ℞ value (central hole)	1.00	1.60
34 (54)	1	Pengö (Al) 1941–1944. National arms. ℞ value within wreath	0.40	0.80
35 (55)	2	Pengö (Al) 1941–1943. National arms within circle. ℞ value in circle	0.60	1.10

75th ANNIVERSARY OF THE BIRTH OF ADMIRAL HORTHY

			VF	XF
36 (57)	5	Pengö (Al) 1943. Bust to left of Miklós Horthy von Nagybánya. ℞ national arms	2.00	4.80
37 (56)	5	Pengö (Al) 1945. Parliament building in Budapest. ℞ national arms, bunch of grapes, ears of corn	1.10	3.00

MAGYAR KÖZTÁRSASÁG
Republic since 2nd February 1946

Various gold coins issued after 1946 never came into circulation, but were exchanged for convertible currencies by the Hungarian official services.

			VF	XF
38 (58)	2	Filler (Br) 1946–1947. Arms of the Republic, inscription MAGYAR ÁLLAMI VÁLTOPÉNZ (small coin of the Hungarian state). ℞ value and ear of corn	0.20	0.30
39 (59)	5	Filler (Al) 1948–1951. Head left of Hungaria. ℞ value with leaf decoration on border	0.40	0.60

			VF	XF
40 (60)	10	Filler (Al–Br) 1946–1950. Dove, inscription MAGYAR ÁLLAMI VÁLTOPÉNZ (small coin of the Hungarian state). ℞ value	0.40	0.60
41 (61)	20	Filler (Al–Br) 1946–1950. Three ears of corn, inscription MAGYAR ÁLLAMI VÁLTOPÉNZ (small coin of the Hungarian state). ℞ value	0.45	0.80
42 (62)	50	Filler (Al) 1948. Blacksmith seated at his anvil. ℞ value within oak wreath	1.00	1.60

			VF	**XF**
43 (63)	1	Forint (Al) 1946–1949. National arms, inscription MAGYAR ÁLLAMI VÁL-TOPÉNZ (small coin of the Hungarian state). R value	0.80	1.60
44 (64)	2	Forint (Al) 1946–1947. National arms. R value	1.00	2.00

45	5	Forint (Ag). Head right of Lajós Kossuth (1802–1894), Governor of Hungary 1848–1849, President of the Hungarian Republic in 1849. R national arms		
		a) (Y 65) 1946, thick flan with edge inscription MUNKA A NEMZETI JOLÉT ALAPJA (Work – the basis of national prosperity)	12.00	18.00
		b) (Y 66) 1947, thinner flan without inscription	3.50	5.50

Of same design: Nos. 77 and 95

COMMEMORATIVE ISSUES (3) FOR THE CENTENARY OF THE 1848 REVOLUTION

46 (67)	5	Forint (Ag) 1948. Head left of Alexander Petöfi (1823–1849), poet (among other works he wrote the National Anthem); he died on 31st July 1849 as a Major in the Revolutionary Army. R value	6.00	11.00
47 (68)	10	Forint (Ag) 1948. Head left of Stephen, Count of Szécheny (1791–1860), liberal political reformer, founder of the Hungarian Academy, Minister of Transport in 1848. R value	9.00	12.00

			VF	XF
48 (69)	20	Forint (Ag) 1948. Head left of Michael Táncsics (1799–1884), revolutionary writer, Member of Parliament 1848–1849. ℞ national arms and value	20.00	26.00

MAGYAR NÉPKÖZTÁRSASÁG – People's Republic

			VF	XF
49 (70)	2	Filler (Al) 1950–1979. Name of state. R value and wreath (central hole)	0.06	0.15
50 (71)	5	Filler (Al) 1953–. Type as No. 39, but with new name of state	0.08	0.20
51 (72)	10	Filler. Type as No. 40, but with new name of state		
		a) (Al) 1950, milled edge, diameter 19 mm	1.60	3.00
		b) (Al) 1951, 1955, 1957–1966, milled edge, diameter 19 mm	0.16	0.35
		c) (Al–Mg) 1967, plain edge, diameter 18 mm	1.20	2.00
		d) (Al–Mg) 1968–1971, plain edge, diameter 18 mm	0.10	0.20
52 (73)	20	Filler. Type as No. 41, but with new name of state		
		a) (Al) 1953–1966, plain edge, diameter 21 mm	0.25	0.40
		b) (Al–Mg) 1967–1974, milled edge, diameter 20 mm	0.15	0.30
53 (74)	50	Filler (Al) 1953–1966. Type as No. 42, but with new name of state	0.30	0.50

			VF	XF
54 (75)	1	Forint (Al) 1949–1952. Arms of the People's Republic. ℞ value	0.35	0.60
55 (76)	2	Forint (Cu–Ni) 1950–1952. Arms of the People's Republic. ℞ value	0.50	0.80

COMMEMORATIVE ISSUES (3) FOR THE 10th ANNIVERSARY OF THE FORINT CURRENCY

		VF	XF
56 (77)	10 Forint (Ag) 1956. The National Museum in Budapest. ℞ value	10.00	12.50

		VF	XF
57 (78)	20 Forint (Ag) 1956. The Szechenyi suspension bridge in Budapest. ℞ arms of the People's Republic	16.00	20.00
58 (79)	25 Forint (Ag) 1956. The Parliament building in Budapest. ℞ arms of the People's Republic over cog-wheel	20.00	25.00
59 (80)	1 Forint. New arms of the People's Republic. ℞ value	0.40	0.80
	a) (Al) 1957–1966, diameter 24 mm		
	b) (Al–Mg) 1967–1970, diameter 22.5 mm	0.30	0.70
60 (81)	2 Forint. New arms of the People's Republic. ℞ value		
	a) (Cu–Ni) 1957–1962	0.80	1.50
	b) (Cu–Ni–Zi) 1963–1966	0.60	1.20

COMMEMORATIVE ISSUES (5) FOR THE 150th ANNIVERSARY OF FRANZ VON LISZT

		Proof
61 (82)	25 Forint (Ag) 1961. Head right of Franz von Liszt (1811–1886), pianist and composer. ℞ value and lyre	25.00

		Proof
62 (83)	50 Forint (Ag) 1961. Type as No. 61	26.00
63 (84)	50 Forint (Au) 1961. Type as No. 61	100.00
64 (85)	100 Forint (Au) 1961. Type as No. 61	150.00
65 (86)	500 Forint (Au) 1961. Type as No. 61	650.00

COMMEMORATIVE ISSUES (5) FOR THE 80th ANNIVERSARY OF THE BIRTH OF BÉLA BARTÓK

66 (87)	25 Forint (Ag) 1961. Head left of Béla Bartók (1881–1945), composer and pioneer of the New Music. ℞ lyre above value	25.00
67 (88)	50 Forint (Ag) 1961. Type as No. 66	28.00
68 (89)	50 Forint (Au) 1961. Type as No. 66	100.00
69 (90)	100 Forint (Au) 1961. Type as No. 66	150.00
70 (91)	500 Forint (Au) 1961. Type as No. 66	650.00

COMMEMORATIVE ISSUES (5) FOR THE 400th ANNIVERSARY OF THE DEATH OF MIKLOS ZRINYI

71 (92) 25 Forint (Ag) 1966. Facing head of Count Miklos Zrinyi (1508–1566), defender of the fortress of Sigeth (Szigetvár), which was besieged and conquered in 1566 by the Turks under Sultan Sulei-

man II (1494–1566). ℞ scene showing
soldiers trying to break out from the
fortress; family arms

			Proof
			25.00
72 (93)	50	Forint (Ag) 1966. Type as No. 71	40.00
73 (94)	100	Forint (Au) 1966. Type as No. 71	175.00
74 (95)	500	Forint (Au) 1966. Type as No. 71	650.00
75 (96)	1000	Forint (Au) 1966. Type as No. 71	2000.00

Nos. 71–75 were issued on polished flans only (proofs).

			XF	Unc
76 (97)	50	Filler (Al–Mg) 1967–. The Elizabeth Bridge in Budapest. ℞ value	0.15	0.30

77 (98)	5	Forint (Cu–Ni–Zi) 1967, 1968. Type as No. 45, but diameter only 27.5 mm, milled edge	1.00	2.00

COMMEMORATIVE ISSUES (5) FOR THE 85th ANNIVERSARY OF THE BIRTH OF ZOLTAN KODÁLY

78 (99) 25 Forint (Ag) 1967. Bust three-quarters
to left of Zoltan Kodály (1882–1967),
composer of modern national Hungar-

				Unc	Proof

ian music; he collected and systematized the folk music of Hungary. ℞ blue peacock (Pavo cristatus – Phasianidae) 10.00

79 (100) 50 Forint (Ag) 1967. Type as No. 78 14.00

80 (101) 100 Forint (Ag) 1967. Type as No. 78 40.00

81 (102) 500 Forint (Au) 1967. Type as No. 78 650.00

82 (103) 1000 Forint (Au) 1967. Type as No. 78 1250.00

COMMEMORATIVE ISSUES (7) FOR THE 150th ANNIVERSARY OF THE BIRTH OF SEMMELWEIS

83 (104) 50 Forint (Ag) 1968. Head right of Dr. Ignatius Philip Semmelweis (1818 to 1865), who discovered the origin of puerperal fever 12.00 16.00

84 (106) 50 Forint (Au) 1968. Type as No. 83 90.00

85 (105) 100 Forint (Ag) 1968. Type as No. 83 25.00 35.00

86 (107) 100 Forint (Au) 1968. Type as No. 83 160.00

87 (108) 200 Forint (Au) 1968. Type as No. 83 300.00

88 (109) 500 Forint (Au) 1968. Type as No. 83 650.00

89 (110) 1000 Forint (Au) 1968. Type as No. 83 1400.00

COMMEMORATIVE ISSUES (2) FOR THE PROCLAMATION OF THE REPUBLIC OF REVOLUTIONARY COUNCILS ON 21st MAY 1919

90 (111) 50 Forint (Ag) 1969. "Revolutionary hold-

	Unc	Proof
ing flag", from a contemporary poster. R emblem of state, value	12.50	18.00
91 (112) 100 Forint (Ag) 1969. Type as No. 90	28.00	35.00

COMMEMORATIVE ISSUES (2) FOR THE 25th ANNIVERSARY OF THE LIBERATION

	Unc	Proof
92 (113) 50 Forint (Ag) 1970. "Allegorical figure of Liberty", the Strobl Monument in Budapest	8.00	12.50
93 (114) 100 Forint (Ag) 1970. Type as No. 92	16.00	25.00

	XF	Unc
94 (115) 2 Forint (Bra) 1970–. Emblem of state and name of country in semi-circular legend above. R value, date	0.40	0.75

	XF	Unc
95 (116) 5 Forint (Ni) 1971–. Lajos Kossuth (1802–1894), Governor of Hungary 1848–1849, President of the Hungarian Republic in 1849. R emblem of state, date and value		
a) 1971–1982; dia. 24 mm	0.60	1.25
b) 1983–; dia. 22 mm	0.50	1.00
96 (117) 10 Forint 1971–. »Allegorical figure of Liberty«, the Strobl Monument in Budapest. R value, emblem of state and date		
a) (Ni) 1971–1982; dia. 27 mm	1.20	1.80
b) (Ni-Bra) 1983–; dia. 25 mm	1.00	1.50

COMMEMORATIVE ISSUES (2) FOR THE 1000th BIRTHDAY OF ST. STEPHEN

97 (118) 50 Forint (Ag) 1972. Equestrian portrait

of Stephen I, the Saint, King of Hungary 955–1038. ℞ contemporary silver denarius. Value, date

	Unc	Proof
	8.00	15.00

98 (119) 100 Forint (Ag) 1972. Portrait of the King. ℞ monogram of the King. Value, date   15.00   25.00

COMMEMORATIVE ISSUE FOR THE CENTENARY OF BUDAPEST BY THE AMALGAMATION OF THE TOWNS OF BUDA (OFEN) AND PEST

99 (120) 100 Forint (Ag) 1972. Clamped parts of cornices as symbol of the union. ℞ value, national emblem, date   10.00   18.00

COMMEMORATIVE ISSUES (2) FOR THE 150th BIRTHDAY OF SANDOR PETÖFI

100 (121)   50 Forint (Ag) 1973. Sandor (Alexander) Petöfi (1823–1849), poet, among others of the National Anthem, fell as a major in the Revolutionary Army on 31st July 1849. ℞ rosette, date, year   7.50   10.00

101 (122) 100 Forint (Ag) 1973. Head similar to No. 100 and quotation from his poem "March Youth", translated: "We have dared to act for the fatherland", including his signature. ℞ national emblem, value, date   15.00   25.00

COMMEMORATIVE ISSUE FOR THE 25th ANNIVERSARY OF THE FOUNDING OF THE COUNCIL FOR MUTUAL ECONOMIC AID (25. 1. 1974)

102 (123) 100 Forint (Ag) 1974. National arms, name of country, value. ℞ the letters KGST

	Unc	Proof
and figures relating to the anniversary, surrounded by coins of the member states of Hungary, the Soviet Union, Rumania, the German Democratic Republic, People's Republic of Mongolia, Poland, Cuba, Czechoslovakia and Bulgaria (arranged clockwise)	12.50	25.00

50th ANNIVERSARY OF HUNGARIAN NATIONAL BANK (2)

103 (124) 50 Forint (Ag) 1974. Building of Hungarian National Bank   7.50   12.50

104 (125) 100 Forint (Ag) 1974   15.00   27.50

Values are given for each coin in U.S. Dollars and reference to Yeoman-numbers.

30th ANNIVERSARY OF THE LIBERATION

	Unc	Proof
105 (126) 200 Forint (Ag) 1975	20.00	27.50

150th ANNIVERSARY OF THE ACADEMY OF SCIENCE

	Unc	Proof
106 (127) 200 Forint (Ag) 1975	20.00	27.50

300th ANNIVERSARY OF THE BIRTH OF RAKOCZI

	Unc	Proof
107 (128) 200 Forint (Ag) 1976. Scene of Francis II Rákóczi on horseback surrounded by serveral followers	20.00	27.50

HUNGARIAN PAINTERS (3)

	Unc	Proof
108 (129) 200 Forint (Ag) 1976. Mihaly Munkácsy	20.00	25.00
109 (130) 200 Forint (Ag) 1976. Pál Szinyei Merse	20.00	25.00
110 (131) 200 Forint (Ag) 1976. Gyula Derkovits	20.00	25.00

				Unc	Proof
111 (132)	200 Forint (Ag) 1977. Adám Mányoki			20.00	25.00
112 (134)	200 Forint (Ag) 1977. Rónai Rippl			20.00	25.00
113 (133)	200 Forint (Ag) 1977. Kosztka Csontváry			20.00	25.00

175th ANNIVERSARY OF THE HUNGARIAN NATIONAL MUSEUM

			Unc	Proof
114 (135)	200 Forint (Ag) 1977		20.00	25.00

FIRST GOLD FORINT

			Unc	Proof
115 (136)	200 Forint (Ag) 1978		15.00	20.00

INTERNATIONAL YEAR OF THE CHILD 1979

			Unc	Proof
116 (137)	200 Forint (Ag) 1979:			
	a) 28 gm., dia. 37 mm		30.00	50.00
	b) 56 gm., dia. 37 mm; Piéfort			180.00

350th ANNIVERSARY OF THE DEATH OF GABOR BETHLEN

	Unc	Proof

117 (138)   200 Forint (Ag) 1979:

    a) 28 gm., dia. 37 mm   20.00   30.00
    b) 56 gm., dia. 37 mm; Piéfort   130.00

13th OLYMPIC WINTER GAMES IN LAKE PLACID (2)

118 (140)   200 Forint (Ag) 1980:
    a) 16 gm., dia. 36 mm   30.00
    b) 32 gm., dia. 36 mm; Piéfort   120.00
119 (141)   500 Forint (Ag) 1980:
    a) 39 gm., dia. 46 mm   45.00
    b) 78 gm., dia. 46 mm; Piéfort   185.00

1st SOVIET-HUNGARIAN SPACE FLIGHT

120 (139)   100 Forint (Ni) 1980   6.00   15.00

100th ANNIVERSARY OF THE BIRTH OF B. BARTOK

121 (144)   500 Forint (Ag) 1981. Béla Bartók (1881–
        1945), composer   35.00   42.00

		XF	Unc
122 (142)	10 Forint (Ni) 1981	1.25	2.00

		Unc	Proof
123 (143)	100 Forint (Ni) 1981	6.00	10.00

1300 YEARS OF BULGARIA

124 (147)   100 Forint (Ni) 1981. Portraits of Alexander
Petöfi (1823–1849), Hungarian poet and
Khristo Botev (1848–1876), Bulgarian
poet   9.00

WORLD SOCCER CHAMPIONSHIP GAMES 1982 IN SPAIN (3)

125 (148)   100 Forint (Cu-Ni) 1982   7.50   12.50

 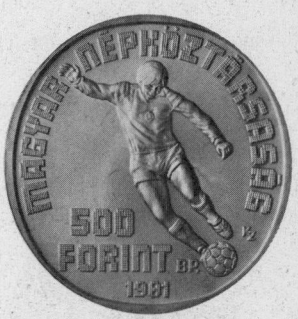

126 (145)	500 Forint (Ag) 1981	27.50	35.00
127 (146)	500 Forint (Ag) 1981	27.50	35.00

		XF	Unc
128 (160)	20 Forint (Cu-Ni) 1982–1984. G. Dózsa	0.75	1.25

			XF	Unc
129 (149)	20	Filler (Al) 1983	0.10	0.25
130 (150)	5	Forint (Ni) 1983	0.30	0.60
131 (151)	10	Forint (Ni) 1983	1.00	1.50

			Unc	Proof
132 (152)	100	Forint (Ni) 1983	7.00	10.00

200th ANNIVERSARY OF THE BIRTH OF BOLIVAR

133 (153)	100	Forint (Ni) 1983. Simón Bolívar (1783–1830), statesman and general, liberator of South America from Spanish rule	7.00	10.00
134 (159)	100	Forint (Ni) 1983. Stephen (István), Count of Széchenyi (1791–1860), liberal political reformer	7.00	10.00

100th ANNIVERSARY OF THE BIRTH OF BELA CZOBEL

135 (155)	100	Forint (Ni) 1983. Béla Czóbel, painter	7.00	10.00

200th ANNIVERSARY OF THE BIRTH OF CSOMA DE KÖRÖSI

136 (156) 100 Forint (German silver) 1984. Alex-   Unc   Proof
        ander (Sándor) Csoma de Körösi
        (1784–1842), philologist   7.00   10.00

OLYMPIC WINTER GAMES IN SARAJEVO

137 (158) 500 Forint (Ag) 1984   45.00

OLYMPIC SUMMER GAMES IN LOS ANGELES

138 (159) 500 Forint (Ag) 1984   45.00

WORLD FORESTRY CONGRESS (2)

139 (161) 20 Forint (Cu-Ni) 1984   2.50
140 (162) 100 Forint (German silver) 1984   10.00

DECADE FOR WOMEN

141 (157) 500 Forint (Ag) 1984   45.00

142	100 Forint (Cu-Ni) 1985. Otter	8.50
143	100 Forint (Cu-Ni) 1985. Turtle	8.50
144	100 Forint (Cu-Ni) 1985. Wildcat	8.50
145	200 Forint (Ag) 1985. Otter	30.00
146	200 Forint (Ag) 1985. Turtle	30.00
147	200 Forint (Ag) 1985. Wildcat	30.00

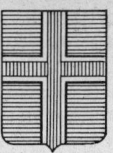

Island   # Iceland   **Islande**

Area: 39,760 sq. mi. Population: 210,000.
This island in the North Atlantic Ocean was colonized in 874 mainly by
the Norwegian Vikings. Iceland became the point of departure for
voyages of discovery to Greenland and North America. In 1262 it came
under the rule of the Norwegian kings. In 1380 Iceland fell to Denmark
at the same time as Norway. On 1st December 1918 it became a sovereign state closely united with Denmark under the King. In 1944, following a referendum, the republic was proclaimed.
Capital: Reykjavík.

100 Aurar = 1 Icelandic Krona

CHRISTIAN X 1912–1944

			VF	XF
1 (1)	1	Eyrir (Br) 1926–1942. Monogram CX, above which crown. ℞ value	1.10	1.50
2 (2)	2	Aurar (Br) 1926–1942. Type as No. 1	1.00	1.50
3 (3)	5	Aurar (Br) 1926–1942. Type as No. 1	1.30	2.00
4 (4)	10	Aurar (Cu-Ni) 1922–1940. Crowned arms, monogram, divided date. Rev. value	2.00	4.00
5 (5)	25	Aurar (Cu-Ni) 1922–1940. Type as No. 4	1.80	3.00
6 (6)	1	Krona (Al-Br) 1925, 1929, 1940. Type similar to No. 4	2.00	3.00

7 (7)	2	Kronur (Al–Br) 1925–1940. Type as No. 6	2.60	4.00

			VF	**XF**
8 (8)	2 Kronur (Br) 1930. Seated figure. ℞ Icelandic cross, representation of animals and hunting scene			65.00
9 (9)	5 Kronur (Ag) 1930. Ulfliot, the law-giver. ℞ decoration: intertwined dragons			160.00

10 (10)	10 Kronur (Ag) 1930. The King of Thule. National arms			200.00
11 (4a)	10 Aurar (Zi) 1942. Type as No. 4		3.00	8.00
12 (5a)	25 Aurar (Zi) 1942. Type as No. 5		4.00	9.00

REPUBLIC since 1944

13 (11)	1 Eyrir (Br) 1946–1966. Coat of arms within wreath. ℞ value		0.15	0.30

14 (12)	5 Aurar (Br) 1946-1966. Type as No. 13		0.20	0.35
15 (13)	10 Aurar (Cu-Ni) 1946-1969. Type as No. 13		0.15	0.30

			XF	**Unc**

16 (13a) 10 Aurar (Al) 1970-. Type as No. 13   0.05   0.10
17 (14)   25 Aurar (Cu-Ni) 1946-1967. Type as No. 13   0.15   0.30

18 (A 15) 50 Aurar (Ni-Bra) 1969-. Coat of arms within
          wreath. R value   0.12   0.25
19 (15)   1 Krona (Al-Br) 1946. Coat of arms. Rev.
          value   0.80   1.80

20 (15a)   1 Krona (Ni-Bra) 1957-1975. Type as No. 19   0.20   0.40
21 (15b)   1 Krona (Al) 1976-. Type as No. 20; 17 mm
          dia.   0.05   0.10
22 (16)   2 Kronur (Al-Br) 1946. Type as No. 19   2.50   4.50
23 (16a)   2 Kronur (Ni-Bra) 1958, 1962, 1963, 1966.
          Type as No. 19   0.50   0.80
24 (18)   5 Kronur (Cu-Ni) 1969-. Type as No. 19   0.20   0.30
25 (19)   10 Kronur (Cu-Ni) 1967-. Type as No. 19   0.35   0.60

26 (21)   50 Kronur·(Cu-Ni) 1970-. Parliament buil-
          ding in Reykjavik. R value   0.60   1.00

150th ANNIVERSARY OF THE BIRTH OF SIGURDSSON

		VF	Unc
27 (17)	500 Kronur (Au) 1961. Jón Sigurdsson (1811–1879), philologist, historian and politician; advocate of Icelandic independence. ℞ national arms	175.00	250.00

COMMEMORATIVE ISSUE FOR THE 50th ANNIVERSARY OF INDEPENDENCE

28 (20)	50 Kronur (Cu–Ni) 1968. Parliament building in Reykjavik; commemorative inscription. ℞ value	1.50	2.00

COMMEMORATIVE ISSUES (3) FOR THE 100th ANNIVERSARY OF THE SETTLEMENT BY NORWEGIAN VIKINGS

29 (22) 500 Kronur (Ag) 1974. Viking woman with
cow. ℞ sea eagle, dragon, bull and

giant in quartered circle, the so-called protectors of the land who in accordance with the legend are reputed to have protected Iceland against an invasion of the Danish King Harald Blatand, value, name of country

	Unc	Proof
	8.00	15.00

30 (23) 1000 Kronur (Ag) 1974. Two vikings, in the background a blazing fire which was lit when taking possession of the country as a boundary of occupation. ℞ as No. 29 — 15.00 — 20.00

31 (24) 10000 Kronur (Au) 1974. Ingulfur (Ingólfr) Arnason from Firdafylke in Norway in his boat, proceeding to toss the two posts of his subsequent raised domicile on to the beach when landing (legend of the foundation of Reykjavik). ℞ as with No. 29 — 200.00 — 250.00

CURRENCY REFORM: 1 new Kronur = 100 old Kronur

			XF	Unc
32 (25)	5	Aurar (Br) 1981–	0.05	0.10
33 (26)	10	Aurar (Br) 1981–	0.05	0.10
34 (27)	50	Aurar (Br) 1981–	0.10	0.15
35 (28)	1	Kronur (Cu-Ni) 1981–	0.15	0.30
36 (29)	5	Kronur (Cu-Ni) 1981–	0.30	0.60
37 (30)	10	Kronur (Cu-Ni) 1984	0.70	1.20

No. 38 omitted.

39 (31) 500 Kronur (Ag) 1986:
      a) .500 silver, 20 g   17.50
      b) .925 silver, 20 g   30.00

Indien   # India   **Inde**

Area: 1,259,797 sq. mi. Population: 748,000,000.

On the basis of the Act of Independence passed by the British Parliament, British India was divided in 1947 into an almost exclusively Mohammedan state (Pakistan) and a predominantly Hindu state (India). On 15th August 1947 India obtained the status of an independent dominion, and since 26th January 1950 it has been a republic within the British Commonwealth. Capital: New Delhi.

3 Pies = 1 Pice (Paisa), 12 Pies = 1 Anna; 16 Annas = 1 Rupee,
15 Rupees = 1 Mohur; since 1st April 1957: 100 Naye Paise =
1 Rupee; since 1st April 1964: 100 Paise = 1 Rupee

EDWARD VII 1901–1910

			VF	XF
1 (27)	$\frac{1}{12}$ Anna (Cu) 1903–1910. Head right of King Edward VII. ℞ value within dotted circle, the whole surrounded by leaf decoration		0.25	0.50
2 (28)	$\frac{1}{2}$ Pice (Cu) 1903–1910		0.30	0.60
3 (29)	$\frac{1}{4}$ Anna (Cu) 1903–1910		0.30	0.60
4 (30)	1 Anna (Cu–Ni) 1907–1910. ℞ value within scroll (scalloped edge)		0.50	1.50
5 (31)	2 Annas (Ag) 1903–1910. ℞ crown above value		1.00	2.00
6 (32)	$\frac{1}{4}$ Rupee (Ag) 1903–1910		1.20	3.00
7 (33)	$\frac{1}{2}$ Rupee (Ag) 1903–1910		3.00	5.00
8 (34)	1 Rupee (Ag) 1903–1910		4.00	6.50

KING GEORGE V 1910–1936

			VF	XF
9 (35)	$\frac{1}{12}$ Anna (Br) 1911–1936. Crowned bust to left of King George V		0.15	0.25
10 (36)	$\frac{1}{2}$ Pice (Br) 1911–1936		0.30	0.50
11 (37)	$\frac{1}{4}$ Anna (Br) 1911–1936		0.30	0.50

			VF	**XF**

12 (38) 1 Anna (Cu–Ni) 1912–1936. ℞ value within scroll (scalloped edge) — 0.30 / 0.60

13 (42) 2 Annas (Ag) 1911–1917. ℞ value within circle, the whole surrounded by floral decoration — 1.00 / 1.50

14 (43) ¼ Rupee (Ag) 1911–1936 — 1.50 / 2.50

15 (44) ½ Rupee (Ag) 1911–1936 — 2.50 / 4.00

16 (45) 1 Rupee (Ag) 1911–1922. Value also given in Persian — 5.00 / 6.50

17 (39) 2 Annas (Cu–Ni) 1918–1936. ℞ large "2" within square (square shape) — 0.60 / 1.20

18 (40) 4 Annas (Cu–Ni) 1919–1921. ℞ large "4" within square (octagonal) — 1.00 / 2.00

19 (41) 8 Annas (Cu–Ni) 1919–1920. Large "8"; value also given in Nagpuri, Persian, Bengali and Tamili — 3.00 / 7.00

20 (46) 15 Rupees (1 Mohur) (Au) 1918. Crowned bust to left of King George V. ℞ value within dotted circle, the whole surrounded by border decoration — 150.00 / 200.00

21 (A 46) 1 £ (Au) 1918. King George V. ℞ St. George and the Dragon — 120.00 / 150.00

Coin No. 21 can only be distinguished from the other similar coins issued at the same time in Great Britain by the mintmark "I".

KING GEORGE VI 1936–1952

22 (47) ¹/₁₂ Anna (Br) 1938–1939. Crowned head left of King George VI. ℞ value within dotted circle, the whole surrounded by border decoration — 0.15 / 0.25

23 (47a) ¹/₁₂ Anna (Br) 1939–1942. Type as No. 22, but low-relief head (second head) — 0.15 / 0.30

			VF	XF
24 (49)	½ Pice (Br) 1938–1940		0.20	0.40
25 (49a)	½ Pice (Br) 1940–1942. Type as No. 22, second head		0.30	0.50
26 (50)	¼ Anna (Br) 1938–1940		0.30	0.50
27 (50a)	¼ Anna (Br) 1940–1942. Type as No. 26, second head		0.30	0.60
28 (51)	1 Pice (Br) 1943–1947. Border decoration. R crown and date (central hole); value also given in Devanagari and Persian		0.15	0.30
29 (52)	½ Anna. R value within scroll			
	a) (Ni-Bra) 1942–1945		0.10	0.25
	b) (Cu-Ni) 1946–1947		0.10	0.25
30 (53)	1 Anna (Cu-Ni) 1938–1940, R value within scroll		0.10	0.20
31 (53)	1 Anna. Type as No. 30, second head			
	a) (Cu-Ni) 1940–1947		0.10	0.20
	b) (Ni-Bra) 1942–1945		0.10	0.20
32 (54)	2 Annas (Cu-Ni) 1939. R large »2« within scroll (square shape)		0.15	0.30
33 (54)	2 Annas. Type as No. 32, second head			
	a) (Cu-Ni) 1939–1947		0.15	0.30
	b) (Ni-Bra) 1942–1945		0.15	0.30
34 (55)	¼ Rupee (Ag) 1939–1940		2.00	3.00
35 (55)	¼ Rupee (Ag) 1939–1945. Type as No. 34, second head		1.60	2.50
36 (56)	½ Rupee (Ag) 1938–1939		4.00	6.00
37 (56)	½ Rupee (Ag) 1939–1945. Type as No. 36, second head		1.80	2.50
38 (57)	1 Rupee (Ag) 1938–1945		3.50	7.00
39 (58)	¼ Rupee (Ni) 1946–1947. R tiger (Panthera tigris – Felidae)		1.00	1.60
40 (59)	½ Rupee (Ni) 1946–1947. Type as No. 39		1.10	1.80

41 (60)	1 Rupee (Ni) 1947. Type as No. 39		1.50	2.60

Values are given for each coin in U.S. Dollars and reference to Yeoman-numbers.

			VF	XF
42 (61)	1	Pice (Br). Capital of the Ashoka column (Edict column) from Sarnat surmounted by three lions with the "Wheel of the Law", today in the National Museum in New Delhi; emblem of the national coat of arms. ℞ horse (Equus caballus caballus — Equidae)		
		a) 1950, thick flan	0.15	0.30
		b) 1951–1955, thin flan	0.05	0.10
43 (62)	½	Anna (Cu–Ni) 1950–1955. ℞ Zebu (square shape)	0.10	0.20

44 (63)	1	Anna (Cu–Ni) 1950–1955. ℞ Zebu (scalloped edge)	0.20	0.40
45 (64)	2	Annas (Cu–Ni) 1950–1954. ℞ Zebu (square shape)	0.20	0.40
46 (65)	¼	Rupee (Ni) 1950–1956. ℞ value with ear of corn on either side	0.25	0.50

47 (66)	½	Rupee (Ni) 1950–1956	0.25	0.50
48 (67)	1	Rupee (Ni) 1950–1954	0.90	1.50

NEW CURRENCY (Decimal System): 100 Naye Paise = 1 Rupee

			VF	XF
49 (68)	1	Naya Paisa. R value		
		a) (Br) 1957–1962	0.10	0.15
		b) (Ni-Bra) 1962–1963	0.10	0.15
50 (69)	2	Naye Paise (Cu-Ni) 1957–1963. R value (scalloped edge)	0.10	0.15
51 (70)	5	Naye Paise (Cu-Ni) 1957–1963 (square shape)	0.10	0.20
52 (71)	10	Naye Paise (Cu-Ni) 1957–1963 (scalloped edge)	0.10	0.20
53 (72)	25	Naye Paise (Ni) 1957–1963	0.20	0.50
54 (73)	50	Naye Paise (Ni) 1960–1963	0.40	0.70
55 (74)	1	Rupee 1962–1984. Value between ears:		
		a) (Ni) 1962, 1970, 1962, 1970–1974,	0.75	1.50
		Proof		1.50
		b) (Cu-Ni) 1975–1984	0.30	0.50

NEW CURRENCY: 100 Paise = 1 Rupee

			VF	XF
56 (75)	1	Paisa (Ni–Bra) 1964. Type as No. 49	0.10	0.20
57 (76)	2	Paise (Cu–Ni) 1964. Type as No. 50	0.10	0.20

			VF	XF
58 (77)	3	Paise (Al) 1964–1971 (hexagonal)	0.08	0.15
59 (78)	5	Paise (Cu-Ni) 1964–1966. Type as No. 51	0.10	0.16
60 (79)	10	Paise (Cu-Ni) 1964–1967. Type as No. 52	0.10	0.20
61 (80)	25	Paise (Ni) 1964–1968. Type as No. 53	0.12	0.25
62 (81)	50	Paise (Ni) 1964–1971. Type as No. 54	0.15	0.30

FOR THE DEATH OF JAWAHARLAL NEHRU (3)

			VF	XF
63 (82)	50	Paise (Ni) 1964. Head left of Jawaharlal Nehru (1889–1964), politican, Prime Minister 1947–1964. R capital of the Ashoka column from Sarnat surmounted by three lions, and value also given in Devanagari	0.40	1.00
64 (82.1)	50	Paise (Ni) 1964. Type as No. 63, but Hindi obverse	0.35	0.80

			VF	XF
65 (83)	1	Rupee (Ni) 1964. Type as No. 63	1.00	2.00
66 (84)	1	Paisa (Al) 1965–. ℞ value (square shape)	0.05	0.10
67 (85)	2	Paise (Al) 1965–. ℞ value (scalloped edge)	0.05	0.10
68 (78)	5	Paise (Al) 1967–1971. Rev. value (square shape)	0.05	0.10

69 (79a)	10	Paise (Ni-Bra) 1968–1971. Type as No. 60	0.10	0.20

70 (86)	20	Paise (Ni-Bra) 1968–1971. Rev. lotus flower, value and date	0.15	0.25

COMMEMORATIVE ISSUES (4) FOR THE CENTENARY OF THE BIRTH OF MAHATMA GANDHI

			XF	Unc
71 (87)	20	Paise (Al–Br) 1969. Head left of Mohandas Karamchand Gandhi (1869–1948), known as Mahatma ("Sublime Soul"), advocate of the non-violent resistance movement "Satyagraha". ℞ emblem of state and value	0.30	0.50
72 (88)	50	Paise (Ni) 1969. Type as No. 71	0.35	0.70
73 (89)	1	Rupee (Ni) 1969. Type as No. 71	0.60	1.00

Values are given for each coin in U.S. Dollars and reference to Yeoman-numbers.

			XF	Unc
74 (90)	10 Rupees (Ag) 1969. Type as No. 71		5.00	10.00

COMMEMORATIVE ISSUES (2) FOR THE FAO COIN PLAN

			XF	Unc
75 (91)	20 Paise (Al-Br) 1970, 1971. Lotus flower between ears of corn; above stylized sun		0.30	0.50
76 (92)	10 Rupees (Ag) 1970, 1971. Type as No. 75		6.00	10.00
77 (A 93)	3 Paise (Al) 1972–. Coat of arms. Rev. value, date; proof			1.50

78 (B 93)	5 Paise (Al) 1972–. Type as No. 77		0.05	0.10
79 (93)	10 Paise (Al) 1971–. National emblem in dotted circle, the whole in wreath of leaf ornaments. R value (rounded serrated edge)		0.05	0.15
80 (94)	25 Paise (Ni-Al) 1972–. National emblem. Value, date, crossed branches		0.15	0.25
81 (95)	50 Paise (Ni-Al) 1972–. Type as No. 78		0.20	0.30

		XF	Unc
82 (96)	50 Paise (Cu–Ni) 1972	0.25	0.50

83 (97)	10 Rupees (Ag) 1972	6.00	9.00

COMMEMORATIVE ISSUES (3) FOR THE FAO COIN PLAN

		XF	Unc
84 (98)	50 Paise (Cu–Ni) 1973. Lettering in square between ears of wheat, date. ℞ national arms, value	0.15	0.30
85 (99)	10 Rupees (Ag) 1973. Type as No. 84	5.50	8.00
86 (100)	20 Rupees (Ag) 1973. Type as No. 84	9.00	12.00

ISSUE FOR THE FAO COIN PLAN (3)

87 (101)	10 Paise (Al) 1974	0.15	0.25
88 (102)	10 Rupees (Cu-Ni) 1974	2.00	3.00
89 (103)	50 Rupees (Ag) 1974	10.00	12.50

INTERNATIONAL WOMEN'S YEAR 1975 AND FAO COIN PLAN (3)

				XF	Unc
90 (104)	10	Paise (Al) 1975		0.15	0.25
91 (105)	10	Rupees (Cu-Ni) 1975		2.00	3.00
92 (106)	50	Rupees (Ag) 1975		12.00	17.50

No. 93 omitted.

ISSUES FOR THE FAO COIN PLAN (4)

94 (107)	5 Paise (Al) 1976. Farm Mechanization	0.15	0.25
95 (108)	10 Paise (Al) 1976. Type as No. 94	0.15	0.25
96 (109)	10 Rupees (Cu-Ni) 1976. Type as No. 94	2.00	3.00
97 (110)	50 Rupees (Ag) 1976. Type as No. 94	9.00	12.50

ISSUES FOR THE FAO COIN PLAN (4)

98 (111)	5 Paise (Al) 1977	0.15	0.25
99 (112)	10 Paise (Al) 1977	0.15	0.25
100 (113)	10 Rupees (Cu-Ni) 1977	2.00	3.00
101 (114)	50 Rupees (Ag) 1977	10.00	15.00

FOR THE FAO COIN PLAN (4)

			XF	Unc
102 (115)	5 Paise (Al) 1978		0.15	0.25
103 (116)	10 Paise (Al) 1978		0.15	0.25
104 (117)	10 Rupees (Cu-Ni) 1978		1.80	3.00

105 (118)	50 Rupees (Ag) 1978		9.00	12.50

INTERNATIONAL YEAR OF THE CHILD (5)

106 (119)	5 Paise (Al) 1979		0.10	0.20
107 (120)	10 Paise (Al) 1979		0.10	0.20
108 (121)	10 Rupees (Cu-Ni) 1979		1.75	2.50
109 (122)	50 Rupees (Ag) 1979		9.00	12.50
				Proof
110 (143)	100 Rupees (Ag) 1981			35.00

RURAL WOMEN'S ADVANCEMENT (4)

			XF	Unc
111 (123)	10 Paise (Al) 1980		0.15	0.20
112 (124)	25 Paise (Cu-Ni) 1980		0.20	0.30
113 (125)	10 Rupees (Cu-Ni) 1980		1.80	3.60
114 (126)	100 Rupees (Ag) 1980		17.50	22.50

WORLD FOOD DAY 1981 (4)

		XF	Unc
115 (127)	10 Paise (Al) 1981	0.10	0.20

116 (128)	25 Paise (Cu-Ni) 1981	0.20	0.30
117 (129)	10 Rupees (Cu-Ni) 1981	2.25	3.50
118 (130)	100 Rupees (Ag) 1981	16.00	22.50

IX ASIAN GAMES (5)

119 (131)	10 Paise (Al) 1982	0.10	0.20
120 (132)	25 Paise (Cu-Ni) 1982	0.20	0.30
121 (134)	2 Rupees (Cu-Ni) 1982	0.50	0.65
122 (135)	10 Rupees (Cu-Ni) 1982		4.00
123 (136)	100 Rupees (Ag) 1982		25.00

WORLD FOOD DAY 1982 (2)

| **124** (139) | 10 Paise (Al) 1982 | 0.10 | 0.20 |

| **125** (138) | 20 Paise (Al) 1982 | 0.20 | 0.50 |

		XF	Unc
126 (142)	50 Paise (Cu-Ni) 1982. Map and flag	0.15	0.30

		XF	Unc
127 (138)	2 Rupees (Cu-Ni) 1982. Type as No. 127	0.25	0.60
128	10 Rupees (Cu-Ni) 1982. Type as No. 127	2.00	3.00
129	100 Rupees (Ag) 1982. Type as No. 127		22.50
130	5 Paise (Al) 1985–. Capital of the Asho-ka column and inscription below	0.10	0.15
131 (141)	10 Paise (Al) 1983–. Arms. Rev. value, date	0.10	0.15
132 (140)	20 Paise (Al) 1982–. Rev. value and date between ornaments	0.10	0.20
133	25 Paise (Cu-Ni)	–.–	–.–
134	50 Paise (Cu-Ni) 1983–. Rev. value with-in ornaments	0.20	0.40
135 (137)	1 Rupee (Cu-Ni) 1983–. Rev. value be-tween ears	0.35	0.65

No. 136 omitted.

FOR THE FAO COIN PLAN

137 (145)	20 Paise (Al) 1983. Rev. fisherman	0.20	0.30

ISSUES OF THE NATIVE AND VASSAL STATES

Bahawalpur

The emirate of Bahawalpur belonged to British India until 1947 when it became part of Pakistan. Its integration into the state of West Pakistan followed on 14th October 1955.

SADIQ MOHAMMED KHAN V 1907–1947

		VF	XF
1 (8)	1 Paisa (Br) 1924 (Hegira Calendar dating 1342). Toughra. ℞ three stylized ears of corn, above which four stars (square shape)	9.00	12.00

2 (9) 1 Paisa (Br) 1925 (H. C. 1343). Toughra within double linear square. ℞ three stylized ears of corn, above which four stars, the whole within double linear square — 12.00 / 30.00

3 (10) 1 Rupee (Ag) 1925 (H. C. 1343). Bust left of Emir Sadiq Mohammed Khan V. ℞ arms — 40.00 / 80.00

	VF	XF

4 (11) 1 Mohur (1 Ashrafi) (Au) 1925 (H. C. 1343). Type as No. 3 — 250.00 / 300.00

5 (12) ½ Pice (Cu) 1940. Bust left of Emir Sadiq Mohammed Khan V (1904 to 1966) wearing fez. ℞ toughra surrounded by stars — 1.00 / 2.00

6 (13) ¼ Anna (Cu) 1940. Type as No. 5 — 2.00 / 4.00

Bikanir

The dating of the coins corresponds to the Samvat calendar.

SRI GANGA SINGHJI 1887–1943
COMMEMORATIVE ISSUE FOR THE 50th YEAR OF REIGN

1 (19) 1 Rupee (Ag) 1937 (S. C. 1994). Bust facing of Maharajah Sri Ganga Singhji. ℞ monogram within wreath, the whole surrounded by inscription and symbols — 12.50 / 20.00

2 (20) ½ Mohur (Au) 1937. ℞ inscription within circle broken by emblems — 120.00 / 140.00

3 (21) 1 Mohur (Au) 1937. Type as No. 2 — 220.00 / 300.00

Bundi

State in Rajasthan. The dating of the coins corresponds to the Samvat calendar. The coins were issued in the name of the reigning British monarch.

MAHARAO RAJAH RAGHUBIR SINGH 1889–1927

			VF	XF
1 (9)	1	Rupee (Ag) 1889–1900 (S. C. 1946 to 1957). Kunjar (Indian dagger) and inscription QUEEN VICTORIA. ℞ inscription in Devanagari	4.00	10.00
2 (10)	1	Rupee (Ag) 1901 (S. C. 1958). Bust of a Yaksha and inscription QUEEN VICTORIA. ℞ inscription in Devanagari	25.00	60.00
3 (12)	¼	Rupee (Ag) 1907–1909 (S. C. 1964 to 1966). Kunjar and inscription EDWARD VII. ℞ inscription in Devanagari	3.00	7.00
4 (13)	½	Rupee (Ag) 1909 (S. C. 1966). Type as No. 3	5.00	9.00
5 (11)	1	Rupee (Ag) 1901–1905 (S. C. 1958 to 1962). Bust of a Yaksha	7.00	10.00
6 (14)	1	Rupee (Ag) 1906–1911 (S. C. 1963 to 1968). Type as No. 3 (the coin can be round or square)	8.00	12.00
7 (15)	¼	Paisa (Cu) 1916–1929 (S. C. 1973 to 1986). Kunjar and inscription GEORGE V. ℞ inscription (square shape)	3.00	5.00
8 (16)	¼	Rupee (Ag) 1916–1924 (S. C. 1973 to 1981). Kunjar	4.50	6.00
9 (17)	½	Rupee (Ag) 1923–1926 (S. C. 1980 to 1983). Type as No. 8	5.00	8.00
10 (18)	1	Rupee (Ag) 1922–1926 (S. C. 1979 to 1983). Type as No. 8 (the coin can be round or square)	8.00	15.00
11 (19)	½	Rupee (Ag) 1925. Date and inscription	20.00	50.00
12 (20)	1	Rupee (Ag) 1925. Type as No. 11	26.00	40.00

Datia

State in the Bundelkhand territory.

MAHARAJAH GOVIND SINGH 1907–1955

1 (1)	½	Mohur (Au) undated. Portrait of the Maharajah. ℞ arms	260.00	300.00

Dungarpur

The dating of the coins corresponds to the Samvat calendar.

LAKSHMAN SINGH 1918–1948

		VF	XF
1 (1)	1 Paisa (Br) 1944 (S. C. 2001). Emblem of state. ℞ inscription (square shape)	15.00	30.00

Gwalior

State in the Malwa territory. The dating of the coins corresponds to the Samvat calendar.

MAHARAJAH MADHAO RAO SINDIA II
1886–1925

1 (45)	½ Pice (Cu) 1901. Cobra (Naja naja — Elapidae or Elaphidae) (in Sanskrit: naga), trident (attribute of the god Shiva) and sceptre, the whole within dotted circle; inscription reading Sri Madhava Rao ma Sinde Alijabahadar in Devanagari. ℞ value and date within floral decoration	1.60	2.50

2 (46)	¼ Anna (Cu) 1901. Type as No. 1	2.00	4.00
3 (48)	¼ Anna (Cu) 1913–1917 (S. C. 1970 to 1974). Bust of the Maharajah wearing turban. ℞ arms of the state	2.00	3.00
4 (47)	⅓ Mohur (Au) 1902 (S. C. 1959). Type similar to No. 3	200.00	240.00

MAHARAJAH GEORGE JIVAJI RAO SINDIA
1925–1961

5 (49)	¼ Anna (Cu) 1929 (S. C. 1986). Bust of the Maharajah. ℞ arms of the state	1.00	1.50
6 (50)	¼ Anna (Cu) 1942. Type as No. 5, but diameter only 19 mm instead of 22 mm	0.80	1.20
7 (51)	½ Anna (Bra) 1942	0.90	1.50

Hyderabad

State in Upper Deccan. In 1948 Hyderabad was integrated into the Dominion of India and in November 1956 was divided into the Union States of Andhra Pradesh, Maisur and Bombay.

NAWAB MIR MAHBUB ALI KHAN BAHADUR, ASAFJAH VI, NIZAM OF HYDERABAD 1869–1911

			VF	XF
1 (37)	¹/₈ Rupee (Ag) 1905 (H. C. 1323). The Char Minar in Hyderabad. ℞ inscription		1.50	3.00
2 (38)	¹/₄ Rupee (Ag) 1905–1911 (H. C. 1323 to 1329)		1.50	3.00
3 (39)	¹/₂ Rupee (Ag) 1910–1911 (H. C. 1328 to 1329)		3.50	6.50

			VF	XF
4 (40)	1 Rupee (Ag) 1903–1911 (H. C. 1321 to 1329)		6.00	8.00
5 (41)	¹/₈ Mohur (Au) 1903–1911 (H. C. 1321 to 1329). Type as No. 1		26.00	35.00
6 (42)	¹/₄ Mohur (Au) 1903–1911 (H. C. 1321 to 1329)		38.00	45.00
7 (43)	¹/₂ Mohur (Au) 1903–1911 (H. C. 1321 to 1329)		60.00	75.00

			VF	XF
8 (44)	1 Mohur (Au) 1903–1911 (H. C. 1321 to 1329)		85.00	100.00

NAWAB MIR USMAN ALI KHAN, ASAF JAH VII, NIZAM OF HYDERABAD & BERAR 1911–1948

			VF	XF
9 (45)	1 Pai (Br) 1920–1935 (H. C. 1338–1353). Toughra. ℞ inscription		0.70	1.00

			VF	XF
10 (46a)	2	Pai (Br) 1912–1932 (H. C. 1330–1349)	1.00	1.50
11 (47)	½	Anna (Br) 1914–1930 (H. C. 1332 to 1348)	1.50	3.00
12 (48)	1	Anna (Cu–Ni) 1920–1936 (H. C. 1338 to 1354). Toughra. ℞ three sections, the central one with value, the other two with inscription surrounded by meander pattern	1.00	2.00
13	1	Anna. Toughra. R value within scroll (square shape) a) (Y 49) (Cu–Ni) 1938–1941 (H. C. 1356 to 1359)	1.00	1.50
		b) (Y 59) (Br) 1943–1950 (H. C. 1361 to 1368)	0.40	0.60
14 (50)	⅛	Rupee (Ag) 1912–1929 (H. C. 1330 to 1347). The Char minaret in Hyderabad. ℞ inscription	1.10	1.60
15 (51)	¼	Rupee (Ag) 1912–1936 (H. C. 1330 to 1354)	1.80	3.00
16 (52)	½	Rupee (Ag) 1912–1924 (H. C. 1330 to 1342)	4.00	7.00
17 (53)	1	Rupee (Ag) 1912–1925 (H. C. 1330 to 1343)	6.00	8.00
18 (54)	⅛	Mohur (Au) 1919–1925 (H. C. 1337 to 1343)	35.00	45.00
19 (55)	¼	Mohur (Au) 1919 (H. C. 1337)	50.00	65.00

			VF	XF
20 (56)	½	Mohur (Au) 1919–1935 (H. C. 1337 to 1353)	70.00	85.00
21 (57a)	1	Mohur (Au) 1925–1926 (H. C. 1343 to 1344)	100.00	120.00
22 (60)	⅛	Rupee (Ag) 1944–1946 (H. C. 1362 to 1364). ℞ value within circle	1.00	2.00
23 (61)	¼	Rupee (Ag) 1944–1946 (H. C. 1362 to 1364). Type as No. 22	1.00	1.50
24 (62)	½	Rupee (Ag) 1945 (H. C. 1363). Type as No. 22	2.00	3.00
25 (63)	1	Rupee (Ag) 1943–1947 (H. C. 1361 to 1365)	6.00	9.00

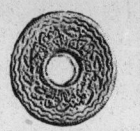

			VF	XF
26 (58)	2	Pai (Br) 1944–1950. Inscription (central hole)	0.50	1.00
27 (64)	⅛	Rupee (Ni) 1947–1950 (H. C. 1365 to 1368)	0.30	0.60
28 (65)	¼	Rupee (Ni) 1947–1950 (H. C. 1365 to 1368)	0.50	0.90
29 (66)	½	Rupee (Ni) 1948 (H. C. 1366)	1.50	3.00

Indore

State in the Malwa territory. The dating of the coins corresponds to the Samvat calendar.

MAHARAJAH SHIVAJI RAO HOLKAR
1886–1903

			VF	XF
1 (10a)	¼	Anna (Cu) 1886–1902 (S. C. 1943 to 1959). Zebu, inscription reading Srimant Maharaja Holkar Sirkar Indore in Devanagari. ℞ value and date within dotted circle, the whole surrounded by leaf decoration	1.00	1.80
2 (11a)	½	Anna (Cu) 1886–1902 (S. C. 1943 to 1959). Type as No. 1	1.20	2.50
3 (19)	1	Rupee (Ag) 1899–1901 (S. C. 1956 to 1958). Facing bust of the Maharajah wearing turban. ℞ emblem of state	110.00	150.00
4 (18)	1	Rupee (Ag) 1904–1911 (S. C. 1961 to 1968). Sun sourrounded by inscription in Devanagari. ℞ inscription within wreath	7.50	10.00

MAHARAJAH YESHVANT RAO HOLKAR II
1926–1961

			VF	XF
5 (20)	¼ Anna (Cu) 1935 (S. C. 1992). Facing bust of the Maharajah within dotted circle. ℞ value and date in dotted circle, the whole surrounded by leaf decoration		1.00	2.00
6 (21)	½ Anna (Cu) 1935 (S. C. 1992). Type as No. 5		2.00	4.00

Jaipur

State in Rajasthan. The dating of the coins corresponds to the year of reign of the ruling monarch.

MAHARAJAH SAWAI MADHO SINGH II
1880–1922

1 (8)	1 Paisa (Br) 5–37 (1880–1916). Inscription in Hindi	1.20	2.50
2 (10)	⅛ Rupee (Ag) 1–29 (1880–1908). Inscription in Hindi	3.00	5.00
3 (11)	¼ Rupee (Ag) 1–43 (1880–1922). Inscription in Hindi surrounded by border decoration	4.00	7.00
4 (12)	½ Rupee (Ag) 1–28 (1880–1907). Type as No. 3	6.00	10.00
5 (13)	1 Rupee (Ag) 1–42 (1880–1921). Type as No. 3	8.00	12.50

MAHARAJAH SAWAI MAN SINGH II
1922–1949

6 (18)	1 Anna (Bra) 1943–1944. Emblem of state within circle. ℞ value in circle	1.00	2.50

7 (19)	1 Anna (Bra) 1944. Bust to right of the Maharajah. Rev. emblem of state	1.00	2.50

Values are given for each coin in U.S. Dollars and reference to Yeoman-numbers.

			VF	XF
8 (20)	2 Annas (Bra) 21 (1942). Inscription in Hindi (square shape)		2.00	4.00
9 (21)	1 Rupee (Ag) 17–28 (1938–1949)		12.50	20.00

Kutch

Until 1947 the coins were issued in the name of the reigning British monarch.

$$24 \text{ Dokda} = 1 \text{ Kori}$$

KHENGARJI III 1876–1942

			VF	XF
1 (71)	3 Dokda (Cu) 1936. Trident and inscription in Devanagari. ℞ kunjar (Indian dagger)		1.50	3.00
2 (73)	1 Kori (Ag) 1936. Inscriptions		2.00	4.00
3 (74)	2½ Kori (Ag) 1936		3.00	6.00

			VF	XF
4 (75)	5 Kori (Ag) 1936		6.00	12.50

VIJAYAARIJI 1942–1947

			VF	XF
5 (77)	1/16 Kori (Cu) 1943–1947. Wreath surrounded by circle and inscription. ℞ trident, half-moon and kunjar surrounded by inscription (central hole)		0.40	0.80
6 (78)	1/8 Kori (Cu) 1943–1944 (central hole)		1.00	2.00
7 (79)	¼ Kori (Cu) 1943–1947 (central hole)		1.20	2.50
8 (80)	½ Kori (Cu) 1943–1946 (central hole)		2.50	4.00

MADANASINHJI 1947

			VF	XF
9 (84)	1 Kori (Ag) 1947. Castle with towers and pinnacles, surrounded by double circle and leaf decoration. ℞ trident, half-moon and kunjar, inscription		11.00	15.00
10 (85)	5 Kori (Ag) 1947		80.00	100.00

Mewar Udaipur

BHUPAL SINGH 1930–1948

			VF	XF
1 (18)	1	Anna (Ag) 1932. The hills of Mewar and inscription within floral border ℞ inscription in four lines with floral border	1.20	2.00
2 (19)	2	Annas (Ag) 1932	1.50	2.50
3 (20)	1/4	Rupee (Ag) 1932	3.00	4.50
4 (21)	1/2	Rupee (Ag) 1932	4.00	6.00
5 (22)	1	Rupee (Ag) 1932	7.00	10.00

Sailana

YESHVANT SINGH 1895–1919

1 (5)	1/4	Anna (Cu) 1908. Crowned bust left of King Edward VII. ℞ value and date within dotted circle, inscription giving name of state in English and Devanagari	7.00	15.00
2 (6)	1/4	Anna (Cu) 1912. Type as No. 1, but with bust of King George V	16.00	25.00

Travancore

State on the south-west coast of the Indian sub-continent. The dating of the coins corresponds in part to the Malabar calendar.

16 Cash = 1 Chuckram, 4 Chuckrams = 1 Fanam,
8 Fanams = 1 Rupee

MAHARAJAH RAMA VARMA IX 1885–1924

1 (29)	1	Cash (Cu) undated (1901). Chank snail (Xancus pyrum – Xancidae), symbol of the Indian god Vishnu. Rev. monogram RV	4.00	8.00
2 (30)	4	Cash (Cu) undated. Type as No. 1	1.50	3.00
3 (31)	8	Cash (Cu) undated. Type as No. 1	1.00	2.00
4 (32)	1	Chuckram (Cu) undated (1901–1903). Type as No. 1, legend »CHUCKRAM ONE«	3.00	6.00
5 (32a)	1	Chuckram (Cu) undated (1924). Type as No. 4, but legend »ONE CHUCKRAM«	1.50	3.00
6 (33)	2	Chuckrams (Ag) 1885–1930	3.00	5.00
7 (34)	1	Fanam (Ag) 1911–1930 (M. C. 1087 to 1106)	4.00	6.00
8 (35)	1/4	Rupee (Ag) 1906–1930 (M. C. 1082 to 1106)	6.50	9.00
9 (36)	1/2	Rupee (Ag) 1910–1931 (M. C. 1086 to 1107)	8.50	12.00

As can be seen from the dates, coins Nos. 1–3 and 6–9 continued to be issued under the era of Maharajah Bala Rama Varma.

			VF	XF
10 (4)	¼	Pagoda (Au) 1885–1924. Chank snail within wreath. ℞ inscription in wreath	80.00	100.00
11 (5)	½	Pagoda (Au) 1885–1924. Type as No. 10	110.00	130.00
12 (6)	1	Pagoda (Au) 1885–1924. Type as No. 10	255.00	280.00
13 (7)	2	Pagoda (Au) 1885–1924. Type as No. 10	375.00	420.00

MAHARAJAH SIR BALA RAMA VARMA X
1924–1949

			VF	XF
14 (41)	1	Cash (Br) undated (1938–1945). Chank snail surrounded by circle and wreath. ℞ monogram BRV and value	0.50	1.00
15 (42)	4	Cash (Br) undated (1938–1945)	0.50	1.00
16 (43)	8	Cash (Br) undated (1938–1945)	1.00	2.00
17 (44)	1	Chuckram (Br) undated (1938–1945). Bust to right of the Maharajah wearing plumed hat. ℞ Chank snail within wreath, value	2.00	4.00
18 (45)	1	Fanam (Ag) 1936–1945 (M. C. 1112 to 1121). Chank snail surrounded by circle and wreath. ℞ value and date	2.00	4.00
19 (46)	¼	Rupee (Ag) 1936–1945 (M. C. 1112 to 1121)	5.00	8.00
20 (47)	½	Rupee (Ag) 1936–1945 (M. C. 1112 to 1121)	5.00	8.00

Indonesien   # Indonesia   **Indonésie**

Area: 735,268 sq. mi. Population: 167,000,000.

The proclamation of the Indonesian Republic within the realm of the former Dutch East Indies took place on 17th August 1945 under the leadership of Sukarno and Hatta. It was only after the end of the Dutch police action to restore the old order, and the Conference to The Hague on 28th December 1949, that Indonesia obtained full sovereignty over all the islands, with the exception of Dutch New Guinea (since 1963 Irian Barat or West Irian). This territory passed to Indonesia only after an interim period.

Capital: Djakarta (formerly Batavia).

100 Sen = 1 Rupiah

				XF	Unc
1 (1)	1	Sen (Al) 1952. Malay inscription. ℞ name of country INDONESIA, rice plant and value (central hole)		0.50	0.80

2 (2)	5	Sen (Al) 1951–1954. Type as No. 1		0.50	0.70
3 (3)	10	Sen (Al) 1951–1954. Garuda bird holding symbolic representation of the Pantjasila (national emblem) over Malay inscription. ℞ value		0.30	0.50
4 (4)	25	Sen (Al) 1952. Type as No. 3		0.40	0.60
5 (5)	50	Sen (Cu-Ni) 1952–1954. Head left of Dipanegara, national hero. ℞ value		0.30	0.60
6 (3a)	10	Sen (Al) 1957. Type as No. 3, but also on the obverse the inscription INDONESIA now in English		0.80	1.50
7 (6)	25	Sen (Al) 1955–1957. Type as No. 4, but also on the obverse the inscription INDONESIA now in English		0.30	0.60
8 (5a)	50	Sen (Cu-Ni) 1954–1957. Type as No. 5, but without Malay inscription:			
		a) 1954		3.00	6.00
		b) 1955, 1957		0.25	0.50

			XF	Unc
9 (7)	50 Sen (Al) 1958–1961. National arms. ℞ value		0.20	0.30

COMMEMORATIVE ISSUES (10) FOR THE 25th ANNIVERSARY OF INDEPENDENCE ON 17th AUGUST 1970

		Proof
10	200 Rupiah (Ag) 1970. Great bird of paradise (Paradisea apoda — Paradisaeidae). ℞ national arms, above which dates 1945–1970. Initials of the Bank of Indonesia, date and value	10.00
11	250 Rupiah (Ag) 1970. Mandjusjri statue in stone, from the temple of Tumpang	15.00

12	500 Rupiah (Ag) 1970. Wajang dancer	25.00

			Proof
13	750	Rupiah (Ag) 1970. Garuda, mythological bird, Balinese chisel work	40.00
14	1 000	Rupiah (Ag) 1970. General Sudirman (1912–1950), leader of the revolt against Dutch domination	60.00
15	2 000	Rupiah (Au) 1970. Type as No. 10	100.00
16	5 000	Rupiah (Au) 1970. Type as No. 11	225.00
17	10 000	Rupiah (Au) 1970. Type as No. 12	450.00
18	20 000	Rupiah (Au) 1970. Type as No. 13	900.00
19	25 000	Rupiah (Au) 1970. Type as No. 14	1100.00

			XF	**Unc**
20 (13)	1	Rupiah (Al) 1970	0.10	0.20
21 (14)	2	Rupiah (Al) 1970	0.15	0.30
22 (15)	5	Rupiah (Al) 1970	0.20	0.40
23 (16)	25	Rupiah (Cu–Ni) 1971	0.25	0.60
24 (17)	50	Rupiah (Cu–Ni) 1971	0.40	0.90

COMMEMORATIVE ISSUE FOR THE FAO COIN PLAN

25 (18)	10	Rupiah (Cu-Ni) 1971, 1973. Value surrounded by rice plant (Oryza sativa – Gramineae) and cotton plant (Gossypium sp. – Malvaceae). Rev. inscription reading Bank Indonesia, value and date	0.20	0.40
26 (19)	100	Rupiah (Cu-Ni) 1973. House with sagging gable roof in the style of the Menangkabau	0.70	1.00

Values are given for each coin in U.S. Dollars and reference to Yeoman-numbers.

ISSUE FOR THE FAO COIN PLAN

		XF	Unc
27 (20)	5 Rupiah (Al) 1974. Family planning	0.20	0.40

SPECIAL ISSUE (3) CONSERVATION COIN COLLECTION

		Unc	Proof
28 (22)	2000 Rupiah (Ag) 1974. Coat of arms, date. ℞ Javan Tiger (Panthera tigris – Felidae)	17.50	22.50
29 (23)	5000 Rupiah (Ag) 1974. ℞ Orang-Utan (Pongo pygmaeus – Pongidae)	25.00	30.00
30 (24)	100000 Rupiah (Au) 1974. ℞ Komodo Dragon (Varanus komodensis – Varanidae)	475.00	550.00

ISSUE FOR THE FAO COIN PLAN (4)

		XF	Unc
31 (21)	10 Rupiah (Brass-clad steel) 1974	0.25	0.50
32 (25)	100 Rupiah (Cu-Ni) 1978	1.10	1.60
33 (26)	5 Rupiah (Al) 1979	0.20	0.40
34 (27)	10 Rupiah (Al) 1979	0.30	0.50

25th ANNIVERSARY OF WORLD WILDLIFE FUND

		Proof
35	10000 Rupiah (Ag) 1986	75.00
36	200000 Rupiah (Au) 1986	–.–

Riau Archipelago

Group of islands between Sumatra and Singapore under Indonesian rule.

			XF	Unc
1 (8)	1 Sen (Al) 1962. Bust left of President Mohammed Ahmad Sukarno (1901 to 1970), known simply as Sukarno. ℞ value within wreath, border inscription: KEPULAUAN RIAU		0.80	1.20

2 (9)	5	Sen (Al) 1962	0.80	1.20
3 (10)	10	Sen (Al) 1962	0.80	1.20
4 (11)	25	Sen (Al) 1962	1.10	1.50
5 (12)	50	Sen (Al) 1962	1.60	2.00

West Irian (Irian Barat)

The former territory of Dutch New Guinea, renamed Irian Barat in 1963, was only added to Indonesia after an interim period. From 1st October 1962 to 1st March 1963, following negotiations, Dutch New Guinea was by treaty placed under the supervision of the United Nations. Since 1963 Irian Barat has been under Indonesian rule.

100 Sen = 1 Irian Barat Rupiah

1 (8a)	1 Sen (Al) 1962. Bust left of President Mohammed Ahmad Sukarno (1901 to 1970). ℞ value within wreath		1.20	1.60
2 (9a)	5	Sen (Al) 1962	1.60	2.00
3 (10a)	10	Sen (Al) 1962	1.80	2.20
4 (11a)	25	Sen (Al) 1962	2.00	2.60
5 (12a)	50	Sen (Al) 1962	2.20	3.00

Area: 630,000 sq. mi. Population: 40,000,000.
Located between the Arrarat highland and the Persian Gulf, this country once produced the powerful empires of the Persians and Medes. This second large Persian empire was created by the Sassanids in 226.
Due to its geographical location and its enormous oil recources, presentday Persia, since 1935 officially called Iran, holds a tremendous interest for the Great Powers.
Capital: Teheran.

50 Dinars = 1 Chahi, 20 Chahis = 1 Kran,
10 Krans = 1 Toman, 100 Dinars = 1 Rial, 20 Rials = 1 Pahlevi,
since 1937: 100 Rials = 1 Pahlevi
20 Rials = 1 Pahlevi, since 1937: 100 Rials = 1 Pahlevi

MUZAFFAR-ED-DIN SHAHINSHAH 1896–1907

			VF	XF
1 (23)	1	Chahi (Cu–Ni) H-C 1318–1323 (1900–1905). Coat of arms (=lion with sword in front of sun). ℞ legend in wreath, with crown above	0.80	1.20
2 (24)	2	Chahis (Cu–Ni) H-C 1318–1324 (1900–1906)	1.20	1.60
3 (25)	1	Chahi (Ag) H-C 1318 (1900). ℞ legend in wreath, with crown above	4.00	7.00
4 (26)	¼	Kran (Ag) H-C 1319 (1901)	7.00	11.00
5 (27)	½	Kran (Ag) H-C 1316–1323 (1898–1905)	8.00	12.00
6 (A 27)	1	Kran (Ag) H-C 1317–1318 (1899–1900)	12.50	20.00
7 (28)	2	Krans (Ag) H-C 1315–1322 (1897–1904)	10.00	16.00
8 (29)	5	Krans (Ag) H-C 1320 (1902)	15.00	25.00
9 (30)	½	Kran (Ag) H-C 1323 (1905). Muzaffar-ed-Din Shahinshah (1853–1907), portrait in wreath. ℞ coat of arms	7.00	12.00
10 (31)	1	Kran (Ag) H-C 1319–1324 (1901–1906)	10.00	16.00
11 (32)	2	Krans (Ag) H-C 1319–1324 (1901–1906)	12.00	20.00
12 (33)	5	Krans (Ag) H-C 1322–1324 (1904–1906)	120.00	170.00

			VF	**XF**
13 (34)	¼ Toman (Au) H-C 1314–1325 (1896–1907). Muzaffar-ed-Din Shahinshah, portrait right. R legend in wreath		65.00	100.00
14 (35)	½ Toman (Au) H-C 1314–1325 (1896–1907)		38.00	45.00
15 (36)	1 Toman (Au) H-C 1314–1325 (1896–1907)		60.00	70.00
16 (37)	2 Tomans (Au) H-C 1314–1325 (1896–1907)		100.00	120.00
17	5 Tomans (Au) H-C 1314–1325 (1896–1907)		–.–	–.–
18	10 Tomans (Au) H-C 1314–1325 (1896–1907)		–.–	–.–

COMMEMORATIVE ISSUES (2) FOR THE BIRTHDAY OF THE SHAHINSHAH

19 (40)	1 Toman (Au) H-C 1322 (1904). Muzaffar-ed-Din Shahinshah, portrait left. R in wreath		80.00	100.00
20 (41)	2 Tomans (Au) H-C 1322 (1904)		100.00	125.00
21 (A 38)	⅕ Toman (Au) H-C 1316–1324 (1898–1906). Coat of arms. R legend in wreath		–.–	–.–
22 (38)	½ Toman (Au) H-C 1316–1324 (1898–1906)		60.00	70.00
23 (39)	1 Toman (Au) H-C 1316–1325 (1898–1907)		90.00	110.00
24	5 Tomans (Au) H-C 1316–1325 (1898–1907)		–.–	–.–
25	10 Tomans (Au) H-C 1316–1325 (1898–1907)		–.–	–.–

MOHAMMED ALI 1907–1909

26 (23)	1 Chahi (Cu–Ni) H-C 1326–1327 (1908–1909). Coat of arms. R legend in wreath		0.80	1.20
27 (24)	2 Chahis (Cu–Ni) H-C 1326–1327 (1908–1909)		1.20	1.60
28 (44)	1 Chahi (Ag) undated		4.50	8.00
29 (45)	¼ Kran (Ag) H-C 1326–1327 (1908–1909)		6.00	10.00
30 (46)	½ Kran (Ag) H-C 1326–1327 (1908–1909)		8.00	12.00
31 (47)	2 Krans (Ag) H-C 1325–1327 (1907–1909)		10.00	16.00
32 (48)	½ Kran (Ag) H-C 1326–1327 (1908–1909). Mohammed Ali Shahinshah (1872–1930), portrait left. R coat of arms		10.00	16.00

				VF	XF
33 (49)	1	Kran (Ag) H-C 1326–1327 (1908–1909)		12.50	20.00
34 (50)	2	Krans (Ag) H-C 1326 (1908)		100.00	150.00
35 (A 50)	5	Krans (Ag) H-C 1327 (1909)		300.00	500.00
36 (56)	½	Toman (Au) H-C 1325 (1907). Coat of arms. ℞ legend in wreath		18.00	25.00
37 (A 56)	1	Toman (Au) H-C 1325 (1907)		55.00	70.00
38	⅕	Toman (Au) H-C 1326 (1908). Mohammed Ali Shahinshah, portrait. ℞ legend in wreath		–.–	–.–
39 (53)	½	Toman (Au) H-C 1326 (1908)		50.00	60.00
40 (54)	1	Toman (Au) H-C 1326 (1908)		50.00	60.00
41 (55)	2	Tomans (Au) H-C 1326 (1908)		–.–	–.–
42	5	Tomans (Au) H-C 1325–1327 (1907–1909). Mohammed Ali Shahinshah, portrait. ℞ coat of arms		–.–	–.–

AHMED SHAH 1909–1925

				VF	XF
43 (64)	1	Chahi Sefid (Ag) H-C 1328–1330. Coat of arms date at bottom. Rev. legend in wreath		2.00	4.00
44 (A 64)	1	Chahi Sefid (Ag) H-C 1332. Type as No. 43, but date in lion's legs		4.00	7.00
45 (65)	¼	Kran (Ag) H-C 1327–1331. Type as No. 43; dia. 15 mm		5.00	8.00
46 (66)	500	Dinars (Ag) H-C 1327–1330; dia. 18 mm		4.00	7.00
47 (67)	1000	Dinars (Ag) H-C 1327–1330; dia. 23 mm		5.00	8.00
48 (68)	2	Krans (Ag) H-C 1327–1329; dia. 28 mm		8.00	12.00
49 (68a)	2000	Dinars (Ag) H-C 1330; dia. 28 mm		8.00	12.00
50 (68b)	2000	Dinars (Ag) H-C 1330–1331. Type as No. 49, but date in lion's legs		8.00	12.00
51 (75)	⅕	Toman (Au) H-C 1329. .900 gold, 0.57 gm.		55.00	70.00
52 (76)	½	Toman (Au) H-C 1328–1329. .900 gold, 1.43 gm.		60.00	80.00
53 (77)	1	Toman (Au) H-C 1329		–.–	–.–
54 (A 70)	1	Chahi Sefid (Ag) H-C 1333–1342		2.50	4.00
55 (B 70)	1	Chahi Sefid (Ag) H-C 1332–1342. Type as No. 54, but date in lion's legs		2.50	4.00
56 (C 70)	¼	Kran (Ag) H-C 1332–1343		3.50	6.00
57 (C 70a)	¼	Kran (Ag) H-C 1334. Typ as No. 56, but date at bottom		10.00	16.00
58 (70)	500	Dinars (Ag) H-C 1331–1343		6.00	10.00
59 (71)	1000	Dinars (Ag) H-C 1331–1344		5.50	8.00
60 (72)	2000	Dinars (Ag) H-C 1330–1344		7.50	9.50
61 (69)	5000	Dinars (Ag) H-C 1331–1344		16.00	30.00

		VF	XF
62 (79)	1/5 Toman (Au) H-C 1332–1341. Ahmed Shah, portrait. Rev. legend	40.00	50.00
63 (80)	½ Toman (Au) H-C (1332–1343)	50.00	60.00

64 (81)	1 Toman (Au) H-C 1333–1343 (1915–1925)	65.00	85.00
65	2 Tomans (Au) H-C 1333–1343 (1915–1925)	125.00	160.00
66 (83)	10 Tomans (Au) H-C 1333–1343 (1915–1925)	–.–	–.–

COMMEMORATIVE ISSUES (6) FOR THE 10th REGNAL ANNIVERSARY

67 (73)	1 Kran (Ag) H-C 1337 (1919). Ahmed Shah, portrait. ℞ coat of arms	16.00	20.00

68 (74)	2 Krans (Ag) H-C 1337 (1919)	18.00	25.00
69	1 Toman (Au) H-C 1337 (1919)	120.00	150.00
70	2 Tomans (Au) H-C 1337 (1919)	185.00	250.00
71	5 Tomans (Au) H-C 1337 (1919)	420.00	500.00
72	10 Tomans (Au) H-C 1337 (1919)	850.00	1000.00

RIZA SHAH PAHLEVI 1925-1941

Upon the introduction of the Solar-Hidshra-calendar (hidshri shamsi) the following dates, 1305-1349, correspond with the years 1924-1971, of the Christian calendar.

			VF	XF
73 (95)	50	Dinars (Cu-Ni) SH 1305-1307. Coat of arms. Rev. legend in wreath	0.80	1.20
74 (96)	100	Dinars (Cu-Ni) SH 1305-1307. Type as No. 73	1.20	2.00
75 (100)	¼	Kran (Ag) SH 1304. Coat of arms. Rev. legend; dia. 15 mm	8.50	12.00
76 (A101)	500	Dinars (Ag) SH 1304	200.00	350.00
77 (101)	1000	Dinars (Ag) SH 1304-1305	5.00	8.00
78 (102)	2000	Dinars (Ag) SH 1304-1305	8.50	12.50
79 (103)	5000	Dinars (Ag) SH 1304-1305	25.00	40.00
80 (119)	1	Toman (Au) SH 1305, .900 gold, 2.87 gm.	200.00	250.00
81 (105)	500	Dinars (Ag) SH 1305	65.00	90.00
82 (106)	1000	Dinars (Ag) SH 1305-1306	6.50	10.00
83 (107)	2000	Dinars (Ag) SH 1305-1306	9.00	12.00
84 (108)	5000	Dinars (Ag) SH 1305-1306	22.00	30.00
85 (116)	1	Pahlevi (Au) SH 1305, .900 gold, 1.91 gm.	120.00	140.00
86 (117)	2	Pahlevis (Au) SH 1305, .900 gold, 3.83 gm.	175.00	200.00
87 (118)	5	Pahlevis (Au) SH 1305, .900 gold, 9.59 gm.	350.00	400.00
88 (A109)	500	Dinars (Ag) SH 1306-1308. Bust of the Shah. Rev. coat of arms	8.50	12.00
89 (109)	1000	Dinars (Ag) SH 1306-1308. Type as No. 88	6.50	9.00
90 (110)	2000	Dinars (Ag) SH 1306-1308. Type as No. 88	8.00	12.00
91 (111)	5000	Dinars (Ag) SH 1306-1308	20.00	32.00
92 (120)	1	Pahlevi (Au) SH 1306-1308. Bust of the Shah. Rev. legend within dotted circle, .900 gold, 1.91 gm.	65.00	90.00
93 (121)	2	Pahlevis (Au) SH 1306-1308. Type as No. 92, .900 gold, 3.83 gm.	70.00	95.00
94 (122)	5	Pahlevis (Au) SH 1306-1308. Type as No. 92, .900 gold, 9.59 gm.	220.00	285.00
95 (93)	1	Dinar (Br) SH 1310. Coat of arms. Rev. value	1.20	2.50
96 (94)	2	Dinars (Br) SH 1310. Type as No. 95	1.20	2.50

			VF	XF
97 (97)	5	Dinars:		
		a) (Cu-Ni) SH 1310	2.50	5.50
		b) (Br) SH 1314	11.50	18.00
98 (98)	10	Dinars:		
		a) (Cu-Ni) SH 1310	3.50	6.00
		b) (Br) SH 1314	6.00	11.50
99 (99)	25	Dinars:		
		a) (Cu-Ni) SH 1310	12.50	20.00
		b) (Br) SH 1314	20.00	32.00
100 (92)	10	Chahis (Br) SH 1314	6.00	11.50
101 (104)	¼	Rial (Ag) SH 1315	2.00	3.20
102 (112)	½	Rial (Ag) SH 1310–1315	3.50	5.50
103 (113)	1	Rial (Ag) SH 1310–1313	4.00	6.50
104 (114)	2	Rials (Ag) SH 1310–1313	6.00	10.00
105 (115)	5	Rials (Ag) SH 1310–1313	16.00	20.00

			VF	XF
106 (123)	½	Pahlevi (Au) SH 1310–1315	85.00	125.00
107 (124)	1	Pahlevi (Au) SH 1310	280.00	400.00
108 (125)	5	Dinars (Al-Br) SH 1315–1320	0.80	1.20
109 (126)	10	Dinars (Al-Br) SH 1315–1320	0.80	1.20
110 (128)	50	Dinars (Al-Br) SH 1315–1320	0.80	1.20

MOHAMMED RIZA PAHLEVI 1941–1978

			VF	XF
111 (125)	5	Dinars (Al–Br) S-HC 1320–1321 (1942–1943). Coat of arms. ℞ value in wreath	0.80	1.20
112 (126)	10	Dinars (Al–Br) S-HC 1320–1321 (1942–1943)	0.80	1.20
113 (127)	25	Dinars (Al–Br) S-HC 1324–1329 (1946–1951)	4.00	6.50
114 (128)	50	Dinars		
		a) (Al–Br) S-HC 1321–1332 (1942–1954)	0.80	1.20
		b) (Cu) S-HC 1322 (1943)	2.50	4.00
115 (129)	1	Rial (Ag) S-HC 1322–1328 (1944–1950)	0.80	1.20
116 (130)	2	Rials (Ag) S-HC 1322–1338 (1944–1960)	1.20	2.00
117 (131)	5	Rials (Ag) S-HC 1322–1331 (1944–1953)	4.00	6.00
118 (132)	10	Rials (Ag) S-HC 1322–1325 (1944–1947)	8.00	12.00

				VF	XF
119	(133)	½	Pahlevi (Au) S-HC 1322–1327 (1944–1949)	50.00	65.00
120	(134)	1	Pahlevi (Au) S-HC 1320–1327 (1942–1949)	75.00	100.00
121	(137)	50	Dinars (Al–Br) S-HC 1333– (1955–)	0.25	0.40
122	(138)	1	Rial (Cu–Ni) S-HC 1331–1339 (1953–1961). Coat of arms. ℞ value	0.60	1.00
123	(139)	2	Rials (Cu–Ni) S-HC 1331–1336 (1953–1958)	0.60	1.00
124	(140)	5	Rials (Cu–Ni) S-HC 1331–1332 (1953–1954)	1.00	1.80
125	(141)	¼	Pahlevi (Au) S-HC 1333 (1955). Mohammed Riza Pahlevi (1919–1980), head left. ℞ coat of arms	25.00	32.00

126	(142)	½	Pahlevi (Au) S-HC 1333 (1955)	50.00	65.00
127	(143)	1	Pahlevi (Au) S-HC 1333 (1955)	100.00	125.00
128	(144)	2½	Pahlevis (Au) S-HC 1339 (1961)	200.00	250.00
129	(145)	5	Pahlevis (Au) S-HC 1339 (1961)	400.00	450.00
130	(A140)	1	Rial (Cu–Ni) S-HC 1337– (1959–). Coat of arms. ℞ value	0.25	0.40
131	(B140)	2	Rials (Cu–Ni) S-HC 1338– (1960–)	0.20	0.35
132	(C140)	5	Rials (Cu–Ni) S-HC 1337– (1959–)	0.25	0.50
133	(D140)	10	Rials (Cu–Ni) S-HC 1334– (1956–)	0.80	1.20

134	(149)	10	Rials (Cu–Ni) S-HC 1345–1352 (1967–1972). Mohammed Riza Pahlevi, head left. ℞ coat of arms	0.80	1.20
135	(151)	20	Rials (Cu–Ni) S-HC 1350–1352. Same type as No. 134	1.00	2.00

			VF	XF
136 (152)	1	Rial (Cu-Ni) S-HC 1350–1354. Similar to No. 137	0.25	0.40
137 (150)	10	Rials (Cu–Ni) S-HC 1348 (1969). Head of the shah, left. ℞ coat of arms, letters "FAO" and dates, surrounded by ears of rice, and a quotation from the Holy Avesta, "sow wheat, and harvest the truth"	1.20	2.00

COMMEMORATIVE COINS (9) FOR THE
2500th ANNIVERSARY OF THE PERSIAN EMPIRE

			Proof
138	25	Rials (Ag) 1971. Column head with averted steer heads above double volutes from the Artaxerxes palace in Susa. Now in the Louvre, Paris (Achaemenidian). ℞ State emblem, with name and title of Mohammed Riza Pahlevi above, value, dates. Wreath of 25 stylized Pahlevi crowns symbolising 25 centuries of monarchy	12.00
139	50	Rials (Ag) 1971. Walking griffin with ram's antlers, glazed brick tile relief, Susa; now in the Louvre, Paris (Achaemenidian). ℞ like No. 138	20.00
140	75	Rials (Ag) 1971. Stone of Cyrus II, the original is in the British Museum, London. Wreath of stylized Pahlevi crowns, imperial emblem. ℞ like No. 138	30.00
141	100	Rials (Ag) 1971. Tatshara (= palace) of Darius I and pillars of the Apadana (= reception hall) in Persepolis (Achaemenidian). ℞ like No. 138	35.00

All valuations in the SCHÖN are stated in U.S. Dollars.

		Proof
142	200 Rials (Ag) 1971. Imperial couple. ℞ like No. 138	65.00
143	500 Rials (Au) 1971. Same type as No. 139	125.00
144	750 Rials (Au) 1971. Same type as No. 140	150.00
145	1000 Rials (Au) 1971. Same type as No. 141	200.00
146	2000 Rials (Au) 1971. Same type as No. 142	450.00

		XF	**Unc**
147 (149a)	10 Rials (Cu-Ni) S-HC 1352-1354 (1973-1975). Type as No. 134, but value in numerals (below lion)	0.40	0.80

148 (151a)	20 Rials (Cu-Ni) S-HC 1352-1354 (1973-1975). Type as No. 147	0.60	1.20

FOR THE 7th ASIAN GAMES IN TEHERAN (2)

			XF	Unc
149 (153)	20	Rials (Cu-Ni) S-HC 1353 (1974). Emblem of the games, Motto: EVER ONWARD	1.50	2.50
150	5	Pahlevis (Au) S-HS 1353		–.–

The new monarchial calender system was adopted in 1976 = MS 2535.

50th ANNIVERSARY OF THE PAHLEVI RULE (6)

151 (154)	1	Rial (Cu-Ni) MS 2535 (1976). Coat of arms. Rev. value, inscription, crown	0.30	0.50
152 (155)	2	Rials (Cu-Ni) MS 2535 (1976). Type as No. 151	0.30	0.50
153 (156)	5	Rials (Cu-Ni) MS 2535 (1976). Type as No. 151	0.50	0.90
154 (157)	10	Rials (Cu-Ni) MS 2535 (1976). Head left, inscription above, date below. Rev. coat of arms, value	0.70	1.00
155 (158)	20	Rials (Cu-Ni) MS 2535 (1976). Type as No. 154	1.10	2.00
156 (159)	5	Pahlevi (Au) MS 3535 (1976).		–.–

ISSUE FOR THE FAO COIN PLAN

157 (160)	20	Rials (Cu-Ni) MS 2535–2536. Type as No. 137	1.00	2.00
158 (137a)	50	Dinars (Brass-coated steel) MS 2535–2537. Type as No. 121	0.40	0.80
159 (A140a)	1	Rial (Cu-Ni) MS 2536. Type as No. 130	0.25	0.50
160 (B140)	2	Rials (Cu-Ni) MS 2536. Type as No. 131	0.40	0.80

			XF	Unc
161 (C140b)	5 Rials (Cu-Ni) MS 2536–2537. Type as No. 132		0.80	1.20
162 (149a)	10 Rials (Cu-Ni) MS 2536–2537. Type as No. 147		1.00	1.60
163 (151a)	20 Rials (Cu-Ni) MS 2536–2537. Type as No. 148		1.20	2.00
164 (141b)	¼ Pahlevi (Au) MS 2536–2538. Type as No. 125		32.00	40.00
165 (142a)	½ Pahlevi (Au) MS 2536–2538. Type as No. 126		65.00	80.00
166 (143a)	1 Pahlevi (Au) MS 2536–2538. Type as No. 127		120.00	140.00
167 (144a)	2½ Pahlevis (Au) MS 2536–2538. Type as No. 128		265.00	300.00
168 (145a)	5 Pahlevis (Au) MS 2536–2538. Type as No. 129		650.00	700.00

50th ANNIVERSARY OF BANK MELLI

169 (162)	20 Rials (Cu-Ni) SH 1357	3.50	4.50

FOR THE FAO COIN PLAN

170 (163)	20 Rials (Cu-Ni) SH 1357	1.00	2.00

ISLAMIC REPUBLIC OF IRAN		XF	Unc
171 (164)	1 Rial (Cu-Ni) SH 1358–1360, 1362	0.25	0.50
172 (165)	2 Rials (Cu-Ni) SH 1358–1360	0.40	0.80
173 (166)	5 Rials (Cu-Ni) SH 1358–1363	0.60	1.20
174 (167)	10 Rials (Cu-Ni) SH 1358–1360	1.00	2.00

175 (168)	20 Rials (Cu-Ni) SH 1358–1361	1.50	3.00

1st ANNIVERSARY OF REVOLUTION (3)

176 (169)	10 Rials (Cu-Ni) SH 1358	2.00	3.00
A176 (A163)	½ Azadi (Au) SH 1358		*80.00*
177 (B163)	1 Azadi (Au) SH 1358		*160.00*

1400th ANNIVERSARY OF MOHAMMED'S FLIGHT

			XF	Unc
178 (170)	20 Rials (Cu-Ni) SH 1358		3.00	4.00

			XF	Unc
179 (171)	1 Rial (Bronze-clad steel) SH 1359		0.50	1.00

2nd ANNIVERSARY OF REVOLUTION

180 (174)	20 Rials (Cu-Ni) SH 1359		3.00	5.00

181 (172)	50 Rials (Al-Br) SH 1360, 1361		1.50	3.00

3rd ANNIVERSARY OF REVOLUTION

				XF	Unc
182 (173)	20 Rials (Cu-Ni) SH 1360			1.00	2.00

MOSLEMS UNITY

			XF	Unc
183 (175)	10 Rials (Cu-Ni) SH 1361		1.00	2.00

Area: 171,599 sq. mi. Population: 14,000,000.
The territory, which was once the centre of the Sassanian Empire, was conquered by the Mongolians in 1258. Then, before the country came under Turkish domination, it was ruled temporarily by Persia. In the years 1915–1917 the British Army of India conquered the Wilayets of Mesopotamia. On 2nd March 1921 Iraq became a British mandate under the League of Nations, and in the same year Faisal I was made King. It has been a republic since 14th July 1958.
Capital: Baghdad.

50 Fils = 1 Dirham, 200 Fils = 1 Ryal, 1000 Fils = 1 Dinar

FAISAL I 1921–1933

			VF	XF
1 (1)	1	Fils (Br) 1931–1933. Head right of King Faisal I (1883–1933). ℞ value, date and inscription in Arabic	1.20	2.00
2 (2)	2	Fils (Br) 1931–1933	2.00	4.00
3 (3)	4	Fils (Ni) 1931–1933 (scalloped)	1.20	2.50
4 (4)	10	Fils (Ni) 1931–1933 (scalloped)	2.00	4.00
5 (5)	20	Fils (Ag) 1931–1933	3.00	4.00
6 (6)	50	Fils = 1 Dirham (Ag) 1931–1933	16.00	10.00
7 (7)	200	Fils = 1 Ryal (Ag) 1932	22.00	35.00

GHAZI I 1933–1939

			VF	XF
8 (8)	1	Fils (Br) 1936–1938. Head left of King Ghazi I (1912–1939). ℞ value, date and inscription in Arabic	0.40	0.80
9 (9)	4	Fils. Type as No. 8, but scalloped		
		a) (Ni) 1938–1939	1.20	2.00
		b) (Cu–Ni) 1938	0.80	1.80
		c) (Br) 1938	0.90	1.80
10 (10)	10	Fils. Type as No. 8, but scalloped		
		a) (Ni) 1937–1938	6.00	10.00
		b) (Cu–Ni) 1938	1.00	3.00
		c) (Br) 1938	0.80	1.25
11 (11)	20	Fils (Ag) 1938	3.00	5.00

			VF	XF
12 (12)	50 Fils (Ag) 1937–1938		5.00	8.00

FAISAL II 1939–1958

			VF	XF
13 (13)	4 Fils (Br) 1943. Young head right of King Faisal II (1935–1958). ℞ value, date and inscription in Arabic (scalloped)		2.50	5.00
14 (14)	10 Fils (Br) 1943. Type as No. 13		3.50	7.00
15 (15)	1 Fils (Br) 1953. Head right of King Faisal II		0.25	0.50
16 (16)	2 Fils (Br) 1953		1.40	2.50

		VF	XF
17 (17)	4 Fils (Cu-Ni) 1953 (scalloped)	0.60	1.20
18 (18)	10 Fils (Cu-Ni) 1953 (scalloped)	0.80	1.50
19 (19)	20 Fils (Ag) 1953	6.50	10.00
20 (20)	50 Fils (Ag) 1953	20.00	28.00
21 (21)	100 Fils (Ag) 1953	20.00	26.00
22 (22)	20 Fils (Ag) 1955. Rev. value and date between branches	4.50	7.50
23 (23)	50 Fils (Ag) 1955. Type as No. 22	7.50	11.00
A24 (A24)	100 Fils (Ag) 1955. Type similar to No. 21; .500 silver		*200.00*

REPUBLIC since 1958

		VF	XF
24 (24)	1 Fils (Br) 1959. National emblem of the Republic. ℞ value within circle (decagonal)	0.25	0.50
25 (25)	5 Fils (Cu–Ni) 1959 (scalloped)	0.30	0.60
26 (26)	10 Fils (Cu–Ni) 1959 (scalloped)	0.50	1.00
27 (27)	25 Fils (Ag) 1959	1.80	2.50
28 (28)	50 Fils (Ag) 1959	3.00	4.00

			VF	**XF**

29 (29) 100 Fils (Ag) 1959 — 5.50 — 7.50

30 (30) 500 Fils (Ag) 1959. Bust in uniform of General Abdul Karim Kassem (1914–1963). R national emblem (medallic issue) — 26.00 — 32.00

31 (31) 5 Fils (Cu-Ni) 1967, 1971, 1974, 1975, 1980, 1981. Date palms (Phoenix dactylifera – Palmae). Rev. value within circle surrounded by Arabic inscription; below, ear of corn and tobacco leaf (scalloped) — 0.25 — 0.40

32 (32) 10 Fils (Cu-Ni) 1967, 1971, 1974, 1975, 1979, 1980, 1981. Type as No. 31 — 0.25 — 0.40

33 (33) 25 Fils (Cu-Ni) 1969, 1970, 1972, 1975, 1980, 1981. Type as No. 31, but round — 0.30 — 0.50

34 (34) 50 Fils (Cu-Ni) 1969, 1970, 1972, 1975, 1980, 1981. Type as No. 33 — 0.60 — 1.00

35 (35) 100 Fils (Cu-Ni) 1970, 1972, 1975, 1979. Type as No. 34 — 0.90 — 1.50

COMMEMORATIVE ISSUE FOR THE FAO COIN PLAN AND FOR THE AGRARIAN REFORM DAY
(September 30, 1970)

	Unc	**Proof**

36 (36) 250 Fils (Ni) 1909. Type as No. 31. Edge inscription »FAO 250« — 3.00 — 15.00

COMMEMORATIVE ISSUE FOR THE PEACE TREATY WITH THE KURDS (March 3, 1970)

	XF	Unc
37 (40) 250 Fils (Ni) 1971. Allegory of Peace (with flying dove)	3.00	5.00

COMMEMORATIVE ISSUES (3) FOR THE GOLDEN JUBILEE OF THE IRAQI ARMY

	Unc	Proof
38 (37) 500 Fils (Ni) 1971. Busts of two soldiers. ℞ value	6.00	8.50
39 (38) 1 Dinar (Ag) 1971. Same type as No. 38	15.00	27.50
40 (39) 5 Dinars (Au) 1971. Same type as No. 38	250.00	300.00

COMMEMORATIVE ISSUE FOR THE SILVER JUBILEE OF THE ARAB SOCIALIST BAATH PARTY (7. 4. 1972)

	XF	Unc
41 (41) 250 Fils (Ni) 1972. Date palm grove. ℞ value in circle, below date 7. 4. 1972; legend "Iraqi Republic" (above) and "Silver Jubilee of the Baath Party (= ABSP)" (below)	4.00	7.50

COMMEMORATIVE ISSUES (2) FOR THE SILVER JUBILEE OF THE IRAQI CENTRAL BANK

42 (42) 250 Fils (Ni) 1972. Date palm grove. ℞ value in circle, below dates; legend "Iraqi Republic" (above) and "Silver

		XF	Unc
	Jubilee of the Central Bank of Iraq"		
	(below)	3.00	5.50
43 (43)	1 Dinar (Ag) 1972. Type as No. 42	17.50	27.50

COMMEMORATIVE ISSUES (3)
FOR THE NATIONALIZATION OF OIL

		Unc	Proof
44 (44)	250 Fils (Ni) 1973	3.00	7.50

| **45** (45) | 500 Fils (Ni) 1973 | 6.00 | 8.50 |

| **46** (46) | 1 Dinar (Ag) 1973 | 17.50 | 28.00 |

ISSUES FOR THE FAO COIN PLAN (2)

		XF	Unc
47 (47)	5 Fils (St) 1975. Type similar to No. 31	0.25	0.40
48 (48)	10 Fils (St) 1975. Type as No. 47	0.30	0.60

INAUGURATION OF THE THATHAR EUPHRATES CANAL

		Unc	Proof
49 (49)	1 Dinar (Ag) 1977		30.00

INTERNATIONAL YEAR OF THE CHILD (4)

50 (50)	250 Fils (Ni) 1979. Head of a child	7.00
51 (51)	1 Dinar (Ag) 1979. Type as No. 50; .900 silver, 31 g	30.00
A51	50 Dinars (Au) 1979. Type as No. 50; .916⅔ gold, 13.7 g	350.00
B51	100 Dinars (Au) 1979. Type as No. 50; .916⅔ gold, 26 g	550.00

FIRST ANNIVERSARY OF THE ASSUMPTION OF PRESIDENCY BY SADDAM HUSSAIN (2)

52 (52)	250 Fils (Ni) 1980. President Saddam Hussain (born 1937)	4.00
A52	50 Dinars (Au) 1980. Type as No. 52	350.00

BATTLE OF QADISSIYA

			XF	Unc
53 (57)	1 Dinar (Ni) 1980		5.00	9.00

		XF	Unc
54 (36a)250 Fils (Ni) 1980, 1981. Type as No. 31 (octagonal)		2.00	3.00

15th CENTURY OF HEGIRA (3)

			Unc	Proof
55 (53)	1 Dinar (Ag) 1980			30.00
56 (55)	50 Dinars (Au) 1980			250.00
57 (56)	100 Dinars (Au) 1980			450.00

50th ANNIVERSARY OF IRAQ AIR FORCE

58 (58)	1 Dinar (Ag) 1981		6.00	
59 (59)	100 Dinars (Au) 1981			650.00

WORLD FOOD DAY 1981

		XF	Unc
60 (54) 250 Fils (Cu-Ni) 1981 (octagonal)		3.00	5.00

			XF	Unc
61 (60)	250 Fils (Cu-Ni) 1982. Date palm. Rev. value (octoganal)		3.00	
62 (61)	1 Dinar (Ni) 1982. Type as No. 61 (decagonal)		7.50	
63	50 Dinars (Au) 1982. Type as No. 61; .916 ⅔ gold, 13.7 g			300.00
64	100 Dinars (Au) 1982. Type as No. 61; .916 ⅔ gold, 26 g			500.00
65	500 Fils (Ni) 1982. Type as No. 31 (square)		2.00	3.00

RESTORATION OF THE HISTORIC CITY OF BABYLON (7)

			Unc	Proof
66	5 Fils 1982. Part of the Ishtar gate (scalloped):			
	a) (Cu-Ni)			2.00
	b) (St)		1.00	
67	10 Fils 1982. Ishtar gate (scalloped):			
	a) (Cu-Ni)			2.00
	b) (St)		1.00	
68	25 Fils (Cu-Ni) 1982. Relief figure of the Lion (round)		1.50	3.00
69	50 Fils (Cu-Ni) 1982. Relief figure of the Bull (round)		2.50	5.00
70	250 Fils (Cu-Ni) 1982. Upper part of the Hammurabi stele (octagonal)		5.00	10.00
71	500 Fils (Ni) 1982. The Lion of Babylon (square)		12.50	17.50
72	1 Dinar (Ni) 1982. The Zigurrat of Babylon (decagonal)		22.50	35.00

Irland   # Ireland   **Irlande**

Eire

Area: 26,600 sq. mi. Population: 4,254,000.
Until the conquest by the Normans there were many Celtic kingdoms in this island. Later Ireland came under British domination. On 16th January 1922, as a result of the Anglo-Irish Treaty, Southern Ireland became a free state with the status of a dominion (Saorstát Eireann). When the Constitution came into force on 29th December 1937, the independent state of Eire was created.
Capital: Dublin.

4 Farthings = 1 Penny, 12 Pence = 1 Shilling,
2 Shillings = 1 Florin, 5 Shillings = 1 Crown, 20 Shillings = 1 £
since 15th February 1971: 100 New Pence = 1 £

Gaelic Legend: SAORSTÁT EIREÁNN

			VF	XF
1 (1)	1	Farthing (Br) 1928–1937. Harp (national emblem). ℞ European woodcock (Scolopax rusticola – Scolopacidae)	1.00	3.00
2 (2)	½	Penny (Br) 1928–1937. ℞ sow (Sus scrofa domestica – Suidae) with piglets	1.50	4.00
3 (3)	1	Penny (Br) 1928–1937. ℞ hen (Gallus gallus domesticus – Phasianidae) with chicks	1.50	4.00
4 (4)	3	Pence (Ni) 1928–1935. ℞ blue hare (Lepus timidus – Leporidae)	1.50	4.00
5 (5)	6	Pence (Ni) 1928–1935. ℞ Irish wolfhound (Canis familiaris leineri – Canidae)	2.00	5.00
6 (6)	1	Shilling (Ag) 1928–1937. ℞ bull	6.00	12.50
7 (7)	1	Florin (Ag) 1928–1937. ℞ Atlantic salmon (Salmo salar – Salmonidae)	8.00	15.00
8 (8)	½	Crown (Ag) 1928–1937. ℞ Irish hunter	12.00	25.00

EIRE

			VF	XF
9 (9)	1	Farthing (Br) 1939–1966. Harp (national emblem), name of country now EIRE. ℞ woodcock	0.50	1.00

			VF	XF
10 (10)	½ Penny (Br) 1939–1967. ℞ sow with piglets		0.40	1.60
11 (11)	1 Penny (Br) 1940–1968. ℞ hen with chicks		0.20	0.40
12 (12)	3 Pence (Ni) 1939, 1940. Blue hare		3.00	7.00
13 (13)	6 Pence (Ni) 1939, 1940. Irish wolfhound		2.50	5.00
14 (14)	1 Shilling (Ag) 1939–1942. Bull		8.00	12.50

			VF	XF
15 (15)	1 Florin (Ag) 1939-1943. Atlantic salmon:			
	a) 1939-1942		8.00	15.00
	b) 1943 (about 30 specimens known)		300.00	550.00
16 (16)	½ Crown (Ag) 1939-1943. Irish hunter:			
	a) 1939-1942		8.00	15.00
	b) 1943		300.00	550.00
17 (12a)	3 Pence (Cu-Ni) 1942-1968. Type as No. 12		0.25	0.40
18 (13a)	6 Pence (Cu-Ni) 1942-1969. Type as No. 13		0.25	0.50
19 (14a)	1 Shilling (Cu-Ni) 1951-1968. Type as No. 14		0.40	0.60
20 (15a)	1 Florin (Cu-Ni) 1951-1968. Type as No. 15		0.60	1.00
21 (16a)	½ Crown (Cu-Ni) 1951-1967. Type as No. 16		1.00	2.00

COMMEMORATIVE ISSUE FOR THE 50th ANNIVERSARY OF THE EASTER UPRISING OF 1916

			XF	**Unc**

22 (17) 10 Shillings (Ag) 1966. Padraig (Patrik) Henry Pearse (1879–1916), author, educator, politician, and fighter for independence; executed 1916. R the dying hero Cuchulainn, Irish legendary hero, with a raven (Corvus corax – Corvidae) on his shoulder ... 6.00 9.00

CURRENCY REFORM (Decimal System): 100 (New) Pence = 1 £

23 (18) ½ Penny (Br) 1971–. Harp (= state emblem). Rev. fabulous creature according to an old Irish manuscript ... 0.05 0.10

24 (19) 1 Penny (Br) 1971–. Rev. fabulous creature according to an old Irish manuscript ... 0.10 0.15

25 (20) 2 Pence (Br) 1971-. Rev. fabulous creature according to an old Irish manuscript ... 0.15 0.25

26 (21) 5 Pence (Cu-Ni) 1969–. Rev. bull ... 0.20 0.35

27 (22) 10 Pence (Cu-Ni) 1969–. Rev. Atlantic salmon ... 0.30 0.60

28 20 Pence (Ni-Bra) 1986–. Rev. Irish hunter ... 0.70 1.25

29 (23) 50 Pence (Cu-Ni) 1970–. Rev. European woodcock; seven-sided ... 1.25 1.75

Usually the commemorative coins of Israel reflect the events of current history. Since 1958, the 10th anniversary of independent Israel, the majority of coins depict the nation's economic, cultural and political accomplishments, but occasionally they contain references to Old Testament times.

Additional commemorative issues, known as Chanukah (Hanukkah) coins, appeared between 1959 and 1963, to celebrate Chanukah, the festival celebrating the lighting of the Menorah for eight days, which lasts from the end of December to the beginning of January. To this day, the nine candles of the candelabra are lighted in increasing numbers on the eight successive days of Chanukah. The coins therefore display symbols of light, such as the Menorah, stars, etc.

A third category of commemorative coins comprises irregular issues, celebrating special events such as the anniverseries of celebrities, institutions, etc.

Since the Israeliate calendar starts with August/September, its conversion into Christian chronology necessarily produces differences whenever the dates are given.

$$1000 \text{ Mils} = 1 \text{ Lira } (\pounds), 1000 \text{ Prutot} = 1 \text{ Lira } (\pounds),$$
$$100 \text{ Agorot} = 1 \text{ Israel } \pounds$$

1 (1)   25 Mils (Al) 1948–1949 = 5708–5709.
         Bunch of grapes (Vitus vinifera – Vitaceae) with vine leaf, in beaded border.
         This design is modelled after a bronze
         Prutot originating in the time of Herod

	VF	XF

Antipas (about the time of the birth of Christ), similar to the later bronze and silver coins from the time of the Second Revolt (132–135 A. D., also called the Bar Kokhba War); compare with No. 7. In the Bible, grapes are one of the seven fruits of the Promised Land. ℞ 25 Mils – 5708–5709 in wreath of two olive branches

12.50 ... 20.00

NEW CURRENCY: 1000 Prutot = 1 Israel £

General characteristics of circulating Prutot coins: usually beaded border on obverse and reverse. On reverse, value, numerals of value, date, in Hebrew, in wreath of olive branches. Already on ancient Jewish coins the beaded border was in use. The two olive branches occur for the first time on the coins of the Hasmonean Dynasty, starting with Yohanan Hyrkanos I (135–104 B. C.). Other coins of the Hasmonean period display also names such as "Yehuda", "Yehonathan", or "Mattathiahu" in wreath of two olive branches.

2 (2)   1 Pruta (Al) 1949 = 5709. Anchor. Design modelled after the coins from the time of King Alexander Yannaeus (103–76 B. C.). The anchor symbolized the Hebrew sovereignty over the coastal towns, and is repeated on the later coins of the Herod Dynasty. ℞ 1 Pruta in wreath of two olive branches

0.50 ... 1.00

3 (3)   5 Prutot (Br) 1949 = 5709. Four-stringed large lyre. This design comes from a vessel of the temple, and was first used

			VF	XF

on coins at the time of the Second Revolt (Bar Kokhba War, 132–135 A.D.). ℞ 5 Prutot – 5709 in wreath of two olive branches .... **0.50** | **1.00**

4 (4) 10 Prutot (Br) 1949 = 5709. Amphora with two handles. Design modelled after a copper coin from the time of the Second Revolt (132–135 A.D.). This ceremonial object was to symbolize the rebuilding of the destroyed temple. ℞ 10 Prutot – 5709 in wreath of two olive branches .... **0.75** | **1.50**

5 (5) 10 Prutot (Al) 1952 = 5712. Jug with one handle between two palm branches. Originally a ceremonial object, the design is borrowed from a silver denar from the time of the Second Revolt (132–135 A.D.). The jug itself was probably used to store oil for the temple lamps. This supposition is reinforced by the palm branch, even though on antique coins it occurs only once, on the right of the jug. ℞ 10 Prutot – 5712 in wreath of olive branches, scalloped ... **0.50** | **1.00**

6 (5) 10 Prutot 1957 = 5717. The design varies only slightly from that on No. 5. Round
a) (Al-Cu-plated) 1957 = 5717 .... **0.50** | **1.00**
b) (Al-Br) 1957 = 5717 .... **0.50** | **1.00**

7 (6) 25 Prutot (Cu–Ni) 1949 = 5709. Bunch of grapes with vine tendrils. The design is modelled after the coins from the time of the Second Revolt (132–135 A.D.). Golden grapes used to decorate the entrance to the inner holy temple, a fact that emphasizes the symbolic significance of the design. The only difference between this coin and No. 1 is that here the grapes are displayed with the tendrils instead of the leaf. ℞ 25 Prutot – 5709 in wreath of two olive branches ... **0.50** | **1.00**

8 (6a) 25 Prutot (Ni–St) 1954 = 5714. Same type as No. 7, but different date .... **0.60** | **1.00**

9 (8) 50 Prutot (Cu–Ni) 1949–1954 = 5709–5714. Vine leaf. Design modelled after a bronze Prutot from the time of the First Revolt against the Romans (66–70 A.D.) and the 3rd year (68 A.D.) of the revolt. ℞ 50 Prutot – 5709 in wreath of two olive branches. With reeded edge .... **1.00** | **2.00**

10 (8a) 50 Prutot (Cu–Ni) 1954 = 5714. Same type as No. 9, but plain edge .... **0.75** | **1.50**

			VF	XF

11 (8b) 50 Prutot (Ni–St) 1954 = 5714. Same type
as No. 9, but plain edge **0.50** **1.00**

12 (10) 100 Prutot (Cu–Ni) 1949 = 5709. Seven-branched date palm (Phoenix dactyli-fera-Palmae) with two date clusters. In Jewish history the date palm is the most commonly recurring symbol and was equally popular with the Romans during their provincial period. On coinage, the date palm first appeared on the issues of King Herod Antipas (4 B.C. – 37 A.D.), and later on those of the Second Revolt (132–135 A.D.). On coins from this time of the so-called Bar Kokhba War, the date palm is the most commonly used symbol. ℞ 100 Prutot – 5709 in wreath of two olive branches **1.00** **2.00**

13 (10a) 100 Prutot (Ni–St) 1954 = 5714. Same design as No. 12, but diameter 25.6 mm instead of 28.5 mm **1.25** **2.50**

14 (12) 250 Prutot (Cu–Ni) 1949 = 5709. Three ears of barley. Design modelled after a silver quarter shekel from the 4th year of the First Revolt against the Romans (69 A.D.). The only coin of this type is owned by the British Museum, London. For similar design compare No. 23. ℞ 250 Prutot – 5709 in wreath of two olive branches **1.50** **2.50**

15 (12a) 250 Prutot (Ag) 1949 = 5709. Same type as No. 14, but with mint mark H below the two olive branches **4.50** **7.50**

Values are given for each coin in U.S. Dollars and reference to Yeoman-numbers.

				VF	XF
16 (14)	500	Prutot (Ag) 1949 = 5709. Three pomegranates (Punica granatum – Punicaceae). Designed after a Jewish shekel from the time of the First Revolt against the Romans (66–70 A.D.). ℞ 500 Prutot – 5709 in wreath of two olive branches. Pomegranates are one of the seven fruits of the Promised Land. During the time of the second temple, as well as in the following periods, this fruit was often used as a decoration		12.00	16.00

COMMEMORATIVE ISSUE FOR THE 10th ANNIVERSARY OF INDEPENDENT ISRAEL

				Unc	Proof
17 (16)	5	£ (Ag) 1958 = 5718. Menorah (= seven-branched candelabrum), old Jewish symbol, now state emblem. This candelabrum with three feet and seven branches symbolizes the number 10 and stems from the time of King Mattathias Antigonus (40–37 B.C., Hasmonean Dynasty)		12.50	400.00

COMMEMORATIVE ISSUE FOR THE
CHANUKAH FESTIVAL (5718)

18 (17)   1 £ (Cu–Ni) 1958 = 5718. Menorah be-   **Unc**   **Proof**
tween two eight-pointed stars, design
modelled after a coin from the time of
King Mattathias Antigonus (Hasmonean Dynasty). Legend: "The Law
(Torah) is Light". ℞ 1 Lira Israelit,
underneath ISRAEL and 5718   4.00   45.00

COMMEMORATIVE ISSUE FOR THE 11th ANNIVERSARY
OF INDEPENDENT ISRAEL
AND THE INGATHERING OF THE EXILES

19 (18)   5 £ (Ag) 1959 = 5719. Eleven immigrants (symbol of 11 years) dancing
around the biblical legend, "Thy children shall return home" – Jer. 31, 17.
℞ value and dates 5708–5719 (= 1948–
1959)   20.00   65.00

COMMEMORATIVE ISSUE FOR THE CHANUKAH FESTIVAL (5720) AND THE 50th ANNIVERSARY OF DEGANIA

20 (19) 1 £ (Cu–Ni) 1959 = 5719. View of the first Kibbutz of Degania. This oldest collective settlement, located on lake Genezareth, was founded by Russian immigrants in 1909. ℞ 1 Lira Israelit – 5720

	Unc	Proof
	5.00	50.00

COMMEMORATIVE ISSUE FOR THE 12th ANNIVERSARY OF INDEPENDENT ISRAEL AND THE 100th BIRTHDAY OF DR. THEODOR HERZL

21 (20) 5 £ (Ag) 1960 = 5720. Dr. Theodor Zeev Herzl (1860–1904), author, lawyer, and co-founder of the Zionist Movement. In the lower left Herzl's famous words: "[If you will it] it is not a legend", next to coat of arms. ℞ 5 Lirot Israeliot

	20.00	60.00

COMMEMORATIVE ISSUE FOR THE 100th BIRTHDAY OF DR. THEODOR HERZL

22 (21) 20 £ (Au) 1960 = 5720. Obverse similar to No. 21. ℞ Menorah (= seven-branched

candelabrum), state emblem, between
two olive branches with name of country
ISRAEL. This Menorah was made after
a relief detail from the Arc of Titus in
Rome, with the caption "The loot
from Israel". Legends surrounded by
two circles: Twenty Israel pounds
(above), the anniversary years 5620–
5720 = 1860–1960 (below)

	XF	Unc
		350.00

NEW CURRENCY: 100 Agorot = 1 Israel £

The new decimal coins utilize an asymmetric design. On the denominations up to 25 Agorot basket-like arches alternate with beaded border
and olive branches giving the edge the almost dynamic appearance of
a perpetual band. On the obverse are partially new designs with
ISRAEL written in Hebrew and Arabic. On the obverse of the high
denominations (designated £), Israel is written in Latin in addition to
the two other languages. The reverse carries the value in numerals as
well as in letters, with the date of coinage underneath.

23 (22)   1 Agora (Al) 1960 = 5720–. Three ears
of barley, design modelled after a bronze
Prutot from the 6th year of the reign
Agrippa I (42/43 B.C.). Barley is one
of the seven fruits of the Promised
Land. ℞ 1 Agora – 5720 in basket-like
arches. Scalloped edge   0.10   0.20

24 (24)   5 Agorot (Al–Br) 1960 = 5720–. Three
ripe pomegranates (Punica granatum –
Punicaceae). On old Hebrew shekels

the pomegranate is shown in different form, see No. 16, but not as mature as on this modern version. ℞ 5 Agorot – 5720 in basket-like arches

	XF	Unc
	0.10	0.25

25(25) 10 Agorot (Al–Br) 1960 = 5720–. Seven-branched date palm with two date clusters. For further details see No. 12. ℞ 10 Agorot – 5720 in basket-like arches 0.10 0.25

26(26) 25 Agorot (Al–Br) 1960 = 5720–. Three-stringed kithara. Design modelled after silver dinars and bronze coins from the time of the Second Revolt (132–135 A.D.). See No. 3. ℞ 25 Agorot – 5720 in basket-like arches 0.10 0.25

27(36) ½ £ (Cu–Ni) 1963 = 5723–. State emblem in olive branches and ISRAEL, see No. 22. On the obverse ISRAEL, for the first time on Israeli coins also in Latin. ℞ ½ Lira Israelit – 5723 0.15 0.35

28 (37)   1 £ (Cu–Ni) 1963 = 5723 – 1967 = 5727, same as No. 27. ℞ 1 Lira Israelit – 5723   0.60   1.20

29 (46)   1 £ (Cu–Ni) 1967 = 5727–. Three pomegranates, coat of arms in lower left. For text see No. 16 or No. 24. ℞ "1" between eight-pointed stars (coins from the time of Alexander Yannaeus, 103 B.C.), underneath: 1 Lira Israelit – 5727   0.25   0.60

COMMEMORATIVE ISSUE FOR THE CHANUKAH FESTIVAL (5721) AND THE 100th BIRTHDAY OF HENRIETTA SZOLD

| | Unc | Proof |

30 (27)   1 £ (Cu–Ni) 1960 = 5721. Seated woman to left holding a lamb in her arms. Legend: Henrietta Szold 5621–5721. HADASSAH – ALIYAT HANOAR (=youth immigration), since the honoured had founded the American Women's Aid Association "Hadassah" and the "Aliyat Hanoar". ℞ Hadassah Medical Centre, located on Mount Scopus west of Jerusalem, opened in 1961, financed by the Zionist Women's organization "Hadassah" in America; architect: Joseph Neufeld, USA. Legend: 1 Lira Israelit – 5721   40.00   200.00

COMMEMORATIVE ISSUE FOR THE 13th ANNIVERSARY OF INDEPENDENT ISRAEL AND FOR "BAR MITZVAH" OF ISRAEL

31 (28)   5 £ (Ag) 1961 = 5721. Ark of the Law   Unc   Proof
with six Torah (= law) scrolls. The
design is borrowed from a golden gob-
let of the third century, now owned
by the Vatican. The term "BAR
MITZVAH" refers to the commencing
of the 13th year of a Jewish boy, when
he comes of age for religious duty and
responsibility, and was therefore chosen
for the celebration of the 13th anniversary of the independence. ℞ olive
branch with ten leaves and three olives
= 13, also a symbolic implication.
Legend: "13th year of the State of
Israel" 5721–1961, underneath 5 Lirot
Israeliot   45.00   75.00

COMMEMORATIVE ISSUE FOR THE CHANUKAH FESTIVAL 5722 (1961) AND FOR THE DEATH OF A HASMONEAN HERO

32 (30)   1 £ (Cu–Ni) 5722 (1961). Combat elephant in asymmetrical pentagon, from
the time of the Hasmonean war when
Elazar (Mattathias), Judas Maccabeus'
brother, fought with his sword against

a heavily armed combat elephant of the
Seleucids. ℞ torch with legend "...and
he gave up his soul in battle", and:

		Unc	Proof
1 Lira Israelit – 5722 = 1961		12.50	22.50

COMMEMORATIVE ISSUE FOR
THE HALF SHEKEL TEMPLE SACRIFICE

33 (29) ½ £ (Cu–Ni) 1961–1962 = 5721–5722.
Old half shekel coin with chalice. Design modelled after a half shekel silver
coin from the third year (= 68 A.D.)
of the First Revolt against the Romans.
Commemorates the half shekel due
which every male Jew above 20 years
of age had to pay yearly to the temple.
℞ legend "Half Israel Pound (Chazi
Lira Israelit)", left 5721 or 5722   15.00   18.00

COMMEMORATIVE ISSUES (2) FOR THE 10th ANNIVERSARY
OF THE DEATH OF ISRAEL'S PRESIDENT

34 (32) 50 £ (Au) 1962 = 5723. Dr. Chaim Weiz-
mann (1874–1952), President from
1948 to 1952, in basket-like arches. ℞
state emblem with legend "Fifty
Israel Pounds – 5713–5723" = 1952–
1962. Diameter 27 mm   400.00

			Unc	**Proof**

35 (33) 100 £ (Au) 1962 = 5723. Same type as No.
34. ℞ but on top "One hundred Israel
Pounds". Diameter 33 mm   550.00

COMMEMORATIVE ISSUE FOR THE 14th ANNIVERSARY OF INDEPENDENT ISRAEL UNDER THE MOTTO "DEVELOPMENT"

36 (31)   5 £ (Ag) 1962 = 5722. Stylized bulldozer,
used in canal construction, in front of
landscape of the Negev desert. Legend:
"…and Israel shall blossom" – Isaiah
27, 6. ℞ stylized equipment of petro-
chemical industry; legend: 5 Israel
Pounds, Israel, 5722–1962   55.00   75.00

COMMEMORATIVE ISSUE FOR THE CHANUKAH FESTIVAL (5723)

37 (34)   1 £ (Cu–Ni) 1962 = 5723. Chanukah
lamp with eight compartments in triangular, basket-like pattern. These Chanukah lamps in the style of the baroque
era originated in seventeenth century
Italian workshops, today owned by the
Jerusalem Museum, therefore legend:
"Chanukia from Italy — 17th century".
℞ 1 Lira Israelit 1962–5723   35.00   55.00

COMMEMORATIVE ISSUE FOR THE 15th ANNIVERSARY
OF INDEPENDENT ISRAEL
UNDER THE MOTTO "SEAFARING"

			Unc	Proof
38 (35)	5 £ (Ag) 1963 = 5723. Ancient galley, designed after a Hasmonean drawing discovered in a tomb. Legend "15th year of Israel's independence". ℞ funnel of a modern Israel ship, in front of the port of Haifa with Mount Carmel, and "5 Lirot Israeliot" 5723–1963		350.00	400.00

COMMEMORATIVE ISSUE FOR THE
CHANUKAH FESTIVAL (5724)

39 (38)	1 £ (Cu–Ni) 1963 = 5724. Chanukah lamp with eight compartments and side wings, accommodating the Islamic style. The original was manufactured during the 18th century in North Africa, and is now owned by the Jerusalem Museum. ℞ 1 Lira Israelit – 1963–5724		35.00	55.00

COMMEMORATIVE ISSUE FOR THE 16th ANNIVERSARY OF INDEPENDENT ISRAEL WITH THE MOTTO "ISRAEL MUSEUM"

			Unc	Proof
40 (39)	5 £ (Ag) 1964 = 5724. Israel Museum in Jerusalem opened in 1964. ℞ capital of an ancient pillar, legends "5 Lirot Israeliot" – 1964–5724		60.00	85.00

COMMEMORATIVE ISSUE: 10 YEARS BANK OF ISRAEL

41 (40)	50 £ (Au) 1964 = 5724. Legend "Ten years Bank of Israel"; pomegranate, surrounded by cornucopias. ℞ state emblem. In circle: "Fifty Lirot Israeliot" 1964–5724		450.00	3000.00

COMMEMORATIVE ISSUE FOR THE 17th ANNIVERSARY OF INDEPENDENT ISRAEL WITH THE MOTTO "THE KNESSET"

42 (41) 5 £ (Ag) 1965 = 5725. Parliament build-   **Unc**   **Proof**
ing in Jerusalem, located opposite from
the Israel Museum, shown on No. 40,
opened in 1965, seat of the legislative
assembly of Israel. ℞ state emblem.
1965–5725 and 5 Lirot Israeliot   15.00   22.50

COMMEMORATIVE ISSUE FOR THE 18th ANNIVERSARY
OF INDEPENDENT ISRAEL
WITH THE MOTTO "ISRAEL LIVES ON"

43 (42) 5 £ (Ag) 1966 = 5726. Design of the
Hebrew words "Am Israel Hai" = The
people of Israel lives on. ℞ 5 Lirot
Israeliot 1966–5726   12.50   20.00

COMMEMORATIVE ISSUE FOR THE 19th ANNIVERSARY
OF INDEPENDENT ISRAEL
WITH THE MOTTO "PORT OF EILAT"

44 (43) 5 £ (Ag) 1967 = 5727. The letters of the
word EILAT stylized to represent har-
bour scene with lighthouse. The gateway to Africa and Asia, the port of
Eilat celebrated its 10th year of existence in 1967. ℞ 5 Lirot Israeliot – 1967–
5727   17.50   25.00

COMMEMORATIVE ISSUES (2) FOR THE VICTORIES OF THE DEFENCE FORCES DURING THE SIX DAY WAR

			Unc	Proof
45 (44)	10	£ (Ag) 1967 = 5727. Westermost part of the Wailing Wall (once the surrounding wall of the old temple, in Jerusalem), destroyed by Titus in 70 A.D. ℞ emblem of the defence forces in front of a star formed of "arrows", symbol of the widely and successfully executed military operations. 10 Lirot Israeliot	10.00	15.00
46 (45)	100	£ (Au) 1967 = 5727. Same type as No. 45, but with smaller diameter and "100 Lirot Israeliot"		600.00

COMMEMORATIVE ISSUES (2) FOR THE 20th ANNIVERSARY OF INDEPENDENT ISRAEL WITH THE MOTTO "JERUSALEM'S RE-UNIFICATION"

47 (47) 10 £ (Ag) 1968 = 5728. Allegory of Mount Zion (Jerusalem) with striking buildings of the modern Jerusalem, state emblem. ℞ facade of the temple of Solomon, designed after a silver sela from

the time of the Second Revolt (132–135
A.D.) and "10 Lirot Israeliot" – 1968–
5728. Diameter 37 mm

48 (48) 100 £ (Au) 1968 = 5728. Same type as No.
47, but with diameter 33 mm, and "100
Lirot Israeliot" on reverse   400.00

COMMEMORATIVE ISSUES (2) FOR THE 21st ANNIVERSARY
OF INDEPENDENT ISRAEL
WITH THE MOTTO "SHALOM"

49 (49) 10 £ (Ag) 1969 = 5729. Allegory of Mount
Zion in the form of a memorial for a
soldier fallen in combat, shaped in the
words "…and no man knoweth the
place of his burial" – Deuteronomy
34, 6. Helmet and olive plant in foreground. ℞ letters of the word "Sha-
lom" (= peace) in shape of the seven-
branched candelabrum, 10 Lirot Israe-
liot – 1969–5729   12.50   17.50
50 (50) 100 £ (Au) 1969 = 5729. Same type as No.
49, but with diameter of 33 mm, and
"100 Lirot Israeliot" on reverse   350.00

COMMEMORATIVE ISSUE PIDYON HABEN –
FOR THE REDEMPTION OF THE FIRST-BORN

51 (51) 10 £ (Ag) 1970 = 5730. Above the quo-   **Unc**   **Proof**
tation "All the first-born of thy sons
thou shalt redeem" – Exodus 34, 20:
stylized imitation of the Tables of the
Law. On the lower edge: Pidyon
Haben – Coin. The redemption of the
first-born carried out by the father
dates back to the time of the Old Testament. According to the law every first-
born son has to be redeemed to the payment of 5 silver pieces. Ŗ coat of arms,
10 Lirot Israeliot – 1970–5730   12.50   15.00

COMMEMORATIVE ISSUE FOR THE 22nd ANNIVERSARY
OF INDEPENDENT ISRAEL
WITH THE MOTTO "100 YEARS MIKVEH ISRAEL"

52 (52) 10 £ (Ag) 1970 = 5730. Plough. Upper
left, four lines of writing "One hundred

	Unc	Proof

years Mikveh Israel"; underneath the plough: Kol Israel Haverim = Israeli World Alliance. ℞ ear of wheat and "10 Lirot Israeliot" with main building of the Mikveh school, an agricultural educational and experimental institute near Jaffa, founded by Charles Netter one hundred years ago. Underneath the centennial dates 5630–5730 = 1870–1970

	12.50	15.00

COMMEMORATIVE ISSUE PIDYON HABEN – FOR THE REDEMPTION OF THE FIRST-BORN

53 (51a) 10 £ (Ag) 1971 = 5731. Similar type as No. 51

	12.50	15.00

COMMEMORATIVE ISSUE FOR THE 23rd ANNIVERSARY OF INDEPENDENT ISRAEL WITH THE MOTTO "SCIENCE IN THE SERVICE OF INDUSTRY"

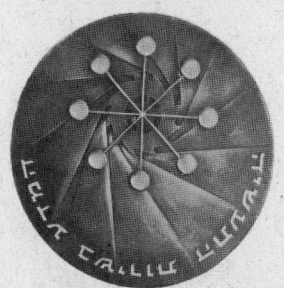 

54 (53) 10 £ (Ag) 1971 = 5731. Molecule, driving cog-wheel. ℞ Nahal Sorek: stylized atomic reactor

	12.50	15.00

COMMEMORATIVE ISSUES (2) FOR THE FIGHT
FOR FREEDOM WITH THE MOTTO
"LET MY PEOPLE GO"

		Unc	Proof
55 (54)	10 £ (Ag) 1971–5731. Sun behind bars. Motto in Hebrew and in English. ℞ coat of arms, 10 Lirot Israeliot – 5731–1971	10.00	15.00

56 (55)	100 £ (Au) 1971–5731. Same type as No. 55, but diameter 30 mm, and "100 Lirot Israeliot" on reverse		400.00

COMMEMORATIVE ISSUE PIDYON HABEN –
FOR THE REDEMPTION OF THE FIRST-BORN

57 (51b)	10 £ (Ag) 1972–5732. Similar to No. 53, but the arms again altered	12.50	15.00

COMMEMORATIVE ISSUE FOR THE 24th ANNIVERSARY
OF INDEPENDENT ISRAEL
WITH THE MOTTO "ISRAEL AVIATION"

58 (56)	10 £ (Ag) 1971–5732. Stylized jet. ℞ numeral 1 in shape of a rocket, blasting off	15.00	22.50

COMMEMORATIVE ISSUE
FOR THE CHANUKAH FESTIVAL 5732

			Unc	Proof
59 (57)	5 £ (Ag) 1972 = 5732. Russian Chanukah candelabra, 20th century. ℞ national arms, 5 Loriot Israeliot		7.50	12.00

COMMEMORATIVE ISSUE PIDYON HABEN –
FOR THE REDEMPTION OF THE FIRST-BORN

| **60** (58) | 10 £ (Ag) 1973 = 5733. Surrounded by five silver shekels, the quotation from the Bible: "All the first-born of thy sons thou shalt redeem" – Exodus 34, 20; the whole within an oval | | 10.00 | 12.50 |

COMMEMORATIVE ISSUES (10)
FOR THE 25th ANNIVERSARY OF THE INDEPENDENCE
OF THE STATE OF ISRAEL

61 (59)	1 Agora (Al) 1973. Type as No. 23, but with additional commemorative inscription "25th Anniversary of the State"	0.25
62 (60)	5 Agorot (Cu–Ni) 1973. Type as No. 24, but with additional inscription as with No. 61	0.50

							Unc	Proof

63 (61)   10   Agorot (Cu–Ni) 1973. Type as No. 25, but with additional inscription as with No. 61   0.75

64 (62)   25   Agorot (Cu–Ni) 1973. Type as No. 26, but with additional inscription as with No. 61   0.90

65 (63)   ½ £ (Cu–Ni) 1973. Type as No. 27, but with additional inscription as with No. 61   1.20

66 (64)   1 £ (Cu–Ni) 1973. Type as No. 29, but with additional inscription as with No. 61   1.50

					Unc	Proof
67 (65)	10	£ (Ag) 1973			10.00	12.50
68 (66)	50	£ (Au) 1973				150.00
69 (67)	100	£ (Au) 1973				225.00
70 (68)	200	£ (Au) 1973				425.00

COMMEMORATIVE ISSUE FOR THE CHANUKAH FESTIVAL

71 (69)   5 £ (Ag) 1973 = 5734. Chanukah candelabra from Mesopotamia, 18th entury, now in the Israel Museum in Jerusalem. ℞ value, name of country, date   7.50   9.00

COMMEMORATIVE ISSUE PIDYON HABEN –
FOR THE REDEMPTION OF THE FIRST-BORN

		Unc	**Proof**
72 (58a) 10 £ (Ag) 1974 = 5734. Type similar to No. 60		10.00	12.50

COMMEMORATIVE ISSUE FOR THE 26th ANNIVERSARY
OF THE INDEPENDENCE OF THE STATE OF ISRAEL

73 (70) 10 £ (Ag) 1974 = 5734	10.00	12.50

COMMEMORATIVE ISSUES (2) FOR THE 1th ANNIVERSARY
OF THE DEATH OF DAVID BEN GURION

74 (71) 25 £ (Ag) 1974 = 5734	12.00	15.00

75 (72) 500 £ (Au) 1974 = 5734	425.00

CHANUKAH FESTIVAL

	Unc	Proof
76 (73) 10 £(Ag) 1974 = 5735. Chanukah candelabra from Damascus, 18th century	8.00	10.00
77 (24a) 5 Agorot (Cu-Ni) 1974 = 5735 – 1976 = 5736. Type as No. 24	0.30	
78 (25a) 10 Agorot (Cu-Ni) 1974 = 5735 – 1976 = 5736. Type as No. 25	0.30	
79 (26a) 25 Agorot (Cu-Ni) 1974 = 5735 –. Type as No. 26	0.40	

PIDYON HABEN – FOR THE REDEMPTION OF THE FIRST- BORN

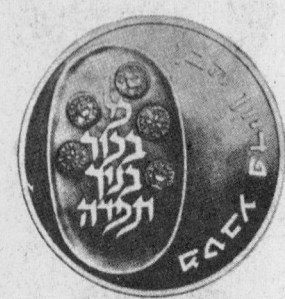 

	Unc	Proof
80 (74) 25 £ (Ag) 1975 = 5735. Type similar to No. 60	12.50	15.00

25th ANNIVERSARY OF ISRAEL BOND PROGRAM (2)

	Unc	Proof
81 (75) 25 £(Ag) 1975 = 5735. Multiple image of the Star of David	12.50	15.00
82 (76) 500 £ (Au) 1975 = 5735. Type as No. 81		350.00

			Unc	Proof
83 (77)	10 £ (Ag) 1975 =5736. Holland Chanukah candelabra, 18th century		8.50	12.00

PIDYON HABEN – FOR THE REDEMPTION OF THE FIRST-BORN

84 (79)	25 £ (Ag) 1976 = 5736. Five pomegranate flowers around a five-pointed star		12.50	17.50

28th ANNIVERSARY OF THE INDEPENDENCE OF THE STATE OF ISRAEL

				Unc	Proof
85 (78)	25	£ (Ag) 1976 = 5736. The words "Strength for Israel" in Hebrew and a stylized Star of David		12.50	17.50
86 (24b)	5	Agorot (Al) 1976 = 5736. Type as No. 24 or 77		0.30	
87 (25b)	10	Agorot (Al) 1977 = 5737. Type as No. 25 or 78		0.40	

CHANUKAH FESTIVAL 5735 AND BICENTENARY OF AMERICAN INDEPENDENCE

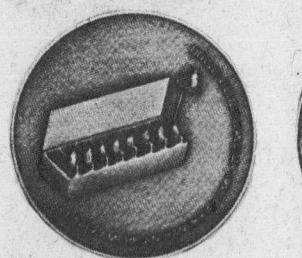 

88 (80)	10	£ (Ag) 1976 = 5737. An early American Chanukah candelabra from the Jewish Museum in New York	25.00	32.00

29th ANNIVERSARY OF THE INDEPENDENCE OF THE STATE OF ISRAEL

89 (81)	25	£ (Ag) 1977 = 5737	11.00	15.00

PIDYON HABEN – FOR THE REDEMPTION OF THE FIRST-BORN

90 (82)	25	£ (Ag) 1977 = 5738. Type similar to No. 84	12.00	16.50

CHANUKAH FESTIVAL 5738

		Unc	**Proof**

91 (83) 10 £ (Cu-Ni) 1977 = 5738. An early
20th century Chanukah candelabra
from Jerusalem, now in the Ha'aretz
Museum in Ramat Aviv .... 6.00 ... 9.00

30th ANNIVERSARY OF THE INDEPENDENCE OF THE STATE OF ISRAEL (2)

92 (84) 50 £ (Ag) 1978 = 5738. Olive tree with
the Hebrew words »ISRAEL'S
THIRTY YEARS« .... 12.50 ... 17.50
93 (85) 100 £ (Au) 1978 = 5738. Type as No. 92 .... 300.00

CHANUKAH FESTIVAL 5739

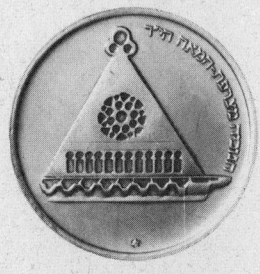 

94 (87) 25 £ (Cu-Ni) 5739/1978.
French Chanukah lamp .... 7.00 ... 10.00

		XF	**Unc**

95 (86) 5 £ (Cu-Ni) 5738, 5739 (1978, 1979) .... 0.75 ... 1.00

31th ANNIVERSARY OF THE INDEPENDENCE OF THE STATE OF ISRAEL – MOTHERHOOD

	Unc	Proof
96 (88) 50 £ (Ag) 1979 = 5740. Mother and child	11.00	18.00

CHANUKAH FESTIVAL 5740

	Unc	Proof
97 (89) 100 £ (Ag) 5740/1979. Egyptian Chanu- kah lamp	15.00	20.00

		Unc	Proof
98 (90)	200 £ (Ag) 1980	20.00	30.00
99 (91)	5000 £ (Au) 1980		450.00

25th ANNIVERSARY OF THE BANK OF ISRAEL (7)

		Unc	Proof
100 (92)	1 Agora (Ni) 1980 = 5740	0.30	1.00
101 (93)	5 Agorot (Ni) 1980 = 5740	0.30	1.00
102 (94)	10 Agorot (Ni) 1980 = 5740	0.30	1.00
103 (95)	25 Agorot (Ni) 1980 = 5740	0.30	1.00
104 (96)	½ £ (Ni) 1980 = 5740	0.60	2.00
105 (97)	1 £ (Ni) 1980 = 5740	2.00	3.00
106 (98)	5 £ (Ni) 1980 = 5740	3.00	5.00

MONETARY REFORM: 10 Agorot = 1 New Agora, 1 Lira (£) =
10 New Agorot

MONETARY SYSTEM commencing February 24th, 1980:
100 (New) Agorot = 1 Shekel

		XF	Unc
107 (99)	1 Agora (Al) 5740–5745 (1980–1985). Date palm	0.05	0.10

		XF	Unc
108 (100)	5 Agorot (Al) 5740–5745 (1980–1985). Menorah	0.05	0.10

		XF	Unc
109 (101)	10 Agorot (Br) 1980–	0.05	0.10

| **110** (102) | ½ Shekel (Cu-Ni) 1980– | 0.10 | 0.15 |
| **111** (106) | 1 Shekel (Cu-Ni) 1981–. Chalice cup | 0.15 | 0.25 |

| **112** (110) | 5 Sheqalim (Cu-Ni-Al) 1981–. Cornu-copia | 1.00 | 1.20 |

| **113** (111) | 10 Sheqalim (Cu-Ni) 1982–. Ancient galley | 1.20 | 1.50 |

100th ANNIVERSARY OF THE BIRTH OF ZEEV JABOTINSKY (2)

			Unc	Proof
114 (103)	25	Sheqalim (Ag) 1980 = 5740. Zeev Jabotinsky (1880–1940), patriot	22.50	30.00
115 (104)	500	Sheqalim (Au) 1980 = 5740. Type as No. 114		400.00

CHANUKAH FESTIVAL 5741

		Unc	Proof
116 (105)	1 Shekel (Ag) 5740/1980. Chanukah Korfu lamp	20.00	30.00

33th ANNIVERSARY OF THE INDEPENDENCE OF THE STATE OF ISRAEL (2)

		Unc	Proof
117 (107)	2 Sheqalim (Ag) 1981 = 5741	30.00	45.00
118 (108)	10 Sheqalim (Au) 1981 = 5741		400.00

CHANUKAH FESTIVAL 5742

		Unc	Proof
119 (109)	1 Shekel (Ag) 5742/1981. Chanukah Polish lamp	22.50	35.00

34th ANNIVERSARY OF THE INDEPENDENCE OF THE STATE OF ISRAEL (2)

			Unc	Proof
120 (112)	2 Sheqalim (Ag) 1982 = 5742. Baron Edmond de Rothschild (1845–1934), banker		18.00	30.00
121 (113)	10 Sheqalim (Au) 1982 = 5742. Type as No. 120			500.00

SITES IN THE HOLY LAND – 1st ISSUE (3)

122 (114)	½ Shekel (Ag) 1982. Qumran caves	12.50	
123 (115)	1 Shekel (Ag) 1982. Type as No. 122		30.00
124 (116)	5 Sheqalim (Au) 1982. Type as No. 122		250.00

HANUKKA FESTIVAL 5743 (2)

125 (117)	1 Shekel (Ag) 1982. Hanukka candelabra from Yemen	20.00

126 (118)	2 Sheqalim (Ag) 1982. Type as No. 125	40.00

35th ANNIVERSARY OF THE INDEPENDENCE OF THE STATE OF ISRAEL AND THE ISRAEL DEFENSE FORCES (3)

127 (119)	1 Shekel (Ag) 1983 = 5743. Sword and olive branch within star of David	25.00

			Unc	Proof
128	(120)	2 Sheqalim (Ag) 1983 = 5743. Type as No. 127		35.00
129	(121)	10 Sheqalim (Au) 1983 = 5743. Type as No. 127		500.00

SITES IN THE HOLY LAND – 2nd ISSUE (3)

			Unc
130	(122)	½ Shekel (Ag) 1983. Herodion ruins	12.50
131	(123)	1 Shekel (Ag) 1983. Type as No. 130	30.00
132	(124)	5 Sheqalim (Au) 1983. Type as No. 130	250.00

HANUKKA FESTIVAL 5744 (3)

			Unc	Proof
133	(125)	1 Shekel (Ag) 1983. Hanukka lamp from Prague, 18th century, showing Moses and his brother Aaron	20.00	
134	(126)	2 Sheqalim (Ag) 1983. Type as No. 133		35.00

			XF	Unc
135	(127)	10 Sheqalim (Cu-Ni) 1983. Type as No. 113, with additional inscription »HANUKKA«	0.85	1.00

80th ANNIVERSARY OF THE DEATH OF DR. TH. HERZL

			XF	Unc
136	(128)	10 Sheqalim (Cu-Ni) 1984. Portrait of Herzl (cf No. 21)	0.85	1.00

36th ANNIVERSARY OF THE INDEPENDENCE OF THE STATE OF ISRAEL (3)

		Unc	Proof
137 (129)	1 Shekel (Ag) 1984 = 5744	35.00	

		Unc	Proof
138 (130)	2 Sheqalim (Ag) 1984 = 5744	45.00	
139 (131)	10 Sheqalim (Au) 1984 = 5744		400.00

		XF	Unc
140 (132)	50 Sheqalim (Br) 1984. Coin design from the 4th year of the First Revolt against the Romans (69/70 AD)	0.75	1.00

		XF	Unc
141 (133)	100 Sheqalim (Cu-Ni) 1984. Coin issued by Mattathias Antigonus depicting a Menorah (cf No. 18)	1.00	1.75

SITES IN THE HOLY LAND – 3rd ISSUE (3)

		Unc	Proof
142 (134)	½ Shekel (Ag) 1984. Valley of Kidron	15.00	

		Unc	Proof
143 (135)	1 Shekel (Ag) 1984. Type as No. 142		30.00
144 (136)	5 Sheqalim (Au) 1984. Type as No. 142		400.00

HANUKKA FESTIVAL 5745 (3)

		Unc	Proof
145 (137)	1 Shekel (Ag) 1984. Menorah from the Theresienstadt Ghetto	20.00	
146 (138)	2 Sheqalim (Ag) 1984. Type as No. 145		45.00

		XF	Unc
147 (139)	100 Sheqalim (Cu-Ni) 1984. Type as No. 141, with additional inscription »HANUKKA«	1.00	2.00

		XF	Unc
148 (140)	50 Sheqalim (Cu-Ni) 1985. David Ben Gurion (1886–1973), politician (cf No. 74)	0.85	1.25
149	100 Sheqalim (Cu-Ni) 5745 (1985). Ze'ev Jabotinsky (cf No. 114)	1.25	1.75

37th ANNIVERSARY OF THE INDEPENDENCE OF THE STATE OF ISRAEL (3)

		Unc	Proof
150 (141)	1 Shekel (Ag) 1985 = 5745. Symbol of the Israel Academy of Sciences and Humanities, a stylized tree with branches containing an atomic-structure Star of David	22.50	
151 (142)	2 Sheqalim (Ag) 1985 = 5745. Type as No. 150	35.00	
152 (143)	10 Sheqalim (Au) 1985 = 5745. Type as No. 150	400.00	
153	1 Shekel (Ag) 1985. Ancient drawing depicting a boat		25.00

		Unc	Proof
154	½ Shekel (Ag) 1985. Capernaum	15.00	

| 155 | 1 Shekel (Ag) 1985. Type as No. 154 | | 35.00 |
| 156 | 5 Sheqalim (Au) 1985. Type as No. 154 | | 325.00 |

HANUKKA FESTIVAL 5746 – 1th ISSUE (3)

| 157 | 1 Shekel (Ag) 5746/1985. Ashkanaz Hanukka lamp | 17.50 | |
| 158 | 2 Sheqalim (Ag) 5746/1985. Type as No. 157 | | 35.00 |

		XF	Unc
159	100 Sheqalim (Cu-Ni) 5746/1985. Type as Nr. 157	1.50	2.50

MONETARY REFORM: 100 Agorot = 1 New Shekel

160	1 Agora (Cu-Al-Ni) 5745–5747 (1985–1987). Ancient galley	0.10	0.15
161	5 Agorot (Cu-Al-Ni) 5745–5747 (1985–1987). Ancient coin	0.10	0.15
162	10 Agorot (Cu-Al-Ni) 5745–5747 (1985–1987). Menorah	0.10	0.20

		XF	Unc
163	½ New Shekel (Cu-Ni-Al) 5745–5747 (1985–1987). Harp	0.40	0.70
164	1 New Shekel (Cu-Ni) 5745–5747 (1985–1987). Lily	0.75	1.25

HANUKKA FESTIVAL 5746 – 2nd ISSUE

		XF	Unc
165	1 New Shekel (Cu-Ni) 5746 (1985). Type as No. 164, with additional inscription »HANUKKA«	0.75	1.25

38th ANNIVERSARY OF THE INDEPENDENCE OF THE STATE OF ISRAEL (3)

		Unc	Proof
166	1 New Shekel (Ag) 5746/1986	17.50	
167	2 New Shegalim (Ag) 5746/1986		35.00
168	10 New Shegalim (Au) 5746/1986		400.00

		XF	Unc
169	½ New Shekel (Cu-Al-Ni) 5746 (1986). Baron Edmond de Rothschild (1845–1934), banker	0.50	0.85

SITES IN THE HOLY LAND – 5th ISSUE (3)

		Unc	Proof
170	½ New Shekel (Ag) 5747/1986. Akko	15.00	

			Proof
171	1 New Shekel (Ag) 5747/1986. Type as No. 170		30.00

		Unc	Proof
172	5 New Shegalim (Au) 5747/1986. Type as No. 170		275.00

HANUKKA FESTIVAL 5747

		Unc	Proof
173	1 Agora (Cu-Al-Ni) 5747 (1986). Typ as No. 160, with additional inscription „HA-NUKKA"	0.10	0.15
174	5 Agorot (Cu-Al-Ni) 5747 (1986). Type as No. 161, with inscription and lamp	0.10	0.15
175	10 Agorot (Cu-Al-Ni) 5747 (1986). Type as No. 162, with inscription and lamp	0.10	9.20
176	½ New Schekel (Cu-Al-Ni) 5747 (1986). Type as No. 163, with inscription and lamp	0.40	0.70
177	1 New Schekel (Cu-Ni) 5747 (1986). Type as No. 165	0.75	1.25

HANUKKA FESTIVAL 5747 (2)

		Unc	Proof
178	1 New Shekel (Ag) 5747/1986. Algerian lamp	20.00	
179	2 New Shegalim (Ag) 5747/1986. Type as No. 178		35.00

39th ANNIVERSARY OF THE INDEPENDENCE OF THE STATE OF ISRAEL AND 20 YEARS UNITED JERUSALEM (3)

		Unc	Proof
180	1 New Shekel (Ag) 5747/1987	20.00	
181	2 New Shegalim (Ag) 5747/1987		35.00
182	10 New Shegalim (Au) 5747/1987		400.00

SITES IN THE HOLY LAND – 6th ISSUE (3)

		Unc	Proof
183	½ New Shekel (Ag) 5748/1987. Jericho	15.00	
184	1 New Shekel (Ag) 5748/1987		30.00
185	5 New Shegalim (Au) 5748/1987		275.00

HANUKKA FESTIVAL 5748 (2)

		Unc	Proof
186	1 New Shekel (Ag) 5748/1987	20.00	
187	2 New Shegalim (Ag) 5748/1987		35.00

Italian Somaliland

Italienisch-Somaliland   **Somalie Italienne**

Having been administered by the Benadir Company, this territory came under Italian jurisdiction in 1905. Since 1960 the former Italian Colony is united with British Somaliland, and thus forming the Republic of Somalia.
Capital: Mogadishu.

100 Bese = 1 Rupia, 100 Centesimi = 1 Lira

VICTOR EMMANUEL III 1905–1944

			VF	XF
1 (1)	1	Besa (Br) 1909–1921. Victor Emmanuel III, head left. ℞ value	18.50	30.00
2 (2)	2	Bese (Br) 1909–1924	22.00	40.00

3 (3)	4	Bese (Br) 1909–1924	28.00	50.00
4 (4)	¼	Rupia (Ag) 1910–1913. Victor Emmanuel III, head right. ℞ crown above value	35.00	70.00
5 (5)	½	Rupia (Ag) 1910–1919	65.00	115.00
6 (6)	1	Rupia (Ag) 1910–1921	80.00	150.00

NEW COINAGE STANDARD: 100 Centesimi = 1 Lira

7 (7)	5	Lire (Ag) 1925. Victor Emmanuel III, crowned portrait right. ℞ crowned coat of arms	90.00	180.00
8 (8)	10	Lire (Ag) 1925	120.00	250.00

Italien   Italy   Italie

Area: 116,286 sq. mi. Population: 59,980,000.
After Italy had been united, the Sardinian king, Victor Emmanuel II acquired the title of »King of Italy«. Following the abdication of Humbert II, the kingdom became a republic in 1946.
Capital: Rome.

100 Centesimi = 1 Lira

VICTOR EMMANUEL III 1900–1946

			VF	XF
1 (35)	1 Centesimo (Br) 1902–1908. Victor Emmanuel III (1869–1947), head left. ℞ value in wreath		0.40	2.50
2 (36)	2 Centesimi (Br) 1903–1908		0.40	2.50
3 (37)	25 Centesimi (Ni) 1902–1903		25.00	60.00
4 (38)	1 Lira (Ag) 1901–1907. Victor Emmanuel III, head right. ℞ crowned heraldic eagle		10.00	32.00
5 (39)	2 Lire (Ag) 1901–1907		25.00	60.00
6 (40)	5 Lire (Ag) 1901 (114 pieces)			*6500.00*
7 (41)	20 Lire (Au). Victor Emmanuel III, head left. ℞ crowned heraldic eagle			
	a) 1902			5000.00
	b) 1902; small anchor – Eritrea gold			6000.00
	c) 1903, 1905		400.00	650.00
	d) 1908, 1910			–.–

		VF	XF
8 (42)	100 Lire (Au) 1903, 1905. Same type as No. 7	3500.00	5800.00
A8	100 Lire (Au) 1903. Victor Emmanuel III,		

			VF	XF
		head facing right. ℞ two female figures, representing the "Italia" and Agriculture. Date MCMIII, value. Rare!	–.–	–.–
9 (43)	1	Centesimo (Br) 1908–1918. ℞ Italia standing	0.80	2.50
10 (44)	2	Centesimi (Br) 1908–1917	0.80	2.50
11 (45)	5	Centesimi (Br) 1908–1918	2.50	6.00
12 (46)	10	Centesimi (Br) 1908	–.–	–.–
13 (47)	20	Centesimi (Ni) 1908–1935. Classical head. ℞ Italia floating in the air, with torch. Coins struck after 1922 were never put into circulation	0.80	1.80
14 (48)	1	Lira (Ag) 1908–1913. Victor Emmanuel III, head right. ℞ Italia riding in quadriga	7.50	15.00
15 (49)	2	Lire (Ag) 1908–1912	8.00	20.00
16 (50)	1	Lira (Ag) 1915–1917. Similar type as No. 14	6.00	25.00
17 (51)	2	Lire (Ag) 1914–1917. Same type as No. 16	7.50	15.00
18 (52)	5	Lire (Ag) 1914. Same type as No. 16		2750.00
19 (53)	10	Lire (Au) 1910–1927. Victor Emmanuel III, head left. ℞ Italia with plough:		
		a) 1910	–.–	–.–
		b) 1912	1200.00	1600.00
		c) 1926, 1927	–.–	–.–
20 (54)	20	Lire (Au) 1910–1927. Same type as No. 19:		
		a) 1910	–.–	–.–
		b) 1912	650.00	800.00
		c) 1926, 1927		–.–

			VF	XF
21 (55)	50	Lire (Au) 1910, 1912, 1926, 1927. Same type as No. 19:		
		a) 1910		–.–
		b) 1912	600.00	850.00
		c) 1926, 1927		–.–
22 (56)	100	Lire (Au) 1910, 1912, 1926, 1927. Same type as No. 19:		
		a) 1910		–.–
		b) 1912	1600.00	2000.00
		c) 1926, 1927		–.–

				VF	XF
23 (57)	10	Centesimi (Br) 1911. Victor Emmanuel III, head left. ℞ allegory of the unification; industrial plants, bow of a ship, plough		3.50	8.00
24 (58)	2	Lire (Ag) 1911. Same type as No. 23		26.00	45.00

25 (59)	5	Lire (Ag) 1911. Same type as No. 23		380.00	550.00
26 (60)	50	Lire (Au) 1911. Same type as No. 23		600.00	850.00
27 (61)	5	Centesimi (Br) 1919–1937. Victor Emmanuel III, head left. ℞ ear of wheat		0.40	1.00
28 (62)	10	Centesimi (Br) 1919–1937. ℞ honey bee (Apis mellifica – Apidae)		0.80	2.00
29 (63)	20	Centesimi (Cu–Ni) 1918–1920. Crowned coat of arms. ℞ value in hexagon		2.00	4.00
30 (64)	50	Centesimi (Ni). ℞ Victor Emmanuel III, head left. ℞ Justitia riding in quadriga, drawn by lions. Coins struck after 1925 were never put into circulation			
		a) 1919–1928. Plain edge		8.00	11.50
		b) 1919–1935. Milled edge		1.60	4.50
31 (65)	1	Lira (Ni) 1922–1935. Seated Italia. ℞ value and coat of arms in wreath. Coins struck after 1928 were never put into circulation		2.00	4.50
32 (66)	2	Lire (Ni) 1923–1935. Victor Emmanuel III, head right. ℞ fasces. Coins struck after 1927 were never put into circulation		4.00	9.00
33 (67)	5	Lire (Ag) 1926–1935. Victor Emmanuel III, head left. ℞ heraldic eagle with fasces. Coins struck after 1930 were never put into circulation		4.50	8.00
34 (68)	10	Lire (Ag) 1926–1934. ℞ biga. Coins struck after 1930 were never put into circulation:			

			VF	XF
		a) 1926	30.00	170.00
		b) 1927	12.50	20.00
		c) 1928, 1929, 1930	20.00	45.00

35 (69) 20 Lire (Ag) 1927–1934. Coins struck after 1928 were never put into circulation — 45.00 | 85.00

36 (72) 20 Lire (Au) 1923. Victor Emmanuel III, head left. ℞ fasces and date October 1922 (first anniversary of the March on Rome) — 350.00 | 500.00

37 (73) 100 Lire (Au) 1923. Same type as No. 36 — 650.00 | 1000.00

COMMEMORATIVE COIN FOR THE 25th YEAR OF REIGN AND 10th ANNIVERSARY OF ENTERING WORLD WAR I

38 (74) 100 Lire (Au) 1925. Victor Emmanuel III, head left. ℞ male figure with flag holding statue of Victory — 1250.00 | 2000.00

39 (70) 50 Lire (Au) 1931–1933. Victor Emmanuel III, head left. ℞ male figure carrying fasces — 125.00 | 200.00

40 (71) 100 Lire (Au) 1931–1933. ℞ Italia standing at bow of galley — 300.00 | 360.00

10th ANNIVERSARY OF THE END OF WORLD WAR I

41 (75) 20 Lire (Ag) 1928. Victor Emmanuel III, with steel helmet. ℞ fasces, lion head, legend and value — 65.00 | 125.00

			VF	**XF**
42 (77)	5	Centesimi (Cu) 1936-1939. Victor Emmanuel III, head right, legend now RE. E. IMP. instead of RE. D. ITALIA. Rev. eagle with spread wings and fasces	0.40	1.60
43 (78)	10	Centesimi (Cu) 1936-1939. Rev. fasces, ear of wheat and oak leaves	0.80	2.00
44 (79)	20	Centesimi (Ni) 1936-1938. Rev. fasces, in front of profiled head. Issues dated 1937 and 1938 were never put into circulation	40.00	85.00
45 (80)	50	Centesimi (Ni) 1936-1938. Rev. eagle with spread wings in front of fasces. Issues dated 1937 and 1938 were never put into circulation	25.00	50.00
46 (81)	1	Lira (Ni) 1936-1938. Rev. eagle with spread wings in front of fasces. Issues dated 1937 and 1938 were never put into circulation	15.00	30.00

47 (82)	2	Lire (Ni) 1936-1938. Rev. eagle in wreath. Issues dated 1937 and 1938 were never put into circulation:		
		a) 1936	22.00	40.00
		b) 1937, 1938	–.–	–.–
48 (89)	5	Lire (Ag) 1936–1941. ℞ mother with children. Coins struck after 1937 were never put into circulation	25.00	48.00
49 (90)	10	Lire (Ag) 1936–1941. ℞ Italia standing at bow of galley. Coins struck after 1936 were never put into circulation	20.00	38.00
50 (91)	20	Lire (Ag) 1936–1941. ℞ quadriga. Coins struck after 1936 were never put into circulation	500.00	650.00
51 (92)	50	Lire (Au) 1936. ℞ Italian eagle over emblems of Italy and Ethiopia, resembling Roman field badge	2000.00	2600.00

				VF	XF
52 (93)	100	Lire (Au) 1936. ℞ male figure carrying fasces; diameter: 25 mm			2600.00	3500.00
53 (93a)	100	Lire (Au) 1937. Same type as No. 52, but; diameter: 20 mm			4000.00	5000.00

Forgeries are known to exist of Nos. 50-53.

			VF	XF
54 (77a)	5 Centesimi (Al-Br) 1939-1943. Type as No. 42		0.40	1.00
55 (78a)	10 Centesimi (Al-Br) 1939-1943. Type as No. 43		0.40	1.00
56 (79a)	20 Centesimi (St) 1939-1943. Type as No. 44		0.40	0.80
57 (80a)	50 Centesimi (St) 1939-1943. Type as No. 45		0.40	1.60
58 (81a)	1 Lira (St) 1939-1943. Type as No. 46		0.80	1.60
59 (82a)	2 Lire (St) 1939-1943. Type as No. 47		1.00	2.00

REPUBLIC since 1946

60 (95)	1 Lira (Al) 1946–1950. Head of goddess Ceres. ℞ orange:	
	a) 1946	6.00	25.00
	b) 1947	12.00	100.00
	c) 1948–1950	1.50	2.50
61 (96)	2 Lire (Al) 1946–1950. Ploughman. ℞ ear of wheat:	
	a) 1946	16.00	40.00
	b) 1947	20.00	90.00
	c) 1948–1950	1.00	4.00
62 (97)	5 Lire (Al) 1946–1950. Head of liberty with torch. ℞ grape (Vitis vinifera – Vitaceae):	
	a) 1946	40.00	165.00
	b) 1947	28.00	60.00
	c) 1948–1950	1.00	3.00

63 (98)	10 Lire (Al) 1946–1950. Pegasus. ℞ olive branch (Olea europea – Oleaceae):	
	a) 1946	16.00	40.00
	b) 1947	160.00	260.00
	c) 1948–1950	2.00	4.00

			VF	XF
64 (99)	1	Lira (Al) 1951–1970. Scale. R cornucopia:		
		a) 1951–1953	0.50	2.50
		b) 1954–1959	0.25	0.80
		c) 1968–1970; in mint sets only		5.00
65 (100)	2	Lire (Al) 1953–1970. Honey bee (Apis mellifica – Apidae). R olive branch:		
		a) 1953–1957, 1959	0.30	0.80
		b) 1958	25.00	60.00
		c) 1968–1970; in mint sets only		3.00
66 (101)	5	Lire (Al) 1951–1973. Oar. R common dolphin (Delphinus delphis – Delphinidae):		
		a) 1951–1955, 1966–1979	0.15	0.30
		b) 1956	5.50	18.00
67 (102)	10	Lire (Al) 1951–. Plough. R ears of wheat:		
		a) 1951–1953	0.80	4.00
		b) 1954	2.00	7.00
		c) 1955–1956, 1965–	0.15	0.30
68 (A102)	20	Lire (Al-Br) 1955–1959, 1968–. Head of Italia. Rev. oak leaves:		
		a) 1955, 1956, 1968; reeded edge	–.–	–.–
		b) 1957–1959; reeded edge	1.50	3.00
		c) 1969–; plain edge	0.15	0.30
69 (103)	50	Lire (St) 1954–. Head of Italia. Rev. blacksmith with anvil:		
		a) 1954-1957, 1959-	0.20	0.40
		b) 1958	3.50	10.00
70 (104)	100	Lire (St) 1955–. Head of Italia. Rev. goddess Ceres with sprig	0.25	0.50

			VF	XF
71 (105)	500	Lire (Ag) 1958–. Portrait of young girl. R fleet of Columbus: Santa Maria, Nina, Pinta:		
		a) 1958–1960	5.00	8.00
		b) 1961	5.50	10.00
		c) 1964, 1965	5.00	8.00
		d) 1966, 1967	5.00	7.00
		e) 1968	25.00	35.00
		f) 1969, 1970, 1980–1986	5.00	8.00

COMMEMORATIVE COIN FOR THE CENTENNIAL
OF ITALY'S UNIFICATION

 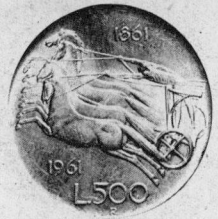

		XF	Unc
72 (106) 500 Lire (Ag) 1961. Seated Italia. R quadriga		5.00	7.00

COMMEMORATIVE COIN FOR THE 700th BIRTHDAY
OF DANTE ALIGHIERI

	XF	Unc
73 (107) 500 Lire (Ag) 19865. Dante Alighieri (1265–1321), poet. R scene from »Inferno«	5.00	7.00

COMMEMORATIVE COIN FOR THE CENTENNIAL OF ROME
AS ITALY'S CAPITAL

	XF	Unc
74 (108) 1000 Lire (Ag) 1970. Concordia, divine personification of civic unity – here symbol of Italy's national unity. R design Michel Angelo's (1538) for the multicoloured stone pattern of the Capitol plaza paving	10.00	15.00

	XF	Unc

75 (109) 100 Lire (St) 1974. Guglielmo Marconi
(1874–1937), physicist   0.35   0.75

76 (110) 500 Lire (Ag) 1974. Bust left. Rev. map of Italy
and surrounding areas under four sets of
concentric circles   27.50

500th ANNIVERSARY OF THE BIRTH OF MICHELANGELO BUONARROTI

77 (111) 500 Lire (Ag) 1975. Michelangelo Buonarroti
(1475–1564), bust facing left   35.00

		XF	Unc
78 (112)	200 Lire (Ni) 1977–	0.40	0.85

FOR THE FAO COIN PLAN

79 (113)	100 Lire (St) 1979	0.35	0.60

F.A.O. AND INTERNATIONAL WOMEN'S DECADE

80 (116)	200 Lire (Al-Br) 1980. Maria Montessori (1870–1952), pedagogue	0.50	0.85

CENTENNIAL OF LIVORNO NAVAL ACADEMY

81 (117)	100 Lire (St) 1981	0.35	0.60

WORLD FOOD DAY

82 (118)	200 Lire (Al-Br) 1981. Rev. Girl with cornucopia	0.50	0.85

2000th ANNIVERSARY OF VERGIL'S DEATH

	XF	Unc
83 (120)500 Lire (Ag) 1981		20.00

84 (119)500 Lire (Acmonital ring/Bronzital centre) 1982–	0.60	1.00

GALILEO GALILEI

85 (122)500 Lire (Ag) 1982. Galileo Galilei (1564–1642), naturalist   20.00

100th ANNIVERSARY OF THE DEATH OF GARIBALDI

86 (121)500 Lire (Ag) 1982. Giuseppe Garibaldi (1807–1882), patriot   20.00

XXIII OLYMPIC SUMMER GAMES LOS ANGELES 1984

		XF	Unc
87	500 Lire (Ag) 1984		22.50

FIRST ITALIAN PRESIDENT OF COMMON MARKET

		Unc	Proof
88	500 Lire (Ag) 1985	20.00	30.00

ETRUSCIAN CULTURE

89	500 Lire (Ag) 1985	20.00

EUROPEAN YEAR OF MUSIC

90	500 Lire (Ag) 1985. Rev. Organ	20.00

COLLEGIO DEL MONDO UNITO DELL'ADRIATICO, DUINO, TRIEST

91	500 Lire (Ag) 1985	20.00

200th ANNIVERSARY OF THE BIRTH OF A. MANZONI

		Unc	Proof
92	500 Lire (Ag) 1985. Alessandro Manzoni (1785–1873), poet	20.00	85.00

WORLD SOCCER CHAMPIONSHIP GAMES IN MEXICO

		Unc	Proof
93	500 Lire (Ag) 1986	20.00	30.00

Previous issues see »Weltmünzkatalog 19. Jahrhundert« (World Coin Catalogue of the 19th Century).

Elfenbeinküste   # Ivory Coast   **Côte d'Ivoire**

Area: 128,364 sq. mi. Population: 8,500,000.
From the end of the last century the Ivory Coast belonged as a French colony to the Union of French West Africa; in 1957 it obtained a high degree of internal autonomy within the structure of the Communauté Française. On 7th August 1960 the Republic was proclaimed. The Ivory Coast is linked with the states of Dahomey, Mauretania, Niger, Upper Volta, Senegal and Togo in the Union Monétaire Ouest-Africaine; the issuing authority for the whole Monetary Union is the Banque Centrale des Etats de l'Afrique de l'Ouest; see also under West Africa.
Capital: Abidjan.

100 Centimes = 1 CFA Franc

1	10 Francs (Ag) 1966. Head right of Dr. Félix Houphouët-Boigny (*1905), Head of State since 1960. ℞ African elephant (Loxodonta africana — Elephantidae) = national arms, within wreath	**Proof**	
		20.00	
2	10 Francs (Au) 1966. Type as No. 1	75.00	
3	25 Francs (Au) 1966. Type as No. 1	150.00	
4	50 Francs (Au) 1966. Type as No. 1	300.00	
5	100 Francs (Au) 1966. Type as No. 1	600.00	

All valuations in the SCHÖN are stated in U.S. Dollars.

Jamaica

Area: 4,411 sq. mi. Population: 2,400,000.
Discovered by Christopher Columbus in 1494, this island became British Territory in 1670. Following the temporary mambership of the West Indian Federation, Jamaica declared her independence on August 6th, 1962. Jamaica is a member of the British Commonwealth.
Capital: Kingston.

4 Farthings = 1 Penny, 12 Pence = 1 Shilling, 20 Shillings = 1 £;
since September 8th, 1969: 100 Cents = 1 Jamaica Dollar

EDWARD VII 1901–1910

			VF	XF
1	1 Farthing (Cu-Ni) Edward VII (1841–1910), crowned head right			
	a) (Y 4) 1902–1903; shading in coat of arms horizontal		5.50	11.00
	b) (Y 7) 1904–1910; shading in coat of arms vertical		3.50	8.00
2	½ Penny (Cu-Ni). Same type as No. 1			
	a) (Y 5) 1902–1904; shading in coat of arms horizontal		5.50	12.00
	b) (Y 8) 1904–1910; shading in coat of arms vertical		3.50	6.00
3	1 Penny (Cu-Ni). Same type as No. 1			
	a) (Y 6) 1902–1904; shading in coat of arms horizontal		6.50	12.00
	b) (Y 9) 1904–1910; shading in coat of arms vertical		3.50	8.00

GEORGE V 1910–1936

			VF	XF
4 (10)	1 Farthing (Cu-Ni) 1914–1934. George V (1865–1936), crowned head left. R coat of arms with American crocodile (Crocodylus acutus – Crocodylidae)		4.00	8.00

Values are given for each coin in U.S. Dollars and reference to Yeoman-numbers.

			VF	XF
5 (11)	½	Penny (Cu–Ni) 1914–1928. Same type as No. 4	3.50	6.00
6 (12)	1	Penny (Cu–Ni) 1914–1928. Same type as No. 4	3.50	6.00

GEORGE VI 1936–1952

			VF	XF
7 (13)	1	Farthing (Ni–Bra) 1937. George VI (1895–1952), crowned head left. ℞ coat of arms	2.00	3.50
8 (14)	½	Penny (Ni–Bra) 1937. Same type as No. 7	2.50	4.00
9 (15)	1	Penny (Ni–Bra) 1937. Same type as No. 7	2.80	4.50
10 (16)	1	Farthing (Ni–Bra) 1938–1947. Same type as No. 7, but larger head	0.50	0.80

			VF	XF
11 (17)	½	Penny (Ni–Bra) 1938–1947. Same type as No. 8, but larger head	0.70	1.50
12 (18)	1	Penny (Ni–Bra) 1938–1947. Same type as No. 8, but larger head	0.80	1.50
13 (19)	1	Farthing (Ni–Bra) 1950–1952. Same type as No. 10, but with new legend KING GEORGE THE SIXTH	0.20	0.40
14 (20)	½	Penny (Ni–Bra) 1950–1952. Same type as No. 11, but with new legend KING GEORGE THE SIXTH	0.25	0.50
15 (21)	1	Penny (Ni–Bra) 1950–1952. Same type as No. 12, but with new legend KING GEORGE THE SIXTH	0.40	1.00

ELIZABETH II since 1952

			VF	XF
16 (22)	½	Penny (Ni–Bra) 1955–1963. Elizabeth II (*1926), crowned head right. ℞ coat of arms	0.20	0.40
17 (23)	1	Penny (Ni–Bra) 1953–1963. Same type as No. 16	0.25	0.55
18 (24)	½	Penny (Ni–Bra) 1964–1966. Elizabeth II, crowned head right. ℞ coat of arms	0.15	0.30
19 (25)	1	Penny (Ni–Bra) 1964–1967. Same type as No. 18	0.25	0.60

COMMEMORATIVE ISSUE FOR THE 8th BRITISH EMPIRE AND COMMONWEALTH GAMES IN KINGSTON ON JAMAICA

			XF	Unc
20 (26)	5 Shillings (Cu–Ni) 1966. Crown between dates, legend surrounded by chain with 10 links. ℞ coat of arms		1.50	3.00

COMMEMORATIVE ISSUES (2) FOR JAMAICA'S 100th YEAR OF COINAGE

21 (27)	½ Penny (Br) 1969. Elizabeth II, crowned head right. ℞ coat of arms, dates 1869–1969, value		0.30	0.80
22 (28)	1 Penny (Br) 1969. Same type as No. 21		0.30	0.80

NEW CURRENCY: 100 Cents = 1 Jamaica Dollar

23 (29)	1 Cent (Br) 1969–1975. Coat of arms. R ackee (Blighia sapida – Sapindaceae)		0.10	0.20

24 (30)	5 Cents (Cu–Ni) 1969–. ℞ American crocodile (Crocodylus acutus – Crocodylidae)		0.10	0.20

		XF	Unc

25 (31) 10 Cents (Cu-Ni) 1969–. R butterfly (Papilio sp. – Papilionidae) on lignum vitae tree, branch with blossoms (Guaiacum officinale – Zygophyllaceae) — 0.20 — 0.40

26 (32) 20 Cents (Cu-Ni) 1969–1976. R blue mahoe (Hibiscus elatus – Malvaceae) — 0.35 — 0.50

27 (33) 25 Cents (Cu-Ni) 1969–. R Jamaica humming bird (Trochilus polytmus – Trochilidae) — 0.50 — 0.75

28 (34) 1 Dollar (Cu-Ni) 1969–1982. Sir William Alexander Bustamante (*1884), Prime Minister 1962–1967. R coat of arms, value:
a) 38 mm dia.; 1969, 1970 — 2.00 — 4.00
b) 38 mm dia.; 1971–1979 — 2.00 — 3.00
c) 34 mm dia.; 1980–1982 — 2.00 — 3.00

COMMEMORATIVE ISSUE FOR THE FAO COIN PLAN

29 (36) 1 Cent (Br) 1971–1974. Coat of arms. R ackee (Blighia sapida – Sapindaceae), motto: »Let us produce more food«, value — 0.15 — 0.30

			Unc	Proof
30 (35)	5	Dollars (Ag) 1971. Norman W. Manley, Prime Minister 1959–1962. Rev. coat of arms, value	15.00	20.00
31 (A36)	5	Dollars (Ag) 1972–. Norman W. Manley, head left:		
		a) .925 silver; 1972, 1973	15.00	20.00
		b) (Cu-Ni), 42 mm dia.; 1974–1979	5.00	
		c) .500 silver, 42 mm dia.; 1974–1979;		12.00
		d) (Cu-Ni), 36 mm dia.; 1980–	6.00	
		e) .500 silver, 36 mm dia.; 1980–		12.50

10th ANNIVERSARY OF INDEPENDENCE (2)

			Unc	Proof
32 (37)	10	Dollars (Ag) 1972. Alexander Bustamante and Norman W. Manley, map of the island. R coat of arms, new memorial legend, value	17.50	22.50

			Unc	Proof
33 (38)	20	Dollars (Au) 1972. Map of the island. Sail boats: »Cardera«, »San Juan« and »Nina«. R like No. 32	135.00	150.00

			Unc	Proof
34 (39)	10	Dollars 1974. Sir Henry Morgan (1635–1688), Lieutenant Governor of Jamaica 1674:		
		a) (Ag)		20.00
		b) (Cu-Ni)	10.00	

			Unc	Proof
35 (40)	10	Dollars 1975. Christopher Columbus (1451–1506), discoverer of the New World. Rev. coat of arms, value:		
		a) (Ag)		25.00
		b) (Cu-Ni)	12.50	
36 (41)	100	Dollars (Au) 1975. Type similar to No. 35	125.00	150.00

ISSUE FOR THE FAO COIN PLAN

			XF	Unc
37 (36a)	1	Cent (Al) 1975–1984. Type as No. 29	0.10	0.25
38 (43)	50	Cents (Cu-Ni) 1975–1984. Marcus Garvey (1887–1940), politician	0.80	1.50

			Unc	Proof
39 (44)	10	Dollars 1976. Admiral Horatio Nelson:		
		a) (Ag)		25.00
		b) (Cu-Ni)	12.50	
40 (45)	100	Dollars (Au) 1976. Admiral Horatio Nelson	175.00	175.00

ISSUE FOR THE FAO COIN PLAN

			XF	Unc
41 (42)	20	Cents (Cu-Ni) 1976–1984. Type as No. 26, but inscription FORESTRY FOR DEVELOPMENT	0.75	1.20

			Unc	Proof
42 (46)	10	Dollars 1977. Admiral George Rodney:		
		a) (Ag)		30.00
		b) (Cu-Ni)	15.00	

JAMAICAN UNITY

			Unc	Proof
43 (47)	10	Dollars 1978 »Out of many, one people«:		
		a) (Ag)		30.00
		b) (Cu-Ni)	15.00	

25th ANNIVERSARY OF THE CORONATION OF HER MAJESTY QUEEN ELIZABETH II (3)

		Unc	Proof
44 (48)	25 Dollars (Ag) 1978. The Queen seated on the Throne in full coronation regalia	90.00	110.00
45 (49)	100 Dollars (Au) 1978. Type as No. 44		200.00
46 (50)	250 Dollars (Au) 1978. Type as No. 44		750.00

10th ANNIVERSARY OF INVESTITURE OF PRINCE CHARLES (3)

47 (52)	25 Dollars (Ag) 1979	90.00	110.00
48 (53)	100 Dollars (Au) 1979		200.00
49 (54)	250 Dollars (Au) 1979		750.00

50 (51)	10 Dollars 1979. Homerus Swallowtails:		
	a) (Ag)		40.00
	b) (Cu-Ni)	20.00	

INTERNATIONAL YEAR OF THE CHILD (2)

51 (55)	10 Dollars (Ag) 1979		25.00
A 51	250 Dollars (Au) 1983. Type as No. 51:		
	a) .900 gold, 11.34 g		400.00
	b) Piéfort, 22.68 g		1500.00

OLYMPIC GAMES (2)

52 (58)	25 Dollars (Ag) 1980	100.00	100.00
53 (59)	250 Dollars (Au) 1980		350.00

			Unc	Proof
54 (56)	10	Dollars 1980. Trochilus polytmus Hummingbirds:		
		a) (Ag)		30.00
		b) (Cu-Ni)	15.00	

10th ANNIVERSARY OF CARIBBEAN DEVELOPMENT BANK

			Unc	Proof
55 (57)	10	Dollars (Ag) 1980.		30.00

WEDDING OF PRINCE CHARLES AND LADY DIANA (3)

			Unc	Proof
56 (60)	10	Dollars (Ag) 1981		25.00
57 (61)	25	Dollars (Ag) 1981		100.00
58 (62)	250	Dollars (Au) 1981		250.00
59 (63)	10	Dollars 1981. American crocodile:		
		a) (Ag)		32.00
		b) (Cu-Ni)	12.50	

WORLD FOOD DAY 1981 (2)

			XF	Unc
60 (64)	20	Cents (Cu-Ni) 1981. Cacao branch	0.60	0.75
61 (65)	1	Dollar (Cu-Ni) 1981. Fruits		7.50

WORLD SOCCER CHAMPIONSHIP GAMES (4)

			Unc	Proof
62 (66)	1	Dollar (Cu-Ni) 1982. Goalkeeper	7.50	
63 (69)	10	Dollars (Ag) 1982		27.50
64 (68)	25	Dollars (Ag) 1982		130.00
65 (70)	250	Dollars (Au) 1982. Type as No. 62		250.00
66 (67)	10	Dollars 1982. Mongoose:		
		a) (Ag)		30.00
		b) (Cu-Ni)	12.50	

ROYAL STATE VISIT (3)

			Unc	Proof
67 (73)	10	Dollars (Ag) 1983. Conjoined heads of Queen Elizabeth II and Prince Philip		40.00
68 (74)	25	Dollars (Ag) 1983. Type as No. 67		125.00
69 (75)	250	Dollars (Au) 1983. Type as No. 67		250.00

21st ANNIVERSARY OF INDEPENDENCE (10)

			Unc	Proof
70 (76)	1	Cent (Al) 1983. Type as No. 37, with additional legend »21ST ANNIVERSARY · INDEPENDENCE	0.30	0.75

		Unc	Proof
71 (77)	5 Cents (Cu-Ni) 1983. Type as No. 24	0.40	1.00
72 (78)	10 Cents (Cu-Ni) 1983. Type as No. 25	0.50	1.00
73 (79)	20 Cents (Cu-Ni) 1983. Type as No. 41	0.60	2.00
74 (80)	25 Cents (Cu-Ni) 1983. Type as No. 27	0.80	2.50
75 (81)	50 Cents (Cu-Ni) 1983. Type as No. 38	1.50	3.50
76 (82)	1 Dollar (Cu-Ni) 1983. Type as No. 28	2.50	8.00
77 (83)	5 Dollars 1983. Type as No. 31:		
	a) (Ag)		15.00
	b) (Cu-Ni)	6.00	
78 (84)	10 Dollars 1983. Rev. Busts of Sir A. Bustamante and N.W. Manley, motto »Onward Together – Land we Love«:		
	a) (Ag)	12.50	
	b) (Cu-Ni)		32.00
79 (85)	100 Dollars (Au) 1983. Type as No. 78		165.00

XXIII OLYMPIC SUMMER GAMES LOS ANGELES 1984 (2)

		Unc	Proof
80	10 Dollars (Ag) 1984		35.00
81 (86)	25 Dollars (Ag) 1984. Sprinter		100.00

DECADE FOR WOMEN (3)

		Unc	Proof
82 (87)	10 Dollars (Ag) 1984		35.00
A 82	25 Dollars (Ag) 1984. Type as No. 82 (about 20 pcs.)		–.–

		Unc	Proof
83 (88)	250 Dollars (Au) 1984. Type as No. 82		225.00

CENTENARY OF THE BIRTH OF A. BUSTAMANTE (2)

		Unc	Proof
84 (91)	1 Dollar (Cu-Ni) 1984. Sir Alexander Bustamante (1884–1977)		10.00
85	100 Dollars (Au) 1984. Type as No. 84; .900 gold, 7.134 g (551 pcs.)		185.00
86 (92)	10 Dollars 1984. Blue marlins (Makaira indica – Istiophoridae):		
	a) (S)		30.00
	b) (Cu-Ni)	12.50	

INTERNATIONAL YEAR OF YOUTH

		Unc	Proof
A 86	10 Dollars (Ag) 1985		40.00

WHALE PROTECTION

87	25 Dollars (Ag) 1985. Humpback whales		100.00

COMMONWEALTH GAMES IN EDINBURGH

88	10 Dollars (Ag) 1986:		
	a) .500 silver, 28.28 g	22.50	
	b) .925 silver, 28.28 g		45.00

WORLD SOCCER CHAMPIONSHIP GAMES IN MEXICO (3)

89	10 Dollars (Ag) 1986		45.00
90	25 Dollars (Ag) 1986		–.–
91	100 Dollars (Ag) 1986		125.00

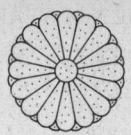

Japan
Nippon, also Nihon

Area: 142,720 sq. mi. Population: 120,050,000.

The Japanese empire has existed since about 660 B. C. until the present day. After the rigid isolation towards the outer world had been given up by the middle of the last century, industrialization also began in Japan which was especially forced very strongly after World War II and allowed Japan to rise to be an economic world power. Capital: Tokyo. The first coins were issued in Japan, patterned on the Cast Chinese cash coins, at the beginning of the 7th Century. Subsequently also silver and gold coins were put into circulation. These old coin shapes were substituted around 1870 by the introduction of modern minted round coins. The dates quoted on the modern coins refer to the era of the reign (Japanese; nengo) of the respective ruling emperor (Japanese: tenno), at the beginning of which the years are once more counted from one. The periods of reign oft the emperors mentioned below fall into the period covered by this catalog.

Mutsuhito, Meiji Era	明治	1868–1912
Yoshihito, Taisho Era	大正	1912–1926
Hirohito, Showa Era	昭禾ロ	1926–.

Upon the introduction of the modern coins the following nominal values and value ratios were laid down:

10 Rin (厘) = 1 Sen (金菱);
100 Sen = 1 Yen (圓 or 円).

During the period covered by this catalog, the following country designations are used on the Japanese coins:

–1945: 大日本
1945–1947:
1947– :日本國 or 日本国

Emperor: Mutsuhito (1868–1912)
Era: Meiji 明月氵台

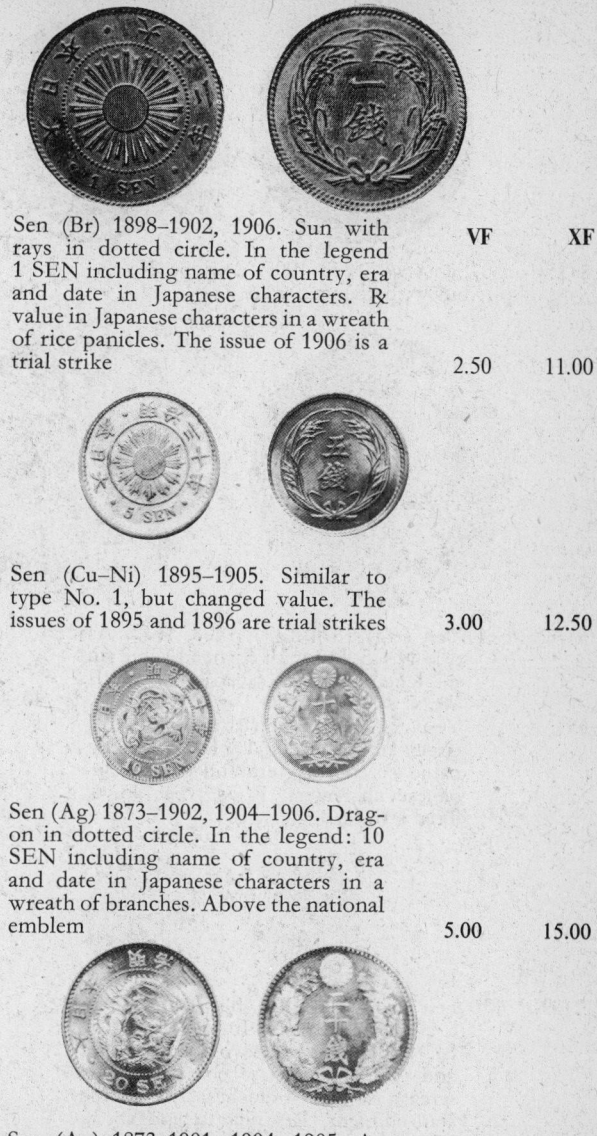

		VF	XF
1 (20)	1 Sen (Br) 1898–1902, 1906. Sun with rays in dotted circle. In the legend 1 SEN including name of country, era and date in Japanese characters. R value in Japanese characters in a wreath of rice panicles. The issue of 1906 is a trial strike	2.50	11.00
2 (21)	5 Sen (Cu–Ni) 1895–1905. Similar to type No. 1, but changed value. The issues of 1895 and 1896 are trial strikes	3.00	12.50
3 (23)	10 Sen (Ag) 1873–1902, 1904–1906. Dragon in dotted circle. In the legend: 10 SEN including name of country, era and date in Japanese characters in a wreath of branches. Above the national emblem	5.00	15.00
4 (24)	20 Sen (Ag) 1873–1901, 1904, 1905. As type No. 3, but with changed value	7.00	20.00

			VF	XF

5 (25)   50 Sen (Ag) 1873–1905. As type No. 3, but with changed value   16.00   25.00

6 (A25)   1 Yen (Ag) 1874–1906, 1908, 1912. As type No. 3, but with changed value (in the legend on the obverse 416. ONE YEN. 900)   40.00   75.00

6a   1 Yen (Ag) 1901. Sun with rays in double circle. In the legend 1 YEN including name of country, era and date in Japanese characters. ℞ as type No. 6. Trial strike!   –.–   –.–

7 (29)   10 Sen (Ag) 1906–1912. Sun with rays in a circle of rosettes. In the legend 10 SEN including name of country, era and date in Japanese characters in a wreath of two branches. Above the state emblem. (℞ similar to type No. 3). The issue of 1906 was not put in circulation.   4.00   6.00

			VF	XF

8 (30)   20 Sen (Ag) 1906–1911. As type No. 7,
but with changed value   5.00   8.00

9 (31)   50 Sen (Ag) 1906–1912. As type No. 7,
but with changed value   9.00   15.00

10 (32)   5 Yen (Au) 1897, 1898, 1903, 1911, 1912.
Sun with rays in octagonal surround.
In the legend name of country, era and
date in Japanese characters. ℞ value in
Japanese characters in a wreath of two
branches. Above the state emblem. (℞
similar to type No. 3)   600.00   750.00

11 (33)   10 Yen (Au) 1897–1904, 1907–1910. As
type No. 10, but with changed value 700.00   850.00

Values are given for each coin in U.S. Dollars and reference to Yeoman-numbers.

			VF	XF

12 (34) 20 Yen (Au) 1897, 1903–1912. As type No. 10, but with changed value — 1750.00 2800.00

Emperor: Yoshihito (1912–1926)

Era: Taisho 大 正

13 (35) 1 Sen (Bro) 1913–1915. As type No. 1, but now with the Japanese characters for the Taisho Era — 2.50 6.00

14 (36) 10 Sen (Ag) 1912–1917. As type No. 7, but now with the Japanese characters for the Taisho Era — 5.00 7.00

15 (37) 50 Sen (Ag) 1912–1917. As type No. 9, but now with the Japanese characters for the Taisho Era — 10.00 16.00

16 (38) 1 Yen (Ag) 1914. Similar to type No. 6, but with the Japanese characters for the Taisho Era — 35.00 60.00

17 (39) 5 Yen (Au) 1912 (?), 1913, 1924. Similar to type No. 10, but now with the Japanese characters for the Taisho Era — 550.00 900.00

18 (40) 20 Yen (Au) 1912–1920. Similar to type No. 12, but now with the Japanese characters for the Taisho Era — 1750.00 2700.00

19 (41) 5 Rin (Br) 1916–1919. Kiri-mon (Paulownia imperiales) = Imperial arms. In the legend: era and date in Japanese characters. ℞ value Japanese characters in the double circle, border in the way of arabesques and two rosettes

	VF	XF
	1.60	3.50

20 (42) 1 Sen (Br) 1916–1924. Similar to type No. 19, but with changed value ... 0.60 ... 2.00

21 (43) 5 Sen (Cu–Ni) 1916–1920. Central hole in octagonal border. In the legend: name of country, era and date in Japanese characters. ℞ value in Japanese characters above leaf decoration. With central round hole. 21 mm dia. The issue of 1916 is a trial strike. ... 4.00 ... 8.00

21a (44) 5 Sen (Cu–Ni) 1920–1923. Similar to type No. 21, but diameter only 18.5 mm ... 0.60 ... 2.00

22 (45) 10 Sen (Cu–Ni) 1920–1923, 1925, 1926. Similar to type No. 21, but with changed value ... 0.80 ... 2.00

22a 10 Sen (Ag) 1918, 1919. Sun with rays with a dove in the centre. In the legend: 10 SEN including name of country in

			VF	**XF**
		Japanese characters. ℞ value in Japanese characters between two phoenixes. Above the state emblem. Both issues were not put in circulation	–.–	–.–
22b	20	Sen (Ag) 1918, 1919, 1921. Similar to type No. 22a, but with changed value. Trial strikes	–.–	–.–

22c	50	Sen (Ag) 1918, 1919. Similar to type No. 22a, but with changed value. Both issues were not put in circulation	–.–	–.–

23(46)	50	Sen (Ag) 1922–1926. Sun with rays in the centre (changed design in respect of type No. 22a). In the legend: name of country, era and date in Japanese characters. ℞ similar to type No. 22a	3.50	6.00

Emperor: Hirohito (1926–)

Era: Showa 昭 和

24(47)	1	Sen (Br) 1927, 1929–1938. As type No. 20, but changed value and now with the Japanese characters for the Showa Era	0.80	1.60
25(48)	5	Sen (Cu–Ni) 1932. As type No. 21a, but now with the Japanese characters for the Showa Era	1.20	2.00
26(49)	10	Sen (Cu–Ni) 1927–1929, 1931, 1932. As type No. 22, but now with the Japanese characters for the Showa Era	0.80	1.80

			VF	XF
27 (50)	50	Sen (Ag) 1928–1938. As type No. 23, but now with the Japanese characters for the Showa Era	4.50	8.00
28 (51)	5	Yen (Au) 1930. As type No. 10, but now with the Japanese characters for the Showa Era	6500.00	11000.000
29 (52)	20	Yen (Au) 1930–1932. As type No. 12, but now with the Japanese characters for the Showa Era	8000.00	12500.00

30 (55)	1	Sen (Bra) 1938. In the centre a bird. Name of country, era and date as legend in Japanese characters. ℞ value in Japanese characters in ornamental border. Above the state emblem, below Kiri-mon (Imperial arms). 23 mm dia.	0.80	2.50
30a	1	Sen (Al) 1938. As type No. 30. Trial strike!	–.–	–.–

31 (56)	1	Sen (Al) 1938–1940. As type No. 30, but 18 mm dia.	0.60	1.30
31a	5	Sen (Cu–Ni) 1933. Name of country, era and date as legend in Japanese characters, right and left with ornamental background. ℞ value in Japanese characters. Above the state emblem, below Kiri-mon (Imperial arms). With central round hole. Trial strike!	–.–	–.–

			VF	XF
32 (53)	5	Sen (Cu–Ni) 1933–1938. Central round hole inside border with eight-curved design. Name of country, era and date as legend in Japanese characters. ℞ value in Japanese characters. Above the state emblem, below a stylized bird. The issue of 1938 was not put in circulation	1.20	2.50
32a	10	Sen (Ni) 1933. As type No. 32, but with changed value. Trial strike!	–.–	–.–

33 (57)	5	Sen (Al–Br) 1938–1940. Name of country, era and date as legend in Japanese characters. Left and right a flower. ℞ value in Japanese characters. Above the state emblem, below Kiri-mon (Imperial arms). With central round hole	0.80	2.00

34 (54)	10	Sen (Ni) 1933–1937. As type No. 31a, but with changed value and no trial strike	1.20	2.50

35 (58)	10	Sen (Al–Br) 1938–1940. Name of country, era and date as legend in Japanese characters. ℞ value in Japanese char-

acters. Above the state emblem, below wavy decoration in front of ray-like background. With central round hole

	VF	XF
	0.80	1.60

36 (59) 1 Sen (Al) 1941–1943. Name of country, era and date as legend in Japanese characters. ℞ Fujiyama (volcano, 12,390 ft., national shrine). Above state emblem, below value in Japanese characters. Weight 0.65 gram 0.60 1.10

36a (59a) 1 Sen (Al) 1943. As type No. 36, but weight only 0.55 gram (thinner planchet) 0.80 1.60

37 (60) 5 Sen (Al) 1940, 1941. Peregrine (Falco peregrinus callidus – Falconidae) (stylized) including name of country, era and date in Japanese characters. ℞ in the centre the state emblem. Above and below value in Japanese characters. Weight 1.2 gram 0.40 1.50

37a (60a) 5 Sen (Al) 1941, 1942. As type No. 37, but weight only 1.0 gram (thinner planchet) 0.80 2.00

37b (60b) 5 Sen (Al) 1943. As type No. 37, but weight only 0.8 gram (thinner planchet) 0.90 2.00

38 (61) 10 Sen (Al) 1940, 1941. In the centre a stylized flower, name of the country, era and date as legend in Japanese characters. ℞ in the centre the state emblem. Above value in Japanese characters, below leaf decoration. Weight 1.5 gram 0.40 1.50

			VF	**XF**

38a (61a) 10 Sen (Al) 1941, 1942. As type No. 38, but weight 1.2 gram (thinner planchet)   0.60   2.00

38b (61b) 10 Sen (Al) 1943. As type No. 38, but weight 1.0 gram (thinner planchet)   0.60   2.00

39 (62) 1 Sen (Zn) 1944, 1945. Name of country, era and date in Japanese characters. ℞ in the centre the state emblem. Above and below value in Japanese characters   0.40   1.10

40 (63) 5 Sen (Zn) 1944. Name of country, era and date as legend in Japanese characters. ℞ right and left value in Japanese characters. Above the state emblem and below Kiri-mon (Imperial arms). With central round hole   0.80   1.60

41 (64) 10 Sen (Zn) 1944. As type No. 40, but with changed value   0.80   1.80

41a 1 Sen (fiber) undated (1945?). In the centre a stylized flower. Name of country as legend in Japanese characters. ℞ Fujiyama including value in Japanese characters. This issue was not put into circulation   –.–   –.–

41b 5 Sen (fiber) 1945. In the centre a stylized flower (changed design in respect of No. 41a). Name of country and date as legend in Japanese characters. ℞ state emblem and value in Japanese characters. This issue was not put into circulation   –.–   –.–

41c 10 Sen (fiber) 1945. In the centre the Imperial arms (Kiri-mon). Name of country, era and date as legend in Japanese characters. In the centre the state emblem. This issue was not put into circulation   –.–   –.–

From No. 42 changed name of country!

42 (65) 5 Sen (Zn) 1945, 1946. In the centre the

numeral »5«. Name of country, era and date as legend in Japanese characters. Rev. in the centre a flying dove (Columba livia domestica – Columbidae). Above the state emblem, below value in Japanese characters   0.25   0.75

43 (68) 10 Sen (Al) 1945, 1946. The numeral '10' in front of a stylized flower. Name of country, era and date as legend in Japanese characters. ℞ rice panicles (Oryza sativa – Gramineae). Above the state emblem, below value in Japanese characters. 22 mm dia.   0.50   1.25

43a 10 Sen (Bra) 1946. As type No. 43, but diameter only 18.5 mm. This issue was not put into circulation   –.–   –.–

44 (67) 50 Sen (Bra) 1946, 1947. In the centre the value 50 SEN in front of a sheaf of corn. Name of country, era and date as legend in Japanese characters. ℞ in the centre the Bird Phoenix. Above the state emblem, below value in Japanese characters. The issue of 1947 was not put into circulation   0.75   2.00

As from No. 45 name of country changed once more.

45 (69) 50 Sen (Bra) 1947, 1948. In the centre the numeral '50' in a circle. Name of country, era and date as legend in Japanese characters. ℞ value in Japanese characters in an open wreath of blooms. Above the state emblem   0.40   1.25

As from No. 46: method of reading the Japanese characters is from left to right!

46 (70) 1 Yen (Bra) 1948–1950. Value 1 YEN
in circle. Name of country, era and date
as legend in Japanese characters. ℞
value in Japanese characters between
branches of blooms

	VF	XF
	0.50	1.25

47 (74) 1 Yen (Al) 1955–. Sapling with branches
and leaves. In the legend: name of
country and value in Japanese characters. ℞ in the centre the numeral '1'
in the circle. Below era and date in
Japanese characters

0.10   0.15

48 (71) 5 Yen (Bra) 1948, 1949. Dove and plum
blossoms in the circle. Name of coun-
try, era and date as legend in Japanese
characters. ℞ Parliament Buildings in
Tokyo in the circle. Ornamental border. Value in Japanese characters

0.50   2.00

49 (72) 5 Yen (Bra) 1949–1958. Name of country,
era and date as legend in Japanese

characters around a central hole. ℞
above rice panicles (Agriculture). In
the centre a cogwheel (Industry). Below
stylized waves (Fisheries) and value in
Japanese characters

	VF	XF
characters...	0.25	1.00

50 (72a)   5 Yen (Bra) 1959–. As type No. 49, but
with slightly changed design   0.10   0.15

50 a   10 Yen (German silver) 1950, 1951. Name
of the country, era and date as legend
in Japanese characters around a central
round hole. ℞ above and below value
in Japanese characters. Left and right
leaf decorations. Both issues were not
put into circulation   –.–   –.–

51 (73)   10 Yen (Br) 1951–1958. Phoenix Hall of
the Byodo-in Temple in Uji near Kyoto.
Name of the country and value as legend in Japanese characters. ℞ the
numeral '10' including the era and date
in Japanese characters in a wreath open
at the top. Edge reeded   0.25   0.75

51 a (73a) 10 Yen (Br) 1959–. As type No. 51, but
with plain edge   0.10   0.20

52 (75) 50 Yen (Ni) 1955–1958. In the centre a chrysanthemum (Chrysanthemum sp. – Compositae). Name of country and value in Japanese characters. ℞ in the centre the numeral '50'. Era and date as legend in Japanese characters

	VF	XF
	0.50	1.00

53 (76) 50 Yen (Ni) 1959–1966. Chrysanthemum, surrounding a central round hole. Name of country and value as legend in Japanese characters. ℞ at the top the numeral '50'. Underneath era and date in Japanese characters

	0.50	1.50

54 (77) 100 Yen (Ag) 1957, 1958. In the centre the Bird Phoenix. Name of country and date as legend in Japanese characters. ℞ ornamental decoration in the form of blooms. The value of 100 YEN as well as era and date in Japanese characters as legend

	1.00	3.00

			XF	Unc

55 (78) 100 Yen (Ag) 1959–1966. Rice panicles.
Name of country and value as legend
in Japanese characters. ℞ in the centre
the numeral '100'. Era and date as
legend in Japanese characters   2.00   4.00

COMMEMORATIVE ISSUES (2)
FOR THE 18th OLYMPIC SUMMER GAMES 1964
IN TOKYO

56 (79) 100 Yen (Ag) 1964. Olympic rings in front
of Olympic flame. Name of country
and date as legend in Japanese characters. ℞ in the centre the numeral '100'.
In the legend at the top TOKYO 1964
and underneath the era in Japanese
characters as well as the numeral '39'
(date)   2.00   3.00

57 (80) 1000 Yen (Ag) 1964. Fujiyama between
cherry blossoms. Name of country
and value as legend in Japanese characters. ℞ the value of 1000 YEN
above the Olympic rings. In the legend

above 1964 TOKYO and below the
era in Japanese characters as well as
the numeral '39' (date). To the right
and left cherry blossoms

	XF	Unc
	22.00	35.00

Forgeries are known to exist of No. 57.

58 (81) 50 Yen (Cu–Ni) 1967–. Above name of
country and below value in Japanese
characters. Right and left chrysanthe-
mums. ℞ above the numeral '50' and
the date in Arabic figures. With central
round hole   0.25   0.35

59 (82) 100 Yen (Cu–Ni) 1967–. In the centre
cherry blossoms. Name of country and
value as legend in Japanese characters.
℞ in the centre the numeral '100',
below the era in Japanese characters
as well as the date in Arabic figures   0.50   0.70

COMMEMORATIVE ISSUE FOR THE EXPO 70 FROM 15th MARCH TO 13th SEPTEMBER 1970 IN OSAKA

60 (83) 100 Yen (Cu–Ni) 1970. Fujiyama (after a
coloured woodcut by Hokusai [1760–
1849]). Above name of country and
below value in Japanese characters. ℞

symbol of the Expo 70. In the legend
above 100 YEN and below the era in
Japanese characters as well as the
numeral '45' (date)

	XF	Unc
	1.25	2.00

COMMEMORATIVE ISSUE
FOR THE 11th OLYMPIC WINTER GAMES FROM
3rd TO 13th FEBRUARY 1972 IN SAPPORO

61 (84) 100 Yen (Cu-Ni) 1972. Olympic Flame and
value in Japanese characters. As legend
the name of country in Japanese characters as well as the place name: SAP-
PORO. R the numeral »100« above
Olympic rings. In the legend the date
1972, the era in Japanese characters
and the numeral »47« (date). At right
and left a stylized ice crystal   2.50   4.50

COMMEMORATIVE ISSUE FOR THE EXPO 75 IN OKINAWA

62 (85) 100 Yen (Cu-Ni) 1975   0.80   1.50

50th ANNIVERSARY OF THE REIGN OF EMPEROR HIROHITO

		XF	Unc
63 (86)	100 Yen (Cu-Ni) 1976. Imperial Palace and Niju bridge	2.00	4.00

64 (87)	500 Yen (Cu-Ni) 1981–. Kiri-mon. Rev. value	3.00	4.00

TSUKUBA EXPO 85

65 (88)	500 Yen (Cu-Ni) 1985. Mt. Tsukuba, plum blossoms below. Rev. Expo 85 logo	3.50	5.00

100th ANNIVERSARY OF GOVERNMENTAL CABINET SYSTEM

66 (89)	500 Yen (Cu-Ni) 1985	3.50	5.00

60 YEARS OF REIGN OF HIROHITO (3)

67 (90)	500 Yen (Cu-Ni) 1986	4.00	6.00
68 (91)	10 000 Yen (Ag) 1986		80.00
69 (92)	100 000 Yen (Au) 1986, 1987		800.00

JAPANESE OCCUPIED TERRITORIES DURING
WORLD WAR II
NETHERLANDS EAST INDIES

The dates on the coins correspond with the Japanese calendar.

					Unc
1 (22)	1	Sen (Al) 2603–2604 (1943–1944). Dragon. R value		60.00	85.00
2 (23)	5	Sen (Zn) 2603 (1943)		–.–	–.–
3 (24)	10	Sen (Zn) 2603–2604 (1943–1944). Sculpture of a dancer. R value		40.00	70.00

No. 2 is not recorded in official documents.
No. 1–3 also exist in silver proof (extremely rare).
The last three Yeoman numbers refer to the »Netherlands Indies« listings.

Kingdom in the Near East.
Capital: Amman.

10 Fils = 1 Piaster, 100 Fils = 1 Dirham, 1000 Fils = 1 Jordan Dinar

ABDALLAH IBN AL HUSSEIN 1946–1951

			VF	XF
1 (1)	1	Fil (Br) 1949. Value in circle, surrounded by ears of wheat with crown above. ℞ value and legend THE HASHEMITE KINGDOM OF THE JORDAN	3.00	6.00
2 (2)	1	Fils (Br) 1949. Same type as No. 1	0.40	0.60
3 (3)	5	Fils (Br) 1949. Same type as No. 1	0.50	0.70
4 (4)	10	Fils (Br) 1949. Same type as No. 1	0.60	0.80
5 (5)	20	Fils (Cu–Ni) 1949. Same type as No. 1	0.60	1.10
6 (6)	50	Fils (Cu–Ni) 1949. Same type as No. 1	1.20	2.50
7 (7)	100	Fils (Cu–Ni) 1949. Same type as No. 1	1.60	3.50

HUSSEIN II since 1952

8 (8)	1	Fils (Br) 1955–1966. Value in circle, surrounded by ears of wheat with crown above. ℞ value and legend THE HASHEMITE KINGDOM OF JORDAN	0.20	0.40
9 (9)	5	Fils (Br) 1955–1967. Same type as No. 8	0.20	0.40
10 (10)	10	Fils (Br) 1955–1967. Same type as No. 8	0.30	0.60
11 (A10)	20	Fils (Cu–Ni) 1964, 1965. Same type as No. 8	3.00	5.00
12 (11)	50	Fils (Cu–Ni) 1955–1966. Same type as No. 8	0.80	1.50
13 (12)	100	Fils (Cu–Ni) 1955–1966. Same type as No. 8	1.20	2.50
14 (13)	1	Fils (Br) 1968. Hussein II (*1935), head right. Rev. value in Arabic and English, dates, surrounded by olive branches between circles; name of country in English	0.15	0.30

		VF	XF

15 (14) 5 Fils (Br) 1968–1975. Same type as No. 14 — 0.10 — 0.20

16 (15) 10 Fils (Br) 1968–1975. Same type as No. 14 — 0.15 — 0.30

17 (16) 25 Fils (Cu-Ni) 1968–1977. Same type as No. 14 — 0.25 — 0.50

18 (17) 50 Fils (Cu-Ni) 1968–1978. Same type as No. 14 — 0.30 — 0.60

19 (18) 100 Fils (Cu-Ni) 1968–1978. Same type as No. 14 — 0.60 — 1.20

20 ½ Dinar (Ag) 1969. Hussein II (*1935). R Al Harraneh (also Qasr el-Kharaneh), desert castle from the Omajjada Era, located 40 miles west of Amman

Proof
30.00

21 ¾ Dinar (Ag) 1969. R birth place of Christ under the Church of Nativity, Bethlehem

45.00

22 1 Dinar (Ag) 1969. R old part of Jerusalem with rock cathedral on Temple Hill (Haram esh-Sharif) — 65.00

23 2 Dinars (Au) 1969. R forum in Jerash (Roman Gerasa). Remainder of the oval-shaped main meeting place, surrounded by Ionic pillars from the time of Roman sovereignty, originated during 1st–2nd century A.D. — 110.00

24 5 Dinars (Au) 1969. R treasury (Arabic:

Khaznet Firaoun) in Petra. Memorial temple cut from pink sandstone, probably dedicated to a Nabatean king. Nabatean architecture with Greek-Roman influence in the style of Sassanidian rock tombs

Proof

250.00

				Proof
25	10 Dinars (Au) 1969. ℞ portrait of Pope Paul VI, visit to Jerusalem on January 5, 1964; Garden of Gethsemane with Mount of Olives and Church of Gethsemane (church of peace among nations, built in 1924)			450.00
26	25 Dinars (Au) 1969. ℞ Jerusalem: rock cathedral with chain cathedral, southern entrance to the temple square			1200.00

			XF	**Unc**
27	(19)	250 Fils (Cu-Ni) 1969. Hussein II, head right. Rev. olive three and dates in circle; name of country, value Quarter Dinar and letters FAO	2.00	3.00
28	(20)	250 Fils (Cu-Ni) 1970, 1974–1976. Type as No. 27, but without FAO	1.25	2.00
A 28		¼ Dinar (Au) 1975. Type as No. 28; .916⅔ gold		–.–

CONSERVATION COMMEMORATIVE (3)

			Unc	Proof
29 (23)	2½	Dinars (Ag) 1977	25.00	35.00
30 (24)	3	Dinars (Ag) 1977	30.00	40.00
31 (25)	50	Dinars (Au) 1977	600.00	700.00

25th ANNIVERSARY OF THE REIGN OF KING HUSSEIN II (2)

32 (21)	¼	Dinar (Cu-Ni) 1977. King's portrait in center of a crowned wing shield, dates, commemorative inscription. Rev. Petra Temple	5.00	
33 (22)	25	Dinars (Au) 1977		275.00

			XF	Unc
34 (26)	1	Fils (Br) 1978. Hussein II, head right	0.15	0.25
35 (27)	5	Fils (Br) 1978. Type as No. 34	0.15	0.25
36 (28)	10	Fils (Br) 1978. Type as No. 34	0.25	0.35
37 (29)	25	Fils (Cu-Ni) 1978, 1981. Type as No. 34	0.40	0.60
38 (30)	50	Fils (Cu-Ni) 1978, 1981, 1984. Type as No. 34	0.60	0.90
39 (31)	100	Fils (Cu-Ni) 1978, 1981. Type as No. 34	0.90	1.60

1400th ANNIVERSARY OF ISLAM (3)

40 (32)	¼	Dinar (Cu-Ni) 1978, 1980, 1981, 1985. Type as No. 28	1.50	2.50

41 (33)	½	Dinar (Cu-Ni) 1980	2.50	4.00

				Proof
42 (35)	10	Dinars (Ag) 1981		50.00
43 (36)	40	Dinars (Au) 1981		950.00

INTERNATIONAL YEAR OF THE CHILD (2)

44 (34)	3	Dinars (Ag) AH 1401/1981:	
		a) .925 silver, 23.33 g	30.00
		b) Piéfort, .925 silver, 46.66 g	150.00
45 (37)	60	Dinars (Au) AH 1401/1981:	
		a) .900 gold, 17.17 g	300.00
		b) Piéfort, .900 gold, 34.35 g (450 pcs.)	1500.00

When the Belgian Congo declared its independence on 30th June 1960, the province of Katanga detached herself from the Congo, and, under Moise Tshombé also became independent. A military intervention, supported by the UN, put a stop to this secession in January 1963. In 1972 the country was renamed Shaba.

Capital: Elisabethville (now: Lubumbashi).

100 Centimes = 1 Franc

			XF	Unc
1 (2)	1	Franc (Br) 1961. Bananas. (Musa x paradisiaca – Musaceae). ℞ Baluba cross or Katanga cross (in Katanga, rich in copper, such Katanga crosses some time possessed monetary character, e.g. also a bride price); value	1.00	2.00

2 (3)	5	Francs (Br) 1961. Same type as No. 1	1.75	5.00
3 (1)	5	Francs (Au) 1961. Same type as No. 1	200.00	250.00

Keeling-Cocos Islands

Group of coral islands located in the Indian Ocean 1,300 miles northwest of Australia. The islands were placed under the administration of Australia in 1955 with the Australian headquarter on West Island. There the Australian currency is accepted as legal tender only. The seat of the Clunies Ross family and the currency area of the rupee is Home Island. The rupee coinage is on a par with the Singapore Dollar. Seventeen different plastic "ivory" tokens and modern plastic tokens of 1913 and 1968 on rupee scale are also known.

100 Cents = 1 Rupee

			XF	Unc
1	5	Cents (Br) 1977. Portrait of John Clunies Ross facing left. Rev. coconut tree, value, date	0.10	0.20
2	10	Cents (Br) 1977. Type as No. 1	0.15	0.30
3	25	Cents (Br) 1977. Type as No. 1	0.20	0.50
4	50	Cents (Br) 1977. Type as No. 1	0.40	0.80
5	1	Rupee (Cu-Ni) 1977. Type as No. 1	1.00	1.50
6	2	Rupees (Cu-Ni) 1977. Type as No. 1	2.00	3.00
7	5	Rupees (Cu-Ni) 1977. Type as No. 1	4.00	7.50

150th ANNIVERSARY KEELING-COCOS ISLANDS (3)

			XF	Proof
8	10	Rupees (Ag) 1977. Type as No. 1, but with commemorative inscription	9.00	10.00
9	25	Rupees (Ag) 1977. Type as No. 8	16.00	22.00
10	150	Rupees (Au) 1977. Type as No. 8: a) .750 gold b) .916⅔ gold	–.– 150.00	–.– 250.00

Kenia **Kenya** Kenya

Area: 224,960 sq. mi. Population: 20,100,000. Formerly a British Colony and Protectorate, Kenya became independent on 12th December 1963. Following the Constitution of December 12, 1964, the country was proclaimed a Republic, and became a member of the British Commonwealth. Capital: Nairobi.
100 Cents = 1 Kenya Shilling, 20 Kenya Shillings = 1 Kenya Pound

			XF	Unc
1 (1)	5	Cents (Ni-Bra) 1966-1968. Jomo Kenyatta (1893-1978), sociologist and president. Rev. coat of arms	0.10	0.50
2 (2)	10	Cents (Ni–Bra) 1966–1968. Syme type as No. 1	0.15	0.50
3 (3)	25	Cents (Cu–Ni) 1966–1967. Same type as No. 1	0.25	0.50
4 (4)	50	Cents (Cu–Ni) 1966–1968. Same type as No. 1	0.30	0.60
5 (5)	1	Shilling (Cu–Ni) 1966–1968. Same type as No. 1	0.40	0.80

			Unc	Proof
6 (6)	2	Shillings (Cu–Ni) 1966–1968. Same type as No. 1	1.00	2.00
7	100	Shillings (Au) 1966	150.00	150.00
8	250	Shillings (Au) 1966	350.00	350.00
9	500	Shillings (Au) 1966	800.00	800.00

			XF	Unc
10 (7)	5	Cents (Ni-Bra) 1969–1971, 1973–1975, 1978. Type as No. 1, but on the obverse THE FIRST PRESIDENT OF KENYA – MZEE JOMO KENYATTA	0.10	0.20

		XF	Unc
11 (8)	10 Cents (Ni-Bra) 1969–1978. Same type as No. 10	0.10	0.25
12 (9)	25 Cents (Cu-Ni) 1969–1973. Same type as No. 10	0.25	0.50
13 (10)	50 Cents (Cu-Ni) 1969–1977. Same type as No. 10	0.30	0.60
14 (11)	1 Shilling (Cu-Ni) 1969–1975. Same type as No. 10	0.40	1.25
15 (12)	2 Shillings (Cu-Ni) 1969–1973. Same type as No. 10	0.90	2.00

COMMEMORATIVE ISSUE FOR THE 10th ANNIVERSARY OF INDEPENDENCE

		Unc	Proof
16 (13)	5 Shillings (Al-Br) 1973. Type as No. 15, but commemorative inscription	10.00	25.00

17 (18)	200 Shillings (Ag) 1979. President Moi. Rev. Arms		55.00
18 (19)	3000 Shillings (Au) 1979		750.00

		XF	Unc
19 (14)	5 Cents (Ni-Bra) 1980, 1984. President Arap Moi	0.50	1.00
20 (15)	10 Cents (Ni-Bra) 1980, 1984, 1986. Type as No. 19	0.75	1.50
22 (16)	50 Cents (Cu-Ni) 1980, 1984. Type as No. 19	1.00	3.00
23 (17)	1 Shilling (Cu-Ni) 1980. Type as No. 19	1.75	4.00
25 (20)	5 Shillings (Cu-Ni) 1985. Type as No. 19	2.50	6.00

Nos. 21 and 24 omitted.

		Proof
26	5 Shillings (Ag) 1985. Type as No. 25; .925 silver, 15.74 g (500 pcs.)	–.–

Kiribati

Area: 290 sq. mi. Population: 53,000.
Kiribati (formerly a part of the Gilbert and Ellice Islands) attained independence on July 12, 1979.
Capital: Bairiki.

100 Cents = 1 Dollar

			Unc	Proof
1 (1)	1 Cent (Br) 1979		0.20	0.75
2 (2)	2 Cents (Br) 1979		0.20	1.50
3 (3)	5 Cents (Cu-Ni) 1979		0.40	2.00
4 (4)	10 Cents (Cu-Ni) 1979		0.60	3.00

			Unc	Proof
5 (5)	20	Cents (Cu-Ni) 1979	1.00	4.00
6 (6)	50	Cents (Cu-Ni) 1979	1.60	6.00
7 (7)	1	Dollar (Cu-Ni) 1979	3.00	8.00
8 (8)	5	Dollars (Ag) 1979	25.00	30.00
9 (9)	150	Dollars (Au) 1979	300.00	325.00

WEDDING OF PRINCE CHARLES AND LADY DIANA (2)

			Unc	Proof
10 (10)	5	Dollars 1981:		
		a) (Ag)		30.00
		b) (Cu-Ni)	6.00	
11 (11)	150	Dollars (Au) 1981	300.00	325.00

ROYAL VISIT

			Unc	Proof
12 (12)	5	Dollars 1982. Rev. Arms, value:		
		a) (Ag)		100.00
		b) (Cu-Ni)	6.00	

5th ANNIVERSARY OF INDEPENDENCE

			Unc	Proof
13 (13)	10	Dollars (Ag) 1984. Rev. Map		30.00

Area: 85,266 sq. mi. Population: 40,453,000.
In 668 the various separate empires were united by Silla, located in the South East. During the years between 1640 and 1885 Korea cut herself off the remaining world, but soon China, Japan, and Russia gained a continuously growing influence in Korea. Finally the territory became a Japanese Protectorate in 1905, but from 1910 to 1945 it held the position of Japanese Province.
Capital: Seoul.

100 Fun = 1 Yang, since 1912: 100 Chon = 1 Won

KUANG-MU ERA 1897–1907

			VF	**XF**
1 (A10)	5	Fun (Cu) 1898–1902. Dragon in dotted circle. ℞ value in wreath	3.00	5.00
2 (B10)	¼	Yang (Cu–Ni) 1897–1901	2.50	4.00
3 (C10)	1	Yang (Ag) 1898	40.00	100.00

NEW CURRENCY: 100 Chon = 1 Won

4 (10)	1	Chon (Br) 1902. Heraldic eagle in dotted circle	750.00	1000.00
5 (11)	5	Chon (Cu–Ni) 1902. Same type as No. 4	750.00	1000.00
6 (12)	½	Won (Ag) 1901. Same type as No. 4	800.00	1200.00
7	½	Dollar (Ag) 1899. Same type as No. 4. Not circulated	–.–	–.–
8	10	Won (Cu) 1901, 1903. Same type as No. 4. Pattern	–.–	–.–
9	20	Won (Cu) 1900, 1902. Same type as No. 4. Pattern	–.–	–.–

Nos. 4–9 are so-called "Russian" issues.

10 (13)	½	Chon (Br) 1906. Phoenix; diameter: 22 mm	3.50	4.50
11 (14)	1	Chon (Br) 1905–1906. Phoenix; diameter: 28 mm	6.00	15.00
12 (B22)	1	Chon (Br) 1907. Same type as No. 11; diameter: 23.5 mm	3.00	6.00

				VF	**XF**
13 (15)	5	Chon (Cu–Ni) 1905–1907. Phoenix; diameter: 21 mm		5.00	10.00
14 (16)	10	Chon (Ag) 1906–1907. Dragon; diameter: 18 mm		12.00	20.00
15 (17)	20	Chon (Ag) 1905–1906; diameter: 22 mm		18.00	30.00
16 (D22)	20	Chon (Ag) 1907. Same type as No. 15; diameter: 20 mm		15.00	25.00
17 (18)	½	Won (Ag) 1905–1906; diameter: 31 mm		40.00	70.00
18 (E22)	½	Won (Ag) 1907. Same type as No. 17; diameter: 26.5 mm		50.00	80.00
19 (20)	10	Won (Au) 1906. Dragon. ℞ value in wreath		8000.00	15000.00
20 (21)	20	Won (Au) 1906		–.–	–.–

YUNG-HI ERA 1907–1910

21 (22)	½	Chon (Br) 1907–1910. Same type as No. 10, but with Chinese characters for the Yung-Hi era; diameter: 19 mm		4.00	8.00
22 (23)	1	Chon (Br) 1907–1910. Same type as No. 12, but with Chinese characters for the Yung-Hi era; diameter: 24 mm		2.50	5.00
23	5	Chon (Cu–Ni) 1909. Same type as No. 13, but with Chinese characters for the Yung-Hi era. Not circulated			*1000.00*
24 (25)	10	Chon (Ag) 1907–1910. Same type as No. 14, but with Chinese characters for the Yung-Hi era; diameter: 18 mm and less. The 1909 issue are only patterns		6.00	10.00
25 (26)	20	Chon (Ag) 1908–1910. Same type as No. 16, but with Chinese characters for the Yung-Hi era; diameter: 20 mm		10.00	18.00
26 (27)	½	Won (Ag) 1907, 1908. Same type as No. 18, but with Chinese characters for the Yung-Hi era; diameter: 26 mm. The 1909 issue are only patterns		60.00	85.00
27 (19)	5	Won (Au) 1908, 1909. Same type as No. 19 and 20		15000.00	28000.00
28	10	Won (Au) 1909. Same type as No. 19, but with Chinese characters for the Yung-Hi era			–.–
29	20	Won (Au) 1908–1910. Same type as No. 20, but with Chinese characters for the Yung-Hi era			–.–

For further issues see *North Korea* or *South Korea*.

Area: 5,000 sq. mi. Population: 1,700,000.
With the declaration of independence on 19th June 1961, the protectorate of 1899 expired.
Capital: Kuwait.

1000 Fils = 1 Kuwait Dinar

ABDULLAH III AS-SALIM AS-SABAH 1950–1965

			XF	Unc
1 (1)	1 Fils (Ni–Bra) 1961. Sambuke = two-masted Arabian dhow (part of the coat of arms). ℞ value in circle, Arabian name of country EMIRATE OF KUWAIT		0.40	0.60
2 (2)	5 Fils (Ni–Bra) 1961. Same type as No. 1		0.60	0.90
3 (3)	10 Fils (Ni–Bra) 1961. Same type as No. 1		0.65	1.00
4 (4)	20 Fils (Cu–Ni) 1961. Same type as No. 1		0.80	1.50
5 (5)	50 Fils (Cu–Ni) 1961. Same type as No. 1		1.20	2.00

6 (6)	100 Fils (Cu-Ni) 1961. Same type as No. 1		1.80	3.00
7 (7)	5 Dinar (Au) 1961. Same type as No. 1			500.00
8 (8)	1 Fils (Ni-Bra) 1962–. Same type as No. 1, but Arabian name of country now AL-KUWAIT		0.25	0.50
9 (9)	5 Fils (Ni-Bra) 1962–. Same type as No. 2, but Arabian name of country now AL-KUWAIT		0.15	0.30
10 (10)	10 Fils (Ni-Bra) 1962–.		0.20	0.40
11 (11)	20 Fils (Cu-Ni) 1962–.		0.25	0.50
12 (12)	50 Fils (Cu-Ni) 1962–.		0.40	0.80
13 (13)	100 Fils (Cu-Ni) 1962–.		0.75	1.50

SABAH III AS-SALIM AS-SABAH 1965–1977

15th ANNIVERSARY OF INDEPENDENCE

		Unc	Proof
14 (14)	2 Dinars (Ag) 1976:		
	a) .500 silver, 28.28 g	50.00	
	b) .925 silver, 28.28 g		85.00

JABIR AL-AHMED AJ-JABIR AS-SABAH since 1978

15th CENTURY OF THE HIJIRA (2)

15 (15) 5 Dinars (Ag) AH 1401 (1981); .925 silver, 28.28 g — 55.00

16 (16) 100 Dinars (Au) AH 1401 (1981); .916⅔ gold, 15.98 g — 450.00

20th ANNIVERSARY OF INDEPENDENCE (2)

17 (17) 5 Dinars (Ag) AH 1401 (1981) — 55.00
18 (18) 100 Dinars (Au) AH 1401 (1981) — 500.00

25th ANNIVERSARY OF INDEPENDENCE AND 25th YEARS OF DINAR-CURRENCY (2)

19 (19) 5 Dinars (Ag) 1986, .925 silver, 33.624 g — 60.00
20 (20) 50 Dinars (Au) 1986 — –.–

Laos　　　　　　　　**Laos**　　　　　　　　**Laos**

Area: 91,428 sq. mi. Population: 3,900,000.
On 7th December 1959, this state, formerly under French protection, became an independent kingdom.
Capital: Vientiane.

100 Centimes = 1 Kip

			XF	Unc
1 (1)	10	Centimes (Al–Mg) 1952. Woman from Laos. ℞ value (center hole)	0.30	0.50
2 (2)	20	Centimes (Al–Mg) 1952. (Center hole)	0.30	0.60
3 (3)	50	Centimes (Al–Mg) 1952. Book of constitution (center hole)	0.80	1.60

COMMEMORATIVE ISSUES (9) FOR THE CORONATION OF HIS MAJESTY THE KING OF LAOS OF NOVEMBER 13, 1971

			Proof
4	1000	Kip (Ag) 1971. Boromo Setha Khatia Suria Vongsa Phra Maha Sri Savang Vatthana (*1907), King since 1959. ℞ state emblem, name of country, value	20.00
5	2500	Kip (Ag) 1971. Same type as No. 4	30.00

6	4000	Kip (Au) 1971. Same type as No. 4	100.00
7	5000	Kip (Ag) 1971. Same type as No. 4	100.00
8	8000	Kip (Au) 1971. Same type as No. 4	140.00
9	10000	Kip (Ag) 1971. Same type as No. 4	150.00
10	20000	Kip (Au) 1971. Same type as No. 4	350.00
11	40000	Kip (Au) 1971. Same type as No. 4	700.00
12	80000	Kip (Au) 1971. Same type as No. 4	1400.00
13	5000	Kip (Ag) 1975. His Majesty the King of Laos and the royal coat of arms. ℞ Wat Phra Kio Museum, Vientiane	40.00

		Proof
14	5000 Kip (Ag) 1975. ℞ young Laotian girl	40.00
15	10000 Kip (Ag) 1975. ℞ Wat Xieng-Thong Sanctuaty (1560) Luang Prabang	90.00
16	50000 Kip (Au) 1975. ℞ That Luang Sanctuary (XVI Century) Vientiane	150.00
17	50000 Kip (Au) 1975. ℞ young Laotian girl	150.00

18	100000 Kip (Au) 1975. ℞ statue of Laotian Buddha	280.00

LAO PEOPLE'S DEMOCRATIC REPUBLIC

NEW MONETARY SYSTEM: 100 Att = 1 Kip

		XF	Unc
19 (4)	10 Att (Al) 1980	0.30	0.50
20 (5)	20 Att (Al) 1980	0.50	0.80
21 (6)	50 Att (Al) 1980	1.10	1.50

10th ANNIVERSARY OF PEOPLE'S REPUBLIC (4)

		Proof
22	50 Kip (Ag) 1985. Arms. Rev. That Ing Hang	45.00
23	50 Kip (Ag) 1985. Rev. That Luang	45.00
24	50 Kip (Ag) 1985. Rev. Vath Pkhu	45.00
25	50 Kip (Ag) 1985. Rev. Plain of Stones, Xieng Khouang	45.00

Lettland Latvia Lettonie
Latvija

Area: 24,600 sq. mi. Population: 2,000,000 (1939).
In the 18th century Latvia and the Baltic Provinces were annexed by Russia. On 18th November 1918, the independent Democratic Republic was proclaimed, and in June of 1940 occupied by Russian troops. With occasional interruptions, Latvia has since been a member state of the Soviet Union.
Capital: Riga.

100 Santimu = 1 Lats

			VF	XF
1.(1)	1	Santims (Br) 1922–1935. Coat of arms. R value	2.50	4.00
2 (2)	2	Santimi (Br) 1922–1932	2.50	4.00
3 (3)	5	Santimi (Br) 1922	3.00	5.00
4 (4)	10	Santimu (Ni) 1922	2.50	4.00
5 (5)	20	Santimu (Ni) 1922	3.50	6.00
6 (6)	50	Santimu (Ni) 1922. Coat of arms. R Latvija, symbol of the Latvian Republic, at the oar of a boat. Value	6.00	11.00
7 (7)	1	Lats (Ag) 1924. Coat of arms. R value in wreath	3.50	6.50
8 (8)	2	Lati (Ag) 1925–1926	5.00	7.50

			VF	XF
9 (9)	5	Lati (Ag) 1929–1932. Head of Latvija. R coat of arms and value	11.00	15.00
10 (10)	1	Santims (Br) 1937–1939. Coat of arms. R value, flanked by ears of wheat	4.00	6.00
11 (11)	2	Santimi (Br)		
		a) 1937, diameter: 19 mm	60.00	100.00
		b) 1938–1939, diameter: 19.5 mm	4.00	6.00

Libanon   # Lebanon   **Liban**

Area: 3,400 sq. mi. Population: 3,500,000.
Until this South West Asian country, located at the eastern end of the Mediterranean, was part of the Turkish Empire. Constituting a French Mandate until 1924, Lebanon and Syria were governed separately between 1924 and 1941. In 1927 the French Confederation created the Republic of Lebanon. The independence was declared on November 26, 1941, the mandatory privileges however, were not transferred to the Lebanese government until 1944. The last occupational forces left the country in 1946.
Capital: Beirut.

100 Piastres = 1 Lebanese Pound (Livre)

ÉTAT DU GRAND LIBAN

			VF	XF
1 (1)	2	Piastres (Al–Br) 1924. Lebanon cedar (Cedrus libani - Pinaceae). ℞ value	3.00	9.00
2 (2)	5	Piastres (Al–Br) 1924	3.00	9.00
3 (3)	2	Piastres (Al–Br) 1925. Lebanon cedar. ℞ galley	8.00	15.00
4 (4)	5	Piastres (Al–Br) 1925–1940	2.50	8.00
5 (6)	1	Piastre (Cu-Ni) 1925–1936. Legend. R lion heads, value (center hole)	1.00	2.00

REPUBLIQUE LIBANAISE

			VF	XF
6 (5)	½	Piastre (Cu-Ni) 1934–1936	2.00	5.00
7 (8)	10	Piastres(Ag) 1929. Lebanon cedar, new name of country. R cornucopias	12.00	25.00
8 (9)	25	Piastres (Ag) 1929–1936	8.00	15.00
9 (10)	50	Piastres (Ag) 1929–1937	12.00	25.00
10 (5a)	½	Piastre (Sn) 1940–1941. Same type as No. 6	1.20	2.50
11 (6a)	1	Piastre (Sn) 1940–1941. Same type as No. 5	2.00	4.00
12 (7)	2½	Piastres (Al–Br) 1940. Legend. ℞ value (center hole)	2.00	4.00
13 (11)	½	Piastre (Bra) without date (1941–1945). Legend. ℞ value, name of country LIBAN (center hole)	2.00	3.50
14 (12)	1	Piastre (Bra) without date (1941–1945)	2.00	3.50
15 (13)	2½	Piastres (Al) without date (1941–1945)	2.00	3.50
16 (14)	5	Piastres (Al) 1952. Lebanon cedar. ℞ galley	2.00	4.00

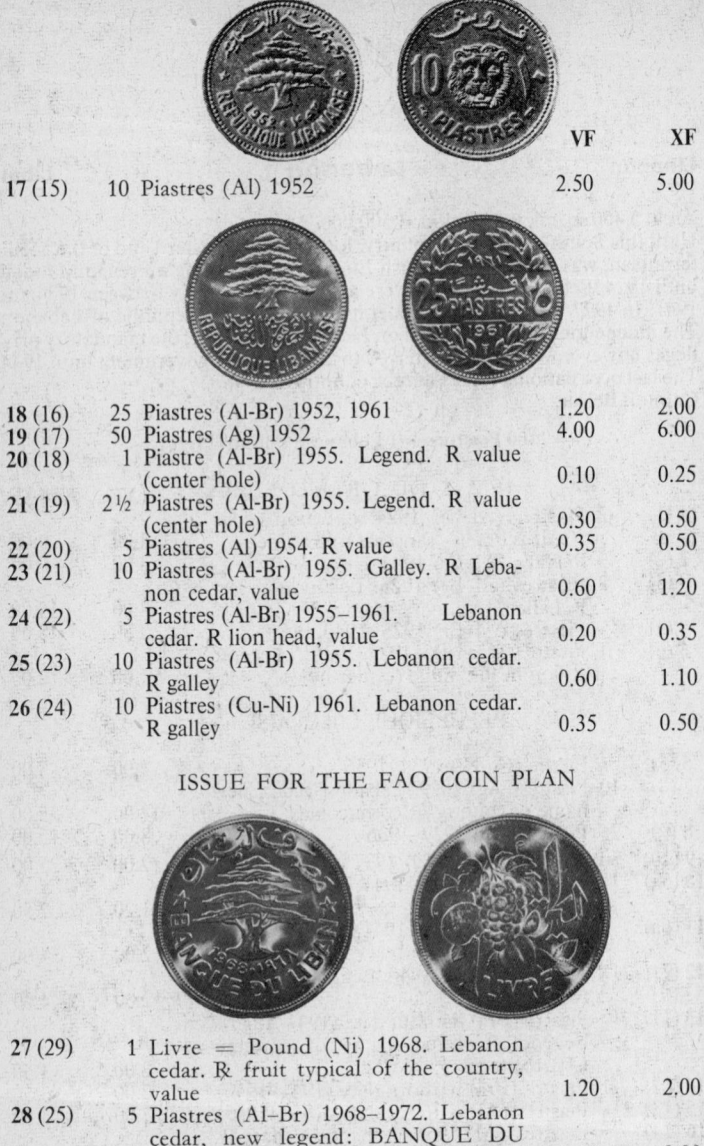

			VF	XF
17 (15)	10	Piastres (Al) 1952	2.50	5.00
18 (16)	25	Piastres (Al-Br) 1952, 1961	1.20	2.00
19 (17)	50	Piastres (Ag) 1952	4.00	6.00
20 (18)	1	Piastre (Al-Br) 1955. Legend. R value (center hole)	0.10	0.25
21 (19)	2½	Piastres (Al-Br) 1955. Legend. R value (center hole)	0.30	0.50
22 (20)	5	Piastres (Al) 1954. R value	0.35	0.50
23 (21)	10	Piastres (Al-Br) 1955. Galley. R Lebanon cedar, value	0.60	1.20
24 (22)	5	Piastres (Al-Br) 1955–1961. Lebanon cedar. R lion head, value	0.20	0.35
25 (23)	10	Piastres (Al-Br) 1955. Lebanon cedar. R galley	0.60	1.10
26 (24)	10	Piastres (Cu-Ni) 1961. Lebanon cedar. R galley	0.35	0.50

ISSUE FOR THE FAO COIN PLAN

27 (29)	1	Livre = Pound (Ni) 1968. Lebanon cedar. R fruit typical of the country, value	1.20	2.00
28 (25)	5	Piastres (Al–Br) 1968–1972. Lebanon cedar, new legend: BANQUE DU LIBAN. R value in laurel wreath	0.12	0.20

			VF	XF
29 (26)	10	Piastres (Al-Br) 1968–1972. Same type as No. 28	0.20	0.30
30 (27)	25	Piastres (Al-Br) 1968–1972, 1980. Same type as No. 28	0.40	0.60

31 (28)	50	Piastres (Ni) 1968–1971, 1975, 1978. Type similar to Nos. 28–30	0.50	1.00
32 (30)	1	Livre (Ni) 1975, 1977, 1980, 1981. Lebanon cedar, date. Rev. value in laurel wreath	0.90	1.50

ISSUE FOR THE FAO COIN PLAN

33 (31)	5	Livres (Ni) 1977	2.50	4.00

			Proof
13th OLYMPIC WINTER GAMES IN LAKE PLACID (3)			
34 (32)	1	Livre (Cu-Ni) 1980	4.00
35 (33)	10	Livres (Ag) 1980	20.00
36 (34)	400	Livres (Au) 1980	250.00

WORLD FOOD DAY 1981

			XF	Unc
37 (35)	10	Livres (Cu-Ni) 1981	4.00	6.00

Area: 11,716 sq. mi. Population: 1,530,000.
The former Basutoland, an enclave in the Eastern Republic of South Africa, was a British High Commission Territory, until it received its independence on 4th October, 1966. Adopting the name of Lesotho, the kingdom became a member of the British Commonwealth.
Capital: Maseru.

100 Cents = 1 Rand, 100 Licente = 1 Maloti

Besides the South African Rand, the Licente coins are legal tender.

				Proof
1	5	Licente (Ag) 1966		8.00
2	10	Licente (Ag) 1966		8.00
3	20	Licente (Ag) 1966		10.00

4	50	Licente (Ag) 1966. Moshoeshoe I (deceased 1870). King and founder of the Basuto Nation. Rev. coat of arms	20.00
5	1	Maloti (Au) 1966	75.00
6	2	Maloti (Au) 1966	150.00
7	4	Maloti (Au) 1966	300.00

ISSUES (5) FOR THE FAO COIN PLAN

8	1	Maloti (Au) 1969	75.00
9	2	Maloti (Au) 1969	150.00

		Unc	Proof
10	4 Maloti (Au) 1969		300.00
11	10 Maloti (Au) 1969		750.00
12	20 Maloti (Au) 1969		1300.00

10th ANNIVERSARY OF INDEPENDENCE AND 45th ANNIVERSARY OF THE COMMONWEALTH (3)

		Unc	Proof
13	10 Maloti (Ag) 1976. King Moshoeshoe II in military uniform. Rev. native woman, wearing a traditional wide hat and robe	22.50	35.00
14	50 Maloti (Au) 1976. Arms. Rev. Queen Elizabeth II	125.00	125.00
15	100 Maloti (Au) 1976. King Moshoeshoe. Rev. Horseman	200.00	175.00

NEW CURRENCY: 100 Lisente = 1 Loti

		XF	Unc
16 (1)	1 Sente (Ni-Bra) 1979–	0.15	0.20
17 (2)	2 Lisente (Ni-Bra) 1979–	0.15	0.20
18 (3)	5 Lisente (Ni-Bra) 1979–	0.20	0.40
19 (4)	10 Lisente (Cu-Ni) 1979–	0.40	0.80
20 (5)	25 Lisente (Cu-Ni) 1979–	0.50	1.00
21 (6)	50 Lisente (Cu-Ni) 1979–	0.60	1.20
22 (7)	1 Loti (Cu-Ni) 1979–	1.00	1.80

		Unc	Proof
23 (8)	10 Maloti (Ag) 1979–1980	10.00	20.00

INTERNATIONAL YEAR OF THE CHILD (3)

		Unc	Proof
24 (9)	10 Maloti (Ag) 1979	20.00	25.00
25 (10)	15 Maloti (Ag) 1979	20.00	25.00
26 (11)	250 Maloti (Au) 1979	500.00	550.00

110th ANNIVERSARY OF THE DEATH OF KING MOSHOESHOE I (3)

		Unc	Proof
27 (12)	50 Maloti (Ag) 1980	30.00	45.00
28 (13)	250 Maloti (Au) 1980	500.00	500.00
29 (14)	500 Maloti (Au) 1980	550.00	550.00

WEDDING OF PRINCE CHARLES AND LADY DIANA (3)

		Unc	Proof
30	30 Maloti (Ag) 1981		25.00
31	250 Maloti (Au) 1981	275.00	275.000
A 31	250 Maloti (Platinum) 1981		400.00

Liberia

Area: 43,000 sq. mi. Population: 2,200,000.

Since 1822 small settlements grew up along the African West Coast, housing former United States slaves, liberated by the American Colonization Society, and other organizations. Following the announcement of the constitution, the actual state was founded in 1847.

Capital: Monrovia.

100 Cents = 1 Liberian Dollar

			VF	XF
1 (4)	1 Cent (Br) 1896–1906. Head of liberty, left. ℞ palm tree (Elaeis guineensis – Palmae), rising sun, value:			
	a) 1896		10.00	20.00
	b) 1906		15.00	30.00
2 (5)	2 Cents (Br) 1896–1906		5.00	10.00
3 (6)	10 Cents (Ag) 1896–1906. ℞ value in wreath		8.00	15.00
4 (7)	25 Cents (Ag) 1896–1906		10.00	25.00

5 (8)	50 Cents (Ag) 1896–1906		18.00	40.00

			VF	XF
6 (9)	½ Cent. African elephant (Loxodonta africana – Elephantidae). ℞ palm tree			
	a) (Bra) 1937		0.40	0.80
	b) (Cu–Ni) 1941		0.30	0.60
7 (10)	1 Cent. Same type as No. 6			
	a) (Bra) 1937		1.20	2.40
	b) (Cu–Ni) 1941		2.00	5.00
8 (11)	2 Cents. Same type as No. 6			
	a) (Bra) 1937		1.60	3.20
	b) (Cu–Ni) 1941		1.00	2.00
	c) (Cu–Ni) 1978		Proof	1.00
9 (12)	1 Cent (Br) 1960–. African elephant. ℞ palm tree, sailing vessel		**Unc**	**Proof**
			0.15	0.50

			VF	XF
10 (13)	5 Cents (Cu–Ni) 1960–. Same type as No. 9		0.25	0.75
11 (14)	10 Cents. Liberian woman. ℞ value in wreath			
	a) (Ag) 1960–1961		3.00	
	b) (Cu–Ni) 1966–		0.30	1.00
12 (15)	25 Cents. Same type as No. 11			
	a) (Ag) 1960–1961		5.00	
	b) (Cu–Ni) 1966–		0.75	1.25

			VF	XF
13 (16)	50 Cents. Same type as No. 11			
	a) (Ag) 1960–1961		8.00	
	b) (Cu–Ni) 1966–		1.00	1.50

14 (17) 1 Dollar. Same type as No. 11
      a) (Ag) 1961–1962   15.00
      b) (Cu–Ni) 1966–   2.00   2.50

	Unc	Proof

15 (27) 20 Dollars (Au) 1964. William Jacanarat Shadrach Tubman (1895–1971), head of government from 1943 to 1971. ℞ coat of arms
      a) mintmark B below date   300.00
      b) mintmark L above date   400.00

70th ANNIVERSARY OF THE BIRTH OF PRESIDENT TUBMAN (3)

16   12 Dollars (Au) 1965. Bust of President Tubman. Rev. coat of arms and value   175.00
17 (28) 25 Dollars (Au) 1965. Head of President Tubman. Rev. Providence Island   350.00   400.00
18   30 Dollars 1965. Type as No. 16   350.00

75th ANNIVERSARY OF THE BIRTH OF PRESIDENT TUBMAN

A18   25 Dollars (Au) 1970   400.00

COMMEMORATIVE ISSUES (4)
FOR THE INAUGURATION INTO OFFICE OF PRESIDENT TOLBERT ON 3rd JAN. 1972

19   2½ Dollars (Au) 1972. The Capitol in Monrovia   75.00
20   5 Dollars (Au) 1972. Sailing boat, motif from the national coat of arms and as legend the national motto   150.00
21   10 Dollars (Au) 1972. Head of Liberty with crown of rays   300.00
22   20 Dollars (Au) 1972. President Tolbert, head facing left. Factual legend. R national coat of arms, name of country, value   550.00

SESQUICENTENNIAL OF FOUNDING OF LIBERIA

23 (A38) 25 Dollars (Au) 1972. Scene at Providence Island   400.00

			Unc	Proof
24 (18)	5	Dollars (Ag) 1973–1978. African elephant and national coat of arms as with No. 15	30.00	15.00

ISSUE FOR THE FAO COIN PLAN

			Unc	Proof
25 (38)	25	Cents (Cu-Ni) 1976–1978. Portrait of President Tolbert. Rev. a woman carrying a basket of food stuffs on her head	1.50	2.50
26 (39)	50	Cents (Cu-Ni) 1976–1978. Rev. coat of arms, value, date	2.00	3.50
27 (40)	1	Dollar (Cu-Ni) 1976–1978. Rev. map of Liberia	3.00	9.00

28 (35)	100	Dollars (Au) 1976		200.00
29 (36)	200	Dollars (Au) 1976		300.00
30 (37)	400	Dollars (Au) 1976		1200.00

130th ANNIVERSARY OF THE REPUBLIC

31 (41)	100	Dollars (Au) 1977	200.00	200.00

ORGANIZATION OF AFRICAN UNITY SUMMIT CONFERENCE IN MONROVIA (10)

32 (12a)	1	Cent (Br) 1979. Type as No. 9, but edge inscription O.A.U. July 1979	–.–
33 (11b)	2	Cents (Cu-Ni) 1979. Type as No. 8c	–.–
34 (13a)	5	Cents (Cu-Ni) 1979. Type as No. 10	–.–

			Proof
35 (14b)	10 Cents (Cu-Ni) 1979. Type as No. 11b		-.-
36 (38a)	25 Cents (Cu-Ni) 1979. Type as No. 25 (FAO issue)		-.-
37 (39a)	50 Cents (Cu-Ni) 1979. Type as No. 26		-.-
38 (40a)	1 Dollar (Cu-Ni) 1979. Type as No. 27		-.-
39 (18a)	5 Dollars (Ag) 1979. Type as No. 24		-,-

Nos. 32–39, Proof Set (1857 sets) 85.00

40 (42)	100 Dollars (Au) 1979. President W. R. Tolbert	200.00
41 (43)	100 Dollars (Au) 1979. African elephant	250.00

			XF	**Unc**
42 (44)	5 Dollars (Cu-Ni) 1982. Monument		7.50	10.00

YEAR OF THE SCOUT (2)

			Unc	**Proof**
43 (45)	20 Dollars (Ag) 1982. Rev. Scouts saluting and flag		20.00	30.00
44 (46)	200 Dollars (Au) 1982. Type as No. 43		300.00	300.00

INTERNATIONAL YEAR OF DISABLED PERSONS (2)

45	20 Dollars (Ag) 1983		20.00	30.00
46	200 Dollars (Au) 1983		275.00	275.00

WORLD FISHERIES CONFERENCE (2)

47	2 Dollars 1983. Arms. Rev. Long-necked Croaker fish (Pseudotolithus typus).		
	a) (Ag)		30.00
	b) (Ag), Pièfort		-.-
	c) (Cu-Ni)	5.00	
48	2 Dollars (Au) 1983. Type as No. 47		1000.00

INTERNATIONAL GAMES

49	25 Dollars (Ag) 1984. Rev. Basketball	-.-

Libyen # Libya Libye

Area: 674,358 sq. mi. Population: 3,860,000.

Formerly under Turkish sovereignty, this North African country came to be governed by Italy in 1911. In 1934, following several military campaigns against the Senussi (1914–1932). Italy succeeded in uniting Cyrenaica and Tripolitania with Fezzan, thus creating the Colony of Libya. On October 7, 1951, the territory became an independent kingdom, and on September 1, 1969 the Libyan Arab Republic.

Capital: Tripolis, future capital: Beida.

10 Millièmes= 1 Piastre, 100 Piastres = 1 £;
since 28th August 1971: 1000 Dirham = 1 Libyan Dinar

			VF	XF
1 (1)	1	Millième (Br) 1952. Idris I (1890–1983), head right. Value in wreath, with crown above	0.20	0.50
2 (2)	2	Millièmes (Br) 1952	0.20	0.50
3 (3)	5	Millièmes (Br) 1952	0.30	0.70
4 (4)	1	Piastre (Cu–Ni) 1952	0.50	1.00
5 (5)	2	Piastres (Cu–Ni) 1952	0.60	1.40
6 (6)	1	Millième (Ni–Bra) 1965. Coat of arms. ℞ value in wreath	0.10	0.30
7 (7)	5	Millièmes (Ni–Bra) 1965 (scalloped)	0.20	0.60
8 (8)	10	Millièmes (Cu–Ni) 1965	0.25	0.70
9 (9)	20	Millièmes (Cu–Ni) 1965	0.50	1.50
10 (10)	50	Millièmes (Cu–Ni) 1965 (scalloped)	0.60	2.00

11 (11)	100	Millièmes (Cu–Ni) 1965	0.80	2.50

LIBYAN ARAB REPUBLIC 1969-1977

NEW CURRENCY: 1000 Dirham = 1 Libyan Dinar

		XF	Unc
12 (12)	1 Dirham (Brass-clad steel) 1975. Coat of arms, date. Rev. value within ornament	3.00	5.00
13 (13)	5 Dirhams (Brass-clad steel) 1975. Type as No. 12	2.50	4.00
14 (14)	10 Dirhams (Cu-Ni-clad steel) 1975. Type as No. 12	2.00	3.50
15 (15)	20 Dirhams (Cu-Ni-clad steel) 1975. Type as No. 12	3.00	6.00
16 (16)	50 Dirhams (Cu-Ni) 1975. Type as No. 12 (scalloped)	4.00	6.50
17 (17)	100 Dirhams (Cu-Ni) 1975. Type as No. 12	4.50	7.00

SOCIALIST PEOPLE'S LIBYAN ARAB JAMAHIRIYA since 1977

18 (18)	1 Dirham (Brass-clad steel) 1979	–.–	–.–
19 (19)	5 Dirhams (Brass-clad steel) 1979	–.–	–.–
20 (20)	10 Dirhams (Brass-clad steel) 1979	–.–	–.–
21 (21)	20 Dirhams (Brass-clad steel) 1979	–.–	–.–
22 (22)	50 Dirhams (Cu-Ni) 1979	–.–	–.–
23 (23)	100 Dirhams (Cu-Ni) 1979	–.–	–.–

INTERNATIONAL YEAR OF DISABLED PERSONS (2)

		Unc	Proof
24 (24)	5 Dinars (Ag) 1981:		
	a) normal thickness	30.00	35.00
	b) Pièfort		75.00
25 (25)	70 Dinars (Au) 1981:		
	a) normal thickness	300.00	300.00
	b) Pièfort		1000.00

All valuations in the SCHÖN are stated in U.S. Dollars.

Liechtenstein

Area: 61 sq. mi. Population: 23,000.

On January 23, 1719, Karl VI combined the immediate states of the empire, Schellenberg, and Vaduz, thus creating the principality of Liechtenstein. A member of the German Confederation (Deutscher Bund) from 1815 to 1866, Liechtenstein formed a customs and tax district with the Austrian Vorarlberg in 1852 (to 1919), and finally entered into the Customs and Monetary Union of Switzerland in 1924.

Capital: Vaduz.

150 Kreuzer = 1½ Gulden = 1 Vereinstaler (Konventionstaler)
100 Heller = 1 Krone; since 1924: 100 Rappen = 1 Franken

JOHANN II 1858–1929

			VF	XF
1 (1)	1	Vereinstaler (Ag) 1862. Johann II, head right. ℞ mantled coat of arms with crown	800.00	1250.00
		Modern special issue in gold, with mint mark "M"		550.00
2 (2)	1	Krone (Ag) 1900–1915	12.00	16.00
3 (3)	2	Kronen (Ag) 1912–1915	16.00	40.00

4 (4)	5	Kronen (Ag) 1900–1915	150.00	170.00
5 (5)	10	Kronen (Au) 1900. Johann II (1840–1929), head left. ℞ coat of arms	1700.00	2200.00

			VF	XF
6 (6)	20	Kronen (Au) 1898. Same type as No. 5	1800.00	2200.00
7 (7)	½	Franken (Ag) 1924	35.00	55.00
8 (8)	1	Franken (Ag) 1924	25.00	35.00
9 (9)	2	Franken (Ag) 1924	35.00	55.00
10 (10)	5	Franken (Ag) 1924	220.00	300.00

FRANZ I 1929–1938

			VF	XF
11 (11)	10	Franken (Au) 1930. Franz I (1853–1938), head right. ℞ coat of arms	650.00	800.00
12 (12)	20	Franken (Au) 1930	700.00	850.00

FRANZ JOSEPH II since 1938

			VF	XF
13 (13)	10	Franken (Au) 1946. Franz Joseph II (*1906), head left. ℞ coat of arms	125.00	140.00
14 (14)	20	Franken (Au) 1946	150.00	175.00
15 (15)	25	Franken (Au) 1956. Franz Joseph II and Princess Georgina (Gina) of Wilczek (*1921). ℞ coat of arms	165.00	185.00
16 (16)	50	Franken (Au) 1956. Same type as No. 15	220.00	230.00

			VF	XF
17 (17)	100	Franken (Au) 1952. Same type as No. 15	1600.00	1800.00

COMMEMORATIVE ISSUES (2) FOR THE CENTENNIAL OF THE BANK OF LIECHTENSTEIN

			Unc
18 (18)	25	Franken (Au) 1961	500.00
19 (19)	50	Franken (Au) 1961	1000.00

Litauen # Lithuania **Lithuanie**
Lietuva

Area: 25,200 sq. mi. Population: 2,550,000 (1938).
Having succeeded in uniting the Lithuanian tribes of the upper Memel
and Duna, Grand Duke Gedimin created the large Lithuanian Empire
during the 14th century. In 1386 Jagaila accepted as Jagiello the Polish
royal dignity, thus creating a basis for unity throughout the empire.
Following the dismemberment of Poland (1772, 1793, 1795), the entire
Lithuanian territory fell to Russia. The independent Republic was
proclaimed on November 2, 1918. The Soviet Republic was created on
July 21, 1940. Since August 3rd of that year, Lithuania has been, with
occasional interruptions, a member state of the Soviet Union.
Capital: Kaunas (Kovno), 1920–1940, provisional capital instead of
Vilna.

100 Centu = 1 Litas

			VF	XF
1 (1)	1	Centas (Al–Br) 1925. Rider on horse-back, "Vytis", principal design of the state of arms. ℞ value	6.00	12.00
2 (2)	5	Centai (Al–Br) 1925	3.50	6.00

3 (3)	10	Centu (Al–Br) 1925	4.00	6.50
4 (4)	20	Centu (Al–Br) 1925	4.50	7.50
5 (5)	50	Centu (Al–Br) 1925	6.50	11.50
6 (6)	1	Litas (Ag) 1925	6.00	9.00
7 (7)	2	Litu (Ag) 1925	8.00	12.00
8 (8)	5	Litai (Ag) 1925	16.00	36.00
9 (9)	1	Centas (Br) 1936	2.50	5.00

10 (10)	2	Centai (Br) 1936	5.00	10.50

		VF	XF
11 (11)	5 Centai (Br) 1936	4.50	7.50
12 (12)	5 Litai (Ag) 1936. Dr. Jonas Basanavicius (1851–1927), doctor of medicine, politician and co-founder of "Auštra", the first newspaper appearing in Lithuanian, in 1883. ℞ rider on horse-back, "Vytis"	7.50	12.00

13 (13)	10 Litu (Ag) 1936. Witold, also Witowt or Vytautas Didysis (c. 1350–1430), Grand Duke of Lithuania 1392–1430. ℞ rider on horse-back, "Vytis"	16.00	26.00

COMMEMORATIVE COIN FOR
THE 20th ANNIVERSARY OF THE REPUBLIC

14 (14)	10 Litu (Ag) 1938. "The three pillars of Grand Duke Gediminas", also found on Lithuanian seals of the 15th century. Name of country, anniversary numerals, commemorative legend. ℞ Anton Smetona (1874 to 1944), President of Lithuania 1919–1921 and 1926–1940	38.00	50.00

Luxemburg **Luxembourg** Luxembourg
Letzeburg

Area: 998 sq. mi. Population: 370,000.

The Duchy of Luxembourg was declared a Grand Duchy in 1815 by a resolution of the Congress of Vienna and in personal union with the Dutch crown and with membership of the Deutsche Bund (German Confederation). At the London Conference of 1839 the great powers decided that the Walloon part as well as a part of the German-speaking territories be detached from Luxembourg. This territorial section was attached to the Belgian Kingdom as "Province de Luxembourg". From 1839 Luxembourg exists as a recognized independent state in its present form.

In 1842 Luxembourg joined the German Customs Union and thus also accepted the responsibilities of the Dresden Monetary Convention of 1838. Upon the restoration of the Customs Union in 1847, Luxembourg left the Dresden Monetary Union. Taking the difficulties into consideration with which the introduction of a new monetary, weights and measures system is connected, the states in the Customs Union declared their willingness to allow the Grand Duchy of Luxembourg to retain the decimal system introduced, as well as the French monetary standard for the duration of the treaty. With the dissolution of the German Confederation in 1867, Luxembourg remeined in the German Customs Union until 1918.

Luxembourg was connected with the Netherlands in a personal union until 1890. When the male line died out of the Dutch royal house, the House of Nassau took over the offices of state in accordance with the right of succession.

The economic union as well as the currency agreement with Belgium were concluded in 1921. The duration of the agreement was initially for 50 years and in 1971 was extended for a further 10 years after previous negotiations.

Capital: Luxembourg.

The gold strikes issued in the Grand Duchy of Luxembourg in the years 1953, 1963 and 1964, weighing 20 francs as well as in 1964 weighing 40 francs must be looked upon as commemorative medallions.

100 Centimes = 1 Luxembourg Franc (Frang)

ADOLPHE 1890–1905

			VF	XF
1 (1)	2½	Centimes (Cu) 1901. Crowned coat of arms. ℞ value in wreath	3.00	6.00
2 (10)	5	Centimes (Cu–Ni) 1901. Adolphe (1817–1905), head right. ℞ value in wreath	1.60	3.20
3 (11)	10	Centimes (Cu–Ni) 1901. Same type as No. 2	1.20	2.50

WILLIAM IV 1905-1912

4 (1)	2½	Centimes (Cu) 1908. Same type as No. 1	3.00	4.50

5 (12)	5	Centimes (Cu-Ni) 1908. William IV (1852-1912), head right. Rev. value in wreath	1.20	2.50

MARIE ADELAIDE 1912–1919

6 (4)	5	Centimes (Z) 1915. Name of country and date. Value (center hole)	4.50	9.00
7 (5)	10	Centimes (Z) 1915. Same type as No. 6	4.00	8.00
8 (6)	25	Centimes (Z) 1916. Same type as No. 6	7.00	12.00
9 (7)	5	Centimes (Fe) 1918. Coat of arms. ℞ value in wreath	4.00	8.00
10 (8)	10	Centimes (Fe) 1918. Same type as No. 9	3.00	6.00

CHARLOTTE 1919–1964

11 (7)	5	Centimes (Fe) 1921, 1922. Same type as No. 9	9.00	12.50
12 (8)	10	Centimes (Fe) 1921, 1923. Same type as No. 10	16.00	30.00

			VF	XF
13 (9)	25	Centimes (Fe) 1919–1922	6.00	12.00
14 (13)	5	Centimes (Cu–Ni) 1924. Crowned monogram. ℞ value in wreath	0.40	0.80
15 (14)	10	Centimes (Cu–Ni) 1924	0.60	1.20
16 (15)	25	Centimes (Cu–Ni) 1927. Crowned coat of arms. ℞ value and oak branch	1.20	2.00
17 (17)	1	Franc (Ni) 1924–1935. Steel worker	1.20	1.80
18 (18)	2	Francs (Ni) 1924. Same type as No. 17	2.50	4.50
19 (19)	5	Francs (Ag) 1929. Charlotte (*1896), head left. ℞ coat of arms	6.50	11.00
20 (20)	10	Francs (Ag) 1929. Same type as No. 19	9.00	15.00
21 (21)	5	Centimes (Br) 1930. Charlotte, head left. ℞ value	0.40	0.80
22 (22)	10	Centimes (Br) 1930. Charlotte, head left. ℞ value	0.40	0.80
23 (15b)	25	Centimes (Br) 1930. Crowned coat of arms. Rev. value and oak branch	1.60	3.00
24 (15a)	25	Centimes (Cu–Ni) 1938. Type as No. 23	2.00	3.50
25 (16)	50	Centimes (Ni) 1930. Steel worker. ℞ value and ears of wheat	1.60	2.50
26 (24)	1	Franc (Cu–Ni) 1939. Crowned monogram. ℞ standing figure, allegory of agriculture	0.80	1.20

COMMEMORATIVE COINS (3)
FOR THE 600th ANNIVERSARY OF THE BATTLE OF CRECY AND IN MEMORY OF THE HEROIC DEATH IN ACTION OF JOHN THE BLIND

			VF	XF
27 (28)	20	Francs (Ag) 1946. Prince Jean, head facing left. Escutcheons: Bourbon/Parma and Luxembourg. ℞ John the Blind (1296 to 26th Aug. 1346), Duke of Luxembourg and King of Bohemia 1310–1346	8.00	16.00
28 (29)	50	Francs (Ag) 1946. Same type as No. 27	15.00	25.00

			VF	XF
29 (30)	100	Francs (Ag) 1946. Same type as No. 27		
		a) with name of engraver	35.00	50.00
		b) without name of engraver (restrike 1964)	70.00	100.00
30 (25)	25	Centimes (Br) 1946, 1947. Crowned coat of arms. Rev. value and oak branch	0.25	0.50
31 (26)	1	Franc (Cu–Ni) 1946–1947. Steel worker. ℞ crowned monogram, value	0.40	0.60
32 (26)	1	Franc (Cu–Ni). Same type as No. 30, but size reduced		
		a) 1952	1.00	1.80
		b) 1953–1964	0.15	0.25
33 (27)	5	Francs (Cu–Ni) 1949. Charlotte, head left. ℞ value between roses, crown above	1.00	1.60
34 (25a)	25	Centimes (Al) 1954-1957, 1960, 1963. Type as No. 30	0.20	0.50
35 (31)	5	Francs (Cu–Ni) 1962. Charlotte, head right. ℞ crowned coat of arms	0.60	1.00
36 (32)	100	Francs (Ag) 1963. Charlotte, head right. ℞ crowned coat of arms	18.00	30.00

COMMEMORATIVE COIN FOR THE MILLENARY OF LUXEMBOURG CITY

37 (33)	250	Francs (Ag) 1963. Charlotte, head right, memorial legend. ℞ medieval fortress and value	110.00	160.00

JEAN since 1964

			XF	Unc
38 (25a)	25	Centimes (Al) 1965, 1967, 1968, 1970, 1972. Type as No. 34	0.10	0.20
39 (34)	1	Franc (Cu-Ni) 1965, 1966, 1968, 1970, 1972, 1973, 1976–1984. Jean (*1921), head left. Rev. crown, value	0.12	0.25

			XF	Unc

40 (35) 5 Francs (Cu-Ni) 1971, 1976, 1979, 1981. Head of Grand Duke Jean. R value, date, flanked by two oak branches ... 0.20 ... 0.40

41 (36) 10 Francs (Ni) 1971, 1972, 1974, 1976, 1977–1980, 1982. Head of Grand Duke Jean. Rev. value between oak leaves, crown above, date ... 0.30 ... 0.60

42 (37) 20 Francs (Ni) 1980–1983. Rev. value between oak leaves ... 0.70 ... 1.00

43 (38) 100 Francs (Ag) 1964. Jean, head left. Rev. crowned coat of arms ... 8.00 ... 12.00

				Proof

44 (25b) 25 Centimes (Ag) 1980. Type as No. 34 ... 17.50
45 (26c) 1 Franc (Ag) 1980. Type as No. 32 ... 25.00
46 (34a) 1 Franc (Ag) 1980. Type as No. 39 ... 25.00
47 (31a) 5 Francs (Ag) 1980. Type as No. 35 ... 36.00
48 (35a) 5 Francs (Ag) 1980. Type as No. 40 ... 36.00
49 (36a) 10 Francs (Ag) 1980. Type as No. 41 ... 50.00
50 (37a) 20 Francs (Ag) 1980. Type as No. 42 ... 60.00

			XF	Unc

51 1 Franc (Cu-Ni) 1986 ... 0.20 ... 0.40
52 5 Francs (Bra) 1986 ... 0.20 ... 0.40
55 50 Francs (Ni) 1987 ... 1.00 ... 1.60

Nos. 53 and 54 omitted.

Macao

Area: 6 sq. mi. Population: 280,000.
An island in the Canton river delta in South China; Macao has been Portuguese Territory since 1557. Maintaining the status of an Overseas Province for centuries, it was only during the years of 1930 to 1951, that Macao held the position of a colony.
Capital: Macao.

100 Avos = 1 Pataca

			VF	XF
1 (1)	5	Avos (Br) 1952. Coat of arms with mural crown. ℞ value	1.20	2.00
2 (2)	10	Avos (Br) 1952	0.60	1.20
3 (3)	50	Avos (Cu-Ni) 1952-1973		
		a) 1952, 20 mm dia.	1.20	2.00
		b) 1972, 1973, 23 mm dia.	0.70	1.20
4 (4)	1	Pataca (Ag) 1952	3.00	4.00

			VF	XF
5 (5)	5	Patacas (Ag) 1952, 1971:		
		a) 1952. Fine silver content 720	5.00	8.00
		b) 1971. Fine silver content 650	3.00	5.00
6 (1a)	5	Avos (Ni-Bra) 1967	0.20	0.40
7 (2a)	10	Avos (Ni-Bra) 1967–1969, 1975, 1976	0.25	0.40
8 (6)	1	Pataca 1968–1980. Type as No. 4:		
		a) (Ni) 1968, 1975	0.60	1.20
		b) (Ni) 1972	–.–	–.–
		c) (Cu-Ni) 1980	0.50	1.00

OPENING OF MACAO-TAIPA BRIDGE

			Unc	Proof
9 (7)	20	Patacas (Ag) 1974. Junk and Macao-Taipa bridge	10.00	27.50

			XF	Unc
10 (A3)	50	Avos (Cu-Ni) 1978. Type as No. 1	0.50	1.00

Nos. 11–13 omitted.

25th ANNIVERSARY OF GRAND PRIX (4)

			Proof
14 (8)	100 Patacas (Ag) 1978. With inscriptions on race car		125.00
15 (9)	500 Patacas (Au) 1978. Type as No. 14		275.00

			Proof
16 (8a)	100 Patacas (Ag) 1978. Type as 14, but without inscriptions on race car		45.00
17 (9a)	500 Patacas (Au) 1978. Type as No. 16		175.00

YEAR OF THE GOAT (2)

			Proof
18 (10)	100 Patacas (Ag) 1979		45.00
19 (11)	500 Patacas (Au) 1979		160.00

YEAR OF THE MONKEY (2)

		Unc	Proof
20 (12)	100 Patacas (Ag) 1980	35.00	45.00
21 (13)	1000 Patacas (Au) 1980		350.00

YEAR OF THE COCKEREL (2)

		Unc	Proof
22 (14)	100 Patacas (Ag) 1981	35.00	45.00
23 (15)	1000 Patacas (Au) 1981	350.00	400.00

		XF	Unc
24 (16)	10 Avos (Al-Br) 1982, 1983	0.10	0.20
25 (17)	20 Avos (Al-Br) 1982, 1983	0.10	0.20
26 (18)	50 Avos (Al-Br) 1982, 1983	0.20	0.40
27 (19)	1 Pataca (Cu-Ni) 1982, 1983	0.30	0.65
28 (20)	5 Patacas (Cu-Ni) 1982, 1983	0.75	1.50

Area: 228,000 sq. mi. Population: 9,100,000.
The world's fourth largest island, off the southeast coast of Africa, in the Indian Ocean. In 1885 France succeeded in establishing a protectorate, and in 1896 Madagascar became a French Colony. After holding the status of an autonomous republic of the French Community, independence was declared on June 26, 1960. The Republic of Madagascar remained a member of the French Community; its name was recently changed to »Repoblika Malagasy«.
Capital: Tananarive.

100 Centimes = 1 Franc, 5 Franc = 1 Ariary

	FRENCH COLONY	VF	XF
1 (1)	50 Centimes (Br) 1943. Gallic rooster. ℞ cross of Lorraine	3.00	7.00
2 (2)	1 Franc (Br) 1943. Same type as No. 1	4.00	7.50
3 (3)	1 Franc (Al) 1948–1958. Marianne, allegory of the French Republic. ℞ heads of zebus	0.60	1.50

4 (4)	2 Francs (Al) 1948. Same type as No. 3	0.40	1.00
5 (5)	5 Francs (Al) 1953. Same type as No. 3	0.60	1.50
6 (6)	10 Francs (Al–Br) 1953. Marianne, head left. ℞ map of Madagascar, zebu horns, value	1.00	2.00
7 (7)	20 Francs (Al–Br) 1953	1.50	3.00

REPUBLIC

8 (8)	1 Franc (St) 1965, 1966, 1970, 1974, 1975, 1977, 1979, 1982. Poinsetta (Euphorbia pulcherrima – Euphorbiaceae). Rev. head of zebu, laurel branches, value	0.75	2.00

			VF	XF

9 (9) 2 Francs (St) 1965, 1970, 1974, 1975, 1983. Same type as No. 8 — 0.75 — 2.00

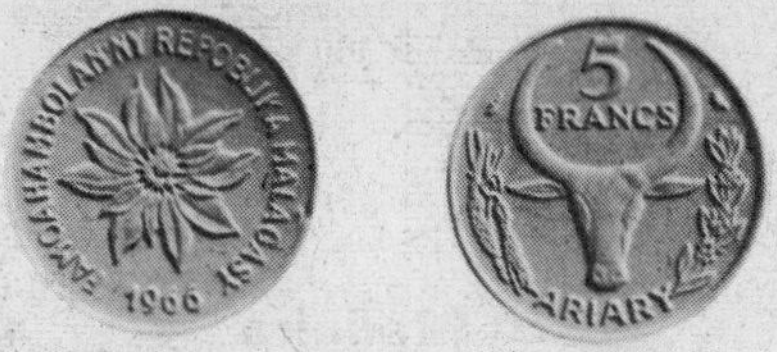

10 (10) 5 Francs (St) 1966–1968, 1970, 1972, 1979, 1983. Same type as No. 8 — 1.75 — 3.50

FAO COIN PLAN AND THE 10th ANNIVERSARY OF INDEPENDENCE (2)

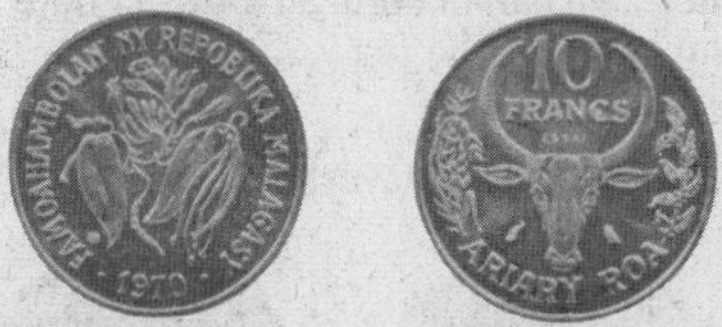

11 (11) 10 Francs (Al-Br) 1970–1976, 1980, 1982. Genuine vanilla (Vanilla planifolia – Orchidaceae) — 0.75 — 1.75

12 (12) 20 Francs (Al-Br) 1970–1976, 1978. Cotton plant (Gossypium sp. – Malvaceae). Rev. like No. 11 — 2.00 — 4.00

DEMOCRATIC REPUBLIC OF MADAGASCAR

FOR THE FAO COIN PLAN (2)

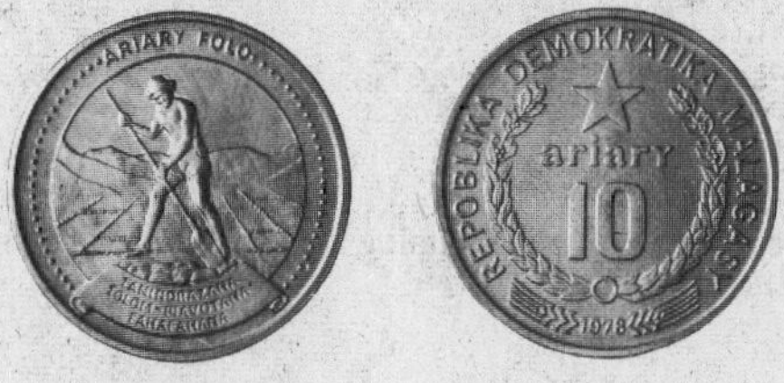

13 (13) 10 Ariary 1978:
  a) (Ag) — — 15.00
  b) (Cu-Ni) — 5.00

14 (14) 20 Ariary 1978:
  a) (Ag) — — 25.00
  b) (Cu-Ni) — 8.00

Area: 307 sq. mi. Population: 280,000.
The island group in the Atlantic was colonized in 1419 and since then considered to be an integrated part of Portugal. British troops occupied the islands in 1801, and again in 1807–14.
Capital: Funchal.

100 Centavos = 1 Escudo

			Unc	Proof
1 (4)	25	Escudos 1981. Gonçalves Zarco, navigator, discoverer of Madeira:		
		a) (Ag)		17.50
		b) (Cu-Ni)	2.50	
2 (5)	100	Escudos 1981. Type as No. 1:		
		a) (Ag)		25.00
		b) (Cu-Ni)	5.00	

Previous issues, see »Weltmünzkatalog 19. Jahrhundert« (World Coin Catalogue of the 19th Century).

Malawi   **Malawi**   **Malawi**

Area: 49,177 sq. mi. Population: 7,000,000.
The former British Protectorate of Nyasaland was renamed Malawi. Between 1953 and 1963 the Central African Federation consisted of Northern Rhodesia, Southern Rhodesia and Nyasaland (called Rhodesia and Nyasaland), but on July 6, 1964, Malawi became independent. On July 6, 1966 Malawi attained the position of a republic within the British Commonwealth.
Capital: Zomba (to be replaced by Lilongwe).

12 Pence = 1 Shilling, 2 Shillings = 1 Florin,
5 Shillings = 1 Crown, 20 Shillings = 1 Malawi Pound;
since February 15, 1971: 100 Tambala = 1 Malawi Kwacha

		XF	Unc
1 (1)	6 Pence (Ni–Bra) 1964. Dr. Hastings Kamuzu Banda (*1906), prime minister. ℞ domestic cock (Gallus gallus domesticus – Phasianidae), emblem of the Malawi Congress Party	1.00	3.00

2 (2)	1 Shilling (Ni–Bra) 1964. ℞ corn cob (Zea mays – Gramineae)	1.50	4.00
3 (3)	1 Florin (Ni–Bra) 1964. ℞ African elephant (Loxodonta africana – Elephantidae)	2.00	6.00
4 (4)	½ Crown (Ni–Bra) 1964. ℞ coat of arms	3.00	7.50

COMMEMORATIVE COIN FOR THE DAY
OF THE REPUBLIC ON JULY 6, 1966

		Proof	
5 (5)	1 Crown (Cu-Ni) 1966	Proof	16.00
6 (6)	1 Penny (Br) 1967, 1968. Value and date. Rev. value	0.50	1.00

NEW CURRENCY: 100 Tambala = 1 Kwacha

			XF	Unc
7 (7)	1	Tambala (Br) 1971–. Dr. Hastings Ka-muzu Banda. R domestic cock (Emblem of the Malawi Congress Party)	0.15	0.25

			XF	Unc
8 (8)	2	Tambala (Br) 1971–. R blue crane (Steganura paradisaea, family of weaver birds – Ploceidae)	0.15	0.30
9 (9)	5	Tambala (Cu-Ni) 1971. R purple heron. (Ardea purpurea – Ardeidae)	0.20	0.40
10 (10)	10	Tambala (Cu-Ni) 1971. R corn cob	0.30	0.60
11 (11)	20	Tambala (Cu-Ni) 1971. R African elephant	0.60	2.00
12 (12)	1	Kwacha (Cu-Ni) 1971. R coat of arms	2.00	4.00

10th ANNIVERSARY OF INDEPENDENCE

			Unc	Proof
13 (13)	10	Kwacha (Ag) 1974. Head right of President Banda. Rev. map, value and independence date between chain, above coat of arms	15.00	25.00

10th ANNIVERSARY OF THE RESERVE BANK OF MALAWI (2)

			Unc	Proof
14 (14)	10	Kwacha (Ag) 1975. Rev. Emblem of the Reserve Bank	15.00	22.50
15	10	Kwacha (Au) 1975. Type as No. 14; .916 ⅔ gold, 49.099 g		1500.00

CONSERVATION COMMEMORATIVE (3)

16 (15)	5	Kwacha (Ag) 1978. Rev. Crawshay's Zebra:		
		a) .925 silver, 25.31 g	20.00	
		b) .925 silver, 28.28 g		40.00
17 (16)	10	Kwacha (Ag) 1978. Rev. Sable Antelope:		
		a) .925 silver, 31.65 g	25.00	
		b) .925 silver, 35.00 g		50.00
18 (17)	250	Kwacha (Au) 1978. Rev. Nyalas (Tragelaphus angari – Bovidae); .900 gold, 33.437 g)	650.00	800.00

Formerly known as Straits Settlements, the Malay States were jointly administered until 1946.
Capital: Kuala Lumpur.
The Straits Dollar, simultaneously valid also in British North Borneo, Brunei and Sarawak, was substituted on 1st April 1946 by the new currency unit, the Malaya Dollar.

100 Cents = 1 Dollar

GEORGE VI 1936–1952

			VF	XF
1 (1)	½	Cent (Br) 1940. George VI, crowned head left. ℞ value and new legend COMMISSIONERS OF MALAYA, date (square)	0.80	1.50
2 (2)	1	Cent (Br) 1939–1941 (square)	0.20	0.60
3 (3)	5	Cents (Cu–Ni) 1939–1945 (round)	0.70	1.50
4 (4)	10	Cents (Cu–Ni) 1939–1945 (round)	1.00	2.00
5 (5)	20	Cents (Cu–Ni) 1939–1945 (round)	2.00	4.00
6 (2a)	1	Cent (Br) 1943–1945 (square; reduced size)	0.20	0.40
7 (7)	5	Cents (Cu–Ni) 1948–1950. George VI, crowned head left; new legend KING GEORGE THE SIXTH (round)	0.30	0.80
8 (8)	10	Cents (Cu–Ni) 1948–1950 (round)	0.40	0.90
9 (9)	20	Cents (Cu–Ni) 1948–1950 (round)	0.60	1.20

For further issues, see under Malaya and British Borneo, Malaysia, Brunei and Singapore.

Values are given for each coin in U.S. Dollars and reference to Yeoman-numbers.

Malaya and British Borneo
Malaya und Britisch-Borneo   Malaisie et Bornéo Britannique

Joint issues of Malaya, Singapore, the British territories on Borneo (Kalimantan) such as Brunei, North Borneo (in 1963 renamed Sabah), and Sarawak.

100 Cents = 1 Dollar

ELIZABETH II 1952–1963

			VF	XF
1 (A1)	1	Cent (Br) 1956–1961. Elizabeth II, head right. ℞ value in circle (square)	0.15	0.30
2 (1)	5	Cents (Cu–Ni) 1953–1961. ℞ value in dotted circle	0.20	0.40
3 (2)	10	Cents (Cu–Ni) 1953–1961. Same type as No. 2	0.40	0.80
4 (3)	20	Cents (Cu–Ni) 1954–1961. Same type as No. 2	0.40	0.80
5 (4)	50	Cents (Cu–Ni) 1954–1961. Same type as No. 2	1.00	2.00
6 (5)	1	Cent (Br) 1962. Crossed Malayan daggers (Kris). ℞ value	0.20	0.30

For further issues see *Brunei*, *Malaysia* and *Singapore*.

Area: 127,334 sq. mi. Population: 15,400,000.
The monarchical, federated State of Malaysia was created on September 16, 1963. Malaysia includes the territories of Malaya (Johor, Kedah, Kelantan, Malakka, Negri, Sembilan, Pahang, Penang, Perak, Perlis, Selangor, and Trengganu), as well as Sabah und Sarawak on Borneo or Kalimantan. Independent by now, Singapore withdrew from the federation on August 9, 1965. Capital: Kuala Lumpur.

100 Sen = 1 Malaysian Dollar (Ringgit)

			XF	Unc
1 (1)	1 Sen 1967–. Parliament building in Kuala Lumpur and state emblem. Rev. value.			
	a) (Bro) 1967, 1968, 1970, 1971, 1973, 1976 (100 pcs.)		0.10	0.20
	1980, Proof only		–.–	–.–
				2.00
	b) (Cu-clad steel) 1973, 1976–1986		0.10	0.15
2 (2)	5 Sen (Cu-Ni) 1967–. Type as No. 1		0.10	0.20
3 (3)	10 Sen (Cu-Ni) 1967–. Type as No. 1		0.12	0.25
4 (4)	20 Sen (Cu-Ni) 1967–. Type as No. 1		0.20	0.30

			XF	Unc
5 (5)	50 Sen (Cu-Ni) 1967–1986. Type as No. 1:			
	a) 1967 – 1969 (»Security edge«)		0.50	1.00
	b) 1971, 1973, 1977–1986 (edge inscription: »BANK NEGARA MALAYSIA«)		0.40	0.75
6 (7)	1 Ringgit (Cu-Ni) 1971, 1980–1982, 1984, 1985. Parliament building in front of arms		0.75	1.50

10th ANNIVERSARY OF THE BANK NEGARA MALAYSIA

			Unc	Proof
7 (6)	1	Dollar 1969. Ismail Nasirudin (* 1907), Sultan (Tuanku) of Trenganu and 4th king (Yang di-Pertuan Agong) of Malaysia. ℞ value in wreath of hibiscus blossoms (Hibiscus rosasinensis – Malvaceae), with state emblem above		
		a) (Ag) .925 silver, 16.85 g		300.00
		b) (German silver)	1.75	

			Unc	Proof
8 (8)	5	Ringgit (= Dollar) (Cu–Ni) 1971. Sultan (Tuanku) Abdul Rahman Putra Al-Haj. ℞ similar to No. 7	4.00	–.–
9 (9)	100	Ringgit (Au) 1971. Same type as No. 8	275.00	1250.00

KUALA LUMPUR ANNIVERSARY

			Unc	Proof
10 (10)	1	Dollar (Cu-Ni) 1972. Emblem, inscription. Rev. value, date	1.50	100.00

CONSERVATION COMMEMORATIVE (3)

			Unc	Proof
11 (11)	15	Ringgit (Ag) 1976. Coat of arms, date. Rev. banteng:		
		a) .925 silver, 25.31 g	20.00	
		b) .925 silver, 28.28 g		25.00

			Unc	Proof
12 (12)	25	Ringgit (Ag) 1976. Rev. rhinoceros hornbill:		
		a) .925 silver, 31.65 g	25.00	
		b) .925 silver, 35.00 g		35.00
13 (13)	500	Ringgit (Au) 1976. Rev. tapir	650.00	750.00

25th ANNIVERSARY OF THE EMPLOYEE PROVIDENT FUND (3)

14 (17)	1	Ringgit (Cu-Ni) 1976	1.25	5.00
15 (18)	25	Ringgit (Ag) 1976	25.00	50.00
16 (19)	250	Ringgit (Au) 1976	180.00	220.00

3rd FIVE-YEAR PLAN 1976/1980 (3)

17 (14)	1	Ringgit (Cu-Ni) 1976	1.25	5.00
18 (15)	10	Ringgit (Ag) 1976:		
		a) .925 silver, 10.82 g	10.00	17.50
		b) .925 silver, 10.43 g (struck in 1980)		17.50
19 (16)	200	Ringgit (Au) 1976; .900 gold, 7.43 g	125.00	150.00

			Unc	Proof
20 (20)	1 Ringgit (Cu-Ni) 1977		1.25	15.00
21 (21)	25 Ringgit (Ag) 1977, 1980. Map of Southeast Asia. Rev. Arms; .925 silver, 35 g:			
	1977		25.00	50.00
	1980			–.–
22 (22)	200 Ringgit (Au) 1977. Bajau Horseman. Rev. Arms; .900 gold, 7.43 g		150.00	200.00

20th ANNIVERSARY OF INDEPENDENCE

		Unc	Proof
23 (23)	1 Ringgit (Cu-Ni) 1977:		
	a) 1977 (as ill.)	1.25	
	b) 1977 FM		15.00

100th ANNIVERSARY OF NATURAL RUBBER PRODUCTION

		Unc
24 (24)	1 Ringgit (Ni) 1977	1.25

20th ANNIVERSARY OF BANK NEGARA MALAYSIA

		Unc	Proof
25 (25)	1 Ringgit 1979. Building of the Bank Negara Malaysia, emblem:		
	a) (Ag) .925 silver, 16.85 g, 1979		20.00
	b) (Ag) 1979 FM (struck in 1980)		–.–
	c) (Cu-Ni) 1979 (as ill.)	1.25	

15th CENTURY OF HEGIRA

 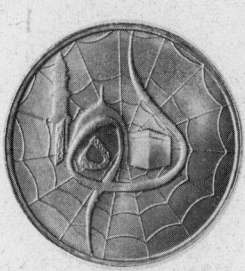

26 (26)	1 Ringgit (Cu-Ni) AH 1401 (1980)	1.50	

FIVE-YEAR PLAN 1981/1985 (3)

27 (27)	1 Ringgit (Cu-Ni) 1981. Tun Hussein Onn	1.25	
28 (28)	20 Ringgit (Ag) 1981. Type as No. 27	8.50	12.50
29 (29)	500 Ringgit (Au) 1981. Type as No. 27	225.00	350.00

25th ANNIVERSARY OF INDEPENDENCE (3)

30 (30)	1 Ringgit (Cu-Ni) 1982. Tunku Abdul Rahman Putra	1.25	7.50
31 (31)	25 Ringgit (Ag) 1982. Type as No. 30	20.00	25.00
32 (32)	500 Ringgit (Au) 1982. Type as No. 30	400.00	450.00

25th ANNIVERSARY OF BANK NEGARA MALAYSIA (2)

			Unc	Proof
33 (33)	1 Ringgit (Cu-Ni) 1984		1.25	

34 (34)	25 Ringgit (Ag) 1984		17.50	27.50

Malediven   # Maldive Islands   **Maldives (Iles)**

Area: 115 sq. mi. Population: 183,000.
Group of 12 atolls in the Indian Ocean, approximately 600 miles west of
Ceylon. British Protextorate since 1887, administrated by Ceylon. Sultanate,
but republic from January 1953 to February 1954. On July 26, 1965 the Maldivs attained full sovereignty, and withdrew from the British Commonwealth. On November 11, 1968 the Maldivs were again proclaimed a republic.
Capital: Malé.

100 Lari = 1 Rupee

MOHAMMED IMAD-EDIN 1900–1904

			VF	XF
1 (1)	1	Larin (Cu, Br, Bra) AH 1318 (1900); dia. 11 mm, 1 g	2.50	5.00
2 (2)	2	Lari (Cu, Br, Bra) AH 1319 (1901); dia. 13 mm, 1.8 g	2.50	5.00
3 (3.1)	4	Lariat (Cu, Br, Bra) AH 1320 (1902); dia. 17 mm, 3.7 g	12.50	25.00
4 (3)	4	Lariat (Cu, Br, Bra) AH 1320 (1902); dia. 17 mm, 3.7 g (without »Sanat«)	2.50	5.00

A4	4	Lariat (Ag) AH 1320 (1902). Type as No. 4; dia. 17 mm, 4.5 g	–.–	–.–

MOHAMMED SHAMS-EDIN 1904–1936

5 (5)	1	Lari (Br) AH 1331 (1913); dia. 13 mm, 0.9 g	2.50	5.00
6 (6)	4	Lariat (Br) AH 1331 (1913); dia. 19 mm, 3.3 g	3.50	6.50

MOHAMMED FARID DIDI 1954–1968

				XF	**Unc**
7 (10)	1 Lari (Br) 1960. Coat of arms. R value (round)			1.00	3.00

| **8** (11) | 2 Lari (Br) 1960 (square) | | | 0.40 | 0.60 |

| **9** (12) | 5 Lari (Ni-Bra) 1960, 1970 (scalloped) | | | 0.40 | 0.70 |
| **10** (13) | 10 Lari (Ni-Bra) 1960 (scalloped) | | | 0.60 | 1.20 |

| **11** (14) | 25 Lari (Ni-Bra) 1960, 1979 (round) | | | 0.70 | 1.50 |
| **12** (15) | 50 Lari (Ni-Bra) 1960, 1979 (round) | | | 1.00 | 2.50 |

| **13** (10a) | 1 Larin (Al) 1970, 1979. Same type as No. 7 | | | 0.20 | 0.40 |

| **14** (11a) | 2 Lari (Al) 1970, 1979. Same type as No. 8 | | | 0.30 | 0.50 |

ISSUES FOR THE FAO COIN PLAN (2)

| **15** (16) | 5 Rupees (Cu-Ni) 1977. Coat of arms, date. Rs. bonito (fish), value | | | 2.50 | 3.50 |
| **16** (17) | 20 Rupees (Ag) 1977. Rev. value between two fishes, one a bonito and the other a bluefin tuna | | | | 12.50 |

FOR THE FAO COIN PLAN (4)

			Unc	Proof
17 (18)	5	Rupees 1978. Lobster:		
		a) (Ag)		30.00
		b) (Cu-Ni)	4.00	
18	5	Rupees (Au) 1978. Type as No. 17		650.00
19 (19)	25	Rupees (Ag) 1978. Dhow (sailing ship)	18.00	40.00
20	25	Rupees (Au) 1978. Type as No. 19		850.00

FOR THE FAO COIN PLAN (2)

21 (20)	10	Rupees 1979:		
		a) (Ag)		25.00
		b) (Cu-Ni)	7.50	
22 (21)	100	Rupees (Ag) 1979:		
		a) .800 silver, 28.3 g	25.00	
		b) .925 silver, 28 g		30.00

INTERNATIONAL YEAR OF THE CHILD

23 (22)	20	Rupees (Ag) 1979:		
		a) normal thickness		25.00
		b) Pièfort		150.00

			XF	Unc
24 (12a)	5	Lari (Al) 1979. Type as No. 9	0.50	1.00
25 (13a)	10	Lari (Al) 1979. Type as No. 10	0.75	1.50

FOR THE FAO COIN PLAN (2)

			Unc	Proof
26 (23)	10	Rupees (Cu-Ni) 1980	7.50	
27 (24)	100	Rupees (Ag) 1980	25.00	40.00

No. 28 omitted.

WORLD FOOD DAY 1981

		Unc	Proof
29 (25) 100 Rufiyaa (Ag) 1981:			
a) .925 silver, 28.28 g			35.00
b) .500 silver, 28.28 g		25.00	

		XF	Unc
30	1 Laari (Al) 1984. Palm tree. Rev. Value (FAO issue)	0.10	0.20
31	5 Laari (Al) 1984. Bonitos. Rev. Value (FAO issue)	0.10	0.20
32	10 Laari (Al) 1984. Sailing ship »Odi«. Rev. Value (FAO issue)	0.20	0.30
33	25 Laari (Ni-Bra) 1984. Mosque. Rev. Value	0.25	0.50
34	50 Laari (Ni-Bra) 1984. Turtle. Rev. Value (FAO issue)	0.50	1.25
35	1 Rufiyaa (Cu-Ni) 1982, 1984. Arms. Rev. Value	1.00	2.00

Nos. 30–35, Proof set, 45.00

WORLD FISHERIES CONFERENCE

		Unc	Proof
36	20 Rufiyaa 1984. Tunny (Thunnus thynnus – Thunnidae):		
	a) (Ag) .925 silver, 28.28 g		30.00
	b) (Cu-Ni)	6.00	

INTERNATIONAL YEAR OF DISABLED PERSONS (2)

		Unc	Proof
37	100 Rufiyaa (Ag) 1984. Rev. International emblem, multiple:		
	a) .925 silver, 28.28 g	25.00	30.00
	b) Piéfort, .925 silver, 56.56 g		110.00
38	100 Rufiyaa (Au) 1984. Rev. Disabled people under umbrella:		
	a) .916⅔ gold, 15.98 g	300.00	350.00
	b) Piéfort, .916⅔ gold, 31.95 g (100 pcs.)		–.–

Area: 464,872 sq. mi. Population: 8,100,000.
Known as French Sudan, this territory belonged to French West Africa until 1958. With Senegal as a temporary member, the Mali Federation was founded in 1959. In 1960 Mali was proclaimed a republic.
Capital: Bamako.

100 Centimes = 1 CFA Franc;
since 2nd July 1962: 100 Centimes = 1 Mali Franc

COMMEMORATIVE ISSUE FOR INDEPENDENCE

			XF	Unc
1	10	Francs (Ag) 1960. Modibo Keita (*1915), President. Appropriate legend INDEPENDANCE 22 SEPT. 1960. ℞ state emblem, name of country, value, motto		20.00

			XF	Unc
2 (1)	5	Francs (Al) 1961. Hippopotamus' head (Hippopotamus amphibius – Hippopotamidae). ℞ value	0.60	1.00
3 (2)	10	Francs (Al) 1961. Horse's head. ℞ value	1.00	2.00
4 (3)	25	Francs (Al) 1961. Lion's head (Panthera leo – Felidae)	1.25	3.00

COMMEMORATIVE ISSUES (4) FOR MODIBO KEITA

				Proof
5	10	Francs (Au) 1967. Modibo Keita (*1915), President. ℞ coat of arms		60.00
6	25	Francs (Au) 1967. Same type as No. 5		150.00
7	50	Francs (Au) 1967. Same type as No. 5		250.00
8	100	Francs (Au) 1967. Same type as No. 5		500.00

			XF	Unc
9 (6)	10	Francs (Al) 1976. Rice plant	0.30	0.60
10 (7)	25	Francs (Al) 1976. Type as No. 9	0.50	1.00

Malta
State Malta; Stat ta'Malta

Area: 122 sq. mi. Population: 386,000.
Group auf islands in the Mediterranean, in British possession since 1800.
On 21st September 1964, Malta became an independent member of the British Commonwealth. The Parliament of Malta decided on 13th December 1974 with 49 to 6 votes that Malta should become a republic, that is with immediate effect. The former Governor-General (since 1971) will be the first president of the republic.
Capital: Valletta (il-Belt Valletta).

4 Farthings = 1 Penny, 12 Pence = 1 Shilling, 20 Shillings = 1 £;
since 16th May 1972: 1000 Mils = 100 Cents = 1 Malta-Pound
Except for the $^1/_3$ Farthing, British coins were legal tender.
Decimal System since 16th May, 1972.

EDWARD VII 1901–1910

			VF	XF
1 (3)	$^1/_3$ Farthing (Br) 1902. Edward VII, head right. ℞ value in wreath, with crown above		2.00	6.00

GEORGE V 1910–1936

2 (4)	$^1/_3$ Farthing (Br) 1913. Georg V, head left. R value in wreath with crown above		2.00	6.00

NEW CURRENCY (Decimal System):
10 Mils = 1 Cent, 100 Cents = 1 Maltese £

3 (5)	2 Mils (Al) 1972, 1976–1981		0.05	0.10
4 (6)	3 Mils (Al) 1972, 1976–1981		0.05	0.10

5 (7)	5 Mils (Al) 1972, 1976–1981		0.05	0.10
6 (8)	1 Cent (Br) 1972, 1975–1981		0.10	0.20

				XF	Unc
7 (9)	2	Cents (Cu-Ni) 1972, 1976–1982		0.10	0.20
8 (10)	5	Cents (Cu-Ni) 1972, 1976–1981		0.20	0.40
9 (11)	10	Cents (Cu-Ni) 1972, 1976–1981		0.40	0.90
10 (12)	50	Cents (Cu-Ni) 1972, 1976–1981		1.40	2.80
11 (13)	1	£ (Ag) 1972. National arms. R Manwel Dimech 1806–1921), politician			8.50
12 (14)	2	£ (Ag) 1972. R Fort St. Angelo			15.00

13 (15) 5 £ (Au) 1972. R Hand holding torch and outline of the islands of Malta and Gozo (Ghawdex)   60.00

14 (16) 10 £ (Au) 1972. R Kenur, a typical Maltese stone charcoal oven   100.00

15 (17) 20 £ (Au) 1972. R blue thrush (Monticola solitarius – Turtidae), national bird; rising sun   200.00

16 (18) 50 £ (Au) 1972. R Neptune, statue in front of the Governor General's Palace in Valletta   450.00

17 (19) 1 £ (Ag) 1973. Coat of arms. Rev. Sir Temi Zammit (1864–1935), historian   10.00

18 (20) 2 £ (Ag) 1973. Rev. Mdina gate   20.00

19 (21) 10 £ (Au) 1973. Rev. watch-tower   60.00

20 (22) 20 £ (Au) 1973. Rev. dolphin fountain   100.00

21 (23) 50 £ (Au) 1973. Rev. castle   250.00

22 (24) 2 £ (Ag) 1974. Coat of arms. Rev. Giov.
Francesco Abela (1582-1655), historian   8.50
23 (25) 4 £ (Ag) 1974. Rev. Cottonera gate   15.00
24 (26) 10 £ (Au) 1974. Rev. National flower   60.00
25 (27) 20 £ (Au) 1974. Rev. boat   100.00

				Unc
26 (28)	50 £ (Au) 1974. Rev. first Maltese coin			250.00
27 (29)	2 £ (Ag) 1975. Coat of arms. Rev. Alfonso Maria Galea (1861–1941), writer and philantropist			12.00
28 (30)	4 £ (Ag) 1975. Rev. St. Agatha's Tower at Qammieh			18.00
29 (31)	10 £ (Au) 1975. Rev. Maltese falcon			75.00
30 (32)	20 £ (Au) 1975. Rev. freshwater crab			150.00
31 (33)	50 £ (Au) 1975. Rev. ornamental stone balcony			300.00

1st ANNIVERSARY OF REPUBLIC OF MALTA

		Unc	Proof
32 (39)	25 Cents 1975–1981. New coat of arms (since Juli 11, 1975), date. Rev. value:		
	a) (Br) 1975		16.00
	b) (Bra) 1975	1.25	
	c) (Cu-Ni) 1976	50.00	5.00
	d) (Cu-Ni) 1977–1981	20.00	4.50
33 (34)	2 £ (Ag) 1975. Type as No. 27, but new coat of arms		Unc 8.50
34 (35)	4 £ (Ag) 1975. Type as No. 28, but new coat of arms		15.00
35 (36)	10 £ (Au) 1975. Type as No. 29, but new coat of arms		75.00
36 (37)	20 £ (Au) 1975. Type as No. 30, but new coat of arms		100.00
37 (38)	50 £ (Au) 1975. Type as No. 31, but new coat of arms		250.00
38 (40)	2 £ (Ag) 1976. Coat of arms. Rev. Guze' Ellul Mercer (1897-1961), politician and writer		8.50
39 (41)	4 £ (Ag) 1976. Rev. fort Manoel gate		13.00
40 (42)	10 £ (Au) 1976. Rev. swallow-tail butterfly		75.00
41 (43)	20 £ (Au) 1976. Rev. storm petrel bird		110.00
42 (44)	50 £ (Au) 1976. Rev. ornamental Maltese door knocker		250.00
43 (45)	1 £ (Ag) 1977	5.00	6.50
44 (46)	2 £ (Ag) 1977	10.00	13.50
45 (47)	5 £ (Ag) 1977	25.00	35.00

	Unc	Proof
46 (48)　25 £ (Au) 1977. Rev. First Gozo coin	125.00	150.00
47 (49)　50 £ (Au) 1977. Rev. Imnara	250.00	300.00
48 (50) 100 £ (Au) 1977. Rev. Sculpture „Les Gav-roches"	500.00	650.00

DEPARTURE OF FOREIGN FORCES

49 (51)　　1 £ (Ag) 1979	7.50	25.00

WORLD FOOD DAY 1981

50 (52)　　2 £ (Ag) 1981. Rev. fishing-boat, value	15.00	12.50

INTERNATIONAL YEAR OF THE CHILD

51 (53)　　5 £ (Ag) 1981. Hopscotch:	
a) normal thickness	30.00
b) Piéfort	125.00

10th ANNIVERSARY OF DECIMALIZATION (9)

			Unc	Proof
52 (54)	2 Mils (Al) 1982. Type as No. 3, but commemorative legend		3.00	1.00
53 (55)	3 Mils (Al) 1982. Type as No. 4		3.00	1.00
54 (56)	5 Mils (Al) 1982. Type as No. 5		3.00	1.50
55 (57)	1 Cent (Br) 1982. Type as No. 6		5.00	1.75
56 (58)	2 Cents (Cu-Ni) 1982. Type as No. 7		5.00	2.50
57 (59)	5 Cents (Cu-Ni) 1982. Type as No. 8		5.00	3.00
58 (60)	10 Cents (Cu-Ni) 1982. Type as No. 9		8.00	3.50
59 (61)	25 Cents (Cu-Ni) 1982. Type as No. 32		10.00	4.50
60 (62)	50 Cents (Cu-Ni) 1982. Type as No. 10		12.00	6.00

INTERNATIONAL YEAR OF DISABLED PERSONS (2)

61 (65)	5 £ (Ag) 1983:		
	a) .925 silver, 28.28 g	30.00	45.00
	b) Piéfort, .925 silver, 56.56 g		175.00
62 (66)	100 £ (Au) 1983. Head, Motto: »Understanding«:		
	a) .916 ⅔ gold, 15.98 g	300.00	350.00
	b) Piéfort, .916 ⅔ gold, 31.95 g (150 pcs.)		–.–

WORLD FISHERIES CONFERENCE (2)

63 (63)	1 £ (Cu-Ni) 1984	5.00	
64 (64)	5 £ (Ag) 1984		35.00

UNITED NATIONS DECADE FOR WOMEN 1976–1985

65 (71)	5 £ (Ag) 1984		30.00

MARITIME HERITAGE (4)

66 (67)	5 £ (Ag) 1984. Rev. »Strangier«, 1813		18.00
67 (68)	5 £ (Ag) 1984. Rev. »Tigre«, 1839		18.00
68 (69)	5 £ (Ag) 1984. Rev. »Wignacourt«, 1844		18.00
69 (70)	5 £ (Ag) 1984. Rev. »Providenza«, 1848		18.00

Mandschukuo   **Manchukuo**   **Mandchoukouo**

Ta Man Zhou Kuo

大 滿 洲 國

Area: 521,360 sq. mi. Population: 43,200,000.

Under the lax central government of the Republic of China Manchuria attained a relatively large measure of independence. This occurred in 1917, under the leadership of Marshal Tschang Tso-lin and his son Tshang Hue-liang. Following the Japanese occupation the State of Manchukuo was established on February 18, 1932, with the annexation of the Chinese Province of Jehol. Under Japanese auspices, Manchukuo is ruled by Pu Yi, the last emperor of the Manchu (Ching) Dynasty, that renounced the Chinese throne in 1911. In 1934 Manchukuo was declared an empire, and Pu Yi proclaimed the emperor.

The empire was dissolved when Soviet troups occupied the territory in August of 1945. Following the Soviet evacuation, Manchukuo was re-incorporated into China.

Capital: Hsinking.

Coin dates are referring to the two reigns:

Ta Tung 大 同 1932–1934

Kang Teh 康 德 1934–1945

The dates were always reckoned from the beginning of the reign.

10 Li 釐 = 1 Fen 分 ; 10 Fen = 1 Chiao 角 ;

100 Fen = 1 Yuan 圓

			VF	XF
1 (1)		5 Li (Cu) 1933, 1934. National flag in dotted circle, name of country, date, and reign in Chinese. On right and left of legend a five-pointed star. ℞ value in Chinese lettering between flower ornament	5.00	9.00
2 (2)		1 Fen (Cu) 1933, 1934. Same type as No. 1	2.00	4.00
3 (3)		5 Fen (Ni) 1933, 1934. Chrysanthemum in center. Name of country, date, and reign in Chinese legend. On left and		

right of legend a five-pointed star. ℞
value in Chinese lettering between two
dragons

	VF	XF
	1.20	2.00

4 (4) 1 Chiao (Ni) 1933, 1934. Same type as
No. 3 — 1.50 — 3.00

5 (5) 5 Li (Cu) 1934–1939. Same type as No. 1,
but new legend on obverse: Chinese
letters for the reign of Kang Teh
instead of Ta Tung — 4.00 — 8.00

6 (6) 1 Fen (Cu) 1934–1939. Same type as No. 2,
but new legend on obverse: Chinese
letters for the reign of Kang Teh
instead of Ta Tung — 2.00 — 4.00

7 (7) 5 Fen (Ni) 1934–1939. Same type as No. 3,
but new legend on obverse: Chinese
letters for the reign of Kang Teh
instead of Ta Tung — 2.00 — 4.00

8 (8) 1 Chiao (Ni) 1934–1939. Same type
as No. 4, but new legend on obverse:
Chinese letters for the reign of Kang
Teh instead of Ta Tung — 2.50 — 4.50

9 (9) 1 Fen (Al) 1939–1943. Stylized flower in

			VF	XF

center. Name of country, date, and
reign on new legend in Chinese. ℞
value in Chinese letters between rice
panicles 2.00 3.50

10(11) 5 Fen (Al) 1940–1943. Number 5 in
circle. Name of country, date, and
reign on new legend in Chinese letters
between flowers 2.00 3.50

11(12) 1 Chiao (Al) 1940–1942. Number 10 in
center. Name of country, date, and
reign on new legend in Chinese letters.
℞ value in Chinese letters between
flowers 2.00 3.50

12(10) 1 Chiao (Ni) 1940. Two winged horses
in centre. Name of country, date, and
reign on new legend in Chinese letters.
℞ value in Chinese letters in circle (sun)
surrounded by rays and clouds. On top,
a stylized flower 2.50 4.50

13(13) 1 Fen (Al) 1943–1944 . . . . 1.60 3.00

14(A13) 5 Fen (Al) 1943–1944. Number 5 in center. Name of country, date, and reign
on new legend in Chinese letters . . 0.80 1.60

**Values are given for each coin in U.S. Dollars and reference to Yeoman-num-
bers.**

			VF	XF
15 (14)	1	Chiao (Al) 1943. Number 10 in center. Name of country, date, and reign on new legend in Chinese letters. ℞ on right and left value in Chinese letters, on top and bottom ornaments	0.80	1.50

			VF	XF
16 (13a)	1	Fen (red fiber) 1945	20.00	40.00
17 (Al3a)	5	Fen (red fiber) 1944	12.50	25.00

Martinique

Area: 421 sq. mi. Population: 290,000.
A French possession since 1635, this island in the Lesser Antilles has been a French Overseas Department since 1946.
Capital: Fort-de-France.

100 Centimes = 1 Franc

			VF	XF
1 (1)	50	Centimes (Cu–Ni) 1897–1922. Bust left. ℞ value within wreath	8.00	20.00

			VF	XF
2 (2)	1	Franc (Cu–Ni) 1897–1922	12.50	30.00

Mauretanien   # Mauritania   **Mauritanie**

Area: 419 000 sq. mi. Population: 1,890,000.

Mauritania, formerly a part of French West Africa, became a French Overseas Territory in 1964 and in 1957 received limited self-government. On 28th Nov. 1958 the establishment of the Islamic Republic of Mauritania took place within the French Community. The country received full independence on 28th Nov. 1960. Initially belonging to the French West African Monetary Area, Mauritania in 1962 became a member of the West African Monetary Union (UMOA) within the Franc zone. The introduction of its own currency took place after leaving the Franc zone on 29th June 1973. The exchange of the new media of exchange was effected in the ratio of 5 CFA-Francs to 1 Ouguiya. Issuing institute is the Banque Centrale de Mauritanie. Thus the CFA-Franc lost its validity in this country.

Capital: Nouakchott.

5 Khoums = 1 Ouguiya

	VF	XF
1 (1) 1/5 Ouguiya (Al) 1973, 1974. National emblem, value, date, name of issuing institution. Rev. Arabic inscriptions	6.00	8.50
2 (2) 1 Ouguiya (Cu-Al-Ni) 1973. Type as No. 1	8.00	12.50
3 (2a) 1 Ouguiya (Cu-Al-Ni) 1974, 1981, 1983, 1986. Type as No. 1, but Rev. two lines inscription	7.00	12.00
4 (3) 5 Ouguiya (Cu-Al-Ni) 1973, 1974, 1981, 1984. Type as No. 1	5.00	8.50
5 (4) 10 Ouguiya (Cu-Ni) 1973, 1974, 1981, 1983. Type as No. 1	5.00	8.50
6 (5) 20 Ouguiya (Cu-Ni) 1973, 1974, 1983. Type as No. 1	8.50	12.50

15th ANNIVERSARY OF INDEPENDENCE

	Proof
7 (6) 500 Ouguiya (Au) 1975	450.00

Mauritius   **Mauritius**   **Maurice**

Area: 808 sq. mi. Population: 1 000,000
Island in the Indian Ocean, east of Madagascar, belonging to the group of
the Mascarenes. Mauritius was discovered in the 16th century by the Portuguese navigator Mascarenhas, and became Dutch Territory in 1598. The
island was named after Prince Maurits of Orange. A British crown colony
since 1810, Mauritius attained its independence on 12th March 1968.
Capital: Port Louis.

100 Cents = 1 Rupee

GEORGE V 1910–1936

			VF	XF
1 (6)	1	Cent (Br) 1911–1924. Crowned portrait of George V, left. ℞ value	2.50	5.00
2 (7)	2	Cents (Br) 1911–1924	3.00	6.00
3 (8)	5	Cents (Br) 1917–1924	6.00	10.00
4 (9)	¼	Rupee (Ag) 1934–1936. ℞ crown above clover, lily, and lotus blossom	4.00	8.00

			VF	XF
5 (10)	½	Rupee (Ag) 1934. Sunda-Sambar (Cervus timorensis – Cervidae)	8.00	14.00
6 (11)	1	Rupee (Ag) 1934. ℞ coat of arms	16.00	28.00

GEORGE VI 1936–1952

			VF	XF
7 (12)	1	Cent (Br) 1943–1947. Crowned head of George VI, left. ℞ value	1.20	2.50
8 (13)	2	Cents (Br) 1943–1947	1.20	2.50
9 (14)	5	Cents (Br) 1942–1945	1.00	2.00
10 (15)	10	Cents (Cu–Ni) 1947 (scalloped)	1.50	3.00
11 (16)	¼	Rupee (Ag) 1938–1946. ℞ crown above clover, lily, and lotus blossom	5.00	10.00
12 (17)	½	Rupee (Ag) 1946. ℞ Sundar-Sambar	12.00	35.00

			VF	XF
13 (18)	1	Rupee (Ag) 1938. ℞ coat of arms	12.00	25.00
14 (23)	1	Cent (Br) 1949–1952. Same type as No. 7, but with legend KING GEORGE THE SIXTH	0.50	1.00
15 (24)	2	Cents (Br) 1949–1952. Same type as No. 8, but with legend KING GEORGE THE SIXTH	0.90	1.70
16 (19)	10	Cents (Cu–Ni) 1952. Same type as No. 10, but with legend KING GEORGE THE SIXTH	1.00	2.00
17 (20)	¼	Rupee (Cu–Ni) 1950–1951. Same type as No. 11, but with legend KING GEORGE THE SIXTH	1.00	2.00
18 (21)	½	Rupee (Cu–Ni) 1950–1951. Same type as No. 12, but with legend KING GEORGE THE SIXTH	1.50	3.50
19 (22)	1	Rupee (Cu–Ni) 1950–1951. Same type as No. 13, but with legend KING GEORGE THE SIXTH	3.50	5.00

ELIZABETH II since 1952

			XF	Unc
20 (25)	1	Cent (Br) 1953–1971, 1975, 1978, 1987. Elizabeth II, crowned head, right. Rev. value, date	0.10	0.20
21 (26)	2	Cents (Br) 1953–1971, 1975, 1978.	0.12	0.25
22 (27)	5	Cents (Br) 1956–1971, 1975, 1978, 1987.	0.25	0.50
23 (28)	10	Cents (Cu–Ni) 1954–1971, 1975, 1978, 1987	0.30	0.60
24 (30)	¼	Rupee (Cu–Ni) 1960–1971, 1975, 1978, 1987. Rev. crown above clover, lilly, and lotus blossom	0.50	1.00
25 (31)	½	Rupee (Cu–Ni) 1965, 1971, 1975, 1978, 1987. Rev. Sunda-Sambar	0.50	1.00
26 (29)	1	Rupee (Cu–Ni) 1956, 1964, 1971, 1975, 1978. Rev. coat of arms	1.00	2.00

			Unc	Proof
27 (32)	10	Rupees 1971. ℞ dodo (Raphus cucullatus – Raphidae), extinct		
		a) (Ag) 20 g		250.00
		b) (Cu–Ni) 17.4 g	4.00	

28 (33)	200	Rupees (Au) 1971. Scene from love-story »Paul et Virginie« (1788) by Bernardin de St.-Pierre	300.00	400.00

CONSERVATION COMMEMORATIVE (3)

29 (34)	25	Rupees (Ag) 1975. Rev. Blue swallow-tail:		
		a) .500 silver, 25.31 g	20.00	
		b) .925 silver, 28.28 g		25.00
30 (35)	50	Rupees (Ag) 1975. Rev. Mauritius kestrel:		
		a) .500 silver, 31.65 g	25.00	
		b) .925 silver, 35.00 g		35.00
31 (36)	1000	Rupees (Au) 1975. Rev. Mauritius fly-catcher	500.00	550.00

SILVER JUBILEE OF HER MAJESTY QUEEN ELIZABETH II

32 (37)	25	Rupees (Ag) 1977:		
		a) .500 silver, 25.31 g	12.50	
		b) .925 silver, 28.28 g		17.50

10th ANNIVERSARY OF INDEPENDENCE (2)

			Unc	Proof
33 (38)	25	Rupees (Ag) 1978	12.50	30.00
34 (39)	1000	Rupees (Au) 1978	300.00	350.00

WEDDING OF PRINCE CHARLES AND LADY DIANA (2)

35 (40)	10 Rupees 1981. Conjoined heads left:		
	a) (Ag)		30.00
	b) (Cu-Ni)	2.50	
36 (41)	1000 Rupees (Au) 1981	500.00	750.00

WORLD FOOD DAY 1981

37 (42)	10 Rupees (Ag) 1981. Rev. Worker cutting sugar cane	20.00	30.00

INTERNATIONAL YEAR OF DISABLED PERSONS (2)

38 (43)	25 Rupees (Ag) 1982:		
	a) .925 silver, 28.28 g	20.00	25.00
	b) Piéfort, .925 silver, 56.56 g		125.00
39 (44)	1000 Rupees (Au) 1982; .916 ⅔ gold, 15.98 g (93 pcs.)	500.00	750.00

Mexiko   # Mexico   **Mexique**

Estados Unidos Mexicanos

Area: 763,944 sq. mi. Population: 77,300,000.
Before the conquest of the Aztec empire by the Spaniards under Ferdinand
Cortés, there existed on Mexican soil, among others, the high cultures of the
Maya, Mixtecs, Olmekes and Toltecs. Mexico later became part of the Spanish colonial empire, from the beginning of the 16th century until it obtained
its independence in 1821. In the 19th century Mexico lost over one-third of
its old territory to the United States of America. The revolution which broke
out in 1910 unleashed a civil war of many years duration, and led in 1917 to
fundamentel changes in the constitution and social reforms.
Capital: Mexico City.

100 Centavos = 1 Peso

REPUBLIC

			VF	XF
1 (3)	1	Centavo (Cu) 1899–1905. Coat of arms: carancho or crested caracara (Polyborus plancus – Falconidae), nopal cactus (Nopalea coccinellifera – Cactaceae), and snake. ℞ number above value		
		a) 1899	150.00	270.00
		b) 1900–1905	1.80	3.60
2 (16)	5	Centavos (Ag) 1898–1905. Coat of arms. ℞ value	3.00	6.00
3 (17)	10	Centavos (Ag) 1898–1905	4.00	7.00
4 (18)	20	Centavos (Ag) 1898–1905	5.50	8.00
5 (20)	1	Peso (Ag) 1898–1909. Coat of arms. ℞ liberty cap in sunburst	12.00	20.00
6 (21)	1	Peso (Au) 1870–1905. Coat of arms. ℞ value in wreath	120.00	150.00
7 (22)	2½	Pesos (Au) 1870–1893	300.00	450.00
8 (23)	5	Pesos (Au) 1870–1905. Coat of arms. ℞ scale of justice, law scroll, with liberty cap above	350.00	450.00
9 (24)	10	Pesos (Au) 1870–1905	500.00	800.00
10 (25)	20	Pesos (Au) 1870–1905	650.00	950.00

Values are given for each coin in U.S. Dollars and reference to Yeoman-numbers.

			VF	**XF**
11 (27)	1	Centavo (Br) 1905–1949. Coat of arms. ℞ value; diameter: 20 mm		
		a) 1905–1914, 1920–1949	0.15	0.25
		b)1915, 1916	25.00	60.00
12 (28)	1	Centavo (Br) 1915. Same type as No. 11, but with diameter: 16 mm	20.00	40.00
13 (29)	2	Centavos (Br) 1905–1941. Diameter: 25 mm		
		a) 1905	180.00	320.00
		b) 1906	10.00	20.00
		c) 1920, 1921, 1924–1941	1.00	2.50
		d) 1922	500.00	1500.00
14 (30)	2	Centavos (Br) 1915. Diameter: 20 mm	6.00	10.00

During the years of the revolution, between 1913 and 1916, some states and other authorities issued revolutionary coins.

			VF	**XF**
15 (31)	5	Centavos (Ni) 1905–1914. Coat of arms. ℞ value in circle	2.00	4.00
16 (39)	10	Centavos (Ag) 1905–1914	2.00	4.00
17 (40)	20	Centavos (Ag) 1905–1914	2.50	4.50
18 (41)	50	Centavos (Ag) 1905–1918	6.00	8.00
19 (42)	1	Peso (Ag) 1910–1914. Liberty on horse-back, rising sun. ℞ coat of arms and value		
		a) 1910–1913	25.00	50.00
		b) 1914	500.00	800.00
20 (32)	5	Centavos (Br) 1914–1935. Coat of arms. ℞ value in wreath	2.50	4.00
21 (33)	10	Centavos (Br) 1919–1935. Same type as No. 20:		
		a) 1919–1921	12.50	30.00
		b) 1935	9.00	20.00
22 (34)	20	Centavos (Br) 1920, 1935:		
		a) 1920	18.00	40.00
		b) 1935	4.00	8.00
23 (55)	2	Pesos (Au) 1919-1948. Coat of arms. Rev. value in wreath		
		a) 1919, 1920, 1944, 1946,1947	30.00	35.00
		b) 1945, official restrike		27.50
		c) 1948		–.–
24 (56)	2½	Pesos (Au) 1918-1948. Coat of arms. Rev. Miguel Hidalgo y Costilla (1753-1811), priest and fighter for independence:		
		a) 1918-1920, 1944, 1946, 1948	35.00	42.00
		b) 1945, official restrike		30.00
		c) 1947	250.00	325.00
25 (57)	5	Pesos (Au) 1905-1955. Same type as No. 24:		
		a) 1905	160.00	250.00
		b) 1906, 1907, 1910, 1918-1920	60.00	70.00
		c) 1955, official restrike		60.00

26 (58)   10 Pesos (Au) 1905-1959. Same type as No. 24:   **VF**   **XF**

a) 1905-1908, 1910, 1916, 1917, 1919   120.00   150.00
b) 1920   320.00   450.00
1959, official restrike   120.00

27 (59)   20 Pesos (Au) 1917-1959. Coat of arms. Rev. Aztec calendar stone, 15th century:

a) 1917-1921   230.00   260.00
b) 1959, official restrike   220.00

28   10 Centavos (Ag) 1919-1935. Coat of arms. Rev. value, date, above liberty cap in sunburst:

a) (Y 43) 1919   16.00   30.00
b) (Y 47) 1925–1928, 1930, 1933–1935   4.00   6.00

29   20 Centavos (Ag) 1919–1943. Type as No. 28:

a) (Y 44) 1919   20.00   40.00
b) (Y 48) 1920, 1921, 1925–1928, 1930, 1933–1935, 1937, 1939–1943   1.50   2.50

30   50 Centavos (Ag) 1918–1945. Type as No. 28:

a) (Y 45) 1918; .800 silver   10.00   20.00
b) (Y 45) 1919; .800 silver   6.00   10.00
c) (Y 49) 1919–1921, 1925; .720 silver   4.00   7.00
d) (Y 49) 1935; .420 silver   3.00   5.00
e) (Y 49) 1937, 1939, 1942–1945; .720 silver   3.00   5.00
f) (Y 49) 1938; .720 silver   12.50   22.00

31   1 Peso (Ag) 1918–1945. Type as No. 28:

a) (Y 46) 1918; .800 silver   35.00   60.00
b) (Y 46) 1919; .800 silver   14.00   25.00
c) (Y 50) 1920; .720 silver   6.00   10.00
d) (Y 50) 1921–1945; .720 silver   5.00   7.00

		VF	XF
32 (51)	2 Pesos (Ag) 1921. Coat of arms. ℞ goddess of victory	32.00	45.00

33 (60)	50 Pesos (Au) 1921–1947. Same type as No. 32:		
	a) 1921-1931, 1944-1946	450.00	550.00
	b) 1943. No value, in its place 37.5 Gr./ORO/PURO twice (see illustration)	450.00	550.00
	c) 1947, official restrike		450.00
34 (52)	50 Centavos (Ag) 1935. Coat of arms. ℞ value with liberty cap above	2.50	4.00
35 (35)	5 Centavos (Cu–Ni) 1936–1942. Coat of arms. ℞ value in circle of pre-Columbian ornaments	0.40	0.80
36 (36)	10 Centavos (Cu–Ni) 1936–1946. Same type as No. 35	0.40	0.80
37 (37)	5 Centavos (Br) 1942–1946, 1951–1955. Coat of arms. ℞ Josefa Ortiz de Dominguez (1773–1829), fighter for independence, facing left	0.20	0.40

Similar design: Nos. 42, 49 and 65.

38 (38)	20 Centavos (Br) 1943–1955. Coat of arms. ℞ Sun Pyramid of Teotihuacán	0.40	0.80

Similar design: No. 51.

39 (53)	1 Peso (Ag) 1947–1949. ℞ José Maria Teclo Morelos y Pavón (1765–1815), priest and fighter for independence		
	a) 1947, 1948	2.00	5.00
	b) 1949 (Beware of counterfeits)		1200.00

			VF	XF
40 (54)	5 Pesos (Ag) 1947–1948. ℞ Cuautémoc († 1525), Huetlatoani (= ruler) of Tenochtitlan, 1520–1525			
			7.50	11.00

			VF	XF
41 (61)	1 Centavo (Bra) 1950–1969. ℞ ear of wheat			
			0.10	0.15
42 (62)	5 Centavos (Cu–Ni) 1950. ℞ Josefa Ortiz de Dominguez			
			1.50	3.00
43 (63)	25 Centavos (Ag) 1950–1953. ℞ scale of justice, law scroll, with liberty cap above			
			0.60	0.80
44 (64)	50 Centavos (Ag) 1950–1951. Cuautémoc. ℞ coat of arms			
			1.10	1.50
45 (65)	1 Peso (Bi) 1950. Coat of arms. ℞ José Maria Teclo Morelos y Pavón			
			2.00	2.60

COMMEMORATIVE COIN FOR THE OPENING OF THE SOUTHERN RAILWAY BETWEEN MEXICO CITY AND YUCATAN

			VF	XF
46 (66)	5 Pesos (Ag) 1950. Engine, rising sun and palm trees. ℞ coat of arms and value			
			30.00	50.00
47 (67)	5 Pesos (Ag) 1951–1954. Miguel Hidalgo y Costilla, facing left, in wreath. ℞ coat of arms			
	a) 1951-1953		7.50	11.00
	b) 1954		45.00	70.00

Similar design: No. 54.

		VF	XF
48 (68)	5 Pesos (Ag) 1953. Miguel Hidalgo y Costilla (1753–1811), priest and fighter for independence in front of church in Dolores, Guanajuato. ℞ coat of arms and value	7.50	11.00

		VF	XF
49 (69)	5 Centavos (Bra) 1954–1969. Coat of arms. ℞ Josefa Ortiz de Dominguez	0.10	0.15
50 (70)	10 Centavos (Br) 1955–1967. Coat of arms. ℞ Benito Juarez	0.10	0.20
51 (71)	20 Centavos (Br) 1955-1971. Coat of arms. ℞ sun pyramid of Teotihuacán	0.15	0.30
52 (72)	50 Centavos (Bra) 1955–1959. Coat of arms. ℞ Cuautémoc	0.30	0.70

		VF	XF
53 (A72)	1 Peso (Ag) 1957–1967. José Maria Teclo Morelos y Pavón. ℞ coat of arms	0.75	1.25

			VF	XF
54 (73)	5	Pesos (Ag) 1955–1957. Miguel Hidalgo y Costilla and new legend INDEPEN-DENCIA Y LIBERTAD-HIDALGO. R Coat of arms	5.00	7.00
55 (74)	10	Pesos (Ag) 1955–1956. Same type as No. 54	7.50	11.00

COMMEMORATIVE ISSUES (3) FOR 100 YEARS MEXICAN CONSTITUTION

56 (75)	1	Peso (Ag) 1957, Benito Juarez (1806–1872), President 1861–1872. R coat of arms	3.00	5.00
57 (76)	5	Pesos (Ag) 1957. Same type as No. 56	6.00	10.00
58 (77)	10	Pesos (Ag) 1957. Same type as No. 56	17.50	27.50

COMMEMORATIVE ISSUE FOR THE 100th BIRTHDAY OF CARRANZA

59 (78)	5	Pesos (Ag) 1959. Venustiano Carranza (1859–1920). R coat of arms	6.00	8.00

COMMEMORATIVE ISSUE FOR THE 150th ANNIVERSARY OF THE WAR OF INDEPENDENCE AND THE 50th ANNIVERSARY OF THE REVOLUTION

60 (79)	10	Pesos (Ag) 1960. Miguel Hidalgo y Costilla and Francisco Indalecio Madero (1873–1913), President 1911–1913. R coat of arms	9.00	12.00
61 (80)	25	Centavos (Cu–Ni) 1964, 1966. Coat of arms. R Francisco Indalecio Madero	0.10	0.20
62 (81)	50	Centavos (Cu–Ni) 1964–1969. Coat of arms. R Cuautémoc	0.10	0.20

COMMEMORATIVE ISSUE FOR THE 19th OLYMPIC SUMMER GAMES OF 1968 IN MEXICO CITY

63 (82) 25 Pesos (Ag) 1968. Maya ball player in

		XF	Unc
front of I-shaped ball court. ℞ coat of arms			
a) Type I, see illustration		6.00	9.00
b) Type II, center ring lowered		12.00	18.00
c) Type III, center ring lowered and snake's tongue curved		15.00	20.00

64 (83) 1 Centavo (Br) 1970–1973. Similar type as No. 41, but changed coat of arms — 0.10 / 0.50

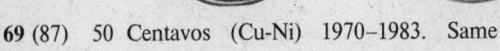

65 (84) 5 Centavos (Al-Br) 1970–1976. Similar type as No. 49, but changed coat of arms — 0.05 / 0.10

66 (91) 10 Centavos (Cu-Ni) 1974–1980. Coat of arms. Rev. corn cob — 0.10 / 0.20

67 (86) 20 Centavos (Br) 1971, 1973, 1974. Similar type as No. 51, but changed coat of arms — 0.15 / 0.30

68 (92) 20 Centavos (Cu-Ni) 1974–1983. Rev. portrait of President Francisco Indalecio Madero — 0.05 / 0.10

69 (87) 50 Centavos (Cu-Ni) 1970–1983. Same

			XF	Unc

type as No. 62, but changed coat of arms — 0.10 — 0.25

70 (88) 1 Peso (Cu-Ni) 1970–1983. New coat of arms, like No. 66. Rev. José Maria Teclo Morelos Pavón — 0.10 — 0.30

71 (89) 5 Pesos (Cu-Ni) 1971–1974, 1976–1978. Vicente Guerrero, General during the War of Independence against Spain

	XF	Unc
1971	0.75	2.00
1972	0.50	1.50
1973	3.00	7.50
1974	0.50	1.75
1976, small date	2.50	5.00
1976, large date	0.50	1.50
1977	0.65	1.50
1978	1.50	6.00

72 (A90) 10 Pesos (Cu-Ni) 1974–1982, 1985. Rev. Miguel Hidalgo y Costilla

	XF	Unc
a) 1974–1977, thin flan, 1.6 mm	0.75	2.00
b) 1978–1982, 1985, thick flan 2.3 mm	0.50	2.50

73 (90) 25 Pesos (Ag) 1972. Benito Juárez (1806 to 1972), statesman, Indian by birth — 5.00 — 8.00

		XF	Unc

74 (93) 100 Pesos (Ag) 1977–1981. Rev. facing portrait of Morelos — 5.00 — 8.00

75 20 Centavos (Br) 1983, 1984. Rev. Olmeco culture — 0.25 — 0.85

76 50 Centavos (St) 1983–1985. Rev. Palenque culture — 0.20 — 0.60

77 5 Pesos (Cu-Ni) 1980–1985. Rev. Quetzalcoatl — 0.25 — 1.50

1100 **Mexico**

		XF	Unc
78	20 Pesos (Cu-Ni) 1980–1984. Rev. Maya culture	0.50	2.25

		XF	Unc
79	50 Pesos (Cu-Ni) 1982–1984. Rev. Coyolxauhqui	1.00	3.25

BULLION ISSUE »LIBERTAD« (4)

A 79	1 Troy Ounce (Ag) 1982–1986. Arms. Rev. goddess of victory; .999 silver, 31.10 g	–.–
A 80	¼ Troy Ounce (Au) 1981. Type as No. A 79; .900 gold, 8.64 g	–.–

		XF	Unc
B 80	½ Troy Ounce (Au) 1981. Type as No. A 79; .900 gold, 17.28 g		–.–
C 80	1 Troy Ounce (Au) 1981. Type as No. A 79; .900 gold, 34.56 g		–.–
81	1 Peso (St) 1984–1987. Rev. Morelos	0.20	0.60

82	5 Pesos (Cu-Al-Ni) 1985. Rev. value, date	0.20	0.60
83	10 Pesos (Bra) 1985, 1987. Rev. Hidalgo	0.25	0.75
84	20 Pesos (Cu-Ni) 1985. Rev. Guadelupe Victoria	0.30	1.00
85	50 Pesos (Cu-Ni) 1984, 1985. Rev. Juarez	0.75	1.50

86	100 Pesos (Cu-Al-Ni) 1984, 1985. Rev. Carranza	1.00	1.75

No. 87 omitted.

88	500 Pesos (Cu-Ni) 1986, 1987. Rev. Francisco Indalecio Madero	3.00	5.00

No. 89 omitted

75th ANNIVERSARY OF REVOLUTION (2)

90	200 Pesos (Cu-Ni) 1985. Portraits of Emiliano Zapata, Francisco Madero, Venustiano Carranza and Pancho Villa	1.00	2.50
			Proof
91	500 Pesos (Ag) 1985. Type as No. 90		45.00

1102   Mexico

		XF	Unc
92	200 Pesos (Cu-Ni) 1985. Portraits of Vincente Guerrero, Ignacio Allende, José Morales and Miguel Hidalgo	1.00	2.50

		Proof
93	1000 Pesos (Au) 1985. Type as No. 92	475.00

XIII WORLD SOCCER CHAMPIONSHIP GAMES IN MEXICO
1st ISSUE (BU only)

		Unc
94	25 Pesos (Ag) 1985. Arms. Rev. Soccer ball behind inscription, legend »PLATA 720«, .720 silver, 7.776 g	8.00

95	50 Pesos (Ag) 1985. Rev. Legs of a soccer player, legend »PLATA 720«, .720 silver, 15.552 g	12.00
96	100 Pesos (Ag) 1985. Rev. Soccer ball, pre-Columbian figure and baroque castouches, legend »PLATA 720«, .720 silver, 31.103 g	18.00
97	250 Pesos (Au) 1985. Rev. soccer ball superimposed on a group of Maya designs, legend »ORO 900«, .900 gold, 8.64 g	200.00

98   500 Pesos (Au) 1985. Rev. Aztec calendar
stone, stylized soccer player, legend
»ORO 900«, .900 gold, 17.28 g

360.00

XIII WORLD SOCCER CHAMPIONSHIP GAMES IN MEXICO
2nd ISSUE (Proof only)
1st series (3)

Nos. 99–114 do not bear any fineness statements.

Proof

99   25 Pesos (Ag) 1985. Rev. pre-Columbian
design, colonial architectural motive
and soccer ball, .925 silver, 8.406 g

16.00

100   50 Pesos (Ag) 1985. Rev. Red Indian ball
player, pre-Columbian goal stone, and
soccer ball, .925 silver, 16.813 g

24.00

101 100 Pesos (Ag) 1985. Rev. goal-keeper with ball on his head, .925 silver, 33.625 g **Proof** 35.00

450th ANNIVERSARY OF MEXIKO CITY MINT (2)

102 250 Pesos (Au) 1985. Rev. »Caballito« design of No. 19 superimposed on a soccer ball, .900 gold, 8.64 g 250.00

103 500 Pesos (Au) 1985. Rev. Soccer ball in front of spanish gold coin of the colonial era, 900 gold, 17.28 g 480.00

2nd series (3)

104 25 Pesos (Ag) 1985. Rev. Soccer ball, inscription below, .925 silver, 8.406 g 16.00

105 50 Pesos (Ag) 1985. Rev. Soccer player in action, .925 silver, 16.813 g 24.00

106 100 Pesos (Ag) 1985. Rev. Soccer ball, pre-Columbian figure and baroque cartouches, .925 silver, 33.625 g 35.00

107 250 Pesos (Au) 1985. Rev. Soccer ball superimposed on a group of Maya designs, .900 gold, 8.64 g 250.00

108 500 Pesos (Au) 1985. Rev. Aztec calendar stone, stylized soccer player, .900 gold, 17.28 g 480.00

		Proof
109	25 Pesos (Ag) 1986. Rev. Ball within the goal, .925 silver, 8.406 g	16.00
110	50 Pesos (Ag) 1986. Rev. Legs of a soccer player, .925 silver, 16.813 g	24.00
111	100 Pesos (Ag) 1986. Rev. goal-keeper holding the ball, .925 silver, 33.625 g	35.00

4th series (3)

112	25 Pesos (Ag) 1986. Rev. Soccer ball behind inscription, .925 silver, 8.406 g	16.00
113	50 Pesos (Ag) 1986. Rev. Three soccer balls, .9.25 silver, 16.813 g	24.00
114	100 Pesos (Ag) 1986. Rev. Soccer ball and globe, .925 silver, 33.625 g	35.00

XIII WORLD SOCCER CHAMPIONSHIP GAMES IN MEXICO
3rd ISSUE

115	200 Pesos (Cu-Ni) 1986. Rev. Three soccer players	0.50	2.00

4th ISSUE (3)

116	200 Pesos (Ag) 1986. Rev. Soccer ball, flanked by the hemispheres, .999 silver, 62.206 g	50.00
117	1000 Pesos (Au) 1986. Type as No. 116, .999 gold, 31.1 g	700.00
118	2000 Pesos (Au) 1986. Type as No. 116, .999 gold, 62.2 g	1400.00

Nos. 116–118 have also been awarded to the winning teams of Argentina, Germany and France.

25th ANNIVERSARY OF WORLD WILDLIFE FUND

119	100 Pesos (Ag) 1986. Rev. Monarch butterfly, .720 silver, 31.103 g	25.00

Monaco

Area: 1.9 sq. km. Population: 26,000.
Principality under French protection.
Capital: Monte Carlo.

100 Centimes = 1 Franc

			VF	XF
		ALBERT I 1889–1922		
1 (1)	100	Francs (Au) 1891–1904. Albert I (1848–1922), head left. ℞ coat of arms	425.00	550.00
		LOUIS II 1922–1949		
2 (2)	50	Centimes (Al–Br) 1924. Archer. ℞ value, coat of arms and legend in circle	10.00	22.00
3 (3)	1	Franc (Al–Br) 1924. Same type as No. 2	8.50	18.00
4 (4)	2	Francs (Al–Br) 1924. Same type as No. 2	12.00	26.00
5 (5)	50	Centimes (Al–Br) 1926. Archer. ℞ value and coat of arms in circle	15.00	26.00
6 (6)	1	Franc (Al–Br) 1926. Same type as No. 5	12.00	25.00
7 (7)	2	Francs (Al–Br) 1926. Same type as No. 5	16.00	28.00
8 (8)	1	Franc. Louis II (1870–1949), head left. ℞ coat of arms		
		a) (Al) undated (1943)	1.20	2.80
		b) (Al–Br) undated (1945)	1.60	2.50
9 (9)	2	Francs. Same type as No. 8		
		a) (Al) undated (1943)	3.50	6.00
		b) (Al–Br) undated (1945)	2.50	4.00
10 (10)	5	Francs (Al) 1945. Same type as No. 8	2.50	4.50
11 (11)	10	Francs (Cu–Ni) 1946. Louis II in uniform, portrait left. ℞ coat of arms	3.00	6.00
12 (12)	20	Francs (Cu–Ni) 1947. Same type as No. 11	4.00	7.00

			VF	XF
13 (13)	10	Francs (Al–Br) 1950–1951. Rainier III (*1923), head left. ℞ coat of arms	2.00	3.00

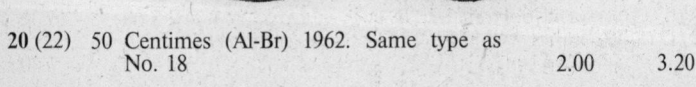

			VF	XF
14 (14)	20	Francs (Al–Br) 1950–1951. Same type as No. 13	1.50	2.50
15 (15)	50	Francs (Al–Br) 1950. ℞ rider on horseback with sword and Grimaldi shield	4.00	7.00
16 (16)	100	Francs (Cu–Ni) 1950. Same type as No. 15	9.00	14.00
17 (17)	100	Francs (Cu–Ni) 1956. Rainier III, head left. ℞ coat of arms	4.00	8.00

CURRENCY REFORM: 100 Old Francs = 1 New Franc

			VF	XF
18 (20)	10	Centimes (Al-Br) 1962, 1974–1979, 1982. Rainier III, head right. Rev. St. Rainier, patron saint of Monaco, crown above arms, value	0.20	0.40
19 (21)	20	Centimes (Al-Br) 1962, 1974–1979, 1982. Same type as No. 18	0.50	1.00

			VF	XF
20 (22)	50	Centimes (Al-Br) 1962. Same type as No. 18	2.00	3.20

		VF	XF
21 (A18)	½ Franc (Ni) 1965–. R crown in front of arms	0.50	1.00
22 (18)	1 Franc (Ni) 1960–. Same type as No. 21	0.80	1.20
23 (19)	5 Franc (Ag) 1960–. Rainier III, head left. R coat of arms	10.00	12.50

COMMEMORATIVE ISSUES (2) FOR THE 10th WEDDING ANNIVERSARY OF THE PRINCE AND THE PRINCESS

		Unc	Proof
24 (23)	10 Francs (Ag) 1966. Prince Rainier III and Princess Gracia Patricia (1929–1982), former film actress Grace Kelly. Rev. crowned coat of arms	35.00	175.00
25 (24)	200 Francs (Au) 1966. Same type as No. 24	550.00	750.00

COMMEMORATIVE COIN FOR THE CENTENNIAL OF THE FOUNDING OF MONTE CARLO

		XF	Unc
26 (25)	10 Francs (Ag) 1966. Charles III (1818–1889), reigned 1856–1889. R crowned coat of arms		30.00
27 (26)	5 Francs (Ni) 1971–. Rainier III, head left. R monogram and crown	1.50	2.50

25th ANNIVERSARY OF REIGN (6)

		Unc	Proof
28 (27)	10 Francs (Cu-Ni) 1974. Head left. Rev. coat of arms, value, date	8.50	
29 (28)	50 Francs (Ag) 1974. Head right. Rev. crowned monograms. Commemorative edge inscription	45.00	
30 (29)	100 Francs (Ag) 1974. Head left. Rev. coat of arms	55.00	
31	1000 Francs (Platinum) 1974. Type as No. 30		*250.00*
32	2000 Francs (Platinum) 1974. Type as No. 30		*500.00*
33	3000 Francs (Au) 1974. Type as No. 30		*750.00*

			XF	Unc
34 (33)	10	Francs (Cu-Ni) 1975–1979, 1981–1983. Head left. Rev. Coat of arms, value, date		5.00
35	50	Francs (Ag) 1975, 1976. Type as No. 29, but plain edge		45.00

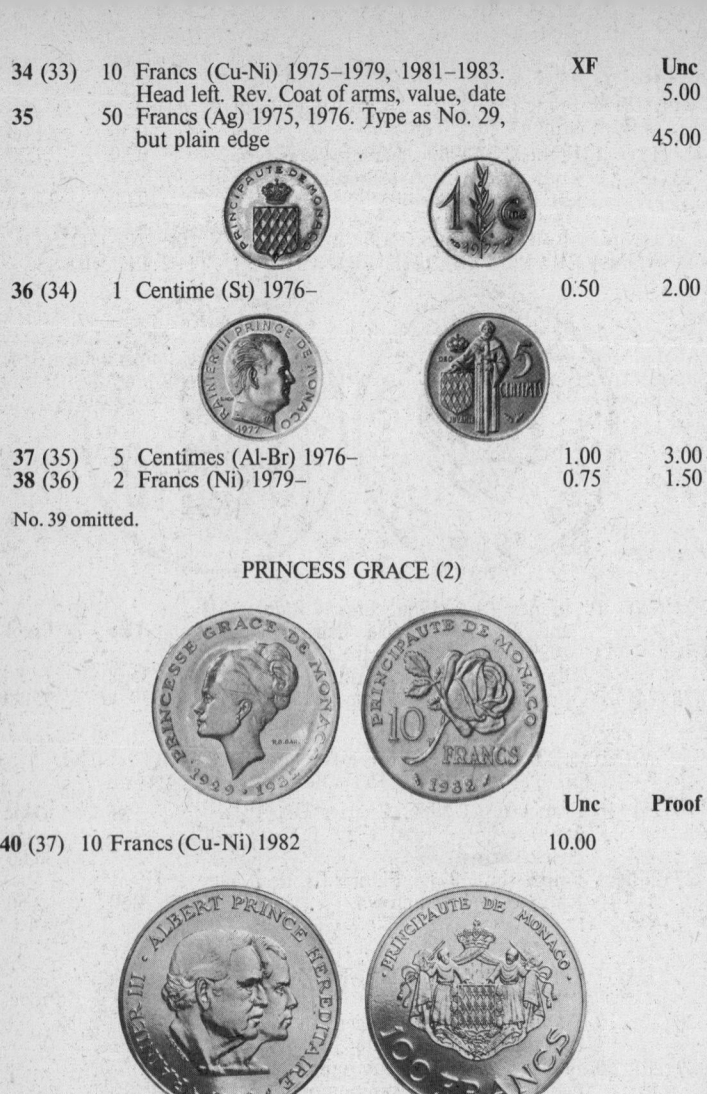

			XF	Unc
36 (34)	1	Centime (St) 1976–	0.50	2.00

37 (35)	5	Centimes (Al-Br) 1976–	1.00	3.00
38 (36)	2	Francs (Ni) 1979–	0.75	1.50

No. 39 omitted.

PRINCESS GRACE (2)

			Unc	Proof
40 (37)	10	Francs (Cu-Ni) 1982	10.00	

41 (38)	100	Francs (Ag) 1982	40.00	50.00

All valuations in the SCHÖN are stated in U.S. Dollars.

Mongolian People's Republic

Mongolische Volksrepublik   **Mongolie**

Bugd Nairamdach Mongol Ard Uls

Area: 625,783 sq. mi. Population: 1,875,000.

At the time of the Chinese revolution, self-government was instituted in Outer Mongolia with the aid of the Kalkha princes. On 10th July 1921 the country declared its independence, and the Mongolian People's Republic was proclaimed on 26th November 1924.

Capital: Ulan Bator.

100 Mongo = 1 Tugrik

Note: The year dates shown on the coins up to and including 1945 refer to the New-Mongolian calendar, beginning with the year 1911.

			VF	XF
1 (1)	1 Mongo (Cu) 1925. Soyombo-emblem (old coat of arms) and old Mongolian legends; year date 15. ℞ value in Mongolian; wreath of wheat ears		10.00	20.00

2 (2)	2 Mongo (Cu) 1925		7.00	12.00

3 (3)	5 Mongo			
	a) (Cu) 1925		10.00	20.00
	b) (Cu) 1925. Variety		35.00	65.00

Coin No. 3b can be recognized by the lack of one ornament in the lower left Mongolian word of the legend on each side of Soyombo-emblem (old coat of arms). The origin of this type is uncertain; according to some sources it is a forgery manufactured in a convent.

			VF	XF
4 (4)	10 Mongo (Ag) 1925		8.00	12.00
5 (5)	15 Mongo (Ag) 1925		8.00	12.00
6 (6)	20 Mongo (Ag) 1925		9.00	13.00

7 (7)	50 Mongo (Ag) 1925		12.00	22.00

8 (8)	1 Tugrik (Ag) 1925		25.00	38.00

9 (10)	1 Mongo (Al–Br) 1937. Same type as No. 1, but year date 27		6.00	10.00

10 (11)	2 Mongo (Al–Br) 1937		6.00	8.00

			VF	XF
11 (12)	5	Mongo (Al–Br) 1937	6.00	9.00

| **12** (13) | 10 | Mongo (Cu–Ni) 1937 | 6.00 | 9.00 |

| **13** (14) | 15 | Mongo (Cu–Ni) 1937 | 6.00 | 9.00 |

14 (15)	20	Mongo (Cu–Ni) 1937	8.00	12.00
15 (16)	1	Mongo (Al–Br) 1945. Coat of arms of Mongolia. Name of country now in Mongolian-Cyrillic lettering, year date 35. ℞ value in wreath	4.50	8.00
16 (17)	2	Mongo (Al–Br) 1945	4.50	8.00

17 (18)	5	Mongo (Al–Br) 1945	4.50	8.00
18 (19)	10	Mongo (Cu–Ni) 1945	4.50	8.00
19 (20)	15	Mongo (Cu–Ni) 1945	4.50	8.00
20 (21)	20	Mongo (Cu–Ni) 1945	4.50	8.00
21 (22)	1	Mongo (Al) 1959. Name of country in Mongolian-Cyrillic lettering. ℞ value in wreath (center hole)	2.50	4.00
22 (23)	2	Mongo (Al) 1959 (center hole)	2.50	4.00

				VF	XF
23 (24)	5	Mongo (Al) 1959 (center hole)		3.00	4.50
24 (25)	10	Mongo (Al) 1959. Coat of arms, name of country now in Mongolian-Cyrillic lettering. ℞ value in wreath		4.00	5.00
25 (26)	15	Mongo (Al) 1959. Same type as No. 24		4.00	6.00
26 (27)	20	Mongo (Al) 1959. Same type as No. 24		4.50	8.00

				XF	Unc
27 (28)	1	Mongo (Al) 1970–. Coat of arms and abbreviation of country name, BNMAU, in Mongolian-Cyrillic letters, year date. Rev. value and ornament		0.60	1.25
28 (29)	2	Mongo (Al) 1970–. Same type as No. 27		0.75	1.50
29 (30)	5	Mongo (Al) 1970–. Same type as No. 27		1.00	2.00
30 (31)	10	Mongo (Al) 1970–. Coat of arms, country name spelt out, year date. Rev. value and leaf ornament		1.50	2.50

				XF	Unc
31 (32)	15	Mongo (Al) 1970–. Same type as No. 30		1.60	2.50
32 (33)	20	Mongo (Cu-N) 1970–. Same type as No. 30		1.75	3.00
33 (34)	50	Mongo (Cu-Ni) 1970–. Same type as No. 30		2.25	4.00

50th ANNIVERSARY OF PEOPLE'S REPUBLIC

			Unc	Proof
34 (35)	1	Tugrik 1971. Equestrian statue of Suche-Bator (1893–1923) and legend 50 Years People's Republic of Mongolia. ℞ coat of arms, country name spelt out, value in words (NEG TOGROG).		
		a) (Cu-Al-Ni)	10.00	
		b) (Cu-Ni)	20.00	
		c) (Ag) 18.4 g		–.–
		d) (Au) 30.3 g (9 pes.)		–.–

50th ANNIVERSARY OF MONGOLIAN STATE BANK

			Unc
35 (36)	10	Tugrik (Cu-Ni) 1974. Building of the State Bank	35.00

CONSERVATION COMMEMORATIVE (3)

			Unc	Proof
36 (37)	25	Tugrik (Ag) 1976. Coat of arms. Argali sheep:		
		a) .925 silver, 25.31 g	22.50	
		b) .925 silver, 28.28 g		30.00
37 (38)	50	Tugrik (Ag) 1976. Rev. Bactrian camel:		
		a) .925 silver, 31.65 g	30.00	
		b) .925 silver, 35.00 g		40.00
38 (39)	750	Tugrik (Au) 1976. Rev. Przewalski's horse	600.00	750.00

INTERNATIONAL YEAR OF THE CHILD (2)

39 (40)	25	Tugrik (Ag) 1980:	
		a) .925 silver, 19.44 g	35.00
		b) Piéfort, .925 silver, 38.88 g	175.00
40 (41)	750	Tugrik (Au) 1980:	
		a) .900 gold, 18.79 g	300.00
		b) Piéfort, .900 gold, 37.59 g	1250.00

No. 41 omitted.

SOVIET-MONGOLIAN SPACE FLIGHT

		XF	Unc
42	1 Tugrik (Cu-Al-Ni) 1981	5.00	7.50

60th ANNIVERSARY OF MONGOLIAN PEOPLE'S REVOLUTION

43 (42)	1 Tugrik (Cu-Al-Ni) 1981	5.00	7.50

60th ANNIVERSARY OF MONGOLIAN STATE BANK

44	1 Tugrik (Cu-Al-Ni) 1984	5.00	7.50

60th ANNIVERSARY OF MONGOLIAN PEOPLE'S REPUBLIC

45	1 Tugrik (Cu-Al-Ni) 1984	5.00	7.50

DECADE FOR WOMEN (2)

		Proof
47	25 Tugrik (Ag) 1984; .925 silver, 19.44 g	35.00
48	250 Tugrik (Au) 1984; .900 gold, 7.13 g	250.00

Montenegro

ЦРНА ГОРА

Area: 5,330 sq. mi. Population: 471,800.

The principality of Montenegro was raised to the status of a kingdom in 1910. The National Assembly then decided in favor of uniting with the state of the Serbs, Croats and Slovenes on November 26, 1918. During World War II, the state of Montenegro (1941-1944) was created, initially under Italian domination, later under German. Subsequently the country again became part of Yugoslavia.

Capital: Cetinje.

100 Para = 1 Perper

PRINCIPALITY

NICHOLAS I 1860–1918

			VF	XF
1 (1)	1	Para (Br) 1906. Crowned heraldic eagle. R value	16.00	35.00
2 (2)	2	Pare (Br) 1906–1908	6.00	12.00
3 (3)	10	Para (Ni) 1906–1908	2.00	4.00
4 (4)	20	Para (Ni) 1906–1908	4.00	7.00
5 (5)	1	Perper (Ag) 1909	8.00	16.00
6 (6)	2	Perpera (Ag) 1910	16.00	30.00
7 (7)	5	Perpera (Ag) 1909	110.00	180.00
8 (8)	10	Perpera (Au) 1910. Nicholas I (1841–1921), Prince of Montenegro, also known as poet and dramatist. R heraldic eagle on mantled arms	325.00	500.00

9 (9)	20	Perpera (Au) 1910	400.00	650.00
10 (10)	100	Perpera (Au) 1910	6000.00	8500.00

KINGDOM

COMMEMORATIVE ISSUES (3) FOR THE 50th ANNIVERSARY OF THE GOVERNMENT

11 (18)	10	Perpera (Au) 1910. Nicholas I, head with laurel wreath. R heraldic eagle on mantled arms	325.00	500.00

			VF	XF
12 (19)	20	Perpera (Au) 1910	400.00	650.00

13 (20)	100	Perpera (Au) 1910	5500.00	8000.00
14 (11)	1	Para (Br) 1913–1914	11.00	25.00
15 (12)	2	Pare (Br) 1913–1914	6.00	12.00
16 (13)	10	Para (Ni) 1913–1914	2.80	5.00

17 (14)	20	Para (Ni) 1913–1914	5.00	10.00
18 (15)	1	Perper (Ag) 1912–1914	15.00	20.00

19 (16)	2	Perpera (Ag) 1914	16.00	22.00
20 (17)	5	Perpera (Ag) 1912–1914	105.00	160.00

Yeoman Numbers

In order to help collectors and dealers, we have added after most SCHÖN numbers the corresponding number assigned by R.S. Yeoman in his wellknown works entitled »A Catalog of Modern World Coins« and »Current Coins of the World«.

Area: 32.5 sq. mi. Population: 18,500.
One of the Leeward Islands and a member of the Caribbean Free Trade
Area (CARIFTA). Montserrat has united with the countries of Antigua,
Barbados, Dominica, Grenada, St. Christopher-(Kitts-)Nevis-Anguilla,
St. Lucia and St. Vincent to form the currency area of the East Carib-
bean Dollar. The issuing authority for the whole of the currency area is
the East Caribbean Currency Authority with its seat in Bridgetown on
the island of Barbados.
Capital: Plymouth.

100 Cents = 1 East Caribbean Dollar

COMMEMORATIVE ISSUE FOR THE INAUGURATION OF THE CARIBBEAN DEVELOPMENT BANK AND THE FAO COIN PLAN

		Unc	Proof
1 (6*)	4 Dollars (Cu–Ni) 1970. Coat of arms. ℞ bananas, sugar cane, value	10.00	30.00

*This number refers to Yeoman's East Caribbean Territories listing.

Marokko   # Morocco   **Maroc**

Al Mamlakah al Maghrebia

Area: c. 174.000 sq. mi. Population: 22,500,000.
After decades as an European protectorate, this North African country was
restored to independence in 1956. Based upon the constitution of 1962,
Morocco is a constitutional democratic and sozial monarchy.
Capital: Rabat.

50 Mazunas = 1 Dirham, 10 Dirhams = 1 Rial, 100 Centimes =
1 Franc; since 17th October 1959: 100 Francs = 1 Dirham

100 Centimes = 1 Dirham

ABD AL AZIZ IV 1894–1908

			VF	XF
1 (14)	1	Mazuna (Br) H-C 1319–1321 (1901–1903). Arabic legend and date in circle, meander ornament. ℞ value in circle; meander ornament	6.00	12.50
2 (15)	2	Mazunas (Br) H-C 1320–1323 (1902–1905)	4.00	8.50
3 (16)	5	Mazunas (Br) H-C 1320–1322 (1902–1904)	2.00	5.00
4 (17)	10	Mazunas (Br) H-C 1320–1323 (1902–1905)	1.25	3.50
5 (9)	½	Dirham (Ag) H-C 1313–1319 (1896–1901)	5.00	10.00
6 (10)	1	Dirham (Ag) H-C 1313–1318 (1896–1900)	6.50	12.00
7 (11)	2½	Dirhams (Ag) H-C 1313–1318 (1896–1900)	12.50	20.00
8 (12)	5	Dirhams (Ag) H-C 1313–1318 (1896–1900)	15.00	30.00
9 (13)	10	Dirhams (Ag) H-C 1313 (1896)	150.00	275.00
10 (18)	1/20	Rial (Ag) H-C 1320–1321 (1902–1904)	4.00	6.50
11 (19)	1/10	Rial (Ag) H-C 1320–1321 (1902–1904)	4.00	8.50
12 (20)	¼	Rial (Ag) H-C 1320–1321 (1902–1904)	8.00	15.00
13 (21)	½	Rial (Ag) H-C 1320–1323 (1902–1906)	12.00	22.00
14 (22)	1	Rial (Ag) H-C 1320–1321 (1902–1904)	35.00	70.00

ABD AL HAFIZ 1908-1912

			VF	XF
15 (23)	¼	Rial (Ag) H–C 1329 (1911)	8.50	18.00
16 (24)	½	Rial (Ag) H–C 1329 (1911)	12.50	30.00
17 (25)	1	Rial (Ag) H–C 1329 (1911)	25.00	55.00

JOUSSEF 1912–1927

			VF	XF
18 (26)	1	Mazuna (Br) H-C 1330 (1912). Over-lapping triangle with date. ℞ pentagram with value	22.00	45.00
19 (27)	2	Mazunas (Br) H-C 1330 (1912)	2.50	5.00
20 (28)	5	Mazunas (Br) H-C 1330–1340 (1912–1922)	1.00	2.50
21 (29)	10	Mazunas (Br) H-C 1330–1340 (1912–1922)	1.25	2.50
22 (30)	¹/₁₀	Rial (Ag) H-C 1331 (1913). Legend in circle, all in star. ℞ date in circle, legend	30.00	50.00
23 (31)	¼	Rial (Ag) H-C 1331 (1913)	12.50	30.00
24 (32)	½	Rial (Ag) H-C 1331–1336 (1913–1918)	12.00	25.00
25 (33)	1	Rial (Ag) H-C 1331–1336 (1913–1918)	30.00	65.00

NEW CURRENCY: 100 Centimes = 1 Franc

			VF	XF
26 (34)	25	Centimes (Cu–Ni) undated (1922–1927). Star, Moorish ornament. ℞ value (center hole)	0.80	1.60
27 (35)	50	Centimes (Ni) undated (1921–1926)	0.80	1.60

			VF	XF
28 (36)	1	Franc (Ni) undated (1922–1925)	1.20	2.00

MOHAMMED BEN JOUSSEF 1927–1956

			VF	XF
29 (37)	5	Francs (Ag) H-C 1347–1352 (1929–1934)	4.50	7.50
30 (38)	10	Francs (Ag) H-C 1347–1352 (1929–1934)	7.50	12.00
31 (39)	20	Francs (Ag) H-C 1347–1352 (1929–1934)	20.00	40.00
32 (40)	50	Centimes (Al–Br) H-C 1364 (1945). Pentagram. ℞ value, dates	0.50	1.50
33 (41)	1	Franc (Al–Br) H-C 1364 (1945)	1.00	2.00
34 (42)	2	Francs (Al–Br) H-C 1364 (1945)	0.60	1.50

		VF	**XF**
35 (43)	5 Francs (Al–Br) H-C 1365 (1946)	1.00	2.00
36 (44)	10 Francs (Cu–Ni) H-C 1366 (1947)	1.00	2.00
37 (45)	20 Francs (Cu–Ni) H-C 1366 (1947)	1.50	3.00
38 (46)	1 Franc (Al) H-C 1370 (1951)	0.10	0.20

39 (47)	2 Francs (Al) H-C 1370 (1951)	0.20	0.40
40 (48)	5 Francs (Al) H-C 1370 (1951)	0.25	0.50
41 (49)	10 Francs (Al–Br) H-C 1371 (1952)	0.40	0.80
42 (50)	20 Francs (Al–Br) H-C 1371 (1952)	0.50	1.00
A43 (A54)	100 Francs (Ag) AH 1370 (1951); .720 silver, 2.2 g		400.00
44 (52)	100 Francs (Ag) AH 1372 (1953); .720 silver, 4 g	4.00	7.50

45 (53)	200 Francs (Ag) H-C 1372 (1953)	6.00	8.00

MOHAMMED V 1956–1961

46 (54)	500 Francs (Ag) H-C 1376 (1956). Mohammed V (1911–1961), sultan of Morocco 1927–1956, King 1956–1961, bust left. ℞ crown in pentagram	15.00	22.50

NEW CURRENCY: 100 Francs = 1 Dirham

47 (55)	1 Dirham (Ag) H-C 1380 (1960). Mohammed V. ℞ coat of arms	2.50	4.00

HASSAN II since 1961

48 (56)	1 Dirham (Ni) 1965, 1968, 1969. Hassan II (*1930), head left. Rev. coat of arms	0.80	1.50
49 (57)	5 Dirhams (Ag) 1965	5.00	8.00

NEW CURRENCY: 100 Centimes (Santimin) = 1 Dirham

			XF	Unc
50 (58)	1 Santim (Al) 1974, 1975. Arms. Rev. Value		0.25	0.40
51 (59)	5 Santimat (Cu-Al-Ni) 1974, 1975, 1978. Rev. Fishery (FAO issue)		0.10	0.25
52 (60)	10 Santimat (Cu-Al-Ni) 1974, 1975, 1978. Rev. Sunflowers (FAO issue)		0.15	0.30
53 (61)	20 Santimat (Cu-Al-Ni) 1974, 1975, 1977, 1978. Head left. Rev. Arms, value		0.20	0.35
54 (62)	50 Santimat (Cu-Ni) 1974, 1978. Type as No. 53		0.30	0.60
55 (63)	1 Dirham (Cu-Ni) 1974, 1978. Type as No. 53		0.50	0.85
56 (72)	5 Dirhams (Cu-Ni) 1980. Type as No. 53		2.00	4.00

				Proof
57 (58a)	1 Santim (Au) 1974. Type as No. 50; .900 gold			300.00
58 (59a)	5 Santimat (Au) 1974. Type as No. 51; .900 gold			300.00
59 (60a)	10 Santimat (Au) 1974. Type as No. 52; .900 gold			400.00
60 (61a)	20 Santimat (Au) 1974. Type as No. 53; .900 gold			500.00
61 (62a)	50 Santimat (Au) 1974. Type as No. 54; .900 gold			500.00
62 (63a)	1 Dirham (Au) 1974. Type as No. 55; .900 gold			600.00

WORLD FOOD CONFERENCE

			Unc	Proof
63 (64)	5 Dirhams 1975. Rev. Dam, sugarbeet, value, date:			
	a) (Ag)			–.–
	b) (Cu-Ni)		10.00	
64	5 Dirhams (Au) 1975. Type as No. 63:			
	a) .900 gold, 23.65 g			750.00
	b) .900 gold, 35.48 g			–.–

20th ANNIVERSARY OF INDEPENDENCE (2)

			Unc	Proof
65 (65)	50 Dirhams (Ag) 1975. Head left. Rev. arms, value, date		30.00	55.00
66	50 Dirhams (Au) 1975. Type as No. 65			–.–

BIRTHDAY OF KING HASSAN II

	Unc	Proof
67 (66) 250 Dirhams (Au) 1975–1979. Rev. arms, value, date	110.00	140.00

INTERNATIONAL WOMEN'S YEAR 1975 (2)

	Unc	Proof
68 (67) 50 Dirhams (Ag) 1975	30.00	65.00
69 50 Dirhams (Au) 1975		–.–

COMMEMORATING THE GREEN MARCH OF 1975 (2)

	Unc	Proof
70 (68) 50 Dirhams (Ag) 1976–1980	30.00	55.00
71 50 Dirhams (Au) 1976–1979		–.–

INTERNATIONAL YEAR OF THE CHILD (2)

	Unc	Proof
72 (70) 50 Dirhams (Ag) 1979	25.00	50.00
73 50 Dirhams (Au) 1979		–.–

BIRTHDAY OF KING HASSAN II (3)

			Unc	Proof
74 (76)	50	Dirhams (Ag) 1979. Rev. arms between map and ear of wheat	30.00	50.00
75	50	Dirhams (Au) 1979		–.–
76 (71)	500	Dirhams (Au) 1979–1984	300.00	350.00

15th CENTURY OF HEGIRA

77 (74)	150	Dirhams (Ag) 1980	30.00	50.00

20th ANNIVERSARY OF REIGN (2)

78 (73)	150	Dirhams (Ag) 1981. Head left. Rev. arms, value, date	35.00	55.00
79	150	Dirhams (Au) 1981. Type as No. 78; .900 gold, 60.14 g (30 pcs.)		2500.00

9th MEDITERRANEAN GAMES IN CASABLANCA AND RABAT

80 (75)	100	Dirhams (Ag) 1983. Emblem of the Games	30.00	55.00

Mosambik　　　　　**Mozambique**　　　　　**Mozambique**

Moçambique

Area: 297,729 sq. mi. Population: 14,100,000.

Since the early years of the 16th Century the Portuguese consolidated their economic influence on the East Coast (cf. Mombasa in the World Coin Catalog of the 19th Century and Zanzibar) in the coastal strip (south of Beira) and the island of Mozambique in the form of fortified settlements and at the same time also penetrated the interior along the path of the Zambesi. The British and Dutch interests in the colonization of Africa adversely affected the already slack Portuguese colonial policy which defended itself by declaring the overseas possessions as overseas provinces. Mozambique and the dependencies were already administered in the early 19th century by a Governor General, in 1891 declared as the "State of East Africa", mainly, however, continued to be described under the usual name. The designation "Portuguese Colony" returned in use, was substituted in 1951 by "Overseas Territory" (Province of Mozambique), in place of which even "Portuguese State of Mozambique" (Estado português de Moçambique) was used. After fighting which extended over more than a decade, one of the indigenous independence movements (Frelimo = Frente de Libertação de Moçambique) (Mozambique Freedom Front) has had the power of government transferred, following upon the fall of the government in the motherland (25th April 1974). On June 25, 1975, Mozambique became full independence. Capital: Lourenco Marques, now Maputo.

100 Centavos = 1 Escudo; 100 Centavos = 1 Mozambique Escudo; 100 Centavos = 1 Metica

For the Escudos circulating in Mozambique there was a legal parity with the Escudo of Portugal of 1:1

			VF	XF
1 (1)	10	Centavos (Br) 1936. Coat of arms. ℞ value	4.00	7.00
2 (2)	20	Centavos (Br) 1936	4.50	8.00
3 (3)	50	Centavos (Cu–Ni) 1936	6.00	9.00
4 (4)	1	Escudo (Cu–Ni) 1936	8.00	10.50
5 (5)	2½	Escudos (Ag) 1935	9.00	12.00
6 (6)	5	Escudos (Ag) 1935	8.00	12.00
7 (7)	10	Escudos (Ag) 1936	18.00	35.00
8 (8)	2½	Escudos (Ag) 1938–1951. ℞ coat of arms with mural crown	5.00	8.00
9 (9)	5	Escudos (Ag) 1938–1949	15.00	22.00

			VF	XF
10 (10)	10	Escudos (Ag) 1938	25.00	45.00
11 (11)	10	Centavos (Br) 1942	3.00	6.00
12 (12)	20	Centavos (Br) 1941	3.00	6.00
13 (13)	50	Centavos (Br) 1945	3.00	6.00
14 (14)	1	Escudo (Br) 1945	3.50	6.00
15 (15)	20	Centavos (Br) 1949–1950	2.00	3.50
16 (16)	50	Centavos (Ni–Br) 1950–1951	2.00	4.00
17 (17)	1	Escudo (Ni–Br) 1950–1951	2.00	4.00
18 (24)	10	Centavos (Br) 1960, 1961	0.20	0.40
19 (25)	20	Centavos (Br) 1961	0.30	0.60
20 (18)	50	Centavos (Br) 1953–1957	0.30	0.50
21 (19)	1	Escudo (Br) 1953–1974	0.30	0.60
22 (20)	2½	Escudos (Cu-Ni) 1952–1973	0.60	1.00

23 (21)	5	Escudos (Ag) 1951, 1960	1.50	2.50
24 (22)	10	Escudos (Ag) 1952–1966	2.50	5.00
25 (23)	20	Escudos (Ag) 1952–1966	6.50	12.00
26 (21a)	5	Escudos (Cu-Ni) 1971, 1973. Same type as No. 23	0.80	1.20
27 (22a)	10	Escudos (Cu-Ni) 1968, 1970, 1974. Same type as No. 24	1.20	2.50
28 (26)	20	Escudos (Ni) 1971–1973. Same type as No. 25	2.50	4.00
29 (25a)	20	Centavos (Br) 1973, 1974. Type as 19, but reduced size	0.20	0.40
30 (18a)	50	Centavos (Br) 1973, 1974. Type as No. 20, but changed diameter and weight	0.25	0.50

PEOPLE'S REPUBLIC OF MOZAMBIQUE

MONETARY REFORM: 100 Centimos = 1 Metica

			XF	Unc
31 (27)	1 Centimo (Al) 1975. Head right of Samora Machel		125.00	225.00
32 (28)	2 Centimos (Br) 1975		125.00	225.00
33 (29)	5 Centimos (Br) 1975		125.00	225.00
34 (30)	10 Centimos (Br) 1975		125.00	225.00
35 (31)	20 Centimos (Cu-Ni) 1975		-.-	-.-
36 (32)	50 Centimos (Cu-Ni) 1975		175.00	300.00
37 (33)	1 Metica (Cu-Ni) 1975		100.00	150.00
38 (34)	2½ Meticas (Cu-Ni) 1975		175.00	300.00

MONETARY REFORM: 100 Centavos = 1 Metical (plural = Meticais)

		XF	Unc
39 (35)	50 Centavos (Al) 1980, 1982	0.35	0.75
40 (36)	1 Metical (Me) 1980, 1982	0.50	1.00
41 (37)	2½ Meticais (Cu-Ni) 1980, 1982	0.75	1.30
42 (38)	5 Meticais (Al) 1980, 1982	1.10	1.75
43 (39)	10 Meticais (Cu-Ni) 1980, 1981	1.50	2.25
44 (40)	20 Meticais (Cu-Ni) 1980	2.50	5.00

5th ANNIVERSARY OF INDEPENDENCE (2)

		Unc	Proof
45 (41)	500 Meticais (Ag) 1980		85.00
46 (42)	5000 Meticais (Au) 1980		500.00

WORLD FISHERIES CONFERENCE (2)

		Unc	Proof
47 (43)	50 Meticais 1984. Xi-Tataru:		
	a) (Ag) normal thickness		35.00
	b) (Ag), Pièfort		100.00
	c) (Cu-Ni)	10.00	
48	50 Meticais (Au) 1984		850.00

			Unc	Proof
49 (44)	250	Meticais 1985. Rev. Map and star:		
		a) (Ag) .925 silver, 28.28 g		45.00
		b) (Cu-Ni)	17.50	
50 (45)	2000	Meticais (Au) 1985. Type as No. 49;		
		916⅔ gold, 17.5 g (100 pcs.)		450.00

Oman ### Muscat and Oman Sultanat d'Oman
Sultanate of Oman

Area: 82,000 sq. mi. Population: 750,000.
Sultanate in the south-east of the Arabian Peninsula.
Capital: Muscat.

4 Baiza = 1 Anna, 64 Baiza = 1 Rupee;
200 Baiza = 1 Muscat Rial.
Since May 7, 1970: 1000 Baiza = 1 Rial Saidi

The Indian Rupee, which had been in circulation for some considerable
time, lost its validity on May 20, 1970. The Maria Theresa Taler (= 450
Baiza, fluctuating rate of exchange) is recognized, together with the
Rial Saidi and its sub-divisions, for private transactions.

FAISAL BIN TURKEE 1888–1913

			VF	XF
1 (1)	$1/_{12}$ Anna (Cu) H-C 1311 (1894). View of the harbour. ℞ lines of lettering in wreath of branches		28.00	50.00
2 (2)	¼ Anna (Cu) H-C 1311 (1894). Same type as No. 1		20.00	45.00
3 (3)	¼ Anna (Cu or Bra) H-C 1312–1319 (1895–1902). Value, legend and date in circle. ℞ legend in wreath		2.00	3.50

SAID BEN TAIMUR 1932–1970

4 (7)	2 Baiza (Cu–Ni) H-C 1365 (1946). jambija and crossed sabers (state emblem), value. ℞ legend and date. Square		1.20	2.00

			VF	XF
5 (8)	5	Baiza (Cu–Ni) H-C 1365 (1946). Scalloped		
6 (10)	20	Baiza (Cu–Ni) H-C 1365 (1946). Square	1.60	2.50
7 (14)	3	Baiza (Br) H-C 1380 (1961). Diameter: 18 mm	2.00	3.50
			1.20	2.00

8 (16)	5	Baiza (Cu–Ni) H–C 1381 (1962). State emblem, legend. ℞ dhow and date in circle, value	2.00	3.00

ISSUES FOR DHUFAR

9 (4)	10	Baiza (Cu–Ni) H–C 1359 (1940). State emblem. ℞ legend	4.50	6.50

10 (5)	20	Baiza (Cu–Ni) H-C 1359 (1940). Square	6.50	9.00
11 (6)	50	Baiza (Cu–Ni) H-C 1359 (1940). Octagonal	8.00	11.00

			VF	XF
12 (11)	½	Rial (Ag) H-C 1367 (1948). State emblem in wreath. ℞ legend in circle, all surrounded by leaves	20.00	30.00
13 (12)	1	Rial (Ag) H-C 1378 (1959). State emblem surrounded by legend and circle; edge decoration: dhow and palm tree, alternating. ℞ value and date	25.00	35.00
14 (13)	3	Baiza (Br) H-C 1378 (1959). Diameter 20 mm	3.00	4.50
15 (15)	½	Rial (Ag) H-C 1380–1381 (1961–1962)	5.50	8.00
16 (17)	15	Rials (Au) H-C 1381 (1962). State emblem, surrounded by new legend and circle; edge decoration: dhow and palm tree, alternating. ℞ value and date	175.00	220.00

NEW CURRENCY: 1000 Baiza = 1 Rial Saidi

In the Sultanate of Muscat and Oman, as well as in the Province of Dhufar, the Rial Saidi is now the only legal tender.

			XF	Unc
17 (18)	2	Baiza (Br) H-C 1390 (1970). State emblem. ℞ value, date	0.10	0.20
18 (19)	5	Baiza (Br) H-C 1390. Same type as No. 17	0.10	0.20
19 (20)	10	Baiza (Br) H-C 1390. Same type as No. 17	0.12	0.25
20 (21)	25	Baiza (Cu–Ni) H-C 1390. Same type as No. 17	0.15	0.30

			XF	Unc
21 (22)	50	Baiza (Cu–Ni) H-C 1390. Same type as No. 17	0.20	0.30
22 (23)	100	Baiza (Cu–Ni) H-C 1390. Same type as No. 17	0.35	0.50

				Proof
23	25	Baiza (Au) H-C 1390. Same type as No. 20		150.00
24	50	Baiza (Au) H-C 1390. Same type as No. 21		200.00
25	100	Baiza (Au) H-C 1390. Same type as No. 22		350.00
26	½	Rial (Au) H-C 1390		500.00
27	1	Rial (Au) H-C 1390		800.00

Area: c. 800,000 sq. mi. Population: 4,000,000.
The Sultanate in central Arabia, independent until 1932, now forms the
core of Saudi Arabia.
Capital: Riyadh.

$$20 \text{ Guerche} = 1 \text{ Riyal}$$

ABDUL AZIZ ABDUR RAHMAN IBN SAUD

There is no evidence of any coins struck for the sultanate. Egyptian or
Turkish silver coins, and even Maria Theresa Talers, were countermarked with the Arab name of Nejd.

		VF	XF
1 (1)	¼ Riyal	25.00	35.00
2 (2)	½ Riyal	35.00	40.00

3 (3a)	1 Riyal	65.00	85.00

Sri Nepála Sarkár

Area: 54,00 sq. mi. Population: 16,500,000.
Kingdom on the south side of the Himalayas, situated between Tibet and India.
Capital: Katmandu.

32 Paise = 16 Dak = 1 Mohar, 100 Paise = 1 Nepalese Rupee

Dates on coins correspond with the Samwat (A.S.) or the Saka Calendar.

PRITHVI BIR BIKRAM SHAH DEV 1881–1911

				VF	XF
1 (1)	¼	Paisa (Cu) 1907–1911 (A.S. 1964–1968). Nepalese inscription around lotus flower, within eight-pointed star, formed of two squares. ℞ trident in center, otherwise similar to obverse		9.00	12.00
2 (A3)	1	Paisa (Cu) 1892–1907 (A.S. 1949–1964). Same type as No. 1		8.00	11.50
3 (B3)	1	Paisa (Cu) 1902–1911 (A.S. 1959–1968). Same type as No. 1		6.50	9.00
4 (4)	1	Dak (Cu) 1891–1911 (A.S. 1948–1968). Same type as No. 1		7.50	10.50
5	8	Dak (Br) 1902 (A. Saka 1824). Same type as No. 1, but with center hole		–.–	–.–
6 (9)	1/64	Mohar (Ag) undated		4.00	6.00
7 (10)	1/32	Mohar (Ag) undated		4.00	6.00
8 (11)	1/16	Mohar (Ag) undated		6.00	8.00
9 (12)	1/8	Mohar (Ag) undated		6.50	9.00
10 (13)	¼	Mohar (Ag) 1881–1911 (A. Saka 1803–1833). Lettering around small circle of arms. ℞ lettering in three lines with central symbol		8.00	10.50
11 (14)	½	Mohar (Ag) 1881–1911 (A. Saka 1803–1833). Same type as No. 10		8.50	12.00
12 (15)	1	Mohar (Ag) 1881–1911 (A. Saka 1803–1833). Lettering in swastika ornament. ℞ lettering in stylized lotus flower		12.00	16.00
13 (16)	2	Mohar (Ag) 1889–1911 (A. Saka 1811–1833). Same type as No. 12, diameter: 25.5 mm		28.00	40.00
14 (17)	4	Mohar (Ag) 1895–1911 (A. Saka 1817–1833). Same type as No. 12, diameter: 29 mm		55.00	75.00

			VF	XF
15 (18)	$1/_{64}$	Mohar (Au) no date	30.00	40.00
16 (19)	$1/_{32}$	Mohar (Au) no date	35.00	48.00
17 (20)	$1/_{16}$	Mohar (Au) no date	40.00	60.00
18 (21)	$1/_8$	Mohar (Au) no date	45.00	72.00
19 (22)	$1/_4$	Mohar (Au) 1886–1911 (A. Saka 1808– 1833). Lettering in quadrangular ar- rangement around small circle of arms, date below. ℞ lettering in lotus flower	65.00	85.00
20 (23)	$1/_2$	Mohar (Au) 1901–1911 (A. Saka 1823– 1833). Same type as No. 19	90.00	100.00
21 (24)	1	Mohar (Au) 1899–1911 (A. Saka 1821– 1833). Same type as No. 19	100.00	120.00
22 (25)	2	Mohar (Au) 1904–1911 (A. Saka 1826– 1833). Same type as No. 19	150.00	170.00
23	4	Mohar (Au) 1911 (A. Saka 1833). Same type as No. 19	–.–	–.–

PATTERN PIECES

The Mohar coinages of 1911 (A. Saka 1833) can also be considered pattern pieces.

			VF	XF
P 1 (5)	$1/_4$	Paisa (Cu) 1911 (A.S. 1968). Nine let- ters in square. ℞ twelve letters in square. Date below. Diameter: 16 mm	8.00	12.00
P 2 (6)	$1/_2$	Paisa (Cu) 1911 (A.S. 1968). Same type as P 1, but diameter: 19 mm	8.00	12.00
P 3 (7)	1	Paisa (Cu) 1911. (A.S. 1968). Same type as P 1, but diameter: 23 mm	9.00	12.50
P 4 (8)	1	Dak (Cu) 1911 (A.S. 1968). Same type as P 1, but diameter: 26.6 mm	10.50	15.00

QUEEN LAKSHMI DEVJESBARI Sovereign in 1914

			VF	XF
24 (A26)	$1/_4$	Mohar (Ag) 1914 (A.S. 1971). Same type as No. 10	10.50	15.00
25 (B26)	1	Mohar (Ag) 1914 (A.S. 1971). Same type as No. 12	12.50	18.50
26 (C26)	1	Mohar (Au) 1914 (A.S. 1971). Same type as No. 12	120.00	150.00

TRIBHUVANA BIR BIKRAM SHAH DEV 1911–1950

			VF	XF
27 (27)	1	Paisa (Cu) 1911–1914 (A.S. 1968– 1971). Same type as No. 3, but crude design. Change in name and date	4.50	6.00
28 (28)	$1/_2$	Paisa (Cu) 1921–1928 (A.S. 1978– 1985). Circle of lettering around crossed kukris (daggers). ℞ circle of lettering around lines of lettering	5.00	8.00

			VF	XF
29 (29)	1 Paisa (Cu) 1918–1929 (A.S. 1975–1986). Same type as No. 28		2.50	4.00
30 (30)	2 Paise (Cu) 1921–1928 (A.S. 1978–1985). Same type as No. 28		3.50	5.00
31 (31)	5 Paise (Cu) 1919–1927 (A.S. 1976–1984). Same type as No. 28		6.00	8.00
32 (32)	¼ Mohar (Ag) 1912–1913 (A.S. 1969–1970). Same type as No. 10		2.50	3.50
33 (33)	½ Mohar (Ag) 1913 (A.S. 1970). Same type as No. 10		3.50	5.00
34 (34)	1 Mohar (Ag) 1912 (A.S. 1969). Same type as No. 12		6.00	8.00
35 (35)	2 Mohar (Ag) 1912–1932 (A.S. 1969–1989). Same type as No. 12		12.00	16.00
36 (36)	4 Mohar (Ag) 1912 (A.S. 1969). Same type as No. 12		28.00	40.00
37 (37)	½ Asarfi (Au) 1938 (A.S. 1995). Same type as No. 19		70.00	85.00
38 (38)	1 Asarfi (Au) 1912–1948 (A.S. 1969–2005). Same type as No. 19		150.00	170.00

39 (39)	1 Tola (Au) 1912–1948 (A.S. 1969–2005). Same type as No. 19		265.00	300.00

NEW CURRENCY: 100 Paise = 1 Rupee

			VF	XF
40 (40)	1 Paisa (Cu) 1933–1939 (A.S. 1990–1996). Type similar to No. 28, but two ears of wheat above kukris		2.50	4.00
41 (41)	2 Paise (Cu) 1935–1939 (A.S. 1992–1996). Same type as No. 40		4.00	6.00
42 (42)	5 Paise (Cu) 1934–1939 (A. S. 1991–1996). Same type as No. 40		5.00	7.00
43 (A42)	¼ Paisa (Cu or Br) 1947 (A.S. 2004)		12.00	16.00
44 (B42)	½ Paisa (Cu or Br) 1947 (A.S. 2004)		12.00	16.00
45 (43a)	1 Paisa (Cu or Br) 1943–1951 (A.S. 2000–2008). Type similar to No. 40, but R with sun, sword and crescent in center		1.50	2.00
46 (44)	2 Paise (Cu or Br) 1935–1953 (A.S. 1992–2010). Same type as No. 45			
	a) (Cu) 1935–1936, diameter: 27 mm		3.50	5.00

			VF	**XF**
		b) (Cu) 1937–1941, diameter: 25 mm	1.50	2.50
		c) (Cu–Br) 1943–1953, diameter: 23 mm	1.50	2.50
47	4	Paise (Ag) 1939	–.–	–.–
48	5	Paise (Cu) 1941 (A. S. 1998). Same type as No. 45	–.–	–.–
49 (45)	5	Paise (Cu–Ni) 1943, 1953 (A. S. 2000, 2010). Obverse similar to No. 48, but hoe instead of kukris. ℞ without inner circle, sword instead of trident	1.20	2.00
50 (46)	20	Paise (Ag) 1935–1953 (A. S. 1992–2010). Trident and legend. ℞ small sword and ears of wheat in stylized lotus flower, with lettering	1.50	2.50
51 (47)	50	Paise (Ag) 1938–1948 (A.S. 1995–2005). Trident in center of swastika ornament with lettering. R same as No. 50	3.00	4.00
51a	50	Paise (Ag) 1949–1953 (A.S. 2006–2010). Type as No. 51, reduced fineness	2.50	3.50

52 (48)	1	Rupee (Ag) 1932–1952 (A.S. 1989–2010). Same type as No. 51	10.00	16.00
53 (50)	¼	Asarfi (Au) 1937	45.00	60.00
54 (51)	½	Asarfi (Au) 1915–1948	70.00	80.00
55 (52)	1	Asarfi (Au) 1935	150.00	180.00
56 (53)	2	Asarfi (Au) 1948	310.00	360.00

GIANENDRA BIR BIKRAM SHAH DEV 1950–1952

57 (54)	50	Paise (Ag) 1950 (A.S. 2007). Same type as No. 51, but name of ruler GIANENDRA	250.00	300.00
58 (55)	1	Rupee (Ag) 1950 (A.S. 2007). Same type as No. 57	16.00	20.00
A58	1	Asarfi (Au) 1950	–.–	–.–
B58	1	Tola (Au) 1950	–.–	–.–

TRIBHUVANA BIR BIKRAM SHAH DEV (2nd reign) 1952–1955

59 (59)	2	Paise (Bra) 1954	1.00	2.00
60	5	Paise (Cu–Ni) 1953. Similar to No. 49	1.20	2.00

			VF	XF

61 (62) 5 Paise (Bra) 1954 (A. S. 2011). Mountains with rising sun and ears of wheat. ℞ Buddha's hand raised to teach … **1.00** **1.50**

62 (63) 10 Paise (Br) 1954 (A. S. 2011). Obverse like No. 61. ℞ kukri (dagger) in front of mountains in circle of ornamental lettering … **1.20** **1.60**

63 (64) 20 Paise (Cu–Ni) 1953–1954 … **3.00** **4.50**

64 (65) 25 Paise (Cu–Ni) A. S. 2011 (1954). Same type as No. 62 … **1.50** **2.50**

65 (56) 50 Paise (Cu–Ni) A. S. 2010–2011 (1953–1954). Tribhuvana Bir Bikram (1906–1955), head in pentagram. ℞ mountains and rising sun, between ears of wheat … **2.00** **3.50**

66 (57) 1 Rupee (Cu–Ni) A. S. 2010–2011 (1953–1954). Same type as No. 65 … **5.00** **7.50**

MAHENDRA BIR BIKRAM 1955–1972

67 (58) 1 Paisa (Bra) A. S. 2012 (1955). Kukri in front of mountains. ℞ mountains and rising sun, between ears of wheat. Date … **1.50** **2.50**

68 (59) 2 Paise (Bra) A. S. 2012–2013 (1955–1956). Same type as No. 67 … **0.40** **0.60**

				VF	XF
69 (61)	4	Paise (Bra) A. S. 2012 (1955). Center hole		1.20	2.50
70 (62)	5	Paise (Br) A. S. 2012-2014 (1955-1957). Buddha's hand raised to teach. Rev. mountains and rising sun, between ears of wheat; 3,89 grams		0.80	1.20
71 (62a)	5	Paise (Cu-Ni) A. S. 2014 (1957). Type as No. 70; 4,04 grams		–.–	–.–
72 (63)	10	Paise (Br) A. S. 2012 (1955). Kukri in front of mountains. ℞ mountains and rising sun, between ears of wheat. Date		1.00	1.50
73 (65)	25	Paise (Cu–Ni) A. S. 2012–2014 (1955–1957). Same type as No. 72		1.20	1.80
74 (82)	25	Paise (Cu-Ni) A. S. 2015-2023 (1958-1966). Trident in circle, all within a tablet. Four characters in line above trident		1.00	1.50
75 (83)	50	Paise (Cu-Ni) A. S. 2011–2023 (1954–1966). Type as No. 74; 25 mm dia.		1.50	3.00
76 (83a)	50	Paise (Cu-Ni) A. S. 2023 (1966). Type as No. 75; 23,5 mm dia.		1.50	3.00
77 (84)	1	Rupee (Cu-Ni) A. S. 2011–2023 (1954–1966). Type as No. 74:			
		a) A. S. 2011, 2012 (1954, 1955); dia. 29,6 mm		3.00	5.00
		b) A. S. 2012–2023 (1955–1966); dia. 28,8 mm		3.00	5.00
78 (84a)	1	Rupee (Cu-Ni) A. S. 2023 (1966). Type as No. 77; 27 mm dia.		3.00	5.00
79 (82a)	25	Paise (Cu-Ni) A. S. 2024-2028 (1967-1971). Type as No. 74, but five characters in line above trident		1.20	2.00
80 (83a)	50	Paise (Cu-Ni) A. S. 2025-2028 (1968-1971). Type as No. 76, but five characters in line above trident:			
		a) A. S. 2025-2026 (1968-1969)		1.50	2.80
		b) A. S. 2027-2028 (1970-1971); proof only			10.00
81 (84b)	1	Rupee (Cu-Ni) A. S. 2025-2028 (1968-1971). Type as No. 78, but five characters in line above trident:			
		a) A. S. 2025-2026 (1968-1969)		3.00	5.00
		b) A. S. 2027-2028 (1970-1971); proof only			14.00
82 (85)	1/5	Asarfi (Au) A. S. 2012 (1955); 2.33 grams		28.00	36.00
83 (86)	¼	Asarfi (Au) A. S. 2012 (1955); 2.91 grams		30.00	40.00

84 (87)	½ Asarfi (Au) 2012-2019 (1955-1962)	40.00	50.00
85 (88)	1 Asarfi (Au) A. S. 2012-2019 (1955-1962)	80.00	96.00
86 (89)	2 Asarfi (Au) A. S. 2012 (1955)	185.00	240.00

COMMEMORATIVE COINS (10) FOR THE CORONATION
OF THE KING AND QUEEN OF NEPAL

		VF	XF
87 (66)	1 Paisa (Bra) A. S. 2013 (1956). Royal crown of the Shah dev Dynasty. Rev. value in circle	2.50	3.50
88 (67)	2 Paise (Bra) A. S. 2013. Type similar to No. 87	2.50	4.00
89 (68)	5 Paise (Br) A. S. 2013. Type similar to No. 87	3.50	5.00
90 (69)	10 Paise (Br) A. S. 2013. Type similar to No. 87	3.50	6.00
91 (70)	25 Paise (Cu-Ni) A. S. 2013. Type similar to No. 87	2.50	4.00
92 (71)	50 Paise (Cu-Ni) A. S. 2013. Type similar to No. 87	2.50	4.00
93 (72)	1 Rupee (Cu-Ni) A. S. 2013. Type similar to No. 87	4.00	6.00
94 (73)	1/6 Asarfi (Au) A. S. 2013. Type similar to No. 87	35.00	48.00
95 (76)	½ Asarfi (Au) A. S. 2013. Type similar to No. 87	80.00	90.00
96 (77)	1 Asarfi (Au) A. S. 2013. Type similar to No. 87	300.00	360.00
97 (78)	1 Paisa (Bra) A. S. 2014-2020 (1957-1963). Trident between moon and sun. Rev. value between branches. Denomination with shading	0.25	0.40
98 (79)	2 Paise (Bra) A. S. 2014-2020 (1957-1963). Rev. value in rhombiodal ornament. Denomination with shading	0.40	0.60
99 (80)	5 Paise (Br) A. S. 2014-2020 (1957-1963). Rev. value on lotus flower with eight leaves. Denomination with shading; 22 mm dia.	0.40	0.60
100 (81)	10 Paise (Br) A. S. 2014-2020 (1975-1963). Rev. value on lotus flower with four leaves	0.50	0.80
101 (78a)	1 Paisa (Bra) A. S. 2021-2022 (1964-1965). Type as No. 97, but large sun with short rays. Denomination without shading	0.25	0.40
102 (79a)	2 Paise (Bra) A. S. 2021-2023 (1964-1966). Type as No. 98, but large sun with short rays. Denomination without shading	0.40	0.60
103 (80a)	5 Paise (Al-Br) A. S. 2021 (1964). Type as No. 99, but large sun with short rays. Denomination without shading	2.50	4.00

				VF	XF
104	(81a)	10	Paise (Al-Br) A. S. 2021 (1964). Type as No. 100, but large sun with short rays; 24.5 mm dia.	3.00	4.00

				VF	XF
105	(80b)	5	Paise (Br) A. S. 2021-2023 (1964-1966). Type as No. 103, but 20.5 mm dia.	0.40	0.60
106	(81b)	10	Paise (Br) A. S. 2021-2023 (1964-1966). Type similar to No. 104. Modified design; 24 mm dia.	0.50	0.80

107	(90)	1	Paisa (Al) A. S. 2023-2028 (1966-1971). Mountains. Rev. national flower	0.15	0.25

108	(91)	2	Paise (Al) A. S. 2023-2028 (1966-1971). Rev. Himalayan Monal (Lophophorus impejanus – Phasianidae)	0.15	0.25
109	(92)	5	Paise (Al) A. S. 2023-2028 (1966-1971). Rev. cow	0.20	0.40

	VF	XF
110 (93) 10 Paise (Bra) A. S. 2023-2028 (1966-1971). Type as No. 109	0.25	0.50

ISSUES FOR THE FAO COIN PLAN (2)

	XF	Unc
111 (98) 10 Paise (Bra) A. S. 2028 (1971). Ear of wheat. Rev. cow	0.15	0.30

	VF	XF
112 (97) 10 Rupees (Ag) A. S. 2025 (1968). King Mahendra with crown of the Shah Dev Dynasty. Rev. trident and Symbols of progress. Motto: FOOD FOR ALL	4.00	7,50

BIRENDRA BIR BIKRAM since 1972

113 (99) 1 Paisa (Al) A. S. 2028–2036 (1972–1979). Type as No. 107; new name of ruler	0.10	0.20
114 (100) 2 Paise (Al) A. S. 2028–2035 (1972–1978), Type as No. 108; new name of ruler	0.15	0.25
115 (101) 5 Paise (Al) A. S. 2028–2038 (1972–1981). Type as No. 109; new name of ruler	0.15	0.35
116 (102) 10 Paise (Bra) A. S. 2028 (1972). Type as No. 115	1.50	3.00

				XF	Unc
117 (103)	25	Paise (Cu-Ni) A. S. 2028–2038 (1972–1981). Trident within circle, letterin in quadrangular arrangement around. Rev. Sword and garlands, value		0.40	0.75
118 (104)	50	Paise (Cu-Ni) A. S. 2028–2040 (1972–1983). Type as No. 117		0.50	1.00
119 (105)	1	Rupee (Cu-Ni) A. S. 2028–2036 (1972–1979). Type as No. 117		1.00	2.00
A120	¼	Asarfi (Au) A. S. 2028–2037 (1972–1980). Type as No. 177; 2.91 grms			90.00
B120	½	Asarfi (Au) A. S. 2028–2037. Type as No. 117; 5.82 grms			150.00
C120	1	Asarfi (Au) A. S. 2028–2037. Type as No. 117; 11.64 grms			380.00
120 (106)	10	Paise (Bra) A. S. 2029–2035 (1972–1978). Mountains. Rev. value between ears		0.20	0.40

ISSUES (2) FOR THE FAO COIN PLAN

121 (107)	5	Paise (Al) A. S. 2031 (1974)		0.10	0.20

			XF	Unc
122 (108)	10	Rupees (Ag) A. S. 2031 (1974)	4.00	7.50

BIRENDRA CORONATION COMMEMORATIVE (10)

			XF	Unc
123 (109)	1	Paisa (Al) A. S. 2031 (1974). Royal crown of the Shah Dev Dynasty. Rev. sword with garland and value in Devanagari	0.10	0.20
124 (110)	5	Paise (Al) A. S. 2031 (1974). Type as No. 123	0.15	0.30
125 (111)	10	Paise (Al) A. S. 2031 (1974). Type as No. 123	0.20	0.40
126 (112)	25	Paise (Cu-Ni) A. S. 2031 (1974). Type as No. 123	0.40	0.80
127 (113)	50	Paise (Cu-Ni) A. S. 2031 (1974). Type as No. 123	0.60	1.20
128 (114)	1	Rupee (Cu-Ni) A. S. 2031 (1974). Type as No. 123	1.10	2.50
129 (115)	25	Rupees (Ag) A. S. 2031 (1974). Type as No. 123	11.00	15.00
130 (116)	¼	Asarfi (Au) A. S. 2031 (1974). Type as No. 123		125.00
131 (117)	½	Asarfi (Au) A. S. 2031 (1974). Type as No. 123		180.00
132 (118)	1	Asarfi (Au) A. S. 2031 (1974). Type as No. 123		360.00

CONSERVATION COMMEMORATIVE (3)

			Unc	Proof
133 (119)	25	Rupees (Ag) A. S. 2031 (1974). Bust right of King Birendra. Rev: Himalayan Monal:		
		a) .500 silver, 25.31 g	17.50	
		b) .925 silver, 28.28 g		25.00
134 (120)	50	Rupees (Ag) A. S. 2031 (1974). Rev. Himalayan Panda:		
		a) .500 silver, 31.65 g	25.00	
		b) .925 silver, 35.00 g		30.00
135 (121)	1	Asarfi (Au) A. S. 2031 (1974). Rev. Indian One-horned Rhinoceros	550.00	650.00

ISSUES FOR THE FAO COIN PLAN AND FOR INTERNATIONAL WOMEN'S YEAR 1975 (3)

			XF	Unc
136 (122)	10	Paise (Bra) A. S. 2032 (1975). Conjoined busts of the royal couple, date. Rev. value between ears	0.15	0.30
137 (123)	1	Rupee (Cu-Ni) A. S. 2032 (1975). Type as No. 136	1.00	1.50
138 (124)	20	Rupees (Ag) A. S. 2032 (1975). Type as No. 136	5.00	9.00

ISSUE FOR THE FAO COIN PLAN (2)

139 (125)	10	Paise (Bra) A. S. 2033 (1976). Head of a Barwal sheep. Rev. value, date	0.15	0.30

140 (126)	20	Paise (Bra) A. S. 2035 (1978)	0.75	1.00

EDUCATION FOR VILLAGE WOMEN (3)

141 (A130)	10	Paise (Al) 1979. Book with inscription	0.25	0.40
142 (130)	50	Rupees (Ag) 1979. Type as No. 141:	**Unc**	**Proof**
		a) .500 silver	12.50	
		b) .925 silver, 25 g, dia. 40 mm		35.00
A142	1	Asarfi (Au) 1979. Type as No. 141		250.00

5th ANNIVERSARY OF CORONATION (2)

143	25	Rupees (Ag) 1979		35.00
144 (127)	1000	Rupees (Au) 1979 (250 pcs.)		300.00

RURAL WOMEN'S ADVANCEMENT (2)

		XF	Unc
146 (131)	5 Rupees (Cu-Ni) A. S. 2037 (1980)	1.50	3.00

INTERNATIONAL YEAR OF THE CHILD (6)

		XF	Unc
147	10 Paise (Bra) 1979. IYC Logo, rising sun	0.30	0.60
148	20 Paise (Bra) 1979. Type as No. 147	0.50	1.00
150	20 Rupees (Ag) 1979. Type as No. 147:		
	a) .500 silver		9.00
	b) .925 silver, proof		40.00
A151	50 Rupees (Ag) 1981		–.–

			Proof
151	100 Rupees (Ag) 1981. King Birendra. Rev. Children filling water in a bottle		40.00
152	1 Asarfi (Au) 1981. Rev. Reading girl		400.00

WORLD FOOD DAY 1981 (4)

		XF	Unc
153 (132)	25 Paise (Bra) 1981. Corn	0.30	0.60
154 (133)	50 Paise (Cu-Ni) 1981. Type as No. 153	0.50	1.00
155 (134)	2 Rupees (Cu-Ni) 1981. Type as No. 153	1.00	2.60
		Unc	Proof
156	100 Rupees (Ag) 1981. Rice cultivation:		
	a) .500 silver, 25 g, 40 mm dia.	20.00	
	b) .925 silver	28.00	32.00

INTERNATIONAL YEAR OF DISABLED PERSONS (3)

		XF	Unc
157 (135)	25 Paise (Bra) 1981. IYDP Logo	0.50	1.00
158 (136)	50 Paise (Cu-Ni) 1981. Type as No. 157	0.80	1.50
159 (137)	50 Rupees (Ag) 1981. Type as No. 157	5.50	10.00

Nos. 149, 160–260 omitted.

NATIONAL BANK SILVER JUBILEE

		XF	Unc
261	5 Rupees (Cu-Ni) 1981	4.00	7.50

10th ANNIVERSARY OF REIGN (2)

		Proof
263	250 Rupees (Ag) 1982. The Royal Couple. Rev. value	40.00
264	1 Asarfi (Au) 1982. Rev. sword and garlands	300.00

		XF	Unc
265	1 Paisa (Al) VS 2039 (1982). Crown of the Shah Dev Dynasty, crossed Kukris and flags below. Rev. value between ears	0.10	0.20
266	5 Paise (Al) VS 2039, 2040 (1982, 1983). Type as No. 265	0.15	0.30
267	10 Paise (Al) VS 2041 (1984). Type as No. 265	0.30	0.50
268	25 Paise (Al) VS 2039, 2040 (1982, 1983). Type as No. 265	0.40	0.75
269	50 Paise (Cu-Ni) VS 2039, 2040 (1982, 1983)	0.50	1.00
270	1 Rupee (Cu-Ni) VS 2040 (1983)	-.-	-.-
271	2 Rupees (Cu-Ni) VS 2040 (1983)	-.-	-.-
272	5 Rupees (Cu-Ni) VS 2040 (1983)	2.50	4.00

ISSUE FOR THE FAO COIN PLAN

		XF	Unc
279	2 Rupees (Cu-Ni) VS 2039 (1982). Fruits	0.60	1.00

YEAR OF THE SCOUT (2)

		Unc	Proof
280	250 Rupees (Ag) VS 2039 (1982). Rev. scouts planting a tree	25.00	30.00
281	1 Asarfi (Au) VS 2039 (1982). Rev. girl-scout	300.00	400.00

30th ANNIVERSARY OF ASCENT OF MT. EVEREST (3)

282	10 Rupees (Cu-Ni) VS 2040 (1983). Rev. Mt. Everest	7.50	
283	100 Rupees (Ag) VS 2040 (1983). Type as No. 282		65.00
284	1 Asarfi (Au) VS 2040 (1983). Type as No. 282		300.00

FAMILY PLANNING (4)

		XF	Unc
285	50 Paise (Cu-Ni) VS 2041 (1984). Value. Rev. family of four, stylized house	0.40	0.70
286	1 Rupee (Cu-Ni) VS 2041 (1984)	0.60	1.25
287	2 Rupees (Cu-Ni) VS 2041 (1984)	0.75	1.50
288	5 Rupees (Cu-Ni) VS 2041 (1984)	1.25	2.50

Niederlande　　　　　**Netherlands**　　　　　**Pays-Bas**

Koningrijk der Nederlanden

Area: 15,780 sq. mi. Population: 14,500,000.
The country is subdivided into the provinces of Drente, Friesland, Gelderland, Groningen, Limburg, North Brabant, North Holland, Overijsel, Zealand, South Holland, and Utrecht.
Capital: Amsterdam, seat of government: Den Haag (The Hague).

100 Cents = 1 Gulden

WILHELMINA 1890–1948

			VF	XF
1 (15)	1 Ducat (Au) 1894–1937. Knight with sword and bundle of arrows. ℞ latin		60.00	80.00

Similar design: Nos. 43,57.

			VF	XF
2 (23)	10 Cents (Ag) 1898, 1901		50.00	70.00
3 (23a)	10 Cents (Ag) 1903		20.00	35.00
4 (23b)	10 Cents (Ag) 1904–1906		15.00	45.00
5 (24)	25 Cents (Ag) 1898–1906:			
	a) 1898		225.00	550.00
	b) 1901–1906		22.50	45.00
6 (25a)	½ Gulden (Ag) 1904–1909		25.00	47.50

		VF	XF
7 (26)	1 Gulden (Ag) 1898, 1901. With mark »100 C« underneath coat of arms	55.00	100.00
8 (26a)	1 Gulden (Ag) 1904–1909. Same type as No. 7, but without mark »100 C«	30.00	60.00
9 (33)	5 Cents (Cu-Ni) 1907–1909. Crown in wreath. ℞ value in wreath	12.50	27.50

			VF	XF
10 (35)	½ Cent (Br) 1909–1940. Heraldic lion. R value in wreath		3.00	8.00
11 (36)	1 Cent (Br) 1913–1941. Type as No. 10		1.20	6.00
12 (37)	2½ Cents (Br) 1912–1941. Type similar to No. 10		2.00	8.00
13 (34)	5 Cents (Cu-Ni) 1913–1940. Orange branch in wreath. Rev. value		4.50	12.00

			VF	XF
14 (39)	10 Cents (Ag) 1910–1925		4.00	16.00
15 (40)	25 Cents (Ag) 1910–1925		10.00	32.00
16 (41)	½ Gulden (Ag) 1910–1919		20.00	40.00

			VF	XF
17 (42)	1 Gulden (Ag) 1910–1917		28.00	45.00

			VF	XF
18 (31)	5 Gulden (Au) 1912. Wilhelmina, head right. R crowned coat of arms		150.00	200.00
19 (30)	10 Gulden (Au) 1911–1913, 1917		95.00	125.00
20 (43)	10 Cents (Ag) 1926–1945		1.00	4.00
21 (44)	25 Cents (Ag) 1926–1945		1.50	6.50
22 (45)	½ Gulden (Ag) 1921–1930		3.00	7.00
23 (46)	1 Gulden (Ag) 1922–1945		5.00	10.00
24 (47)	2½ Gulden (Ag) 1929–1943		12.50	20.00

			VF	XF
25 (32)	10 Gulden (Au) 1925–1933		100.00	140.00

				VF	XF
26 (48)	1	Cent (Z) 1941–1944. Cross. ℞ value and ears of wheat		0.40	1.20
27 (49)	2½	Cents (Z) 1941–1942. Ornamentation. ℞ value and ears of wheat		6.00	12.00
28 (50)	5	Cents (Z) 1941–1943. Crossed horse's heads. ℞ value		3.50	11.00
29 (51)	10	Cents (Z) 1941–1943. Stylized tulips. ℞ value		1.20	3.50
30 (52)	25	Cents (Z) 1941–1943. Vessel. ℞ value		4.00	7.50
31 (53)	1	Cent (Br) 1948. Wilhelmina, head left. ℞ value		0.40	0.80
32 (54)	5	Cents (Br) 1948. ℞ value		0.40	1.50
33 (55)	10	Cents (Ni) 1948. ℞ crown above value		0.40	1.20
34 (56)	25	Cents (Ni) 1948		0.40	2.00

JULIANA 1948–1980

				XF	Unc
35 (57)	1	Cent (Br) 1950–1980. Juliana, head right. R value		0.10	0.20
36 (58)	5	Cents (Br) 1950–1980.		0.10	0.20
37 (59)	10	Cents (Ni) 1950–1980.		0.10	0.20

38 (60)	25	Cents (Ni) 1950–1980		0.15	0.25

39 (61)	1	Gulden (Ag) 1954–1967		4.00	7.00
40 (61a)	1	Gulden (Ni) 1967–1980. Same type as No. 39		0.50	0.80
41 (62)	2½	Gulden (Ag) 1959–1966		9.00	12.50
42 (62a)	2½	Gulden (Ni) 1969–1980. Same type as No. 41 but smaller diameter		1.20	2.00
43 (15)	1	Ducat (Au) 1960–1978. Type as No. 1:			
		1960			500.00
		1972, 1978			100.00
		1974, 1975			80.00
		1976			200.00

Similar design: No. 57.

COMMEMORATIVE ISSUE FOR THE 25th ANNIVERSARY OF THE END OF WORLD WAR II

			XF	Unc
44 (64)	10	Gulden (Ag) 1970	12.50	17.50

COMMEMORATIVE ISSUE FOR THE 25th ANNIVERSARY OF THE REIGN ON 4th SEPT. 1973

45 (65)	10	Gulden (Ag) 1973. Juliana, head facing right. ℞ crowned armorial shield, date, value	12.50	20.00

400th ANNIVERSARY OF THE UNION OF UTRECHT

46 (66)	2½	Gulden (Cu-Ni) 1979	1.00	1.50

BEATRIX since 1980

47 (67)	1	Gulden (Cu-Ni) 1980	0.60	0.75
48 (68)	2½	Gulden (Cu-Ni) 1980	1.25	1.75

			XF	Unc
49 (69)	5 Cent (Br) 1982–. Beatrix, head facing left. Rev. value, date		0.05	0.10
50 (70)	10 Cent (Ni) 1982–		0.05	0.10
51 (71)	25 Cent (Ni) 1982–		0.15	0.20

		XF	Unc
52 (72)	1 Gulden (Ni) 1982–	0.50	0.65
53 (73)	2½ Gulden (Ni) 1982–	0.90	1.25

No. 54 omitted

DUTCH-AMERICAN FRIENDSHIP

		Unc	Proof
55 (74)	50 Gulden (Ag) 1982	35.00	55.00

400th ANNIVERSARY OF DEATH OF WILLIAM OF ORANGE

		Unc	Proof
56 (75)	50 Gulden (Ag) 1984	30.00	45.00
57	1 Ducat (Au) 1985. Type as No. 1		85.00

400 YEARS OF THE DUTCH-DUCAT-TYP (4)

58	1 Ducat (Au) 1986, 1988. Type similar to No. 1; .983 gold, 3.494 g		90.00

		Unc	Proof
A 59	5 Daalder (Ag) 1986. Knight standing. Rev. Ship; .999 silver, 155.5 g	185.00	
B 59	5 Daalder (Au) 1986; .999 gold, 155.5 g (50 pcs.)	–.–	
59	2 Ducats (Au) 1986. Type as No. 58		–.–

Netherlands Antilles

Niederländische Antillen   **Antilles Néerlandaises**

Nederlandse Antillen

Area: 336 sq. mi. Population: 225,000.
Group of islands, comprising the islands of Curaçao, Aruba, Bonaire,
Saint Martin, Saint Eustatius, and Saba. After the statute of 1954, this
group constitutes part of the kingdom of the Netherlands.
Capital: Willemstad.

100 Cents = 1 Gulden

JULIANA since 1948

			VF	XF
1 (1)	1	Cent (Br) 1952–1970. Heraldic lion. ℞ value within wreath	0.40	1.20
2 (2)	2½	Cents (Br) 1956–1965	0.40	1.20
3 (3)	5	Cents (Cu-Ni) 1957–1970. Orange branch (Citrus sinensis – Rutaceae) within circle. ℞ value	0.50	1.20
4 (4)	1/10	Gulden (Ag) 1954–1970	1.20	2.80
5 (5)	¼	Gulden (Ag) 1954–1970	2.50	6.00
6 (6)	1	Gulden (Ag) 1952–1970	6.50	10.50
7 (7)	2½	Gulden (Ag) 1964	11.50	18.00

			XF	Unc
8 (8)	1	Cent (Br) 1970–1978. Crowned coat of arms, name of country, date. R value	0.10	0.20
9 (9)	2½	Cents (Br) 1970–1978. Same type as No. 8	0.15	0.25
10 (10)	5	Cents (Cu-Ni) 1971–1980. Same type as No. 8 (Square with rounded corners)	0.20	0.30
11 (11)	10	Cents (Cu-Ni) 1970–1980. Same type as No. 8	0.25	0.40

			XF	Unc
12 (12)	25	Cents (Ni) 1970–1980. Same type as No. 8	0.30	0.60
13 (13)	1	Gulden (Ni) 1970–1980. Juliana, Queen of the Netherlands, head right. R crowned coat of arms, value	1.00	2.00

COMMEMORATIVE ISSUE FOR THE 25th ANNIVERSARY OF THE REIGN ON 4th SEPT. 1973

			Unc	Proof
14 (14)	25	Gulden (Ag) 1973. Juliana, head facing right. R Juliana and Prince Consort Bernhard in the State Coach upon the occasion of their visit to the island of Curacao while crossing the "Queen Emma Bridge"; legend in papiamento, the local vernacular; names of the individual islands. Edge inscription DIOS KU NOS	22.50	30.00

BICENTENARY OF AMERICAN INDEPENDENCE (2)

15 (15)	25	Gulden (Ag) 1976. Head right of Queen Juliana. Rev. the ship "Andrew Doria"; 45 mm dia.	50.00	50.00
16 (16)	200	Gulden (Au) 1976. Type as No. 16	175.00	185.00
17 (17)	25	Gulden (Ag) 1977. Peter Stuyvesant	220.00	
18 (18)	200	Gulden (Au) 1977. Peter Stuyvesant	225.00	175.00

			XF	Unc
19 (19)	2½	Gulden (Cu-Ni) 1978–1980	2.00	3.50

BANK COMMEMORATIVE (2)

			Unc	Proof
20 (20)	10	Gulden (Ag) 1978	17.50	30.00
21 (21)	100	Gulden (Au) 1978	120.00	150.00

			XF	Unc
22 (8a)	1 Cent (Al) 1979, 1980. Type as No. 8		0.10	0.20
23 (9a)	2½ Cents (Al) 1979, 1980. Type as No. 9		0.20	0.30

INTERNATIONAL YEAR OF THE CHILD

		Unc	Proof
24 (22)	25 Gulden (Ag) 1979:		
	a)		55.00
	b) Pièfort		175.00

25th ANNIVERSARY OF THE ROYAL STATUTE

25 (23)	50 Gulden (Au) 1979	65.00	65.00
26 (24)	300 Gulden (Au) 1980:		
	a) Mintmark	200.00	200.00
	b) W/o Mintmark	450.00	

	BEATRIX since 1980	XF	Unc
27 (8a)	1 Cent (Al) 1981–1985. Type as No. 8	0.10	0.20
28 (9a)	2½ Cent (Al) 1981–1985. Type as No. 9	0.15	0.25
29 (10)	5 Cent (Cu-Ni) 1981–1985. Type as No. 10	0.20	0.30
30 (11)	10 Cent (Ni) 1981–1985. Type as No. 11	0.25	0.40
31 (12)	25 Cent (Ni) 1981–1985. Type as No. 12	0.30	0.60
32 (26)	1 Gulden (Ni) 1980–1985. Beatrix, head facing left. Rev. arms. value, date	0.50	1.00
33 (27)	2½ Gulden (Ni) 1980–1985. Type as No. 32	1.50	2.50
		Unc	Proof
34 (30)	5 Gulden (Au) 1980		125.00
35 (31)	10 Gulden (Au) 1980		250.00
36 (25)	50 Gulden (Ag) 1980	55.00	55.00

DUTCH-AMERICAN FRIENDSHIP

37 (28)	50 Gulden (Ag) 1982. Rev. Peter Stuyvesant, flags	40.00

MIKVE ISRAEL EMANUEL SYNAGOGUE

38 (29)	50 Gulden (Ag) 1982	65.00

Netherlands East Indies

Niederländisch-Indien　　　　　　　**Indes Néerlandaises**

Nederlandsch Indië

The establishment of the Netherlands East Indian Company in 1602
resulted in the first trading posts in the area of today's Indonesia. From
1942 to 1945 the entire territory was occupied by the Japanese.
Dutch administration, limited since 1945 to only part of the island state,
ended completely with the establishment of the Indonesian Republic,
and the Conference of The Hague on December 28, 1949.
Capital: Djakarta (Dutch: Batavia).

100 Cents = 1 Gulden

			VF	XF
1 (1)	½	Cent (Cu) 1856–1909. Crowned coat of arms. ℞ legend in Malayan and Javanese	1.20	2.00
2 (2)	1	Cent (Cu) 1855–1912	0.80	1.20
3 (3)	2½	Cents (Cu) 1856–1913	1.20	2.00
4 (5)	¹⁄₁₀	Gulden (Ag) 1854–1901	3.00	4.50
5 (6)	¼	Gulden (Ag) 1854–1901	4.00	6.50
6 (7)	¹⁄₁₀	Gulden (Ag) 1903–1909	3.50	5.50
7 (8)	¼	Gulden (Ag) 1903–1909	3.50	5.50
8 (14)	¹⁄₁₀	Gulden (Ag) 1910–1945	1.60	2.00
9 (15)	¼	Gulden (Ag) 1910–1945	1.60	2.00

			VF	XF
10 (17)	5	Cents (Cu–Ni) 1913–1922. Crown above rice panicles. ℞ garudas, mythological birds (center hole)	0.80	1.20
11 (18)	½	Cent (Br) 1914–1945	0.40	0.60
12 (19)	1	Cent (Br) 1914–1929	0.50	0.80
13 (20)	2½	Cents (Br) 1914–1945	0.60	0.80
14 (21)	1	Cent (Br) 1936–1945. Rice panicles. ℞ legends (center hole)	0.25	0.40

For Japanese Occupation issues see at the end of the section for Japan.

Area: 9,401 sq. mi. Population: 120,000.
Located in the Pacific, north of New Zealand, this island has been French
territory since 1854. Together with the Loyalties, and other small island
groups, it constitutes a French Overseas Department.
Capital: Nouméa.

100 Centimes = 1 CFP Franc

			VF	XF
1 (1)	50 Centimes (Al) 1949. Marianne, sitting, allegory of the Republic of France. ℞ Kagu (Rhynochetos jubatus – Rhynochetidae)		0.60	1.00
2 (2)	1 Franc (Al) 1949. Same type as No. 1		0.70	1.20
3 (3)	2 Francs (Al) 1949. Same type as No. 1		0.80	1.50
4 (4)	5 Francs (Al) 1952. Same type as No. 1		1.50	2.00

5 (5)	10 Francs (Ni) 1967, 1970. Head of Marianne, allegory of the Republic of France. ℞ Melanesian pirogue	1.20	1.80

6 (6)	20 Francs (Ni) 1967, 1970. ℞ zebus	1.60	2.50

			VF	XF
7 (7)	50	Francs (Ni) 1967. Rev. natives' hut, surrounded by trees	3.00	5.00

			VF	XF
8 (A5)	1	Franc (Al) 1971. Type as No. 1, but inscription REPUBLIQUE FRANÇAISE	0.50	1.00
9 (B5)	2	Francs (Al) 1971. Type as No. 8	0.50	1.00

			XF	Unc
10 (A5a)	1	Franc (Al) 1972–. Type as No. 8, but I.E.O.M. added	0.20	0.40
11 (B5a)	2	Francs (Al) 1973–. Type as No. 9, but I.E.O.M. added	0.40	0.70
12 (5a)	10	Francs (Ni) 1972, 1973, 1977, 1979. Type as No. 5, but I.E.O.M. added	0.80	1.30
13 (6a)	20	Francs (Ni) 1972, 1977, 1979. Type as No. 6, but I.E.O.M. added	1.50	2.00
14 (7a)	50	Francs (Ni) 1972, 1979. Type as No. 7, but I.E.O.M. added	2.00	4.00
15 (8)	100	Francs (Ni) 1976, 1979. Type as No. 14	2.50	5.50

Newfoundland

Area: 152,734 sq. mi. Population: 515,000.
Newfoundland was discovered by John Cabot in 1497, and adjudicated
to England in 1713. In 1855 Newfoundland attained the status of a
dominion, and joined the Canadian Confederacy on 11th December
1948.
Capital: St. John's.

100 Cents = 1 Dollar

EDWARD VII 1901–1910

			VF	XF
1 (7)	1 Cent (Br) 1904–1909. Crowned portrait of Edward VII, right. R value in letters, crown and date in circle		6.00	10.00
2 (8)	5 Cents (Ag) 1903–1908. R value and date in circle		12.00	30.00
3 (9)	10 Cents (Ag) 1903–1904		9.00	25.00
4 (10)	20 Cents (Ag) 1904		20.00	75.00
5 (11)	50 Cents (Ag) 1904–1909		17.50	50.00

GEORGE V 1910–1936

6 (12)	1 Cent (Br) 1913–1936. Crowned portrait of George V, left. R value in letters and date in circle		2.00	5.00

7 (13)	5 Cents (Ag) 1912–1929. R value and date in circle	**VF**	**XF**
		6.00	20.00
8 (14)	10 Cents (Ag) 1912–1919	5.00	12.50
9 (15)	20 Cents (Ag) 1912	12.00	40.00
10 (16)	25 Cents (Ag) 1917–1919	7.50	15.00

11 (17)	50 Cents (Ag) 1911–1919	12.00	35.00

GEORGE VI 1936–1952

12 (18)	1 Cent (Br) 1938–1947. Crowned portrait of George VI, left. Rev. red sarracenia (Sarracenia purpurea – Sarraceniaceae)	0.80	1.60
13 (19)	5 Cents (Ag) 1938–1947. Rev. value and date in circle	2.00	4.00
14 (20)	10 Cents (Ag) 1938–1947	2.00	4.00

Yeoman Numbers

In order to help collectors and dealers, we have added after most SCHÖN-numbers the corresponding number assigned by R. S. Yeoman in his wellknown works entitled »A Catalog of Modern World Coins« and »Current Coins of the World«.

This former German protectorate was under mandate after 1921. Its status was changed in 1946, when it became an Australian Trust Territory.

12 Pence = 1 Shilling, 20 Shillings = £ 1

GEORGE V 1921–1936

			VF	XF
1 (1)	½ Penny (Cu–Ni) 1929. Crown and crossed maces. ℞ ornamentation in cross (center hole)		350.00	450.00

			VF	XF
2 (2)	1 Penny (Cu–Ni) 1929. Crown and crossed maces. ℞ ornamentation in cross (center hole)		350.00	450.00
3 (3)	3 Pence (Cu–Ni) 1935. Crown, monogram. ℞ square above a quadrangle, standing on its tip (center hole)		6.00	10.50
4 (4)	6 Pence (Cu–Ni) 1935. Crown, monogram. ℞ rosette (center hole)		4.00	8.00
5 (5)	1 Shilling (Ag) 1935–1936. Crown and crossed maces. ℞ ornamentation in cross (center hole)		4.00	6.00

EDWARD VIII 1936

6 (6)	1 Penny (Br) 1936. Crown above native carving, monogram. ℞ idol of the native ancestor worship (center hole)		3.50	6.00

			VF	XF
7 (7)	1	Penny (Br) 1938–1944. Same type as No. 6, but with monogram of George VI	2.50	4.00
8 (8)	3	Pence (Cu–Ni) 1944. Same type as No. 3 but with monogram of George VI	3.00	4.50

9 (9)	6	Pence (Cu–Ni) 1943. Same type as No. 4 but with monogram of George VI	4.00	7.50
10 (10)	1	Shilling (Ag) 1938–1945. Same type as No. 5 but with monogram of George VI	2.00	3.00

Values are given for each coin in U.S. Dollars and reference to Yeoman-numbers.

New Hebrides

Neue Hebriden   **Nouvelles Hébrides**

Area: 5,700 sq. mi. Population: 80,000.
Melanese island group in the South West Pacific, including the Banks
and Torres Islands, and, since the treaties of 1906 and 1914 to 1922,
constituting an Anglo-French Condominium.
Capital: Port Vila.

100 Centimes = 1 New Hebrides Franc

In addition to the N. H. Franc, the Australian Dollar is also in circulation as common legal tender.

			VF	XF
1 (1)	10	Francs (Ni) 1967, 1970. Head of Marian-ne, allegory of the French Republic. R native mask, flanked by cowry, taken from the shells of a giant clam (Tridac-na gigas – Tridacnidae)	1.20	1.60

2 (2)	20	Francs (Ni) 1967, 1970. Same type as No. 1	1.80	2.00

3 (3)	100	Francs (Ag) 1966. R carved ceremonial staff of natives	15.00	20.00
4 (4)	1	Franc (Ni-Bra) 1970. Head of Marianne, date. Rev. Frigate Bird (Fregata minor – Fregatidae), value	0.25	0.50
5 (5)	2	Francs (Ni-Bra) 1970. Type as No. 4	0.25	0.50
6 (6)	5	Francs (Ni-Bra) 1970. Type as No. 5	0.50	1.00

			VF	XF
7 (4a)	1	Franc (Ni-Bra) 1975, 1978, 1979. Type as No. 4, but I.E.O.M. added	0.30	0.40
8 (5a)	2	Francs (Ni-Bra) 1973, 1975, 1978, 1979. Type as No. 5, but I.E.O.M. added	0.35	0.50
9 (6a)	5	Francs (Ni-Bra) 1975, 1979. Type as No. 6, but I.E.O.M. added	0.40	0.80
10 (1a)	10	Francs (Ni) 1973, 1975, 1979. Type as No. 1, but I.E.O.M. added	1.00	1.50
11 (2a)	20	Francs (Ni) 1973, 1975, 1979. Type as No. 2, but I.E.O.M. added	2.00	2.50

			VF	XF
12 (7)	50	Francs (Ni) 1972, 1979. Type as No. 3, but I.E.O.M. added	2.50	3.50

			XF	Unc
13 (3)	100	Francs (Ag) 1979. Type as No. 3, but I.E.O.M. added	10.00	17.50

INTERNATIONAL YEAR OF THE CHILD

14 (8)	500	Francs (Ag) 1979:		
		a) (Ag) .925 silver, 20,3 g		125.00
		b) (Cu–Al–Ni) 16 g, reeded edge	125.00	

For later issues, see under Vanuatu.

Neuseeland   # New Zealand   **Nouvelle Zélande**

Area: 103,738 sq. mi. Population: 3,400,000.
British crown colony 1840–1907, dominion 1907–1953, monarchist
state in the British Commonwealth since 1953 with a parliamentary constitution. The Crown is represented by a Governor General. Administratively the Cook Islands, Niue and the Tokelau Islands also belong
to New Zealand. In the Antarctic the Ross Dependency comes under
the jurisdiction of New Zealand.
Capital: Wellington.

12 Pence = 1 Shilling, 2 Shillings = 1 Florin, 5 Shillings =
1 Crown, 20 Shillings = 1 Pound (£)
since 10th July 1967: 100 Cents = 1 New Zealand Dollar ($)

GEORGE V 1910–1936

			VF	XF
1 (1)	3 Pence (Ag) 1933–1936. Georg V, crowned bust, facing left. R Maori war clubs			
	a) 1933, 1934, 1936		5.00	10.00
	b) 1935		140.00	250.00

			VF	XF
2 (2)	6 Pence (Ag) 1933–1936. R huia bird (Heteralocha acutirostris – Callaeidae): sacred bird of the Maoris (extinct!)		4.00	12.00
3 (3)	1 Shilling (Ag) 1933–1935. R Maori war- rior		5.00	25.00

			VF	XF
4 (4)	1	Florin (Ag) 1933–1936. ℞ kiwi bird (Apteryx australis – Apterygidae)	9.00	40.00
5 (5)	½	Crown (Ag) 1933–1935. ℞ arms	12.00	45.00

COMMEMORATIVE ISSUE FOR THE 25th JUBILEE OF REIGN OF KING GEORGE V AND THE TREATY OF WAITANGI IN THE YEAR 1840

			Unc	Proof
6 (6)	1	Crown (Ag) 1935. ℞ Maori chief and William Hobson († 1842), Captain in the Royal Navy and plenipotentiary of the British Crown	2000.00	2500.00

GEORGE VI 1936–1952

			VF	XF
7 (7)	½	Penny (Br) 1940–1947. George VI, head towards left. ℞ tiki, demigod and idol of the Maoris	1.00	2.00

				VF	XF
8 (8)	1	Penny (Br) 1940–1947. ℞ parson bird or tui (Prosthemadura novaeseelandiae – Meliphagidae)			1.00	3.00
9 (9)	3	Pence (Ag) 1936–1946. ℞ Maori war clubs			2.00	4.00
10 (10)	6	Pence (Ag) 1937–1946. ℞ huia bird			2.00	4.00
11 (11)	1	Shilling (Ag) 1937–1946. ℞ Maori warrior			3.50	6.00
12 (12)	1	Florin (Ag) 1937–1946. ℞ kiwi bird			6.50	30.00
13 (13)	½	Crown (Ag) 1937–1946. ℞ arms			8.50	35.00

COMMEMORATIVE ISSUE FOR THE CENTENARY OF THE FOUNDING OF THE BRITISH COLONY ON THE BASIS OF THE TREATY OF WAITANGI

			VF	XF
14 (14)	½	Crown (Ag) 1940. ℞ Maori woman against background of a city	22.50	40.00
15 (9a)	3	Pence (Cu–Ni) 1947. Type as No. 9	0.80	2.00
16 (10a)	6	Pence (Cu–Ni) 1947. Type as No. 10	1.25	5.00
17 (11a)	1	Shilling (Cu–Ni) 1947. Type as No. 11	3.00	12.00
18 (12a)	1	Florin (Cu–Ni) 1947. Type as No. 12	4.00	17.50
19 (13a)	½	Crown (Cu–Ni) 1947. Type as No. 13	5.00	20.00
20 (20)	½	Penny (Br) 1949–1952. Type as No. 7, but inscription KING GEORGE THE SIXTH	0.60	1.20
21 (21)	1	Penny (Br) 1949–1952. Type as No. 8, but inscription KING GEORGE THE SIXTH	0.80	1.20
22 (22)	3	Pence (Cu–Ni) 1948–1952. Type as No. 15, but inscription KING GEORGE THE SIXTH	0.60	1.20
23 (23)	6	Pence (Cu–Ni) 1948–1952. Type as No. 16, but inscription KING GEORGE THE SIXTH	0.80	1.60
24 (24)	1	Shilling (Cu–Ni) 1948–1952. Type as No 17, but inscription KING GEORGE THE SIXTH	2.50	20.00
25 (25)	1	Florin (Cu–Ni) 1948–1951. Type as No 18, but inscription KING GEORGE THE SIXTH	2.00	5.00

26 (26)	½ Crown (Cu–Ni) 1948–1951. Type as No 19, but inscription KING GEORGE THE SIXTH	**VF**	**XF**
		4.00	7.00

COMMEMORATIVE ISSUE FOR THE PROPOSED ROYAL VISIT

		XF	**Unc**
27 (27)	1 Crown (Ag) 1949. ℞ fern leaf	15.00	25.00

ELIZABETH II since 1952

28 (28)	½ Penny (Br) 1953–1965. Queen Elizabeth II, head towards right. ℞ tiki	0.20	0.40
29 (29)	1 Penny (Br) 1953–1965. ℞ parson bird or tui	0.30	0.60
30 (30)	3 Pence (Cu–Ni) 1953–1965. ℞ Maori war clubs	0.40	0.70
31 (31)	6 Pence (Cu–Ni) 1953–1965. ℞ huia bird	0.50	1.00
32 (32)	1 Shilling (Cu–Ni) 1953–1965. ℞ Maori warrior	1.00	2.00
33 (33)	1 Florin (Cu–Ni) 1953–1965. ℞ kiwi	1.00	2.00
34 (34)	½ Crown (Cu–Ni) 1953–1965. ℞ arms	1.50	3.00
35 (35)	1 Crown (Cu–Ni) 1953. ℞ Royal monogram and crown above a Maori design	8.00	12.50

NEW CURRENCY: 100 Cents = 1 New Zealand Dollar

36 (36)	1 Cent (Br) 1967–. ℞ stylized fern leaf	0.10	0.15
37 (37)	2 Cents (Br) 1967–. ℞ kowhai (Sophora microphylla – Leguminosae)		
	a) Obverse with date	0.15	0.25
	b) without date: muled with obverse of Bahamas No. 2		30.00
38 (38)	5 Cents (Cu–Ni) 1967–. ℞ tuatara (Sphenodon punctatus – Sphenodontidae or Rhynchocephalidae)	0.15	0.30

39 (39)	10 Cents (Cu–Ni) 1967-1969. Rev. a Maori carved head or koruru	0.50	1.00

			XF	**Unc**
40 (40)	20	Cents (Cu–Ni) 1967–. ℞ kiwi (Apteryx australis – Apterygidae)	0.20	0.40
41 (41)	50	Cents (Cu–Ni) 1967–. ℞ H. M. S. "Endeavour", sailing ship of the English circumnavigator James Cook (1728–1779)	0.50	0.80
42 (42)	1	Dollar (Cu–Ni). Rev. arms:		
		a) 1967, lettered edge	1.50	3.00
		b) 1971 –, reeded edge	2.00	6.00

COMMEMORATIVE ISSUES (2) OF THE BI-CENTENARY OF THE DISCOVERY OF NEW ZEALAND BY CAPTAIN JAMES COOK ON 7th OCTOBER 1769

43 (43)	50	Cents (Cu–Ni) 1969. Type as No. 41, but edge inscription COOK BI-CENTENARY 1769–1969	2.00	4.50
44 (44)	1	Dollar (Cu–Ni) 1969. James Cook (1728 to 1779), English circumnavigator, map of New Zealand of 1769 and H. M. S. "Endeavour". Variants	1.50	3.00

COMMEMORATIVE ISSUE FOR THE VISIT OF THE ROYAL FAMILY

45 (45)	1	Dollar (Cu–Ni) 1970. Elizabeth II. ℞ Mt. Cook or Aorangi, 12,346 feet	1.50	3.00

46 (39a)	10	Cents (Cu–Ni) 1970–. Type as No. 39, but without inscription ONE SHILLING	0.15	0.25

COMMEMORATIVE ISSUE FOR THE 10th BRITISH EMPIRE AND COMMONWEALTH GAMES IN CHRISTCHURCH (24. 1. – 2. 2. 1974)

			Unc	**Proof**
47 (47)	1	Dollar 1974:		
		a) (Ag)		40.00
		b) (Cu-Ni)	2.50	

			Unc	Proof
48 (48)	1 Dollar 1974:			
	a) (Ag)			225.00
	b) (Cu-Ni)		12.00	

25th ANNIVERSARY OF THE SILVER JUBILEE OF HER MAJESTY QUEEN ELIZABETH II AND WAITANGI DAY

49 (49)	1 Dollar 1977:			
	a) (Ag)			25.00
	b) (Cu-Ni)		7.50	

25th ANNIVERSARY OF CORONATION

50 (50)	1 Dollar 1978. Parliament building:			
	a) (Ag)			20.00
	b) (Cu-Ni)		3.50	
51 (51)	1 Dollar 1979:			
	a) (Ag)			17.50
	b) (Cu-Ni)		3.00	

52 (52)	1 Dollar 1980:			
	a) (Ag)			20.00
	b) (Cu-Ni)		4.00	

			Unc	Proof
53 (53)	1 Dollar 1981:			
	a) (Ag)			20.00
	b) (Cu-Ni)		3.00	

54 (54)	1 Dollar 1982. Takahe:			20.00
	a) (Ag)			
	b) (Cu-Ni)		3.50	

ROYAL VISIT

55 (55)	1 Dollar 1983. Conjoined heads of Prince Charles and Lady Diana:			
	a) (Ag)			40.00
	b) (Cu-Ni)		7.50	

50 YEARS OF NEW ZEALAND COINAGE

56 (56)	1 Dollar 1983. Rev. arms, different coins:			
	a) (Ag)			22.50
	b) (Cu-Ni)		3.00	
57	1 Dollar 1984. Rev. Chatham Island Black robin bird:			
	a) (Ag)			20.00
	b) (Cu-Ni)		4.00	
58	1 Dollar 1985. Rev. Black stilt:			
	a) (Ag)			20.00
	b) (Cu-Ni)		3.50	

ROYAL VISIT

59	1 Dollar 1986:			
	a) (Ag)			25.00
	b) (Cu-Ni)		4.00	

Nicaragua   # Nicaragua   **Nicaragua**

Area: 57,100 sq. mi. Population: 3,400,000.
Republic in Central America. From 1823 to 1839 it was a member of the
Confederacy of the Central American States.
Capital: Managua.

100 Centavos = 1 Cordoba

			VF	XF
1 (10)	½	Centavo (Br) 1912–1937. Coat of arms. ℞ value within wreath	1.50	2.50
2 (11)	1	Centavo (Br) 1912–1940	1.20	2.00
3 (12)	5	Centavos (Cu–Ni) 1912–1940	1.00	1.60
4 (13)	10	Centavos (Ag) 1912–1936. Francisco Hernández de Córdoba (1476–1526), Spanish conqueror, governor. ℞ sunburst over crests of hills	2.00	5.00
5 (14)	25	Centavos (Ag) 1912–1936	3.00	10.00
6 (15)	50	Centavos (Ag) 1912, 1929	10.00	30.00
7 (16)	1	Córdoba (Ag) 1912	75.00	150.00
8 (17)	5	Centavos (Cu–Ni) 1946–1956. Edge inscription: B. N. N. (Banco Nacional de Nicaragua)	0.25	0.40
9 (18)	10	Centavos (Cu–Ni) 1939–1956	0.40	0.60
10 (19)	25	Centavos (Cu–Ni) 1939–1956	0.50	0.80

			VF	XF
11 (20)	50	Centavos (Cu–Ni) 1939–1956	0.80	1.20
12 (21)	1	Centavo (Bra) 1943. Coat of arms. ℞ value within wreath	1.00	1.60
13 (22)	5	Centavos (Bra) 1943. Same type as No. 8, but with reeded edge	1.10	1.50
14 (23)	10	Centavos (Bra) 1943. Same type as No. 9, but with reeded edge	1.50	2.50
15 (24)	25	Centavos (Bra) 1943. Same type as No. 10, but with reeded edge	1.60	2.80

			VF	XF
16 (17a)	5	Centavos (Cu–Ni) 1962, 1964, 1965. Same type as No. 8, but with edge inscription: B. C. N. (Banco Central de Nicaragua)	0.10	0.20
17 (18a)	10	Centavos (Cu–Ni) 1962, 1964, 1965. Same type as No. 16	0.25	0.40
18 (19a)	25	Centavos (Cu–Ni) 1964, 1965. Same type as No. 16	0.40	0.60
19 (20a)	50	Centavos (Cu–Ni) 1965. Same type as No. 16	0.60	1.10

100th ANNIVERSARY OF THE BIRTH OF RUBÉN DARÍO

20 (29)	50	Córdobas (Au) 1967. Rubén Darío (1867-1916), poet. Rev. coat of arms, value	Proof	550.00
21 (17b)	5	Centavos (Cu-Ni) 1972. Same type as No. 16, but reeded edge	0.10	0.20
22 (18b)	10	Centavos (Cu-Ni) 1972. Same type as No. 21	0.20	0.40
23 (19b)	25	Centavos (Cu-Ni) 1972. Same type as No. 21	0.50	0.70
24 (20b)	50	Centavos (Cu-Ni) 1972. Same type as No. 21	0.80	2.00
25 (25)	1	Córdoba (Cu-Ni) 1972. Same type as No. 21	1.20	2.50

ISSUES FOR THE FAO COIN PLAN (2)

26 (27)	5	Centavos (Al) 1974. Coat of arms, below PRODUZCAMOS MAS ALIMENTOS	0.10	0.25
27 (28)	10	Centavos (Al) 1974. Map of Nicaragua, below PRODUZCAMOS MAS ALIMENTOS	0.30	0.50
28 (26)	5	Centavos (Al) 1974. Type as No. 26, but without PRODUZCAMOS MAS ALIMENTOS	0.10	0.25

29 (A26)	10	Centavos (Al) 1974. Type as No. 27, but without PRODUZCAMOS MAS ALIMENTOS	0.40	0.80
30 (A26a)	10	Centavos (Cu-Ni) 1975, 1978. Type as No. 29	0.40	0.80
31 (30)	20	Córdobas (Ag) 1975. Peace and Progress	Unc 9.00	Proof 12.50

			Unc	Proof
32 (A31)	50	Córdobas (Ag) 1975. "The Bud" painting by Annigoni (Rebirth of Managua)	12.50	20.00
33 (31)	50	Córdobas (Ag) 1975. Liberty Bell (U. S. Bicentennial)	15.00	25.00

34 (A32)	100	Córdobas (Ag) 1975. Globe with flags (Tribute to world for help received)	30.00	45.00
35 (32)	100	Córdobas (Ag) 1975. Woman and Astronaut (U. S. Bicentennial)	35.00	50.00
36 (33)	200	Córdobas (Au) 1975. The "Pieta" by Michelangelo	65.00	65.00
37 (34)	500	Córdobas (Au) 1975. Colonial church "La Merced"	150.00	175.00
38 (A34)	500	Córdobas (Au) 1975. "The Bud" painting by Annigoni (Rebirth of Managua)	140.00	160.00

39 (35)	1000	Córdobas (Au) 1975. Liberty Bell (U.S. Bicentennial)	175.00	250.00

			Unc	Proof
40 (36)	2000 Córdobas (Au) 1975. Woman and Astronaut (U.S. Bicentennial)		375.00	500.00

FIRST ANNIVERSARY OF REVOLUTION (7)

			Unc	Proof
41 (43)	500 Córdobas (Ag) 1980. Cesar Augusto Sandino			20.00
42 (44)	500 Córdobas (Ag) 1980. Carlos Fonseca			20.00
43 (45)	500 Córdobas (Ag) 1980. Rigoberto Lopez Perez			20.00
44 (43a)	500 Córdobas (Au) 1980. Type as No. 41			400.00
45 (44a)	500 Córdobas (Au) 1980. Type as No. 42			350.00
46 (45a)	500 Córdobas (Au) 1980. Type as No. 43			350.00
47 (46)	1000 Córdobas (Au) 1980. Rebels. Rs. Sandino and Fonseca			500.00

			XF	Unc
48 (40)	5 Centavos (Al) 1981. Cesar Augusto Sandino (1895–1934), revolutionary		0.15	0.30
49 (41)	10 Centavos (Al) 1981. Type as No. 48		0.15	0.30
50 (42)	25 Centavos (Ni) 1981. Type as No. 48		0.30	0.60
51 (37)	50 Centavos 1980, 1982, 1983. Type as No. 48:			
	a) (Cu-Ni) 1980		0.30	0.60
	b) (Nickel-clad steel) 1982, 1983		0.30	0.60
52 (38)	1 Córdoba 1980, 1983–1985. Type as No. 48:			
	a) (Cu-Ni) 1980, 1983		0.60	1.00
	b) (Nickel-clad steel) 1984, 1985		0.60	1.00

53 (39)	5 Córdoba (Cu-Ni) 1980, 1984. Type similar to No. 48		1.00	2.00

Area: 458,976 sq. mi. Population: 6,200,000.
Formerly a part of French West Africa, Niger became an autonomous republic in 1958, and independent on August 3, 1960.
Capital: Niamey.

100 Centimes = 1 CFA Franc

COMMEMORATIVE ISSUES (6) FOR INDEPENDENCE

			Proof
1	10 Francs (Au) 1960		75.00
2	25 Francs (Au) 1960		160.00
3	50 Francs (Au) 1960		300.00
4	100 Francs (Au) 1960		600.00
5	500 Francs (Ag) 1960. Diori Hamani (*1916), Head of State and Prime Minister. ℞ coat of arms and flags, value		20.00
6	1000 Francs (Ag) 1960. Same type as No. 5		35.00

7	10 Francs (Ag) 1968. Lion (Panthera leo – Felidae). ℞ coat of arms and flags, motto, value, date		
		a) normal thickness	35.00
		b) double thickness. Pattern	80.00
8	10 Francs (Au) 1968		70.00
9	25 Francs (Au) 1968		150.00
10	50 Francs (Au) 1968		280.00
11	100 Francs (Au) 1968		550.00

Nigeria **Nigeria** Nigérie

Area: 339,168 sq. mi. Population: 100,000,000.
As a crown colony, Nigeria used the coins of British West Africa until 1959.
On October 1, 1960, Nigeria became an independent state and a member of
the Commonwealth.
Capital: Lagos.

12 Pence = 1 Shilling, 20 Shillings = £ 1;
since January 1, 1973: 100 Kobo = 1 Naira

ELIZABETH II since 1952

			XF	Unc
1 (1)	½ Penny (Br) 1959. Star, name of country. ℞ crown, legend, value (center hole)		0.15	0.40
2 (2)	1 Penny (Br) 1959–1961. Same type as No. 1		0.20	0.40
3 (3)	3 Pence (Ni–Bra) 1959. Elizabeth II, crowned head, right. ℞ cotton plant (Gossypium sp. – Malvaceae) (dodecagonal)		0.50	1.00
4 (4)	6 Pence (Cu–Ni) 1959. ℞ cocoa beans (Theobroma cacao – Sterculiaceae)		0.50	1.00
5 (5)	1 Shilling (Cu–Ni) 1959, 1961, 1962. ℞ palm branches (Elaeis guineensis – Palmae)		0.60	1.00
6 (6)	2 Shillings (Cu–Ni) 1959. ℞ flowers		0.70	1.50

			XF	Unc

New currency: 100 Kobo = 1 Naira

			XF	Unc
7 (7)	½	Kobo (Br) 1973. State arms, name of country, date. R cotton plants, value	0.15	0.25
8 (8)	1	Kobo (Br) 1973, 1974. R two oil derricks	0.20	0.30
9 (9)	5	Kobo (Cu-Ni) 1973, 1974, 1976. Cocoa fruit (Theobroma cacao – Sterculiaceae)	0.40	0.60
10 (10)	10	Kobo (Cu-Ni) 1973, 1974, 1976. R two oil palms	0.60	1.00
11 (11)	25	Kobo (Cu-Ni) 1973, 1975. R groundnuts (Arachis hypogaea – Leguminosae) and seco (groundnuts packed in bags for export and heaped into a pyramid)	1.20	2.00

Nordkorea   # North Korea   **Corée du Nord**

Tschoson Mindshudshuy Inmin Konghwaguk

Area: 46,812 sq. mi. Population: 15,000,000.
Under Japanese administration until 1945. The northern part of the country was proclaimed as the People's Republic of North Korea on September 12, 1948. The border between North and South Korea falls approximately on the 38th degree of latitude.
Capital: Pyongyang.

100 Chon = 1 Won

		VF	XF
1 (1)	1 Chon (Al) 1959, 1970. Coat of arms of the People's Republic. R value	1.00	2.00
2 (2)	5 Chon (Al) 1959, 1974. Same type as No. 1	1.10	2.50

		VF	XF
3 (3)	10 Chon (Al) 1959. Same type as No. 1	1.50	3.00

		VF	XF
4 (4)	50 Chon (Al) 1978. Tscholima with rising sun in background. Rev. coat of arms	3.00	6.00

Nordvietnam   **North Vietnam**   **Vietnam du Nord**

Viet-nam Dan-chu Cong-hoa

Area: 63,344 sq. mi. Population: 21,900,000.
Annam, Tongking, and Cochinchina were parts of former French Indo-china. Following a plesbiscite, these territories merged into the Republic of Vietnam, under President Ho Chi Minh, recognized by France within the frame-work of the Indochina Federation, and the Union Française. However, instead of constructive collaboration, severe discrepancies developed, leading to a break with France, and ultimately to the Indo-china war. Ho Chi Minh's political power was limited to the North, and a few southern territories, areas not yet reoccupied by the French after the defeat of Japan. After the Geneva Indochina agreement effected an armistice in Vietnam, the 17th parallel became the demarcation line between North and South Vietnam.
Capital: Hanoi.

100 Xu = 1 Hao = 1 Dong

			VF	XF
1 (1)	20 Xu (Al) 1945. Star, surrounded by name of country. ℞ value		18.00	35.00
2 (2)	5 Hao (Al) 1946. Copper censer, surrounded by name of country. ℞ value in star			
	a) value incused		8.00	20.00
	b) value raised		7.00	18.00
3 (3)	1 Dong (Al) 1946. Ho Chi Minh (1890–1969), president from 1945–1969. ℞ value		60.00	110.00
4 (4)	HAI (2) Dong (Br) 1946. Ho Chi Minh. ℞ value in letters and star in wreath		40.00	65.00
A4	20 Việt (Au) 1948. Ho Chi Minh. Rev. Value, rice; .900er gold, 8.2 g		–.–	
5 (5)	1 Xu (Al) 1958. Coat of arms. ℞ value (center hole)		1.00	2.00

		VF	XF
6 (6)	2 Xu (Al) 1958. Same type as No. 5	1.20	2.50
7 (7)	5 Xu (Al) 1958. Same type as No. 5	1.20	2.50

			VF	Unc
8 (8)	1 Xu (Al) undated (1975)		1.20	2.00

9 (9)   2 Xu (Al) 1975   1.20   2.00

10 (10)   5 Xu (Al) undated (1975)   1.20   2.00

11 (11)   1 Hao (Al) 1976. Coat of arms. Rev. value
and inscription NGAN HANG NHA
NUOC VIET-NAM (State Bank of Viet-
nam)   1.20   2.00
12 (12)   2 Hao (Al) 1976. Type as No. 11   1.20   2.00
13 (13)   5 Hao (Al) 1976. Type as No. 11   1.50   3.00

14 (14)   1 Dong (Al) 1976   6.50   12.00

Norwegen **Norway** Norvége
Norge, Noreg

Area: 125,068 sq. mi. Population: 4,146,000.
From 1387 to 1814 Norway was united with Denmark. The subsequent union with Sweden continued until June 7, 1905, when the kingdom became independent.
Capital: Oslo.

100 Øre = 1 Krone

OSCAR II 1872–1905

		VF	XF
1 (19)	1 Øre (Br) 1876–1902. Crowned arms. ℞ value in wreath	4.00	8.00
2 (20)	2 Øre (Br) 1876–1902	4.50	9.00
3 (21)	5 Øre (Br) 1875–1902	5.00	10.00
4 (22)	10 Øre (Ag) 1875–1903. Monogram. ℞ crowned arms	11.00	18.00
5 (24)	25 Øre (Ag) 1896–1904. Arms	8.00	14.00
6 (25)	50 Øre (Ag) 1877–1904. Oscar II (1829–1907), head left. ℞ arms in wreath	12.00	25.00
7 (26)	1 Krone (Ag) 1877–1904	20.00	45.00
8 (27)	2 Kroner (Ag) 1878–1904	50.00	100.00
9 (28)	10 Kroner (Au) 1877–1902. Oscar II, head right. ℞ arms in wreath	350.00	500.00

10 (29)	20 Kroner (Au) 1876–1902	300.00	450.00

HAAKON VII 1905–1957

11 (30)	1 Øre (Br) 1906–1907. Crowned shield, monogram. ℞ value in wreath	6.00	10.00

			VF	XF
12 (31)	2	Øre (Br) 1906–1907	6.00	11.00
13 (32)	5	Øre (Br) 1907	7.50	15.00

ISSUES FOR INDEPENDENCE (3)

			VF	XF
14 (33)	2	Kroner (Ag) 1906. Memorial legend. ℞ shield with mantle and crown (civil issue)	90.00	125.00
15 (33a)	2	Kroner (Ag) 1907. Same type as No. 14, but smaller shield (civil issue)	160.00	220.00
16 (34)	2	Kroner (Ag) 1907. Same type as No. 15, but crossed rifles under legend, symbol of defence vigilance (military issue)	300.00	400.00
17 (35)	1	Øre (Br) 1908–1952. Crown above monogram. ℞ value	0.40	0.80
18 (36)	2	Øre (Br) 1909–1952	0.40	0.80
19 (37)	5	Øre (Br) 1908–1952	0.80	1.20
20 (38)	10	Øre (Ag) 1909–1919	4.00	6.50
21 (39)	25	Øre (Ag) 1909–1919. Crowned monogram in shape of cross. ℞ heraldic lion	10.50	16.00
22 (40)	50	Øre (Ag) 1909–1919. Haakon VII, head right. ℞ shield	8.00	12.00
23 (41)	1	Krone (Ag) 1908–1917. ℞ order of Saint Olaf	16.00	25.00

			VF	XF
24 (42)	2	Kroner (Ag) 1908–1917. ℞ crowned shield with order of Saint Olaf, surrounded by arms	25.00	45.00

			VF	XF
25 (43)	10	Kroner (Ag) 1910. Haakon VII (1872–1957), crowned head right. ℞ Olaf II Haraldson, the Saint (995–1030), King of Norway 1016–1030	200.00	250.00
26 (44)	20	Kroner (Au) 1910. Same type as No. 25	275.00	300.00

COMMEMORATIVE ISSUE FOR THE CENTENNIAL
OF THE CONSTITUTION OF NORWAY

		VF	XF
27 (45)	2 Kroner (Ag) 1914. Standing Norwegia. ℞ crowned shield	40.00	65.00
28 (35a)	1 Øre (E) 1918–1921. Crowned monogram and crown. ℞ value	7.50	12.00
29 (36a)	2 Øre (E) 1917–1920	8.00	13.00
30 (37a)	5 Øre (E) 1917–1920	18.00	30.00
31 (46)	10 Øre (Cu–Ni) 1920–1923. Crowned monogram	8.00	13.00
32 (49)	10 Øre (Cu–Ni) 1924–1951. Crown. ℞ value (center hole)	0.30	0.50
33 (47)	25 Øre (Cu–Ni) 1921–1923. Crowned monogram. ℞ heraldic lion	13.00	22.00
34 (47a)	25 Øre (Cu–Ni) 1921–1923 (center hole)	2.00	4.50
35 (50)	25 Øre (Cu–Ni) 1924–1950. Crowned monogram in shape of cross. ℞ crown	0.40	0.80
36 (48)	50 Øre (Cu–Ni) 1920–1923. Crowned monogram in shape of cross. ℞ crowned shield	12.00	22.00
37 (48a)	50 Øre (Cu–Ni) 1920–1923 (center hole)	4.00	8.00
38 (51)	50 Øre (Cu–Ni) 1926–1949. Crowned monogram in shape of cross. ℞ crown (center hole)	0.90	2.00
39 (52)	1 Krone (Cu–Ni) 1925–1951. Crowned monogram in shape of cross. ℞ crown with order of Saint Olaf (center hole)	1.00	2.00
40 (53)	1 Øre (E) 1941–1945. Shield. ℞ value	0.80	1.60
41 (54)	2 Øre (E) 1943–1945	1.20	2.00
42 (55)	5 Øre (E) 1941–1945	1.20	2.00
43 (56)	10 Øre (Z) 1941–1945	1.50	3.20
44 (57)	25 Øre (Z) 1943–1945	3.00	6.00
45 (58)	50 Øre (Z) 1941–1945	3.00	7.50
46 (49a)	10 Øre (Ni–Bra) 1942	30.00	70.00
47 (50a)	25 Øre (Ni–Bra) 1942	30.00	70.00
48 (51a)	50 Øre (Ni–Bra) 1942	60.00	100.00

The coins Nos. 46–48 were issued by the Government in exile, in London.

		VF	XF
49 (59)	1 Øre (Br) 1952–1957	0.10	0.40
50 (60)	2 Øre (Br) 1952–1957	0.10	0.40
51 (61)	5 Øre (Br) 1952–1957	0.10	0.40
52 (62)	10 Øre (Cu–Ni) 1951–1957	0.20	0.40
53 (63)	25 Øre (Cu–Ni) 1952–1957	0.40	0.80

54 (64)	50 Øre (Cu–Ni) 1953–1957	0.60	1.00
55 (65)	1 Krone (Cu–Ni) 1951–1957	0.80	1.60

OLAF V since 1957

56a 56b

56 (66) 1 Øre (Br) 1958–1972. Crown above
monogram OV. ℞ squirrel (Sciurus
vulgaris – Sciuridae)
a) 1958. Legend small (pattern)   –.–   –.–
b) 1958–1972. Legend larger   0.20   0.40

57a 57b

57 (67) 2 Øre (Br). Moor hen (Lyrurus tetrix –
Tetraonidae)
a) 1958. Legend small   2.00   3.50
b) 1959-1967, 1969-1972. Legend larger 0.20 0.40
c) 1968 (3,467 pieces)   450.00

		VF	XF
58 (68)	5 Øre (Br) 1958–1973. Olaf V (*1903), head left. ℞ elk (Alces alces – Cervidae)	0.20	0.40

		VF	XF
59 (69)	10 Øre (Cu–Ni). ℞ honey bee (Apis melifica – Apidae)		
	a) 1958. Legend small	2.50	4.50
	b) 1959–1973. Legend larger	0.20	0.40

		VF	XF
60 (70)	25 Øre (Cu–Ni) 1958–1973. ℞ Siberian tit (Parus cinctus – Paridae)	0.20	0.40

		VF	XF
61 (71)	50 Øre (Cu–Ni) 1958–1973. ℞ elkhound or grahound (Canis familiaris intermedius – Canidae)	0.25	0.50

		VF	XF
62 (72)	1 Krone (Cu–Ni) 1958–1973. ℞ Norwegian fjord horse	0.40	0.80

			VF	**XF**
63 (73)	5 Kroner (Cu–Ni) 1963–1973. ℞ crowned arms		1.20	2.50

COMMEMORATIVE ISSUE FOR THE 150th ANNIVERSARY OF NORWAY SIGNING THE CONSTITUTION

			XF	**Unc**
64 (74)	10 Kroner (Ag) 1964. Crowned shield. ℞ farm house in Eidsvoll, where the constitution was signed		9.00	12.50

COMMEMORATIVE ISSUE FOR THE 25th ANNIVERSARY OF THE END OF WORLD WAR II

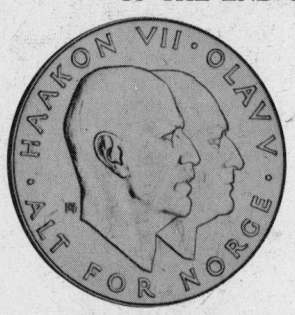 

65 (75)	25 Kroner (Ag) 1970. Haakon VII and Olaf V, heads right. ℞ legend, value		11.00	16.00

66a

66b

66 (76)	5 Øre (Br) 1973–1983. Norwegian armorial lion with axe. R value, name of coun-	

try, date, mint mark:		
a) 1973	0.20	0.40
b) 1974–1983. Design variety	0.05	0.10

67 (77)	10 Øre (Cu-Ni) 1974–. Crowned monogram	0.10	0.20

68 (78)	25 Øre (Cu-Ni) 1974–1983. Crowned monograms placed in the shape of a cross	0.10	0.20

69 (79)	50 Øre (Cu-Ni) 1974–. Crowned shield	0.15	0.30

70 (80)	1 Krone (Cu-Ni) 1974–. Olaf V, head facing left, motto. R crown, value	0.25	0.50
71 (81)	5 Kroner (Cu-Ni) 1974–. R crowned shield, value, date	0.70	1.40

100th ANNIVERSARY OF KRONE SYSTEM

			XF	Unc
72 (82)	5 Kroner (Cu-Ni) 1975. Crowned coat of arms, value. Rev. sitting mintmaker superimposed on a lever balance		1.00	2.00

150th ANNIVERSARY OF NORWEGIAN EMMIGRATION TO AMERICA

73 (83)	5 Kroner (Cu-Ni) 1975. Norwegian lion with axe, value. Rev. The imagined likeness of the sloop "Restauration". In the lower segment the words VEIEN MOT VEST (the road westward)	1.00	2.00

350th ANNIVERSARY OF THE NORWEGIAN ARMY

74 (84)	5 Kroner (Cu-Ni) 1978. Sword dividing crowned monograms of Kings Christian IV and Olaf V; above the word HÆREN. Norwegian lion with axe, value	1.00	2.00

75th ANNIVERSARY OF THE BIRTH OF KING OLAV V

		XF	Unc
75 (85) 50 Kroner (Ag) 1978. Head left of the King. Rev. King's signature, stylized flower, value			17.50

35th ANNIVERSARY OF THE END OF WORLD WAR II

76 (86) 200 Kroner (Ag) 1980. View of the Norwegian castle Akershus 35.00

25th ANNIVERSARY OF KING OLAV'S REIGN

77 (87) 100 Kroner (Ag) 1982. Head of the King. Rev. helmeted arms 18.00

78 (88) 10 Kroner (Ni-Bra) 1983–. Rev. value, date .... 1.50 / 2.50

300th ANNIVERSARY OF THE MINT OF KONGSBERG

79 (89)   5 Kroner (Cu-Ni) 1986 .... 1.50 / 2.50

Oman

Sultanate of Oman

Sultanat Oman   **Sultanat d'Oman**

Area: 82,000 sq. mi. Population: 1,200,000.
Sultanate in the south-east of the Arabian Peninsula (formerly Muscat and
Oman).
Capital: Muscat.

1000 Baiza = 1 Rial Omani

QABUS SA'ID since 1970

			Proof
1 (7)	15 Rials Omani (Au) H-C 1391 (1971). .917 gold, 7.99 gm.		–.–
2 (2)	25 Baiza (Au) H-C 1394 (1974). National arms. Rs. value and date; .917 gold, 5.96 gm.		–.–
3 (3)	50 Baiza (Au) H-C 1394 (1974). Type as No. 2; .917 gold, 12.89 gm.		–.–
4 (4)	100 Baiza (Au) H-C 1394, 1395 (1974, 1975). Type as No. 2; .917 gold, 22.74 gm.		–.–
5 (5)	½ Rial Omani (Au) H-C 1394, 1397 (1974, 1977). Type similar as No. 2; .917 gold, 25.6 gm.		–.–
6 (6)	1 Rial Omani (Au) H-C 1394, 1397 (1974, 1977). Type as No. 5; .917 gold, 46.65 gm.		*1000.00*

ISSUE FOR THE FAO COIN PLAN

		XF	**Unc**
7 (1)	10 Baiza (Br) H-C 1395 (1975). Date palms (Phoenix dactylifera – Palmae). Rev. value, date	0.25	0.50

			XF	Unc
8 (8)	5	Baiza (Br) H-C 1395 (1975). National arms. Rs. value and date	0.10	0.20
9 (9)	10	Baiza (Br) H-C 1395 (1975). Type as No. 8	0.15	0.30
10 (10)	25	Baiza (Cu-Ni) H-C 1395 (1975). Type as No. 8	0.30	0.70
11 (12)	50	Baiza (Cu-Ni) H-C 1395 (1975). Type as No. 8	0.50	0.90

			Unc	Proof
12 (11)	25	Baiza (Au) H-C 1395 (1975). Type as No. 10		–.–
13 (13)	50	Baiza (Au) H-C 1395, 1397 (1975, 1977). Type as No. 11		– –

CONSERVATION COMMEMORATIVE (3)

			XF	Unc
14 (14)	2½	Rials (Ag) 1977	30.00	40.00
15 (15)	5	Rials (Ag) 1977	40.00	50.00
16 (16)	75	Rials (Au) 1977	600.00	850.00

FAO COIN ISSUES (2)

			XF	Unc
17 (17)	½	Rial (Cu-Ni) 1978	2.00	3.00
18 (18)	1	Rial (Cu-Ni) 1978	6.00	10.00
19 (19)	¼	Rial (Al-Br) 1980. Arms. Rev. value		1.25
20 (20)	½	Rial (Al-Br) 1980. Type as No. 19		2.00

Pakistan

Area: 310,236 sq. mi. Population: 98,000,000.
Republic in the western part of the Indian subcontinent, consisting to 1971
of the provinces of West and East Pakistan (now Bangladesh).
Capital: Rawalpindi, the future capital: Islamabad.

3 Pies = 1 Pice, 4 Pice = 1 Anna, 16 Annas = 1 Rupee;
since January 1st, 1961: 100 Paisa = 1 Pakistan Rupee

			VF	XF
1 (1)	1	Pice (Br) 1948–1952. Legend with name of country. ℞ value (center hole)	0.60	2.00
2 (2)	½	Anna (Cu–Ni) 1948–1951. Toughra. ℞ state emblem (crescent and star)	0.15	0.30
3 (3)	1	Anna (Cu–Ni) 1948–1952. Toughra. ℞ crescent, facing right (scalloped)	0.30	0.80
4 (3a)	1	Anna (Cu–Ni) 1950. ℞ crescent, facing left (scalloped)	9.00	16.00
5 (4)	2	Anna (Cu–Ni) 1948–1951. ℞ crescent, facing right (square)	0.25	0.50
6 (4a)	2	Anna (Cu–Ni) 1950. ℞ crescent, facing left (square)	12.00	20.00
7 (5)	¼	Rupee (Ni) 1948–1951. ℞ crescent, facing right	0.40	0.60
8 (5a)	¼	Rupee (Ni) 1950. ℞ crescent, facing left	18.00	28.00
9 (6)	½	Rupee (Ni) 1948–1951. Type as No. 7	0.80	1.20
10 (7)	1	Rupee (Ni) 1948–1949. Type as No. 7	1.50	2.50
11 (8)	1	Pie (Br) 1951–1957. Toughra and state emblem. R. value	0.15	0.25

12 (9)	1	Pice (Ni–Bra) 1953–1959. Toughra and state emblem. ℞ value between ears of wheat	0.10	0.25

			VF	XF
13 (10)	½	Anna (Ni–Bra) 1953–1958 (square)	0.10	0.25

14 (11)	1	Anna (Cu–Ni) 1953–1958 (scalloped)	0.20	0.30
15 (12)	2	Annas (Cu–Ni) 1953–1959. ℞ value in wreath (square)	0.40	0.75

NEW CURRENCY: 100 Paisa = 1 Rupee

16 (13)	1	Pice (Br) 1961. Toughra and state emblem. ℞ value	0.10	0.20
17 (13a)	1	Paisa (Br) 1961–1963. Type as No. 16	0.10	0.20
18 (14)	5	Pice (Ni–Bra) 1961. ℞ sailing boat (pallar) with value on sail (square)	0.20	0.40

19 (14a)	5	Paise (Ni–Bra) 1961–1963. ℞ pallar with value on sail (square)	0.10	0.20
20 (15)	10	Pice (Cu–Ni) 1961. ℞ value in wreath (scalloped)	0.30	0.60

21 (15a)	10	Paisa (Cu–Ni) 1961-1963. Rev. value in wreath (scalloped)	0.40	0.60
22 (18)	1	Paisa (Br) 1964-1965. Rev. value between ears of wheat (round)	0.25	0.50
23 (18a)	1	Paisa (Ni–Bra) 1965-1966. Type as No. 22	0.10	0.20
24 (19)	2	Paisa (Br) 1964-1966 (scalloped)	0.10	0.25
25 (23)	2	Paisa (Al) 1966-1968 (round)	0.10	0.20

			VF	XF
26 (20)	5 Paisa (Ni-Bra) 1964-1974 (square)	0.10	0.25
27 (21)	10 Paisa (Cu-Ni) 1964-1968 (scalloped)	0.15	0.40
28 (16)	25 Paisa (Ni) 1963-1967 (round)	0.15	0.40

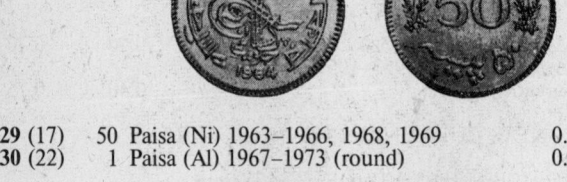

| 29 (17) | 50 Paisa (Ni) 1963–1966, 1968, 1969 | 0.40 | 0.80 |
| 30 (22) | 1 Paisa (Al) 1967–1973 (round) | 0.10 | 0.20 |

31 (19a)	2 Paisa (Al) 1968-1974. Type as No. 25, but scalloped	0.10	0.20
32 (21a)	10 Paisa (Cu-Ni) 1969-1974	0.10	0.25
33 (24)	25 Paisa (Cu-Ni) 1967-1974. Obverse like No. 28. Rev. value in Persian on right and left flower; below "25"	0.20	0.40
34 (25)	50 Paisa (Cu-Ni) 1969-1974. Same type as No. 33	0.30	0.60

ISSUE FOR THE FAO COIN PLAN (4)

		XF	Unc
35 (26)	1 Paisa (Al) 1974–1979. Cotton	0.10	0.25
36 (27)	2 Paisa (Al) 1974–1976. Rice	0.10	0.25
37 (28)	5 Paisa (Al) 1974–1981. Sugar-cane	0.15	0.30
38 (29)	10 Paisa (Al) 1974–1981. Ears	0.15	0.30

39 (30)	25 Paisa (Cu-Ni) 1975–1981	0.15	0.30
40 (31)	50 Paisa (Cu-Ni) 1975–1981	0.25	0.50
41 (51)	1 Rupee (Cu-Ni) 1979–1981; Ø 26.5 mm	0.40	0.90

CONSERVATION COMMEMORATIVE (3)

		Unc	Proof
42 (32)	100 Rupees (Ag) 1976. Rev. Tropogan Pheasant:		
	a) .925 silver, 25.31 g	30.00	
	b) .925 silver, 28.28 g		40.00
43 (33)	150 Rupees (Ag) 1976. Rev. Gavial Crocodile:		
	a) .925 silver, 31.65 g	30.00	
	b) .925 silver, 35.00 g		45.00
44 (34)	3000 Rupees (Au) 1976. Rev. Astor Markhor Goat	550.00	750.00

100th ANNIVERSARY OF THE BIRTH OF MOHAMMAD ALI JINNAH (3)

		Unc	Proof
45 (35)	50 Paisa (Cu-Ni) 1976	0.60	
46 (36)	100 Rupees (Ag) 1976	30.00	40.00
47 (37)	500 Rupees (Au) 1976	100.00	125.00

ISLAMIC SUMMIT CONFERENCE (3)

48 (38)	1 Rupee (Cu-Ni) 1977	0.80	
49 (39)	100 Rupees (Ag) 1977	28.00	35.00
50 (40)	1000 Rupees (Au) 1977	175.00	200.00

100th ANNIVERSARY OF THE BIRTH OF MOHAMMAD IQBAL (3)

51 (41)	1 Rupee (Cu-Ni) 1977	0.80	
52 (42)	100 Rupees (Ag) 1977	15.00	20.00
53 (43)	500 Rupees (Au) 1977	85.00	100.00

WORLD FOOD DAY

		XF	Unc
54 (46)	1 Rupee (Cu-Ni) 1981	0.70	1.10

1400th ANNIVERSARY OF MOHAMMED'S FLIGHT (2)

55 (44)	50 Paisa (Cu-Ni) 1981	0.20	0.35
56 (45)	1 Rupee (Cu-Ni) 1981	0.60	1.00

		XF	Unc
57 (47)	5 Paisa (Al) 1981–1985	0.10	0.15

		XF	Unc
58 (48)	10 Paisa (Al) 1981–1984	0.10	0.15
59 (49)	25 Paisa (Cu-Ni) 1982–1986	0.20	0.25
60 (50)	50 Paisa (Cu-Ni) 1981–1985	0.20	0.25

		XF	Unc
61 (51a)	1 Rupie (Cu-Ni) 1981–1984; Ø 25 mm	0.30	0.65

Between 1918 and 1948 Palestine was under British mandate. After the repeal of the mandate, and the withdrawal of the troops, the State of Israel was proclaimed on May 14, 1948.

1000 Mils = £ 1

			VF	XF
1 (1)	1	Mil (Br) 1927–1947. Arab name of country, also English and Hebrew name. ℞ olive branch, and value	0.80	1.60
2 (2)	2	Mils (Br) 1927–1947	0.60	2.00

			VF	XF
3 (3)	5	Mils (center hole)		
		a) (Cu–Ni) 1927–1941, 1946, 1947	0.90	2.00
		b) (Br) 1942–1944	1.60	3.00
4 (4)	10	Mils (center hole)		
		a) (Cu–Ni) 1927–1941, 1946, 1947	1.60	2.50
		b) (Br) 1942–1943	5.50	9.00
5 (5)	20	Mils (center hole)		
		a) (Cu–Ni) 1927–1941	6.00	10.00
		b) (Br) 1942–1944	9.00	16.00
6 (6)	50	Mils (Ag) 1927–1942. Olive branch. ℞ value	4.50	8.00
7 (7)	100	Mils (Ag) 1927–1942. Olive branch. ℞ value in circle	7.50	16.00

Area: 28,575 sq. mi. Population: 2,200,000.
Formerly a member of the Columbian Confederacy, the country declared its independence in 1903.
Capital: Panama City.

100 Centesimos = 1 Balboa

			VF	XF
1 (5)	2½	Centesimos (Ag) 1904. Vasco Núñez de Balboa (ca. 1475–1517), Spanish conqueror, reached the Gulf of San Miguel in the Pacific on September 29, 1513. ℞ coat of arms. So-called Panama pill.	16.00	28.00
2 (6)	5	Centesimos (Ag) 1904–1916:		
		a) 1904	8.00	12.00
		b) 1916	140.00	200.00
3 (7)	10	Centesimos (Ag) 1904	10.00	22.00
4 (8)	25	Centesimos (Ag) 1904	15.00	30.00
5 (9)	50	Centesimos (Ag) 1904–1905	40.00	70.00
6 (1)	½	Centesimo (Cu–Ni) 1907. ℞ value in letters	1.50	3.00
7 (2)	2½	Centesimos (Cu–Ni) 1907. Coat of arms. ℞ value in letters: DOS Y MEDIOS CENTESIMOS	3.00	7.00
8 (2a)	2½	Centesimos (Cu–Ni) 1916. Same type as No. 7, value in letters, but this time: DOS Y MEDIO CENTESIMOS	4.00	15.00

9 (3)	2½	Centesimos (Cu–Ni) 1929. Balboa, bust left. ℞ value in letters	5.50	18.00
10 (4)	5	Centesimos (Cu–Ni) 1929–1932. Coat of arms. ℞ value	4.00	8.00

			VF	XF
11 (10)	1	Centesimo (Cu) 1935–1937. Urraca, cazique (Indian chief) of Burica (Costa Rica); portrait left. R value in letters	2.00	4.00
12 (11)	1¼	Centesimos (Cu) 1940. Balbao, portrait left. R. value in letters	1.50	2.50
13 (12)	2½	Centesimos (Cu-Ni) 1940	1.20	2.50
14 (13)	1/10	Balboa. Balboa, portrait left. Rs coat of arms:	3.50 1.00	6.00 1.50
		a) Y 13 (Ag) 1930–1934	0.15	0.25
		b) Y 13 (Ag) 1947–1962		
		c) Y 13a (Cu-Ni) 1966–1972	8.00	18.00
15 (14)	¼	Balboa. Type as No. 14:	4.00	7.00
		a) Y 14 (Ag) 1930–1934	0.30	0.50
		b) Y 14 (Ag) 1947–1962		
		c) Y 14a (Cu-Ni) 1966–1972		
16 (15)	½	Balboa. Type as No. 14:		
		a) Y 15 (Ag) 1930–1934	8.00	12.00
		b) Y 15 (Ag) 1947–1962	4.00	8.00
		c) Y 15a (Cu-Ni) 1966–1972	1.50	3.00
17 (16)	1	Balboa (Ag) 1931–1947. R allegory of the Republic and coat of arms	15.00	20.00

COMMEMORATIVE ISSUES (5) FOR THE 50th ANNIVERSARY OF THE REPUBLIC

			VF	XF
18 (17)	1	Centesimo (Cu) 1953. Same type as No. 11, but with addition of CINCUENTENARIO. R date and value	0.30	0.60
19 (18)	1/10	Balboa (Ag) 1953. Same type as No. 14, but with addition of CINCUENTENARIO	1.00	2.50
20 (19)	¼	Balboa (Ag) 1953. Same type as No. 15, but with addition of CINCUENTENARIO	3.00	5.50
21 (20)	½	Balboa (Ag) 1953. Same type as No. 16, but with addition of CINCUENTENARIO	5.00	8.00

			XF	Unc
22 (21)	1	Balboa (Ag) 1953. Same type as No. 17, but with addition of CINCUENTE-NARIO	18.00	25.00
23 (22)	1	Centesimo (Cu) 1961–1977. Same type as No. 18, but without CINCUENTE-NARIO	0.10	0.20
24 (23)	5	Centesimos (Cu-Ni) 1961. Coat of arms. R value	0.60	1.20
25 (23a)	5	Centesimos (Cu-Ni) 1962–1975. Same type as No. 24, but with coat of arms narrower, and number smaller	0.15	0.30
26 (24)	1/10	Balboa (Ag) 1961. Same type as No. 19, but with laurel branches in place of CINCUENTENARIO	1.20	2.00
27 (25)	¼	Balboa (Ag) 1961. Same type as No. 20, but with laurel branches in place of CINCUENTENARIO	3.50	5.00
28 (26)	½	Balboa (Ag) 1961, 1962, 1970. Same type as No. 21, but with laurel branches in place of CINCUENTENARIO	5.50	8.00
29 (27)	1	Balboa (Ag) 1966–1974. Type as No. 14: a) 1966 b) 1966–1972, Proof only	15.00	18.00 20.00

COMMEMORATIVE ISSUE FOR THE 11th CENTRAL AMERICAN AND CARIBBEAN ATHLETIC GAMES OF 1970, IN PANAMA

			Unc	Proof
30 (28)		5 Balboas (Ag) 1970. Man throwing a discus, memorial legend. ℞ coat of arms, value	10.00	15.00

COMMEMORATIVE ISSUE FOR THE 150th ANNIVERSARY OF INDEPENDENCE FROM SPAIN

31 (29)	20 Balboas (Ag) 1971. Simón Bolívar (1783–1830), statesman and general, liberator of South America from Spanish rule. ℞ national coat of arms and value		40.00	55.00

			Unc	Proof
32 (30)	20	Balboas (Ag) 1972–1976. Type as No. 33, but legend reads on the obverse SIMON BOLIVAR 1783–1830	40.00	55.00

FOR THE FAO COIN PLAN (2)

33 (31)	2½	Centesimos (Br) 1973, 1975. Coat of arms, value. Rev. rice (Oryza sativa – Gramineae)	0.30	
34 (32)	5	Balboas (Ag) 1972. Type as No. 33	17.50	40.00

500th ANNIVERSARY OF THE BIRTH OF VASCO NUNEZ DE BALBOA (2)

35 (41)	100	Balboas (Au) 1975–1977. Coat of arms. Rev. Head of Vasco Nunez de Balboa	115.00	125.00

36 (42)	500	Balboas (Au) 1975–1977. Balboa kneeling holding sword	550.00	550.00

			XF	Unc
37 (33)	1	Centesimo (Br) 1975–. Head of Urraca, Indian chief of Burica	0.40	1.00
38 (34)	2½	Centesimos (Cu-Ni) 1975–. Head of Victoriano Lorenzo, Indian chief	0.60	1.50
39 (35)	5	Centesimos (Cu-Ni) 1975–. Head of Carlos J. Finlay	1.00	2.00
40 (36)	10	Centesimos (Cu-Ni) 1975–. Head of Manuel E. Amador	1.10	2.20
41 (37)	25	Centesimos (Cu-Ni) 1975–. Head of Justo Arosemena	1.25	2.40

			XF	Unc
42 (38)	50	Centesimos (Cu-Ni) 1975–. Head of Fernando de Lesseps	1.50	2.70
43 (39)	1	Balboa 1975–. Vasco Nunez de Balboa:		
		a) (Cu-Ni) 1975–1982	4.00	8.00
		b) (Ag .925) 1975–1979; proof only		20.00
		c) (Ag .500) 1981, 1982; proof only		20.00
44 (40)	5	Balboas 1975–. Head of Belisario Porras:		
		a) (Cu-Ni) 1975–1982	10.00	17.50
		b) (Ag .925) 1975–1979; proof only		28.00
		c) (Ag .500) 1981, 1982; proof only		28.00
45 (39b)	1	Balboa (Cu-Ni) 1975, 1976. Type as No. 43b (with .925 silver fineness on reverse)		30.00
46 (40b)	5	Balboas (Cu-Ni) 1975, 1976. Type as No. 44 b (with .925 silver fineness on reverse)		40.00
A46	5	Balboas (Cu-Ni) 1982. Type as No. 44c (with .500 silver fineness on reverse)		40.00

150th ANNIVERSARY OF THE PAN-AMERICAN CONGRESS

			Unc	Proof
47 (43)	150	Balboas (Platinum) 1976. Bust left of Simon Bolivar	250.00	200.00
48 (44)	20	Balboas (Ag) 1977, 1979. Vasco Nuñez de Balboa	75.00	65.00

75th ANNIVERSARY OF INDEPENDENCE (10)

49 (45)	1	Centesimo (Br) 1978	0.60	2.00
50 (46)	2½	Centesimos (Cu-Ni) 1978	0.80	2.00
51 (47)	5	Centesimos (Cu-Ni) 1978	1.00	2.00
52 (48)	10	Centesimos (Cu-Ni) 1978	1.10	2.00
53 (49)	25	Centesimos (Cu-Ni) 1978	1.25	2.50
54 (50)	50	Centesimos (Cu-Ni) 1978	1.60	4.00
55 (51)	1	Balboa 1978:		
		a) (Cu-Ni)	10.00	
		b) (Ag)		22.00
56 (52)	5	Balboas 1978:		
		a) (Cu-Ni)	20.00	
		b) (Ag)		20.00
57 (53)	20	Balboas (Ag) 1978	85.00	75.00
58 (54)	75	Balboas (Au) 1978. Rev. flag	140.00	110.00

PANAMA CANAL TREATY RATIFICATION

59 (55)	10	Balboas 1978. Map:		
		a) (Cu-Ni)	12.50	
		b) (Ag)		40.00

FOR PEACE AND PROGRESS

60 (56)	100	Balboas (Au) 1978. Dove-Orchid	175.00	125.00

			Unc	Proof
61 (57)	500	Balboas (Au) 1978. Rev. Globe with North and South America	600.00	600.00
62 (58)	500	Balboas (Au) 1979. Golden Jaguar	850.00	850.00

PANAMA CANAL TREATY IMPLEMENTATION (3)

63 (59)	5	Balboas (Ag) 1979	30.00
64 (60)	10	Balboas (Ag) 1979	55.00
65 (61)	200	Balboas (Platinum) 1979. Panama Canal Treaties	300.00

PRE-COLUMBIAN ART – 1st ISSUE

66 (62)	100	Balboas (Au) 1979. Golden Turtle	275.00	150.00

SIMON BOLIVAR DEATH SESQUICENTENARIUM (10)

67 (33.1)	1	Centesimo (Br) 1980. Edge inscription »1830 SIMON BOLIVAR 1980«. Type as No. 37		5.00
68 (34.1)	2½	Centesimos (Cu-Ni) 1980. Type as No. 38		6.00
69 (35.1)	5	Centesimos (Cu-Ni) 1980. Type as No. 39		7.00
70 (36.1)	10	Centesimos (Cu-Ni) 1980. Type as No. 40		8.00
71 (37.1)	25	Centesimos (Cu-Ni) 1980. Type as No. 41		9.00
72 (38.1)	50	Centesimos (Cu-Ni) 1980. Type as No. 42		10.00
73 (39c)	1	Balboa (Ag) 1980. Type as No. 43c		40.00
74 (40c)	5	Balboas (Ag) 1980. Type as No. 44c		45.00
75 (63)	20	Balboas (Ag) 1980. Simon Bolivar on horseback	175.00	300.00
76 (66)	150	Balboas (Au) 1980. Simon Bolivar	280.00	175.00

SPORTS IN PANAMA (3)

77 (A63)	5	Balboas (Ag) 1980. Champions of boxing	50.00
78 (B63)	10	Balboas (Ag) 1980. Balseria game	65.00
79 (A67)	200	Balboas (Platinum) 1980. Type as No. 77	300.00

		Unc	Proof

PRE-COLUMBIAN ART – 2nd ISSUE

80 (64) 100 Balboas (Au) 1980. Golden Condor — 375.00 / 200.00

PANAMA CANAL CENTENNIAL

			Unc	Proof
81 (65)	100	Balboas (Au) 1980. Fernando de Lesseps	250.00	120.00
82 (67)	500	Balboas (Au) 1980. White herons	900.00	900.00
83 (68)	20	Balboas (Ag) 1981. Simon Bolivar on horseback, flags around	150.00	225.00
84 (69)	20	Balboas (Au) 1981. Rev. Butterfly	100.00	70.00

PRE-COLUMBIAN ART – 3rd ISSUE

85 (A70)	100	Balboas (Au) 1981. Cocle Indian ceremonial mask	250.00	180.00
86 (70)	500	Balboas (Au) 1981. Rev. Sailfish	900.00	900.00

CHRISTMAS 1981

87 (71)	50	Balboas (Au) 1981. Rev. Dove	160.00	125.00
88 (72)	20	Balboas (Ag) 1982. Balboa with flag as discoverer of the Pacific		225.00

PRE-COLUMBIAN ART – 4th ISSUE

89 (73) 100 Balboas (Au) 1982. Indian design — 280.00 / 200.00

O. TORRIJOS DEATH COMMEMORATIVES (2)

90 (A74)	1	Balboa (Cu-Ni) 1982–1984. General Omar Torrijos H.	5.00	–.–
91 (74)	500	Balboas (Au) 1982. Type as No. 90	900.00	900.00
92 (75)	20	Balboas (Au) 1982. Hummingbird	100.00	70.00

WORLD SOCCER CHAMPIONSHIP GAMES 1982 IN SPAIN (2)

93 (76)	5	Balboas (Ag) 1982		40.00
94 (77)	10	Balboas (Ag) 1982		50.00

CHRISTMAS 1982

95 (78) 50 Balboas (Au) 1982 — 180.00 / 100.00

PRE-COLUMBIAN ART – 5th ISSUE

			Unc	Proof
96 (79)	100	Balboas (Au) 1983. Cocle Indian birds		180.00
97 (80)	500	Balboas (Au) 1983. Butterfly		850.00

INTERNATIONAL YEAR OF THE CHILD 1979

			Unc	Proof
98 (81)	10	Balboas (Ag) 1982		40.00
99 (82)	20	Balboas (Au) 1983. Banded Butterfly fish		70.00
100 (83)	50	Balboas (Au) 1983		125.00
101 (22)	1	Centesimo (Br) 1983, 1984. Type as No. 23		1.25
102 (84)	2½	Centesimos (Cu-Ni) 1983, 1984. Arms between branches. Rev. Head of Victoriano Lorenzo		1.50
103 (85)	5	Centesimos (Cu-Ni) 1983, 1984. Rev. value		2.50
104 (86)	1/10	Balboa (Cu-Ni) 1983, 1984. Rev. Vasco Nuñez de Balboa, value		3.00
105 (87)	¼	Balboa (Cu-Ni) 1983, 1984. Type as No. 104		4.00
106 (88)	½	Balboa (Cu-Ni) 1983, 1984. Type as No. 104		6.50
107 (89)	1	Balboa (Ag) 1983, 1984. Type as No. 104		20.00
108 (90)	5	Balboas (Ag) 1983, 1984. Type as No. 104		27.00

BICENTENARY OF BIRTH OF SIMON BOLIVAR

			Unc	Proof
109 (91)	20	Balboas (Ag) 1983. Bust of Bolivar	150.00	100.00

PRE-COLUMBIAN ART – 6th ISSUE

			Unc	Proof
110 (92)	100	Balboas (Au) 1984. Indian art	275.00	175.00
111	20	Balboas (Ag) 1984. Vasco Nuñez de Balboa and Red Indian. »Descubridor del Pacifico«		125.00
112	20	Balboas (Au) 1984. Puma. 500 fine, 2.14 g	175.00	100.00
113	500	Balboas (Au) 1984. Eagle with motto on band	1000.00	900.00

CHRISTMAS 1984

			Unc	Proof
114 (95)	50	Balboas (Au) 1984. Lion and lamb living together in peace		100.00
115 (97)	20	Balboas (Au) 1985. Harpy Eagle		75.00

Papua New Guinea

Papua-Neuguinea   **Papoua Nouvelle Guinée**

Area: 183,540 sq. mi. Population: 3,100,000.

The largest island in the world after Greenland has been known geographically since the 16th century, but was hardly developed up to the 19th century and also later on only slightly opened up. Partycularly Dutch interests on the western half fluctuated between commercial and political activities. In the 19th century the Netherlands declared their claims regarding the western half, whereupon a British man-of-war proclaimed British rule over the Southeast; Germany followed soon after (cf. New Guinea). The island was partly named Papua according to the inhabitants, partly New Guinea due to its supposed similarity with West African coastlines. In Port Moresby, after British New Guinea had been declared a Crown Colony in 1888, an administrator under the control of the Governor of Queensland was appointed; after the formation of the Australian Federation, the latter were also entrusted with the administration of the territory now called »Papua« on 1st Sept. 1906. The Territory of Papua was united with the Territory of New Guinea (see New Guinea) in 1949 to form a new Territory of Papua and New Guinea which, since 24th June 1971 is called Papua New Guinea (without the word "Territory" and without „and"), was permitted to elect in March 1972 a House of Deputies received internal autonomy in December 1973 and was to receive full independence at the end of 1974.

Capital: Port Moresby.

100 Toea = 1 Kina

			Unc	Proof
1 (1)	1	Toea (Br) 1975-	0.10	1.00
2 (2)	2	Toea (Br) 1975-	0.15	1.20
3 (3)	5	Toea (Cu-Ni) 1975-	0.25	1.50
4 (4)	10	Toea (Cu-Ni) 1975-	0.45	2.00
5 (5)	20	Toea (Cu-Ni) 1975-	1.00	3.00
6 (6)	1	Kina (Cu-Ni) 1975-	3.00	4.50
7 (7)	5	Kina 1975-		
		a) (Cu-Ni)	10.00	
		b) (Ag)		18.00
8 (8)	10	Kina 1975-		
		a) (Cu-Ni)	15.00	
		b) (Ag)		25.00

INDEPENDENCE COMMEMORATIVE

9 (9)	100	Kina (Au) 1975. Prime Minister Michael		
		T. Somare. Rev. bird of Paradise	165.00	165.00

1st ANNIVERSARY OF INDEPENDENCE

				Unc	Proof
10 (10)	100	Kina (Au) 1976		200.00	150.00

SILVER JUBILEE OF THE REIGN OF HER MAJESTY QUEEN ELIZABETH II

				Unc	Proof
11 (11)	10	Kina 1977:			
		a) (Cu-Ni)		40.00	
		b) (Ag)			25.00
12 (12)	100	Kina (Au) 1977		200.00	175.00
13 (13)	100	Kina (Au) 1978		300.00	300.00
14 (14)	100	Kina (Au) 1979		250.00	175.00

SOUTH PACIFIC FESTIVAL OF ARTS (2)

				Unc	Proof
15 (15)	50	Toea (Cu-Ni) 1980:			
		a) 1980			7.50
		b) 1980 FM		22.50	17.50
16 (16)	100	Kina (Au) 1980			150.00

5th ANNIVERSARY OF INDEPENDENCE

				Unc	Proof
17 (17)	100	Kina (Au) 1980		300.00	185.00

INTERNATIONAL YEAR OF THE CHILD 1979

				Unc	Proof
18 (19)	5	Kina (Ag) 1981:			
		a) normal thickness		30.00	
		b) Pièfort			150.00
19 (18)	100	Kina (Au) 1981. Prime Minister, Sir Julius Chan			250.00

DEFENCE OF THE KOKODA TRAIL 1942

				Unc	Proof
20 (20)	5	Kina 1982. Soldiers:			
		a) (Cu-Ni)		10.00	
		b) (Ag)			40.00

ROYAL VISIT 1982 (2)

			Unc	Proof
21 (21)	10	Kina 1982. Conjoined heads:		
		a) (Cu-Ni)	20.00	
		b) (Ag)		65.00
22 (22)	100	Kina (Au) 1982. Type as No. 21		275.00

10th ANNIVERSARY OF THE BANK OF PAPUA NEW GUINEA (2)

			Unc	Proof
23 (23)	5	Kina 1983. National Bank building:		
		a) (Cu-Ni)	10.00	
		b) (Ag)		40.00
24 (24)	100	Kina (Au) 1983. Emblem of National Bank (with central hole)		300.00

PARLIAMENT BUILDING

			Proof
25 (25)	5	Kina (Ag) 1984	40.00

VISIT OF POPE JOHN PAUL II

			Proof
26 (26)	10	Kina (Ag) 1984	60.00

100th ANNIVERSARY OF PROTECTORATE FOUNDING

			Proof
27 (27)	100	Kina (Au) 1984. Flags of Great Britain and Germany	300.00

DECADE FOR WOMEN

			Proof
28 (28)	5	Kina (Ag) 1984. Coffee gathering	30.00

All valuations in the SCHÖN are stated in U.S. Dollars

Paraguay

Republica del Paraguay

Area: 157,000 sq. mi. Population: 3,700,000.
The town of Asunción, founded on August 15, 1537, soon became the center
of colonization of the upper La Plata territory and later the center of the
Jesuit state. After the uprising against Spain, Paraguay became a republic on
May 14, 1811.
Capital: Asunción.

100 Centavos = 1 Peso,
since 5th October 1943: 100 Centimos = 1 Guarani

			VF	XF
1 (6)	5	Centavos (Cu–Ni) 1900–1903. Coat of arms showing lion with liberty cap (= state emblem). ℞ value within wreath	3.20	6.00
2 (7)	10	Centavos (Cu–Ni) 1900–1903	4.50	7.50
3 (8)	20	Centavos (Cu–Ni) 1900–1903	5.00	8.00
4 (9)	5	Centavos (Cu–Ni) 1908. Star within wreath. ℞ value	10.00	25.00
5 (10)	10	Centavos (Cu–Ni) 1908	15.00	25.00
6 (11)	20	Centavos (Cu–Ni) 1908	5.00	11.50
7 (12)	50	Centavos (Cu–Ni) 1925	2.00	3.00
8 (13)	1	Peso (Cu–Ni) 1925	2.50	4.50
9 (14)	2	Pesos (Cu–Ni) 1925	3.50	5.50
10 (15)	5	Pesos (Cu–Ni) 1939	3.50	5.50

11 (16)	10	Pesos (Cu–Ni) 1939	4.50	6.50
12 (17)	50	Centavos (Al) 1938	1.00	2.00
13 (18)	1	Peso (Al) 1938	2.00	3.00
14 (19)	2	Pesos (Al) 1938	3.00	5.00

			VF	XF
15 (20)	1	Centimo (Al–Br) 1944–1950. Flower. ℞ value within wreath	0.40	0.60
16 (21)	5	Centimos (Al–Br) 1944–1947. Passion-flower (Passiflora sp. – Passifloraceae). ℞ value within wreath	0.50	0.80

			VF	XF
17 (22)	10	Centimos (Al–Br) 1944–1947. Orchid. ℞ value within wreath	0.25	0.50
18 (23)	25	Centimos (Al–Br) 1944–1951. Orchid. ℞ value within wreath	0.60	1.00
19 (24)	50	Centimos (Al–Br) 1944–1951. Coat of arms. ℞ value within wreath	0.80	1.50
20 (25)	10	Centimos (Al–Br) 1953 (scalloped)	0.20	0.30
21 (26)	15	Centimos (Al–Br) 1953	0.25	0.40
22 (27)	25	Centimos (Al–Br) 1953	0.25	0.50

			VF	XF
23 (28)	50	Centimos (Al–Br) 1953	0.40	0.80

COMMEMORATIVE COINS (2) FOR PRESIDENT STROESSNER'S 4th TERM IN OFFICE 1968–1973

			XF	Unc
24 (29)	300	Guaranies (Ag) 1968. Alfredo Stroessner (*1912), military officer and politician, President since 1954. ℞ state emblem and motto; name of country, value. Edge inscription: CENTENARIO DE LA EPOPEYA NACIONAL	10.00	17.50
25 (30)	10000	Guaranies (Au) 1968. Same type as No. 24		1800.00

26	150	Guaranies (Ag) 1972. President Stroessner	30.00
27	1500	Guaranies (Au) 1972. Type as No. 26	200.00
28	3000	Guaranies (Au) 1972. Type as No. 26	400.00
29	4500	Guaranies (Au) 1972. Type as No. 26	600.00
30	150	Guaranies (Ag) 1972. Munich Olympics 1972 – sprinter	30.00

31	1500	Guaranies (Au) 1972. Type as No. 30	200.00
32	3000	Guaranies (Au) 1972. Type as No. 30	400.00
33	4500	Guaranies (Au) 1972. Type as No. 30	600.00
34	150	Guaranies (Ag) 1972. Munich Olympics 1972 – footballer	30.00
35	1500	Guaranies (Au) 1972. Type as No. 34	200.00
36	3000	Guaranies (Au) 1972. Type as No. 34	400.00
37	4500	Guaranies (Au) 1972. Type as No. 34	600.00
38	150	Guaranies (Ag) 1972. Munich Olympics 1952 – long-jumper	30.00
39	1500	Guaranies (Au) 1972. Type as No. 38	200.00
40	3000	Guaranies (Au) 1972. Type as No. 38	400.00
41	4500	Guaranies (Au) 1972. Type as No. 38	600.00
42	150	Guaranies (Ag) 1972. Munich Olympics 1972 – high-jumper	30.00
43	1500	Guaranies (Au) 1972. Type as No. 42	200.00
44	3000	Guaranies (Au) 1972. Type as No. 42	400.00
45	4500	Guaranies (Au) 1972. Type as No. 42	600.00
46	150	Guaranies (Ag) 1972. Munich Olympics 1972 – hurdler	30.00
47	1500	Guaranies (Au) 1972. Type as No. 46	200.00
48	3000	Guaranies (Au) 1972. Type as No. 46	400.00
49	4500	Guaranies (Au) 1972. Type as No. 46	600.00
50	150	Guaranies (Ag) 1973. Munich Olympics 1972 – boxer	30.00
51	1500	Guaranies (Au) 1973. Type as No. 50	200.00
52	3000	Guaranies (Au) 1973. Type as No. 50	400.00
53	4500	Guaranies (Au) 1973. Type as No. 50	600.00
54	150	Guaranies (Ag) 1973. Marshal José F. Estigarribia (1888–1940), president 1939–1940	30.00
55	1500	Guaranies (Au) 1973. Type as No. 54	200.00
56	3000	Guaranies (Au) 1973. Type as No. 54	400.00
57	4500	Guaranies (Au) 1973. Type as No. 54	600.00

				Proof
58	150	Guaranies (Ag) 1973. Marshal Solano López (1827–1870), president 1862 to 1870		30.00
59	1500	Guaranies (Au) 1973. Type as No. 58		200.00
60	3000	Guaranies (Au) 1973. Type as No. 58		400.00
61	4500	Guaranies (Au) 1973. Type as No. 58		600.00
62	150	Guaranies (Ag) 1973. General José E. Diaz		30.00
63	1500	Guaranies (Au) 1973. Type as No. 62		200.00
64	3000	Guaranies (Au) 1973. Type as No. 62		400.00
65	4500	Guaranies (Au) 1973. Type as No. 62		600.00
66	150	Guaranies (Ag) 1973. General Bernardino Caballero (1831–1885), president 1880–1885		30.00
67	1500	Guaranies (Au) 1973. Type as No. 66		200.00
68	3000	Guaranies (Au) 1973. Type as No. 66		400.00
69	4500	Guaranies (Au) 1973. Type as No. 66		600.00
70	150	Guaranies (Ag) 1973. Seated woman, Teotihuacán culture, highland of Mexico, c. 100 B. C. – 400 A. D.		30.00
71	1500	Guaranies (Au) 1973. Type as No. 70		200.00
72	3000	Guaranies (Au) 1973. Type as No. 70		400.00
73	4500	Guaranies (Au) 1973. Type as No. 70		600.00
74	150	Guaranies (Ag) 1973. Vessel, polychrome decoration, Huaxtec culture of the northern Gulf coast of Mexico		30.00
75	1500	Guaranies (Au) 1973. Type as No. 74		200.00
76	3000	Guaranies (Au) 1973. Type as No. 74		400.00
77	4500	Guaranies (Au) 1973. Type as No. 74		600.00
78	150	Guaranies (Ag) 1973. Four-legged earthenware vessel in the shape of a jaguar, polychrome decoration, Mixtec cuture, c. 900–1494 A. D.		30.00

79	1500	Guaranies (Au) 1973. Type as No. 78		200.00
80	3000	Guaranies (Au) 1973. Type as No. 78		400.00
81	4500	Guaranies (Au) 1973. Type as No. 78		600.00
82	150	Guaranies (Ag) 1973. Vessel, Tolul style of Veracruz		30.00
83	1500	Guaranies (Au) 1973. Type as No. 82		200.00
84	3000	Guaranies (Au) 1973. Type as No. 82		400.00
85	4500	Guaranies (Au) 1973. Type as No. 82		600.00

86	150	Guaranies (Ag) 1973. "Smiling face", culture of Veracruz	30.00
87	1500	Guaranies (Au) 1973. Type as No. 86	200.00
88	3000	Guaranies (Au) 1973. Type as No. 86	400.00
89	4500	Guaranies (Au) 1973. Type as No. 86	600.00
90	150	Guaranies (Ag) 1973. Albrecht Dürer (1471–1528), painter, graphic artist, author on the arts	30.00
91	1500	Guaranies (Au) 1973. Type as No. 90	200.00
92	3000	Guaranies (Au) 1973. Type as No. 90	400.00
93	4500	Guaranies (Au) 1973. Type as No. 90	600.00
94	150	Guaranies (Ag) 1973. Johann Wolfgang von Goethe (1749–1832), poet	30.00
95	1500	Guaranies (Au) 1973. Type as No. 94	200.00
96	3000	Guaranies (Au) 1973. Type as No. 94	400.00
97	4500	Guaranies (Au) 1973. Type as No. 94	600.00
98	150	Guaranies (Ag) 1973. Abraham Lincoln (1809–1865), 16th President of the United States of America	30.00
99	1500	Guaranies (Au) 1974. Type as No. 98	200.00
100	3000	Guaranies (Au) 1974. Type as No. 98	400.00
101	4500	Guaranies (Au) 1974. Type as No. 98	600.00
102	150	Guaranies (Ag) 1974. Ludwig van Beethoven (1770–1827), composer	30.00
103	1500	Guaranies (Au) 1974. Type as No. 102	200.00
104	3000	Guaranies (Au) 1974. Type as No. 102	400.00
105	4500	Guaranies (Au) 1974. Type as No. 102	600.00
106	150	Guaranies (Ag) 1974. Otto von Bismarck (1815–1898), founder of the second German Reich	30.00
107	1500	Guaranies (Au) 1974. Type as No. 106	200.00
108	3000	Guaranies (Au) 1974. Type as No. 106	400.00
109	4500	Guaranies (Au) 1974. Type as No. 106	600.00
110	150	Guaranies (Ag) 1974. Albert Einstein (1879–1955), physicist	30.00
111	1500	Guaranies (Au) 1974. Type as No. 110	200.00
112	3000	Guaranies (Au) 1974. Type as No. 110	400.00
113	4500	Guaranies (Au) 1974. Type as No. 110	600.00
114	150	Guaranies (Ag) 1974. Giuseppe Garibaldi (1807–1882), Italian hero in the struggle for freedom	30.00
115	1500	Guaranies (Au) 1974. Type as No. 114	200.00
116	3000	Guaranies (Au) 1974. Type as No. 114	400.00
117	4500	Guaranies (Au) 1974. Type as No. 114	600.00
118	150	Guaranies (Ag) 1974. Alessandro Manzoni (1785–1873), Italian poet	30.00
119	1500	Guaranies (Au) 1974. Type as No. 118	200.00
120	3000	Guaranies (Au) 1974. Type as No. 118	400.00
121	4500	Guaranies (Au) 1974. Type as No. 118	600.00
122	150	Guaranies (Ag) 1974. William Tell, the hero of the well-kown Swiss legend	30.00

			Proof
123	1500	Guaranies (Au) 1974. Type as No. 122	200.00
124	3000	Guaranies (Au) 1974. Type as No. 122	400.00
125	4500	Guaranies (Au) 1974. Type as No. 122	600.00
126	150	Guaranies (Ag) 1974. John F. Kennedy (1917–1963), 35th President of the United States of America	30.00
127	1500	Guaranies (Au) 1974. Type as No. 126	200.00
128	3000	Guaranies (Au) 1974. Type as No. 126	400.00
129	4500	Guaranies (Au) 1974. Type as No. 126	600.00
130	150	Guaranies (Ag) 1974. Konrad Adenauer (1876–1967), first German Federal chancellor	30.00
131	1500	Guaranies (Au) 1974. Type as No. 130	200.00
132	3000	Guaranies (Au) 1974. Type as No. 130	400.00
133	4500	Guaranies (Au) 1974. Type as No. 130	600.00
134	150	Guaranies (Ag) 1974. Winston Churchill (1874–1965), British statesman	30.00
135	1500	Guaranies (Au) 1974. Type as No. 134	200.00
136	3000	Guaranies (Au) 1974. Type as No. 134	400.00
137	4500	Guaranies (Au) 1974. Type as No. 134	600.00
138	150	Guaranies (Ag) 1974. Pope John XXIII, Roncalli (1881–1963)	30.00
139	1500	Guaranies (Au) 1974. Type as No. 138	200.00
140	3000	Guaranies (Au) 1974. Type as No. 138	400.00
141	4500	Guaranies (Au) 1974. Type as No. 138	600.00
142	150	Guaranies (Ag) 1975. Pope Paul VI, Montini (1897-1978)	30.00
143	1500	Guaranies (Au) 1975. Type as No. 142	200.00
144	3000	Guaranies (Au) 1975. Type as No. 142	400.00
145	4500	Guaranies (Au) 1975. Type as No. 142	600.00
146	150	Guaranies (Ag) 1975. Bridge of Friendship	30.00
147	1500	Guaranies (Au) 1975. Type as No. 146	200.00
148	3000	Guaranies (Au) 1975. Type as No. 146	400.00
149	4500	Guaranies (Au) 1975. Type as No. 146	600.00
150	150	Guaranies (Ag) 1975. Parliament building in Asunción	30.00

151	1500	Guaranies (Au) 1975. Type as No. 150	200.00
152	3000	Guaranies (Au) 1975. Type as No. 150	400.00

			Proof
153	4500 Guaranies (Au) 1975. Type as No. 150		600.00
154	150 Guaranies (Ag) 1975. Church of San Roque in Yaguaron		30.00
155	1500 Guaranies (Au) 1975. Type as No. 154		200.00
156	3000 Guaranies (Au) 1975. Type as No. 154		400.00
157	4500 Guaranies (Au) 1975. Type as No. 154		600.00
158	150 Guaranies (Ag) 1975. Ruin of the church of Humaitá		30.00
159	1500 Guaranies (Au) 1975. Type as No. 158		200.00
160	3000 Guaranies (Au) 1975. Type as No. 158		400.00
161	4500 Guaranies (Au) 1975. Type as No. 158		600.00
162	150 Guaranies (Ag) 1975. US research program „Apollo 11"		30.00
163	1500 Guaranies (Au) 1975. Type as No. 162		200.00
164	3000 Guaranies (Au) 1975. Type as No. 162		400.00
165	4500 Guaranies (Au) 1975. Type as No. 162		600.00
166	150 Guaranies (Ag) 1975. US research program "Apollo 15"		30.00
167	1500 Guaranies (Ag) 1975. Type as No. 166		200.00
168	3000 Guaranies (Au) 1975. Type as No. 166		400.00
169	4500 Guaranies (Au) 1975. Type as No. 166		600.00

		XF	**Unc**
170 (31)	1 Guarani (St) 1975, 1976. Soldier. Rev. tobacco plant	0.05	0.10
171 (32)	5 Guaranies (St) 1975. A young woman holding a vessel in her right arm. Rev. cotton	0.10	0.15
172 (33)	10 Guaranies (St) 1975, 1976. Portrait of General Garay. Rev. cow's head	0.20	0.30
173 (34)	50 Guaranies (St) 1975. Marshal José Felix Estigarribia	0.60	0.90

FOR THE FAO COIN PLAN (3)

174 (35)	1 Guarani (St) 1978, 1980, 1984, 1986	0.05	0.10
175 (36)	5 Guaranies (St) 1978, 1980, 1984	0.10	0.15
176 (37)	10 Guaranies (St) 1978, 1980, 1984, 1986	0.20	0.30
177 (38)	50 Guaranies (St) 1980, 1986	0.50	1.00

Peru   **Peru**   **Pérou**

Area: 514,060 sq. mi. Population: 19,700,000.
Before the conquest by the Spaniards under Francisco Pizarro (1531–1534),
Peru was the central province of the Inka empire. The province created in
1542, and governed by a viceroy of Peru, comprised initially almost the
whole of Spanish South America. The provinces of New Granada and Rio
de la Plata were only detached in the 18th century. During the early years of
the battles of independence in South America, Peru was the focal point of
Spanish domination. The Republic was proclaimed on 28th July 1821, after
the entry of General José de San Martín into Lima.
Capital: Lima.

10 Centavos = 1 Dinero,
100 Centavos = 10 Dineros = 1 Sol de Oro

			VF	XF
1 (9a)	1	Centavo (Br) 1975–1878, 1919. Date above sunburst. R value in wreath	1.20	2.00
2 (11)	1	Centavo (Br) 1901–1941. Date at bottom	1.00	1.50
3 (12)	1	Centavo (Br) 1876–1937. Date at bottom CENTAVO curved	1.00	2.00
4 (11a)	1	Centavo (Br) 1941–1944. Date at bottom CENTAVO straight	0.80	1.60
5 (12a)	1	Centavo (Br) 1941–1949. Date at bottom CENTAVO curved	0.40	0.80

			VF	XF
6 (10a)	2	Centavos (Br) 1876–1895, 1919. Date above sunburst. R value in wreath	1.00	1.60
7 (13)	2	Centavos (Br) 1917–1941. Date at bottom, CENTAVOS curved	0.50	0.80
8 (13a)	2	Centavos (Br) 1941–1949. Date at bottom, CENTAVOS curved. Same type as No. 7, but thinner planchet	0.40	0.60
9 (14)	½	Dinero (Ag) 1863–1917. Figure of Liberty, seated. R coat of arms	1.50	2.50

			VF	XF
10 (15)	1	Dinero (Ag) 1864–1916	2.50	3.50
11 (16)	1/5	Sol (Ag) 1863–1967	3.50	5.00
12 (17)	½	Sol (Ag) 1864–1917	8.00	12.00
13 (18)	1	Sol (Ag) 1864–1916	16.00	28.00
14 (20)	1/5	Libra (Au) 1906–1969. Head right of Manco Capac, founder of the Inca empire. R coat of arms	27.50	35.00
15 (21)	½	Libra (Au) 1902–1969. Same type as No. 14	60.00	70.00
A15 (22)	1	Libra (Au) 1898–1969. Same type as No. 14	120.00	140.00
B15 (23)	1	Sol (Ag) 1910	40.00	60.00
16 (24)	5	Soles (Au) 1910. Coat of arms. R motto and value	100.00	130.00
17 (31)	5	Centavos. Head of Liberty, right; date spelled out. R value and branch		
		a) (Cu-Ni) 1918–1941	0.25	0.40
		b) (Bra) 1942–1944	0.25	0.40
18 (32)	10	Centavos. Same type as No. 17		
		a) (Cu-Ni) 1918–1941	0.40	0.60
		b) (Bra) 1942–1944	0.50	0.80
19 (33)	20	Centavos. Same type as No. 17		
		a) (Cu-Ni) 1918–1941	0.40	0.80
		b) (Bra) 1942–1944	1.00	2.00
20 (34)	½	Sol (Ag) 1922–1935	5.00	8.00
21 (36)	1	Sol (Ag) 1923–1935. Coat of arms, new legend: REPUBLICA PERUANA LIMA 5 DECIMOS FINO, date. R allegory of the Liberty, UN SOL in exergue	7.50	11.00

			VF	XF
21a (35)	1	Sol (Ag) 1923. Same type as No. 21, but no Fineness	45.00	75.00

Yeoman Numbers

In order to help collectors and dealers, we have added after most SCHÖN-numbers the corresponding number assigned by R. S. Yeoman in his wellknown works entiles »A Catalog of Modern World Coins« and »Current Coins of the World«.

22 (37)	50 Soles (Au) 1930–1931, 1967–1969. Manco Capac, founder of the Inca empire in the 11th century. R Inca ornament:	**XF**	**Unc**
	a) 1930–1931	650.00	1000.00
	b) 1967–1969		600.00

			VF	**XF**
23 (43)	½	Sol (Bra) 1935–1965. Coat of arms. R value in circle, new legend: EL BANCO CENTRAL DE RESERVA DEL PERU	0.30	0.50
24 (44)	1	Sol (Bra) 1943–1965	0.50	0.70
25 (41)	1	Centavo (Sn) 1950–1965. Sunburst. R value in wreath	0.30	0.60
26 (42)	2	Centavos (Sn) 1950–1956	0.30	0.60
27 (38)	5	Centavos (Bra). Head of Liberty, right. Name of country, date. R value and branch		
		a) 1945–1951	0.20	0.40
		b) 1951–1965, thinner planchet	0.15	0.25
28 (39)	10	Centavos (Bra). Same type as No. 27		
		a) 1945–1950	0.25	0.40
		b) 1951–1965, thinner planchet	0.15	0.25
29 (40)	20	Centavos (Bra). Same type as No. 27		
		a) 1942–1951	0.40	0.60
		b) 1951–1965	0.10	0.20
30 (48)	5	Soles (Au) 1956–1969. Coat of arms. R Liberty seated		50.00
31 (49)	10	Soles (Au) 1956–1969		75.00
32 (50)	20	Soles (Au) 1950–1969		150.00
33 (51)	50	Soles (Au) 1950–1969		400.00
34 (52)	100	Soles (Au) 1950–1969		700.00

35 (45)	5 Centavos (Al–Br) 1954. Ramón Castilla (1797–1867), president 1845–1851 and 1855–1862. ℞ value in wreath, and torch	**VF**	**XF**
		2.50	5.00
36 (46)	10 Centavos (Al–Br) 1954. Same type as No. 35	2.50	5.00

37 (47)	20 Centavos (Al–Br) 1954. Same type as No. 35	4.00	8.00

COMMEMORATIVE COINS (8) FOR THE 400th ANNIVERSARY OF THE LIMA MINT

		XF	**Unc**
38 (53)	5 Centavos (Bra) 1965. 8-Reales-coin of 1565	0.10	0.20
39 (54)	10 Centavos (Bra) 1965. Same type as No. 38	0.25	0.50
40 (55)	25 Centavos (Bra) 1965. Same type as No. 38	0.30	0.60
41 (56)	½ Sol (Bra) 1965. Same type as No. 38	0.40	0.70
42 (57)	1 Sol (Bra) 1965. Same type as No. 38	0.50	0.80
43 (58)	20 Soles (Ag) 1965. Same type as No. 38	6.50	9.00
44 (59)	50 Soles (Au) 1965. Same type as No. 38		400.00
45 (60)	100 Soles (Au) 1965. Same type as No. 38		800.00

COMMEMORATIVE COINS (3) FOR THE CENTENNIAL OF THE UNSUCCESSFUL SIEGE OF CALLAO BY THE SPANISH FLEET ON 2nd MAY 1866

46 (61)	20 Soles (Ag) 1966. Victoria, from the Victory Monument in Lima. ℞ coat of arms	12.00	20.00
47 (62)	50 Soles (Au) 1966		550.00
48 (63)	100 Soles (Au) 1966		825.00

49 (64) 5 Centavos (Bra) 1966–. Coat of arms.   **XF**   **Unc**
R flowers of the chinabark tree (Chin-
chona sp. – Rubiaceae)
  a) 1966–1968, reeded edge   0.15   0.25
  b) 1969–1975, plain edge   0.10   0.20

50 (65) 10 Centavos (Bra) 1966-1975. Type as No. 49:
  a) 1966-1968, reeded edge   0.20   0.30
  b) 1969-1975, plain edge   0.15   0.25

51 (66) 25 Centavos (Bra) 1966-1975. Type as No. 49:
  a) 1966-1968, reeded edge   0.25   0.40
  b) 1969-1975, plain edge   0.20   0.35

52 (67) ½ Sol (Bra) 1966–1975. R vicugna (Lama
vicugna – Camelidae)   0.30   0.50

53 (68) 1 Sol (Bra) 1966–1975. Type as No. 52   0.30   0.70

54 (69) 5 Soles (Cu-Ni) 1969. Coat of arms. R
cup (Keru) of the Inca era   0.50   1.00

			XF	Unc
55 (70)	10 Soles (Cu-Ni) 1969. ℞ stylized fish from pre-Columbian design		1.00	2.00

COMMEMORATIVE ISSUE (3) FOR THE 150th ANNIVERSARY OF INDEPENDENCE

56 (71) 5 Soles (Cu–Ni) 1971. Coat of arms. ℞ Tupác Amarú (c. 1740–1781), descendent of the Inca rulers, leader of the great Indian rebellion (1780/81); executed in 1781 for treason 1.00 2.00

57 (72) 10 Soles (Cu–Ni) 1971. Same type as No. 56 1.25 2.50

58 (73) 50 Soles (Ag) 1971. Same type as No. 56 9.00 15.00

59 (74) 5 Soles (Cu-Ni) 1972–1975. Type similar to No. 57, but without legend 0.50 0.75

60 (75) 10 Soles (Cu-Ni) 1972–1975. Same type as No. 59 1.00 1.50

COMMEMORATIVE ISSUE FOR THE 100th ANNIVERSARY OF THE PERUVIAN-JAPANESE TRADE AGREEMENT

61 (76) 100 Soles (Ag) 1973. National coat of arms and anniversary dates. ℞ chrysanthemum (Chrysanthemum sp. – Compositae), value, functional legend 10.00 15.00

AVIATION HEROES

			XF	Unc
62 (77)	200	Soles (Ag) 1974–1978. Conjoined heads left of Jorge Chavez and José Quinones	10.00	15.00

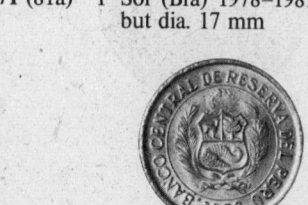

63 (78)	10	Centavos (Bra) 1975. Coat of arms. Rev. value	0.10	0.20
64 (79)	20	Centavos (Bra) 1975. Type as No. 63	0.10	0.20
65 (80)	½	Sol (Bra) 1975–1977. Type as No. 63	0.20	0.30

66 (81)	1	Sol (Bra) 1975, 1976. Type similar to No. 63	0.20	0.40
67 (82)	5	Soles (Cu-Ni) 1975–1977. Type similar to No. 59	0.30	0.60

150th ANNIVERSARY OF THE BATTLE OF AYACUCHO (3)

68 (84)	½	Sol (Au) 1976. Ayacucho monument; 9.25 grams		200.00
69 (85)	1	Sol (Au) 1976. Type as No. 68; 23.4 grams		450.00
70 (83)	400	Soles (Ag) 1976. Type as No. 68		20.00
71 (81a)	1	Sol (Bra) 1978–1981. Type as No. 66, but dia. 17 mm	0.20	0.30

72 (86)	5	Soles (Bra) 1978–1983. Coat of arms. Rev. value	0.30	0.50

		XF	Unc
73 (75a) 10 Soles (Bra) 1978–1983. Type as No. 59		0.40	0.85

NATIONAL CONGRESS

	XF	Unc
74 (95) 1000 Soles (Ag) 1979	6.00	10.00

No. 75 omitted.

100th ANNIVERSARY OF THE BATTLE OF IQUIQUE

	Unc
76 (88) 5000 Soles (Ag) 1979	25.00

100th ANNIVERSARY OF THE PACIFIC WAR (6)

		XF	Unc
77 (89)	50000 Soles (Au) 1979. Alfonso Ugarte		300.00
78 (90)	50000 Soles (Au) 1979. Elias Aguirre		300.00
79 (91)	50000 Soles (Au) 1979. F. Garcia Calderon		
80 (92)	100000 Soles (Au) 1979. Francisco Bologne- se		300.00 550.00
81 (93)	100000 Soles (Au) 1979. Andrés A. Cáceres		550.00
82 (94)	100000 Soles (Au) 1979. Miguel Grau		550.00
83 (96)	50 Soles (Cu-Al-Ni) 1979–1983	0.25	0.50

		XF	Unc
84 (97)	100 Soles (Cu-Ni) 1980, 1982	0.40	0.75

100th ANNIVERSARY OF THE BATTLE OF LA BRENA

	Unc
85 (98) 10000 Soles (Ag) 1982. Bust of Andrés Av- elino Cáceres (1836–1924), General	15.00

WORLD SOCCER CHAMPIONSHIP GAMES 1982 IN SPAIN (2)

			Proof
86 (99)	5000 Soles (Ag) 1982		40.00
87 (100)	5000 Soles (Ag) 1982		40.00

150th ANNIVERSARY OF THE BIRTH OF M. L. GRAU (4)

		XF	**Unc**
88 (101)	10 Soles (Bra) 1984. Miguel L. Grau (1834–1879), Admiral	0.15	0.35
89	50 Soles (Bra) 1984, 1985. Type as No. 88	0.30	0.50
90 (102)	100 Soles (Bra). 1984. Type as No. 88	0.40	0.75
91 (103)	500 Soles (Bra) 1984, 1985. Type as No. 88	0.60	1.25

MONETARY REFORM: 100 Céntimos = 1 Inti

		XF	**Unc**
92	1 Céntimo (Cu-Al-Ni) 1985. Miguel L. Grau	0.10	0.20
93	5 Céntimos (Cu-Al-Ni) 1985. Type as No. 92	0.10	0.20
94	10 Céntimos (Cu-Al-Ni) 1985–1987. Type as No. 92	0.15	0.25
95	20 Céntimos (Cu-Al-Ni) 1985–1987. Type as No. 92	0.20	0.35
96	50 Céntimos (Cu-Al-Ni) 1985–1987. Type as No. 92	0.25	0.40
97	1 Inti (Cu-Al-Ni) 1985–1987	0.35	0.70
98	100 Intis (Ag) 1986		10.00
99	200 Intis (Ag) 1986		18.00

Pilipinas

Area: 115,700 sq. mi. Population: 54,700,000.
The Philippines were discovered by Magellan in 1521. The group of islands, situated in the Malayan archipelago, was a Spanish possession until 1898 when it was ceded to the United States of America after the Peace of Paris. In 1916 the Philippines obtained limited self-government and, in 1935, were awarded dominion status with the designation of Commonwealth of the Philippines. The island nation became independent on 4th July 1946. Capital: Manila.

100 Centavos = 1 Peso, since 1967: 100 Sentimos = 1 Piso

UNDER AMERICAN SOVEREIGNTY

			VF	XF
1 (14)	½	Centavo (Br) 1903–1908. Blacksmith with anvil, Mt. Mayon, 7,926 feet, volcano on Luzon. ℞ coat of arms	1.50	4.00
2 (15)	1	Centavo (Br) 1903–1936	1.50	4.50

3 (16)	5	Centavos (Cu–Ni) 1903–1928	1.00	2.50
4 (17)	5	Centavos (Cu–Ni) 1930–1935. Same type as No. 3, but smaller diameter	2.00	5.00
5	10	Centavos (Ag). Walking Philippina		
		a) (Y 18) 1903–1906	4.00	8.00
		b) (Y 22) 1907–1935	2.00	3.00
6	20	Centavos (Ag). Same type as No. 5		
		a) (Y 19) 1903–1906	4.00	6.00
		b) (Y 23) 1907–1929	3.00	4.00
7	50	Centavos (Ag). Same type as No. 5		
		a) (Y 20) 1903–1906	10.00	18.00
		b) (Y 24) 1907–1921	7.00	9.00

		VF	XF
8	1 Peso (Ag). Same type as No. 5		
	a) (Y 21) 1903–1906	12.50	20.00
	b) (Y 25) 1907–1912	7.50	12.50

COMMONWEALTH OF THE PHILIPPINES 1935–1946

COMMEMORATIVE ISSUES (3) FOR THE ESTABLISHMENT OF THE COMMONWEALTH OF THE PHILIPPINES ON NOVEMBER 15th, 1935

9 (26) 50 Centavos (Ag) 1936. Frank Murphy (1890–1949), American civil governor and ambassador, Manuel L. Quezón (1878–1944), lawyer and politician; 1st President of the Commonwealth. ℞ coat of arms ... 28.00 50.00

		VF	XF
10 (27)	1 Peso (Ag) 1936. Franklin D. Roosevelt (1882–1945) and President Quezón	50.00	85.00
11 (28)	1 Peso (Ag) 1936. F. Murphy and President Quezón	50.00	85.00
12 (29)	1 Centavo (Br) 1937–1944. Blacksmith with anvil, Mt. Mayon, 7,926 feet, volcano on Luzon. ℞ coat of arms	0.10	0.20
13 (30)	5 Centavos. Same type as No. 12		
	a) (Y 30) (Cu-Ni) 1937–1941	1.20	2.50
	b) (Y 30a) (Ni-St) 1944–1945	0.10	0.20

			VF	XF
14 (31)	10	Centavos (Ag) 1937–1945	0.80	1.20
15 (32)	20	Centavos (Ag) 1937–1945	1.20	2.00
16 (33)	50	Centavos (Ag) 1944–1945	3.00	5.00

REPUBLIC since 1946
COMMEMORATIVE ISSUES (2) FOR GENERAL MACARTHUR

			XF	Unz
17 (34)	50	Centavos (Ag) 1947. General Douglas MacArthur (1888–1964), commander-in-chief of the American Forces in the Pacific during World War II. ℞ coat of arms	5.00	8.00
18 (35)	1	Peso (Ag) 1947. Same type as No. 17	10.00	15.00
19 (36)	1	Centavo (Br) 1958–1963. Blacksmith with anvil, Mt. Mayon, 7,926 feet, volcano on Luzon. R coat of arms	0.10	0.20
20 (37)	5	Centavos (Bra) 1958–1966	0.20	0.30
21 (38)	10	Centavos (Cu–Ni–Sn) 1958–1966. Walking Philippina	0.25	0.40
22 (39)	25	Centavos (Cu–Ni–Sn) 1958–1966	0.40	0.60
23 (40)	50	Centavos (Cu–Ni–Sn) 1958–1964	0.80	1.20

COMMEMORATIVE ISSUES (2) FOR THE 100th BIRTHDAY OF DR. JOSÉ RIZAL

24 (41)	½	Peso (Ag) 1961. José Rizal, Doctor of Medicine (1861–1896), national hero; executed as a rebel; head left. ℞ coat of arms	4.50	8.50

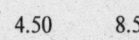

25 (42)	1	Peso (Ag) 1961. José Rizal, portrait	9.00	12.50

COMMEMORATIVE ISSUE FOR THE 100th BIRTHDAY OF ANDRES BONIFACIO

		XF	Unc
26 (43)	1 Peso (Ag) 1963. Andres Bonifacio (1863–1897), national hero	9.00	12.50

COMMEMORATIVE ISSUE FOR THE 100th BIRTHDAY OF APOLINARIO MABINI

27 (44)	1 Peso (Ag) 1964. Apolinario Mabini (1864–1903), national hero	9.00	12.50

COMMEMORATIVE ISSUE FOR THE 25th ANNIVERSARY OF THE BATTLE OF BATAAN

28 (45)	1 Peso (Ag) 1967. Sword in flames surrounded by laurel wreath. ℞ coat of arms	9.00	12.50

NEW CURRENCY: 100 Sentimos = 1 Piso

29 (46)	1 Sentimo (Al) 1967–1974. King Lapu-Lapu. R coat of arms, legend in Tagalog	0.05	0.10
30 (47)	5 Sentimos (Bra) 1967–1974. Melchora Aquino (1812–1919), patriot. R same as No. 29	0.05	0.10

31 (48)   10 Sentimos (Cu-Ni-Sn) 1967–1974. Francisco

				XF	Unc
			Baltazar (1788–1862), poet. R same as No. 29	0.10	0.20
32	(49)	25	Sentimos (Cu-Ni-Sn) 1967–1974. Juan Luna (1857–1899), painter. R same as No. 29	0.20	0.30
33	(50)	50	Sentimos (Cu-Ni-Sn) 1967–1975. Marcelo H. del Pilar (1850–1886), lawyer and journalist. R same as No. 29	0.30	0.60

COMMEMORATIVE ISSUE FOR THE 100th BIRTHDAY OF EMILIO AGUINALDO

				XF	Unc
34	(51)	1	Piso (Ag) 1969. Emilio Aguinaldo (1869–1964), General and leader of the rebellious Philippinos from 1898 to 1901. R coat of arms, name of country, value PISO	9.00	12.50

COMMEMORATIVE ISSUES (3) FOR THE VISIT OF POPE PAUL VI

				XF	Unc
35	(52)	1	Piso (Ni) 1970. Pope Paul VI, portrait right. R Ferdinand E. Marcos, portrait left. Value	1.20	2.50
36	(52a)	1	Piso (Ag) 1970. Type as No. 35, but plain edge	9.00	12.50
37	(52b)	1	Piso (Au) 1970. Same type as No. 35		550.00
38	(53)	1	Piso (Cu-Ni) 1972, 1974. José Rizal, Doctor of Medicine. Rev. coat of arms	0.50	1.00

			XF	Unc
39 (54)	25	Piso (Ag) 1974	10.00	15.00

3rd ANNIVERSARY OF THE NEW SOCIETY (2)

40 (62)	50	Piso (Ag) 1975. Head left of President Ferdinand E. Marcos. Rev. coat of arms, value	18.00	25.00

41 (63)	1000	Piso (Au) 1975. Type as No. 40	175.00	200.00
42 (55)	1	Sentimo (Al) 1975–1978. King Lapulapu	0.05	0.10
43 (56)	5	Sentimos (Bra) 1975–1978. Melchora Aquino (scalloped)	0.05	0.10
44 (57)	10	Sentimos (Cu-Ni) 1975–1978. Francisco Baltasar	0.10	0.20
45 (58)	25	Sentimos (Cu-Ni) 1975–1978. Juan Luna	0.15	0.30
46 (59)	1	Piso (Cu-Ni) 1975–1978. José Rizal	0.50	1.00
47 (60)	5	Piso (Ni) 1975–1978, 1982. Head left of President Ferdinand E. Marcos	Unc 1.50	Proof 10.00
48 (61)	25	Piso (Ag) 1975. Emilio Aguinaldo	9.00	15.00

ISSUE FOR THE FAO COIN PLAN

49 (64)	25	Piso (Ag) 1976. Rice harvest	12.50	20.00

I.M.F. MEETING IN MANILA (2)

			Unc	Proof
50 (65)	50 Piso (Ag) 1976		17.50	17.50
51 (66)	1500 Piso (Au) 1976		300.00	325.00

5th ANNIVERSARY OF THE NEW SOCIETY (2)

52 (69)	1500 Piso (Au) 1977		300.00	325.00
53 (70)	5000 Piso (Au) 1977		1200.00	1200.00

RICE CULTIVATION

54 (67)	25 Piso (Ag) 1977. Banawie Rice Terraces		12.50	27.50

INAUGURATION OF NEW MINT FACILITIES (2)

55 (68)	50 Piso (Ag) 1977		17.50	22.50
56 (73)	1500 Piso (Au) 1978		300.00	325.00

100th ANNIVERSARY OF THE BIRTH OF MANUEL L. QUEZON (2)

57 (71)	25 Piso (Ag) 1978		12.50	17.50
58 (72)	50 Piso (Ag) 1978		15.00	20.00

UN CONFERENCE ON TRADE AND DEVELOPMENT

59 (74)	25 Piso (Ag) 1979		15.00	20.00

INTERNATIONAL YEAR OF THE CHILD

60 (75)	50 Piso (Ag) 1979		20.00	20.00

			Unc	Proof
61 (55a)	1	Sentimo (Al) 1979–1982. Type as No. 42, but redesigned seal	1.00	2.00
62 (56a)	5	Sentimos (Bra) 1979–1982. Type as No. 43, but redesigned seal	1.00	2.50
63 (57a)	10	Sentimos (Cu-Ni) 1979–1982. Type as No. 44, but redesigned seal	1.00	3.00
64 (58a)	25	Sentimos (Cu-Ni) 1979–1982. Type as No. 45, but redesigned seal	1.50	4.00
65 (59a)	1	Piso (Cu-Ni) 1979–1982. Type as No. 46, but legend ISANG BANSA ISANG DIWA below shield	2.50	5.00
66 (60a)	5	Piso (Ni) 1979–1982. Type as No. 47, but legend ISANG BANSA ISANG DIWA	3.50	8.50

100th ANNIVERSARY OF THE BIRTH OF GENERAL MACARTHUR (2)

67 (76)	25	Piso (Ag) 1980	20.00	40.00
68 (77)	2500	Piso (Au) 1980		500.00

WORLD FOOD DAY 1981

69 (78)	25	Piso (Ag) 1981	12.50	20.00

VISIT OF POPE JOHN PAUL II (2)

70 (79)	50	Piso (Ag) 1981	20.00	50.00
71 (80)	1500	Piso (Au) 1981		450.00

40th ANNIVERSARY OF THE BATTLE OF BATAAN-CORREGIDOR (2)

72 (81)	50	Piso (Ag) 1982. Conjoined heads	15.00	40.00
73 (82)	1500	Piso (Au) 1982. Type as No. 72	250.00	350.00

PRESIDENTS MARCOS AND REAGAN

			Unc	Proof
74 (91)	25 Piso (Ag) 1982. Conjoined heads		65.00	500.00

			XF	Unc
75 (84)	1 Sentimo (Al) 1983–1985. King Lapu-Lapu. Rev. Seashell (Voluta imperiaes)		0.05	0.10
76 (85)	5 Sentimo (Al) 1983–1985, 1987. Melchora Aquino. Rev. Waling-Waling orchid		0.05	0.10
77 (86)	10 Sentimo (Al) 1983–1985. Francisco Baltasar. Rev. Pygmy-Goby fish (Pandaka pygmea)		0.10	0.15
78 (87)	25 Sentimo (Bra) 1983–1985. Juan Luna. Rev. Butterfly (Graphium idaeoides) (F.A.O. issue)		0.10	0.20
79 (88)	50 Sentimo (Cu-Ni) 1983–1985. Marcelo H. del Pilar. Rev. Monkey-eating eagle			
	a) inscription PITHECOBHAGA, 1983		0.80	2.00
	b) inscription PITHECOPHAGA, 1983–1985		0.20	0.50
80 (89)	1 Piso (Cu-Ni) 1983–1985. José Rizal. Rev. Tamaraw bull (Anoa mindorensis) (F.A.O. issue)		0.40	0.65
81 (90)	2 Piso (Cu-Ni) 1983–1985. Andres Bonifacio. Rev. Coconut palm (Cocos nucifera – Palmae)		0.60	1.00

75th ANNIVERSARY OF NATIONAL UNIVERSITY

			Unc	Proof
82 (92)	100 Piso (Ag) 1983		12.50	35.00

AQUINO VISIT (2)

			Unc
83	25 Piso (Ag) 1986. Corazon C. Aquino. Rev. Ronald W. Reagan; .925 silver, 28.28 g		35.00
84	2500 Piso (Au) 1986. Type as No. 83; .500 gold, 15 g		400.00

Polen   # Poland   **Pologne**

Polska

Area: 120,330 sq. mi. Population: 37,100,000.

The first historical ruler of Poland was Duke Mieszko of the House of Piasts. The eventful history comprises the greatness and decline of the Polish state. The Piasts were superseded at the end of the 14th century by the Jagiello dynasty; after the Jagiellos became extinct, the Polish aristocracy elected foreign princes as their kings. In the more recent past, the rule of Jan III Sobieski (1674–1696) can be described as a glorious climax in Polish history, who by virtue of his victory over the Turks before the gates of Vienna was acclaimed as the hero of the occident. The years 1772, 1793 and 1795 brought the partition of Poland and thus the temporary ceasing of the independent state. The Duchy of Warsaw created in 1807, the later Congress Poland, must be considered as a transition stage up to the foundation of the republic. Although the Central Powers had supported the creation of a kingdom in 1916, the republic was proclaimed on November 11, 1918. During 1939 to 1944 Central Poland came under the German State as a government of occupation. After the end of the Second World War, the People's Republic was created.

Capital: Warsaw.

100 Fenigów = 1 Marka, since 1923: 100 Groszy = 1 Zloty

INTERIM 1917–1918

			VF	XF
1 (4)	1	Fenig (Fe) 1918. Polish eagle, with crown above. ℞ value and legend KROLESTWO POLSKIE	6.00	16.00
2 (5)	5	Fenigów (Fe) 1917–1918. Same type as No. 1	1.50	3.50
3 (6)	10	Fenigów. Same type as No. 1		
		a) (Fe) 1917, 1918	1.50	3.50
		b) (Sn) 1917	50.00	75.00
4 (7)	20	Fenigów. Same type as No. 1		
		a) (Fe) 1917, 1918	3.50	6.50
		b) (Sn) 1917	55.00	80.00

			VF	XF
5 (8)	1	Grosz (Br) 1923–1939. Heraldic eagle. Ŗ value	0.40	0.60
6 (9)	2	Grosze (Br) 1923–1939	0.60	1.00

Of practically all Polish coins, struck since 1923, pattern pieces exist as counterparts, distributed by the Bank of Poland. These coins usually bear the word PROBA, and are distinguished by more or less changed designs. Besides these pattern pieces, another group of issues was struck but for several reasons never officially distributed; these include numbers 15–17 from 1925, and the 10 Zlotych and 20 Zlotych coins struck for the 20th anniversary of the People's Republic of Poland, in 1964.

7 (10)	5	Groszy (Br) 1923–1939	0.30	0.60
8 (11)	10	Groszy (Ni) 1923. Ŗ value in wreath	0.25	0.40
9 (12)	20	Groszy (Ni) 1923	0.40	0.60

10 (13)	50	Groszy (Ni) 1923	0.50	0.80
11 (14)	1	Zloty (Ni) 1929. Ŗ value in ornament	1.50	2.00

12 (15)	1	Zloty (Ag) 1924–1925. Ŗ peasant girl, ears of wheat		
		a) 1924, Hôtel des Monnaies, Paris: low relief strike, torches right and left of date	16.00	25.00
		b) 1925, Royal Mint, London: high relief strike, dot behind date	15.00	20.00

Three official silver pattern pieces are dated 1924, all of identical design and denomination.

13 (16)   2 Zlote (Ag) 1924–1925. Same type as   **VF   XF**
No. 12
a) 1924, Hôtel des Monnaies, Paris:
low relief strike, torches right and
left of date   35.00   45.00
b) 1924, Royal Mint, London: low
relief strike, mint mark: small H in-
stead of torches   40.00   75.00
c) 1924, United States Mint, Philadel-
phia: without mint mark, but invert-
ed reverse   35.00   55.00
d) 1925, Royal Mint, London: dot
behind date   28.00   36.00
e) 1925, United States Mint, Philadel-
phia: without mint mark   55.00   70.00

Six official pattern pieces were struck in 1924, five in silver, and one in
brass. Except for one silver strike all bear identical designs, denominations are identical. There is one official silver pattern piece from 1925,
of identical design and denomination. Further official pattern pieces
are two silver and one bronze coin from 1927, all bearing identical
design and denomination.

14 (18)   5 Zlotych (Ag) 1928, 1930–1932. Nike.
℞ heraldic eagle and value
a) 1928, Munt Belgie: without mint
mark   65.00   90.00
b) 1928, 1930–1932, Warsaw: dot left
of Nike's foot   190.00   280.00

Three official pattern pieces are dated 1927, two in silver and one in
bronze, only slightly differing in design, but of identical denomination. There is one official silver pattern piece in high relief strike, of
identical design and denomination, issued in 1928.

COMMEMORATIVE ISSUE FOR THE ADOPTION OF THE CONSTITUTION

				VF	**XF**
15 (17)	5	Zlotych (Ag) 1925. Heraldic eagle. ℞ allegory by S. Lewandowski; "Mother Polonia, right hand on eagle shield, receives constitution from an elected representative"		700.00	800.00

No. 15 did not circulate. There are eight types, all of identical design and denomination: in high relief two pieces of gold, two pieces of silver and one of brass, in low relief two pieces of silver and one of tombac.

				VF	**Unc**
16 (32)	10	Zlotych (Au) 1925. Boleslaw I. Chrobry (967–1025), duke since 992, first king of Poland 1024/25		75.00	100.00

One official pattern piece from 1925 was struck in bronze of identical design and denomination.

17 (33)	20	Zlotych (Au) 1925		120.00	150.00

Two offical pattern pieces were struck in 1925, one in bronze and one in nickel, both bear identical designs and denomination.
Coins No. 16 and 17 never circulated, but could be purchased until 1939 from the Bank Polski by furnishing the gold and paying the cost of coinage.

COMMEMORATIVE COIN FOR THE CENTENNIAL
OF THE POLISH UPRISING OF 1830

	VF	XF
18 (19) 5 Zlotych (Ag) 1930. Flag, memorial legend, dates. Rev. Heraldic eagle and value	75.00	125.00

Two strikes are to be distinguished: one low and one high relief.
An official bronze pattern piece from 1930, with high relief, identical design and denomination, was struck for the same event.

| **19** (20) 2 Zlote (Ag) 1932–1934. Woman's head with wreath of clover, allegory of the republic. ℞ heraldic eagle and value | 3.00 | 6.00 |

Two official pattern pieces date from 1933, one each in silver and in bronze, both of identical design and denomination.

| **20** (21) 5 Zlotych (Ag) 1932–1934. Same type as No. 19 | 6.00 | 15.00 |

The coins of 1932 were struck in Warsaw with a mint mark in the left claw of the eagle, London strikes are without mint mark.
Two official pattern pieces are dated 1933, one each in silver and in bronze, both of identical design and denomination.

| **21** (22) 10 Zlotych (Ag) 1932–1933. Same type as No. 19 | 10.00 | 25.00 |

The coins of 1932 were struck in Warsaw with the mint mark in the left claw of the eagle, London strikes are without mintmark.
Two offical pattern pieces are dated 1932, one each in silver and in bronze, also one official bronze pattern piece dated 1933, all are of identical design and face denomination.

Values are given for each coin in U.S. Dollars and reference to Yeoman-numbers.

COMMEMORATIVE COIN FOR THE 250th ANNIVERSARY
OF THE LIBERATION OF VIENNA

			VF	XF
22 (23)	10 Zlotych (Ag) 1933. Jan III Sobieski (1624–1696), king from 1674 to 1696, liberated Vienna from the Turkish siege in 1683. ℞ heraldic eagle and value		30.00	85.00

Three official silver pattern pieces from 1933, one on square planchet (klippe), all of identical design and denomination, commemorate the same event.

COMMEMORATIVE COIN FOR THE 70th ANNIVERSARY
OF THE JANUARY REBELLION OF 1863

		VF	XF
23 (24)	10 Zlotych (Ag) 1933. Romuald Traugutt (1826–1864), patriot and leader of the rebellion. ℞ heraldic eagle and value	22.50	60.00

Three official silver pattern pieces from 1933, one on square planchet, all of identical design and denomination, commemorate the same event.

COMMEMORATIVE COINS (2) FOR THE FOUNDING OF THE
POLISH LEGION

		VF	XF
24 (25)	5 Zlotych (Ag) 1934. Jósef Pilsudski (1867–1935), marshal and statesman. ℞ heraldic eagle, with emblem below	9.00	25.00

Three official pattern pieces from 1934, two of silver and one of bronze, all of identical design and denomination, commemorate the same event.

	VF	XF
25 (26) 10 Zlotych (Ag) 1934. Same type as No. 24	18.00	50.00

Four official pattern pieces from 1934, three of silver, one square planchet, and one of bronze, all of identical design and denomination, commemorate the same event.

	VF	XF
26 (27) 2 Zlote (Ag) 1934, 1936. J. Pilsudski. ℞ heraldic eagle	5.00	12.00
27 (28) 5 Zlotych (Ag) 1934–1936, 1938. Same type as No. 26	7.50	18.00
28 (29) 10 Zlotych (Ag) 1934–1939. Same type as No. 26	17.50	35.00
29 (30) 2 Zlote (Ag) 1936. Heraldic eagle. ℞ three-masted sailing vessel "Dar Pomorza", value	5.00	12.00

There are two official silver pattern pieces dated 1936 of identical design and denomination.

An additional official pattern piece was struck from the original dies at the Warsaw mint, in 1958, in aluminum.

	VF	XF
30 (31) 5 Zlotych (Ag) 1936. Same type as No. 29	12.50	35.00

Four official pattern pieces were struck in 1936, two in silver, one square planchet (klippe), also of silver and one square planchet of bronze, all of identical design and denomination.

For coins of the military government (Generalgouvernement), circulating between 1939 and 1944, see under German Occupations of World War II.

			VF	XF
31 (39)	1	Grosz (Al) 1949. Heraldic eagle. ℞ value	0.10	0.25
32 (40)	2	Grosze (Al) 1949	0.40	0.80
33 (41)	5	Groszy 1949		
		a) (Br)	1.00	2.00
		b) (Al)	1.00	2.50
34 (42)	10	Groszy 1949		
		a) (Cu–Ni)	1.50	3.00
		b) (Al)	0.80	1.50
35 (43)	20	Groszy 1949		
		a) (Cu–Ni)	2.00	4.00
		b) (Al)	0.80	1.50
36 (44)	50	Groszy 1949		
		a) (Cu–Ni)	1.50	3.00
		b) (Al)	1.00	2.00
37 (45)	1	Zloty 1949		
		a) (Cu–Ni)	2.50	5.00
		b) (Al)	1.50	2.50

Since 1965 some regular coins as well as commemorative coins, bear the Warsaw mintmark MW.

			VF	XF
38 (A46)	5	Groszy (Al) 1958–. Same type as No. 33, but with new legend POLSKA RZECZPOSPOLITA LUDOWA	0.10	0.20
39 (AA47)	10	Groszy (Al) 1961–. Heraldic eagle. ℞ value and laurel branch	0.15	0.30
40 (A47)	20	Groszy (Al) 1957–	0.20	0.30
41 (48)	50	Groszy (Al) 1957–	0.25	0.40

			VF	XF
42 (49)	1	Zloty (Al) 1957–	0.40	0.60
43 (46)	2	Zlote (Al) 1958–1974. Heraldic eagle. R fruits and ears of wheat	0.60	1.00

			VF	XF
44 (47)	5 Zlotych (Al) 1958–1960, 1971–1976. Rev. fisherman		0.60	1.10

45 (50)   10 Zlotych (Cu-Ni) 1959–1973. Heraldic eagle. R Tadeusz Kosciuszko (1746–1817), General and fighter for independence

a) 1959, 1960, 1966, diameter: 31 mm   1.00   2.00
b) 1969–1973, diameter: 28 mm   0.80   1.25

Of No. 45 a exist two official nickel pattern pieces, one from 1958 with a slightly different design and one from 1959 with identical design, both of identical denomination.

46 (51)   10 Zlotych (Cu-Ni). Nikolaus Kopernikus (1473–1543). theologian and astronomer

a) 1959, 1965, diameter: 31 mm   2.00   3.00
b) 1967–1969, diameter: 28 mm   1.00   1.50

Of No. 46 a exist one official nickel pattern piece from 1959 of identical design and denomination.

COMMEMORATIVE COIN FOR THE 600th ANNIVERSARY
OF THE JAGIELLO UNIVERSITY IN CRACOW

47 (52)   10 Zlotych (Cu-Ni) 1964. Kasimir the Great (1309–1370), founder of the Cra-

	VF	XF
cow University. ℞ heraldic eagle and value		
a) raised memorial legend	1.00	2.00
b) incused memorial legend	1.00	2.00

Two official nickel pattern pieces, dated 1964, one each with raised and incused memorial legend, both of same design and denomination, commemorate the same event. Two more official nickel pattern pieces of 1964, one each with crowned and uncrowned heraldic eagle, are of identical denomination.

COMMEMORATIVE COINS (2): 700 YEARS WARSAW

48 (54) 10 Zlotych (Cu–Ni) 1965. Nike of Warsaw,
modern large monument for the libera-
tion of Warsaw in 1945. ℞ heraldic eagle
and value   1.00   1.80

Four official nickel pattern pieces from 1965, one of identical and three of different design, but all of identical denomination, commemorate the same event.

49 (55) 10 Zlotych (Cu–Ni) 1965. Eagle. ℞ Sigis-
mund (Zygmunt) pillar in Warsaw and
value   1.00   1.80

One official nickel pattern piece of 1965, with identical design and denomination, commemorates the same event.

50 (56) 10 Zlotych (Cu–Ni) 1966. Same type as
and egde inscription W DWUSETNA
ROCZNICE MENNICY WAR-
SZAWSKIEJ

	VF	XF
	1.60	4.00

One official nickel pattern piece, dated 1966, of identical design and
denomination, commemorates the same event.

COMMEMORATIVE COIN FOR THE MILLENIUM
OF POLAND

51 (57) 100 Zlotych (Ag) 1966. Heraldic eagle, city
arms arranged in circle. ℞ Mieszko I
and his Bohemian wife Dabrówka;
value

10.00	18.00

Two official silver pattern pieces, dated 1966, of different design but
identical denomination commemorate the same event. Eight additional
nickel pattern pieces were struck in 1966, one of identical and seven of
different design, but all of identical denomination.

COMMEMORATIVE COIN FOR THE 20th ANNIVERSARY
OF SWIERCZEWSKI'S DEATH

52 (58) 10 Zlotych (Cu–Ni) 1967. Karol Swierc-
zewski, called General Walter (1896–
1947), politician, Deputy Defense Minister 1943–1947. ℞ heraldic eagle

1.00	2.00

COMMEMORATIVE COIN FOR THE 100th BIRTHDAY
OF MARIE CURIE

53 (59) 10 Zlotych (Cu–Ni) 1967. Heraldic eagle. **VF** **XF**
Ṛ Marie Curie, former Sklodowska
(1867–1934), 1903 Nobel Prize winner
for physics (discovery of polonium and
radium) and for chemistry 1911   0.90   1.80

COMMEMORATIVE COIN FOR THE 25th ANNIVERSARY
OF THE POLISH PEOPLE'S ARMY

54 (60) 10 Zlotych (Cu–Ni) 1968. Polish eagle as
army emblem. Ṛ profiled head of sol-
dier; memorial legend, value   0.80   1.50

COMMEMORATIVE COIN:
25 YEARS PEOPLE'S REPUBLIC OF POLAND

55 (61) 10 Zlotych (Cu–Ni) 1969. Heraldic eagle
in circle, surrounded by legend. Ṛ sheaf
of wheat in circle, surrounded by leg-
end; value   0.80   1.50

COMMEMORATIVE ISSUE FOR THE 25th ANNIVERSARY
OF THE END OF WORLD WAR II

			VF	XF
56 (62)	10	Zlotych (Cu–Ni) 1970. City arms of the seven district capitals in the Northern and Western areas with border marker, and dates below: 1945–1970. ℞ heraldic eagle with breast shield; value	0.80	1.50

ISSUE FOR THE FAO COIN PLAN

57 (63)	10	Zlotych (Cu–Ni) 1971. Ear of barley (Hordeum sp. – Gramineae) in front of East Atlantic turbot (Bothus maximus – Bothidae). ℞ heraldic shield, value	0.80	1.50

Two official cupro-nickel pattern pieces, dated 1971, of different design but identical denomination commemorate the same event.

COMMEMORATIVE ISSUE FOR THE 50th ANNIVERSARY
OF THE THIRD SILESIAN UPRISING

58 (64)	10	Zlotych (Cu–Ni) 1971. Detail from insurrection monument in Katowice, cross of insurgents, date and inscription. ℞ heraldic eagle, date, value	0.80	1.50

COMMEMORATIVE ISSUE FOR FRÉDÉRIC CHOPIN

Proof

59 (66)   50 Zlotych (Ag) 1972, 1974. Frédéric
Chopin (1810–1849), famous pianist   10.00

For the same event there is an official pattern piece of 1972 in silver
with a changed design and the same face value.

COMMEMORATIVE ISSUE FOR THE 50 YEARS
CELEBRATION OF THE PORT OF GDYNIA (GDINGEN)

		XF	Unc
60 (65)	10 Zlotych (Cu–Ni) 1972. City coat of arms above outline of the coastline.		
	℞ heraldic eagle, legend, date, value	1.00	1.60

COMMEMORATIVE ISSUE FOR THE 500th BIRTHDAY
OF NIKOLAUS KOPERNIKUS

Proof

61 (68)   100 Zlotych (Ag) 1973, 1974. Nikolaus Kopernikus (1473–1543), theologian and
astronomer   12.50

62 (67)   20 Zlotych (Cu-Ni) 1973, 1974, 1976.
Heraldic eagle, legend, date. R corn-
field in front of skyscraper under construction

	XF	Unc
	0.80	1.20

COMMEMORATIVE ISSUE
30 YEARS POLISH PEOPLE'S REPUBLIC

63 (72) 200 Zlotych (Ag) 1974. Outline of the
Polish frontier and functional legend.
R heraldic eagle, name of country,
value, date

	Unc	Proof
	8.50	15.00

COMMEMORATIVE ISSUE FOR M. NOWOTKO

64 (69) 20 Zlotych (Cu-Ni) 1974–1977. Marceli
Nowotko (1893–1942), leading activist
of the revolutionary movement, First
Secretary of the Central Committee of
the Polish Labour Party

	XF	Unc
	0.80	1.20

Poland   1251

25th ANNIVERSARY OF THE COMECON

				XF	Unc
65 (70)	20	Zlotych (Cu-Ni) 1974. In a circle formed of sun-flower leaves and one half of cog-wheel, inscription. Rev. heraldic eagle, value		1.00	1.60

40th ANNIVERSARY OF THE DEATH OF MARIE CURIE

			Proof
66 (71)	100	Zlotych (Ag) 1974. Marie Curie, former Sklodowska (1867-1934). Head left with radiation running from the symbol of the element Ra	12.50

RECONSTRUCTION OF THE ROYAL CASTLE IN WARSAW

67 (76)	100	Zlotych (Ag) 1974. The frontal view of the royal castle in Warsaw, Sigismund III's column in front of it	12.50

		XF	Unc
68 (73)	10 Zlotych (Cu-Ni) 1975–1978, 1981–1984. Boleslaw Prus (1847–1912), writer	0.60	0.90

		XF	Unc
69 (74)	10 Zlotych (Cu-Ni) 1975–1977. Adam Mickiewicz (1798–1855), poet	0.60	0.90

		Proof
70 (77)	100 Zlotych (Ag) 1975. Ignacy Jan Paderewski (1860–1941), pianist, composer, politician	12.50

		XF	Unc
68 (73)	10 Zlotych (Cu-Ni) 1975–1978, 1981–1984. Boleslaw Prus (1847–1912), writer	0.60	0.90

30th ANNIVERSARY OF THE END OF WORLD WAR II

			Unc	Proof
72 (79)	200	Zlotych (Ag) 1975. Coinjoined heads left	10.00	15.00

INTERNATIONAL WOMEN'S YEAR 1975

			XF	Unc
73 (75)	20	Zlotych (Cu-Ni) 1975. A woman's profile, in her hair the emblem of a stylized dove of peace	1.00	2.00

74 (80)	2	Zlote (Bra) 1975–1987. Heraldic eagle. Rev. value and stylized corn-ears	0.25	0.50

75 (81)	5	Zlotych (Bra) 1975–1977, 1979–1987. Rev. value	0.45	0.80

76 (82) 100 Zlotych (Ag) 1976. Tadeusz Kościuszko **Proof**
(1746-1817), General and fighter for
independence 12.50
77 (83) 500 Zlotych (Au) 1976, 1977. Type as No. 76 500.00

78 (84) 100 Zlotych (Ag) 1976. Kazimierz Pulaski
(1747-1779), fighter for independence 12.50
79 (85) 500 Zlotych (Au) 1976, 1977. Type as No. 78 500.00

FOR THE OLYMPIC GAMES 1976 IN MONTREAL

80 (86) 200 Zlotych (Ag) 1976. Olympic rings and
torch 12.00

81 (87) 100 Zlotych (Ag) 1977. Bison 15.00

82 (88) 100 Zlotych (Ag) 1977. Henryk Sienkiewicz
(1846-1916), writer, 1905 Nobel Prize
winner 15.00

83 (89) 100 Zlotych (Ag) 1977 Wladyslaw Reymont
(1867-1925), story-teller, 1924 Nobel
Prize winner 15.00

84 (90) 2000 Zlotych (Au) 1977. Frédéric Chopin
(1810-1849), pianist 150.00
85 (91) 100 Zlotych (Ag) 1977. Royal castle in Crakow 15.00
86 (92) 100 Zlotych (Ag) 1978. Adam Mickiewicz
(1798-1855), poet 17.50

ENVIRONMENT PROTECTION

				Proof
87 (93)	100	Zlotych (Ag) 1978. Elk		15.00

			XF	Unc
88 (95)	20	Zlotych (Cu-Ni) 1978. Maria Konopnicka (1842–1910)	1.00	2.00

100th ANNIVERSARY OF THE BIRTH OF JANUSZ KORCZAK

			Proof
89 (94)	100	Zlotych (Ag) 1978	15.00

FIRST POLISH COSMONAUT

			XF	Unc
90 (97)	20	Zlotych (Cu-Ni) 1978	1.00	2.00

ENVIRONMENT PROTECTION

			Proof
91 (96)	100	Zlotych (Ag) 1978. Beaver	16.00
92 (98)	100	Zlotych (Ag) 1979. Henryk Wieniawski (1835–1880), composer	16.00

INTERNATIONAL YEAR OF THE CHILD

			XF	Unc
93 (99)	20	Zlotych (Cu-Ni) 1979	1.00	2.00

			Unc	Proof
94 (106)	2000	Zlotych (Au) 1979. Nikolaus Koperni-kus (1473–1543), theologian and astro-nomer		150.00
95 (103)	100	Zlotych (Ag) 1979. Dr. Ludwig Zamen-hof (1859–1917)		16.00

ENVIRONMENT PROTECTION (2)

96 (104)	100	Zlotych (Ag) 1979. Lynx		15.00
97 (105)	100	Zlotych (Ag) 1979. Chamois		15.00

DUKE MIESZKO (3)

98 (100)	50	Zlotych (Cu-Ni) 1979. Duke Mieszko (960–992)	3.00	
99 (101)	200	Zlotych (Ag) 1979. Type as No. 98		22.00

			Unc	Proof

100 (102) 2000 Zlotych (Au) 1979. Type as No. 98   200.00
101 (107) 2000 Zlotych (Au) 1979. Marie Curie   200.00

13th OLYMPIC WINTER GAMES 1980 IN LAKE PLACID (3)

102 (110a) 200 Zlotych (Ag) 1980. Ski-jumper   22.00

103 (110) 200 Zlotych (Ag) 1980. Type as No. 102,
       but torch added   22.00
104 (111) 2000 Zlotych (Au) 1980   200.00

22nd OLYMPIC GAMES 1980 IN MOSCOW (2)

105 (108) 20 Zlotych (Cu-Ni) 1980. Runner and
       olympics rings   8.00
106 (109) 100 Zlotych (Ag) 1980   18.00

No. 107 omitted.

108 (112) 20 Zlotych (Cu-Ni) 1980. Sailing vessel
       »Dar Pomorza«   2.00

450th ANNIVERSARY OF THE BIRTH OF JAN KOCHANOWSKI

109 (120) 100 Zlotych (Ag) 1980. Jan Kochanowski
       (1530–1584), poet   15.00

KING BOLESLAW I CHROBRY (3)

				Unc	Proof
110 (114)	50	Zlotych (Cu-Ni) 1980. King Boleslaw I Chrobry		2.00	
111 (115)	200	Zlotych (Ag) 1980. Type as No. 110			15.00
112 (116)	2000	Zlotych (Au) 1980. Type as No. 110			200.00

ENVIRONMENT PROTECTION

113 (121)	100	Zlotych (Ag) 1980. Heath cock			15.00
114 (117)	50	Zlotych (Cu-Ni) 1980. King Kazimierz		2.00	
115 (118)	200	Zlotych (Ag) 1980. Type as No. 114			15.00

No. 116 omitted.

117 (122)	50	Zlotych (Cu-Ni) 1981. General Sikorski		2.50	
118 (123)	100	Zlotych (Ag) 1981			15.00

119 (124)	50	Zlotych (Cu-Ni) 1981. King Boleslaw II		2.50	
120 (125)	200	Zlotych (Ag) 1981. Type as No. 119			15.00

WOLD SOCCER CHAMPIONSHIP GAMES 1982 IN SPAIN

121 (130)	200	Zlotych (Ag) 1981			22.00

ENVIRONMENT PROTECTION

122 (126)	200	Zlotych (Ag) 1981. Horse			15.00

WORLD FOOD DAY

123 (127)	50	Zlotych (Cu-Ni) 1981		2.50	

KING WLADYSLAW I (2)

			Unc	Proof
124 (128)	50	Zlotych (Cu-Ni) 1981. King Wladyslaw I. Herman (1079–1102)	2.50	
125 (129)	200	Zlotych (Ag) 1981. Type as No. 124		16.00

KING BOLESLAW III KRZYWOUSTY (2)

126 (133)	50	Zlotych (Cu-Ni) 1982. King Boleslaw III (1102–1138)	3.00	
127 (132)	200	Zlotych (Ag) 1982. Type as No. 126		20.00

ENVIRONMENT PROTECTION

128 (141)	100	Zlotych (Ag) 1982. Stork		20.00

VISIT OF POPE JOHN PAUL II (6)

129 (136)	100	Zlotych (Ag) 1982, 1983. Bust left	22.50	30.00

			Unc	Proof
130 (137)	200 Zlotych (Ag) 1982, 1983. Type as No. 129		35.00	40.00
131 (144)	1000 Zlotych (Ag) 1982, 1983. Type as No. 129		40.00	40.00
132 (138)	1000 Zlotych (Au) 1982, 1983. Half bust		175.00	175.00
133 (139)	2000 Zlotych (Au) 1982, 1983. Type as No. 132		275.00	275.00
134 (140)	10000 Zlotych (Au) 1982, 1983. Type as No. 132		1100.00	1100.00

300th ANNIVERSARY OF THE LIBERATION OF VIENNA (2)

135 (145)   50 Zlotych (Cu-Ni) 1983. Jan III Sobieski
(1624–1696), king from 1674 to 1696   1.50

136 (143)   200 Zlotych (Ag) 1983. Type as No. 135   18.00

150th ANNIVERSARY OF WIELKIEGO THEATRE

137 (142)   50 Zlotych (Cu-Ni) 1983. General view of
the theatre   3.00

OLYMPIC WINTER GAMES IN SARAJEVO

138   200 Zlotych (Ag) 1984   20.00

OLYMPIC SUMMER GAMES IN LOS ANGELES (2)

139 (150)   200 Zlotych (Ag) 1984. Hurdler   30.00

		Unc	Proof
140	500 Zlotych (Ag) 1983. Gymnast. Pattern!		55.00
141 (146)	50 Zlotych (Cu-Ni) 1983. Ignacy Lukasiewicz	4.00	

ENVIRONMENT PROTECTION

			Unc	Proof
142 (147)	100 Zlotych (Ag) 1983. Bear			20.00
143	100 Zlotych (Cu-Ni) 1984. Wincenty Witos (1874–1945), politician		3.00	

30 YEARS POLISH PEOPLE'S REPUBLIC

		Unc
144	100 Zlotych (Cu-Ni) 1984. Inscription	3.00

ENVIRONMENT PROTECTION

		Proof
145 (154)	500 Zlotych (Ag) 1984. Swan	27.50

		XF	Unc
146 (152)	10 Zlotych (Cu-Ni) 1984–1987. Heraldic eagle, name of country, date. Rev. value	0.25	0.40
147 (153)	20 Zlotych (Cu-Ni) 1984–1987. Type as No. 146	0.50	0.75

KING PRZEMYSLAW II (2)

		Unc	Proof
148 (155)	100 Zlotych (Cu-Ni) 1985. King Przemyslaw II (1295–1296)	3.00	

		Proof
149 (156)	500 Zlotych (Ag) 1985. Type as No. 148	27.50

UNITED NATIONS 40th ANNIVERSARY

		Unc	Proof
150 (158) 500 Zlotych (Ag) 1985. Symbol			27.50

HOSPITAL FOR POLISH MOTHERS

	Unc	Proof
151 (157) 100 Zlotych (Ni-Fe) 1985	3.00	

ENVIRONMENT PROTECTION

	Unc	Proof
152 (159) 500 Zlotych (Ag) 1985. Squirrel		27.50

WORLD SOCCER CHAMPIONSHIP GAMES IN MEXICO

	Unc	Proof
153 500 Zlotych (Ag) 1986		27.50

WLADISLAW I LOKIETEK (2)

	Unc	Proof
154 (160) 100 Zlotych (Cu-Ni) 1986	3.00	
155 (161) 500 Zlotych (Ag) 1986		25.00

ENVIRONMENT PROTECTION

	Unc	Proof
156 (162) 500 Zlotych (Ag) 1986. Owl		27.50

Area: 35,490 sq. mi. Population: 10,300,000.
In the Age of Discoveries, the kingdom of Portugal was one of the leading
seafaring nations. Since 1910 the country situated on the Iberian Peninsula
has a republican form of government.
Capital: Lisbon.

1000 Reis = 1 Milreis, 100 Centavos = 1 Escudo

CARLOS I 1889–1908

			VF	XF
1 (15)	5	Reis (Br) 1890–1906. Carlos I (1863–1908), head right. ℞ value in wreath	2.50	5.00
2 (16)	10	Reis (Br) 1891–1892	2.50	4.00
3 (17)	20	Reis (Br) 1891–1892	2.00	4.00
4 (18)	50	Reis (Cu–Ni) 1900. Crowned arms. ℞ value	2.50	4.00
5 (19)	100	Reis (Cu–Ni) 1900	2.00	3.00
6 (21)	100	Reis (Ag) 1890–1898. Carlos I, head right. ℞ value in wreath	20.00	35.00
7 (22)	200	Reis (Ag) 1891–1903. Same type as No. 6	22.00	38.00
8 (23)	500	Reis (Ag) 1891–1908. ℞ crowned arms	18.00	28.00
9 (24)	1000	Reis (Ag) 1899–1900. ℞ Shield on crowned ermine mantle:		
		a) 1899	40.00	65.00
		b) 1900	1500.00	1800.00

MANUEL II 1908–1910

			VF	XF
10 (28)	5	Reis (Br) 1910. Manuel II (1888–1932), head left. ℞ value in wreath	2.50	4.50
11 (29)	100	Reis (Ag) 1909–1910. ℞ crown above value, all in wreath	4.00	6.50
12 (30)	200	Reis (Ag) 1909	10.00	16.00
13 (31)	500	Reis (Ag) 1908–1909	20.00	32.00

COMMEMORATIVE ISSUES (2) FOR THE CENTENNIAL OF THE WAR AGAINST NAPOLEON

			VF	XF
14 (32)	500	Reis (Ag) 1910. Manuel II. ℞ crowned arms	90.00	120.00
15 (33)	1000	Reis (Ag) 1910	100.00	130.00

COMMEMORATIVE ISSUE FOR MARQUIS DE POMBAL

			VF	XF
16 (34)	500 Reis (Ag) 1910. Manuel II. ℞ Goddess of Victory with crowned shield and monument of Marquis de Pombal (1699–1782), rebuilder of Lisbon after the earthquake of 1755		35.00	55.00

REPUBLIC since 1910

		VF	XF
17 (48)	10 Centavos (Ag) 1915. Head of Liberty. ℞ coat of arms, surrounded by laurel branches	2.50	4.00
18 (49)	20 Centavos (Ag) 1913–1916	15.00	25.00
19 (50)	50 Centavos (Ag) 1912–1916	9.00	16.00

20 (51)	1 Escudo (Ag) 1915–1916	26.00	40.00

COMMEMORATIVE ISSUE FOR THE FOUNDING OF THE REPUBLIC, ON OCTOBER 5, 1910

21 (47)	1 Escudo (Ag) undated (1914). Allegory of the Republic with torch. ℞ coat of arms in wreath	40.00	52.00
22 (36)	1 Centavo (Br) 1917–1922. Coat of arms. ℞ value	0.80	2.00
23 (35)	2 Centavos (Fe) 1918. Same type as No. 22	75.00	110.00
24 (37)	2 Centavos (Br) 1918–1921. Same type as No. 22	2.00	3.50
25 (42)	4 Centavos (Cu–Ni) 1917–1919. Head of Liberty, left. ℞ value	0.80	1.60
26 (38)	5 Centavos (Br) 1920–1922. Same type as No. 22	2.50	4.00
27 (39)	5 Centavos (Br) 1924–1927. Same type as No. 25	0.80	1.60
28 (43)	10 Centavos (Cu–Ni) 1920–1921. Same type as No. 25	4.00	6.50
29 (40)	10 Centavos (Br) 1924–1940. Same type as No. 25	1.50	4.00

			VF	XF
30 (44)	20	Centavos (Cu–Ni) 1920–1922. Same type as No. 25	3.00	4.50
31 (41)	20	Centavos (Br) 1924–1925. Same type as No. 25	2.50	4.00
32 (45)	50	Centavos (Al–Br) 1924–1926. Allegory of the Republic. ℞ coat of arms in wreath	8.00	12.00
33 (46)	1	Escudo (Al–Br) 1924–1926	12.00	20.00
34	5	Escudos (Au) 1920. Allegory of the Republic. ℞ coat of arms and value Coin No. 34 is a pattern piece and did not circulate.	–.–	–.–

35 (54)	50	Centavos (Ni–Bra) 1927–1968. Head of Liberty, right. ℞ coat of arms in wreath	0.15	0.25
36 (55)	1	Escudo (Ni–Bra) 1927–1968	0.25	0.50

COMMEMORATIVE ISSUE FOR THE BATTLE OF OURIQUE 1139

37 (56)	10	Escudos (Ag) 1928. Knight on horseback. ℞ coat of arms	22.00	35.00
38 (57)	2.50	Escudos (Ag) 1932–1951. Sailing vessel, 15th century. ℞ coat of arms	1.50	2.00
39 (58)	5	Escudos (Ag) 1932–1951	3.00	4.00

			VF	XF
40 (59)	10 Escudos (Ag) 1932–1948		8.00	16.00
41 (60)	X (10) Centavos (Br) 1942–1969. Quinas cross. ℞ value		0.10	0.20
42 (61)	XX (20) Centavos (Br) 1942–1969		0.15	0.25

COMMEMORATIVE ISSUE FOR THE 25th ANNIVERSARY OF THE FINANCE REFORM

			VF	XF
43 (62)	20 Escudos (Ag) 1953. Sitting figure. ℞ shield with Quinas cross above globe		12.00	18.00
44 (63)	10 Escudos (Ag) 1954–1955. Sailing vessel, 15th century. ℞ shield with Quinas cross above globe		7.50	12.00

COMMEMORATIVE ISSUES (3) FOR THE 500th ANNIVERSARY OF THE DEATH OF HENRY THE NAVIGATOR

			VF	XF
45 (64)	5 Escudos (Ag) 1960. Henry the Navigator (Dom Enrique el Navegador) 1394–1460, promoter of Portuguese seafaring and discoverer of West Africa. ℞ coat of arms		2.50	4.00
46 (65)	10 Escudos (Ag) 1960		15.00	20.00
47 (66)	20 Escudos (Ag) 1960		28.00	40.00

		XF	Unc
48 (67)	2.50 Escudos (Cu-Ni) 1963–. Sailing vessel, 15th century. R coat of arms	0.15	0.40
49 (68)	5 Escudos (Cu-Ni) 1963–. Type as No. 48	0.30	0.60

COMMEMORATIVE ISSUE FOR THE OPENING OF THE SALAZAR-BRIDGE

50 (69)	20 Escudos (Ag) 1966. Salazar-Bridge crossing the Tejo near Lisbon. R coat of arms	3.50	5.50

COMMEMORATIVE ISSUE FOR THE 500th BIRTHDAY OF PEDRO ALVARES CABRAL

51 (70)	50 Escudos (Ag) 1968. Pedro Alvares Cabral (c. 1468–1526), navigator, discoverer of Brazil. R crowned coat of arms, value	6.00	8.00

52 (72)	20 Centavos (Br) 1969–. Quinas Cross, name of country, date. R value, olive branches	0.05	0.10

		XF	Unc
53 (73)	50 Centavos (Br) 1969–1979 Obverse as No. 52. ℞ value, ears of wheat	0.10	0.15
54 (74)	1 Escudo (Br) 1969–1980. Type as No. 53	0.15	0.25

COMMEMORATIVE ISSUE FOR THE 500th BIRTHDAY OF VASCO DA GAMA

		XF	Unc
55 (75)	50 Escudos (Ag) 1969. Vasco da Gama (1469–1524), navigator, discovered the sea route to India in 1497/98. ℞ coat of arms, value	8.00	10.00

100th BIRTHDAY OF MARSHAL CARMONA

		XF	Unc
56 (76)	50 Escudos (Ag) 1969. Marshal Oscar Fragoso de Carmona (1869–1951), politician, president 1928–1951. R coat of arms, value	7.00	10.00
57 (71)	10 Centavos (Al) 1969–1979. Type as No. 52:		
	1969		85.00
	1970		–.–
	1971–1979	0.05	0.10
58 (A68)	10 Escudos (Cu-Ni) 1969–1974. Type as No. 48:		
	1969		–.–
	1971–1974	0.40	0.85

125 YEARS BANK OF PORTUGAL

		XF	Unc
59 (77)	50 Escudos (Ag) 1971. Stylized tree, date 1846 · 1971. R arms, value	7.00	10.00

COMMEMORATIVE ISSUE 400 YEARS
HEROIC EPIC "THE LUSIADS" BY CAMOES

		XF	Unc
60 (78)	50 Escudos (Ag) 1972. Angel with quill pen and laurel wreath in front of lyre. ℞ Quinas cross, bearing the book "Os Lusiadas", decorated with the sign of the cross of the crusaders	6.00	8.00

1974 REVOLUTION COMMEMORATIVE (2)

		Unc	Proof
61 (79)	100 Escudos (Ag) 1974	6.00	9.00
62 (80)	250 Escudos (Ag) 1974	10.00	20.00

		XF	Unc
63 (81)	25 Escudos (Cu-Ni) 1977–. Classical head. Rev. coat of arms, value:		
	a) 1977, 1978; 9.5 g, dia. 26.25 mm	0.60	1.00
	b) 1980–, 11 gm., dia. 28.5 mm	0.50	0.80

100th ANNIVERSARY OF THE DEATH OF
ALEXANDRE HERCULANO (3)

		Unc	Proof
64 (82)	2½ Escudos (Cu-Ni) 1977. Alexandre Herculano (1810–1877), poet	0.40	2.00
65 (83)	5 Escudos (Cu-Ni) 1977. Type as No. 64	0.90	4.50
66 (84)	25 Escudos (Cu-Ni) 1977. Type as No. 64	1.20	6.50

INTERNATIONAL YEAR OF THE CHILD

		XF	Unc
67 (101)	25 Escudos (Cu-Ni) 1979. Rev. Mother and Child	0.75	1.25

Portugal 1271

400th ANNIVERSARY OF THE DEATH OF CAMOES

		Unc	Proof
68 (89)	1000 Escudos (Ag) 1980. Rev. Luis Vaz de Camões (1524/25–1580), poet	15.00	45.00
		XF	**Unc**
69 (85)	1 Escudo (Ni-Bra) 1981–1985. Arms, date. Rev. value	0.10	0.20

INTERNATIONAL YEAR OF THE DISABLED (2)

70 (96)	25 Escudos (Cu-Ni) 1981 [82]. Rev. Antonio Feliciano de Castilho		1.00
71 (97)	100 Escudos (Cu-Ni) 1981 [82]. Rev. Jacobo Rodrigues Pereira		3.00

WORLD ROLLER HOCKEY CHAMPIONSHIP (4)

72 (90)	1 Escudo (Ni-Bra) 1982	0.15	0.30

73   74

73 (91)	2½ Escudos (Cu-Ni) 1982	0.15	0.30
74 (92)	5 Escudos (Cu-Ni) 1982	0.30	0.60
75 (93)	25 Escudos (Cu-Ni) 1982	0.85	1.50

WORLD FOOD DAY 1983 (3)

76 (98)	2½ Escudos (Cu-Ni) 1983. Rev. maize	0.20	0.50
77 (99)	5 Escudos (Cu-Ni) 1983. Rev. cow	0.35	0.75
78 (100)	25 Escudos (Cu-Ni) 1983. Rev. fish	0.85	1.50

EUROPEAN ART EXHIBITION (3)

	Unc	Proof
79 (86) 500 Escudos (Ag) 1983	6.50	20.00
80 (87) 750 Escudos (Ag) 1983	10.00	27.50
81 (88)1000 Escudos (Ag) 1983	12.50	35.00

WORLD FISHERIES CONFERENCE

82 (94) 250 Escudos 1984. Rev. fish swarm:

a) (Ag) .925 silver, 23.00 g		35.00
b) (Cu-Ni)	4.00	

10th ANNIVERSARY OF REVOLUTION

	XF	Unc
83 (95) 25 Escudos (Cu-Ni) 1984	1.00	2.00

50th ANNIVERSARY OF THE DEATH OF F. PESSOA

	Unc	Proof
84 (104)100 Escudos 1985. Rev. Fernando Pessoa (1888–1935), poet and writer:		
a) (Ag) .925 silver, 16.5 g		25.00
b) (Cu-Ni)	4.00	

600th ANNIVERSARY OF THE BATTLE OF ALJU BARROTA (2)

85 (111) 25 Escudos 1985. Rev. Dom João I:		
a) (Ag) .925 silver, 11 g	–.–	–.–
b) (Cu-Ni)	–.–	
86 (112)100 Escudos 1985. Rev. Dom Nuno Alvares Pereira:		
a) (Ag) .925 silver, 16.5 g	–.–	–.–
b) (Cu-Ni)	–.–	

Portugal   1273

800th ANNIVERSARY OF THE DEATH OF
KING ALFONSO HENRIQUES

87 (110)100 Escudos 1985:
a) (Ag) .925 silver, 16.5 g   –.–   –.–
b) (Cu-Ni)   –.–

DECADE FOR WOMEN (2)

Proof

88 1000 Escudos (Ag) 1985: .925 silver,
23.33 g   –.–
89 10000 Escudos (Au) 1985: .900 gold, 7.13 g   –.–

Portuguese Guinea

Portugiesisch-Guinea   **Guineé Portugaise**

Area: 13,948 sq. mi. Population: 530,000.
The territory until 1879 administratively dependent on the Cape Verde
Islands, then became an individual colony, but in 1951 – the same as
the other Portuguese colonies – was reorganized as an·(overseas)
province. It is the first Portuguese overseas territory which has succeeded – after the proclamation of the Republic on 23rd Sept. 1973 –
in being given complete independence and sovereignty from 10th Sept.
1974 as Guinea-Bissau together with membership of the United Nations.
Champion of the movement was and is the P(artido) A(fricano da)
I(ndependencia de) G (uiné e) C(abo Verde).
Capital: Bissau.

100 Centavos = 1 Escudo

			VF	XF
1 (1)	5	Centavos (Br) 1933. Head of liberty, left. ℞ value	30.00	60.00
2 (2)	10	Centavos (Br) 1933	6.00	17.50
3 (3)	20	Centavos (Br) 1933	4.00	10.00
4 (4)	50	Centavos (Ni–Br) 1933. Head of liberty, right. ℞ coat of arms	12.00	30.00
5 (5)	1	Escudo (Ni–Br) 1933	4.00	10.00

500th ANNIVERSARY OF DISCOVERY (2)

6 (6)	50	Centavos (Br) 1946. Coat of arms with mural crown of the colonies and com-memorative legend. ℞ value and dates 1446–1946	2.50	5.00

			VF	**XF**
7 (7)	1	Escudo (Cu–Ni) 1946	2.50	5.00

			VF	XF
8 (8)	50	Centavos (Br) 1952. Coat of arms with mural crown. ℞ value	0.80	1.40
9 (9)	2.50	Escudos (Cu–Ni) 1952	1.20	3.00
10 (10)	10	Escudos (Ag) 1952	6.50	12.50
11 (11)	20	Escudos (Ag) 1952	10.00	17.50

			Unc
12 (12)	10	Centavos (Al) 1973	2.00
13 (13)	20	Centavos (Br) 1973	3.00
14 (8a)	50	Centavos (Br) 1973	–.–
15 (14)	1	Escudo (Br) 1973	5.00
16 (15)	5	Escudos (Cu-Ni) 1973	6.00
17 (10a)	10	Escudos (Cu-Ni) 1973	7.50

Portuguese India

Inde Portugaise

Area: 1426 sq. mi. Population: 720,000 (1966),
Around 1500 the Portuguese captured several economically interesting
places in eastern India within the scope of their overseas activities,
where they installed viceroys. The second in this line, Alfonso de
Albuquerque, captured the city of Goa on the west coast on 25th Nov.
1510 and made it the centre of the dispersed Portuguese acquisitions.
Of these colonial possessions, the so-called Estado da India, there
remained in the 19th century apart from Goa only the towns of Daman
(Damão in Portuguese, captured 1559) and Diu (captured 1536), situated
five degrees of latitude to the north on both sides of the Gulf of Cambay.
Goa was the seat of the viceroy since 1559, the residence, however,
being transferred from this city in 1759 for climatic reasons to the
nearby Pangim (also called Nova Goa). The widespread autonomy
conferred in 1951 and its own constitution (of 1955) did not save
Portuguese India from the capture by Indian troops on the 17th/18th
Dec. 1961. A plesbiscite legalized the integration in India retrospectively
for the 20th Dec. 1961, but was only recognized by treaty on 31st Dec.
1974. The three widely dispersed territories since then form a territory
of the Indian Union under the names of Goa, Daman and Diu.
Capital: Pangim (Nova Goa).

16 Tangas = 1 Rupia, 100 Centavos = 1 Escudo

CARLOS I 1889–1908

			VF	XF
1 (15)	$1/_{12}$	Tanga (Br) 1901–1903. Carlos I (1863–1908), head right. ℞ crowned arms	3.00	4.50
2 (16)	$1/_8$	Tanga (Br) 1901–1903	2.50	4.00
3 (17)	$1/_4$	Tanga (Br) 1901–1903	1.50	2.50
4 (18)	$1/_2$	Tanga (Br) 1901–1903	2.00	3.50
5 (19	1	Rupia (Ag) 1903, 1904	12.00	18.00

ISSUES OF THE PORTUGUESE REPUBLIC

6 (20)	1 Rupia (Ag) 1912. Head of Republic, left. ℞ value in wreath	35.00	52.00

			VF	XF
7 (21)	1	Tanga (Br) 1934. Provisional coat of arms above date. ℞ coat of arms above value	3.00	7.00
8 (22)	2	Tangas (Cu–Ni) 1934	4.00	10.00
9 (23)	4	Tangas (Cu–Ni) 1934	5.00	10.00
10 (24)	½	Rupia (Ag) 1936. Coat of arms over cross. ℞ coat of arms (Old Portugal)	12.00	20.00
11 (25)	1	Rupia (Ag) 1935	12.00	16.00
12 (26)	1	Tanga (Br) 1947. Coat of arms with mural crown of the colonies. ℞ value	1.00	1.50
13 (27)	¼	Rupia (Cu–Ni) 1947, 1952	1.50	2.00
14 (28)	½	Rupia (Cu–Ni) 1947, 1952	2.00	3.00
15 (29)	1	Rupia (Ag) 1947. Coat of arms over cross. ℞ coat of arms with mural crown	7.50	10.00
16 (26a)	1	Tanga (Br) 1952. Same type as No. 12, but smaller diameter	1.20	2.00
17 (29a)	1	Rupia (Cu–Ni) 1952	4.50	7.50

NEW CURRENCY: 100 Centavos = 1 Escudo

18 (34)	10	Centavos (Br) 1958–1961. Coat of arms with mural crown. ℞ value	0.60	0.80

19 (35)	30	Centavos (Br) 1958–1959	0.80	1.20
20 (36)	60	Centavos (Cu–Ni) 1958–1959	1.20	1.80
21 (37)	1	Escudo (Cu–Ni) 1958–1959	1.50	2.00
22 (38)	3	Escudos (Cu–Ni) 1958–1959	2.00	3.50
23 (39)	6	Escudos (Cu–Ni) 1959	3.50	5.00

Katar   # Qatar   Qatar

Area: c. 8000 sq. mi. Population: 140,000.
The emirate of Qatar, situated on a peninsula in the Persian Gulf, placed itself under British protection since 1896 and on 3rd Nov. 1916 concluded an exclusive treaty of protection with Great Britain. The Emir declared the independence of the "State of Qatar" on 1st Sept. 1971 and on 3rd Sept. 1971 concluded a new treaty of friendship with Great Britain. Until 1959 the Indian rupee was also in circulation in Qatar, but was then substituted by the Gulf-Rupee. From June 1966 until the introduction of the Qatar and Dubai Riyal (QDR) in September 1966, the Saudi-Riyal was legal tender. Due to the participation of Dubai in the founding of the United Arab Emirates on 2nd Dec. 1971 Dubai left the monetary union with Qatar; the latter's legal tender were legally valid until 18th Aug. 1973, being exchanged at the rate of 1 QDR to 1 QR.
Capital: Doha.

100 Dirham = 1 Qatar-Riyal

			XF	Unc
1 (1)	1	Dirham (Br) 1973. Arab dhow and two palms, dates. R value and name of country STATE OF QATAR	0.10	0.20
2 (2)	5	Dirham (Br) 1973, 1978. Type as No. 1	0.15	0.30
3 (3)	10	Dirham (Br) 1972, 1973. Type as No. 1	0.30	0.50
4 (4)	25	Dirham (Cu-Ni) 1973, 1976, 1981. Type as No. 1	0.35	0.70
5 (5)	10	Dirham (Cu-Ni) 1973, 1978. Type as No. 1	0.70	1.10

Katar und Dubai **Qatar and Dubai** **Qatar et Dubai**

Despite of the fact that the emirate of Qatar and the sheikdom of Dubai have merged under a Monetary Union, the two territories are governed independently from each other.

Qatar: Under British patronage since 1916, this sultanate, located on the Persian Gulf, declared its independence on 1st Sept. 1971.
Capital: Doha.

Dubai: The sheikdom is situated on the south shore of the Persian Gulf and represents one of the seven Trucial States.
Capital: Dubai.

100 Dirhams = 1 Qatar and Dubai Riyal

			XF	Unc
1 (1)	1	Dirham (Br) 1966. Slender horned gazelle (Gazella leptoceros – Bovidae). R value and name of country	0.20	0.30
2 (2)	5	Dirhams (Br) 1966, 1969	0.25	0.60
3 (3)	10	Dirhams (Br) 1966	0.30	0.60
4 (4)	25	Dirhams (Cu-Ni) 1966, 1969	0.50	1.20

5 (5)	50	Dirhams (Cu–Ni) 1966	0.90	1.50

Ras El Khaimah   **Ras Al Khaima**   **Ras Al Khaima**

Area: 642 sq. mi. Population: 34,000.
The sheikdom of Ras Al Khaima is one of the seven Trucial States on the
Persian Gulf and the Gulf of Oman. Since February 1972 Ras Al Khaima
is a member state of the "United Arab Emirates" (UAE).
Capital: Ras Al Khaima.

100 Dirham = 1 Rial or Riyal

SAKER BEN MOHAMMED AL KAISIMI

			Unc	Proof
1	1	Rial (Ag) 1969. Crossed jambijas over crossed flags (= state emblem), dates. ℞ value, name of country	5.00	
2	2	Rials (Ag) 1969. Same type as No. 1	8.00	
3	5	Rials (Ag) 1969. Same type as No. 1	12.00	
4	7½	Riyals (Ag) 1970		30.00
5	10	Riyals (Ag) 1970		30.00
6	10	Riyals (Ag) 1970		30.00
7	15	Riyals (Ag) 1970		40.00
8	50	Riyals (Au) 1970		180.00
9	75	Riyals (Au) 1970		260.00
10	100	Riyals (Au) 1970		360.00
11	150	Riyals (Au) 1970		550.00
12	200	Riyals (Au) 1970		700.00
13	50	Dirhams (Cu–Ni) 1970. Value in Arabic, in circle. ℞ Berber falcon (Falco peregrinoides – Falconidae)	3.00	
14	2½	Riyals (Ag) 1970. Sheikh Saker. ℞ Berber falcon, value	10.00	
15	7½	Riyals (Ag) 1970. Type as No. 14	20.00	

COMMEMORATIVE ISSUE FOR THE FIRST ANNIVERSARY OF THE DEATH OF DWIGHT D. EISENHOWER

| **16** | 10 | Riyals (Ag) 1970. Dwight D. Eisenhower (1890–1969), 34th President of the United States of America | 26.00 | |

Réunion

Area: 970 sq. mi. Population: 470,000.
French territory since 1643, the island of Réunion carried the name "Ile
Bourbon" until 1848. In 1946 Réunion became a French Overseas
Department.
Capital: Saint-Denis.

100 Centimes = 1 CFA Franc

			VF	XF
1 (8)	1	Franc (Al) 1948–. Head of Marianne, allegory of the French Republic	0.25	0.40
2 (9)	2	Francs (Al) 1948–	0.40	0.60

3 (10)	5	Francs (Al) 1955	0.60	1.00
4 (11)	10	Francs (Al–Br) 1955–1964	0.90	1.20
5 (12)	20	Francs (Al–Br) 1955–1964	1.00	1.50
6 (13)	50	Francs (Ni) 1962–	1.20	1.60
7 (14)	100	Francs (Ni) 1964–	1.80	2.50

Previous issues, see "Weltmünzkatalog 19. Jahrhundert" (World Coin
Catalogue of the 19th Century)

Rhodesien # Rhodesia **Rhodésie**

Area: 150,333 sq. mi. Population: 5,690,000 (1979).

The territories of Northern and Southern Rhodesia were united under the administration of the British South Africa Company from 1889 to 1923. From 1953 to 1963 Southern Rhodesia together with Northern Rhodesia and Nyasaland belonged to the Central African Federation. October 1964 renaming of Southern Rhodesia as Rhodesia. On November 11, 1965 Rhodesia declared its independence and on March 2, 1970 became a republic.

Capital: Salisbury.

12 Pence = 1 Shilling, 10 Cents = 1 Shilling, 20 Shillings = 1 £; since February 17, 1970: 100 Cents = 1 Rhodesian Dollar

		VF	XF
1 (A1)	3 Pence (Cu–Ni) 1968. ℞ 3 spear points	0.30	0.60
2 (1)	6 Pence = 5 Cents (Cu–Ni) 1964. Queen Elizabeth II. ℞ flame lily (Gloriosa sp. – Liliaceae)	0.50	0.80
3 (2)	1 Shilling = 10 Cents (Cu–Ni) 1964. ℞ coat of arms	1.00	1.60
4 (3)	2 Shillings = 20 Cents (Cu–Ni) 1964. ℞ large Zimbabwe bird	1.50	2.50

5 (4)	2½ Shillings = 25 Cents (Cu–Ni) 1964. ℞ Sable antelope (Hippotragus niger – Bovidae)	2.00	3.50

			Proof
6 (A5)	10 Shillings (Au) 1966. ℞ sable antelope		150.00
7 (B5)	1 £ (Au) 1966. ℞ heraldic lion		300.00
8 (C5)	5 £ (Au) 1966. ℞ coat of arms		1000.00

CURRENCY REFORM (Decimal System):
100 Cents = 1 Rhodesian Dollar

			XF	Unc
9 (5)	½ Cent (Br) 1970–1977:			
	a) 1970–1972, 1975		0.10	0.20
	b) 1973 (28 pieces)			500.00
	c) 1977 (10 pieces)			1000.00

			XF	Unc
10 (6)	1 Cent (Br) 1970–1977		0.10	0.20

			XF	Unc
11 (7)	2½ Cents (Cu-Ni) 1970		0.30	0.50
12 (8)	5 Cents (Cu-Ni) 1973. Coat of arms. Rev. flame lily (gloriosa sp.-Liliaceae), country name, date, value		0.30	0.50

			XF	Unc
13 (9)	5 Cents (Cu-Ni) 1975–1977. Coat of arms, country name. Rev. flame lily, date, value:			
	a) 1975, 1976		0.40	1.00
	b) 1977		2.00	5.00
14 (10)	10 Cents (Cu-Ni) 1975, 1976		0.50	1.00
15 (11)	20 Cents (Cu-Ni) 1975–1977		0.75	1.50
16 (12)	25 Cents (Cu-Ni) 1975, 1976		1.00	2.00

Rhodesia and Nyasaland

In 1953 the colony of Southern Rhodesia and the protectorates of Northern Rhodesia and Nyasaland merged into the Central African Federation, which was dissolved again in 1963.

12 Pence = 1 Shilling, 2 Shillings = 1 Florin,
5 Shillings = 1 Crown, 20 Shillings = 1 £

ELISABETH II 1952–1963

			VF	XF
1 (1)	½ Penny (Br) 1955–1964. Giraffes (Giraffa camelopardalis – Giraffidae) and crown. ℞ value and ornamentations (center hole)		0.40	0.60

2 (2)	1 Penny (Br) 1955–1963. African elephants (Loxodonta africana – Elephantidae) and crown. ℞ value and ornamentations (center hole)		0.50	0.80
3 (3)	3 Pence (Cu–Ni) 1955–1964. Elisabeth II, head right. ℞ flame lily (Gloriosa sp. – Liliaceae)		0.60	0.90
4 (4)	6 Pence (Cu–Ni) 1955–1963. ℞ lion (Panthera leo – Felidae)		1.10	1.60
5 (5)	1 Shilling (Cu–Ni) 1955–1957. ℞ antilope (Hippotragus niger – Bovidae)		2.00	3.00
6 (6)	2 Shillings (Cu–Ni) 1955–1957. ℞ African fish eagle (Haliaetus vocifer Accipitridae) with fish		3.50	6.50

		VF	XF
7 (7)	½ Crown (Cu–Ni) 1955–1957. ℞ coat of arms	7.50	10.50

Rumänien　　　　　　**Rumania**　　　　　　**Roumanie**

Romania

Area: 91,700 sq. mi. Population: 22,800,000.
The principalities of Moldavia and Wallachia which orginated in the 14th
century, came under Turkish suzerainty at the beginning of the 15th century.
In 1881 Rumania was raised to the status of a kingdom, after the two principalities had already had the opportunity of untiting in 1859, which then as-
sumed the name of Rumania on January 24, 1862. Micheal, the last king,
had to abdicate in 1947; in 1948 the country became a People's Republic.
Capital: Bukarest.

100 Bani = 1 Leu

		CAROL I 1881–1914	VF	XF
1 (24)	50	Bani (Ag) 1894–1901. Carol I (1839– 1914), head left. ℞ value and date in wreath	3.50	5.50
2 (25)	1	Leu (Ag) 1894–1901. ℞ coat of arms, value and date	5.50	10.50
3 (26)	2	Lei (Ag) 1894–1901. Same type as No. 1	22.00	40.00
4 (23a)	5	Lei (Ag) 1901. Same type as No. 1	40.00	90.00
5 (29)	1	Ban (Cu) 1900	1.50	3.50
6 (30)	2	Bani (Cu) 1900	1.50	3.50
7 (31)	5	Bani (Cu-Ni) 1900. Crown and date in wreath. ℞ value	1.50	3.50
8 (32)	10	Bani (Cu-Ni) 1900. Same type as No. 7	2.00	4.50
9 (33)	20	Bani (Cu-Ni) 1900. Same type as No. 7	`15.00	25.00
10 (34)	5	Bani (Cu-Ni) 1905–1906. Ribbon with name of country, crown above. ℞ value and date (center hole)	0.40	1.20
11 (35)	10	Bani (Cu-Ni) 1905–1906. Same type as No. 10	1.20	2.50
12 (36)	20	Bani (Cu-Ni) 1905–1906. Same type as No. 10	1.50	3.50

COMMEMORATIVE ISSUES (7) FOR THE 40th REGNAL ANNIVERSARY OF CAROL I

13 (37)	1	Leu (Ag) 1906. Karl Eitel Friedrich of Hohenzollern-Sigmaringen (1839– 1914), Prince (Domnul) of Rumania	

			VF	XF
	from 1866 to 1881, King (Rege) of the country, as Carol I, from 1881 to 1914		15.00	25.00
14 (38)	5 Lei (Ag) 1906. Same type as No. 13		50.00	90.00

15 (39)   12½ Lei (Au) 1906. Portrait in uniform. Rev. crowned eagle   125.00   175.00

16 (41)	20 Lei (Au) 1906. Same type as No. 13	220.00	275.00
17 (40)	25 Lei (Au) 1906. Same type as No. 15	240.00	300.00

18 (43)   50 Lei (Au) 1906. Carol I, portrait in uniform. ℞ Carol I on horseback   425.00   650.00

			VF	**XF**
19 (42)	100	Lei (Au) 1906. Same type as No. 13	1200.00	1600.00
20 (44)	50	Bani (Ag) 1910–1914. Carol I, head left. R crown above olive branch	3.00	4.50
21 (45)	1	Leu (Ag) 1910–1914. R woman in national costume	4.00	6.50
22 (46)	2	Lei (Ag) 1910–1914. Same type as No. 21	5.50	9.00

FERDINAND I 1914–1927

23 (47)	25	Bani (Al) 1921. Eagle above name of country and date. R value and crown (center hole)	0.80	1.50
24 (48)	50	Bani (Al) 1921. Same type as No. 23	1.20	2.00
25 (49)	1	Leu (Cu–Ni) 1924. Coat of arms and date. R value in wreath	0.40	0.80
26 (50)	2	Lei (Cu–Ni) 1924. Same type as No. 25	0.80	1.50

COMMEMORATIVE COINS (4) FOR THE CORONATION OF FERDINAND I

27 (51)	20	Lei (Au) 1922. Ferdinand I, head with laurel wreath. R crowned coat of arms with value	260.00	320.00
28 (52)	25	Lei (Au) 1922. Ferdinand I (1865–1927) in coronation robe. R Queen Mary (1875–1938) in coronation robe	300.00	400.00
29 (53)	50	Lei (Au) 1922. Same type as No. 28	500.00	650.00
30 (54)	100	Lei (Au) 1922. Same type as No. 27	1400.00	1800.00

MICHAEL I 1927–1930

31 (55)	5	Lei (Br) 1930. Michael I as a boy. R coat of arms and value	1.20	2.00

		VF	XF

32 (56) 20 Lei (Br) 1930. ℞ allegory of the unity of the country — 5.50 · 9.00

CAROL II 1930–1940

33 (57) 1 Leu (Ni–Bra). Crown and date, surrounded by name of country and wreath
  a) 1938, diameter: 21 mm (pattern) — 10.00 · 15.00
  b) 1938–1941, diameter: 18 mm — 0.40 · 1.20

34 (58) 10 Lei (Ni–Bra) 1930. Carol II (1893–1953), head left. ℞ crowned double-headed eagle and shield with monogram — 1.20 · 2.50

35 (59) 20 Lei (Ni–Bra) 1930. Same type as No. 34 — 1.50 · 3.50

36 (60) 50 Lei (Ni) 1937–1938. Carol II in full-dress uniform. ℞ coat of arms in wreath — 2.00 · 4.00

37 (62) 100 Lei (Ag) 1932. Carol II, head right. ℞ coat of arms in wreath — 16.00 · 25.00

38 (61) 100 Lei (Ni) 1936–1938. Carol II, head left — 2.00 · 3.50

39 (63) 250 Lei (Ag) 1935. Carol II, head left. ℞ crowned eagle with shield — 22.00 · 40.00

40 (64) 250 Lei (Ag) 1939–1940. Carol II, head right. ℞ crowned coat of arms and wreath of wheat and grapes — 12.00 · 20.00

COMMEMORATIVE ISSUES (4) FOR THE 100th BIRTHDAY OF CAROL I, ON APRIL 20, 1839

			VF	XF
41 (65)	20	Lei (Au) 1939. Carol II, head right. ℞ crowned coat of arms	600.00	800.00
42 (66)	20	Lei (Au) 1939. ℞ heraldic eagle	350.00	500.00
43 (67)	100	Lei (Au) 1939. Same type as No. 41	3000.00	5000.00
44 (68)	100	Lei (Au) 1939. Angel with sword, and coat of arms	3000.00	5000.00

COMMEMORATIVE ISSUES (4) FOR THE 10th REGNAL ANNIVERSARY OF CAROL II

45 (71)	20	Lei (Au) 1940. Carol II, head right. ℞ monogram with crown, surrounded by laurel wreath with heraldic ornamentation	260.00	325.00
46 (72)	20	Lei (Au) 1940. R crown above monogram, surrounded by chain	260.00	325.00
47 (A71)	100	Lei (Au) 1940. Same type as No. 45	1500.00	2000.00
48 (A72)	100	Lei (Au) 1940. Same type as No. 46	1800.00	2200.00

MICHAEL I 1940–1947

49 (73)	2	Lei (Sn) 1941. Crown. ℞ value in wreath	2.00	4.00
50 (74)	5	Lei (Sn) 1942. ℞ value and ears of wheat	1.50	3.00
51 (75)	20	Lei (Sn) 1942–1944. ℞ value in wreath	2.00	3.00
52 (76)	100	Lei (Ni–St) 1943–1944. Michael I (1921–1970), head right. ℞ value in wreath, with crown above	1.00	2.50
53 (77)	200	Lei (Ag) 1942. ℞ coat of arms	4.00	5.00
54 (78)	250	Lei (Ag) 1941. Michael I, head left. ℞ crowned coat of arms and wreath, surrounded by wheat and grapes; edge inscription NIHIL SINE DEO (Nothing without God)	8.00	12.50
55 (78a)	250	Lei (Ag) 1941. Same type as No. 54, but edge inscription TOTUL PENTRU TARA	20.00	40.00
56 (79)	500	Lei (Ag) 1941. Stephan III the Great (Stefan cel Mare) (1433–1504), Prince of the Moldavia 1457–1504, kneeling, with model of church	15.00	25.00

COMMEMORATIVE ISSUE FOR THE REUNION WITH TRANSYLVANIA

A56	20	Lei (Au) 1944. Heads of Prince Michael, King Ferdinand I and King Michael. ℞ 11 coat of arms	75.00	100.00
57 (81)	200	Lei (Bra) 1945. Michael I, head right. ℞ value and date in wreath, crown above	4.00	8.00
58 (80)	500	Lei (Ag) 1944. Michael I, head left. ℞ crowned coat of arms	5.00	8.00

			VF	XF
59 (82)	500	Lei (Bra) 1945. Same type as No. 58	6.00	9.00
60 (83)	500	Lei (Al) 1946. Michael I, head right. ℞ value in wreath, with name of country above	3.00	5.00
61 (84)	2000	Lei (Bra) 1946. ℞ crowned coat of arms	4.00	6.00

			VF	XF
62 (85)	10 000	Lei (Bra) 1947. ℞ crowned shield, olive branches and value	4.00	7.00
63 (86)	25 000	Lei (Ag) 1946. Same type as No. 62	5.00	10.00
64 (87)	100 000	Lei (Ag) 1946. ℞ Romania, allegory of the state with crowned coat of arms and dove of peace	12.00	25.00

CURRENCY REFORM of August 15, 1947:
20 000 old Lei = 1 new Leu

			VF	XF
65 (88)	50	Bani (Bra) 1947. Crown. ℞ value	1.50	3.00
66 (89)	1	Leu (Bra) 1947. Crowned coat of arms. ℞ value in wreath of wheat	2.00	4.00
67 (90)	2	Lei (Br) 1947. Same type as No. 66	2.50	4.50

			VF	XF
68 (91)	5	Lei (Al) 1947. Michael I, head right. ℞ value and ears of wheat	3.00	5.00

PEOPLE'S REPUBLIC
Republica Populara Romana since 1948

			VF	XF
69 (92)	1	Leu (Al-Br) 1949-1951. Oil derrick in front of rising sun. Rev. value, date	1.50	3.00
70 (93)	2	Lei (Al-Br) 1950, 1951. Typical fruits of the country. Rev. value, date	1.50	3.00
71 (92a)	1	Leu (Al) 1951-1952. Type as No. 69:		
		a) 1951	1.50	2.00
		b) 1952	2.50	5.00

			VF	**XF**
72 (93a)	2	Lei (Al) 1951-1952. Type as No. 70:		
		a) 1951	1.50	2.00
		b) 1952	2.50	5.00

73 (94)	5	Lei (Al) 1948–1951. Coat of arms of the People's Republic. ℞ value in wreath	2.00	4.00
74 (95)	20	Lei (Al) 1951. ℞ blacksmith with anvil in front of industrial plant	10.00	16.00

Change to gold currency on Januar 28, 1952

75 (96)	1	Ban (Al-Br) 1952. Coat of arms. Rev. value, date	0.25	0.50
76 (97)	3	Bani (Al-Br) 1952. Type as No. 75	0.80	1.50
77 (98)	5	Bani (Al-Br) 1952. Type as No. 75	1.00	2.50
78 (99)	10	Bani (Cu-Ni) 1952. Coat of arms. Rev. value in wreath	1.00	3.00

79 (100)	25	Bani (Cu-Ni) 1952. Type as No. 78	1.00	2.50
80 (96a)	1	Ban (Al-Br) 1953, 1954. Type as No. 75, but new coat of arms (star at top of arms)	0.80	1.50
81 (97a)	3	Bani (Al-Br) 1953, 1954. Type as No. 80	0.40	0.80
82 (98a)	5	Bani (Al-Br) 1953-1957. Type as No. 80	0.50	1.00
83 (99a)	10	Bani (Cu-Ni) 1953-1955. Type as No. 78, but new coat of arms (star at top of arms)	0.50	1.00
84 (100a)	25	Bani (Cu-Ni) 1953-1955. Type as No. 83	1.00	1.50

			VF	XF
85 (99b)	10	Bani (Cu-Ni) 1955, 1956. Type as No. 83, but country name ROMINA	0.40	0.80
86 (100b)	25	Bani (Cu-Ni) 1955. Type as No. 85	0.50	1.00
87 (101)	50	Bani (Cu-Ni) 1955, 1956. Type similar to No. 74	0.80	2.00

88 (103)	15	Bani (Ni-St) 1960. Rev. value in wreath	0.30	0.60

89 (104)	25	Bani (Ni-St) 1960. Rev. value above tractor and ears of wheat	0.40	1.00
90 (102)	5	Bani (Ni-St) 1963. Coat of arms. Rev. value, date	0.15	0.40

91 (105)	1	Leu (Ni-St) 1963. Rev. tractor in front of mountain landscape and rising sun	0.70	1.50

92 (106)	3	Lei (Ni-St) 1963. Rev. oil refinery	0.90	1.70

RUMANIAN SOCIALIST REPUBLIC
Republica Socialista Romania

					VF	XF
93 (107)	5	Bani (Ni-St) 1966. New coat of arms (with ROMANIA on ribbon in arms)			0.10	0.20
94 (108)	15	Bani (Ni-St) 1966. Type as No. 88, but new coat of arms			0.15	0.30
95 (109)	25	Bani (Ni-St) 1966. Rev. similar to No. 89			0.20	0.40
96 (110)	1	Leu (Ni-St) 1966. Rev. similar to No. 91			0.40	0.80
97 (111)	3	Lei (Ni-St) 1966. Rev. similar to No. 92			0.60	1.30

			VF	XF
98 (107a)	5 Bani (Al) 1975. Type as No. 93		0.10	0.20

			VF	XF
99 (108a)	15 Bani (Al) 1975. Type as No. 94		0.20	0.30
100 (109a)	25 Bani (Al) 1982. Type as No.95		0.30	0.50

			VF	XF
101 (112)	5 Lei (Al) 1978		1.00	2.00

2050th ANNIVERSARY OF FOUNDING OF AN INDEPENDENT DACER STATE (4)

			Proof
102 (115)	50 Lei (Ag) 1983		35.00
103 (113)	100 Lei (Ag) 1982, 1983		65.00
104 (114)	500 Lei (Au) 1982, 1983		450.00
105 (116)	1000 Lei (Au) 1983		800.00

РОССИЯ · СССР

Area: 6,591,090 sq. mi. Population: 280,000,000.

Until February 1917 Russia was an empire ruled by a tsar and then a bourgeois republic. After the October Revolution of 1917, the Russian Soviet Federal Socialist Republic (RSFSR) was created. On December 30, 1922 the Union of Soviet Socialist Republics (USSR) was founded which consisted of the RSFSR, the T(ranscaucasian)SFSR, the U(krainian)SSR and the W(hite Russian)SSR. Later on the Usbek, Turkmen (1924) and Tadzhik SSR (1929) joined the Union. Further Union Republics originated 1940/41 out of the Baltic states and the Moldavian territory as well as Karelia, which, however, after World War II lost the status of an autonomous republic.

Capital: St. Petersburg (Leningrad), since 1922 Moscow.

100 Kopeks (КОПЕЙКИ) = 1 Rouble (РУБЛЬ)

NICOLAS II 1894–1917

The minor coins minted under Nicolas II exhibit in the main the same patterns as those of his predecessor Alexander III (1881–1894) and were struck in St. Petersburg practically without exception. The designation of this mint with С. П. Б. was omitted on the pieces between 1915 and 1917, perhaps because a part of the coinage was ordered to be struck in Osaka.

			VF	XF
1 (47)	¼	Kopek (Cu). Monogram of Nicholas II, between crown and laurel branches. ℞ value and date		
		a) 1894–1914, with mint mark	3.00	6.00
		b)1915–1916, without mint mark	6.00	10.00
2 (48)	½	Kopek (Cu) 1894–1916. Same type as No. 1		
		a) 1894–1914, with mint mark	3.00	6.00
		b) 1915–1916, without mint mark	4.00	7.50
3 (9)	1	Kopek (Cu). Crowned double-headed eagle. ℞ value in circle and wreath		
		a) 1894–1914, with mint mark	2.00	3.50
		b) 1915–1916, without mint mark	2.00	3.50

			VF	XF
4 (10)	2	Kopeks (Cu). Same type as No. 3		
		a) 1894–1914, with mint mark	2.00	3.50
		b) 1915–1916, without mint mark	2.00	3.50
5 (11)	3	Kopeks (Cu). Same type as No. 3		
		a) 1894–1914, with mint mark	2.00	3.50
		b) 1915–1916, without mint mark	2.00	3.50
6 (12)	5	Kopeks (Cu). Same type as No. 3		
		a) 1911–1912, with mint mark	3.50	6.00
		b) 1916, without mint mark	80.00	115.00
7 (19a)	5	Kopeks (Ag). Crowned double-headed eagle. ℞ value and date in wreath, crown above		
		a) 1897–1914, with mint mark	1.50	2.50
		b) 1915, without mint mark	1.50	2.50
8 (20a)	10	Kopeks (Ag). Same type as No. 7		
		a) 1895–1914, with mint mark	1.50	2.50
		b) 1915–1917, without mint mark	1.50	2.50
9 (21a)	15	Kopeks (Ag). Same type as No. 7		
		a) 1896–1914, with mint mark	2.50	4.00
		b) 1915–1917, without mint mark	2.50	4.00
10 (22a)	20	Kopeks (Ag). Same type as No. 7		
		a) 1901–1914, with mint mark	2.50	4.00
		b) 1914–1917, without mint mark	2.50	4.00
11 (57)	25	Kopeks (Ag). 1895–1901. Nicholas II (1868–1918), head left. ℞ crowned double-headed eagle	15.00	30.00
12 (58)	50	Kopeks (Ag) 1895–1914. Same type as No. 11	10.00	20.00

			VF	XF
13 (59)	1	Rouble (Ag). Same type as No. 11		
		a) 1895–1913	12.00	25.00
		b) 1914 (900 pieces), 1915 (600 pieces)	300.00	380.00
14 (62)	5	Roubles (Au) 1897–1911. Same type as No. 11	60.00	80.00
15 (63)	7½	Roubles (Au) 1897. Same type as No. 11	160.00	180.00
16 (64)	10	Roubles (Au) 1895–1911. Same type as No. 11	110.00	130.00

				VF	**XF**

17 (65)   15 Roubles (Au) 1897. Same type as No. 11   130.00   165.00

18 (A65)   25 Roubles (Au). Same type as No. 11:
        a) 1896 (300 pieces)   *3000.00*   *4000.00*
        b) 1908 (175 pieces)   *4000.00*   *5000.00*

19 (B65)   37½ Roubles with additional value 100
Franc as double currency (Au) 1902.
Same type as No. 11   6000.00   8000.00

COMMEMORATIVE COIN FOR THE CENTENNIAL OF NAPOLEON'S DEFEAT

20 (68)   1 Rouble (Ag) 1912. Memorial legend.
℞ crowned double-headed eagle on
St. George's shield, surrounded by six
provincial arms   125.00   185.00

COMMEMORATIVE COIN FOR ALEXANDER III

21 (69)   1 Rouble (Ag) 1912. Alexander III
(1845–1894), tsar 1881–1894. ℞ monu-
ment of the ruler   400.00   600.00

COMMEMORATIVE COIN FOR THE 300th ANNIVERSARY OF THE HOUSE OF ROMANOFF

				VF	XF

22 (70)   1 Rouble(Ag) 1913. Nicholas II and Michael Feodorovich (1596–1645), first tsar of the Romanoff Dynasty, reigned 1613–1645. ℞ crowned double-headed eagle   16.50   30.00

COMMEMORATIVE COIN FOR THE 200th ANNIVERSARY OF THE NAVAL BATTLE OF GANGUT

23 (71)   1 Rouble (Ag) 1914. Peter I, the Great (1672–1725), portrait right. ℞ crowned double-headed eagle   900.00   1500.00

RUSSIAN SOVIET FEDERAL SOCIALIST REPUBLIC
Name of country: РСФСР

24 (80)   10 Kopeks (Ag) 1921–1923. Arms of the Soviet Republic. Value in wreath   2.00   4.00

25 (81)   15 Kopeks (Ag) 1921–1923. Same type as No. 24   3.50   5.00

26 (82)   20 Kopeks (Ag) 1921–1923. Same type as No. 24   4.50   6.50

27 (83)   50 Kopeks (Ag) 1921–1922. Coat of arms. ℞ value in star, date below, all in circle and wreath   7.50   15.00

				VF	**XF**

28 (84)   1   Rouble (Ag) 1921–1922. Same type as No. 27   15.00   22.50

29 (85)   10   Roubles = Chervonetz (Au) 1923, 1925, 1975–1982. Sowing farmer. Rev. coat of arms. The issue of 1925 is a pattern piece:

    a) 1923   225.00   300.00
    b) 1925, pattern   –.–   –.–
    c) 1975–1982   80.00   100.00

UNION OF SOVIET SOCIALIST REPUBLICS
Name of country: CCCP

30 (75)   ½   Kopek (Cu) 1925–1928. Name of country CCCP in circle. ℞ value spelt out   5.00   10.00

31 (76)   1   Kopek (Cu) 1924–1925. Coat of arms with new legend and name of country CCCP. ℞ value in wreath of wheat ears   3.00   9.00

32 (77)   2   Kopeks (Cu) 1924, 1925. Same type as No. 31. Year 1925 is very rare   7.00   15.00

33 (78)   3   Kopeks (Cu) 1924. Same type as No. 31   5.00   10.00

34 (79)   5   Kopeks (Cu) 1924. Same type as No. 31   8.00   20.00

35 (86)   10   Kopeks (Ag) 1924–1931. Same type as No. 31   2.00   4.00

36 (87)   15   Kopeks (Ag) 1924–1931. Same type as No. 31   2.50   4.00

37 (88)   20   Kopeks (Ag) 1924–1931. Same type as No. 31   2.50   4.00

38 (89)   50   Kopeks (Ag) 1924–1927. Blacksmith with anvil. ℞ coat of arms and value in letters   5.00   8.00

			VF	XF
39 (90)	1	Rouble (Ag) 1924. Workman and farmer in front of landscape and rising sun	10.00	15.00

40 (91)	1	Kopek (Al–Br) 1926–1935. Coat of arms with new legend and name of country CCCP. ℞ value in wreath	0.50	1.50
41 (92)	2	Kopeks (Al–Br) 1926–1935. Same type as No. 40	0.80	1.50
42 (93)	3	Kopeks (Al–Br) 1926–1935. Same type as No. 40	0.50	1.50
43 (94)	5	Kopeks (Al–Br) 1926–1935. Same type as No. 40	0.80	1.50
44 (95)	10	Kopeks (Cu–Ni) 1931–1934. Coat of arms with new legend without name of country. ℞ workman, shield with value	0.40	1.25
45 (96)	15	Kopeks (Cu–Ni) 1931–1934. Same type as No. 44	0.60	1.20
46 (97)	20	Kopeks (Cu–Ni) 1931–1934. Same type as No. 44	0.80	1.20

Coins No. 47 to 74 can be distinguished by the number of ribbons on wreath around arms. The number of ribbons stands for the number of republics existing at the time of issue. Usually the coins have a rough rim, smooth rims are very rare and high in demand, and forgeries exist.

47 (98)	1	Kopek (Al–Br) 1935–1936. Coat of arms with three ribbons on each side, name of country below, but without new legend. ℞ value and date in wreath	2.00	4.50

			VF	XF
48 (99)	2	Kopeks (Al–Br) 1935–1936. Same type as No. 47	1.50	5.00
49 (100)	3	Kopeks (Al–Br) 1935–1936. Same type as No. 47	2.00	5.00
50 (101)	5	Kopeks (Al–Br) 1935–1936. Same type as No. 47	5.00	12.00
51 (102)	10	Kopeks (Cu–Ni) 1935–1936. Coat of arms with three ribbons on each side. ℞ shield with value surrounded by ears of wheat, oak branches and date	0.40	0.80
52 (103)	15	Kopeks (Cu–Ni) 1935–1936. Same type as No. 51	1.00	1.50
53 (104)	20	Kopeks (Cu–Ni) 1935–1936. Same type as No. 51	1.20	1.80
54 (105)	1	Kopek (Al–Br) 1937–1946. Same type as No. 47, but coat of arms with five ribbons on each side	0.30	0.60
55 (106)	2	Kopeks (Al–Br) 1937–1946. Same type as No. 48, but coat of arms with five ribbons on each side	0.30	0.60
56 (107)	3	Kopeks (Al–Br) 1937–1946. Same type as No. 49, but coat of arms with five ribbons on each side	0.30	0.60
57 (108)	5	Kopeks (Al–Br) 1937–1946. Same type as No. 50, but coat of arms with five ribbons on each side	0.30	0.60
58 (109)	10	Kopeks (Cu–Ni) 1937–1946. Same type as No. 51, but coat of arms with five ribbons on each side	0.30	0.60
59 (110)	15	Kopeks (Cu–Ni) 1937–1946. Same type as No. 52, but coat of arms with five ribbons on each side	0.30	0.60

			VF	XF
60 (111)	20	Kopeks (Cu–Ni) 1937–1946. Same type as No. 53, but coat of arms with five ribbons on each side	0.60	1.10
61 (112)	1	Kopek (Al–Br) 1948–1956. Same type as No. 47, but coat of arms with eight ribbons on left and seven on right side	0.30	0.60
62 (113)	2	Kopeks (Al–Br) 1948–1956. Same type as No. 48, but coat of arms with eight ribbons on left and seven on right side	0.30	0.60

			VF	XF
63 (114)	3	Kopeks (Al–Br) 1948–1956. Same type as No. 49, but coat of arms with eight ribbons on left and seven on right side	0.30	0.50
64 (115)	5	Kopeks (Al–Br) 1948–1956. Same type as No. 50, but coat of arms with eight ribbons on left and seven on right side	0.40	0.80
65 (116)	10	Kopeks (Cu–Ni) 1948–1956. Same type as No. 51, but coat of arms with eight ribbons on left and seven on right side	0.30	0.50
66 (117)	15	Kopeks (Cu–Ni) 1948–1956. Same type as No. 52, but coat of arms with eight ribbons on left and seven on right side	0.40	0.80
67 (118)	20	Kopeks (Cu–Ni) 1948–1956. Same type as No. 53, but coat of arms with eight ribbons on left and seven on right side	0.60	1.10
68 (119)	1	Kopek (Al–Br) 1957–1960. Same type as No, 47, but coat of arms with seven ribbons on each side	0.80	2.00
69 (120)	2	Kopeks (Al–Br) 1957–1960. Same type as No. 48, but coat of arms with seven ribbons on each side	0.80	2.00
70 (121)	3	Kopeks (Al–Br) 1957–1960. Same type as No. 49, but coat of arms with seven ribbons on each side	1.50	3.00
71 (122)	5	Kopeks (Al–Br) 1957–1960. Same type as No. 50, but coat of arms with seven ribbons on each side	1.20	2.60
72 (123)	10	Kopeks (Cu–Ni) 1957–1960. Same type as No. 51	0.50	0.80
73 (124)	15	Kopeks (Cu–Ni) 1957–1960. Same type as No. 52	0.60	1.20
74 (125)	20	Kopeks (Cu–Ni) 1957–1960. Same type as No. 53	0.80	1.50

CURRENCY REFORM
of January 1, 1961: 10 old Roubles = 1 new Rouble

75 (126)	1	Kopek (Bra) 1961–. State emblem. ℞ value and date in wreath	0.15	0.30
76 (127)	2	Kopeks (Bra) 1961–	0.15	0.30
77 (128)	3	Kopeks (Bra) 1961–	0.20	0.40
78 (129)	5	Kopeks (Bra) 1961–	0.30	0.60
79 (130)	10	Kopeks (Ni–Bra) 1961–	0.30	0.60

80 (131)	15	Kopeks (Ni–Bra) 1961–	0.40	0.75

			VF	**XF**
81 (132)	20	Kopeks (Ni–Bra) 1961–	0.40	0.80
82 (133)	50	Kopeks (Ni–Bra)		
		a) 1961, edge plain	1.50	2.50
		b) 1964–, edge with value in letters and date	0.80	1.50
83 (134)	1	Rouble (Ni–Bra)		
		a) 1961, edge plain	2.50	4.00
		b) 1964–, edge with value in letters and date	1.60	2.50

The 50 Kopeks, and the 1, 2, 3, and 5 Roubles pieces, bearing the same design as Nos. 82 and 83 (Ni–Bra) 1958, are pattern pieces. Other patterns are the 5 Kopeks (Al) 1953, with same obverse as No. 78, but reverse with value above oak branches and hammer and sickle, and 50 Kopeks (Br) 1953, identical with No. 82.

COMMEMORATIVE COIN FOR THE 20th ANNIVERSARY OF THE END OF WORLD WAR II

84 (135)	1	Rouble (Ni–St) 1965. Berlin-Treptow: statue of soldier by E. Vouchetich. ℞ state emblem and value in letters	2.50	4.00

COMMEMORATIVE COINS (5) FOR THE 50th ANNIVERSARY OF THE OCTOBER REVOLUTION

85 (136)	10	Kopeks (Ni–St) 1967. State emblem in circle of rays, dates. ℞ Moscow: monument	0.25	0.40

86 (137) 15 Kopeks (Ni–St) 1967. Moscow: "laborer and female farm laborer", monument by Vera Muchina; dates. ℞ state emblem and value

	VF	XF
	0.40	0.60

87 (138) 20 Kopeks (Ni–St) 1967. State emblem, dates, legend "50 years of Soviet power". ℞ Small cruiser "Aurora"   0.50   0.80

88 (139) 50 Kopeks (Ni–St) 1967. Lenin statue in front of hammer and sickle. ℞ state emblem and value in letters   1.10   1.60

89 (140)   1 Rouble (Ni–St) 1967. Same type as No. 88   3.00   4.50

Values are given for each coin in U.S. Dollars and reference to Yeoman-numbers.

COMMEMORATIVE COIN FOR LENIN'S
100th BIRTHDAY

90 (141) 1 Rouble (Ni–St) 1970. Vladimir Ilyich
Lenin (1870–1924), actually Ulyanov;
Soviet Russian politician, leader of the
world's proletariat. ℞ state emblem,
value, memorial legend

	XF	Unc
	2.00	3.00

30th ANNIVERSARY OF THE END OF WORLD WAR II

91 (142) 1 Rouble (German silver) 1975. Monument
in Wolgograd   2.00   3.00

60th ANNIVERSARY OF THE OCTOBER REVOLUTION

92 (143) 1 Rouble (German silver) 1977. Bust of
Lenin and small cruiser "Aurora". Rev.
coat of arms, value   1.60   2.50

	XF	Unc

93 (144) 1 Rouble (German silver) 1977. Emblem of the Olympic games 1980. Rev. coat of arms, value   1.80   3.00

94   95

	Unc	Proof

94 (145) 5 Roubles (Ag) 1977. City view of Kiev   15.00   17.50
95 (146) 5 Roubles (Ag) 1977. City view of Leningrad   15.00   17.50

96   97

96 (147) 5 Roubles (Ag) 1977. City view of Minsk   15.00   17.50
97 (148) 5 Roubles (Ag) 1977. City view of Tallinn (Reval)   15.00   17.00

98   99

			Unc	Proof
98 (149)	10 Roubles (Ag) 1977. City view of Moscow		25.00	35.00
99 (150)	10 Roubles (Ag) 1977. Map of Soviet Union		25.00	35.00
100 (151)	100 Roubles (Au) 1977. Globe and palm branch		250.00	300.00

101 (152)	150 Roubles (Platinum) 1977. Olympic emblem	300.00	350.00

102 (153)	1 Rouble (German silver) 1978	3.00

1308   **Russia**

	Unc	Proof
103 (A163) 100 Roubles (Au) 1978	225.00	280.00

		Unc	Proof
104 (162)	100 Roubles (Au) 1978	225.00	280.00
105 (154)	5 Roubles (Ag) 1978	10.00	20.00
106 (155)	5 Roubles (Ag) 1978	10.00	20.00
107 (158)	10 Roubles (Ag) 1978	20.00	30.00
108 (159)	10 Roubles (Ag) 1978	20.00	30.00
109 (160)	10 Roubles (Ag) 1978	20.00	30.00

110 111

		Unc	Proof
110 (156)	5 Roubles (Ag) 1978	10.00	18.00
111 (157)	5 Roubles (Ag) 1978	10.00	18.00

		Unc	Proof
112 (161)	10 Roubles (Ag) 1978	20.00	30.00

113

114

113 (168)	10 Roubles (Ag) 1978	20.00	30.00
114 (169)	10 Roubles (Ag) 1978	20.00	30.00

115 (163)	150 Roubles (Platinum) 1978	300.00	350.00

1310   **Russia**

			Unc	**Proof**
116 (173)	100	Roubles (Au) 1979	225.00	330.00

| **117** (174) | 100 | Roubles (Au) 1979 | 225.00 | 330.00 |

| **118** (164) | 1 | Rouble (German silver) 1979 | 3.00 | |
| **119** (165) | 1 | Rouble (German silver) 1979 | 3.00 | |

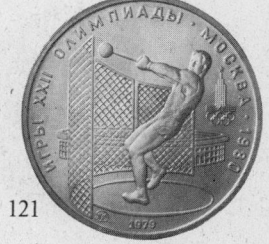

120 121

| **120** (166) | 5 | Roubles (Ag) 1979 | 10.00 | 18.00 |
| **121** (167) | 5 | Roubles (Ag) 1979 | 10.00 | 18.00 |

122

123

			Unc	Proof
122 (170)	10 Roubles (Ag) 1979		20.00	30.00
123 (171)	10 Roubles (Ag) 1979		20.00	30.00

124 (172)	10 Roubles (Ag) 1979		20.00	30.00

125 (175)	150 Roubles (Platinum) 1979. Ancient wrestlers		320.00	350.00

			Unc	Proof
126 (176)	150	Roubles (Platinum) 1979	320.00	350.00
127 (186)	100	Roubles (Au) 1980	225.00	330.00
128 (177)	1	Rouble (German silver) 1980	3.00	
129 (178)	1	Rouble (German silver) 1980	3.00	
130 (181)	5	Roubles (Ag) 1980	10.00	18.00
131 (187)	10	Roubles (Ag) 1980	20.00	30.00
132 (183)	10	Roubles (Ag) 1980	20.00	30.00
133 (185)	10	Roubles (Ag) 1980	20.00	30.00
134 (182)	5	Roubles (Ag) 1980	10.00	18.00
135 (179)	5	Roubles (Ag) 1980	10.00	18.00
136 (180)	5	Roubles (Ag) 1980	10.00	18.00

137 (187)	150	Roubles (Platinum) 1980	400.00	425.00

20th ANNIVERSARY OF MANNED SPACE FLIGHT

			XF	Unc
138 (188)	1	Rouble (German silver) 1981. Juri A. Gagarin (1934–1968), cosmonaut	2.50	4.00

RUSSO-BULGARIAN FRIENDSHIP

			Proof
139 (189)	1	Rouble (German silver) 1981. Flags above clasped hands	6.00

60th ANNIVERSARY OF THE SOVIET STATE

140 (190)   1 Rouble (German silver) 1982. Lenin statue in front of rising sun   **Proof** 6.00

KARL MARX DEATH CENTENNIAL

141 (191)   1 Rouble (German silver) 1983. Karl Marx (1818–1883), socialist ideologist   6.00

20th ANNIVERSARY OF FIRST WOMAN IN SPACE

142 (192)   1 Rouble (German silver) 1983. Valentina V. Tereshkova   6.00

400th ANNIVERSARY OF THE DEATH OF I. FEDOROV

143 (193)   1 Rouble (German silver) 1983. Ivan Fedorov (1510–1583), Russia's first printer, detail from a monument in Moscow   6.00

SESQUICENTENARY OF THE BIRTH OF D.I. MENDELEJEV

144 (194)   1 Rouble (German silver) 1984. Dimitriy Ivanovich Mendelejev (1834–1907), chemist   6.00

125th ANNIVERSARY OF THE BIRTH OF A.S. POPOV

145 (195)　1 Rouble (German silver) 1984. Alexander Stepanovich Popov (1859–1906), physicist

Proof

6.00

185th ANNIVERSARY OF THE BIRTH OF A.S. PUSHKIN

146 (196) 1 Rouble (German silver) 1984. Alexander Sergejevich Pushkin

6.00

115th ANNIVERSARY OF LENIN'S BIRTH

147 (197) 1 Rouble (German silver) 1985. Vladimir Ilyich Lenin (1870–1924)

6.00

40th ANNIVERSARY OF THE END OF WORLD WAR II

148 (198) 1 Rouble (German silver) 1985. Star of Order, branch, dates

6.00

12th WORLD FESTIVAL OF THE YOUTH AND THE STUDENTS IN MOSCOW

149 (199) 1 Rouble (German silver) 1985. Festival Logo

6.00

165th ANNIVERSARY OF THE BIRTH OF F. ENGELS

Proof

150 (200) 1 Rouble (German silver) 1985. Rev.
Friedrich Engels (1820–1895), politi-
can and socialist theoretian   6.00

INTERNATIONAL YEAR OF THE PEACE

151 (201) 1 Rouble (German silver) 1986. Rev.
Emblem   6.00

275th ANNIVERSARY OF THE BIRTH OF M. V. LOMONOSOV

152 (202) 1 Rouble (German silver) 1986. Rev.
M. V. Lomonosov (1711–1765), phi-
losopher and savant   6.00

130th ANNIVERSARY OF THE BIRTH OF K. E. ZIOLKOVSKI

153 (205) 1 Rouble (German silver) 1987   6.00

175th ANNIVERSARY OF THE BATTLE OF BORODINO (2)

154 (203) 1 Rouble (German silver) 1987   6.00

Proof

155 (204) 1 Rouble (German silver) 1987   6.00

70th ANNIVERSARY OF THE OCTOBER REVOLUTION (3)

156 (206) 1 Rouble (German silver) 1987   6.00

Proof

157   3 Roubles (German silver) 1987   –.–

158   5 Roubles (German silver) 1987   –.–

ARMAWIR MONEY

			VF	XF
1 (1)	1	Rouble (Cu) 1918. Double-headed eagle without crown. Legend, signifying the Armawir Branch of the state bank as issuer. ℞ value between branches	55.00	80.00

			VF	XF
2 (2)	3	Roubles (Cu) 1918. Same type as No. 1		
		a) diameter: 28 mm	90.00	120.00
		b) diameter: 31 mm	160.00	180.00
3 (3)	5	Roubles (Cu) 1918. Same type as No. 1	140.00	160.00

The 1 Rouble piece is known with and without mint mark I. S. (= Sadler) on the tail of the eagle. Pattern pieces: 3 Roubles (Ag), 10 Pieces, and 5 Roubles (Al).

KHWAREZM SOVIET PEOPLE'S REPUBLIC

			VF	XF
1 (1)	20	Roubles (Br) 1920–1921. Name of country and date (Mohammedan calendar 1338–1339) in Turkish. ℞ value in Russian and Turkish	52.00	75.00

		VF	XF
2 (2)	25 Roubles (Br) 1921. Similar type as No. 1	40.00	60.00
3 (3)	100 Roubles (Br) 1921. Similar type as No. 1	40.00	60.00

| 4 (4) | 500 Roubles (Br) 1921–1922. Similar type as No. 1 | 62.00 | 85.00 |

ISSUES FOR SPITSBERGEN

1	10 Kopeks (Al–Br) 1946. Legend: Island of Spitsbergen in Russian, date. ℞ value and name of issuing authority ARKTIKUGOL in Cyrillic lettering	25.00	40.00
2	15 Kopeks (Al–Br) 1946. Same type as No. 1	25.00	40.00
3	20 Kopeks (Cu–Ni) 1946. Same type as No. 1	35.00	50.00
4	50 Kopeks (Cu–Ni) 1946. Same type as No. 1	35.00	50.00

Ruanda # Rwanda République Rwandaise

Area: 10,169 sq. mi. Population: 6,200,000.

A Republic in central equatorial Africa, that formerly belonged to German East Africa, and later became part of the Belgian Trust Territory of Ruanda-Urundi. An independent republic since July 1, 1962, Rwanda merged with Burundi under a monetary union, with the Rwanda-Burundi Franc as the basic unit. Compare Burundi, Rwanda, and Burundi (joint issues), and emissions prior to the independence, also, check under Belgian Congo, years 1952 to 1960.

Capital: Kigali.

100 Centimes = 1 Rwanda Franc

			VF	XF
1 (1)	1	Franc (Cu–Ni) 1964, 1965. Gregoire Kayibanda (*1925), President. ℞ coat of arms and value	0.30	0.80
2 (2)	5	Francs (Br) 1964	0.60	1.20
3 (3)	10	Francs (Cu–Ni) 1964	0.90	2.00

			Proof
4	10	Francs (Au) 1965	75.00
5	25	Francs (Au) 1965	125.00
6	50	Francs (Au) 1965	250.00
7	100	Francs (Au) 1965	450.00

ISSUE FOR THE FAO COIN PLAN

8 (4)   2 Francs (Al) 1970. Boy filling coffee

	VF	XF

basket, symbol of the Rwanda Savings
Bank. Motto: AUGMENTONS LA
PRODUCTION. ℞ coat of arms, value 0.30 0.60

9 (5) ½ Franc (Al) 1970   0.30 0.60

10 (6) 1 Franc (Al) 1969. G. Kayibanda, head
right. ℞ coat of arms, value   0.30 0.60

COMMEMORATIVE COIN FOR THE 10th ANNIVERSARY OF INDEPENDENCE AND THE FAO COIN PLAN

11 (7) 200 Francs (Cu–Ni) 1972. Scene of wel-
come on the occasion of the Declara-
tion of Independence on 1st July 1962
in front of the national flag of Ruanda.

	XF	Unc

     ℞ agricultural worker cultivating rice 9.00 15.00

12 (8) 1 Franc (Al) 1974. Millet 0.30 0.80

13 (9) 5 Francs (Br) 1974. Branch of a coffee tree 0.40 1.80

14 (10) 10 Francs (Cu–Ni) 1974. Branch of a coffee
tree 1.20 4.00

15 (11) 20 Francs (Bra) 1977 1.00 2.00
16 (12) 50 Francs (Bra) 1977 1.25 2.50

Rwanda and Burundi

Ruanda und Burundi   **Rwanda et Burundi**

The common administration of Ruanda-Urundi terminated with the
Declaration of Independence of 1st July 1962. Although on 22nd Sept.
1962 the Rwanda and Burundi Franc had been created as a new common
currency unit for the two states of Rwanda and Burundi (formerly
Urundi) which had now become independent, the existing economic
and monetary union was already cancelled on 30th Sept. 1964.

100 Centimes = 1 Rwanda and Burundi Franc

			XF	Unc
1 (1)	1	Franc (Bra) 1960–1961. Lion (Panthera leo – Felidae). ℞ value and name of country RWANDA * BURUNDI	0.60	1.20

St. Christopher-Nevis-Anguilla
St. Christopher-Nevis-Anguilla · Saint-Christophe-Nevis-Anguilla

Area: 168 sq. mi. Population: 65,000.
Group of islands in the Lesser Antilles. Member of the Caribbean Free
Trade Area (CARIFTA). In 1967 Anguilla broke off relations with the
neighboring islands, see also under Anguilla. St. Christopher-Nevis-
Anguilla is united with the countries of Antigua, Barbados, Dominica,
Grenada, Montserrat, St. Lucia and St. Vincent in the currency area of
the East Caribbean Dollar. The issuing authority for the whole of the
currency area is the East Caribbean Currency Authority with its seat in
Bridgetown on the island of Barbados.
Capital: Basseterre on the island of St. Christopher (also known as
St. Kitts).

100 Cents = 1 East Caribbean Dollar

COMMEMORATIVE ISSUE FOR THE INAUGURATION OF THE CARIBBEAN DEVELOPMENT BANK AND THE FAO COIN PLAN

		Unc	Proof
1 (3*)	4 Dollars (Cu–Ni) 1970. Coat of arms with shield supporters and helmet decoration. ℞ bananas, sugar cane, value	10.00	22.50

*This number refers to Yeoman's East Carribean Territories listings.
For further issues see »St. Kitts and Nevis«.

St. Christopher and Nevis

St. Christopher und Nevis   **Saint-Christophe et Nevis**

The caribbean islands of St. Christopher (St. Kitts) and Nevis attained independence on September 19th, 1983. In addition the name of country was renamed from St. Kitts and Nevis to St. Christopher and Nevis.
Capital: Basseterre on St. Christopher.

100 Cents = 1 East Caribbean Dollar

INDEPENDENCE ATTAINMENT

		Unc	Proof
1	20 Dollars 1983. Elizabeth II, portrait right. Rev. sailing vessel and map of the islands:		
	a) (Ag)		40.00
	b) (Cu-Ni)	15.00	

ROYAL VISIT (2)

		Unc	Proof
2	10 Dollars 1985. Rev. Arms:		
	a) (Ag) .925 silver, 28.28 g		50.00
	b) (Cu-Ni)	6.00	
3	500 Dollars (Au) 1985. Type as No. 2; .916⅔ gold, 47.54 g (250 pes.)		1000.00

St. Helena   # St. Helena   **Ste. Hélène**

Area: 47 sq. mi. Population: 5,300.

St. Helena was discovered by the Portuguese on 21st May 1502 (the day of St. Helena). In 1588 the British were on the island, in 1633 the Dutch. The British East India Company were granted the Royal Charter in 1673 by the British King Charles II, permitting the this Company to occupy the island officially and to administer it. Since 1834 St. Helena is a Crown Colony.

Capital: Jamestown.

100 New Pence = 1 £

ELIZABETH II since 1952

COMMEMORATIVE COIN FOR THE TERCENTENARY OF THE GRANTING OF THE ROYAL CHARTER TO THE BRITISH EAST INDIA COMPANY

					Unc	Proof
1 (1)	25 Pence 1973. Elizabeth II facing right. R Sailing ship (17th entury):					
	a) (Ag)					25.00
	b) (Cu-Ni)				3.00	

SILVER JUBILEE OF THE REIGN OF HER MAJESTY
QUEEN ELIZABETH II

			Unc	Proof
2 (2)	25 Pence 1977:			
	a) (Ag)			25.00
	b) (Cu-Ni)		3.00	

St. Helena   1325

25th ANNIVERSARY OF THE CORONATION OF HER MAJESTY QUEEN ELIZABETH II

			Unc	Proof
3 (3)	1 Crown 1978:			
	a) (Ag)			25.00
	b) (Cu-Ni)		3.00	

80th BIRTHDAY OF QUEEN MOTHER

			Unc	Proof
4 (4)	25 Pence 1980:			
	a) (Ag)			30.00
	b) (Cu-Ni)		3.00	

WEDDING OF PRINCE CHARLES AND LADY DIANA

			Unc	Proof
5 (5)	25 Pence 1981:			
	a) (Ag)			30.00
	b) (Cu-Ni)		3.00	

INTERNATIONAL YEAR OF THE SCOUT (2)

			Unc	Proof
6 (6)	25 Pence (Ag) 1983		20.00	30.00
7 (7)	2 £ (Au) 1983		300.00	325.00

150th ANNIVERSARY OF COLONY (2)

8 (8) 50 Pence 1984. Rev. New arms:
a) (Ag) — 35.00
b) (Cu-Ni) 5.00

9 (8b) 50 Pence (Au) 1984. Type as No. 8 — 900.00

10 (9) 50 Pence 1984. Portrait of Prince Andrew:
a) (Ag) normal thickness — 40.00
b) (Ag) Piéfort — 400.00
c) (Cu-Ni) 5.00

St. Helena and Ascension

			Unc	Proof
1 (1)	1 Penny (Br) 1984		0.10	1.00
2 (2)	2 Pence (Bro) 1984		0.15	1.25
3 (3)	5 Pence (Cu-Ni) 1984		0.20	1.50
4 (4)	10 Pence (Cu-Ni) 1984		0.30	1.75
5 (5)	50 Pence (Cu-Ni) 1984		0.75	2.25

6 (6)	1 £ (Ni-Bra) 1984		1.50	3.50
7 (6a)	1 £ (Ag) 1984. Type as No. 6:			
	a) normal thickness			30.00
	b) Piéfort			–.–

PRINCE ANDREW'S MARRIAGE (2)

8 (7)	50 Pence 1986. Busts of the Couple:			
	a) (Ag) .925 silver, 28.28 g			40.00
	b) (Ag) Piéfort, .925 silver, 56.56 g			–.–
	c) (Cu-Ni)		5.00	
9	50 Pence (Au) 1986. Type as No. 8; .916⅔ gold, 47.54 g (50 pes.)			1000.00

St. Kitts and Nevis

St. Kitts und Nevis   **Saint-Kitts et Nevis**

After the separation of Anguilla the country St. Christopher-Nevis-Anguilla
was renamed St. Kitts and Nevis. Independence was attained on September
19th, 1983.
Capital: Basseterre on St. Christopher.

100 Cents = 1 East Caribbean Dollar

BI-CENTENARY OF THE BATTLE OF THE SAINTS

		Unc	Proof
1	20 Dollars 1982:		
	a) (Ag)		40.00
	b) (Cu-Ni)	10.00	

BI-CENTENARY OF THE SIEGE OF BRIMSTONE HILL

		Unc	Proof
2	100 Dollars (Au) 1982		200.00

Further issues see »St. Christopher and Nevis«.

STLUCIA

St. Lucia   **St. Lucia**   **Sainte-Lucie**

Area: 233 sq. mi. Population: 130,000.
An island in the group of the Lesser Antilles (Windward Islands). Discovered by Columbus in 1502, it became a British colony in 1814. On March 1, 1967 St. Lucia obtained internal autonomy; member of the Caribbean Free Trade Area (CARIFTA). St. Lucia is united with the countries of Antigua, Barbados, Dominica, Grenada, Montserrat, St. Christopher-Nevis-Anguilla and St. Vincent in the currency area of the East Caribbean Dollar. The issuing authority for the whole of the currency area is the East Caribbean Currency Authority in Bridgetown on the island of Barbados.
Capital: Castries.

100 Cents = 1 East Caribbean Dollar

COMMEMORATIVE ISSUE FOR THE INAUGURATION
OF THE CARIBBEAN DEVELOPMENT BANK AND THE FAO
COIN PLAN

		Unc	Proof
1 (7*)	4 Dollars (Cu–Ni) 1970. Coat of arms with shield supporters and helmet decoration. ℞ bananas, sugar cane, value	10.00	30.00

*This number refers to Yeoman's East Carribean Territories listings.

BI-CENTENARY OF THE BATTLE OF THE SAINTS

		Unc	Proof
2	10 Dollars 1982:		
	a) (Ag)		40.00
	b) (Cu-Ni)	8.00	

ROYAL VISIT (2)

		Unc	Proof
3	10 Dollars 1985. Rev. Arms:		
	a) (Ag) .925 silver, 28.28 g		40.00
	b) (Cu-Ni)	8.00	
4	500 Dollars (Au) 1985. Type as No. 3, .916⅔ gold, 47.54 g (250 pcs.)		1000.00

St. Pierre and Miquelon

Area: 96,5 sq. mi. Population: 6,000.
Island group south-west of Newfoundland, French territory.
Capital: St. Pierre.

100 Centimes = 1 Franc

			XF	Unc
1 (1)	1 Franc (Al) 1948. Head of Marianne, allegory of the Republic of France. ℞ schooner		2.00	4.00

2 (2)	2 Francs (Al) 1948		2.50	5.00

St. Thomas and Prince Islands
St. Thomas und Prinzeninsel   St. Thomas et Prince

Area: 372 sq. mi. Population: 70,000.
The island discovered in 1470 on St. Thomas's Day (21st December) was
named after this day and the neighbouring island »Prince Island« in honour
of King Alfons V. At certain higher levels of administration, Luanda in Angola was the competent authority, apart from which the colony (since 1951 a
province) had a large measure of autonomy. The waterwheel in the coat of
arms is the personal emblem of King Alfons V. The Democratic Republic of
Sao Tomé and Principe was declared on July 12, 1975.
Capital: São Tomé.

100 Centavos = 1 Escudo; 100 Centimos = 1 Dobra

1 (1)	10	Centavos (Ni–Br) 1929. Head of Liberty. ℞ coat of arms in front of globe, value	3.50	8.00
2 (2)	20	Centavos (Ni–Br) 1929	3.50	8.00
3 (3)	50	Centavos (Ni–Br) 1928–1929		
		a) 1928	40.00	55.00
		b) 1929	6.00	12.00
4 (4)	1	Escudo (Cu–Ni) 1939. Coat of arms with mural crown. ℞ value	4.00	10.00
5 (7)	2½	Escudos (Ag) 1939, 1948. ℞ coat of arms in front of cross of Jerusalem	6.00	10.00
6 (8)	5	Escudos (Ag) 1939, 1948	8.00	20.00
7 (9)	10	Escudos (Ag) 1939	22.00	45.00
8 (5)	50	Centavos (Ni–Br) 1948	5.00	15.00

9 (6)	1	Escudo (Ni–Br) 1948. Same type as No. 4	6.00	15.00
10 (10)	50	Centavos (Cu–Ni) 1951	4.00	8.00
11 (11)	1	Escudo (Cu–Ni) 1951	6.00	15.00
12 (12)	2½	Escudos (Ag) 1951	4.00	8.00

			VF	XF
13 (13)	5 Escudos (Ag) 1951. 25 mm dia.		6.50	10.00
14 (14)	10 Escudos (Ag) 1951		8.00	16.00
15 (15)	10 Centavos (Br) 1962		1.00	1.60

16 (16)	20 Centavos (Br) 1962	1.00	1.50
17 (17)	50 Centavos (Br) 1962	0.80	1.20
18 (18)	1 Escudo (Br) 1962	1.00	1.50
19 (19)	2½ Escudos (Cu–Ni) 1962	1.50	2.50
20 (20)	5 Escudos (Ag) 1962. Type as No. 13, but 22 mm dia.	5.00	8.00

COMMEMORATIVE ISSUE FOR THE 5th CENTENARY OF THE DISCOVERY OF THE ISLANDS

21 (21)	50 Escudos (Ag) 1970. Coat of arms (the revised city coat of arms of São Tomé and the city coat of arms of Santo Antonio do Principe, granted on 25th May 1954) above stylized waves. ℞ the 5 miniature shields from the coat of arms of Portugal, laid on the Cross of Jerusalem, value	8.00	12.00
22 (15a)	10 Centavos (Al) 1971	0.20	0.30
23 (16a)	20 Centavos (Br) 1971	0.20	0.40
24 (17a)	50 Centavos (Br) 1971	0.30	0.50
25 (20a)	5 Escudos (Cu–Ni) 1971	0.65	1.00
26 (A21)	10 Escudos (Cu–Ni) 1971	0.90	1.80
27 (B21)	20 Escudos (Cu–Ni) 1971	2.50	4.00

			XF	Unc
28 (22)	50	Centimos (Al-Br) 1977. Coat of arms, date. Rev. fish, value	0.10	0.20
29 (23)	1	Dobra (Al-Br) 1977. Cocoa beans on stem	0.15	0.30
30 (24)	2	Dobras (Cu-Ni) 1977. Goats	0.30	0.50
31 (25)	5	Dobras (Cu-Ni) 1977. Maize	0.40	0.70
32 (26)	10	Dobras (Cu-Ni) 1977. Chicken, eggs	0.80	1.50
33 (27)	20	Dobras (Cu-Ni) 1977. Fruits typical of the country	1.20	2.50

			Unc	Proof
34	250	Dobras (Ag) 1977. Friendship	40.00	45.00
35	250	Dobras (Ag) 1977. Folklore	40.00	45.00
36	250	Dobras (Ag) 1977. Globe	40.00	45.00
37	250	Dobras (Ag) 1977. Mother and child	40.00	45.00
38	250	Dobras (Ag)1977. We and the world	40.00	45.00
39	2500	Dobras (Au) 1977. Type as No. 34	200.00	200.00
40	2500	Dobras (Au) 1977. Type as No. 35	200.00	200.00
41	2500	Dobras (Au) 1977. Type as No. 36	200.00	200.00
42	2500	Dobras (Au) 1977. Type as No. 37	200.00	200.00
43	2500	Dobras (Au) 1977. Type as No. 38	200.00	200.00

FAO WORLD FISHERIES CONFERENCE 1983–84

44 (28) 100 Dobras 1984:
    a) (Ag) .925 silver, 28.28 g — 30.00
    b) (Ag) Piéfort, .925 silver, 56.56 g (600 pcs.) — –.–
    c) (Cu-Ni) — 5.00
45 100 Dobras (Au) 1984. Type as No. 44; .916⅔ gold, 47.54 g (100 pcs.) — 500.00

INTERNATIONAL GAMES

46 20 Dobras (Cu-Ni) 1984 — –.–

10th ANNIVERSARY OF INDEPENDENCE (2)

47 (29) 100 Dobras 1985:
    a) (Ag) .925 silver, 28.28 g — 40.00
    b) (Cu-Ni) — 5.00
48 100 Dobras (Au) 1985. Type as No. 47; .916⅔ gold, 47.54 g (50 pcs.) — 1200.00

Area: 150 sq. mi. Population: 116,000.
Part of the Lesser Antilles; member of the Caribbean Free Trade Area
(CARIFTA). On October 27, 1967 St. Vincent obtained internal autonomy.
St. Vincent is united with the countries of Antigua, Barbados, Dominica,
Grenada, Montserrat, St. Christopher-Nevis-Anguilla and St. Lucia in the
currency area of the East Caribbean Dollar. The issuing authority for the
whole of the currency area is the East Caribbean Currency Authority with
its seat in Bridgetown on the island of Barbados. Capital: Kingstown.

100 Cents = 1 East Caribbean Dollar

INAUGURATION OF THE CARIBBEAN DEVELOPMENT BANK AND THE FAO COIN PLAN

			Unc	Proof
1 (8*)	4 Dollars (Cu–Ni) 1970. Coat of arms.		10.00	30.00
	℞ bananas, sugar cane, value			

*This number refers to Yeoman's East Caribbean Territories listings.

St. Vincent and the Grenadines

		Unc	Proof
1	10 Dollars 1985:		
	a) (Ag) .925 silver, 28.28 g		50.00
	b) (Cu-Ni)	5.00	
2	500 Dollars (Au) 1985. Type as No. 1;		
	.916⅔ gold, 47.54 g (250 pcs.)		1200.00

Salvador

Republica de El Salvador

Area: 8,260 sq. mi. Population: 5,600,000.
The territory of the smallest republic of Central America was conquered for Spain by Pedro Alvaredo, as early as 1526. After withdrawing from the confederacy of the Central American States (Provincias Unidas del Centro de América), the country declared its independence in 1841.
Capital: San Salvador.

8 Reales = 100 Centavos = 1 Peso, 100 Centavos = 1 Colón

			VF	XF
1 (1)	1	Centavo (Cu-Ni) 1889–1913. Francisco Morazán y Quesada (1792–1842), military leader and national hero of the Honduras, President of the Republik of Central America 1829–1840. Head left. R value within wreath	3.00	6.00
2 (2)	3	Centavos (Cu-Ni) 1889–1913	3.00	8.00
3 (3)	50	Centavos (Ag) 1892–1894. Christopher Columbus (1451–1506), discoverer of the New World	12.00	25.00
4 (7)	1	Peso (Ag) 1892–1914	14.00	30.00
5 (15)	¼	Real (Cu) 1909. Old coat of arms. Rev. value within wreath	40.00	80.00
6 (22)	5	Centavos (Ag) 1911. Old coat of arms. R value in wreath	4.00	7.50
7 (23)	10	Centavos (Ag) 1911. Same type as No. 6	4.00	6.50
8 (24)	25	Centavos (Ag) 1911. Same type as No. 6	6.50	10.50
9 (16)	1	Centavo (Cu-Ni) 1915–1936. Francisco Morazán, head left. R value within wreath	1.50	3.00
10 (17)	3	Centavos (Cu-Ni) 1915. Same type as No. 9	3.00	8.00
11 (18)	5	Centavos (Cu-Ni) 1915–1925. Same type as No. 9	1.00	2.00

REPUBLICA DE EL SALVADOR

12 (25)	5	Centavos (Ag) 1914. New coat of arms. R value within wreath	3.00	6.00
13 (26)	10	Centavos (Ag) 1914. Same type as No. 12	3.50	6.00

			VF	XF
14 (21)	10	Centavos (Cu-Ni) 1921-1972, 1977. Francisco Morazán. Rev. value within wreath		
A14 (21a)	10	Centavos (German silver) 1952. Same type as No. 14	0.40	0.70
			0.50	0.90
15 (27)	25	Centavos (Ag) 1914. Same type as No. 12	5.50	9.00

COMMEMORATIVE ISSUES (2) FOR THE 4th CENTENNIAL OF THE FOUNDING OF SALVADOR

16 (30)	1	Colón (Ag) 1925. Alfonso Quiñónez Molina (1873–1950), President from 1914 to 1915, and 1923 to 1927, and Pedro Alvaredo (c. 1486–1541), Spanish Conquistador. ℞ coat of arms	110.00	200.00
17 (29)	20	Colónes (Au) 1925. Same type as No. 16	2500.00	3500.00
18 (19)	1	Centavo (Cu–Ni) 1940. Francisco Morazán. ℞ value within wreath	2.50	5.00
19 (19a)	1	Centavo (Br) 1942–	0.15	0.25

20 (20)	5	Centavos (Cu-Ni) 1940-1976	0.30	0.60
A20 (20a)	5	Centavos (German silver) 1944, 1948, 1950, 1952. Same type as No. 20	0.40	0.80
21 (28)	25	Centavos (Ag) 1943–1944	3.50	5.50
22 (31)	25	Centavos (Ag) 1953. José Matias Delgado (1768–1833), President in 1823. ℞ value within wreath	1.50	3.00
23 (32)	50	Centavos (Ag) 1953	2.50	3.50
24 (33)	25	Centavos (Ni) 1970. Same type as No. 22	0.30	0.60
25 (34)	50	Centavos (Ni) 1970. Same type as No. 24	0.40	0.80

26	1	Colón (Ag) 1971. Coat of arms. Dr. José Simeón Cañas y Villacorta (1767–1838), priest, and one of the early contenders, fighting for the abolition of slavery. ℞ "La Fecundida" of Salvador Dali (*1904), surrealistic painter. Value	**Proof** 10.00

27	5	Colónes (Ag) 1971. Coat of arms. ℞ statue of liberty pillar. José Simeón Cañas y Villacorta. Value	15.00
28	25	Colónes (Au) 1971. Same type as No. 26	100.00
29	50	Colónes (Au) 1971. Same type as No. 27	175.00
30	100	Colónes (Au) 1971. Obverse like No. 26. ℞ map of America with special consideration given to Salvador	250.00
31	200	Colónes (Au) 1971. Obverse like No. 26. ℞ colonial church of Panchimalco	450.00

			XF	Unc
32 (19b)	1	Centavos (Bra) 1976. Type as No. 19	0.15	0.25
33 (A20)	2	Centavos (Bra) 1974. Type as No. 32	0.15	0.30
34 (B20)	3	Centavos (Bra) 1974. Type as No. 32	0.20	0.40
35 (20b)	5	Centavos (Ni-clad steel) 1975. Type as No. 32	0.35	0.70
36 (21b)	10	Centavos (Ni-clad steel) 1975. Type as No. 32	0.50	1.00

INTERAMERICAN BANKER'S CONFERENCE (2)

			Unc	Proof
37 (35)	25	Colónes (Ag) 1977	20.00	80.00
38 (36)	250	Colónes (Au) 1977	300.00	350.00
			XF	**Unc**
39	1	Colón (Cu-Ni) 1984, 1985. Christopher Columbus	0.90	1.25

San Marino

Repubblica di San Marino

Area: 23 sq. mi. Population: 19,000.
This tiny republic, located south-west of Rimini, was, through the
establishment of a customs union, connected with Italy in 1862. The
independence is guaranteed by comity contracts.
Capital: San Marino.

100 Centesimi = 1 Lira; 1 Gold Escudo = 15,000 Lire

			VF	**XF**
1 (3)	50	Centesimi (Ag) 1898. Crowned coat of arms with "Tre Penne" in wreath. ℞ value in wreath	25.00	45.00
2 (4)	1	Lira (Ag) 1898–1906	30.00	60.00
3 (5)	2	Lire (Ag) 1898–1906	60.00	90.00
4 (6)	5	Lire (Ag) 1898. St. Marinus	160.00	250.00
5 (12)	10	Lire (Au) 1925. Tre Penne. ℞ St. Marinus	900.00	1200.00

6 (13)	20	Lire (Au) 1925	1500.00	1800.00

7 (9)	5	Lire (Ag) 1931–1938. Head of Liberty with helmet. ℞ plough	15.00	20.00

				VF	XF

8(10)   10 Lire (Ag) 1931–1938. Standing Liberty, half. ℞ crowned coat of arms   20.00   30.00

9(11)   20 Lire (Ag) 1931–1938. St. Marinus. ℞ three ostrich feathers above pinnacle, crown:

a) 1931–1933, 1935, 1936; 15 grams	100.00	140.00
b) 1935; 20 grams	500.00	600.00
c) 1937; 20 grams	300.00	450.00
d) 1938; 20 grams	700.00	850.00

10(14)   5 Centesimi (Br) 1935–1938. Crowned coat of arms in wreath. ℞ value   2.50   4.00

11(15) 10 Centesimi (Br) 1935–1938   2.50   4.00

12(16)   1 Lira (Al) 1972. Bust of St. Marinus   1.25   2.00

13(17)   2 Lire (Al) 1972. Type similar to No. 12   1.25   2.00

14(18)   5 Lire (Al) 1972. Type as No. 12   0.30   0.60

15(19) 10 Lire (Al) 1972. Cow with suckling calf   0.30   0.60

16(20) 20 Lire (Al–Bro) 1972. Garibaldi with woman   0.30   0.60

17(21) 50 Lire (St) 1972. Saint Marinus and a woman   0.30   0.60

18(22) 100 Lire (St) 1972. Saint Marinus in a boat   0.60   1.00

				XF	Unc
19 (23)	500	Lire (Ag) 1972. Mother and child		7.00	10.00
20 (24)	1	Lira (Al) 1973. Arms, name of country, date. ℞ Girl with national flag, date, value		1.00	1.25
21 (25)	2	Lire (Al) 1973. ℞ pelican (Pelecanus sp. – Pelecanidae), feeding its young with the blood torn with its own beak from wounds in accordance with the Christian legend		1.00	1.25
22 (26)	5	Lire (Al) 1973. ℞ Heads of five men, stars as border		0.30	0.50
23 (27)	10	Lire (Al) 1973. ℞ Man with torch forcing back four-headed dragon with his shield		0.30	0.50
24 (28)	20	Lire (Al–Bro) 1973. ℞ man rescuing old man and child from the flames		0.30	0.50
25 (29)	50	Lire (St) 1973. ℞ girl with sword holding scales with three people in each scale pan		0.30	0.50
26 (30)	100	Lire (St) 1973. ℞ Ulysses while passing the Columns of Hercules		0.30	0.50
27 (31)	500	Lire (Ag) 1973. ℞ girl with dove		7.00	10.00
28 (32)	1	Lira (Al) 1974		1.00	1.25
29 (33)	2	Lire (Al) 1974		1.00	1.25
30 (34)	5	Lire (Al) 1974		0.30	0.50

ISSUE FOR THE FAO COIN PLAN

				XF	Unc
31 (35)	10	Lire (Al) 1974. Honey bee (FAO issue)		0.50	0.70
32 (36)	20	Lire (St) 1974		0.30	0.50
33 (37)	50	Lire (St) 1974		0.30	0.50
34 (38)	100	Lire (St) 1974		0.30	0.50
35 (39)	500	Lire (Ag) 1974		6.50	8.50
36 (40)	1	Scudo (Au) 1974		Proof	75.00
37 (41)	2	Scudi (Au) 1974		Proof	125.00
38 (42)	1	Lira (Al) 1975		0.80	1.60
39 (43)	2	Lire (Al) 1975		0.80	1.60
40 (44)	5	Lire (Al) 1975		0.40	0.80
41 (45)	10	Lire (Al) 1975		0.40	0.80
42 (46)	20	Lire (Al-Br) 1975 (FAO issue)		0.50	1.00
43 (47)	50	Lire (St) 1975		0.40	0.80
44 (48)	100	Lire (St) 1975		0.40	0.80
45 (49)	500	Lire (Ag) 1975		7.00	10.00

		XF	Unc
46 (50)	500 Lire (Ag) 1975	9.00	12.50
47 (A41) 1	Scudo (Au) 1975	Proof	75.00
48 (B41) 2	Scudi (Au) 1975	Proof	125.00
49 (51) 1	Lira (Al) 1976	0.80	1.60
50 (52) 2	Lire (Al) 1976	0.80	1.60
51 (53) 5	Lire (Al) 1976 (FAO issue)	0.50	1.00
52 (54) 10	Lire (Al) 1976	0.20	0.40
53 (55) 20	Lire (Al-Br) 1976	0.25	0.50
54 (56) 50	Lire (St) 1976	0.80	1.50
55 (57) 100	Lire (St) 1976	0.90	1.80
56 (58) 500	Lire (Ag) 1976	9.00	12.00
57 (A60) 1	Scudo (Au) 1976	Proof	100.00
58 (B60) 2	Scudi (Au) 1976	Proof	175.00
59 (C60) 5	Scudi (Au) 1976	Proof	900.00
60 (59) 500	Lire (Ag) 1976	12.00	20.00
61 (60) 1	Lira (Al) 1977 (FAO issue)	0.50	1.00
62 (61) 2	Lire (Al) 1977	0.50	1.00
63 (62) 5	Lire (Al) 1977	0.25	0.50
64 (63) 10	Lire (Al) 1977	0.15	0.30
65 (64) 20	Lire (Al-Br) 1977	0.20	0.40
66 (65) 50	Lire (St) 1977	0.20	0.40
67 (66) 100	Lire (St) 1977	0.30	0.60
68 (67) 100	Lire (St) 1977	0.30	0.60
69 (68) 500	Lire (Ag) 1977	7.00	10.00

600th ANNIVERSARY OF THE BIRTH OF F. BRUNELLESCO

		XF	Unc
70 (69) 1000 Lire (Ag) 1977. Filippo Brunellesco (1377-1446), architect and author		9.00	12.50

			Proof
71 (70)	1	Scudo (Au) 1977. Democrazia	75.00
72 (71)	2	Scudi (Au) 1977	125.00
73 (72)	5	Scudi (Au) 1977	350.00

150th ANNIVERSARY OF THE BIRTH OF LEO TOLSTOI

			Unc
74 (82)	1000	Lire (Ag) 1978. Leo Tolstoi (1828–1910), Russian writer	16.00

			Proof
75 (75)	1	Scudo (Au) 1978. Miss Liberta	75.00
76 (84)	2	Scudi (Au) 1978	125.00
77 (85)	10	Scudi (Au) 1978	800.00

			XF	Unc
78 (73)	1	Lira (Al) 1978	0.25	0.40
79 (74)	2	Lire (Al) 1978	0.25	0.40
80 (75)	5	Lire (Al) 1978	0.15	0.30
81 (76)	10	Lire (Al) 1978	0.15	0.30

82 (77)	20	Lire (Al-Br) 1978	0.15	0.30
83 (78)	50	Lire (St) 1978	0.15	0.30
84 (79)	100	Lire (St) 1978 (FAO issue)	0.30	0.60
85 (80)	200	Lire (Al-Br) 1978	0.60	1.25
86 (81)	500	Lire (Ag) 1978	7.00	10.00

EUROPEAN UNITY

			XF	Unc
87 (95)	1000 Lire (Ag) 1979		10.00	12.50

				Proof
88 (96)	1 Scudo (Au) 1979. PACE (Peace)			75.00
89 (97)	2 Scudi (Au) 1979			125.00
90 (A97)	5 Scudi (Au) 1979			300.00

			XF	Unc
91 (86)	1 Lira (Al) 1979		0.60	0.80
92 (87)	2 Lire (Al) 1979		0.60	0.80
93 (88)	5 Lire (Al) 1979		0.20	0.40
94 (89)	10 Lire (Al) 1979		0.20	0.40

			XF	Unc
95 (90)	20 Lire (Al-Br) 1979		0.20	0.40
96 (91)	50 Lire (St) 1979		0.40	0.80
97 (92)	100 Lire (St) 1979		0.60	1.00
98 (93)	200 Lire (Al-Br) 1979 (FAO issue)		0.80	2.00
99 (94)	500 Lire (Ag) 1979		7.00	10.00

1500th ANNIVERSARY OF THE BIRTH OF ST. BENEDICT

100 (107)	1000 Lire (Ag) 1980			12.50

OLYMPIC GAMES 1980 IN MOSCOW (9)

			XF	Unc
101 (98)	1	Lira (Al) 1980	0.60	0.80
102 (99)	2	Lire (Al) 1980	0.60	0.80
103 (100)	5	Lire (Al) 1980	0.60	0.80
104 (101)	10	Lire (Al) 1980	0.60	0.80
105 (102)	20	Lire (Al-Br) 1980	0.60	0.80
106 (103)	50	Lire (St) 1980	0.60	0.80
107 (104)	100	Lire (St) 1980	0.70	1.20
108 (105)	200	Lire (Al-Br) 1980	0.90	2.20
109 (106)	500	Lire (Ag) 1980	10.00	14.00

			Proof
110 (108)	1	Scudo (Au) 1980	75.00
111 (109)	2	Scudi (Au) 1980	125.00
112 (110)	5	Scudi (Au) 1980	265.00

2000th ANNIVERSARY OF VIRGIL'S DEATH (3)

			XF	Unc
113 (112)	500	Lire (Ag) 1981		12.00
114 (113)	500	Lire (Ag) 1981		12.00
115 (114)	1000	Lire (Ag) 1981		20.00
116 (115)	1	Scudo (Au) 1981		75.00
117 (116)	2	Scudi (Au) 1981		125.00
118 (A116)	5	Scudi (Au) 1981		300.00

WORLD FOOD DAY (9)

119 (117)	1	Lira (Al) 1981	0.60
120 (118)	2	Lire (Al) 1981	0.60
121 (119)	5	Lire (Al) 1981	0.60
122 (120)	10	Lire (Al) 1981	0.60
123 (121)	20	Lire (Al-Br) 1981	0.60
124 (122)	50	Lire (St) 1981	0.60
125 (123)	100	Lire (St) 1981	1.00
126 (124)	200	Lire (Al-Br) 1981 (FAO issue)	1.25
127 (125)	500	Lire (Ag) 1981	15.00

			Unc
128 (126)	1 Scudo (Au) 1982	75.00
129 (127)	2 Scudi (Au) 1982	125.00
130 (139)	5 Scudi (Au) 1982	265.00

SOCIAL CONQUESTS (9)

			Unc
131 (130)	1 Lira (Al) 1982	0.35
132 (131)	2 Lire (Al) 1982	0.35
133 (132)	5 Lire (Al) 1982	0.35
134 (133)	10 Lire (Al) 1982	0.60
135 (134)	20 Lire (Al-Br) 1982	0.60
136 (135)	50 Lire (St) 1982	0.70
137 (136)	100 Lire (St) 1982	1.00
138 (137)	200 Lire (Al-Br)	1.25
139 (138)	500 Lire (St/Al-Br)	2.00

CENTENNIAL OF DEATH OF GARIBALDI (2)

			Unc	**Proof**
140 (128)	500 Lire (Ag) 1982. Capitano Reggente Domenico Maria Belzoppi	10.00	40.00
141 (129)	1000 Lire (Ag) 1982. Giuseppe Garibaldi (1807–1882), Italian hero	18.00	60.00

NUCLEAR WAR THREAT (9)

			Unc
142 (140)	1 Lira (Al) 1983. Rev. Beast of war	0.30
143 (141)	2 Lire (Al) 1983. Rev. Two arms	0.30
144 (142)	5 Lire (Al) 1983. Rev. Arm in window	0.30
145 (143)	10 Lire (Al) 1983. Rev. Two arms in frame	0.30
146 (144)	20 Lire (Al-Br) 1983. Rev. Torch above man	0.30
147 (145)	50 Lire (St) 1983. Rev. Beast above woman	0.60
148 (146)	100 Lire (St) 1983. Rev. Beast above man and woman	1.00
149 (147)	200 Lire (Al-Br) 1983. Rev. Rider spearing victim	1.25
150 (148)	500 Lire (St/Al-Br) 1983. Rev. Three horses above two people	1.75

500th ANNIVERSARY OF BIRTH OF RAFFAEL (2)

			Unc	**Proof**
151 (151)	500 Lire (Ag) 1983	10.00	27.50
152 (152)	1000 Lire (Ag) 1983	18.00	50.00

PERPETUAL LIBERTY (3)

				Unc
153 (149)	1	Scudo (Au) 1983		70.00
154 (150)	2	Scudi (Au) 1983		125.00
155 (153)	5	Scudi (Au) 1983		250.00
156 (154)	1	Lira (Al) 1984. Hippocrates		0.30
157 (155)	2	Lire (Al) 1984. Leonardo da Vinci		0.30
158 (156)	5	Lire (Al) 1984. Galileo Galilei		0.30
159 (157)	10	Lire (Al) 1984. Alessandro Volta		0.30
160 (158)	20	Lire (Al-Br) 1984. Louis Pasteur		0.30
161 (159)	50	Lire (St) 1984. Marie Sklodowska Curie and Pierre Curie		0.60
162 (160)	100	Lire (St) 1984. Guglielmo Marconi		1.00
163 (161)	200	Lire (Al-Br) 1984. Enrico Fermi		1.25
164 (162)	500	Lire (St/Al-Br) 1984. Albert Einstein		1.75

XXIII OLYMPIC SUMMER GAMES LOS ANGELES 1984 (2)

			Unc	Proof
165 (163)	500	Lire (Ag) 1984	10.00	20.00
166 (164)	1000	Lire (Ag) 1984	20.00	40.00
			Unc	
167	1	Scudo (Au) 1984	75.00	
168	2	Scudi (Au) 1984	120.00	
169	5	Scudi (Au) 1984	265.00	
170	1	Lira (Al) 1985	0.30	
171	2	Lire (Al) 1985	0.30	
172	5	Lire (Al) 1985	0.30	
173	10	Lire (Al) 1985	0.30	
174	20	Lire (Al-Br) 1985	0.30	
175	50	Lire (St) 1985	0.60	
176	100	Lire (St) 1985	1.00	
177	200	Lire (Al-Br) 1985	1.25	
178	500	Lire (St/Al-Br) 1985	1.75	

INTERNATIONAL YOUTH YEAR (3)

			Unc
179	1	Scudo (Au) 1985	70.00
180	2	Scudi (Au) 1985	110.00
181	5	Scudi (Au) 1985	250.00

EUROPEAN MUSIC YEAR (2)

			Unc	Proof
182	500	Lire (Ag) 1985. Johann Sebastian Bach (1685–1750), composer	10.00	25.00
183	1000	Lire (Ag) 1985	18.00	45.00

Sarawak

Area: c. 47,000 sq. mi. Population: 862,000.
The Rajah of Sarawak, Sir Charles Johnson Brooke, formally placed his principality in 1888 under British protection. Due to the disastrous consequences of the Japanese occupation during World War II, the last rajah relinquished independence in favour of the colonial status in 1946. From 17th May 1946 until 1963 the country was a Crown Colony in Northwest Borneo. On 31st August 1963 Sarawak received self-government; thereupon it joined the Federation of Malaysia on 16th September of the same year. Together with Sabah it constitutes the section of East Malaysia.
Capital: Kuching.
Sarawak belonged to the currency area of the Straits-Dollar. The adoption of the Malaya-Dollar (1st April 1946) and subsequently of the Malaysia-Dollar is based on traditional economic and political interdependences.

100 Cents = 1 Straits Dollar

SIR CHARLES JOHNSON BROOKE 1868–1917

			VF	XF
1 (8)	1 Cent (Cu) 1892–1897. Sir Charles Johnson Brooke (1829–1917), raja of Sarawak, crossed flags. ℞ value in wreath (center hole)		5.00	10.00
2 (9)	5 Cents (Ag) 1900–1915. Sir Charles Johnson Brooke. ℞ value in circle of knotted cord		12.00	18.00
3 (10)	10 Cents (Ag) 1900–1915		15.00	20.00

4 (11)	20 Cents (Ag) 1900–1915	18.00	32.00
5 (12)	50 Cents (Ag) 1900–1906	35.00	52.00

			VF	XF
6 (13)	½ Cent (Br) 1933. Sir Charles Vyner Brooke (1874–1963), raja. ℞ value in wreath		2.00	3.00
7 (15)	1 Cent (Cu–Ni) 1920. Same type as No. 6		12.00	18.00

8 (14)	1 Cent (Br) 1927–1941. Same type as No. 6		1.50	2.50
9 (18)	5 Cents (Ag) 1920. ℞ value in circle of knotted string		55.00	80.00
10 (16)	5 Cents (Cu–Ni) 1920–1927. Same type as No. 6		3.00	4.50
11 (19)	10 Cents (Ag) 1920. Same type as No. 9		22.00	35.00
12 (17)	10 Cents (Cu–Ni) 1920–1934. Same type as No. 6		2.50	3.50
13 (20)	20 Cents (Ag) 1920–1927. Same type as No. 9		15.00	22.00
14 (21)	50 Cents (Ag) 1927. Same type as No. 9		22.00	35.00

Values are given for each coin in U.S. Dollars and reference to Yeoman-numbers.

Al-Mamlakah Al'Arabiya As-Sa'udiya

Area: c. 800,000 sq. mi. Population: 8,500,000.
The ruler of the Wahhabis, Ibn Saud, united Asir and Hejaz with his
ancestral country, the Nejd, and in 1927 ordered to be proclaimed "King
of the Hejaz, the Nejd, and its dependent territories". Since September
20, 1932 the country's name is Saudi Arabia. After the end of the war
with the Yemen, the Nedjran was incorporated in 1934. Due to the
information, partly in dispute, concerning the location of the border
between Saudi Arabia and its neighboring countries, and thus of its
area, the figure concerning the latter can only be approximate.
Capital: Rijadh.

5 Halala = 1 Girsh, 20 Girsh = 1 Saudi Ryal,
40 Saudi Ryals = 1 Pound

ABDUL-AZIZ IBN ABDUL-RAHMAN AL-FAISAL AL-SAUD 1927–1953

			VF	XF
1 (1)	¼ Girsh (Cu) H-C 1343 (1925). Toughra. R value		8.00	12.00
2 (2)	½ Girsh (Cu) H-C 1343 (1925)		6.00	10.00
A2 (3)	¼ Girsh (Cu-Ni) H-C 1344–1348 (1926–1930)		5.00	10.00
B2 (4)	½ Girsh (Cu-Ni) H-C 1344–1348 (1926–1930)		6.50	12.00
3 (A3)	½ Girsh (Br) H-C 1344 (1926). Toughra. R value in circle, surrounded by new legend		3.60	8.00
4 (5)	1 Girsh (Cu–Ni) H-C 1344–1348 (1926–1930). New legend. R value above large date		8.00	12.50
5 (6)	¼ Girsh (Cu–Ni) H-C 1346–1356 (1928–1937). New legend. R value, date		2.50	5.00
6 (7)	½ Girsh (Cu–Ni) H-C 1346–1356 (1928–1937)		5.50	10.00
7 (8)	1 Girsh (Cu–Ni) H-C 1346–1356 (1928–1937)		6.00	10.00
8 (9)	¼ Girsh (Cu–Ni) H-C 1356– (1937–). Same type as No. 5		0.50	1.00
9 (10)	½ Girsh (Cu-Ni) H-C 1356– (1937–). Same type as No. 6		0.50	1.00
10 (11)	1 Girsh (Cu–Ni) H-C 1356–1372 (1937–1953). Same type as No. 7		0.60	1.20

11 (12) ¼ Ryal (Ag) H-C 1346–1348 (1928–1930). Lettering in dotted circle, surrounded by legend. Crossed daggers, flanked by palm trees (state emblem), on lower edge. ℞ lettering and date in dotted circle, surrounded by legend, on lower edge small box with value, flanked by palm trees

12 (13) ½ Ryal (Ag) H-C 1346–1348 (1928–1930). Same type as No. 11

	VF	XF
No. 11	35.00	55.00
No. 12	60.00	100.00

13 (14) 1 Ryal (Ag) H-C 1346–1348 (1928–1930). Same type as No. 11 — 50.00 — 75.00

14 (18) ¼ Ryal (Ag) H-C 1354–1370 (1935–1951). Same type as No. 11, but smaller diameter — 4.00 — 6.50

15 (19) ½ Ryal (Ag) H-C 1354–1370 (1935–1951). Same type as No. 12, but smaller diameter — 6.00 — 10.00

16 (20) 1 Ryal (Ag) H-C 1354–1370 (1935–1951). Same type as No. 13, but smaller diameter — 8.00 — 12.00

17 (A21) ¼ Girsh (Cu–Ni) H-C 1365 (1946). No. 8 counterstamped "65" — 7.00 — 10.00

18 (B21) ½ Girsh (Cu–Ni) H-C 1365 (1946). No. 9 counterstamped "65" — 7.00 — 10.00

19 (C21) 1 Girsh (Cu–Ni) H-C 1365 (1946). No. 10 counterstamped "65" — 7.00 — 10.00

20 (23) 1 Pound (Au) H-C 1370 (1951). Same type as No. 11 — 110.00 — 135.00

			VF	XF
21 (30)	1 Halala (Br) H-C 1383 (1964). Coat of arms, surrounded by legend. ℞ value, date			
			0.10	0.25
22 (A23)	1 Girsh (Cu–Ni) H-C 1376– (1957–). Same type as No. 21			
			0.20	0.30
23 (24)	2 Girsh (Cu–Ni) H-C 1376– (1957–). Same type as No. 21			
			0.25	0.40

		VF	XF
24 (25)	4 Girsh (Cu–Ni) H-C 1376– (1957–). Same type as No. 21		
		0.40	0.80
25 (26)	¼ Ryal (Ag) H-C 1374 (1955). Same type as No. 14		
		2.00	4.00
26 (27)	½ Ryal (Ag) H-C 1374 (1955). Same type as No. 15		
		4.00	6.50

		VF	XF
27 (28)	1 Ryal (Ag) H-C 1374 (1955). Same type as No. 16		
		6.50	10.00

	VF	XF
28 (29) 1 Pound (Au) H-C 1377 (1957). Same type as No. 21	120.00	145.00

FAISAL 1964-1975
ISSUES (2) FOR THE FAO COIN PLAN

29 (A31)   25 Halala (Cu-Ni) H-C 1392 (1972). National coat of arms and the quotation from the Koran "Feed the poor and distressed". Rev. value   .0.40   0.80

30 (31)   50 Halala = ½ Riyal (Cu-Ni) H-C 1392 (1972). Type as No. 29   0.70   1.40

31 (32)   5 Halala (Cu-Ni) H-C 1392 (1972). National coat of arms, Arabic inscription. R value, date   0.15   0.30

32 (33)   10 Halala (Cu-Ni) H-C 1392 (1972). Type as No. 31   0.20   0.35

33 (34)   25 Halala (Cu-Ni) H-C 1392 (1972). Type as No. 31   0.25   0.50

34 (35)   50 Halala (Cu-Ni) H-C 1392 (1972). Type as No. 31   0.30   0.60

KHALID 1975–1982

			XF	Unc
35 (37)	5 Halala (Cu-Ni) AH 1397, 1400 (1977, 1980)		0.50	1.00
36 (38)	10 Halala (Cu-Ni) AH 1397, 1400 (1977, 1980)		0.50	1.00

			XF	Unc
37 (39)	25 Halala (Cu-Ni) AH 1397, 1400 (1977, 1980)		0.30	0.75
38 (40)	50 Halala (Cu-Ni) AH 1397, 1400 (1977, 1980)		0.50	1.00
39 (36)	100 Halala = 1 Riyal (Cu-Ni) AH 1396, 1400 (1976, 1980)		1.00	1.75

FOR THE FAO COIN PLAN (3)

40 (42)	5	Halala (Cu-Ni) H-C 1398 (1978)	0.25	0.50
41 (43)	10	Halala (Cu-Ni) H-C 1398 (1978)	0.50	1.00
42 (41)	100	Halala (Cu-Ni) H-C 1398 (1978)	1.00	1.75

Senegal   # Senegal   **Sénégal**

Area: 76,084 sq. mi. Population: 6,800,000.
Formerly a part of French West Africa, Senegal became an autonomous Republic in 1958, and entered into a federation with Mali, the former French Sudan, in 1960. However, this alliance was a rather short one, and upon its dissolution the country reached total independence.
Capital: Dakar.

100 Centimes = 1 CFA Franc

COMMEMORATIVE ISSUES (4) FOR THE 8th ANNIVERSARY OF INDEPENDENCE ON APRIL 4, 1960

			Proof
1	10	Francs (Au) 1968. Coat of arms. ℞ value, date, inscription INDEPENDANCE 4 AVRIL 1960	60.00
2	25	Francs (Au) 1968	140.00
3	50	Francs (Au) 1968	280.00
4	100	Francs (Au) 1968	560.00

25th ANNIVERSARY OF THE EURAFRIQUE PROGRAM (6)

			Unc	Proof
5	50	Francs (Ag) 1975. Leopold Sedar Senghor. Rev. Mercator's projections of North Africa and Europe; pirogue	50.00	70.00
6	150	Francs (Ag) 1975. Rev. Mercator's projections of North Africa and Europe; white pelican	100.00	120.00
7	250	Francs (Au) 1975. Rev. coat of arms	110.00	135.00
8	500	Francs (Au) 1975. Type as No. 7	200.00	220.00
9	1000	Francs (Au) 1975. Type as No. 7	400.00	420.00
10	2500	Francs (Au) 1975. Type as No. 7	900.00	900.00

All valuations in the SCHÖN are stated in U.S. Dollars.

Serbia

СРБИЈА

In 1878 the Berlin Congress granted full independence to the Principality fo Serbia. In 1882 Prince Milan accepted the royal status. In the fall of 1918 the South Slavs of the Austro-Hungarian area and Montenegro united with Serbia, comprising the new kingdom. During World War II, from 1941 to 1944, Serbia became a separate state under German sovereignty. After this relatively short period under foreign government, the unity of the Yugoslavi state was restored.
Capital: Belgrade (Beograd).

100 Para (ПАРА) = 1 Dinar (ДИНАР)

PETER I 1903–1918

			VF	XF
1 (13)	2	Pare (Br) 1904. Crowned heraldic eagle. ℞ value	2.50	5.00
2 (14)	5	Para (Cu–Ni) 1904–1917	1.00	2.00
3 (15)	10	Para (Cu–Ni) 1912–1917	1.50	2.50

			VF	XF
4 (16)	20	Para (Cu–Ni) 1912–1917	2.00	3.50
5 (19)	50	Para (Ag) 1904–1915. Peter I (1844–1921), head right. ℞ value in wreath with crown above	4.00	5.00
6 (20)	1	Dinar (Ag) 1904–1915	5.00	6.50
7 (21)	2	Dinara (Ag) 1904–1917	8.00	10.50

COMMEMORATIVE ISSUE FOR THE CENTENNIAL
OF THE REBELLION AGAINST TURKISH RULE
AND FOR THE REINSTATEMENT OF THE HOUSE
OF KARAGEORGEVICH

			VF	XF
8 (22)	5	Dinara (Ag) 1904. George Petrovich (Karageorge) 1766–1817, prince and national hero, and Peter I, head left. ℞ arms on mantle, dates 1804–1904	40.00	60.00
9 (23)	50	Para (Z) 1942. Heraldic eagle. ℞ value and date between ears of wheat	6.00	9.00

10 (24)	1	Dinar (Z) 1942	1.50	3.50
11 (25)	2	Dinara (Z) 1942	1.50	3.50
12 (26)	10	Dinara (Z) 1942	3.50	4.50

Values are given for each coin in U.S. Dollars and reference to Yeoman-numbers.

Seychellen   **Seychelles**   **Seychelles**

Area: 156 sq. mi. Population: 66,000.
Island group in the Indian Ocean, discovered by the Portuguese during the 16th century; British territory since 1794. The Seychelles was granted limited internal self-government in 1970, and attained independence on June 28, 1976.
Capital: Port Victoria.

100 Cents = 1 Rupee

			VF	XF
		GEORGE VI 1936–1952		
1 (1)	10	Cents (Cu–Ni) 1939–1944. George VI, crowned head, left. R value (scalloped)	4.00	10.00
2 (2)	25	Cents (Ag) 1939–1944	6.00	20.00
3 (3)	½	Rupee (Ag) 1939	10.00	45.00
4 (4)	1	Rupee (Ag) 1939	12.00	50.00
5 (5)	1	Cent (Br) 1948. George VI, new legend KING GEORGE THE SIXTH. R value in dotted circle	0.40	1.20
6 (6)	2	Cents (Br) 1948	0.50	1.20

			VF	XF
7 (7)	5	Cents (Br) 1948	0.60	1.50
8 (8)	10	Cents (Cu–Ni) 1951 (scalloped)	2.50	4.00
9 (9)	25	Cents (Cu–Ni) 1951	2.50	4.00

			VF	XF
		ELIZABETH II since 1952		
10 (14)	1	Cent (Br) 1959–1969. Elizabeth II, crowned head, right. R value	0.40	0.80
11 (15)	2	Cents (Br) 1959–1969	0.50	1.00
12 (16)	5	Cents (Br) 1964–1971	0.40	0.80

			VF	XF
13 (10)	10 Cents (Ni-Bra) 1953–1974		0.30	0.80
14 (11)	25 Cents (Cu-Ni) 1954–1974		0.50	1.00
15 (12)	½ Rupee (Cu-Ni) 1954–1974		0.60	1.20
16 (13)	1 Rupee (Cu-Ni) 1954–1974		1.00	2.00

ISSUES (2) FOR THE FAO COIN PLAN

			XF	Unc
17 (17)	1 Cent (Al) 1972. R̶ head of a cow		0.10	0.20
18 (18)	5 Cents (Al) 1972, 1975. Rev. head of cabbage (scalloped)		0.10	0.20

			Unc	Proof
19 (19)	5 Rupees 1972–1974:			
	a) (Cu-Ni) 1972		3.00	
	b) (Ag), 1972, 1974			50.00
20 (20)	10 Rupees 1974:			
	a) (Cu-Ni)		4.00	
	b) (Ag)			30.00

INDEPENDENCE

		Unc	Proof
21 (21)	1 Cent (Al) 1976. Profile of President Mancham. Rev. boueteur fish	0.20	1.50
22 (22)	5 Cents (Al) 1976. Rev. bourgeois fish	0.20	1.50
23 (23)	10 Cents (Ni-Bra) 1976. Rev. sailfish	0.40	2.00
24 (24)	25 Cents (Cu-Ni) 1976. Rev. black parrot	0.60	2.00
25 (25)	50 Cents (Cu-Ni) 1976. Rev. vanilla orchid	0.80	2.50
26 (26)	1 Rupee (Cu-Ni) 1976. Rev. triton conch shell	1.00	5.00
27 (27)	5 Rupees (Cu-Ni) 1976. Rev. coco-de-mer palm tree:		
	a) (Ag)		18.00
	b) (Cu-Ni)	2.00	
28 (28)	10 Rupees 1976. Turtle:		
	a) (Ag)		25.00
	b) (Cu-Ni)	4.00	
29 (29)	1000 Rupees (Au) 1976	300.00	400.00

SILVER JUBILEE OF THE REIGN OF HER MAJESTY QUEEN ELIZABETH II

30 (30)	25 Rupees (Ag) 1977. President Mancham. Rev. orb, commemorative inscription, value	12.50	20.00

		XF	Unc
31 (31)	1 Cent (Al) 1977		0.20
32 (32)	5 Cents (Al) 1977 (FAO issue)		0.40
33 (33)	10 Cents (Ni-Bra) 1977 (FAO issue)		0.40
34 (34)	25 Cents (Cu-Ni) 1977		0.60
35 (35)	50 Cents (Cu-Ni) 1977		0.80
36 (36)	1 Rupee (Cu-Ni) 1977		1.20
37 (37)	5 Rupees (Cu-Ni) 1977		2.00
38 (38)	10 Rupees (Cu-Ni) 1977		4.00

CONSERVATION COMMEMORATIVE (3)

		Unc	Proof
39 (39)	50 Rupees (Ag) 1977	20.00	35.00
40 (40)	100 Rupees (Ag) 1977	35.00	50.00
41 (41)	1500 Rupees (Au) 1977	600.00	750.00

INTERNATIONAL YEAR OF THE CHILD

42 (42)	50 Rupees (Ag) 1980		40.00

FOR THE FAO COIN PLAN (2)

		XF	Unc
43 (43)	5 Cents (Al-Br) 1981	0.15	0.30
44 (44)	10 Cents (Al-Br) 1981	0.20	0.50

Area: 965 sq. mi. Population: 35,000.
The Sheikdom of Sharjah is one of the seven Trucial States in Pacified
Oman. The enclaves of Dhiba, Kalba and Khor Fakkan belong administratively to Sharjah. Since December 2, 1971 Sharjah is a member
state of the "United Arab Emirates" (UAE).

100 Naye Paise = 1 Rupee, 20 Piastre = 1 Rial,
since 1966: 100 Dirham = 1 Sharjah Riyal

SAKER BEN MOHAMMED AL KAISIMI until 1965

COMMEMORATIVE COIN FOR JOHN F. KENNEDY

		Unc	Proof
1	5 Rupees (Ag) 1964. John Fitzgerald Kennedy (1917–1963), 35th President of the United States of America. ℞ crossed flags (state emblem of the sheikdom)	12.00	

KHALED BEN MOHAMMED AL KAISIMI since 1965

2	1 Riyal (Ag) 1969–. Mona Lisa, also called La Gioconda, wife of the Marchese Francesco del Giocondo; after a painting by Leonardo da Vinci (1452–1519), Louvre, Paris. ℞ state emblem, name of country, value	15.00	
3	2 Riyals (Ag) 1969–. Jules-Rimet cup between laurel branches in front of stylized globe. Football. Referring to the soccer world championship in Mexico City, 1970. ℞ like No. 2	30.00	

| 4 | 5 Riyals (Ag) 1969–. Napoleon Bonaparte (1769–1821), Emperor of France 1804–1815. ℞ like No. 2 | **Proof** 40.00 |

5	10 Riyals (Ag) 1969–. Simón Bolivar (1783–1830), statesman and General, liberated South America from the Spanish. ℞ like No. 2	60.00
6	25 Riyals (Au) 1969–. Same type as No. 2	150.00
7	50 Riyals (Au) 1969–. Same type as No. 3	300.00
8	100 Riyals (Au) 1969–. Same type as No. 4	400.00
9	100 Riyals (Au) 1969–. Same type as No. 5	400.00
10	200 Riyals (Au) 1969–. Sheik Khaled Ben Mohammed Al Kaisimi (*1931). ℞ like No. 2	700.00

Area: 27,925 sq. mi. Population: 3,650,000.

Formerly a British Crown Colony, Sierra Leone became an independent member of the Commonwealth of Nations on April 27, 1961. In April 1971, this West African country was proclaimed a Republic by Dr. Siaka Stevens.

Capital: Freetown.

100 Cents = 1 Leone, 50 Leone = 1 Golde

1

2

			XF	Unc
1 (1)	½ Cent (Br) 1964–. Sir Milton Margai (1895–1964), President of the Council and co-founder of the independent state. ℞ Bonga fish (Ethmalosa dorsalis – Clupeidae)		0.10	0.20
2 (2)	1 Cent (Br) 1964–. ℞ palm branches and fruit stalks (Elaeis guineensis – Palmae)		0.15	0.30

3

4

5

			XF	Unc
3 (3)	5 Cents (Cu–Ni) 1964–. ℞ kapok tree (Ceiba pentandra – Bombacaceae)		0.20	0.40
4 (4)	10 Cents (Cu–Ni) 1964–. ℞ value, surrounded by cocoa beans		0.30	0.60
5 (5)	20 Cents (Cu–Ni) 1964–. ℞ heraldic lion		0.50	0.90

6 (6)	1 Leone (Cu–Ni) 1964–. Coat of arms with lions supporting shield	**Unc**	**Proof** 10.00

Nos. 7–11 omitted.

5th ANNIVERSARY OF INDEPENDENCE (3)

12 (7)	¼ Golde (Au) 1966. Lion's head (Pan-thera leo – Felidae). ℞ map	225.00	275.00
13 (8)	½ Golde (Au) 1966. Same type as No. 12	450.00	550.00
14 (9)	1 Golde (Au) 1966. Same type as No. 12	900.00	1200.00

Nos. 15–18 omitted.

REPUBLIC

		XF	**Unc**
19 (14)	½ Cent (Br) 1980. Dr. Siaka Stevens (*1905), President since 1971. Rev. Arms.	0.15	0.25
20 (15)	1 Cent (Br) 1980. Type as No. 19	0.20	0.35
21 (16)	5 Cents (Cu-Ni) 1980, 1984, Type as No. 19	0.25	0.50
22 (17)	10 Cents (Cu-Ni) 1978, 1980, 1984. Type as No. 19	0.40	0.75
23 (18)	20 Cents (Cu-Ni) 1978, 1980, 1984. Type as No. 19	0.65	1.25

		XF	Unc
24 (11)	50 Cents (Cu-Ni) 1972, 1980, 1984. Type as No. 19	1.25	3.00

10th ANNIVERSARY OF THE BANK OF SIERRA LEONE

		Unc	Proof
25 (12)	1 Leone 1974. Rev. lion with mountains in background:		
	a) (Cu-Ni)	2.50	
	b) (Ag)		22.00
26 (B 22)	10 Golde (Au) 1975. Dr. Siaka Stevens	950.00	1200.00

FAO REGIONAL CONFERENCE FOR AFRICA

		XF	Unc
31 (13)	2 Leones (Cu-Ni) 1976. Agricultural labour	2.00	4.00

		XF	Unc
32 (20)	1 Leone 1980:		
	a) (Cu-Ni)	3.00	
	b) (Ag)		40.00
33 (21)	5 Golde (Au) 1980	350.00	450.00

Singapur   # Singapore   **Singapour**

Republic of Singapore

Area: 220 sq. mi. Population: 2,650,000.

Republic at the southern tip of the Malacca peninsula, consisting of the island of Singapore and a few small islands. Singapore became British in 1819 and until 1946 belonged to the Crown Colony of the Straits Settlements; from 1946–1957 a separate British Crown Colony, in 1957 internal self-government, in 1959 an autonomous state. From 1963 until August 8, 1965 Singapore was a part of Malaysia and has been independent since August 9, 1965. The Republic of Singapore is a member of the British Commonwealth.

Capital: Singapore.

100 Cents = 1 Singapore Dollar

			XF	Unc
1 (1)	1 Cent 1967–. Fountain in front of high-rise appartment building:			
	a) (Br) 1967-1975		0.05	0.10
	b) (Copper-clad steel) 1976–		0.05	0.10
2 (2)	5 Cents (Cu–Ni) 1967–. Great white egret (Casmerodius albus – Ardeidae)		0.05	0.15

3 (3)	10 Cents (Cu–Ni) 1967. Stylized great crowned seahorse (Hippocampus kuda – Syngnathidae)		0.10	0.25

4 (4)	20 Cents (Cu–Ni) 1967–. Swordfish (Xiphias gladius – Xiphiidae)		0.20	0.40
5 (5)	50 Cents (Cu–Ni) 1967–. Zebra fish (Pterois volitans – Scorpaenidae)		0.40	0.70

			Unc	Proof
6 (6)	1 Dollar (Cu-Ni) 1967-. "Lion", Symbol of Singapore (Sanskrit = lion city). Rev. value:			
	a) (Cu-Ni) 1967–		1.20	
	b) (Ag) 1975–			30.00

COMMEMORATIVE ISSUE FOR THE 150th ANNIVERSARY OF THE CITY OF SINGAPORE

		Unc	Proof
7 (7)	150 Dollar (Au) 1969. Shield with shield supporters. ℞ lighthouse, value	400.00	1500.00

ISSUE FOR THE FAO COIN PLAN

		XF	Unc
8 (8)	5 Cents (Al) 1971	0.15	0.30

		Unc	Proof
9 (9)	10 Dollars (Ag) 1972. Coat of arms. R eagle, value	25.00	85.00
10 (9a)	10 Dollars (Ag) 1973, 1974. Type similar to No. 9. but the word »Singapore« in reserved position	17.50	30.00

7th SOUTH EAST ASIAN PENINSULAR GAMES

			Unc	Proof
11 (10)	5 Dollars (Ag) 1973. National arms. ℞ emblem of the games above the National Stadium of Singapore		10.00	65.00

10th ANNIVERSARY OF THE REPUBLIC OF SINGAPORE (4)

		Unc	Proof
12 (11)	10 Dollars (Ag) 1975. Steamship at quayside	12.50	25.00
13 (12)	100 Dollars (Au) 1975. High-rise buildings	125.00	175.00
14 (13)	250 Dollars (Au) 1975. four hands clasped together	300.00	450.00
15 (14)	500 Dollars (Au) 1975. Head of a lion	550.00	900.00

16 (15)	10 Dollars (Ag) 1976, 1977. Type as No. 12, but without commemorative inscription	12.50	25.00

10th ANNIVERSARY OF THE ASEAN PACT

17 (16)	10 Dollars (Ag) 1977	12.50	25.00
18 (17)	10 Dollars 1978–1980. Two communications satellite radio antenna:		
	a) (Ag) 1978, 1979	12.50	25.00
	b) (Cu-Ni) 1980	8.00	

INTERNATIONAL FINANCIAL CENTER

19 (18)	50 Dollars (Ag) 1980, 1981	30.00	50.00

YEAR OF THE ROOSTER (2)

			Unc	Proof
20 (19)	10	Dollars 1981:		
		a) (Ag)		50.00
		b) (Cu-Ni)	8.00	
21 (20)	500	Dollars (Au) 1981		650.00
22 (1b)	1	Cent (Ag) 1981. Type as No. 1		10.00
23 (2a)	5	Cents (Ag) 1981. Type as No. 2		10.00
24 (3a)	10	Cents (Ag) 1981. Type as No. 3		10.00
25 (4a)	20	Cents (Ag) 1981. Type as No. 4		10.00
26 (5a)	50	Cents (Ag) 1981. Type as No. 5		15.00
27 (21)	5	Dollars 1981. Changi Airport:		25.00
		a) (Ag)		
		b) (Cu-Ni)	4.50	

YEAR OF THE DOG (2)

28 (22)	10	Dollars 1982:		
		a) (Ag)		35.00
		b) (Cu-Ni)	8.00	
29 (23)	500	Dollars (Au) 1982		600.00
30 (24)	5	Dollars 1982. Benjamin Sheares Bridge:		
		a) (Ag)		22.50
		b) (Cu-Ni)	4.00	

YEAR OF THE PIG (2)

31 (35)	10	Dollars 1983:		
		a) (Ag)		35.00
		b) (Cu-Ni)	8.00	
32 (26)	500	Dollars (Au) 1983		600.00

Slowakei   # Slovakia   **Slovaquie**
Slovensko

An independent Slovakia arose in March 1939 which followed Germany
very closely in respect of foreign policy and the army. Since 1945
Slovakia is once more a state within the republic of Czechoslovakia.
Capital: Bratislava.

100 Halierov = 1 Koruna

			VF	XF
1 (S19b)	5	Halierov (Sn) 1942. Coat of arms, surrounded by name of country. ℞ value	10.00	18.00
2 (S20)	10	Halierov (Br) 1939, 1942. Coat of arms. ℞ castle of Pressburg (Bratislava)	1.20	2.00
3 (S21)	20	Halierov (Br) 1940–1942. Coat of arms. R Bishop's Castle, built on the identical spot where between 832/33 the first Christian church stood on Slovakian soil	2.00	3.00
4 (S22)	50	Halierov (Cu-Ni) 1940-1941. Coat of arms. Rev. plough:		
		a) 1940	25.00	50.00
		b) 1941	2.00	3.00
5 (S23)	1	Koruna (Cu–Ni) 1940–1942, 1944–1945. Coat of arms. ℞ ears of wheat	1.50	2.50

6 (S24)	5	Korun (Ni) 1939. Coat of arms. ℞ Andrej Hlinka (1864–1938), priest and leader of the Catholic autonomous Slovakian People's Party	2.50	3.50

COMMEMORATIVE ISSUE FOR THE ELECTION
OF TISO AS PRESIDENT

			VF	XF
7 (S26)	20 Korun (Ag) 1939. Coat of arms. ℞ Dr. Jozef Tiso (1887–1947), President 1939–1945		**12.50**	**20.00**

			VF	XF
8 (S27)	20 Korun (Ag) 1941. St. Cyrill (827–869) and St. Methodius (815–885), propagators of the Cyrillic alphabet		6.00	9.00
9 (S21a)	20 Halierov (Al) 1942, 1943. Type as No. 3		1.25	2.50
10 (S22b)	50 Halierov (Al) 1943, 1944. Type as No. 4		1.50	3.00
11 (S25)	10 Korun (Ag) 1944. Pribina (+861), Slovakian Prince at the cornerstone laying of the first Christian church on Slovakian soil in Nitra (832). In the background: priest with church model and soldier with drawn sword		5.00	10.00

COMMEMORATIVE ISSUE FOR THE 5th ANNIVERSARY
OF THE SLOVAKIAN REPUBLIC

			VF	XF
12 (S28)	50 Korun (Ag) 1944. Coat of arms. ℞ Dr. Jozef Tiso		5.50	10.00

Values are given for each coin in U.S. Dollars and reference to Yeoman-numbers.

Salomon-Inseln   # Solomon Islands   **Salomon (Iles)**

Area: 11,500 sq. Population: 275,000.
The Solomon Islands, located in the Southwest Pacific east of Papua New Guinea,
were discovered by the Spanish navigator Alvaro de Mendaña. The former British
protectorate achieved self government in 1975 and full independence in 1978.
Capital: Honiara, on the island of Guadalcanal.

100 Cents = 1 Dollar

SELF GOVERNMENT COMMEMORATIVE (2)

		Proof
1	30 Dollars (Ag with gilt Cuscus) 1975. Coat of arms, name of country, value, fineness. Rev. Cuscus	60.00
2	30 Dollars (Ag gilt) 1975. Rev. Solomon Mamaloni, Chief Minister	60.00

FOR THE FAO COIN PLAN

		XF	Unc
3 (1)	1 Cent (Br) 1977–1983. Bust right of the Queen, date. Rev. native food bowl	0.15	0.20
4 (2)	2 Cents (Br) 1977–1983. Rev. eagle with spread wings and perched on a war club	0.15	0.20
5 (3)	5 Cents (Cu-Ni) 1977–1983. Rev. native mask	0.15	0.30
6 (4)	10 Cents (Cu-Ni) 1977–1983. Rev. a walking sea spirit	0.20	0.40
7 (5)	20 Cents (Cu-Ni) 1977–1983. Rev. a traditional intricate design showing four monkeys in the center	0.35	0.60
8 (6)	1 Dollar (Cu-Ni) 1977–1983. Rev. Nusu-Nusu head (war canoe figure head)	1.25	2.50
9 (7)	5 Dollars 1977–1983. Rev. Bokolo, an ornamental object fashioned from fossilized clam shell:		
	a) (Ag)		35.00
	b) (Cu-Ni)	25.00	

	Unc	Proof
10 (10) 10 Dollars 1979–1982:		
a) (Ag)		40.00
b) (Cu-Ni) .	20.00	

CORONATION SILVER JUBILEE

11 (8) 5 Dollars (Ag) 1978		25.00

ATTAINMENT OF SOVEREIGNTY ON JULY 7, 1978

	Unc	Proof
12 (9) 100 Dollars (Au) 1978; .900 gold, 9.37 g	225.00	200.00
13 (11) 100 Dollars (Au) 1980. Native art	200.00	125.00
14 (12) 100 Dollars (Au) 1981. Shark		260.00

40th ANNIVERSARY OF THE BATTLE OF GUADALCANAL (2)

	Unc	Proof
15 (13) 5 Dollars 1982. Three soldiers:		
a) (Ag)		30.00
b) (Cu-Ni)	15.00	
16 (14) 100 Dollars (Au) 1982		250.00

30th ANNIVERSARY OF CORONATION

17 (15) 5 Dollars (Ag) 1983		30.00

5th ANNIVERSARY OF INDEPENDENCE (2)

	Unc	Proof
18 (16) 10 Dollars 1983. Rev. Flag and arms:		
a) (Ag)		50.00
b) (Cu-Ni)	20.00	
19 (17) 100 Dollars (Au) 1983. Type as No. 18 (seven-sided)		250.00

INTERNATIONAL YEAR OF THE CHILD

20 (18) 5 Dollars (Ag) 1983. Rev. three children in a boat:		
a)		30.00
b) Pièfort		75.00

XXIII OLYMPIC SUMMER GAMES LOS ANGELES 1984 (3)

	Unc	Proof
21 (19) 1 Dollar (Cu-Ni) 1984. Rev. two runners	5.00	
22 (20) 10 Dollars (Ag) 1984. Type as No. 21		40.00
23 (21) 100 Dollars (Au) 1984. Rev. weight-lifter		250.00
24 (22) 5 Dollars (Ag) 1985. Decade for Women		45.00

Somalia # Somalia **Somalie**

Area: 246,000 sq. mi. Population: 5,700,000.

The former protectorate of Italian Somaliland was united with Ethiopia in 1936 to form Italian East-Africa, and occupied by British troops in 1941. After the withdrawal of the British troops, the territory came under U. N. trusteeship and was administered by Italy from 1950 until its independence on June 26, 1960. On July 1, 1960 British Somaliland united with the republic as Somalia. A democratic republic since October 21, 1969.

Capital: Mogadishu.

100 Centesimi = 1 Somalo,
since 1962: 100 Centesimi = 1 Somali Shilling (Scellino)

			VF	XF
1 (1)	1	Centesimo (Br) 1950. African elephant (Loxodonta africana – Elephantidae). ℞ value in circle	0.50	1.00
2 (2)	5	Centesimi (Br) 1950. Same type as No. 1	0.75	2.00

3 (3)	10	Centesimi (Br) 1950. Same type as No. 1	1.50	4.00
4 (4)	50	Centesimi (Ag) 1950. Crescents and star above lioness (Panthera leo – Felidae). ℞ value in dotted circle	6.00	11.00

5 (5)	1	Somalo (Ag) 1950. Same type as No. 4	5.00	10.00

COMMEMORATIVE ISSUES (5) FOR THE 5th ANNIVERSARY OF INDEPENDENCE, IN 1965

			Proof
6	20	Shillings (Au) 1965. Aden Abdulla Osman (*1908), 1st President 1960–1967. ℞ coat of arms, value	75.00
7	50	Shillings (Au) 1965. Same type as No. 6	150.00
8	100	Shillings (Au) 1965. Same type as No. 6	250.00
9	200	Shillings (Au) 1965. Same type as No. 6	550.00
10	500	Shillings (Au) 1965. Same type as No. 6	1500.00

			XF	Unc
11 (6)	5	Centesimi (Br) 1967–. Coat of arms. ℞ denomination in English, Italian and Arabic	0.15	0.40
12 (7)	10	Centesimi (Br) 1967–. Same type as No. 11	0.20	0.60
13 (8)	50	Centesimi (Cu–Ni) 1967–. Same type as No. 11	10.00	30.00
14 (9)	1	Shilling (Cu–Ni) 1967–. Same type as No. 11	8.00	20.00

DEMOCRATIC REPUBLIC

COMMEMORATIVE ISSUE FOR THE 2nd CONFERENCE OF THE FOOD AND AGRICULTURAL ORGANIZATION (FAO) OF THE UNITED NATIONS

15 (10)	5	Shillings (Cu–Ni) 1970. Coat of arms with leopards supporting the shield. ℞ ox (Bos primigenius taurus), sheep (Ovis ammon aries) and goat (Capra aegagrus hircus), all of the Bovidae family. Plants: corn (Zea mays) and genuine millet (Panicum miliaceum), both from the family of wheats – Gramineae. Bananas and grapefruits	5.00	50.00

			Proof
16	20 Shillings (Au) 1970. Coat of arms. ℞ model of an atom. Value		75.00
17	50 Shillings (Au) 1970. ℞ half-portrait of a man with censer. Value		150.00
18	100 Shillings (Au) 1970. ℞ Somali woman with bananas (Musa x paradisiaca – Musaceae), grapefruit (Citrus paradisi – Rutaceae), and cotton balls (Gossypium sp. – Malvaceae) in basket. Value		250.00

19	200 Shillings (Au) 1970. ℞ Dromedary (Camelus dromedarius – Camelidae), with heavy burden, pack-animal of the Somali nomads. Value		550.00
20	500 Shillings (Au) 1970. ℞ new parliament building in Mogadishu and map of Somalia. Value		1500.00

1st ANNIVERSARY OF THE REVOLUTION (3)

21	50 Shillings (Au) 1970. Ear of corn	150.00
22	100 Shillings (Au) 1970. Hand, helmet and rifle	250.00
23	200 Shillings (Au) 1970. Monument	550.00

ISSUES FOR THE FAO COIN PLAN (4)

			XF	Unc
24 (11)	5 Senti (Al) 1976. Coat of arms. Rev. fruits, value, date		0.15	0.30
25 (12)	10 Senti (Al) 1976. Rev. sheep, value, date		0.20	0.40
26 (13)	50 Senti (Cu-Ni) 1976. Type as No. 24		0.30	0.60
27 (14)	1 Shilling (Cu-Ni) 1976. Type as No. 25		0.60	1.20

			Unc	Proof
28 (15)	10	Shillings 1979:		
		a) (Ag)		40.00
		b) (Cu-Ni)	3.00	
29 (16)	10	Shillings 1979:		
		a) (Ag)		40.00
		b) (Cu-Ni)	3.00	
30 (17)	10	Shillings 1979:		
		a) (Ag)		40.00
		b) (Cu-Ni)	3.00	
31 (18)	10	Shillings 1979:		
		a) (Ag)		40.00
		b) (Cu-Ni)	3.00	
32 (19)	10	Shillings 1979:		
		a) (Ag)		40.00
		b) (Cu-Ni)	3.00	
33 (20)	1500	Shillings (Au) 1979	300.00	300.00
34 (21)	1500	Shillings (Au) 1979	300.00	300.00
35 (22)	1500	Shillings (Au) 1979	300.00	300.00
36 (23)	1500	Shillings (Au) 1979	300.00	300.00
37 (24)	1500	Shillings (Au) 1979	300.00	300.00

INTERNATIONAL YEAR OF THE DISABLED (2)

38 (26)	150	Shillings (Ag) 1983. Rev. Ibado Ibdi Mohamed, portrait left:		
		a) normal thickness	30.00	35.00
		b) Pièfort		–.–
39 (27)	1500	Shillings (Au) 1983. Rev. Four children with Koran	300.00	300.00

WORLD FISHERIES CONFERENCE (2)

40 (28)	25	Shillings 1984. Rev. Sea-turtle:		
		a) (Ag)		40.00
		b) (Ag), Pièfort		–.–
		c) (Cu-Ni)	5.00	
41	25	Shillings (Au) 1984. Type as No. 40		1300.00

South Africa
Suid-Africa

Area: 472,733 sq. mi. (exl. S.W. Africa). Population: 28,900,000.

The Union of South Africa was formed on May 31, 1910 by the integration of the Cape Province which had already become British in 1814 and of Natal as well as the republics of the Orange Free State and the Transvaal captured in the Boer War. On May 31, 1961 the Union of South Africa left the British Commonwealth and since that time carries the title of the Republic of South Africa.

Capital: Pretoria.

12 Pence = 1 Shilling, 2 Shillings = 1 Florin,
20 Shillings = 1 £, since 1961: 100 Cents = 1 Rand

The currency area of the Rand also includes Southwest Africa (Namibia), Botswana (to 1976), Lesotho, Swaziland and Transkei.

GEORGE V 1910–1936

			VF	XF
1 (11)	¼ Penny (Br) 1923–1926. George V, crowned portrait left. ℞ 2 sparrows (Passer domesticus – Fringillidae) on acacia branches: compare Matthew 10, 29 = "Are not two sparrows sold for a farthing? And one of them shall not fall on the ground without your Father."		4.00	8.00
2 (11a)	¼ Penny (Br) 1928–1931. Same type as No. 1, but value instead of "¼ Penny ¼" only "¼ Penny"		3.00	7.00
3 (12)	½ Penny (Br) 1923–1926. R »½ Penny ½«		20.00	40.00
4 (12a)	½ Penny (Br) 1928–1931. Same type as No. 3, but value instead of "½ Penny ½", only "½ Penny"		17.50	35.00
5 (13)	1 Penny (Br) 1923–1924. ℞ sailing vessel		8.00	18.00
6 (13a)	1 Penny (Br) 1926–1930. Same type as No. 5, but value instead of »1 Penny 1«, only »Penny«		7.00	15.00
7 (15)	3 Pence (Ag) 1923–1925. ℞ value in wreath		9.00	22.00
8 (17)	3 Pence (Ag) 1925–1930. ℞ Protea cynaroides – Proteaceae, surrounded by three brushwood bundles		5.00	20.00

			VF	**XF**
9 (16)	6	Pence (Ag) 1923–1924. ℞ value in wreath	15.00	30.00
10 (18)	6	Pence (Ag) 1925–1930. ℞ Protea cynaroides – Proteaceae	8.00	20.00
11 (19)	1	Shilling (Ag) 1923–1924. ℞ allegory of Hope	12.50	30.00
12 (19a)	1	Shilling (Ag) 1926–1930. Same type as No. 11, but value instead of "1 Shilling 1", only "Shilling"	15.00	50.00
13 (20)	1	Florin (Ag) 1923–1930. ℞ coat of arms	15.00	45.00
14 (21)	2½	Shillings (Ag) 1923–1925. ℞ crowned coat of arms	12.50	35.00
15 (21a)	2½	Shillings (Ag) 1926–1930. Same type as No. 14, but value instead of "2½ Shillings 2½", only "2½ Shillings"	20.00	75.00
16 (A21)	½	Sovereign (Au) 1923–1926. George V. ℞ St. George fighting the dragon	90.00	125.00
17 (22)	1	Sovereign (Au) 1923–1932	120.00	150.00

There are many coins issued by Great Britain which appeared at the same time with identical designs. Coins No. 16 and 17 can only be distinguished from those by their mint mark SA.

			VF	**XF**
18 (23)	¼	Penny (Br) 1931–1936. ℞ sparrows. Value now "D" instead of "Penny"	2.00	5.00
19 (24)	½	Penny (Br) 1931–1936. ℞ sailing vessel "Dromedaris"	6.00	18.00
20 (25)	1	Penny (Br) 1931–1936. ℞ sailing vessel	2.00	7.50
21 (26)	3	Pence (Ag) 1931–1936. ℞ Protea cynaroides – Proteaceae, surrounded by three bundles of brushwood	4.00	10.00
22 (27)	6	Pence (Ag) 1931–1936. ℞ Protea cynaroides – Proteaceae, surrounded by six bundles of brushwood	5.00	15.00
23 (28)	1	Shilling (Ag) 1931–1936. ℞ allegory of Hope	6.00	20.00
24 (29)	2	Shillings (Ag) 1931–1936. ℞ coat of arms	9.00	20.00
25 (30)	2½	Shillings (Ag) 1931–1936. ℞ crowned coat of arms	12.00	25.00

GEORGE VI 1936–1952

			VF	**XF**
26 (31)	¼	Penny (Br) 1937–1947. George VI, head left. ℞ sparrows	0.30	0.75

			VF	XF
27 (32)	½	Penny (Br) 1937–1947. ℞ sailing vessel	0.40	1.00
28 (33)	1	Penny (Br) 1937–1947. ℞ sailing vessel	0.60	1.20
29 (34)	3	Pence (Ag) 1937–1947. ℞ Protea cyna-roides – Proteaceae, surrounded by three bundles of brushwood	1.00	2.00
30 (35)	6	Pence (Ag) 1937–1947	1.00	2.50
31 (36)	1	Shilling (Ag) 1937–1947. ℞ allegory of Hope	2.00	4.00
32 (37)	2	Shillings (Ag) 1937–1947. ℞ coat of arms	4.00	8.50
33 (38)	2½	Shillings (Ag) 1937–1947. ℞ crowned coat of arms	5.00	10.00

COMMEMORATIVE ISSUE FOR THE VISIT OF THE ROYAL FAMILY

			VF	XF
34 (39)	5	Shillings (Ag) 1947. ℞ Springbok (Antidorcas marsupialis – Bovidae)	8.50	15.00
35 (40)	¼	Penny (Br) 1948–1950. Same type as No. 26, but legend GEORGIUS SEXTUS REX	0.40	0.90
36 (41)	½	Penny (Br) 1948–1952	0.40	0.90
37 (42)	1	Penny (Br) 1948–1950	0.60	1.20
38 (43)	3	Pence (Ag) 1948–1952	0.65	1.30
39 (44)	6	Pence (Ag) 1948–1950	1.50	3.00
40 (45)	1	Shilling (Ag) 1948–1950	3.00	7.00
41 (45a)	1	Shilling (Ag) 1951–1952	3.00	6.00
42 (46)	2	Shillings (Ag) 1948–1950	10.00	15.00

			VF	XF
43 (47)	2½	Shillings (Ag) 1948–1950	60.00	125.00
44 (47a)	2½	Shillings (Ag) 1951–1952	5.00	10.00
45 (48)	5	Shillings (Ag) 1948–1950. ℞ Spring-bok	8.00	12.00
46 (57)	½	Sovereign (Au) 1952. ℞ Springbok	Proof	110.00
47 (58)	1	Sovereign (Au) 1952	Proof	150.00
48 (49)	¼	Penny (Br) 1951–1952	0.35	0.70
49 (50)	1	Penny (Br) 1951–1952	0.50	1.00
50 (51)	6	Pence (Ag) 1951–1952	1.00	2.00
51 (52)	2	Shillings (Ag) 1951–1952	2.50	5.00
52 (53)	5	Shillings (Ag) 1951	8.00	12.00

COMMEMORATIVE ISSUE FOR THE FOUNDING OF CAPE TOWN BY JAN VAN RIEBEECK (1619–1677)

53 (56)	5	Shillings (Ag) 1952. ℞ sailing vessel in front of the Cape of Good Hope	8.00	12.00

ELIZABETH II 1952–1961

54 (59)	¼	Penny (Br) 1953–1960. Elizabeth II, head right. ℞ sparrows	0.30	0.50
55 (60)	½	Penny (Br) 1953–1960. ℞ sailing vessel	0.40	0.60
56 (61)	1	Penny (Br) 1953–1960. ℞ sailing vessel	0.40	0.70
57 (62)	3	Pence (Ag) 1953–1960. ℞ Protea cyna-roides – Proteaceae, surrounded by three bundles of brushwood	0.70	1.00
58 (63)	6	Pence (Ag) 1953–1960	1.00	2.00
59 (64)	1	Shilling (Ag) 1953–1960. ℞ allegory of Hope	2.00	3.00
60 (65)	2	Shillings (Ag) 1953–1960. ℞ coat of arms	3.00	6.00
61 (66)	2½	Shillings (Ag) 1953–1960. ℞ crowned coat of arms	4.00	6.00
62 (67)	5	Shillings (Ag) 1953–1959. Springbok	6.00	8.50
63 (68)	½	£ (Au) 1953–1960. Elizabeth II, head right. ℞ springbok	Proof	110.00
64 (69)	1	£ (Au) 1953–1960	Proof	150.00

COMMEMORATIVE ISSUE FOR THE 50th ANNIVERSARY OF THE SOUTH AFRICAN UNION

			VF	XF
65 (70)	5	Shillings (Ag) 1960. ℞ parliament building	7.50	12.00

REPUBLIC since 1961

NEW CURRENCY: 100 Cents = 1 Rand
Bilingual Legends

66 (71)	½ Cent (Bra) 1961–1964. Jan Anthoniszoon van Riebeeck (1619–1677), Dutchman, founder of Cape Town, colonizer and governor of the Cape Colony. ℞ sparrows	0.20	0.50
67 (72)	1 Cent (Bra) 1961–1964. ℞ covered wagon from the Voortrekker time	0.20	0.50
68 (73)	2½ Cents (Ag) 1961–1964. ℞ Protea cynaroides – Proteaceae	0.60	1.50
69 (74)	5 Cents (Ag) 1961–1964. ℞ Protea cynaroides – Proteaceae, surrounded by five bundles of brushwood	0.50	1.20
70 (75)	10 Cents (Ag) 1961–1964. ℞ allegory of Hope	1.00	1.75

71 (76)	20 Cents (Ag) 1961–1964. ℞ coat of arms	2.00	3.00
72 (77)	50 Cents (Ag) 1961–1964. ℞ springbok	6.00	9.00
73 (78)	1 Rand (Au) 1961–1971. ℞ springbok	65.00	70.00

74 (79)	2 Rand (Au) 1961–1971. ℞ springbok Name of country in English	125.00	140.00
75 (80)	1 Cent (Br) 1965–1969. ℞ sparrows	0.05	0.10
76 (81)	2 Cents (Br) 1965–1969. ℞ white-tailed gnu (Connochaetes taurinus – Bovidae)	0.05	0.10
77 (82)	5 Cents (Ni) 1965–1969. ℞ blue crane (Anthropoides paradisea – Gruidae)	0.10	0.20
78 (83)	10 Cents (Ni) 1965–1969. ℞ Aloe sp. – Liliaceae	0.15	0.30
79 (84)	20 Cents (Ni) 1965–1969. ℞ Protea cynaroides and Protea repens – Proteaceae	0.25	0.50

			VF	**XF**
80 (85)	50 Cents (Ni) 1965–1969. Jan van Riebeeck. ℞ Zantedeschia elliottiana –Araceae; Strelitzia reginae – Musaceae and Agapanthus sp. – Liliaceae		0.50	1.00
81 (86)	1 Rand (Ag) 1965–1968. ℞ springbok Name of country in Afrikaans		7.50	10.00
82 (80a)	1 Cent (Br) 1965–1969		0.05	0.10
83 (81a)	2 Cents (Br) 1965–1969		0.05	0.10
84 (82a)	5 Cents (Ni) 1965–1969		0.10	0.20
85 (83a)	10 Cents (Ni) 1965–1969		0.15	0.30
86 (84a)	20 Cents (Ni) 1965–1969		0.25	0.50
87 (85a)	50 Cents (Ni) 1965–1969		0.50	1.00
88 (86a)	1 Rand (Ag) 1965–1968		6.00	8.00

COMMEMORATIVE ISSUES (2) FOR THE 1st ANNIVERSARY OF THE DEATH OF DR. H. F. VERWOERD

89 (87)	1 Rand (Ag) 1967. Dr. Hendrik Frensh Verwoerd (1901–1966), Prime Minister from 1958 to 1966. ℞ springbok; Calvin's motto: "SOLI DEO GLORIA", name of country in English		6.00	8.00
90 (87a)	1 Rand (Ag) 1967. Dr. Hendrik F. Verwoerd; name of country in Afrikaans		6.00	8.00
A90 (104)	1 Kruger Rand (Au) 1967– Name of country in English			*450.00*
91 (88)	1 Cent (Br) 1968. Charles Robert Swart (*1894), 1st President of the Republic of South Africa, from 1961 to 1967. ℞ sparrows		0.05	0.10

			VF	XF
92 (89)	2 Cents (Br) 1968. ℞ white-tailed gnu		0.05	0.10
93 (90)	5 Cents (Ni) 1968. ℞ blue crane		0.05	0.10
94 (91)	10 Cents (Ni) 1968. ℞ Aloe		0.10	0.20
95 (92)	20 Cents (Ni) 1968. ℞ Protea cynaroides and Protea repens – Proteaceae		0.25	0.50
96 (93)	50 Cents (Ni) 1968. ℞ Zantedeschia elliottiana – Araceae; Strelitzia and Agapanthus		0.50	1.00

Name of country in Afrikaans

			VF	XF
97 (88a)	1 Cent (Br) 1968		0.05	0.10
98 (89a)	2 Cent (Br) 1968		0.05	0.10
99 (90a)	5 Cents (Ni) 1968		0.05	0.10
100 (91a)	10 Cents (Ni) 1968		0.10	0.20
101 (92a)	20 Cents (Ni) 1968		0.25	0.50
102 (93a)	50 Cents (Ni) 1968		0.50	1.00

			XF	Unc
103 (94)	1 Rand (Ag) 1969. Dr. Theophilus Ebenhaezer Dönges, elected President. ℞ state emblem, value; name of country in English		6.00	8.00

			XF	Unc
104 (94a)	1 Rand (Ag) 1969. Same type as No. 103, but name of country in Afrikaans		6.00	8.00
105 (95)	½ Cent (Br) 1970–1975. Coat of arms with shield supporters, date, name of country in two languages. R sparrows, value		0.05	0.10
106 (96)	1 Cent (Br) 1970–1975. Same type as No. 105		0.05	0.10
107 (97)	2 Cents (Br) 1970–1975. R same type as No. 92		0.05	0.10
108 (98)	5 Cents (Ni) 1970–1975. R same type as No. 93		0.15	0.30
109 (99)	10 Cents (Ni) 1970–1975. R same type as No. 94		0.20	0.40
110 (100)	20 Cents (Ni) 1970–1975. R same type as No. 95		0.30	0.60
111 (101)	50 Cents (Ni) 1970–1975. R same type as No. 96		0.50	1.00
112 (102)	1 Rand (Ag) 1970–1975. R springbok		7.50	10.00

COMMEMORATIVE ISSUE FOR THE 50th ANNIVERSARY OF THE PRETORIA MINT (1923–1973)

			Unc	Proof
113 (103)	1 Rand (Ag) 1974		12.50	15.00

			XF	Unc
114 (105)	½ Cent (Br) 1976. Jacobus Johannes Fouché, President of the Republic of South Africa, from 1968 to 1974. Rev. sparrows		0.05	0.10
115 (106)	1 Cent (Br) 1976. Type as No. 114		0.05	0.10
116 (107)	2 Cents (Br) 1976. Rev. white-tailed gnu		0.05	0.10
117 (108)	5 Cents (Ni) 1976. Rev. blue crane		0.10	0.20
118 (109)	10 Cents (Ni) 1976. Rev. aloe		0.15	0.30
119 (110)	20 Cents (Ni) 1976. Rev. Protea cynaroides and Protea repens – Proteaceae)		0.20	0.40

120 (111)	50 Cents (Ni) 1976. Rev. Zantedeschia elliottiana – Araceae; Strelizia and Agapanthus		0.50	1.00

121 (102a)	1 Rand (Ni) 1977, 1978, 1980, 1981, 1983–1985. Type as No. 112		1.00	2.00

			XF	Unc
122 (112)	½	Cent (Br) 1979. Dr. Nicolaas Diederichs (1903–1978), President of the Republic	0.10	0.15
123 (113)	1	Cent (Br) 1979	0.15	0.25
124 (114)	2	Cents (Br) 1979	0.20	0.30

			XF	Unc
125 (115)	5	Cents (Ni) 1979	0.25	0.40
126 (116)	10	Cents (Ni) 1979	0.30	0.50
127 (117)	20	Cents (Ni) 1979	0.50	0.80
128 (118)	50	Cents (Ni) 1979	0.90	1.20
129 (119)	1	Rand 1979:		
		a) (Ag)	Proof	17.50
		b) (Ni)	1.25	2.00

			XF	Unc
130 (120)	1/10	Kruger Rand (Au) 1980–		45.00
131 (121)	¼	Kruger Rand (Au) 1980–		90.00
132 (122)	½	Kruger Rand (Au) 1980–		225.00
133 (123)	½	Cent (Br) 1982. Balthasar J. Vorster (1915–1983), President of the Republic. Rev. Sparrows	Proof	1.00
134 (124)	1	Cent (Br) 1982. Type as No. 133	0.10	0.15
135 (125)	2	Cents (Br) 1982. Rev. White-tailed gnu	0.15	0.20
136 (126)	5	Cents (Ni) 1982. Rev. Blue crane	0.20	0.30
137 (127)	10	Cents (Ni) 1982. Rev. Aloe	0.25	0.35
138 (128)	20	Cents (Ni) 1982. Rev. Protea cynaroides and Protea repens	0.40	0.65
139 (129)	50	Cents (Ni) 1982. Rev. Zantedeschia, Strelizia and Agapanthus	0.80	1.25
140 (130)	1	Rand 1982. Rev. Springbok:		
		a) (Ag)	Proof	17.50
		b) (Ni)	1.50	2.00
141	1	Rand 1985. Marais Viljoen (*1915), President of the Republic. Rev. Springbok:		
		a) (Ag)	Proof	17.50
		b) (Ni)	1.50	2.00

			Unc	Proof
142	1	Rand (Ag) 1985. Parliament	10.00	12.50
143	1	Kruger Rand (Au) 1985. Parliament		850.00

South Arabia

Südarabische Föderation   **Arabie du Sud (Fédération)**
Federation of South Arabia

Area: 61,890 sq. mi. Population: 1,250,000.
Several sultanates and emirates of the West Aden protectorate united
to form the South Arabian Federation in 1959/60. The Crown Colony of
Aden together with the islands of Sokotra and Abd-el-Kuri joined the
federation only in 1963.
Capital: Al Ittihad.

		1000 Fils = 1 Dinar	**VF**	**XF**
1 (1)	1 Fils (Al) 1964. Star. ℞ crossed daggers (jambijas)		0.30	0.80
2 (2)	5 Fils (Br) 1964		0.40	0.80
3 (3)	25 Fils (Cu–Ni) 1964. ℞ dhow, Arabian sailing vessel		0.60	1.50

4 (4)	50 Fils (Cu–Ni) 1964		0.90	1.80

All valuations in the SCHÖN are stated in U.S. Dollars.

Südrhodesien **Southern Rhodesia** **Rhodésie du Sud**

In 1889 Southern and Northern Rhodesia were united under the administration of the British South African Company; since October 1st, 1923,
the two territories are governed separately.
Capital: Salisbury.

12 Pence = 1 Shilling, 2 Shillings = 1 Florin,
5 Shillings = 1 Crown, 20 Shillings = 1 £

GEORGE V 1923–1936

			VF	XF
1 (1)	½ Penny (Cu–Ni) 1934–1936. Crown above stylized rose. ℞ value and ornamentations (center hole)		3.00	6.00

			VF	XF
2 (2)	1 Penny (Cu–Ni) 1934–1936 (center hole)		2.00	3.00
3 (3)	3 Pence (Ag) 1932–1936. George V, crowned portrait, left. ℞ three spear tips		4.00	12.50
4 (4)	6 Pence (Ag) 1932–1936. ℞ crossed axes		5.00	18.00
5 (5)	1 Shilling (Ag) 1932–1936. ℞ large Zimbabwe bird (= soap stone sculpture)		6.00	18.00
6 (6)	2 Shillings (Ag) 1932–1936. ℞ sable antelope (Hippotragus niger – Bovidae)		12.00	25.00
7 (7)	½ Crown (Ag) 1932–1936. ℞ coat of arms		15.00	30.00

GEORGE VI 1936–1952

			VF	XF
8 (8)	½ Penny (Cu–Ni) 1938–1939. Crown above stylized rose. ℞ value and ornamentations (center hole)		2.00	6.00
9 (9)	1 Penny (Cu–Ni) 1937–1942 (center hole)		1.50	5.00

			VF	XF
10 (8a)	½ Penny (Br) 1942–1944 (center hole)		1.00	3.00
11 (9a)	1 Penny (Br) 1942–1947 (center hole)		1.00	2.00
12 (12)	3 Pence (Ag) 1937. ℞ three spear tips		4.00	10.00
13 (13)	6 Pence (Ag) 1937. ℞ crossed axes		5.00	12.00
14 (14)	1 Shilling (Ag) 1937. ℞ large Zimbabwe bird		8.00	12.00
15 (15)	2 Shillings (Ag) 1937. ℞ sable antelope		12.00	25.00

			VF	XF
16 (16)	½ Crown (Ag) 1937. ℞ coat of arms		15.00	30.00
17 (17)	3 Pence. ℞ three spear tips			
	a) (Ag) 1939–1946		3.50	6.00
	b) (Cu–Ni) 1947		1.00	3.00
18 (18)	6 Pence. ℞ crossed axes			
	a) (Ag) 1939–1946		4.00	12.00
	b) (Cu–Ni) 1947		2.00	5.00
19 (19)	1 Shilling. ℞ large Zimbabwe bird			
	a) (Ag) 1939–1946		7.50	15.00
	b) (Cu–Ni) 1947		2.00	6.00
20 (20)	2 Shilling. ℞ sable antelope			
	a) (Ag) 1939–1946		12.00	25.00
	b) (Cu–Ni) 1947		6.00	15.00
21 (21)	½ Crown. ℞ coat of arms			
	a) (Ag) 1938–1946		15.00	22.00
	b) (Cu–Ni) 1947		5.00	8.00
22 (27)	½ Penny (Br) 1951–1952. Same type as No. 10, but with legend KING GEORGE THE SIXTH		1.00	2.00
23 (28)	1 Penny (Br) 1949–1952. Same type as No. 11, but with legend KING GEORGE THE SIXTH		1.00	2.00
24 (29)	3 Pence (Cu–Ni) 1948–1952		1.00	3.00
25 (30)	6 Pence (Cu–Ni) 1948–1952		1.00	3.00
26 (31)	1 Shilling (Cu–Ni) 1948–1952. ℞ large Zimbabwe bird		2.00	5.00
27 (32)	2 Shillings (Cu–Ni) 1948–1952		2.50	6.00
28 (33)	½ Crown (Cu–Ni) 1948–1952		4.00	7.50

COMMEMORATIVE COIN FOR THE
100th BIRTHDAY OF C. RHODES

			VF	XF
29 (34)	1	Crown (Ag) 1953. ℞ Cecil Rhodes (1853–1902), British South African chief economist and statesman, colonial pioneer, portrait above arms of Southern Rhodesia, Northern Rhodesia, and Nyasaland	10.00	20.00
30 (35)	¹/₂	Penny (Br) 1954. Crown above stylized rose. ℞ value with ornamentations (center hole)	2.00	3.00
31 (36)	1	Penny (Br) 1954	3.00	8.00
32 (37)	2	Shillings (Cu–Ni) 1954. Elizabeth II. ℞ sable antelope	50.00	110.00
33 (38)	¹/₂	Crown (Cu–Ni) 1954. ℞ coat of arms	12.00	20.00

Values are given for each coin in U.S. Dollars and reference to Yeoman-numbers.

Südjemen   # Southern Yemen   **Yemen du Sud**
Democratic Yemen

Area: 61,890 sq. mi. Population: 2,250,000.

Southern Yemen is the successor of the South Arabian Federation. The former Federation was transformed into a centrally governed state on 26th November 1967 by proclaiming the People's Republic. The old sultanates and emirates were replaced by 10 provinces with governors. On the occasion of the festivities for the third anniversary of independence, 1970, the designation of state "Democratic Yemen" was adopted, which meant the first step towards the aspired union with the Republic of Yemen.

Capital: Al Ittihad.

1000 Fils = 1 Southern Yemen Dinar;
since 1972: 1000 Fils = 1 Yemen Dinar

			VF	**XF**
1 (2)	5 Fils (Br) 1971. Star and name of the country, DEMOCRATIC YEMEN. ℞ crossed daggers, value, date		0.70	1.50
2 (3)	2½ Fils (Al) 1973. Rev. Orchid		4.00	8.00

3 (4)	5 Fils (Al) 1973. Rev. Cancer		3.00	6.50

4 (5)   25 Fils (Cu-Ni) 1976, 1977, 1979, 1981, 1982. Star and name of the country, PEOPLE'S DEMOCRATIC REPUBLIC OF YEMEN. Rev. Dhow, Arabian sailing vessel

	VF	XF
	1.50	3.00

5 (6)   50 Fils (Cu-Ni) 1976, 1977, 1979, 1981, 1984. Type as No. 4   2.50   5.00

10th ANNIVERSARY OF INDEPENDENCE (2)

		VF	XF
6 (7)	250 Fils (Cu-Ni) 1977	12.50	30.00
7 (8)	5 Dinars (Ag) 1977	Proof	80.00
8 (9)	10 Fils (Al) 1981	3.50	6.00
9 (10)	100 Fils (Cu-Ni) 1981	5.00	8.00
10 (11)	250 Fils (Cu-Ni) 1981	8.00	16.00

INTERNATIONAL YEAR OF THE DISABLED (2)

		Unc	Proof
11 (12)	2 Dinars (Ag) 1981. Abdullah Baradoni, blind poet:		
	a) normal thickness	30.00	40.00
	b) Pièfort		80.00
12 (13)	50 Dinars (Au) 1981. Arms:		
	a) normal thickness	300.00	350.00
	b) Pièfort		800.00

Taihan   # South Korea   **Südkorea**

Corée du Sud

Area: 38,452 sq. mi. Population: 42,500,000.
In the southern part of the country administered by Japan until 1945, the
Republic of Korea was proclaimed on August 15, 1948. The border between
North and South Korea is formed approximately by the 38th parallel. The
dates on the coins correspond in part to Korean chronology.
Capital: Seoul.

100 Hwan = 1 Won, since June 10, 1962: 100 Jeon = 1 Won

			VF	XF
1 (1)	10 Hwan (Bra) 4292–4294 (1959–1961). Rose of Sharon = hibiscus (Hibiscus syriacus – Malvaceae), national flower of South Korea. ℞ value and date		0.25	0.50
2 (2)	50 Hwan (Ni–Bra) 4292–4294 (1959–1961). Turtle boat, iron clad war vessel of Admiral Lee Shun-shin (1545–1598), appointed to ward off the Hideyoshi invasion from 1592 to 1598. ℞ value		0.40	0.80

			VF	XF
3 (3)	100 Hwan (Cu–Ni) 4292 (1959). Syngman Rhee (1875–1965), President 1948–1960. ℞ phoenix, value		1.00	2.00

Values are given for each coin in U.S. Dollars and reference to Yeoman-numbers.

			VF	XF
4 (4)	1	Won (Bra) 1966, 1967. Rose of Sharon. Rev. value	0.20	0.40
5 (4a)	1	Won (Al) 1968–1970, 1974–1982. Same type as No. 4	0.10	0.20
6 (5)	5	Won (Br) 1966–1970. Turtle boat. Rev. value	0.15	0.30
7 (5a)	5	Won (Bra) 1970–1972, 1977–1979, 1982. Type as No. 6	0.15	0.40

8 (6)	10	Won (Br) 1966–1970. Prabhuta-vatna-stupa in Pulguksa, 8th century, great Silla dynasty. Rev. value	0.20	0.40
9 (6a)	10	Won (Bra) 1970–1982. Type as No. 8	0.10	0.20

10 (7)	100	Won (Cu-Ni) 1970–1982. Admiral Lee Shun-shin. Rev. value, date	0.30	0.75

			Proof
11	50	Won (Ag) 1970–. Kwan Sun Yu (1904–1920) with national flag (Taegukki), girl student, fought for an independent Korea	*50.00*
12	100	Won (Ag) 1970–. Admiral Lee Shun-shin (also SUN SIN LEE) (1545–1598) and turtle boat	*75.00*
13	200	Won (Ag) 1970–. Seladon vase, porcelain, Koryo dynasty, 11th century	*110.00*
14	250	Won (Ag) 1970–. Tschang Hi Park (*1917), President since 1961. ℞ hibiscus flower between two phoenixes, state emblem, value	*150.00*

15	500	Won (Ag) 1970–. Kyongju: Bodhisattva from the Sokkuram (cave temple). ℞ state emblem surrounded by hibiscus branches, value	**Proof**
			275.00
16	1000	Won (Ag) 1970–. Soldiers in front of fluttering South Korean and UN flags. Flags of the 16 countries supporting South Korea in the Korean war (1950–1953)	
			500.00
17	1000	Won (Au) 1970–. Seoul: Namdae-Mun (= Southern gate), built at the beginning of the Yi dynasty (1396)	
			500.00

18	2500	Won (Au) 1970–. Queen Sunduk (reign: 632–647), wearing the precious gold crown of the Silla dynasty	750.00
19	5000	Won (Au). Turtle boats of Admiral Lee Shun-shin. ℞ like No. 13	1000.00
20	10000	Won (Au) 1970–. Same type as No. 12	3000.00
21	20000	Won (Au) 1970–. Gold crown from the golden crown tomb in Kyongju, 5th to 6th century, of the Silla dynasty, today in Seoul, National Museum	4200.00
22	25000	Won (Au) 1970–. King Sedschong (1397–1450), creator of the Korean phonetic alphabet	8500.00

COMMEMORATIVE ISSUE FOR THE FAO COIN PLAN

			XF	Unc
23 (A7)	50	Won (Cu-Ni) 1972–1974, 1977–1982. Rice. Rev. value, date	0.25	0.50

30th ANNIVERSARY OF LIBERATION

| 24 (8) | 100 | Won (Cu-Ni) 1975 | 0.90 | 1.75 |

			Unc	Proof
25 (9)	500 Won (Ni) 1978		4.00	60.00

26 (10)	5000 Won (Ag) 1978	50.00	125.00

1th ANNIVERSARY OF THE 5th REPUBLIC (3)

27 (11)	100 Won (Cu-Ni) 1981. Hibiscus flower	1.00	30.00
28 (12)	1000 Won (Cu-Ni) 1981. Bird of paradise	5.00	45.00
29 (13)	20000 Won (Ag) 1981. Military forces	50.00	65.00
30 (15)	1000 Won (Cu-Ni) 1982. Dancers	3.00	25.00
31 (16)	10000 Won (Ag) 1982. Namdae-Mun	20.00	50.00
32 (17)	20000 Won (Ag) 1982. Olympic flame	40.00	75.00

33 (18)	1 Won (Al) 1983–1985. Hibiscus flower	0.05	0.10
34 (19)	5 Won (Bra) 1983. Turtle boat	0.05	0.10
35 (20)	10 Won (Bra) 1983, 1985–1987. Pra-bhuta-vatna-Stupa	0.10	0.20
36 (21)	50 Won (Cu-Ni) 1983–1985. Rice (FAO issue)	0.25	0.50
37 (22)	100 Won (Cu-Ni) 1983–1986. Admiral Lee Shunshin	0.40	0.75
38 (14)	500 Won (Cu-Ni) 1982–1984. Manchu-rian crane	1.00	2.50

		Unc	Proof
39 (23)	1000 Won (Cu-Ni) 1983. Drummer	3.00	15.00
40 (24)	10000 Won (Ag) 1983. Building and birds	20.00	32.00
41 (25)	20000 Won (Ag) 1983. Wrestlers	40.00	45.00

200 YEARS OF CATHOLIC CHURCH IN KOREA (2)

42 (26)	1000 Won (Cu-Ni) 1984.	5.00
43 (27)	10000 Won (Ag) 1984.	40.00

Nos. 44–46 omitted.

10th ASIAN GAMES SEOUL 1986 (5)

47 (31)	1000 Won (Cu-Ni) 1986. Rev. Masked dancer	5.00	7.50
48 (32)	10000 Won (Ag) 1986 Rev. Badminton	25.00	35.00
49 (33)	10000 Won (Ag) 1986. Rev. Soccer	25.00	35.00
50 (34)	20000 Won (Ag) 1986. Rev. Runner with torch	40.00	50.00
51 (35)	20000 Won (Ag) 1986. Rev. Pulguksa temple	40.00	50.00

OLYMPIC GAMES 1988 IN SEOUL (3rd ISSUE) (32)
1st Series

52	1000 Won (Cu-Ni) 1987. Arms, Hibiscus flower. Rev. Basketball	5.00	8.00
53	2000 Won (Cu-Ni) 1987. Rev. Boxing	10.00	18.00
54	5000 Won (Ag) 1986. Rev. Tiger Mascot		20.00
55	5000 Won (Ag) 1986. Rev. Rope Pulling		20.00
56	10000 Won (Ag) 1986. Rev. Runner		35.00
57	10000 Won (Ag) 1987. Rev. Diving		35.00
58	25000 Won (Au) 1986. Rev. Falk Dancing		400.00
59	50000 Won (Au) 1986. Rev. Turtle ship		850.00

2nd Series

60	1000 Won (Cu-Ni) 1987. Rev. Tennis	5.00	8.00
61	2000 Won (Cu-Ni) 1987. Rev. Judo	10.00	18.00
62	5000 Won (Ag) 1987. Rev. Stadium		20.00
63	5000 Won (Ag) 1987. Rev. Badminton		20.00
64	10000 Won (Ag) 1987. Rev. Volleyball		35.00
65	10000 Won (Ag) 1987. Rev. Archery		35.00
66	25000 Won (Au) 1987. Rev. Dancing		400.00
67	50000 Won (Au) 1987. Rev. Great South Gate, Seoul		850.00

3rd Series

		Unc	Proof
68	1000 Won (Cu-Ni) 1988. Handball	5.00	8.00
69	2000 Won (Cu-Ni) 1988. Wrestlers	10.00	18.00
70	5000 Won (Ag) 1988.		20.00
71	5000 Won (Ag) 1988		20.00
72	10000 Won (Ag) 1988		35.00
73	10000 Won (Ag) 1988		35.00
74	25000 Won (Au) 1988		400.00
75	50000 Won (Au) 1988		850.00

4th Series

		Unc	Proof
76	1000 Won (Cu-Ni) 1988. Rev. Ping-pong	5.00	8.00
77	2000 Won (Cu-Ni) 1988. Rev. Weight Lifting	10.00	18.00
78	5000 Won (Ag) 1988		20.00
79	5000 Won (Ag) 1988		20.00
80	10000 Won (Ag) 1988		35.00
81	10000 Won (Ag) 1988		35.00
82	25000 Won (Au) 1988		400.00
83	50000 Won (Au) 1988		850.00

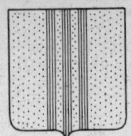

Südvietnam   # South Vietnam   **Viet-Nam du Sud**

Viet-Nam Cong Hoa

Area: 66,281 sq. mi. Population: 19,200,000.
After the coming into force of the armistice in Vietnam based on the
Geneva Indochina Agreement of 1954, the Republic of Vietnam was
formed south of the 17th parallel, when the Emperor Bao Dai had been
deposed in 1955. After a long conflict South Vietnam surrendered to North Vietnam
in 1975, and in 1976, both parts were united into the single socialist Republic of
Vietnam.

Capital: Saigon.

100 Xu or Su (= Cent) = 1 Dong (= Vietnam Piastre)

BAO DAI

		VF	**XF**
1 (1)	10 Su (Al–Bra) 1953. Vietnamese women. ℞ rice plant (Oryza sativa – Gramineae) and value	0.50	1.00
2 (2)	20 Su (Al–Bra) 1953. Same type as No. 1	0.50	1.00
3 (3)	50 Xu (Al–Br) 1953. Vietnamese women. ℞ sea dragon between value	1.20	2.40

REPUBLIC

4 (4)	50 Su (Al–Bra) 1960. Ngo Dinh Diem (1901–1963), President from 1955 to 1963. ℞ bamboo (belonging to the grass family, Gramineae), value	1.00	2.00

			VF	XF
5 (5)	1	Dong (Cu–Ni) 1960. Same type as No. 4	0.30	0.75
6 (6)	50	Xu (Al) 1963	0.75	1.00

			VF	XF
7 (7)	1	Dong (Cu–Ni). Rice plant. R value:		
		a) (Cu–Ni) 1964	0.30	1.00
		b) (Ni–St) 1971	0.20	0.50
8 (8)	5	Dong. (Scalloped)		
		a) (Cu–Ni) 1964	1.00	2.00
		b) (Ni–St) 1971	0.30	0.60
9 (9)	10	Dong:		
		a) (Cu–Ni) 1964	0.60	1.25
		b) (Ni–St) 1968–1970	0.20	0.50

			VF	XF
10 (10)	20	Dong (Ni) 1968. Vietnamese woman in rice field. New legend NGAN-HANG QUOC-GIA VIET-NAM, date R value	0.50	1.25

FOR THE FAO COIN PLAN (4)

			VF	XF
11 (12)	1	Dong (Al) 1971. Rice plant, date. R value	0.25	0.50
12 (13)	10	Dong (Brass-clad-steel) 1974	0.30	0.60
13 (11)	20	Dong (Ni) 1968. Same type as No. 10 but with new legend CHIEN-DICH THE GIOI CHONG NAN DOI	1.50	3.00
14 (14)	50	Dong (Nickel-clad-steel) 1975. Cultivation of rice		*950.00*

Spanien   # Spain   **Espagne**

Area: 194,232 sq. mi. Population: 38,500,000.
State on the Iberian peninsula including the Balearic and Canary Islands.
Capital: Madrid.

$$100 \text{ Centimos} = 1 \text{ Peseta}$$

Note: From 1947 to 1982, most Spanish coins bear two dates. The larger is the year of authorization, while the actual year of striking is incused on one or two six-pointed stars. In this catalogue, the latter appears in parentheses.

ALFONSO XIII 1886–1931

			VF	XF
1 (87)	50 Centimos (Ag) 1896–1900. Alfonso XIII (1886–1941), first under regency of his mother, took over the reign in 1902; head left. ℞ crowned arms between pillars		4.00	10.00
2 (88)	1 Peseta (Ag) 1896–1901		4.50	12.00
3 (89)	5 Peseta (Ag) 1896–1899		15.00	28.00
4 (91)	20 Pesetas (Au) 1904. Alfonso XIII, portrait in uniform, right. ℞ mantled arms with crown		1500.00	2000.00
5 (96)	1 Centimo (Br) 1906. Alfonso XIII, portrait in uniform, right. ℞ crowned arms, value		3.00	4.50
6 (97)	2 Centimos (Br) 1904–1905		2.50	4.00
7 (92)	50 Centimos (Ag) 1904–1910. Alfonso XIII, head left. ℞ crowned arms between pillars		4.00	7.50
8 (94)	1 Peseta (Ag) 1902–1905		8.00	12.00

9 (95)	2 Pesetas (Ag) 1905		12.00	22.00

			VF	XF
10 (98)	1	Centimo (Br) 1911–1913. Alfonso XIII, portrait in uniform, left. ℞ crowned arms, value	2.50	4.50
11 (99)	2	Centimos (Br) 1911–1912	2.50	4.50
12 (93)	50	Centimos (Ag) 1910	4.50	10.00
13 (100)	25	Centimos (Ni–Bra) 1925. Sailing vessel. ℞ value between branches, crown above	1.50	4.00
14 (101)	25	Centimos (Cu–Ni) 1927. Hammer, olive branch, crown. ℞ ears of wheat, value (center hole)	1.20	3.50
15 (102)	50	Centimos (Ag) 1926. Alfonso XIII, head left. ℞ crowned arms	4.50	11.00

REPUBLIC

16 (103)	5	Centimos (Fe) 1937. Head of Hispania. ℞ value in wreath	2.00	4.50
17 (107)	25	Centimos (Ni–Br) 1934. Hispania with olive branch. ℞ ears of wheat and olive branch in front of cog-wheel (center hole)	0.60	1.20
18 (104)	25	Centimos (Br) 1938. Intertwined chains. ℞ value (center hole)	2.00	4.00
19 (105)	50	Centimos (Br) 1937. Seated Hispania with olive branch. ℞ value	1.50	3.50

20 (108)	1	Peseta (Ag) 1933. Seated Hispania with olive branch. ℞ coat of arms with mural crown, between pillars	7.50	12.50
21 (106)	1	Peseta (Bra) 1937. Head of Hispania. ℞ bunch of grapes	0.60	1.50

NATIONAL GOVERNMENT

22 (109) 25 Centimos (Cu–Ni) 1937. Name of country in sun rays, and emblem of the Falange "yoke and arrows" (= at the same time recalling the great national history). ℞ coat of arms, olive branch (center hole)

	VF	XF
22 (109)	1.20	2.50

23 (110) 5 Centimos (Al) 1940–1953. Lancer. ℞ crowned coat of arms between Hércules pillars, with eagle above. The details on the arms illustrate the integration of the historic territories: castle = Castile, lion = León, poles = Aragon, net = Navarre, pomegranate = Granada   0.20   0.40

24 (111) 10 Centimos (Al) 1940–1953. Same type as No. 23   0.25   0.50

25 (112) 1 Peseta (Al-Br) 1944. Coat of arms. Rev. value surrounded by coat of arms   0.50   1.00

MONARCHY

Spain was converted to a monarchy on April 1, 1947, under a regency.

26 (115) 50 Centimos (Cu–Ni) 1949 (51). Anchor, rope and steering wheel (symbolic of Spain as a seafaring nation). R coat of arms, yoke and arrows. Arrows pointing down (center hole)   5.50   8.00

27 (116) 50 Centimos (Cu–Ni) 1949 (51–62), 1963 (63–65). Same type as No. 26, but arrows pointing up (center hole)   0.25   0.40

28 (113) 1 Peseta (Al-Br) 1947 (48–56), 1953 (54–63), 1963 (63–67). Francisco Franco y Bahamonde (1892–1975). General and statesman, since 1938 with the title Caudillo. R coat of arms   0.15   0.25

29 (114) 2½ Pesetas (Al-Br) 1953 (54–71)   0.60   1.20

30 (117) 5 Pesetas (Cu–Ni) 1949 (49–52)   2.50   6.00

31 (121) 10 Centimos (Al) 1959. General Franco, head right. R value, surrounded by olive leaves   0.10   0.20

32 (124) 50 Centimos (Al-Mg) 1966 (67–75). R ear of wheat, value   0.10   0.20

			VF	XF
33 (125)	1	Peseta (Al-Br) 1966 (67–75). R coat of arms, value	0.10	0.20
34 (118)	5	Pesetas (Cu-Ni) 1957 (58–75). R coat of arms in front of eagle	0.25	0.50

			VF	XF
35 (119)	25	Pesetas (Cu-Ni) 1957 (58–75)	0.50	1.00
36 (120)	50	Pesetas (Cu-Ni) 1957 (58–75)	1.30	2.60
37 (122)	100	Pesetas (Ag) 1966. R crowned five-sectional coat of arms. Three crosses of the San Fernando Order, seperating value, yoke, and arrows	10.00	12.50

JUAN CARLOS I since 1975

			XF	Unc
38 (126)	50	Centimos (Al) 1975 (76). Head left of the King, date. Rev. laurel branch	0.10	0.20
39 (127)	1	Peseta (Al-Br) 1975 (76–79), 1980 (81). Rev. coat of arms	0.10	0.20
40 (128)	5	Pesetas (Cu-Ni) 1975 (76–79), 1980 (81). Rev. coat of arms	0.25	0.50
41 (129)	25	Pesetas (Cu-Ni) 1975 (76–79), 1980 (81). Rev. crown	0.55	1.10
42 (130)	50	Pesetas (Cu-Ni) 1975 (76–79), 1980 (81). Type as No. 40	1.25	2.50
43 (131)	100	Pesetas (Cu-Ni) 1975 (76). Rev. coat of arms	2.00	3.60
44	100	Pesetas (Au) 1977, 1978 (medallic issue)		600.00

WORLD SOCCER CHAMPIONSHIP GAMES 1982 IN SPAIN (6)

			XF	Unc
45 (132)	50	Centimos (Al) 1980 (80–82)	0.30	0.70

			XF	Unc
46 (133)	1	Peseta (Al-Br) 1980 (80–82)	0.40	0.80
47 (134)	5	Pesetas (Cu-Ni) 1980 (80–82)	0.50	1.00
48 (135)	25	Pesetas (Cu-Ni) 1980 (80–82)	0.60	1.25
49 (136)	50	Pesetas (Cu-Ni) 1980 (80–82)	0.90	2.00
50 (137)	100	Pesetas (Cu-Ni) 1980 (80)	2.00	3.20
51 (140)	1	Peseta (Al) 1982–1987	0.05	0.10
52 (141)	2	Pesetas (Al) 1982, 1984, 1985	0.10	0.15
53 (128A)	5	Pesetas (Cu-Ni) 1982–1985	0.10	0.20
54 (143)	10	Pesetas (Cu-Ni) 1983–1985	0.10	0.20
55 (129A)	25	Pesetas (Cu-Ni) 1982–1985	0.35	0.70
56 (130A)	50	Pesetas (Cu-Ni) 1982–1985	0.50	1.00

			XF	Unc
57 (139)	100	Pesetas (Al-Br) 1982–1987	1.25	2.00
58 (146)	200	Pesetas (Cu-Ni) 1986, 1987	1.75	2.80
59	500	Pesetas (Cu-Ni) 1986	5.00	9.00

No. 60 omitted.

NUMISMATIC EXPOSITION 1987 IN MADRID (2)

		Proof
61	1 Peseta (Al) 1987. Type as No. 51, but »E-87« added	8.00
62	200 Pesetas (Cu-Ni) 1987. Type as No. 58, but »E-87« added	12.00

ISSUES FOR VIZCAYA (EUZKADI)

During the time of the civil war the province of Vizcaya constituted an autonomous territory. Capital: Bilbao.

		VF	XF
1 (1)	1 Peseta (Ni) 1937. Head of Liberty right, new legend GOBIERNO DE EUZKADI. ℞ value and date in wreath	2.50	5.00
2 (2)	2 Pesetas (Ni) 1937	2.50	5.00

Area: 25,384 sq. mi. Population: 16,100,000.
Island in the Indian Ocean off the southern tip of India, Ceylon became a
sovereign member of the British Commonwealth on 4th February 1948. As
of 22nd May 1972 Ceylon has declared itself a republic and declared its former name, in Singhalese, to be Sri Lanka, the latter also to be used exclusively on an international basis. Since 22nd May 1972 the monetary unit is
called the Sri Lanka Rupee.
Capital: Colombo.

100 Cents = 1 Sri Lanka Rupee

			VF	XF
1 (1)	1 Cent (Al-Mg) 1975 –. Coat of arms.			
		Rev. value	0.05	0.10
2 (2)	2 Cents (Al-Mg) 1975		0.10	0.20
3 (3)	5 Cents (Ni-Me) 1975		0.15	0.30
4 (4)	10 Cents (Ni-Me) 1975		0.20	0.35
5 (5)	25 Cents (Cu-Ni) 1975		0.25	0.40
6 (6)	50 Cents (Cu-Ni) 1972		0.40	0.80

			VF	XF
7 (7)	1 Rupie (Cu-Ni) 1972–		0.90	1.20

NON-ALIGNED NATIONS CONFERENCE 1976 (2)

			VF	XF
8 (8)	2 Rupees (Cu-Ni) 1976. Conference building		1.00	2.00
9 (9)	5 Rupees (Ni) 1976. Type as No. 8		1.50	3.50

INVESTITURE OF PRESIDENT JAYAWARDENE

			VF	XF
10 (10)	1 Rupee (Ni) 1978		0.60	1.50

			VF	XF
11 (3a)	5 Cents (Al) 1978. Type as No. 3		0.10	0.25
12 (4a)	10 Cents (Al) 1978. Type as No. 4		0.10	0.25

MAHAWELI DAM

13 (11)	2 Rupees (Cu-Ni) 1981	0.75	1.50

UNIVERSAL ADULT FRANCHISE

14 (12)	5 Rupees (Cu-Ni) 1981	0.90	2.00
15 (5a)	25 Cents (Ni) 1982. Type as No. 5	0.30	0.60
16 (6a)	50 Cents (Ni) 1982. Type as No. 6	0.35	0.75
17 (7a)	1 Rupee (Ni) 1982. Type as No. 7	0.50	0.90
18 (13)	2 Rupees (Cu-Ni) 1984	0.65	1.25
19 (14)	5 Rupees (Ni-Bra) 1984, 1986	0.90	1.50

INTERNATIONAL YEAR OF SHELTER FOR THE HOMELESS

20	10 Rupees (Cu-Ni) 1987. IYSH logo (square)	1.50	2.75

Straits Settlements

Straits Settlements   **Établissements du Détroit**

Under the name of the "Straits Settlements" the British created in 1867 a Crown Colony out of smaller territories previously acquired around 1800 with the centre in the city of Singapore (= Lion City) situated on the Malayan peninsula purchased from the Sultan of Johore in 1824 by the British East India Company. On the Malayan peninsula only Penang and the town of Malacca were true components of the Straits Settlements. But the expansion in the direction of Siam by subordinating the Malayan princes under British rule or protection, extended the area of the Governor General far towards the North.
Capital: Singapore.
The Straits-Dollar was introduced on 25th June 1903 and was not only valid in the states of the Malayan peninsula, but also in British North Borneo, Brunei, the island of Labuan near Borneo, the Cocos Islands as well as on Christmas Island south of Java and in Sarawak. The Straits Dollar corresponded in fineness and weight to the up to then conventional Mexican Piaster.

100 Cents = 1 Straits Dollar

EDWARD VII 1901–1910

			VF	XF
1 (17)	¼	Cent (Cu) 1905–1908. Edward VII, crowned head, right. ℞ value in dotted circle	5.00	12.00
2 (18)	½	Cent (Cu) 1908	4.00	10.00
3 (19)	1	Cent (Cu) 1903–1908	3.00	8.00
4 (20)	5	Cents (Ag) 1902–1910	3.50	7.00
5 (21)	10	Cents (Ag) 1902–1910	4.00	6.00
6 (22)	20	Cents (Ag) 1902–1910	6.50	11.00
7 (23,24)	50	Cents (Ag)		
		a) 1902–1903	30.00	60.00
		b) 1907–1908, smaller diameter	9.00	18.00
8 (25)	1	Dollar (Ag) 1903–1904, 1907–1909. ℞ value, also in Malayan and Chinese		
		a) 1903–1904	15.00	30.00
		b) 1907–1909, smaller diameter	10.00	20.00

			VF	**XF**
9 (27)	¼	Cent (Cu) 1916. George V, crowned head, left. ℞ value	2.00	4.00
10 (28)	½	Cent (Cu) 1916	2.50	5.00
11 (29)	½	Cent (Br) 1932 (scalloped)	1.50	3.50
12 (30)	1	Cent (Br) 1919-1926	0.80	2.00
13 (31)	5	Cents (Cu-Ni) 1920	8.00	25.00
14 (32)	5	Cents (Ag) 1918-1935	2.00	3.50
15 (34)	10	Cents (Ag) 1916-1927	2.00	3.50
16 (35)	20	Cents (Ag) 1916-1935	3.50	5.50
17 (36)	50	Cents (Ag) 1920-1921	5.00	10.00

18 (37)	1 Dollar (Ag) 1919-1920		18.00	22.00

For further issues see under **Malaya, Malaysia, North Borneo** and **Singapore.**

Sudan   # Sudan   **Soudan**

The Sudan

Area: 967,500 sq. mi. Population: 21,500,000.

The Anglo-Egyptian Condominium established over the Sudan on 19th January 1899 existed until its unilateral abrogation by Egypt on 18th October 1951. The present day Sudan Republic was declared independent with effect of 1st January 1956 and on 25th May 1969 declared a "Democratic Republic". With the introduction of the Sudanese Pound on 8th April 1957, the Egyptian Pound was superseded in circulation. Capital: Khartoum.

10 Millièmes = 1 Gersh (internationally called Piaster),
100 Gersh = 1 Sudanese Pound

			VF	XF
1 (34)	1	Millième (Br) 1956–. 'Flying postman' on dromedary (Camelus dromedarius-Camelidae). Ŗ value	0.10	0.20
2 (35)	2	Millièmes (Br) 1956– (scalloped)	0.20	0.30
3 (36)	5	Millièmes (Br) 1956– (scalloped)	0.25	0.40
4 (37)	10	Millièmes (Br) 1956–	0.30	0.45
5 (38)	2	Piastres (Cu-Ni)		
		a) 1956. 17.5 mm dia.	1.00	1.50
		b) 1963–. 20 mm dia.	0.40	0.60

6 (39)	5	Piastres (Cu-Ni) 1956–	0.50	0.80
7 (40)	10	Piastres (Cu-Ni) 1956–	1.00	2.00
8 (41)	20	Piastres (Cu-Ni) 1967-1969; proof only		5.00

9 (42)	25	Piastres (Cu–Ni) 1968. Flying postman; inscription FAO. ℞ value. The legend reads 'Let us work together towards providing food for all'	**Proof** 18.00	

DEMOCRATIC REPUBLIC since 1969

10 (A43)	1	Millième (Br) 1970, 1971. Type as No. 1, but inscription "Democratic Republic" added	2.00
11 (B43)	2	Millièmes (Br) 1970, 1971. Type as No. 10	2.00

12 (C43)	5	Millièmes (Br) 1970, 1971. Type as No. 10	2.00
13 (D43)	10	Millièmes (Br) 1970, 1971. Type as No. 10	2.00
14 (E43)	2	Piastres (Cu-Ni) 1970, 1971. Type as No. 10 20 mm dia.	2.20
15 (F43)	5	Piastres (Cu-Ni) 1970, 1971. Type as No. 10	2.50
16 (G43)	10	Piastres (Cu-Ni) 1970, 1971. Type as No. 10	4.00
17 (H43)	20	Piastres (Cu-Ni) 1970, 1971. Type as No. 10	15.00

COMMEMORATIVE COINS (5) FOR THE SECOND ANNIVERSARY OF THE REVOLUTION

			XF	**Unc**
18 (43)	5	Millièmes (Br) 1971. New state emblem (model of a secretary bird, Sagittarius serpentarius – Sagittariidae) between year dates. Legend. ℞ value between cotton blossoms. Legend	0.15	0.30

			XF	Unc
19 (44)	10	Millièmes (Br) 1971. Same type as No. 11	0.20	0.40
20 (45)	2	Piastres (Cu–Ni) 1971. Same type as No. 11	0.25	0.50
21 (46)	5	Piastres (Cu–Ni) 1971. Same type as No. 11	0.40	0.80
22 (47)	10	Piastres (Cu–Ni) 1971. Same type as No. 11	0.80	1.50

ISSUES FOR THE FAO COIN PLAN (2)

| 23 (48) | 5 | Millièmes (Br) 1972, 1973. New state emblem (model of a secretary bird. ℞ value, cotton, with inscription "Grow more food" | 0.25 | 0.50 |

24 (49)	50	Piastres (Cu–Ni) 1972. ℞ man ploughing with oxen, and inscription "Let us increase production"	4.00	5.00
25 (50)	5	Millièmes (Bra) 1975. Type similar to No. 18		4.00
26 (51)	10	Millièmes (Br) 1972. Type similar to No. 25 (scalloped)		4.00
27 (51a)	10	Millièmes (Bra) 1975. Type as No. 25 (scalloped)		4.00
28 (52)	2	Piastres (Cu–Ni) 1975. Type as No. 25		4.00
29 (53)	5	Piastres (Cu–Ni) 1975. Type as No. 25		6.00
30 (54)	10	Piastres (Cu–Ni) 1975. Type as No. 25		2.00

ISSUES FOR THE FAO COIN PLAN (5)

			XF	Unc
31 (58)	5	Millièmes (Bra) 1976. Coat of arms between ears. date. Rev. value between cotton	0.20	0.40
32 (59)	10	Milliémes (Bra) 1976. Type as No. 31 (scalloped)	0.25	0.50
33 (60)	2	Piastres (Cu-Ni) 1976. Type as No. 31	0.40	0.80
34 (61)	5	Piastres (Cu-Ni) 1976. Type as No. 31	0.55	1.10
35 (62)	10	Piastres (Cu-Ni) 1976. Type as No. 31	1.00	2.00

CONSERVATION COMMEMORATIVE (3)

			Unc	Proof
36 (55)	2½	Pounds (Ag) 1976	20.00	25.00
37 (56)	5	Pounds (Ag) 1976	35.00	45.00
38 (57)	100	Pounds (Au) 1976	550.00	700.00

20th ANNIVERSARY OF INDEPENDENCE (5)

			XF	Unc
A 39 (89)	5	Millièmes (Bra) 1976	-.-	-.-
39 (63)	10	Millièmes (Bra) 1976	0.20	0.45
40 (64)	2	Piastres (Cu-Ni) 1976	0.30	0.50
41 (65)	5	Piastres (Cu-Ni) 1976	0.50	0.90
42 (66)	10	Piastres (Cu-Ni) 1976	0.70	1.50

ESTABLISHMENT OF ARAB COOPERATIVE

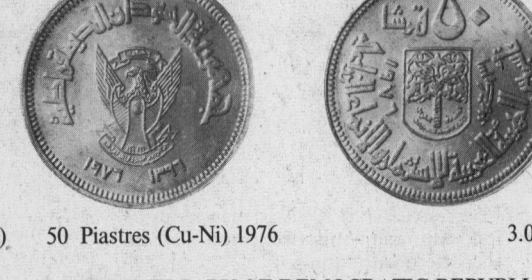

43 (67)	50 Piastres (Cu-Ni) 1976	3.00	4.00

8th ANNIVERSARY OF DEMOCRATIC REPUBLIC AND FOR THE FAO COIN PLAN

44 (68)	50 Piastres (Cu-Ni) 1977	3.00	4.00

COUNCIL OF ARAB ECONOMIC UNITY (2)

45 (86)	5 Piastres (Cu-Ni) 1978. Clasped hands	1.00	2.00
A 45 (90)	10 Piastres (Cu-Ni) 1978. Type as No. 45	-.-	-.-

Surinam
Suriname

Area: 55,143 sq. mi. Population: 420.000.
Surinam (Netherlands Guyana) was given the status of an autonomous territory in 1948 and self-government in 1950. Since 1954 Surinam has been an overseas territory of the Kingdom of the Netherlands. Full independence was achieved on Nov. 25, 1975.
Capital: Paramaribo.

100 Cent = 1 Surinam Gulden

WILHELMINA 1890-1948

			VF	XF
1 (36a)	1	Cent (Bra) 1943. Type as No. 11 of the Netherlands, but mintmark P (= Philadelphia)	2.50	5.00
A1 (34a)	5	Cent (Cu-Ni) 1943. Type as No. 13 of the Netherlands	4.50	7.50
2 (43a)	10	Cent (Ag) 1942. Type as No. 20 of the Netherlands, but mintmark P	4.00	7.50
3 (44a)	25	Cent (Ag) 1942. Type as No. 21 of the Netherlands, but mintmark P	7.50	12.50

JULIANA 1948-1975

			VF	XF
4 (36b)	1	Cent (Br) 1957, 1959. 1960. Type as No. 11 of the Netherlands	1.20	3.50

			VF	XF
5 (2)	1	Cent (Br) 1962, 1966, 1970, 1972. Coat of arms. Rev. value, date	0.15	0.25

			VF	XF
6 (3)	5 Cent (Ni-Bra) 1962, 1966, 1971–1972. Type similar to No. 5 (square)		0.15	0.30
7 (4)	10 Cent (Cu-Ni) 1962, 1966, 1971, 1972, 1974. Type as No. 5		0.20	0.40
8 (5)	25 Cent (Cu-Ni) 1962, 1966, 1972, 1974. Type as No. 5		0.50	1.00
9 (6)	1 Gulden (Ag) 1962, 1966. Juliana, Queen of the Netherlands:			
	a) 1962		5.00	9.00
	b) 1966		80.00	125.00

INDEPENDENCE

			XF	Unc
10 (2a)	1 Cent (Al) 1974–1983. Type as No. 5		0.05	0.10
11 (3a)	5 Cent (Al) 1976, 1978, 1979, 1980, 1982, 1983. Type as No. 6		0.10	0.20
12 (4)	10 Cent (Cu-Ni) 1976, 1978, 1979, 1982, 1983. Type as No. 7		0.15	0.30
13 (5)	25 Cent (Cu-Ni) 1976, 1979, 1982, 1983. Type as No. 8		0.40	0.65

1st ANNIVERSARY OF INDEPENDENCE (3)

			Unc	Proof
14 (7)	10 Gulden (Ag) 1975. Hand holding flag over map		10.00	20.00
15 (8)	25 Gulden (Ag) 1976. Type as No. 14		22.00	30.00
16 (9)	100 Gulden (Au) 1976. Type as No. 14		165.00	200.00

1st ANNIVERSARY OF REVOLUTION (2)

			Unc	Proof
17 (10)	25 Gulden (Ag) 1981. Monument, value. Rev. Popular uprising		27.50	45.00
18 (11)	200 Gulden (Au) 1981. Type as No. 17		150.00	200.00

10th ANNIVERSARY OF INDEPENDENCE AND 5th ANNIVERSARY OF REVOLUTION (2)

19	25 Gulden (Ag) 1985		35.00	
20	250 Gulden (An) 1985			300.00

Area: 6,704 sq. mi. Population: 650,000.

Belonging to the Ndwandwe group of the Zulus, the Swazi owe their name to Chief Mswazi, head of the government in 1839. Swaziland joined Transvaal in 1894, and became a British Protectorate in 1906. Swaziland attained the right of self-government in April 1967, and its independence on September 6, 1968.

Capital: Mbabane.

100 Cents = 1 Luhlanga, 25 Luhlanga = 1 Lilangeni;
since Sept. 6, 1974: 100 Cents = 1 Lilangeni (Plural: Emalangeni)

Swaziland belongs to the currency area of the South African Rand; the Luhlanga corresponds to the Rand.

SOBHUZA II 1921–1982
INDEPENDENCE COMMEMORATIVE (6)

		Proof
1	5 Cents (Ag) 1968. Sobhuza II (1899–1982), bust of the King. Rev. Swazi shield and spears (= state emblem), value in letters	5.00
2	10 Cents (Ag) 1968. Same type as No. 1	8.00
3	20 Cents (Ag) 1968. Same type as No. 1	15.00
4	50 Cents (Ag) 1968. Same type as No. 1	50.00

5	1 Luhlanga (Ag) 1968. Same type as No. 1	65.00
6	1 Lilangeni (Au) 1968. ℞ coat of arms with lion and elephant supporting shield	700.00

		XF	Unc
7 (1)	1 Cent (Br) 1974, 1979, 1982. Rev. Ananas	0.15	0.25

			XF	**Unc**
8 (2)	2 Cents (Br) 1974, 1979, 1982. Rev. Trees		0.15	0.30
9 (3)	5 Cents (Cu-Ni) 1974, 1975, 1979. Rev. Arum lily		0.25	0.50

			XF	Unc
10 (4)	10 Cents (Cu-Ni) 1974, 1979. Rev. Sugarcane		0.35	0.70
11 (5)	20 Cents (Cu-Ni) 1974, 1975, 1979. Rev. Elephant's head		0.50	1.00
12 (6)	50 Cents (Cu-Ni) 1974, 1975, 1979, 1981. Rev. Arms		1.00	2.00
13 (7)	1 Lilangeni (Cu-Ni) 1974, 1979. Rev. Mother and child		2.00	4.00

75th ANNIVERSARY OF THE BIRTH OF KING SOBHUZA II
1st ISSUE (7)

			Proof
14	5 Emalangeni (Ag) 1974		25.00
15	7½ Emalangeni (Ag) 1974		40.00
16	15 Emalangeni (Ag) 1974		75.00
17 (8)	5 Emalangeni (Au) 1974		125.00
18 (9)	10 Emalangeni (Au) 1974		225.00
19 (10)	20 Emalangeni (Au) 1974		400.00
20 (11)	25 Emalangeni (Au) 1974		600.00

75th ANNIVERSARY OF THE BIRTH OF KING SOBHUZA II
2nd ISSUE (3)

		Unc	Proof
21	10 Emalangeni (Ag) 1975	25.00	30.00
22 (12)	50 Emalangeni (Au) 1975	75.00	100.00
23	100 Emalangeni (Au) 1975	150.00	200.00

FOR THE FAO COIN PLAN (3)

			XF	Unc
24 (13)	1 Cent (Br) 1975. Type as No. 7, but inscription FOOD FOR ALL		0.15	0.30
25 (14)	2 Cents (Br) 1975. Type as No. 8, but inscription INCREASE EXPORTS		0.20	0.40
26 (15)	10 Cents (Cu-Ni) 1975. Type as No. 10, but inscription FOOD FOR ALL		0.35	0.70

INTERNATIONAL WOMEN'S YEAR 1975

		XF	Proof
27 (16)	1 Lilangeni (Cu-Ni) 1975	3.00	5.00

FOR THE COIN PLAN

28 (17)	1 Lilangeni (Cu-Ni) 1976	3.00	5.00

SILVER JUBILEE OF HER MAJESTY QUEEN ELIZABETH II

29	5 Emalangeni (Au) 1978. Sobhuza II. Rev. Elizabeth II; .999 gold, 31.1 g	600.00

80th ANNIVERSARY OF THE BIRTH OF KING SOBHUZA II (2)

		Unc	Proof
30	1 Lilangeni (Au) 1979	275.00	300.00
31	2 Emalangeni (Au) 1979	550.00	600.00

WORLD FOOD DAY 1981 (2)

32 (21)	20 Cents (Cu-Ni) 1981	1.50	
33 (22)	1 Lilangeni (Cu-Ni) 1981:		
	a) (Ag)	15.00	20.00
	b) (Cu-Ni)	4.00	

DIAMOND JUBILEE OF KING SOBHUZA II (3)

34 (18)	2 Emalangeni 1981. Rev. Orchid blossoms:		
	a) (Ag)		35.00
	b) (Cu-Ni)	8.00	
35 (19)	25 Emalangeni (Ag) 1981. Rev. Parrot	50.00	65.00
36 (20)	250 Emalangeni (Au) 1981. Rev. Elephant	400.00	450.00

MSWATI III since 1986
ACCESSION OF KING MSWATI III (MAKHOSETIVE) (2)

37	25 Emalangeni (Ag) 1986. Queen Mother Mtombi. Rev. Prince Makhosetive Dlamini (*1967), Crown Prince since 1982, King since 1986		45.00
38	250 Emalangeni (Au) 1986. Type as No. 37	400.00	450.00

		XF	Unc
39	1 Cent (Br) 1986. Mswati III. Rev. Ananas	0.15	0.25

No. 40 omitted.

		XF	Unc
41	5 Cents (Cu-Ni) 1986. Rev. Arum lily	0.25	0.50
42	10 Cents (Cu-Ni) 1986. Rev. Sugar-cane	0.35	0.70
43	20 Cents (Cu-Ni) 1986. Rev. Elephant's head	0.50	1.00
44	50 Cents (Cu-Ni) 1986. Rev. Arms	1.00	2.00
45	1 Lilangeni (Ni-Bra) 1986. Rev. Queen Mother Mtombi ans Mswati as a boy	2.00	4.00

Schweden   **Sweden**   **Suède**

Sverige

Area: 173,629 sq. mi. Population: 8,370,000.
Kingdom on the eastern part of the peninsula of Scandinavia.
Capital: Stockholm.

100 Öre = 1 Krona

OSKAR II 1872-1907

			VF	XF
1 (14)	1	Öre (Br) 1877–1905. Crowned monogram. ℞ value and date, surrounded by three crowns	4.50	9.00
2 (15)	2	Öre (Br) 1877–1905	4.50	9.00
3 (16)	5	Öre (Br) 1889–1905	5.00	10.00
4 (27)	10	Öre (Ag) 1880–1904. ℞ value, date	5.00	10.00
5 (28)	25	Öre (Ag) 1880–1905	7.50	15.00
6 (29)	1	Krona (Ag) 1890–1904. Oskar II, (1829–1907), King of Norway 1872–1905 (abdicated), King of Sweden (1872–1907). ℞ crowned arms	10.00	20.00
7 (30)	2	Kronor (Ag) 1890–1904	15.00	35.00
8 (24a)	5	Kronor (Au) 1901. Oskar II, head right. ℞ value and crowns in wreath	100.00	120.00
9 (25b)	10	Kronor (Au) 1901	125.00	150.00

10 (26b)	20	Kronor (Au) 1900–1902	225.00	250.00
11 (32)	1	Öre (Br) 1906–1907. Legend SVERIGES VAL	2.50	5.00
12 (33)	2	Öre (Br) 1906–1907. Same type as No. 11	3.00	6.00

		VF	XF
13 (34)	5 Öre (Br) 1906–1907. Same type as No. 11	2.60	5.50
14 (35)	10 Öre (Ag) 1907. Crowned monogram, three crowns, legends SVERIGES VAL. ℞ value in wreath	3.50	6.50
15 (36)	25 Öre (Ag) 1907. Same type as No. 14	4.00	8.00
16 (37)	50 Öre (Ag) 1906–1907. Same type as No. 14	6.00	12.00
17 (38)	1 Krona (Ag) 1906–1907. Oskar II, head left. ℞ crowned arms	10.00	20.00
18 (39)	2 Kronor (Ag) 1906–1907	20.00	40.00

COMMEMORATIVE ISSUE FOR THE GOLDEN WEDDING ANNIVERSARY

		VF	XF
19 (40)	2 Kronor (Ag) 1907. Oskar II, and Queen Sofia. ℞ crowned arms	18.00	25.00

GUSTAF V 1907–1950

		VF	XF
20 (44)	1 Öre (Br) 1909–1950. Crowned monogram. ℞ three crowns, value	0.60	1.20
21 (45)	2 Öre (Br) 1909–1950	0.60	1.20

		VF	XF
22 (46)	5 Öre (Br) 1909–1950	1.20	1.60
23 (47)	10 Öre (Ag) 1909–1942. Crowned arms. ℞ value	1.20	2.50
24 (48)	25 Öre (Ag) 1910–1941. ℞ value in wreath	2.50	4.00

		VF	XF
25 (49)	50 Öre (Ag) 1911–1939. ℞ value in wreath	4.00	6.50

		VF	XF
26 (50)	1 Krona (Ag) 1910–1942	4.00	6.50
27 (51)	2 Kronor (Ag) 1910–1940	7.00	12.00
28 (52)	1 Öre (Fe) 1917–1919. Same type as No. 20	5.00	8.00
29 (53)	2 Öre (Fe) 1917–1919. Same type as No. 21	10.50	16.00
30 (54)	5 Öre (Fe) 1917–1919. Same type as No. 22	25.00	42.00
31 (55)	10 Öre (Ni–Br) 1920–1947. Crowned monogram. ℞ value	0.80	1.50
32 (56)	25 Öre (Ni–Br) 1921–1947. Rev. value surrounded by ears of wheat	1.25	2.50
33 (57)	50 Öre (Ni-Br) 1920-1947	1.60	3.00

		VF	XF
34 (62)	5 Kronor (Au) 1920. Gustav V (1858–1950), head right. ℞ value, three crowns, branches	110.00	160.00
35 (63)	20 Kronor (Au) 1925. ℞ crowned coat of arms, date	650.00	800.00

COMMEMORATIVE ISSUE FOR THE
400th ANNIVERSARY OF THE WAR OF LIBERATION
LED BY GUSTAF VASA

		VF	XF
36 (58)	2 Kronor (Ag) 1921. Gustaf Erikson Vasa (1496–1560), regent from 1521 to 1523, King from 1523 to 1560. ℞ crowned arms	17.50	25.00

Values are given for each coin in U.S. Dollars and reference to Yeoman-numbers.

COMMEMORATIVE ISSUE FOR THE 300th ANNIVERSARY
OF THE DEATH OF GUSTAF II ADOLF

			VF	**XF**
37 (59)	2 Kronor (Ag) 1932. Gustaf II Adolf (1594–1632), head with wreath, right. ℞ memorial legend on tablet		15.00	20.00

COMMEMORATIVE ISSUE FOR THE
500th ANNIVERSARY OF THE SWEDISH RIKSDAG

38 (60)	5 Kronor (Ag) 1935. Gustaf V, head left. ℞ coat of arms		16.00	22.00

COMMEMORATIVE ISSUE FOR THE 300th ANNIVERSARY
OF THE FOUNDING OF THE COLONY NEW SWEDEN
ON THE DELAWARE RIVER, BY PETER MINUIT
(MINNEWIT)

39 (61)	2 Kronor (Ag) 1938. Gustaf V, head left. ℞ Calmare Nyckel, sailing vessel of the emigrants; crown		8.50	12.50
40 (69)	1 Öre (Fe) 1942–1950. Crowned monogram. ℞ three crowns, value		1.00	2.00
41 (70)	2 Öre (Fe) 1942–1950		1.50	3.00
42 (71)	5 Öre (Fe) 1942–1950		3.00	6.00
43 (64)	10 Öre (Ag) 1942–1950. Crown. ℞ value		1.50	2.50
44 (65)	25 Öre (Ag) 1942–1950		2.00	3.50
45 (66)	50 Öre (Ag) 1943–1950		3.00	4.50
46 (67)	1 Krona (Ag) 1942–1950. Gustaf V, head left. ℞ crowned arms		4.00	7.00
47 (68)	2 Kronor (Ag) 1942–1950		5.00	6.50

GUSTAF VI ADOLF 1950–1973

48 (72)	1 Öre (Br) 1952–1971. Crown above king's name. ℞ value		0.15	0.25
49 (73)	2 Öre (Br) 1952–1971		0.15	0.25

			VF	XF
50 (74)	5 Öre (Br) 1952–1971		0.20	0.40
51 (75)	10 Öre (Ag) 1952–1962. Crown. ℞ value		0.80	1.60
52 (76)	25 Öre (Ag) 1952–1961		1.20	2.00

		VF	XF
53 (77)	50 Öre (Ag) 1952–1961	1.80	3.50
54 (78)	1 Krona (Ag) 1952–1968. Gustaf VI Adolf, head left. ℞ crowned arms	1.80	3.50

		VF	XF
55 (79)	2 Kronor (Ag) 1952–1967	3.60	6.00
56 (80)	5 Kronor (Ag) 1954–1955, 1971	5.50	11.00

COMMEMORATIVE ISSUE FOR THE
70th BIRTHDAY OF THE KING

57 (81)	5 Kronor (Ag) 1952. Gustaf VI, Adolf (1882–1973), head left. ℞ crowned monogram	**VF**	**XF**
		35.00	60.00

COMMEMORATIVE ISSUE FOR THE 150th ANNIVERSARY OF THE SWEDISH CONSTITUTION REFORM

58 (82)	5 Kronor (Ag) 1959. Gustaf VI Adolf. ℞ constitutionalists, book with constitution on platform with state emblem	8.50	12.00

COMMEMORATIVE ISSUE FOR THE 80th BIRTHDAY OF THE KING

59 (86)	5 Kronor (Ag) 1962. Gustaf VI Adolf (1882–1973), head left. Rev. Pallas Athena with Bird of Wisdom, the owl (little owl ˈ= Athene noctua – Strigidae), symbolic of the king's archeologic and scientific interests	45.00	65.00
60 (83)	10 Öre (Cu–Ni) 1962–1973. Crown above monogram. ℞ value	0.10	0.20
61 (84)	25 Öre (Cu–Ni) 1962–1973	0.15	0.30

			VF	XF
62 (85)	50 Öre (Cu–Ni) 1962–1973	0.30	0.60
63 (78a)	1 Krona (Cu–Ni) 1968–1973. Same type as No. 54	0.40	0.75
64 (79a)	2 Kronor (Cu–Ni) 1968–1971. Same type as No. 55	1.00	2.00

COMMEMORATIVE ISSUE FOR THE 100th ANNIVERSARY OF THE CONSTITUTION REFORM AND THE INTRODUCTION OF THE TWO-CHAMBER LEGISLATURE

| **65** (87) | 5 Kronor (Ag) 1966. Gustaf VI Adolf. ℞ tablet with memorial legend, surrounded by laurel branches | 4.50 | 6.00 |

| **66** (88) | 5 Öre (Br) 1972, 1973. Three crowns, name of country. ℞ value, date | 0.12 | 0.25 |

| **67** (89) | 5 Kronor (Cu–Ni) 1972. Gustaf VI Adolf. ℞ crowned coat of arms, motto, value | 1.50 | 2.50 |

			VF	XF
68 (90)	10 Kronor (Ag) 1972		7.00	12.00

CARL XVI GUSTAF since 1973

CONSTITUTIONAL REFORM

			XF	Unc
69 (97)	50 Kronor (Ag) 1975. Three crowns, value Rev. raised hands, symbolic for the consent			30.00

70 (91)	5 Öre (Al-Br) 1976-. Crowned monogram, divided date. Rev. value, country name		0.12	0.20
71 (92)	10 Öre (Cu-Ni) 1976-		0.12	0.20
72 (93)	25 Öre (Cu-Ni) 1976-		0.15	0.25
73 (94)	50 Öre (Cu-Ni) 1976-		0.25	0.40
74 (95)	1 Krona (Cu-Ni) 1976-. Head left of the King, inscription CARL XVI GUSTAF SVERIGE, date. Rev. crowned coat of arms, inscription FÖR SVERIGE I TIDEN, value		0.40	0.60
75 (96)	5 Kronor (Cu-Ni) 1976-. Crowned monogram, curved SVERIGE and date. Rev. value		1.25	2.50

FOR THE WEDDING OF KING CARL XVI GUSTAV ON JUNE 6, 1976

76 (97)	50 Kronor (Ag) 1976. King Carl XVI Gustav and Queen Silvia. Rev. National arms, value			15.00

SWEDISH ROYAL SUCCESSION LAW

77 (99) 200 Kronor (Ag) 1980. Head left. Rev. Inscription, value ... **Unc** 40.00

10th ANNIVERSARY OF REIGN

78 (100) 200 Kronor (Ag) 1983. Head left. Rev. National arms, date, value ... 40.00

PARLIAMENT

79 (101) 100 Kronor (Ag) 1983 ... 18.00

STOCKHOLM CONFERENCE

		Unc
80 (102)	100 Kronor (Ag) 1984	18.00

INTERNATIONAL YOUTH YEAR

81 (103)	100 Kronor (Ag) 1985	18.00

EUROPEAN MUSIC YEAR

82 (104)	100 Kronor (Ag) 1985	18.00

INTERNATIONAL YEAR OF THE FOREST

83 (105)	100 Kronor (Ag) 1985	18.00

350th ANNIVERSARY OF THE FOUNDING OF THE COLONY NEW SWEDEN ON THE DELAWARE RIVER (2)

84	100 Kronor (Ag) 1988; .925 silver, 16 g	–.–
85	1000 Kronor (Au) 1988; .900 gold, 5.8 g	–.–

Schweiz   # Switzerland   **Suisse**
Helvetia

Area: 16,500 sq. mi. Population: 6,467,000.
The dissociation from the German Nation within the Holy Roman
Empire which had already taken place in 1499 was only recognized in
1648. The original cantons of Uri, Schwyz and Unterwalden constituted
the nucleus of an independent Switzerland. Strict neutrality is maintained, enabling numerous international organizations to set up their
headquarters there.
Capital: Berne.

100 Rappen (Centimes) = 1 Franken (Franc)

The Cantons of Switzerland

Aargau   Appenzell*   Basel-Land   Basel-Stadt   Bern   Fribourg

Genf   Glarus   Graubünden   Jura   Luzern   Neuenburg   Nidwalden

Obwalden   St. Gallen   Schaffhausen   Schwyz   Solothurn   Thurgau

Ticino   Uri   Valais   Vaud   Zug   Zürich

* Appenzell-Ausserrhoden: In the case of Appenzell-Innerrhoden and
of the whole canton the initials VR are omitted.

			VF	**XF**
1 (18)	1	Rappen (Br) 1850–1941. Swiss cross on shield, the whole within wreath. ℞ value in wreath		
		a) 1850–1895, 1897–1938, 1940, 1941	0.50	1.00
		b) 1896 (only 36 pieces struck)	–.–	–.–
		c) 1939	12.00	20.00
2 (19)	2	Rappen (Br) 1850–1941		
		a) 1850–1893, 1897–1941	0.50	1.00
		b) 1896 (only 20 pieces struck)	–.–	–.–
3 (20)	5	Rappen (Bi) 1850–1877		
		a) 1850–1851, 1872–1874, 1876–1877	12.00	20.00
		b) 1850, without mint mark	450.00	800.00
		c) 1851, mint mark BB	320.00	600.00
4 (21)	10	Rappen (Bi) 1850–1876		
		a) 1850–1851, 1871, 1873, 1876	300.00	550.00
		b) 1875	16.50	30.00
5 (22)	20	Rappen (Bi) 1850–1859	15.00	27.50
6 (26)	½	Franken (Ag) 1850, 1851. Seated figure of Helvetia. ℞ value within wreath	90.00	165.00
7 (27)	1	Franken (Ag) 1850–1861. Type as No. 6:		
		a) 1850, 1851, 1861	55.00	90.00
		b) 1857 (only 526 pieces struck)	–.–	–.–
		c) 1860	300.00	500.00
8 (28)	2	Franken (Ag) 1850–1863. Type as No. 6:		
		a) 1850, 1863	260.00	425.00
		b) 1857 (only 622 pieces struck)	–.–	–.–
		c) 1860, 1862	100.00	165.00

9 (29)	5	Franken (Ag) 1850–1874. Type as No. 6:		
		a) 1850–1874	130.00	225.00
		b) 1873	750.00	1250.00
10 (23)	5	Rappen 1879–. Female head right. ℞ value within wreath		
		a) (Cu–Ni) 1879, 1887, 1889	25.00	55.00
		b) (Cu–Ni) 1880–1905	8.00	20.00
		c) (Cu–Ni) 1896 (only 16 pieces struck)	–.–	–.–

		VF	XF
d) (Cu-Ni) 1906–1931, 1940, 1942– 1980		0.05	0.15
e) (Ni) 1932–1939, 1941		0.30	1.00
f) (Al-Br) 1981–		0.05	0.10

11 (24) 10 Rappen 1879–. Type as No. 10:

		VF	XF
a) (Cu–Ni) 1879		18.00	35.00
b) (Cu-Ni) 1880–1899		5.00	20.00
c) (Cu-Ni) 1896 (only 16 pieces struck)		–.–	–.–
d) (Cu-Ni) 1900–1931, 1940–		0.05	0.10
e) (Ni) 1932–1939		0.50	1.25

12 (25) 20 Rappen 1881–. Type as No. 10:

		VF	XF
a) (Ni) 1881–1938		0.25	0.50
b) (Cu-Ni) 1939–		0.10	0.20

13 (30) ½ Franken (Ag) 1875–1967. Standing figure of Helvetia. ℞ value within wreath:

		VF	XF
a) 1875–1894		30.00	65.00
b) 1896 (only 28 pieces struck)		–.–	–.–
c) 1898–1967		1.50	2.00
d) 1901		70.00	125.00

14 (31) 1 Franken (Ag) 1875–1967. Type as No. 13:

		VF	XF
a) 1875–1880		55.00	100.00
b) 1886–1901		18.00	45.00
c) 1896 (only 28 pieces struck)		–.–	–.–
d) 1903–1967		2.00	3.00

15 (32)   2 Franken (Ag) 1874–1967. Type as
No. 13:

		VF	**XF**
a) 1874–1894		40.00	115.00
b) 1896 (only 20 pieces struck)		–.–	–.–
c) 1901		650.00	1000.00
d) 1903–1967		3.50	6.50

16 (33)   5 Franken (Ag) 1888–1916. Female head
left. ℞ Swiss cross on shield, above
with star, value, the whole within
wreath:

a) 1888, 1900, 1916	500.00	1100.00
b) 1889-1892, 1904, 1907-1909	110.00	260.00
c) 1894, 1895	275.00	600.00
d) 1896 (only 2000 pieces struck)	–.–	–.–
e) 1912	900.00	1600.00

17 (40)   20 Franken (Au) 1883–1896. Female head
left. ℞ Swiss cross on shield, above
with star, value, the whole within
wreath:

	VF	XF
a) 1883–1896	110.00	125.00
b) 1888	6000.00	8500.00

18 (41) 20 Franken (Au) 1897–1949. Female bust left of "Vreneli". ℞ Swiss cross on shield, value, date:

	VF	XF
a) 1897–1949	90.00	110.00
b) 1926	150.00	200.00

19 (42) 10 Franken (Au) 1911–1922

	VF	XF
a) 1911	165.00	250.00
b) 1912–1922	100.00	125.00

20 (43) 100 Franken (Au) 1925. Type as No. 19 — 6000.00 | 8500.00

21 (23b) 5 Rappen (Bra) 1918. Type as No. 10 — 10.00 | 20.00

22 (24b) 10 Rappen (Bra) 1918–1919. Type as No. 11

	VF	XF
a) 1918	20.00	30.00
b) 1919	45.00	90.00

23 (34) 5 Franken (Ag) 1922, 1923. Bust of shepherd to right. ℞ Swiss cross on shield, value "5 Fr.", date. Diameter: 37 mm — 50.00 | 85.00

24 (34a) 5 Franken (Ag) 1924–1928. Type as No. 23, but value "5 FR":

	VF	XF
a) 1924	200.00	420.00
b) 1925, 1926	80.00	150.00
c) 1928	2500.00	4500.00

25 (36) 5 Franken (Ag) 1931–1967, 1969. Type as No. 24, but diameter: 31 mm:

	VF	XF
a) 1931–1951	6.00	10.00
b) 1952	40.00	75.00
c) 1953–1967, 1969	3.00	6.00

COMMEMORATIVE MEDALS (2)
FOR THE RIFLEMENS MEETING IN FRIBOURG

			VF	XF
26 (44)	5 Franken (Ag) 1934. Standing soldier. Ŗ crowned arms within wreath		40.00	70.00
27 (45)	100 Franken (Au) 1934		1750.00	2200.00

COMMEMORATIVE ISSUE FOR
THE CONFEDERATION ARMAMENT FUND

		VF	XF
28 (46)	5 Franken (Ag) 1936. Kneeling female figure with sword and dove held level. Ŗ steel helmet above inscription within square	25.00	45.00

COMMEMORATIVE MEDALS (2)
FOR THE RIFLEMENS MEETING IN LUCERNE

29 (47)   5 Franken (Ag) 1939. Kneeling figure r.

			VF	XF
	shooting. ℞ legend reading EINER FÜR ALLE, ALLE FÜR EINEN (One for all, all for one)		40.00	70.00
30 (48)	100 Franken (Au) 1939		650.00	900.00

COMMEMORATIVE ISSUE FOR THE 600th ANNIVERSARY OF THE BATTLE OF LAUPEN

31 (49)	5 Franken (Ag) 1939. Male figure facing. ℞ Swiss cross	350.00	600.00

COMMEMORATIVE MEDAL FOR THE SWISS NATIONAL EXPOSITION IN ZÜRICH

32 (50)	5 Franken (Ag) 1939. Agricultural scene, below which hands clasped. ℞ national arms over inscription	85.00	135.00

COMMEMORATIVE ISSUE FOR THE 650th ANNIVERSARY OF THE CONFEDERATION

33 (51)   5 Franken (Ag) 1941. Oath scene at the

				VF	XF
		Rütli. Three standing figures representing the original cantons of Uri, Schwyz and Unterwalden. ℞ inscription		45.00	80.00
34 (18a)	1	Rappen (Sn) 1942–1946. Type as No. 1		0.50	1.00
35 (19a)	2	Rappen (Sn) 1942–1946. Type as No. 2			
			a) 1942–1945	1.00	1.80
			b) 1946	10.00	18.00

COMMEMORATIVE ISSUE FOR THE 500th ANNIVERSARY OF THE BATTLE OF ST. JAKOB AN DER BIRS

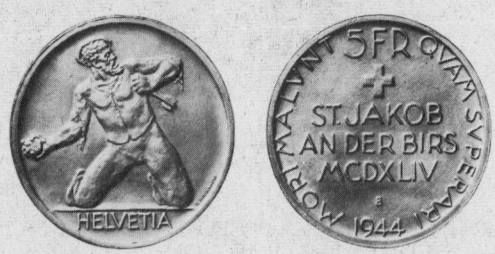

36 (52)	5	Franken (Ag) 1944. Warrior fighting. ℞ inscription	40.00	75.00

COMMEMORATIVE ISSUE FOR THE CENTENNIAL OF THE SWISS CONFEDERATION

37 (53)	5	Franken (Ag) 1948. Group representing mother and child. ℞ inscription, Swiss cross	15.00	25.00
38	25	Franken (Au) 1955–1959. William Tell holding crossbow. ℞ value	–.–	–.–
39	50	Franken (Au) 1955–1959. Oath scene at the Rütli. Three standing figures representing the original cantons of Uri, Schwyz and Unterwalden. ℞ value	–.–	–.–

Coins Nos. 32 and 33 have not yet been issued.

40 (54)	1	Rappen (Br) 1948–. Swiss cross. ℞ value and ear of corn	0.02	0.04

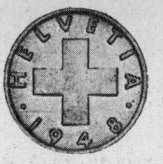 

		VF	XF
41 (55)	2 Rappen (Br) 1948–1974	0.02	0.04

COMMEMORATIVE ISSUE FOR THE CENTENARY OF THE RED CROSS

			VF	XF
42 (56)	5 Franken (Ag) 1963. Nurse standing and patient on stretcher, in form of cross. R value		12.50	20.00
43 (30a)	½ Franken (Cu-Ni) 1968–1982. As No. 13		0.25	0.40
44 (31a)	1 Franken (Cu-Ni) 1968–1982. As No. 14		0.45	0.65
45 (32a)	2 Franken (Cu-Ni) 1968–1982. As No. 15		0.80	1.20
46 (36a)	5 Franken (Cu-Ni) 1968, 1970–. As No. 25		2.20	2.60

COMMEMORATIVE ISSUE FOR THE 100th ANNIVERSARY OF THE REVISION OF THE CONSTITUTION
(29th May 1874)

		Unc	Proof
47 (57)	5 Franken (Cu-Ni) 1974	5.00	15.00

EUROPEAN MONUMENT PROTECTION YEAR

		Unc	Proof
48 (58)	5 Franken (Cu-Ni) 1975	5.00	20.00

500th ANNIVERSARY OF THE BATTLE OF MURTEN

| **49** (59) | 5 Franken (Cu-Ni) 1976 | 5.00 | 15.00 |

150th ANNIVERSARY OF THE DEATH OF J. H. PESTALOZZI

| **50** (60) | 5 Franken (Cu-Ni) 1977 | 6.00 | 30.00 |

150th ANNIVERSARY OF THE BIRTH OF HENRY DUNANT

| **51** (61) | 5 Franken (Cu-Ni) 1978 | 5.00 | 17.50 |

100th ANNIVERSARY OF THE BIRTH OF ALBERT EINSTEIN (2)

| **52** (62) | 5 Franken (Cu-Ni) 1979. Portrait | 7.50 | 100.00 |
| **53** (63) | 5 Franken (Cu-Ni) 1979. Formula | 6.00 | 50.00 |

HODLER COMMEMORATIVE

| **54** (64) | 5 Franken (Cu-Ni) 1980. Ferdinand Hodler (1853–1918), painter | 5.00 | 25.00 |

STANS CONVENTION OF 1481

| **55** (65) | 5 Franken (Cu-Ni) 1981 | 5.00 | 20.00 |

100th ANNIVERSARY OF GOTTHARD RAILWAY

			Unc	Proof
56 (66)	5 Franken (Cu-Ni) 1982		5.00	25.00
57	½ Franken (Cu-Ni) 1983–. Type as No.		**XF**	**Unc**
	13, but 23 stars instead of 22 stars		0.30	0.40
58	1 Franken (Cu-Ni) 1983–. Type as No. 57		0.50	0.60
59	2 Franken (Cu-Ni) 1983–. Type as No. 57		0.90	1.00

100th ANNIVERSARY OF THE BIRTH OF E. ANSERMET

		Unc	Proof
60 (67)	5 Franken (Cu-Ni) 1983. Ernest Anser-met (1883–1969), composer	5.00	20.00

100th ANNIVERSARY OF THE BIRTH OF A. PICCARD

		Unc	Proof
61	5 Franken (Cu-Ni) 1984. Auguste Piccard (1884–1962), physicist: Balloon and submarine	5.00	20.00

EUROPEAN MUSIC YEAR

62	5 Franken (Cu-Ni) 1985	5.00	20.00

600th ANNIVERSARY OF THE BATTLE NEAR SEMPACH

63	5 Franken (Cu-Ni) 1986	5.00	20.00

100th ANNIVERSARY OF THE BIRTH OF LE CORBUSIER

64	5 Franken (Cu-Ni) 1987. Le Corbusier (1887–1965), architect and sculptor	5.00	20.00

			Unc	Proof
SH 1	50	Franken (Ag) 1984. William Tell and son. Rev. figure of Helvetia		
			50.00	225.00
SH 2	1000	Franken (Au) 1984. Type as No. SH 1		900.00

SH 3	50	Franken (Ag) 1985. Crossbowman. Rev. Crossed rifles		
			50.00	
SH 4	1000	Franken (Au) 1985. Type as No. SH 3		850.00

Syrien   **Syria**   **Syrie**

Area: 12,234 sq. mi. Population: 10,200,000.
Following the collapse of the Ottoman Empire, Syria became a French Mandate, and later on, in 1944, independent. From 1958 to 1961 Syria belonged to the United Arab Republic.
Capital: Damascus.

100 Piastres = 1 Lira (£)

SYRIAN STATE 1920-1944

			VF	XF
1 (1)	½	Piastre (Cu–Ni) 1921. Value within wreath. ℞ value	2.50	4.00
2 (2)	2	Piastres (Al–Br) 1926	3.50	6.00
3 (3)	5	Piastres (Al–Br) 1926–1940	1.50	2.50
4 (4)	½	Piastre (Ni–Bra) 1935–1936	1.50	2.50
5 (5)	1	Piastre:		
		a) (Ni–Bra) 1929–1936	1.20	2.00
		b) (Sn) 1940	1.20	2.00
6 (6)	2½	Piastres (Al–Br) 1940	2.50	4.00
7 (7)	10	Piastres (Ag) 1929. Rosette design	6.00	11.00
8 (8)	25	Piastres (Ag) 1929–1938	11.00	16.00

9 (9)	50	Piastres (Ag) 1929–1937	16.00	20.00
10 (10)	1	Piastre (Bra) undated (1942)	2.50	4.00
11 (11)	2½	Piastres (Al) undated (1943)	2.50	4.00

SYRIAN REPUBLIC 1944-1958

12 (12)	2½	Piastres (Cu–Ni) 1948–1956. Coat of arms. ℞ value	0.40	0.80
13 (13)	5	Piastres (Cu–Ni) 1948–1956	0.40	0.80
14 (14)	10	Piastres (Cu–Ni) 1948–1956	0.40	0.80
15 (15)	25	Piastres (Ag) 1947	2.60	4.50
16 (16)	50	Piastres (Ag) 1947	3.50	6.50

				VF	XF
17 (17)	1	Lira (Ag) 1950		6.50	11.00
18 (18)	½	£ (Au) 1950. Coat of arms. ℞ legend in quadrangle		85.00	110.00
19 (19)	1	£ (Au) 1950		110.00	150.00

UNITED ARAB REPUBLIC 1958–1961

			VF	XF
20 (21)	2½	Piastres (Al–Br) 1960. New coat of arms. ℞ value	0.20	0.40
21 (22)	5	Piastres (Al–Br) 1960	0.30	0.60
22 (23)	10	Piastres (Al–Br) 1960	0.40	0.80
23 (A19)	25	Piastres (Ag) 1958. ℞ value and ears of wheat, surrounded by cog-wheel	1.50	4.00
24 (B19)	50	Piastres (Ag) 1958	2.50	6.50

COMMEMORATIVE ISSUE FOR THE FOUNDING OF THE UNITED ARAB REPUBLIC ON MARCH 1, 1958

			VF	XF
25 (20)	50	Piastres (Ag) 1959. Coat of arms. ℞ value, date, and commemorative legend	5.00	10.00

SYRIAN ARAB REPUBLIC since 1961

			VF	XF
26 (24)	2½	Piastres (Al-Br) 1962, 1965. Coat of arms of the Republic. Rev. value	0.10	0.20
27 (25)	5	Piastres (Al-Br) 1962, 1965	0.15	0.25
28 (26)	10	Piastres (Al-Br) 1962, 1965	0.30	0.45
29 (27)	25	Piastres (Ni) 1968	0.40	0.60
30 (28)	50	Piastres (Ni) 1968	0.60	0.90
31 (29)	1	Lira (Ni) 1968, 1971	1.00	1.40

			XF	Unc
32 (31)	5	Piastres (Bra) 1971. With design of olives and wheat and inscription "Food for All"	0.25	0.40

33 (30)	1	Lira (Ni) 1968. Coat of arms. R̷ pair of hands holding sign reading "Campaign against Hunger"; above five ears of wheat	1.20	2.00

COMMEMORATIVE ISSUES (3) FOR THE
25th ANNIVERSARY OF THE BAATH PARTY

34 (32)	25	Piastres (Ni) 1972. New coat of arms (without stars in the breast-shield), date. Rev. torch, value	0.40	0.60
35 (33)	50	Piastres (Ni) 1972. Type similar to No. 34	0.60	0.80
36 (34)	1	Lira (Ni) 1972. Type similar to No. 34	1.00	1.50
37 (35)	2½	Piastres (Bra) 1973. Type similar to No. 26 (without stars in the breast-shield)	0.10	0.15
38 (36)	5	Piastres (Al-Br) 1974. Type similar to No. 27 (without stars in the breast-shield)	0.12	0.20
39 (37)	10	Piastres (Al-Br) 1974. Type similar to No. 28 (without stars in the breast-shield)	0.25	0.40

					XF	Unc
40 (38)	25	Piastres (Ni) 1974. Type similar to No. 29 (without stars in the breast-shield)			0.35	0.50
41 (39)	50	Piastres (Ni) 1974. Type similar to No. 30 (without stars in the breast-shield)			0.50	0.75
42 (40)	1	Lira (Ni) 1974. Type similar to No. 31 (without stars in the breast-shield)			0.80	1.20

FOR THE FAO COIN PLAN (5)

43 (41)	5	Piastres (Bra) 1976. Rev. Euphrates Dam	0.10	0.15
44 (42)	10	Piastres (Bra) 1976. Type as No. 43	0.15	0.25
45 (43)	25	Piastres (Ni) 1976. Type as No. 43	0.20	0.40
46 (44)	50	Piastres (Ni) 1976. Type as No.43	0.30	0.60
47 (45)	1	Lira (Ni) 1976. Type as No. 43	0.40	0.80

RE-ELECTION OF HAFEZ AL-ASAD

48 (46)	1	Lira (Ni) 1978. Coat of arms. Rev. Portrait	1.00	1.50
49 (25a)	5	Piastres (Bra) 1979	0.15	0.25
50 (26a)	10	Piastres (Bra) 1979	0.15	0.25
51 (47)	25	Piastres (Ni) 1979	0.25	0.35

52 (48)	50	Piastres (Ni) 1979	0.40	0.55
53 (49)	1	Lira (Ni) 1979	0.60	0.80

Taiwan   # Taiwan   **Formose**
Nationalist China

Area: 13,890 sq. mi. Population: 18,900,000.

From 1895 to 1942 Taiwan came under a governor general as a Japanese outlying possession. Since Taiwan had only temporarily been a part of the Japanese state, the return of the country to China took place in 1945. The Kuomintang government under Chiang Kai-shek retreated to the island in 1949 before the troops of Mao Tse-tung. On March 1, 1950 the Chinese Nationalist Republic was proclaimed.
Capital: Taipeh.

10 Cents = 1 Chiao, 100 Cents = 1 Taiwan Dollar

			VF	XF
1 (531)	1 Chiao (Br) 1949. Chiang Kai-shek (1886–1975), President. ℞ map of Formosa		0.30	0.50
2 (533)	1 Chiao (Al) 1955		0.15	0.25

3 (534)	2 Chiao (Al) 1950		0.20	0.40
4 (532)	5 Chiao (Ag) 1949		3.00	6.00
5 (535)	5 Chiao (Bra) 1954		0.20	0.40
6 (536)	1 Dollar (Ag) 1960. Plum blossom (Prunus sp. – Rosaceae). ℞ orchid (Dendrobium sp. – Orchidaceae)		0.50	0.90

COMMEMORATIVE ISSUES (6) FOR THE 100th BIRTHDAY OF DR. SUN YAT-SEN

7 (537)	5 Dollars (Cu–Ni) 1965. Dr. Sun Yat-sen (1866–1925). ℞ mausoleum in Nanking		1.50	2.50
8 (538)	10 Dollars (Cu–Ni) 1965. Same type as No. 7		2.00	3.00

			VF	XF
9 (539)	50	Dollars (Ag) 1965. Dr. Sun Yat-sen. ℞ sambar (Cervus = Rusa unicolor – Cervidae), with Manchurian crane above	10.00	12.50
10 (540)	100	Dollars (Ag) 1965. Same type as No. 9	12.00	16.00
11 (541)	1000	Dollars (Au) 1965. Dr. Sun Yat-sen, in profile. ℞ value between branches	–.–	–.–
12 (542)	2000	Dollars (Au) 1965. Same type as No. 11	–.–	–.–

COMMEMORATIVE ISSUES (2) FOR THE 80th BIRTHDAY OF CHIANG KAI-SHEK

13 (543)	1	Dollar (Cu–Ni) 1966. Chiang Kai-shek (1886-1975). ℞ value	0.60	0.80
14 (544)	2000	Dollars (Au) 1966. Chiang Kai-shek. ℞ Manchurian cranes (Grus japonensis – Gruidae), promising happiness and long life		550.00
15 (545)	1	Chiao (Al) 1967–. Orchid (Phalaenopsis sp. – Orchidaceae). ℞ value	0.12	0.20
16 (546)	5	Chiao (Al–Br) 1967. Orchid (Cattleya hybr. – Orchidaceae). ℞ value	0.30	0.60

COMMEMORATIVE ISSUE FOR THE FAO COIN PLAN AND FOR THE 24th ANNIVERSARY OF THE FAO (16. 10. 1969)

17 (547)	1	Dollar (Cu–Ni) 1969. Plum blossom, surrounded by Chinese writing with implication toward the FAO campaign. ℞ female farm laborer and tractor; value	0.65	1.25

18 (548)	5	Dollars (Cu-Ni) 1970–1979. Chiang Kai-shek, head left. Rev. value in circle of ornamentions	0.50	1.00

90th ANNIVERSARY OF THE BIRTH OF CHIANG-KAI-SHEK

			Unc
19 (549)	150 Dollars (Ag) 1976		15.00

Note: with the coinage appearing upon the occasion of the 60th birthday of the Republic in silver and gold, according the official information, these are medals.

70th ANNIVERSARY OF THE FOUNDING OF THE REPUBLIC OF CHINA (4)

		XF	Unc
20 (550)	½ Dollar (Al-Br) 1981	0.15	0.30
21 (551)	1 Dollar (Al-Br) 1981	0.15	0.30
22 (552)	5 Dollars (Cu-Ni) 1981	0.30	0.60
23 (553)	10 Dollars (Cu-Ni) 1981	0.50	1.00

Tansania   # Tanzania   **Tanzanie**

Area: 363,700 sq. mi. Population: 21,300,000.

The Republic of Tanganyika and the People's Republic of Zanzibar with Pemba united to form the United Republic of Tanganyika-Zanzibar on April 26, 1964; renaming of the state designation in October of the same year to Tanzania.

Capital: Dar-es-Salaam.

100 Senti (Cents) = 1 Tanzania Shilingi (Shilling)

			XF	Unc
1 (1)	5 Senti (Br) 1966–1983. Julius Kambarage Nyerere (*1921), President of State. ℞ Indo-Pacific sailfish (Istiophorus gladius – Istiophoridae)		0.05	0.15
2 (11)	10 Senti (Ni-Bra) 1977–1982. ℞ Zebra (scalloped)		0.10	0.25

3 (2)	20 Senti (Ni-Bra) 1966–. ℞ ostrich (Struthio camelus – Struthionidae)		0.15	0.30
4 (3)	50 Senti (Cu-Ni) 1966–. ℞ Smith's red hare (Pronolagus crassicaudatus – Leporidae)		0.25	0.50
5 (4)	1 Shilingi (Cu-Ni) 1966–. ℞ Freedom torch		0.40	1.00

No. 6 omitted.

10th ANNIVERSARY OF THE INDEPENDENCE OF TANGANYIKA AND FAO COIN PLAN

		XF	Unc
7 (5)	5 Shilingi (Cu-Ni) 1971. Portrait of President Nyerere, dates 1961–1971. ℞ value in circle, surrounded with bananas, millet, maize and a zebu (decagonal)	1.00	2.00

ISSUE FOR THE FAO COIN PLAN

		XF	Unc
8 (5a)	5 Shilingi (Cu-Ni) 1972, 1973, 1980. President Nyerere, similar to No.1.℞ value in circle, surrounded with bananas, millet, maize and a zebu (decagonal)	1.00	2.00

CONSERVATION COMMEMORATIVE (3)

		Unc	Proof
9 (6)	25 Shilingi (Ag) 1974. Rev. southern giraffe	20.00	25.00
10 (7)	50 Shilingi (Ag) 1974. Rev. black rhino	35.00	40.00
11 (8)	1500 Shilingi (Au) 1974. Rev. cheetah	500.00	600.00

10th ANNIVERSARY OF THE BANK OF TANZANIA

		Unc	Proof
12 (9)	5 Shilingi (Cu-Ni) 1976. Building of the Bank of Tanzania (decagonal)	1.50	–.–

10th FAO REGIONAL CONFERENCE FOR AFRICA

13 (10)	5 Shilingi (Cu-Ni) 1978	3.00	22.50

20th ANNIVERSARY OF INDERPENDENCE (3)

			Unc	Proof
14 (12)	20 Shilingi 1981. Bust of President Nyerere. Rev. Arms, value:			
	a) (Ag)			27.50
	b) (Cu-Ni)		15.00	
15 (13)	200 Shilingi (Ag) 1981. Type as No. 14		50.00	70.00
16 (14)	2000 Shilingi (Au) 1981. Type as No. 14		300.00	350.00

U.N. DECADE FOR WOMEN (2)

17	100 Shilingi (Ag) 1984		45.00
18	1000 Shilingi (Au) 1984		185.00

Nos. 19–20 omitted.

25th ANNIVERSARY OF WORLD WILDLIFE FOUND (2)

21	100 Shilingi (Ag) 1986		–.–
22	2000 Shilingi (Au) 1986		–.–

Nos. 23–27 omitted.

28	1 Shilingi (Ni plated St) 1987. Ali Hassan Mwinyi, President of State. Rev. as No. 5		–.–
29	5 Shilingi (German silver) 1987. Rev. as No. 8		–.–
30	10 Shilingi (Cu-Ni) 1987. Obv. as No. 14. Rev. Arms		–.–

Thailand   **Thailand**   **Thailande**

Area: 198,247 sq. mi. Population: 51,700,000.

The Thai people originating from South China, pressed back the Khmer and founded the kingdom of Sukothai. After changeable battles, particularly also with the Burmese, Chao Phraya Chakri in 1782 founded the Chakri Dynasty as King Rama I which has been governing until the present day. In place of the old state designation of Siam, the name of Thailand (Land of the Free People) is being used since 1939. Capital: Bangkok.

64 Att = 8 Füang, 1 Füang = $^1/_8$ Baht, 1 Salüng = $^1/_4$ Baht,
1 Solot = $^1/_2$ Att = $^1/_{128}$ Baht, 1 Sio = 2 Att,
100 Satangs or Stangs = 1 Baht (Bat)

CHULALONGKORN (RAMA V) 1868–1910

			VF	XF
1 (21)	1 Solot (Br) 1887–1905. Rama V (1853–1910), portrait left. ℞ heavenly nymph with shield		2.50	3.00
2 (22)	1 Att (Br) 1887–1905		2.50	4.00
3 (23)	1 Sio (Br) 1887–1905		3.00	5.00
4 (32)	1 Füang (Ag) 1876–1908. Rama V, portrait left. ℞ coat of arms			
	a) 1876–1902 (undated)		3.00	4.00
	b) 1902–1908		6.00	8.00
5 (33)	1 Salüng (Ag) 1876–1908			
	a) 1876–1901 (undated)		8.00	12.00
	b) 1901–1908		10.00	15.00

6 (34)	1 Baht (Ag) 1878–1907			
	a) 1878–1900 (undated)		6.00	10.00
	b) 1901–1907		8.00	12.00

		VF	XF
7 (39)	1 Baht (Ag) 1908. Rama V, portrait left. ℞ three-headed elephant	160.00	200.00
8 (35)	1 Satang (Br) 1908–1937. Common cobra (Naja naja – Elapidae or Elaphidae); (Sanskrit: naga). ℞ kongchak, mythological weapon of the Hindu God Vishnu (a disc with very sharp teeth) (center hole)	0.40	0.60
9 (36)	5 Satangs (Ni) 1908–1937. Same as No. 8	0.50	0.80
10 (37)	10 Satangs (Ni) 1908–1937. Same as No. 8	0.50	0.80

VAJIRAVUDH (RAMA VI) 1910–1925

		VF	XF
11 (43)	1 Salüng (Ag) 1913, 1917–1919, 1924–1925. Rama VI (1881–1925), portrait right. ℞ three-headed elephant	4.00	7.50
12 (44)	2 Salüng (Ag) 1913, 1919–1921	5.00	8.00

| **13** (45) | 1 Baht (Ag) 1913–1918 | 8.00 | 12.00 |

PRAJADHIPOK (RAMA VII) 1925–1935

		VF	XF
14 (48)	25 Satangs (Ag) 1929. Rama VII (1893–1941), portrait left. ℞ Asiatic elephant (Elephas maximus – Elephantidae)	6.00	9.00
15 (49)	50 Satangs (Ag) 1929	8.00	12.00

ANANDA MAHIDOL (RAMA VIII) 1935–1946

		VF	XF
16 (50)	½ Satang (Br) 1937	0.40	0.60
17 (51)	1 Satang (Br) 1939	0.50	0.70
18 (54)	1 Satang (Br) 1941. Decorative design. ℞ name of country, value (center hole)	0.60	1.00
19 (55)	5 Satangs (Ag) 1941	2.00	3.00
20 (56)	10 Satangs (Ag) 1941	3.00	5.00
21 (A56)	20 Satangs (Ag) 1942	6.00	8.00
22 (57)	1 Satang (Zn) 1942 (without center hole)	0.25	0.40
23 (58)	5 Satangs (Zn) 1942 (center hole)	0.50	0.80
24 (59)	10 Satangs (Zn) 1942 (center hole)	1.00	1.50

		Value and date in Arabic numerals	VF	XF
25 (60)	1	Satang (Zn) 1944 (without hole)	0.25	0.40
26 (61)	5	Satangs (Zn) 1944–1945 (with center hole)		
		a) 1944–1945, thick flan	0.50	0.80
		b) 1945, thin flan	0.60	1.00
27 (62)	10	Satangs (Zn) 1944–1945 (center hole)		
		a) 1944, thick flan	1.20	1.60
		b) 1945, thin flan	1.40	1.80

			VF	XF
28 (63)	20	Satangs (Zn) 1945	2.00	2.50
29 (64)	5	Satangs (Zn) 1946. Rama VIII (1925–1946), as child, portrait left. ℞ garuda, mythological bird	2.00	3.00
30 (65)	10	Satangs (Zn) 1946	2.50	3.50
31 (66)	25	Satangs (Zn) 1946	4.00	6.00
32 (67)	50	Satangs (Zn) 1946	9.00	12.00
33 (68)	5	Satangs (Zn) 1946. Rama VIII, portrait left	0.40	0.60
34 (69)	10	Satangs (Zn) 1946	0.50	0.80
35 (70)	25	Satangs (Zn) 1946	0.50	0.80
36 (71)	50	Satangs (Zn) 1946	0.90	1.20

PHUMIPHOL ADULYADET (RAMA IX) since 1946

			VF	XF
37 (72)	5	Satangs (Zn) 1950. Rama IX (*1927), in uniform decorated with one medal. ℞ coat of arms	0.25	0.40
38 (72a)	5	Satangs (Al–Br) 1950	0.25	0.40
39 (73)	10	Satangs (Zn) 1950	0.40	0.60
40 (73a)	10	Satangs (Al–Br) 1950	0.40	0.60
41 (76)	25	Satangs (Al–Br) 1950	0.50	0.80
42 (77)	50	Satangs (Al–Br) 1950	0.60	1.00
43 (78)	5	Satangs 1957. Rama IX in uniform decorated with three medals. ℞ coat of arms		
		a) (Al–Br)	0.10	0.20
		b) (Br)	0.10	0.20
44 (79)	10	Satangs 1957		
		a) (Al–Br)	0.20	0.40
		b) (Br)	0.35	0.50
45 (80)	25	Satangs (Al–Br) 1957	0.40	0.60
46 (81)	50	Satangs (Al–Br) 1957	0.55	0.80
47 (82)	1	Baht (Cu–Ni–St) 1957	1.50	2.00

		VF	**XF**

48 (83)   1 Baht (Cu–Ni) 1961. Rama IX and
Queen Sirikit. ℞ coat of arms   1.20   2.00

49 (84)   1 Baht (Cu–Ni) 1962. Rama IX, legend,
arranged in semicircle   1.00   1.50

COMMEMORATIVE ISSUES (2) FOR THE KING'S 36th BIRTHDAY

50 (85)   1 Baht (Cu–Ni) 1963. Rama IX. ℞ royal
insignia   0.40   0.70

51 (86)   20 Baht (Ag) 1963   6.50   12.00

COMMEMORATIVE ISSUE FOR THE 5th ASIAN GAMES FROM DECEMBER 9 TO DECEMBER 20, 1966, IN BANGKOK

52 (87)   1 Baht (Cu–Ni) 1966. Rama IX and
Queen Sirikit. ℞ emblem of the games,
Motto: EVER ONWARD   0.40   0.60

COMMEMORATIVE ISSUES (3) FOR QUEEN SIRIKIT'S 36th BIRTHDAY, ON AUGUST 12, 1968

		Unc

53 (88)   150 Baht (Au) 1968. Queen Sirikit Kitiya-
kara (*1932), portrait right. ℞ crowned
monogram in wreath, value below   60.00

54 (89)   300 Baht (Au) 1968. Same type as No. 53   120.00

55 (90)   600 Baht (Au) 1968. Same type as No. 53   225.00

COMMEMORATIVE ISSUE FOR THE 6th ASIAN GAMES IN BANGKOK

56 (91)   1 Baht (Cu–Ni) 1970. Similar to No. 52   0.30   0.50

COMMEMORATIVE ISSUES (3) FOR 25 YEARS OF REIGN ON JUNE 9, 1971

			XF	Unc
57 (92)	10 Baht (Ag) 1971. Rama IX, bust right. Ŗ royal insignia		2.00	3.00

58 (93)	400 Baht (Au) 1971. Same type as No. 57		100.00
59 (94)	800 Baht (Au) 1971. Same type as No. 57		200.00

COMMEMORATIVE ISSUE FOR THE 20th ANNIVERSARY OF THE WORLD FELLOWSHIP OF BUDDHISTS

60 (95)	50 Baht (Ag) 1971. Rama IX. Ŗ the buddhists wheel of the law (The Dhamachakr)	10.00	16.00

COMMEMORATIVE ISSUE FOR THE 21st BIRTHDAY OF CROWN PRINCE VAJIRALONGKORN

61 (97)	1 Baht (Cu–Ni) 1972	0.20	0.40
62 (98)	5 Baht (Cu–Ni) 1973	0.60	1.00

COMMEMORATIVE ISSUE FOR THE FAO COIN PLAN

63 (96)	1 Baht (Cu–Ni) 1973. Design shows the State Ploughing Ceremony, and ancient festival of Hindu origin which is now officially celebrated each year as a symbol government action for agricultural development. This coin was released on State Ploughing Day, 7 May 1973. The inscription reads 'FAO Thailand – With the improvement of agriculture the country prospers'	0.20	0.40

COMMEMORATIVE ISSUE FOR THE 25th ANNIVERSARY OF THE WORLD HEALTH ORGANIZATION (WHO)

64 (99)	1 Baht (Cu–Ni) 1973. Ŗ Emblem of the WHO	0.20	0.40

100th ANNIVERSARY OF THE NATIONAL MUSEUM

65 (101)	50 Baht (Ag) 1974	6.00	9.00
66 (100)	1 Baht (Cu–Ni) 1974	0.25	0.40

			Unc	Proof
CONSERVATION COMMEMORATIVE (3)				
67 (102)	50	Baht (Ag) 1975. Rev. Sumatran rhino	20.00	25.00
68 (103)	100	Baht (Ag) 1975. Rev. Brow-antlered deer	35.00	40.00
69 (104)	2500	Baht (Au) 1975. Rev. whiteeyed river martin	400.00	600.00

8th ASIAN GAMES IN BANGKOK

			XF	Unc
70 (105)	1	Baht (Cu-Ni) 1975. Conjoined heads of the royal couple	0.25	0.40

100th ANNIVERSARY OF THE FINANCE MINISTRY

71 (106)	100	Baht (Ag) 1975	18.00	25.00

75th ANNIVERSARY OF THE BIRTH OF PRINCESS MOTHER (2)

72 (107)	1	Baht (Cu-Ni) 1976. Bust of Princess Mother. Rev. emblem	0.25	0.40
73 (108)	150	Baht (Ag) 1976. Type as No. 72	15.00	18.00

74 (110)	1	Baht (Cu-Ni) 1977. Head left of the King. Rev. royal barque	0.20	0.30

FOR THE FAO COIN PLAN (2)

75 (112)	1	Baht (Cu-Ni) 1977. Rice goddess	0.25	0.40
76 (113)	150	Baht (Ag) 1977. Elephants	15.00	18.00

GRADUATION OF PRINCESS SIRINTHORN (3)

			XF	**Unc**
77 (114)	1	Baht (Cu-Ni) 1977	0.25	0.40
78 (115)	10	Baht (Ni) 1977	0.60	1.00
79 (116)	150	Baht (Ag) 1977	15.00	18.00

No. 80 omitted.

WEDDING OF CROWN-PRINCE VIJIRALONGKORN (3)

81 (117)	10 Baht (Ni) 1977. Conjoined busts of Crown Prince Vijiralongkorn and Princess Soamsawali	0.60 1.00
82 (118)	150 Baht (Ag) 1977. Type as No. 81	15.00 18.00
83 (119)	2500 Baht (Au) 1977. Type as No. 81	180.00
84 (109)	25 Satangs (Bra) 1977	0.10 0.20

85 (111)	5 Baht (Cu-Ni) 1977; dia. 30 mm	0.40 0.65

50th ANNIVERSARY OF THE BIRTH OF THE KING (2)

86 (120)	5 Baht (Cu-Ni) 1977. Bust of the King. Rev. Royal monogram	0.40 0.65
87 (122)	5000 Baht (Au) 1977. Type as No. 86	350.00

INVESTITURE OF PRINCESS SIRINTHORN (3)

88 (124)	1 Baht (Cu-Ni) 1978. Bust of the Princess. Rev. Monogram	0.25 0.40
89 (125)	150 Baht (Ag) 1978. Type as No. 88	15.00 18.00
90 (126)	2500 Baht (Au) 1978. Type as No. 88	180.00

9th WORLD ORCHID CONFERENCE IN BANGKOK

91 (123)	150 Baht (Ag) 1978. Bust of the King. Rev. orchid blossoms	15.00 18.00

GRADUATION OF PRINCE VIJIRALONGKORN (3)

					XF	Unc
92 (127)	1	Baht (Cu-Ni) 1978. Bust of the Prince. Rev. Emblem of the staff college			0.25	0.40
93 (128)	150	Baht (Ag) 1978. Type as No. 92			15.00	18.00
94 (129)	3000	Baht (Au) 1978. Type as No. 92				180.00

8th ASIAN GAMES (2)

			XF	Unc
95 (130)	1	Baht (Cu-Ni) 1978. Conjoined busts of the Royal couple	0.25	0.40
96 (131)	5	Baht (Cu-Ni) 1978. Type as No. 95	0.60	1.00

ROYAL CRADLE CEREMONY (2)

			XF	Unc
97 (132)	5	Baht (Cu-Ni) 1979	0.50	0.70

			XF	Unc
98 (133)	200	Baht (Ag) 1979	12.50	16.50

GRADUATION OF PRINCESS CHULABHORN (3)

			XF	Unc
99 (134)	2	Baht (Cu-Ni) 1979	0.30	0.50
100 (135)	10	Baht (Cu-Ni) 1979	0.60	1.00
101 (136)	300	Baht (Ag) 1979	26.00	30.00

		XF	Unc
102 (137)	5 Baht (Cu-Ni) 1980	0.40	0.60
103 (138)	600 Baht (Ag) 1980		45.00
104 (139)	9000 Baht (Au) 1980		350.00

80th ANNIVERSARY OF THE BIRTH OF KING'S MOTHER (2)

105 (140)	5 Baht (Cu-Ni) 1980. Bust of King's mother	0.40	0.60
106 (141)	10 Baht (Cu-Ni) 1980. Type as No. 105	0.80	1.30

RAMA VII CONSTITUTIONAL MONARCHY

107 (144)	5 Baht (Cu-Ni) 1980. Crowned monogram	0.30	0.60

30th ANNIVERSARY OF THE WORLD FELLOWSHIP OF BUDDHISTS

108 (145)	10 Baht (Cu-Ni) 1980. The Buddhist's wheel of the law	0.80	1.00

109 (168)	50 Satangs (Al-Br) 1978, 1980. Type as No. 84	0.15	0.25

KING RAMA VI BIRTH CENTENNIAL (3)

110 (142)	5 Baht (Cu-Ni) 1981. Bust of King Rama VI	0.30	0.50

			XF	Unc
111 (143)	600	Baht (Ag) 1981. Type as No. 110		45.00
112 (A143)	9000	Baht (Au) 1981. Type as No. 110	400.00	450.00

KING RAMA IX ANNIVERSARY OF REIGN (3)

			XF	Unc
113 (146)	10	Baht (Cu-Ni) 1981. Conjoined busts	0.70	1.00
114 (147)	600	Baht (Ag) 1981. Type as No. 113		35.00
115 (148)	9000	Baht (Au) 1981. Type as No. 113		400.00

INTERNATIONAL YEAR OF THE CHILD (2)

			Proof
116 (152)	200	Baht (Ag) 1981. Dancing girl:	
		a) normal thickness	35.00
		b) Pièfort	–.–
117 (153)	4000	Baht (Au) 1981. Loy-Krathong Festival	400.00

200th ANNIVERSARY OF BANGKOK (3)

			XF	Unc
118 (149)	5	Baht (Cu-Ni) 1982. Conjoined busts. Rev. Trident and chakra		0.60
119 (150)	600	Baht (Ag) 1982. Type as No. 118		40.00
120 (151)	9000	Baht (Au) 1982. Type as No. 118		500.00

50th ANNIVERSARY OF THE BIRTH OF QUEEN SIRIKIT (3)

			Unc	Proof
121 (154)	10	Baht (Ni) 1982. Bust of the Queen. Rev. Crowned monogram	1.00	
122 (155)	600	Baht (Ag) 1982. Type as No. 121	40.00	50.00
123 (156)	9000	Baht (Au) 1982. Type as No. 121	500.00	

WORLD FOOD DAY (2)

			XF	Unc
124 (157)	1	Baht (Cu-Ni) 1982. Rev. Ananas, rice, fish	0.15	0.30
125 (158)	5	Baht (Cu-Ni) 1982. Type as No. 124	0.30	0.60
126 (159)	1	Baht (Cu-Ni) 1982. Rev. Palace	0.15	0.30
127 (160)	5	Baht (Cu-Ni) 1982. Rev. Garuda	0.30	0.60

75th YEAR OF WORLD SCOUTING (2)

			Unc	Proof
128 (161)	5	Baht (Cu-Ni) 1982	0.60	
129 (162)	10	Baht (Ni) 1982	1.00	–.–

CENTENARY OF THAI POSTAL SERVICE

	Unc	Proof
130 (163) 10 Baht (Ni) 1983. Rev. Emblem	1.00	10.00

CENTENARY OF THAI POSTAGE STAMPS

131 (164) 600 Baht (Ag) 1983. Rev. Stamps, value	30.00	80.00

700th ANNIVERSARY OF THAI ALPHABET (3)

132 (165) 10 Baht (Ni) 1983. Monument	1.00	
133 (166) 600 Baht (Ag) 1983. Type as No. 132	30.00	80.00
134 (167) 6000 Baht (Au) 1983. Type as No. 132	400.00	750.00

INTERNATIONAL YEAR OF THE DISABLED (2)

135 (169) 250 Baht (Ag) 1983. Rev. Emblem	30.00	
136 (170) 2500 Baht (Au) 1983	350.00	300.00

84th ANNIVERSARY OF THE BIRTH OF KING'S MOTHER (3)

137 (171) 5 Baht (Cu-Ni) 1984. Bust of King's mother. Rev. Emblem		0.80
138 (172) 10 Baht (Ni) 1984. Type as No. 137	1.50	
139 (173) 600 Baht (Ag) 1984. Type as No. 137		40.00
140 (174) 6000 Baht (Au) 1984. Type as No. 137	400.00	650.00

72nd ANNIVERSARY OF GOVERNMENT SAVINGS BANK

141 (175) 10 Baht (Ni) 1985	2.00	12.50

INTERNATIONAL YOUTH YEAR

		Unc	Proof
142 (176)	2 Baht (Cu-Ni) 1985	0.75	

XIII SEA GAMES IN BANGKOK

| **143** (177) | 2 Baht (Cu-Ni) 1985. Emblem of the games | | 0.75 |

Area: c. 471,700 sq. mi. Population: 1,280,000.
Since the reign of the Chinese Tang Dynasty (618 to 906), Tibet has been to a varying degree under the cultural and political influence of China. Under the Ching Dynasty (1644 to 1911) China was able to consolidate this influence considerably at first, but towards the end of the dynasty this influence, however, diminished very largely under the reign of weak emperors. After the supersession of the empire in China by the republic (1911/12), Tibet considered itself released from Chinese suzerainty. The independence of Tibet guaranteed in 1914 by Great Britain, India, and Russia was not acknowledged by China. For the purpose of counteracting increasing foreign influence in Tibet, the troops of the People's Republic of China occupied the country step by step in 1950 to 1951. Based upon the Peking agreements of May 23, 1951, Tibet was incorporated in the People's Republic of China as an autonomous region.
Capital: Lhasa.

10 Skarung = 1 Shokang, 15 Skarung = 1 Tangka
10 Shokang = 1 Srang, 3 Tangka = 1 Indian Rupee

			VF	XF
1 (1)	¼	Rupee (Ag) 1903 (undated). Portrait with cap, left ℞ name of province (Szechuan) in 4 Chinese letters, surrounded by leaf decorations. Rosette in center. Diameter: 19.5 mm. Several variations	32.00	40.00

Coins Nos. 1 to 4 were struck in the Chinese Province of Szechuan, for the frontier territory of Szechuan and Tibet. There are also gold strikes of Nos. 1, 2, and 3.

| 2 (2) | ½ | Rupee (Ag) 1903 (undated). Like No. 1, but diameter: 25.5 mm. Several variations | 35.00 | 45.00 |

			VF	XF
3 (3)	1	Rupee (Ag) 1903 (undated). Like No. 1, but diameter: 30 mm. Several variations	15.00	18.00
4	2½	Rupee (Ag) 1903 (undated). Like No. 1, but diameter: 38 mm	–.–	–.–

5 (13)	1	Tangka (Ag) 18th century to 1948 (undated). Stylized lotus flower, surrounded by 8 Tibetan letter groups. ℞ Buddhist symbol in center, surrounded by 8 more symbols	5.00	8.00
6 (4)	1	Skarung (Cu) (undated). Dragon in dotted circle and new legend in Tibetan letters ℞ name of country, denomination, and regnal era "Hsüan Tung" in 4 Chinese letters. In center stylized lotus flower in dotted circle	18.00	25.00
7 (5)	1	Shokang (Ag) 1910 (?) (undated) Similar to No. 6	18.00	25.00
8 (6)	2	Shokang (Ag) 1910 (?) (undated). Similar to No. 6	22.00	35.00
9	1	Shokang (Ag) 1908, 1909. Two squares in double circle. Tibetan letters between the squares. Buddhist symbol in center. 8 stars framing the double circle. ℞ In center two circles inside a double circle. Between the circles twice 8 dots. 8 groups of Tibetan letters constituting legend. Edge: 8 stars inside a double circle and in one outer circle	65.00	90.00

			VF	**XF**
10 (8)	5	Shokang (Ag) 1908, 1909 (?). Similar to No. 9, but 16 stars in outer circle	20.00	30.00
11 (9)	1	Srang (Ag) 1908 Similar to No. 9, but 24 stars in outer circle	160.00	220.00
12	5	Shokang (Ag) 1908–1912. Stylized flower in center, surrounded by 8 Tibetan letter groups. ℞ Buddhist symbol in center, surrounded by 8 more symbols	–.–	–.–
13	1	Tael (Ag) 1908 (undated). 8 Chinese letters and denomination. ℞ name of country and value in 4 Chinese letters	–.–	–.–
14 (10)	2½	Skarung (Cu) 1909. Lion in circle and 8 Tibetan letter groups. ℞ in center Buddhist symbol in double circle. Legend in Tibetan letters	12.00	16.00
15 (A10)	5	Skarung (Cu) 1909	12.00	16.00
16 (11)	7½	Skarung (Cu) 1909	20.00	26.00
17 (12)	1	Srang (Ag) 1909. Stylized lion in circle, surrounded by 8 Tibetan letter groups. ℞ in center Buddhist symbol in circle, surrounded by legend in Tibetan letters. All surrounded by 8 Buddhist symbols	385.00	450.00
18 (14)	1	Tangka (Ag) 1910. Obverse similar to No. 9, but dotted circle instead of stars around the edge. ℞ in center a stylized flower with 8 petals, surrounded by one dotted and one regular circle	6.00	9.00
19 (16)	2½	Skarung (Cu) 1914–1916. Lion in circle and 8 Tibetan letter groups. ℞ double circle in center, surrounded by two groups of 8 dots each, all surrounded by one dotted and one regular circle. Legend in Tibetan letters	4.00	6.00
20 (17)	5	Skarung (Cu) 1913–1918. Obverse similar to No. 19. ℞ stylized flower in double circle and legend in Tibetan letters	3.50	5.00
21 (18)	5	Shokang (Ag) 1914–1918. Stylized lion in circle, surrounded by 8 Tibetan letter groups. ℞ in center Buddhist symbol in circle, surrounded by legend in Tibetan letters (date and value). All surrounded by 8 Buddhist symbols	11.00	16.00
22 (22)	20	Srang (Au) 1917–1920. Stylized lion and Tibetan letters (date) in circle. Surrounded by 8 Buddhist symbols. ℞ in center stylized flower in circle. Legend in Tibetan letters, name of country, value	620.00	800.00
23 (A19)	2½	Skarung (Cu) 1918–1919. Stylized lion and legend in Tibetan letters. ℞ in		

center a Buddhist symbol, surrounded
by Tibetan letters and arabesques.
(Scalloped)

	VF	XF
	35.00	48.00

24 (19) 5 Skarung (Cu) 1918–1925. Stylized lion
and legend in Tibetan letters. ℞ Tibet-
an letters in circular design, legend in
Tibetan letters
2.60   4.00

25 (20) 7½ Skarung (Cu) 1918–1925. Stylized lion
in dotted circle and legend in Tibetan
letters. ℞ in center 3 curved lines in
circle, surrounded by 8 dots in dotted
circle. Legend in Tibetan letters. (Scalloped)
2.60   4.00

26 (21) 1 Shokang (Cu) 1918–1922. Lion in circle
and legend in 8 Tibetan letter groups.
℞ Tibetan letters in one regular and one
dotted circle. Legend in Tibetan letters
3.50   5.00

27 (21a) 1 Shokang (Cu) 1923–1928. Similar to
No. 26, but lettering variety
4.00   6.50
27a (32a) 5 Shokang (Ag) 1930. Diameter 24 mm
–.–   –.–

28 (23) 1 Shokang (Cu) 1932–1938. Stylized lion, sun, and clouds in circle. Legend in Tibetan letters. ℞ Tibetan letters and arabesques in circle. Legend in Tibetan letters and 5 rosettes

	VF	XF
	2.50	3.50

29 (24) 1½ Srang (Ag) 1935–1937. Stylized lion, 5 mountain peaks, two suns, and clouds in circle. In legend 4 Tibetan letter groups, and 4 Buddhist symbols. ℞ arabesques in circle. Legend in Tibetan letters, and Buddhist symbols

	VF	XF
	6.00	8.00

30 (25) 3 Srang (Ag) 1933, 1934 (?). Stylized lion and clouds in circle. In legend 4 Tibetan letter groups, and 4 Buddhist symbols. ℞ Tibetan letters, value, and arabesques in circle. Legend in 3 Tibetan letter groups, and 3 Buddhist symbols

	VF	XF
	12.00	16.00

Values are given for each coin in U.S. Dollars and reference to Yeoman-numbers.

				VF	XF
31 (26)	3	Srang (Ag) 1935–1938. Stylized lion, 5 mountain peaks, 2 suns, and clouds in circle. In legend 4 Tibetan letter groups, and 4 Buddhist symbols. ℞ arabesques in circle. In legend 4 Tibetan letter groups, date, 2 rosettes with 8 petals, and 2 Buddhist symbols		12.00	16.00
32 (27)	3	Shokang (Cu) 1946. Stylized lion, 5 mountain peaks, and 2 suns in circle. In legend 4 Tibetan letter groups, and 4 Buddhist symbols. ℞ Tibetan letters and arabesques in circle. Legend in Tibetan letters and 6 Buddhist symbols		7.50	10.50
33	1	Tangka (Ag) 1946–1948 (undated). In center Yin-Yang symbol in 2 circles. In legend 8 Tibetan letter groups. ℞ arabesques in circle, surrounded by 8 Buddhist symbols		9.00	12.00

				VF	XF
34 (28)	5	Shokang (Cu) 1947–1949. Lion, 3 mountain peaks, 2 suns, and clouds. ℞ Tibetan letters in circle surrounded by 8 Tibetan letter groups		2.60	4.00
35 (28a)	5	Shokang (Cu) 1950–1951. Like No. 34, but sun and moon instead of 2 suns		3.50	5.00

				VF	XF
36 (29)	10	Srang (Ag) 1948, 1949. Lion with 3 mountain peaks and 2 suns in circle. In legend 8 Tibetan letter groups, name of country. ℞ Buddhist symbols and Tibetan letters, date, value in circle. In legend 8 Tibetan letter groups, name of country		18.00	25.00
37 (29a)	10	Srang (Ag) 1950, 1951. Like No. 36, but sun and moon instead of 2 suns		18.00	25.00
38 (30)	10	Srang (Ag) 1950, 1951. Lion, 3 mountain peaks, and 2 suns in circle. In legend 8 Tibetan letter groups. ℞ 3 lines of Tibetan letters in circle. In legend 8 Tibetan letter groups		18.00	25.00

Values are given for each coin in U.S. Dollars and reference to Yeoman-numbers.

Area: 6,970 sq. mi. Population: 574,000.
While the western part, including the village of Kupang, belonged to Indonesia since 1947, the north-eastern part of the island of Timor remained Portuguese. In 1952 Portugal changed the colony into an Overseas Province. In 1976 Portuguese Timor was annexed by Indonesia.
Capital: Dili.

100 Avos = 1 Pataca; since 1958: 100 Centavos = 1 Escudo

			VF	XF
1 (1)	10	Avos (Br) 1945–1951. Cross. ℞ value	7.50	11.00
2 (2)	20	Avos (Ni–Br) 1945. Head of Liberty. ℞ coat of arms in wreath and value	40.00	55.00
3 (3)	50	Avos (Ag) 1945–1951. Coat of arms on cross. ℞ value	18.00	26.00

NEW CURRENCY: 100 Centavos = 1 Escudo

			VF	XF
4 (4)	10	Centavos (Br) 1958. Coat of arms with mural crown. ℞ value	4.00	8.00
5 (5)	30	Centavos (Br) 1958	2.00	4.00
6 (6)	60	Centavos (Cu–Ni) 1958	2.50	4.00
7 (7)	1	Escudo (Cu–Ni) 1958	2.50	4.00
8 (8)	3	Escudos (Ag) 1958	4.50	7.50
9 (9)	6	Escudos (Ag) 1958	7.50	11.00
10 (10)	10	Escudos (Ag) 1964	8.00	12.00
11 (12)	20	Centavos (Br) 1970. Coat of arms with mural crown. ℞ value	0.40	0.80
12 (13)	50	Centavos (Br) 1970. Same type as No. 11	0.40	0.80
13 (14)	1	Escudo (Br) 1970. Same type as No. 11	1.20	2.50
14 (15)	2,50	Escudos (Cu–Ni) 1970	1.20	2.50
15 (16)	5	Escudos (Cu–Ni) 1970	1.60	2.80
16 (17)	10	Escudos (Cu–Ni) 1970	2.50	4.00

Area: 20,000 sq. mi. Population: 2,930,000.

The former German protectorate was occupied by the British and French in August 1914 and in 1920 partitioned as a mandate between Great Britain and France under the League of Nations. The British part which was incorporated in the Gold Coast, also remained, after a plebiscite in 1957, with that state which had become independent under the name of Ghana. The French part received limited autonomy in 1957 and became independent on April 27, 1960.

Capital: Lomé.

100 Centimes = 1 Franc

			VF	XF
1 (1)	50	Centimes (Al–Br) 1924–1926. Laureate head of Marianne, symbol of the French Republic. ℞ value and palm leaves	4.00	10.00
2 (2)	1	Franc (Al–Br) 1924–1925	5.00	12.00
3 (3)	2	Francs (Al–Br) 1924–1925	8.00	18.00
4 (4)	1	Franc (Al) 1948. ℞ slender-horned gazelle (Gazella leptoceros – Bovidae)	6.50	16.00

			VF	XF
5 (5)	2	Francs (Al) 1948	20.00	35.00
6 (6)	5	Francs (Al–Br) 1956	2.00	5.00

			Proof
7	2500	Francs (Ag) 1977	65.00
8	5000	Francs (Ag) 1977	100.00
9	10000	Francs (Au) 1977	130.00
10	15000	Francs (Au) 1977	130.00
11	25000	Francs (Au) 1977	250.00
12	50000	Francs (Au) 1977	500.00

Tokelau Islands

Area: 4 sq. mi. Population: 2,000.
Tokelau or Union Islands located in the South Pacific. The group, a New Zealand Territory, consists of Atafu, Fakaofo and Nikunono.

100 Cents = 1 Dollar

			Unc	Proof
1 (1)	1	Tala 1978:		
		a) (Ag)		35.00
		b) (Cu-Ni)	6.00	
2 (2)	1	Tala 1979:		
		a) (Ag)		30.00
		b) (Cu-Ni)	5.00	
3 (3)	1	Tala 1980:		
		a) (Ag)		30.00
		b) (Cu-Ni)	5.00	
4 (4)	1	Tala 1981:		
		a) (Ag)		30.00
		b) (Cu-Ni)	5.00	

			Unc	Proof
5 (5)	1	Tala 1982:		
		a) (Ag)		35.00
		b) (Cu-Ni)	5.00	
6 (6)	1	Tala (Cu-Ni) 1983	7.50	
7 (7)	5	Tala (Ag) 1983		60.00
8	5	Tala (Ag) 1984. Fishermen; .925 silver, 27.21 g	25.00	50.00

Nos. 9–11 omitted.

OLYMPIC GAMES 1988

			Unc	Proof
12	5	Tala (Ag) 1988. Throwing the javolin		60.00

Friendly Islands

Area: 270 sq. mi. Population: 100,000.
The Tonga Islands (Friendly Islands) united as a kingdom in 1845, were
under British protection since 1900. The first king of the united island
realm was George Tupou I (1845–1893). On June 4, 1970 the Polynesian
kingdom became independent.
Capital: Nuku'alofa.

1 Koula = 16 British Pounds; since 1967: 100 Seniti =
1 Pa'anga (Tonga Dollar), 100 Pa'anga = 1 Hau

SALOTE TUPOU III 1918–1965

			Proof
1 (1)	¼	Koula (Au) 1962. Salote Tupou III (1900–1965), head right. ℞ coat of arms	200.00
2 (2)	½	Koula (Au) 1962. Salote Tupou III, standing	400.00
3 (3)	1	Koula (Au) 1962	800.00

TAUFA'AHAU TUPOU IV since 1965

CURRENCY REFORM (Decimal System):
100 Seniti = 1 Pa'anga, 100 Pa'anga = 1 Hau

			XF	Unc
4 (4)	1	Seniti (Br) 1967. Salote Tupou III, head right. ℞ giant tortoise (family Testudinidae)	0.20	0.40
5 (5)	2	Seniti (Br) 1967. ℞ giant tortoise	0.30	0.50
6 (6)	5	Seniti (Cu–Ni) 1967. ℞ value in wreath	0.30	0.60
7 (7)	10	Seniti (Cu–Ni) 1967	0.50	0.90
8 (8)	20	Seniti (Cu–Ni) 1967. Coat of arms	0.90	1.20
9 (9)	50	Seniti (Cu–Ni) 1967	1.20	2.00

			XF	Unc
10 (10)	1	Pa'anga (Cu–Ni) 1967	3.50	4.50

COMMEMORATIVE ISSUES (7) FOR THE CORONATION OF TAUFA'AHAU TUPOU IV ON 4th JULY, 1967

			XF	Unc
11 (11)	20	Seniti (Cu–Ni) 1967. Taufa'ahau Tupou IV, head right, memorial legend, edge decor: crowns. ℞ coat of arms	2.00	4.00
12 (12)	50	Seniti (Cu–Ni) 1967	3.00	6.00
13 (13)	1	Pa'anga (Cu–Ni) 1967	3.50	7.00
14 (14)	2	Pa'anga (Cu–Ni) 1967	4.50	9.00
15 (15)	¼	Hau (Pd) 1967		250.00
16 (16)	½	Hau (Pd) 1967		500.00
17 (17)	1	Hau (Pd) 1967		1000.00
18 (18)	1	Seniti (Br) 1968. Taufa'ahau Tupou IV, head right. ℞ giant tortoise	0.15	0.30
19 (19)	2	Seniti (Br) 1968, 1974. ℞ giant tortoise	0.20	0.40
20 (20)	5	Seniti (Cu–Ni) 1968, 1974. ℞ value between leaves	0.25	0.50
21 (21)	10	Seniti (Cu–Ni) 1968, 1974	0.40	0.70
22 (22)	20	Seniti (Cu–Ni) 1968, 1974. ℞ coat of arms	0.60	0.90
23 (23)	50	Seniti (Cu–Ni) 1968	0.85	1.50
24 (24)	1	Pa'anga (Cu–Ni) 1968, 1974	1.50	3.50
25 (25)	2	Pa'anga (Cu–Ni) 1968, 1974	3.00	6.00

COMMEMORATIVE ISSUES (7) FOR THE 50th BIRTHDAY OF TAUFA'AHAU TUPOU IV

			Proof
26 (11a)	20	Seniti (Cu–Ni). Type as No. 11, but with countermark 1918/monogram/TT IV/1968	6.00
27 (12a)	50	Seniti (Cu–Ni). Type as No. 12, but countermark as No. 26	10.00
28 (13a)	1	Pa'anga (Cu–Ni). Type as No. 13, but with countermark as No. 26	15.00
29 (14a)	2	Pa'anga (Cu–Ni). Type as No. 14, but with countermark as No. 26	40.00
30 (5a)	¼	Hau (Pd). Type as No. 15, but with countermark as No. 26	200.00
31 (6a)	½	Hau (Pd). Type as No. 16, but with countermark as No. 26	400.00

32(7a) 1 Hau (Pd). Type as No. 17, but with **Proof**
countermark as No. 26 **800.00**

COMMEMORATIVE ISSUES (2) FOR THE FIRST SCIENTIFIC OIL SEARCH IN TONGA

Unc

33 (24a) 1 Pa'anga (Cu–Ni, gilded). Type as No. 24,
but with countermark OIL SEARCH
1969 and oil derrick left and right side
of date 10.00

34(25a) 2 Pa'anga (Cu–Ni, gilded). Type as No.
25, but with countermark as No. 33 20.00

COMMEMORATIVE ISSUES (2) FOR JOINING THE BRITISH COMMONWEALTH

35(24b) 1 Pa'anga (Cu–Ni). Type as No. 24,
but with countermark COMMON-
WEALTH MEMBER 1970 left and
right side of date 10.00

36(25b) 2 Pa'anga (Cu–Ni). Type as No. 25, but
with countermark as No. 35 20.00

COMMEMORATIVE ISSUES (2) FOR THE 5th ANNIVERSARY OF THE DEATH OF QUEEN SALOTE TUPOU III

37(9a) 50 Seniti (Cu–Ni) 1970. Type as No. 9, but
with countermark 10.00

38(10a) 1 Pa'anga (Cu–Ni) 1970. Type as No. 10,
but with countermark 20.00

COMMEMORATIVE ISSUES (2) FOR INVESTITURE 1971

39(24c) 1 Pa'anga (Cu–Ni, gilded). Type as No.
24, but with countermark INVESTI-
TURE 1971 10.00

40(25a) 2 Pa'anga (Cu–Ni, gilded). Type as No.
25, but with countermark as No. 39 20.00

			XF	Unc
41 (18a)	1	Seniti (Bra) 1974. Type as No. 18	0.10	0.20
42 (23a)	50	Seniti (Cu-Ni) 1974. Type as No. 23 (12-sided)	0.80	1.50

FOR THE FAO COIN PLAN (8)

			XF	Unc
43 (26)	1	Seniti (Br) 1975, 1979	0.10	0.20
44 (27)	2	Seniti (Br) 1975, 1979	0.10	0.20
45 (28)	5	Seniti (Cu-Ni) 1975, 1977–1979	0.15	0.30
46 (29)	10	Seniti (Cu-Ni) 1975, 1977–1979	0.25	0.50
47 (30)	20	Seniti (Cu-Ni) 1975, 1977–1979	0.45	0.90
48 (31)	50	Seniti (Cu-Ni) 1975, 1977, 1978	0.70	1.40
49 (32)	1	Pa'anga (Cu-Ni) 1975	2.00	4.00
50 (33)	2	Pa'anga (Cu-Ni) 1975–1977	3.50	7.50

CONSTITUTION CENTENNIAL (7)

			Unc
51 (34)	5	Pa'anga (Ag) 1975	22.00
52 (35)	10	Pa'anga (Ag) 1975	40.00
53 (36)	20	Pa'anga (Ag) 1975	150.00
54 (37)	25	Pa'anga (Au) 1975	100.00
55 (38)	50	Pa'anga (Au) 1975	200.00
56 (39)	75	Pa'anga (Au) 1975	300.00
57 (40)	100	Pa'anga (Au) 1975	500.00

FOR THE FAO COIN PLAN

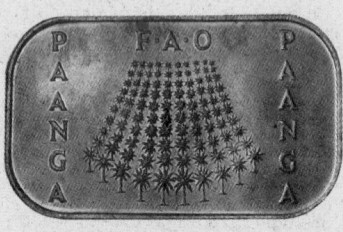

			XF	Unc
58 (41)	1	Pa'anga (Cu-Ni) 1977	1.60	3.00

60th ANNIVERSARY OF THE BIRTH OF TAUFA'AHAU TUPOU IV (2)

			Unc	Proof
59 (42)	1	Pa'anga 1978. Type as No. 58, but DIAMOND-BIRTHDAY/1918–1978« added:		
		a) (Ag)		22.00
		b) (Cu-Ni)	3.00	

		Unc	Proof
60 (43)	2 Pa'anga 1978. Type as No. 50, but »DIAMOND-BIRTHDAY/1918–1978« added:		
	a) (Ag)		80.00
	b) (Cu-Ni)	6.00	

FOR THE FAO COIN PLAN (2)

		Unc	Proof
61 (44)	1 Pa'anga 1979. Type as No. 58, but »DECADE OF PROGRESS 1969–1979« added. Rev. inscription »F.A.O. TECH-NICAL/COOPERATION PROGRAM-ME« added:		
	a) (Ag)		75.00
	b) (Cu-Ni)	7.00	
62 (45)	2 Pa'anga 1979:		
	a) (Ag)		40.00
	b) (Cu-Ni)	7.00	

FAO COIN PLAN AND RURAL WOMEN'S ADVANCEMENT (4)

63 (46)	1 Pa'anga 1980. Head of Salote Tupou III. Rev. woman in front of a cabin:		
	a) (Ag)		50.00
	b) (Cu-Ni)	4.00	
64 (47)	2 Pa'anga 1980. Type as No. 62, but without »DECADE . . .«:		
	a) (Ag)		70.00
	b) (Cu-Ni)	8.00	
65 (48)	10 Pa'anga (Au) 1980. Feminal symbol on dove		60.00
66 (49)	20 Pa'anga (Au) 1980. Feminal symbol on dove		100.00

ROYAL WEDDING AND CENTENARY OF TONGA-U.K. FRIENDSHIP TREATY (3)

67 (50)	½ Hau (Ag) 1981. Rev. Prince Charles and Lady Diana	60.00	60.00
68 (51)	1 Hau (Au) 1981. Type as No. 67	200.00	225.00

69 (52)	5 Hau (Au) 1981. Type as No. 67	400.00	450.00

WORLD FOOD DAY 1981 (8)

			XF	Unc
70 (53)	1	Seniti (Br) 1981		0.15
71 (54)	2	Seniti (Br) 1981		0.15
72 (55)	5	Seniti (Cu-Ni) 1981		0.15
73 (56)	10	Seniti (Cu-Ni) 1981		0.30
74 (57)	20	Seniti (Cu-Ni) 1981		0.60
75 (58)	50	Seniti (Cu-Ni) 1981		1.25

			Unc	Proof
76 (59)	1	Pa'anga 1981:		
		a) (Ag)		30.00
		b) (Cu-Ni)	3.00	
77 (60)	2	Pa'anga 1981:		
		a) (Ag)		60.00
		b) (Cu-Ni)	5.00	

COMMONWEALTH GAMES (3)

78 (61)	10	Pa'anga (Ag) 1982	50.00	60.00
79 (62)	1	Hau (Au) 1982		300.00
80	5	Hau (Au) 1982		–.–

CHRISTMAS 1982 (3)

81 (63)	1	Pa'anga 1982:		
		a) (Ag)		40.00
		b) (Cu-Ni)	3.00	10.00
82 (63b)	1	Pa'anga (Au) 1982		500.00
83 (63c)	1	Pa'anga (Platinum) 1982		900.00

CHRISTMAS 1983 (3)

84 (64)	1	Pa'anga 1983:		
		a) (Ag)		35.00
		b) (Cu-Ni)	2.00	
85 (64b)	1	Pa'anga (Au) 1983		500.00
86 (64c)	1	Pa'anga (Platinum) 1983		900.00

CHRISTMAS 1984 (3)

87 (65)	1	Pa'anga 1984:		
		a) (Ag)		35.00
		b) (Cu-Ni)	2.00	
88 (65b)	1	Pa'anga (Au) 1984		500.00
89 (65c)	1	Pa'anga (Platinum) 1984		900.00

Transvaal
Zuid Afrikaansche Republiek
Südafrikanische Republik   République Sudafricaine (Transvaal)

Boers dissatisfied with British rule in the Cape Colony, migrated via Natal into the deserted areas north of the Waal river and founded in 1852 the "South African Republic" by the integration of the smaller Free States of Potschefstroom, Zoutpansberg and Lyndenburg, which was called "Transvaal" abroad and from the British aspect due to its geographical position. Great Britain which had immediately recognized this republic, occupied its area from 1877 to 1881, but again recognized its independence in 1881. In the treaty of 27th February 1884 Great Britain alse recognized the name "South African Republic". The Boer War which broke out in 1899 ended on 31st May 1902 with the recognition of the annexation by Great Britain on the part of the Boers. After administering the Transvaal for several years as a Crown Colony, it was integrated as a province of the newly formed Union of South Africa in 1910, whose further development towards the sovereign republic has very strongly been determined by the Boer element of the province of Transvaal.

Capital: Pretoria.

12 Pence = 1 Shilling, 20 Shillings = 1 Pound (Pond)

With the law of 1891 the Pond was declared as the chief gold coin and on a par with the British gold sovereign.

PAUL KRÜGER 1883–1902

			VF	XF
1 (1)	1 Penny (Br) 1891–1898. Paul Krüger (1825–1904), called Ohm Krüger, President of the Republic. ℞ devided coat of arms		4.00	10.00
2 (2)	3 Pence (Ag) 1892–1897. ℞ value in wreath		8.00	12.50
3 (3)	6 Pence (Ag) 1891–1897		7.00	10.00

			VF	XF
4 (4)	1	Shilling (Ag) 1892–1897	10.00	18.00
5 (5)	2	Shillings (Ag) 1892–1897. ℞ coat of arms	12.50	20.00
6 (6)	2½	Shillings (Ag) 1892–1897	15.00	22.00
7 (7)	5	Shillings (Ag) 1892. ℞ covered wagon with one shaft (bottom section of coat of arms)	175.00	200.00
8 (7a)	5	Shillings (Ag) 1892. ℞ covered wagon with two shafts (bottom section of coat of arms)	250.00	360.00
9 (8)	½	£ (Au) 1893–1897. ℞ covered wagon with one shaft	140.00	160.00
10 (8a)	½	£ (Au) 1892. ℞ covered wagon with two shafts		250.00

			VF	XF
11 (9)	1	£ (Au) 1892–1900. ℞ covered wagon with one shaft	140.00	175.00
12 (9a)	1	£ (Au) 1892. ℞ covered wagon with two shafts	200.00	350.00
13 (10)	1	Pond (Au) 1902. ZAR, abbreviation of the name of the country, date. ℞ value in letters	1500.00	2500.00

Values are given for each coin in U.S. Dollars and reference to Yeoman-numbers.

Trinidad and Tobago

Trinidad und Tobago   **Trinité et Tobago**

Area: 1980 sq. mi. Population: 1,100,000.
The island of Trinidad was discovered by Christopher Columbus in
1498. Until captured by the British, Trinidad was a Spanish possession. Together with Tobago, Trinidad has formed an independent state
within the British Commonwealth since August 31, 1962.
Capital: Port of Spain.

100 Cents = 1 Trinidad Tobago Dollar

			XF	Unc
1 (1)	1	Cent (Br) 1966–1973. Coat of arms; crest: hummingbird (Polytmus guainnumbi – Trochilidae). R value	0.05	0.10
2 (2)	5	Cents (Br) 1966–1973. Same type as No. 1	0.10	0.20
3 (3)	10	Cents (Cu-Ni) 1966–1973. Same type as No. 1	0.15	0.30
4 (4)	25	Cents (Cu-Ni) 1966–1973. Same type as No. 1	0.30	0.60
5 (5)	50	Cents (Cu-Ni) 1966–1971. Same type as No. 1	0.50	1.00

			Unc	Proof
6 (6)	1	Dollar (Cu-Ni) 1970, 1971. Same type as No. 1:		
		a) 1970		20.00
		b) 1971	3.00	6.00

ISSUE FOR THE FAO COIN PLAN

			XF	Unc
7 (7)	1	Dollar (Ni) 1969. Coat of arms, name of country, date. R value, cocoa beans on a branch (Theobroma cacao – Sterculiaceae), motto: FOOD FOR ALL	3.00	6.50

			Unc	Proof
8 (8)		5 Dollars 1971-1975. Rev. red-tailed guan (Ortalis ruficauda - Cracidae), national bird of Tobago, called the "Cocrico"		
		a) (Ag) 1971, 1973-1975		35.00
		b) (Cu-Ni) 1974, 1975	10.00	

COMMEMORATIVE ISSUES (8) FOR THE 10th ANNIVERSARY OF INDEPENDENCE

			Unc	Proof
9 (9)	1 Cent	(Bro) 1972. Type as No. 1, but with additional commemorative legend	0.20	1.00
10 (10)	5 Cents	(Bro) 1972. Type as No. 9	0.25	1.10
11 (11)	10 Cents	(Cu-Ni) 1972. Type as No. 9	0.50	1.50
12 (12)	25 Cents	(Cu-Ni) 1972. Type as No. 9	0.80	2.00
13 (13)	50 Cents	(Cu-Ni) 1972. Type as No. 9	1.50	2.50
14 (14)	1 Dollar	(Cu-Ni) 1972	4.50	9.00
15 (15)	5 Dollars	(Ag) 1972. Type as No. 8, but with additional commemorative legend	28.00	30.00
16 (16)	10 Dollars	(Ag) 1972. R map of the islands	32.00	36.00
17 (9a)	1 Cent	(Br) 1973. Type as No. 9, but without commemorative inscription	1.00	2.00
18 (21)	50 Cents	(Cu-Ni) 1973–1976. Rev. Drums of a steel band, called »pans«	1.40	2.50
19 (22)	1 Dollar	(Cu-Ni) 1973–1975	3.50	6.00
20 (23)	10 Dollars	1973–1975. Type as No. 16, but without commemorative inscription:		
		a) (Ag) 1973–1975	32.00	35.00
		b) (Cu-Ni) 1974, 1975	15.00	28.00
21 (17)	1 Cent	(Br) 1974, 1975	0.20	1.00
22 (18)	5 Cents	(Br) 1974, 1975	0.25	1.00
23 (19)	10 Cents	(Cu-Ni) 1974, 1975	0.50	1.20
24 (20)	25 Cents	(Cu-Ni) 1974, 1975	0.80	2.00
25 (24)	100 Dollars	(Au) 1976		80.00
26 (17a)	1 Cent	(Br) 1976–1980. Type as No. 17, but inscription »Republic of . . .«	0.10	1.00
27 (18a)	5 Cents	(Br) 1976–1980	0.20	1.50
28 (19a)	10 Cents	(Cu-Ni) 1976–1980	0.40	1.50
29 (20a)	25 Cents	(Cu-Ni) 1976–1980	1.00	2.50
30 (21a)	50 Cents	(Cu-Ni) 1976–1980	1.30	4.00
31 (22a)	1 Dollar	(Cu-Ni) 1976–1980	7.00	8.00
32 (8)	5 Dollars	1976–1980:		
		a) (Y 8b) (Ag)		30.00
		b) (Y 8c) (Cu-Ni)	40.00	
33 (23)	10 Dollars	1976–1980:		
		a) (Y 23b) (Ag)		35.00
		b) (Y 23c) (Cu-Ni)	50.00	
34 (7a)	1 Dollar	(Cu-Ni) 1979. FAO issue	6.00	
35 (25)	25 Dollars	(Ag) 1980. Development Bank		30.00

All valuations in the SCHÖN are stated in U.S. Dollars.

Tristan da Cunha

Area: 45sq. mi. Population: 300.
Tristan da Cunha is midway between Africa, South America and Antarctica and 1,320 miles from St. Helena of which it became a dependency in 1938. It is a volcano (which last erupted in 1961) rising to a height of 6,760 feet above the Atlantic. Up to now, the circulating coinage has been British. Tristan da Cunha has also used South African currency up to 1961.

100 Pence = 1 £

ELIZABETH II since 1952

SILVER JUBILEE OF THE REIGN OF HER MAJESTY QUEEN ELIZABETH II

			Unc	Proof
1 (1)	25 Pence 1977:			
	a) (Ag)			32.50
	b) (Cu-Ni)		2.50	

25th ANNIVERSARY OF THE CORONATION OF HER MAJESTY QUEEN ELIZABETH II

2 (2)	1 Crown 1978:			
	a) (Ag)		20.00	35.00
	b) (Cu-Ni)		3.00	

80th BIRTHDAY OF QUEEN MOTHER

3 (3)	1 Crown 1980:			
	a) (Ag)			30.00
	b) (Cu-Ni)		2.50	

WEDDING OF PRINCE CHARLES AND LADY DIANA

4 (4)	1 Crown 1981:			
	a) (Ag)			30.00
	b) (Cu-Ni)		3.00	

INTERNATIONAL YEAR OF THE SCOUT (2)

5 (5)	1 Crown (Ag) 1982	25.00	30.00
6 (6)	2 £ (Au) 1982	300.00	350.00

Area: 48,000 sq. mi. Population: 7,100,000.

In 1881 Tunisia became a French protectorate and in 1946 an associated state of the French Union. Since 1956 the country has been independent. In the following year, after Bey Mohammed Lamine had been deposed, the country became a republic.

Capital: Tunis.

100 Centimes = 1 Tunisian Franc, 1000 Millimes = 1 Tunisian Dinar

ALI BAI 1882–1902

			VF	XF
1 (11)	1	Centime (Br) 1891. Arabic legend between branches. ℞ name of country and denomination in French; date	4.00	6.00
2 (12)	2	Centimes (Br) 1891. Type as No. 1	4.00	6.00
3 (13)	5	Centimes (Br) 1891–1893. Type as No. 1	1.50	2.00
4 (14)	10	Centimes (Br) 1891–1893. Type as No. 1	1.50	2.50

			VF	XF
5 (15)	50	Centimes (Ag) 1891–1902:		
		a) 1891	4.00	6.00
		b) 1892–1902	40.00	55.00
6 (16)	1	Franc (Ag) 1891–1902. Type as No. 5:		
		a) 1891–1892	5.50	10.00
		b) 1893–1902	80.00	110.00
7 (17)	2	Francs (Ag) 1891–1902. Type as No. 5:		
		a) 1891–1892	8.00	12.00
		b) 1893–1902	120.00	160.00

			VF	XF
8 (18)	10	Francs (Au) 1891–1902. Type as No. 5:		
		a) 1891	65.00	80.00
		b) 1892–1902	300.00	400.00
9 (19)	20	Francs (Au) 1891–1902. Type as No. 5:		
		a) 1891–1892, 1897–1901	110.00	120.00
		b) 1893	140.00	160.00
		c) 1894–1896, 1902	520.00	650.00

MOHAMMED AL HADI BEI 1902–1906

			VF	XF
10 (20)	5	Centimes (Br) 1903–1904. Type as No. 3	1.50	2.60
11 (21)	10	Centimes (Br) 1903–1904. Type as No. 4	4.00	6.50
12 (22)	50	Centimes (Ag) 1903–1906. Type as No. 5	40.00	55.00
13 (23)	1	Franc (Ag) 1903–1906. Type as No. 6:		
		a) 1903, 1905, 1906	70.00	90.00
		b) 1904	4.50	6.50
14 (24)	2	Francs (Ag) 1903–1906. Type as No. 7:		
		a) 1903, 1905, 1906	120.00	160.00
		b) 1904	8.00	12.00
15 (25)	10	Francs (Au) 1903–1906. Type as No. 8	300.00	400.00
16 (26)	20	Francs (Au) 1903–1906. Type as No. 9:		
		a) 1903–1904	120.00	140.00
		b) 1905–1906	520.00	650.00

MOHAMMED EN-NACEUR BEI 1906–1922

			VF	XF
17 (27)	5	Centimes (Br) 1907–1917. Type as No. 3	1.70	2.50
18 (28)	10	Centimes (Br) 1907–1917. Type as No. 4	2.60	4.00
19 (29)	50	Centimes (Ag) 1907–1921. Type as No. 5:		
		a) 1907, 1912, 1914–1917	3.50	5.00
		b) 1908–1911, 1913, 1918–1921	36.00	55.00
20 (30)	1	Franc (Ag) 1907–1921. Type as No. 6:		
		a) 1907–1908, 1911–1912, 1914–1918	4.00	6.00
		b) 1909–1910, 1913, 1919–1921	80.00	110.00
21 (31)	2	Francs (Ag) 1907–1921. Type as No. 7:		
		a) 1907, 1909–1910, 1913, 1917–1921	120.00	160.00
		b) 1908, 1911–1912, 1914–1916	6.50	9.00
22 (32)	10	Francs (Au) 1907–1921. Type as No. 8:		
		a) 1907	550.00	600.00
		b) 1908–1921	250.00	320.00
23 (33)	20	Francs (Au) 1907–1921. Type as No. 9:		
		a) 1907, 1909–1921	550.00	600.00
		b) 1908	400.00	500.00

| **24** (34) | 5 | Centimes (Cu–Ni) 1918–1920. Arabic |

			VF	XF
		legend. ℞ French legend. Date between branches. Diameter 19 mm, 3 g (with hole)	0.40	0.80
25 (34a)	5	Centimes (Cu–Ni) 1920. Type as No 24, but diameter 17 mm and weight 2 g (with hole)	1.50	2.50
26 (35)	10	Centimes (Cu–Ni) 1918–1920. Type as No. 24 (with hole)	0.40	0.80
27 (36)	25	Centimes (Cu–Ni) 1918–1920. Type as No. 24 (with hole):		
		a) 1918	2.50	4.00
		b) 1919–1920	1.20	1.60

MOHAMMED AL-HABIB BEI 1922–1929

28 (41)	50	Centimes (Ag) 1922–1928. Type as No. 6	35.00	48.00
29 (42)	1	Franc (Ag) 1922–1928. Type as No. 6	75.00	100.00
30 (43)	2	Francs (Ag) 1922–1928. Type as No. 7	110.00	130.00
31 (44)	10	Francs (Au) 1922–1928. Type as No. 8	280.00	400.00
32 (45)	20	Francs (Au) 1922–1928. Type as No. 9	400.00	500.00
33 (40)	10	Centimes (Ni–Br) 1926. Type as No. 26 (with hole)	1.20	2.00

AHMED BEI 1929–1942

34 (46)	5	Centimes (Cu–Ni) 1931, 1933, 1938. Type as No. 25	0.40	0.80
35 (47)	10	Centimes (Cu–Ni) 1931, 1933, 1938. Type as No. 26 (with hole)	0.80	1.20
36 (48)	25	Centimes (Cu–Ni) 1931, 1933, 1938. Type as No. 27	1.50	2.00

37 (37)	50	Centimes (Al–Bro) 1921, 1926, 1933, 1941, 1945. Date between tied laurel branches, above name of country in French. ℞ value between palm branches, above BON POUR	0.40	0.80
38 (38)	1	Franc (Al–Bro) 1921, 1926, 1941, 1945. Type as No. 37	0.70	1.20
39 (39)	2	Francs (Al–Bro) 1921, 1924, 1926, 1941, 1945. Type as No. 37	1.00	2.00

			VF	XF

40 (49) 10 Francs (Ag) 1930–1934:

    a) 1930, 1932, 1934 — 26.00 — 40.00

    b) 1931, 1933 — 85.00 — 115.00

41 (50) 20 Francs (Ag) 1930–1934. Type as No. 40:

    a) 1930, 1932, 1934 — 35.00 — 55.00

    b) 1931, 1933 — 250.00 — 320.00

42 (57) 100 Francs (Au) 1930–1937 — 135.00 — 160.00

43 100 Francs (Au) 1938–1942. Type as No. 42, but large date in place of value — 400.00 — 520.00

44 (51) 5 Francs (Ag) AH 1353, 1355 (1934, 1936) — 4.00 — 6.50

45 (52) 10 Francs (Ag) AH 1353–1356 (1934–1938). Type as No. 44:

    a) AH 1353 (1934) — 6.00 — 9.00

    b) AH 1354–1356 (1936–1938) — 80.00 — 120.00

			VF	XF
46 (53)	20 Francs (Ag) AH 1353–1356 (1934– 1938). Type as No. 44:			
	a) AH 1353 (1934)		10.00	15.00
	b) AH 1354–1356 (1936–1938)		260.00	300.00

47 (54)	5 Francs (Ag) 1939		4.00	6.50
48 (55)	10 Francs (Ag) 1939–1942. Type as No. 47:			
	a) 1939		8.00	12.00
	b) 1940–1942		80.00	110.00
49 (56)	20 Francs (Ag) 1939–1942. Type as No. 47:			
	a) 1939		16.00	26.00
	b) 1940–1942		260.00	300.00
50 (58)	10 Centimes (Sn) 1941–1942 (with hole)		0.40	0.80
51 (59)	20 Centimes (Sn) 1942		2.50	4.00

MOHAMMED AL MONCEF BEI 1942–1943

52	100 Francs (Au) 1943. Type as No. 43		–.–	–.–

MOHAMMED LAMINE BEI 1943–1957

53 (60)	10 Centimes (Sn) 1945		25.00	40.00
54 (61)	20 Centimes (Sn) 1945. Type as No. 51		27.00	45.00

			VF	XF
55 (62)	5	Francs (Al–Br) 1946	2.50	3.00

56 (63)	5	Francs (Cu–Ni) 1954, 1957	0.40	0.60
57 (64)	20	Francs (Cu–Ni) 1950, 1957. Type as No. 56	0.60	1.00
58 (65)	50	Francs (Cu–Ni) 1950, 1957. Type as No. 56	1.10	1.60
59 (66)	100	Francs (Cu–Ni) 1950, 1957. Type as No. 56	2.50	4.00
60	100	Francs (Au) 1943–1955. Type as No. 43	400.00	520.00

61	10	Francs (Ag) 1943–1944. Type as No. 48	75.00	110.00
62	20	Francs (Ag) 1943–1944. Type as No. 61	265.00	320.00

63	10	Francs (Ag) 1945–1955. Type as No. 61, but large date in place of value	40.00	55.00

			VF	XF
64	20	Francs (Ag) 1945–1955. Type as No. 63	75.00	110.00
65	10	Francs (Ag) 1956. Legend ROYAUME DE TUNISIE	–.–	–.–

66	20	Francs (Ag) 1956. Type as No. 65	–.–	–.–
67	100	Francs (Au) 1956	–.–	–.–

REPUBLIC since 1957

1000 Millimes = 1 Dinar

			XF	Unc
68 (67)	1	Millime (Al-Mg) 1960. Cork oak (Quercus suber – Fagaceae). Rev. value in wreath	0.15	0.25
69 (68)	2	Millimes (Al-Mg) 1960. Same type as No. 33	0.15	0.30
70 (69)	5	Millimes (Al-Mg) 1960. Same type as No. 33	0.25	0.50

71 (70)	10	Millimes (Bra) 1960	0.30	0.60
72 (71)	20	Millimes (Bra) 1960. Type as No. 71	0.60	1.00
73 (72)	50	Millimes (Bra) 1960. Type as No. 71	0.80	1.25
74 (73)	100	Millimes (Bra) 1960. Type as No. 71	1.25	2.50

		XF	Unc
75 (74)	½ Dinar (Cu-Ni) 1968	1.50	2.50

COMMEMORATIVE ISSUES (5) FOR THE 10th ANNIVERSARY OF THE REPUBLIC

		Proof
76	2 Dinars (Au) 1967. Habib Ibn Ali Bour-guiba (*1903), President since 1957. ℞ Kairuan, minaret of the Grand Mosque	75.00
77	5 Dinars (Au) 1967. Same type as No. 76	175.00
78	10 Dinars (Au) 1967. Same type as No. 76	300.00
79	20 Dinars (Au) 1967. Same type as No. 76	600.00
80	40 Dinars (Au) 1967. Same type as No. 76	1200.00

COMMEMORATIVE ISSUES (10) FOR THE HISTORY OF TUNISIA

81 1 Dinar (Ag) 1969. President Bourguiba.
℞ Phoenician sailing vessel with oars.
On the sail is the symbol of Tanit, the

patron goddess of Carthage, also ruler of the moon and goddess of fertility; reference to the Phoenicians who colonized the North African coast, founded Carthage in 814 B. C., and maintained a fleet as early as 650 B. C. Carthage became center of the Empire in 332 B. C. when Alexander the Great drove the Phoenicians to the western areas of the Mediterranean. Following there were the three Punic Wars against the rising Roman power   50.00

82   1 Dinar (Ag) 1969. ℞ Venus. Goddess of horticulture. Originates partly from the Punic goddess Aphrodite, from Mount Eryx in northern Sicily, which was for a time stronghold of the Carthaginian Empire. During the Second Punic War Venus became a patron goddess of Rome, and Carthage finally had to renounce northwestern Sicily. Venus, shown with the Ribbon of Love, is also the goddess of beauty. According to mythology, she sprang from the foam of the sea. Her son was Aeneas (see No. 87)   30.00

83   1 Dinar (Ag) 1969. ℞ Neptune, in vessel, drawn by four sea-horses. He is accompanied by a Triton (merman) on his left, and a mermaid on his right. While Venus was the goddess of fertility, Neptune (Greek: Poseidon) was the god of the seas, responsible for successful seafaring and fishing, (see the attributes in his hands), and therefore much respected by the Mediterranean people   30.00

84   1 Dinar (Ag) 1969. ℞ Hannibal (246–183

Proof

B. C.), son of Hamilcar Barca. Next to his father, he was the most successful Carthaginian commander. Hero of the Second Punic War, he became, only 25 years old, the Commander-in-Chief in Spain. In Spain in 219 B. C. he conquered the Roman stronghold of Saguntum and thus began the Second Punic War (218–201 B. C.). The coin pictures Hannibal leading his troops (50,000 men, 9,000 horsemen, and 37 war elephants) over the Pyrenees and the Alps towards Italy. This resulted in the most crushing defeat ever suffered by Rome (battle of Cannae). In 211 B. C., after years of fighting, Hannibal finally approached Rome. Since a reasonable peace treaty could not be realized, Hannibal finally had to leave Italy in 203 B. C. Following the decisive battle at Zama (202 B. C.), Carthage lost her predominance in the western Mediterranean region

30.00

85   1 Dinar (Ag) 1969. ℞ Masinissa (after 240–148 B. C.) Berber Prince and King of East Numidia. Supported the Carthaginians in their fight against the Romans in Spain. After the year 206 B. C. he sided with Rome, and united East and West Numidia in 201 B. C., thus becoming Carthage's principal opponent. His cavalry conquered large Carthaginian territories, thus causing the Third Punic War (149–146 B. C.), and the destruction of Carthage. Coin design: Masinissa's profile, Numidian horseman, and map of Greater Numi-

dia which extended from Mauretania
to Cyrenaica and included Carthage,
the later Roman Province of Africa,
today's Tunisia (see No. 86)

86   1 Dinar (Ag) 1969. ℞ Jugurtha. Jugurtha
above map of Numidia. A scale behind
his portrait shows a Numidian coin
balancing the Capitoline she-wolf, the
emblem of Rome. (The coin pictures
a horse in front of a palm tree, symbolic
of stock-farming and fruit growing).
The adopted son of Micipsa (who is a
son of the obove mentioned Masinissa),
outwitted Micipsa's own sons, taking
their inheritances as well as their lives.
When he defeated the Italic people he
became a danger to the Romans, a fact
that led to the so-called Juguthine War
(111–105 B. C.). His successful briberies
among leading Romans culminated in
his exclamation, "Oh venal city (Ro-
ma), how soon you shall be lost, if you
will find a buyer."

30.00

87   1 Dinar (Ag) 1969. ℞ Vergilius. Publius

Vergilius Marco (70–19 B. C.), greatest Roman poet of the Augustan times. Also called Virgil. Pictured between Clio, the muse of history, and Melpomene, the muse of vocal music, Virgil is writing his National Epos, the Aeneid. Since Aeneas is considered the ancestor of the Romans, the poem tells the story from the Trojan War to the founding of Rome. The first chapter is about a storm that brought Aeneas' fleet after a seven year odyssey, to the Court of Queen Dido, the legendary founder of Carthage. The four-volume educational poem " Georgica" made Virgil famous in Africa, which was at that time the granary of Rome. It deals with the art of agriculture, the cultivation of trees, stock-raising, and beekeeping. The design on the coin is modelled after and 2nd century Roman floor mosaic from Hadrumetum (Sousse), today in the Bardo Museum, Tunis

30.00

88 1 Dinar (Ag) 1969. ℞ Sbeitla – Sufetula. A portal with three arches built at former Roman Sufetula in honor of Emperor Antoninus Pius (150 A. D.). View of the ruins of the three Capitoline Temples near the Forum 30.00

89 1 Dinar (Ag) 1969. ℞ El Djem –Thysdrus. Amphitheatre. Because of its dimensions, the African Romans called it Colosseum. It was built around 240 A. D., in what is today El Djem (Roman: Thysdrus) by the emperors Gordianus I and III. Measuring 485×400 feet, with an arena of 214×124 feet. It seats approx. 35,000 people. As the second largest amphitheatre of the Roman Empire it is a silent witness of North African wealth. 30.00

90 1 Dinar (Ag) 1969. ℞ St. Augustinus. St. Aurelius Augustinus was one of the Latin ecclesiastical teachers of ancient times. Born in Tagaste (Numidia) in 354 A. D., he was Bishop in Hippo Regius/Bône, today's Annaba (Algeria) from 396 until his death in 430. As teacher of rhetoric in Carthage and Tagaste he founded the Augustinian philosophy, a sort of Christian Platonism, also known as Neo-Platonism.

	Unc	Proof

Therefore, the bishop is portrayed on the coin sitting behind his desk in front of a bust of Plato. In the background are the ruins of the early Christian Basilica of St. Cyprian at Carthage, excavated in 1915

30.00

2nd CONFERENCE OF THE F.A.O.

91 (75) 1 Dinar (Ag) 1970   12.00   *70.00*

20th ANNIVERSARY OF INDEPENDENCE

92 (76) 5 Dinars (Ag) 1976   30.00

FOR THE FAO COIN PLAN (2)

	XF	Unc
93 (77) ½ Dinar (Cu-Ni) 1976, 1983		5.00
94 (78) 1 Dinar (Cu-Ni) 1976, 1983		6.50

Nos. 95–99 omitted.

1500   **Tunisia**

25th ANNIVERSARY OF INDEPENDENCE (3)

		Proof
100 (81) 5 Dinars (Au) 1981		*250.00*
101 (82) 10 Dinars (Au) 1981		*400.00*
102 (83) 10 Dinars (Au) 1981		*400.00*

INTERNATIONAL YEAR OF THE CHILD (2)

103 (79) 5 Dinars (Ag) 1982:	
a) normal thickness	40.00
b) Pièfort	120.00
104 (80) 75 Dinars (Au) 1982	400.00

Türkei   # Turkey   **Turquie**

Türkiye Cümhuriyeti

Area: 296,108 sq. mi. Population: 52,000,000.

From the nucleus of the once powerful Ottoman Empire, the modern Turkish state originated after the collapse as a sequel of World War I on October 29, 1923. Mustafa Kemal Pasha (Atatürk) was at the head of the National Turks during the time of the struggle for independence from 1919 to 1923. As the country's president, Kemal Pasha championed vigorously reforms and created a state on the lines of a Western pattern. Mustapha Kemal Pasha was given the surname of Atatürk (= Father of the Turks).

Capital: Ankara.

40 Para = 1 Piastre, 100 Piastres = 1 Lira or Pound,
100 Kurus = 1 Lira

			VF	XF
1 (43)	5	Para (Ni) 1910–1914 Toughra. Ⱥ value	0.80	1.50
2 (44)	10	Para (Ni) 1910–1915	0.80	1.50
3 (45)	20	Para (Ni) 1910–1914	0.80	1.50
4 (46)	40	Para (Ni) 1911–1913	1.50	2.50
5 (47)	1	Piastre (Ag) 1909–1911. Toughra, surrounded by stars	2.50	4.00
6 (48)	2	Piastres (Ag) 1909–1914	3.50	4.50
7 (49)	5	Piastres (Ag) 1909–1915	5.50	8.00
8 (50)	10	Piastres (Ag) 1909–1915	16.00	26.00
9 (51)	20	Piastres (Ag) 1916–1918	40.00	60.00
10 (F51)	12½	Piastres (Au) H-C 1327 (1909). Toughra, surrounded by stars and olive branches		160.00
11 (53)	25	Piastres (Au) H-C 1327 (1909)	52.00	65.00
12 (54)	50	Piastres (Au) H-C 1327 (1909)	85.00	105.00
13 (55)	100	Piastres (Au) H-C 1327 (1909)	100.00	120.00
14 (56)	250	Piastres (Au) H-C 1327 (1909)	620.00	800.00
15 (57)	500	Piastres (Au) H-C 1327 (1909)	800.00	1150.00
16 (58)	40	Para (Cu–Ni) 1921	2.00	3.00
17 (59)	2	Piastres (Ag) 1918–1919		250.00
18 (60)	5	Piastres (Ag) 1918–1919		260.00
19 (61)	10	Piastres (Ag) 1918–1919		300.00
20 (62)	20	Piastres (Ag) 1918–1919		250.00
21 (63)	25	Piastres (Au) 1919–1921	60.00	105.00
22 (64)	50	Piastres (Au) 1919–1921	220.00	260.00
23 (65)	100	Piastres (Au) 1919–1921	140.00	160.00
24 (66)	250	Piastres (Au) 1919–1921	120.00	140.00

			VF	XF
25 (67)	500	Piastres (Au) 1919–1921	1200.00	1550.00

Numbers 26–69 omitted.

REPUBLIC since 1923

			VF	XF
70 (68)	100	Para (Al–Br) H-C 1340–1342 (1922–1924). Ear of wheat. ℞ oak branch, value, state emblem above	6.00	12.00
71 (69)	5	Piastres (Al–Br) H-C 1340–1341 (1922–1923)	3.00	5.00
72 (70)	10	Piastres (Al–Br) H-C 1340–1341 (1922–1923)	3.00	5.50
73 (71)	25	Piastres (Ni) H-C 1341 (1923)	7.50	12.00
74 (68a)	100	Para (Al–Br) 1926	8.00	12.00
75 (69a)	5	Piastres (Al–Br) 1926	3.50	6.00
76 (70a)	10	Piastres (Al–Br) 1926	3.00	4.50
77 (71a)	25	Piastres (Ni) 1928	6.00	12.00
78 (72)	25	Piastres (Au) 1926–1929	80.00	120.00
79 (73)	50	Piastres (Au) 1926–1928	90.00	120.00
80 (74)	100	Piastres (Au) 1926–1928	300.00	400.00
81 (75)	250	Piastres (Au) 1926–1928	600.00	800.00

82 (76)	500	Piastres (Au) 1926–1929	600.00	800.00
83 (77)	25	Piastres (Au) 1927–1928	120.00	160.00
84 (78)	50	Piastres (Au) 1927–1928. Same type as No. 83	170.00	220.00

				VF	XF
85 (79)	100	Piastres (Au) 1927–1928. Same type as No. 39		270.00	300.00
86 (80)	250	Piastres (Au) 1927–1928. Same type as No. 39		420.00	520.00
87 (81)	500	Piastres (Au) 1927–1928. Same type as No. 39		600.00	900.00

NEW CURRENCY: 100 Kurus = 1 Lira

				VF	XF
88 (82)	100	Kurus (Ag) 1934. Mustafa Kemal (1881–1938), called Atatürk (= Father of the Turks), 1st President 1923–1938. ℞ crescent and star (state emblem) and value		18.00	30.00
89 (83)	25	Kurus (Ag) 1935–1937. ℞ ear of wheat and value		5.00	10.00
90 (84)	50	Kurus (Ag) 1935–1937		8.00	13.00
91 (85)	1	Lira (Ag) 1937–1939		12.00	18.00
92 (87)	1	Kurus (Cu–Ni) 1936–1937		8.00	13.00
93 (88)	5	Kurus (Cu–Ni) 1935–1943		2.50	4.50
94 (89)	10	Kurus (Cu–Ni) 1935–1940		2.50	4.00
95 (90)	1	Kurus (Cu–Ni) 1938–1944		1.50	3.00
96 (91)	10	Para (Al–Br) 1940–1942		1.50	3.00
97 (92)	25	Kurus (Ni–Br) 1944–1946		2.50	4.00
98 (100)	25	Piastres (Au) 1943–. Head of Atatürk. Rev. Writing surrounded by wreath and 2 figures when added provide the exact year of minting, e.g. 1923 + 20 = 1943. No value; dia. 14.75 mm		22.00	25.00
99 (101)	50	Piastres (Au) 1943–. Type as No. 98; dia. 18 mm		35.00	48.00
100 (102)	100	Piastres (Au) 1943–. Type as No. 98; dia. 22 mm		90.00	100.00
101 (103)	250	Piastres (Au) 1943–. Type as No. 98; dia. 27.2 mm		190.00	210.00
102 (104)	500	Piastres (Au) 1943–. Type as No. 98; dia. 35 mm		400.00	450.00

			VF	XF
103	25	Piastres (Au) 1938–. Head of Atatürk in circle of stars and ornaments. Rev. Writing and year in circle of stars and ornaments. No value; dia. 18 mm	25.00	28.00
104	50	Piastres (Au) 1938–. Type as No. 103; dia. 22.5 mm	48.00	55.00
105	100	Piastres (Au) 1938–. Type as No. 103; dia. 31 mm	90.00	100.00
106	250	Piastres (Au) 1938–. Type as No. 103; dia. 43.5 mm	220.00	250.00
107	500	Piastres (Au) 1938–. Type as No. 103; dia. 46.5 mm	410.00	460.00
108 (86)	1	Lira (Ag) 1940–1941. Ismet Inönü (1884–1973), 2nd President 1938–1950	10.00	18.00
109 (A99)	25	Piastres (Au) 1943–1949. Head of Ismet Inönü. Rev. Writing surrounded by wreath and 2 figures, their addition provides the exact year of minting, e.g. 1923 + 20 = 1943. No value; dia. dia. 14.75 mm	30.00	40.00
110 (B99)	50	Piastres (Au) 1943–1950. Type as No. 109; dia. 18 mm	50.00	60.00
111 (C99)	100	Piastres (Au) 1943–1950. Type as No. 109; dia. 22 mm	95.00	105.00
112 (D99)	250	Piastres (Au) 1943–1947. Type as No. 109; dia. 27.2 mm	220.00	260.00
113 (E99)	500	Piastres (Au) 1943–1948. Type as No. 109; dia. 35 mm	400.00	450.00

LUXURY STRIKES (5)

			VF	XF
114	25	Piastres (Au) 1943–1949. Head of Ismet Inönü in circle of stars and ornaments. Rev. Writing and year in circle of stars and ornaments. No value; dia. 18 mm	90.00	120.00
115	50	Piastres (Au) 1943–1949. Type as No. 114; dia. 22.5 mm	130.00	150.00
116	100	Piastres (Au) 1943–1950. Type as No. 114; dia. 31 mm	130.00	150.00
117	250	Piastres (Au) 1943–1950. Type as No. 114; dia. 43.5 mm	250.00	270.00
118	500	Piastres (Au) 1943–1948. Type as No. 114; dia. 46.5 mm	500.00	600,00
119 (A92)	½	Kurus (Bra) 1948		450.00
120 (93)	1	Kurus (Bra) 1947–1951	0.20	0.40
121 (94)	2½	Kurus (Bra) 1948–1951	0.80	1.60
122 (95)	5	Kurus (Bra) 1949–1957	0.80	1.60
123 (96)	10	Kurus (Bra) 1949–1956	1.20	2.50
124 (97)	25	Kurus (Bra) 1948–1956	1.20	2.50
125 (98)	50	Kurus (Ag) 1947–1948	5.00	7.00

		VF	XF
126 (99)	1 Lira (Ag) 1947–1948	5.00	8.00
127 (110)	1 Lira (Cu–Ni) 1957. Mustafa Kemal, called Atatürk. ℞ value in wreath	1.60	3.00
128 (111)	5 Kurus (Br) 1958–1968	0.20	0.40
129 (112)	10 Kurus (Br) 1958–1968	0.25	0.50
130 (113)	25 Kurus (St) 1959–1966. Peasant woman	0.40	0.60
131 (114)	1 Lira (St) 1959–1967. Atatürk	0.50	0.80
132 (115)	2½ Lira (St) 1960–. Atatürk in uniform:		
	a) 1960–1968; 12 gm.	0.80	2.00
	b) 1969–; 9 gm.	0.40	0.80

		VF	XF
133 (116)	10 Lira (Ag) 1960–. Atatürk. R emblem of the National Unity Committee and date May 27, 1960 = the day when General Cemal Gürsel came to power	10.50	16.00
134 (117)	1 Kurus (Bra) 1961–1963. Olive branch	0.25	0.35
135 (117a)	1 Kurus (Br) 1963–1974	0.10	0.20
136 (111a)	5 Kurus (Br) 1969–1973. Same type as No. 128, but reduced weight	0.10	0.20
137 (112a)	10 Kurus (Br) 1969–1973. Same type as No. 129	0.10	0.20
138 (113a)	25 Kurus (St) 1966–1978. Same type as No. 130	0.30	0.50
139 (114a)	1 Lira (St) 1967–1980. Same type as No. 131, but lower weigth	0.30	0.50

ISSUES (2) FOR THE FAO COIN PLAN

		XF	Unc
140	10 Kurus (Br) 1971–1974. Atatürk on tractor (symbolical for progress). R Ears of wheat (Triticum aestivum – Grami- neae), value, date:		
	a) (Y A118) 1971, 1972; 3.40 gm.	0.35	0.50
	b) 1973; 3.40 gm.		12.50
	c) (Y A118a) 1974; 2.50 gm.	1.75	3.50

	XF	Unc
141 (118) 2½ Lira (St) 1970. Atatürk at wheel of tractor. Motto: "The plough is superior to the sword". R value and date between tied ears of wheat and laurel branches	0.60	1.25

COMMEMORATIVE ISSUE FOR THE 50th ANNIVERSARY OF THE TURKISH PARLIAMENT

	Unc	Proof
142 (119) 25 Lira (Ag) 1970. Atatürk. R Parliament building in Ankara, value	10.00	20.00

143 (A113) 50 Kurus (Ac) 1971–1977. Anatolic bride. Rev. Value, date	0.15	0.30

COMMEMORATIVE ISSUE FOR THE 900th ANNIVERSARY OF THE VICTORY OF THE SELJUKS OVER THE BYZANTINES

144 (120) 50 Lira (Ag) 1971. Alparslan (reigned

		Unc	Proof

from 1063 to 1073), was victorious at Manzikert on Lake Wan over the Byzantines led by Romanos IV. ℞ Asia Minor with marking of the battle-field   12.00   27.50

COMMEMORATIVE ISSUE FOR THE 50th ANNIVERSARY OF KEMAL ATATÜRK'S ENTRY INTO SMYRNA

145 (121)   50 Lira (Ag) 1972. Equestrian statue of Atatürk. ℞ scene of battle   12.00   27.50

50th ANNIVERSARY OF THE REPUBLIC (3)

			XF	Unc
146 (122)	50 Lira (Ag) 1973			10.00
147 (123)	100 Lira (Ag) 1973. Type as No. 146			18.00

148 (124)	500 Lira (Au) 1973. Type similar to No. 146			120.00
149 (111b)	5 Kurus (Br) 1974. Type as No. 136; 1.35 gr.		0.10	0.30

			XF	Unc
150 (112b)	10 Kurus (Br) 1974. Type as No. 137; 2.5 gr.		0.10	0.30
151 (125)	5 Lira (St) 1974–1979. Atatürk on horse-back		0.80	1.20
152 (117b)	1 Kurus (Al) 1975–1977. Type as No. 134		0.05	0.10
153 (111b)	5 Kurus (Al) 1975–1977. Type as No. 128		0.05	0.15
154 (112b)	10 Kurus (Al) 1975–1977. Type as No. 129		0.10	0.20

FOR THE FAO COIN PLAN (2)

155 (126)	5 Kurus (Al) 1975. Anatolic bride		0.60	1.80
156	10 Kurus (Al) 1975, 1976. Type as No. 140		0.30	0.60

FOR THE FAO COIN PLAN (3)

157 (128)	5 Kurus (Al) 1976			1.80
158 (129)	10 Kurus (Al) 1976			3.00

159 (127)	5 Lira (St) 1976			12.50

FOR THE FAO COIN PLAN (3)

160	2½ Lira (St) 1977			10.00
161	5 Lira (St) 1977			10.00
162	50 Lira (Ag) 1977			18.00

		Unc	Proof
163	150 Lira (Ag) 1978	20.00	100.00

705th ANNIVERSARY OF THE DEATH OF MEVLANA (3)

		Unc	Proof
164	200 Lira (Ag) 1978. Mevlana Jelal ed-Din Rumi (1207–1273), mystic poet	12.00	17.50
165	500 Lira (Au) 1978 (900 pieces)		225.00
166	1000 Lira (Au) 1978 (450 pieces)		550.00

FOR THE FAO COIN PLAN (8)

		Unc
167	50 Kurus (St) 1978. Type as No. 159	2.00
168	1 Lira (St) 1978. Type as No. 159	3.00
169	2½ Lira (St) 1978. Type as No. 159	6.00
170	5 Lira (St) 1978. Type as No. 142	8.00
171	150 Lira (Ag) 1978. Type as No. 142	12.00

1510   Turkey

		Proof
172	150 Lira (Ag) 1978. Type as No. 171, but edge inscription FAO and arabesques	50.00

173	500 Lira (Au) 1978. Mother and child		300.00
174	1000 Lira (Au) 1978. Anatolic bride		550.00

		XF	**Unc**
175	1 Kurus (Br) 1979. Anatolic bride. Rev. olive branch	0.15	0.30
176	1 Kurus (Al) 1979. Type as No. 175	0.15	0.30

FOR THE FAO COIN PLAN (10)

		XF	**Unc**
177	50 Kurus (St) 1979. Type as No. 142	0.15	0.30
178	1 Lira (St) 1979. Type as No. 142	0.30	0.50
179	2½ Lira (St) 1979. Anatolic bride. Rev. value	0.40	0.80
180	5 Lira (St) 1979. Type as No. 179	0.80	1.25
181	150 Lira (Ag) 1979. Type as No. 179, reeded edge	7.50	10.00

		Proof
A 181	150 Lira (Ag) 1979. Type as No. 179, edge inscription FAO and arabesques	50.00
182	500 Lira (Au) 1979. Anatolic bride	225.00
183	1000 Lira (Au) 1979. Mother and child	400.00

INTERNATIONAL YEAR OF THE CHILD (2)

		XF	**Unc**
184	500 Lira (Ag) 1979. Five children in front of mosque	35.00	60.00
185	10,000 Lira (Au) 1979. Type as No. 184:		
	a) normal thickness		400.00
	b) Pièfort		–.–

		XF	Unc
186	5 Kurus (Br) 1980. Fishermen within a flounder. Rev. oak branch		1.50
187	10 Kurus (Br) 1980. Anatolic bride. Rev. corn-ears	0.15	0.30
188	50 Kurus (St) 1980. Anatolic bride. Rev. value in wreath	0.15	0.30
189	1 Lira (St) 1980. Type as No. 188	0.40	0.80
190	2½ Lira (St) 1980. Fishermen within a flounder. Rev. value in wreath		3.00
191	5 Lira (St) 1980. Type as No. 190		6.00
192	500 Lira (Ag) 1980. Mother and child		12.00
A 192	500 Lira (Ag) 1980. Type as No. 192, edge inscription FAO and arabesques		35.00
193	500 Lira (Au) 1980. Type as No. 192	Proof	225.00
194	1 Lira (Al) 1981. Atatürk left. Rev. value in wreath	0.15	0.30
195	5 Lira (Al) 1981. Equestrian statue of Atatürk. Rev. value in wreath	0.20	0.40
196	10 Lira (Al) 1981. Atatürk, uniformed half bust. Rev. value in wreath	0.60	1.00

ATATÜRK BIRTH CENTENNIAL (4)

197	½ Lira (Ag) 1981. Atatürk, head right. Rev. State emblem (crescent facing right) above globe		12.50
198	1 Lira (Ag) 1981. Type as No. 197		27.50
199	½ Lira (Au) 1981. Type as No. 197		225.00
200	1 Lira (Au) 1981. Type as No. 197		400.00

WORLD FOOD DAY 1981 AND 1982 (2)

		XF	Unc
201	20 Lira (Al) 1981. She-goat with kid. Rev. value in wreath, crescent facing right	0.80	1.25

		Unc	Proof
202	1500 Lira (Ag) 1981, 1982. Type as No. 201	22.50	30.00

INTERNATIONAL YEAR OF DISABLED PERSONS (2)

			Unc	Proof
203	3000	Lira (Ag) 1981:		
		a) normal thickness	30.00	40.00
		b) Pièfort		80.00
204	30,000	Lira (Au) 1981:		
		a) normal thickness		350.00
		b) Pièfort		500.00

			XF	Unc
205	1	Lira (Al) 1982. Atatürk left. Rev. value in wreath, crescent facing right	0.15	0.30
206	5	Lira (Al) 1982. Equestrian statue of Atatürk. Rev. value in wreath, crescent facing right	0.25	0.40
207	10	Lira (Al) 1982. Atatürk, uniformed half bust. Rev. value in wreath, crescent facing right	0.60	1.00

WORLD SOCCER CHAMPIONSHIP GAMES IN SPAIN (4)

			Unc	Proof
208	100	Lira (Cu-Ni) 1982. Soccer player. Rev. soccer ball, combined with globe and date	5.00	
209	500	Lira (Ag) 1982. Soccer player. Rev. emblem and map of Spain on globe		35.00
210	500	Lira (Ag) 1982. Soccer ball. Rev. goalkeeper		35.00
211	5000	Lira (Au) 1982. Soccer player. Rev. soccer ball, combined with globe and ISPANYA '82		225.00

15th CENTURY OF HEGIRA

			Unc	Proof
212	100,000	Lira (Au) 1982. Mosque of Sultan Ahmed I (1603–1617). Rev. seal of Mohammed		1200.00

YEAR OF THE SCOUT (2)

			Unc	Proof
213	3000	Lira (Ag) 1982	35.00	50.00
214	30,000	Lira (Au) 1982	350.00	400.00

WORLD FOOD DAY 1983

215	1500	Lira (Ag) 1983. She-goat with kid. Rev. value, date	50.00

		XF	Unc
216	500 Lira (Cu-Ni) 1983. First coin in the world: Lydia BC. 640 Anatolia	5.00	6.50

60th ANNIVERSARY OF REPUBLIC

			Unc
217	3000 Lira (Ag) 1983. Atatürk. Rev. crowd		27.50

WORLD CONFERENCE ON FISHERIES (2)

		Unc	Proof
218	500 Lira 1984. Turbot (Bothus maximus – Bothidae):		
	a) (Ag)		50.00
	b) (Cu-Ni)	6.00	
219	500 Lira (Au) 1984. Type as No. 218		1200.00

XIV OLYMPIC WINTER GAMES SARAJEVO 1984

		Unc
220	5000 Lira (Ag) 1984	40.00

XXIII OLYMPIC SUMMER GAMES LOS ANGELES 1984

		Unc
221	5000 Lira (Ag) ND (1984). Olympic flame	40.00
222	5000 Lira (Ag) 1984	40.00

DECADE FOR WOMEN (2)

		Proof
222	5000 Lira (Ag) 1984. Woman holding emblem	35.00
223	50,000 Lira (Au) 1984. Type as No. 222	250.00

		XF	Unc
226	1 Lira (Al) 1984–1986. Atatürk left. Rev. value in wreath	0.10	0.20
227	5 Lira (Al) 1984–1986. Type as No. 226	0.15	0.25

		XF	Unc
228	10 Lira (Al) 1984–1987. Type as No. 226	0.15	0.25
229	20 Lira (Ni) 1984. Type as No. 226	0.25	0.50
230	25 Lira (Al) 1984–1987. Type as No. 226	0.25	0.50
231	50 Lira (St) 1984–1987. Type as No. 226	0.35	0.75
232	100 Lira (St) 1984–1987. Type as No. 226	0.50	1.00

Turks and Caicos Islands

Turks- und Caicos-Inseln   **Turks et Caicos (Iles des)**

Area: 166 sq. mi. Population: 8000.
The Turks and Caicos Islands form the southeastern group of the Bahamas.

12 Pence = 1 Shilling, 20 Shillings = 1 £

			Unc	Proof
1 (1)	1	Crown (Cu–Ni) 1969. Elizabeth II. ℞ coat of arms with heraldic designs: queen conch (Strombus gigas – Strombidae), lobster (Palinurus argus – Palinuridae), Turks's head cactus (Melocactus communis – Cactaceae); helmet decoration: brown pelican (Pelecanus occidentalis – Pelecanidae); shield supporters: red flamingos (Phoenicopterus ruber ruber – Phoenicopteridae)	4.00	10.00

100th ANNIVERSARY OF THE BIRTH OF SIR WINSTON CHURCHILL (3)

			Unc	Proof
2 (2)	20	Crowns (Ag) 1974. Bust of Sir Winston Churchill	15.00	25.00
3 (3)	50	Crowns (Au) 1974. Type as No. 2	80.00	90.00
4 (4)	100	Crowns (Au) 1974. Type as No. 2	150.00	150.00
5 (5)	1	Crown (Cu–Ni) 1975–1977. Rev. map	3.00	7.00
6 (6)	5	Crowns (Ag) 1975–1977. Rev. Turk's head cactus	10.00	12.50
7 (14)	10	Crowns (Ag) 1976, 1977. Rev. salt windmill	25.00	35.00
8 (9)	25	Crowns (Au) 1975, 1976. Rev. coat of arms:		
		a) 1975; 17 mm dia.	50.00	50.00
		b) 1976, 1977; 19 mm dia.	50.00	50.00

AGE OF EXPLORATION (4)

		Unc	Proof
9 (7)	10 Crowns (Ag) 1975. Two spacecraft in orbit	35.00	45.00
10 (8)	20 Crowns (Ag) 1975. Christopher Columbus	40.00	50.00
11 (10)	50 Crowns (Au) 1975. Type as No. 9	150.00	125.00
12 (11)	100 Crowns (Au) 1975. Type as No. 8	200.00	200.00

BICENTENARY OF AMERICAN INDEPENDENCE (2)

13 (12)	20 Crowns (Ag) 1976. King Georg III and George Washington	40.00	50.00
14 (13)	50 Crowns (Au) 1976. Type as No. 12	150.00	140.00

QUEEN VICTORIA COMMEMORATIVE (3)

15 (15)	20 Crowns (Ag) 1976. Four portraits of Queen Victoria	40.00	50.00
16 (16)	50 Crowns (Ag) 1976. Type as No. 15	65.00	80.00
17 (17)	100 Crowns (Au) 1976. Type as No. 15	200.00	220.00

SILVER JUBILEE OF HER MAJESTY QUEEN ELIZABETH II (2)

18 (18)	25 Crowns (Ag) 1977	50.00	75.00
19 (19)	50 Crowns (Au) 1977	100.00	120.00

GEORGE III PORTRAITS

20 (20)	20 Crowns (Ag) 1977	40.00	50.00
21 (21)	50 Crowns (Ag) 1977	70.00	75.00
22 (22)	100 Crowns (Au) 1977	200.00	220.00

11th COMMONWEALTH GAMES (2)

23 (23)	20 Crowns (Ag) 1978		50.00
24 (24)	100 Crowns (Au) 1978		175.00

25th ANNIVERSARY OF CORONATION (20)

		Proof
25 (25)	25 Crowns (Ag) 1978. The lion of England	50.00
26 (26)	25 Crowns (Ag) 1978. The griffin of Edward III	50.00
27 (27)	25 Crowns (Ag) 1978. The red dragon of Wales	50.00
28 (28)	25 Crowns (Ag) 1978. The white greyhound of Richmond	50.00
29 (29)	25 Crowns (Ag) 1978. The unicorn of Scotland	50.00
30 (30)	25 Crowns (Ag) 1978. The white horse of Hanover	50.00
31 (31)	25 Crowns (Ag) 1978. The black bull of Clarence	50.00
32 (32)	25 Crowns (Ag) 1978. The yale of Beaufort	50.00
33 (33)	25 Crowns (Ag) 1978. The falcon of the Plantagenets	50.00
34 (34)	25 Crowns (Ag) 1978. The white lion of Mortimer	50.00
35 (35)	50 Crowns (Au) 1978. Type as No. 25	150.00
36 (36)	50 Crowns (Au) 1978. Type as No. 26	150.00
37 (37)	50 Crowns (Au) 1978. Type as No. 27	150.00
38 (38)	50 Crowns (Au) 1978. Type as No. 28	150.00
39 (39)	50 Crowns (Au) 1978. Type as No. 29	150.00
40 (40)	50 Crowns (Au) 1978. Type as No. 30	150.00
41 (41)	50 Crowns (Au) 1978. Type as No. 31	150.00
42 (42)	50 Crowns (Au) 1978. Type as No. 32	150.00
43 (43)	50 Crowns (Au) 1978. Type as No. 33	150.00
44 (44)	50 Crowns (Au) 1978. Type as No. 34	150.00

10th ANNIVERSARY OF INVESTITURE OF CHARLES AS PRINCE OF WALES (2)

		Proof
45 (45)	10 Crowns (Ag) 1979	40.00
46 (46)	100 Crowns (Au) 1979	200.00

LORD MOUNTBATTEN (4)

47 (47)	5 Crowns (Ag) 1980:	
	a) normal thickness	25.00
	b) Piéfort	100.00
48 (48)	10 Crowns (Ag) 1980:	
	a) normal thickness	40.00
	b) Piéfort	140.00

			Proof
49 (49)	20 Crowns (Ag) 1980:		
	a) normal thickness		45.00
	b) Piéfort		180.00
50 (50)	100 Crowns (Au) 1980:		
	a) normal thickness		300.00
	b) Piéfort		700.00

WEDDING OF PRINCE CHARLES AND LADY DIANA (2)

51 (52)	10 Crowns (Ag) 1981	30.00
52 (51)	100 Crowns (Au) 1981. Conjoined heads	250.00

		XF	Unc
53 (53)	¼ Crown (Cu-Ni) 1981. Elizabeth II. Rev. lobster	0.60	0.90
54 (54)	½ Crown (Cu-Ni) 1981. Rev. salt windmill	1.00	1.25

INTERNATIONAL YEAR OF THE CHILD

		Proof
55 (55)	10 Crowns (Ag) 1982:	
	a) normal strike	35.00
	b) Pièfort	120.00

WORLD SOCCER CHAMPIONSHIP GAMES 1982 (3)

56 (56)	10 Crowns (Ag) 1982	40.00
57 (57)	10 Crowns (Ag) 1982	40.00
58	100 Crowns (Au) 1982	200.00

XXIII. OLYMPIC SUMMER GAMES LOS ANGELES 1984

59	10 Crowns (Ag) 1984	40.00

DECADE FOR WOMEN 1976–1985 (2)

60	10 Crowns (Ag) 1985	30.00
61	100 Crowns (Au) 1985	200.00

Area: 65,800 sq. mi. Population: 192,000.
This country, also known by the name of Tannu Tuva, used to belong
as the northern part of Mongolia to the Chinese, later to the Czarist
sphere of influence, and in September 1921 became the independent
Tuvin Aratic Republic (TAR = People's Republic Tuva). Since October 11, 1944, Tuva is an autonomous region within the association of
states within the Soviet Union.
Capital: Kyzyl.

100 KΘPEJEH (≐ Kopeks) = 1 AKSA (= Rouble)

			VF	XF
1 (1)	1	KΘPEJEH (Al-Br) 1934. Designation of state in a circle inscription in Tuvinian-Latin letters. Ŗ value and date	40.00	60.00
2 (2)	2	KΘPEJEH (Al-Br) 1934. Type as No. 1	40.00	60.00
3 (3)	3	KΘPEJEH (Al-Br) 1934. Type as No. 1	40.00	60.00
4 (4)	5	KΘPEJEH (Al-Br) 1934. Type as No. 1	40.00	60.00
5 (5)	10	KΘPEJEH (Cu-Ni) 1934. Type as No. 1	40.00	60.00
6 (6)	15	KΘPEJEH (Cu-Ni) 1934. Type as No. 1	50.00	70.00
7 (7)	20	KΘPEJEH (Cu-Ni) 1934. Type as No. 1	50.00	65.00

**Values are given for each coin in U.S. Dollars and reference to Yeoman-
numbers.**

Area: 10 sq. mi. Population: 9,000.

In October 1975, the nine Ellice Islands (formerly a part of the Gilbert and Ellice Colony) gained self government and became British Dependency of Tuvalu. Full independence was attained on October 1st, 1978.
Capital: Funafuti.   100 Cents = 1 Dollar

			Unc	Proof
1 (1)	1	Cent (Br) 1976, 1981, 1985. Bust right of the Queen. Rev.	0.15	1.00
2 (2)	2	Cents (Br) 1976, 1981, 1985	0.20	1.00
3 (3)	5	Cents (Cu-Ni) 1976, 1981, 1985	0.40	1.50
4 (4)	10	Cents (Cu-Ni) 1976, 1981, 1985. Rev. crab	0.50	2.00
5 (5)	20	Cents (Cu-Ni) 1976, 1981, 1985. Rev. flying fish	0.80	2.50
6 (6)	50	Cents (Cu-Ni) 1976, 1981, 1985. Rev. octopus	1.50	3.00
7 (7)	1	Dollar (Cu-Ni) 1976, 1981. Rev. sea-turtle	4.00	5.00
8 (8)	5	Dollars (Ag) 1976. Rev. outrigger canoe		40.00
9 (9)	50	Dollars (Au) 1976. Rev. native's hut		300.00

1th ANNIVERSARY OF INDEPENDENCE

10 (10)	10	Dollars 1979. Two-masted sailing vessel »Rebecca«:		
		a) .925 silver		55.00
		b) .500 silver	25.00	

80th BIRTHDAY OF QUEEN MOTHER

11 (11)	10	Dollars 1980. Portrait of Queen Mother.		
		a) .925 silver		30.00
		b) .500 silver	15.00	

WEDDING OF PRINCE CHARLES AND LADY DIANA (2)

12 (12)	5	Dollars 1981:		
		a) (Ag)		35.00
		b) (Cu-Ni)	4.00	
13 (14)	50	Dollars (Au) 1981. Type as No. 12		300.00

DUKE OF EDINBURGH'S AWARD SILVER JUBILEE

14 (13)	10	Dollars 1981:		
		a) .925 silver		30.00
		b) .500 silver	20.00	

ROYAL VISIT

15 (15)	10	Dollars 1982:		
		a) .925 silver		35.00
		b) .500 silver	22.50	

Uganda

Uganda   **Uganda**   **Ouganda**

Area: 93,981 sq. mi. Population: 15,500,000.
This former British protectorate in East Africa became an independent republic within the framework of the British Commonwealth on October 9, 1962.
Capital: Kampala.

100 Cents = 1 Uganda Shilling

			XF	Unc
1 (1)		5 Cents (Br) 1966, 1974–1976. Value in letters. R numeral of value between elephant's tusks	0.10	0.20
2 (2)		10 Cents (Br) 1966–1976. Same tpye as No. 1	0.15	0.30
3 (3)		20 Cents (Br) 1966, 1974. Same type as No. 1	0.25	0.40
4 (4)		50 Cents (Cu-Ni) 1966–1976. Coat of arms. R crested crane (Balearica pavonina gibberifrons – Balearicidae) and mountains	0.30	0.50
5 (5)		1 Shilling (Cu-Ni) 1966–1976	0.40	1.00

6 (6)		2 Shillings (Cu–Ni) 1966	1.00	2.50

All valuations in the SCHÖN are stated in U.S. Dollars.

7 (7) 5 Shillings (Cu–Ni) 1968. On the left of the coat of arms a southern Uganda buffon's kob (Adenota kob thomasi – Bovidae), supporting the shield, coffee branch below (Coffea arabica – Rubiaceae), on the right the shield is supported by an eastern crowned crane, below cotton plant. (Gossypium sp. – Malvaceae). ℞ cattle: cow with calf. Legend reads "Produce more food – FAO Coin Plan"

	Unc	Proof
	3.50	10.00

VISIT OF POPE PAUL VI TO KAMPALA, ON JULY 31, 1969 (10)

8   2 Shillings (Ag) 1969–. Portrait of Pope Paul VI, right, with cap; papal arms; martyr shrine. ℞ coat of arms, value 12.00

9   5 Shillings (Ag) 1969–. Crested crane and hippopotamus in African landscape. R like No. 8 .... 20.00

10 10 Shillings (Ag) 1969–. Martyr shrine in Namugongo near Kampala, built in honour of the 22 Uganda martyrs (1885/87). ℞ like No. 8 .... 25.00

11 20 Shillings (Ag) 1969–. Pope Paul VI, in blessing gesture. Map of Africa and Southern Europe, with itinerary Rome – Libya – Sudan – Kampala. ℞ like No. 8 .... 40.00

				Proof
12	25	Shillings (Ag) 1969–. Pope Paul VI in front of stylized globe, marking the Pope's visits during the past pontificate: Jerusalem 1964, Bombay 1964, New York 1965, Fatima 1967, Constantinople 1967, Bogotá 1968, Geneva 1969, Kampala 1969. ℞ like No. 8			60.00
13	30	Shillings (Ag) 1969–. Same type as No. 8			85.00
14	50	Shillings (Au) 1969–. Same type as No. 10			125.00
15	100	Shillings (Au) 1969–. Same type as No. 11			275.00
16	500	Shillings (Au) 1969–. Same type as No. 12			1200.00
17	1000	Shillings (Au) 1969–. Same type as No. 8			2500.00

			Unc
18 (8)	5	Shillings (Cu-Ni) 1972. Same type as No. 4 (heptagonal)	160.00

OAU CONFERENCE KAMPALA 1975

			Unc	Proof
A18	1 £ (Au) 1975. Idi Amin, bust. Rev. arms			1000.00
B18	1 £ (Au) 1975. Idi Amin as Field Marshall		225.00	

WEDDING OF PRINCE CHARLES AND LADY DIANA SPENCER (3)

			Unc	Proof
19 (9)	10	Shillings (Cu-Ni) 1981	5.00	
20 (10)	100	Shillings (Ag) 1981		40.00
21 (11)	1000	Shillings (Au) 1981		185.00

UGANDA – PEARL OF AFRICA (2)

			Unc	Proof
22 (12)	500	Shillings (Ag) 1981. African Elephants	125.00	160.00
23 (13)	5000	Shillings (Au) 1981. Crested Crane	700.00	700.00

INTERNATIONAL YEAR OF DISABLED PERSONS (2)

			Unc	Proof
24 (14)	200	Shillings (Ag) 1981:		
		a)	25.00	30.00
		b) Pièfort		80.00
25 (15)	2000	Shillings (Au) 1981	300.00	350.00

Umm Al Kiwain   # Umm al Qiwain   **Oumm Al Qiwain**

Area: 290 sq. mi. Population: 3700.
The Sheikdom of Umm al Qiwain is one of the seven Trucial States in Pacified Oman. Since December 2, 1971 Umm al Qiwain is a member state of the "United Arab Emirates" (UAE).
Capital: Umm al Qiwain.

100 Dirham = 1 Umm al Qiwain Riyal
AHMAD BEN RASHID AL-MAALLA

			Proof
1	1	Riyal (Ag) 1970. Old cannon. ℞ state emblem, value	12.50
2	2	Riyals (Ag) 1970. Portuguese fort of the 19th century, and cannon. ℞ like No. 1	20.00

3	5	Riyals (Ag) 1970. Gazelle (Gazella gazella – Bovidae). ℞ like No. 1	40.00
4	10	Riyals (Ag) 1970. Abu Simbel, seated statues of Rameses II from the northern facade of the Great Rock Temple (19th Dynasty, c. 1250 B. C.). ℞ like No. 1	55.00
5	25	Riyals (Au) 1970. Same type as No. 1	150.00
6	50	Riyals (Au) 1970. Same type as No. 2	285.00
7	100	Riyals (Au) 1970. Same type as No. 3	450.00
8	200	Riyals (Au) 1970. Sheik Ahmed Ben Rashid Al Maalla. ℞ like No. 1	700.00

United Arab Emirates

Vereinigte Arabische Emirate   **Émirats Arabes Unis**

The sheikdoms of Abu Dhabi, Ajman, Dubai, Fujairah, Sharjah and Umm al Qaiwain proclaimed the Federation of Arab Emirates on 2nd December 1971. The residence of Sheikh Sajed bin Sultan in Abu Dhabi was declared the provisional capital. By mid-February 1972 the seventh Gulf sheikdom, Ras al Khaimah, joined the federation.

100 Fils = 1 Dirham

ISSUES (2) FOR THE FAO COIN PLAN

			XF	Unc
1 (1)	1	Fils (Br) 1973, 1975. Date palms (Phoenix dactylifera – Palmae) with legend "Increase Food Production"	0.30	0.60

			XF	Unc
2 (2)	5	Fils (Br) 1973. Mata Hari fish (Lethrinus nebulosus – Lithrinidae) with legend "Cleaner seas, more food for mankind"	0.30	0.60
3 (3)	10	Fils (Ni–Bra) 1973. Arab dhow	0.40	0.60
4 (4)	25	Fils (Cu-Ni) 1973. Arab dune gazelle		
5 (5)	50	Fils (Cu-Ni) 1973, 1982. Oil derricks	0.80	1.20
6 (6)	1	Dirham (Cu-Ni) 1973, 1982. Jug	1.00	2.00

INTERNATIONAL YEAR OF THE CHILD (2)

			Proof
7 (7)	50	Dirhams (Ag) 1980:	
		a)	35.00
		b) Pièfort	125.00
8 (8)	750	Dirhams (Au) 1980:	
		a)	350.00
		b) Pièfort	1600.00

United States of America

Vereinigte Staaten von Amerika　　　　**États-Unis d'Amérique**

Area: 3,619,615 sq. mi. Population: 241,000,000.
The United States of America are a presidential republic in accordance with
the Federal Constitution of 1787.
Capital: Washington, D.C.

10 Cents = 1 Dime, 25 Cents = Quarter Dollar,
50 Cents = Half Dollar, 100 Cents = 1 Dollar,
10 Dollars = 1 Eagle

Mints and mintmarks:

CC = Carson City, Nevada. 1870-1893.
D　= Denver, Colorado. 1906 to date.
O　= New Orleans, Louisiana. 1838-1909.
P　= Philadelphia, Pennsylvania. 1793 to date. Coins struck at Philadelphia
　　　(with some exceptions) do not carry a mintmark.
S　= San Francisco, California. 1854 to date.
W = West Point. 1984 to date.
L　= the initial of the engraver, Longacre.

1 (2b)　　1 Cent (Br) 1864–1909. Head of Red In-
　　　　　dian squaw with plumes. R denomina-
　　　　　tion in words, surrounded by laurel
　　　　　wreath. A small shield at the top. **Indian
　　　　　Head Cent:**

	Mintage	Fine	VF	XF
1864	39,233,714	8.00	16.00	30.00
1864 L		40.00	90.00	140.00
1865	35,429,286	6.00	15.00	30.00
1866	9,826,500	25.00	50.00	75.00
1867	9,821,000	25.00	50.00	75.00
1868	10,266,500	25.00	50.00	75.00
1869/8	6,420,000	165.00	300.00	450.00
1869		50.00	85.00	150.00
1870	5,275,000	35.00	60.00	110.00
1871	3,929,500	40.00	76.00	110.00
1872	4,042,000	60.00	100.00	160.00
1873	11,676,500	12.00	20.00	45.00
1874	14,187,500	10.00	18.00	40.00
1875	13,528,000	10.00	30.00	40.00
1876	7,944,000	18.00	30.00	50.00
1877	852,500	300.00	500.00	700.00
1878	5,799,850	22.00	42.00	60.00
1879	16,231,200	7.00	14.00	20.00
1880	38,964,955	3.00	5.00	12.00
1881	39,211,575	2.50	5.00	12.00
1882	38,581,100	2.50	5.00	12.00
1883	45,589,109	2.50	5.00	12.00
1884	23,261,742	4.00	9.00	18.00
1885	11,765,384	7.00	12.00	25.00
1886	17,654,290	5.00	8.00	17.50
1887	45,226,483	2.00	4.00	10.00
1888	37,494,414	2.00	4.00	10.00
1889	48,869,361	2.00	4.00	10.00
1890	57,182,854	2.00	4.00	10.00
1891	47,072,350	2.00	4.00	10.00
1892	37,649,832	2.00	4.00	10.00
1893	46,642,195	2.00	4.00	10.00
1894	16,752,132	4.00	6.00	15.00
1895	38,343,636	1.50	3.00	6.00
1896	39,057,293	1.50	3.00	6.00
1897	50,466,330	1.50	3.00	6.00
1898	49,823,079	1.50	3.00	6.00
1899	53,600,031	1.50	3.00	6.00
1900	66,833,764	1.50	3.00	6.00
1901	79,611,143	1.50	3.00	6.00
1902	87,376,722	1.50	3.00	6.00
1903	85,094,493	1.50	3.00	6.00
1904	61,328,015	1.50	3.00	6.00
1905	80,719,163	1.50	3.00	6.00
1906	96,022,255	1.50	3.00	6.00
1907	108,138,618	1.50	3.00	6.00
1908	32,327,987	1.50	3.00	6.00
1908 S	1,115,000	16.00	30.00	50.00
1909	14,370,645	2.00	4.00	9.00
1909 S	309,000	110.00	150.00	220.00

2 (14)   5 Cents (Cu-Ni) 1883–1913. Head of the Goddess of Liberty facing left. R Roman numeral in laurel wreath, name of country, coin designation CENTS a bottom. **Liberty Head Nickel:**

	Mintage	Fine	VF	XF
1883 NC	5,479,519	4.00	6.00	10.00
1883 WC	16,032,983	10.00	18.00	35.00
1884	11,273,942	12.00	20.00	40.00
1885	1,476,490	400.00	550.00	700.00
1886	3,330,290	90.00	135.00	225.00
1887	15,263,652	10.00	16.00	32.00
1888	10,720,483	12.00	20.00	38.00
1889	15,881,361	10.00	16.00	32.00
1890	16,259,272	12.00	18.00	35.00
1891	16,834,350	8.50	16.00	32.00
1892	11,699,642	9.00	17.50	35.00
1893	13,370,195	8.50	16.00	32.00
1894	5,413,132	12.50	22.00	50.00
1895	9,979,884	8.00	15.00	30.00
1896	8,842,920	9.00	17.50	32.00
1897	20,428,735	4.00	8.00	20.00
1898	12,532,087	4.00	8.00	20.00
1899	26,029,031	3.00	8.00	18.00
1900	27,255,995	3.00	8.00	18.00
1901	26,480,213	3.00	8.00	18.00
1902	31,480,579	3.00	8.00	18.00
1903	28,006,725	3.00	8.00	18.00
1904	21,404,984	3.00	9.00	20.00
1905	29,827,276	3.00	8.00	18.00
1906	38,613,725	2.50	7.00	18.00
1907	39,214,800	2.50	7.00	18.00
1908	22,686,177	2.50	7.00	18.00
1909	11,590,526	3.00	8.00	18.00
1910	30,169,353	2.50	7.00	18.00
1911	39,559,372	2.50	7.00	18.00
1912	26,236,714	2.50	7.00	18.00
1912 D	8,474,000	6.00	12.00	40.00
1912 S	238,000	60.00	140.00	340.00
1913	only 5 pieces known.			

3 (15) 1 Dime (Ag) 1892–1916. Laurel-wreathed head of the Goddess of Liberty facing right. R denomination in words in wreath. **Barber Dime:**

	without mintmark		D		O		S	
	VF	XF	VF	XF	VF	XF	VF	XF
1892	10.00	20.00			15.00	30.00	60.00	90.00
1893	15.00	25.00			35.00	50.00	20.00	30.00
1894	35.00	70.00			110.00	220.00	Proof	–.–
1895	100.00	185.00			250.00	380.00	40.00	65.00
1896	20.00	35.00			100.00	175.00	75.00	120.00
1897	8.00	20.00			90.00	185.00	30.00	50.00
1898	7.00	18.00			25.00	45.00	20.00	35.00
1899	7.00	18.00			25.00	45.00	20.00	30.00
1900	7.00	18.00			27.50	50.00	10.00	25.00
1901	7.00	18.00			18.00	40.00	110.00	200.00
1902	7.00	18.00			15.00	27.50	27.50	55.00
1903	7.00	18.00			10.00	22.50	85.00	140.00
1904	7.00	18.00					65.00	120.00
1905	7.00	18.00			15.00	25.00	12.00	25.00
1906	7.00	18.00	10.00	20.00	18.00	27.50	12.00	25.00
1907	7.00	18.00	10.00	22.50	9.00	20.00	12.00	25.00
1908	7.00	18.00	8.00	20.00	20.00	32.00	10.00	22.50
1909	7.00	18.00	20.00	40.00	15.00	25.00	20.00	35.00
1910	7.00	18.00	15.00	26.00			15.00	25.00
1911	7.00	17.00	8.00	18.00			8.00	18.00
1912	7.00	17.00	8.00	18.00			9.00	20.00
1913	7.00	17.00					45.00	90.00
1914	7.00	17.00	8.00	18.00			9.00	25.00
1915	7.00	17.00					10.00	30.00
1916	7.00	17.00					8.00	18.00

4 (16) Quarter Dollar (Ag) 1892–1916. Laurel-wreathed head of the Goddess of Liberty facing right. R state coat of arms of the Union and thirteen stars, symbolizing the thirteen original States. **Barber Quarter:**

	without mintmark		D		O		VF S	XF
1892	17.50	40.00			20.00	55.00	45.00	85.00
1893	17.50	40.00			20.00	55.00	25.00	60.00
1894	17.50	40.00			20.00	50.00	22.50	55.00
1895	17.50	40.00			20.00	50.00	25.00	65.00
1896	20.00	45.00			35.00	90.00	750.00	1250.00
1897	15.00	38.00			40.00	110.00	40.00	90.00
1898	15.00	38.00			25.00	65.00	22.00	48.00
1899	15.00	38.00			22.50	55.00	28.00	60.00
1900	15.00	38.00			27.50	65.00	20.00	50.00
1901	15.00	38.00			55.00	120.00	2400.00	3600.00
1902	15.00	38.00			25.00	55.00	27.50	70.00
1903	15.00	38.00			25.00	55.00	30.00	75.00
1904	15.00	38.00			38.00	85.00		
1905	15.00	38.00			25.00	55.00	22.50	45.00
1906	15.00	38.00	18.00	40.00	20.00	45.00		
1907	15.00	38.00	18.00	45.00	17.50	40.00	18.00	48.00
1908	15.00	38.00	17.50	40.00	17.50	40.00	28.00	70.00
1909	15.00	38.00	17.50	40.00	65.00	160.00	18.00	45.00
1910	15.00	38.00	18.00	45.00				
1911	15.00	38.00	18.00	45.00			18.00	45.00
1912	15.00	38.00					18.00	48.00
1913	120.00	380.00	18.00	45.00			850.00	1500.00
1914	15.00	38.00	17.50	38.00			80.00	200.00
1915	15.00	38.00	17.50	40.00			20.00	45.00
1916	15.00	38.00	17.50	45.00				

5 (17)   Half Dollar (Ag) 1892–1915. Laurel-wreathed head of the Goddess of Liberty facing right. R state coat of arms of the Union and thirteen stars. **Barber Half:**

	without mintmark		D		O		S	
1892	50.00	160.00			225.00	350.00	225.00	350.00
1893	50.00	160.00			85.00	240.00	200.00	320.00
1894	50.00	160.00			60.00	180.00	55.00	200.00
1895	45.00	150.00			50.00	165.00	80.00	210.00
1896	50.00	160.00			100.00	250.00	170.00	300.00
1897	40.00	120.00			210.00	375.00	180.00	340.00
1898	40.00	120.00			75.00	200.00	50.00	170.00
1899	40.00	120.00			70.00	220.00	50.00	165.00
1900	40.00	120.00			70.00	215.00	55.00	175.00
1901	40.00	120.00			70.00	240.00	120.00	350.00
1902	40.00	120.00			45.00	165.00	50.00	175.00
1903	40.00	120.00			45.00	165.00	50.00	190.00
1904	40.00	120.00			75.00	250.00	125.00	320.00
1905	70.00	210.00			85.00	220.00	50.00	175.00
1906	40.00	120.00	45.00	130.00	50.00	140.00	50.00	155.00
1907	40.00	120.00	45.00	130.00	45.00	130.00	60.00	200.00

	without mintmark		D		O		VF / S	XF / S
1908	40.00	140.00	55.00	130.00	55.00	135.00	60.00	170.00
1909	40.00	120.00			70.00	240.00	50.00	160.00
1910	65.00	210.00					45.00	160.00
1911	40.00	120.00	45.00	150.00			45.00	150.00
1912	40.00	120.00	45.00	125.00			45.00	150.00
1913	80.00	210.00	50.00	150.00			65.00	175.00
1914	140.00	270.00					50.00	160.00
1915	85.00	250.00	40.00	125.00			45.00	130.00

6 (18) 1 Dollar (Ag) 1878–1921. Head of Liberty. **Morgan Dollar:**

	without mintmark		CC		O		S	
1878	18.00	25.00	27.50	35.00			16.00	20.00
1879	15.00	18.00	70.00	180.00	15.00	20.00	15.00	20.00
1880	14.00	19.00	50.00	80.00	14.00	19.00	15.00	20.00
1881	14.00	19.00	80.00	100.00	14.00	19.00	14.00	19.00
1882	14.00	19.00	35.00	50.00	14.00	19.00	14.00	19.00
1883	14.00	19.00	35.00	50.00	14.00	19.00	14.00	20.00
1884	14.00	19.00	40.00	65.00	14.00	19.00	15.00	25.00
1885	14.00	19.00	150.00	190.00	14.00	19.00	20.00	28.00
1886	14.00	19.00			14.00	19.00	35.00	50.00
1887	14.00	19.00			14.00	19.00	20.00	28.00
1888	14.00	19.00			14.00	19.00	20.00	28.00
1889	14.00	19.00	350.00	700.00	14.00	19.00	30.00	45.00
1890	14.00	19.00	35.00	48.00	15.00	22.00	22.00	30.00
1891	20.00	24.00	35.00	48.00	20.00	24.00	22.00	28.00
1892	22.00	28.00	55.00	90.00	22.00	28.00	75.00	175.00
1893	60.00	100.00	150.00	320.00	85.00	180.00	1500.00	3500.00
1894	260.00	400.00			20.00	27.50	35.00	70.00
1895	Proof	–.–			80.00	175.00	150.00	320.00
1896	14.00	19.00			15.00	20.00	40.00	100.00

	without mintmark		D		O		S	
1897	14.00	19.00			18.00	26.00	20.00	28.00
1898	14.00	19.00			14.00	19.00	20.00	28.00
1899	65.00	90.00			14.00	18.00	30.00	40.00
1900	14.00	19.00			14.00	19.00	18.00	26.00
1901	40.00	50.00			14.00	18.00	30.00	40.00
1902	18.00	26.00			14.00	18.00	60.00	100.00
1903	18.00	26.00			200.00	300.00	60.00	165.00
1904	19.00	28.00			14.00	18.00	50.00	120.00
1921	14.00	18.00	14.00	18.00			14.00	18.00

7 (22)   2½ Dollars (Au) 1840–1907. Head of Liberty with diadem. Rev. state coat of arms. **Quarter Eagle:**

	without mintmark		C		D		O	
1840	225.00	375.00	460.00	860.00	1300.00	3000.00	240.00	360.00
1841		30,000.00	380.00	760.00	1000.00	2800.00		
1842	500.00	1000.00	700.00	1300.00	900.00	2000.00	280.00	750.00
1843	220.00	285.00	420.00	780.00	550.00	860.00	220.00	280.00
1844	340.00	600.00	400.00	700.00	550.00	850.00		
1845	200.00	250.00			550.00	850.00	1000.00	1700.00
1846	275.00	500.00	750.00	125.00	650.00	1000.00	240.00	360.00
1847	230.00	300.00	360.00	680.00	550.00	850.00	240.00	400.00
1848	500.00	800.00	400.00	780.00	500.00	850.00		
CAL.	4500.00	9000.00						
1849	250.00	360.00	400.00	850.00	650.00	1250.00		
1850	200.00	280.00	400.00	850.00	500.00	950.00	250.00	400.00
1851	200.00	250.00	400.00	850.00	550.00	1000.00	200.00	250.00
1852	220.00	280.00	350.00	800.00	650.00	1350.00	200.00	280.00
1853	200.00	240.00			600.00	1350.00		
1854	190.00	240.00	400.00	800.00	2500.00	4600.00	190.00	240.00
S		25,000.00						
1855	200.00	240.00	1100.00	2000.00	3000.00	4800.00		
1856	200.00	240.00	600.00	1000.00	6000.00	10,000.00	220.00	400.00
S	220.00	340.00						
1857	200.00	260.00			900.00	1450.00	200.00	285.00
S	200.00	285.00						
1858	200.00	260.00	400.00	750.00				

	without mintmark		C/D		S	
1859	200.00	240.00	D:1100.00	2100.00	260.00	400.00
1860	200.00	260.00	C: 450.00	900.00	200.00	290.00
1861	200.00	230.00			350.00	600.00
1862	200.00	230.00			650.00	950.00
1863	Proof	50,000.00			260.00	680.00
1864	1400.00	4000.00				
1865	1100.00	1850.00			200.00	350.00
1866	450.00	850.00			200.00	450.00
1867	260.00	500.00			200.00	450.00
1868	250.00	360.00			210.00	400.00
1869	250.00	360.00			210.00	280.00
1870	275.00	380.00			200.00	240.00
1871	250.00	365.00			210.00	275.00
1872	265.00	500.00			210.00	275.00
1873	200.00	240.00			220.00	360.00
1874	250.00	400.00				
1875	Proof	5000.00			200.00	370.00
1876	230.00	340.00			200.00	270.00
1877	420.00	650.00			200.00	240.00
1878	200.00	225.00			200.00	225.00
1879	200.00	225.00			210.00	275.00
1880	230.00	420.00				
1881	1300.00	2250.00				
1882	260.00	410.00				
1883	260.00	425.00				
1884	260.00	425.00				
1885	700.00	1300.00				
1886	250.00	410.00				
1887	260.00	410.00				
1888	260.00	400.00				
1889	260.00	400.00				
1890	260.00	400.00				
1891	260.00	400.00				
1892	260.00	440.00				
1893	240.00	275.00				
1894	250.00	410.00				
1895	190.00	240.00				
1896	185.00	220.00				
1897	190.00	240.00				
1898	185.00	220.00				
1899	185.00	225.00				
1900	185.00	220.00				
1901	185.00	220.00				
1903	185.00	220.00				
1904	185.00	220.00				
1905	185.00	220.00				
1906	185.00	220.00				
1907	185.00	220.00				

8 (23a)   5 Dollars (Au) 1866–1908. Head of Liberty facing left. Rev. state coat of arms and motto: IN GOD WE TRUST. **Half Eagle:**   VF   XF

	without mintmark		CC		S	
1866	450.00	775.00			550.00	950.00
1867	450.00	750.00			725.00	1300.00
1868	450.00	875.00			400.00	1000.00
1869	620.00	900.00			550.00	1050.00
1870	550.00	875.00	2000.00	4000.00	875.00	1500.00
1871	620.00	950.00	800.00	1200.00	400.00	800.00
1872	500.00	775.00	750.00	1350.00	400.00	1000.00
1873	230.00	400.00	800.00	1400.00	550.00	1000.00
1874	500.00	800.00	600.00	900.00	650.00	1200.00
1875	Proof	70,000.00	840.00	1250.00	540.00	1250.00
1876	850.00	1150.00	700.00	1050.00	1000.00	1850.00
1877	750.00	1000.00	750.00	1150.00	380.00	620.00
1878	165.00	250.00	1400.00	2650.00	165.00	250.00
1879	165.00	210.00	380.00	780.00	200.00	260.00
1880	165.00	200.00	360.00	670.00	165.00	200.00
1881	165.00	200.00	400.00	700.00	165.00	200.00
1882	165.00	200.00	285.00	350.00	165.00	200.00
1883	165.00	200.00	400.00	720.00	230.00	285.00
1884	175.00	200.00	450.00	800.00	200.00	300.00
1885	160.00	190.00			160.00	190.00
1886	175.00	220.00			160.00	200.00
1887	Proof	28,000.00			160.00	190.00
1888	210.00	260.00			270.00	325.00
1889	300.00	575.00				
1890	400.00	620.00	260.00	300.00		
1891	175.00	210.00	230.00	285.00		
1892	160.00	185.00	250.00	300.00	200.00	260.00
O	450.00	650.00				
1893	160.00	185.00	230.00	300.00	200.00	235.00
O	240.00	310.00				
1894	160.00	185.00			320.00	475.00
O	200.00	360.00				
1895	160.00	185.00			260.00	350.00
1896	185.00	230.00			260.00	325.00
1897	160.00	185.00			185.00	280.00
1898	160.00	185.00			175.00	210.00
1899	160.00	185.00			170.00	200.00
1900	160.00	185.00			185.00	250.00

	without mintmark		CC		D		VF S	XF S
1901	160.00	185.00					160.00	185.00
1902	165.00	190.00					16.00	185.00
1903	165.00	190.00					165.00	190.00
1904	160.00	185.00					200.00	230.00
1905	165.00	190.00					200.00	230.00
1906	160.00	185.00			160.00	185.00	170.00	200.00
1907	160.00	185.00			160.00	185.00		
1908	160.00	185.00						

9 (24a)   10 Dollars (Au) 1866–1907. Head of Liberty facing left. Rev. state coat of arms and motto: IN GOD WE TRUST. **Eagle:**

	without mintmark		CC		O		S	
1866	700.00	850.00					650.00	1100.00
1867	850.00	1400.00					1400.00	2750.00
1868	600.00	800.00					680.00	1300.00
1869	800.00	1500.00					850.00	1400.00
1870	700.00	1100.00	2200.00	4400.00			600.00	1550.00
1871	1150.00	1600.00	1100.00	2000.00			680.00	1350.00
1872	1750.00	3400.00	1000.00	2200.00			650.00	1275.00
1873	2700.00	4500.00	1000.00	2000.00			660.00	1150.00
1874	340.00	400.00	660.00	1600.00			580.00	1250.00
1875		90000.00	850.00	1500.00				
1876	1400.00	3000.00	1200.00	2800.00			650.00	1350.00
1877	1400.00	2600.00	950.00	1500.00			700.00	1400.00
1878	330.00	400.00	1400.00	2000.00			600.00	950.00
1879	270.00	320.00	2800.00	4500.00	1600.00	3000.00	265.00	300.00
1880	240.00	280.00	450.00	600.00	360.00	500.00	265.00	300.00
1881	220.00	260.00	400.00	500.00	400.00	500.00	220.00	260.00
1882	220.00	260.00	500.00	660.00	450.00	560.00	320.00	400.00

	without mintmark		CC		O		S	
1883	265.00	300.00	440.00	560.00	2000.00	3000.00	320.00	380.00
1884	320.00	380.00	480.00	565.00			300.00	360.00
1885	270.00	320.00					265.00	300.00
1886	320.00	380.00					235.00	280.00
1887	265.00	310.00					265.00	300.00
1888	300.00	370.00			235.00	280.00	235.00	280.00
1889	400.00	500.00					235.00	280.00
1890	300.00	380.00	310.00	385.00				
1891	265.00	310.00	265.00	300.00				
1892	235.00	280.00	325.00	400.00	275.00	325.00	300.00	350.00
1893	235.00	280.00	335.00	420.00	265.00	310.00	300.00	350.00
1894	235.00	280.00			235.00	280.00	280.00	375.00
1895	235.00	280.00			235.00	280.00	380.00	650.00
1896	265.00	300.00					360.00	450.00
1897	235.00	280.00			265.00	300.00	275.00	350.00
1898	235.00	280.00					265.00	300.00
1899	235.00	280.00			285.00	330.00	275.00	350.00
1900	265.00	300.00					275.00	350.00
1901	235.00	280.00			270.00	320.00	235.00	280.00
1902	265.00	300.00					235.00	280.00
1903	265.00	300.00			235.00	280.00	275.00	350.00
1904	235.00	280.00			300.00	360.00		
1905	265.00	300.00					270.00	320.00
1906	265.00	300.00			275.00	350.00	275.00	340.00
1906 D	235.00	280.00						
1907	235.00	280.00					300.00	360.00
1907 D	265.00	300.00						

10 (25) 20 Dollars (Au) 1866–1907. Head of Liberty facing left. Rev. state coat of arms and motto: IN GOD WE TRUST. **Double Eagle:**

	without mintmark		CC		O		S	
1866	560.00	660.00					580.00	700.00
1867	500.00	560.00					570.00	680.00
1868	640.00	780.00					560.00	665.00
1869	560.00	670.00					550.00	625.00
1870	570.00	720.00	16,500.00	25,000.00			540.00	625.00
1871	600.00	720.00	1500.00	3000.00			540.00	625.00
1872	500.00	585.00	900.00	1200.00			550.00	630.00
1873	500.00	560.00	900.00	1100.00			560.00	630.00
1874	560.00	660.00	600.00	850.00			500.00	585.00
1875	560.00	660.00	590.00	720.00			520.00	600.00
1876	500.00	600.00	600.00	750.00			520.00	600.00
1877	550.00	625.00	600.00	760.00			485.00	550.00
1878	530.00	610.00	780.00	950.00			500.00	600.00
1879	540.00	670.00	850.00	1100.00	2600.00	3800.00	500.00	610.00
1880	540.00	660.00					540.00	660.00
1881	2500.00	5800.00					550.00	660.00
1882		12,000.00	600.00	750.00			530.00	625.00
1883		65,000.00*	600.00	750.00			520.00	625.00
1884		52,000.00*	640.00	720.00			500.00	575.00
1885		8,000.00	950.00	1600.00			500.00	600.00
1886		9,000.00						
1887		35,000.00*					500.00	600.00
1888	500.00	600.00					500.00	600.00
1889	500.00	600.00	650.00	875.00			485.00	550.00
1890	540.00	640.00	640.00	725.00			540.00	640.00
1891		3400.00	1300.00	2000.00			475.00	540.00
1892		1300.00	650.00	750.00			485.00	550.00
1893	475.00	540.00	650.00	750.00			485.00	550.00
1894	475.00	540.00					485.00	550.00
1895	475.00	540.00					475.00	540.00
1896	475.00	540.00					485.00	550.00
1897	475.00	540.00					475.00	540.00
1898	500.00	575.00					475.00	540.00
1899	475.00	540.00					475.00	540.00
1900	465.00	525.00					485.00	550.00
1901	465.00	525.00					485.00	550.00

* N.B. Proofs only.

	without mintmark		D		S	
1902	485.00	550.00			500.00	560.00
1903	465.00	525.00			485.00	550.00
1904	465.00	525.00			465.00	525.00
1905	500.00	600.00			485.00	550.00
1906	485.00	550.00	485.00	550.00	485.00	550.00
1907	465.00	525.00	485.00	550.00	465.00	525.00

COMMEMORATIVE ISSUE FOR LAFAYETTE

			XF	**Unc**
11 (C2)	1 Dollar (Ag) 1900. Double portrait: George Washington and Marie Joseph Paul Roch Yves Gilbert Motier, Marquis de Lafayette (1757–1834), French Liberal and friend of Washington, supported the American battle of independence against Britain. ℞ equestrian statue of Lafayette in Paris (1900), a gift of the American people		300.00	400.00

COMMEMORATIVE ISSUES (2) FOR THE LOUISIANA PURCHASE IN THE YEAR 1803

12 (C59)	1 Dollar (Au) 1903. Thomas Jefferson (1743–1826), 3rd President. ℞ denomination, date, laurel wreath	200.00	400.00

13 (C60)	1 Dollar (Au) 1903. William McKinley (1843–1901), 25th President 1897–1901.	**XF**	**Unc**
	R denomination, date, laurel wreath	200.00	400.00

COMMEMORATIVE ISSUE FOR THE EXPOSITION
UPON THE OCCASION OF THE 100th ANNIVERSARY OF
DESPATCHING THE LEWIS AND CLARK
EXPEDITION FOR THE EXPLORATION OF THE LOUISIANA
TERRITORY PURCHASED FROM FRANCE IN 1803

14 (C58)	1 Dollar (Au) 1904–1905. Captain Meriwether Lewis (1774–1809). R Lt. William Clark (1770–1838):		
	a) 1904	300.00	600.00
	b) 1905	300.00	600.00

15 (26) 1 Cent (Br) 1909–1958. Abraham Lincoln (1809–1865), 16th President 1861–1865. R denomination in words between ears of corn. **Lincoln Cent:**

	without mintmark		D		S	
					VF	**XF**
1909	0.70	1.40			60.00	85.00
1910	0.75	1.50			10.00	18.00
1911	2.00	4.00	10.00	25.00	18.00	30.00
1912	3.00	6.00	11.00	21.00	15.00	25.00
1913	3.50	7.00	10.00	18.00	12.00	20.00
1914	4.00	8.00	180.00	350.00	15.00	25.00
1915	12.00	25.00	6.00	12.00	12.00	20.00
1916	1.00	2.00	3.50	7.00	3.50	7.00
1917	1.00	2.00	3.00	6.00	3.00	6.00
1918	1.00	2.00	3.00	6.00	3.00	6.00
1919	1.00	2.00	2.60	5.50	1.50	3.00
1920	1.00	2.00	2.00	4.00	2.00	4.00
1921	2.00	4.00			6.00	12.00
1922	300.00	500.00	8.00	16.00		
1923	1.00	2.00			7.50	14.00
1924	1.75	3.50	15.00	42.00	3.50	7.00
1925	1.00	2.00	2.00	4.00	2.00	4.00
1926	1.00	2.00	1.50	3.00	6.00	12.00
1927	1.00	2.00	1.30	3.00	2.00	4.00
1928	0.80	1.60	0.80	2.00	1.20	2.50
1929	0.60	1.20	0.60	1.20	0.60	1.20
1930	0.50	1.00	0.50	1.00	0.50	1.00
1931	0.50	1.00	3.50	7.00	30.00	50.00
1932	1.50	3.00	1.50	3.00		
1933	1.00	2.00	2.00	4.00		
1934	0.25	0.50	0.60	1.20		

	without mintmark		D		S	
1935	0.20	0.40	0.20	0.40	0.25	0.50
1936	0.15	0.30	0.20	0.40	0.25	0.50
1937	0.15	0.30	0.15	0.30	0.20	0.40
1938	0.15	0.30	0.30	0.60	0.35	0.70
1939	0.10	0.20	0.40	0.80	0.20	0.40
1940	0.10	0.20	0.10	0.20	0.10	0.20
1941	0.10	0.20	0.10	0.20	0.15	0.30
1942	0.10	0.20	0.10	0.20	0.20	0.40
1944	0.10	0.20	0.10	0.20	0.10	0.20
1945	0.10	0.20	0.10	0.20	0.10	0.20
1946	0.10	0.20	0.10	0.20	0.10	0.20
1947	0.10	0.20	0.10	0.20	0.10	0.20
1948	0.10	0.20	0.10	0.20	0.30	1.00
1949	0.10	0.20	0.10	0.20	0.50	2.50
1950	0.10	0.20	0.10	0.20	0.10	0.20
1951	0.10	0.20	0.10	0.20	0.10	0.20
1952	0.10	0.20	0.10	0.20	0.10	0.20
1953	0.05	0.10	0.05	0.10	0.10	0.20
1954	0.15	0.30	0.05	0.10	0.10	0.20
1955	0.05	0.10	0.05	0.10	0.10	0.20
1956	0.10	0.20	0.10	0.20		
1957	0.10	0.20	0.10	0.20		
1958	0.10	0.20	0.10	0.20		

16 (27) 5 Cents (Cu-Ni) 1913. Head of Red Indian facing right. Rev. bison (Bison bison – Bovidae), on a mound. **Buffalo Nickel** (Variety 1–Mound Type):

	Mintage	Fine	VF	XF
1913	30,993,520	4.00	7.00	12.00
1913 D	5,337,000	8.00	12.00	20.00
1913 S	2,105,000	12.00	22.00	40.00

17 (27a) 5 Cents (Cu-Ni) 1913–1938. Type as No. 16, but bison on a level. **Buffalo Nickel** (Variety 2–Line Type):

	without mintmark		D		S	
1913	6.00	10.00	65.00	95.00	120.00	175.00
1914	7.00	14.00	70.00	100.00	18.00	32.00
1915	6.00	12.00	30.00	55.00	45.00	90.00
1916	3.00	6.00	20.00	35.00	16.00	30.00
1917	5.00	10.00	35.00	75.00	32.00	55.00
1918	6.00	12.50	35.00	75.00	35.00	80.00
1919	4.00	8.00	65.00	100.00	38.00	80.00
1920	3.50	8.00	65.00	100.00	30.00	80.00
1921	7.00	15.00			110.00	270.00
1923	3.00	6.00			25.00	55.00
1924	4.00	9.00	45.00	70.00	180.00	360.00
1925	3.00	10.00	50.00	85.00	20.00	45.00
1926	2.50	5.00	40.00	90.00	80.00	260.00
1927	2.50	5.00	12.00	30.00	20.00	55.00
1928	2.00	4.00	4.00	10.00	5.00	10.00
1929	2.00	4.00	3.00	10.00	2.00	6.00
1930	2.00	4.00			3.00	7.00
1931					5.50	12.00
1934	1.50	4.00	2.50	5.00		
1935	1.00	2.00	1.50	3.00	1.00	2.00
1936	0.70	1.50	1.00	2.00	1.00	2.00
1937	0.70	1.50	0.80	2.00	1.00	1.60
1938			0.80	1.60		

18 (28) 1 Dime (Ag) 1916–1945. Head of figure of Liberty with winged helmet; due to the similarity with the messenger of the gods, however, generally designated as »Mercury Dime«. Rev. fasces: **VF**   **XF**

	without mintmark		D		S	
1916	5.00	9.00	1000.00	1500.00	5.00	12.00
1917	4.00	8.00	12.50	30.00	4.00	8.00
1918	9.00	20.00	8.50	18.00	6.00	12.00
1919	4.00	8.00	15.00	27.50	12.00	25.00
1920	3.00	6.00	5.00	12.00	6.00	12.00
1921	120.00	350.00				

	without mintmark		D		S	
1923	2.00	5.00			10.00	20.00
1924	4.00	7.00	8.00	16.00	7.00	15.00
1925	3.00	6.00	26.00	60.00	8.50	17.00
1926	3.00	5.00	7.50	15.00	33.00	80.00
1927	2.00	4.00	16.00	32.00	7.00	15.00
1928	2.00	4.00	15.00	30.00	6.00	12.00
1929	2.00	4.00	4.00	8.00	2.00	4.00
1930	2.00	4.00			5.50	12.00
1931	3.00	6.00	15.00	30.00	5.00	10.00
1934	1.00	2.00	2.00	4.00		
1935	1.00	2.00	3.00	6.00	1.00	3.00
1936	1.00	2.00	2.00	4.00	2.00	4.00
1937	1.00	2.00	1.00	2.00	1.00	2.00
1938	1.00	2.00	1.00	2.00	1.00	3.00
1939	1.00	2.00	1.00	2.00	1.00	2.00
1940	1.00	2.00	1.00	2.00	1.00	2.00
1941	1.00	2.00	1.00	2.00	1.00	2.00
1942	1.00	2.00	1.00	2.00	1.00	2.00
1943	0.50	1.00	1.00	2.00	1.00	2.00
1944	0.50	1.00	1.00	2.00	1.00	2.00
1945	0.50	1.00	1.00	2.00	1.00	2.00

19 (29) Quarter Dollar (Ag) 1916–1917. Standing figure of Liberty. R Bald Eagle (National bird = Haliaetus leucocephalus – Accipitridae). **Standing Liberty Quarter** (Variety 1):

	Mintage	VF	XF
a) 1916	52,000	1500.00	2500.00
b) 1917	8,792,000	27.50	60.00
c) 1917 D	1,509,200	50.00	90.00
d) 1917 S	1,952,000	45.00	80.00

20 (29a) Quarter Dollar (Ag) 1917–1930. Type as No. 19, R however with differing arrangement of wording and three stars underneath the Bald Eagle. **Standing Liberty Quarter** (Variety 2):

	without mintmark		D		S	
1917	25.00	40.00	60.00	120.00	50.00	90.00
1918	35.00	60.00	50.00	100.00	30.00	65.00
1919	45.00	80.00	160.00	260.00	125.00	220.00
1920	20.00	45.00	80.00	140.00	30.00	60.00
1921	150.00	225.00				
1923	20.00	50.00			200.00	320.00
1924	20.00	50.00	65.00	115.00	32.00	60.00
1925	15.00	30.00				
1926	15.00	30.00	30.00	70.00	30.00	75.00
1927	15.00	30.00	40.00	85.00	175.00	550.00
1928	15.00	30.00	22.00	50.00	20.00	46.00
1929	15.00	30.00	18.00	45.00	20.00	48.00
1930	15.00	30.00			20.00	50.00

21 (30) Half Dollar (Ag) 1916–1947. Walking figure of Liberty in front of rising sun. Rev. Bald Eagle. **Walking Liberty Half:** **VF** **XF**

	without mintmark		D		S	
1916	100.00	200.00	60.00	130.00	200.00	320.00
1917			70.00	140.00	120.00	285.00
1917	15.00	30.00	40.00	100.00	20.00	42.00
1918	50.00	125.00	55.00	135.00	20.00	42.00
1919	90.00	340.00	120.00	400.00	90.00	350.00
1920	18.00	45.00	90.00	280.00	40.00	120.00
1921	400.00	1000.00	500.00	1250.00	250.00	1100.00
1923					40.00	140.00
1927					25.00	75.00
1928					30.00	90.00
1929			18.00	65.00	20.00	65.00
1933					18.00	45.00

	without mintmark		D		S	
1934	10.00	20.00	15.00	35.00	13.00	26.00
1935	10.00	20.00	15.00	35.00	10.00	30.00
1936	10.00	18.00	10.00	28.00	10.00	28.00
1937	10.00	18.00	15.00	35.00	10.00	28.00
1938	10.00	18.00	40.00	100.00		
1939	10.00	18.00	10.00	18.00	10.00	22.00
1940	10.00	18.00			10.00	20.00
1941	8.00	12.00	8.00	12.00	10.00	15.00
1942	8.00	12.00	8.00	12.00	9.00	14.00
1943	8.00	12.00	8.00	12.00	8.00	12.00
1944	8.00	12.00	8.00	12.00	8.00	12.00
1945	8.00	12.00	8.00	12.00	8.00	12.00
1946	8.00	12.00	8.00	12.00	8.00	12.00
1947	8.00	12.00	8.00	12.00		

22 (31) 1 Dollar (Ag) 1921–1935. Peace type, head of Liberty with halo. R seated eagle with motto: E PLURIBUS UNUM. **Peace Dollar:**   VF   XF

	without mintmark		D		S	
1921	30.00	50.00				
1922	12.00	18.00	15.00	20.00	15.00	20.00
1923	12.00	18.00	12.00	20.00	12.00	20.00
1924	13.00	18.00			18.00	25.00
1925	12.00	16.00			13.00	18.00
1926	14.00	18.00	15.00	20.00	14.00	18.00
1927	18.00	25.00	18.00	28.00	18.00	26.00
1928	110.00	150.00			18.00	24.00
1934	18.00	25.00	18.00	25.00	40.00	150.00
1935	15.00	20.00			15.00	20.00

23 (32)   2½ Dollars (Au) 1908–1929. Head of Red Indian. R Golden Eagle (Aquila chrysaëtos – Accipitridae). Incused legend. **Quarter Eagle – Indian Head:**   **VF**   **XF**

	without mintmark		D	
1908	180.00	210.00		
1909	180.00	210.00		
1910	180.00	210.00		
1911	180.00	210.00	650.00	950.00
1912	180.00	210.00		
1913	180.00	210.00		
1914	200.00	230.00	180.00	210.00
1915	180.00	210.00		
1925			180.00	210.00
1926	180.00	210.00		
1927	180.00	210.00		
1928	180.00	210.00		
1929	180.00	210.00		

24 (33)   5 Dollars (Au) 1908–1929. Head of Red Indian facing left. Rev. golden Eagle. **Half Eagle – Indian Head:**

	without mintmark		D		O		S	
1908	200.00	250.00	200.00	250.00			300.00	450.00
1909	200.00	250.00	200.00	250.00	400.00	900.00	300.00	425.00
1910	200.00	250.00	225.00	280.00			270.00	325.00
1911	200.00	250.00	380.00	500.00			225.00	280.00
1912	200.00	250.00					275.00	350.00
1913	200.00	250.00					300.00	400.00
1914	210.00	265.00	210.00	265.00			225.00	285.00
1915	210.00	265.00					270.00	325.00
1916							225.00	285.00
1929		360.00						

25 (34)   10 Dollars (Au) 1907–1908. Head of Liberty with Red Indian ceremonial head dress. Rev. Golden Eagle. **Eagle – Indian Head:**

	VF	XF
a) 1907	480.00	550.00
b) 1908	540.00	620.00
c) 1908 D	525.00	600.00

26 (34a)   10 Dollars (Au) 1908–1933. Type as No.   **VF**   **XF**
25, but with motto: IN GOD WE
TRUST. **Eagle – Indian Head.**

	without mintmark		D		S	
1908	480.00	525.00	550.00	620.00	580.00	680.00
1909	490.00	550.00	535.00	600.00	515.00	580.00
1910	480.00	525.00	480.00	525.00	490.00	540.00
1911	465.00	500.00	700.00	950.00	500.00	550.00
1912	480.00	525.00			510.00	565.00
1913	465.00	500.00			550.00	650.00
1914	480.00	525.00	465.00	500.00	480.00	525.00
1915	480.00	525.00			510.00	565.00
1916					465.00	500.00
1920						8000.00
1926	465.00	500.00				
1930						5000.00
1932	465.00	500.00				
1933		50000.00				

27 (35)   20 Dollars (Au) 1907. Standing figure of
Liberty. R Golden Eagle in flight in
front of rising sun, date in Roman numerals. **Double Eagle** (Saint-Gaudens
Type):   2800.00   4500.00

28 (35a) 20 Dollars (Au) 1907–1908. Type as No. 27, but date in Arabic numerals.
Double Eagle (Saint-Gaudens Type):

	VF	**XF**
	550.00	620.00

29 (35b) 20 Dollars (Au) 1908–1933. Type as No. 28, motto: IN GOD WE TRUST.
Double Eagle (Saint-Gaudens Type):

	without mintmark		D		S	
1908	500.00	600.00	500.00	600.00	700.00	1000.00
1909	560.00	620.00	650.00	750.00	500.00	600.00
1910	500.00	600.00	500.00	600.00	500.00	600.00
1911	500.00	600.00	500.00	600.00	500.00	600.00
1912	500.00	600.00				
1913	500.00	600.00	500.00	600.00	500.00	600.00
1914	500.00	600.00	500.00	600.00	500.00	600.00
1915	500.00	600.00			500.00	600.00
1916					500.00	600.00
1920	500.00	600.00				7500.00
1921		9000.00				
1922	500.00	600.00			580.00	675.00
1923	500.00	600.00	500.00	600.00		
1924	500.00	600.00		1000.00		1200.00
1925	500.00	600.00		1300.00	700.00	900.00
1926	500.00	600.00	850.00	1200.00	750.00	1000.00
1927	500.00	600.00		270000.00		3200.00
1928	500.00	600.00				
1929		4500.00				
1930					6000.00	10000.00
1931	4500.00	7000.00	4000.00	6500.00		
1932	5000.00	9000.00				

1933: None placed in circulation.

COMMEMORATIVE ISSUES (5) UPON THE OCCASION OF THE PANAMA-PACIFIC EXPOSITION OF 1915 IN SAN FRANCISCO FOR THE OPENING OF THE PANAMA CANAL

			VF	XF
30 (C39)	Half Dollar (Ag) 1915. "Columbia" strewing flowers with small angel child and horn of plenty; in the background, rising sun over Golden Gate Bay. ℞ eagle with USA coat of arms between oak and laurel leaves		175.00	260.00

31 (C62)	1	Dollar (Au) 1915. Portrait of a Panama Canal worker. ℞ denomination in words. Two bottle-nosed dolphins or porpoises, symbolizing the two oceans	185.00	360.00

32 (C63) 2½ Dollars (Au) 1915. "Columbia" on sea-horse. ℞ eagle with raised wings on column with motto: E PLURIBUS UNUM | **VF** 400.00 | **XF** 700.00

33 (C65) 50 Dollars (Au) 1915. Head of Minerva. ℞ Great Horned Owl (Bubo virginianus – Strigidae) on pine branch; in the 8 corners: bottle-nosed dolphins or porpoises; octagonal | 12000.00 | 16000.00

34 (C64) 50 Dollars (Au) 1915. Type as No. 33, but circular and without the bottle-nosed dolphins | 17000.00 | 20000.00

COMMEMORATIVE ISSUE FOR WILLIAM MCKINLEY

35 (C61) 1 Dollar (Au) 1916–1917. William McKinley (1843–1901), 25th President, head facing left. ℞ McKinley-shrine in Niles, Ohio | 150.00 | 350.00

COMMEMORATIVE ISSUE FOR THE 100th ANNIVERSARY OF THE STATE OF ILLINOIS

36 (C28) Half Dollar (Ag) 1918. Abraham Lincoln (1809–1865), 16th President. Head facing right. ℞ eagle of the coat of arms, escutcheon, rising sun (seal of the State of Illinois) | 40.00 | 65.00

COMMEMORATIVE ISSUE 100 YEARS OF MAINE

		VF	XF
37 (C31)	Half Dollar (Ag) 1920. Coat of arms of the State of Maine, above the motto DIRIGO (I show the way). ℞ legend in wreath of fir branches with cones attached	65.00	80.00

COMMEMORATIVE ISSUE FOR THE 300th ANNIVERSARY OF THE LANDING OF THE PILGRIM FATHERS ON THE CAPE COD PENINSULA, MASSACHUSETTS, ON DECEMBER 22, 1620

38 (C40)	Half Dollar (Ag) 1920–1921. Portrait of Bradford, the first governor (1589–1657). ℞ "Mayflower"		
	a) 1920	35.00	45.00
	b) 1921, with date in the field of the obv.	65.00	100.00

COMMEMORATIVE ISSUE 100 YEARS OF ALABAMA
(1819–1919)

39 (C4) Half Dollar (Ag) 1921. William Wyatt

	VF	XF

Bibb (1781–1820), doctor, first governor, and Thomas Erby Kilby (1865–1943), governor in 1920. ℞ large eagle on escutcheon
a) with 2 x 2 (22nd State of the Union)   110.00   160.00
b) without 2 x 2   70.00   90.00

COMMEMORATIVE ISSUE 100 YEARS OF MISSOURI

40 (C34) Half Dollar (Ag) 1921. Forest runner of the early 19th century with racoon fur cap. ℞ Red Indians and forest runners of the times
a) with 2 * 4 (24th State of the Union)   240.00   320.00
b) without 2 * 4   180.00   260.00

COMMEMORATIVE ISSUES (2) FOR THE 100th BIRTHDAY OF ULYSSES S. GRANT

41 (C22) Half Dollar (Ag) 1922. Ulysses Simpson Grant (1822–1885), 18th President 1869 – 1877. ℞ block house under trees – birthplace of Grant in Point Pleasant, Ohio
a) with star   300.00   420.00
b) without star   40.00   55.00
42 (C56) 1 Dollar (Au) 1922. Type as No. 41
a) with star   550.00   625.00
b) without star   550.00   625.00

COMMEMORATIVE ISSUE FOR THE 100th ANNIVERSARY
OF THE PROCLAMATION OF THE MONROE DOCTRINE

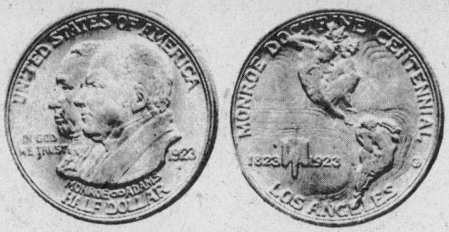

43 (C35) Half Dollar (Ag) 1923. Double portrait: James Monroe (1758–1831), 5th President from 1817 to 1825; in accordance with the doctrine named after him, European powers were to be prevented from exercising their influence on the political affairs of the states of the two Americas under the call of "America for the Americans", and John Quincy Adams (1767–1848), 6th President, who took a decisive part in formulating the Monroe Doctrine. ℞ two female figures, representing North and South America

	VF	XF
	25.00	35.00

COMMEMORATIVE ISSUE FOR THE 300th ANNIVERSARY
OF THE LANDING OF THE
HUGENOTS AND WALLOONS IN AMERICA

44 (C25) Half Dollar (Ag) 1924. Gaspard de Coligny (1519–1572), French admiral and leader of the Hugenots and William I of Orange, called the Silent (1533–1584), stadholder of the Netherlands. Both personalities bear no relation to the cause of this commemoration; as representatives and martyrs of the Protestant faith, their portraits were chosen symbolically. ℞ emigrants' ship the "Nieu Nederland"   50.00   65.00

COMMEMORATIVE ISSUE FOR THE 75th ANNIVERSARY OF THE ENTRY OF CALIFORNIA INTO THE UNION AS A FEDERAL STATE

		VF	XF
45 (C11)	Half Dollar (Ag) 1925. Gold washer of 1849. ℞ striding grizzly bear (Ursus arctos – Ursidae), state symbol	60.00	85.00

COMMEMORATIVE ISSUE FOR THE 150th ANNIVERSARY OF THE BATTLE OF LEXINGTON AND CONCORD

46 (C27)	Half Dollar (Ag) 1925. The "Minute Man", volunteer of the American Revolution, after a bronze statue by Daniel Chester French in Concord. ℞ "Old Belfry" in Lexington	30.00	40.00

COMMEMORATIVE ISSUE FOR THE PROJECTED STONE MOUNTAIN MEMORIAL IN GEORGIA IN HONOR OF THE CONFEDERATE ARMY

| | **VF** | **XF** |

47 (C48) Half Dollar (Ag) 1925. Equestrian statues of Generals Robert Edward Lee (1807–1870) and Thomas "Stonewall" Jackson (1824–1863). ℞ Bald Eagle with outspread wings on mountain top. The Stone Mountain is situated some 15 miles east of Atlanta, Georgia and represents the largest block of massive granite on the North American continent. The projected memorial is being hewn out of rock on the north-east side of the mountain as the "largest sculpture in the world". Work commenced in 1920, was abandoned in 1930 and only recommenced in recent times

20.00 30.00

COMMEMORATIVE ISSUE 100 YEARS OF FORT VANCOUVER

48 (C50) Half Dollar (Ag) 1925. John McLoughlin (1784–1857), doctor, explorer, agent of the Hudson Bay Company for the District of Columbia, leader of the first settlers on the Oregon Trail towards the Far Northwest, built Fort Vancouver on the Columbia River in 1825. ℞ forest runner of the early 19th century with levelled rifle, in the background high mountain landscape and Fort Vancouver

180.00 300.00

COMMEMORATIVE ISSUE FOR THE OREGON TRAIL

49 (C38) Half Dollar (Ag) 1926–1939. Mountain

Red Indian with plumes, gazing towards the East, in front of a map of the USA. ℞ Conestoga Wagon drawn by oxen on its way to the Far Northwest. The 2000 miles long Oregon Trail, leading from East to West through the North-American Continent, was of decisive importance for the settlement of the Far Northwest during the 19th century

	VF	XF
	65.00	90.00

COMMEMORATIVE ISSUES (2) FOR THE 150th ANNIVERSARY OF THE SIGNING OF THE DECLARATION OF INDEPENDENCE

50 (C46) Half Dollar (Ag) 1926. George Washington (1732–1799), 1st President and Calvin Coolidge (1872–1933), 30th President. ℞ cracked Freedom Bell (Liberty Bell) in the Independence Hall in Philadelphia, Pa.   25.00   35.00

51 (C66) 2½ Dollars (Au) 1926. Goddess of Liberty, standing, with torch and scroll. ℞ Independence Hall of the Union in Philadelphia, Pa.   280.00   350.00

All valuations in the SCHÖN are stated in U.S. Dollars.

COMMEMORATIVE ISSUE FOR THE 150 YEARS
OF VERMONT AND THE BATTLE OF BENNINGTON

			VF	**XF**
52 (C51)	Half Dollar (Ag) 1927. Ira Allen (1751–1814), politician, founder of Vermont. ℞ puma (Puma concolor – Felidae)		125.00	175.00

COMMEMORATIVE ISSUE FOR THE REDISCOVERY
OF HAWAII BY CAPTAIN JAMES COOK 150 YEARS AGO

53 (C23)	Half Dollar (Ag) 1928. James Cook (1728–1779), British world circumnavigator. ℞ Hawaii island chief in festive garb; to the left village near Diamond Hill on Waikiki Beach, to the right coconut palm tree	580.00	750.00

54 (37)   5 Cents (Cu-Ni) 1938–1965. Thomas Jefferson (1743–1826), 3rd President 1801–1809. R »Monticello«, Thomas Jefferson's residence. **Jefferson Nickel:**

	without mintmark		D		S	
1938	0.25	0.50	1.20	2.40	1.80	3.60
1939	0.25	0.25	5.00	10.00	1.00	2.00
1940	0.15	0.30	0.20	0.40	0.30	0.60
1941	0.15	0.30	0.15	0.30	0.20	0.40
1942	0.20	0.40	1.20	2.50		
1946	0.05	0.10	0.15	0.30	0.20	0.40
1947	0.10	0.20	0.10	0.20	0.15	0.30
1948	0.10	0.20	0.20	0.40	0.20	0.40
1949	0.10	0.20	0.15	0.30	0.35	0.70
1950	0.30	0.60	5.00	10.00		
1951	0.10	0.20	0.10	0.20	0.40	0.80
1952	0.10	0.20	0.30	0.60	0.10	0.20
1953	0.10	0.20	0.10	0.20	0.15	0.30
1954	0.05	0.10	0.05	0.10	0.10	0.20
1955	0.20	0.40	0.05	0.10		
1956	0.05	0.10	0.05	0.10		
1957	0.05	0.10	0.05	0.10		
1958	0.05	0.10	0.05	0.10		
1959	0.05	0.10	0.05	0.10		
1960	0.05	0.10	0.05	0.10		
1961	0.05	0.10	0.05	0.10		
1962	0.05	0.10	0.05	0.10		
1963	0.05	0.10	0.05	0.10		
1964	0.05	0.10	0.05	0.10		
1965	0.05	0.10				

55 (39)   Quarter Dollar (Ag) 1932–1964. George   **VF**   **XF**
           Washington (1732–1799), 1st President
           1789–1797. Rev. Bald Eagle. **Washington
           Quarter:**

Values are given for each coin in U.S. Dollars and reference to Yeoman-numbers.

	without mintmark		D		S	
1932	7.00	10.00	100.00	170.00	80.00	125.00
1934	7.00	10.00	10.00	20.00		
1935	6.00	10.00	10.00	20.00	7.00	12.00
1936	6.00	10.00	16.00	35.00	6.00	10.00
1937	6.00	10.00	7.00	11.00	10.00	20.00
1938	10.00	16.00			7.00	13.00
1939	7.00	10.00	8.00	11.00	8.00	11.00
1940	7.00	10.00	9.00	14.00	7.00	10.00
1941	2.00	4.00	2.00	4.00	2.00	4.00
1942	2.00	3.00	2.00	3.00	2.00	3.00
1943	2.00	3.00	2.00	3.00	2.00	3.00
1944	2.00	3.00	2.00	3.00	2.00	3.00
1945	2.00	3.00	2.00	3.00	2.00	3.00
1946	2.00	3.00	2.00	3.00	2.00	3.00
1947	2.00	3.00	2.00	3.00	2.00	3.00
1948	2.00	3.00	2.00	3.00	2.00	3.00
1949	2.00	3.00	2.00	3.00		
1950	2.00	3.00	2.00	3.00	2.00	3.00
1951	2.00	3.00	2.00	3.00	2.00	3.00
1952	2.00	3.00	2.00	3.00	2.00	3.00
1953	2.00	3.00	2.00	3.00	2.00	3.00
1954	2.00	3.00	2.00	3.00	2.00	3.00
1955	2.00	3.00	2.00	3.00		
1956	2.00	3.00	2.00	3.00		
1957	2.00	3.00	2.00	3.00		
1958	2.00	3.00	2.00	3.00		
1959	2.00	3.00	2.00	3.00		
1960	2.00	3.00	2.00	3.00		
1961	2.00	3.00	2.00	3.00		
1962	2.00	3.00	2.00	3.00		
1963	2.00	3.00	2.00	3.00		
1964	2.00	3.00	2.00	3.00		

All valutions in the SCHÖN are stated in U.S. Dollars.

COMMEMORATIVE ISSUE FOR THE 200th BIRTHDAY
OF DANIEL BOONE

56 (C9)   Half Dollar (Ag) 1934–1938. Daniel Boone (1734–1820), most famous American forest runner, entered world literature as the hero of a novel, Nat Bumppo (Leather Stocking) by James Fenimore Cooper. ℞ Daniel Boone parleying with the Shawnee Chief "Black Fish"

	VF	XF
a) 1934–1938	60.00	90.00
b) 1935, also with supplementary date "1934" on ℞ (see illustration)	75.00	120.00

COMMEMORATIVE ISSUE FOR THE 300th ANNIVERSARY
OF THE FOUNDING OF MARYLAND

57 (C32)   Half Dollar (Ag) 1934. Cecil Calvert (1580–1632), the later Lord Baltimore, founder of the colony. ℞ coat of arms of Maryland   85.00   125.00

COMMEMORATIVE ISSUE FOR THE CENTENARY OF THE FOUNDING OF THE REPUBLIC OF TEXAS

58 (C49)   Half Dollar (Ag) 1934–1938. Eagle in front of five-peaked star; this star was the distinctive sign of the Republic of Texas. ℞ kneeling guardian angel above the mission station "Alamo" between portraits of Sam Houston (1793–1863), political and military leader on the road to independence, 1st President of the Republic, later US senator and Governor of Texas, and Stephan Austin (1793–1836), co-founder of the Republic, distinguished politician and colonizer; above flags. Texas seceded from Mexico in 1835 and became an independent republic; as late as 1845 Texas joined the Union as the 28th State

	VF	XF
	80.00	125.00

COMMEMORATIVE ISSUE FOR THE CENTENARY OF THE STATE OF ARKANSAS

59 (C7)   Half Dollar (Ag) 1935–1939. Double por-

trait: Red Indian chief of 1836 and young American woman of 1936. ℞ eagle in front of Arkansas emblem

	VF	XF
	60.00	90.00

COMMEMORATIVE ISSUE FOR THE 300th ANNIVERSARY OF THE FOUNDING OF THE COLONY OF CONNECTICUT

60 (C17) Half Dollar (Ag) 1935. "The Charter Oak", underneath which the first colonists were handed the Charter, at one time also served as a hideout; destroyed by lightning in 1856. ℞ eagle

150.00   200.00

COMMEMORATIVE ISSUE 150 YEARS OF HUDSON, N. Y.

61 (C24) Half Dollar (Ag) 1935. The "Half Moon", sailing ship of the explorer and discoverer Hendrick Hudson. ℞ Neptune with trident, astride a bottle-nosed dolphin or porpoise (Tursiops truncatus – Delphinidae) = the seal of the town of Hudson

350.00   450.00

COMMEMORATIVE ISSUE FOR THE CALIFORNIA-PACIFIC EXPOSITION IN SAN DIEGO

62 (C45) Half Dollar (Ag) 1935–1936. Seated female figure with spear and grizzly bear, coat of arms of the State of California. ℞ observation tower and cupola of the California Hall at the exposition; Gulf States of the Union

	VF	XF
	50.00	75.00

COMMEMORATIVE ISSUE 400 YEARS OF THE "OLD SPANISH TRAIL"

63 (C47) Half Dollar (Ag) 1935. Emblem of the leader of the expedition, Cabeza de Vaca ("Cow's Head"). De Vaca was one of the four survivors who after eight years of traveling on foot reached the West Coast of the Continent from Florida. ℞ Yucca tree with map of the Gulf States and route taken by the expedition

	400.00	600.00

COMMEMORATIVE ISSUE FOR THE 250th ANNIVERSARY
OF THE GRANTING OF THE FREEDOM
OF THE CITY TO ALBANY, N. Y.

64 (C5)   Half Dollar (Ag) 1936. Canadian (American) beaver (Castor fiber canadensis – Castoridae), gnawing a maple branch. ℞ Governor Thomas Dongan of New York granting the freedom of the city; handing the document to Peter Schuyler, the first mayor of Albany and his Secretary Robert Livingston

	VF	XF
	165.00	240.00

COMMEMORATIVE ISSUE FOR THE OPENING OF THE
BAY BRIDGE BETWEEN SAN FRANCISCO AND OAKLAND

65 (C8)   Half Dollar (Ag) 1936. Grizzly bear (Ursus arctos – Ursidae). ℞ Oakland Bay Bridge with historical "Ferry Tower" in the foreground

	45.00	85.00

COMMEMORATIVE ISSUE 100 YEARS
OF BRIDGEPORT, CONNECTICUT

66 (C10)   Half Dollar (Ag) 1936. P. T. Barnum (1810–1891), circus king and prominent citizen of Bridgeport. ℞ stylized eagle

	90.00	135.00

COMMEMORATIVE ISSUE 50 YEARS OF THE MUSIC CENTER CINCINNATI, OHIO

	VF	XF
67 (C12) Half Dollar (Ag) 1936. Stephen Collins Foster (1826–1864), interpreter of American folk songs (Oh! Suzanna). ℞ kneeling female figure with lyre, as allegory of music	200.00	260.00

COMMEMORATIVE ISSUE 100 YEARS OF CLEVELAND, OHIO, AND JUBILEE EXPOSITION

68 (C13) Half Dollar (Ag) 1936. Moses Cleaveland (1754–1806), general, city founder. ℞ map of the Great Lakes region, with the nine largest cities marked by stars and a circle based on Cleveland	50.00	75.00

COMMEMORATIVE ISSUE 150 YEARS OF COLUMBIA, S. C.

69 (C14) Half Dollar (Ag) 1936. Goddess of Justice with sword and balance between the old (1786) and new (1936) State Capitol. ℞ palm (emblem of the State)	265.00	225.00

		VF	**XF**
70 (C18)	Half Dollar (Ag) 1936. The "Kalmar Nyckel", Swedish emigrants' ship. ℞ "Old Swedes' Church" in Wilmington, erected at the point of landing	165.00	225.00

COMMEMORATIVE ISSUE 100 YEARS OF ELGIN, ILLINOIS

71 (C19)	Half Dollar (Ag) 1936. Idealized head of a pioneer. ℞ pioneer family, group taken from a monument in Elgin. The date 1673 has no relation to the occasion of the anniversary, but designates the year in which the explorers Louis Jolyet and Jacques Marquette (1637–1675) set foot in the territory of Illinois for the first time	145.00	200.00

COMMEMORATIVE ISSUE FOR THE BATTLE OF GETTYSBURG, PA., IN 1863

72 (C20)	Half Dollar (Ag) 1936. Double portrait: soldier of the Confederate States and soldier of the Union army. ℞ fasces between the coat of arms of the Union and the Confederation	165.00	225.00

COMMEMORATIVE ISSUE FOR THE JUBILEE OF THE FIRST COLONIZATION OF LONG ISLAND 300 YEARS AGO

		VF	XF
73 (C29)	Half Dollar (Ag) 1936. Dutch colonist and Red Indian. ℞ Dutch merchantman	45.00	70.00

COMMEMORATIVE ISSUE 150 YEARS OF LYNCHBURG, VIRGINIA

74 (C30)	Half Dollar (Ag) 1936. Portrait: Senator Carter Glass (1858–1946). ℞ standing figure of Liberty with the old Town Hall of Lynchburg in the background	125.00	185.00

COMMEMORATIVE ISSUE 200 YEARS OF NORFOLK, VIRGINIA

75 (C37)   Half Dollar (Ag) 1936. Seal of the city of

	VF	**XF**

Norfolk with a sailing ship as center piece. ℞ the Mace, granted the city in 1753   225.00   480.00

COMMEMORATIVE ISSUE FOR THE TERCENTENARY OF THE FOUNDING OF PROVIDENCE, RHODE ISLAND

76 (C42)   Half Dollar (Ag) 1936. Founder of the town and colony, Roger Williams (1604–1684), landing from a canoe and being received by Red Indians. ℞ coat of arms of the Colony of Rhode Island: "Hope" inscribed above an anchor   65.00   100.00

COMMEMORATIVE ISSUE FOR THE ARKANSAS CENTENARY

77 (C7)   Half Dollar (Ag) 1936. Senator Joseph T. Robinson (1872–1937). ℞ same as No. 59   60.00   95.00

COMMEMORATIVE ISSUE FOR THE CENTENARY OF WISCONSIN TERRITORY

78 (C54)   Half Dollar (Ag) 1936. Seal of the Terri-

tory (arm with pick axe). ℞ American
badger (Taxidae taxus – Mustelidae) on
tree trunk

	VF	XF
	140.00	210.00

COMMEMORATIVE ISSUE FOR THE TERCENTENARY
OF YORK COUNTY, MAINE

79 (C55)   Half Dollar (Ag) 1936. Seal of York
County, Maine. ℞ Brown's Garrison
(fort on the Red Indian frontier), situated on the Saco river   130.00   200.00

COMMEMORATIVE ISSUE FOR THE 75th ANNIVERSARY
OF THE BATTLE OF ANTIETAM CREEK, MARYLAND
SEPTEMBER 17, 1862

80 (C6)   Half Dollar (Ag) 1937. Double portrait
of generals McClellan (1826–1885)
(Union) and Lee (Confederation). ℞
Burnside Bridge, fought over, strate-
gically important point in this battle   200.00   340.00

COMMEMORATIVE ISSUE FOR THE 350th ANNIVERSARY
OF THE SETTLING OF ROANOKE ISLAND, N. C.

81 (C43)   Half Dollar (Ag) 1937. Sir Walter Raleigh (1552–1618), seafarer, explorer, writer, founded the first settlement of whites in 1584 on the Roanoke Island, extending in front of what was to be North Carolina. ℞ Eleanor Dare holding her daughter Virginia in her arms, the first white child to be born in America

	VF	XF
	85.00	130.00

COMMEMORATIVE ISSUE FOR THE 250th ANNIVERSARY OF THE FOUNDING OF NEW ROCHELLE, N. Y. BY THE HUGENOTS

82 (C36)   Half Dollar (Ag) 1938. The Hugenots acquired the land for their settlement from Lord John Pell; the contract of sale provided for a fattened calf to be given away each year on a certain day. J. Pell with a calf is represented on the obverse. ℞ stylized lily, part of the State coat of arms

200.00	275.00

83 (26a)   1 Cent (Zn-coated St) 1943. Abraham Lincoln (1809–1865), 16th President. Rev. value between ears of corn:

a) 1943	0.15	0.30
b) 1943 D	0.15	0.30
c) 1943 S	0.15	0.30

84 (37a)   .5 Cents (Bi) 1942-1945. Thomas Jefferson (1743-1826), 3rd President. Rev. Monticello, Jefferson's residence:

	D		P		S	
1942			1.60	3.20	0.70	1.50
1943	0.80	2.00	0.70	1.40	0.50	1.20
1944	0.50	1.20	0.50	1.20	0.50	1.20
1945	0.50	1.50	0.50	1.00	0.50	1.00

85 (38)   1 Dime (Ag) 1946–1964. Franklin Delano Roosevelt (1882–1945), 32nd President 1933–1945. Rev. torch between branches. **Roosevelt Dime:**

	without mintmark		D		S	
					VF	XF
1946	0.70	1.20	0.70	1.20	0.70	1.20
1947	0.70	1.20	0.90	2.00	0.70	1.20
1948	0.70	1.20	0.90	2.00	0.70	1.20
1949	2.00	4.00	0.90	2.00	2.50	5.00
1950	0.70	1.20	0.70	1.20	1.50	2.50
1951	0.70	1.20	0.70	1.20	0.90	2.00
1952	0.70	1.20	0.70	1.20	0.90	2.00
1953	0.70	1.20	0.70	1.20	0.70	1.20
1954	0.70	1.20	0.70	1.20	0.70	1.20
1955	1.00	2.00	0.80	1.50	0.70	1.20
1956	0.70	1.20	0.70	1.20		
1957	0.70	1.20	0.70	1.20		
1958	0.70	1.20	0.70	1.20		
1959	0.70	1.20	0.70	1.20		
1960	0.70	1.20	0.70	1.20		
1961	0.70	1.20	0.70	1.20		
1962	0.70	1.20	0.70	1.20		
1963	0.70	1.20	0.70	1.20		
1964	0.70	1.20	0.70	1.20		

86 (40)   Half Dollar (Ag) 1948–1963. Benjamin Franklin (1706–1790), diplomat, scientist, inventor and writer. ℞ Liberty Bell:

	without mintmark		D		S	
1948	4.00	8.00	4.00	8.00		
1949	7.00	10.00	8.00	11.00		
1950	4.00	9.00	4.00	9.00	10.00	20.00
1951	4.00	9.00	4.50	8.00	3.00	6.00
1952	4.00	7.00	4.00	7.00	4.00	7.00
1953	4.00	7.00	4.00	7.00	4.00	7.00
1954	4.00	6.50	4.00	6.50	4.00	6.50
1955	4.00	6.50				
1956	4.00	6.50				
1957	3.50	6.00	3.50	6.00		
1958	3.50	6.00	3.50	6.00		
1959	3.50	6.00	3.50	6.00		
1960	3.50	6.00	3.50	6.00		
1961	3.50	6.00	3.50	6.00		
1962	3.50	6.00	3.50	6.00		
1963	3.50	6.00	3.50	6.00		

COMMEMORATIVE ISSUE FOR THE CENTENARY OF THE STATE OF IOWA

87 (C26)	Half Dollar (Ag) 1946. Coat of arms Eagle (State Seal). ℞ Old State Capitol in Iowa City	VF	XF
		50.00	85.00

Values are given for each coin in U.S. Dollars and reference to Yeoman-numbers.

88 (C52) Half Dollar (Ag) 1946–1951. Booker Taliaferro Washington (1856–1915), born a negro slave, pedagogue, reformer of the educational system for colored people. ℞ Tuskagee College, and birthplace of B. T. Washington in Virginia and inscription: FROM SLAVE CABIN TO HALL OF FAME

	VF	XF
	10.00	15.00

COMMEMORATIVE ISSUE FOR WASHINGTON
AND CARVER

89 (C53) Half Dollar (Ag) 1951–1954. Double portrait: Booker T. Washington and George Washington Carver (1864–1943), biologist, chemist and philantropist. ℞ map of the USA

10.00   14.00

90 (36) 1 Cent (Br) 1959-. Abraham Lincoln. Rev. Hall of Remembrance:

	without mintmark		D		S
1959	0.05	0.10	0.05	0.10	
1960	0.05	0.10	0.05	0.10	
1961	0.05	0.10	0.05	0.10	
1962	0.05	0.10	0.05	0.10	
1963	0.05	0.10	0.05	0.10	
1964	0.05	0.10	0.05	0.10	
1965	0.05	0.10			

	without mintmark		D		S	
1966	0.05	0.10				
1967	0.05	0.10				
1968	0.05	0.10	0.05	0.10	0.05	0.10
1969	0.05	0.10	0.05	0.10	0.05	0.10
1970	0.05	0.10	0.05	0.10	0.05	0.10
1971	0.05	0.10	0.05	0.10	0.05	0.10
1972	0.05	0.10	0.05	0.10	0.05	0.10
1973	0.05	0.10	0.05	0.10	0.05	0.10
1974	0.05	0.10	0.05	0.10	0.05	0.10
1975	0.05	0.10	0.05	0.10	Proof	10.00
1976	0.05	0.10	0.05	0.10	Proof	2.50
1977	0.05	0.10	0.05	0.10	Proof	2.50
1978	0.05	0.10	0.05	0.10	Proof	4.00
1979	0.05	0.10	0.05	0.10	Proof	2.00
1980	0.05	0.10	0.05	0.10	Proof	2.00
1981	0.05	0.10	0.05	0.10	Proof	2.00
1982	0.05	0.10	0.05	0.10	Proof	3.00
1983	0.05	0.10	0.05	0.10	Proof	10.00
1984	0.05	0.10	0.05	0.10	Proof	12.50
1985	0.05	0.10	0.05	0.10	Proof	12.50
1986	0.05	0.10	0.05	0.10	Proof	9.00
1987	0.05	0.10	0.05	0.10	Proof	9.00

91 5 Cents (St, Cu-Ni plated) 1966-. Thomas Jefferson. Rev. Monticello: **VF** **XF**

	without mintmark		D		S	
1966	0.05	0.10				
1967	0.05	0.10				
1968			0.05	0.10	0.05	0.10
1969			0.05	0.10	0.05	0.10
1970			0.05	0.10	0.05	0.10
1971	0.05	0.10	0.05	0.10	Proof	2.00
1972	0.05	0.10	0.05	0.10	Proof	2.00
1973	0.05	0.10	0.05	0.10	Proof	2.00
1974	0.05	0.10	0.05	0.10	Proof	2.50
1975	0.05	0.10	0.05	0.10	Proof	2.00
1976	0.05	0.10	0.05	0.10	Proof	1.50
1977	0.05	0.10	0.05	0.10	Proof	1.50
1978	0.05	0.10	0.05	0.10	Proof	1.50
1979	0.05	0.10	0.05	0.10	Proof	1.50
1980	0.05	0.10	0.05	0.10	Proof	1.25
1981	0.05	0.10	0.05	0.10	Proof	1.00
1982	0.05	0.10	0.05	0.10	Proof	2.00
1983	0.05	0.10	0.05	0.10	Proof	1.50
1984	0.05	0.10	0.05	0.10	Proof	1.50
1985	0.05	0.10	0.05	0.10	Proof	1.50
1986	0.05	0.10	0.05	0.10	Proof	1.50
1987	0.05	0.10	0.05	0.10	Proof	1.50

92 1 Dime (St, Cu-Ni plated) 1965-. Franklin Delano Roosevelt. Rev. torch between branches:

	without mintmark		D		S	VF	XF
1965	0.10	0.20					
1966	0.10	0.20					
1967	0.10	0.20					
1968	0.10	0.20	0.10	0.20	Proof	0.85	
1969	0.10	0.20	0.10	0.20	Proof	0.85	
1970	0.10	0.20	0:10	0.20	Proof	0.85	
1971	0.10	0.20	0.10	0.20	Proof	0.85	
1972	0.10	0.20	0.10	0.20	Proof	0.85	
1973	0.10	0.20	0.10	0.20	Proof	0.85	
1974	0.10	0.20	0.10	0.20	Proof	1.00	
1975	0.10	0.20	0.10	0.20	Proof	1.25	
1976	0.10	0.20	0.10	0.20	Proof	0.85	
1977	0.10	0.20	0.10	0.20	Proof	0.85	
1978	0.10	0.20	0.10	0.20	Proof	1.00	
1979	0.10	0.20	0.10	0.20	Proof	1.25	
1980	0.10	0.20	0.10	0.20	Proof	1.00	
1981	0.10	0.20	0.10	0.20	Proof	1.00	
1982	0.10	0.20	0.10	0.20	Proof	1.00	
1983	0.10	0.20	0.10	0.20	Proof	1.50	
1984	0.10	0.20	0.10	0.20	Proof	1.00	
1985	0.10	0.20	0.10	0.20	Proof	1.00	
1986	0.10	0.20	0.10	0.20	Proof	1.00	
1987	0.10	0.20	0.10	0.20	Proof	1.00	

93 Quarter Dollar (St, Cu-Ni plated) 1965-. George Washington. Rev. Bald Eagle:

						VF	XF
1965	0.25	0.40					
1966	0.25	0.50					
1967	0.25	0.50					
1968	0.30	0.60	0.40	0.90	Proof	1.00	
1969	0.30	0.50	0.40	1.00	Proof	1.00	
1970	0.30	0.50	0.30	0.50	Proof	1.00	
1971	0.30	0.50	0.30	0.50	Proof	1.00	
1972	0.30	0.50	0.30	0.50	Proof	1.00	
1973	0.25	0.40	0.25	0.45	Proof	1.00	
1974	0.25	0.40	0.25	0.40	Proof	1.00	
1977	0.25	0.40	0.25	0.40	Proof	1.00	

	without mintmark		D		S	
1978	0.25	0.40	0.25	0.45	Proof	1.00
1979	0.25	0.40	0.25	0.40	Proof	1.00
1980	0.25	0.40	0.25	0.40	Proof	1.00
1981	0.25	0.40	0.25	0.40	Proof	1.00
1982	0.25	0.40	0.25	0.40	Proof	1.00
1983	0.25	0.40	0.25	0.40	Proof	1.50
1984	0.25	0.40	0.25	0.40	Proof	1.00
1985	0.25	0.40	0.25	0.40	Proof	1.00
1986	0.25	0.40	0.25	0.40	Proof	1.00
1987	0.25	0.40	0.25	0.40	Proof	1.00

94 (41)　　Half Dollar. John Fitzgerald Kennedy　　**VF**　　**XF**
(1917-1963), 35th President 1961-1963.
Rev. Great Seal of the USA:

	Silver Coinage					
	without mintmark		D		S	
1964	5.00	6.00	5.00	6.00		
	Silver Clad Coinage (Clad 40% Silver)					
1965	0.80	2.00				
1966	0.80	2.00				
1967	0.80	2.00				
1968			0.70	1.80	Proof	4.00
1969			0.70	1.80	Proof	4.00
1970			10.00	20.00	Proof	12.00

	without mintmark		D		P	S	
	Cupro Nickel	Clad Copper	Cupro Nickel	Clad Copper			
1971	0.60	1.00	0.60	1.00		Proof	3.00
1972	0.60	1.00	0.60	1.00		Proof	3.00
1973	0.60	1.00	0.60	1.00		Proof	3.00
1974	0.60	0.90	0.60	0.90		Proof	3.50
1977	0.60	0.90	0.60	0.90		Proof	2.00
1978	0.60	0.90	0.60	0.90		Proof	4.00
1979	0.60	0.90	0.60	0.90		Proof	2.50
1980			0.60	0.90	0.75	Proof	2.00
1981			0.60	0.90	0.75	Proof	2.00
1982			0.60	0.90	0.75	Proof	9.00
1983			0.60	0.90	0.75	Proof	10.00
1984				1.00	0.75	Proof	5.00
1985				0.75	0.75	Proof	5.00
1986				0.75	0.75	Proof	5.00
1987				4.00	4.00	Proof	5.00

95 (A48) 1 Dollar 1971–. Dwight Eisenhower (1890–1969), 34th President from 1953 to 1961. R̷ Bald Eagle with olive branch in his fangs, gliding down on to moonscape; in the lunar sky the (waning) Earth. Representation following the emblem of spaceship »Apollo 11«, with which humans landed for the first time on the moon on July 21, 1969. **Eisenhower Dollar.**

	without mintmark		D		S	
	Silver Clad Coinage (Clad 40% Silver)					
1971					6.00	7.00
1972					6.00	7.00
1973					6.00	7.00
1974					6.00	7.00
1976					7.50	10.00
	Cupro-Nickel Clad Copper					
1971	1.50	2.50	2.00	3.00		
1972	1.50	2.50	1.40	1.80		
1973	9.00	14.00	9.00	14.00	Proof	4.00
1974	1.50	2.00	1.50	2.00	Proof	4.00
1976	2.00	3.00	1.50	2.00	Proof	4.00
1977	1.50	2.00	1.50	2.00	Proof	4.00
1978	1.50	2.00	1.50	2.00	Proof	6.00

BICENTENARY OF AMERICAN INDEPENDENCE (3)

96 (67) Quarter Dollar 1976. George Washington.
Rev. Revolutionary War drummer:

	without mintmark		D		S	VF	XF
Clad Metal	0.30	0.50	0.30	0.50	Proof:		2.00
.400 Silver					Proof:		4.00

97 (68) Half Dollar 1976. John Fitzgerald Kennedy. Rev. Independence Hall in Philadelphia (cf. No. 51):

.400 Silver Clad Metal	without mintmark		D		S	
	0.70	1.00	0.70	1.00	4.00 Proof:	6.50 2.00

98 (69) 1 Dollar 1976. Dwight David Eisenhower. Rev. Liberty Bell. **Bicentennial Dollar:** VF XF

.400 Silver Clad Metal	without mintmark		D		S	
	1.50	2.00	1.50	2.00	Proof: Proof:	12.50 5.00

99 1 Dollar (Cu-Ni) 1979–1981. Susan B. Anthony (1820–1906), suffragette. **Anthony Dollar:** 1.25 1.50

250th ANNIVERSARY OF THE BIRTH OF GEORGE WASHINGTON

		Unc	Proof
100 (C70)	Half Dollar (AG) 1982. Mount Vernon. Rev. Washington on horseback. **Washington Half**	16.00	17.00

23rd OLYMPIC SUMMER GAMES 1984 IN LOS ANGELES (3)

101 (C71) 1 Dollar (Ag) 1983. Bald eagle. Rev.
Discus thrower, olympic rings.
Discus Thrower Dollar:
a) 1983 D (174,014)   55.00
b) 1983 P (294,543)   42.00
c) 1983 S (174,014)   55.00
d) 1983 S (1,577,014)   25.00

		Unc	Proof

102 (C72) 1 Dollar (Ag) 1984. Bald eagle. Rev.
Olympic Coliseum Gateway.
Gateway Dollar:

	Unc	Proof
a) 1984 D (116,675)	42.00	
b) 1984 P (217,954)	30.00	
c) 1984 S (116,675)	42.00	
d) 1984 S (1,801,210)		22.50

103 (C73) 10 Dollars (Au) 1984. Great Seal of the
USA. Rev. Two runners bearing the
olympic torch aloft, olympic rings:

	Unc	Proof
a) 1984 D (34,533)		650.00
b) 1984 P (33,309)		875.00
c) 1984 S (48,551)		550.00
d) 1984 W (75,886)		285.00
e) 1984 W (381,085)	375.00	

STATUE OF LIBERTY (3)

104 (C74) Half Dollar (Cu-Ni) 1986. A ship of
immigrants steaming into New
York harbor, Statue of Liberty, rising sun. Rev. An immigrant family

	Unc	Proof
	7.00	9.00

		Unc	Proof
105 (C75)	1 Dollar (Ag) 1986. Statue of Liberty in the foreground, with the Ellis Island Immigration building standing behind her. Rev. Liberty torch	25.00	27.50

		Unc	Proof
106 (C76)	5 Dollars (Au) 1986. View of Statue of Liberty's crowned head from below. Rev. American eagle in flight:		
	a) 1986 W (171,797)	500.00	
	b) 1986 W (137,841)		400.00

BULLION ISSUE »Silver American Eagle«

		Unc	Proof
107	1 Dollar (Ag) 1986 –. Walking Liberty in front of rising sun (cf. No. 21). Rev. Arms:		
	a) 1986 (5,393,005)	15.00	
	b) 1986 S (1,384,855)		40.00
	c) 1987	10.00	
	d) 1987 S		30.00

BULLION ISSUE »American Eagle« (4)

		Unc	Proof
108	5 Dollars (Au) 1986 –. Standing Liberty – »Saint Gaudens Type« (cf. Nos. 27-29). Rev. Family of American eagles; .916⅔ gold. 3.39 g:		
	a) 1986 (852,500)	55.00	
	b) 1987 –	52.00	
109	10 Dollars (Au) 1986 –. Type as No. 108; .916⅔ gold, 6.79 g:		
	a) 1986 (587,000)	130.00	
	b) 1987 –	125.00	

		Unc	Proof

110 25 Dollars (Au) 1986 –. Type as No. 108; .916⅔ gold, 16.97 g:
a) 1986 (486,500) — 260.00
b) 1987 – 250.00

111 50 Dollars (Au) 1986 –. Type as No. 108; .916⅔ gold, 33.93 g:
a) 1986 (1,312,500) — 500.00
b) 1986 W — — 700.00
c) 1987 – 475.00

200th ANNIVERSARY OF CONSTITUTION (2)

112 1 Dollar (Ag) 1987. Sheaf of parchment and a quill pen with the inscription »We the People«. Rev. Cross-section of Americans from past and present in a dramatic parade through history — 30.00 35.00

| 113 | 5 Dollars (Au) 1987. American eagle holding a quill pen. Rev. A quill with the inscription »We the People« | 200.00 | 225.00 |

OLYMPIC GAMES 1988 (2)

| 114 | 1 Dollar (Ag) 1988 | –.– | –.– |
| 115 | 5 Dollars (Au) 1988 | –.– | –.– |

All valuations in the SCHÖN are stated in U.S. Dollars.

Uruguay

Republica Oriental del Uruguay

Area: 72,180 sq. mi. Population: 3,000,000.
The Republic of Uruguay extends to the North of the Rio de la Plata
(River Plate) between the river Uruguay and the Atlantic Ocean.
Capital: Montevideo.

100 Centésimos = 1 Peso

			VF	XF
1 (15)	1	Centésimo (Cu–Ni) 1901, 1909, 1924, 1936. Sun. ℞ value in wreath	0.80	1.60
2 (16)	2	Centésimos (Cu–Ni) 1901, 1909, 1924, 1936, 1941	0.80	1.20
3 (17)	5	Centésimos (Cu–Ni) 1901, 1909, 1924, 1936, 1941	0.80	1.20
4 (20)	20	Centésimos (Ag) 1920. José Artigas (1764–1850), General, fighter for independence; Dictator from 1813 to 1820. ℞ coat of arms	6.00	10.50
5 (22)	50	Centésimos (Ag) 1916–1917	9.00	15.00
6 (23)	1	Peso (Ag) 1917	45.00	85.00

COMMEMORATIVE ISSUES (3) FOR THE CENTENNIAL OF THE CONSTITUTION

			VF	XF
7 (18)	10	Centésimos (Al–Br) 1930. Head of Liberty. ℞ puma (Puma concolor–Felidae), value, and memorial legend	4.00	8.00

			VF	XF
8 (21)	20	Centésimos (Ag) 1930. Allegory of the Republic and shield with memorial legend. ℞ ears of wheat, value	6.00	10.50

			VF	XF
9 (24)	5	Pesos (Au) 1930. José Artigas, head right. ℞ laurel branches, rays of the rising sun, memorial legend, value	160.00	200.00
10 (16a)	2	Centésimos (Br) 1943, 1944, 1945, 1946, 1947, 1948, 1949, 1951. Same type as No. 2	0.40	0.60
11 (17a)	5	Centésimos (Br) 1944, 1946, 1947, 1948, 1949, 1951. Same type as No. 3	0.50	0.80
12 (19)	10	Centésimos (Al–Br) 1936. Same type as No. 7, but without memorial legend	4.50	8.00
13 (25)	20	Centésimos (Ag) 1942. Head of Liberty, right. ℞ ears of wheat	3.50	6.00
14 (26)	50	Centésimos (Ag) 1943. ℞ value	4.00	7.00
15 (27)	1	Peso (Ag) 1942. José Artigas, head right. ℞ puma	8.00	12.00
16 (28)	1	Centésimo (Cu–Ni) 1953. José Artigas. ℞ value in wreath	0.25	0.40
17 (29)	2	Centésimos (Cu–Ni) 1953	0.25	0.40
18 (30)	5	Centésimos (Cu–Ni) 1953	0.25	0.40
19 (31)	10	Centésimos (Cu–Ni) 1953–1959	0.40	0.65
20 (32)	20	Centésimos (Ag) 1954. ℞ five ears of wheat	2.00	4.00
21 (33)	2	Centésimos (Ni–Bra) 1960. José Artigas. ℞ value in wreath	0.20	0.30
22 (34)	5	Centésimos (Ni–Bra) 1960	0.25	0.40
23 (35)	10	Centésimos (Ni–Bra) 1960	0.25	0.40
24 (36)	25	Centésimos (Cu–Ni) 1960. ℞ coat of arms	0.40	0.60
25 (37)	50	Centésimos (Cu–Ni) 1960	0.50	0.80
26 (38)	1	Peso (Cu–Ni) 1960	0.80	1.20

Values are given for each coin in U.S. Dollars and reference to Yeoman-numbers.

COMMEMORATIVE ISSUE FOR THE 150th ANNIVERSARY OF REVOLUTION AGAINST SPAIN

			VF	**XF**
27 (39)	10	Pesos (Ag) 1961. Gaucho, head right. ℞ value in wreath, memorial legend	7.00	12.00
28 (40)	20	Centésimos (Al) 1965. José Artigas. ℞ value in wreath	0.15	0.25
29 (41)	50	Centésimos (Al) 1965	0.20	0.30
30 (42)	1	Peso (Al–Br) 1965. ℞ coat of arms	0.30	0.50
31 (43)	5	Pesos (Al–Br) 1965	0.50	0.80

32 (44)	10	Pesos (Al–Br) 1965	1.00	1.50
33 (45)	1	Peso (Al–Br) 1968. José Artigas. ℞ ceibo (Erythrina crista-galli – Leguminosae) = national flower; value	0.10	0.20
34 (46)	5	Pesos (Al–Br) 1968. Same type as No. 33	0.20	0.40

35 (47)	10	Pesos (Al–Br) 1968. Same type as No. 33	0.35	0.60

				VF	XF
36 (48)	1	Peso (Al–Br) 1969. Sun, date. ℞ ceibo		0.10	0.20
37 (49)	5	Pesos (Al–Br) 1969. Same type as No. 36		0.25	0.40

				VF	XF
38 (50)	10	Pesos (Al–Br) 1969. Same type as No. 36		0.40	0.60
39 (51)	20	Pesos (Cu–Ni) 1970. Coat of arms. ℞ ears of wheat, value		0.45	0.80

				VF	XF
40 (52)	50	Pesos (Cu–Ni) 1970. Same type as No. 39		0.70	1.20

ISSUE FOR THE FAO COIN PLAN

				XF	Unc
41 (53)	1000	Pesos (Ag) 1969. Man, nature and agriculture, by Uruguayan sculptor Francisco Matta Vilaró. Legend reads "FAO – Fiat Panis". ℞ sun with twelve rays, value. Gold and copper trial strikes also known!		12.00	15.00

COMMEMORATIVE ISSUE FOR THE 100th BIRTHDAY OF J. E. RODO

42 (54)	50	Pesos (Cu–Ni) 1971. José Enrique	

Rodó (1871–1917), philosopher and writer. Gold and copper trial strikes also known!

	XF	Unc
	0.80	1.50

43 (A53) 100 Pesos (Cu–Ni) 1973. Bust of José Artigas. ℞ value, date — 0.70 — 1.10

CURRENCY REFORM: 1000 Old Pesos = 1 New Peso (Nuevo Peso)

			XF	Unc
44	(54)	5 Nuevo Pesos (Al-Br) 1975	2.50	5.00
45	(A55)	1 Centésimo (Al) 1977	0.12	0.25
46	(B55)	2 Centésimos (Al) 1977, 1978	0.12	0.25
47	(C55)	5 Centésimos (Al) 1977, 1978	0.12	0.25
48	(55)	10 Centésimos (Al-Br) 1976–1978, 1981	0.15	0.30
49	(56)	20 Centésimos (Al-Br) 1976–1978, 1981	0.20	0.40
50	(57)	50 Centésimos (Al-Br) 1976–1978, 1981	0.40	0.70
51	(58)	1 Nuevo Peso (Al-Br) 1976–1978	0.70	1.25

250th ANNIVERSARY OF THE FOUNDING OF MONTEVIDEO

52	(60)	5 Nuevo Pesos (Al-Br) 1976	3.00	6.50
53	(61)	1 Nuevo Peso (Cu-Ni) 1980	0.30	0.60
54	(62)	5 Nuevo Peso (Cu-Ni) 1980	0.70	1.50
55	(63)	10 Nuevo Peso (Cu-Ni) 1980	1.00	2.00
56	(63a)	10 Nuevo Peso (Au) 1980	Proof	*500.00*

WORLD FOOD DAY 1981 (2)

		XF	Unc
57 (64)	2 Nuevo Pesos (Al-Br) 1981. Five ears of wheat	0.50	0.75
58 (64a)	2 Nuevo Pesos (Au) 1981. Type as No. 57	Proof	500.00

HYDROELECTRIC DAM »SALTO GRANDE« (4)

		Unc	Proof
59 (65)	100 Nuevo Pesos (Ag) 1981	7.50	20.00
60 (65a)	100 Nuevo Pesos (Au) 1981		*350.00*
61 (66)	5000 Nuevo Pesos (Ag) 1981		25.00
62 (66a)	5000 Nuevo Pesos (Au) 1981		*500.00*
63 (67)	1 Nuevo Peso (Ag) 1981. National flag		*50.00*
64 (68)	5 Nuevo Pesos (Ag) 1981. Coat of arms		*60.00*
65 (69)	10 Nuevo Pesos (Ag) 1981. José Artigas		*70.00*

ROYAL VISIT (2)

66 (70)	2000 Nuevo Pesos (Ag) 1983. Conjoined heads of the Spanish Queen and the King. Rev. two coats of arms	75.00
67 (71)	20,000 Nuevo Pesos (Au) 1983. Type as No. 66	500.00

HYDROELECTRIC DAM »9 de Febrero de 1973« (2)

68 (72)	500 Nuevo Pesos (Ag) 1983	20.00
69 (73)	20,000 Nuevo Pesos (Au) 1983	500.00

25th INTERAMERICAN BANKERS' CONFERENCE AT PUNTA DEL ESTE, MARCH 1984 (3)

70 (74)	2000 Nuevo Pesos (Ag) 1984. Reproduction of an 1844 Peso from Uruguay	50.00
71 (75)	20,000 Nuevo Pesos (Au) 1984. Reproduction of an 1854 40-Reales-piece from Uruguay	500.00
72 (76)	2000 Nuevo Pesos (Ag) 1984. Coat of arms	50.00

WORLD FISHERIES CONFERENCE (2)

73 (77)	20 Nuevo Pesos 1984:		
	a) (Ag) 11.66 g		30.00
	b) (Ag) 23.32 g, Pièfort		–.–
	c) (Cu-Ni)	5.00	
74 (77b)	20 Nuevo Pesos (Au) 1984		500.00

Area: 5,700 sq. mi. Population: 135,000.

Formerly a Anglo-French condominium, the group of the New Hebrides Islands located in the South West Pacific attained independence on July 30th, 1980 and were renamed Vanuatu.

Capital: Port Vila.

1st ANNIVERSARY OF INDEPENDENCE (2)

			Unc	Proof
1 (1)	50	Vatu 1981:		
		a) (Ag)		40.00
		b) (Cu-Ni)	2.00	
2 (2)	10,000	Vatu (Au) 1981. Coconut crab on island	400.00	450.00

			Unc
3 (3)	1	Vatu (Ni-Bra) 1983. Coat of arms. Rev. sea shell	0.30

			Unc
4 (4)	2	Vatu (Ni-Bra) 1983. Type as No. 3	0.40
5 (5)	5	Vatu (Ni-Bra) 1983. Type as No. 3	0.50

ISSUES FOR THE FAO-COIN-PLAN (3)

			Unc
6 (6)	10	Vatu (Cu-Ni) 1983. Rev. coconut crab	0.60
7 (7)	20	Vatu (Cu-Ni) 1983. Type as No. 6	0.80
8 (8)	50	Vatu (Cu-Ni) 1983. Rev. yam	1.25

Vatikanstadt   # Vatican City   **Vatican**

Stato della Cittá del Vaticano

Area: 109 acres. Population: 1025.
The Vatican City not only possesses its own railway station and a radio
transmitter, but also has currency and postal privileges. In the Lateran
Treaty of February 11, 1929, ratified on June 7, 1929, the sovereignty
of the Pope over the Vatican City with the Vatican enclaves was recog-
nized by Italy. In the Vatican City there are also the Vatican Collections
(Collection of Antiquities, Vatican Library, Vatican Archives, Vatican
Picture Gallery).

100 Centesimi = 1 Vatican Lira

POPE PIUS XI 1922–1939

			VF	XF
1 (1)	5	Centesimi (Br) 1929–1937. Coat of arms. ℞ olive branch:		
		a) 1929	26.00	42.00
		b) 1930–1937	6.50	9.00
2 (2)	10	Centesimi (Br) 1929–1938. ℞ St. Peter, portrait right:		
		a) 1929	20.00	35.00
		b) 1930–1937	6.00	9.00
3 (3)	20	Centesimi (Ni) 1929–1937. ℞ St. Paul, portrait left:		
		a) 1929	20.00	35.00
		b) 1930–1937	3.00	4.50
4 (4)	50	Centesimi (Ni) 1929–1937. ℞ Arch-angel Michael:		
		a) 1929	20.00	35.00
		b) 1930–1937	3.50	5.50

			VF	XF
5 (5)	1	Lira (Ni) 1929–1937. ℞ Virgin Mary:		
		a) 1929	20.00	35.00
		b) 1930–1937	4.00	6.50

		VF	**XF**

6 (6) 2 Lire (Ni) 1929–1937. ℞ Virgin Mary:

a) 1929 — 25.00 — 36.00

b) 1930–1937 — 6.50 — 9.00

7 (7) 5 Lire (Ag) 1929–1937. Pius XI, Ratti (1857–1939), portrait right. ℞ St. Peter in a boat:

a) 1929 — 26.00 — 40.00

b) 1930–1937 — 12.00 — 16.00

8 (8) 10 Lire (Ag) 1929–1937. ℞ sitting Madonna with child:

a) 1929 — 30.00 — 50.00

b) 1930–1937 — 15.00 — 18.00

9 (9) 100 Lire (Au). Rev. standing Christ:

a) 1929, 1931-1935, diameter 23.5 mm — 300.00 — 350.00

b) 1930, diameter 23.5 mm — 800.00 — 1000.00

c) 1936, diameter 20.5 mm — 320.00 — 400.00

d) 1937, diameter 20.5 mm — 2600.00 — 3000.00

e) 1938, diameter 20.5 mm — –.–

SEDE VACANTE 1939

10 (20) 5 Lire (Ag) 1939. Coat of arms of Cardinal Pacelli. ℞ dove — 10.00 — 16.00

11 (21) 10 Lire (Ag) 1939. Same type as No. 10 — 12.50 — 18.00

			VF	XF
12 (22)	5	Centesimi (Br) 1939–1941. Coat of arms. ℞ olive branch	7.50	11.50
13 (23)	10	Centesimi (Br) 1939–1941. ℞ St. Peter, portrait right	7.50	11.50
14 (24)	20	Centesimi. ℞ St. Paul, portrait left		
		a) (Ni) 1939	8.00	12.00
		b) (St) 1940–1941	1.60	3.00
15 (25)	50	Centesimi. ℞ Archangel Michael		
		a) (Ni) 1939	5.50	8.00
		b) (St) 1940–1941	1.60	2.80
16 (26)	1	Lira. ℞ Virgin Mary		
		a) (Ni) 1939	8.00	12.00
		b) (St) 1940–1941	2.50	3.50
17 (27)	2	Lire. ℞ Virgin Mary		
		a) (Ni) 1939	10.00	13.00
		b) (St) 1940–1941	2.50	3.50
18 (28)	5	Lire (Ag) 1939–1941. Pius XII, Pacelli (1876–1958), portrait left. ℞ St. Peter in boat	8.00	12.00
19 (29)	10	Lire (Ag) 1939–1941. ℞ seated Madonna with child	60.00	80.00

			VF	XF
20 (30)	100	Lire (Au) 1939–1941. ℞ standing Christ	300.00	400.00
21 (31)	5	Centesimi (Bra) 1942–1946. ℞ dove	60.00	75.00
22 (32)	10	Centesimi (Bra) 1942–1946. ℞ dove	50.00	65.00
23 (33)	20	Centesimi (St) 1942–1946. Coat of arms. ℞ Justice	2.00	3.00
24 (34)	50	Centesimi (St) 1942–1946. Same type as No. 23	2.00	3.00
25 (35)	1	Lira (St) 1942–1946. Same type as No. 23	2.00	3.00
26 (40)	1	Lira (Al) 1947–1949. Same type as No. 23	15.00	18.50
27 (36)	2	Lire (St) 1942–1946. Same type as No. 23	3.00	4.00

			VF	XF
28 (41)	2	Lire (Al) 1947–1949. Same type as No. 23	12.00	26.00

				VF	**XF**
29 (37)	5	Lire (Ag) 1942–1946. ℞ Caritas		70.00	90.00
30 (42)	5	Lire (Al) 1947–1949. Same type as No. 29		10.00	12.50
31 (38)	10	Lire (Ag) 1942–1946. Same type as No. 29		120.00	145.00
32 (43)	10	Lire (Al) 1947–1949. Same type as No. 29		10.00	13.00
33 (39)	100	Lire (Au) 1942–1949. Same type as No. 29		300.00	350.00

COMMEMORATIVE ISSUE (5) FOR THE HOLY YEAR

34 (44)	1	Lira (Al) 1950. Coat of arms. ℞ Holy Portal	6.00	9.00
35 (45)	2	Lire (Al) 1950. Pius XII, portrait right. ℞ peace dove in front of St. Peter's Cathedral	6.00	9.00
36 (46)	5	Lire (Al) 1950. Pius XII, portrait left. ℞ procession	4.00	5.00
37 (47)	10	Lire (Al) 1950. Same type as No. 38	6.00	8.00

38 (48)	100	Lire (Au) 1950. The Pope's portrait with tiara. ℞ Pius XII opening Holy Portal	200.00	260.00
39 (49)	1	Lira (Al) 1951–1958. Coat of arms. ℞ Temperantia	1.00	2.00
40 (50)	2	Lire (Al) 1951–1958. Same type as No. 41	1.00	2.00
41 (51)	5	Lire (Al) 1951–1958. ℞ Justitia	1.00	2.00
42 (52)	10	Lire (Al) 1951–1958. ℞ Prudentia	1.00	2.00
43 (A52)	20	Lire (Al–Br) 1957–1958	2.50	3.50
44 (54)	50	Lire (St) 1955–1958. ℞ Spes	1.60	2.80
45 (55)	100	Lire (St) 1955–1958. Fides	2.60	3.50
46 (53)	100	Lire (Au) 1951–1956. ℞ Caritas	450.00	600.00
47 (A53)	100	Lire (Au) 1957–1958. ℞ coat of arms	300.00	400.00

COMMEMORATIVE ISSUE FOR THE 20th ANNIVERSARY OF THE PONTIFICATE

48 (56)	500	Lire (Ag) 1958. Pius XII, portrait left. ℞ coat of arms	30.00	45.00

SEDE VACANTE 1958

		VF	XF
49 (57) 500 Lire (Ag) 1958. Dove. ℞ coat of arms		12.00	17.50

POPE JOHN XXIII 1958–1963

			VF	XF
50 (58)	1	Lira (Al) 1959–1962. Coat of arms. ℞ Temperantia	6.00	10.00
51 (59)	2	Lire (Al) 1959–1962. Rev. Fortitudo	6.00	10.00

			VF	XF
52 (60)	5	Lire (Al) 1959–1962. John XXIII, Roncalli (1881–1963), portrait right. Rev. Justitia	6.00	9.00
53 (61)	10	Lire (Al) 1959–1962. Rev. Prudentia	4.00	6.50
54 (62)	20	Lire (Al-Br) 1959–1962. Rev. Caritas	3.50	5.00
55 (63)	50	Lire (St) 1959–1962. Rev. Spes	1.20	1.60
56 (64)	100	Lire (St) 1959–1962. Rev. Fides	1.50	2.00
57 (66)	100	Lire (Au) 1959. Rev. coat of arms	1000.00	1250.00

		VF	XF
58 (65) 500 Lire (Ag) 1959–1962. ℞ coat of arms:			
a) 1959, 1961–1962		18.00	27.50
b) 1960		100.00	125.00

COMMEMORATIVE ISSUES (8) FOR THE 2nd ECUMENICAL COUNCIL OF THE VATICAN

		VF	XF
59 (67)	1 Lira (Al) 1962. Coat of arms. ℞ dove, symbolizing the Holy Ghost	2.60	4.50
60 (68)	2 Lire (Al) 1962	2.60	4.50
61 (69)	5 Lire (Al) 1962	1.80	3.50
62 (70)	10 Lire (Al) 1962	0.80	1.50
63 (71)	20 Lire (Al) 1962	0.80	1.50
64 (72)	50 Lire (St) 1962. ℞ John XXIII, head of the Council	0.80	1.50
65 (73)	100 Lire (St) 1962. Same type as No. 64	1.20	1.80

66 (74)	500 Lire (Ag) 1962. Same type as No. 64	22.00	30.00

SEDE VACANTE 1963

67 (75)	500 Lire (Ag) 1963. Coat of arms. ℞ dove	8.00	10.00

POPE PAUL VI 1963-1978

		VF	XF
68 (76)	1 Lira (Al) 1963–1965. Coat of arms. ℞ Temperantia	4.00	5.00
69 (77)	2 Lire (Al) 1963–1965. Coat of arms. ℞ Fortitudo	4.00	5.00
70 (78)	5 Lire (Al) 1963–1965. Paul XI, Montini (1963-1978), portrait right. R. Justitia	2.00	3.00
71 (79)	10 Lire (Al) 1963–1965. ℞ Prudentia	2.00	3.00
72 (80)	20 Lire (Al–Br) 1963–1965. ℞ Caritas	1.20	1.60
73 (81)	50 Lire (St) 1963–1965. ℞ Spes	0.80	1.20
74 (82)	100 Lire (St) 1963–1965. Fides	0.40	1.20
75 (83)	500 Lire (Ag) 1963–1965. ℞ coat of arms	16.00	20.00
76 (84)	1 Lira (Al) 1966. 4th year of the pontificate. Head of Paul VI, left, with cappa and miter. ℞ shepherd, carrying a lamb on his back: "I am the Good Shepherd", John 10, 2, motto of Pope Paul VI	1.00	2.00
77 (85)	2 Lire (Al) 1966. Same type as No. 76	1.00	2.00
78 (86)	5 Lire (Al) 1966. Same type as No. 76	0.80	1.20
79 (87)	10 Lire (Al) 1966. Same type as No. 76	0.40	0.80
80 (88)	20 Lire (Al–Br) 1966. Same type as No. 76	0.80	1.20
81 (89)	50 Lire (St) 1966. Same type as No. 76	0.40	0.80
82 (90)	100 Lire (St) 1966. Same type as No. 76	0.40	0.80
83 (91)	500 Lire (Ag) 1966. Same type as No. 76	12.00	16.00

			VF	XF

84 (92) 1 Lira (Al) 1967. Coat of arms of Pope
Paul VI. ℞ crossed keys above Holy
Sword in front of rising sun   1.20   2.00

85 (93) 2 Lire (Al) 1967. Coat of arms of Pope
Paul VI. ℞ tiara (symbol of the educational, pastoral and ministerial duties
of the pope) above upside-down cross
with ropes (allegory of St. Peter's cruci-
fication with head down – John 21, 18);
key on right and left side of cross con-
nected with ropes and tiara bows   1.20   2.00

86 (94) 5 Lire (Al) 1967. Portrait of the Pope,
right, with pileolus (cap) and mozzetta
(short-hooded cape) and stole. ℞ St.
Peter's key and sword in front of rising
sun (sword as St. Paul's instrument of
torture – 1900th anniversary of his
martyrdom)   0.80   1.20

87 (95) 10 Lire (Al) 1967. Portrait of the Pope,
left. ℞ like No. 85   0.40   0.80

88 (96) 20 Lire (Al–Br) 1967. Portrait of the Pope,
right. ℞ sword in front of rising sun
between the Saints Peter to the left and
Paul to the right; crossed keys symbolizing the papal banning and redeem-
ing power, as a direct successor to St.
Peter – Matthew 16, 19 (1900th anniversary of the martyrdom of St. Peter
and St. Paul)   0.40   0.80

89 (97) 50 Lire (St) 1967. Portrait of the Pope,
right. ℞ Damascus Hour: conversion
of Saulus – apostle 9, 3 to 4; Saulus on
horseback   0.40   0.80

90 (98) 100 Lire (St) 1967. Portrait of the Pope,
left. ℞ the Pope holding the highest

	VF	XF

ecclesiastical professorial chair, giving
an ex-cathedra explanation   0.40   0.80

91 (99) 500 Lire (Ag) 1967. Portrait of the Pope,
left. ℞ like No. 88   14.00   20.00

COMMEMORATIVE ISSUES (8)
FOR THE 6th ANNIVERSARY OF THE PONTIFICATE
AND FOR THE FAO COIN PLAN

92 (100) 1 Lira (Al) 1968. Portrait of the Pope
with pileolus and mozzetta. ℞ wheat
in form of a cross, in front of sun, symbolizing the fertility in Christian faith   1.20   2.00

93 (101) 2 Lire (Al) 1968. ℞ Feeding of the Five
Thousand   1.20   2.00

94 (102) 5 Lire (Al) 1968. ℞ Our Lady of the
Harvest   1.20   2.00

95 (103) 10 Lire (Al) 1968. Same type as No. 93   0.40   0.80
96 (104) 20 Lire (Br) 1968. Same type as No. 92   0.40   0.80
97 (105) 50 Lire (St) 1968. Same type as No. 94   0.40   0.80
98 (106) 100 Lire (St) 1968. Same type as No. 93   0.40   0.80
99 (107) 500 Lire (Ag) 1968. Same type as No. 92   14.00   20.00

COMMEMORATIVE ISSUES (8) FOR THE 7th ANNIVERSARY OF THE PONTIFICATE

			VF	XF
100 (108)	1	Lira (Al) 1969. Pope Paul VI, with miter. ℞ angel	1.00	2.00
101 (109)	2	Lire (Al) 1969	1.00	2.00
102 (110)	5	Lire (Al) 1969	0.80	1.20
103 (111)	10	Lire (Al) 1969	0.40	0.80
104 (112)	20	Lire (Al–Br) 1969	0.40	0.80
105 (113)	50	Lire (St) 1969	0.20	0.40
106 (114)	100	Lire (St) 1969	0.30	0.60

		VF	XF
107 (115) 500	Lire (Ag) 1969	10.00	13.00

COMMEMORATIVE ISSUES (8) FOR THE 8th to 15th ANNIVERSARY OF THE PONTIFICATE

			VF	XF
108 (116)	1	Lira (Al) 1970-1977. Coat of arms of Pope Paul VI. Rev. palm leaf (date palm-Phoenix dactylifera - Palmae)	0.80	1.20
109 (117)	2	Lire (Al) 1970-1977. Rev. lamb (Ovis ammon aries - Bovidae)	0.80	1.20
110 (118)	5	Lire (Al) 1970-1977. Rev. pelican (Pelecanus sp. - Pelicanidae), according to Christian legend it feeds it's young ones with the blood drawn from the self-inflicted chest wounds	0.40	0.60
111 (119)	10	Lire (Al) 1970-1977. Rev. fish	0.40	0.60
112 (120)	20	Lire (Al-Br) 1970-1977. Rev. red deer (Cervus elaphus - Cervidae)	0.30	0.40
113 (121)	50	Lire (St) 1970-1976. Rev. olive branch (Olea europaea - Oleaceae)	0.20	0.30
114 (122)	100	Lire (St) 1970-1977. Rev. domestic pigeon (Columba livia domestica - Columbidae) and olive branch	0.20	0.30
115 (123)	500	Lire (Ag) 1970-1976. Rev. grape (Vitis vinifera - Vitaceae) and ear of barley (Hordeum sp. - Gramineae)	9.00	12.00

HOLY YEAR 1975 (8)

				XF	Unc
116 (124)	1	Lira (Al)	1975	1.00	2.00
117 (125)	2	Lire (Al)	1975	1.00	2.00
118 (126)	5	Lire (Al)	1975	0.50	1.00
119 (127)	10	Lire (Al)	1975	0.50	1.00
120 (128)	20	Lire (Al-Br)	1975	0.80	1.50
121 (129)	50	Lire (St)	1975	0.80	1.50
122 (130)	100	Lire (St)	1975	0.80	1.50
123 (131)	500	Lire (Ag)	1975	13.00	20.00
124 (A121)	50	Lire (St)	1977	1.00	1.50

125 (132)	500	Lire (Ag)	1977	11.00	16.00

16th ANNIVERSARY OF THE PONTIFICATE (7)

126 (133)	5	Lire (Al)	1978	0.50	1.00
127 (134)	10	Lire (Al)	1978	0.50	1.00
128 (135)	20	Lire (Al-Br)	1978	0.60	1.00
129 (136)	50	Lire (St)	1978	0.90	1.50
130 (137)	100	Lire (St)	1978	1.00	2.00
131 (138)	200	Lire (Al-Br)	1978	1.50	2.50
132 (139)	500	Lire (Ag)	1978	12.00	15.00

SEDE VACANTE 1978 (I)

133 (140)	500	Lire (Ag)	1978	15.00	18.00

POPE JOHN PAUL I 1978

			XF	Unc
134 (142)	1000 Lire (Ag) 1978			22.50

SEDE VACANTE 1978 (II)

135 (141)	500 Lire (Ag) 1978	12.00	15.00

POPE JOHN PAUL II since 1978

136 (143)	10 Lire (Al) 1979–1980	0.30	0.50
137 (144)	20 Lire (Al-Br) 1979–1980	0.30	0.50
138 (145)	50 Lire (St) 1979–1980	0.30	0.50
139 (146)	100 Lire (St) 1979–1980	0.40	0.60
140 (147)	200 Lire (Al-Br) 1979–1980	0.60	1.25
141 (148)	500 Lire (Ag) 1979–1980	12.00	15.00

3rd ANNIVERSARY OF THE PONTIFICATE (6)

142 (155)	10 Lire (Al) 1981	0.30	0.50
143 (156)	20 Lire (Al-Br) 1981	0.30	0.50
144 (157)	50 Lire (St) 1981	0.30	0.50
145 (158)	100 Lire (St) 1981	0.40	0.60
146 (159)	200 Lire (Al-Br) 1981	0.60	1.25
147 (160)	500 Lire (Ag) 1981	11.00	15.00

4th ANNIVERSARY OF THE PONTIFICATE (7)

148 (161)	10 Lire (Al) 1982	0.20	0.40
149 (162)	20 Lire (Al-Br) 1982	0.30	0.50
150 (163)	50 Lire (St) 1982	0.30	0.50
151 (164)	100 Lire (St) 1982	0.40	0.60
152 (165)	200 Lire (Al-Br) 1982	0.60	1.20
153 (166)	500 Lire (Steel ring/Al-Br centre)	0.65	1.25
154 (167)	1000 Lire (Ag) 1982	10.00	12.50

		XF	Unc
155 (168)	500 Lire (Ag) 1983	9.00	12.00
156 (169)	1000 Lire (Ag) 1983	12.00	15.00

5th ANNIVERSARY OF THE PONTIFICATE (7)

		XF	Unc
157 (170)	10 Lire (Al) 1983	0.20	0.40
158 (171)	20 Lire (Al-Br) 1983	0.25	0.50
159 (172)	50 Lire (St) 1983	0.25	0.50
160 (173)	100 Lire (St) 1983	0.30	0.60
161 (174)	200 Lire (Al-Br) 1983	0.50	0.80
162 (175)	500 Lire (Steel ring/Al-Br centre) 1983	0.60	1.00
163 (176)	1000 Lire (Ag) 1983	12.00	15.00

6th ANNIVERSARY OF THE PONTIFICATE (7)

		XF	Unc
164 (177)	10 Lire (Al) 1984	0.20	0.40
165 (178)	20 Lire (Al-Br) 1984	0.25	0.50
166 (179)	50 Lire (St) 1984	0.25	0.50
167 (180)	100 Lire (St) 1984	0.30	0.60
168 (181)	200 Lire (Al-Br) 1984	0.50	0.80
169 (182)	500 Lire (Steel ring/Al-Br centre) 1984	0.60	1.00

170	1000 Lire (Ag) 1984	12.00	15.00

ANNIVERSARY OF BIRTH OF VIRGIN MARY

171 (184)	500 Lire (Ag) 1984		25.00

All valuations in the SCHÖN are stated in U.S. Dollars.

Venezuela　　　　**Venezuela**　　　　**Vénézuéla**

Area: 352,150 sq. mi. Population: 15,900,000.
Republic in northern South America.
Capital: Caracas.

100 Centavos (Centimos) = 1 Bolívar

ESTADOS UNIDOS DE VENEZUELA

			VF	XF
1 (25)	1	Centavo (Cu–Ni) 1876–1877. Coat of arms. ℞ value in wreath	8.00	18.00
2 (26)	2½	Centavos (Cu–Ni) 1876–1877	12.00	25.00
3 (27)	5	Centimos (Cu–Ni) 1896–1938	0.60	1.00
4 (28)	12½	Centimos (Cu–Ni) 1896–1938	1.00	2.00
5 (19)	⅕	Bolívar (Ag) 1879. Simón Bolívar (1783–1830), liberated South America from the Spanish government. ℞ coat of arms	350.00	600.00
6 (20)	¼	Bolívar (Ag) 1894–1948	1.25	2.50
7 (21)	½	Bolívar (Ag) 1879–1936	2.50	5.00
8 (22)	1	Bolívar (Ag) 1879–1936	3.50	6.00
9 (23)	2	Bolivares (Ag) 1879–1936	6.00	9.00

10 (24)	5	Bolivares (Ag) 1879–1936	15.00	20.00
11 (31)	10	Bolivares (Au) 1930	90.00	110.00
12 (32)	20	Bolivares (Au) 1879–1912	140.00	180.00
13 (17)	25	Bolivares (Au) 1875	275.00	400.00
14 (33)	100	Bolivares (Au) 1886–1889	550.00	850.00

Further gold pieces, 5, 50, and 100 Bolivares, with the date 1875 are extremely rare pattern pieces.

			VF	**XF**
15 (29)	5	Centimos (Bra) 1944. Coat of arms. ℞ value in wreath	3.00	6.50
16 (29a)	5	Centimos (Cu–Ni) 1945–1948	0.25	0.50
17 (30)	12½	Centimos (Bra) 1944	15.00	35.00
18 (30a)	12½	Centimos (Cu–Ni) 1945–1948	0.30	0.75
19 (21a)	½	Bolivar (Ag) 1944–1946. Same type as No. 7	2.00	3.00
20 (22a)	1	Bolivar (Ag) 1945. Same type as No. 8	4.00	6.00
21 (23a)	2	Bolivares (Ag) 1945. Same type as No. 9	5.50	7.00

REPUBLICA DE VENEZUELA

			VF	**XF**
22 (38)	5	Centimos (Cu–Ni) 1958–1971. Rev. value in wreath		
		a) 1958	0.20	0.30
		b) 1964, 1965, 1971	0.10	0.20
23 (39)	12½	Centimos (Cu–Ni) 1958, 1969	0.20	0.30

			VF	**XF**
24 (35)	25	Centimos (Ag) 1954	0.80	1.20
25 (35a)	25	Centimos (Ag) 1960. Same type as No. 24, but narrow shield	0.80	1.20
26 (40)	25	Centimos (Ni) 1965	0.20	0.40
27 (36)	50	Centimos (Ag) 1954	1.60	2.60
28 (36a)	50	Centimos (Ag) 1960. Same type as No. 27, but narrow shield	1.60	2.60
29 (41)	50	Centimos (Ni) 1965, 1985	0.40	0.60
30 (37)	1	Bolivar (Ag) 1954	3.00	4.50

			VF	**XF**
31 (37a)	1	Bolivar (Ag) 1960, 1965. Same type as No. 30, but Bolívar's head slightly altered	3.00	4.00
32 (42)	1	Bolivar (Ni) 1967	0.60	1.00
33 (A37)	2	Bolivares (Ag) 1960, 1965	5.00	7.00
34 (43)	2	Bolivares (Ni) 1967	1.00	1.80

			XF	Unc
35 (A40)	10	Centimos (Cu-Ni) 1971. National coat of arms, name of country, date. R denomination between laurel branches tied underneath	0.20	0.30
36 (44)	5	Bolivares (Ni) 1973. Type as No. 31	2.00	3.00

COMMEMORATIVE ISSUE FOR SIMON BOLIVAR

37 (45)	10	Bolivares (Ag) 1973	15.00	22.00
38 (49)	5	Centimos 1974, 1976, 1977, 1983. Coat of arms, date. Rev. value:		
		a) (Copper-clad steel) 1974, 1976, 1977	0.10	0.20
		b) (Nickel-clad steel) 1983, 1986	0.10	0.20

CONSERVATION COMMEMORATIVE (3)

			Unc	Proof
39 (46)	25	Bolivares (Ag) 1975. Rev. Jaguar:		
		a) .925 silver, 25.31 g	25.00	
		b) .925 silver, 28.28 g		35.00
40 (47)	50	Bolivares (Ag) 1975. Rev. Giant armadillo:		
		a) .925 silver, 31.65 g	30.00	
		b) .925 silver, 35 g		40.00
41 (48)	1000	Bolivares (Au) 1975. Rev. Cock of the Rock	500.00	700.00

NATIONALIZATION OF OIL INDUSTRY

42 (54)	500	Bolivares (Au) 1975. Oil derricks; .900 gold, 33.47 g (100 pcs.)		–.–

			XF	Unc
43 (50)	25	Centimos (Ni) 1977, 1978:		
		a) 1977; 26.8 gm., 1.18 mm thick	0.15	0.30
		b) 1978; 26.5 gm., 1.07 mm thick	0.15	0.30

			XF	Unc
44 (52)	1 Bolivar (Ni) 1977		0.50	1.00
45 (53)	5 Bolivares (Ni) 1977, 1978		1.80	2.50

150th ANNIVERSARY OF INDEPENDENCE (2)

			Proof
46 (55)	75 Bolivares (Ag) 1980. Antonio José de Sucre		15.00
47 (56)	100 Bolivares (Ag) 1980. Simón Bolivar		30.00

200th ANNIVERSARY OF BIRTH OF A. BELLO

48 (57)	100 Bolivares (Ag) 1981. Andrès Béllo (1781–1865), poet. Rev. monogram	22.50

200th ANNIVERSARY OF BIRTH OF S. BOLIVAR (2)

49 (58)	100 Bolivares (Ag) 1983. Simón Bolivar (1783–1830), liberator. Rev. National bank building	25.00
50 (59)	3000 Bolivares (Au) 1983. Type as No. 49	550.00

200th ANNIVERSARY OF THE BIRTH OF J. M. VARGAS

51 (60)	100 Bolivares (Ag) 1986. Dr. José Maria Vargas (1786–1854), politician and statesman. Rev. University of Caracas building	20.00

All valuations in the SCHÖN are stated in U.S. Dollars.

West African States

Westafrikanische Staaten   Afrique de l'Ouest

The West African Monetary Union (UMOA) within the Franc Area comprises the states of Dahomey (now Benin), Jvory Coast, Mauritania (up to June 1973), Niger, Upper Volta, Senegal and Togo.

100 Centimes = 1 CFA Franc

			XF	Unc
1 (1)	1	Franc (Al) 1961–1976. Dune gazelle (Gazella leptoceros – Bovidae). Rev. gold weight of the Ashanti, 17th to 18th century, between value	0.20	0.40
2 (2)	5	Francs (Al-Br) 1960–1984	0.50	0.80
3 (3)	10	Francs (Al-Br) 1959–1981	0.60	1.20
4 (A3)	25	Francs (Al-Br) 1970–1978. Dune gazelle. Rev. Ashanti gold weight between value	1.00	1.60

ISSUE FOR THE FAO COIN PLAN

5 (5)	50	Francs (Cu-Ni) 1972–1984. Rev. rice, millet, groundnuts, cocoa and coffee. Value and date	0.60	1.20
6 (4)	100	Francs (Ni) 1967–1982. Ashanti gold weight. Rev. value	1.60	2.50

10th ANNIVERSARY OF THE WEST AFRICAN MONETARY UNION

7 (6)	500	Francs (Ag) 1972	35.00	50.00
8 (7)	1	Franc (Cu-Ni) 1976–1980, 1982, 1984. Obv. as No. 6. Rev. value, date, inscription UNION MONETAIRE OUEST AFRICAINE	0.20	0.30
9 (8)	25	Francs (Al-Br) 1980–1982	0.80	1.20
10 (9)	10	Francs (Al-Br) 1981, 1982	0.50	0.75

20th ANNIVERSARY OF THE WEST AFRICAN MONETARY UNION (2)

11 (10)	5000	Francs (Ag) 1982		27.50
12 (11)	5000	Francs (Au) 1982		*400.00*

Area: 1,133 sq. mi. Population: 164,000.

Group of islands in the Pacific with Savaii, Upolu, Manong and Apolima. The former German protectorate came under New Zealand administration as a League of Nations mandate in 1919 and from 1946–1962 under UN trusteeship. Since January 1, 1962 Western Samoa is an independent chiefs aristocracy.

Capital: Apia, on the island of Upolu.

100 Sene = 1 Tala (Dollar)

MALIETOA TANUMAFILI since 1963

		XF	Unc
1 (1)	1 Sene (Br) 1967. Malietoa Tanumafili II. Head of State. ℞ value in wreath	0.10	0.20
2 (2)	2 Sene (Br) 1967	0.15	0.30
3 (3)	5 Sene (Cu–Ni) 1967	0.20	0.40
4 (4)	10 Sene (Cu–Ni) 1967	0.40	0.70
5 (5)	20 Sene (Cu–Ni) 1967	0.50	1.00
6 (6)	50 Sene (Cu–Ni) 1967, but with scroll	1.20	1.80

7 (7)	1 Tala (Cu–Ni) 1967. Type as No. 6	2.50	4.00

COMMEMORATIVE ISSUE FOR THE 75th ANNIVERSARY OF STEVENSON'S DEATH

		Unc	Proof
8 (8)	1 Tala (Cu–Ni) 1969. Robert Louis Stevenson (1850–1894), writer. Best known publication: "Treasure Island". He lived for many years in Vailima, Samoa, where he is also laid to rest. ℞ coat of arms, value	5.00	75.00

COMMEMORATIVE ISSUE FOR JAMES COOK

9 (9)	1 Tala (Cu–Ni) 1970. James Cook (1728–1779), British circumnavigator		5.00	50.00

COMMEMORATIVE ISSUE FOR THE VISIT OF POPE PAUL VI IN SAMOA ON NOVEMBER 29, 1970

10 (10)	1 Tala (Cu–Ni) 1970	5.00	65.00

COMMEMORATIVE ISSUE FOR THE 250th ANNIVERSARY OF THE DISCOVERY OF SAMOA BY JACOB ROGGEVEEN (JUNE 14, 1722)

11 (11)	1 Tala (Cu–Ni) 1972	5.00	70.00

			Unc	Proof
12 (12)	1	Tala 1974. Boxer, functional legend, date. Rev. national coat of arms, name of coutry, value:		
		a) (Ag)		180.00
		b) (Cu-Ni)	5.00	

			XF	Unc
13 (13)	1	Sene (Br) 1974	0.10	0.15
14 (14)	2	Sene (Br) 1974	0.15	0.25
15 (15)	5	Sene (Cu-Ni) 1974	0.20	0.30
16 (16)	10	Sene (Cu-Ni) 1974	0.35	0.50
17 (17)	20	Sene (Cu-Ni) 1974	0.45	0.80
18 (18)	50	Sene (Cu-Ni) 1974	1.20	1.80
19 (19)	1	Tala (Cu-Ni) 1974	1.80	3.50

BICENTENARY OF AMERICAN INDEPENDENCE (2)

			Unc	Proof
20 (20)	1	Tala 1976. Rev. Paul Revere on horse:		
		a) (Ag)		60.00
		b) (Cu-Ni)	4.00	
21 (21)	100	Tala (Au) 1975. Type as No. 20		250.00

OLYMPIC GAMES 1976 IN MONTREAL (2)

			Unc	Proof
22 (22)	1	Tala 196. Rev. Weightlifter:		
		a) (Ag)		45.00
		b) (Cu-Ni)	4.00	
23 (23)	100	Tala (Au) 1976. Type as No. 22		250.00

SILVER JUBILEE OF THE REIGN OF HER MAJESTY QUEEN ELIZABETH II (2)

			Unc	Proof
24 (24)	1	Tala 1977. Rev. Bust of Queen Elizabeth II over island scene:		
		a) (Ag)		50.00
		b) (Cu-Ni)	6.00	
25 (25)	100	Tala (Au) 1977. Type as No. 24		260.00

LINDBERGH COMMEMORATIVE (2)

			Unc	Proof
26 (26)	1	Tala 1977. Bust of Charles Lindbergh below »Spirit of St. Louis«:		
		a) (Ag)		35.00
		b) (Cu-Ni)	5.00	
27 (27)	100	Tala (Au) 1977. Type as No. 26		250.00

50th ANNIVERSARY OF THE FIRST TRANSPACIFIC FLIGHT (2)

			Unc	Proof
28 (28)	1	Tala 1978. Rev. Head of Kingsford Smith and Pacific map:		
		a) (Ag)		30.00
		b) (Cu-Ni)	5.00	
29 (29)	100	Tala (Au) 1978. Type as No. 28		250.00

COMMONWEALTH GAMES (2)

			Unc	Proof
30 (30)	1	Tala 1978. Rev. Three runners:		
		a) (Ag)		30.00
		b) (Cu-Ni)	5.00	
31 (31)	100	Tala (Au) 1978. Type as No. 30		275.00

200th ANNIVERSARY OF THE DEATH OF JAMES COOK (3)

			Unc	Proof
32 (32)	1	Tala (Cu-Ni) 1979. Rev. Head of James Cook and his ship H.M.S. »Endeavour«	5.00	
33 (33)	10	Tala (Ag) 1979. Type as No. 32:		
		a) silver content 925		35.00
		b) silver content 500	20.00	
34 (34)	100	Tala (Au) 1979		300.00

OLYMPIC GAMES 1980 IN MOSCOW (3)

			Unc	Proof
35 (35)	1	Tala (Cu-Ni) 1980. Rev. Hurdler	6.00	
36 (36)	10	Tala (Ag) 1980. Type as No. 35:		
		a) silver content 925		35.00
		b) silver content 500	20.00	
37 (37)	100	Tala (Au) 1980. Type as No. 35	225.00	175.00

FOR THE FAO COIN PLAN (2)

			Unc	Proof
38 (38)	1	Tala (Cu-Ni) 1980. Rev. Cocos palm	5.00	
39 (39)	10	Tala (Ag) 1980. Type as No. 38		25.00

GOVERNOR WILHELM SOLF (3)

			Unc	Proof
40 (40)	1	Tala (Cu-Ni) 1980. Rev. Dr. Wilhelm Solf (1862–1936), German Governor	5.00	
41 (41)	10	Tala (Ag) 1980. Type as No. 40:		
		a) silver content 925		35.00
		b) silver content 500	20.00	
42 (42)	100	Tala (Au) 1980. Type as No. 40	225.00	175.00

WEDDING OF PRINCE CHARLES AND LADY DIANA (4)

		Unc	Proof
43 (43)	1 Tala (Cu-Ni) 1981. Conjoined heads	5.00	
44 (44)	10 Tala (Ag) 1981. Type as No. 43		30.00
45 (45)	100 Tala (Au) 1981. Type as No. 43	200.00	150.00
46 (46)	1000 Tala (Au) 1981. Type as No. 43		1000.00

INTERNATIONAL YEAR OF DISABLED PERSONS (3)

47 (47)	1 Tala (Cu-Ni) 1981. President Franklin Delano Roosevelt	5.00	
48 (48)	10 Tala (Ag) 1981. Type as No. 47		30.00
49 (49)	100 Tala (Au) 1981. Type as No. 47	200.00	150.00

XII COMMONWEALTH GAMES 1982 BRISBANE, AUSTRALIA (3)

50 (50)	1 Tala (Cu-Ni) 1982. Rev. Javelin-throwing	5.00	
51 (51)	10 Tala (Ag) 1982. Type as No. 50		30.00
52 (52)	100 Tala (Au) 1982. Type as No. 50	200.00	150.00

7th SOUTH PACIFIC GAMES 1983 APIA (4)

53 (53)	1 Tala (Cu-Ni) 1983. Sprinter	5.00	
54 (54)	10 Tala (Ag) 1983. Type as No. 53		35.00
55 (55)	100 Tala (Au) 1983. Type as No. 53		200.00
56 (56)	1000 Tala (Au) 1983. Type as No. 53		1000.00

57 (57)	1 Tala 1984. Malietoa Tannmafili II. Rev. Arms, value, date (sevensided):		
	a) (Ag) Piéfort		80.00
	b) (Cu-Ni)	5.00	
	c) (Cu-Al-Ni)	3.00	

XXIII OLYMPIC SUMMER GAMES 1984 LOS ANGELES (4)

58 (58)	1 Tala (Cu-Ni) 1984. Boxer	5.00	
59 (59)	10 Tala (Ag.) 1984. Type as No. 58		35.00
60 (60)	100 Tala (Au) 1984. Type as No. 58	300.00	225.00
61 (61)	1000 Tala (Au) 1984. Type as No. 58		1000.00

BULLION ISSUE »KON-TIKI«

62 (62)	25 Tala (Ag) 1986. Sailing raft »Kon-Tiki«; .999 silver, 155.5 g		125.00

Area: 61,890 sq. mi. Population: 6,000,000.
The Imamate, under Osman governorship since 1517, obtained its independence in 1918. On September 27, 1962, upon the death of Imam Ahmed, his son and successor, Mohammed el-Badr was deposed a few days after his accession by a coup d'etat of the army, and the republic was proclaimed. The Imam who had excaped, however, succeeded in rallying devoted tribal warriors and to keep parts of the impassable hill country under his control.
Capital: San'a and Taiz.

2 Halala = 1 Bogash, 40 Bogash = 1 Imadi;
since 1962: 40 Bogash = 1 Riyal

YAHYA BIN MOHAMMED HAMID AL-DIN 1918–1948

			VF	XF
1 (1)	½ Halala (Br) A.H. 1342–1346 (1924–1928). Legend and crescent. ℞ legend		8.00	16.00
2 (2)	1 Halala (Br) A.H. 1322–1361 (1904–1944)		2.00	4.50
3 (3)	1 Bogash (Br) A.H. 1341–1367 (1923–1948)		2.50	5.00
4 (4)	1/20 Imadi (Ag) A.H. 1337–1366 (1919–1948)		8.00	12.00
5 (5)	1/10 Imadi (Ag) A.H. 1337–1366 (1919–1948)		5.50	8.00
6 (8)	⅛ Imadi (Ag) A.H. 1339 (1920)		130.00	220.00

| 7 (6) | ¼ Imadi (Ag) A.H. 1344–1366 (1926–1948) | | 6.50 | 10.50 |
| 8 (7) | 1 Imadi (Ag) A.H. 1344 (1926) | | 16.00 | 28.00 |

AHMED HAMID AL-DIN 1948–1962

9 (11)	1 Halala. Legend and crescent. ℞ legend			
	a) (Br) A.H. 1368–1381 (1949–1962)		1.50	2.50
	b) (Al) A.H. 1374–1378 (1955–1959)		0.80	1.60

				VF	XF
10 (12)	1	Bogash			
		a) (Br) A.H. 1368–1379 (1949–1960)		2.00	3.00
		b) (Al) A.H. 1374–1376 (1955–1957)		0.80	2.00

			VF	XF
11 (13)	1/16	Imadi (Ag) A.H. 1367–1374 (1948–1955). Pentagon	4.00	6.50
12 (14)	1/8	Imadi (Ag) A.H. 1367–1380 (1948–1961)	4.00	6.00
13 (15)	1/4	Imadi (Ag) A.H. 1367–1377 (1948–1958)	5.00	8.00
14 (16)	1/2	Imadi (Ag) A.H. 1367–1379 (1948–1960)	8.00	16.00
15 (17)	1	Imadi (Ag) A.H. 1367–1380 (1948–1961)	16.00	22.00
16 (G15)	1/4	Imadi (Au) A.H. 1370–1377 (1951–1958). Crescent and legend. ℞ legend	180.00	240.00
17 (G16)	1/2	Imadi (Au) A.H. 1370 (1951)	300.00	360.00
18 (G17)	1	Imadi (Au) A.H. 1377 (1958)	720.00	840.00

			VF	XF
19 (18)	1	Halala (Al) no date (1956)	1.20	2.50
20 (19)	1	Bogash (Al) no date (1956)	1.60	3.50

REPUBLIC since 1962

			VF	XF
21 (20)	1	Halala (Br) A.H. 1382 (1963). Hand holding torch	0.80	1.20
22 (21)	1	Halala (Br) A.H. 1382 (1963). Flag with star in circle	1.50	2.50
23 (32)	1/2	Bogash (Br) A.H. 1382 (1963). Flag with star in circle	2.80	5.00
24 (22)	1	Bogash (Bra) A.H. 1382 (1963)	1.50	2.50
25 (23)	1/20	Riyal (Ag) A.H. 1382 (1963)	2.00	3.50
26 (24)	1/10	Riyal (Ag) A.H. 1382 (1963)	2.50	4.00
27 (25)	1/5	Riyal (Ag) A.H. 1382 (1963)	4.00	6.00

			VF	XF
28 (A25)	¼	Riyal (Ag) A.H. 1382 (1963)	8.00	12.00
29 (26)	½	Bogash (Al–Br) A.H. 1382 (1963). Coffee plant (Coffea arabica – Rubiaceae), branch	0.40	0.60

30 (27)	1	Bogash (Al–Br) A.H. 1382 (1963)	0.50	0.80
31 (A27)	2	Bogash (Al–Br) A.H. 1382 (1963)	0.80	1.50
32 (28)	5	Bogash (Ag) A.H. 1382 (1963)	1.60	3.20
33 (29)	10	Bogash (Ag) A.H. 1382 (1963)	2.50	4.00
34 (30)	20	Bogash (Ag) A.H. 1382 (1963)	5.00	8.00

35 (31)	1	Riyal (Ag) A.H. 1382 (1963). Coffee plant, branch	9.00	12.00

COMMEMORATIVE ISSUES (10) FOR THE 1st MANNED MOON LANDING ON JULY 20, 1969, AND IN MEMORY OF QADHI MOHAMMED MAHMUD AZZUBAIRI

| 36 | 1 | Riyal (Ag) 1969. Man riding on drome- |

dary. ℞ state emblem, value, date, name
of country

37   2 Riyals (Ag) 1969. Lion's head. ℞ like
No. 36

27.50

38   2 Riyals (Ag) 1969. Cape Kennedy: take-
off of "Apollo 11" on July 16, 1969. ℞
like No. 36

30.00

39   2 Riyals (Ag) 1969. US moon research
programme, 3rd section "manned
landing". Apollo programme. Astro-
nauts examining the ground, moon capsule "Apollo 11" and date of the landing, July 20, 1969. Globe. ℞ like No. 36

30.00

				Proof
40	5	Riyals (Au) 1969. Head of falcon. ℞ like No. 36			**125.00**
41	10	Riyals (Au) 1969. Arabian slender-horned gazelles. ℞ like No. 36			200.00
42	20	Riyals (Au) 1969. Same type as No. 36			350.00
43	20	Riyals (Au) 1969. Same type as No. 39			350.00
44	30	Riyals (Au) 1969. Qadhi Mohammed Mahmud Azzubairi, fighter for independence			600.00
45	50	Riyals (Au) 1969. Lion. ℞ like No. 36			800.00
46 (33)	1	Fils (Al) 1974, 1980. Coat of arms. Rev. value, date	**XF** 0.15		**Unc** 0.25
47 (34)	5	Fils (Bra) 1974, 1980. Type as No. 46	0.25		0.40
48 (35)	10	Fils (Bra) 1974, 1980. Type as No. 46	0.30		0.60
49 (36)	25	Fils (Cu-Ni) 1974, 1979, 1980. Type as No. 46	0.40		0.80
50 (37)	50	Fils (Cu-Ni) 1974, 1979, 1980. Type as No. 46	0.50		1.00
51 (42)	1	Rial (Cu-Ni) 1976, 1980. Type as No. 46	2.00		3.50

FOR THE FAO COIN PLAN (6)

52 (43)	1	Fils (Al) 1978 (7,050 pieces)		7.50
53 (38)	5	Fils (Bra) 1974	0.25	0.40
54 (39)	10	Fils (Bra) 1974	0.30	0.60
55 (40)	25	Fils (Cu-Ni) 1974	0.40	0.80
56 (41)	50	Fils (Cu-Ni) 1974	0.50	1.00

57 (44)	1	Rial (Cu-Ni) 1978 (7,050 pieces)		12.50

				Unc	Proof
58	2½	Riyals (Ag) 1975. Oil Exploration		–.–	60.00

			Unc	Proof
59	5 Riyals (Ag) 1975. Mona Lisa		–.–	–.–
60	10 Riyals (Ag) 1975. XXI Olympiad Montreal 1976		35.00	50.00
61	15 Riyals (Ag) 1975. Jerusalem		–.–	–.–
62	20 Riyals (Au) 1975. Mosque		200.00	250.00
63	25 Riyals (Au) 1975. Oil Exploration		200.00	250.00
64	50 Riyals (Au) 1975. Mona Lisa		250.00	250.00
65	75 Riyals (Au) 1975. Oil Exploration		300.00	400.00
66	100 Riyals (Au) 1975. Jerusalem		350.00	425.00

INTERNATIONAL YEAR OF THE DISABLED

67	(46)	25 Riyals (Ag) 1982	25.00	35.00

20th ANNIVERSARY OF THE GLORIOUS REVOLUTION (2)

68	(47)	25 Riyals (Ag) 1982	45.00
69	(48)	500 Riyals (Au) 1982	400.00

INTERNATIONAL YEAR OF THE CHILD

70	(45)	25 Riyals (Ag) 1983	40.00

ROYALIST ISSUES UNDER MOHAMMED EL-BADR

During his flight, Imam Mohammed el-Badr succeeded in assembling loyal warriors from the desolate areas north and east of Yemen. With their help he resisted the republican government, which was supported by Egyptian troops at that time. The circulating currency consisted mainly of Maria Theresa Talers, Saudi Arabian Riyals, Indian Rupees, and Gold Sovereigns.

COMMEMORATIVE ISSUE FOR SIR WINSTON CHURCHILL

			Unc
1	1 Riyal (Ag) 1965. Sir Winston Churchill (1874–1965). British statesman		12.00

Jugoslawien   # Yugoslavia   **Yougoslavie**

Area: 98,740 sq. mi. Population: 23,500,000.

Alexander as Regent united Serbia, Croatia and Slovenia to form a kingdom on December 1, 1918, which has been named Yugoslavia since 1929. On November 29, 1943 the Federal Republic of Yugoslavia was created which was transformed into a Federal People's Republic on November 29, 1945.

Capital: Belgrade (Beograd).

100 Para = 1 Dinar

			VF	XF
	PETER I 1918–1921			
1 (1)	5	Para (Sn) 1920. Crowned arms. ℞ value	8.00	18.00
2 (2)	10	Para (Sn) 1920. Same type as No. 1	4.00	7.50
3 (3)	25	Para (Ni–Br) 1920	1.50	4.00
	ALEXANDER I 1921–1934			
4 (4)	50	Para (Ni–Br) 1925. Alexander I (1888–1934), Regent 1918–1921, King 1921–1934. ℞ value in wreath, crown above above	0.80	2.00
5 (5)	1	Dinar (Ni–Br) 1925. Same type as No. 4	1.00	2.00
6 (6)	2	Dinara (Ni–Br) 1925. Same type as No. 4	2.50	3.50
7 (7)	10	Dinara (Ag) 1931. Alexander I, head left. ℞ crowned heraldic eagle	4.00	8.00
8 (8)	20	Dinara (Ag) 1931. Same type as No. 7	10.50	20.00
9 (9)	50	Dinara (Ag) 1932. Same type as No. 7	32.00	70.00

10 (10)	20	Dinara (Au) 1925. Same type as No. 4	175.00	200.00
11 (A11)	1	Dukat (Au) 1931–1934	75.00	100.00
12 (12)	4	Dukats (Au) 1931–1933	700.00	1000.00

PETER II 1934–1945

			VF	XF
13 (13)	25	Para (Br) 1938. Wreath, crown above. ℞ value (center hole)	2.50	4.50
14 (14)	50	Para (Al–Br) 1938. Crown. ℞ value	1.00	1.50
15 (15)	1	Dinar (Al–Br) 1938	1.00	1.50

			VF	XF
16	2	Dinara (Al-Br) 1938		
		a) (Y 16) large crown (see illustration)	1.00	1.50
		b) (Y 17) small crown	5.00	15.00
17 (18)	10	Dinara (Ni) 1938. Peter II (1923–1970), head right	1.00	2.50
18 (19)	20	Dinara (Ag) 1938. Peter II, head left	4.00	6.00

			VF	XF
19 (20)	50	Dinara (Ag) 1938. Peter II, head right	6.00	12.00

PEOPLE'S REPUBLIC since 1945

			VF	XF
20 (21)	50	Para (Sn) 1945. Coat of arms of the People's Republic. ℞ value	1.20	3.00
21 (22)	1	Dinar (Sn) 1945	0.80	2.50
22 (23)	2	Dinara (Sn) 1945	1.20	2.50
23 (24)	5	Dinara (Sn) 1945	1.50	2.80
24 (25)	50	Para (Al) 1953. Coat of arms, new legend FEDERATIVNA NARODNA REPUBLIKA JUGOSLAVIJA. ℞ value	0.10	0.20
25 (26)	1	Dinar (Al) 1953. Cyrillic legend	0.10	0.25
26 (27)	2	Dinara (Al) 1953	0.15	0.30
27 (28)	5	Dinara (Al) 1953. Cyrillic legend	0.25	0.40

			VF	XF
28 (29)	10	Dinara (Al–Br) 1955. Coat of arms. ℞ female farm worker with sheaf of wheat	0.20	0.40
29 (30)	20	Dinara (Al–Br) 1955. ℞ factory worker, section of a cog-wheel, symbolizing the industrialization	0.30	0.60
30 (31)	50	Dinara (Al-Br) 1955. R male and female worker, section of cog-wheel, and ear of wheat	0.50	1.00
31 (32)	1	Dinar (Al) 1963. Coat of arms, new legend SOCIJALISTIKA FEDERATIVNA REPUBLIKA JUGOSLAVIJA. ℞ value	0.10	0.20
32 (33)	2	Dinara (Al) 1963	0.15	0.25
33 (34)	5	Dinara (Al) 1963	0.20	0.35
34 (35)	10	Dinara (Al–Br) 1963	0.20	0.40
35 (A35)	20	Dinara (Al–Br) 1963	0.30	0.60
36 (B35)	50	Dinara (Al–Br) 1963	0.40	0.75

CURRENCY REFORM: 100 old Dinara = 1 new Dinar

37 (36)	5	Para (Al–Br) 1965	0.15	0.30

38 (37)	1	Dinar (Cu-Ni) 1965	0.50	1.00
39 (38)	5	Para (Al-Br) 1965, 1973–1980. Coat of arms. New legend SFR JUGOSLAVIJA	0.05	0.10
40 (39)	10	Para (Al-Br) 1965, 1973–1981	0.10	0.20
41 (40)	20	Para (Al-Br) 1965, 1973–1981	0.15	0.30
42 (41)	50	Para (Al-Br) 1965, 1973–1981	0.30	0.60

43 (42)	1	Dinar (Cu–Ni) 1968	0.40	0.80

COMMEMORATIVE ISSUES (6) FOR THE 25th ANNIVERSARY OF THE YUGOSLAV FEDERATED REPUBLIC

44 (48)	20	Dinara (Ag) 1968. Monument in Jaice, Bosnia. ℞ state emblem, value, name of country	**Proof** 20.00

45 (49)	50	Dinara (Ag) 1968. Josip Broz Tito (*1892), President since 1953. ℞ like No. 44	45.00
46 (50)	100	Dinara (Au) 1968. Same type as No. 44	200.00
47 (51)	200	Dinara (Au) 1968. Same type as No. 45	400.00
48 (52)	500	Dinara (Au) 1968. Same type as No. 44	1000.00
49 (53)	1000	Dinara (Au) 1968. Same type as No. 45	1800.00

COMMEMORATIVE ISSUES (2) FOR THE FAO COIN PLAN

			XF	**Unc**
50 (43)	2	Dinara (Cu–Ni) 1970. State emblem. ℞ value in circular inscription, date, and FIAT PANIS above. FAO between ears of wheat	0.30	0.60

51 (44)	5	Dinara (Cu–Ni) 1970. Same type as No. 50	0.60	1.25

						XF	Unc
52 (A45)	1	Dinar (Cu-Ni) 1973–1981				0.20	0.40
53 (45)	2	Dinara (Cu-Ni) 1971–1981. Type as No. 52				0.20	0.40
54 (46)	5	Dinara (Cu-Ni) 1971–1981. Type as No. 52				0.30	0.60
55 (A47)	10	Dinara (Cu-Ni) 1976–1981. Type as No. 52				0.50	1.00

30th ANNIVERSARY OF THE END OF WORLD WAR II

			XF	Unc
56 (47)	5	Dinara (Cu-Ni) 1975. Type as No. 54, but commemorative legend	0.60	1.00

FOR THE FAO COIN PLAN (2)

			XF	Unc
57 (54)	1	Dinar (Cu-Ni) 1976. Type as No. 50	0.15	0.25
58 (55)	10	Dinara (Cu-Ni) 1976. Type as No. 50	0.60	1.00

85th ANNIVERSARY OF THE BIRTH OF J. B. TITO

			Unc	Proof
59 (56)	200	Dinara (Ag) 1977. Bust of J. B. Tito	22.00	35.00

8th MEDITERRANEAN GAMES AT SPLIT 1979 (11)

		Proof
60 (57)	100 Dinara (Ag) 1978	18.00
61 (58)	150 Dinara (Ag) 1978	25.00
62 (59)	200 Dinara (Ag) 1978	35.00
63 (60)	250 Dinara (Ag) 1978	40.00
64 (61)	300 Dinara (Ag) 1978	50.00
65 (62)	350 Dinara (Ag) 1978	60.00
66 (63)	400 Dinara (Ag) 1978	70.00
67 (64)	1500 Dinara (Au) 1978	200.00
68 (65)	2000 Dinara (Au) 1978	275.00
69 (66)	2500 Dinara (Au) 1978	350.00
70 (67)	5000 Dinara (Au) 1978	650.00

VUKOVAR CONGRESS (3)

		Unc	Proof
71 (68)	500 Dinara (Ag) 1980		20.00
72 (69)	1000 Dinara (Ag) 1980		30.00
73 (70)	1500 Dinara (Ag) 1980		40.00

TITO'S DEATH

74 (71)	1000 Dinara (Ag) 1980	35.00	40.00

WORLD TABLE TENNIS CHAMPIONSHIP GAMES 1981 (3)

75 (72)	500 Dinara (Ag) 1981		20.00
76 (73)	1000 Dinara (Ag) 1981		30.00
77 (74)	1500 Dinara (Ag) 1981		40.00

40th ANNIVERSARY OF UPRISING

78 (75)	1000 Dinara (Ag) 1981		30.00

INTERNATIONAL CANOEING CHAMPIONSHIP (2)

				Proof
79 (76)	1000	Dinara (Ag) 1982		25.00
80 (77)	1500	Dinara (Ag) 1982		35.00

			XF	**Unc**
81 (78)	25	Para (Br) 1982, 1983. Arms, name of country. Rev. Value, date	0.10	0.15
82 (79)	50	Para (Br) 1982–1984. Type as No. 81	0.10	0.15
83 (80)	1	Dinar (Ni-Bra) 1982–1984. Type as No. 81	0.10	0.15
84 (81)	2	Dinara (Ni-Bra) 1982–1984. Type as No. 81	0.10	0.15
85 (82)	5	Dinara (Ni-Bra) 1982–1984. Type as No. 81	0.15	0.30
86 (83)	10	Dinara (Cu-Ni) 1982–1984. Type as No. 81	0.30	0.50

OLYMPIC WINTER GAMES IN SARAJEVO – 1st ISSUE (4)

			Proof
87 (84)	100	Dinara (Ag) 1982. Ice hockey	27.50
88 (85)	250	Dinara (Ag) 1982. Sarajevo view	35.00
89 (86)	500	Dinara (Ag) 1982. Downhill skiing	45.00
90 (87)	5000	Dinara (Au) 1982. Emblem of the games	225.00

OLYMPIC WINTER GAMES IN SARAJEVO – 2nd ISSUE (7)

91 (88)	100	Dinara (Ag) 1983. Figure skating	27.50
92 (89)	250	Dinara (Ag) 1983. Goddes of Lepinski Vir	35.00
93 (90)	500	Dinara (Ag) 1983. Ski jumping	45.00
94 (92)	100	Dinara (Ag) 1983. Bobsledding	27.50
95 (93)	250	Dinara (Ag) 1983. Radimlja tombs	35.00
96 (94)	500	Dinara (Ag) 1983. Biathlon	45.00
97 (91)	5000	Dinara (Au) 1983. Bust of J. B. Tito	225.00

40th ANNIVERSARY OF THE BATTLES OF NERETVA AND SUTJESKA (2)

			XF	**Unc**
98	10	Dinara (Cu-Ni) 1983. Neretva bridge	0.50	0.80
99	10	Dinara (Cu-Ni) 1983. Sutjeska monument	0.50	0.80

OLYMPIC WINTER GAMES IN SARAJEVO – 3rd ISSUE (7)

				Proof
100 (96)	100	Dinara (Ag) 1984. Speed skating		22.50
101 (97)	250	Dinara (Ag) 1984. Jajce village		30.00
102 (98)	500	Dinara (Ag) 1984. Cross country skiing		40.00
103 (99)	100	Dinara (Ag) 1984. Pairs figure skating		22.50
104 (100)	250	Dinara (Ag) 1984. J. B. Tito		30.00
105 (101)	500	Dinara (Ag) 1984. Slalom		40.00
106 (95)	5000	Dinara (Au) 1984. Olympic flame		225.00

WORLD SKI JUMPING CHAMPIONSHIPS (4)

			Proof
107 (104)	500 Dinara (Ag) 1985. Flying Herons		22.50

108   109

			XF	Unc
108 (106)	1000 Dinara (Ag) 1985. Slovenian Cradle			30.00
109 (105)	1000 Dinara (Ag) 1985. Stanko Bloudek			30.00
110 (107)	10000 Dinara (Au) 1985. Type as No. 107			240.00
111 (108)	20 Dinara (German silver) 1985, 1986. Type as No. 81		0.25	0.50
112 (109)	50 Dinara (German silver) 1985, 1986. Type as No. 81		0.50	1.00
113 (110)	100 Dinara (German silver) 1985, 1986. Type as No. 81		0.85	1.75

All valuations in the SCHÖN are stated in U.S. Dollars.

Saire

Zaire

République du Zaïre

Area: 902,080 sq. mi. Population: 32,500,000.
The new name of Zaire was adopted by Congo (Kinshasa) on October 27, 1971.
Capital: Kinshasa.

100 Sengi = 1 Likuta, 100 Makuta = 1 Zaire
(Makuta = plural of Likuta)

			XF	Unc
1 (3)	5	Makuta (Cu-Ni) 1977. Bust of President Mobutu. Rev. value	0.60	1.25
2 (4)	10	Makuta (Cu-Ni) 1973, 1975, 1976, 1978. Bust of President Mobutu. Rev. coat of arms, value, date	1.25	2.00
3 (5)	20	Makuta (Cu-Ni) 1973, 1976. Bust of President Mobutu. Rev. arm holding torch	1.50	3.00

CONSERVATION COMMEMORATIVE (3)

			Unc	Proof
4 (8)	2,50	Zaires (Ag) 1975. Rev. Mountain gorilla:		
		a) .925 silver, 25.31 g	20.00	
		b) .925 silver, 28.28 g		22.00
5 (9)	5	Zaires (Ag) 1975. Rev. Okapi:		
		a) .925 silver, 31.65 g	30.00	
		b) .925 silver, 35 g		40.00
6 (10)	100	Zaires (Au) 1975. Rev. Leopard	600.00	750.00

			XF	Unc
7	1	Zaire (Cu-Ni) 1987. President Mobutu. Rev. Value	–.–	–.–
8	5	Zaire (Cu-Ni) 1987. Type as No. 7	–.–	–.–

Sambia # Zambia **Zambia**

Area: c. 288,130 sq. mi. Population: 6,800,000.

The former Northern Rhodesia was a part of the Central African Union with the designation of Rhodesia and Nyasaland from 1953 to 1963. Under the name of Zambia the country became independent on October 24, 1964. The Republic of Zambia is a member of the British Commonwealth.

Capital: Lusaka.

12 Pence = 1 Shilling, 20 Shillings = 1 £,
since January 16, 1968: 100 Ngwee = 1 Kwacha

			XF	Unc
1 (1)	6 Pence (Ni–Bra) 1964. Coat of arms. ℞ morning glory flower (Ipomoea sp. – Convolvulaceae)		0.60	1.00
2 (2)	1 Shilling (Ni–Bra) 1964. ℞ crowned hornbill (Tockus = Lophoceros albo-terminatus – Bucerotidae)		1.20	2.00
3 (3)	2 Shillings (Ni–Bra) 1964. ℞ bohor reedbuck (Redunca redunca – Bovidae)		1.80	3.50

COMMEMORATIVE ISSUE FOR THE FIRST ANNIVERSARY OF INDEPENDENCE

		Unc	Proof
4 (4)	5 Shillings (Ni) 1965. Kenneth David Kaunda (*1924), President of State. ℞ coat of arms	6.00	10.00

		XF	Unc
5 (5)	1 Penny (Br) 1966 (center hole)	0.50	0.80
6 (6)	6 Pence (Cu–Ni) 1966. Kenneth David Kaunda. ℞ morning glory flower	0.40	0.80
7 (7)	1 Shilling (Cu–Ni) 1966. Crowned hornbill	0.70	1.20
8 (8)	2 Shillings (Cu–Ni) 1966. ℞ bohor reedbuck	1.50	3.00

NEW CURRENCY (Decimal System): 100 Ngwee = 1 Kwacha

		XF	Unc
9 (9)	1 Ngwee 1968–1983. Rev. aardvark (Orycteropus afer – Orycteropidae):		
	a) (Br) 1968, 1969, 1972, 1978	0.35	1.00
	b) (Cu-clad steel) 1983	0.20	0.50

		XF	Unc
10 (10)	2 Ngwee 1968–1983. Rev. martial eagle (Polemaëtus bellicosus – Accipitridae):		
	a) (Br) 1968, 1978	0.25	0.40
	b) (Cu-clad steel) 1983	0.25	0.40

		XF	Unc
11 (11)	5 Ngwee (Cu-Ni) 1968, 1972, 1978. Rev. morning glory flower	0.30	0.50

		XF	Unc
12 (12)	10 Ngwee (Cu-Ni) 1968, 1972, 1978. ℞ crowned hornbill	0.50	0.90

13 (13)	20 Ngwee (Cu-Ni) 1968, 1972, 1978. ℞ bohor reedbuck	0.80	1.80

ISSUE FOR THE FAO COIN PLAN

		XF	Unc
14 (14)	50 Ngwee (Cu-Ni) 1969. Kenneth David Kaunda, head right. Rev. maize (Zea mays – Gramineae)	2.00	3.50
15 (15)	50 Ngwee (Cu-Ni) 1972	2.50	4.00

SECOND REPUBLIC 13th DECEMBER 1972

16 (16)	50 Ngwee (Cu-Ni) 1972, 1978	2.50	4.00

10th ANNIVERSARY OF INDEPENDENCE

		Unc	Proof
17 (17)	1 Kwacha (Ag) 1974	30.00	40.00

CONSERVATION COMMEMORATIVE (3)

18 (18)	5 Kwacha (Ag) 1979	22.50	30.00
19 (19)	10 Kwacha (Ag) 1979	30.00	45.00
20 (20)	200 Kwacha (Au) 1979	600.00	750.00

INTERNATIONAL YEAR OF THE CHILD

21 (21)	10 Kwacha (Ag) 1980		35.00

WORLD FOOD DAY 1981

		XF	Unc
22 (22)	20 Ngwee (Cu-Ni) 1981	1.00	1.50

Area: 640 sq. mi. Population: 330,000.

A Portuguese rule over this island lasting 150 years, during which the town of Zanzibar was founded, ended with its recapture by the Arabs from Oman. The Imam of Muscat, Seyyid Said, became Sultan in Zanzibar in 1833, transferred his main seat there in 1840 and extended his rule to the East African coastal strip from Lindi beyond Kilwa in the south, then Mombasa in the north as far as Lamu and Mogadishu. After his death in 1856, the Sultanate of Zanzibar separated from the Imamate in Muscat, but remained in the same dynasty with a common ruling regarding the succession to the throne. The agreement between the German Reich and Great Britain regarding the delimitation of their mutual interests in the so-called Heligoland/Zanzibar Treaty of 1890 robbed the Sultan of his influence over the African coast, but left him the Island of Pemba and placed him under the protection of British rule. The independence granted the Sultanate on 10th December 1963 lasted only one month. Since 12th January 1964 Zanzibar is a republic which united on 27th April 1964 with Tanganyika to form the United Republic of Tanganyika-Zanzibar – since 3rd November 1964 known as Tanzania.

Capital: Zanzibar.

100 Cents = 1 Rupee

ALI BEN HAMOUD 1902–1911

			VF	XF
1 (8)	1 Cent (Br) 1908. Arabic legend. ℞ cocos palm (Cocos nucifera-Palmae)		160.00	200.00

2 (9)	10 Cents (Br) 1908		200.00	250.00
3 (10)	20 Cents (Ni) 1908		250.00	300.00

Previous issues, see "Weltmünzkatalog 19. Jahrhundert" (World Coin Catalogue of the 19th Century)

Values are given for each coin in U.S. Dollars and reference to Yeoman-numbers.